"No ot. [...]
pleasure to read.
— Gene Shalit on the *Today Show*

★ ★ ★ ★ ★ (5-star rating) "Crisply written and remarkably personable. Cleverly organized so you can pluck out the minutest fact in a moment. Satisfyingly thorough."
— *Réalités*

"The information they offer is up-to-date, crisply presented but far from exhaustive, the judgments knowledgeable but not opinionated."
— *New York Times*

"The individual volumes are compact, the prose succinct, and the coverage up-to-date and knowledgeable . . . The format is portable and the index admirably detailed."
— *John Barkham Syndicate*

"They contain an amount of information that is truly staggering, besides being surprisingly current."
— *Detroit News*

"These guides address themselves to the needs of the modern traveler demanding precise, qualitative information . . . Upbeat, slick, and well put together."
— *Dallas Morning News*

". . . Attractive to look at, refreshingly easy to read, and generously packed with information."
— *Miami Herald*

"These guides are as good as any published, and much better than most."
— *Louisville* (Kentucky) *Times*

Stephen Birnbaum Travel Guides

Acapulco
Bahamas, Turks & Caicos
Barcelona
Bermuda
Boston
Canada
Cancun, Cozumel, and Isla Mujeres
Caribbean
Chicago
Disneyland
Eastern Europe
Europe
Europe for Business Travelers
Florence
France
Great Britain
Hawaii
Ireland
Italy
Ixtapa & Zihuatanejo
London
Los Angeles
Mexico
Miami
New York
Paris
Portugal
Rome
San Francisco
South America
Spain
United States
USA for Business Travelers
Venice
Walt Disney World
Western Europe

CONTRIBUTING EDITORS

Lawrence Baker, Janet Bennett, Ron Berler, John Bowen, David Breakstone, Bob Brooke, Bob Butler, Carol Cantner, Kevin Causey, Kim Christ, Dan Christopherson, James Cortese, Scott Craven, Teresa Day, Brenda Fine, Sam Fletcher, Kathryn Gress, Laura Hambleton, Helen Heath, Rosemary Peters Hinkle, Dan Hintz, Martin Hintz, Deb Holland, Mark Holland, Bob Hoover, Kate Imbrie, Arline Inge, Bill Jamison, Irene Jerison, Steve Kaplan, Laura Kelly, Elliot S. Krane, Sara Laschever, Pam Lechtman, Wendy Lefkon, Kitty Marciniak, Erica Meltzer, Eleanor Morris, Laurie Nadel, June Naylor, Lawrence Parent, Richard J. Pietschmann, Patricia Tunison Preston, Caryn Reading, Holly Remy, Grace Renshaw, Stacy Ritz, Steve Roberts, Dawna Robertson, Frank Rosci, John Rudolph, William Schemmel, Jennifer Schmits, Joan Scobey, Allan Seiden, Art Siemering, Tracy Smith, Janet Steinberg, Philip Storey, Rick Sylvain, Warren Thompson, Ward Triplett, Ginny Turner, Jan Walker, Abigail Wenger, Loralee Wenger, Leslie Westbrook, Bob Whitaker, Don Woodward, Bill Wrenn, Sonya Zalubowski, Christine Zust

SYMBOLS Gloria McKeown
MAPS B. Andrew Mudryk, Paul J. Puliese

A Stephen Birnbaum Travel Guide

Birnbaum's USA for BUSINESS TRAVELERS 1992

Stephen Birnbaum
Alexandra Mayes Birnbaum
EDITORS

Lois Spritzer
EXECUTIVE EDITOR

Laura L. Brengelman
Managing Editor

Mary Callahan
Ann-Rebecca Laschever
Julie Quick
Beth Schlau
Dana Margaret Schwartz
Associate Editors

 HarperPerennial
A Division of HarperCollins*Publishers*

FIRST EDITION

ISSN: 0749-2561 (Stephen Birnbaum Travel Guides)
ISSN: 0883-251X (USA for Business Travelers)
ISBN: 0-06-278018-2 (pbk.)

91 92 93 94 95 96 CC/HC 10 9 8 7 6 5 4 3 2 1

Contents

A Word from the Editor

If there's one curse common to all business travelers, it's got to be that oft-heard comment of non-traveling associates that goes, "Oh, you've got such a great job; you get to see all of the country/continent/world." Envy seeps through every syllable; the only problem is that the perception of the speaker is almost entirely incorrect.

Anyone who has ever been on the road for business — whether the territory covered domestic or international destinations — knows that jet planes long ago eliminated what little romance ever existed in connection with on-the-job travel. Schedules are more hectic and more compressed, so it's hardly unusual to hear about a busy executive taking advantage of the differences between time zones by leaving New York at 5 o'clock in the afternoon for an 8 PM dinner in Los Angeles, then catching the "Red Eye" back to New York to be at a mid-Manhattan desk by 9 AM (Eastern Time) the next day. It may sound very romantic in the telling, but it's more often the case that travelers arrive feeling stiff, rumpled, and exhausted — rather as though they've been shipped home in a plain white envelope.

Even for a business traveler who actually gets to spend the night in an unfamiliar city, the thought of really looking around is seldom even considered. To begin with, reliable local information is usually notable by its absence, and while the busy business traveler carries a briefcase full of important papers, these documents rarely include any information whatever about local life and environment. There's nothing about a particularly evocative downtown restaurant, or a nearby theater whose regional troupe presents truly notable performances, or a perfect site from which to view a unique panorama of the cityscape. More often, the business traveler moves from airport to taxicab to meeting to hotel, feet seldom touching the ground, and the only non-commercial human contact is an occasional monosyllabic exchange with a room-service waiter. What a waste!

For though contemporary business travel schedules are understandably tight, I suspect that there's often a bit of spare time perfect for working out, taking a peek at a local landmark, or savoring a bite of the regional delicacy — momentarily casting off the pressures of the day. It makes all the difference between having actually *been* to a city or merely having passed through.

Even in the case of business activities — including such simple matters as finding a temporary secretary or a convenient place to make a photocopy — not knowing the city can make awesome endeavors out of otherwise minor chores. Sending a package across town can suddenly seem the equivalent of scaling Everest, while getting a page translated into (or out of) a foreign language borders on the impossible.

The purpose of this special guide for the business traveler is, therefore, to eliminate such frustrations, as well as to give an often harried and harassed stranger a satisfying glimpse of what various cities have to offer — beyond boardrooms and sales calls. We have organized our material into the most manageable size and format, eliminating superfluous data in favor of succinct descriptions of what we think is best and really worth seeing and doing. Scanning the pages that follow should provide insights into each city that are sufficiently specific to make any business traveler's stay more productive — and more enjoyable.

Let me point out that every good travel guide is a living enterprise; that is, no part of this text is in any way cast in bronze. In each annual revision, we will refine, expand, and further hone all our material to serve your needs even better. To this end, no contribution is of greater value to us than your reaction to what we have written as well as information reflecting your experiences while trying our suggestions. We earnestly and enthusiastically solicit your comments on this book *and* your opinions and perceptions about places you have recently visited. In this way, we are able to provide the best sorts of information — including the actual experiences of the traveling public — to make that experience more readily available to others.

We sincerely hope to hear from you, and ask that you address your letters to 60 E. 42nd St., New York, NY 10165.

— STEPHEN BIRNBAUM

Birnbaum's USA for BUSINESS TRAVELERS 1992

ATLANTA

AT-A-GLANCE

SEEING THE CITY: The view from the 70th floor of the *Peachtree Plaza* hotel's revolving *Sun Dial* restaurant is, in a word, spectacular. When the weather is clear, your eye sweeps from the planes arriving and taking off at Hartsfield International Airport (to the south) to the Blue Ridge Mountains (in the north). The *Sun Dial* can be reached only by an 80-second ride in one of the two glass elevators that skim up and down in the glass tubes affixed to the outside of the building. You will have to order something to eat or drink to spend any time there, and it's a good idea to make a reservation first. Open daily till 1:45 AM for cocktails. Peachtree at International Blvd. (phone: 589-7506).

SPECIAL PLACES: You can walk around downtown Atlanta without much difficulty, but be warned, the streets aren't laid out in a neat, orderly grid. They roughly follow the paths of early — and now extinct — rail lines, because the early streets ran parallel to the old tracks. The result is a tangled web that often leaves visitors confused, as much by the erratic pattern as by the fact that at least half the streets seem to be named Peachtree, Circle, or Hills.

The good news is that the public transportation system — *MARTA* — is excellent, especially if you are downtown or near Peachtree Street. Most of *MARTA*'s bus routes begin at rapid-rail stations in the downtown area. Call 848-4711 for information.

DOWNTOWN

Peachtree Center – Designed by celebrated local architect John Portman, Peachtree Center is the heart of modern Atlanta. The ensemble of contemporary buildings includes several office towers; the Atlanta Merchandise Mart and Apparel Mart; and the *Marriott Marquis, Hyatt Regency,* and *Westin Peachtree Plaza* hotels, all linked by aerial skyways and landscaped plazas. The 3-story *Peachtree Center Gallery* offers a variety of shopping, dining, and entertainment options. *MARTA*'s Peachtree Center rapid-rail station is also part of the complex.

Woodruff Park – A few blocks south of Peachtree Center, Woodruff Park is a gift from Atlanta's best-known anonymous donor, the late Coca-Cola millionaire Robert W. Woodruff, whose considerable civic generosity has done more to change the face of the city than cosmetic surgery has done for Hollywood. (Emory University's medical school is another major beneficiary of his largesse.) At lunch, hundreds of office workers, street people, wandering preachers, and Hare Krishna folk swarm into the park — a gentle crowd. Grab a hot dog or a plate of shrimp fried rice at *Tokyo Shapiro's* (62 Peachtree St.), across from the park, and settle down on the grass. Peachtree, Edgewood, Pryor, and Auburn Sts.

APEX Museum (African-American Panoramic Experience Museum) – An excellent introduction to the neighboring Martin Luther King, Jr. National Historic District, this museum focuses on African-American art as well as Atlanta's black history. Permanent displays on

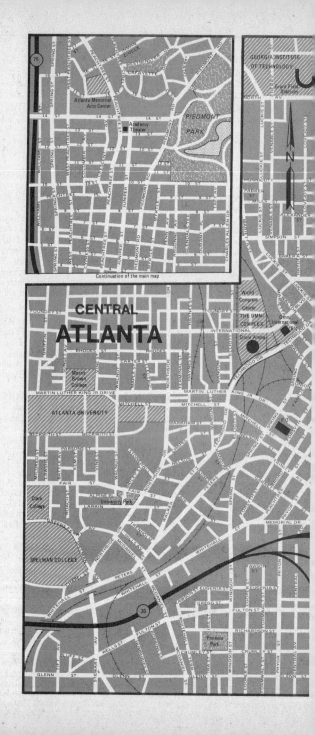

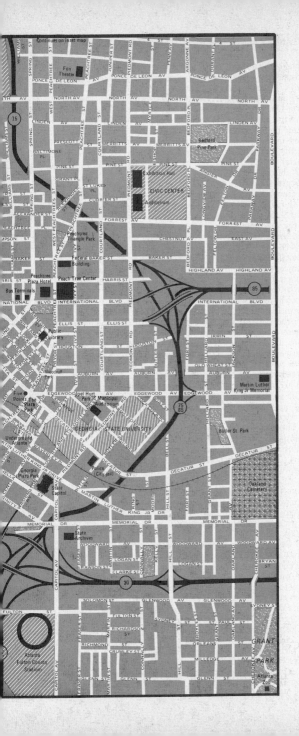

local black culture and African arts and crafts are augmented by changing exhibitions by national and regional artists. Open daily. Admission charge. 135 Auburn Ave. (phone: 521-2654).

Martin Luther King Jr. Historic District – Within a 5-block National Historic District near downtown are sites associated with the life and times of the late Nobel Peace Prize winner. These include his birthplace; Ebenezer Baptist Church, where he preached with his father; his tomb, guarded by an eternal flame and inscribed with the words "Free At Last"; the Interfaith Peace Chapel; a community center; and the Center for Social Change, which displays related papers, films, and memorabilia. Auburn Ave. at Boulevard NE (phone: 524-1956).

Georgia Capitol – Completed in 1889 and crowned by a dome of North Georgia gold, the classically styled capitol contains the governor's office, the *Hall of Fame* with busts of notable Georgians, and the *Museum of Science and Industry.* Visitors may watch democracy in action when the Georgia Assembly convenes from January through March. Guided tours on weekdays. No admission charge. Capitol Sq. (phone: 656-2844).

Federal Reserve Bank – Remember when dollar bills were silver certificates, not Federal Reserve notes? The dollar was worth a dollar in silver then. Not these days. But we're not complaining much — Federal Reserve notes seem to work just as well. To see where they're made, walk over to Marietta Street, 2 blocks east of the CNN Center, and look at the Corinthian-columned Federal Reserve Bank. Although the building is new, the Federal Reserve System's Sixth District headquarters has been here since 1914. Tours of the bank's operations and its *Money Museum* are available on Tuesdays, Wednesdays, and Thursdays, but you must call in advance to schedule a visit. No admission charge. 104 Marietta St. NW (phone: 521-8500).

SciTrek Museum – Atlanta's science and technology museum invites visitors to push buttons, turn cranks and dials, make electricity, and learn the secrets of more than 100 machines and gadgets. Open daily. Admissions charge. Civic Center Exhibition Hall, 395 Piedmont Ave. at Ralph McGill Blvd. (phone: 522-5500).

Fox Theater – One of the last of the opulent 1920s "picture palaces," the beautifully restored *Fox* is a fabulous blend of Egyptian-Moorish-Byzantine-Hollywood design. A vintage movie series, with newsreels and cartoons, is a summer highlight, but the theater's calendar mostly is taken up with touring Broadway musicals and concerts of all sorts. A portion of every ticket sold goes toward ongoing restoration costs. The *Fox* seats 4,518, making it the country's second largest operating theater after *Radio City Music Hall* in New York City. Tours of the hall are conducted daily except Sundays, April through October. Admission varies with the event. Peachtree St. at Ponce de Leon Ave. (phone: 881-2000).

CNN Center, Omni Coliseum, Georgia World Congress Center – Clustered at the southern edge of downtown, the three large structures are the center of the city's convention industry. At CNN Center — a modern megastructure formerly known as Omni International — visitors may tour the Cable News Network studios, watch CNN newscasts, and then enjoy a glass of ale at cheery *Reggie's British Pub.* The deluxe *Omni at CNN Center* hotel at the center's southern end is connected with the Georgia World Congress Center, Atlanta's major convention complex. The adjacent *Omni Coliseum* is the scene of basketball games, rodeos, circuses, and other events (CNN, phone: 827-1500; *Coliseum,* phone: 681-2100; Congress, phone: 656-7600).

Carter Presidential Center – Four connected circular buildings, set among 30 acres of trees, lakes, and Japanese gardens 2 miles east of downtown, contain documents, photos, and memorabilia of Jimmy Carter's White House years. The complex includes the *Jimmy Carter*

Library and Museum. Highlights of the center include a re-creation of the Oval Office, elaborate state gifts to the Carters and other first families, and multimedia presentations on the presidency, human rights, and the environment, among other topics. A gift shop and an attractive restaurant overlook the gardens. Open daily. Admission charge. N. Highland and Cleburne Aves. (phone: 331-0296).

New Georgia Railroad – Vintage steam-powered trains make excursions around the city and to Stone Mountain Park on Saturdays. The Zero Mile Post, next to the New Georgia depot, marks the spot where two rail lines were joined in the northwest Georgia wilderness during the 1830s, giving birth to the city. Dinner served on the train Thursdays, Fridays, and Saturdays. Admission charge. 90 Central Ave., near Underground Atlanta (phone: 656-0769).

Underground Atlanta – The city's most eclectic shopping and amusement area — housing a total of 100 stores and an assortment of 22 bars, restaurants, and nightclubs, and 20 fast-food establishments — reopened in 1989 at a cost of $142 million. After a dismal debut 22 years ago (intended as a symbol of revitalization, the original Underground became a haven for rowdy teenagers and other undesirables and was closed down in 1980), the 3-level (1 aboveground, 2 underground) complex, done in turn-of-the-century style, takes up 6 city blocks. The current incarnation is on the right track — bright, climate-controlled, and secure. Shops, bars, and restaurants open daily from 10 AM until after midnight. Martin Luther King, Jr., Dr. and Peachtree St.

Atlanta Heritage Row – Part of the Underground complex, this museum celebrates Atlanta's colorful past. Exhibits and films located in successive rooms within one building highlight the city's founding as a railroad center in the 1830s; its emergence from the ashes of the Civil War; Dr. Martin Luther King and the civil rights movement; and the city's successful bid for the *1996 Summer Olympic Games.* Open daily. Admission charge. 55 Upper Alabama St. (phone: 584-7879).

World of Coca-Cola Pavilion – A tribute to one of the world's favorite soft drinks. The 3-story facility displays the most innovative outdoor neon sign ever created for the company — an 11-ton extravaganza that hangs 18 feet above the entrance. The pavilion contains more than 1,000 exhibits that chronicle the history of the Coca-Cola Company. A replica of a 1930s vintage soda fountain, complete with a "soda jerk," is part of the exhibit and multimedia and interactive exhibits transport visitors into a Coke-filled future. Open Mondays through Saturdays, 10 AM to 9:30 PM; Sundays, noon to 6 PM. Admission is $2.50 for adults, $2 for senior citizens, $1.50 for children age 6 through 12, and free for children under 6. Martin Luther King, Jr., Dr. and Central Ave. (phone: 676-5151).

ENVIRONS

The Wren's Nest – The charming name was given to this Victorian cottage by its famous owner, Joel Chandler Harris, best known as the creator of Brer Fox, Brer Rabbit, and the other immortal Southern animal characters of the *Uncle Remus* stories. The house has original furnishings and lots of memorabilia from the life of the Atlanta storyteller. Closed Monday. Admission charge. 1050 Gordon SW (phone: 753-7735).

Chattahoochee Nature Center – The center is actually a 7-acre nature preserve on the peaceful banks of the Chattahoochee River, with animal exhibits and classes for both children and adults. Open daily. Admission charge. 9135 Willeo Rd., Roswell, 20 miles north of downtown (phone: 992-2055).

Piedmont Park – Three miles north of downtown, Piedmont is a spacious green place for swimming, tennis, jogging, picnics, and observing Atlantans at leisure. The *Atlanta Arts Festival* is held here annually in early May, and the *Atlanta Symphony* presents outdoor concerts in summer. The Atlanta Botanical Garden, on 60 acres in the park, has greenhouses, a Japanese garden, rose gardens, a Fragrance Garden for the blind, and the new Dorothy Chapman Fugua Conservatory, with hundreds of tropical, desert, and endangered plants. Open daily. Admission charge for botanical garden. Piedmont Ave. between 10th and 14th Sts. (phone: 876-5858).

Zoo Atlanta – An ambitious revitalization program has turned the once-depressing local zoo into an outstanding animal sanctuary. The highlight is the 5-acre Ford African Rain Forest, where several families of silverback gorillas and orangutans live in surroundings strikingly similar to their former natural habitats. The star is silverback Willie B. Open daily. Admission charge. Grant Park, 800 Cherokee Ave., 3 miles from downtown (phone: 624-5678).

Cyclorama – The dramatic circular painting of the Civil War Battle for Atlanta (50 feet high and 400 feet in circumference) has been beautifully restored and enhanced by new sound and lighting effects. Admission charge for both the Cyclorama and the zoo (see above). Grant Park, 800 Cherokee Ave., 3 miles from downtown (phone: 658-7625).

Fernbank Science Center – Often overlooked by non-parents, the center has the Southeast's third-largest planetarium, an observatory, and a nature trail leading through 70 acres of unspoiled forest. A see-and-touch museum, an electronic microscope laboratory, a meteorological laboratory, and an experimental garden also on the premises make this a fascinating place to spend an afternoon. Open daily. Admission charge. 156 Heaton Park Dr. NE (phone: 378-4311).

High Museum of Art – The magnificent building is an architectural masterpiece in its own right, with an exterior of dazzling white enamel tiles and a central atrium flooded with natural light. It houses collections of American, European, and African art and a fine assemblage of decorative arts. Peachtree and 16th Sts. (phone: 892-3600). The *High*'s downtown branch, in the Georgia-Pacific Center, has changing exhibitions of regional, national, and international art. Open weekdays. No admission charge. 133 Peachtree St. (phone: 577-6940).

Robert W. Woodruff Arts Center – Originally dedicated to the 122 Atlanta art patrons who died in a 1962 air crash in Paris, the center was renamed in honor of the Coca-Cola patriarch and arts benefactor. It is the home of the *Atlanta Symphony Orchestra*, the *Alliance Theater*, the *Atlanta Children's Theater*, and the Atlanta College of Art. 1280 Peachtree St. NE (phone: 892-3600).

Atlanta Historical Society – Proceed north along Peachtree Road to West Paces Ferry Road. Turn left and look for Andrews Drive, site of the society's 18-acre complex. Its showpiece is Swan House, built in 1928 and designed by well-known Atlanta architect Philip Shutze in the Anglo-Palladian style. A magnificent exercise in a popular Italian Renaissance mode, it is handsomely furnished in 18th-century antiques, many of which belonged to the former owners, prominent Atlantans Mr. and Mrs. Edward Inman. Also on the grounds is the Tullie Smith house, an authentic 1840s "plantation plain" Georgia farmhouse reconstructed on the property with all its attached buildings. Nearby is the Inmans' coach house, now a pleasant restaurant, gift shop, and art gallery. The *McElreath Memorial Hall*, which houses the society's museum and its extensive collection on Atlanta's history, most of which is available to the public, is here, too. A nature trail has been marked so that you can learn about the region's ecology. Open daily. Admission charge. 3101 Andrews Dr. NW (phone: 261-1837).

Six Flags Over Georgia – Just outside the Perimeter Highway (I-285), this 269-acre amusement park has over 100 rides and live shows, including the Great American Scream Machine (one of the fastest, tallest, and longest roller coasters in the world) and the Great Gasp parachute jump (666 feet tall), which includes a 30-foot free-fall. During the summer, there's a free fireworks display at closing time (11 PM). Open daily, late May through *Labor Day;* weekends, late March through November. Admission charge. 12 miles west of Atlanta on I-20 (phone: 739-3400).

Stone Mountain Park – There's a bit of something for everybody here: a cable car ride to the top, an old steam train, hiking trails, a lake where you can ride a riverboat or canoe, an 18-hole golf course, and an antebellum plantation. And that's not all. This is Mt. Rushmore South. The Confederate heroes Jefferson Davis, Robert E. Lee, and Stonewall Jackson have been drilled into the sheer face of a giant mass of exposed granite. The enormous bas-relief was begun — but not finished — by Gutzon Borglum, who went on to carve Mt. Rushmore. Resort facilities include campgrounds, restaurants, and motels. Open daily. Admission charge. 16 miles northeast of Atlanta on Rte. 78 (phone: 498-5690).

White Water Park – A relaxing relief from Atlanta's steamy summers, this attractive, well-maintained oasis offers a variety of cooling experiences, headed by an enormous wave pool and water slides designed for the adventurous as well as the timid. A children's area has numerous activities for youngsters. There are lockers, showers, snack bars, and a picnic area. Open daily from May to September. Admission charge. At 250 N. Cobb Pkwy. (US 41), Marietta (phone: 424-9283).

Kennesaw Mountain National Battlefield Park – The mountain and 2,800-acre park were the scene of one of the most important engagements in the Battle of Atlanta campaign. Attractions include a Civil War museum and defense lines. Open daily. No admission charge. Off I-75; 25 miles from downtown, near Marietta (phone: 427-4686). Also in the vicinity is the *Big Shanty Museum* in Kennesaw. Its locomotive *General* was involved in a famous Civil War spy chase and was the subject of the Walt Disney movie *Great Locomotive Chase.* Open daily. Admission charge (phone: 427-4686).

American Adventures – A turn-of-the-century theme prevails throughout this charming entertainment park. Indoor and outdoor activities include miniature golf, a go-cart racetrack, a penny arcade, carousels, and other amusements. Open daily. No admission charge to park, but there are individual charges for each attraction. North Cobb Pkwy., Marietta, off I-75 at exit 13 (phone: 424-9283).

Tara – Just about everybody comes to Atlanta looking for the legendary white-columned mansion. But, alas, Tara never existed, except in Margaret Mitchell's imagination and on David O. Selznick's movie sets. *Gone With the Wind* is shown frequently at *CNN Cinemas* (CNN Center downtown; phone: 577-6928). Memorabilia and foreign editions of *GWTW* are on display in the Margaret Mitchell Room of the Atlanta Public Library, Peachtree and Forsyth Sts. (phone: 730-1700).

■ **EXTRA SPECIAL:** Just 35 miles northeast of Atlanta, Lanier Islands have been developed into a resort area. The 1,200 acres of hills and woods contain golf courses, tennis courts, and horseback riding and camping facilities. There also are sailboats and houseboats for rent. (Manmade Lake Lanier has 540 miles of shoreline.) Stouffer's *Pine Isle Resort* hotel is on the grounds, too. Open daily. A parking permit is $3 daily. On I-85 (Lanier Islands information, phone: 945-6701).

SOURCES AND RESOURCES

TOURIST INFORMATION: For general information, brochures, and maps, contact the Atlanta Chamber of Commerce (235 International Blvd., Atlanta, GA 30303; phone: 880-9000) or Atlanta Convention and Visitors Bureau (235 Peachtree St. NE, Suite 1414; phone: 521-6600). Exhibitions on Georgia tourism and industry are at the World Congress Center (Marietta and Magnolia Sts. NW; phone: 656-7600). A covered pedestrian bridge links the center to the *Omni International* hotel. Foreign visitors information is available from the Georgia Council for International Visitors (999 Peachtree St.; phone: 873-6170). Contact the Georgia state hotline (phone: 404-656-3590) for maps, calendars of events, health updates, and travel advisories.

Georgia Off the Beaten Path (Globe Pequot Press, 1989; $8.95) offers an insider's look at attractions, dining, nightlife, and shopping in Atlanta and elsewhere in Georgia.

Local Coverage – *Atlanta Constitution,* morning daily; *Atlanta Journal,* evening daily; *Atlanta* magazine, monthly.

■ **Note:** CNN (Cable News Network), which has emerged as a strong competitor in the network news race, has its headquarters at 1 CNN Center (phone: 827-1500). Its thorough and dedicated news reporting during the war in the Gulf in 1991 transformed its status; millions of viewers now tune in daily.

Television Stations – WSB Channel 2–ABC; WAGA Channel 5–CBS; WXIA Channel 11–NBC.

Radio Stations – AM: WSB 750 (contemporary music); WGST 920 (news/talk). FM: WABE 90 (classical music/news); WCLK 91.9 (jazz); WVEE 103.3 (urban contemporary).

Food – *Atlanta* magazine contains listings of most of the established restaurants and some newcomers. The Weekend section of the combined Saturday *Atlanta Journal-Constitution* offers complete dining, entertainment, and special events listings.

TELEPHONE: The area code for Atlanta is 404.
  Sales Tax – State and city sales tax is 6%; the hotel tax is 13%.

CLIMATE: Atlanta's temperatures vary from moderate winters to comfortable springs and falls to hot and humid summers. Winter is generally mild, but temperatures occasionally do drop to near zero, with sleet and light snow. May, September, October, and November tend to be the sunniest months. While Atlanta isn't exactly what you'd call dry, the average humidity hovers at 60%, which isn't intolerable either.

GETTING AROUND: Airport – Atlanta is served by Hartsfield International Airport, one of the world's largest and busiest. The airport's two terminals (North and South) are connected by a speedy and efficient subway system with trains that run every 2 minutes. Except during rush hours, it's about a 20-minute trip between the airport and downtown. (Changing traffic patterns make it easier to get *to* the airport in the morning and *from* the airport to downtown in late afternoon.) The flat taxi rate from the airport to downtown hotels is $15 for one person, $16 for two, $17 for three. *Atlanta Airport Shuttle* vans (phone: 766-5312) charge $8 one way, $14 round trip to downtown hotels, and $12 one way, $20 round trip to Emory University and Lenox Square. *Northside Airport Express* (phone: 455-1600) has bus service to several suburban terminals for $15 each way. Travelers without much luggage can take *MARTA* (*Metropolitan Atlanta Rapid Transit Authority*) trains from the airport to downtown in about 12 minutes for $1 one way (call 848-4711 for information).

Bus – *MARTA* is the backbone of Atlanta's public transportation system. Bus routes interlace the city, with frequent stops at downtown locations. Exact fare ($1) required. A new rapid-rail system now runs 12 miles east-west and 12 miles north-south, connecting at the Five Points station downtown. When complete, the system will have 60 miles of tunnel and grade-level track. Each station has been designed by a different architect and decorated with murals, photos, and collages. *MARTA* maintains information booths at the intersection of Peachtree and West

Peachtree, near the *Hyatt Regency* hotel and at Broad and Walton NE (phone: 848-4711).

Car Rental – All major national firms are represented.

Taxi – Atlanta isn't known for its efficient taxi services. Many are unclean, mechanically suspect, and often manned by drivers unfamiliar with local geography. *Yellow Cab* (phone: 521-0200) and *London Taxi* (phone: 681-2280) are among the more reliable.

 VITAL SERVICES: Audiovisual Equipment – *Southern Business Communications* (6090 McDonough Dr.; phone: 449-4088); *Corporate Audio-Visual Services* (580 Dutch Valley Rd.; phone: 881-8234).

Business Services – *Team Concept,* 1925 Century Center NE (phone: 325-9754).

Dry Cleaner/Tailor – *One-Hour Valet,* 64 Peachtree St. (phone: 584-0254).

Limousine – *Atlanta Livery* (620 Peachtree St., Suite 300; phone: 872-8282); *Davis Limousine Service* (446 Martin St. SE; phone: 524-3413).

Mechanics – *Don Davis Gulf Service* (359 W. Ponce de Leon Ave., Decatur; phone: 378-6751); *Joe Winkler's Gulf Station* (2794 Clairmont Rd. NE; phone: 636-2940).

Medical Emergency – *Piedmont Hospital,* 1968 Peachtree Rd., NE (phone: 350-3297).

Messenger Services – *Central Delivery Service* (phone: 892-1350); *Flash Courier Service* (phone: 873-5052).

National/International Courier – *Federal Express* (phone: 321-7566); *DHL Worldwide Courier Express* (phone: 997-1635).

Pharmacy – *Treasury Drug Store,* open 24 hours; Ponce de Leon Ave. NE at N. Highland, about 3 miles from downtown (phone: 876-0381).

Photocopies – *Kinko's* (Peachtree and 5th Sts.; phone: 876-4752); *Center Office Supply & Printing* (225 Peachtree St.; phone: 681-3889).

Post Office – Downtown, 240 Peachtree St (phone: 522-1196).

Professional Photographer – *Ron Sherman Photography* (340 Spring Creek Rd., Roswell; phone: 993-5491); *Richard Magruder Photography* (2156 Snapfinger Rd., Decatur; phone: 289-8985).

Secretary/Stenographer – *Norrell Services* (phone: 525-5451); *The Message Board* (phone: 688-6505).

Teleconference Facilities – *Atlanta Hilton, Hyatt Regency, Westin Peachtree Plaza, Radisson Inn* (see *Checking In* for all).

Translator – *Berlitz* (phone: 261-5062); *International Language School Service* (phone: 252-3829).

Typewriter Rental – *Atlanta Typewriter Co.,* 1-week minimum (phone: 892-7585).

Western Union/Telex – 2221 Peachtree Rd. (phone: 350-9177 or 800-325-6000).

Other – *Peachtree Suite Word Processing* (phone: 525-8221); *Tourgals* (phone: 262-7660) and *Presenting Atlanta,* convention services and consultants (phone: 231-0200).

 SPECIAL EVENTS: The best time to visit Atlanta is during the spring *Dogwood Festival,* the second week in April, when the city explodes in color and celebration (phone: 525-6145). During the summer months, the *Atlanta Symphony Orchestra* plays outdoors in Piedmont Park on Sunday evenings. The *Arts Festival of Atlanta* takes place in Piedmont Park in September, as does the *Atlanta Greek Festival,* a potpourri of Greek costumes, movies, gifts, art, dances, and food (Greek Orthodox Cathedral of the Annunciation, 2500 Clairmont Rd. NE; phone: 633-5870). For those who regard beautiful flower gardens an event at any time of the year, visit the tranquil *Callaway Gardens* in Pine Mountain, Georgia (phone: 663-2281 or 800-282-8181).

MUSEUMS: The *Jimmy Carter Library and Museum,* the *Fernbank Science Center,* the *Hall of Fame* and *Museum of Science and Industry* in the capitol, the *High Museum of Art,* the *McElreath Memorial Hall,* the *Money Museum,* the *APEX Museum,* the *SciTrek Museum,* the *Woodruff Arts Center,* and the *World of Coca-Cola Pavilion* are described in *Special Places.* Another museum of note is:

Emory University Museum of Art and Archaeology – Greek and Roman coins, amphora, an Egyptian mummy; art ranging from the American Southwest to Southeast Asia, China, and Japan; and works by Dali, Kandinsky, and Matisse are displayed in this attractive museum. Closed Sundays and Mondays. No admission charge. Emory University, N. Decatur and Oxford Rds. (phone: 727-7522).

 MAJOR COLLEGES AND UNIVERSITIES: There are eight important institutions of higher education in the metro area, each contributing to the cultural, as well as the academic, climate. They are Clark Atlanta University (223 Chestnut SW; phone: 880-8000); Atlanta College of Art (1280 Peachtree NE; phone: 898-1164); Agnes Scott College (E. College Dr., Decatur; phone: 371-6285); Emory University (famous for its medical program; 1380 S. Oxford Rd. NE; phone: 727-6123); Georgia Institute of Technology (225 North Ave. NW; phone: 894-2500); Georgia State University (University Plaza NE; phone: 651-2000); Interdenominational Theological Center (671 Beckwith SW; phone: 527-7700); and Oglethorpe University (4484 Peachtree Rd. NE; phone: 261-1441).

SHOPPING: Atlanta offers a taste of Fifth Avenue, Rodeo Drive, and the rainbow's end. Huge department stores, malls, galleries, food and flea markets, and antiques centers offer a world of tempting merchandise. Upscale shopping abounds in the affluent Buckhead neighborhood, along Peachtree Road, and about 6 to 8 miles north of downtown, where local branches of *Gucci, Tiffany, Neiman Marcus, Saks Fifth Avenue,* and *Lord & Taylor* are the venerable institutions for southern spending. In *Underground Atlanta*'s festival-style downtown complex, scores of shops and vending carts feature apparel, gifts, food, and wine. The reborn in-town neighborhood of Virginia/Highland is a place to shop for antiques, high fashion, African, Latin, and Irish imports, and other offbeat items. Shops are interspersed by trendy and ethnic restaurants and bars.

DeKalb Farmers Market – This enormous indoor market, which extends over 3 blocks, all but bursts with stalls of exotic fruits, seafood, herbs, spices, breads, and other delicacies from around the world. Patrons and clerks jointly form a mini-United Nations. 3000 E. Ponce de Leon Ave., Decatur (phone: 377-6400).

Lenox Square – Atlanta's splashiest mall, where *Neiman Marcus, Macy's, Alfred Dunhill Tobacco Shop, Benetton, Burberry's,* and numerous California, European, and New York specialty shops reside. And if you'd like a rest between eye-gorging expeditions, there are numerous restaurants and bars from which to choose. Peachtree and Lenox Rds. (phone: 233-6767).

Muse's – Fashionable men's and women's togs with a conservative bent. 52 Peachtree St. (phone: 522-5400).

Peachtree Center – A more unusual array of shops, as well as old standbys, like *Brooks Brothers,* office buildings, *Hyatt Regency* and *Marriott Marquis* hotels, and the *MARTA* Peachtree Center rapid rail station. 225 Peachtree St. (phone: 659-0800).

SPORTS AND FITNESS: A major league city, Atlanta is the home of the *Braves* and the nest of the *Falcons* and *Hawks.*
Baseball – Atlanta *Braves* play at *Atlanta–Fulton County Stadium,* 521 Capitol Ave. SW (phone: 522-7630).

Basketball – The Atlanta *Hawks'* home games are played at the *Omni*, 100 Techwood Dr. NW (phone: 827-3800).

Bicycling – Bikes (and roller skates) may be rented at *Skate Escape*, 1086 Piedmont Ave. NE, across from Piedmont Park (phone: 892-1292).

Fishing – There's good fishing at Lake Allatoona, Lake Lanier, and Lake Jackson. Fishing permits are necessary and can be purchased at *K-Mart, Wal-Mart,* and at hunting and fishing supply stores.

Fitness Centers – The *YMCA* (phone: 588-9622) has modern health centers throughout the metro area. *Colony Square Athletic Club* offers racquetball and aerobics classes (1197 Peachtree at 14th St.; phone: 881-1632).

Football – The Atlanta *Falcons* (phone: 261-5400) play at the *Atlanta–Fulton County Stadium.*

Golf – The best public courses are at *Stone Mountain Park* (phone: 498-5690) and *Bobby Jones Golf Course* (384 Woodward Way; phone: 355-1009).

Jogging – Run along Peachtree Street or Piedmont Road to Piedmont Park, about 1½ miles, and enter at 10th or 14th Street; roads in the park are closed to traffic. You also can run just past 14th Street to the Ansley Park and Sherwood Forest areas of Atlanta and along the wide residential streets. For more information, call *Atlanta Track Club* (phone: 231-9064).

Tennis – The best clay courts are at the *Bitsy Grant Tennis Center* (2125 Northside Dr. NW; phone: 351-2774). Lanier Islands and Stone Mountain have good outdoor tennis courts, too. There are excellent public courts at the *Blackburn Tennis Center* (3501 Ashford-Dunwoody Rd.; phone: 451-1061) and at the *DeKalb Tennis Center* (off Clairmont Rd., in suburban Decatur; phone: 325-2520).

Whitewater Rafting – Burt Reynolds (with some help from poet and novelist James Dickey) made North Georgia whitewater famous in the movie *Deliverance.* For an urban alternative, rent a raft at the Chattahoochee River Park at Highway 41 in NW Atlanta during the summer.

THEATER: For complete performance schedules, check the local publications listed above. Among the best-known theatrical companies are the *Alliance Theater* and *Studio Theater* at the *Woodruff Arts Center* (Peachtree and 15th Sts.; phone: 892-2414); and *Theatrical Outfit* (Peachtree and 10th Sts.; phone: 872-0665). *Seven Stages Theater* (1105 Euclid Ave.; phone: 522-0911) offers topical, offbeat plays. The *Center for Puppetry Arts* (1404 Spring St.; phone: 873-3089) has performances and exhibitions. The nationally honored *Atlanta Ballet* (phone: 892-3303) has a repertoire of classical and contemporary works. *Agatha's A Taste of Mystery* (693 Peachtree St.; phone: 875-1610) is a dinner-theater where intrigue and suspense luckily are served after your meal.

MUSIC: The *Atlanta Symphony Orchestra* (phone: 892-3600) plays virtually year-round at the *Woodruff Arts Center* and gives a variety of indoor and outdoor concerts. Chamber music groups include the *Atlanta Virtuosi* (phone: 938-8611) and *Atlanta Chamber Players* (phone: 892-8681).

NIGHTCLUBS AND NIGHTLIFE: Atlanta's nightlife covers the spectrum, with most places open nightly until 3 or 4 AM. There's excellent jazz at *Dante's Down the Hatch* (Underground Atlanta; phone: 577-1800; and 3380 Peachtree St.; phone: 266-1600). Blues heads the menu at *Blues Harbor* (Underground Atlanta; phone: 524-3001). Name comedians are featured at *The Punch Line* (280 Hildebrand Dr.; phone: 252-LAFF). *Blind Willie's* (830 N. Highland Ave.; phone: 873-2583) highlights New Orleans blues and food; *County Cork Pub* (52 E. Andrews Dr.; phone: 262-2227) has Irish singers. British ales, darts, and a sing-along piano draw big crowds to *Churchill Arms,* across the street from the *County Cork* (phone: 233-5633). Cabaret-style shows are presented at *Upstairs at Gene and Gabe's* (1578 Piedmont Rd.; phone: 892-2261). The best places to meet and mingle are *Peachtree Café* (268 E. Paces Ferry Rd.; phone: 233-4402) and *J. Paul's* (3060 Peachtree St.; phone: 233-4840). The most convivial old-fashioned neighborhood bars are *Manuel's Tavern* (602 N. Highland Ave.; phone: 525-3447) and *P.J. Haley's Club* (1799 Briarcliff Rd.; phone: 874-3116). *Reggie's British Pub* (in the CNN Center, downtown; phone: 525-1437) is a jolly good spot for a glass of ale, a steak-and-kidney pie, and a rousing game of darts. The *Cotton Club* (1021 Peachtree St.; phone: 874-2523) is a high-energy forum for the latest pop, rock, blues, and jazz.

BEST IN TOWN

CHECKING IN: Today, Atlanta visitors can pick and choose from among one of the broadest accommodations assortments in the country. The largest selections are in the downtown convention district; the uptown Buckhead commercial area, near Hartsfield International Airport, and in commercial areas such as *I-285/Perimeter Mall* in northern DeKalb County and the *Cumberland Mall/Galleria* area of Cobb County. Remember to book early from fall through spring, when major conventions may virtually have everything locked up. It's also possible to stay in a bed and breakfast establishment very inexpensively. These are private homes, all of which rent rooms with adjacent baths, and they're scattered throughout the city. For information and reservations: *Bed & Breakfast Atlanta* (1801 Piedmont Ave. NE, Suite 208, Atlanta 30324; phone: 875-0525). Expect to pay $100 and up for a double in hotels we've classified as expensive; between $60 and $80 at places in the moderate category; under $60 in inexpensive places. All telephone numbers are in the 404 area code unless otherwise indicated. All hotels carry CNN (Cable News Network).

Atlanta Hilton & Towers – The 3-winged, 30-story, 1,250-room building has a group of small courtyards, each 7 stories tall. Restaurants at the top include *Trader Vic's* and *Nikolai's Roof* (see *Eating Out*). The hotel provides 144 rooms for guests in wheelchairs or with other disabilities. Amenities include a health club, pool, 49 meeting rooms, concierge, A/V equipment, photocopiers, computers, and express checkout. 255 Courtland St. (phone: 659-2000; 800-445-8667; Telex: 804370; Fax: 404-222-2868). Expensive.

Hyatt Regency – This John Portman-designed hotel provoked the interior atrium craze in the mid-1960s. Each of the 1,358 rooms in the main building has an outside balcony as well as a window overlooking the inner atrium. The adjoining tower has 200 additional rooms. The 327-foot-high revolving rooftop restaurant, *Polaris,* is reached via glass elevator. Amenities include a concierge, 37 meeting rooms, secretarial services, A/V equipment, photocopiers, computers, AP-Dow Jones business news, and express checkout. 265 Peachtree NE (phone: 577-1234; 800-233-1234; Telex: 542485; Fax: 404-588-4137). Expensive.

Nikko Atlanta – Asian elegance and luxury are highly visible in this 440-room, Japanese-owned hotel which debuted in 1990. One of its restaurants, *Cassis,* serves French and Mediterranean dishes, while its other eatery, *Kamogawa,* proffers Japanese fare. Amenities include a health club, pool, concierge, conference center, secretarial services, A/V equipment, photocopiers, computers, and express checkout. 3300 Peachtree Rd. (phone: 365-8100; 800-NIKKO-US; Fax: 404-233-5686). Expensive.

Omni at CNN Center – Attached to the CNN Center mega-structure, it has a surprisingly dignified atmosphere. Many of the 500 rooms, furnished with discreet, European charm, have balconies overlooking all or part of the 14-story, 5½-acre *Omni* atrium. Amenities include a concierge desk, 18 meeting rooms, secretarial services, A/V equipment, photocopiers, computers, and express checkout. Marietta St. and Techwood Dr. (phone: 659-0000; 800-843-6665; Fax: 404-659-1621). Expensive.

Ritz-Carlton, Atlanta – With its European decor and elegant extras, this luxury property, with 472 rooms, is especially attractive to those whose business takes them to the nearby downtown financial district. It's right next door to the Georgia-Pacific Center. The *Dining Room* is one of the city's leading restaurants (see *Eating Out*). Amenities include 24-hour room service, concierge, 15 meeting rooms, secretarial services, A/V equipment, photocopiers, computers, and express checkout. 181 Peachtree St. NE (phone: 659-0400; 800-241-3333; Telex: 543291; Fax: 404-688-0400). Expensive.

Ritz-Carlton, Buckhead – Probably Atlanta's most fashionable stopping place; the plush dining rooms (see *Eating Out*) and lounges are *the* places to see and be seen by local and visiting celebrities. The 574 rooms and suites are handsomely appointed. In the heart of the city's most upscale shopping, dining, and nightlife neighborhood. Amenities include an indoor pool and health club, 24-hour room service, concierge, 26 meeting rooms, secretarial services, A/V equipment, photocopiers, computers, and express checkout. 3434 Peachtree Rd. NW (phone: 237-2700; 800-241-3333; Telex: 549521; Fax: 404-239-0078). Expensive.

Stouffer Waverly – In the heart of a suburban shopping and office complex, this deluxe, 545-room property has first class dining, entertainment, and shopping, as well as a complete health club. Amenities include 24-hour room service, concierge, 22 meeting rooms, secretarial services, A/V equipment, photocopiers, and express checkout. 2450 Galleria Pkwy. NW (phone: 953-4500; 800-468-3571; Telex: 804323; Fax: 404-589-7586). Expensive.

Swisshôtel Atlanta – Elegant and efficient Swiss hotel-keeping and Biedermeier-style furnishings classify this newly opened, 358-room property as top-drawer. This establishment's dining spots prepare both international and American dishes. Amenities include 24-hour room service, concierge, 15 meeting rooms, secretarial services, A/V equipment, photocopiers, computers, and express checkout. 3391 Peachtree Rd. (phone: 365-0065; Fax: 404-365-8787). Expensive.

Westin Peachtree Plaza – The world's tallest hotel, this 73-story structure has a half-acre lagoon in its 7-story lobby, which has recently undergone much-needed renovations. Regrettably, the 1,124 guestrooms in its glass silo are far less spacious and most are barely adequate. Atop the cylindrical structure is the *Sun Dial* restaurant and lounge, our choice for the best bird's-eye view of the city and the surrounding countryside, though better food can be found in the hotel's *Savannah Fish Company* restaurant (see *Eating Out*). Amenities include 24-hour room service, concierge, 40 meeting rooms, A/V equipment, photocopiers, computers, and express checkout. 210 Peachtree St. (phone: 659-1400; 800-228-3000; Telex: 804323; Fax: 404-589-7586). Expensive.

Comfort Inn Downtown – Formerly the *Ibis* hotel, this 260-room property has attractive facilities, a restaurant, a lounge, and a pool. Amenities include small meeting rooms and photocopiers. 101 International Blvd. (phone: 524-5555; 800-535-0707; Fax: 404-221-0702). Expensive to moderate.

Atlanta Peachtree TraveLodge – For those looking for a smaller place, this 56-room facility might do. It's not elegant, but it is comfortable. A swimming pool, too. 1641 Peachtree St. (phone: 873-5731). Moderate.

Dunwoody – Formerly the *Radisson Dunwoody,* this 391-room motor hotel is convenient to the northeast metro area's business district. Two outdoor swimming pools grace the property, as well as tennis courts, a restaurant, and a lounge. Amenities include 12 meeting rooms, A/V equipment, and photocopiers. I-285 at Chamblee-Dunwoody Rd. exit (phone: 394-5000; Fax: 404-394-5000, ext. 7698). Moderate.

Days Inn – The Atlanta-based chain offers basic, clean accommodations at very reasonable rates. Most inns (actually very conventional hotels and motels) have a swimming pool, playground, family restaurant, color TV sets; some have kitchenettes. Ten Atlanta locations, and the high-rise downtown, a block from the *Peachtree Plaza* (300 Spring St.; phone: 523-1144), may be the best value in the city. For information on the others, call 320-2000 or 800-325-2525. Moderate to inexpensive.

EATING OUT: Atlanta's hundreds of restaurants, cafés, and trendy grills and bistros specialize in everything from traditional Southern home cooking to American regional dishes and an astonishing variety of international cuisines. Two people can expect to pay between $80 and $100 for dinner in restaurants in our expensive category; from $45 to $75 in the moderate range; and $20 to $35 in the inexpensive category. Prices do not include wine, drinks, or tips. All telephone numbers are in the 404 area code unless otherwise indicated.

Bone's – The place in town for prime beef and fresh seafood in clubby, convivial surroundings. It's very popular among executives and savvy out-of-towners. Lunch on weekdays only; dinner daily. Reservations advised. Major credit cards accepted. 3130 Piedmont Rd. (phone: 237-2663). Expensive.

La Grotta – An elegant Northern Italian dining room. Delicious veal, pasta, and seafood dishes are matched by some of Atlanta's most professional service. Dinner only; closed Sundays. Reservations advised. Major credit cards accepted. Two locations: 2637 Peachtree Rd. NE (phone: 231-1368) and 647 Atlanta St. (US 19), Roswell (phone: 998-0645). Expensive.

Hedgerose Heights Inn – Pheasant, veal, beef, seafood, and fowl are served with either a French, Swiss, or German flair, and complemented by a fine wine list and very good service. Dinner only; closed Sundays and Mondays. Reservations advised. Major credit cards accepted. 490 E. Paces Ferry Rd. (phone: 233-7673). Expensive.

Nikolai's Roof – With decor and atmosphere suggesting Czarist opulence, the *Atlanta Hilton*'s rooftop restaurant was originally intended to heighten the establishment's prestige, not to serve as a big money-making operation — which is why it seats only 67 diners. Waiters dressed in Cossack attire recite the evening's five-course menu from memory. The food is French, but then the old Russian courts were also shamelessly Francophilic. Open daily; dinner only. Reservations advised. Major credit cards accepted. *Atlanta Hilton,* Courtland and Harris NE (phone: 659-2000). Expensive.

103 West – A creative array of richly sauced dishes and superior wines are complemented by Victorian floral prints, potted palms, and marble-topped tables. A memorable dining experience. Dinner only; closed Sundays. Reservations advised. Major credit cards accepted. 103 West Paces Ferry Rd. (phone: 233-5993). Expensive.

Pano's & Paul's – A classy spot hidden in a shopping center. Continental and American food is served, but the kitchen promises it will prepare anything if requested far enough in advance. Dinner only; closed Sundays. Reservations advised. Major credit cards accepted. *West Paces Shopping Center* (phone: 261-3662). Expensive.

Patio By the River – Enviably situated on the banks of the Chattahoochee River, it marries a pretty setting of Regency antiques and white lace napery to expert French cooking. Grilled salmon with shallot brown butter sauce and triple-cut lamb chops are standouts. Closed Sundays; no lunch Saturdays. Reservations advised. Major credit cards accepted. 4199 Paces Ferry Rd. NW (phone: 432-2808). Expensive.

Ritz-Carlton, Buckhead – Dinner here is a carefully orchestrated affair, with menus composed by Chef Guenter Seeger. The food is creative and memorable — melon soup with lobster and mint, rack of lamb with Vidalia onions and tomato coulis, and for dessert, cherries gratinéed with cinnamon ice cream. Closed Sundays. Reservations advised. Major credit cards accepted. 3340 Peachtree Rd. NE (phone: 237-2700). Expensive.

Savannah Fish Company – Fish and shellfish, flown in fresh from the Gulf of Mexico, the Pacific, and the North Atlantic, are the hallmark of this cozy restaurant in the *Peachtree Plaza* hotel. Open daily. Reservations for lunch only. Major credit cards accepted. Peachtree St. and International Blvd. (phone: 589-7456). Expensive.

Chef's Café – One of Atlanta's exemplary small eating places, with sensational crab cakes, homemade soup, rich pasta, unusual sandwiches, and salads. Dinner daily, with a Sunday brunch. Reservations advised. Major credit cards accepted. 2115 Piedmont Rd. (phone: 872-2284). Expensive to moderate.

Morton's of Chicago – Steaks and lots of them are the raison d'être of this Chicago steakhouse offshoot. The porterhouse weighs in at 24 ounces and comes with a suitably sized doggie bag. The grilled fish, veal, and lamb chops are all excellent. Lunch served on weekdays; dinner daily. Reservations advised. Major credit cards accepted. Marquis One Tower, 245 Peachtree Center Ave. (phone: 577-4366). Expensive to moderate.

Azalea – Trendy fare that imaginatively fuses dishes from Italy, Thailand, China, and California to produce some unorthodox but delicious alliances. Dinner daily. No reservations. Major credit cards accepted. 3167 Peachtree Rd. (phone: 237-9939). Moderate.

Buckhead Diner – Gleaming stainless steel, neon, and leather are the signatures of this sleek, super-chic 1990s eatery that has become a haven for the city's movers and shakers and hip out-of-towners. The menu is a trendy array of pasta, salads, seafood, and meat entrées. Valet parking. Open daily. No reservations. Major credit cards accepted. 3073 Piedmont Rd. (phone: 262-3336). Moderate.

Camille's – Perpetually packed, very New Yorkish Italian café, serving big platters of pasta, seafood, veal, and chicken dishes in rich red sauces. In warm weather, take a sidewalk table and watch the crowd go by. Open daily for dinner. No reservations. Major credit cards accepted. 1186 N. Highland Ave. (phone: 872-7203). Moderate.

Dante's Down the Hatch – A late-night niche with a faithful coterie. Jazz lovers come to hear *Paul Mitchell's Trio* and assorted combos. The fondue/wine/cheese menu is an attraction on its own, and so is owner Dante Stephenson, who's usually there to recommend a vintage from his personally selected list. Open daily for dinner. Reservations advised. Major credit cards accepted. 3380 Peachtree Rd. (phone: 266-1600) and Underground Atlanta (phone: 577-1800). Moderate.

Gojinka – It's Atlanta's most authentic Japanese restaurant, claim local and visiting Asians, who rave about the sushi and sashimi. Very good tempura, sukiyaki, and yakitori, too. Dinner daily; closed Sundays. No reservations. Major credit cards accepted. 5269 Buford Hwy., *Pinetree Plaza Shopping Center,* Doraville (phone: 458-0558). Moderate.

Indigo Coastal Grill – Like a laid-back trip to the Caribbean, this spiffy little neighborhood café specializes in fresh seafood, conch chowder, and Key lime pie. Dinner daily; closed Sundays. No reservations. Major credit cards accepted. 1409 N. Highland Ave. (phone: 876-0676). Moderate.

Lombardi's – Underground Atlanta's best full-service restaurant. A very good range of Italian dishes and a great wine list are served in a cheerful, low-key setting. Lunch and dinner daily. No reservations. Major credit cards accepted. Upper Level, Underground Atlanta (phone: 522-6568). Moderate.

Partners Morningside Café – In a small room decorated with artworks, an upwardly mobile crowd dines on seafood and pasta. Closed Mondays. No reservations. Major credit cards accepted. 1397 Highland Ave. (phone: 875-0202). Moderate.

The Peasant Group – Some of Atlanta's favorite dining places are among the locally owned *Peasant* restaurants, which feature innovative American/continental meals served in a stylish and relaxed atmosphere. The group includes: the *Pleasant Peasant* (555 Peachtree St.; phone: 874-3223); the *Country Place* (Colony Sq., Peachtree and 14th Sts.; phone: 881-0144); *Dailey's* (17 International Blvd., downtown; phone: 681-3303); *Winfield's* (100 Galleria Pkwy., Smyrna; phone: 955-5300); *Buck's* (Underground Atlanta; phone: 525-2825; and 116 E. Ponce de Leon Ave., Decatur; phone: 373-7797); the *Peasant Uptown* (Phipps Plaza, Peachtree and Lenox Rds.; phone: 261-6341); and the *Public House* (605 Atlanta St., Roswell; phone: 992-4646). Check each location for its operating days. No reservations. Major credit cards accepted. Moderate.

Sierra Grill – A contemporary Southwestern café serving an inventive menu of grilled quail and smoked chicken soup, among other tangy delights. The ambience is bright with folk art from New Mexico and Arizona lining the walls. Open daily; no lunch Saturdays or Sundays. Reservations for large groups advised. Major credit cards accepted. 1529 Piedmont Rd. at Monroe Dr. (phone: 873-5630). Moderate.

Skeeter's Mesquite Grill – Texas steakhouse, complete with country and western on the jukebox and faded denim on the patrons. Though the emphasis is on steaks, the grilled Cajun redfish is pretty tasty. Open daily. No reservations. Major credit cards accepted. 2892 N. Druid Hills Rd. (phone: 636-3817) and 3505 Satellite Blvd., Duluth (phone: 476-3131). Moderate.

A Taste of New Orleans – Delectable creole and Cajun dishes done with a traditional French Quarter flair in a casually sophisticated atmosphere. Open daily for dinner. No reservations. Major credit cards accepted. 889 W. Peachtree St. (phone: 874-5535). Moderate.

Honto – Hong Kong–style seafood dishes lure local Asians and other fanciers of Asian cooking for such delicacies as Dungeness crab with ginger and scallions, mussels in black bean sauce, and salt-and-pepper squid. Open daily. No reservations. Major credit cards accepted. 3295 Chamblee-Dunwoody Rd. (phone: 458-8088). Moderate to inexpensive.

Colonnade – A cheerful local landmark that's renowned for its friendly service and delicious steaks, seafood, fried chicken, vegetables, and other American and Southern favorites. Open daily. No reservations or credit cards accepted. 1879 Cheshire Bridge Rd. (phone: 874-5642). Inexpensive.

Dai Nam Vietnamese Cuisine – This shopping center hideaway presents first-rate Vietnamese fare. The mussels are a delicious treat. Open daily. No reservations. No credit cards accepted. *Parkside Shopping Center,* 5920 Roswell Rd. (phone: 256-2340). Inexpensive.

Delectables – One of downtown's best little luncheon cafés, this attractive eatery — on the lower level of the Atlanta-Fulton Public Library — specializes in sandwiches, homemade soup, salads, and pastries. Lunch only; closed Saturday and Sunday. No reservations or credit cards accepted. 1 Margaret Mitchell Square, at the corner of Carnegie Way and Fairlie St. (phone: 681-2909). Inexpensive.

Harold's Barbecue – This quintessential Southern barbecue shack is a local legend for its grilled pork and beef sandwiches and hearty Brunswick stew. Closed Sundays. No reservations or credit cards accepted. 171 McDonough Blvd. (phone: 627-9268). Inexpensive.

Huey's – An upbeat café with an outdoor terrace, featuring New Orleans gumbo, po' boys, coffee, and beignets (deep-fried New Orleans doughnuts). Popular late-night retreat. Open daily. No reservations or credit cards accepted. 1816 Peachtree Rd. (phone: 873-2037). Inexpensive.

King & I – Spicy, exotic Thai dishes have made this friendly place a popular destination for adventurous Atlantans. Open daily. No reservations. Major credit cards accepted. Ansley Sq. at Piedmont Ave. and Monroe Dr. (phone: 892-7743). Inexpensive.

Mary Mac's Tea Room – Southern home cooking, chapter and verse. State-of-the-art fried chicken, turnip greens, cornbread, cobblers, and other traditional southern favorites are prepared to perfection in a maze of bustling dining rooms. Open for lunch and dinner on weekdays only. No reservations or credit cards accepted. 224 Ponce de Leon Ave., near downtown (phone: 875-4337). Inexpensive.

Mirror of Korea – Zesty soup, grilled meat, seafood, and sushi, all accompanied by kimchee, that fiery Korean staple. Open daily. No reservations. Major credit cards accepted. 1047 Ponce de Leon Ave. at North Highland Ave. (phone: 874-6243). Inexpensive.

Rio Bravo – These cantinas, with campy Old Mexico decor, serve very good Tex-Mex victuals. Open daily. No reservations. Major credit cards accepted. Three locations: 3172 Roswell Ave. (phone: 262-7431); 5565 New Northside Dr. (phone: 952-3241); 1570 Holcomb Bridge Rd. (phone: 642-0838). Inexpensive.

El Toro – A group of spicy spots that serve the zippiest enchiladas, tacos, burritos, and other Tex-Mex dishes served hereabouts. Open daily. No reservations. Major credit cards accepted. 4300 Buford Hwy. NE (phone: 321-9502); 5288 Buford Hwy. NE (phone: 455-9677); 1775 Lawrenceville Hwy., Decatur (phone: 294-8478); and 10 other locations. Inexpensive.

Touch of India – The city's most expertly prepared tandoori dishes and curries. Open daily. No reservations. Major credit cards accepted. 962 Peachtree St., near 10th St. (phone: 876-7777), and 2065 Piedmont Rd. (phone: 876-7775). Inexpensive.

Varsity – It's a scene right out of *American Graffiti* — a drive-in with singing car hops, an air of bedlam, and a menu of such all-American favorites as hot dogs, hamburgers, and sandwiches. Open daily. No reservations or credit cards accepted. 61 North Ave. NW (phone: 881-1706). Inexpensive.

BALTIMORE

AT-A-GLANCE

SEEING THE CITY: Baltimore offers its finest panoramic view from the Top of the World Trade Center at the Inner Harbor (Pratt St., between South and Gay Sts.). Downstream lies Ft. McHenry, where the successful American repulsion of British forces in 1814 inspired Francis Scott Key to compose "The Star-Spangled Banner." To the northwest, the buildings and plazas of Charles Center stand out against the surrounding cityscape. To the east lie Little Italy, Fell's Point, and Canton.

SPECIAL PLACES: Most of the notable sights in Baltimore are concentrated in a few nicely designed areas. Consequently, the best way to see the city is by walking. Buses and taxis, which serve the entire city, are convenient, but parking in the lots downtown is neither difficult nor expensive.

CHARLES CENTER AND DOWNTOWN

Charles Center – Built during the past 2 decades, Charles Center is a 33-acre plot of new office buildings, luxury apartment towers, overhead walkways, fountains, and plazas. It's bounded by Lombard Street on the south, Saratoga Street on the north, Hopkins Place and Liberty Street on the west, and Charles Street on the east. (One of the city's oldest and grandest thoroughfares, Charles Street is also being revitalized, with shops and restaurants opening their doors to new business.)

Within the complex is One Charles Center, a 24-story tower of bronze-covered glass designed by Mies van der Rohe. Star performers, such as Rudolph Nureyev and Lauren Bacall have performed inside its *Morris Mechanic Theater.* Charles and Baltimore Sts.

Hopkins Plaza is the scene for many events, ranging from concerts by the *Baltimore Symphony Orchestra* to performances by lesser-known jazz ensembles and chamber groups (between Hopkins Pl., Charles, Baltimore, and Lombard Sts.). Center Plaza features a 33-foot bronze sculpture in the shape of a flame, designed by Francesco Somaini and presented to the city by the Gas and Electric Company (north of Fayette St. between Liberty and Charles Sts.). Pedestrian ramps link Charles Center to the *Convention Center* and to the *Baltimore Arena,* a sawtooth-roofed building that hosts professional soccer, circuses, ice hockey games, and rock concerts. 201 W. Baltimore St. (phone: 347-2010).

Edgar Allan Poe Home and Grave – Poe lived here in the 1830s; he visited Baltimore again in 1849 long enough to die and be buried. His grave is nearby, in the Westminster Presbyterian Church Cemetery at Fayette and Greene Sts. Home visiting hours are noon to 3:45 PM Wednesdays through Saturdays. Admission charge. 203 N. Amity St. (phone: 396-7932, for information); graveyard tours are given on the first and third Friday evenings of the month and on Saturday mornings from April through October (phone: 328-2070).

City Hall – Still in use, the domed building is a monument to mid-Victorian design and craftsmanship. 100 N. Holliday St. For tour information, call 396-1151.

Lexington Market – Since 1782 this colorful indoor marketplace has provided stalls for independent merchants, who sell a variety of goods. An addition, the *Arcade,* opened in October 1982, as the market celebrated its 200th anniversary. Today, 100 kiosks and shops are in operation. Lunch on Maryland seafood at its best — in the rough and at relatively little expense — at *John W. Faidley Seafood,* one of the largest raw oyster bars in the world. The crab cakes are divine, the clam chowder superb, and the beer is cold from the tap. 400 W. Lexington and Eutaw Sts.

MOUNT VERNON PLACE

This 19th-century bastion of Baltimore aristocracy now houses much of the 20th century's counterculture, with an array of boutiques, plant stores, restaurants, and natural food shops. Reminders of bygone days remain in the lovely 19th-century merchant prince housefronts, the stately squares, and outstanding cultural institutions.

Walters Art Gallery – This extensive collection, owned by the Walters family (who also owned railroads) and bequeathed to the city, offers an impressive span of art from ancient Near Eastern, Byzantine, and classical archaeological artifacts to medieval European illuminated manuscripts and painted panels, Italian Renaissance paintings, and 20th-century works. The gallery's Asian collection of Indian, Japanese, Chinese, and Southeast Asian art moved last year to Hackerman House, a historic 1850s mansion overlooking Mt. Vernon Place. Closed Mondays; no admission charge on Wednesdays. Charles and Centre Sts. (phone: 547-9000).

Maryland Historical Society – Examples of 18th- and 19th-century clothing, furniture, and silver, plus general exhibitions. Its library is rich in genealogical material. Closed Mondays. Admission charge. 201 W. Monument St. (phone: 685-3750).

Peabody Institute and Conservatory of Music – Worth a visit simply for a look at the magnificently designed library. Amid pillars and balconies, this 19th-century interior holds 300,000 volumes on tiered iron stacks that spiral upward 6 stories. Free student concerts. Mount Vernon Pl. at Monument and N. Charles Sts. (phone: 659-8164; for concert information, 659-8124).

Washington Monument – The very first Washington Monument, designed by Robert Mills and completed in 1842. Washington's statue stands atop the monument. Admission charge. Mount Vernon Pl. (phone: 396-7939).

NORTH

Baltimore Museum of Art – The home of the *Harbor City Ballet,* which performs in the *Meyerhoff Auditorium,* and noted for two especially fine collections: the Cone collection of the French post-Impressionist period, with a wealth of Matisse works (the Cone collection also includes much of the art collection of the late Gertrude Stein); and the Wurtzburger collections of primitive art and modern sculpture. There also are restored rooms from 17th- and 18th-century Maryland mansions, a wing featuring American decorative arts, an outdoor sculpture garden, and the *Museum Café.* Closed Mondays. Admission charge for those 22 and over; no charge on Thursdays. Art Museum Dr. near N. Charles and 31st Sts. (phone: 396-7101).

INNER HARBOR

Harborplace – The dazzling kingpin in Baltimore's renaissance, Harborplace is carrying the heart of the city's business southward. A plethora of shops, restaurants, and market stalls — about 140 in all — fill its two glass-enclosed pavilions, known as *The Gallery.* On the first floor of the Light Street Pavilion is a marketplace where vendors hawk

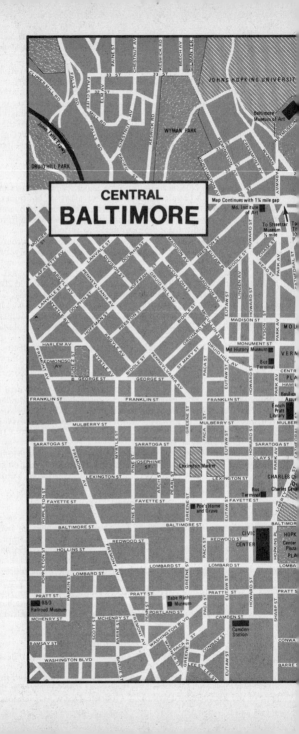

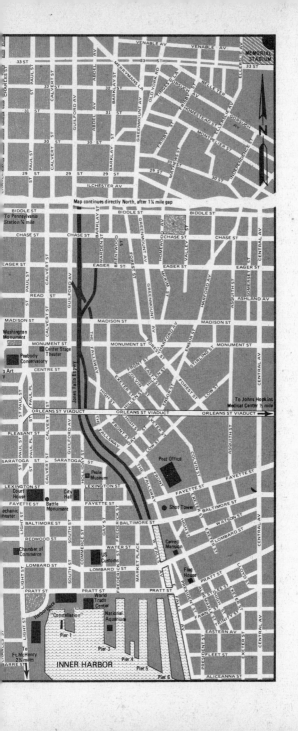

all manner of comestibles, while the upper level is chockablock with small eateries serving a diverse range of foodstuffs — everything from hot dogs to knishes. And whether you're looking for a crab mallet or a collector's comic book, chances are it's in the *Sam Smith Market*, where merchants sell a raft of unusual wares from their pushcarts and kiosks (also on the second floor). The Pratt Street Pavilion has its share of restaurants, boutiques, and specialty stores. Pratt and Light Sts. (phone: 332-4191).

National Aquarium – The aquarium has an impressive series of audiovisual displays on marine life, with a total of 5,000 specimens on 7 different levels. The $35 million Aquatic Educational Resource Center features 3 beluga whales and 6 Atlantic bottle-nosed dolphins, along with educational presentations, audiovisual displays, and behavioral studies. "People movers" carry visitors between levels, which include shark and dolphin pools, puffins living in a reproduction of their natural habitat, the largest coral reef in the US, and a reconstruction of Maine's coast with a hands-on display of shellfish and other shoreline creatures. Finally, on the top floor, visitors can wander through a tropical rain forest. Open daily. Admission charge. Pier 3, Inner Harbor (phone: 576-3810).

Fort McHenry National Monument and Historic Shrine – Here in 1814, a young Maryland lawyer witnessed the successful resistance of American forces to heavy British mortar bombardment and was so inspired by the sight of the Stars and Stripes still fluttering against the morning sky that he wrote "The Star-Spangled Banner." Visitors can see the fort, the old powder magazine, the officers' quarters, the enlisted men's barracks, and then walk along Francis Scott Key's famed ramparts overlooking the harbor. Open daily. During the summer on weekend afternoons, drills and military ceremonies modeled after those of 1814 are performed by uniformed soldiers and sailors. No admission charge. South of Inner Harbor, at the end of E. Fort Ave. (phone: 962-4299).

US Frigate *Constellation* – The US Navy's oldest warship (1797), the *Constellation* (named by George Washington), defeated the French frigate *L'Insurgente* in America's first important victory at sea and was in service through World War II. Now the ship has daily tours. A new visitors' center provides an introduction to the ship through films and "living history" presentations. Admission charge. Pier 1, Inner Harbor (phone: 539-1797).

Maryland Science Center and Planetarium – One of 25 full-size science centers in the country, covering everything from the vastness of outer space in the planetarium to the complexity of inner space in the walk-through model of a single human cell. There is a 400-seat IMAX (maximum image) movie theater with a 5-story screen capable of producing vivid sensations of movement so that the viewer feels part of the action. Admission charge. At the southwest corner of the Inner Harbor (phone: 685-2370).

■ **EXTRA SPECIAL:** Just 30 miles south of Baltimore on Route 2 (Ritchie Hwy.) lies Annapolis, Maryland's capital, where the charm of the first peacetime capital of the US is still preserved. Around town are lovely 18th-century buildings, including the old State House, still in use today, the Hammond-Harwood House, a Georgian home designed by William Buckland, and the campus of St. John's College, which appears much as it did to its most famous alumnus, Francis Scott Key. Also interesting is the US Naval Academy. The remains of John Paul Jones lie in the crypt of the chapel. The full brigade of midshipmen passes in formal parade review most Wednesdays at 3:30 PM on Worden Field. In town, the harbor is flanked by boutiques and restaurants.

SOURCES AND RESOURCES

TOURIST INFORMATION: The Baltimore Area Visitors Center offers useful tourist information, such as directions, maps, and brochures, as well as a listing of daily events. 300 W. Pratt St. and at a kiosk at the Inner Harbor during the summer (phone: 800-282-6632). Contact the Maryland state hotline (phone: 301-333-6611) for maps, calendars of events, health updates, and travel advisories.

Baltimore, Annapolis and Chesapeake Country Guidebook by James F. Waesche (Bodine and Associates; $4.95) is a good guide to Baltimore and the surrounding area.

Local Coverage – The *Baltimore Sun,* published twice daily and on Sundays, lists upcoming events. The weekly *City Paper,* which is free, offers a refreshing alternative and great classifieds. *Baltimore* is a monthly magazine with features on city life, restaurant listings, and calendars of events. All are available at newsstands. *Baltimore Scene* magazine and *Guest Informant in Baltimore* are comprehensive, free, tourist publications, available in hotels and from the Baltimore Area Convention and Visitors Association.

Television Stations – WMAR Channel 2–NBC; WBAL Channel 11–CBS; WJZ Channel 13–ABC; WMPB Channel 67–PBS.

Radio Stations – AM: WBAL 1090 (news/talk); WFBR 1300 (pop music); WWIN 1400 (urban contemporary). FM: WJHU 88.1 (classical/jazz); WYST 92.3 (adult contemporary/light rock); WLIF 101.9 (easy listening/news).

TELEPHONE: All telephone numbers are in the 301 area code unless otherwise indicated.

    Sales Tax – The state sales tax is 5%.

CLIMATE: Baltimore weather is fickle, neither the rigorous clime of the North nor the mild South. Unpredictable rain and frequent changes in wind direction make umbrellas advisable, particularly in the summer and early fall. In the summer, the weather can be hot and muggy, though the Chesapeake Bay exerts a modifying influence and brings relief with nighttime breezes. The winter is cold with moderate snowfall. Spring is windy and pleasant.

GETTING AROUND: Airport – Baltimore/Washington, DC International Airport (or BWI) is usually a 20-minute ride from downtown Baltimore via the Baltimore-Washington Expressway; taxi fare should run about $12. Train service is available from the airport to the city's downtown station for $2.70 one way; a shuttle bus transfers passengers from the air terminal to the airport train station. Trains run twice in early morning and five times in late afternoon. *Airport Connection* (phone: 859-0008), with a desk on the airport's lower level, charges $5 for transportation to most downtown hotels.

Bus – The *Mass Transit Administration* covers the entire metropolitan area. Route information and maps are available at the *MTA*'s main office (300 W. Lexington St.; phone: 539-5000; for the hearing-impaired, 539-3497). The *MTA* Tourist Passport is a 1-day pass, good from midnight to midnight for unlimited downtown travel on buses, the subway, and trolleys. The $2.25 pass is available, along with a comprehensive map, from many downtown hotels.

Car Rental – All the major national firms are represented.

Subway – The *Metro Rail* system offers limited access to much of the downtown area. Free parking and bus shuttle service is available from most stations. Trains operate from 5 AM to 10:30 PM on weekdays, from

8 AM to 10:30 PM on weekends. Base fare is 90¢. There is an additional charge for trips into the outer zones (phone: 333-2700).

Taxi – Cabs may be hailed on the street but are usually called by phone. Major companies are *Yellow Cab* (phone: 685-1212), *Diamond* (phone: 947-3333), *Sun* (phone: 235-0300), and *BWI Airport Cab* (phone: 859-1100).

 VITAL SERVICES: Audiovisual Equipment – *Avcom* (phone: 752-7838); *Audio Visual Service* (phone: 467-3620).

 Baby-sitting – *Elizabeth Cooney Personnel Agency* (phone: 323-1700).

Business Services – *Able Temporaries,* 2 N. Charles St. (phone: 685-8189).

Dry Cleaner/Tailor – *Apex Cleaners,* shoe repair also, 218 E. Baltimore St. (phone: 752-3979).

Limousine – *Limousine by Renoff* (phone: 366-2600).

Mechanic – *Plotkin's of Franklin Street,* 600 W. Franklin St. (phone: 728-5533).

Medical Emergency – *University Hospital,* 22 Greene St. (phone: 528-6722).

Messenger Services – *Central Delivery Service* (phone: 247-9500); *Carl Messenger Service* (phone: 685-3220).

National/International Courier – *Federal Express* (phone: 792-8200); *DHL Worldwide Courier Express* (phone: 768-3756).

Pharmacy – *Drug Fair,* 7 AM to 8 PM, 17 W. Baltimore St. (phone: 539-0838).

Photocopies – *Copy Cat Instant Press,* 211 E. Baltimore St. (phone: 837-6411); *Day Speedy Printing,* 106 E. Lombard St. (phone: 539-8500).

Post Office – The central office, open 24 hours, is at 900 E. Fayette St. (phone: 962-2492).

 SPECIAL EVENTS: The *Maryland House and Garden Pilgrimage* lavishly demonstrates Baltimoreans' pride in their own backyards. This statewide event for garden lovers, held during the last week of April and the first week of May, is a series of self-guided tours through a group of outstanding homes and gardens. For details, contact the *Pilgrimage* offices (1105A Providence Rd., Towson, MD 21204; phone: 821-6933). Merriment abounds in May during the *Preakness Festival Week* of outdoor concerts, exhibitions, and performances preceding the famous horse race. Numerous ethnic fairs take place in warm weather and are held at a variety of locations (see newspapers for listings). These festivities culminate in September in the *City Fair,* with everything from Old Country food to top-name entertainers. The *Harborlights Music Festival* is held every summer, usually June through August, at Baltimore's 2,000-seat *Pier 6 Pavilion.* Many concerts — from symphony to pop — are given. The *Baltimore Jazz Festival,* dedicated to native son Eubie Blake, is held in early September (Pier 6 at Pratt St.; phone: 625-4230).

■ **EXTRA SPECIAL:** For those intrigued by the thought of a cruise along Chesapeake Bay, there are many charter boat companies in the area. The bay is one of the most scenic waterways in the country, with its little coves and harbors and quaint islands. *Chesapeake Marine Tours* (Box 3350, Annapolis, MD 21403; phone: 268-7600) offers a variety of cruises; its day-long trip starts at Annapolis on the west side of the bay to St. Michaels on the eastern shore, where passengers can delve into Chesapeake's maritime history, have lunch, and meander about before reboarding. The *Clipper Cruise Line* (7711 Bonhomme Ave.; phone: 314-727-2929 or 800-325-0010) and *Tauck Tours* (11 Wilton Rd., Westport, CT; phone: 203-226-6911 or 800-468-2825) both offer 8-day cruise/tour combinations, with visits to Washington, DC, colonial Williamsburg, and Baltimore.

MUSEUMS: The fine collections of the *Baltimore Museum of Art,* the *Maryland Historical Society,* the *Maryland Science Center,* and the *Walters Art Gallery* are described in *Special Places.* Some other museums of note are the following:

Babe Ruth Birthplace and Maryland Baseball Hall of Fame – Cooperstown, New York, may have the fame, but baseball buffs will find everything authentic here, from photos of the Babe to taped interviews and *Orioles* memorabilia. Open daily. Admission charge. 216 Emory St. (phone: 727-1539).

Baltimore City Life Museums – Baltimore has organized its small museums into an integrated collection; each museum represents a facet of the city's culture and history. At the *Peale Museum* (225 Holliday St.), enjoy the collected works of the Peale family, early American portrait painters, and see how Baltimore grew during the 19th and 20th centuries in the exhibition "Rowhouse: A Baltimore Style of Living." Get acquainted with Baltimore's most famous literary son at the *H. L. Mencken House* on Union Square (1524 Hollins St.). Stroll through the *Carroll Mansion,* the elegant townhouse of a signer of the Declaration of Independence (800 E. Lombard St.). Dig into the city's past at the *Center of Urban Archaeology* (802 E. Lombard St.). Visit a 19th-century artisan's family through a dramatic living history presentation at the *1849 House* (50 Albermarle St., corner of E. Lombard). Celebrate Baltimore's renaissance at the *Courtyard Exhibition Center* (44-48 Albemarle St.). For more information, call 396-3523.

Baltimore Maritime Museum – The submarine USS *Torsk* and the lightship *Chesapeake* are open for tours Thursdays through Mondays in winter, daily in summer. Admission charge. Pier 4 at Pratt St. (phone: 396-5528).

B&O Railroad Museum – The most extensive collection of railroad memorabilia in the US and the second largest train exhibition in the world. It includes the nation's first passenger and freight station as well as related exhibits. Closed Mondays and Tuesdays. Admission charge. 901 W. Pratt St. (phone: 237-2387).

City Fire Museum – Once the oldest engine house in the nation, now filled with old equipment, artifacts, and photos of the aftermath of the Great Baltimore Fire of 1904. Open Sundays from 1 to 4 PM. 414 N. Gay St. (phone: 727-2414).

Lacrosse Hall of Fame Museum – Baltimore is the cradle of lacrosse, and displayed here are memorabilia and records of all levels. Closed on weekends. On Johns Hopkins' Homewood Campus in the *Newton H. White Athletic Center* (phone: 235-6882).

Peale Museum – Tom Thumb's brown velvet suit and the Feejee Mermaid of P.T. Barnum days are now displayed here, along with other quirky exhibits such as a fake mastodon skeleton that glows eerily in the museum's gas lighting. Open daily. Admission charge. 800 E. Lombard St. (phone: 396-1149).

Streetcar Museum – Home of the nation's first electric streetcar, this museum features a mile-and-a-quarter ride on a vintage streetcar, an exploration of the original carhouse, and exhibits of antique vehicles. Open Sundays from noon to 5 PM, and Thursdays and Saturdays in summer. 1901 Falls Rd. (phone: 547-0264).

MAJOR COLLEGES AND UNIVERSITIES: Johns Hopkins University (34th and Charles Sts.; phone: 338-8000) and Johns Hopkins Hospital and Medical School (600 N. Wolfe; phone: 955-5000) are internationally renowned. Other notable schools are the Peabody Institute and Conservatory of Music (Mount Vernon Pl.; phone: 659-8100), Morgan State University (Hillen Rd. and Cold Spring La.; phone: 444-3333), and Loyola (Charles St. and Cold Spring La.; phone: 323-1010). Goucher College is in suburban Towson (Dulaney Valley Rd.; phone: 337-6000).

SPORTS AND FITNESS: Baseball – The *Orioles* play their home games at *Memorial Stadium*. Tickets for good seats may be hard to get (phone: 338-1300). Note that a new *Orioles* stadium will open late this year; the 47,000-seat park will be located down by the harbor.

Bicycling – A brochure and map describing bicycle routes through the countryside are available from the *Bicycle Affairs Office*, Maryland State Highway Admin. (707 N. Calvert St., Baltimore, MD 21202; phone: 800-252-8776). Bicycles can be rented from *Cross-Country Cycling Center* (11612 Reisterstown Rd., Reisterstown; phone: 833-4444) or *Race Pace* (8450 Baltimore National Pike, Ellicott City; phone: 461-7878).

Boating – Middle Branch Park is the site of the *Baltimore Rowing and Resource Center,* a unique facility that includes boat storage and a fishing pier (phone: 396-3838).

Fitness Center – The *Druid Hill YMCA* opens its pool and equipment to visitors. 1609 Druid Hill Ave. (phone: 728-1600).

Golf – The best public course is the 18-hole *Pine Ridge,* 3 miles north on Dulaney Valley Road (exit 27 on the Baltimore Beltway; phone: 252-1408). There are others at Forest Park (Hillside and Forest Park Aves.; phone: 448-0300) and Carroll Park (Monroe and Washington Blvd.).

Hockey – The minor league *Skipjacks* play at the *Baltimore Arena.* 201 W. Baltimore (phone: 727-0703).

Horse Racing – The season runs from March through June, and September through mid-October. The high point is the running of the *Preakness,* which, along with the *Kentucky Derby* and the *Belmont Stakes,* make up the Triple Crown for 3-year-olds. At the *Pimlico* racecourse, Belvedere and Park Heights Aves. (phone: 542-9400).

Jogging – Run around the lake in Druid Hill Park. The Baltimore Area Visitors Center can provide a list of other routes.

Lacrosse – The Johns Hopkins *Blue Jays* (*Homewood Field,* Charles St. and University Pkwy.; phone: 235-6882) are among the tops in the ranks of collegiate stickmen. Seats usually are available.

Soccer – Watch the *Blast* indoors from January to April at the *Baltimore Arena.* 201 W. Baltimore (phone: 397-2010).

Steeplechase – As for another specialty, point-to-point races (with timber barrier jumps) are run in the valleys north of the city (Western Run, Worthington, Long Green) on Saturday afternoons during April and May.

Tennis – There are many courts in the city's parks. The best are at Clifton Park, Harford Rd., and 33rd St. (phone: 396-6101 for permit).

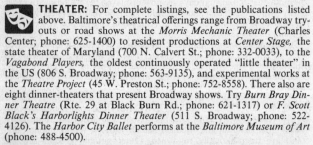 **THEATER:** For complete listings, see the publications listed above. Baltimore's theatrical offerings range from Broadway tryouts or road shows at the *Morris Mechanic Theater* (Charles Center; phone: 625-1400) to resident productions at *Center Stage,* the state theater of Maryland (700 N. Calvert St.; phone: 332-0033), to the *Vagabond Players,* the oldest continuously operated "little theater" in the US (806 S. Broadway; phone: 563-9135), and experimental works at the *Theatre Project* (45 W. Preston St.; phone: 752-8558). There also are eight dinner-theaters that present Broadway shows. Try *Burn Bray Dinner Theatre* (Rte. 29 at Black Burn Rd.; phone: 621-1317) or *F. Scott Black's Harborlights Dinner Theater* (511 S. Broadway; phone: 522-4126). The *Harbor City Ballet* performs at the *Baltimore Museum of Art* (phone: 488-4500).

MUSIC: The *Baltimore Symphony Orchestra,* which is highly regarded nationally, performs at the *Joseph Meyerhoff Symphony Hall,* where the music can be appreciated in series concerts throughout the year (1212 Cathedral St.; phone: 837-5691). The *Balti-*

more Opera performs in the *Lyric Opera House* (phone: 685-5086). For those more attuned to a syncopated beat, try to catch the *Left Bank Jazz Society* (call 945-2266 to learn where they're performing). Other musical programs are presented by well-known visiting artists; check the newspapers.

NIGHTCLUBS AND NIGHTLIFE: The city's only comedy club, the *Charm City Comedy Club,* presents stand-up comics from New York and LA, including those from top late-night TV shows (102 Water St.; phone: 576-8558); closed Sundays, cover charge Fridays and Saturdays.

BEST IN TOWN

CHECKING IN: There is an increasing number of luxury hotels and several less costly ones downtown. Expect to pay $80 and up for a double we list as inexpensive, and $45 to $70 in the moderate range. Note that there is free parking at many of the hotel chains downtown. For reservations, contact the *Maryland Reservation Center* (phone: 800-654-9303), *The Traveler in Maryland* (phone: 269-6232), or for bed and breakfast accommodations, contact *Amanda's Bed and Breakfast and Reservation Service* (1428 Park Ave.; phone: 225-0001). All telephone numbers are in the 301 area code unless otherwise indicated. All hotels carry CNN (Cable News Network).

Baltimore Marriott Inner Harbor – Within walking distance of Harborplace downtown, this 531-room property is ideal for business travelers and, due to its convenient location, also a good bet for tourists. It has several restaurants and lounges with entertainment. Room service is available until 11 PM, and a concierge desk, 20 meeting rooms, and secretarial services round out the list of business conveniences. Pratt and Eutaw Sts. (phone: 962-0202 or 800-654-2000; Fax: 301-962-0202, ext. 2044). Expensive.

Cross Keys Inn – Five miles from downtown (12 minutes via I-83, Jones Falls Expressway). A stop on the airport limousine run, it has a quiet atmosphere and is adjacent to the boutiques and specialty shops of *Cross Keys Village Square.* There's a good restaurant, a coffee shop, a lounge with entertainment, and a pool. There are 9 meeting rooms, and room service delivers until 11 PM. 5100 Falls Rd. (phone: 532-6900; Fax: 301-532-2903). Expensive.

Hyatt Regency, Baltimore – A glossy waterfront hostelry with 500 rooms, 27,000 square feet of meeting space, and a path connecting it to Harborplace and the *Baltimore Convention Center.* It's also only a short walk to the *National Aquarium* and the *Maryland Science Center.* Recreational facilities include tennis courts, jogging track, and swimming pool, and there's a coffee shop (with a waterfall) for snacks, a dining room in a park like setting, and a formal restaurant on the rooftop level. Twenty-four-hour room service, a concierge desk, secretarial services, and express checkout are among the business amenities. 300 Light St., Inner Harbor (phone: 528-1234 or 800-228-9000; Fax: 301-685-3362). Expensive.

Marriott's Hunt Valley Inn – In a suburban industrial complex where office buildings and factories are attractively landscaped and discreetly set apart from one another, this 392-room spot is the place to stay if embarking on the Maryland House and Garden Pilgrimage or attending the spring's timber races in hunt country. In addition to the restaurant, bar, and breakfast-luncheon parlor, recreational facilities are available — a pool, golf and tennis courts. Room service is available until 11 PM, and there are secretarial services and 20 meeting rooms available to assist with business needs. 245 Shawan Rd. at I-83, in the Hunt Valley Cockeysville Business Park (phone: 785-7000; Fax: 301-785-0341). Expensive.

Peabody Court – The same people responsible for the splendid restoration of Washington, DC's *Hay-Adams* hotel have brought similar distinctive qualities to this property in Baltimore's historic Mount Vernon Square. It has been transformed into a European-style hotel with fine service, antique decor, and a superb restaurant, *The Conservatory* (see *Eating Out*). Room service is available until midnight, and the hotel offers 8 meeting rooms, a concierge, and secretarial services. Mount Vernon Pl. (phone: 727-7101 or 800-732-5301; Fax: 301-789-3312). Expensive.

Stouffer Harborplace – A contemporary high-rise, containing 622 rooms, on the Inner Harbor at Harborplace, it is convenient to the aquarium, science center, and other attractions. *Windows* restaurant looks out over the harbor and features local seafood and continental dishes; 2 lounges (one with a piano bar) have live entertainment nightly. The decor is typically Stouffer's — elegant. Room service is available 24 hours a day. Business amenities include a concierge desk, 20 meeting rooms, and secretarial services. There's also express checkout. 202 E. Pratt St. (phone: 547-1200, 800-325-5000, or 800-HO-TELS-1; Fax: 301-539-5780). Expensive.

Tremont – Four blocks south of Mount Vernon Square, just off Charles Street, it caters to a clientele consisting mostly of executives looking for the privacy and amenities of an "all suites" hotel. Another attractive feature is guest privileges at the nearby *Downtown Athletic Club*. Room service is available until 10 PM, and there are 3 meeting rooms. 8 E. Pleasant St. (phone: 576-1200; Fax: 301-685-4215). Expensive.

Admiral Fell Inn – Contemporary bed and breakfast establishment with 37 rooms of various shapes and sizes carved out of 3 buildings. All rooms are named for famous city residents and feature four-poster beds. There's a small restaurant, continental breakfast, honor bar, and all-day coffee service for guests. Free van to town or summer ferry to Inner Harbor. One meeting room is available for business functions, and room service can be ordered until 10 PM. Fell's Point, 888 S. Broadway (phone: 522-7377 or 800-292-4667; Fax: 301-522-0707). Expensive to moderate.

Sheraton Johns Hopkins Inn – The most convenient, respectable hotel for visitors to Johns Hopkins Hospital or School of Medicine, near colorful Fell's Point. The 162-room property has a restaurant, a lounge, a pool, and 5 meeting rooms. 400 N. Broadway (phone: 675-6800). Moderate.

Shirley House – This 1880s hotel has been restored to its former elegance. Run as a bed and breakfast establishment, it offers guests a continental breakfast each morning and a complimentary glass of wine before bed. Spacious rooms have high ceilings, antique furnishings, and imported Victorian wallpaper. Connecting doors facilitate a variety of room arrangements. There is 1 meeting room. 205 Madison St. (phone: 728-6550). Moderate.

EATING OUT: Dedicated eaters find happiness in Baltimore. From its regional specialty, seafood in the rough, to the authentic dishes of its Little Italy, there are restaurants to suit most palates and pocketbooks. Our selections range in price from $60 or more for a dinner for two in the expensive range, $35 to $50 in the moderate range, and $30 or less in the inexpensive range. Prices do not include drinks, wine, or tips. All telephone numbers are in the 301 area code unless otherwise indicated.

Conservatory at the Peabody Court – Even if the food were merely mediocre, a meal here would be enjoyable simply for the lovely view overlooking Mount Vernon's cultural institutions. Fortunately, the menu is quite commendable. Specialties include Virginia squab with poached quail eggs and new potatoes stuffed with escargots. Closed Mondays. Reservations necessary. Major credit cards accepted. Mount Vernon Pl. (phone: 727-7101). Expensive.

Orchid – Baltimore's first French and Oriental restaurant offers an award-winning menu of fresh meat, seafood, and crisp vegetables, in a marriage that combines the best of both worlds — creamy French sauces and fresh Oriental seasonings. Open daily. Reservations necessary. Major credit cards accepted. Downtown near all attractions, 419 N. Charles St. (phone: 837-0080). Expensive.

Prime Rib – A hangout for figures in the city's political and entertainment worlds. Its prime ribs are great, but no more so than the crab imperial. This is a surprisingly dressy place; jackets (not ties) required. Dinner nightly. Reservations advised. Major credit cards accepted. 1101 N. Calvert St., in Horizon House (phone: 539-1804). Expensive to moderate.

Haussner's – Everything abounds in this German restaurant, from the fat Tyrolean dumplings to the draft Bavarian beer to the Barbizon paintings and busts of Roman emperors that cover the walls. The museum downstairs has a ball of string 300 miles long. Don't ask; we're just reporting the facts. Open Tuesdays through Saturdays for lunch and dinner. Reservations accepted for lunch only. Major credit cards accepted. 3242 Eastern Ave. (phone: 327-8365). Moderate.

Maison Marconi – The interior may not be pleasing to the eye, but the artistry is on the plate. The restaurant where Baltimoreans head in a steady stream. The specialty of this Franco-Italian eatery is filet of sole prepared in a variety of delicious ways. Lunch and dinner; closed Sundays and Mondays. No reservations. Major credit cards accepted. 106 W. Saratoga St. (phone: 727-9522). Moderate.

Olde Obrycki's Crab House – Roll back your sleeves, put on your bib, grab a mallet, and you're ready for a bout at *Obrycki's.* Be prepared to spend all evening battling steamed crabs. There's plenty of support along the way in the warm family atmosphere. Open April through November only; closed Mondays; weekends, dinner only. Reservations advised. Major credit cards accepted. 1729 E. Pratt St., Fell's Point. (phone: 732-6399). Moderate.

Sabatino's – A good late-night dining spot in the heart of Baltimore's Little Italy. Veal and shrimp marsala are the specialties, appreciated by the locals, who refer to the place familiarly as "Sabby's." Open daily for lunch and dinner. Reservations advised. Major credit cards accepted. 901 Fawn St., Little Italy (phone: 727-9414). Moderate.

Attman's – Baltimoreans boast that this bastion of cold cuts and appetizers rivals anything New York can offer. They point to the consummate corned beef that has been delighting deli devotees for generations. The sheer size of sandwiches here makes it an authentic lure. Open daily. Reservations unnecessary. No credit cards acccepted. 1019 E. Lombard St. (phone: 563-2666). Inexpensive.

John W. Faidley Seafood – In the past 100 years, it has established itself as the place for oysters, crabs, and clams brought in fresh daily from the bay. The downtown lunch crowd regards a visit to *Faidley's* in Lexington Market — a vast assemblage of butchers and merchants — as the ultimate adventure. Open from 9 AM to 6 PM. Closed Sundays. No credit cards accepted. Paca at Lexington St. (phone: 727-4898). Inexpensive.

■ **Note: Harborplace:** In addition to 33 food stalls, where visitors can find everything from Buffalo wings to chocolate-covered strawberries, the following restaurants have good food, harbor views, and moderate prices. In the Light Street Pavilion are *The American Café*, with a light

American menu and frequent live entertainment (phone: 962-8800); *City Lights,* featuring seafood and homemade desserts (phone: 244-8811); *Phillips Harborplace,* with Chesapeake Bay seafood and a piano bar (phone: 685-6600); and *W. Brokke's,* with homemade soups, good salads, and desserts (phone: 539-3810). In the Pratt Street Pavilion are *Tandoor,* featuring Northern Indian dishes cooked in tandoori ovens (phone: 547-0575); *Taverna Athena,* with authentic Greek food (phone: 547-8900); and *Bamboo House,* with Chinese food (phone: 625-1191).

BOSTON

AT-A-GLANCE

SEEING THE CITY: There are two unparalleled posts from which to view Boston: the John Hancock Tower's 60th-floor Observatory, and the 50th-floor Prudential Skywalk. The Hancock Tower offers a spectacular panorama that even includes the mountains of southern New Hampshire (weather permitting), telescopes, recorded commentaries, a topographical model of Boston in 1775 (which is a must — we promise you'll be surprised), and a 7-minute film of a helicopter flight over the city. (200 Clarendon St.; Copley Sq.; phone: 247-1977. Take the *Green Line* on the subway system to Copley Square, or the *Orange Line* to the Back Bay station.) Open daily. Admission charge. Like the Hancock, the Prudential Skywalk at the Prudential Center (800 Huntington Ave.; phone: 236-3318) offers an excellent 360° view, but the Pru also has a restaurant and bar, *The Top of the Hub,* on the 52nd floor. (*Green Line* to the Copley Place or Prudential stop.) Skywalk and restaurant are open daily. Admission charge.

SPECIAL PLACES: Boston is best seen on foot; the city is compact, and driving, even for residents, is hair-raising.
Freedom Trail – The city has made it both easy and fun to track down the important sites from its colonial and Revolutionary past. Just follow the red brick (or red paint) line set into the sidewalk; it takes about 2 hours to walk its length without stops or side trips. To begin, take the *Green* or *Red Line* to Park Street and go to the visitors' information center on the Common, which has maps available. Or you can take a double-decker bus tour (see *Getting Around*).

Boston Common – A pastoral green, this is the nation's oldest park, set up in 1634. The earliest Bostonians brought their cows and horses here to graze. Today, you'll find their descendants engaging in free-form pastimes that range from music making to baseball and skateboarding. We suggest starting your walking tour here. (It's advisable not to walk alone — and especially not at night — since the Common is often inadequately patrolled; you can park underneath the green in the Underground Parking Garage, open 24 hours daily.) For information about activities on the Common, call 536-4100.

State House – Facing the Beacon Street entrance to the Common, the gold-domed State House designed by Charles Bulfinch dates to 1795. The gold leaf was added in 1874. You can enter through the side door of the right wing (the main door is hardly ever used). Inside, you can pick up pamphlets in Doric Hall and visit the *Archives Museum* in the basement. It contains American historical documents, among them the original Massachusetts constitution, the oldest written constitution in the world (phone: 727-2816). There also is a library (phone: 727-2590). Closed weekends. No admission charge. Beacon St. (phone: 727-2121).

Park Street Congregational Church and Granary Burying Ground – Built in 1809, the church witnessed William Lloyd Garrison's famous antislavery address in 1829 and heard the first singing of "My country, 'tis of thee" 2 years later. Open Tuesdays through Saturdays, July and August; otherwise by appointment. 1 Park St. (phone: 523-

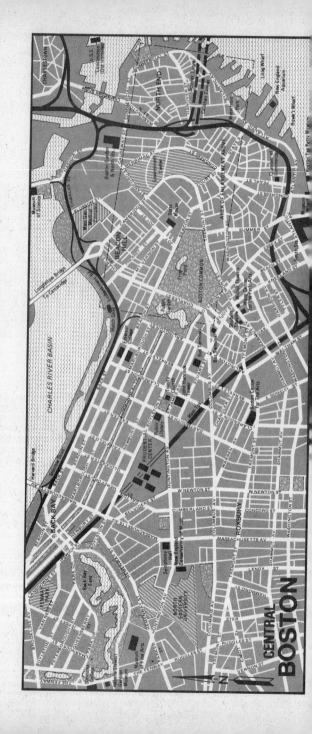

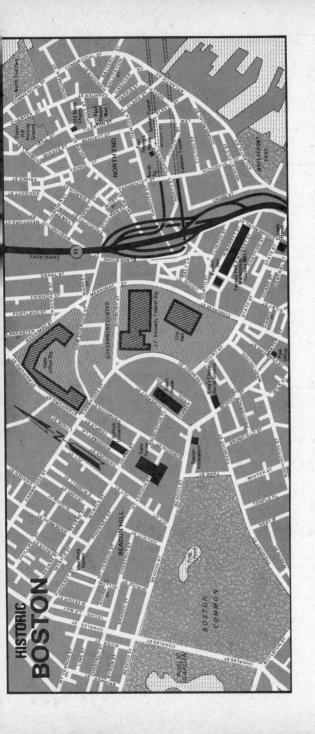

3383). In the 1660 cemetery next door are the graves of such Revolutionary notables as John Hancock, Samuel Adams, Thomas Paine, Paul Revere, and the parents of Benjamin Franklin. Look for the grave of Mary Goose, believed to be Mother Goose. Open daily.

City Hall – The focal point of the Government Center plaza, Boston's looming concrete City Hall (1968), designed by Kallmann, McKinnell, & Knowles, is considered a landmark of modern architecture, although the local populace loves to revile it. City Hall sits in the middle of an 8-acre plaza that is often the scene of civic celebrations and politicking. Congress St. (phone: 725-4000).

Old State House – The 18th-century seat of government, which sits in the middle of State Street, surrounded by modern towers of law and finance, served both the English colony and American state of Massachusetts until Bulfinch's State House was built. Unfortunately, this museum of Boston history is closed for renovation until 1993 (206 Washington St.; phone: 242-5655). Next door is a National Park Service visitors' center, which provides useful information about Boston and sites in outlying areas. There are free guided tours of the nearby portions of the Freedom Trail, April through December. Open daily. 15 State St. (phone: 242-5642 or 223-5200).

Faneuil Hall Marketplace – These three large buildings have been a market since 1826 and still house 11 of the original tenants. Redesigned and opened between 1976 and 1978, the market has become a much-copied prototype of urban renewal. Over a million people per month — natives and tourists — partake of its multiplicity of stalls, restaurants, and shops. Plan to spend time wandering around and sampling its food, drink, and chic wares. An information booth in the South Market area stands inside the South Canopy in winter, and outside in summer. The market takes its official name from adjacent Faneuil (pronounced *Fan*'l) Hall, a historic meeting house. Open daily (phone: 523-3886).

Beacon Hill – Walk along Mt. Vernon Street to see the stately old townhouses that were (and are today) the pride of the first families of Boston. Look for the famous brass knockers, the charming carriage houses, and the intimate backyard gardens. A few blocks down is Louisburg Square, a rectangle of terribly proper houses facing a tiny park; this was once home to Louisa May Alcott and Jenny Lind, among others. Cobblestoned Acorn Street, parallel to Mt. Vernon and Chestnut, is the most photographed in town.

North End – Paul Revere's House and Old North Church are both snugly tucked away among the narrow red brick streets of the North End, a colorful, Italian-American community with a lively street life and some excellent little restaurants (see *Eating Out*). To experience *la dolce vita,* stop at the *Café Paradiso* (255 Hanover St.; phone: 742-1768) for cannoli, cappuccino, and people watching.

Paul Revere's House – In addition to having housed the legendary Revolutionary hero, this place has the distinction of being the oldest wooden house in Boston. Before Revere lived here, one of the previous occupants was a sea captain who spent time in a Puritan pillory for "lewd and vicious behavior." Revere moved here in 1770 with his wife, mother, and five children. He had seven more children by his second wife, which is why his house was the only one on the block that didn't have to quarter British soldiers. Open daily. Admission charge. 19 North Sq. (phone: 523-2338).

Old North Church – Affectionately known as Old North, the official name of the church is Christ Church, built in 1723. On the night of April 18, 1775, sexton Robert Newman hung two lanterns outside to warn Bostonians that the British were coming by sea. His action and Paul Revere's famous ride were later immortalized by poet Henry Wadsworth Longfellow in a poem that you probably read in school. (The line you will want to remember is: "One if by land, two if by sea.") The church's original clock still ticks in the back and services are still held every Sunday. Open daily. No admission charge. 193 Salem St. (phone: 523-6676).

Waterfront – Walk along Waterfront Park, with its invigorating views of the harbor and browse in the many new shops set in the renovated wharf buildings. On Long Wharf, the pier behind the aquarium, you'll find the Custom House, built between 1845 and 1847, the ferry (summer only) across Cape Cod Bay to Provincetown, and boats for harbor cruises and fishing excursions. For information, contact *Bay State Cruise Company* (phone: 723-7800), which provides service from *Memorial Day* to *Columbus Day* (and sometimes on warm weekends during the winter) out of 2 locations, Long Wharf and Commonwealth Pier. Boats take passengers on day trips to George's Island and the Inner Harbor; Nantasket Beach and the Outer Harbor; and Provincetown, at the tip of Cape Cod. *Boston Harbor Cruises* (phone: 227-4300) sends boats out among the harbor islands seasonally from April to November, and runs the Navy Yard water shuttle to Charlestown year-round. For $1, this is a great way to get from the aquarium to the Charlestown Navy Yard, where you can see "Old Ironsides" (the USS *Constitution*), the adjoining museum, the Bunker Hill Pavilion, or Bunker Hill itself. *Massport* (phone: 800-235-6426) runs a water shuttle from Rowes Wharf to Logan Airport (a 7-minute ride), except in winter.

New England Aquarium – One of the world's top collections of marine life, it served as the model for the *National Aquarium* in Baltimore. Taking center stage is the 180,000-gallon Giant Ocean Tank, the home of 1,000 aquatic specimens and a 4-story coral reef. Divers regularly feed the multitudes of turtles, fish, and sharks, so they don't dine on each other. Exhibits re-creating environments such as tropical marine, northern waters, and a tidepool surround the saltwater tank. Penguins cavort in their own habitat called the Penguin Tray, and seals and dolphins perform aboard the floating pavilion *Discovery,* next door to the main building. A variety of films are shown in the auditorium, and there's an interesting gift shop. *Blue Line,* Aquarium stop. Open daily. Admission charge; children under 3 free; Thursdays after 4, free to all. Central Wharf, Waterfront (phone: 973-5200).

BACK BAY

Arlington is the first of an alphabetically ordered series of streets created when the Back Bay was filled in during the mid-1800s. Broad streets and avenues were laid out in an orderly fashion, and along them wealthy Bostonians built palatial homes, churches, and public institutions. This area is a joy to walk and gives a better feeling of Victorian Boston than any other part of the city.

Public Garden – A treasure among city parks and a Boston tradition since 1861, the garden has fountains, formal gardens, and trees labeled for identification. A special treat is a ride on the Swan Boats, past the geese and ducks on the lake (open daily, mid-April through *Labor Day,* except on windy or rainy days; admission charge, group rates available; call 522-1966). Across Charles Street from the Common. Open daily. No admission charge.

Commonwealth Avenue – Intended to replicate the broad boulevards of 19th-century Paris, with their mansard-roofed, stately homes, Commonwealth Avenue has fulfilled its early promise. Stroll down the shady mall, with its statues of famous Bostonians. In April, the magnolias are a special treat. On the corner of Clarendon Street stands the First Baptist Church, a splendid Romanesque structure designed by H. H. Richardson and completed in 1882. Open daily. No admission charge. 110 Commonwealth Ave. (phone: 267-3148).

Newbury Street – This is where fashionable Bostonians shop. There are many art galleries and boutiques as well as a variety of restaurants and several outdoor cafés.

Copley Square – Seagoing vessels used to drop their anchors in Copley Square; now it harbors Richardson's magnificent Trinity Church. Open daily. No admission charge (phone: 536-0944). The Boston Public Library, founded in 1852, is the oldest municipally supported library in the country. The main Copley Square building, completed in 1895, was designed by the famous New York firm of McKim, Mead & White, and is considered one of the first outstanding examples of the Renaissance Beaux Arts style in the US. Step inside the Copley Square entrance for a quiet moment in the lovely central courtyard. (The 1972 addition was designed by Philip Johnson.) Closed Sundays (phone: 536-5400). Across Dartmouth Street from the *Copley Plaza* is Copley Place, a complex of hotels, fashionable shops (*Neiman Marcus, Tiffany, Godiva Chocolatiers, Williams-Sonoma,* and the like), restaurants, 11 movie theaters (phone: 266-2533), and an indoor waterfall (phone: 375-4400).

OTHER SPECIAL PLACES

John F. Kennedy Library – Designed by I. M. Pei, this presidential library sits on the edge of a point of land projecting into Dorchester Bay, with a magnificent view of the Boston skyline and out to sea. The museum includes a half-hour film and an exhibit of documents, photographs, and memorabilia of JFK and his administration. There's also a section on his brother Robert F. Kennedy. By car, take I-93 south to exit 15 and follow the signs to the library. Or take the *Red Line* (Ashmont or Quincy train) to the JFK/UMass station; a shuttle bus takes you to the library. Open daily except certain holidays. Admission charge for adults; children under 16 free (phone: 929-4567).

Museum of Fine Arts – This is one of the world's great art museums, with comprehensive exhibits from every major period and in every conceivable medium. The Monets are especially dazzling. Special shows come and go frequently, many of them mounted in the new West Wing, designed by I. M. Pei. Films, classical music, lectures, and superb activities for children make this a multimedia magnet for everyone. Restaurant, snack bar, museum shop, and library. Take the E train (*Green Line*) to Museum/Ruggles St. stop. Closed Mondays; open Wednesdays (the West Wing is open late on Thursdays and Fridays, too). Admission charge except Wednesday afternoons from 4 to 6 PM. 465 Huntington Ave., along the Fenway (phone: 267-9377 or 267-9300).

Isabella Stewart Gardner Museum – Mrs. Gardner, the wife of a Boston Brahmin, built this lovely Venetian palazzo, which she filled with her extraordinary collections of tapestries, sculpture, stained glass, fine furniture, and paintings by masters like Rembrandt, Titian, and Sargent. A major burglary in March 1990 somewhat diminished the collection, but there are still plenty of beautiful works on view. The courtyard is filled with blooms year-round. Free chamber music concerts are frequently held in the Tapestry Room, except in July and August (call ahead for the schedule). A small café serves superb light lunches, in the garden in summer. Take the E train (*Green Line*), to Museum/Ruggles St. stop. Closed Mondays. Admission charge; children under 12 free. 280 The Fenway (phone: 566-1401 or 734-1359 for concert information).

Institute of Contemporary Art – Exciting contemporary art in several media, including an interesting film series, set in the halls of a 19th-century police station. *Green Line,* Hynes Auditorium/ICA stop. Closed Mondays and Tuesdays. Hours vary seasonally; check before you go. Admission charge. 955 Boylston (phone: 266-5151).

Museum of Science and the Charles Hayden Planetarium – A wide variety of superb exhibitions illustrate the fields of medicine, technology, and space. Many of them involve viewer participation. You can watch a model of the ocean and a simulated lunar module in action. There's a special medical wing with anatomical and medical history and nutrition displays. The *Omni Theater* has a gigantic screen that nearly surrounds viewers with images and sounds from scientific or scenic films. There's also a splendid gift shop and cafeteria. Lechmere train (*Green Line*), Science Park stop. Closed Mondays. Admission charge; separate admission for *Omni Theater*, advance reservations suggested. Science Park, Charles River Dam (phone: 523-6664 or 589-0100).

Computer Museum – In addition to a collection of vintage computers that reveal the progress of artificial-intelligence machines — from huge, room-size monsters to modern laptops — this delightful museum now has a 2-story-tall computer through which you can walk. The keys are a foot wide, the disks are 6 feet across, and the "microchip" is the biggest in the world — 7½ feet square. Exhibits explain how the different parts of a computer work, and visitors can even run a simple program. Closed Mondays. Admission charge; group rates available. 300 Congress St., Museum Wharf (phone: 423-6758 or 426-2800).

Boston Tea Party Ship and Museum – Board the *Brig Beaver II,* a full-size working replica of one of the three original ships at the Boston Tea Party. If you feel like it, you can even throw a little tea into Boston Harbor. The adjacent museum houses historical documents relevant to the period, as well as films and related exhibits. *Red Line,* South Station stop. Open daily. Admission charge. Congress St. Bridge at Fort Point Channel (phone: 338-1773).

USS *Constitution* – View famous "Old Ironsides," the oldest commissioned ship in the US Navy and the proud winner of 40 victories at sea (phone: 242-5670). The adjacent shoreside museum displays related memorabilia and a slide show. City Square bus stop. Museum open daily. Admission charge. Boston Naval Shipyard, Charlestown (phone: 241-9078).

Bunker Hill Pavilion – Witness a vivid multimedia reenactment of the Battle of Bunker Hill on 14 screens, with 7 sound channels. Bet you thought the Americans won. Open daily, with shows every half hour. Admission charge. Adjacent to USS *Constitution* (phone: 241-7575).

Arnold Arboretum – Contained in these 265 acres of beautifully landscaped woodland and park are over 14,000 trees, shrubs, and vines, most of them labeled by their assiduous Harvard caretakers. Six miles from downtown Boston; the main gate and visitors' center are 100 yards south of the rotary junction of Routes 1 and 203. Take the *Green Line,* Arborway bus No. 39 from Copley Square stop, or *Orange Line,* Forest Hills stop. The visitors' center shop has a large selection of books on botany and horticulture. Open daily sunrise to sunset. No admission charge. The Arborway, Jamaica Plain (phone: 524-1717 or 524-1718).

Frederick Law Olmsted National Historic Site – Olmsted, the premier 19th-century landscape designer best known for Central Park in New York City and Prospect Park in Brooklyn, is honored through archives that include plans, drawings, and photographs. There are tours of the house occupied by Olmsted and his two sons. Olmsted also designed the nearby Brookline Reservoir and Boston's "Emerald Necklace" of green spaces, which tie the city to the suburbs. He helped design the Arnold Arboretum as well. Open Fridays through Sundays. Admission charge. 99 Warren St., Brookline (phone: 566-1689).

CAMBRIDGE

Harvard Square – Just across the Charles River from Boston, Cambridge has always had an ambience and identity all its own. Catering equally to the academic and professional communities, the Square is a lively combination of the trendy, traditional, and "upscale." It has the greatest concentration of bookstores in the country (many are open daily until late into the evening), movie options that range from vintage films like *Casablanca* to the latest from Hollywood and abroad, and the ever-present street musicians. When hunger pangs strike, everything from muffins to nouvelle cuisine awaits — with an authentic Italian ice to top it off. Take the *Red Line* headed toward Alewife (the last stop) and get off at the Harvard Square stop.

Harvard Yard – This tree-filled enclave is the focal point of the oldest (1636) and most prestigious university in the country (the Law School is nearby, the Business School just across the river, the Medical School a bus ride away in Boston). Notice especially Massachusetts Hall (1720; Harvard's oldest building), Bulfinch's University Hall, and in the adjoining quadrangle, Widener Library and H. H. Richardson's Sever Hall. Campus tours are given year-round; check at the information office in Holyoke Center (phone: 495-1573).

Arthur Sackler Museum and Fogg Museum – The *Sackler*'s 1985 postmodern building designed by James Stirling joins the *Fogg*'s neo-Georgian building to house Harvard's impressive collection of paintings, drawings, prints, sculpture, and silver, as well as changing exhibitions. Closed Mondays and weekends in summer. Admission charge. 32 Quincy St. (phone: 495-9400).

Harvard University Museums – On 1 short block parallel to Oxford Street is this complex housing the *Comparative Zoology, Peabody* (anthropology), *Geology,* and *Botanical* museums. The *Peabody* houses extensive anthropological and archaeological collections, with an emphasis on South American Indians. There are also exhibitions on Africa and evolution as well as a fine gift shop. The *Botanical* houses a famous collection of glass flowers handmade for Harvard by a German father and son, Leopold and Rudolph Blaschka, between 1887 and 1936. Renowned for their scientific accuracy as well as their beauty, they are worth a special visit. Reservations must be made for either group (phone: 495-2341) or individual (phone: 495-3045) tours for any of the museums. Open daily. Admission charge except on Saturdays from 9 to 11 AM. 26 Oxford St. (phone: 495-3045).

Longfellow National Historic Site – George Washington and his troops billeted at this Tory Row house, built in 1759, at the beginning of the Revolutionary War. In 1843, Longfellow's father-in-law bought the house for the poet and his wife as a wedding gift. Longfellow was then a professor at Harvard and lived here until his death in 1882. (His children lived in neighboring Brattle Street homes.) Open daily; summer concerts. Admission charge. 105 Brattle St. (phone: 876-4491).

Radcliffe Yard – One of the Seven Sister colleges, Radcliffe has evolved from its historical role as "Harvard's Annex" to its current position, with its undergraduates fully integrated into the life of the university. Radcliffe offers special alternative programs for women at the graduate level and those involved in career changes. Its Schlesinger Library has one of the country's top collections on the history of women in America as well as an important culinary collection. Open weekdays. No admission charge. 3 James St. (phone: 495-8647).

Old Burying Ground – Back on Garden Street, walk past Christ Church to the Old Burying Ground, also known as God's Acre, where the graves go back to 1635. Many Revolutionary War heroes and Harvard presidents are buried here. On the Garden Street fence, there's a mileage marker dating to 1754.

Massachusetts Institute of Technology – The foremost scientific school in the country, MIT opened its doors in Boston in 1865 and moved across the river to its Cambridge campus in 1916. In addition to its world-famous laboratories and graduate schools in engineering and science, its professional schools include the Sloan School of Management, the Joint Center for Urban Studies (with Harvard), and the School of Architecture. Architect I. M. Pei is an alumnus; next to his Green

Building for the earth sciences stands Calder's stabile *The Big Sail,* one of a superb collection of outdoor sculptures on the campus. Also worth noting are Saarinen's chapel and the Kresge Auditorium, just across from the main entrance on Massachusetts Avenue. The main MIT museum (265 Mass. Ave., phone: 253-4429) contains permanent collections and changing exhibits of contemporary art and technology. Closed Mondays; admission charge. The *Compton Gallery* (77 Mass. Ave.) features changing technical exhibitions. Open weekdays; free. The Wiesner Building (20 Ames St., phone: 253-4680), is another I. M. Pei landmark worth a visit for its arresting interior and the often provocative changing exhibitions, three galleries of which are in the *List Visual Arts Center.* Open daily, no admission charge. MIT campus tours are given year-round on weekdays at 10 AM and 2 PM. *Red Line,* Kendall Square/MIT stop or No. 1 Dudley bus, headed toward Harvard Sq., 77 Mass. Ave. (phone: 253-4795).

Mt. Auburn Cemetery – The first garden cemetery in the United States, this rural retreat in the midst of Cambridge is bliss to the senses. Founded in 1831, Mt. Auburn's 170 beautifully landscaped acres include hills, ponds (4), magnificent trees (over 3,500 of them, including 575 varieties), and an observation tower. Visitors are encouraged to walk or drive around, and bird watchers find it especially appealing. Among the many famous people buried here are Mary Baker Eddy, Henry Wadsworth Longfellow, Julia Ward Howe, Oliver Wendell Holmes, and Winslow Homer. An hour's stroll might be the pinnacle of a sightseeing day. Open daylight hours year-round; tower open in fair weather from early spring to late fall. Stop for a map at the north entrance. 580 Mt. Auburn St. (phone: 547-7105).

■ **EXTRA SPECIAL:** About 18 miles north of Boston on Route 107 is the town of Salem. The capital of the Massachusetts Bay Colony from 1626 to 1630, and again, briefly, in 1774 when the British closed Boston Harbor after the Boston Tea Party, Salem earned a bitter name in American history as the scene of the witch trials, in which a group of women and children accused over 100 villagers of witchcraft. The hysterical allegations resulted in the deaths of 25 of the accused. Several of the judges bitterly regretted their roles subsequently. Salem is also the site of Nathaniel Hawthorne's House of the Seven Gables (54 Turner St.; phone: 744-0991). Open daily. Admission charge. Hawthorne worked in the Salem Custom House and wrote his classic *The Scarlet Letter* at 14 Mall Street. Like Boston, Salem has a history trail winding through its streets and port. Visit the Salem Maritime National Historic Site, run by the National Park Service, for information, maps, and a variety of seasonal tours. 174 Derby St. Open daily (phone: 508-744-4323 or 508-745-1470).

While you're in the neighborhood, stop at the *Witch Museum* (19½ Washington Sq. N.; phone: 508-744-1692). Closed *Thanksgiving, Christmas, New Year's.* Admission charge. The Witch House, site of some of the interrogations, radiates a claustrophobic, spooky feeling still, especially at night. Open daily March to mid-December; other times by appointment. Admission charge (310½ Essex St.; phone: 508-744-0180). You can get in the mood for this tour by picking up a copy of Arthur Miller's play *The Crucible.*

The *Peabody Museum* (161 Essex St.; phone: 508-745-1876) has fascinating scrimshaw carvings and nautical regalia from the early days of shipping and far-off ports. Closed *Thanksgiving, Christmas, New Year's.* Admission charge. For a cruise in the harbor, walk down to Salem Willows Pier; *Pier Transit Cruises* (phone: 508-744-6311; 800 696-6311).

A few miles east of Salem, the sailboating town of Marblehead has myriad colonial houses, places to sit and look at the harbor, lots of boats, and shops selling New England seascapes and elegant, old-fashioned furnishings. Toward evening, you can watch fishermen unloading the day's catch.

SOURCES AND RESOURCES

 TOURIST INFORMATION: For tourist information, maps, and brochures, visit one of the visitor information centers — at City Hall, Boston Common or the Hancock Tower — or call 536-4100. The Boston Convention and Tourist Bureau (PO Box 490, Prudential Plaza W., Boston, MA 02199) has multilingual maps and brochures and is open weekdays. Contact the Massachusetts state hotline (phone: 617-727-3201) for maps, calendars of events, health updates, and travel advisories.

The *Visitor's Channel* of the Panorama Television Network, Channel 12, is offered on local hotel television sets. This 24-hour station provides weather updates every 15 minutes, as well as travel advisories, traffic information, and half-hour specials on special attractions within Boston and day trips outside the city.

A comprehensive guidebook is *In and Out of Boston (With or Without Children)* by Bernice Chesler (Globe Pequot Press; $9.95).

Local Coverage – *Boston Herald,* morning daily; *Christian Science Monitor,* weekday mornings; *Boston Globe,* morning daily; *Boston Phoenix,* weekly, comes out on Fridays; *Boston* magazine, monthly.

Television Stations – WBZ Channel 4–NBC; WCVB Channel 5–ABC; WHDH Channel 7–CBS.

Radio Stations – AM: WEEI 590 (news); WBZ 1030 (pop). FM: WROR 93.5 (pop); WJIB 98 (pop).

Food – *Robert Nadeau's Guide to Boston Restaurants* by Mark Zanger (World Food Press; $3.95), *Boston* magazine's listings, and Robert Levey's restaurant columns in the *Boston Globe.*

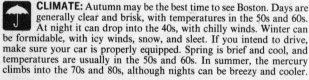 **TELEPHONE:** The area code for Boston is 617 unless otherwise indicated. *Note:* Much of the surrounding area is served by the 508 area code.

Sales Tax – The city sales tax is 5%, as is the hotel tax.

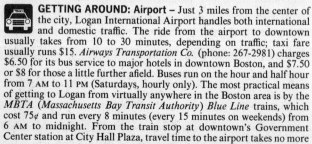 **CLIMATE:** Autumn may be the best time to see Boston. Days are generally clear and brisk, with temperatures in the 50s and 60s. At night it can drop into the 40s, with chilly winds. Winter can be formidable, with icy winds, snow, and sleet. If you intend to drive, make sure your car is properly equipped. Spring is brief and cool, and temperatures are usually in the 50s and 60s. In summer, the mercury climbs into the 70s and 80s, although nights can be breezy and cooler.

GETTING AROUND: Airport – Just 3 miles from the center of the city, Logan International Airport handles both international and domestic traffic. The ride from the airport to downtown usually takes from 10 to 30 minutes, depending on traffic; taxi fare usually runs $15. *Airways Transportation Co.* (phone: 267-2981) charges $6.50 for its bus service to major hotels in downtown Boston, and $7.50 or $8 for those a little further afield. Buses run on the hour and half hour from 7 AM to 11 PM (Saturdays, hourly only). The most practical means of getting to Logan from virtually anywhere in the Boston area is by the *MBTA (Massachusetts Bay Transit Authority) Blue Line* trains, which cost 75¢ and run every 8 minutes (every 15 minutes on weekends) from 6 AM to midnight. From the train stop at downtown's Government Center station at City Hall Plaza, travel time to the airport takes no more than 30 minutes. A water shuttle operated by *Massport* (phone: 800-235-6426) also connects the downtown area with Logan (except in winter, when service is suspended). Boats cross the harbor from Rowes Wharf (400 Atlantic Ave.) to the airport every half hour during rush periods; the trip takes about 10 minutes and costs $7 ($3 for seniors and children under 12).

Bus, Trolley, and Train – The *Massachusetts Bay Transit Authority* (*MBTA*) operates a network of trolleys and subways (referred to by locals as "the T," for trolley) with four major lines, the *Red, Blue, Green, and Orange.* The *MBTA* also runs the city's bus system. Compared to the mass transit systems in most major American cities, Boston's is a bargain: 50¢ for buses, and 75¢ for the T. Exact change required. Three-day visitor's passes are $8, and 7-day passes are $16, which also allow you to ride free on all *MBTA* conveyances — trolleys, subways, trains, and buses. At North Station or the Back Bay Station (phone: 722-5218). Service is fairly frequent during the day, less frequent at night, and nonexistent after about 12:30 AM. *MBTA* stations are marked with large, white circular signs bearing a giant "T." For schedules, directions, time-tables, and maps, call 722-3200. For charter tours, complete with sight-seeing guides, call *Complete Transportation Services,* 800-346-9595.

■ **Note:** Electronic video machines placed on various street corners now assist wandering visitors trying to get their bearings or searching for a particular spot in the area. A combination keyboard and video screen will show the address and telephone number. Or you can ask for a selection of shops and restaurants in the area, and the machine will present a detailed list. Other computer terminals located at Logan Airport provide information on cultural and tourist events throughout New England.

Car Rental – All major national firms are represented. Among the least expensive are *Budget* (with locations at 95 Brighton Ave. in Allston; 24 Eliot St., Park Square, downtown; 150 Huntington Ave.; 133 Federal St., Post Office Square, in the Financial District; 220 Massachusetts Ave. in Cambridge; and at Logan Airport; phone: 800-848-8005); and *American International* (Logan Airport; phone: 569-3550; 200 Stuart St.; phone: 542-4196; or 200 Milk St.; phone: 423-3550).

Taxi – Boston has several taxi fleets, and you can hail them on the street, pick them up at taxi stands downtown, or call for them. *Boston Cab* (phone: 536-5010); *Independent Taxi Operators Assn.* (phone: 426-8700); *Town Taxi* (phone: 536-5000); *Checker Taxi* (phone: 536-7000); *Yellow Cab* (Cambridge; phone: 547-3000); *Ambassador/Brattle Taxi* (Cambridge; phone: 492-1100).

 VITAL SERVICES: Audiovisual Equipment – *Massachusetts Audio Visual Equipment Co.* (phone: 646-5410); *Audio Visual Communications* (phone: 329-6644).

Baby-sitting – *Child Care Resource Center* (552 Mass. Ave., Cambridge; phone: 547-9861); *Parents in a Pinch* (45 Bartlett Crescent, Brookline; phone: 739-5437).

Business Services – *Bette James & Associates,* 1430 Mass. Ave., Cambridge (phone: 661-2622).

Computer Rental – *Computer Factory* at three locations (2 Liberty Square; phone: 542-4554; 660 Summer St.; phone: 348-2911; and One Kendall Sq., Cambridge; phone: 225-0246).

Dry Cleaner/Tailor – *Sarni Original Dry Cleaners,* 1 Winter Pl. (phone: 338-8170) and many other locations.

Limousine – *Carey of Boston* (phone: 623-8700); *Classic Limo* (phone: 266-3980); *Waites Transportation, Inc.* (phone: 567-5867 or 567-0420).

Mechanic – Ray and Tom Magliozzi (they're the amusing "Car Guys" on National Public Radio), at the *Good News Garage,* will repair anything for a fair price. 75 Hamilton St., Cambridge, between Central Square and MIT (phone: 354-5383).

Medical Emergency – *Massachusetts General Hospital,* Fruit St., off Cambridge St. (phone: 726-2000).

Messenger Services – *Beacon Hill Courier Service* (phone: 742-1358); *Boston Cab Association* (phone: 536-5010); *Central Delivery Service,* 24-hour service (phone: 395-3213); *Town Taxi* (phone: 536-5000).

National/International Courier – *Federal Express* (phone: 391-4760); *DHL Worldwide Express* (phone: 846-8770 or 800-225-5345).

Pharmacy – *Phillips Drug,* open 24 hours (155 Charles St.; phone: 523-1078 or 523-4372); *CVS Pharmacy,* open 24 hours (Porter Sq., Cambridge; phone: 876-5519).

Photocopies – *Copy Cop* has many locations, including 815 Boylston St. (phone: 267-9267) and 85 Franklin St. (phone: 451-0233).

Post Office – Downtown, John W. McCormack Station at Post Office SW. and Devonshire St. (phone: 654-5180).

Professional Photographer – *Atlantic Photo Service* (669 Boylston St.; phone: 267-7480); *Fay Foto Service* (45 Electric Ave.; phone: 267-2000).

Secretary/Stenographer – *A-Plus Secretarial Office,* 4 Brattle St., Cambridge (phone: 491-2200).

Teleconference Facilities – The *Charles, Colonnade, Hyatt Regency Cambridge;* the *Marriott* hotels in Cambridge, Copley Place, and Long Wharf; the *Meridien, Omni Parker House,* and the *Royal Sonesta* (see *Best in Town,* below).

Translator – *Berlitz* (437 Boylston St.; phone: 266-6858); *Boston Language Institute* (636 Beacon St.; phone: 262-3500).

Typewriter Rental – *Cambridge Typewriter Co.,* 2-day minimum, 102 Massachusetts Ave., Arlington (phone: 354-6258).

Western Union/Telex – Many locations around the city (phone: 800-325-6000).

Other – *HQ, Headquarters Company,* word processing, telex, facsimile, conference rooms (phone: 451-2589); *Meeting House Offices,* office space, word processing, photocopying, postage meter (phone: 367-7171).

 SPECIAL EVENTS: The *Chinese New Year* is celebrated in Chinatown every February. *Patriots' Day* is observed the third Monday in April, which is also when the famous *Boston Marathon* is run. The *Battle of Bunker Hill* is commemorated on June 17. *Saint's Day* celebrations occur every weekend during July and August on Hanover Street in the North End. Male and female rowers compete in the *Head of the Charles Races* the last Sunday in October. In even-numbered years, the *Harvard-Yale Football Game* is held in Cambridge; this year on November 21.

 MUSEUMS: For descriptions of *Bunker Hill Pavilion,* the *Fogg Museum, Gardner Museum, Museum of Fine Arts, Museum of Science,* and other major museums, see *Special Places.* Other fine museums worth visiting include the following:

Boston Center for the Arts – Multi-use arts complex in a city block of historic buildings. 539 Tremont St. (phone: 426-5000 or 426-7700).

Carpenter Center for the Visual Arts – Le Corbusier's only building in the US; at Harvard University. Rotating exhibitions are presented, as well as four or five film series running simultaneously during the school year. 24 Quincy St., Cambridge (phone: 495-3251).

Children's Museum – Museum Wharf, 300 Congress St. (phone: 426-8855).

Gibson House – Victorian era. 137 Beacon St. (phone: 267-6338).

Museum of Afro-American History – 46 Joy St. (phone: 742-1854).

Ralph Waldo Emerson Memorial House – 28 Cambridge Turnpike, Concord (phone: 508-369-2236).

Society for the Preservation of New England Antiquities – 141 Cambridge St. (phone: 227-3956).

MAJOR COLLEGES AND UNIVERSITIES: Boston is the country's consummate college town, with tens of thousands of students, professors, and visitors from all over the world pouring onto the campuses every academic year. There are literally dozens of educational institutions, including many of the aristocratic New England prep schools. Check the bulletin boards and college newspapers for listings of campus events; Harvard University (see *Special Places*) is the most prestigious in the country (Harvard Sq., Cambridge; phone: 495-1000). MIT (see *Special Places*) produces scientists in all fields, many of whom continue in government research and consulting positions (77 Mass. Ave., Cambridge; phone: 253-1000). In Boston itself, Boston University, with its many colleges and graduate schools, sprawls around Kenmore Square; Charles River Campus (phone: 353-2000). Boston College is an excellent liberal arts college as well as a sports hub in Chestnut Hill (phone: 552-8000). Other schools: Brandeis University (415 South St., Waltham; phone: 736-2000); Emerson College (100 Beacon St.; phone: 578-8500); Emmanuel College (400 The Fenway; phone: 277-9540); Endicott College (376 Hale St., Beverly; phone: 927-0585); Lesley College (29 Everett St., Cambridge; phone: 868-9600); Simmons College (300 The Fenway; phone: 738-2000); Suffolk University (8 Ashburton Pl.; phone: 573-8000); Tufts University (Medford-Somerville; phone: 628-5000); University of Massachusetts/Boston (Park Sq. and Columbia Point; phone: 287-5000); Wellesley College (Wellesley; phone: 235-0320); Wheaton College (Norton; phone: 508-285-7722); Wheelock College (150 The Riverway; phone: 734-5200).

SHOPPING: The best upscale shopping and browsing is found along Newbury Street, where art galleries, fine jewelry, handicrafts, expensive antiques, cosmopolitan restaurants, and cafés flourish. In the Back Bay, Newbury Street runs from Arlington Street at the Public Garden to Massachusetts Avenue. The best traditional New England shopping can be found on Charles Street. This graceful, winding, gaslit street on Beacon Hill looks and feels the way one imagines "Old Boston" to have been. Antiques, prints, books (old and new), and many intimate restaurants and cafés are located here, from Beacon on the Common to Cambridge Street on the back side of Beacon Hill. Two of the more famous spots, offering everything from antique furniture and housewares to clothes and jewelry, are *George Gravery Antiques* (122 Charles St.; phone: 227-1593) and *Boston Antique Cooperative* (119 Charles St.; phone: 227-9810). Below is a list of some of Boston's favorite emporia:

Bailey's of Boston – One of Boston's original, homemade, hand-dipped chocolate businesses now lures local chocoholics to make the short trip to the nearby western suburb of Belmont (just beyond Cambridge on Concord Ave.) to get a chocolate fix. Don't miss the heavenly fudge. 21 Leonard St., Belmont (phone: 484-8264).

Brattle Book Shop – This Dickensian-style bookstore located near the Boston Common is an antiquarian book lover's Elysian Fields. More than 200,000 used, out of print, and rare books populate the 3-story building, with original manuscripts and authors' autographs for sale. Open Monday through Saturday from 9 AM to 5:30 PM. 9 West St. (phone: 542-0210; 800-447-9595).

DeLuca's Market – When almost every food emporium is now either part of a chain or homogenized to anonymity, it's a pleasure to find a friendly, family-run food market devoted to high quality and personal service. 11 Charles St. (phone: 523-4343). Also in the Back Bay at 239 Newbury St. (phone: 262-5990).

Filene's Basement – For the best bargains in town, where else can one find markdowns from every state in the union and nearly every country in the world? Take the *Red* or *Orange* lines to Downtown Crossing. 426 Washington St. (phone: 348-7966).

Harvard Book Store Café – Fine books combined with a classic café and restaurant, which is open-air in the warm months. 190 Newbury St. (phone: 536-0095).

Louis of Boston – Trendy, elegant menswear designed to make a statement. Also on the premises are *Café Louis,* a continental bistro, and a hair salon called *The Cutting Room.* 234 Berkeley St., Back Bay (phone: 965-6100). Second location at *The Mall at Chestnut Hill* (phone: 965-6100).

Museum of Science Gift Shop – For children who have everything: toys, gifts, and artifacts. Science Park (phone: 723-2500).

Out of Town News – A periodical lover's dream, staffed by folks who know when and where every journal under the sun is published: from a Des Moines Sunday paper to a magazine from Cairo. Harvard Sq. (phone: 354-7777).

Toscanini's – Ice cream heaven. Rumor has it that Bostonians eat more ice cream per capita than the residents of any other city. In a blizzard or in balmy weather, it's packed. The ice cream is made on the premises and features exotic foreign flavors such as Italian *nocciola* and *gianduia,* and Indian cardamom-pistachio, mango, and saffron. 899 Main St., Central Sq., Cambridge (phone: 491-5877), and also in the MIT Student Center (phone: 494-1640).

Tower Records – CDs, tapes, LPs, housed in a dazzling 3-story space at 360 Newbury St., on the corner of Mass. Ave. (phone: 247-5900).

Victorian Bouquet Ltd. – Especially noteworthy for its spectacular flower arrangements and cordial, thoughtful staff. 53A Charles St. (phone: 367-6648).

Words Worth Bookstore – A bookworm and gift-giver's paradise packed with every hard- and soft-cover book you can imagine, almost all substantially discounted. 30 Brattle St., Cambridge, near Harvard Sq. (phone: 354-5201).

SPORTS AND FITNESS: No doubt about it, Boston is one of the all-time great professional sports towns.

Baseball – The *Red Sox* play at *Fenway Park,* 24 Yawkey Way. *Green Line,* Kenmore stop (phone: 267-8661).

Basketball – The *Celtics* play at *Boston Garden,* 150 Causeway St. *Green* and *Orange* lines, North Station stop (phone: 523-3030 or 523-6050).

Fishing – *Boston Harbor Fishing* for fishing charters, clambakes, or evening cruises (619 E. Broadway, South Boston; phone: 268-2244); *Atlantic/Yankee Fishing Fleet* for charters April through November (79 Essex Ave., Gloucester; phone: 508-283-0313; 800-942-5464); or *Captain's Fishing Parties and Boat Livery,* half- and full-day charters (Plum Island Pr., Newburyport; phone: 508-462-3441).

Fitness Center – *Fitcorp Fitness and Physical Therapy Center* has a track and workout equipment available (133 Federal St.; phone: 542-1010); there's also the *Boston Health and Swim Club* (1079 Commonwealth Ave., Brighton; phone: 254-1711 and 695 Atlantic Ave.; phone: 439-9600); and *Le Pli* (5 Bennett St., Charles Sq., Cambridge; phone: 547-4081).

Football – The New England *Patriots* play at *Sullivan Stadium,* Rte. 1, Foxboro (phone: 508-262-1776; 800-543-1776).

Golf – There's a city course in Hyde Park, where the Parks and Recreation Department offers golf instruction. Contact *George Wright Pro Shop* (420 West St., Hyde Park; phone: 361-8313 or 361-9679); you also can play or take lessons at the *Fresh Pond* golf club (691 Huron Ave., Cambridge; phone: 354-9130 or 354-8870).

Hockey – The *Bruins* play at *Boston Garden,* 150 Causeway St. *Green* and *Orange* lines, North Station stop (phone: 227-3200).

Jogging – Run along the banks of the Charles River on Memorial or Storrow Drive.

Racing – Greyhounds race at *Wonderland Park,* Revere. (phone: 284-1300).

Sailing – You can rent boats from *Marblehead Rental Boat Co.* (83 Front St., Marblehead; phone: 631-2259), and in Boston at the *Boston Sailing Center* (54 Lewis Wharf; phone: 227-4198).

Skiing – There's cross-country skiing at Weston Ski Track on *Leo J. Martin Golf Course* (Park Rd., Weston; phone: 894-4903) and at *Lincoln Guide Service* (152 Lincoln Rd., Lincoln; phone: 259-9204). Lessons available.

Tennis – There are courts at *Charles River Park* tennis club, 35 Lomasney Way (phone: 742-8922).

THEATER: For information on performance schedules, check the local publications listed above.

Catch a Broadway show before it gets to Broadway. Trial runs often take place at the *Shubert Theatre* (265 Tremont St.; phone: 426-4520); the *Colonial Theatre* (106 Boylston St.; phone: 426-9366); the *Wilbur Theatre* (246 Tremont St.; phone: 423-4008); and the *Wang Center for the Performing Arts* (268 Tremont St.; phone: 800-223-0120). Or check out the *Charles Playhouse* (74 Warrenton St.; phone: 426-6912). This is a much smaller and often livelier place, hosting consistently interesting contemporary plays. The *Lyric Stage* (54 Charles St.; phone: 742-1790) performs new, experimental works — often satiric and political — with aplomb. The *American Repertory Theatre* (64 Brattle St., Cambridge; phone: 547-8300), one of the East Coast's premier repertory companies, is based at Harvard's *Loeb Drama Center* and features an ever-changing bill of plays during the school year. In addition, there are dozens of smaller theater groups, including several affiliated with colleges, such as Boston University's *Huntington Theatre Company* (264 Huntington Ave. in Back Bay; phone: 266-3913). The *Boston Ballet Company* gives performances at the *Wang Center* (see above; call 542-3945 for ballet information). Tickets for theatrical and musical events can be purchased through the *Out of Town Ticket Agency* (in the center of Harvard Square, now on the mezzanine level of that subway station of the *Red Line;* phone: 492-1900); *Ticketron* (phone: 720-3400); or *Bostix* (day of the play), *Faneuil Hall Marketplace* (phone: 723-5181).

MUSIC: Almost every evening, Bostonians can choose from among several classical and contemporary musical performances, ranging from the most delicate chamber music to the most ferocious acid rock. The *Boston Symphony Orchestra,* usually under the baton of Seiji Ozawa, performs at *Symphony Hall,* September through April (301 Mass. Ave.; phone: 266-1492). (In summer, they're at the *Tanglewood Music Festival* in Lenox, MA) Selected members of the *Boston Symphony* make up the *Boston Pops Orchestra,* which performs less weighty orchestrations of popular music, under the direction of John Williams, at *Symphony Hall,* April through July (phone: 266-1492), and gives free outdoor concerts in the *Hatch Shell* on the Charles River Esplanade in June and July. The *Opera Company of Boston,* with Sarah Caldwell, has an elegant home (539 Washington St.; phone: 426-2786). For jazz, try *Nightstage* (823 Main St., Cambridge; phone: 497-8200), *Ryles* (Inman Sq., Cambridge; phone: 876-9330), *Sculler's Jazz Lounge* in the *Guest Quarters Suite* hotel (400 Soldiers Field Rd.; phone: 783-0090), and the *Regattabar* (in the *Charles* hotel, Cambridge; phone: 864-1200), the premier jazz club in the area. Top-name blues and pop musicians play here, too. For folk music, visit *Passim's* (47 Palmer St.,

Cambridge; phone: 492-7679), and for bluegrass, visit *Harpers Ferry* (158 Brighton Ave.; phone: 254-9734).

NIGHTCLUBS AND NIGHTLIFE: A sophisticated and well-heeled crowd gathers nightly in the elegant *Plaza Bar* to listen to topnotch entertainers, *Copley Plaza* hotel (phone: 267-5300), or at the *Palm Court* at *Cricket's* (101 *Faneuil Hall Marketplace;* phone: 720-5570). TV celebrities, professional athletes, and those who want to meet them hang out at tiny, cozy *Daisy Buchanan's* (240A Newbury St. at Fairfield St.; phone: 247-7416). *Narcissus* features dancing to new wave music, has a video performance center, and is available for private parties (535 Commonwealth Ave., Kenmore Square; phone: 536-1950). Devotees of hard rock should try the *Channel Club* (25 Necco St., right beside the Fort Point Channel of the harbor; phone: 451-1905). A rather disheartening sight is the *Bull and Finch* bar of television's "Cheers" fame. Only the façade of this tourist trap (84 Beacon St.; phone: 227-9600) is used for the show; the bar's interior is filled with enough kitsch to send "Cheers" fans running out the door.

BEST IN TOWN

CHECKING IN: Boston has some fine, old, gracious hotels with the history and charm you'd expect to find in this dignified New England capital. But Boston is in the midst of a hotel building boom, and there are now many modern places offering standard contemporary accoutrements. Expect to pay $150 or more for a double room at those places noted as expensive; between $100 and $150 in the moderate category; and inexpensive, under $100. Many of these hotels offer special weekend packages for relatively low rates. Reservations always are required, so write or call well in advance. For bed and breakfast accommodations, contact *Bed & Breakfast Associates of Bay Colony* (PO Box 166, Babson Park, Boston, MA 02157; phone: 449-5302); *Greater Boston Hospitality* (Box 1142, Brookline, MA 02146; phone: 277-5430); *Bed and Breakfast Cambridge & Greater Boston* (Box 665, Cambridge, MA 02140; phone: 576-1492); or write to the Massachusetts Division of Tourism (100 Cambridge St., 13th Floor, Boston, MA 02202) for its *Spirit of Massachusetts Bed & Breakfast Guide.* All telephone numbers are in the 617 area code unless otherwise indicated.

Boston Harbor – A distinctive tower rising 16 stories above the bustle of Rowes Wharf, this striking development resides on the waterfront, overlooking the harbor and the airport. There are 230 rooms, the glass-enclosed *Harborview Lounge,* and the elegant, paneled *Rowes Wharf* restaurant with its handsome bar. Visit the *Rotunda Observatory,* a doughnut-shaped space above the hotel's great arched entrance that has magnificent views of both city and sea. The health club includes a 60-foot pool and a spa with a sauna. Water taxis zip guests to and from the airport in less than 10 minutes. Amenities include 24-hour room service, concierge, secretarial services, A/V equipment, photocopiers, computers, CNN, and express checkout. 70 Rowes Wharf (phone: 439-7000; 800-752-7077; Fax: 617-330-9450; Telex: 920027). Expensive.

Bostonian – Understated and small (152 rooms), this beautifully appointed hotel is across from the shopping and entertainment activities of *Faneuil Hall Marketplace* and just 2 blocks from the North End and the revitalized waterfront. It's glass-enclosed rooftop *Seasons* restaurant discreetly overlooks the colorful bustle below, and is one of the best in Boston. There is 24-hour room service, concierge, secretarial services, A/V equipment, photocopiers, computers, CNN, and express checkout. North and Blackstone Sts. at *Faneuil Hall Marketplace* (phone: 523-3600 or 800-343-0922; Fax: 617-523-2454; Telex: 948159). Expensive.

Charles – Between the Charles River and Harvard Square, this handsome red brick building is the centerpiece of the Charles Square complex. The 296 rooms are well-decorated, and those on the 10th floor have teleconferencing and telecommunications facilities. Relaxation can be sedentary in the pleasant *Bennett Street Café* or elegant *Rarities* restaurant, or more active at the lavish *Le Pli* health spa, complete with an indoor pool. The *Regattabar* features live jazz by top names nightly Tuesdays through Saturdays. Amenities include 24-hour room service, concierge, full conference facilities, secretarial services, A/V equipment, photocopiers, CNN, and express checkout. One Bennett St., Cambridge (phone: 864-1200 or 800-882-1818; Fax: 617-864-5715.) Expensive.

Colonnade – The management at this distinguished 288-room property tries very hard to emulate the tradition of European luxury. There are large rooms, a (seasonal) rooftop pool, *Zachary's* restaurant, and the classy *Promenade Café*. The hotel is near the Prudential Center, Copley Square, and Newbury Street. Amenities include 24-hour room service, concierge, 8 meeting rooms, secretarial services, A/V equipment, photocopiers, computers, CNN, and express checkout. 120 Huntington Ave. (phone: 424-7000 or 800-962-3030; Fax: 617-424-1717; Telex: 940565). Expensive.

Copley Plaza – This large (340 rooms), elegant, old establishment is on one of Boston's handsomest squares adjacent to the Boston Public Library, H. H. Richardson's landmark Trinity Church, and I. M. Pei's famous (some say notorious) John Hancock Building. It's convenient to the South End and the Prudential Center as well as Copley Place and Newbury Street shopping. Among its restaurants, *Copley's* is a New England-style brasserie, while the *Plaza Dining Room* is grand in the continental tradition. The high-ceilinged, dark-panelled *Plaza Bar* is one of the most beautiful in the city, and features some of the great names in jazz. Amenities include 24-hour room service, concierge, 12 meeting rooms, secretarial services, A/V equipment, photocopiers, computers, CNN, and express checkout. 138 St. James Ave., Copley Sq. (phone: 267-5300 or 800-826-7539; Fax: 617-267-7668). Expensive.

Four Seasons – Over $80 million was spent on this 15-story luxury property across from the Public Garden. Fresh flowers fill the rich wood and marble lobby, and 19th-century artwork complements the decor. Its 285 elegant rooms and suites each have a bar and 3 phones. There also are 2 restaurants: *Aujourd'hui,* one of Boston's best (see *Eating Out*), and the more informal *Bristol Lounge,* which features a Viennese dessert buffet Friday and Saturday nights from 9 PM to midnight. The full-service health club includes a pool, sauna, and whirlpool baths. Amenities include 24-hour room service, concierge, 8 meeting rooms, secretarial services, A/V equipment, photocopiers, computers, and express checkout. 200 Boylston St. (phone: 338-4400 or 800-332-3442; Fax: 617-423-0154; Telex: 853349). Expensive.

Guest Quarters Suite – A distinctive property on the Charles River with 10 conventional guestrooms and 310 luxurious suites and *Sculler's Grille* restaurant. Complimentary breakfast is served on weekends. *Sculler's Jazz Lounge* is one of the city's premier jazz venues, and showcases both national and local talent. Health club facilities include a pool, a whirlpool bath, sauna, and exercise machines. At the junction of two major traffic arteries, it is particularly attractive to businesspeople traveling by car. Amenities include room service until 11 PM, concierge, 7 meeting rooms, secretarial services, A/V equipment, photocopiers, computers, CNN, a garage, and express checkout. 400 Soldiers Field Rd., at the Cambridge/Allston exit of I-90, the Mass. Pike (phone: 783-0090 or 800-424-2900; Fax: 617-783-0897). Expensive.

Hyatt Regency, Cambridge – Some 469 rooms surround an atrium with fountains, greenery, and glass-walled elevators. The revolving rooftop restaurant offers a spectacular view of Boston, especially at sunset. Health club facilities are complemented by an indoor pool, sauna, whirlpool bath, and steamroom. Amenities include 24-hour room service, concierge, 4 meeting rooms, secretarial services, A/V equipment, photocopiers, CNN, and express checkout. On the Charles River, near MIT and Harvard (not easily accessible by public transportation). 575 Memorial Dr., Cambridge (phone: 492-1234, 800-233-1234; Fax: 617-491-6906; Telex: 921409). Expensive.

Lafayette – Centrally located in Downtown Crossing and part of the Lafayette Place complex of shops, restaurants, and an outdoor skating rink, this luxury hotel offers European elegance and service. The 487 beautifully appointed rooms are grouped around four atriums. As befits a member of the Swissôtel group, the main dining room is called the *Café Suisse;* for formal dining, the classic *Le Marquis de Lafayette* restaurant offers creative continental fare. A lap pool, sun terrace, and saunas are available. Amenities include 24-hour room service, concierge, 16 meeting rooms, secretarial services, A/V equipment, photocopiers, computers, CNN, and express checkout. 1 Ave. de Lafayette (phone: 451-2600 or 800-992-0124; Fax: 617-451-21989; Telex: 853840). Expensive.

Marriott, Cambridge – The fifth Marriott in Greater Boston is in the heart of the Kendall Square construction boom near MIT. This understated yet posh 431-room property features a comfortable restaurant and lounge, an indoor pool, and a health club with a whirlpool bath and saunas. Amenities include room service until midnight, concierge, 6 meeting rooms, secretarial services, A/V equipment, photocopiers, personal computers, CNN, and express checkout. 2 Cambridge Center (phone: 494-6600 or 800-228-9290; Fax: 617-494-6600). Expensive.

Marriott, Copley Place – This 1,147-room giant is a focal point of the Copley Place development. Among its premium facilities are 3 restaurants, 3 bars, and the largest ballroom and most expansive exhibition area in any Boston hotel. For relaxation, there's an indoor pool, health club, and gameroom. Amenities include 24-hour room service, concierge, 36 meeting rooms, A/V equipment, photocopiers, computers, CNN, and express checkout. 110 Huntington Ave. (phone: 236-5800 or 800-228-9290; Fax: 617-236-9378; Telex: 6712126). Expensive.

Marriott, Long Wharf – A striking 5-story atrium is the centerpiece of this big, downtown property (412 rooms) at the foot of State Street. The *Harbor Terrace Sea Grille* requires a jacket and tie, while the more casual *Rachel's Lounge* provides taped contemporary music for dancing nightly. A ballroom, an indoor-outdoor pool, and a health club offer multiple diversions. Amenities include 24-hour room service, concierge, 5 meeting rooms, A/V equipment, photocopiers, CNN, and computers. 296 State St. (phone: 227-0800 or 800-228-9290; Fax: 617-227-2867). Expensive.

Meridien – Distinctive red awnings mark this splendid renovation of the landmark Federal Reserve Bank Building in the heart of the financial district. The 1922 Renaissance revival structure was transformed with as little exterior alteration as possible; hence, there are 326 chic rooms and 22 stylish suites, in 153 styles. Surrounded by greenery in a 6-story atrium is the French bistro *Café Fleuri;* its Sunday Jazz Brunch has been voted Boston's best every year since 1985. *Julien's* (see *Eating Out*), the elegant dining room, honors the city's first French restaurant of 1794. Its contemporary French menu is the inspiration of consulting chef Olivier Roellinges, chef-owner of *de Bircourt* in Brittany. For chocolate lovers, the hotel is the banquet host for a delectable all-you-can-eat buffet of chocolate desserts on Saturday afternoons from 2:30 to 5:30 PM. Other activities for the restless can be pursued at the health club with indoor pool, whirlpool, and a full workout room, and lobby shops. Across from the hotel, the recently redesigned Post Office Square park offers a lovely, tree-shaded retreat among the brick and stone of the Financial District. Amenities include 24-hour room service; concierge; a variety of meeting and function rooms; secretarial services; A/V equipment, photocopiers, computers, French news telexed in daily from the hotel's Paris headquarters, CNN, and express checkout. 250 Franklin St., Post Office Sq. (phone: 451-1900 or 800-453-4300; Fax: 617-423-2844; Telex: 940194). Expensive.

Omni Parker House – Right on the historic Freedom Trail, this 541-room hostelry is within easy walking distance of Beacon Hill, the Common, and *Faneuil Hall Marketplace.* The hotel's main restaurant (there are 2) is *Parker's* (where Boston cream pie and Parker House rolls were invented); the *Last Hurrah,* a jolly Victorian room in the basement, is livelier, with good food and a swing band. Amenities include room service until midnight, concierge, 14 meeting rooms, secretarial services, A/V equipment, photocopiers, computers, CNN, and express checkout. 60 School St. (phone: 227-8600 or 800-THE-OMNI; Fax: 617-742-5729). Expensive.

Ritz-Carlton – The great lady of Boston hotels, quietly elegant, impeccably correct, and conveniently across from the Public Garden, its 278 rooms are a few steps from Newbury Street shops. The bar is the best place in town for a drink, and the upstairs dining room is superb (see *Eating Out*). Amenities include 24-hour room service, concierge, 6 meeting rooms, secretarial services, A/V equipment, photocopiers, computers, CNN, and express checkout. 15 Arlington St. (phone: 536-5700 or 800-241-3333; Fax: 617-536-1335; Telex: 940591). Expensive.

Royal Sonesta – Tasteful renovations and sparkling additions to this flagship of the Sonesta chain have boosted its room count to 400. There are also 5 eye-catching suites along with the newest outpost of *Davio's* (see *Eating Out*), one of the area's best Northern Italian restaurants. There's also a fully outfitted health club with a pool. Amenities include room service until 1 AM, concierge, numerous meeting rooms, secretarial services, A/V equipment, photocopiers, computers, CNN, and express checkout. 5 Cambridge Pkwy. (near Kendall Sq.), Cambridge (phone: 491-3600 or 800-SONESTA; Fax: 617-661-5956). Expensive.

Sheraton Boston – A huge, 1,252-room modern hotel in the Prudential Center, surrounded by fine places to shop. Its 3 restaurants, 2 cocktail lounges, and a year-round pool and health club provide plenty of diversion. Amenities include 24-hour room service, concierge, 40 meeting rooms, secretarial services, A/V equipment, photocopiers, computers, CNN, and express checkout. 39 Dalton St., Prudential Center (phone: 236-2000 or 800-325-3535; Fax: 617-236-1702; Telex: 940034). Expensive.

Westin, Copley Place – This opulent 36-story, 804-room property is one of two hotels in burgeoning Copley Place, a $500-million development adjacent to Copley Square. Its *Turner Fisheries* restaurant serves award-winning clam chowder in a town renowned for its chowder. There's also a fully outfitted health club with a pool, saunas, and a masseuse. Amenities include 24-hour room service, concierge, secretarial services, A/V equipment, photocopiers, computers, CNN, and express checkout. 10 Huntington Ave. (phone: 262-9600 or 800-228-3000; Fax: 617-451-2750). Expensive.

57 Park Plaza Howard Johnson's – They're pretty much the same everywhere. This one offers free parking, a year-round pool, and a location convenient to downtown. There are 353 rooms, with amenities such as a concierge, secretarial services, A/V equipment, photo-copiers, computers, CNN, and express checkout. 200 Stuart St. (phone: 482-1800 or 800-654-2000; Fax: 617-451-2750). Moderate.

Holiday Inn–Boston Government Center – In Boston's old West End, convenient to Beacon Hill, the Freedom Trail, *Faneuil Hall Market-place,* and the Massachusetts General Hospital medical complex, this 15-story, familiar replica of the national chain offers 301 guestrooms (including some on a deluxe Executive Level), an outdoor pool, and 2 restaurants (notably, the *James Michael*). 5 Blossom St. (phone: 742-7630 or 800-HOLIDAY; Fax: 617-742-4192). Moderate.

Sheraton Commander – A comfortable 178-room hotel (newly reno-vated) directly on the Cambridge Common, within easy walking dis-tance of Harvard University and Harvard Square. This is where many visiting scholars stay. There's a fitness room and sundeck with lovely views of Cambridge. Amenities include room service until 1 AM, con-cierge, 5 meeting rooms, secretarial services, A/V equipment, photo-copiers, personal computers, CNN, and express checkout. 16 Garden St., Cambridge (phone: 547-4800 or 800-325-3535; Fax: 617-868-8322). Moderate.

Tremont House – Small and centrally located, this refurbished and restored landmark in the theater district boasts 281 rooms. There are 2 clubs for music (*Roxy's* for big band and top 1940s sounds, and the *Juke Box,* for more casual 1950s and 1960s tunes) and an already famous *Stage Deli* (of New York) eatery. Amenities include a con-cierge desk, CNN, and 10 conference rooms. 275 Tremont St. (phone: 426-1400 or 800-228-5151; Fax: 617-482-6730). Moderate.

Chandler Inn – Modest and comfortable, conveniently located between Copley and Park Squares, near Copley Place, it has 56 rooms and provides a continental breakfast in its *Fritz Café,* where weekend brunch is available. Amenities also include a concierge desk, 4 meeting rooms, A/V equipment, CNN, and photocopiers. 26 Chandler St. at Berkeley St. (phone: 482-3450 or 800-842-3450). Inexpensive.

Howard Johnson's – Right on the Charles River, this modern, 205-room facility is a few minutes' drive from both Harvard and MIT (not easily accessible by public transportation). Amenities include a con-cierge desk, 4 meeting rooms, CNN, and photocopiers. 777 Memorial Dr. (phone: 492-7777 or 800-654-2000; Fax: 617-492-7777, ext. 1799). Inexpensive.

EATING OUT: Bostonians dine out less frequently than their New York friends, but when they do, they have their choice of several excellent restaurants. Expect to pay $100 or more for two at one of the places we've noted as expensive; between $50 and $100, moderate; and $50 or under, inexpensive. Prices do not include drinks, wine, or tips. All telephone numbers are in the 617 area code unless otherwise indicated.

Aujourd'hui – The lovely, second-story centerpiece of the *Four Seasons,* this hotel dining room has few peers for ambience, food, or wine. The American-cum-continental menu, changing seasonally, features appe-tizing "alternative cuisine" specials that are both good and good for you. Excellent service. Open daily, 8 AM to 10 PM. Reservations ad-vised. Major credit cards accepted. 200 Boylston St. (phone: 451-1392). Expensive.

Bay Tower Room – Featuring a breathtaking view of Boston Harbor from 33 stories high, this restfully elegant dining room is the perfect setting for special occasion suppers and banquets. The American and continental specialties change seasonally. Piano music is featured dur-ing early evening hours, with a live combo taking over later on Fridays and Saturdays. Open Mondays through Saturdays, 5:30 to 10 or 11 PM; open on Sundays for special functions. Reservations necessary.

Major credit cards accepted. 60 State St. (phone: 723-1666). Expensive.

Le Bocage – Some of the most consistently delectable French food available in New England. Both Gallic regional and classic entrées grace the menu, which changes to suit the season. A bright, efficient staff and a fine wine cellar add to the pleasurable dining. Closed Sundays. Reservations advised. Major credit cards accepted. 72 Bigelow Ave., Watertown (phone: 923-1210). Expensive.

Chez Nous – Sophisticated French fare is served in a luxurious yet intimate setting. The service is truly accommodating, and in the tradition of quiet, elegant establishments, nearly invisible. Daily fresh fish, rack of lamb Provençal, beef tenderloin spiced with thyme and port, and roast duck garnished with green peppercorns and cognac are all menu standouts. Closed Sundays. Reservations advised. Major credit cards accepted. 147 Huron Ave., Cambridge (phone: 864-6670). Expensive.

L'Espalier – Its legion of devotees would not ever choose any other polished, contemporary French restaurant for supper. Whether it's foie gras, veal, lobster, venison, or wine one craves, the French accents are unmistakable, authentic, and flavorful. This eatery resides in a beautiful Back Bay townhouse with 3 elegant, intimate dining rooms. Closed Sundays. Reservations advised. Major credit cards accepted. 30 Gloucester St. (phone: 262-3023). Expensive.

Jasper's – Chef Jasper White has an inventive touch and a national reputation, manifested skillfully in his unique treatment of such items as squab breasts and venison. Another excellent combination is the cape scallops with sun-dried tomatoes. He also makes his own pasta and serves it with equal flair. Closed Sundays. Reservations advised. Major credit cards accepted. 240 Commercial St. (phone: 523-1126). Expensive.

Julien's – The grandeur of the decor, with its high ceilings, walls with ivy-bedecked trellises, and graceful Queen Anne chairs, in no way inhibits the dining atmosphere. Situated in the Members Court of what was the old Federal Reserve Building (now the *Meridien* hotel), this dining spot produces such culinary novelties as halibut with Caribbean spices and duck with spiced figs and candied turnips. Open daily. Reservations advised. Major credit cards accepted. 240 Commercial St. (phone: 523-1126). Expensive.

Michela's – Housed in a huge, converted building in the Kendall Square area of Cambridge, this chic eatery draws the cognoscenti from all around Boston to sample American food with a distinct Northern Italian accent. Choose either the dining room proper or the café (which doesn't take reservations). The menus are completely different, but not the panache with which the food is prepared. Closed Sundays. Reservations strongly advised for the dining room, especially on weekend nights. Major credit cards accepted. 1 Atheneum St., Cambridge (phone: 225-2121). Expensive.

Ritz-Carlton Dining Room – Large, lovely, serenely elegant, and one of only two places in town where you can enjoy a view of the Public Garden while dining with old-fashioned formality. The cuisine is continental, very good, and is served by an expert staff. Men must wear jackets and ties. Open daily. Reservations advised. Major credit cards accepted. 15 Arlington St. (phone: 536-5700). Expensive.

798 Main Street – An understated, tranquil space enlivened by bouquets of fresh flowers, it serves some of the city's best continental fare from a menu that changes constantly. Specialties include crab and scallop casserole, braised venison, maple barbecued chicken, and wild mushroom stew. Closed Sundays and Mondays. Reservations advised. Major credit cards accepted. 798 Main St., Kendall Sq., Cambridge (phone: 492-9500 or 876-8444). Expensive.

Anthony's Pier 4 – Sometimes overrun with tourists, this Boston institution has a dramatic location on the harbor and a commodious waterfront deck where you can have drinks and enjoy the view while you wait for your table. Good seafood, generous servings. Open daily. Reservations advised. Major credit cards accepted. At 140 Northern Ave. (phone: 423-6363). Expensive to moderate.

Biba – Facing the Public Garden, this dramatic 2-level restaurant and bar is the creation of Lydia Shire, one of Boston's most admired young chefs. The inventive, six-part menu affords amazing choices for varying appetites and changing seasons. The sweetbreads are heavenly. The wine list is remarkable in both range and price. Open daily, 11:30 AM to 9:30 or 10:30 PM (no lunch on Saturdays; snack menu available at bar). Reservations necessary. Major credit cards accepted. 272 Boylston St. (phone: 426-7878). Expensive to moderate.

Café Budapest – Decorated in the lavish Eastern European tradition, and renowned for fine continental and Hungarian cooking. On weeknights this is a wonderful place to linger over superb strudel and some of the best coffee anywhere. To be avoided on Saturday nights, when no reservations are accepted and hordes of hungry diners sometimes wait hours for tables. Open daily. Reservations advised. Major credit cards accepted. 90 Exeter St. (phone: 266-1979). Expensive to moderate.

Davio's – The crown prince of Northern Italian cooking in this area. Regional and continental entrées are consistently well prepared, highlighted by veal chops, homemade pasta, and "upscale," luscious pizza combinations. Good wines, good service, lovely, elegant surroundings. Open daily. Reservations advised. Major credit cards accepted. Three locations: 269 Newbury St. (phone: 262-4810); 204 Washington St. in Brookline Village (phone: 738-4810); and in the *Royal Sonesta,* 5 Cambridge Pkwy., Cambridge (phone: 661-4810). Expensive to moderate.

Hampshire House – Thoroughly evocative of 19th-century Boston is this former mansion overlooking the Public Garden. The paneled, clubby café-bar, the *Oak Room Lounge,* has piano music (except on Sundays and Mondays), moose heads on the wall, and a fire blazing in the winter. It offers a simple continental menu and a range of lighter fare. In the refined, eminently Victorian dining room, more elegant American fare, such as New York strip steak and chicken Divan, are served. The basement houses the tacky *Bull and Finch Pub,* a boisterous meeting, eating, and drinking place that was the inspiration for the television series "Cheers," and is now, predictably, jam-packed with tourists. Open daily. Reservations necessary. Major credit cards accepted. 84 Beacon St. (phone: 227-9600). Expensive to moderate.

Harvest – A colorful dining room, lively bar, café, and (weather permitting) a secluded outdoor patio, all tucked into a back corner of the former Design Research complex in Harvard Square. The dining room menu features nicely executed international dishes in its nouvelle cuisine repertoire, fine salads, wines, and desserts. The café serves bistro fare. Open daily. Reservations advised. Major credit cards accepted. 44 Brattle St. (phone: 492-1115). Expensive to moderate.

Locke-Ober Café – A splendid, albeit somewhat stuffy, tradition in probably the best known of Boston's top dining places. Though it was once an exclusive male bastion, today both sexes can eat in the handsome *Men's Grill,* with its glowing mahogany bar lined with massive silver tureens, its stained glass, snowy linens, and indefatigable gray-haired waiters. The food is identical in the less distinguished upstairs room — heavy on continental dishes and seafood. Open daily. Reservations necessary. Major credit cards accepted. 3 Winter Pl. (phone: 542-1340). Expensive to moderate.

Maison Robert – Among the finest French restaurants in the country, with food, drink, ambience, and service all worthy of top ranking. Owner-chef Lucien Robert has taught many of the French chefs in Boston and continues to prepare sauces for fish, fowl, and meat that defy imitation. Two dining areas, *Ben's Café* downstairs (on the patio in summer) and the elegant *Bonhomme Richard* upstairs, are open for lunch and dinner. Closed Sundays. Reservations necessary. Major credit cards accepted. 45 School St. in the old City Hall (phone: 227-3370). Expensive to moderate.

St. Cloud – One of the first culinary outposts in the now-trendy South End, and still one of the best. Steamed mussels with tomato, fennel, and saffron broth, grilled tenderloin of beef with balsamic vinegar sauce, and roasted Maine lobster with chive broth and corn and pepper flan are some of the wonderful dishes. The menu changes seasonally. Open daily. Reservations advised. Major credit cards accepted. 557 Tremont St. (phone: 353-0202). Expensive to moderate.

Upstairs at the Pudding – Set in the old upstairs dining room of Harvard's famous *Hasty Pudding Club* (the walls are lined with original, hand-painted showbills from the club's productions of years past), this elegant place reeks of old Ivy, but the food is decidedly contemporary — and first-rate. Harvard singing groups frequently perform at Sunday brunch. Open daily. Reservations advised. Major credit cards accepted. 10 Holyoke St., Cambridge (phone: 864-1933). Expensive to moderate.

Another Season – An intimate spot on Beacon Hill with murals evoking turn-of-the-century Paris, its menu changes monthly and features inventive continental cooking. Fresh seafood, a vegetarian entrée, and a marvelous array of desserts always are available. There's also an inexpensive prix fixe menu that has a weekly culinary theme such as Eastern Europe or a New England Harvest. Dinner only; closed Sundays. Reservations advised. Major credit cards accepted. 97 Mt. Vernon St. (phone: 367-0880). Moderate.

Cajun Yankee – The granddaddy of the New England crawdaddy crowd, this down-home, creole place is perpetually packed. All the Cajun staples are here — blackened fish, jambalaya, sweet potato pie — in spicy, pungent abundance. Beverages are correspondingly "down south," thirst-quenching. Closed Sundays and Mondays. Reservations advised on weekends. Major credit cards accepted. 1193 Cambridge St., Inman Sq., Cambridge (phone: 576-1971). Moderate.

Changsho – The food served in the new home of this Cambridge institution is still the best Chinese cooking you'll find outside New York's Chinatown, but the restaurant has moved from its tiny, crowded storefront into a strikingly elegant — and much larger — space a block away. Open daily. No reservations. Major credit cards accepted. 1712 Massachusetts Ave., Cambridge (phone: 547-6565). Moderate.

Chart House – In the oldest building on the waterfront, its interior is a strikingly handsome arrangement of lofty spaces, natural wood, exposed red brick, and comfortable captain's chairs. The menu lists abundant portions of steaks and seafood, with all the salad you can eat included in the reasonable prices. Open daily. Reservations advised on weekend nights. Major credit cards accepted. 60 Long Wharf (phone: 227-1576). Moderate.

Cornucopia – Off the beaten track between the Common and Lafayette Place is the historic home of the Peabody family. Here Nathaniel Hawthorne married Sophia, and Elizabeth opened the bookstore that became the meeting place for such literati as Emerson and Thoreau. Today, it has been renovated to accommodate a striking restaurant that features an eclectic blend of regional and ethnic dishes. The menu changes seasonally. Lunch, weekdays only; dinner, Tuesdays through Saturdays. Reservations advised. Major credit cards accepted. 15 West St. (phone: 338-4600). Moderate.

Dali – Garlic braids hanging from the ceiling, white plaster walls daubed with kitschy swirls, and waiters in red jackets and black cummerbunds are not the only things that make this *tapas* bar seem authentic: The kitchen turns out Spanish specialties seldom seen outside Iberia. From the marinated olives served with drinks to the changing list of *tapas* (hors d'oeuvres) and entrées such as *pescado al sal* (whole snapper baked in a salt crust) or *conejo escabechado* (rabbit braised in red wine with juniper berries), dining here is a delicious adventure. There's usually a wait for a table (no reservations), but if you're not in a hurry, order a pitcher of sangria and have another dish of olives. Closed Sundays. Reservations advised. Major credit cards accepted. 415 Washington St., Somerville (phone: 661-3254). Moderate.

Dover Grille – An understated, relaxed, beautifully appointed seafood restaurant and lounge in Brookline, just a clamshell's throw from both Fenway Park and the Harvard Medical School. Marvelous grilled entrées, especially salmon and swordfish, are specialties, as well as bountiful salads and superb desserts. "Early Catch" specials are available weeknights from 5 to 6 PM. Open daily. Reservations advised. Major credit cards accepted. 1223 Beacon St. (phone: 566-7000). Moderate.

East Coast Grill – You might not expect great Southern barbecue around Beantown, but this coolly stylish Inman Square grill repeatedly wins national praise and prizes — and the crowds waiting to be seated testify to the attitude of the locals. In addition to authentic North Carolina shredded pork barbecue, Texas brisket barbecue, and Memphis-style dry-rub ribs, you can get a great spit-roasted chicken, imaginative duck and lamb dishes, and delectable grilled swordfish paired with something spicy — ginger-scallion relish or a mayonnaise of smoked *chipotle* chilies. And if the food isn't hot enough for you, the owners thoughtfully leave a bottle of their Inner Beauty Hot Sauce on every table. Open daily. No reservations (and there's usually a good wait). Major credit cards accepted. 1271 Cambridge St., Cambridge (phone: 491-6568). Moderate.

Genji – An intimate Japanese restaurant in the Back Bay that serves beautifully prepared traditional fare, including tantalizing tempura and sushi. A picturesque, private tearoom can be reserved for special occasions. The service is friendly and informative. Try the complete dinner, which is sumptuous and very reasonably priced. Open daily for lunch and dinner. Reservations advised. Major credit cards accepted. 327 Newbury St. (phone: 267-5656). Moderate.

Hamersley's Bistro – For real home-style cooking, head to this lively place in the heart of the South End. Owner Gordon Hamersley dishes up a hearty bouillabaisse, wonderful cassoulet, and excellent roast chicken. Open daily. Reservations advised. Visa and MasterCard accepted. 578 Tremont St. (phone: 267-6068). Moderate.

Legal Sea Foods – If you don't mind waiting in line (no reservations), you'll find fresh and well-prepared seafood that we think is the best in Boston. Open daily. Major credit cards accepted. Four locations: *Park Plaza Hotel,* corner of Columbus and Arlington (phone: 426-4444); in the *Chestnut Hill Shopping Mall,* 43 Boylston St. (phone: 277-7300); and 5 Cambridge Center, Kendall Sq., Cambridge (phone: 864-3400); and Copley Place (phone: 266-7775). Moderate.

Milk Street Café – Its original home sandwiched into a sparkling niche of the financial district, this bustling vegetarian and fish cafeteria presents superb breakfasts and lunches. The muffins, smoked salmon platter, flavorful soups, and generous, artful quiche are perennial pleasers. Open weekdays until 3 PM. Reservations advised. No credit cards accepted. Two locations: 50 Milk St. (phone: 542-2433); 101 Main St., Kendall Sq., Cambridge, near MIT (phone: 491-8286). Moderate.

Olives – Superb Tuscany-influenced Italian food served in a soothing dove-colored dining room with comfortable banquettes. Try the grilled lobster with white bean *raviolone* and artichoke sauce or the *tortelli* of butternut squash with brown butter and sage. Open Tuesdays through Saturdays. Reservations advised for groups of 6 or more. Visa and MasterCard accepted. 67 Main St., Charlestown (phone: 242-1999). Moderate.

Rebecca's – White walls, blond wood furniture, and works by local artists dominate the comfortable, modern decor. The menu, described as "new American," borrows from French, Greek, Indian, and Italian cuisines. Open daily. No reservations. Major credit cards accepted. 21 Charles St. (phone: 742-9747). Moderate.

St. Botolph – Actually a restored 19th-century brick townhouse, this 2-story eatery sports a contemporary interior with exposed brick walls and a continental menu with good, fresh seafood. Lunch served weekdays; dinner nightly; brunch on Sundays. Reservations advised. Major credit cards accepted. 99 St. Botolph St. (phone: 266-3030). Moderate.

Skipjack's Seafood Emporium – With a dazzling location in Copley Square, this mariner's delight features an extensive array of innovative seafood dishes (they claim to serve the widest variety of seafood in New England). Snapper Veracruz, grilled cilantro shrimp, and blackened redfish are just three of the outstanding choices. For dieters, a spa menu is available, which offers 10 items of 400 calories or less. The wine list is extensive and carefully assembled. Special Sunday jazz brunch is a treat (from 11 AM to 3 PM). Open daily, 11AM to 11PM. Reservations advised. Major credit cards accepted. 500 Boylston St., Copley Square, Back Bay (phone: 536-3500); 2 Brookline Pl., Brookline (phone: 232-8887). Moderate.

Durgin-Park – Though famed for generous servings of traditional Yankee roast beef, prime ribs, oyster stew, Boston baked beans, and Indian pudding (among the reasons Native Americans lost this land), the kitchen now is way below par. However, its long, communal tables are still crowded with convivial diners and brusque, no-nonsense waitresses. Open daily. No reservations or credit cards accepted. Two locations: 340 *Faneuil Hall Marketplace* (phone: 227-2038) and Copley Place (phone: 266-1964). Moderate to inexpensive.

Rubin's Kosher Delicatessen – One of only two kosher restaurants in Boston, its chopped liver, potato *latkes* (pancakes), and lean pastrami (hot or cold) are the genuine articles. Open Sundays through Thursdays; closes Fridays at 3 PM. Reservations unnecessary. Major credit cards accepted. 500 Harvard St., Brookline (phone: 566-8761). Moderate to inexpensive.

Stage Deli – The Boston–New York "deli wars" have found a savory, satisfying harmony in this bright, bustling little eatery in the theater district. From corned beef and chopped liver worth the name to authentic egg creams and ultra-rich cheesecake, all the required deli delights are available at tables and for takeout. Open daily. No reservations. Major credit cards accepted. 275 Tremont St. (phone: 523-DELI). Moderate to inexpensive.

Ye Olde Union Oyster House – It's the real thing: Boston's oldest restaurant. Daniel Webster himself used to guzzle oysters at the wonderful mahogany oyster bar, where skilled shuckers still pry them open before your eyes. Full seafood lunches and dinners are served upstairs, amid well-worn colonial ambience. (One booth is dedicated to John F. Kennedy, once a frequent diner.) Don't miss the seafood chowder. Open daily. No reservations. Major credit cards accepted. 41 Union St. (phone: 227-2750). Moderate to inexpensive.

Elsie's Lunch – This storefront shop, a block from Harvard Yard, has been serving food and drink to famished Harvard students for longer than anyone can remember. A great place to go when your feet are tired, or when you just want to fill up. Open daily. No reservations or credit cards accepted. 71 Mt. Auburn St., Cambridge (phone: 354-8781 or 354-8362). Inexpensive.

Jake and Earl's Dixie BBQ – If you feel more like jumping in a taxi, grabbing some great takeout, and heading back to your hotel, aim for this place next door to the *East Coast Grill*. It's owned by the same duo, and it's equally passionate about authenticity-in-barbecue. In addition to doing all the smoking for its sibling next door, this spot offers up its own list of spicy specialties. The half-jerk chicken is hot and juicy, the daily specials, such as a barbecued bologna sandwich, are always original and surprisingly good, and for $3.95, the pulled-pork sandwich (it comes with a moist hunk of cornbread, fresh cole-slaw, rich and spicy beans, and a slice of watermelon) is a bargain-hunter's bargain. The Elvis memorabilia (from license plates to an assortment of plastic and plaster busts) will keep you entertained while you're waiting, which is never long. Open daily. Reservations unnecessary. Most major credit cards accepted. 1273 Cambridge St., Cambridge (phone: 491-7427). Inexpensive.

- **Sinfully Sweet:** While you're in Cambridge, stop in at *Rosie's Bakery and Desert Shop,* a brightly lit storefront bakery in Inman Square, for a prizewinning brownie, an indescribably rich concoction delicately named a "Chocolate Orgasm," or a slice of the best poppyseed cake — well, anywhere. A great place to order cakes for special occasions, too, should you find yourself in Boston with something to celebrate. Open daily. Major credit cards accepted. 243 Hampshire St., Cambridge (phone: 491-9488). Moderate.

- **NORTH END RESTAURANTS:** Modestly priced Italian meals are available in dozens of little restaurants in Boston's oldest section, the North End. *Felicia's* is popular with Hub celebrities, and Felicia herself, a local personality, oversees the preparation of the food. Open daily. Reservations advised. Major credit cards accepted (145A Richmond St.; phone: 523-9885). *Lucia's* is a warm neighborhood restaurant that unfailingly provides satisfying Italian food. Open daily. Reservations advised. Major credit cards accepted (415 Hanover St.; phone: 523-9148). Many locals swear the town's best pizza is tossed and baked at *Circle Pizza* (361 Hanover St.; phone: 367-2353). Others claim the *European* restaurant produces an even better pie, and it also has a large menu designed for the entire family. Open daily. Reservations advised. Major credit cards accepted (218 Hanover St.; phone: 523-5694). *Mother Anna's* (211 Hanover St.; phone: 523-8496) and *Ida's* (3 Mechanic St.; phone: 523-0015) are small, home-style eateries noted for a fiercely loyal clientele and for authentic dishes cooked to order. Both are open daily, take reservations, and do not accept credit cards. All are moderate to inexpensive.

CHARLESTON, SC

AT-A-GLANCE

SEEING THE CITY: Charleston is set in that sea-level peninsula of southeastern South Carolina known as the Low Country. There are no hills from which to get a good view of the city. Nicknamed the Holy City because of its many church spires, Charleston's best view is from the ground, looking up, especially at night, when floodlights illuminate the church spires.

Guided bus or van tours are available from *Adventure Sightseeing* (phone: 762-0088), *Talk of the Towne* (phone: 577-0634), and *Gray Line Bus Tours* (phone: 722-4444). To see the city from the harbor, take a *Gray Line* water tour, departing at 2 PM daily (more often in summer) from the City Marina on Lockwood Blvd. (phone: 722-1112). It's also possible to rent a tape cassette from *Charles Towne Tours* (phone: 723-5133) for a walking or driving tour. Narrated tours in horse-drawn carriages are provided by *Charlestown Carriage Co.* (phone: 577-0042), *Palmetto Carriage Tours* (phone: 723-8145), and *Old South Carriage Co.* (phone: 723-9712) from 9 AM to dusk, with night rates as well; reservations accepted. Walking tours are conducted by *Charleston Tea Party* (phone: 577-5896) and *Civil War Walking Tours* (phone: 722-7033). Take a bicycle tour with a map and a bike from the *Bicycle Shop* (phone: 722-8168).

SPECIAL PLACES: The old city is approximately 7 square miles, and even a 5-day visit could be spent walking without covering the same street twice. An evening stroll is most popular with residents.

Ft. Sumter – A national monument, the fort where the first shots of the Civil War were fired in 1861 sits on a small manmade island at the entrance to Charleston's harbor. Under federal attack from 1863 to 1865, Ft. Sumter withstood the longest siege in warfare. The Confederates gave up the fort in February 1865. To the Union, it represented secession and treachery; to the Confederates, it meant resistance and courage. The fort can be reached only by boat. *Ft. Sumter Tours* leave City Marina (17 Lockwood Blvd.) at 2:30 PM in winter, three times daily in summer. One tour leaves Patriot's Point daily at 2:30 PM; three times daily in summer. Admission charge (phone: 722-1691).

Charles Towne Landing – Charleston was called Charles Towne in 1670 when the first permanent English settlers arrived. Now a state park, Charles Towne Landing has a number of restored houses, a full-scale replica of a 17th-century trading vessel, open-air pavilion with underground displays of artifacts found during archaeological excavations, and an animal forest with indigenous animals. Plenty of picnic tables, bike trails, and tram tours, too. The museum sustained structural damage during Hurricane Hugo and at press time is still closed, although all other facilities are once again open. The reopening date for the museum is still uncertain. Open daily 9 AM to 5 PM. Admission charge. 1500 Old Towne Rd. (phone: 556-4450).

Magnolia Plantation and Gardens – World famous for its abundance of colors and scents, Magnolia Gardens' 30 acres abound with 900

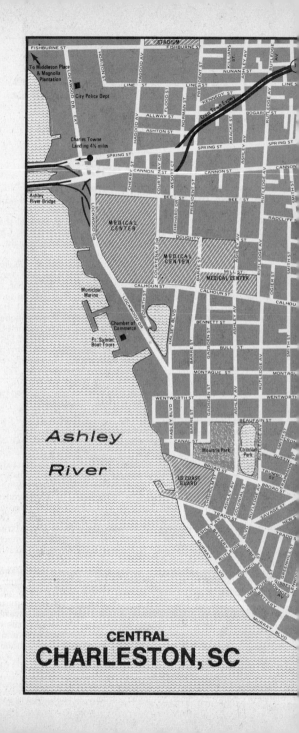

CENTRAL
CHARLESTON, SC

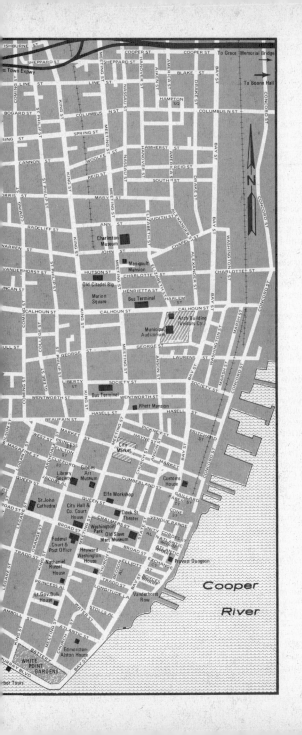

different varieties of camellias, 250 varieties of azaleas, and dozens of different exquisite plants, shrubs, and flowers. Listed in the National Register of Historic Places, Magnolia Plantation has been the home of the Drayton family since the 1670s. In addition to the boat tours, a small zoo, and a ranch exhibiting a breed of miniature horse, Magnolia Gardens offers canoeing, bird watching, and bike trails through its 400-acre wildlife refuge. One of the newest additions to the plantation is the Audubon Swamp Garden, a separate, very secluded 60-acre cyprus swamp. Though this area remained virtually untouched by Hurricane Hugo, the rest of the grounds did suffer. Seventy percent of the damage consisted of the loss of a great number of pine trees, but the only physical evidence of this is the absence of the once dominating shade that the trees used to provide, as more than 12,000 azaleas and numerous new trees have been planted in their stead. Open all year, from 8 AM to 5 PM, except *Christmas.* Admission charge. 10 miles northwest on Rte. 61 (phone: 571-1266).

Boone Hall – If you ever imagined yourself as one of those romantic characters in *Gone With the Wind,* Boone Hall is the place to live out your dream. This 738-acre estate, formerly a cotton plantation, closely resembles MGM's movie set (or is it the other way around?). Settled by Major John Boone in 1681, Boone Hall underwent $1.5 million worth of reconstruction after Hurricane Hugo struck here. About 300 acres of timberland were lost, as well as 200 acres of the famous pecan groves. Roofs were replaced on the buildings, including the original slave houses. Open daily except *Thanksgiving* and *Christmas.* Admission charge. Seven miles north on Rte. 17 (phone: 884-4371).

Drayton Hall – The only pre-Revolutionary mansion remaining on the Ashley River, this National Historic Landmark is one of the finest surviving examples of Georgian Palladian architecture. The mansion is unfurnished, but its tower offers a special look at colonial South Carolina. A victim of Hugo, 70 of its beautiful old trees came down, but only one window of the house was broken. Open daily, except *Thanksgiving, Christmas,* and *New Year's Day.* Admission charge. Nine miles northwest of downtown on Hwy. 61 (phone: 766-0188).

Charleston Museum – This oldest municipal museum in the country has impressive collections of arts, crafts, furniture, textiles, and implements from South Carolina's early days. Special film shows. Open daily except holidays. Admission charge. 360 Meeting St. (phone: 722-2996).

Old Exchange and Provost Dungeon – Another grim reminder of what history was really like. The Provost Dungeon dates to 1780. Here, the British imprisoned American patriots during the Revolutionary War, and exhibits show how they were treated during their detention. Attached to the Provost are excavations from the Half Moon Battery (ca. 1690), the original city wall built by the British. Closed Sundays and major holidays. Admission charge. East Bay St. at Broad, under the Exchange Bldg. (phone: 792-5020).

Elfe Workshop – Thomas Elfe was an 18th-century cabinetmaker whose individual pieces now sell for as much as $80,000. Built between 1750 and 1760, the mansion has small rooms and reproduction furnishings that may make you wonder if Thomas Elfe really was one. You can ask. The guides are friendly and well-informed and give three morning tours on weekdays. Closed Sundays. Admission charge. 54 Queen St. (phone: 722-2130).

■ **EXTRA SPECIAL:** At Middleton Place, about 15 miles north of Charleston via Rte. 61, the self-sustaining world of a Carolina Low Country plantation is re-created daily by people in 18th-century costume. Built in 1755, Middleton Place features the oldest landscaped gardens in the country, laid out by Henry Middleton in 1741. The 1,000-year-old Middleton Oak, which sustained only minor damage from Hurricane Hugo, and the oldest camellias in the New World flourish on the lush grounds. Arthur Middleton, a signer of the Declaration of Independence, is buried here. A national historic landmark, Middleton House is the site of the *Spoleto Festival Finale* in June and *Plantation Days* (a dramatization of life on a plantation) in November. As a result of Hurricane Hugo, the plantation suffered the loss of nearly 500 trees, including the largest eastern red cedar in the US. As a result of countless volunteers, however, the plantation now looks as if it were untouched by the storm. Open daily from 9 AM to 5 PM. Admission charge (phone: 556-6020).

SOURCES AND RESOURCES

TOURIST INFORMATION: The visitors' information center now has a new home (375 Meeting St.; Charleston, SC 29401; phone: 722-8338) where you can get advice or brochures on tours, hotels, and restaurants. The staff will assist you in making reservations. Open daily. A half-hour multimedia presentation about the city, *Charleston Adventure,* is shown frequently at the visitors' information center. Admission charge (phone: 723-5225). In the historic district, The *Preservation Society of Charleston* (147 King St. at Queen St.; phone: 723-4381) also offers information and tours, and has a gift shop. The historical film *Dear Charleston* is shown hourly for an admission charge. The *Historic Charleston Foundation* museum shop at 108 Meeting St. (phone: 724-8484) offers information and tickets to area attractions. The *Historic Charleston Foundation Preservation Center* (phone: 723-3646) sells licensed reproductions of furniture and accessories at *Historic Charleston Reproductions* (105 Broad St.; phone: 723-8292). Contact the South Carolina state hotline (phone: 803-734-0122) for maps, calendars of events, health updates, and travel advisories.

For information on events and performance schedules, call the visitors' information center (phone: 722-8338) or the Charleston County Parks and Recreation Commission (phone: 762-2172).

Local Coverage – *Charleston News & Courier,* morning daily; *Evening Post,* evening daily.

Television Stations – WCBD Channel 2–ABC; WCIV Channel 4–NBC; WCSC Channel 5–CBS; WITV Channel 7–PBS.

Radio Stations – AM: WBAL 730 (rhythm & blues); WTMA 1250 (country music). FM: WSCI 89.3 (classical/jazz); WAVF 96.1 (rock 'n' roll); WXLY 102 (classic rock).

TELEPHONE: The area code for Charleston is 803.
Sales Tax – The sales tax in Charleston is 5%.

CLIMATE: Charleston's average temperature is 65F. Winters are mild, summers hot. March and April are the best spring months to visit, when the city is most accessible by foot and everything green and growing is abloom. In the fall, October and November are ideal.

GETTING AROUND: Airport – Charleston International Airport is a 20-minute drive from downtown; taxi fare should run about $15. *LowCountry Limousine* provides van service from the airport to the downtown hotels for $8 (phone: 767-7117).

Bus – The *South Carolina Electric and Gas Company* operates the city bus system (665 Meeting St.; phone: 722-2226). The *Downtown Area Shuttle* (*DASH*) operates on weekdays (phone: 724-7368).

Car Rental – Major national agencies are represented at the airport.

Taxi – Taxis are rather inexpensive and a better bet than buses; they must be ordered by phone. Call *Yellow Cab* (phone: 577-6565) or *Eveready Cab Co.* (phone: 722-8383).

 VITAL SERVICES: For information about local services, call the Chamber of Commerce (phone: 577-2510).

Business Services – For any work involving office automation, call *Norell Temporary Services* (phone: 554-4933).

Mechanics – *Jennings Exxon* (102 E. Bay St.; phone: 722-3957) or *Rumph's Auto Service* (45 Romney St.; phone: 722-7398).

Medical Emergency – *Charleston Memorial Hospital,* 326 Calhoun St. (phone: 577-0600).

Messenger Services – *Yellow Cab* (phone: 577-6565); *Bullet Deliveries of Charleston* (phone: 763-4129).

National/International Courier – *Federal Express* (phone: 767-0275; 800-238-5355); *DHL World Courier Express* (phone: 800-227-6177).

Pharmacy – *Prescription Center,* Mondays through Fridays, 9AM to 8 PM; Saturdays 9 AM to 6 PM; will deliver (107 Rutledge Ave; phone: 722-7398).

Photocopies – *American Speedy Printing Center* (1660 Sam Rittenberg Blvd.; phone: 571-7556); *Kinko's Copies* (King and Calhoun Sts.; phone: 723-5130).

Post Office – Central, Broad, and Meeting Sts. (phone: 724-4333).

Professional Photographer – *Larry Workman Photography* (phone: 723-3667); *Alterman Studios* (phone: 577-0647).

Secretary/Stenographer – *Norell Services,* for office automation work (phone: 554-4933).

Translator – *Interpreter's Guide* available from the Chamber of Commerce (phone: 577-2510).

Typewriter Rental – *Ideal Business Machines* (3250 Tile Dr.; phone: 747-6097).

Western Union/Telex – Many offices are located about town (800-325-6000).

Other – *Creative Charleston Experiences,* meeting planning, catered dinners in antebellum homes, office space (phone: 766-4861).

 SPECIAL EVENTS: The *Southeastern Wildlife Exhibition* draws over 40,000 visitors to its conservation and wildlife artwork exhibits during the second week of February, at 15 different locations downtown (phone: 723-1748). *Spoleto Festival USA,* 17 days of chamber music, dance, jazz, opera, and theater, begins every year in late May. For schedule information, call 722-2764. An array of local events, many free, make up *Piccolo Spoleto,* which coincides with the main festival (phone: 724-7305). During the *Festival of Houses and Gardens,* from mid-March to mid-April, more than 90 private homes and gardens are open to the public. Admission charge (phone: 723-1623). The Preservation Society conducts *Candlelight Tours of Homes & Gardens* in September and October. Admission charge (phone: 722-4630).

MUSEUMS: The *Charleston Museum* is described under *Special Places.* Some other notable museums include the following:

Beth Elohim Archives Room – Artifacts relating to the oldest continuous Hebrew congregation in the US. 90 Hasell St. (phone: 723-1090).

Gibbes Museum of Art – A fine collection by 18th- and 19th-century American painters, local and regional art, and portrait miniatures. 135 Meeting St. (phone: 722-2706).

Patriots Point Maritime Museum – On Highway 17N, just across the Cooper River, this US naval history museum features the aircraft carrier USS *Yorktown* and several other ships (phone: 884-2727).

HISTORIC HOUSES: Except where noted, the houses listed below are open daily except holidays. Admission charges.

    Aiken-Rhett Mansion (1817) – Open Wednesday through Sunday. 48 Elizabeth St. (phone: 723-1159).

    Calhoun Mansion (1876) – 16 Meeting St. (phone: 722-8205).

    Edmonston-Alston House (1828) – 21 E. Battery St. (phone: 722-7171).

    Heyward-Washington House (1770) – 87 Church St. (phone: 722-0354).

    Joseph Manigault House (1803) – 350 Meeting St. (phone: 723-2926).

    Nathaniel Russell House (1808) – 51 Meeting St. (phone: 723-1623).

MAJOR COLLEGES AND UNIVERSITIES: The Citadel Military College of South Carolina, founded in 1842, is one of the few state-run military schools in the country. A full-dress parade takes place Fridays during the school year at 3:45 PM. West end of Hampton Park (phone: 792-5006). The Citadel Memorial Archives has Civil War memorabilia relating to its graduates. Open daily except holidays. No admission charge (phone: 792-6846).

SPORTS AND FITNESS: Biking – Many of Charleston's parks have bike trails. Bikes may be rented from the *Bicycle Shop* (283 Meeting St.; phone: 722-8168) or *Charleston Carriage Co.* (96 N. Market St.; phone: 577-0042).

    Fishing – The Isle of Palms fishing pier is open spring through fall; generally it's crowded, but in fact, the fishing is unexceptional. For really good surf fishing, try Capers Island and Dewees Island. Charter boats for deep-sea fishing are available through the Municipal Marina, but the best fishing is in the estuarine creeks that swim with bass, sheepshead, flounder, and trout (in fall and winter). In summer and fall the creeks are full of crabs. Crab, oyster, and creek fishing are especially good on Capers, Dewees, Bulls, Kiawah, and Seabrook Islands. There are some public oyster beds closer to Charleston. For fishing and hunting regulations, write: *South Carolina Wildlife Resources Dept.,* PO Box 167, Columbia, SC 29202.

    Fitness Centers – *Roper Health & Fitness Club* has Nautilus and freeweight equipment, aerobics classes, racquetball courts, and a swimming pool. Open from 5:30 AM to 10:30 PM weekdays, shorter hours on weekends. 910 Hwy. 17 Bypass in Mt. Pleasant (phone: 884-2120).

    Golf – There are public courses at Patriots Point (phone: 881-0042) and Shadowmoss (phone: 556-8251). Kiawah (which will host the this year's *Ryder Cup*) and Seabrook Islands have fine resort golf courses, but one of the most popular golfing areas in the country, Myrtle Beach, is only 98 miles north of Charleston on Route 17. This year-round resort, whose non-golf-related facilities have grown increasingly tacky, has 28 golf courses, many of them first rate. Even better is Hilton Head Island, with more than 20 golf courses of its own, including *Harbour Town Golf Links* (phone: 671-2446), home of the annual *Heritage Golf Classic*. The resort accommodations offered on Hilton Head are far classier and more comfortable than those in and around Myrtle Beach. Daufaskie Island, reached by ferry from Hilton Head, is another first-rate golfing destination.

    Jogging – Run around Colonial Lake, on Ashley Avenue; for a nice 5-mile loop, run from Lockwood Drive to Battery, up East Bay Street, turn left onto Broad Street, right onto Meeting Street, and left onto Calhoun, which intersects with Lockwood.

    Sailing – Both crewed and bareboat sailboat charters, as well as sport fishing excursions, are available through *Bohicket Yacht Charters,* 20 miles from Charleston, between Kiawah and Seabrook islands (phone: 768-7294).

Swimming – Close to the city, Sullivan's Island and the Isle of Palms have fairly nice beaches, crowded in summer. Folly Beach, at the end of Folly Road (Rte. 171), usually gets a good crowd even though it's not well kept. North of Charleston, Capers Island and Dewees Island have more secluded beaches, probably because they're only accessible by boat. Both are state wildlife refuges.

Tennis – The courts at the resorts on Kiawah and Seabrook Islands are open to the public but can be expensive, and resort guests have priority. Try *Shadowmoss Plantation Golf & Country Club* (20 Dunvegan Dr.; phone: 556-8251) for inexpensive public courts.

THEATER: Built in 1736, the 463-seat *Dock Street Theater* — the oldest in the country — stages frequent performances of original drama, Shakespeare, Broadway, and 18th-century classics. It's advisable to call in advance for up-to-date information and performance times. Tours of the theater are conducted sporadically during the week. Admission charge. (On the corner of Church and Queen Sts.; phone: 723-5648 or 724-7308). The *Robert Ivey Ballet* presents major concerts in the spring and fall at the College of Charleston's *Simons Center for the Performing Arts,* and at other venues around the city and state (Savannah Hwy., Charleston; phone: 556-1343).

MUSIC: For *Community Concert Association* and *Symphony Orchestra* schedules, call the visitors' information center (phone: 722-8338). The *Spoleto Festival USA,* 17 days of chamber music, dance, jazz, opera, and theater, begins every year in late May (phone: 722-2764).

NIGHTCLUBS AND NIGHTLIFE: A great "happy hour" in town is at the *Jukebox* (4 Vendue Range; phone: 723-3431). Also downtown is *Tingle's* (in the *Sheraton Charleston Hotel,* 170 Lockwood Dr.; phone: 723-3000); and, for an intimate atmosphere, try the *Best Friend Bar* (in the *Mills House* hotel, 115 Meeting St.; phone: 577-2400). *Myskyn's Tavern* (5 Faber St.; phone: 577-5595) hosts jazz groups. *East Bay Trading Company* (corner of E. Bay and Queen Sts.; phone: 722-0722) is a converted warehouse filled with fun antiques and an unusual bar. Right next door is *Fanigan's* (159 E. Bay St.; phone: 722-6916), a favorite spot for businesspeople. Centrally located *Café 99* (99 Market St.; phone: 577-4499) features an outdoor patio, raw bar, and live entertainment. The best nightspot north of town is the *Windjammer* (1008 Ocean Blvd.; phone: 886-8596), a beer-and-billiards beach bar on the Isle of Palms.

BEST IN TOWN

CHECKING IN: Expect to pay $90 and up for a double room in one of the places we've noted as expensive; $60 to $90 at places listed as moderate; and under $60, inexpensive. For bed and breakfast accommodations, contact *Historic Charleston Bed & Breakfast* (43 Legare St., Charleston, SC 29401; phone: 722-6606). All telephone numbers are in the 803 area code unless otherwise indicated.

Battery Carriage House – On the Battery and facing the harbor, this sophisticated inn with 8 rooms provides guests with four-poster beds, continental breakfast in bed, and turn-down service at night. You can sip complimentary wine in the hospitality room or in the wisteria-draped, walled garden. 20 S. Battery (phone: 723-9881 between 10 AM and 5 AM). Expensive.

Hawthorne Suites at the Market – An elegant property that resides in the heart of the historic district. Opened in 1991, one of its many beauties is the entranceway, an 1874 portico. Its 164 one- and two-bedroom suites, furnished with antique reproductions, are also equipped with kitchens. Other niceties are the courtyard, heated pool, fitness facilities, and breakfast delivered to your room. Amenities include concierge, 2 meeting rooms, secretarial services, photocopiers, and express checkout. 181 Church St. (phone: 577-2644; 800-527-1130; Fax: 803-577-2697). Expensive.

Indigo Inn – In a restored tobacco warehouse, it's furnished with 18th-century reproductions; 29 of its 40 rooms have 2 four-poster queen-size beds. Very service-oriented staff — they'll even bring you take-out food from neighboring restaurants. Centrally located at 1 Maiden La. (phone: 577-5900; 800-845-7639; Fax: 803-577-0378). Expensive.

John Rutledge House Inn – The former home of a signer of the Constitution, this property has been meticulously restored, right down to the intricately carved mantels. Its 19 rooms and 3 suites boast astonishingly lovely parquet wooden floors and antique reproductions. Relax in the ballroom with complimentary sherry. Amenities include breakfast delivered to your room with a morning newspaper, and turn-down service. 116 Broad St. (phone: 723-7999; 800-476-9791). Expensive.

Lodge Alley Inn – Quiet and tasteful, this hostelry is in Charleston's best shopping and sightseeing area. It has 34 rooms, each with a fireplace, as well as 37 one- and two-bedroom suites and a penthouse. The elegant *French Quarter* serves delicious viands, as does the *Charleston Tea Party Lounge*. Amenities include room service, which is available only for breakfast; 1 meeting room. 195 E. Bay (phone: 722-1611; 800-845-1004; Fax: 803-722-1611, ext. 7777). Expensive.

Mills House – A topnotch 214-room property operated by Holiday Inn, it is a Charleston classic. Its antebellum decor reflects its 19th-century history, and, fittingly, it's in the center of the historic district. The *Barbados Room* restaurant specializes in tableside preparation of continental food; you'll definately want to make reservations for the famous Sunday buffet. Amenities include room service until 10 PM, concierge, 1 meeting room, secretarial services, and photocopiers. 115 Meeting St. (phone: 577-2400 or 800-874-9600; Fax: 803-722-2112). Expensive.

Omni Charleston Place – This glitzy hotel is the centerpiece of an impressive arcade of stylish shops and restaurants located in the historic district. It has 440 rooms, plus an indoor pool, spa, and fitness facilities. The *Palmetto Café* features fine continental dining, and *Louis' Bar & Grill* is open for dinner. Amenities include 24-hour room service, concierge, 1 meeting room, secretarial services, photocopiers, and express checkout. 130 Market St. (phone: 722-4900; 800-THE-OMNI; Fax: 803-722-0728). Expensive.

Planters Inn – Also in Charleston's historic district, this is the city's most elegant hostelry. The building dates to the 1800s and was thoroughly renovated, under strict government rules, to maintain its original appearance. The public rooms are filled with antiques and the 43 spacious guestrooms (some with fireplaces) are furnished in period reproductions, including four-poster beds. The renowned *Robert's of Charleston* restaurant (see *Eating Out*) is located here. Breakfast is delivered to rooms. The hotel has 1 meeting room. 112 N. Market St. (phone: 722-2345 or 800-845-7082; Fax: 803-577-2125). Expensive.

Sheraton Charleston – Near the historic district on the banks of the Ashley River, some of its 350 rooms have balconies with river views. Its restaurant, *Albemarle's*, emphasizes seafood and beef and offers a good selection of wines. Other facilities include a pool, tennis courts, and jogging track. Amenities include room service until 10 PM, 1 meeting room, secretarial services, and photocopiers. 170 Lockwood

Dr. (phone: 723-3000; 800-325-3535; Fax: 803-723-3000, ext. 1595). Expensive.

Two Meeting Street Inn – A real "find" in Charleston, built in 1891 and similar to a European pension, it has been a guest home for more than 60 years. Nine spacious rooms and a wide second-floor verandah overlook White Point Gardens and the harbor. It's furnished with family antiques, silver, and Oriental rugs. 2 Meeting St. (phone: 723-7322). Expensive.

Best Western King Charles Inn – In the center of the historic district, it reflects old Charleston in the decor of its 90 newly redecorated rooms. There's free parking and a dining room for breakfast. 237 Meeting St. (phone: 723-7451; 800-528-1234; Fax: 803-577-0361). Moderate.

Days Inn Meeting St. – The best deal in the historic district: 124 rooms, a restaurant, and a pool. Free parking. 155 Meeting St. (phone: 722-8411; 800-325-2525; Fax: 803-723-5361). Moderate.

Heart of Charleston – Well run and conscientiously managed, the best thing about this 106-room contemporary motel is the people who own it. Within easy walking distance of the historic, residential, and shopping districts, there is a swimming pool and restaurant. 200 Meeting St. (phone: 723-3451; 800-845-2504; Fax: 803-577-0361). Moderate.

EATING OUT: Charleston used to be known as the kind of place where "you couldn't get a decent hot dog unless you knew somebody," but the times they are a-changin', and there are now more than enough interesting restaurants to whet any palate. Prices range from expensive ($40 or more for dinner for two without drinks, wine, or tips) to moderate ($25 to $35) to inexpensive (under $25). All telephone numbers are in the 803 area code unless otherwise indicated.

82 Queen – There used to be just one restaurant at this address, but its popularity prompted the management to open another, humbler version just down the street, at the corner of King and Queen Streets. It's called the *82 Queen Café and Deli* (phone: 723-4993) and serves only lunch. Its parent restaurant, a lovely 18th-century townhouse with a garden court, specializes in seafood and boasts of 3 separate bars, one of which is the *Wine Bar* — a nice spot for a pre- or post-dinner glass of wine. Open daily. Reservations advised at *82 Queen,* but not taken at *82 Queen Café and Deli.* Major credit cards accepted at both. 82 Queen St. (phone: 723-7591). Expensive.

Louis' Charleston Grill – Owner-chef Louis Osteen's cooking has long and loudly been lauded since he opened in Charleston Place. The menu offers a range of Low Country entrées, focusing especially on fresh seafood. An Italian marble floor and a jazz combo lend an elegant and festive air. Closed Sundays. Reservations advised. Major credit cards accepted. 224 Kings St. (phone: 577-4522). Expensive.

Le Midi – The first thing diners see as they walk in this country-style French eatery is the chef at work in his exhibition kitchen. All 20 to 25 entrées are served with sauces made to order; the flounder in brown butter is a perennial favorite. Closed Sundays. Reservations advised for parties of six or more. Major credit cards accepted. 337 King St. (phone: 577-5571). Expensive.

Restaurant Million – One of Charleston's dining gems is a nouvelle French establishment housed in a beautifully restored old tavern. Of the three prix fixe menus, try *Le Menu Gourmand* for its smoked salmon ravioli and loin of lamb with garlic. Open daily. Reservations necessary. Major credit cards accepted. 2 Unity Alley (phone: 577-7472). Expensive.

Robert's of Charleston – One of the city's top dining spots, which proffers a prix fixe dinner of mouth-watering beef tenderloin. Its home is in the elegant *Planter's Inn* in the market area, and features a pianist and vocalist each evening. Closed Sundays and Mondays. Reservations necessary. Major credit cards accepted. 112 N. Market St. (phone: 577-7565). Expensive.

Colony House – A recently renovated formal dining room and a courtyard make it hard to believe that this was once a warehouse. This dining spot specializes in Low Country cooking, superb broiled and baked seafood, with a few steaks as well. Open daily. Reservations advised. Major credit cards accepted. 35 Prioleau St. (phone: 723-3424). Moderate.

East Bay Trading Company – Whimsical antiques decorate this converted warehouse. The menu features beef dishes, seafood, soup, and homemade desserts (including ice cream). Closed Sundays in winter. Reservations unnecessary. Major credit cards accepted. Corner of E. Bay and Queen Sts. (phone: 722-0722). Moderate.

Garibaldi's – This small café serves what may be best described as Italian home cooking with big-city service. A wide range of pasta dishes are offered daily, as are regular specials, including seafood. Open daily. Reservations advised. Major credit cards accepted. 49 S. Market St. (phone: 723-7153). Moderate.

Jilich's on East Bay – In yet another restored warehouse, this establishment specializes in Southern regional cooking, with emphasis on charcoal-grilled seafood. About 10 to 12 entrées are offered each evening. Closed Sundays. Reservations advised. Major credit cards accepted. 188 E. Bay St. (phone: 577-4342). Moderate.

Marianne – The regular dinner menu is French and excellent: beef, veal, seafood, and lamb, including a good wine list. A late supper also is available from 10:30 PM to 1:30 AM and features appetizers, soup, steaks, and omelettes. Open daily (on Sundays, only dinner is served, from 5 to 11 PM). Reservations advised. Major credit cards accepted. 235 Meeting St. (phone: 722-7196). Moderate.

Poogan's Porch – Fresh seafood and Low Country fare in an old Charleston house, with floral wallpaper and ceiling fans. Grilled alligator is a popular appetizer. Open daily. Reservations necessary. Major credit cards accepted. 72 Queen St. (phone: 577-2337). Moderate.

Port City Café & Club – This restaurant-cum-nightspot opened last year in the market area. Downstairs, the contemporary-styled dining area features regional Italian cuisine — *osso bucco* is a specialty. Upstairs, top-40 recorded music keeps the crowd dancing until the wee hours. Closed Sunday. Reservations advised on weekends. Major credit cards accepted. 36 N. Market St. (phone: 577-5000). Moderate.

Shem Creek Bar and Grill – Grilled seafood, along with chicken and prime ribs, in a casual atmosphere overlooking the creek. Open daily with late-night offerings from 10:30 to 2 AM. Reservations unnecessary. Major credit cards accepted. 508 Mill St. (phone: 884-8102). Moderate.

Gaulart & Maliclet – A local hangout, this tiny bistro serves simple French fare, with an emphasis on the fresh — seafood, a variety of healthy salads, and sandwiches on baguettes and croissants are some of the items on the menu. Open daily except Sundays. No reservations. Major credit cards accepted. 98 Broad St. (phone: 577-9797). Moderate to inexpensive.

Pinckney's – A mom-and-pop café whose seafood gumbo is highly touted by the artists and musicians who make up a good part of the clientele. Closed Sundays and Mondays. No reservations or credit cards accepted. 18 Pinckney St. (phone: 577-0961). Moderate to inexpensive.

Joe's Seafood Emporium – Overlooking Shem Creek and specializing in charcoal-grilled, broiled, and fried seafood dishes served in a casual atmosphere. Chicken and prime ribs also are offered, and there's a good selection of sandwiches at lunchtime. Open daily. Reservations advised on weekends. Major credit cards accepted. 130 Mill St., Mt. Pleasant (phone: 884-3410). Inexpensive.

Martha Lou's – This small eatery serves Southern soul food: fried chicken, pork chops, white rice, collard greens, and the like. For the price, the food can't be beat. Closed Sundays. No reservations or credit cards accepted. 1068 Morrison Dr. (phone: 577-9583). Inexpensive.

CHICAGO

AT-A-GLANCE

 SEEING THE CITY: The 110-story Sears Tower (Wacker and Adams Sts.; phone: 875-9696) maintains a Skydeck on the 103rd floor. Open daily from 9 AM to midnight. Admission charge. For a view from the north, visit the John Hancock Building (fifth largest in the world), fondly nicknamed "Big John." On the 95th floor are a bar and restaurant (875 Michigan Ave.; phone: 751-3681). Open daily. Admission charge. For a river view, *Wendella Sightseeing* (400 N. Michigan Ave.; phone: 337-1446) takes you by boat on the Chicago River and into Lake Michigan. Daily, May through September. Admission charge. For an enjoyable, informative custom tour of Chicago (individuals or groups), contact *Charlotte Kirshbaum* (399 Fullerton, Chicago, IL 60614; phone: 477-6509). Clients must provide their own vehicles.

 SPECIAL PLACES: A sophisticated public transport system makes it easy to negotiate Chicago's streets. You can explore the Loop, the lakefront, and suburbs by El train, subway, and bus (fare: $1.25).

THE LOOP

The Loop generally refers to Chicago's business district, which is encircled by the elevated train known as the "El."

ArchiCenter – The *Exhibition Gallery* has changing shows that span a wide range of architectural topics. Guided walking tours of the Loop (and other neighborhoods) daily, May through November; Fridays through Mondays at 1 PM the rest of the year. Chicago Highlights bus tours, Saturdays, April through November. Fees range from $6 to $17. 330 S. Dearborn, 1st Floor (phone: 922-3431).

Art Institute of Chicago – Founded as an art school in 1879, the *Art Institute* houses an outstanding collection of Impressionist and post-Impressionist paintings, Japanese prints, Chinese sculpture and bronzes, and Old Masters. In the Columbus Drive Addition, you can see the reconstructed trading room of the old Chicago Stock Exchange. In the west wall of the upper level McKinlock Court Galleries are Chagall's stained glass America windows. The $23-million Rice Building houses Edward Hopper's *Nighthawks,* Grant Wood's *American Gothic,* Vincent van Gogh's *Bedroom at Arles,* and Toulouse-Lautrec's *Ballet Dancers* as well as exhibitions of European and American decorative arts and sculpture. Open daily. Admission charge except on Tuesdays. Michigan Ave. at Adams St. (phone: 443-3600 or for recorded information 443-3500).

Chicago Board of Trade – The largest grain exchange in the world. Stand in the visitors' gallery and watch traders gesticulating on the floor, runners in colored jackets delivering orders, and an electronic record of all the trades displayed overhead. A larger trading floor has been built to accommodate expanding markets. Open weekdays, 8 AM to 2 PM. Explanations begin at 9:15 AM, movies at 10, 11, noon, and 12:30. No admission charge. Jackson at La Salle St. (phone: 435-3590).

Chicago Mercantile Exchange and International Monetary Market – The show is much the same, only here you can sit down. Trading here does not stop suddenly. Each commodity has its own opening and

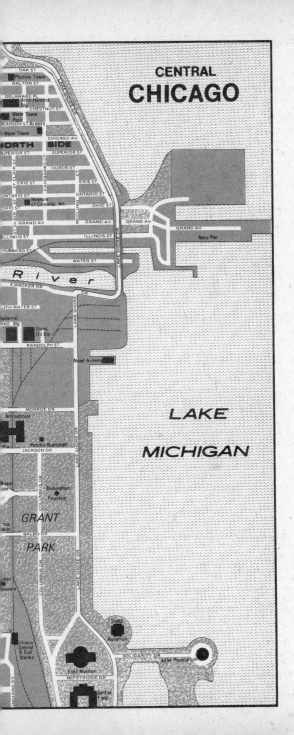

closing time. Open weekdays, 7:30 AM to 3:15 PM. No admission charge. 30 S. Wacker Dr. (phone: 930-8249).

Marshall Field — Chicago's most famous department store. When it was built in 1892 — before electric lighting was common — it was designed in sections, with shopping areas on balconies overlooking a skylit central courtyard. Later, the skylights were covered, one by a vivid blue and gold Louis Tiffany mosaic you can see by entering on the corner of Washington and State Sts. The *Crystal Palace*, on the third floor, serves unbelievable ice cream sundaes. Frango mint ice cream (a subtle mix of coffee, chocolate, malt, and mint) is a tradition, as are its chocolates. Open Mondays through Saturdays and the first Sunday of every month. Wabash, State, Randolph, and Washington Sts. (phone: 781-1000).

NEAR SOUTH SIDE

Adler Planetarium — Exhibitions on everything from surveying and navigation instruments to modern space exploration devices, plus a real moon rock and an antique instrument collection that is one of the three best in the world — the best in the Western Hemisphere. You can see it all before or after the sky shows, which are what most people come for. There are new shows every 3 months, one for adults and one for children 5 and younger. Open daily, 9:30 AM to 4:30 PM Mondays to Thursdays, until 9 PM Fridays, and until 5 PM weekends. Admission charge to the sky shows only. 1300 S. Lake Shore Dr. on Museum Point (phone: 322-0304).

Field Museum of Natural History — Of the endless exhibitions on anthropology, botany, zoology, and geology, one of the most famous is the pair of fighting elephants in the Main Hall. Other standouts include the hands-on Place for Wonder, where youngsters can touch a fish skeleton from the dinosaur age and try on ethnic masks; the Plants of the World Hall; with reproductions of about 500 plants from around the globe; the renovated Gem Hall; the full-scale model of a Pawnee earth lodge, where there are daily programs on Indian life; a full-size, 3-level ancient Egyptian tomb; and an exhibition, Maritime Peoples of the Northwest Coast. The Hall of Chinese Jade and the display of Japanese lacquerware are also outstanding. Open daily. Admission charge except on Thursdays. S. Lake Shore Dr. at Roosevelt Rd. (phone: 922-9410).

Shedd Aquarium — The largest aquarium in the world, this one has more than 200 fish tanks and a collection of over 7,000 specimens: sturgeon from Russia, Bahamian angelfish, Australian lungfish, and a coral reef where divers feed the fish several times a day. Open from 9 AM to 5 PM daily, March through October, 10 AM to 5PM daily through February, closed *Christmas* and *New Year's Day*. Admission charge. Museum Point at 1200 S. Lake Shore Dr. (phone: 939-2426).

NEAR NORTH SIDE

Chicago Academy of Sciences — Particularly lively exhibitions on the natural history of the Great Lakes area, especially the reconstruction of a 300-million-year-old forest that once stood near the present site, complete with gigantic insects and carnivorous dragonflies. There also are a "walk-through" cave and canyon. Open daily. Admission charge except on Mondays. In Lincoln Park at 2001 N. Clark St. (phone: 549-0606).

Chicago Historical Society — Pioneer crafts demonstrations and a Chicago Fire slide show make this one of Chicago's most fascinating museums. New galleries focus on the city's beginnings and explore 19th-century American life through furniture and decorative objects. Open daily. Admission charge except on Mondays. Clark St. and North Ave. (phone: 642-4600).

International College of Surgeons Hall of Fame — Full of medical curiosities: old examining tables, artificial limbs, an amputation set from the Revolution, a "bone crusher" used for correcting bow legs between 1918 and 1950 (!). Finally, there's a fascinating display of prayers and oaths taken by doctors in different countries. Open from 10 AM to 4 PM Tuesdays to Saturdays, 11 AM to 5 PM Sundays; closed Mondays. No admission charge. 1524 N. Lake Shore Dr. (phone: 642-3555).

Lincoln Park Conservatory – Changing floral displays and a magnificent permanent collection that includes orchids, a 50-foot fiddle-leaf rubber tree from Africa with giant leaves, fig trees, and more ferns than you could ever imagine. Open daily. No admission charge. In Lincoln Park, Stockton Dr. at Fullerton (phone: 294-4770).

Lincoln Park Zoo – The best thing about this zoo is that it has the largest group of great apes in captivity, now in a renovated Great Ape House. The renovated Lion House reopened in 1990 and the Bird House in 1991. There are, of course, the standard houses of monkey, tiger, lion, bear, and bison, plus the zoo's popular farm. Open daily from 9 AM to 5 PM. No admission charge. 2200 Cannon Dr., Lincoln Park (phone: 294-4660).

Museum of Contemporary Art – This small museum offers lively changing exhibitions, both retrospectives of contemporary artists and surveys of 20th-century art movements and avant-garde phenomena. The museum also features shows by Chicago artists, symposia, and other special events. Closed Mondays. Admission charge except on Tuesdays. 237 E. Ontario (phone: 280-2660).

Water Tower – Now a landmark, the sole survivor of the Great Fire of 1871 serves as a visitors' center. Open daily except holidays. N. Michigan and Chicago Aves.

Water Tower Place – This incredible, vertical shopping mall gets busier and better every year. Asymmetrical glass-enclosed elevators shoot up through a 7-story atrium, past shops selling dresses, books, gift items plus restaurants and a movie theater. Branches of *Marshall Field*, *FAO Schwarz*, and *Lord & Taylor* are here, along with the lovely *Ritz-Carlton* hotel, stretching 20 stories above its 12th-floor lobby in the tower. Its skylit *Greenhouse* is great for tea or cocktails after a hard day of shopping. Michigan Ave. at Pearson St.

NORTH SIDE

Graceland Cemetery – Buried here are hotel barons, steel magnates, architects Louis Sullivan and Daniel Burnham — enshrined by tombs and miniature temples, and overlooking islands, lakes, hills, and views. A photographer killed while recording the controversial demolition of Sullivan's celebrated Chicago Stock Exchange is buried in a direct line with the grave of Sullivan himself. Guidebooks (65¢) and maps (10¢) may be obtained from the gatekeepers. Open daily. Sunday tours by prior arrangement. 4001 N. Clark St. (phone: 525-1105).

SOUTH SIDE

Museum of Science and Industry – Some 2,000 exhibits explain the principles of science in such a lively way that the museum is Chicago's number one attraction. The newest draw is the *Omnimax Theater*, which has an admission charge. Longtime favorites: Colleen Moore's fairy castle of a dollhouse with real diamond "crystal" chandeliers, the cunning Sears circus exhibit, a working coal mine, a walk-through human heart, and a captured German submarine. Open daily except *Christmas*, but a madhouse on weekends. No admission charge. S. Lake Shore Dr. at 57th St. (phone: 684-1414).

Pullman Community – Founded by George Pullman in 1880 as the nation's first company town, this early example of comprehensive urban planning is now a city, state, and national landmark. Walking tours conducted on the first Sunday of the month from May through October give you the story in detail; at other times you can find the Green Stone Church and other important sites on maps available at the *Florence* hotel, a Pullman-era structure that serves as a visitors center of sorts (and provides lunch on weekdays, breakfast and lunch on Saturdays, and brunch on Sundays). A number of the many privately owned row houses are open for special house tours held annually on the second weekend in October. West of the Calumet Expy. between 111th and 115th Sts. (phone: 785-8181).

WEST

Garfield Park Conservatory – Here are 4½ acres under glass. The Palm House alone is 250 feet long, 85 feet wide, and 65 feet high; it looks like the tropics. There's a fernery luxuriant with greenery, mosses, and pools of water lilies. The Cactus House has 85 genera, 400 species. At *Christmas,* poinsettias bloom; in February, azaleas and camellias; at *Easter,* lilies and bulb plants; and in November, mums. Open daily, 9 AM to 5 PM. No admission charge. 300 N. Central Park Blvd. (phone: 533-1281).

OUTSKIRTS

Brookfield Zoo – Some 200 acres divided by moats and natural-looking barriers make this one of the most modern zoos in the country. There is an indoor rain forest, special woods for wolves, a bison prairie, a replica of the Sahara, and a dolphin show. The Tropic World features South American, Asian, and African birds, primates, and other animals. Open daily. Admission charge except on Tuesdays. 1st Ave. at 31st St. in Brookfield, 15 miles west of the Loop. Take Rte. 290 or I-55 to 1st Ave. Exit (phone: 708-242-2630).

Six Flags Great America – An extravagant roller coaster and a double-tiered carousel are the highlights of this theme park featuring over 130 rides, shows, and attractions. Musical shows are performed throughout the season, and there's a special giant participatory play area for kids. It is also home to the world's largest motion picture experience. Open daily beginning the week before *Memorial Day* through *Labor Day;* weekends May through September. Admission charge. I-94 at Rte. 132 in Gurnee (phone: 708-249-1776 or, for recorded information, 708-249-2020).

Lizzadro Museum of Lapidary Art – The collection of Oriental jade carvings is one of the most extensive in the US. About 150 exhibits show off cameos, gemstones, minerals, and fossils. Closed Mondays. Admission charge except on Fridays. 220 Cottage Hill, Elmhurst (phone: 708-833-1616).

Oak Park – Twenty-five buildings in this suburb, most of them remarkably contemporary looking, show the development of Frank Lloyd Wright's prairie-style architecture. The architect's residence/workshop and Unity Temple are open to the public, and there are daily tours (except on holidays). Admission charge. Edgar Rice Burroughs's and Ernest Hemingway's homes are here, too, along with numerous gingerbread and turreted Queen Anne palaces. The Oak Park Tour Center, based in the Frank Lloyd Wright Home and Studio, operates most area walking tours as well as a visitors' center (at 158 N. Forest), where you can see photo exhibitions and take in an orientation program. At the *Wright Plus Festival,* the third Saturday in May, ten private homes are open to the public. For more information, call the Oak Park Visitor Center (phone: 708-848-1500).

■ **EXTRA SPECIAL:** You don't have to go very far from downtown to reach the North Shore suburbs. Follow US 41 or I-94 north. US 41 takes you past Lake Forest, an exquisite residential area, and Lake Bluff, site of the Great Lakes Naval Station. In Waukegan, *Mathon's* seafood restaurant has been delighting crustacean addicts since before World War II (2 blocks east of Sheridan Rd. near the lake on Clayton St.; phone: 708-662-3610; closed Mondays). Heading inland from Waukegan on Route 120 will take you directly to lake country, past Gages Lake and *Brae Loch* golf course (Rte. 45, Wildwood; phone: 708-223-5542), Grays Lake, and Round Lake where Route 120 becomes Route 134, continuing on to Long Lake, Duck Lake, and the three large lakes — Fox, Pistakee, and Grass, near the Wisconsin border. All of these lakes offer water sports, fishing, golf, and tennis. On the northern border with Wisconsin, the 4,900-acre Chain O'Lakes State Park has campsites and boat rental facilities. Pick up Wilson Road north at Long Lake, then take Route 132 past Fox Lake. This will take you to US 12, which runs to Spring Grove and the state park (phone: 708-587-5512).

SOURCES AND RESOURCES

 TOURIST INFORMATION: The Chicago Tourism Council's Visitor Information Center, in the historic Water Tower (806 N. Michigan Ave. and Pearson St., Chicago, IL 60611; phone: 280-5740) distributes a downtown map that pinpoints major attractions and hotels. Chicago Visitor Eventline gives taped information on theater, sports, and special events (phone: 225-2323). Also get copies of the Chicago Transit Authority brochures: the *Chicago Street Directory*, which locates streets by their distance from State or Madison; the *CTA Route Map* of bus, subway, and El routes; and the *CTA Downtown Transit Map*. These are available at El and subway stations. For details, contact the Illinois Travel Information Center (310 S. Michigan Ave.; phone: 793-2094). Contact the Illinois state hotline (phone: 800-223-0121) for maps, calendars of events, health updates, and travel advisories.

A 24-hour hotline is available for quick and up-to-date information on restaurants, nightclubs, hotels, sports, comedy clubs, special events, and more (phone: ITS-CHGO, or 800-747-CHGO, from out-of-town). For information on flights arriving and departing O'Hare International Airport, delays, and even baggage carousel information, call 900-786-8686; the cost is 75¢ per minute.

The best local guidebook is *Chicago Magazine's Guide to Chicago* (Chicago Guide; $8.95), an insider's look at the city for residents and visitors alike. For self-guided walking tours, see Ira J. Bach's architecturally oriented *Chicago on Foot* (Chicago Review; $14.95).

Local Coverage – *Sun-Times,* morning daily; *Tribune,* morning daily; *Reader,* weekly; *Chicago* magazine, monthly.

Television Stations – WBBM Channel 2–CBS; WMAQ Channel 5–NBC; WLS Channel 7–ABC; WTTW Channel 11–PBS; WGN Channel 9 — superstation; WFLD Channel 32–FOX.

Radio Stations – AM: WGN 720 (talk/sports); WBBM 780 (news); WLUP 1000 (rock); WMAQ 670 (news). FM: WBEZ 91.5 (news); WBBM 96.3 (talk/news); WLUP 97.9 (rock); WFMT 98.7 (classical); WKQX 101.1 (classic rock); WGCI 107.5 (pop/rap).

Food – *The New Good (But Cheap) Chicago Restaurant Book* by Jill and Ron Rohde (Ohio University Press; $4.95) and *Chicago* magazine's section of restaurant reviews.

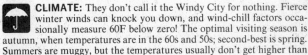 **TELEPHONE:** The area code for Chicago is 312. The area code for all of Chicago's suburbs is 708.
Sales Tax – City sales tax is 8%.

CLIMATE: They don't call it the Windy City for nothing. Fierce winter winds can knock you down, and wind-chill factors occasionally measure 60F below zero! The optimal visiting season is autumn, when temperatures are in the 60s and 50s; second-best is spring. Summers are muggy, but the temperatures usually don't get higher than the 80s.

 GETTING AROUND: Airport – O'Hare International Airport is about 25 miles west of the Loop and, depending on traffic, a 30- to 60-minute ride by cab; the fare should run about $25. *Conti-*

nental Air Transport (phone: 454-7800) charges $12.50 for van service to the airport from 24 city locations (including all the major hotels). The trip takes almost an hour, and vans run approximately every 30 minutes. Ask your hotel concierge for *Continental*'s return schedule. *Chicago Transit Authority* (phone: 836-7000 or 800-972-7000) *O'Hare Line* trains run from several downtown and North Side spots to O'Hare's main terminal in approximately 35 minutes; the fare is $1.25.

Midway Airport, which handles an increasing volume of domestic traffic, is 8 miles south of the Loop. A taxi ride to Midway from the Loop will take from 10 to 20 minutes and cost about $10. The No. 62 *Archer Express* bus (heading south) can be picked up from any stop along State St. in the Loop; transfer at Cicero Avenue to any southbound bus — they stop inside the airport. This ride takes about 30 minutes and costs $1.25. *Continental Air Transport* (phone: 454-7800) also provides van service to the airport from the *Palmer House, Hyatt Regency,* and *Marriott* hotels; schedules vary according to flights. The run to the airport takes about 40 minutes, and the cost is $9.50.

Bus, Subway, and El – *Chicago Transit Authority* operates bus, subway, and El services. For information, call 836-7000. There's also a do-it-yourself tour on public transport. One good round trip by public transportation starts in the Loop, goes through Lincoln Park, past the Historical Society, and into New Town on the No. 151 bus. When you've ridden enough, get off and catch the same bus going in the opposite direction. On Sundays and holidays, there is also a "Culture Bus," which stops at the *Art Institute,* the *Field Museum,* the *Shedd Aquarium,* the *Adler Planetarium,* the *Museum of Science and Industry,* the *Oriental Institute,* and the *DuSable Museum of African-American History.* It operates every half-hour from 11 AM to 5 PM, May through September.

Car Rental – All major national firms are represented.

Taxi – Cabs can be hailed in the street or picked up at stands in front of the major hotels. You also can call one of Chicago's taxi services: *Yellow* and *Checker Cabs* (phone: 829-4222); *Flash Cab* (phone: 561-1444); *American United* (phone: 248-7600).

Train – METRA offers commuter service between the city and its suburbs. Trains depart from the Chicago and Northwestern Station (500 W. Madison) to the north and northwest suburbs, from Union Station (210 S. Canal) to the west and southwest suburbs, and from the Randolph Street (151 E. Randolph) and La Salle Street stations for the south suburbs (phone: 322-6777, 836-7000, or 800-972-7000). *Amtrak* (phone: 800-872-7245) departs from the Union Street Station. *American European Express* (phone: 226-5558) offers luxury overnight rail service 2 days a week between Chicago and Washington, DC, fashioned after Europe's *Orient Express.* The oversize presidential cabin ($829 per person, one way, double occupancy) has side-by-side lower berths, a private shower, a vanity, access to a club car decorated with hand-tooled leather-covered walls and hand-painted ceiling, plus first-rate dining with fine china and crystal goblets. Pricey, but fun; the west (Chicago) to east (DC) direction offers the best scenery during daylight hours.

 VITAL SERVICES: Audiovisual Equipment – *Audio Visual Systems* (phone: 733-3370); *Audio Visual Techniques, Inc.* (phone: 527-0050).

Baby-sitting – Check at your hotel for reliable services.

Business Services – *International Office Centers,* 203 N. LaSalle, Suite 2100 (phone: 346-2030).

Dry Cleaner/Tailor – *Astor Cleaners,* 939 N. State (phone: 787-3914).

Limousine – *Airport Express Limousine Service,* 24 hours (phone: 227-1000).

Mechanic – *Amoco* station, 8 AM to 10 PM (600 W. Randolph; phone: 332-8256); *Passaglia's,* Mondays through Fridays, 7:30 AM to 9 PM; Saturdays, 8 AM to 6 PM (520 N. Wells; phone: 337-4884).

Medical Emergency Service – *Northwestern Memorial Hospital,* Superior St. and Fairbanks Court (phone: 908-5222).

Messenger Services – *Chicago Messenger Service* (phone: 666-6800); *Cannonball Messenger Service* (phone: 829-1234).

National/International Courier – *Federal Express* (phone: 559-9000); *DHL Worldwide Courier Express* (phone: 708-456-3200).

Pharmacy – *Walgreen's Drugs* is open from 7 AM to midnight, 1130 N. State St. (phone: 787-7035).

Photocopies – *Modern Impressions* (105 W. Madison St.; phone: 368-8445); *Aims Copy Services* (69 W. Washington; phone: 332-2604).

Post Office – Located in the Loop (211 S. Clark St.; phone: 427-4225); there is a second branch (227 E. Ontario; phone: 642-7697).

Professional Photographer – *Photo Ideas* (phone: 666-3100); *Stuart-Rodgers-Reilly Photographers* (phone: 787-8696).

Secretary/Stenographer – *A Avenue Typing Service* (phone: 329-1223); *International Office Center* (phone: 346-2030 and 714-8222).

Teleconference Facilities – *Drake, Palmer House, Sheraton-Plaza, Bismarck* (see *Best in Town,* below).

Translator – *Berlitz* (phone: 782-6820); *Joan Masters & Sons* (phone: 787-3009).

Typewriter Rental – *Benbow Office Machines,* 2-week minimum (phone: 427-5969); *Mid-City Typewriter Exchange,* 1-week minimum (phone: 666-0745).

Western Union/Telex – Many locations around the city (phone: 800-325-6000).

Other – *H.Q. Headquarters Company* (phone: 372-2525 or 642-5100), word processing, telex, facsimile, conference rooms; *A.S.A.P. Word Processing* (phone: 558-9333); *Business Center,* desk space and typewriters, conference rooms, photocopying, in the *O'Hare Hilton* (phone: 686-8000); *Woodstock Conference Center,* modern facilities for groups of up to 50 in 80-acre rustic setting, 50 miles from O'Hare and equidistant from Chicago, Milwaukee, and Madison (in Woodstock, Illinois; phone: 815-338-3600).

SPECIAL EVENTS: Summertime is festival time. In June, the beat of rhythm and blues fills the air at the *Chicago Blues Festival* in Grant Park. Also in June is the *Old Town Art Fair,* held in Lincoln Park. In July, sailboats race on Lake Michigan; and in August, the *Western Open Golf Tournament* is played at the *Cog Hill* golf club in Lemont. The *Arlington Million,* the world's richest thoroughbred race, is held the last week of August at *Arlington Park.* The *Ravinia Festival,* a series of outdoor concerts by the *Chicago Symphony Orchestra* and other headliners, runs throughout the summer in Highland Park (phone: RAVINIA). The first week in September heralds a jazz festival in the *Grant Park Bandshell* (free). September also brings the *Chicago Tribune*'s annual *Ribfest,* the largest spareribs-cooking competition in the country. Grant Park, north of the *Field Museum of Natural History.*

MUSEUMS: Chicago is paradise if you like going to museums. Those described in *Special Places* have plenty of company, including the following:

Balzekas Museum of Lithuanian Culture – 6500 S. Pulaski Rd. (phone: 582-6500).

Chicago Architecture Foundation, Glessner House – 1800 S. Prairie Ave. (phone: 326-1393).

DuSable Museum of African-American History – In Washington Park, at 740 E. 56th Pl. (phone: 947-0600).

Jane Addams's Hull House – A National Historic Landmark. 800 S. Halsted St. at Polk St. (phone: 413-5353).

Oriental Institute at University of Chicago – 1155 E. 58th at University (phone: 702-9521).

Polish Museum of America – 984 N. Milwaukee Ave. (phone: 384-3352).

Spertus Museum of Judaica – 618 S. Michigan Ave. (phone: 922-9012).

Ukrainian Institute of Modern Art – 2320 W. Chicago Ave. (phone: 227-5522).

Vietnam War Museum – Uniforms, weapons, photographs, and art work done by American soldiers while they served in Vietnam are among the exhibits here. 5002 N. Broadway Ave. (phone: 728-6111).

Great sculpture and art also can be seen in the plazas of downtown skyscrapers: Bertoia's spellbinding *Sounding Sculpture,* at the Standard Oil Bldg. (200 E. Randolph); *Flamingo,* a stabile by Alexander Calder, at Federal Center Plaza (Adams and Dearborn); Calder's gaily colored mobile *Universe,* in the Sears Tower lobby (Wacker and Adams); sculptor Claes Oldenburg's 101-foot-high baseball bat, *Batcolumn* (600 W. Madison); Chagall's *Four Seasons* mosaic, at First National Plaza (Monroe and Dearborn).

■ **Note:** If you're at First National Plaza at noon, you might catch a free concert. *Chicago's Picasso* (its formal title because no one could agree on a name), a giant sculpture, is at the Richard J. Daley Plaza (on Washington and Clark near the Chagall). There are free concerts at the Richard J. Daley Plaza every weekday, weather permitting. Joan Miró's *Chicago* sculpture mural is across the street from Daley Plaza. Buckingham Fountain, a Chicago landmark in Grant Park at Congress Parkway, is illuminated from May to September.

MAJOR COLLEGES AND UNIVERSITIES: Although far too big to be called a college town, Chicago has many fine universities. The University of Chicago, known for its economics and social science departments, has its main entrance at 5801 S. Ellis Ave. (phone: 753-1234); De Paul University (25 E. Jackson and in Lincoln Park at 2323 N. Seminary; phone: 341-8000); Illinois Institute of Technology (3300 S. Federal; phone: 567-3000); Lake Forest College (Sheridan Rd., Lake Forest; phone: 708-234-3100); Loyola University (820 N. Michigan; phone: 670-3000; and 6525 Sheridan Rd.; phone: 274-3000); Northwestern University (Chicago Ave. and Lake Shore Dr.; phone: 908-8649; and in Evanston; phone: 708-491-5000); Roosevelt University (430 S. Michigan Ave.; phone: 341-3500); University of Illinois at Chicago (601 S. Morgan; phone: 996-3000).

SHOPPING: Some of Chicago's best sights are indoors, along the aisles of the city's many shops and department stores. Los Angeles boasts Rodeo Drive, and New York has Fifth Avenue. In Chicago, the chic shopping district is North Michigan Avenue, between the Chicago River and Oak Street — a stretch known as the Magnificent Mile — where you can find *Carson Pirie Scott* (phone: 641-7000), *Burberrys* (phone: 787-2500), *Hammacher Schlemmer* (phone: 664-9292), *Saks Fifth Avenue* (phone: 944-6500), *Lord & Taylor* (phone: 787-7400), *I. Magnin* (phone: 751-0500), *Tiffany's* (phone: 944-7500), *Neiman Marcus* (phone: 642-5900), and Chicago's doyenne, *Marshall Field* (phone: 781-1234). The last of these is in Water Tower Place (845 N. Michigan Ave.), a 7-story shopper's paradise that houses, among others, *Eddie Bauer* (phone: 337-4353), *FAO Schwarz* (phone: 787-8894), *Laura Ashley* (phone: 951-8004), and *Banana Republic* (phone: 642-7667); *Bloomingdale's* (phone: 440-4460) anchors the street's newest shopping mall (900 N. Michigan), a 6-story Whitman's sampler of tony shops, including *Gucci* (phone: 664-5504), *Aquascutum of London* (phone: 787-0225), *Henri Bendel* (phone: 642-0140), and to quell hunger pangs, a branch of New York's *Carnegie Deli* (phone: 337-5665).

Although much of the city's best downtown shopping is concentrated along the Magnificent Mile, the burgeoning loft area west of the Loop is increasingly being filled with eclectic shops. One of the most interesting is *City* (361 W. Chestnut St.; phone: 664-9581), which sells avant-garde furniture. The *Mallers Building* (67 E. Madison) has 13 floors of retail and wholesale jewelers, and the *5 N. Wabash Building* has 17 floors of stores specializing in watches, necklaces, and precious stones.

 SPORTS AND FITNESS: Plenty of major-league action in town.
Baseball – The *White Sox* play at the new *Comiskey Park* (35th and Shields, off the Dan Ryan Expy.; phone: 924-1000). Seating 43,500 spectators, this state-of-the-art park is equipped with more efficient escalators and elevators, plus numerous services and concessions for the fans. The *Cubs* play at *Wrigley Field* (Addison and Clark; phone: 281-5050), now occasionally at night.

Basketball – The 1991 NBA champion *Bulls* play at *Chicago Stadium,* 1800 W. Madison (phone: 733-5300).

Bicycling – Chicago has a glorious bike path along the shore of Lake Michigan, running from the Loop to the North side — about 6 miles. You can rent bikes in summer from the concession at Lincoln Park.

Fishing – After work, people flock to the rocks along the shore, casting nets for smelt. The rocks around Northwestern University at Evanston are especially popular. There's also an artificial island, attainable by footbridge, around Northwestern.

Fitness Centers – *Body Elite* (445 W. Erie; phone: 664-5710) and *Combined Fitness Centre* (1235 N. LaSalle; phone: 787-8400) both allow non-members for a fee.

Football – The NFL *Bears* (phone: 663-5100) play at *Soldier Field.*

Golf – Chicago has 18 public golf courses, some along the lakeshore. The most accessible municipal course is *Waveland* in Lincoln Park. *Brae Loch* in Wildwood (phone: 708-223-5542) is mentioned under *Special Places.* The Chicago Park District offers golf instruction. For information, call 294-2274.

Hiking – *Windy City Grotto,* the Chicago Chapter of the *National Speleological Society,* organizes frequent field trips to cave country in southern Indiana and Missouri. For information, contact *Windy City Speleonews* (c/o Bill Mixon, 5035 N. South Drexel, Chicago, IL 60615). *Chicago Mountaineering Club* organizes weekend expeditions and teaches safe climbing techniques. They meet at the *Field Museum* every second Monday. For information, write to them (PO Box 1025, Chicago, IL 60690). The *Sierra Club* (53 W. Jackson; phone: 431-0158) also organizes outings.

Hockey – The NHL *Black Hawks* play in *Chicago Stadium* from September through April (phone: 733-5300).

Horse Racing – Horses race at four tracks in the Chicago area:

> *Arlington Park,* Euclid Ave. and Wilke Rd., Arlington Heights (phone: 708-255-4300)
>
> *Hawthorne,* 3501 S. Laramie, Cicero (phone: 708-780-3700)
>
> *Maywood Park,* North and 5th Aves., Maywood (phone: 708-626-4816)
>
> *Sportsman's Park,* 3301 S. Laramie, Cicero (phone: 708-242-1121)

Jogging – Run along Lake Shore Drive to Lincoln Park; there is a 5-mile track inside the park. Or simply do as many Chicagoans do and jog along the lakefront, accessible via numerous pedestrian walkways.

Polo – Summers at the *Oak Brook Polo Club* (1000 Oak Brook Rd., Oak Brook; phone: 708-571-7656); during winter you can play indoors at the *Chicago Armory* (Chicago Ave. and Fairbanks).

Sailing – Lake Michigan offers superb sailing, but as experienced sailors can tell you, the lake is deceptive. Storms of up to 40 knots can blow in suddenly. Check with the Coast Guard before going out (phone: 219-949-7440). You can rent boats and take sailing lessons from *City Sailors* (phone: 975-0044). There are a few marinas between the Loop and Evanston; others, along suburban shores. Highland Park is one of the most popular city marinas.

Skiing – There are more than 50 ski clubs in the Chicago area. For information, contact the *Chicago Metro Ski Council,* PO Box 7926, Chicago, IL 60680 (phone: 346-1268).

Swimming – Beaches line the shore of Lake Michigan. Those just to the north of the Loop off Lake Shore Drive are the most popular and often the most crowded. Oak Street Beach along the "Gold Coast" is the most fashionable beach. If you go farther north, you'll find fewer people. The Chicago Park District offers swimming lessons at some of the 72 city pools. The best are at Wells Park and Gill Park. For information, call 294-2333.

Tennis – The city has 708 outdoor municipal courts. The best are at Randolph and Lake Shore Drive, just east of the Loop (phone: 294-4792). For other tennis information, call 294-2314.

THEATERS: For schedules and ticket information, consult the publications noted above or visit the *HOT TIX* booth (at State St. and Madison; phone: 977-1755), where theater tickets can be purchased at half price on the day of the performance. Many Broadway shows play Chicago before heading to the Big Apple. The main Chicago theaters are the *Shubert* (22 W. Monroe; phone: 977-1700); *Civic* (20 N. Wacker Dr.; phone: 346-0270); *Goodman* (200 S. Columbus Dr.; phone: 443-3800); *Blackstone Theater* (60 E. Balbo; phone: 977-1700); and the *Apollo Theater Center* (2540 N. Lincoln; phone: 935-6100).

Among Chicago's thriving Off-Loop theaters are the *Organic Theater* (3319 N. Clark; phone: 327-5588); *Goodman Studio Theater* (200 S. Columbus; phone: 443-3800); *Victory Gardens Theater* (2257 N. Lincoln; phone: 549-5788), which is dedicated to the promotion of Chicago playwrights; *Steppenwolf Theater* (1650 N. Halsted; phone: 335-1650); *Wisdom Bridge Theater* (1559 W. Howard; phone: 743-6442); the *Royal George Theater* (1641 N. Halstead; phone: 988-9000); and the *Body Politic Theater* (2261 N. Lincoln; phone: 871-3000).

There are several good dinner-theaters as well: *Drury Lane South* (2500 W. 95th, Evergreen Park; phone: 708-779-4000); *Pheasant Run Theater* (Pheasant Run Lodge, Rte. 64, St. Charles; phone: 708-584-1454); and the *Candlelight Playhouse,* the first dinner-theater in the country (5620 S. Harlem Ave. in Summit; phone: 708-496-3000).

MUSIC: Chicago isn't the musical desert that the Midwest once was thought to be. Good music (and lots of it) can be heard all over the place. The world-renowned *Chicago Symphony Orchestra* plays at *Orchestra Hall* from September through June (220 S. Michigan; phone: 435-8111), and at *Ravinia Festival* in Highland Park, late June through August (phone: RAVINIA). Argentine-born conductor Daniel Barenboim, the former artistic director of Paris's *Bastille Opera,* succeeded Sir Georg Solti as the symphony's conductor last year. Outdoor concerts also are heard in the *Petrillo Music Shell,* behind the *Art Institute* (between Jackson and Monroe on Columbus Dr.; phone: 294-2420). The *Lyric Opera of Chicago* performs at the *Civic Opera House* (20 N. Wacker; phone: 332-2244). The *Auditorium Theatre,* a landmark designed by Louis Sullivan (70 E. Congress; phone: 922-2110), is another major hall.

NIGHTCLUBS AND NIGHTLIFE: Take in Chicago's blues, folk, and jazz scene in informal pubs, cafés, and taverns. Among them are *Park West* (322 W. Armitage; phone: 929-5959); *B.L.U.E.S.* (2519 N. Halsted; phone: 528-1012); *Old Town School of Folk Music* (909 W. Armitage; phone: 525-7793); *The Vic* (3145 N. Sheffield; phone: 472-0366); *Buddy Guy's Legends* (754 S. Wabash; phone: 427-0333); *Andy's* (11 W. Hubbard; phone: 642-6805); *Jazz Showcase at the Blackstone* (636 S. Michigan; phone: 427-4300); *Green Mill* (4802 N. Broadway; phone: 878-5552); and *Byfields* (in the *Omni Ambassador East* hotel, 1301 N. State Pkwy.; phone: 787-6433). *Pop's for Champagne*

(2934 N. Sheffield Ave.; phone: 472-1000) is an unusual jazz nightclub with a formal French garden and a grand variety of champagnes to sip or drain from your glass as you relax. *Toulouse* (49 W. Division St.; phone: 944-2606) has an intimate piano bar where Cole Porter's or Noël Coward's songs are heard; and *Yvette* (1206 N. State St.; phone: 280-1700) has enthusiastic twin piano duets. *Jukebox Saturday Night* (2251 N. Lincoln; phone: 525-5000) is the place to dance to vintage 1950s and 1960s rock 'n' roll. The *Second City* revue ensemble performs original, improvisational, and satirical skits (1616 N. Wells; phone: 337-3992). Comedians on the way to becoming household names are at *Catch A Rising Star* (1151 E. Wacker Dr.; phone: 565-4242); *Zanies* (1548 N. Wells; phone: 337-4027); *Funny Firm* (318 W. Grand; phone: 321-9500); and the *Chicago Improv* (504 N. Wells; phone: 527-2500), which also presents top national talent.

BEST IN TOWN

CHECKING IN: There are quite a number of interesting hotels in Chicago, varying in style from the intimate clubbiness of the *Tremont* and *Whitehall* to the supermodern elegance of the *Ritz-Carlton*. Unless otherwise noted, all listed here have at least one restaurant; the choice of eating places normally increases with the price of a room and the size of the hotel. Big hotels have shops, meeting places, nightly entertainment. Rates in Chicago are higher than in most other midwestern cities: Expect to pay $150 to $220 for doubles in expensive hotels; $85 to $145 in those classified as moderate; and from $40 to $85 in those listed as inexpensive. If money is no object, ask for a room with a view. "Near North Side" hotels are close to New Town, Lincoln Park, and Water Tower Place; Loop locations (about 10 minutes away by taxi) are convenient to businesses and the fine, old downtown department stores. For bed and breakfast accommodations, contact *Bed and Breakfast Chicago* (PO Box 14088, Chicago, IL 60614; phone: 951-0085). All telephone numbers are in the 312 area code unless otherwise indicated.

Chicago Hilton and Towers – In 1985, about $180 million — the most ever spent on a hotel renovation — transformed this 30-story landmark building into a good-looking, modern property. The former *Conrad Hilton* now features 1,620 rooms, the most lavish of which is the 2-story Conrad Hilton Suite for $4,000 a night. Restored to their 1927 grandeur are the Great Hall and the Versailles-inspired Grand Ballroom. Facilities include a fitness center with an indoor running track, sundeck, exercise equipment, swimming pool, saunas, and whirlpool baths; there's also a computerized business center. Sometimes large groups of enthusiastic convention goers make it difficult to feel comfortable without a name tag. The Tower rooms are the most elegantly furnished, and have the added convenience of their own registration and checkout desk (on the 24th floor) — not an insignificant bonus when the hordes line up at the lobby cashier each AM. There's a 140,000-square-foot convention center, a self-parking garage, and 21 rooms equipped for handicapped guests. For a fee, a telephone answering machine can be hooked up to your room phone. Amenities include 24-hour room service, concierge, 46 meeting rooms, secretarial services, A/V equipment, photocopiers, computers, CNN, and express checkout. 720 S. Michigan Ave. (phone: 922-4400; Fax: 312-922-5240; Telex: 62975566). Expensive.

Drake – A 535-room institution, with a graciousness not often found in hotels these days. The *Cape Cod Room* is Chicago's finest seafood eatery (see *Eating Out*). There is 24-hour room service, concierge, 19 meeting rooms, secretarial services, A/V equipment, photocopiers, computers, CNN, and express checkout. Near North Side. N. Michigan Ave. at Lake Shore Dr. and Walton Pl. (phone: 787-2200; Fax: 312-787-1431; Telex: 27028). Expensive.

Fairmont – Opulent and sophisticated, its 700 rooms and suites look out at the city skyline and Lake Michigan, and feature such appointments as marble bathrooms equipped with a TV set, telephone, and lighted dressing table. The hotel's supper club, *Moulin Rouge,* features top-name entertainment. There's also a bank of 12 meeting rooms with teleconference facilities and a spectacular penthouse boardroom with a panoramic view of the lake. Amenities include 24-hour room service, concierge, A/V equipment, photocopiers, computers, CNN, and express checkout. 200 N. Columbus Dr. (phone: 565-8000; Fax: 312-856-9020; Telex: 936092). Expensive.

Four Seasons – One of the city's newest luxury hotels occupies 19 floors of a stunning high-rise that also is home to the local branch of *Bloomingdale's.* There are 343 rooms (more than a third boast separate sitting rooms), an opulent Presidential Suite, and 16 residential apartments in this member of what is arguably the best managed hotel group in the world. Guest facilities include two-line telephones, lighted makeup mirrors, a spa, sauna, and indoor swimming pool. Other amenities are 24-hour room service, concierge, 12 meeting rooms, secretarial services, A/V equipment, photocopiers, computers, CNN, and express checkout. This is a luxury hotel worth the adjective. 120 E. Delaware Pl. (phone: 280-8800 or 800-332-3442; Fax: 312-280-9184; Telex: 00214923). Expensive.

Hyatt Regency Chicago – The 2,000 rooms in its two ultramodern towers recently underwent a $20-million refurbishing. Conveniently located between the Loop and N. Michigan Ave. Fine dining at *Truffles.* Amenities include 24-hour room service, concierge, 102 meeting rooms, secretarial services, A/V equipment, photocopiers, computers, CNN, and express checkout. 151 E. Wacker Dr. (phone: 565-1000, 800-233-1234, or 800-228-9000; Fax: 312-565-2966; Telex: 256237). Expensive.

Hyatt Regency O'Hare – Ideal for a comfortable overnight stop between planes. There are 1,100 rooms and a health club. Amenities include 24-hour room service, concierge, 48 meeting rooms, secretarial services, A/V equipment, photocopiers, computers, CNN, and express checkout. South River Rd. exit off Kennedy Expy. (phone: 708-696-1234, 800-233-1234, or 800-228-9000; Fax: 708-696-1418; Telex: 282503). Expensive.

Inter-Continental – Two year's worth of restoration enhanced the sophisticated Biedermeier-style rooms and suites that distinguished the old *Medinah Athletic Club.* Built prior to the crash of 1929, the club has been transformed into a 517-room hotel overlooking Michigan Avenue. Butlers serve afternoon tea in a lobby sitting room. There is a concierge desk, as well as 11 meeting rooms, secretarial services, A/V equipment, photocopiers, computers, and express checkout. 505 N. Michigan Ave. (phone: 944-4100 or 800-327-0200; Fax: 312-944-3050; Telex 62654670). Expensive.

Mayfair Regent – Unlike most of the new high-rise hotels opening these days, this one is small enough to offer the ultimate in comfort and style — the ratio of employees to guests is 1 to 1. Dinner here is an elegant affair: The rooftop *Ciel Bleu* offers classic French food and romantic views of Lake Michigan (particularly pleasant at breakfast); the *Palm,* on the ground floor, has steaks as prime as those served by its New York counterpart (see *Eating Out*). Amenities include 24-hour room service, concierge, 4 meeting rooms, secretarial services, A/V equipment, photocopiers, computers, CNN, and express checkout. 181 E. Lake Shore Dr. (phone: 787-8500; 505-243-6466, collect, from Alaska; 800-545-4000 elsewhere in the US; Fax: 312-664-6194; Telex: 256266). Expensive.

Nikko Chicago – This elegant, 425-room hotel overlooking the Chicago

River was built by Nikko Hotels International, Japan's largest hotel chain. Japanese touches abound — landscaped indoor gardens, native artwork, even Japanese suites with tatami sleeping rooms. A 3-floor amenity area includes a 2-story executive lounge, a business center with computer terminals, a business library, and a health club. Other pluses are 24-hour room service, concierge, 6 meeting rooms, secretarial services, A/V equipment, photocopiers, computers, CNN, and express checkout. 320 N. Dearborn St. (phone: 744-1900; Fax: 312-527-2650; Telex: 276536). Expensive.

Omni Ambassador East – Now part of the Omni Classic chain, this lovely old hotel hasn't lost an ounce of charm. It still houses the famous *Pump Room* restaurant (see *Eating Out*), a Chicago institution whose entryway is lined with photos of famous guests, who always dine in booth one. Convenient location in the Gold Coast area, close to Lincoln Park, Rush Street, and the Magnificent Mile of Michigan Avenue. (Not affiliated with the *Ambassador West,* across the street.) Amenities include 24-hour room service, concierge, 9 meeting rooms, secretarial services, A/V equipment, photocopiers, computers, CNN, and express checkout. 1301 N. State Pkwy. (phone: 787-7200; Fax: 312-787-4760; Telex: 9102212120). Expensive.

Palmer House – A busy, 1,800-room giant, this is another Chicago tradition. The sumptuous *Empire Room* is a visual delight. You also can dine here at the *Palmer Steak House* and *Trader Vic's.* Amenities include a concierge desk, 38 meeting rooms, secretarial services, A/V equipment, photocopiers, computers, CNN, and express checkout. In the Loop on the State Street mall. Monroe St. between State and Wabash (phone: 726-7500; Fax: 312-917-1735; Telex: 382182). Expensive.

Park Hyatt – Small, with 255 elegant rooms and suites, and as convivial as it is convenient to N. Michigan Ave. and the historic Water Tower. The hotel offers 24-hour room service, concierge, 4 meeting rooms, secretarial services, A/V equipment, photocopiers, computers, and express checkout. 800 N. Michigan Ave. (phone: 280-2222; Fax: 312-280-1963; Telex: 256216). Expensive.

Ritz-Carlton – Contemporary and chic, this beautifully appointed 430-room luxury establishment, a member of the fine Four Seasons chain, rises 20 stories above its 12th-floor lobby. In the spectacular Water Tower Place complex, it has all the accoutrements of elegance, including a fine health club and skylit indoor swimming pool. Amenities include 24-hour room service, concierge, 6 meeting rooms, secretarial services, A/V equipment, photocopiers, computers, CNN, and express checkout. Near North Side. 160 E. Pearson (phone: 266-1000; Fax: 312-266-1194; Telex: 00206014). Expensive.

Sheraton-Plaza – The 233 rooms and 100 suites at this gem recently were remodeled and offer a residential decor with such in-room amenities as refreshment centers, coffee machines, and complimentary cable channels. Facilities include a rooftop, outdoor swimming pool, health club privileges at a nearby private facility plus a lobby-level restaurant and bar. Business pluses are a concierge desk, 10 meeting rooms, secretarial services, A/V equipment, photocopiers, computers, CNN, and express checkout. Just off Michigan Avenue. 160 E. Huron St. (phone: 787-2900; Fax: 312-787-6093). Expensive.

Tremont – The paneled lobby, with its elaborate moldings and chandeliers, is more like a private sitting room than a public foyer. The 139 rooms offer traditional elegance. The hotel, which changed ownership from John B. Coleman to Rank North America, is also the home of *Cricket's,* one of Chicago's best restaurants (see *Eating Out*). Amenities include 24-hour room service, concierge, 4 meeting rooms, secretarial services, A/V equipment, photocopiers, computers, CNN, and express checkout. 100 E. Chestnut (phone: 751-1900 or 800-621-8133; Fax: 312-280-1304). Expensive.

21 East Kempinski – This Magnificent Mile hostelry boasts an elegant 4-story atrium lobby and 247 rooms, including 6 duplex penthouse suites, overlooking the city and Lake Michigan. There is a piano bar and formal dining in *Café 21*, which serves Southwestern fare. Amenities include 24-hour room service, concierge, 6 meeting rooms, secretarial services, A/V equipment, photocopiers, computers, CNN, and express checkout. 24 E. Bellevue Pl. (phone: 266-2100; Fax: 312-266-2103). Expensive.

Westin Chicago – This deluxe, near-North Side hotel has 742 rooms and a health club with sauna and steamroom. The *Chelsea* restaurant serves continental fare and the *Lion Bar* is a popular spot that's generally crowded with businesspeople. Amenities include 24-hour room service, concierge, 18 meeting rooms, secretarial services, A/V equipment, photocopiers, CNN, and express checkout. Near the *Drake* and the Hancock Center. N. Michigan Ave. at Delaware (phone: 943-7200; Fax: 312-943-9347; Telex: 206593). Expensive.

Whitehall – Devoted to detail and known for its elegance and its careful, courteous service. Its excellent restaurant is open only to members and registered guests. Its 223 rooms are decorated in the style of an English country manor. Amenities include 24-hour room service, concierge, 6 meeting rooms, secretarial services, A/V equipment, photocopiers, computers, and express checkout. 105 E. Delaware Pl. (phone: 944-6300; Fax: 312-280-1304). Expensive.

Richmont – A somewhat moderately priced alternative near the Magnificent Mile. There are 193 guestrooms, a meeting room, and the *Rue St. Clair* lobby bar, which looks like a French bistro but serves American fare. Amenities include A/V equipment, photocopiers, and CNN. 162 E. Ontario St. (phone: 787-3580 or 800 621-8055; Fax: 312-787-1299). Expensive to moderate.

Allerton – Close to museums and shopping on Michigan Avenue, 10 minutes from the Loop. The 380-room property is an economical but quite pleasant choice — and a steal in this location. There's also a good restaurant, *L'Escargot* (see *Eating Out*). Amenities include 10 meeting rooms, secretarial services, A/V equipment, and photocopiers. 701 N. Michigan Ave. (phone: 440-1500; Fax: 312-440-1819). Moderate.

Bismarck – The *Walnut Room* serves breakfast and lunch, and the *Chalet* is where guests go for dinner. There are 525 rooms and some nice suites. Amenities include 19 meeting rooms, secretarial services, A/V equipment, photocopiers, and express checkout. 171 W. Randolph at La Salle (phone: 236-0123; Fax: 312-236-3177). Moderate.

Congress – Not as large as the nearby *Palmer House* (800 rooms), but this unit of the Best Western chain has a well-deserved reputation for personal attention. It also boasts fine views of Lake Michigan and Grant Park. The hotel offers 24-hour room service, 22 meeting rooms, A/V equipment, and photocopiers. 520 S. Michigan Ave. (phone: 427-3800; Fax: 312-427-3972; Telex: 4330281). Moderate.

Days Inn Lake Shore Drive – The best things about this 586-room property are its setting opposite the lake and Navy Pier and its relatively low rates, which are even more reasonable considering the outdoor pool. Amenities include 5 meeting rooms, A/V equipment, photocopiers, CNN, and express checkout. 644 N. Lake Shore Dr. (phone: 943-9200; Fax: 312-649-5580; Telex: 4973443). Moderate.

Holiday Inn City Centre – Architecturally more interesting than you might expect. Swimming pools and a health club, indoor tennis courts, racquetball, and free parking make this establishment's 500 rooms almost a bargain. Amenities include a concierge desk, 11 meeting rooms, A/V equipment, photocopiers, CNN, and express checkout. 300 E. Ohio (phone: 787-6100; Fax: 312-787-6259). Moderate.

Holiday Inn of Elk Grove – Convenient to O'Hare. With 159 rooms and a domed indoor pool, it's an economical choice for an overnight stop.

Small pets are welcome. Amenities include 5 meeting rooms, A/V equipment, photocopiers, CNN, express checkout, and transportation to the airport. 1000 Busse Rd. (phone: 708-437-6010; Fax: 708-806-9369). Moderate.

Avenue – This budget motel has only 78 rooms and few amenities, but it's close to town. 1154 S. Michigan Ave. (phone: 427-8200). Inexpensive.

Grove – An outdoor pool and low (for Chicago) prices make this 40-room motel a real find. Restaurant nearby. A half-hour drive from the Loop (longer in rush hour). 9110 Waukegan Rd., Morton Grove (phone: 708-966-0960). Inexpensive.

EATING OUT: The city's restaurant business is booming, and some of the finest cooking in America can be found here. Expect to pay from $60 and up for two at those restaurants we've noted as expensive; between $40 and $60, for moderately priced meals; and under $40 at our inexpensive choices. Prices do not include drinks and wine, tips or taxes. All telephone numbers are in the 312 area code unless otherwise indicated.

Ambria – Everything about this place charms, from the comfortable setting to the menu's sophisticated variations on nouvelle cuisine. Dinner might begin with a salad of sliced duck, pine nuts, and fresh pears with red currant dressing, or a tropical lobster salad. Desserts are simply remarkable. There's also a *dégustation* dinner for 4 or more with samplings of many dishes. Closed Sundays. Reservations necessary. Major credit cards accepted. 2300 N. Lincoln Park W. (phone: 472-5959). Expensive.

Biggs – In a restored Victorian mansion. The prix fixe menu changes every day, but the selection often includes beef Wellington, duck à l'orange, roast rack of lamb *persillade*, fettuccine with lobster and scallops, and tenderloin tips sautéed with fresh mushrooms and served on wild rice. There's an extensive wine list. Open daily for dinner. Reservations necessary. Major credit cards accepted. 1150 N. Dearborn (phone: 787-0900). Expensive.

Café Provençal – An intimate room on a quiet north suburban Evanston street. It offers some of the most painstakingly prepared French dishes in the area — the Wisconsin pheasant with rosemary-honey glaze and the New York foie gras with Cortlandt apples are particularly recommended. Closed Sundays. Reservations advised. Major credit cards accepted. 1625 Hinman St., Evanston (phone: 475-2233). Expensive.

Charlie Trotter's – The menu changes daily in this adventuresome, 2-room nouvelle cuisine restaurant, the civilized home of some of the city's most imaginative dishes. Appetizers range from caviar-topped sea scallops to sweetbreads with pancetta, radicchio, shredded potato, sweet peppers, and sharp cilantro butter presented in a crisp potato shell. Entrées are equally varied: tender venison, smoked quail with hazelnuts. Service is excellent; the wine list is extensive. Closed Sundays and Mondays. Reservations necessary. Major credit cards accepted. 816 W. Armitage (phone: 248-6228). Expensive.

Le Ciel Bleu – Overlooking the Oak Street beach and the Lake Michigan shoreline, this delightful eating establishment in the *Mayfair Regent* hotel favors a menu with dishes from Provence and Northern Italy. The seafood soup *niçoise* and angel hair pasta with wild mushrooms and thyme are not to be missed. Open daily. Reservations necessary. Major credit cards accepted. 181 E. Lake Shore Dr. (phone: 951-2864). Expensive.

Cricket's – In the style of the old *"21" Club* in New York, with red-checkered tablecloths, bare floors, low ceilings, and walls festooned with corporate memorabilia, and a menu that includes chicken hash Mornay and various daily specials. A very good choice for Sunday brunch. Open daily. Reservations necessary. Major credit cards accepted. *Tremont Hotel,* 100 E. Chestnut (phone: 280-2100). Expensive.

Everest Room – An elegant French restaurant with a commanding view from atop LaSalle Street, Chicago's Wall Street. The cornucopia of original dishes reflect the chef's Alsatian roots. Try the roast filet of sea bass wrapped in crisp shredded potatoes. Closed Sundays and Mondays. Reservations necessary. Major credit cards accepted. 440 S. LaSalle (phone: 663-8920). Expensive.

Le Français – For years, Jean Bouchet made this one of America's finest French restaurants. Today the kitchen is in the hands of Roland and Mary Beth Liccioni, and the still-excellent fare has a somewhat lighter touch to it. The pastries are superb! Closed Sundays. Reservations necessary. Major credit cards accepted. 269 S. Milwaukee, Wheeling; take Kennedy Expy. to Rte. 294 north, Willow exit (phone: 708-541-7470). Expensive.

Gene and Georgetti – In an old, woodframe building near the Merchandise Mart, hearty sirloin, T-bone steaks, and animated conversation mingle. This eatery also dishes up popular Italian dishes and huge salads. Closed Sunday. Reservations unnecessary. Major credit cards accepted. 500 N. Franklin (phone: 527-3718). Expensive.

Gordon – When Gordon Sinclair's culinary imagination ignites, his clientele is happy to eat the superlative results. Grilled Norwegian salmon with Chinese mustard glaze or charred lamb with minted couscous and eggplant and garlic are beautifully balanced by such desserts as lemon soufflé with warm caramel sauce. Open daily. Reservations advised. Major credit cards accepted. 500 N. Clark St. (phone: 467-9780). Expensive.

Jackie's – An intimate 50-seat neighborhood spot, serving some of the finest nouvelle cooking in the city. Consider delicate orange-honey-glazed squab served with Chinese vermicelli and cabbage garnished with cashews and cloud-ear mushrooms. Closed Sundays and Mondays. Reservations necessary. Major credit cards accepted. 2478 N. Lincoln (phone: 880-0003). Expensive.

Jimmy's Place – Opera fans (and aficionados) can experience the glory of Verdi, Puccini, and Mozart while dining on medaillons of veal, spicy shrimp ragout in sesame crêpes, and veal sweetbreads atop grilled, smoked leeks. Closed Sundays. Reservations advised. Major credit cards accepted. 3420 N. Elston Ave. (phone: 539-2999). Expensive.

Morton's of Chicago – Another fine steak-and-potatoes establishment whose loyal returnees gulp down everything from kosher hot dogs to chicken in the pot to fabulous cheesecake. Open daily. Reservations advised. Major credit cards accepted. 1050 N. State St. (phone: 266-4820). Expensive.

Nick's Fishmarket – The number of choices on the menu is bewildering, but the work of choosing is worth the effort. The cold appetizer assortment of shellfish is always a good bet, and try the pan-fried whole baby salmon or an abalone dish for an entrée. Closed Sundays. Reservations necessary. Major credit cards accepted. First National Plaza, Monroe St. (phone: 621-0200). Expensive.

95th – For food with a view, this is your best bet. An American regional cuisine menu that changes seasonally. Open daily for lunch and dinner; dinner only on Saturdays; brunch and dinner Sundays. Reservations advised. Major credit cards accepted. 95th Floor, John Hancock Center, 172 E. Chestnut St. (phone: 787-9596). Expensive.

Palm – Owned by the same people who run the well-known New York restaurants called *Palm* and *Palm, Too,* this eatery has a similar decor of sawdust-covered floors and walls hung with drawings of regular patrons. Also like its East Coast counterparts, the kitchen here specializes in producing great steaks and lobsters. Closed Sundays. Reservations necessary. Major credit cards accepted. *Mayfair Regent Hotel,* 181 E. Lake Shore (phone: 944-0135). Expensive.

Le Perroquet – Subtle, sumptuous; one of the best dining places around. Expect a parade of delectable wonders such as *moules* or a *soufflé de crevettes Madras* as hors d'oeuvres; salmon mousseline, venison filet, or quail as entrées; pastries to follow. Closed Sundays. Reservations necessary. Major credit cards accepted. 70 E. Walton (phone: 944-7990). Expensive.

Pump Room – A winning formula of fine food, diligent service, and lovely decor have made this a legend among Chicago restaurants. Continental dishes are the mainstays, but there are some nouvelle cuisine specialties; both are complemented by the restaurant's good wine list. Open daily. Reservations necessary. Major credit cards accepted. 1301 N. State Pkwy. (phone: 266-0360). Expensive.

Seasons – This opulent, urbane room features some of the most inventive nouvelle preparations in the city. Try the quail with game-sausage stuffing or the venison. Open daily. Reservations necessary. Major credit cards accepted. *Four Seasons Hotel,* 120 E. Delaware (phone: 280-8800). Expensive.

Spiaggia – Expertly prepared Northern Italian food — including unique pasta dishes, veal, and a grilled fish of the day — served in a beautiful setting. Open daily except Sunday lunch. Reservations advised. Major credit cards accepted. 980 N. Michigan (phone: 280-2750). Expensive.

Printer's Row – Chef Michael Foley awakens sluggish palates with his delicious fare. Choose to dine in the snug wine library, an intimate room lined with bookcases (including Michael's cookbooks), another cozy room decorated with a hunting motif, or the main dining area. The roast pheasant with *jus au natural* and five kinds of onions, as well as the grilled salmon with a basil cream sauce and sun-dried tomato pasta, are true standouts. Chocoholics should dive into the chocolate terrine studded with fresh raspberries or the white and dark chocolate cheesecake with amaretto sauce. Closed Sundays. Reservations advised. Major credit cards accepted. 550 S. Dearborn St. (phone: 461-0780). Expensive to moderate.

Butcher Shop Steakhouse – A unique dining experience, where you have your steak and cook it, too. In this latest, growing trend, guests select a filet or T-bone and pop it on the grill themselves. For those who prefer full service, the kitchen happily will oblige (there's an additional $2 charge if you leave the cooking to them). Open daily. Reservations advised. Major credit cards accepted. 358 W. Ontario (phone: 440-4900). Moderate.

Cape Cod Room – An institution, this seafood spot serves reliable fresh pompano, lobster, and other finny fare. Closed *Christmas.* Reservations necessary. Major credit cards accepted. *Drake Hotel,* 140 E. Walton (phone: 787-2200). Moderate.

Chestnut Street Grill – The Frank Lloyd Wright and Louis Sullivan ornamentation are as distinctive as the house specialty, grilled seafood. Try the swordfish or the tuna. The desserts are sinful, especially the cappuccino-candy ice cream. Open daily. Reservations advised. Major credit cards accepted. Mezzanine level, Water Tower Place (phone: 280-2720). Moderate.

The Eccentric – *Chicago Bears* Coach Mike Ditka was the first Chicago celebrity to open a successful restaurant. Sportscaster Harry Carey was next. This one's Oprah Winfrey's. It lives up to its name: lots of wild colors, paintings by local artists, an amalgam of French, English, American, and Italian cooking styles, and such dishes as cold fruit soup with chili peppers. Don't pass up Oprah's lumpy mashed potatoes with horseradish. Open daily. No reservations. Major credit cards accepted. 159 W. Erie (phone: 787-8390) Moderate.

L'Escargot – Unpretentious and pleasant, with an emphasis on provincial French cooking, including a cassoulet — white. beans, sausage, pork, and goose. There's always fresh fish and homemade pastries on the menu. Open daily. Reservations advised. Major credit cards accepted. *Allerton Hotel,* 701 N. Michigan (phone: 337-1717). Moderate.

Hatsuhana – Delicious sushi and sashimi; tables as well as counter seating available. Open daily. Reservations advised. Major credit cards accepted. 160 E. Ontario (phone: 280-8287). Moderate.

Lawry's The Prime Rib – The specialty here is prime ribs, served in three thicknesses with Yorkshire pudding and a big fresh salad with Lawry's special Famous French dressing and Lawry's seasoned salt. Open daily for dinner; weekdays for lunch. Reservations necessary. Major credit cards accepted. 100 E. Ontario (phone: 787-5000). Moderate.

Lou Mitchell's – For those who consider the idea of awakening before noon a barbaric proposal, make an exception and head for this outstanding breakfast spot. The doors open at 5:30 AM. Freshly squeezed orange juice is followed by perfectly prepared pancakes, omelettes served in the pan, and freshly baked biscuits, and fantastic coffee. Formica tabletops, eccentric waitresses, and a low-key clientele complete the picture. Closed Sundays. Reservations advised. Major credit cards accepted. 563 W. Jackson Blvd. (phone: 939-3111). Moderate.

Prairie – Quite possibly where the term Midwestern cooking was coined, this intimate dining spot offers fine regional fare. The decor is elegant and uncluttered, à la Frank Lloyd Wright, and the open kitchen is a fine place to pick up on new cooking techniques as you watch your food in transit between the cutting board and your plate. Whitefish smothered with onions, crisp bacon, puréed squash, and smoked whitefish caviar is just one of the thoughtfully prepared entrées, and those willing to chance an extra pound should try the warm carrot raisin cake with bourbon glaze and sugarplums. Closed Sundays. Reservations advised. Major credit cards accepted. 500 S. Dearborn (phone: 663-1143). Moderate.

Salvatore's – Diners at this handsome Italian restaurant may sit in a garden atrium or in one of two dining rooms. The menu features 14 kinds of homemade pasta and fresh fish specials that change daily, but the kitchen is most proud of its *castelle di vitello* (roasted milk-fed veal) and *fettuccine alla Caroline* (green noodles with pine nuts, mushrooms, spinach, and cheese). Among the choices on the wine list are 114 varieties from Italy. Open daily. Reservations advised. Major credit cards accepted. 525 W. Arlington Pl. (phone: 528-1200). Moderate.

Scoozi – A cavernous former garage that's been turned into a smashing gathering place with evocative period decor. Besides the chef's daily specials, the unusually large menu includes provincial Italian specialties such as a 3-foot-long pizza served on wooden planks (calorie counters, fear not; they do come smaller), ossobuco (braised veal shanks), and pheasant that is smoked on the premises and served with a choice of soft, baked, or sautéed polenta (the Italian version of grits). Open weekdays for lunch, daily for dinner. Reservations for lunch only. Major credit cards accepted. 410 W. Huron (phone: 943-5900). Moderate.

Shaw's Crab House – A mammoth, immensely popular pre–World War II–style seafood house. Don't miss the stone or soft-shell crabs if they're in season. The pecan pie may be Chicago's best. Open daily. Reservations for lunch only. Major credit cards accepted. 21 E. Hubbard (phone: 527-2722). Moderate.

La Strada – An Italian place with a reputation for its tableside preparation of such specialties as veal Forestiera, rich with mushrooms and artichokes in wine sauce. Other highlights include eggplant *involtini* and carpaccio. Closed Sundays. Reservations advised. Major credit cards accepted. 151 N. Michigan (phone: 565-2200). Moderate.

Terczaki's – Traditional American food just like mom used to make.

Open nightly. Reservations advised on weekends. Major credit cards, *except* American Express, accepted. 2635 N. Halsted (phone: 404-0171). Moderate.

Szechwan House – The hot and sour soup and the crispy duck are just as appetizing as the chef's more unusual dishes, such as snails in spicy sauce and deep-fried ground shrimp wrapped in seaweed. Open daily. Reservations advised. Major credit cards accepted. 600 N. Michigan (phone: 642-3900). Moderate to inexpensive.

Ann Sather's – There actually are two: The original institution may be the world's only Swedish restaurant in a former funeral home. It is on West Belmont Avenue near other Chicago institutions, such as *Wrigley Field* and the *Steppenwolf Theater*. The menu varies from time-honored Swedish dishes to hearty American fare: pork sausage patties and rich country gravy, beefsteak and eggs with cinnamon rolls. Brunch is particularly good. Open daily. Reservations unnecessary. MasterCard and Visa accepted. 929 W. Belmont Ave. (phone: 348-2378) and 5207 N. Clark St. (phone: 271-6677). Inexpensive.

Army & Lou's – This hangout for Chicago aldermen serves the best soul food in the city. Try the greens and neck bones, the Northern beans with hamhocks, the smothered chicken and corn bread dressing, or better yet, the $30 Taste of Soul, which includes everything from chicken to catfish to chitlins and more hamhocks. Closed Tuesdays. Reservations advised. Major credit cards accepted. 422 E. 75th (phone: 483-6550). Inexpensive.

Beau Thai – One of Lincoln Park's fine collection of Southeast Asian eateries. Specialties include *pad thai,* a warm noodle dish; duck Beau Thai, cooked with cashews and vegetables; and sweet, creamy cold Thai coffee for dessert. Closed Mondays. Reservations accepted on weekends only. Major credit cards accepted. 2525 N. Clark (phone: 348-6938). Inexpensive.

Berghoff – Another Chicago tradition. Although the service is rushed, the meals are bountiful and the selection wide-ranging: ragout, Wiener schnitzel, steaks, and seafood. Closed Sundays. Reservations accepted for five or more. Major credit cards accepted. 17 W. Adams (phone: 427-3170). Inexpensive.

Blue Mesa – Southwestern cooking is one of this city's latest dining crazes, and Santa Fe–style reigns in this comfortable room of white-washed adobe and bleached pine. Lovers of wonderfully pulpy guacamole and steaks smothered in green chilies and onions will be quite content. Open daily. Reservations necessary for parties of 8 or more. Major credit cards accepted. 1729 N. Halsted (phone: 944-5990). Inexpensive.

Bub City – A rollicking, mammoth, down-home Texas eating house, featuring shrimp and crab barbecue and "Big Easy" bayou music to wash it all down. This is one loud, entertaining joint. Wear denim. Open daily. No reservations. Major credit cards accepted. 901 W. Weed (phone: 266-1200). Inexpensive.

Café Ba-Ba-Reeba! – A boisterous, informal Spanish *tapas* restaurant/bar with an authentic feel. Dining here involves tossing back dry sherry with bites of hot and cold *tapas.* The tender squid, stuffed with its own ground meat and crunchy pistachios, is especially good. Open Tuesday through Saturday for lunch, daily for dinner. Reservations accepted for lunch only. Major credit cards accepted. 2024 N. Halsted (phone: 935-5000). Inexpensive.

Carson's – Probably the best spareribs in the city. Salads with a creamy, anchovy-flavored dressing and tangy au gratin potatoes are the other lures. Don't dress up, for bibs (supplied) are essential. Open daily. No reservations, so expect to wait. Major credit cards accepted. 612 N. Wells St. (phone: 280-9200). Inexpensive.

Ed Debevic's – The creation of Rich Melman, king of Chicago restaurateurs — a 1950s diner that has crowds lining up outside. Burgers, chili, malts, fries, and a rollicking *American Graffiti* atmosphere. Open daily. No reservations or credit cards accepted. 640 N. Wells (phone: 664-1707). Inexpensive.

Febo's – A real "old neighborhood" restaurant where the Northern Italian cooking tastes as if it came out of a family kitchen. Try the antipasto, followed by linguine Alfredo, cannelloni, tortellini, or chicken Alfredo in mushrooms and lemon-herb wine sauce. Closed Sundays. Reservations necessary on weekends. Major credit cards accepted. 2501 S. Western (phone: 523-0839). Inexpensive.

Frontera Grill and Topolobampo – A pair of upscale Mexican dining rooms. *Frontera* specializes in tempting appetizer platters of guacamole, deep-fried chicken taquitos, and ceviche. *Topolobampo* offers, among other treats, roast pork loin with red-chili apricot sauce and pumpkin purée. Closed Sundays and Mondays. Reservations advised. Major credit cards accepted. 445 N. Clark St. (phone: 661-1434). Inexpensive.

Greek Islands – You can find thoughtfully prepared dishes such as gyros, squid, lamb, and fresh broiled red snapper at this simple eatery. The decor isn't elegant, but the food is delicious. Open daily. Reservations unnecessary. Major credit cards accepted. 200 S. Halsted (phone: 782-9855). Inexpensive.

Hard Rock Café – Yes, Chicago has one, too. The walls of this hip hamburger emporium are covered with an assortment of rock music artifacts and declarations of world peace. Chili and grilled burgers lead the menu. Wash it all down with a fruit and honey "health shake." At the very least, a good addition to any trendy T-shirt collection. Open daily. Reservations unnecessary. Major credit cards accepted. 63 W. Ontario (phone: 943-2252). Inexpensive.

Jerome's – The room is warmly decorated and the service draws little complaint, but the food is the real attraction. In addition to a regular selection of meat, poultry, and fish, the kitchen turns out fresh bread and desserts and six to eight special dishes every day. Open daily. Reservations advised. Major credit cards accepted. 2450 N. Clark (phone: 327-2207). Inexpensive.

A visit to this city's eating establishments wouldn't be complete without a taste of Chicago's famous deep-dish pizza — layer upon layer of toppings baked in a deep-dish pan. The pioneer of this pizza fit for Goliath was *Pizzeria Uno* (29 E. Ohio St., phone: 321-1000), a place whose food more than makes up for its lack of atmosphere. Also in the area is *Pizzeria Due* (619 N. Wabash Ave; phone: 943-2400), serving the same hearty pizza. *Gino's East* (160 E. Superior St.; phone 943-1124) uses cornmeal crusts to vary the flavor. Two other places to try this local delicacy are *Giordano's of Lincoln Park* (1840 N. Clark St.; phone: 944-6100) and *Eduardo's Natural Pizza* (9300 Skokie Blvd., Skokie; phone: 708-674-0008). The latter eatery also serves the latest fad in pizza-noshing, stuffed pizza — a thick, gooey pie-like creation. Both are open daily. Reservations unnecessary. Major credit cards accepted.

■ **Hot Dog!:** If all of the above fail to seduce your culinary sensibilities, the *Wieners Circle* is a terrific alternative for those with the I-can't-get-a-good-hot-dog blues. The special (and novel) concoction of the house is the "chardog," a half-pound of spicy beef on a soft bun with onions, tomatoes, cucumbers, pickles, mustard, relish, and perhaps the kitchen sink. Ignore the seedy atmosphere and utter lack of decor, and concentrate on the perfect french fries and charcoal-broiled cheddar burgers. Open daily. Reservations unnecessary. No credit cards accepted. 2622 N. Clark St. (phone: 477-7444).

CINCINNATI

AT-A-GLANCE

SEEING THE CITY: For the best view of Cincinnati, go to the top of the Carew Tower. You may see the original seven hills on which the town is said to have been built. Admission charge. Children under 6 free. Groups of 20 or more get in for half price but must call at least 1 week in advance. 5th and Vine Sts. (phone: 241-3888).

Another popular way to see the city is by riverboat. *BB Riverboats'* vessels are available for 1- to 2-hour sightseeing, luncheon, dinner, and moonlight cruises, or day-long adventures. They are moored at Madison Avenue at Covington Landing (just across the river from Cincinnati; phone 606-261-8500). Or try *Barleycorn's Riverboats* (Ludlow, KY; phone: 606-581-0300).

SPECIAL PLACES: Pedestrians can traverse the city above the traffic via a Skywalk system that is totally covered. In many areas, it is enclosed and climate-controlled.

Cincinnati Art Museum – Following the renovation which was completed this year, this outstanding collection of paintings, sculpture, prints, and decorative arts fills more than 100 galleries and exhibition rooms (with an exceptionally fine section on ancient Persia). Ancient musical instruments, costumes, and textiles also are on view. Closed Mondays and holidays. Admission charge except on Saturdays. Eden Park (phone: 721-5204).

Museum Center at Union Terminal – This collective center is the home of the *Cincinnati Historical Society Museum and Library,* the *Cincinnati Museum of Natural History,* and an Omnimax movie theater. Open Monday through Saturday from 9AM to 5 PM, Friday from 9 AM to 9 PM; and Sunday from 11 AM to 5 PM. Admission charge. 1301 Western Ave.; Ezzard Charles Drive exit off I-75 (phone: 287-7000).

Harriet Beecher Stowe House – The author of *Uncle Tom's Cabin* resided here for 4 years. In addition to a collection of Stowe memorabilia, the house has a number of exhibitions on black history. Open Tuesdays through Thursdays, 10 AM to 4 PM. No admission charge. 2950 Gilbert Ave. (phone: 632-5120).

Taft Museum – William Howard Taft used this house, the home of his older half brother, for formal occasions during his presidency. Once nicknamed "the Little White House," it is now a museum of paintings, Chinese porcelain, and Duncan Phyfe furniture. Portraits and landscapes by Rembrandt, Turner, Goya, Gainsborough, and Corot line the walls. Open daily. Contributions requested. 316 Pike (phone: 241-0343).

Riverfront Stadium – Cincinnati is the self-proclaimed baseball capital of the world, and sports fans will enjoy touring the dugouts and back rooms of this 60,000-seat, artificial-turf stadium. Tours by appointment during baseball season. Admission charge. 201 E. Pete Rose Way (phone: 352-5400; 352-5456 for tours.).

Contemporary Arts Center – "What is art?" is a puzzler as old as the Cincinnati hills, and the *Contemporary Arts Center* keeps many people in this good city wondering. Not only are there constantly changing modern paintings and sculpture, the center features multimedia ex-

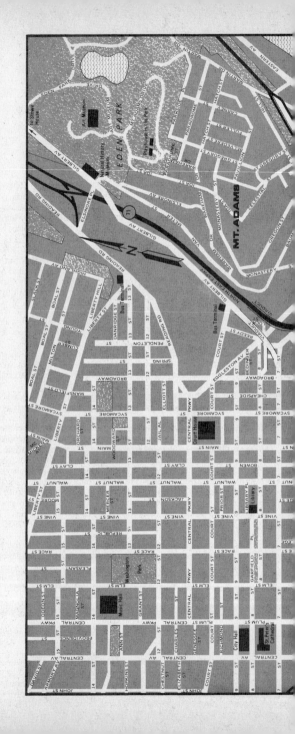

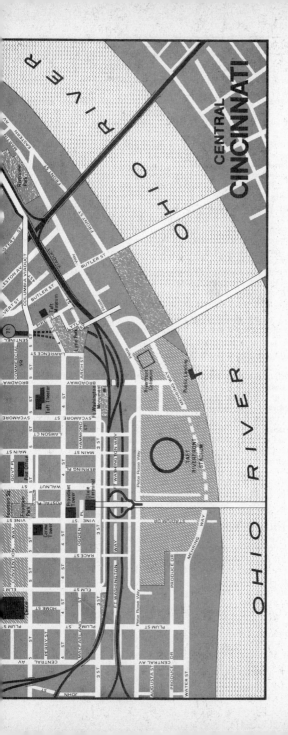

hibits aimed at dazzling the mind, the eye, and the mind's eye. Closed Sundays. Admission charge except on Mondays. 115 E. 5th St. (phone: 721-0390).

Cincinnati Fire Museum – All kinds of old fire engines and paraphernalia in a 1907 firehouse listed on the National Register of Historic Places. Closed Mondays and holidays. Admission charge; children under 2 free. 315 W. Court St. (phone: 621-5553).

Cincinnati Zoo – The second-oldest zoo in the nation, known for its expertise in the propagation of rare and endangered species. There are more than 6,000 animals here. The most popular exhibits are the rare white Bengal tigers, the Bird of Prey Flight Cage, Outdoor Gorilla Exhibit, Children's Zoo, Insectarium, and the new Cat House. Open daily. Admission charge. 3400 Vine St. (phone: 281-4700).

Sharon Woods Village – Life in 19th-century Ohio, with a representative group of pre-1880 buildings in a village setting. Open Wednesdays through Sundays, May through October and during the post-*Thanksgiving* and pre-*Christmas* holidays. Admission charge. Sharon Woods, off Rte. 42 (phone: 563-9484).

Krohn Conservatory – One of the largest public greenhouses in the world, it contains 1,500 labeled specimens of tropical plants and seasonal flowers. Displays change six times a year. Open daily from 10 AM to 5 PM, with extended hours during the *Christmas* and *Easter* seasons. Voluntary admission charge. Eden Park (phone: 352-4086).

■ **EXTRA SPECIAL:** Just 25 miles north of Cincinnati is small-town America at its best. Lebanon, Ohio — where the movie *Harper Valley PTA* was shot — is the home of the *Golden Lamb Inn,* Ohio's oldest operating inn, now also a Shaker museum and a first-rate restaurant (phone: 621-8373). While in Lebanon, visit the *Warren County Historical Society Museum* (phone: 932-1817), which also has a major Shaker collection.

Just a couple of hours south of Cincinnati lies the best horse-breeding region in the US — Kentucky bluegrass country. The drive on I-71/75 takes you through very green rolling hills and beautiful breeding farms. Stop for lunch (except Mondays) or dinner (first seating is at 6 PM) at the relaxing *Beaumont Inn,* just west of Lexington, Kentucky, in Harrodsburg. Reservations recommended. Open mid-March through mid-December (phone: 606-734-3381).

SOURCES AND RESOURCES

TOURIST INFORMATION: For maps and brochures, write or visit the Greater Cincinnati Convention and Visitors Bureau (300 W. 6th St., Cincinnati, OH 45202; phone: 621-2142; 800-344-3445). It also can provide self-guided walking tour maps. Contact the Ohio state hotline (phone: 800-BUCKEYE) for maps, calendars of events, health updates, and travel advisories.

The best guide to events and places of interest is *Cincinnati* magazine, monthly, available at newsstands.

Local Coverage – *Cincinnati Enquirer,* morning daily and Sundays; *Cincinnati Post,* afternoon daily.

Television Stations – WLWT Channel 5–NBC; WCPO Channel 9–CBS; WKRC Channel 12–ABC; WCET Channel 48–PBS.

Radio Stations – AM: WKRC 550 (adult contemporary music and sports); WLW 700 (sports/talk); WCKY 1530 (talk). FM: WGUC 90.9 (classical); WWEZ 92.5 (soft rock); WRRM 98 (adult contemporary); WUBE 105 (country).

Food – *Cincinnati* magazine's annual restaurant guide, available from the Chamber of Commerce, gives the best information on where to dine. The *Cincinnati Enquirer, Post,* and *Cincinnati* magazine feature occasional restaurant columns and guides, too.

 TELEPHONE: The area code for Cincinnati is 513.
  Sales Tax – The city sales tax is 5½%.

 CLIMATE: Cincinnati has four distinct seasons. Crisp winter temperatures average 31F, and summer temperatures average 75.6F. Blossomy springs and blazing falls, however, are more amenable, and a drive through the surrounding countryside in either season is a joy. Keep raingear handy in the spring and fall.

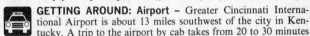 **GETTING AROUND: Airport** – Greater Cincinnati International Airport is about 13 miles southwest of the city in Kentucky. A trip to the airport by cab takes from 20 to 30 minutes and should cost around $20 for 1 to 5 passengers. *Jet Port Express* (phone: 606-283-3702) provides both bus and limo transportation between the airport and Cincinnati's leading hotels. Buses shuttle between the airport and downtown hotels every half hour (every hour on Saturdays) and the fare is $8 one way or $12 round trip.

  Bus – *Queen City Metro* operates an excellent bus service. The bus stop signs carry numbers of the routes that stop there. Route maps are available from *Queen City Metro,* 6 E. 4th St. (phone: 621-4455).

  Car Rental – Major car rental agencies are represented at the Greater Cincinnati International Airport.

  Horse-drawn Carriages – Several companies operate non-motorized transport in the Fountain Square area. Rates vary with the carriage and route. Board carriages at Fountain Square.

  Taxi – Call *Yellow Cab* (1767 Queen City Ave.; phone: 241-2100), or go to any of the major hotels, where cabs line up.

 VITAL SERVICES: Audiovisual Equipment – *Cavalier/David Douglas Audio Visual* (phone: 421-1300).

  Baby-sitting – *Rock-a-Bye Sitters Registry,* 432 Walnut St. (phone: 721-7440).

  Business Services – *Secretarial Office Services* are at two locations (21 E. Court St.; phone: 632-5345 and Carew Tower; phone: 381-2277).

  Dry Cleaner/Tailor – *Teasdale Renton Cleaners,* 236 E. 6th St. (phone: 241-4074).

  Limousine – *Adams Superior Limousine Service* (phone: 396-7433); *Washington Limousine Service* (phone: 221-0074).

  Mechanic – *Certified Car Care,* 412 Liberty St., between Central Ave. and John St. (phone: 721-2886).

  Medical Emergency – *Jewish Hospital Medical Center,* 8 AM to 6 PM, Monday through Friday, 417 Vine St., across from *Westin Hotel* (phone: 241-3322).

  Messenger Services – *Cincinnati Express* (phone: 542-1900).

  National/International Courier – *Federal Express,* closed Sundays (phone: 530-5660); *DHL Worldwide Express* (phone: 800-225-5345).

  Pharmacy – *Walgreen's,* weekdays from 7 AM to 6 PM, Saturdays from 9 AM to 5 PM. Closed on Sundays. 121 E. 5th St. (phone: 721-0840).

  Photocopies – *Quik Graphics,* 615 Main St. (phone: 241-5100).

  Post Office – Downtown, 5th and Walnut Sts. (phone: 684-5664).

  Professional Photographer – *Corporate Group* (phone: 241-8273); *Mayhew & Peper Photographers* (phone: 421-0111).

  Secretary/Stenographer – *Secretarial Office Service* (phone: 381-2277 or 632-5345); *Cin-Tel Corporation* (phone: 621-7723).

  Teleconference Facilities – *Terrace Hilton* (see *Best in Town,* below).

  Translator – *Berlitz* (phone: 381-4650); *Inlingua* (phone: 721-8782).

Typewriter Rental – *Scot Business Machines,* 1-week minimum (phone: 421-9030); *Peter Paul Office Equipment,* 1-week minimum (phone: 721-0865).

Western Union/Telex – Many locations around town (phone: 800-325-6000).

Other – *American Training Center,* teaches word processing and computer software (phone: 791-8298).

 SPECIAL EVENTS: Ever since 1873, Cincinnati has held its annual *May Festival,* a series of choral and instrumental musical concerts at *Music Hall* (1243 Elm; phone: 381-3300). The *Ameri-Flora* international floral and garden show, will be held this year in Columbus (about a 2 hours' drive north of the city); it is part of the quincentennial celebration of Christopher Columbus's voyage to the US (phone: 645-1900). In summer (usually July) the *Jack Nicklaus Sports Center* at Kings Island (3565 Kings Mill Rd.; phone: 381-3300) hosts the *Senior PGA Tour Classic* and in August, the annual *ATP Tournament.* (3565 Kings Mills Rd.; phone: 398-5200). In mid-September, Cincinnati celebrates its German heritage with an *Oktoberfest,* along the lines of the famous Munich festival, in and around Fountain Square. In mid-October, *Tall Stacks* — 18 sternwheelers offering tours and cruises up and down the river — will return to Public Landing (Port of Cincinnati). From *Thanksgiving* weekend through December, *Winterfest* is held at Kings Island, and includes ice skating, musicals, crafts displays, holiday food, and what is claimed to be the world's largest *Christmas* tree.

 MUSEUMS: Cincinnati's major museums — *Cincinnati Art Museum, Cincinnati Fire Museum, Contemporary Arts Center, Harriet Beecher Stowe House, Museum Center at Union Terminal,* and *Taft Museum* — are described in detail under *Special Places.*

 MAJOR COLLEGES AND UNIVERSITIES: The University of Cincinnati (Clifton; phone: 556-6000) has 36,000 students. Other notable schools are Xavier University (3800 Victory Pkwy.; phone: 745-3000); the College of Mount St. Joseph (5701 Delhi Rd.; phone: 244-4200); and the Art Academy of Cincinnati (Eden Park; phone: 721-5205).

 SPORTS AND FITNESS: Not only is Cincinnati one of the country's most enthusiastic baseball cities, it also favors football.

Baseball – The Cincinnati *Reds* (phone: 421-REDS), *World Series* champs in 1990, play at *Riverfront Stadium* (phone: 421-7337).

Basketball – University of Cincinnati *Bearcats* (phone: 556-2287) and Xavier University *Musketeers* (745-3411).

Bicycling – There is a 6.2-mile (10-km) bike trail at *Airport Playfield,* Lunken Airport (Wilmer Ave.; phone: 321-6500). Call to see if rental bikes are available in summer months.

Fishing – There's moderately good fishing at Lake Isabella, Winton Woods (the largest of the county lakes), and in the Ohio River. Serious Cincinnati sportfishers drive 4 hours to Lake Cumberland and Kentucky Lake in southern Kentucky.

Fitness Center – The *YMCA* provides a pool, sauna, equipment, and a track, as well as an outdoor jogging map. 1105 Elm St. (phone: 241-5348).

Football – The NFL *Bengals* play at *Riverfront Stadium* (phone: 621-3550).

Golf – For spectators and golfers, the *Jack Nicklaus Sports Center* (3565 Kings Mills Rd.; phone: 398-5200) is among the best. Also consider the *Glenview* and *Neumann* city courses or county links in Winton Woods and Sharon Woods parks.

Horse Racing – Enthusiasts should check out the action at *River Downs* (6301 Kellogg Ave.; phone: 232-8000) and *Turfway Racecourse*

(7500 Turfway Rd., Florence, KY; phone: 606-371-0200; 800-733-0200).

Jogging – For a 6-mile jaunt, follow tree-lined Central Parkway to Ludlow Street and come back; or run back and forth across the Ohio River Suspension Bridge, designed by Brooklyn Bridge builder John A. Roebling. The Cincinnati Recreation Commission publishes a free brochure, *Healthline Fitness Course,* available at the convention and visitors bureau.

Swimming – A good public pool is *Sunlite Pool* at Coney Island just before River Downs (on Rte. 50; phone: 232-8230). Call first to make sure it's open. There are lake beaches at nearby Hueston Woods in Butler County and Caesar's Creek in Warren County.

THEATER: Cincinnati has two major theaters. The *Taft* features touring companies, and has a spring, fall, and winter season (5th and Sycamore; phone: 721-0411). *Playhouse in the Park* is a professional regional theater specializing in contemporary and classic productions, as well as world premieres. It also stages two musicals during its year-round season. (Mt. Adams Circle, Eden Park; phone: 421-3888). The University of Cincinnati produces plays during the spring, summer, and fall on its *Showboat Majestic* (moored downtown; phone: 241-6550).

MUSIC: The internationally famous *Cincinnati Symphony Orchestra,* founded in 1895, has a September to May season at *Music Hall* (1243 Elm; phone: 381-3300); its summer home is the *Riverbend Music Center* (6295 Kellogg Ave.; phone: 381-3300 or 232-6220). The *College Conservatory of Music* is one of the nation's oldest and most prominent professional music schools, on the University of Cincinnati campus (Corbett Drive; phone: 556-4183). The *Cincinnati Opera* (phone: 241-ARIA), the second-oldest opera company in the US, performs at the downtown *Music Hall,* as does the *Cincinnati Ballet,* whose performance of *The Nutcracker* each December adds to Cincinnati's holiday tradition at the *Music Hall* (1243 Elm St.; phone: 621-5219 or 621-1110).

NIGHTCLUBS AND NIGHTLIFE: Cincinnati is pretty much a couples' town. The most popular nightspots are *Caddy's* (phone: 721-3636) and *Flanagan's Landing* (phone: 421-4055); both are on W. Pete Rose Way. Just across the Ohio River, on the Kentucky riverfront, are *Covington Landing Entertainment Complex,* with a variety of nightclubs, bars, and eateries (phone: 261-1212), *Barleycorn's Yacht Club* (phone: 606-291-8504), *Newport Beach* — an open-air disco (phone: 606-581-9000) — and the *Waterfront* (phone: 606-581-1414). Cincinnati hotel bars that swing into the wee hours: *Joe's Bar* (*Terrace Hilton*), *Fifth and Vine Street Bar* (*Westin*), *Champs* (*Hyatt*), *Palm Court* (*Netherland*), *Top of the Crown* (*Clarion*), and the *Cricket* (*Cincinnatian*). There also are numerous nightspots atop Mt. Adams.

BEST IN TOWN

CHECKING IN: The Cincinnati hotel scene has improved dramatically during the past decade, and accommodations now rival those of any US city of comparable size. Expect to pay between $100 and $195 for a double at any hotel listed as expensive; $70 to $100 at any in the moderate category. For bed and breakfast lodging, contact the *Ohio Valley Bed and Breakfast* (6876 Taylor Mill Rd., Independence, KY 41051; phone: 606-356-7865). All telephone numbers are in the 513 area code unless otherwise indicated.

Cincinnatian – This restored 100-year-old landmark provides European-style elegance that has earned it a reputation as the city's premier hotel. There are 147 well-appointed rooms, some with balconies overlooking an 8-story atrium. Its *Palace* restaurant serves American regional food. Amenities include 24-hour room service, concierge, 4 meeting rooms, secretarial services, A/V equipment, photocopiers, computers, CNN, and express checkout. One block from Fountain Square. 601 Vine St. (phone: 381-3000; Fax: 513-651-0256; Telex: 205234). Expensive.

Clarion – Corporate executives stay at this very modern, 887-room downtown place with a heated outdoor swimming pool, health club, sauna, lounge, restaurant, barber, beauty shop, and valet parking. There's a panoramic view from its *Top of the Crown* restaurant. Amenities include room service until 2 AM, concierge, 14 meeting rooms, secretarial services, A/V equipment, photocopiers, computers, CNN, and express checkout. 141 W. 6th St. (phone: 352-2100; Fax: 513-352-2148). Expensive.

Embassy Suites – This comfortable suite hotel has a spectacular view of the Ohio River and downtown Cincinnati. The *Riverpointe Grill* features fresh seafood, chicken, Black Angus beef, and specialty desserts. Piano entertainment nightly in *Riverpointe Lounge.* Amenities include room service until 10 PM, concierge on weekends, 1 meeting room, secretarial services, A/V equipment, photocopiers, computers, CNN, and express checkout. 10 E. RiverCenter Blvd. (phone: 261-8400; Fax: 606-261-8486). Expensive.

Garfield House – This all-suite hotel — located 2 blocks north of Fountain Square — has spacious suites, separate living rooms, and fully equipped kitchens with microwave ovens. Complimentary breakfast is served daily, and there is a coffee shop that serves sandwiches. There also is a complete health club. Room service is available until 10 PM. There is 1 meeting room, secretarial services, A/V equipment, CNN, and photocopiers. Two Garfield Place (phone: 421-3355; Fax: 513-421-3729). Expensive.

Hyatt Regency – It has 485 rooms, 22 suites, and a complete health club, including an indoor swimming pool. *Champs* restaurant features seafood and steaks; *Findlay's* has more casual dining and a country breakfast on weekends. Amenities include room service until midnight, concierge, 18 meeting rooms, secretarial services, A/V equipment, photocopiers, CNN, and express checkout. Valet parking. 151 W. 5th St. (phone: 579-1234; Fax: 513-579-0107). Expensive.

Omni Netherland Plaza – One of the city's finest, it's connected by the Skywalk to the *Convention Center,* with lots of meeting space of its own (18 meeting rooms; capacity for 1,200). In addition to its 621 rooms, suites are available (some are lovely duplexes). Dining can be either formal at *Orchids at the Palm Court* or a bit more casual at the *Café at the Palm Court.* Amenities include room service until midnight, concierge, A/V equipment, photocopiers, computers, CNN, and express checkout. 35 W. 5th St. (phone: 421-9100; Fax: 513-421-4291). Expensive.

Terrace Hilton – In addition to 350 rooms and suites, this attractive hotel has several restaurants: the *Gourmet* on the top floor, the *Terrace Garden* on the 8th floor, and the very popular *Joe's Bar,* an intimate, rustic place on ground level that serves delicious deli sandwiches. Amenities include room service until 10 PM, concierge, 7 meeting rooms, secretarial services, A/V equipment, photocopiers, CNN, and express checkout. 15 W. 6th St. (phone: 381-4000; Fax: 513-381-5158). Expensive.

Westin – Overlooking Fountain Square, this 17-story downtown property has 450 rooms and 18 suites. *Del's Steaks and Chops* restaurant is one of the city's best. The *Fifth Street Market* offers casual dining for breakfast and lunch. There's also a swimming pool, fitness center, whirlpool, and sauna. Additional amenities include 24-hour room service, concierge, 17 meeting rooms, secretarial services, A/V equipment, photocopiers, computers, CNN, and express checkout. Fountain Sq. (phone: 621-7700; Fax: 513-421-6869; Telex: 241496). Expensive.

Holiday Inn, Queensgate – It's not in the greatest neighborhood, but if you're looking for a 244-room, functional place to rest your head, this could be it. It has a swimming pool, dining room, bar, and nightclub. Amenities include room service until 10 PM, concierge, 4 meeting rooms, secretarial services, A/V equipment, photocopiers, CNN, and express checkout. 8th and Linn (phone: 241-8660; Fax: 513-651-2042; Telex: 6512042). Moderate.

Kings Island Inn – A favorite of golfers, since it's near the Jack Nicklaus course, this Alpine chalet–style hostelry offers good accommodations in an attractive setting. In addition to its 288 rooms with queen-size beds, it has indoor and outdoor pools, playground, tennis courts, gameroom, cocktail lounge with entertainment, dining room, and bus service to *Kings Island* theme park. There are also 2 new conference centers, as well as room service until 10 PM, concierge desk during the summer season, secretarial services, A/V equipment, photocopiers, CNN, and express checkout. 5691 Kings Island Dr., Mason (phone: 241-5800; Fax: 513-398-1095). Moderate.

Vernon Manor – A tasteful restoration of a once-faded beauty. Handsome Victorian decor in the bar, restaurant, and other public space; 166 elegant sleeping rooms; barbershop and flower shop; complimentary morning coffee and newspaper. Amenities include room service until 10:30 PM, concierge, 9 meeting rooms, secretarial services, A/V equipment, photocopiers, CNN, and express checkout. Two miles from downtown, at 400 Oak St. (phone: 281-3300; Fax: 513-281-8933). Moderate.

EATING OUT: Cincinnati's most notable gastronomic eccentricity is its chili, which usually is served over spaghetti, to which may be added cheese ("three-way"), cheese and raw onions ("four-way"), or cheese, raw onions, and beans ("five-way"). Many of the city's finest restaurants are found in its hotels. (See *Checking In*). At our expensive listings, expect to pay at least $50 to $75 for two; between $25 and $50 at those places designated moderate; under $25 at places listed as inexpensive. Prices do not include drinks, wine, or tips. All telephone numbers are in the 513 area code unless otherwise indicated.

Maisonette – It may be in an unlikely spot, but it's one of the best French restaurants in the country. Its food has consistently won major awards and the service is friendly and warm. Jacket and tie required. Lunch weekdays; dinner nightly except Sundays. Reservations required. Major credit cards accepted. 114 E. 6th St. (phone: 721-2260). Expensive.

Restaurant at the Phoenix – In what was once an exclusive turn-of-the-century men's club. Elegant dining in the *President's Dining Room* (the former library) or the spacious, less formal *Chef's Dining Room* (adjoining the glass-walled kitchen, through which diners can watch the food being prepared). An excellent contemporary American menu is offered. Lunch weekdays; dinner Tuesdays through Saturdays. Reservations recommended. Major credit cards accepted. 812 Race St. (phone: 721-2255). Expensive.

Stobart's – A premier dining facility (at Covington Landing), favorites are sautéed shrimp with macadamia-nut pesto and salmon sautéed in rice paper. Sinful *Stobart's* pie is matched only by the panoramic view. Open daily. Reservations advised. Major credit cards accepted. Covington Landing at RiverCenter (phone: 431-8526). Expensive.

Waterfront – Afloat directly across the Ohio River from downtown

Cincinnati, it offers a spectacular skyline view along with its culinary specialties — fresh grilled seafood, raw bar, and steaks. Open daily for dinner. Reservations necessary. Major credit cards accepted. 14 Pete Rose Pier, Covington, KY (phone: 606-581-1414). Expensive.

Crockett's American River Café – Enveloped in glass from floor to ceiling, this place (near *Riverfront Stadium*) has a spectacular view of downtown Cincinnati. The casual topside bar serves light fare, and has a raw bar. The river-level main dining room features fresh seafood, steaks, and their signature blackened scallops. Open daily. Reservations advised. Major credit cards accepted. Boat dock, 1 Riverboat Row, Newport, KY (phone: 606-581-2800). Moderate.

Forest View Gardens – Waiters and waitresses sing your favorite show tunes and serve tasty German food in a garden setting. Its *Dining Room/Showplace* is open for dinner only, Thursdays through Sundays; reservations necessary. Its *Edelweiss Room* is open for lunch on weekdays from 11 AM to 2 PM, and for dinner Tuesdays through Sundays from 5 to 7 PM; reservations unnecessary. Live entertainment on Fridays and Saturdays in summer; reservations advised. Major credit cards accepted. 4508 N. Bend Rd., a 20-minute drive from downtown (phone: 661-6434). Moderate.

Mike Fink – An authentic riverboat, moored on the Kentucky side of the Ohio River, it is famous for its raw bar, in addition to traditional tableside service. Open daily for lunch and dinner. Reservations advised. Major credit cards accepted. At the foot of Greenup St., Covington, KY (phone: 606-261-4212). Moderate.

Montgomery Inn at the Boathouse – The latest jewel in the Cincinnati restaurant king's, Ted Gregory, crown. The barbecue loin back ribs and chicken are laudable, and the wonderful view attracts celebrity crowds. Open daily. Reservations advised. Major credit cards accepted. 925 Eastern Ave., adjacent to Sawyer Point (phone: 721-7427). Moderate.

La Normandie Grill – Adjacent to the *Maisonette,* this steakhouse is renowned for its chops and fresh seafood. Casual conviviality is its hallmark. Closed Sundays. Reservations unnecessary. Major credit cards accepted. 118 E. 6th St. (phone: 721-2761). Moderate.

Precinct – A good choice for an evening of dining and chatting with friends over what some say are the best steaks in town. Other selections include veal, pasta, prime ribs, and fresh seafood. There's also a lively nightspot on the second floor. Open daily for dinner only. Reservations necessary. Major credit cards accepted. 311 Delta Ave. at Columbia Pkwy., 5 minutes from downtown (phone: 321-5454). Moderate.

Steamboat's Steakhouse – Aboard *The Spirit of America,* the mammoth sidewheeler moored at Covington Landing, there is a gallery of river history served along with great food, like thick, T-bone cut lamb chops with blackberry *demi-glacé.* Open daily. Reservations advised. Major credit cards accepted. Covington Landing at RiverCenter (phone: 431-8530). Moderate.

Barleycorn's – This riverfront dining spot across from the stadium has a wonderful view of the Cincinnati skyline. The fare is casual — the Buffalo chicken wings are favorites. Open daily. Reservations unnecessary. Major credit cards accepted. 201 Riverboat Row, Newport, KY (phone: 606-291-8504). Inexpensive.

Izzy's – A unique Cincinnati experience for 8 decades, serving world-famous corned beef, potato pancakes, homemade soups, kosher dill pickles, and sauerkraut. The original is at 819 Elm St. — serving lunch only (phone: 721-4241) — with another at 610 Main St. (phone: 241-6246), which is open until 9 PM; both are closed Sundays. Reservations unnecessary. No credit cards accepted. Inexpensive.

Rookwood Pottery – Atop Mt. Adams, in the original kilns of the historic Rookwood Pottery building, patrons devour gigantic burgers and overindulge at the do-it-yourself ice cream sundae bar. Open daily. Reservations unnecessary. No credit cards accepted. 1077 Celestial (phone: 721-5456). Inexpensive.

- **What's Hot:** Sensational, soul-satisfying chili, rich with meat, kidney beans, tomato sauce, and spices, has been a mainstay of the Cincinnati diet, dating back to when immigrant Greek restaurant owners cooked up a batch in case they ran out of other fare to serve customers. Now there are innumerable chains devoted exclusively to this hearty dish, including *Skyline Chili* (109 Illinois Ave.; phone: 761-4371) and *Goldstar Chili* (5204 Beachmont Ave.; phone: 231-4541). The secret behind the unique taste may never be revealed, for chili makers everywhere guard their recipes, but rumor has it that chocolate is the newest ingredient.

CLEVELAND

SEEING THE CITY: *Stouffer's Top of the Town* restaurant offers a panoramic view of Cleveland, the downtown, the nearby *Galleria,* and Lake Erie with its recreation and shipping activity (1301 E. 9 St.; phone: 771-1600). The Terminal Tower (Public Sq.; phone: 621-7981) observation deck is open weekends from 11 AM to 3:30 PM; call for holiday hours. Small admission charge. *Trolley Tours* (phone: 771-4484) conducts city tours daily, April to November; reservations necessary.

SPECIAL PLACES: Many of Cleveland's most interesting sights are concentrated in the few areas served by public transportation. You'll want to stroll around, particularly in the University Circle area, which is the cultural heart of Cleveland, and in the lovely suburbs of Shaker Heights and Chagrin Falls.

DOWNTOWN

Public Square – In the heart of the business area, the Public Square is a good place to get one's bearings in Cleveland past and present. Statues pay tribute to the city's founder Moses Cleaveland; to the populist reform mayor Tom Johnson; and to Cleveland's Civil War dead with the Soldiers and Sailors Monument. Dominating the square are the world headquarters of BP America and the 52-story Terminal Tower, built by the Van Sweringen brothers on the eve of the stock market crash that leveled their vast empire. Terminal Tower is the nucleus of the $400 million Tower City Center, and the *Ritz-Carlton* hotel. Bounded by Euclid Ave., Superior Ave., and Ontario St.

The *Goodtime II*–Boat Tour – The tour on the river is the best introduction to "the Flats" or industrial valley along the river basin where Rockefeller and shipping magnates Sam Mather and Mark Hanna made their fortunes. The 500-passenger boat goes down the Cuyahoga as far as the steel mills. Departures daily from May through October. Admission charge. E. 9th St. Pier (phone: 481-5001).

The Arcade – This 19th-century marketplace is a multitiered structure topped by a stunning block-long skylight of steel and glass. Bookstores, boutiques, eateries, and galleries line the arcade. At lunchtime, local musicians offer free classical, pop, and jazz concerts. 401 Euclid Ave. (phone: 621-8500).

The Mall – A spacious rectangular mall is the location of all the government and municipal buildings and a plaza with a fountain. Buildings include City Hall, the Court House, the Public Library (which has over 3 million volumes and many WPA murals), and Public Auditorium overlooking *Cleveland Stadium,* home of the *Indians* and *Browns.* Bounded by Lakeside Ave., St. Clair Ave., E. 6th and E. 4th Sts.

UNIVERSITY CIRCLE AREA

Cleveland Museum of Art – Among the best museums in the country, this Greek-style marble building contains extensive collections of many periods and cultures; it's particularly strong on the medieval period, Oriental art, and paintings of Masters including Rembrandt, Rubens, and Picasso. Overlooks the Fine Arts Gardens of Wade Park, with its seasonal flower displays. The auditorium features free films, lectures, and concerts. Closed Mondays. No admission charge. 11150 East Blvd. at University Circle (phone: 421-7340).

Western Reserve Historical Society – The largest collection of Shaker memorabilia in the world is here, including inventions such as the clothes pin, the ladderback chair, and various farming implements and furnishings. There's also an extensive genealogical collection and exhibitions on Indians and pioneers. Closed Mondays. Admission charge. 10825 East Blvd. (phone: 721-5722). At the same location and part of the Historical Society is the *Crawford Auto Aviation Museum,* with 200 antique autos and old airplanes. Displays trace the evolution of the automobile and describe Cleveland's prominence as an early car manufacturing center. Visitors can see how the old cars are given a new lease on life at the museum's restoration shop. Closed Mondays. Admission charge. 10825 East Blvd. at University Circle (phone: 721-5722).

Cleveland Museum of Natural History – Exhibitions of armored fish and sharks found preserved in Ohio shales, a 70-foot mounted dinosaur, skeletons of mastodon and mammoth, and Lucy, the most complete fossil evidence of early man. The museum also has a planetarium and observatory. Open daily. Admission charge. Wade Oval Dr. at University Circle (phone: 231-4600).

Cleveland Children's Museum – Features permanent and temporary exhibits that explore science and nature. Open daily. Admission charge. At 10730 Euclid Ave. (phone: 791-KIDS).

Rockefeller Park – This 296-acre park features the Shakespeare and Cultural Gardens, a series of gardens, landscape architecture, and sculptures representing the 20 nationalities that settled the city. Between East Blvd. and Martin Luther King Jr. Dr. The City Greenhouse displays include a Japanese Garden, tropical plants, and a Talking Garden (with audio descriptions of plants for blind visitors.) Open daily. No admission charge. 750 E. 88th St. (phone: 664-3103).

Little Italy – This ethnic neighborhood, just around the corner from University Circle, is knotted with artists' galleries and studios, especially along Murray Hill Road. Gallery walks are regularly held here. If the consumption of hot, fresh doughnuts is one of your early-morning imperatives, visit *Presti's,* at 1211 Mayfield Rd.

EAST SIDE

Cleveland Health Education Museum – A first of its kind, the museum has exhibitions on the workings of the human body and health maintenance. You can see everything here from the walk-through model of a human eye to Juno, the transparent woman, and the inspiring Wonder of New Life display. Open daily. Admission charge. 8911 Euclid Ave. (phone: 231-5010).

Lakeview Cemetery – The plantings here are beautiful, the view fine, and the company illustrious. Among the natives buried here are President Garfield (you can't miss the monument), Mark Hanna (the US senator), John Hay (secretary of state under McKinley), and John D. Rockefeller (father of the fortune). The Garfield Monument offers a great view of downtown. Open daily, April through November. No admission charge. 12316 Euclid Ave. (phone: 421-2665).

Coventry Road – Cleveland's answer to New York's Greenwich Village. Boutiques and shops offer unique fashions and arts. Sip unusual teas and coffees at *Arabica* (2785 Euclid Heights Blvd.), late at night, or try a sandwich and a milk shake at *Tommy's,* a local institution (1820 Coventry Rd.).

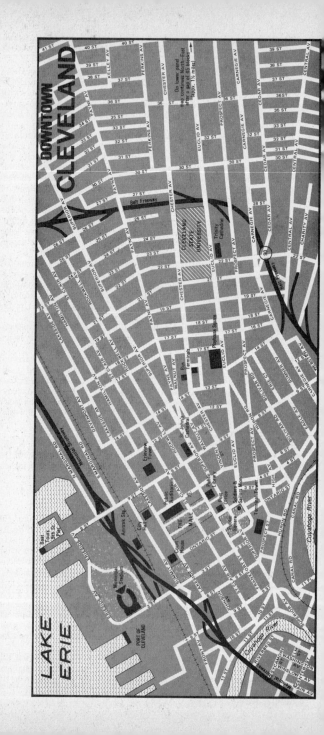

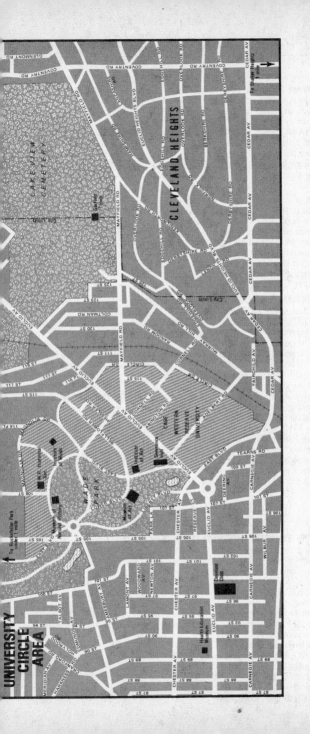

WEST SIDE

West Side Market – One of the largest Old World indoor markets in the country and a historic landmark. Fresh produce, meats, and baked goods are sold year-round on Mondays, Wednesdays, Fridays, and Saturdays. 1979 W. 25th St. at Lorain Ave. (phone: 664-3386).

NASA Lewis Research Center – The NASA complex and its visitors' center offer exhibitions, lectures, and films on aeronautics, energy, space travel, and communications. There also are tours of a propulsion systems laboratory and a supersonic wind tunnel. Open daily. No admission charge. 21000 Brookpark Rd. (phone: 267-1187).

SHAKER HEIGHTS

One of the most affluent suburbs in America, Shaker Heights was developed in the early 1900s by brothers O. P. and M. J. Van Sweringen and now houses Cleveland's elite in lovely old homes on wide, winding, tree-lined streets. The area was originally Shaker Lakes, the rural commune established by the 19th-century religious sect that left American industrial life for a religious regime featuring strict celibacy. Today, all that remains of the Shakers are the *Shaker Historical Museum,* with its collection of artifacts (16740 South Park; phone: 921-1201), and the Shaker Cemetery (Lee Rd. at Chagrin Blvd.).

■ **EXTRA SPECIAL:** *The Pro Football Hall of Fame,* in Canton, is 53 miles south of Cleveland on I-77 (2121 Harrison Ave.; phone: 456-8207). Inside there are all kinds of mementos of the game and its players — uniforms, helmets, team pictures, a recording of Jim Thorpe's voice, a film on football, and a research library. Open daily. Admission charge. On the way, stop at Hale Farm Village (2686 Oak Hill Rd., Bath; phone: 575-9137, Cleveland; 666-3711, Akron), where you'll find homesteads, crafts shops, and a working farm typical of those of the Western Reserve between 1825 and 1850. Closed Mondays. Admission charge. You also can stop in Akron, rubber manufacturing capital of the world, for a tour of the Stan Hywet Hall and Gardens (714 N. Portage Path, Akron; phone: 836-5533). Completed in 1915 by Frank A. Seiberling, founder of the Goodyear and Seiberling Rubber companies, the building is an excellent example of Tudor revival architecture, and the 65-room house contains original antique furnishings and artworks of the 14th through 18th centuries. The 70 acres of gardens are best in spring, when thousands of tulips bloom. Closed Mondays. Admission charge for house tour.

SOURCES AND RESOURCES

TOURIST INFORMATION: The Cleveland Convention and Visitors Bureau (3100 Tower City Center, Cleveland, OH 44113; phone: 621-7981; for events, 621-8860) is best for brochures, maps, and other information. For information on entertainment and dining, call 663-PAGE. Contact the Ohio state hotline (phone: 800-BUCKEYE) for maps, calendars of events, health updates, and travel advisories.

Local Coverage – *Cleveland Plain Dealer,* morning daily; *Northern Ohio LIVE,* monthly; *Cleveland* magazine, monthly. All are available at newsstands.

Television Stations – WKYC Channel 3–NBC; WEWS Channel 5–ABC; WJW Channel 8–CBS; WVIZ Channel 25–PBS.

Radio Stations – AM: WWWE 1100 (talk); WERE 1360 (talk). FM: WCLV 95.5 (classical); WMMS 100.7 (rock).

Food – Check the monthly restaurant listings in *Northern Ohio LIVE* and *Cleveland Magazine.*

TELEPHONE: The area code for Cleveland is 216.
Sales Tax – The city sales tax is 7%.

 CLIMATE: Cleveland has cold and snowy winters that are followed by brief springs that give brief respite from damp winters and humid summers. Fall is generally the most pleasant season, with mild, sunny weather that often extends through November.

 GETTING AROUND: Airport – Cleveland Hopkins International Airport is a 20- to 30-minute drive from downtown; taxi fare should run about $15. The *Regional Transit Authority's Airport Rapid Transit* train runs from the airport to downtown's Terminal Tower in the same amount of time but costs only $1.
Bus – *Regional Transit Authority (RTA)* serves both downtown and the outlying areas. Complete route and tourist information is available from the downtown office, 615 W. Superior Ave. (phone: 621-9500).
Car Rental – Cleveland is served by the major national firms.
Taxi – Cabs can be hailed in the street in the downtown area around Public Square or ordered on the phone. *Yellow-Zone Cab* (phone: 623-1500) and *AmeriCab* (phone: 881-1111) are the major operators.
Train – *Rapid Transit* trains serve the city's east and west sides.

 VITAL SERVICES: Audiovisual Equipment – *Presentation Techniques* (phone: 566-0053); *Hughie's Audio Visual Center* (phone: 241-7731).
Baby-sitting – *Ba-B-Sit Service Enterprises,* 592 Cahoon Rd. (phone: 871-9595).
Business Services – *Kelly Services,* 1111 Superior Ave. (phone: 771-2800).
Dry Cleaner/Tailor – *Avon Cleaners,* 1830 Superior Ave. (phone: 771-3636).
Limousine – *American Academy Limousine Service* (phone: 221-9330).
Mechanic – *Park Auto Repair Co.,* 2163 Hamilton Ave. (phone: 241-7390).
Medical Emergency – *St. Vincent Charity Hospital,* 2351 E. 22nd St. (phone: 363-2536).
Messenger Services – *Star Delivery Service* (phone: 241-2410); *Bonnie Speed Delivery* (phone: 696-6033).
National/International Courier – *Federal Express* (phone: 800-238-5355); *DHL Worldwide Courier Express* (phone: 800-225-5345).
Pharmacy – *Leader Drug* is open 24 hours, 1400 E. 9th St. (phone: 621-0132).
Photocopies – *Rapid Printing & Copy Center,* after hours by arrangement (426 Superior Ave.; phone: 621-9777); *Original Copy Centers* (3311 Perkins Ave.; phone: 881-3500).
Post Office – There is a central office (2400 Orange Ave.; phone: 443-4059); also a branch office (1200 Huron Rd.; phone: 443-4315).
Professional Photographer – *Shuba & Associates* (phone: 351-5080).
Secretary/Stenographer – *Secretariat Inc.,* word processing (phone: 234-4913).
Teleconference Facilities – *Marriott Inn, Sheraton Cleveland City Centre,* (see *Best in Town,* below).
Translator – *Berlitz* (phone: 861-0950); *Language Bank of Cleveland* (phone: 781-4560).
Typewriter Rental – *Cleveland Typewriter,* 2-week minimum (phone: 771-1155).
Western Union/Telex – Many offices located around the city (phone: 800-325-6000).

SPECIAL EVENTS: The *May Show Exhibit* at the *Museum of Art* kicks off spring and summer events, followed by the *All Nations Festival* in June, and the *Budweiser Grand Prix, Annual Rib Burn-Off,* and *Riverfest* on the river, in July. In August, the *Feast of the Assumption* is celebrated in Little Italy. Fall festivities include the *Cleveland Air Show* and *Oktoberfest.*

 MUSEUMS: The *Cleveland Children's Museum,* the *Cleveland Health Education Museum,* the *Cleveland Museum of Art,* the *Cleveland Museum of Natural History,* the *Shaker Historical Museum,* and the *Western Reserve Historical Society* are all described above in *Special Places.* At the new *Rock 'n' Roll Hall of Fame,* next to the Tower City development and designed by I. M. Pei, visitors can view memorabilia relating to the lives and careers of Elvis Presley, Chuck Berry, Buddy Holly, and other inductees. Between 2nd and 3rd Sts., downtown (phone: 781-7625).

 MAJOR COLLEGES AND UNIVERSITIES: Cleveland has close to 20 colleges and universities, including Case Western Reserve University (University Circle), a leading research institution (phone: 368-2000); Cleveland State University (downtown; phone: 687-2000); Baldwin-Wallace College (Berea; phone: 826-2900); and John Carroll University (University Heights; phone: 397-1886).

 SPORTS AND FITNESS: Baseball – The American League's *Indians* play at *Cleveland Municipal Stadium* from April to September. W. 3rd St. and Erieside Ave. (phone: 861-1200).

Basketball – The *Cavaliers* play at the *Coliseum* from mid-October to early April. I-271 and Rte. 303, Richfield (phone: 659-9100).

Bicycling – You can rent bikes from *U-Rent-Um of America* (15400 Brookpark Rd; phone: 676-6776) or *Easy Rider Bicycle Shop* (3974 E. 131st St.; phone: 752-1555). The Cuyahoga Falls Reservation nearby has good biking trails.

Fitness Centers – The *13th Street Racquetball Club* has exercise equipment and a track (1901 E. 13th St.; phone: 696-1365). *One Fitness Center* has a track, a swimming pool, and exercise equipment (1375 E. 9th St.; phone: 781-5510).

Football – The *Browns* play pro ball at the *Municipal Stadium* (phone: 696-3800).

Golf – Punderson State Park has the best public 18-hole golf course, at Rtes. 44 and 87 (phone: 564-5465).

Jogging – Run along Euclid Avenue to Public Square and on to the Flats; stop in at *Koening Sporting Goods* at the *Galleria* (phone: 575-9900). Run at Cleveland State University at Euclid and Prospect.

Tennis – The best public courts are at Cain Park in Cleveland Heights, Superior Rd. at Lee Rd. (phone: 371-3000).

 THEATER: For current offerings and performance times, check the publications listed above. Cleveland has a variety of theatrical offerings, some locally produced, others traveling shows, even some pre-Broadway tryouts. Best bets for shows: *Cleveland Play House* (8500 Euclid Ave; phone: 795-7000); *Karamu House* (2355 E. 89th St.; phone: 795-7070); *Great Lakes Theater Festival, Ohio Theatre* (1501 Euclid Ave.; phone: 241-5490); *Eldred Theatre* (2070 Adelbert Rd.; phone: 368-6262.) For the avant-garde, *Cleveland Public Theater* (6415 Detroit Ave.; phone: 631-2727) offers eclectic performances. For big-name entertainment, try the *Front Row Theatre* (6199 Wilson Mills Rd. in Highland Heights; phone: 449-5000) or the *Playhouse Square Center* (1511 Euclid Ave.; phone: 241-6000). Also, the *Cleveland Ballet* (1 Playhouse Sq.; phone: 621-2260) is a must for dance lovers.

MUSIC: The *Cleveland Orchestra* performs with noted soloists and guest conductors from October to mid-May in *Severance Hall* (11001 Euclid Ave. at East Blvd.; phone: 231-1111). From

June to September, it plays at *Blossom Music Center* (1145 W. Steels Corner Rd., Cuyahoga Falls; phone: 566-9330), as do pop and rock bands.

NIGHTCLUBS AND NIGHTLIFE: Favorites are *Peabody's,* for folk or blues (2140 S. Taylor Rd.; phone: 321-4072); *Club Isabella,* for jazz (2025 Abington Rd.; phone: 229-1177); and *Aquilon,* a European-style disco (1575 Merwin; phone: 781-1575). The *Hilarities Comedy Club* (1230 W. 6th St.; 781-7733), which offers local and national talent, is open Tuesdays through Saturdays.

BEST IN TOWN

CHECKING IN: Cleveland has many accommodations that are attractive, comfortable, and reasonably priced. In addition to the usual chains, there is an assortment of modern, locally owned hotels. Our selections range in price from $100 or more for a double room in the expensive category, $60 to $90 in the moderate range, and under $50, inexpensive. A company called *Private Lodgings* (PO Box 18590, Cleveland, OH 44118; phone: 321-3213) finds private residences in a variety of price ranges for those who'd rather not stay at a hotel. All telephone numbers are in the 216 area code unless otherwise indicated.

Marriott Inn – Near the airport, Cleveland's best motor inn (400 rooms). Its many recreational features include an indoor pool, therapy pool, sauna, miniature golf, putting green, volleyball, badminton. There is a free airport bus, lounge with entertainment, a coffee shop, 2 dining rooms, a concierge desk, 7 meeting rooms, A/V equipment, photocopiers, CNN, and express checkout. 4277 W. 150th St. (phone: 252-5333 or 800-228-9290; Fax: 216-251-1508). Expensive.

Ritz-Carlton – Opened in 1990, it has 208 rooms and 19 suites with panoramic views of the city. There are banquet facilities, a ballroom, 2 restaurants, and an extensive fitness center with indoor pool, sauna, steam room, and a spa. Special amenities include twice-daily maid service, turndown service, and terry cloth robes in all the rooms. Other pluses are 24-hour room service, concierge, 6 meeting rooms, secretarial services, A/V equipment, photocopiers, CNN, and express checkout. 1515 W. 3rd St. (for more information, call 623-1230; Fax: 216-623-1492). Expensive.

Sheraton Cleveland City Centre – With a 22-story tower commanding a good view of Lake Erie, this luxury hotel is near the *Convention Center.* The facilities include indoor parking, a coffee shop, a lounge with entertainment, and a pleasant dining room, plus attentive service. 475 rooms. Amenities include room service until 1 AM, concierge, 6 meeting rooms, secretarial services, A/V equipment, photocopiers, computers, CNN, and express checkout. 777 St. Clair Ave. (phone: 771-7600; Fax: 216-771-5219). Expensive.

Stouffer Tower City Plaza – Always a surprise to guests, since its look and feel are so unlike most other members of this chain. Special feature: a 10-story atrium complete with waterfall and swimming pool. There are 493 rooms and luxury suites, and 3 eating facilities; very good Sunday brunch. Other amenities include 24-hour room service, concierge, 4 meeting rooms, A/V equipment, photocopiers, computers, CNN, and express checkout. 24 Public Square (phone: 696-5600, 800-325-5000, or 800-HOTELS-1; Fax: 216-696-3102; Telex: 752889). Expensive.

Clinic Center – This modern 358-room high-rise is near the famous Cleveland Clinic. Features include foreign-language interpreters, color TV sets, a coffee shop, bistro, and an exquisite dining room. Other amenities include 3 meeting rooms, secretarial services, A/V equipment, photocopiers, CNN, and express checkout. E. 96th St. and Carnegie Ave. (phone: 791-1900; Fax: 216-791-7065). Expensive to moderate.

Glidden House – This stately mansion on University Circle has been transformed into an elegant bed and breakfast inn. There are 52 rooms and 8 suites. Within walking distance of the city's finest cultural institutions. Amenities include 2 meeting rooms, secretarial services, photocopiers, and CNN. 1901 Ford Drive (phone: 231-8900; Fax: 216-231-2130). Moderate.

Harley West – Close to the airport, this 235-room hostelry also has in- and outdoor swimming pools, sauna, basketball, and free airport limousine service. Amenities include 12 meeting rooms, secretarial services, A/V equipment, photocopiers, and CNN. 17000 Bagley Rd., near I-71 (phone: 243-5200 or 800-321-2323; Fax: 216-243-5200, ext. 740). Moderate.

Holiday Inn, Lakeside City Center – A downtown high-rise overlooking Lake Erie and close to the stadium and *Galleria*. It has 400 rooms and features a pool, sauna, exercise room, 2 restaurants, a café and cocktail lounge, free parking, and airport shuttle. Special services are provided for Executive Floor guests. Other amenities include room service until midnight, 7 meeting rooms, A/V equipment, photocopiers, CNN, and express checkout. 1111 Lakeside Ave. (phone: 241-5100 or 800-HOLIDAY; Fax: 216-241-7437). Moderate.

Alcazar – European-style residential property nestled in the trendy Cedar Hill area, 4 miles east of downtown. There are 110 rooms and 180 suites. Features include a full-service restaurant, heated garage, beauty salon, and laundromat. Surrey and Derbyshire Rds., Cleveland Heights (phone: 321-5400). Inexpensive.

EATING OUT: Cleveland caters to the taste of more than 100 different nationalities that have distinctive old country recipes and appetites. Restaurants reflect this background with fine ethnic foods and a wide range of styles: haute cuisine in shimmering elegance to solid hamburgers in a casual atmosphere. Our selections range in price from $60 or more for a dinner for two in the expensive range, $30 to $60 in the moderate, and $30 or less in the inexpensive range. Prices do not include drinks, wine, or tips. All telephone numbers are in the 216 area code unless otherwise indicated.

Baricelli Inn – Cheers for the imaginative Midwestern fare served here. Owned by the Minnillo family, chef and son Paul delivers dishes such as corn chowder with Cape Cod oysters and sautéed red snapper in black currant butter. Closed Sundays. Reservations necessary. Major credit cards accepted. 2203 Cornell Blvd. (phone: 791-6500). Expensive.

Giovanni's – Pasta is prepared in delectable ways; the veal and sweetbreads are equally satisfying. Decor is elegant, so dress accordingly. Closed Sundays. Reservations necessary. Major credit cards accepted. 2550 Chagrin Blvd., Beachwood (phone: 831-8625). Expensive.

Z Contemporary Cuisine – Delectable West Coast–inspired fare, emphasizing grilled meats and fish. A house specialty is grilled chicken breast and skinny fried potatoes. Salads, pasta, and rich desserts are also worthwhile. Closed Sundays. Reservations necessary. Major credit cards accepted. 20600 Chagrin Blvd., Shaker Heights (phone: 991-1580). Expensive.

Hyde Park Grille – The place for hearty meat eaters. Choose from tender steaks, filet mignon with king crab and béarnaise sauce, or an elegantly presented chateaubriand for two. All steaks are served with delicately deep-fried onion crisps. Dark green upholstery and dark paneling complete the clubhouse atmosphere. Open daily. Reservations advised. Major credit cards accepted. 1825 Coventry Rd., Cleveland Heights (phone: 321-6444). Expensive to moderate.

Café Brio – Fresh California-style fare blends perfectly with an open, airy decor. Make a meal of the raw bar and appetizers or enjoy an excellent Caesar salad, southwestern pizza, grilled chicken breast, or linguine with pesto and pine nuts. Nice selection of international wines. Open daily. Reservations advised. Major credit cards accepted. 5433 Mayfield Rd., Lyndhurst (phone: 473-1670). Moderate.

Lopez y Gonzalez – Hearty portions of all-time Mexican favorites — *tacos al carbón,* for example — are washed down with a glass of Mexican beer or, better still, an oversize margarita. Mesquite-smoked game hen and duck and fresh fish dishes round out the menu. Closed Sundays. Reservations advised. Major credit cards accepted. 2066 Lee Rd., Cleveland Heights (phone: 371-7611). Moderate.

Pearl of the Orient – Chinese food carefully presented, particularly the Peking duck; also worth noting is the hot and sour soup. Open daily. Reservations necessary. Major credit cards accepted. 20121 Van Aken Blvd., Shaker Heights (phone: 751-8181). Moderate.

Sammy's – Wooden beams and brick walls make this converted warehouse a gem. The menu has such offerings as chicken in phyllo with vegetables, and medallions of veal in port wine. Desserts include *boule de neige,* a concoction of rum and chocolate espresso cake with whipped cream. Great raw seafood bars and live jazz nightly, too. Closed Sundays. Reservations advised. Major credit cards accepted. 1400 W. 10th St. (phone: 523-5560). Moderate.

Shujiro – Japanese simplicity is the keynote here, as demonstrated by such dishes as a delicate shrimp tempura and the house specialty, scampi. Sushi is also popular. Open daily. Reservations advised. Major credit cards accepted. 2206 Lee Rd., Cleveland Heights (phone: 321-0210). Moderate.

That Place on Bellflower – In a charming century-old carriage house, this is the *fleur-de-lis* of Cleveland's French restaurants. Specialties are veal Oscar and fresh salmon renaissance. In the summer, dining is alfresco. Reservations advised. Major credit cards accepted. 11401 Bellflower Rd., at University Circle (phone: 231-4469). Moderate.

Mad Greek – Moussaka, *pastitsio* (Greco specialties), shish kabob, and Greek wine and liqueurs. Rustic inn atmosphere, with dining in the courtyard, weather permitting. Open daily. No reservations. Major credit cards accepted. Cedar Rd. at Fairmont Blvd. (phone: 421-3333). Moderate to inexpensive.

Noggins – The eclectic menu includes homemade pasta and fresh seafood; good wines. Open daily. Reservations advised for six or more. Major credit cards accepted. 20110 Van Aken Blvd., Shaker Heights (phone: 752-9280). Moderate to inexpensive.

Balaton – The atmosphere isn't much — bright lights and paper placemats — but the Hungarian food is the real thing. Specialties include homemade soups and strudel, dumplings, and Wiener schnitzel. No alcoholic beverages. Closed Sundays and Mondays. No reservations or credit cards. 12523 Buckeye Rd. (phone: 921-9691). Inexpensive.

Corky & Lenny's – With a name like this, it could only be a deli, and it is. Cleveland residents claim that it's the best kosher-style deli outside New York City. Has the standard deli fare and plenty of the hustle-bustle as well. No reservations or credit cards accepted. 13937 Cedar Rd., University Heights (phone: 321-3310). Inexpensive.

Miracles – A friendly, neighborhood eatery, with fast service and good food. The menu ranges from Central European *kielbasa* and potato pancakes to Middle Eastern fare and hearty soups. The frozen vanilla custard is a must. Closed Mondays. Reservations advised. Major credit cards accepted. 2391 W. 11th St. (phone: 621-6419). Inexpensive.

DALLAS

AT-A-GLANCE

SEEING THE CITY: For the best view of Dallas, go to the top of Reunion Tower on Reunion Boulevard (400 S. Houston St.; phone: 651-1234), alongside the huge mirror-faced *Hyatt Regency* hotel, also a Dallas landmark. The tower has a revolving cocktail lounge, restaurant, and observation deck. Admission charge. Another option is to take *Gray Line*'s downtown All About Dallas or Southfork Ranch tours, or a combination package that visits both places. Motorcoach pickups at major downtown hotels (phone: 398-1234).

SPECIAL PLACES: Although attractions in Dallas are spread out, the museums are clustered together at Fair Park (located at 1300 Robert B. Cullum Blvd., 2 blocks south of Interstate 30 and 3 miles east of downtown Dallas). Several amusement park complexes are in Arlington, 15 miles west of Dallas.

Fair Park – For two incredibly jammed weeks in October, Fair Park is the scene of the *Texas State Fair,* held from late September through late October, with all the superlatives you would associate with such an event: biggest, best, highest, widest, etc. Fair Park hosts 24 attractions; included among them are seven museums of science, history, and technology (phone: 670-8400). For the rest of the year, Fair Park is the home of the *Cotton Bowl,* the site of the *New Year's Day* college football game, and *Fair Park Coliseum.* Grand Ave. For information on *State Fair* activities, call 670-8400.

Museum of Natural History – In order to attract the *Texas Centennial Exposition* to Dallas in 1936, the city fathers built a group of museums at Fair Park. The *Museum of Natural History,* a neo-classical, cream limestone building, contains a variety of fauna and flora from the Southwest. There are some interesting zoology and botany exhibitions, too. Open daily. No admission charge. Ranger Circle, Fair Park (phone: 670-8457).

Aquarium – This one isn't the biggest or the best in the country, but it's the only one in Dallas. There are more than 300 species of native freshwater fish, cold- and tropical-water creatures — finned, scaled, and amphibious. If you like watching the fish and sea animals being fed, be sure to get here early — around 9 AM. Open daily. No admission charge. 1st St. and Martin Luther King Ave. (phone: 670-8441).

Garden Center and Science Place I and II – Next to the aquarium, the Garden Center has delightful tropical flowers and plants with braille markers. Open daily. No admission charge (phone: 428-7476). Just down the street, *Science Place* features exhibitions on technology, energy, ecology, and health. A planetarium show enraptures planet watchers and stargazers. Closed Mondays. Admission charge. Fair Park (phone: 428-7200).

Midway and the Hall of State – As you walk along the Midway during the week, you will find it hard to imagine the frenetic carnival activity for which it is known. If you're here during the *State Fair* or on weekends May through September, you'll probably be swept into the frenzy, stopping only long enough to try winning a stuffed animal or doll at a shooting gallery or pitch 'n' toss. There is an assortment of spine-chilling, scream-inducing, turn-you-upside-down-and-inside-out rides for those who like thrills. There are also great food stands here — Greek, barbecue, and Mexican. At one end of the Midway, the *Hall of State* has paintings devoted to the heroes of Texas. It was built in 1936, for the *Texas Centennial.* Open daily. No admission charge. The Midway (phone: 670-8400).

Age of Steam Museum – Will bring a lump to the throat of anyone who ever loved an old train, with steam engines and other railroad nostalgia. Open Thursdays and Fridays 9 AM to 1 PM, Saturdays and Sundays 11 AM to 5 PM. Admission charge. The Midway (phone: 421-8754).

DOWNTOWN DALLAS

Here among the tall skyscrapers of the central business district are the Kennedy Memorial, the Arts District, Thanksgiving Square Park (Pacific, Bryan, and Ervan Sts.), and an intriguing 2-mile network of underground walkways lined with shops and restaurants.

Texas School Book Depository and Sixth Floor Museum – Known to millions of people around the world as the place where Lee Harvey Oswald hid, the Texas School Book Depository is the most-photographed site in Texas. Open daily except major holidays. Admission charge; there is an additional charge for a 35-minute audio tour. 506 Elm, at Houston (phone: 633-6659; 653-6657 for groups). The new *Sixth Floor Museum* (located on the sixth floor of the Depository; hence, the name), a project of the Dallas County Historical Foundation, is a permanent exhibition which examines the life, death, and legacy of John F. Kennedy. Historic photographs, artifacts, interpretive displays, videos, and award-winning films evoke powerful feelings of an unforgettable chapter in American history. Open Sunday through Friday, 10 AM to 6 PM; Saturday from 10 AM to 7 PM. Admission charge. 506 Elm Street, with an entrance on Houston Street between Elm and Pacific (phone: 653-6666).

John F. Kennedy Memorial – A monument near where Kennedy was assassinated. Four unconnected, 30-foot high walls surround an area for meditation which is open to the sky and marked only by a center stone slab. Main and Market Sts. (phone: 653-6659).

Union Station – This renovated 1916 rail station, which currently houses a snack bar and a visitors' center, is such a treat that travelers on *Amtrak* trains disembark just to view it (phone: 746-6600).

Morton H. Meyerson Symphony Center – Completed in 1989 and designed by I. M. Pei, who was also the architect for Dallas' cantilevered City Hall, the center is a major facility for music and the performing arts. A computer was used to determine the unusual structural shapes and supports, which were constructed to "uplift" audiences. Flora and Pearl Sts. (phone: 692-0203).

Dallas Museum of Art – The keystone of Dallas's downtown Arts District houses the permanent collection of pre-Columbian art, African sculpture, and 19th-century modern and contemporary works that have been moved from the old museum at Fair Park. The Sculpture Garden, featuring works by Henry Moore and Ellsworth Kelly, is an urban oasis, replete with cascades and shade trees. The Reves Collection, hung in a reconstructed Italian villa within the museum, and the Bybee Collection (furniture) are worth investigating. The Dallas skyline is an impressive backdrop to the building designed by Edward Larrabee Barnes. Closed Mondays. No admission charge, although a fee is charged for the Reves Collection and special exhibits. 1717 N. Harwood (phone: 922-1220).

West End MarketPlace – In the West End historic district, this one-time warehouse boasts more than 125 shops, pushcart vendors, and

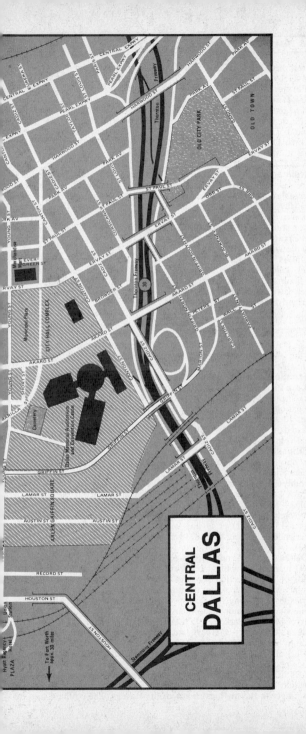

CENTRAL
DALLAS

refreshment stands. Open daily. Market St. at Munger Ave. (phone: 954-4350).

Farmers' Market – This is raunchy, down-home, earthy Texas. From 6 AM, farmers drive into town in their trusty ole pickups to sell the fruit and vegetables of their labor. The market consists of a tin-roof shelter and dozens of stalls, with any number of colorful characters standing around. The vegetables are fresher and a bit cheaper than anywhere else in town. Open daily. In May, there's a flower festival, in September a fall harvest, and in November an arts and crafts fair. 1010 S. Pearl (phone: 748-2082).

Neiman Marcus – The shrine of commercial elegance, this specialty store has been known to induce orgies of spending. If you have an insatiable craving for wave-making machines, a computer chess game, or a biorhythm calculator, this is the place to satisfy it. These games, however, are among the more conservative items in stock. The really exotic stuff is offered in the *Christmas* catalogue. Three locations: Main and Ervay (downtown), NorthPark, and the *Prestonwood Mall* (phone: downtown, 741-6911).

Dallas Arboretum – Sixty-six acres on the eastern shore of White Rock Lake are dedicated to the display, education, and research of horticulture. Just minutes from downtown are fragrant gardens, rolling green lawns, and tall shade trees. Open daily. Admission charge. 8525 Garland Rd. (phone: 327-8263).

ELSEWHERE

Outside the central business district lie the many other attractions that make Dallas a never-ending place of excitement, from a ranch located on the outskirts of town to the recreated natural environment of the Dallas Zoo.

Frontiers of Flight Museum – This newly opened aviation museum at Love Field Airport highlights the history of flight in Dallas from Fair Park's turn-of-the-century barnstormers to D/FW's current prowess as the nation's leading "port of the air." Open Tuesday through Saturday from 10 AM to 5 PM, Sunday from 1 to 5 PM. No admission charge. Located just above the main terminal lobby. Mockingbird La., Love Field (phone: 350-3600).

Biblical Arts Center – Artworks from the Old Masters to contemporary spiritual art and archaeological artifacts are used to help people understand the places, people, and events portrayed in the Bible. Closed Mondays. No admission charge. 7500 Park Lane (phone: 691-4661).

Park Lane Equestrian – Imagine a ranch within the city limits of Dallas — 300 acres under the shadow of downtown skyscrapers and completely surrounded by an urban scene. Visitors can set out on horseback ($15 an hour) or in hay wagons ($150 an hour) for a country experience in the big city. 8713 Park Lane (phone: 349-2002 or 340-9593).

Dallas Zoo – A refurbished and comfortable environment for the 1,600 mammals, reptiles, and birds that live within its 70 acres. The Wilds of Africa section provides the zoo's several species of African animals with 25 acres that simulate their natural habitat. A monorail carries visitors along the treetops high over the Wilds of Africa for a prime view of the animals in their environment. Open daily. Admission charge. Marsalis Park, 621 E. Clarendon Dr. (phone: 946-5154).

Texas Stadium – *Cowboys* fans go crazy here. This open 65,100-seat stadium packs 'em in during home games. It's constructed to give you the feel of being in a theater or auditorium rather than a stadium, but critics point out that with the dome partially open, part of the field is always in shadow. Hwy. 183 at Loop 12 in Irving (phone: 438-7676).

Which Way to Southfork? – The question most asked by visitors is how to get to the mythical home of the Ewings. The building seen on

TV's "Dallas" actually does exist. Formerly a private home, it was purchased by a real estate investor to be transformed into a hotel of sorts — you can't rent a room, but you can rent the entire house for $2,500 a night! The ranch itself is now a tourist attraction, replete with party barns and other amusements. There's trouble in paradise, however, as Southfork's proprietor declared bankruptcy last year, and it was recently sold. And though the television series has ended, plans to continue tours of the ranch seem likely. Open daily. Admission charge. Take Hwy. 75 north to Parker Rd. in Plano, then drive 5½ miles east to FM 2551. (phone: 442-6536).

ARLINGTON

Six Flags Over Texas – A theme amusement park, *Six Flags Over Texas* motifs are based on different periods in Texas history: Spanish, Mexican, French, Republic of Texas, Confederacy, and the period since the Civil War. You can get a panoramic view of the Dallas and Ft. Worth skylines from a 300-foot-high observation deck on top of an oil derrick. A narrow-gauge railway runs around the 145-acre grounds. Open weekends spring and fall, daily June through August. Admission charge. I-30 at Hwy. 360 (phone: 817-640-8900).

Wet 'n Wild – This Texas-size family recreation park attracts huge crowds on blistering summer weekends (weekdays are a bit less jammed). Waterslides, inner-tube chutes, surfing pools, and children's play areas provide heat relief for all ages. Open daily, June through August; weekends only, May and September. Admission charge. Two locations: across I-30 from *Texas Stadium* at 1800 E. Lamar Blvd. (phone: 265-3356) and 12715 LBJ Expy., near the intersection of I-635 and Northwest Hwy. (phone: 271-5637).

GRAND PRAIRIE

International Wildlife Park – A drive-through wildlife preserve, the only one of its kind in the Southwest. Thousands of animals roam freely around the 350-acre tract, and visitors can stop at many points along the 6 miles of safari trails. Open daily. Admission charge. I-30 and Belt Line (phone: 263-2203 or 263-2201).

■ **EXTRA SPECIAL:** Dallas before its skyscrapers and highways was a simpler place whose lifestyle was reflected in unique architectural styles that combined Victorian grace with the less refined influence of the prairie. One of the few places still able to convey a sense of those earlier, unhurried days is Old City Park, an oasis of greenery and history close to downtown. Restored Victorian houses, a railroad depot, pioneer log cabins, and other historically significant structures have been moved in from various locales in North Texas and are open for exploration. Luncheon at *Brent Place,* located on the property, is a treat. Closed Mondays. Admission charge. Gano and St. Paul (phone: 421-5141).

SOURCES AND RESOURCES

 TOURIST INFORMATION: For brochures, maps, and general information, contact the Dallas Convention and Visitors Bureau, open 8:30 AM to 5 PM (1201 Elm St., Suite 2000, Dallas, TX 75270; phone: 746-6677); the Dallas Visitor Information Center in Union Station, open 9 AM to 5 PM (400 S. Houston; phone: 746-6603), a restored 1924 railroad terminal that also houses restaurants and *Amtrak* headquarters; or West End MarketPlace, open Monday through Saturday from 11 AM to 8 PM; Sundays noon to 8 PM (603 Munger). Call the Special Events Info-Line for daily information on Dallas events (phone: 214-746-6679). Contact the Texas state hotline (phone: 800-8888-TEX) for maps, calendars of events, health updates, and travel advisories.

The best guides are Guide, a section in Friday's *Dallas Morning News,* and Datebook, in the *Dallas Times Herald* every Friday. Another good source of information is the *Dallas Observer* weekly tabloid.

Local Coverage – *Dallas Times Herald,* morning and evening daily; *Dallas Morning News,* morning daily; and *D* magazine, monthly.

Television Stations – KDFW Channel 4–CBS; KXAS Channel 5–NBC; WFAA Channel 8–ABC; KERA Channel 13–PBS.

Radio Stations – AM: WBAP 820 (country music); KRLD 1080 (news); KVIL 1150 (contemporary); KLIF 1190 (talk). FM: KERA 90.1 (eclectic); KSCS 96.3 (country); WRR 101.1 (classical); KMGC 102.9 (light rock); KVIL 103.7 (soft pop).

Food – *D* magazine's restaurant section (monthly); the Dallas restaurant guide in *Texas Monthly* magazine; and listings in Friday's newspapers.

 TELEPHONE: The area code for Dallas is 214.

Sales Tax – There is an 8% sales tax on most goods and services, including dining. Hotel room tax is 13%.

 CLIMATE: Summers are blisteringly hot and humid, with temperatures over 100F. Sudden thunderstorms punctuate the dry, blazing heat. From October to January, the weather is mild, although it can be in the 70s one day and in the 30s the next. From January to March, there are occasional sharp cold snaps and high winds (and once in a great while, some ice and snow), and between March and June you can expect rain and dust storms. (For local weather, call 787-1700. For temperature — and time — call 844-4444.)

GETTING AROUND: Airport – Dallas/Ft. Worth Airport (or D/FW), the country's largest, is approximately 20 miles from downtown Dallas. In light traffic, the drive into the city takes about a half hour; cab fare will run about $25. The inner-city Love Field Airport serves Texas and surrounding states. Cab fare between Love Field and downtown is about $10. Most major hotels offer free shuttle service. Companies providing transportation to area hotels include *SuperShuttle* (phone: 817-329-2000) and *Limaxi* (phone: 748-6294).

Bus – *Dallas Area Rapid Transit* (*DART*) operates the bus service. For information, call 979-1111.

Car Rental – All major national firms are represented. A car is necessary in Dallas.

McKinney Avenue Trolley – Recently installed, the trolley serves downtown, the Arts District (including the *Dallas Museum of Art* and the *Morton Meyerson Symphony Center*), and the McKinney Strip. Stops are made along the 2.8 route on McKinney Avenue and St. Paul Street (phone: 220-0610). The fare is 50¢; a 1-day pass costs $2; a 3-day pass costs $5. The trolley runs Sundays through Thursdays from 10 AM to 10 PM; and Fridays and Saturdays until midnight.

Taxi – There are taxi stands at most major hotels, but the best way to get one is to call *Yellow Cab* (phone: 426-6262).

 VITAL SERVICES: Audiovisual Equipment – *Bauer/Southam Audio Video* (phone: 630-6700).

Baby-sitting – *Babysitters of Dallas,* 2703 Fondren (phone: 692-1354).

Business Services – *Kelly Services,* 500 N. Akard, and several other locations (phone: 740-3666).

Limousine – *Dallas Limousine Service* (phone: 484-5770).

Mechanics – For American cars, *Exxon Car Care* (Hillcrest and

Arapaho; phone: 233-7034); for foreign cars, *Fischer's Foreign Car Service* (4770 Memphis; phone: 630-2807). In emergencies, *AAA Emergency Road Service* (phone: 526-7911).

Medical Emergency – *Baylor University Medical Center,* 3500 Gaston Ave. (phone: 820-0111).

Messenger Services – *Big D Messenger Service* (phone: 744-4726); *On Time Delivery Service* (phone: 869-0500).

National/International Courier – *DHL Worldwide Express* (phone: 471-1999); *Federal Express,* several locations (phone: 358-5271).

Pharmacy – *Eckerd Drugs,* at five locations, open 24 hours daily (phone: 272-0411).

Photocopies/Fax – *Quick Print,* 14 locations with pickup and delivery (phone: 741-1425).

Post Office – Downtown, 400 N. Erway St. (phone: 953-3045).

Professional Photographer – *Dallas Photo Referral,* matches projects with photographers (phone: 699-1850).

Secretary/Stenographer – *A-AAA Answering Secretary* (phone: 363-6400).

Teleconference Facilities – *Adolphus, Hyatt Regency, Plaza of the Americas* (see *Best in Town,* below), and the *Summit* (phone: 243-3363).

Translator – *Berlitz* (phone: 380-1693).

Typewriter Rental – *Office Stores, Inc.,* leases and delivers IBM machines (phone: 458-1286).

Western Union/Telex – Many offices located around the city (phone: 991-5440).

Other – *Meeting Management Associates* (phone: 386-9403).

SPECIAL EVENTS: The *Texas State Fair* runs from late September through late October in Fair Park (phone: 565-9931). Other special events this year: the *Byron Nelson Golf Classic* in mid-May (phone: 742-3896); and *Artfest* at Fair Park, during the *Memorial Day* weekend (phone: 361-2011). The *Shakespeare Festival of Dallas* takes place during the last week in June through July (phone: 559-2778). *Dallas Summer Musicals* are held from June through August (phone: 691-7200). College football teams face off annually at the *Cotton Bowl* on *New Year's Day.* For information about events, call 746-6679.

MUSEUMS: The *Age of Steam Museum,* the *Dallas Museum of Art,* the *Sixth Floor Museum, Frontiers of Flight Museum,* the *Museum of Natural History,* and the *Science Place* are all discussed in detail in *Special Places.*

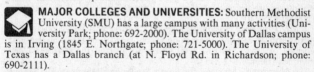

MAJOR COLLEGES AND UNIVERSITIES: Southern Methodist University (SMU) has a large campus with many activities (University Park; phone: 692-2000). The University of Dallas campus is in Irving (1845 E. Northgate; phone: 721-5000). The University of Texas has a Dallas branch (at N. Floyd Rd. in Richardson; phone: 690-2111).

SHOPPING: Despite our well-masticated stereotypes of Texan attire, from the ten-gallon hat on downward, cosmopolitan chic decidedly has replaced cowboy dandy. Shopping in Dallas has emerged as a pastime pursued in the toniest of shops.

While local bus routes stop at major shopping areas, it's easier to drive around Dallas. The city can be split into five main shopping districts — downtown, uptown, Park Cities, Northpark, and North Dallas, home to the *Galleria.*

DOWNTOWN

Cajun Connection – Dedicated cooks intrigued by Cajun cooking can browse through a wide selection of cookbooks, housewares, and creole spices. In the *West End MarketPlace,* Market at Munger (phone: 954-1772).

Dallas Maverick's Locker Room – Just the place to find a present for an avid sports fan, and upon occasion, hometown players stop in to sign a few autographs. In the *West End MarketPlace* (phone: 871-9088).

Dallas Museum of Art – Costume jewelry, gold earrings encrusted with semi-precious stones, and clay ornaments are enticing, as is the vast collection of art books, posters, and children's books. 1717 N. Harwood (phone: 922-1271).

Neiman Marcus – Top-drawer goods have long been de rigueur at this venerable, elegant store (see *Special Places*). Designer clothing, the finest china, crystal, and home furnishings make it a standout. 1618 Main St. (phone: 741-6911).

Wild Bill's Official Western Wear – For those who crave to be outfitted to the teeth in impeccably western gear can try on a pair of leather Roy Rogers gloves with a long, leather fringe or a Texas belt buckle. Less orthodox, but guaranteed to garner notice, are the snakeskin tennis shoes. In the *West End MarketPlace* (phone: 954-1050).

UPTOWN

Adams-Middleton Gallery – Renowned for its fine collections of paintings and sculpture. 3000 Maple (phone: 871-7080).

Afterimage Gallery – Local photographers and artists display and sell their works here. At the Quadrangle, 2828 Routh St. (phone: 871-9140).

Aldredge Book Store – Treasured tomes from as recently as last year to as far back as the 16th century will undoubtedly lure those in love with old bindings, marbelized endpaper, and silk bookmarkers. Out of print and second-hand books are also available. 2909 Maple (phone: 871-3333).

David Thomas Design – The gentleman who claims to have everything will undoubtedly be surprised by a gift of a stuffed and mounted African giraffe or lion, a zebra-skin rug, or a lizard or alligator picture frame. Needless to say, the prices can hardly be described as rock bottom. At the Quadrangle, 2800 Routh St. (phone: 754-8714).

Heirloom House – Oriental rugs and 18th- and 19th-century English and European furniture are the highlights at Dallas's oldest antiques shop. 2521 Fairmount (phone: 871-0012).

Invision – Beautiful blown-glass paperweights, pottery, and wood sculptures are on tasteful display. At the Quadrangle, 2800 Routh St. (phone: 855-1405).

Lady Primrose Shopping English Countryside – Devotees of English antiques will find an amazing selection procured from the remotest corners of Great Britain. 2200 Cedar Springs, in the *Crescent Hotel* complex (phone: 871-8333).

La Mariposa – Mexican and South American clothing are all the rage here. Other notable items are the collection of folk art, as well as a certain armadillo — a bright sculptured piece with pink nails, turquoise and red shell, and yellow and green spotted torso. 2817 Routh St. (phone: 871-9103).

Militaria – This military arts gallery offers such items as a Royal Irish Rifleman's uniform, modern toy soldiers, historical statuettes, and books from all over the world. 2615 Fairmount (phone: 871-1565).

Peregrine Gallery – Recent items for sale have included Eskimo animal icons and totems to antique and contemporary works. 2200 Cedar Springs, in the *Crescent Hotel* complex (phone: 871-3770).

Stanley Korshak – European designer menswear, including Giorgio Armani. 2200 Cedar Springs, in the *Crescent Hotel* complex (phone: 871-3600).

Uncommon Market – Antique lighting fixtures, plus home accessories. 2701 Fairmount (phone: 871-2775).

PARK CITIES

Collector's Covey – Bronze wildlife sculptures, decoys, and limited edition animal and bird prints are very enticing. 15 Highland Park Village (phone: 521-7880).

Highland Park Village – Built in 1931 and purported to be America's oldest shopping center, it has achieved status as Dallas's equivalent of Rodeo Drive. Among the more famous boutiques here are *Ann Taylor, Chanel, Godiva Chocolatier, Hermès, Polo/Ralph Lauren, Victor Costa,* and *William Noble Jewels.* Mockingbird and Preston Sts. (phone: 559-2740).

La Crème Coffee and Tea – Your nostrils will flare happily to inhale the delicious scent of hand-blended coffees. Unusual teas also are available, as are a variety of coffee makers, teapots, and mugs to hold whichever brew you favor. 4448 Lovers La. (phone: 369-4188).

Lou Lattimore – The local grande dame of women's fashion, which includes *la plus haute couture* of Paris, Italy, and New York. 4320 Lovers La. (phone: 369-8585).

NORTHPARK

Neiman Marcus – A cornerstone of the *Northpark Mall,* this is another branch of the famous store (the original is located downtown). Everything from furs to perfume to Neiman's own cactus salsa or barbecue sauce. 400 Northpark Center (phone: 363-8311).

Woolf Brothers – Classic, conservative menswear by Burberrys, among others. In the *Northpark Mall,* 400 Northpark Center (phone: 369-8811).

NORTH DALLAS

The Galleria – An enormous, 4-level, skylit mall that has lots of stylish shops: *Saks Fifth Avenue, Tiffany & Co., Gumps,* and *Macy's.* Best of all, valet parking is available at the *Westin* hotel on the mall's west side. *Gerlo Scherer* features the chic fashion of German designer Jil Sander, who specializes in silk and cashmere suits for women. Handsome stationery, sleek desk accessories, and fine writing implements such as Mont Blanc and Waterman pens are sold at *William Ernest Brown.* Need a new pair of specs while in town? *Optica* has a great selection of eyewear, including frames from Porsche, Ferre, and Paloma Picasso. 13350 Dallas Pkwy.

Olla Podrida – This classic, albeit unusual Dallas landmark, which was originally an artisans' showplace, is packed with wonderful boutiques along its polished wood stairways and greenery. *The Bunker* has military paraphernalia, while *The Clockworks* has wonderful watches and antique timepieces. *De Falco Winemaker* offers a good selection of international wine; as well as homemade varieties. *Earthen Vessels and Treasures* features oddities of Southwestern art, while *The Patchworks* proffers unusual women's clothing. For the small of stature and age, *Through The Looking Glass* presents ornate dollhouses and other miniatures. Lovers of stained glass and handblown art should visit the *Kitrell Glassworks.*

Cowboy boots are certainly the staple of attire as far as Texans are concerned, and visitors longing to be one of the crowd can drive up to the *Ponder Boot Company* (phone: 817-479-2611 for directions), located about an hour's drive north of Dallas in Ponder. They specialize in custom-made boots and western wear. Or try *Just Justin* in Dallas proper (1505 Wycliff; phone: 630-2858) for off-the-rack western outfits, boots, and belts at discounted prices.

SPORTS AND FITNESS: Dallas has enough professional sports to satisfy just about everyone:

Baseball – The Texas *Rangers* play at *Arlington Stadium,* 1600 Copeland Rd., Arlington (phone: 273-5100).

Basketball – Dallas's NBA team, the *Mavericks,* plays at *Reunion Arena,* 777 Sports St. (phone: 658-7068).

Bicycling – Dallas has some pretty trails in the White Rock Lake–East Dallas area and at Bachman Lake, off Northwest Highway near Love Field. For information, call 946-BIKE.

Fitness Centers – The *Downtown YMCA* has an indoor and an outdoor pool, tracks, squash and racquetball courts, exercise equipment, and a sauna (601 N. Akard at Ross, across from the *Fairmont;* phone: 954-0500). *Dr. Kenneth Cooper's Aerobics Center* (12230 Preston Rd.; phone: 386-0306) now has a Guest Lodge available for those who wish to stay overnight (phone: 800-527-0362).

Football – The *Cowboys* play at *Texas Stadium* (Texas 183 at Loop 12, Irving; phone: 556-2500). The *Cotton Bowl* is held every *New Year's Day* at Fair Park (phone: 638-BOWL).

Golf – There are several municipal courses in Dallas. *Tenison Memorial* (3501 Samuell; phone: 670-1402) is best known as the home of Lee Trevino. Many hotels also have courses and the Dallas Convention and Visitors Bureau has a complete listing of area golf courses.

Ice Skating – *Ice Capades Chalets* run two skating rinks; one in the *Galleria Mall* (13350 Dallas Pkwy.; phone: 387-5533) and the other in the *Preston Wood Mall* (530 Beltline Rd.; phone: 980-8988). *America's Ice Gardens* also has a huge rink (700 N. Pearle St.; phone: 922-9800).

Jogging – For a 6-mile stint, head north on Akard, right onto Cedar Springs, then take Turtle Creek Boulevard, left onto Avondale, left onto Oak Lawn, left onto Irving, back to Turtle Creek, and retrace your steps home. Or take a bus (40 Bachman Bank or 43 Park Forest) to Bachman Lake for a 3-mile course, or to White Rock Lake (60 White Rock North on Commerce or East St.) for a 10-mile course.

Rodeo – Professional cowhands compete at the *Mesquite Championship Rodeo* Friday and Saturday evenings, April through September. LBJ Freeway and Military Parkway Exit in Mesquite (phone: 285-8777).

Soccer – The *Sidekicks* play at *Reunion Arena,* 777 Sports St. (phone: 361-5425).

Tennis – Tennis is a year-round sport here, and it's terrifically popular. There are around 204 municipal courts. The best are at Samuell Grand (at 6200 Grand Ave.; phone: 670-1374) and at Fretz Park (Hillcrest and Beltline; phone: 233-8921).

 THEATER: For a complete up-to-date listing on performance schedules, see the publications listed above. The major Dallas theaters are *Theatre Three* (2800 Routh; phone: 871-3300); *Dallas Theater Center* (3636 Turtle Creek Blvd.; phone: 526-8857). The beautifully restored *Majestic Theatre* (1925 Elm; phone: 880-0137) stages a variety of fine arts events. Several "underground" theater companies perform in the Deep Ellum area.

 MUSIC: Dallas's *Morton H. Meyerson Symphony Center,* designed by architect I. M. Pei, was completed in 1989 at a cost of $81.5 million. It is home to the *Dallas Symphony Orchestra,* which gives concerts in the center's 2,066-seat *Eugene McDermott Concert Hall* (2301 Flora St.; phone: 670-3600). For information on opera, call the *Dallas Opera* (phone: 871-0090); and *Rainbow-Ticketmaster* (phone: 787-2000) for pop-rock concerts.

NIGHTCLUBS AND NIGHTLIFE: Dallas crowds are so notoriously fickle that between the time of writing and the time of printing, everyone may have boogied on down the road to another hangout. Regardless of what's hot and what's not, there's never far to go. Nightlife in Dallas finds four major centers. One is Greenville Avenue, a north-south artery chockablock with restaurants and night-clubs on the east side. *Poor David's* (1924 Greenville; phone: 821-9891) features every style of music, from reggae to jazz, and *Studebakers,* with a 1950s theme at *Northpark East Shopping Center* (phone: 696-2475), is one of the Greenville area's popular discos. There's country-and-western dancing at *Borrowed Money* (9100 N. Central; phone: 361-9996).

A second area is the West End Historical District, a downtown district of renovated warehouses (one, *Dallas Alley,* contains eight clubs; phone: 988-WEST). McKinney Avenue is the third major nightlife center. It runs south to downtown and features some of the best restaurants, along with the tourists' favorite, *Hard Rock Café* (2601 McKinney; phone: 827-8282).

For something more avant-garde, head down to the fourth area, Deep Ellum/Near Ellum, a bohemian district where many blues musicians performed in the 1930s. At *Club Dada* (2720 Elm; phone: 744-3232), poetry, classical guitar, rockabilly, and Middle Eastern jazz can be heard. The *Video Bar* (2610 Elm; phone: 939-9113) offers the best in music videos. *Club Clearview* (2806 Elm; phone: 939-0006) is the place for underground music. Near Fair Park, where some of the uprooted artists moved, are the *State Bar* (3611 Parry; phone: 821-9246), a restaurant/gathering place for the "in" crowd; and *Bar of Soap,* a bar/laundromat with live music (3615 Parry; phone: 823-6617).

BEST IN TOWN

CHECKING IN: Dallas is the third most popular convention city in the country and has a considerable number of comfortable accommodations. Some hotels cater almost exclusively to conventions, so it may be difficult to book as an individual. It will save a lot of trouble if you inquire ahead of time. For something different and a little less expensive, try *Bed & Breakfast Texas Style,* a fast-growing service that offers lodging in private homes. Contact *Ruth Wilson* (4224 W. Redbird La., Dallas 75237; phone: 298-5433 or 298-8586) for information. Dallas also has an international youth hostel at the University of Dallas (phone: 438-6061). At the hotels below, expect to spend $105 and up a night for a double at those places we call expensive; between $60 and $90, moderate; $40 and under, inexpensive. All telephone numbers are in the 214 area code unless otherwise indicated.

Adolphus – Built in 1912, this elder giant among Dallas hotels is listed on the National Register of Historic Places. The decor is turn-of-the-century elegant; rooms are large and individually appointed in the finest of taste. Its *French Room* (see *Eating Out*) is one of the city's classiest restaurants, and the *Palm Bar* is a favorite lunch spot. Also available is 24-hour room service. Business amenities include 16 meeting rooms, concierge and secretarial services, A/V equipment, photocopiers, computers, and express checkout. 1321 Commerce (phone: 742-8200; 800-441-0574 in Texas; 800-221-9083 elsewhere in the US; Fax: 214-747-3532; Telex: 284530). Expensive.

Crescent Court – Designed by award-winning architect Philip Johnson, this Rosewood Group property lives up to its reputation for high style and excellent service. The soaring Great Hall lobby of this impressive 190-room, 28-suite extravaganza links an 18-story office tower (with the hottest private club in town) to an elegant courtyard of ultra-chic shops and galleries whose centerpiece is a 5-story fountain. The spacious, airy rooms were designed with style as well as comfort in mind. And to ensure the enjoyment of its guests, the hotel offers a wide range of amenities and services, among them a 24-hour concierge, 24-hour room service, phones in bathrooms, baby-sitting service, a pool, a spa, a lobby lounge, the *Beau Nash* for formal dining, and the *Conservatory* for breakfast and lunch, in addition to extensive conference facilities and 5 meeting rooms. Other pluses are A/V equipment and photocopiers. Free shuttle service to downtown. 400 Crescent Ct. (phone: 871-3200 or 800 654-6541; Fax: 214-871-3245; Telex: 8713272). Expensive.

Embassy Suites – The 244 one- and two-bedroom suites with kitchens are standard in this Spanish-style hotel built around a soaring atrium. Convenient to downtown. Meeting rooms hold up to 100 people, and there's express checkout. Two locations: 2730 Stemmons Fwy. (phone: 630-5332; Fax: 214-620-3446) and 3880 W. Northwest Hwy. at Love Field (phone: 357-4500; Fax: 214-357-0683). Expensive.

Fairmont – This Dallas favorite celebrated its 20th anniversary in 1989 by renovating throughout. Its white marble façade was replaced with Texas pink granite and there's now an elegant entrance and porte cochère. All 550 rooms were redone, and the restaurants are as fine as ever (see the *Pyramid Room* in *Eating Out*). Room service responds around the clock. Among the business amenities are 24 meeting rooms, both concierge and secretarial services, A/V equipment, photocopiers, computers, and express checkout. In the Arts District, within walking distance of the West End. 1717 N. Akard St. (phone: 720-2020 or 800-527-4727; Fax: 214-720-5282). Expensive.

Four Seasons – Numerous awards for its conference facilities have been bestowed on this 315-room property. Other amenities on its 400 acres include a spa and sports club, two 18-hole golf courses, 4 restaurants, tennis courts and a tennis stadium, racquetball and squash courts, a jogging track, 2 pools and 24-hour room service. There also are special golf and fitness packages. Near the airport at 4150 N. MacArthur Blvd., Irving (phone: 717-0700 or 800-332-3442). Expensive.

Grand Kempinski – In far North Dallas and an attraction in itself. There is 24-hour room service, a concierge floor, tennis and racquetball courts, indoor and outdoor pools, and fine restaurants, all lending it a resort ambience. Other amenities are secretarial services, A/V equipment, photocopiers, and computers. Express checkout. 15201 Dallas Pkwy. (phone: 386-6000 or 800-426-3135; Fax: 214-991-6937). Expensive.

Hyatt Regency – One of Dallas's most popular establishments, it has an eye-catching silver-burnished exterior that mirrors the downtown skyline, a soaring atrium lobby, a rooftop restaurant with a dynamite view, and a health club. Room service is on call 24 hours a day. Fifteen meeting rooms are available for business needs, as well as concierge and secretarial services, A/V equipment and photocopiers. Express checkout. 300 Reunion Blvd. (phone: 651-1234 or 800-233-1234; Fax: 214-651-0018; Telex: 732748). Expensive.

Hyatt Regency D/FW – A popular convention spot. In addition to meeting rooms, it has a swimming pool, bar, and 24-hour café. The hotel's golf and racquet sports facilities, just 10 minutes away (free shuttle service provided), includes 2 topnotch 18-hole golf courses, 4 outdoor lighted tennis courts, 3 indoor courts, and 10 racquetball courts. Dallas/Ft. Worth Airport (phone: 453-1234 or 800-233-1234; Fax: 214-456-8668). Expensive.

Loews Anatole – The red brick exterior doesn't look much like a Dallas hotel, but many residents find it a welcome change from the monolithic rectangles of sparkling tinted glass. Its 2 atriums house 16 restaurants and lounges (its *L'Entrecôte* — see *Eating Out* — is one of the best French restaurants in the city) and 13 shops, tennis and racquetball courts, and the *Verandah Club Spa* on 50 acres of grounds. Around-the-clock room service is available. Other amenities include 26 meeting rooms, a concierge desk, secretarial services, A/V equipment, photocopiers, computers, and express checkout. 2201 Stemmons Fwy. (phone: 748-1200 or 800-223-0888; Fax: 214-761-7520). Expensive.

Mansion on Turtle Creek – Dallas's most elegant address exudes the kind of luxury and taste that make it worthy of its membership in the Relais & Châteaux group. Custom-made furnishings, opulent bathrooms, attentive service, and the *Mansion* restaurant (see *Eating Out*) make this the best of the city's deluxe hotels. Twenty-four hour room service is available. Business functions can be conducted in any one of 5 meeting rooms. Secretarial services, A/V equipment, photocopiers, computers, a concierge desk, and express checkout are pluses. 2821 Turtle Creek Blvd. (phone: 559-2100; 800-442-3408 in Texas; 800-527-5432 in other states; Fax: 214-528-4187; Telex: 794946). Expensive.

Marriott Mandalay at Las Colinas – This 27-story enclave dedicated to luxury is in Las Colinas, a business center west of Dallas. Convenient to both the Dallas/Ft. Worth Airport and downtown, it has a fine restaurant, *Enjolie,* a health club, and a heated pool. Among the amenities are 24-hour room service, 19 meeting rooms, a concierge desk, A/V equipment, photocopiers, and express checkout. 221 E. Las Colinas Blvd., Irving (phone: 556-0800 or 800-228-9290; Fax: 214-556-0729). Expensive.

Plaza of the Americas – Part of the British Trusthouse Forte chain, its management was given carte blanche to hire the best help available — and that they did, from the staff at the coffee shop to the chef in the posh *Café Royal,* which features nouvelle cuisine and a well-stocked wine cellar. The property also boasts an ice skating arena, 16 restaurants, and 25 shops. Room service is available around the clock. Business facilities include 9 meeting rooms, secretarial and concierge services, A/V equipment, photocopiers, computers, and express checkout. 650 N. Pearl Expy. at Bryan St. (phone: 979-9000 or 800-223-5672; Fax: 214-953-1931; Telex: 791620). Expensive.

Stouffer Dallas – Likened by some local pundits to a giant tube of lipstick, this 30-story, elliptically shaped hotel of Texas pink granite occupies an enviable site between Market Hall and the Apparel Mart. Its 542 rooms include 30 suites; there also are 2 restaurants, 24-hour room service, a rooftop health club, heated lap pool, nonsmoking rooms, and morning coffee and a newspaper with each wake-up call. Shuttle to D/FW Airport. Eight meeting rooms, a concierge desk, A/V equipment, and photocopiers all serve business needs. Express checkout. 2222 Stemmons (phone: 631-2222 or 800-HOTELS-1; Fax: 214-634-9319; Telex: 910240). Expensive.

Westin Galleria – Elegant, with 440 balconied rooms, it opens onto that large, posh shopping mall, the *Galleria,* which houses some 200 shops and cinemas. Amenities include a pool, jogging track, saunas, exercise facilities, parking garage, and 3 restaurants. Convenient to North Dallas business districts. Room service is available around the clock. Business pluses include 16 meeting rooms, both concierge and secretarial services, A/V equipment, photocopiers, and computers. Express checkout. 13340 Dallas Pkwy. (phone: 934-9494 or 800-228-3000; Fax: 214-851-2869; Telex: 463182). Expensive.

Aristocrat – An old downtown establishment built by Conrad Hilton in 1925, and renovated in 1985 with sparkling results. Suites designed for a business clientele. Reasonably priced for its location. Among the amenities are a concierge desk, secretarial services, A/V equipment, and express checkout. 1933 Main St. (phone: 741-7700 or 800-231-4235; Fax: 214-939-3639). Expensive to moderate.

Omni Melrose – A small, premier place dating from the 1920s, its 185 rooms give it the hospitable feel of a country estate. A cozy, English-style lounge and an Art Deco restaurant, the *Garden Court,* add to its appeal. Six meeting rooms, A/V equipment, and photocopiers are available. Express checkout. 3015 Oak Lawn Ave. (phone: 521-5151; or 800-843-6664; Fax: 214-521-2470). Expensive to moderate.

Courtyard by Marriott – Spacious rooms with king-size beds that surround pleasant courtyards, each of which has an indoor or outdoor pool. Other amenities include secretarial services, 2 meeting rooms, and express checkout. Six locations in the Dallas area: 2383 Stemmons Trail (phone: 352-7676; Fax: 214-352-4914); 2930 Forest Lane (phone: 620-8000; Fax: 214-620-9267); 4615 Proton Dr., Addison (phone: 490-7390; Fax: 214-490-0002); 1151 West Walnut Hill, Irving (phone: 550-8100); 1000 S. Sherman, Richardson (phone: 235-5000; Fax: 214-235-3423); 4901 Plano Pkwy., Plano (phone: 867-8000; Fax: 214-596-4009). For central reservations call 800-321-2211. Moderate to inexpensive.

Amerisuites – These bright, modern rooms, perfect for families, also have a large kitchenette. City bus transportation is within 2 blocks, and there is complimentary airport transportation. There is a meeting room available, as well as secretarial services, photocopiers, and computers. 3950 Airport Frwy., Irving (phone: 790-1950; Fax: 214-790-4750). Inexpensive.

La Quinta Motor Inns – If you're looking for a clean, inconspicuous place to sleep, try any of this chain's 12 motels throughout the area, including the airport. Nonsmoking rooms and free local calls. Twenty-four hour room service is a plus, as are the meeting rooms, with a capacity of 30 to 40 (the number of rooms differs with each location), a concierge desk, secretarial services, photocopiers, and express checkout. Call 800-531-5900 for all locations. Inexpensive.

EATING OUT: Restaurant dining in Dallas has become as sophisticated as that in any major American city in the last few years, with an emphasis on Southwest cooking (in which Dallas restaurants lead the way). Expect to spend $60 or more for two in those places we've listed as expensive; between $30 and $60, moderate; under $30, inexpensive. Prices do not include wine, drinks, or tips. (Parts of Dallas are "dry," but alcoholic beverages generally are available with an inexpensive club membership.) All telephone numbers are in the 214 area code unless otherwise indicated.

Actuelle – The American-inspired menu changes seasonally in this dining oasis under a glass cupola. The atmosphere is distinctly modern and the food artistically presented. Open for lunch weekdays. Closed Sundays. Reservations advised. Major credit cards accepted. 2800 Routh, in the Quadrangle (phone: 855-0440). Expensive.

Café Royal – The 4-course, prix fixe meal is very French and very refined. Quiet and elegant, the dining room is suited for both romance and business. Open for lunch weekdays, dinner daily. Closed Sundays. Reservations advised. Major credit cards accepted. 650 N. Pearl, in the *Plaza of the Americas Hotel* (phone: 979-9000). Expensive.

L'Entrecôte – The menu has a pronounced French accent, with entrées garnished with a garden of edible flowers. Dinner only. Closed Tuesdays. Reservations necessary. Major credit cards accepted. 2201 Stemmons Fwy., in the *Loews Anatole Hotel* (phone: 761-7410). Expensive.

French Room – The most lavish dining room in the city, swathed in rich Louis XIV decor. The menu is a combination of classic French and slightly nouvelle. Closed Sundays. Reservations advised. Major credit cards accepted. Located in the *Adolphus Hotel,* 1321 Commerce (phone: 742-8200). Expensive.

Mansion – As implied in the name, it's a handsomely refurbished private mansion. Quiet elegance, Southwestern cuisine, polished service, and a VIP crowd make dining here a memorable experience. Open daily. Reservations necessary. Major credit cards accepted. In the *Mansion on Turtle Creek,* 2821 Turtle Creek (phone: 526-2121). Expensive.

Medieval Inn – A six-course meal eaten with a "king," his minstrel, jester, magician, and a host of singing "wenches" guarantees an evening of roisterous entertainment and plenty of food. There's also the *Pub*, where you can quaff a pint of ale and throw a few darts. Open Thursday through Saturday. Reservations advised. Major credit cards accepted. 7102 Greenville Ave. (phone: 363-1114). Expensive.

Old Warsaw – One of the oldest restaurants in Dallas, it features continental cooking with such selections as Dover sole, chateaubriand, and rack of lamb. Various pâtés also are offered. Dinner only. Open daily. Reservations necessary. Major credit cards accepted. 2610 Maple (phone: 528-0032). Expensive.

Pyramid Room – This dining room, in the *Fairmont* hotel, has expanded its predominantly French menu by adding a number of Southwestern dishes. Open daily. Reservations necessary. Major credit cards accepted. 1717 N. Akard St. (phone: 720-5949). Expensive.

Riviera – The South of France is the inspiration for this superb gem with a distinct — but not overwhelming — continental atmosphere. Dinner only. Open daily. Reservations advised. Major credit cards accepted. 7709 Inwood (phone: 351-0094). Expensive.

Routh Street Café – This wonderfully innovative place uses regional produce in preparing superb Southwestern dishes. The five-course, prix fixe menu changes daily. Dinner only. Closed Sundays and Mondays. Reservations necessary. Major credit cards accepted. 3005 Routh St. (phone: 871-7161). Expensive.

Café Pacific – An interesting variety of American and European dishes are served in an attractive brass and glass setting. The clam chowder and seafood sauté are especially good. One of the most extensive and reasonably priced wine lists in town. Open daily. Reservations advised. Major credit cards accepted. 24 *Highland Park Shopping Village* (phone: 526-1170). Expensive to moderate.

Uncle Tai's – Some of the best Oriental food in Dallas is served at this elegant spot in the city's glitziest shopping mall. The crispy beef is a must; the two-color chicken Hunan style is extraordinary. Open daily. Reservations advised. Major credit cards accepted. The *Galleria*, 13350 Dallas Pkwy. at LBJ (phone: 934-9998). Expensive to moderate.

Baby Routh – More casual than its older sister, the *Routh Street Café*, it serves excellent Southwestern fare, including catfish, a regional favorite. Open daily. Reservations advised. Major credit cards accepted. 2708 Routh (phone: 871-2345). Moderate.

Chimney – Swiss-Austrian establishment with one of the more esoteric menus found in the Southwest. Tournedos of Montana venison are a specialty, along with Wiener schnitzel, veal Zürich, and naturschnitzel (veal cutlet cooked in its natural broth with lemon and other natural ingredients). Closed Sundays. Reservations advised. Major credit cards accepted. 9739 N. Central Expy. at Walnut Hill, in *Willow Creek Shopping Center* (phone: 369-6466). Moderate.

Deep Ellum Café – Casual, comfortable atmosphere, located in a one-time hot spot for jazz — hence the name. The menu is broad, everything from Vietnamese salads to chicken with dill dumplings, to superb Southern-fried steaks. Lunch weekdays; brunch Sundays. Reservations advised. Major credit cards accepted. 2704 Elm St. (phone: 741-9012). Moderate.

Dick's Last Resort – For a boisterous evening of another kind, this West End MarketPlace eatery serves up Cajun-influenced food in tin buckets, 74 varieties of beer, and lively music. Open daily. Reservations unnecessary. Major credit cards accepted. 1701 N. Market, Suite 110 (phone: 747-0001). Moderate.

Hard Rock Café – Dine in the Supreme Court of Rock 'n' Roll, a renovated Baptist church landmark where everything is authentic — the walls are hung with such memorabilia as Jimi Hendrix's lead guitar and another upon which Elvis strummed a few chords. Try such specialties as the baked potato soup or the grilled fajitas. Portions are generous. Open daily. Reservations unnecessary. Major credit cards accepted. 2601 McKinney Ave. (phone: 855-0007). Moderate.

Lombardi la Trattoria – Great food and good service have made this perhaps the most popular Italian eatery in Dallas. The pasta and seafood dishes are standouts. Closed Sundays. Reservations advised. Major credit cards accepted. 2916 N. Hall St. (phone: 954-0803). Moderate.

Mario's Chiquita – This isn't a Tex-Mex Americanized food joint — everything here is really Mexican. The *carne asada* Tampico-style is a filet sliced to triple its usual length and broiled over a hickory fire, then served with green peppers, onions, and soft tacos topped with ranchero sauce. Far and away one of the finest Mexican eateries north of the border. Open daily. No reservations. Some credit cards accepted. 4514 Travis Walk, Suite 105 (phone: 521-0721) or 221 W. Parker Rd., Plano (phone: 423-2977). Moderate.

Newport's – In a remodeled brewery in downtown's West End is a wharfside seafood restaurant with pier. The brewery's old well remains open in the brick interior, with scuba divers occasionally searching for purses lost by patrons. Grilled seafood is especially good. Lunch weekdays; dinner daily. Reservations advised. Major credit cards accepted. 703 McKinney (phone: 954-0220). Moderate.

Ranchman's Café – About an hour's drive north of Dallas is the town of Ponder (pop. 208) and one of the most splendid little hometown cafés in Texas; it's less than 40 years old. Its old wooden screen doors open into a room with longhorns and stirrups on the wall and an authentic country-and-western jukebox. Specialties are chicken-fried steaks, T-bone steaks, French fries, and possibly the best pecan pie in the country, along with other home-baked fruit pies. Open daily. Reservations unnecessary. No credit cards accepted. Bailey St. (phone: 817-479-2221). Moderate.

St. Martin's – A well-chosen, reasonably priced wine list coupled with imaginatively prepared seafood specialties make this intimate place a favorite with those who like to linger over a meal. Open daily. Reservations advised. Major credit cards accepted. 3022 Greenville (phone: 826-0940). Moderate.

Trail Dust Steak House – Exactly the kind of place visitors expect in Texas. The waitresses wear cowgirl garb, a country-and-western band entertains, and the food is straight off the ranch: steaks, red beans, potatoes, and salad. Don't wear a tie; if you do, the staff will cut it off and add it to the collection on the walls. Open daily. Reservations advised for large parties only. Major credit cards accepted. 10841 Composite, at the Walnut Hill exit off Stemmons Fwy. (phone: 357-3862). Moderate to inexpensive.

Dickey's Barbecue – An unpretentious decor, but superior barbecued meats. The ribs, sausages, and beef are outstanding. Four locations (three are closed Sundays; North Central is open all week). No reservations. Some credit cards accepted. 4610 N. Central (phone: 823-0240); E. 14th and Ave. M, Plano (phone: 423-9960); 7770 Forest (phone: 223-3721); and 14885 Inwood, Addison (phone: 239-8547). Inexpensive.

Dixie House – This chain of amiable eateries serves such down-home staples as chicken-fried steaks, fried chicken, pot roast, and fresh vegetable dishes including black-eyed peas, okra, and greens. Homemade bread and pastries top off the satisfying menu. Several locations: 2822 McKinney (phone: 871-1173); 3647 W. Northwest Hwy. (phone: 353-0769); 6400 Gaston Ave. (phone: 826-2412); 14925 Midway (phone: 239-5144); and 7778 Forest Lane (phone: 361-7221). Open daily. Reservations unnecessary. Major credit cards accepted. Inexpensive.

Hoffbrau – At this popular, casual steakhouse, the beef is served drenched in butter sauce and accompanied by salad, bread, and potatoes. Open daily. Reservations unnecessary. Major credit cards accepted. 3205 Knox St. (phone: 559-2680). Inexpensive.

Joey Tomato's Atlantic City – This Italian dining spot boasts spaghetti dishes prepared eight different ways, as well as great steaks and seafood. The big, shiny tomato over the front door makes this place hard to miss, even from the trolley. Open daily. Reservations unnecessary. Major credit cards accepted. 3232 McKinney Ave. (phone: 754-0380). Inexpensive.

Mia's – A casual, family-run place well known for Tex-Mex specialties, particularly chiles relleños. Closed Sundays. Reservations unnecessary. No credit cards accepted. 4322 Lemmon (phone: 526-1020). Inexpensive.

On the Border – Visit for a taste of Tex-Mex, particularly the fajitas, which are served sizzling on a hot platter and accompanied by a host of condiments. Outdoor tables placed on a good people watching corner supplement those in the spacious dining rooms inside, where a sometimes boisterous atmosphere prevails. Special Sunday brunch menu. Open daily. Reservations unnecessary. Major credit cards accepted. 3302 Knox St. (phone: 528-5900). Inexpensive.

S&D Oyster House – The decor will remind you of almost every cozy little seafood joint you ever found along the Gulf Coast. It's almost always crowded. Offerings include raw oysters, boiled and fried shrimp, and three kinds of broiled fresh fish. A house specialty is seafood gumbo. Only beer and wine are served. Closed Sundays. Reservations unnecessary. Major credit cards accepted. 2701 McKinney Ave. (phone: 880-0111). Inexpensive.

Solly's Bar-B-Que – Family owned since 1945, many down-home boys swear by its extensive menu and ample portions. Closed Sundays. Reservations unnecessary. Some credit cards accepted. 4801 Belt Line Rd. (phone: 387-2900). Inexpensive.

Sonny Bryan's – Few would argue that it serves the best barbecue in Dallas, although some might take exception to the small, drab interior where school desks substitute for tables. Open daily. No reservations or credit cards accepted. 2202 Inwood Rd. (phone: 357-7120) Inexpensive.

DENVER

AT-A-GLANCE

SEEING THE CITY: The best view of Denver is from the top of the capitol rotunda, where you can see the Rockies to the west, the Great Plains stretching, like an ocean, to the east, and Denver itself sprawled below. On the 13th step of the capitol is an inscription noting that you are exactly 1 mile above sea level. Between E. 14th and E. Colfax Aves. (phone: 866-2604).

SPECIAL PLACES: It's a pleasure to walk around Denver. The downtown section has a number of Victorian mansions as well as the city's public institutions and commercial buildings.

US Mint – Appropriately enough for a city that made its fortune in gold, Denver still has more of it than anyplace else in the country (except Ft. Knox). On the outside, the Mint is a relatively unimpressive white sandstone Federal building with Doric arches over the windows. Inside, you can see money being stamped and printed and catch a glimpse of gold bullion, although the stuff on display is only a fraction of the total stored here. Most impressive is the room full of money just waiting to be counted. Open from 8 AM to 3:30 PM (9 AM to 3:30 PM on Wednesdays); closed on weekends; 20-minute tours begin on the half hour. No admission charge. Delaware St. between Colfax and 14th (phone: 844-3582).

Denver Art Museum – That imposing, rather odd building sparkling in the sun down the street from the Mint is the *Denver Art Museum,* a supermodern structure covered with a million glittering glass tiles. Designed by Gio Ponti, its interior is just as spectacular as its exterior. Be sure to visit the American Indian collection on the second floor — it has superlative costumes, basketry, rugs, and totem poles. Stop for lunch or a snack at the terrace restaurant, weather permitting. Closed Mondays. Admission $1.50 to $3; children under 6, free; Saturday mornings, no charge for Colorado residents. 100 W. 14th Ave. and Bannock St. (phone: 575-2793).

Denver Public Library – This $3-million building houses a vast collection, including books, photographs, and historical documents related to the history of the West. The lower level, known as the basement, contains a splendid children's collection. Exhibitions on western life are on the main floor, and rare book lovers willing to hunt for the special collections will be delighted. Open daily. No admission charge. 1357 Broadway (phone: 571-2345).

Colorado State History Museum – This popular attraction features exhibitions on people who've contributed to Colorado history, period costumes from the early frontier days, and Indian relics. Many of the costumes were donated by members of old Denver families whose ancestors actually wore them. Life-size dioramas show how gold miners, pioneers, and Mesa Verde cliff dwellers used to live. Open daily. Admission $1.50 to $3; no charge for children under 6. 1400 Broadway (phone: 866-3682).

Capitol – The rotunda looks like the dome of the Capitol in Washington, DC, coated with $50,900 worth of Colorado gold leaf; the impressive marble staircases rate a look even if you don't want to climb to the top. There are 45-minute tours between 9:15 AM and 3 PM. Closed Saturdays (December through May) and all Sundays. No admission charge. Between E. 14th Ave. and Colfax, at Sherman Ave. (phone: 866-2604).

Molly Brown House – When gold miner Johnny Brown and his wife Molly moved into their Capitol Hill mansion, Denver society snubbed them as nouveau riche. But Molly earned her place in city history, and, ironically, it's her former house that is now high on the "most visited" list. She is remembered for her earthy flair and keen intelligence and for taking charge of a lifeboat when the *Titanic* sank, commanding the men to row while she held her chinchilla cape over a group of children to keep them warm — which is how she came to be known as the "unsinkable Molly Brown." Closed Mondays, September through May. Admission $1 to $3; no charge for children under 6. 1340 Pennsylvania St. (phone: 832-4092).

Financial District – Seventeenth Street is the center of Denver's financial district, and there are quite a number of tall, modern bank buildings that will give you a proper sense of the economic stability and strength that characterizes such areas. During summer lunch hours, street musicians give concerts in the plazas outside the United Bank Center and the First Interstate Bank of Denver.

Larimer Street – Walk along the *16th Street Mall* to Larimer, Denver's most interesting shopping street. You'll pass the Daniels and Fisher Tower, a 1920s landmark said to be a copy of the campanile in Venice. It used to be the tallest building in town, but it has been overshadowed by more modern edifices. Larimer Street is lined with fascinating art galleries, curio shops, silversmiths, and cafés. Most interesting is Larimer Square, where various restaurants, crafts shops, and wine bars have been restored so that they retain the flavor of Denver's past (between 14th and 15th Sts.).

City Park – A 640-acre park with two lakes, spreading lawns, Denver's *Museum of Natural History* (known for its exhibitions of animals in natural settings), and the Denver Zoo. The museum was the first in the country to use curved backgrounds with reproductions of mountain flowers, shrubs, and smaller animals to give a feeling of the natural environment. Displays of fossils, minerals, gold coins, and birds, and the newest exhibit, the Hall of Life, attempts to unravel the mysteries of the human machine. Open daily. Admission charge (phone: 322-7009). The museum also houses the popular *Gates Planetarium* (phone: 370-6351) and the *IMAX Theatre* (phone: 370-6300), its newest addition. Both open daily. Admission charge. The Denver Zoo (phone: 331-4110) has designed a number of natural mountain environments for its animals. Open daily. Admission $4; children under 6, free.

Hyland Hills Water World – Colorado is not the place for an ocean vacation, but this is one spot where you can body-surf a mile above sea level. There are 24 exciting rides, 2 ocean-wave pools, and a special area for small children. Open daily from *Memorial Day* to *Labor Day*. Admission charge. 1850 W. 89th Ave. (phone: 427-7873).

Children's Museum – A kid-size basketball court, a miniature grocery store, and a real television studio will enthrall youngsters, as will the mini ski mountain, where kids can try out Colorado trails. Open daily. Admission charge. 2121 Crescent Dr., I-25 at 23rd Ave. (phone: 433-7444).

Elitch Gardens – This is one of America's oldest amusement parks, and it has retained all of its charm over the years. The park is clean, the gardens are attractive, and the rides will have the kids asking for more. Grounds-only and all-rides admissions available. Open May through September. 4621 W. 38th Ave. (phone: 455-4771).

Coors Brewery – For beer enthusiasts, the Coors Brewery in Golden (just 20 minutes from downtown Denver), will explain the entire brewing

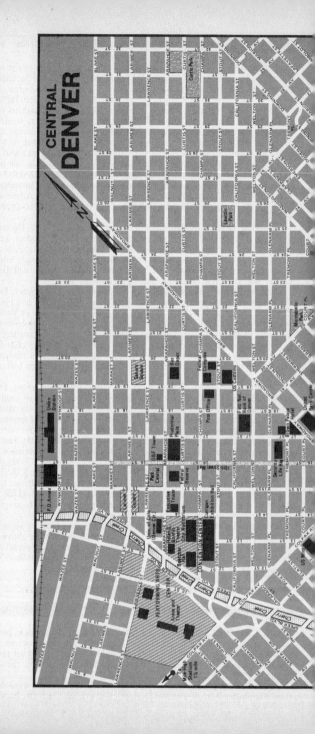

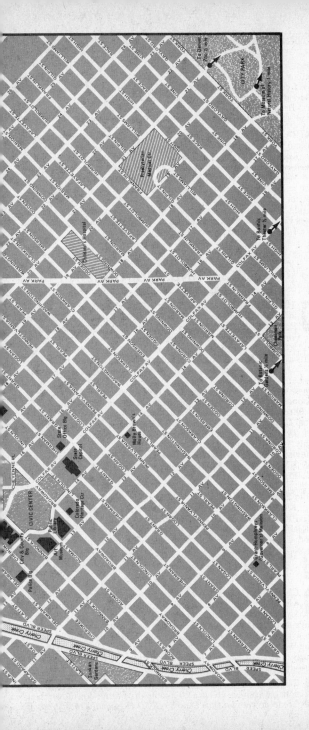

process. Visitors can see thousands of six-packs flash by every minute and enjoy an ice-cold mug of — what else — Coors beer. The 30-minute tour is free, and is offered every 10 to 15 minutes from 8:30 AM to 4:30 PM, Monday through Saturday. For information and directions, contact Coors Brewing Company, Guest Relations/Tours, Mail BC 200, Golden, CO 80401 (phone: 303-277-BEER).

■ **EXTRA SPECIAL:** There are so many gorgeous places to explore around Denver that it's almost unfair to single out any one in particular. Rocky Mountain National Park is, however, one of the most spectacular scenic areas of the US, and it's a perfect choice for a day trip. Within its 264,000 acres are dozens of mountains over the 12,000-foot mark, among them Bighorn Mountain and Longs Peak. The interior of the park offers the opportunity to cross the Continental Divide. You can rent horses and camping equipment in the town of Estes Park, at the northeast corner of the national park. To get there, take I-25 north for 50 miles, then Rte. 34 west.

SOURCES AND RESOURCES

 TOURIST INFORMATION: For brochures, maps, and general information, contact the Denver Metro Convention and Visitors Bureau (225 W. Colfax Ave., Denver, CO 80202; phone: 892-1112). For information on skiing, contact *Colorado Ski Country USA* in town (1560 Broadway, Suite 1440, Denver, CO 80202; phone: 837-0793), or at its airport booth. Contact the Colorado state hotline (phone: 800-433-2656) for maps, calendars of events, health updates, and travel advisories.

Denver magazine is the best guide to the Denver area; it's available at newsstands. Friday editions of the *Denver Post* and *Rocky Mountain News* have complete entertainment and activity guides.

Local Coverage – *Denver Post* and *Rocky Mountain News,* morning dailies; *Denver* magazine and *Colorado Homes & Lifestyles* magazine, monthly.

Television Stations – KCNC Channel 4–NBC; KRMA Channel 6–PBS; KMGH Channel 7–CBS; KUSA Channel 9–ABC; KBDI Channel 12–PBS; KTVD Channel 20–Independent; KDVR Channel 31–FOX.

Radio Stations – AM: KHOW 630 (music/talk); KOA 850 (talk/sports); KYGO 950 (country music); KDEN 1340 (news). FM: KCFR 90.1 (NPR/classical); KHIH 94.7 (jazz/new age); KVOD 99.5 (classical); KRFX 103.5 (classic rock); KAZY 106.7 (rock).

Food – *Denver* magazine has a complete listing of area restaurants.

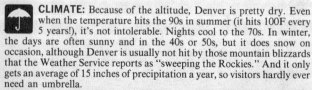 **TELEPHONE:** The area code for Denver is 303.
Sales Tax – The city sales tax is 7.2%; the hotel tax is 11.9%.

 CLIMATE: Because of the altitude, Denver is pretty dry. Even when the temperature hits the 90s in summer (it hits 100F every 5 years!), it's not intolerable. Nights cool to the 70s. In winter, the days are often sunny and in the 40s or 50s, but it does snow on occasion, although Denver is usually not hit by those mountain blizzards that the Weather Service reports as "sweeping the Rockies." And it only gets an average of 15 inches of precipitation a year, so visitors hardly ever need an umbrella.

GETTING AROUND: Airport – Denver's Stapleton International Airport is about a 20-minute drive from downtown; taxi fare to downtown runs $8 to $9. *RTD (Regional Transportation*

District) buses leave for downtown Denver every half hour from the airport terminal's east entry; fare is $1 during rush periods, 50¢ at other times.

Bus – *RTD* runs buses throughout the Denver area. For information, contact the Downtown Information Center, 626 16th St. (phone: 299-6000).

Car Rental – All major national firms are represented.

Taxi – Taxis cannot be hailed in the streets. Call *Yellow Cab* (phone: 777-7777), *Zone Cab* (phone: 861-2323), or *Metro Taxi* (phone: 333-3333). There are cab stands at the airport, bus station, Union Station, and at most major hotels.

 VITAL SERVICES: Audiovisual Equipment – *Colorado Visual Aids* (phone: 778-1111).
    Baby-sitting – *Rent a Mom,* 1873 S. Bellaire (phone: 691-5099).

Business Services – *Record Executive Services,* 11000 E. Yale Ave. (phone: 771-8686).

Dry Cleaner/Tailor – *Colorado Lace* (200 E. 7th St.; phone: 837-1338); and other downtown locations.

Limousine – *Colorado Limousine* (phone: 832-7155).

Mechanic – *May D & F Goodyear Auto Center,* 14th St. and Tremont Pl. (phone: 573-1502).

Medical Emergency – *Denver General Hospital Emergency Service,* 8th and Cherokee Sts. (phone: 893-6000).

Messenger Services – *Express Messenger* (phone: 936-0200); *Speedy Messenger* (phone: 292-6000).

National/International Courier – *Federal Express* (phone: 892-7981); *DHL Worldwide Courier Express* (phone: 388-9212).

Pharmacy – *Walgreen's Pharmacy,* 7 AM to 7 PM. 801 16th St. and Stout (phone: 571-5314).

Photocopies – *City-Wide Printing* (1240 14th St.; phone: 623-7414); *Sir Speedy* (1438 Tremont Pl. and other downtown locations; phone: 534-2529).

Post Office – Terminal Annex, open daily 24 hours, 1595 Wynkoop St. (phone: 297-6455).

Professional Photographer – *CoMedia* (phone: 832-2299); *Mile High Photo Co.* (phone: 744-6104).

Secretary/Stenographer – *Record Executive Services* (phone: 771-8686).

Teleconference Facilities – *Brown Palace* (see *Best in Town,* below); *Hyatt Regency Denver* (phone: 295-1200); *Hilton* (phone: 779-6161).

Translator – *Berlitz* (phone: 399-8686); *Rocky Mountain Translations* (phone: 449-6954).

Typewriter Rental – *Aurora Business Machines,* 10-day minimum (phone: 364-7426).

Western Union/Telex – Many locations around the city (phone: 800-325-6000).

 SPECIAL EVENTS: The *National Western Stock Show and Rodeo* in January lasts 2 weeks and attracts cowfolk from all over. The *Denver Art Museum*'s annual exhibition of western art runs from January through March. *Easter* Sunrise Service at *Red Rocks Natural Amphitheater* attracts thousands. In July and August, the University of Colorado at Boulder presents its annual *Shakespeare Festival.* And Larimer Square is the site of the *Oktoberfest* in guess what month? September!

 MUSEUMS: For a complete description of the *Colorado State History Museum, Denver Art Museum, Molly Brown House,* the *Children's Museum,* and *Museum of Natural History,* see *Special Places.* Other notable museums to visit:

Buffalo Bill Museum – Interesting, especially for children. Buffalo Bill is buried on the grounds. Lookout Mountain (phone: 526-0747).

Colorado Railroad Museum – 17155 W. 44th Ave. (phone: 279-4591).

Kidsport – The *Children's Museum* installed this center at the airport to amuse little ones with lots of energy between planes. There are exhibits on travel, the dynamics of flight, diet and fitness, and there's even a climbing wall where youngsters move horizontally across a wall by gripping exposed pegs in a simulation of mountain climbing. No admission charge. Stapleton International Airport (phone: 333-6507).

MAJOR COLLEGES AND UNIVERSITIES: The University of Denver makes its home in the city proper (at S. University Blvd. and E. Evans Ave.; phone: 871-2000). The University of Colorado is 20 miles northwest of the city (on Rte. 36, in Boulder; phone: 492-0111). The US Air Force Academy's bright, clean, spacious campus is 60 miles south of Denver (on I-25, near Colorado Springs; phone: 719-472-1818).

SHOPPING: Denver rapidly is becoming a shoppers' paradise and soon may rival Dallas as a regional retail center. In 1990, Denver added *Neiman Marcus, Lord & Taylor,* and *Saks Fifth Avenue,* all at the *Cherry Creek Mall.* Several old favorites are going strong, such as downtown's spectacular *Tabor Center,* home to *Brooks Brothers, Sharper Image,* and others; and *Cherry Creek North,* located just across 1st Avenue from the mall and featuring dozens of quaint shops, boutiques, and the shelf-brimming bookstore — there are over 400,000 books — *The Tattered Cover* (2955 E. 1st Ave.; phone: 322-7727), rated by many as among the best in the country.

SPORTS AND FITNESS: Baseball – The AAA American League *Zephyrs* play at *Mile High Stadium,* 1700 Federal Blvd. (phone: 433-8645).

Basketball – The NBA *Nuggets* play at *McNichols Sports Arena,* 1635 Clay St. (phone: 893-3865).

Bicycling – Bicycle tours can be arranged by *Two Wheel Tours,* 2949 E. Cresthill (phone: 798-4609).

Fishing – There's good fishing at Dillon Reservoir, 70 miles west of Denver on I-70, and Cherry Creek Reservoir, just 8 miles southeast of the city on I-225.

Fitness Centers – The *Indian Springs Resort* has relaxing, hot mineral baths (302 Soda Creek Rd., 1 block south of Miner St., in Idaho Springs; phone: 623-2050). The *International Athletic Club* welcomes guests from several downtown hotels; it has exercise classes, tracks, racquetball and squash courts, sauna, and massage (1630 Welton; phone: 623-2100).

Football – The NFL *Broncos* (phone: 433-7466) play at *Mile High Stadium,* 1700 Federal Blvd. (phone: 433-7466).

Golf – Among the 50 golf courses in the area, the best public courses are *Kennedy* (10500 E. Hampden Ave.; phone: 751-0311), *Park Hill* (3500 Colorado Blvd.; phone: 333-5411), and *Wellshire* (3333 S. Colorado Blvd.; phone: 757-1352).

Hockey – The University of Denver *Pioneers* play at the *DU Arena,* E. Jewell Ave. and S. Gaylord Way (phone: 871-2336).

Jogging – Follow the Highline Canal trail; or run in Washington Park, which is 4½ miles from downtown, or in City Park, 2 miles from downtown.

Racing – Greyhounds race at *Mile High Kennel Club* from June through August, 6200 Dahlia Rd. (phone: 288-1591). No one under 21 is admitted.

Skiing – Colorado ski country is famous all over the world. The slopes closest to the city are in *Loveland Basin* (60 miles west on I-70); *Keystone and Arapahoe Basin, Breckenridge,* and *Copper Mountain* (all from 15 to 25 miles farther on I-70); and *Winter Park* (west on I-70, then north on Rte. 40). Former President Ford used to give news conferences on the slopes at *Vail,* a resort 100 miles west of Denver on I-70, and now has a house at Beaver Creek. Internationally acclaimed *Aspen* and *Snowmass* are about 190 miles southwest of Denver (on I-70 and Hwy. 82). *Crested Butte* (237 miles southwest) and *Steamboat Springs* (163 miles northwest) are growing in popularity.

Tennis – The best public courts are at *Gates Tennis Center,* 100 S. Adams St. (phone: 355-4461).

THEATER: For complete up-to-the-minute listings on theatrical and musical events, see local publications listed above. The University of Colorado at Boulder — about 20 miles northwest of Denver — hosts a *Shakespeare Festival* every summer (see *Special Events*). The *Denver Center for the Performing Arts* presents Broadway productions as well as those of local companies (14th and Curtis Sts.; phone: 893-4000). The *Country Dinner Playhouse,* a dinner-theater, presents light offerings and musicals throughout the year (6875 S. Clinton in Englewood, just south of Denver; phone: 799-1410).

MUSIC: Two outdoor amphitheaters feature summer rock concerts: *Red Rocks,* which provides a spectacular mountain setting (12 miles west of Denver off I-70; phone: 575-2637), and *Fiddler's Green* (12 miles south of downtown, off I-25 in the Denver Tech Center; phone: 741-5000). Most large indoor concerts are held at *McNichols Arena* (1635 Clay St.; phone: 572-4703). The *Colorado Symphony* performs classical and pop concerts November through May at *Boettcher Hall* (14th and Arapahoe Sts.; phone: 595-4388).

NIGHTCLUBS AND NIGHTLIFE: The well-dressed crowd can find jazz at *El Chapultepec* (1962 Market St.; phone: 295-9126). Comedy is king at *Comedy Works* (1226 15th St.; phone: 595-3637). Singles and rockers have an almost limitless choice all over town. Among the best are *Panama Reds* (phone: 695-1750) and *Basin's Up* (in Larimer Square; phone: 623-2104).

BEST IN TOWN

CHECKING IN: Denver's plentiful hotel facilities often provide great lodging values compared to those in other major US cities. Expect to pay between $100 and $195 for a double room at those places we've listed as expensive; between $60 and $100 at those in the moderate category; and about $50 at places noted as inexpensive. All telephone numbers are in the 303 area code unless otherwise indicated.

Brown Palace – Built in the 1890s, it was one of the first hotels to have a multi story atrium lobby with balconies rimming it on every floor. The 231 rooms have been remodeled several times, and the whole place still has a certain faded glamour. Business amenities include 13 meeting rooms, secretarial services, A/V equipment, CNN, and photocopiers. 17th St. and Tremont Pl. (phone: 297-3111; Fax: 303-293-9204). Expensive.

Hyatt Regency Denver – In the middle of downtown, this 26-story, 540-room property boasts superior restaurants, a rooftop recreational complex with pool, tennis court, and jogging track, and lavish room amenities. Thirteen meeting rooms, secretarial services, A/V equipment, photocopiers, and CNN are available. 1750 Welton St. (phone: 295-1200; Fax: 303-292-2472). Expensive.

Loews Giorgio – This hotel has risen rapidly in stature since its opening in 1987. The only Colorado member of the Loews chain, it boasts 200 rooms and an Italian motif. From the imported Italian marble and original artwork in the public areas to the romantic Italian atmosphere of the guestrooms, this is one of Denver's best. The library, bar, and *Tuscany* restaurant are quiet and relaxed, and all guests have free access to the nearby *Cherry Creek Sporting Club*. Business amenities include 2 meeting rooms, photocopiers, and CNN. Close to Cherry Creek shopping area. S. Colorado Blvd. and E. Mississippi Ave. (phone: 782-9300; Fax: 303-758-6542). Expensive.

Oxford Alexis – A short stroll from the shopping attractions of the *Tabor Center,* Writer Square, and historic Larimer Square, this 82-room place is a bit of history unto itself, having opened in 1891. A $12-million restoration (in 1979) turned it into a Denver showplace. Restaurant, bar. 17th St. and Wazee (phone: 628-5400; Fax: 303-628-5413). Expensive.

Radisson Denver – Once slightly tired, this former *Hilton* recently completed over $20 million in renovations. The largest hostelry downtown, it has 750 rooms, *Finnegan's* authentic Irish pub and restaurant, and *Katie's Ice Cream Parlor.* There is also a rooftop pool, health club, shops, and an on-site business center, which offers photocopying and secretarial services. Other amenities include 27 meeting rooms, A/V equipment, and CNN. 16th and Court Place (phone: 893-3333). Expensive.

Sheraton DTC – The Denver Tech Center's largest hotel and one of its better values, with 623 rooms, racquetball courts, a 24-hour deli, and *Campari's* Italian restaurant, which is highly recommended. Amenities include 24 meeting rooms, secretarial services, A/V equipment, photocopiers, and CNN. There is also a commercial airport shuttle for $7. 4900 DTC Pkwy. (phone: 779-1100; Fax: 303-779-1100). Expensive.

Stouffer Concourse – The best of the bunch along "Airport Row," with 400 rooms. Its bars and restaurants offer a stylish atmosphere, though the food is not quite so good. Business amenities include 19 meeting rooms, A/V equipment, photocopiers, and CNN. 3801 Quebec St. (phone: 399-7500). Expensive.

Westin Tabor Center – The centerpiece of the *Tabor Center,* this office-hotel-retail complex is in Denver's *16th Street Mall.* Its *Augusta* restaurant is among the best of a number of excellent downtown restaurants. There is also a pool, sauna, racquetball courts, and a fitness center. CNN, too. 16th and Lawrence Sts. (phone: 572-9100; Fax: 303-572-7288). Expensive.

Clarion Hotel/Denver Southeast – Across from Centennial Airport, a popular roost for executives with private planes, it offers beautiful southwestern decor and room appointments for a relatively low price. Amenities include use of a nearby athletic club, an outdoor pool, and helicopter shuttle to the airport. CNN. 7770 Peoria St. (phone: 790-7770; Fax: 303-790-7770, ext. 726). Moderate.

Marriott Courtyard – A "few frills" entry on the Denver lodging scene that's not to be overlooked. If you can forgo a bellman or room service, you can secure a Marriott-style room (including CNN) and access to a restaurant for a lot less money. Two-room suites are only about $20 more than a standard room. Two locations: Stapleton Airport, 7415 E. 42st Ave. (phone: 333-3303); Southeast, I-25 and Arapahoe Rd. (phone: 721-0300; Fax: 303-721-0037). Moderate.

Queen Anne Inn – Denver's best-known bed and breakfast spot is just 4 blocks from the downtown *16th Street Mall.* Proprietors Charles and Ann Hillestad restored this 1879 Victorian home into a 10-unit treasure: Each unit has a unique decor, private bath, and telephone. The historic surrounding neighborhood is re-emerging after years of decline. No smokers or children under 15. CNN. 2147 Tremont Pl. (phone: 296-6666). Moderate.

Comfort Inn–Downtown – Originally part of the *Brown Palace,* this 230-room structure was converted into a separate establishment for budget-conscious travelers. Complimentary breakfast and access to health club provided. CNN. 17th St. and Tremont Pl. (phone: 296-0400). Inexpensive.

EATING OUT: Denver seems to be a magnet for great chefs and adventurous restaurateurs. While beef is king, there are enough places featuring nouvelle cuisine, southwestern fare, pizza, and just plain good eats to keep everyone happy. For two people, expect to pay $60 or more for dinner at restaurants listed as expensive, $40 to $50 at places in the moderate category, and $30 or less at those listed as inexpensive. Prices do not include wine, drinks, or tips. Except where noted otherwise, all restaurants are open for lunch and dinner. All telephone numbers are in the 303 area code unless otherwise indicated.

Buckhorn Exchange – Established in 1893 by a former scout for Buffalo Bill Cody, it's in the National Register of Historic Places. Festooned with scores of hunting trophies, the restaurant's game dishes — elk, buffalo, and quail, among others — continue to make history today. For those who aren't "game," more standard fare, such as generous beef cuts, are available. Don't pass up the navy bean soup or home-made apple pie with ice cream and hard cinnamon sauce. Open daily for dinner, lunch weekdays. Reservations advised. Major credit cards accepted. Near downtown, 1000 Osage (phone: 534-9505). Expensive.

Cliff Young's – If you're looking for pampered extravagance with well-prepared food, this is among the best. Try the herb-encrusted rack of lamb. Located just east of downtown. Open daily for dinner; lunch on Fridays only. Reservations essential. Major credit cards accepted. 1700 E. 17th Ave. (phone: 831-8900). Expensive.

The Fort – Near the foothills southwest of Denver, it's where locals take out-of-towners to show off Denver's pioneer spirit. Frontier recipes have been adapted to modern tastes, including elk, Buffalo Boodie Sausage, and Rocky Mountain Oysters (bull's testicles). Try a combination to get a sampling. The restaurant is a replica of Colorado's famous Bent's Fort. In warm weather, make sure you get a seat on the patio: the scenery is fantastic. Dinner nightly. Reservations necessary. Major credit cards accepted. US 285 at Colorado Hwy. 8 (phone: 697-4771). Expensive.

Fresh Fish Company – What's in a name? Everything. The seafood here is so fresh you might think they pulled the swordfish from the Colorado River. The truth is that the fish is flown in daily from all over, so the menu items include Maine lobster, Florida stone crab, Canadian walleye, and Hawaiian ahi, among others. Everything is cooked over imported Mexican mesquite wood. Those who are health and weight conscious can choose "Healthmark" entrées, which are low in fat, cholesterol, and sodium. No Saturday lunch. Reservations accepted for 5 or more. Major credit cards accepted. 7800 E. Hampden Ave. (phone: 740-9556). Moderate.

Beau Jo's – Ideal for a family outing, this chain of pizza places serves up the Rockies' best mountain pie. Diners choose the ingredients of their "pie," beginning with style of pie and thickness of dough, right down to variety and quantity of cheese. Pies are "weighed" and charged accordingly. Beer and wine available. Takeout available. Idaho Springs (phone: 573-6924) branch is popular as an après-ski stopover. Open daily. No reservations. Major credit cards accepted. Other locations include 2700 S. Colorado Blvd. (phone: 758-1519) and 7805 Wadsworth Blvd. (phone: 420-8376). Inexpensive.

Bonnie Brae Tavern – In a city where most pizza seems to come from a "hut" or a "domino," this is one pizza place Denverites like to boast about. The setting is rustic and there's usually a wait for a table, but no one seems to mind. No reservations. 740 S. University Blvd. (phone: 777-2262). Inexpensive.

Le Central – Casual, affordable, and French. A real local favorite, where the menu — written on large blackboards — changes daily and the accepted dress ranges from blue jeans to suits and dresses. The service is wonderful, although some may feel rushed by the way one course quickly follows the last. Entrées include chicken, veal, filet, and lots of fish, with prices of just $6.50 to $10.50. Save room for dessert. Opt for the nonsmoking sections and ignore the vinyl tablecloths. Reservations accepted for parties of six or more. No credit cards accepted. Near downtown, 112 E. 8th Ave. (phone: 863-8094). Inexpensive.

La Loma – Started in 1974 as a family enterprise, the intimate, friendly atmosphere and authentic Mexican fare still prevail. Offered here are diverse Mexican selections, from enchiladas and tacos to more ambitious fare, including Mexican camarónes, large Gulf shrimp sautéed in seasoned butter, and fajitas, charbroiled chicken or steak bits with grilled onions, marinated in salsa and served with corn tortillas and beans. Try the fried ice cream. Open daily. No reservations. Major credit cards accepted. Near downtown, 2527 W. 26th Ave. (phone: 433-8307). Inexpensive.

My Brother's Bar – The best hamburger in town is found here, just a few blocks north of downtown. Try the jalapeño burger. Don't look for a sign out front — there's never been one. Closed Sundays. Reservations accepted for six or more. American Express not accepted. 2376 15th St. (phone: 455-9991). Inexpensive.

Pour La France Cafés – There are several of these comfortable, casual, bistro-like eateries in town. Menus combine the best of French and American cooking and brunch is special: Grand Marnier French toast, garnished with bananas and strawberries; shrimp and crabmeat quiche; and eggs Arnold (poached eggs on a butter croissant, with avocado and hollandaise sauce). All the cafés have bakeries. Closed Sunday and Monday evenings. No reservations. Visa and MasterCard accepted. Three locations: 730 S. University Blvd. (phone: 744-1888); 8101 E. Belleview Ave. (phone: 220-8820); and at the *Denver Jet Center* at Centennial Airport (lunch through 6 PM), 7625 S. Peoria St. (phone: 790-4321). Inexpensive.

DETROIT

AT-A-GLANCE

SEEING THE CITY: The best view of the city is from the top of the 73-story *Westin* hotel. Part of the Renaissance Center, it is one of the city's most dramatic creations. Views are from the hotel's top three floors, called the *Summit,* with a revolving restaurant and cocktail lounge and an observation deck ($3 if you're not dining or a hotel guest). Ever-changing views are possible from the People Mover (phone: 962-7245); fare 50¢. There are great skyline views of Detroit from rooms in the *Windsor Hilton,* the *Compri* hotel, and from Dieppe Gardens, a riverside park at the foot of Ouellette Avenue, Windsor's main street. *Detroit Upbeat* (phone: 341-6808) offers dozens of tours of Detroit and southeast Michigan.

SPECIAL PLACES: Down on the ground, Civic Center is a good place to begin sightseeing. We've divided the city into Civic Center, Cultural Center, and Other Special Places.

CIVIC CENTER

Renaissance Center – Detroit's very own Oz, this city-within-the-city dominates Detroit's skyline. Dining, entertainment, boutiques, and more have made RenCen tick since it opened in 1977. The huge complex is tied together by a maze of walkways, atriums, gardens — even an indoor lake. Prediction: With seven circular buildings to stroll around, first-timers will get lost. Everybody does. Group tours are available (phone: 591-3611). Jefferson Ave. between Randolph and Beaubien Sts.

Millender Center – Tethered to RenCen by an arcing skywalk over Jefferson Avenue, Millender is a smaller version of the office-shopping complex without the dizzying confusion. Both the Millender Center and the abutting *Omni* hotel boast quality shops and restaurants.

Philip A. Hart Plaza – Detroit's riverfront playground, designed by the international sculptor Isamu Noguchi. What it lacks in grass, this paved esplanade makes up for in action. The $30-million Dodge Fountain spouts 30 computer-controlled water displays. It's also the home of Detroit's summer riverfront festivals of food and entertainment. In winter, there's an ice skating pavilion, à la Rockefeller Center. The Detroit River is alongside, with Windsor, Ontario, on the far bank.

The Fist – Robert Graham's downtown sculpture of the fist and forearm of legendary Detroit boxer Joe Louis is a split decision. Supporters say it celebrates Detroit's fighting spirit, while the non-admirers feel that a city with a high crime rate hardly needs a 4-ton fist in its midst. At Woodward and Jefferson.

Detroit People Mover – An elevated, 2.9-mile cement ribbon wraps around downtown, carrying pedestrians in automated, weatherproof cars from city squares to RenCen, Cobo Center to Greektown. Complete 13-station loop takes 14 minutes and costs 50¢.

Washington Boulevard Trolley – A charming, antique trolley car wends its way south from Grand Circus Park along Washington Boulevard and east to RenCen. (The conductor wears 1890 regalia.) The trolley runs past St. Aloysius Church, Cobo Center, the visitors' informa-

CENTRAL
DETROIT

(Above) CULTURAL CENTER

(Below) DOWNTOWN AND CIVIC CENTER

Detroit River

tion center, and the Mariner's Church on its way to the Renaissance Center.

CULTURAL CENTER

Detroit Institute of Arts – An unusual collection of Old Masters and modern artists lines the walls, halls, and gardens here. Visitors can examine Peter Breughel's Flemish masterpiece *Wedding Dance* and Mexican artist Diego Rivera's gripping, provocative frescoes on the industrial life of Detroit. In the garden is a bust of Lincoln by Gutzon Borglum, Mt. Rushmore's sculptor. Closed Mondays and Tuesdays. Admission charge. 5200 Woodward Ave. (phone: 833-7900).

Detroit Public Library – This Italian Renaissance, white Vermont marble building houses books, paintings, stained glass windows, and mosaics. The *Burton Historical Museum,* an archive of material related to Detroit history, is one of the library's special collections. Closed Sundays and holidays. No admission charge. Woodward and Kirby Aves. (phone: 833-1000).

Detroit Historical Museum – The early days of Detroit are shown by models of early streets and railroads, period rooms, and exhibitions on horseless carriages and automobiles. In the basement stands a permanent display of actual storefronts from bygone eras. Closed Mondays, Tuesdays, and holidays. Donations suggested. Woodward and Kirby Aves. (phone: 833-1805).

Wayne State University – Known for its innovative architecture rather than its football. A lot of buildings have gone up since 1960, among them a medical center attached to the Wayne State Medical School, reputed to be one of the best in the country. If you enjoy a college atmosphere, take a stroll on the campus. 650 W. Kirby (phone: 577-2424).

Detroit Science Center – The hands-on displays here allow visitors to demonstrate scientific principles for themselves. This $5-million complex also features a domed space theater. Closed Mondays. Admission charge. 5020 John R St. (phone: 577-8400).

Children's Museum – A planetarium and collections of puppets and small animals. Kids love the life-size sculpture of the horse near the entrance — it's made out of automobile bumpers. Closed Sundays. No admission charge. 67 E. Kirby Ave. (phone: 494-1210).

Museum of African American History – Black heritage explored through art and artifacts. Closed Mondays and Tuesdays. Donations accepted. 301 Douglass (phone: 833-9800).

OTHER SPECIAL PLACES

Belle Isle – This beautiful island park in the middle of the Detroit River was originally allocated for pasture by M. Cadillac himself. About 2 miles long, Belle Isle has a children's zoo; the *Dossin Great Lakes Museum,* with displays of model ships (phone: 267-6440); and the *Belle Isle Aquarium* (267-7159). It's also a good place for picnics, biking, canoeing, and jogging. South of Jefferson, across the Gen. Douglas MacArthur Bridge (recreation office, phone: 224-1100).

Boblo Boats – Every day between *Memorial Day* and *Labor Day,* two 1,200-passenger steamers leave Detroit for Boblo Island. The 26-mile boat ride takes about 1½ hours each way — the most pleasant way to see industrial Detroit and Canada. At Boblo Island, there's a large amusement park and local craftwork. At the foot of Clark Ave., 2 blocks south of I-75. 4401 W. Jefferson (phone: 843-8800).

Cranbrook – Stroll through 49 acres of gardens surrounding an English manor. Catch a laser light show in a planetarium. Visit a nature center or browse through an art museum or science exhibition. It's all part of this internationally known center for the arts, education, science, and culture. A maple sugar festival, concerts, and other special events make Cranbrook a compelling place, worth the 25-mile drive north from Detroit. Lone Pine Rd., Bloomfield Hills (phone: 645-3000).

Star of Detroit – Restaurants/bars that are tugboats, sidewheelers, or otherwise waterbound are anchored in the Detroit River between Detroit and Windsor. The *Star* one-ups the rest by offering lunch, dinner, Sunday brunch, and cocktail cruises. Entertainment and dancing. Operates in the summer from the foot of Hart Plaza (phone: 259-9160).

Greenfield Village and Henry Ford Museum – Legend has it that when Henry Ford couldn't find a copy of McGuffey's *Reader,* he feared such examples of Americana would disappear entirely unless he founded a museum. The result is here — and as you might expect, it has dozens of splendid, antique automobiles and thousands of 19th- and 20th-century machines. Next-door Greenfield Village is a collection of transplanted houses of historical interest. Henry Ford couldn't be stopped — he bought McGuffey's school and had it reconstructed, along with Thomas Edison's Menlo Park laboratory and the first boardinghouse to have electricity. An English shepherd's cottage and Noah Webster's house are also here. Separate admissions for Greenfield Village and *Henry Ford Museum;* combination tickets available. South of Michigan Ave. between Oakwood Blvd. and Southfield Fwy., Dearborn (phone: 271-1620).

Eastern Market – A carnival of sights, smells, and sounds, this has been a farmers' market since 1892. Saturdays are great fun, watching shoppers haggle over prices with merchants selling the freshest produce, meats, fish, poultry, and cheeses. Russell at Fisher Fwy. (phone: 833-1560).

Fox Theatre – The cavernous *Fox* is part theater, part fantasyland. An $8 million restoration of C. Howard Crane's 1928 movie palace has brought name acts back to the great stage and suburbanites back downtown. The gilded lobby is eye-popping, with red-eyed griffins and faux marble columns. The golden elephant above the proscenium and the stained glass chandelier that hangs above 4,800 seats are remnants from the original theater. 2211 Woodward St. (phone: 567-6000).

Greektown – A downtown enclave of restaurants serving authentic Greek fare. Quaint shops, bakeries, and Old St. Mary's Church make an interesting stroll. *Trappers Alley* is a 5-level mall full of restaurants, specialty shops, and *Monroe's* disco. Monroe St. between Beaubien and St. Antoine.

Motown Museum – To pop music fans, this brick and stucco building, called Hitsville, USA, turned out more gold than Ft. Knox. Motown memories abound in the museum including Berry Gordy Jr.'s original studio, where the *Supremes,* Stevie Wonder, the *Temptations,* the *Four Tops,* and others recorded. Michael Jackson, the museum's biggest benefactor, donated $125,000 to fund more displays. Open daily. Admission charge. 2648 W. Grand Blvd. (phone: 875-2264).

Detroit Zoological Park – The first zoo in the US to use barless dwellings is home to hundreds of species of animals in a setting of lakes and flower gardens. Open daily in summer, Wednesdays through Sundays in winter. Admission $5 adults, $2.50 children ages 5 through 12. In Royal Oak at Woodward and I-696 (phone: 398-0903).

Plant Tours – Watch Cadillacs being born at General Motors' futuristic Detroit-Hamtramck Assembly Plant (adjacent to I-94, I-75). Except for a 6-week midsummer downtime, 90-minute walking tours are offered at no charge on Tuesdays and Wednesdays at 9 AM, Thursdays at noon (phone: 972-6000 for reservations). With advance notice, you can tour the high-tech Mazda plant in Flat Rock (phone: 782-7800). Tours of Windsor's Hiram Walker Canadian Club Distillery are held twice daily during summers only (phone: 965-6611 for reservations). *Michigan Thanksgiving Day Parade Co.* (9600 Mt. Elliott; phone: 923-7400) leads guided tours among the floats, balloons, and papier-mâché heads. Reservations necessary January through September, other times for groups only.

Birmingham – Detroit's hip, village-like northern suburb is the place to hang out, shop, have drinks, and be seen. A neighborhood of parks, trendy stores, de rigueur eateries, a theater with stage shows, and the ritzy homes of social climbers. Fifteen miles north of downtown Detroit, where Woodward forks at Hunter.

■ **EXTRA SPECIAL:** Detroit's biggest tourist attraction is just a mile away: Canada. In just a few minutes, you can enter a different country, and you don't even need a passport if you're a US citizen — just a birth certificate. Don't expect any drastic change from Detroit, however. Windsor, Ontario, just across the river, is another automobile-producing city, with Canadian GM, Chrysler, and Ford plants. If you're looking for bargains, Ontario is a great place to buy English woolens, glassware, and china. The city is literally on Detroit's doorstep, and you can get there by bus or taxi to the tunnel or by the Ambassador Bridge.

SOURCES AND RESOURCES

TOURIST INFORMATION: The Metropolitan Detroit Convention and Visitors Bureau maintains a 24-hour "What's Line" directory of events and distributes free brochures and maps. 2 Jefferson Ave., Detroit, MI 48226 (phone: 567-1170). Contact the Michigan state hotline (phone: 800-543-2937) for maps, calendars of events, health updates, and travel advisories.

Detroit Visitor's Guide (Metropolitan Detroit Convention and Visitors Bureau; free) is the best guide to the area. Pick up a free *Detroit Monitor* or the more avant-garde *Metro Times* for about-town happenings and attractions.

Local Coverage – *Detroit Free Press,* morning weekdays; *Detroit News,* morning and afternoon weekdays, combined papers weekends; *Royal Oak Tribune* and *Oakland Press* (Pontiac, both afternoon). *Key* (free) and *Travel Host* magazines are available at hotels. *Detroit Monthly* is the popular city magazine.

Television Stations – WJBK Channel 2–CBS; WDIV Channel 4–NBC; WXYZ Channel 7–ABC; WKBD Channel 50–FOX; WTVS Channel 56–PBS.

Radio Stations – AM: WJR 760 (news/talk); WWJ 950 (news); WXYT 1270 (talk); WCKL 800 (big band). FM: WLTI 93.1 (adult contemporary music); WOMC 104.3 (oldies); WQRS 105.1 (classical music); WJZZ 105.9 (jazz).

TELEPHONE: The area code for Detroit is 313.

Sales Tax – The city sales tax is 4%; hotel tax ranges from 5% to 11%, depending on the size and location of the establishment.

CLIMATE: Seasons usually procrastinate in Detroit. You might miss spring if you blink, and summer doesn't really peak until July. Autumn can be a day. The local joke is that if you don't like the weather, stick around because it'll change again in about 5 minutes. Temperatures range into the 70s and 80s in summer. Subfreezing temperatures are often the rule in January and February.

GETTING AROUND: Airport – Detroit Metropolitan Wayne County Airport handles most of the city's air traffic and is about a 30-minute drive from downtown; taxi fare to downtown runs approximately $25. *Commuter Transportation* (phone: 941-3252) provides bus transport to the downtown area from the airport's north and south terminals for $13.

 Southwest Airlines (phone: 562-1221 or 800 531-5601) serves 24 cities from the regional City Airport, 7 miles from downtown. *Kirby Tours* (phone: 278-2224) offers shuttle service between the airports and hotels ($12–$30 each way; add $5 to or from a home or business). *Commuter Transportation* (see above) has van service between Metro and area hotels; one-way fares from $9.50 to $20.50; Metro to City Airport, $13.50. Cab fare runs $12.

Car Rental – All the major national firms are represented.

Taxi – Cabs can be hailed in the street or picked up at the stands in front of hotels. Some of the cabs are licensed to cross over to Canada. If you prefer to call for a cab, we suggest *Checker* (phone: 963-7000).

 VITAL SERVICES: Audiovisual Equipment – *Allied Audio Visual* (phone: 568-0855); *Gavco* (phone: 567-2155).
    Business Services – For photocopying, try *NRC* (at RenCen; phone: 259-5066); *Silver's* (151 W. Fort; phone: 963-0000) has stationery and supplies.

Dry Cleaner/Tailor – *Renaissance Dry Cleaners,* Renaissance Center (phone: 568-8566).

Limousine – *Detroit Limousine Service* (phone: 471-0980).

Mechanic – *Downtown Auto Service,* 1200 Cass Ave. (phone: 963-2744).

Medical Emergency – *New Detroit Receiving Hospital,* 4201 St. Antoine St. (phone: 745-3000).

Messenger Services – *Pony Express* (phone: 965-7420).

National/International Courier – *Federal Express* (phone: 961-8771); *DHL Worldwide Courier Express* (phone: 942-6500).

Pharmacy – *Perry Drugs,* weekdays, 7 AM to 7 PM; Saturdays, 8 AM to 6 PM, 1124 Griswold St. (phone: 964-5020).

Photocopies – *National Reproductions Corp. (NRC),* pickup and delivery (433 E. Larned St.; phone: 961-5252, and Renaissance Center; phone: 259-5066); *Duffy's Printing & Copying* (Renaissance Center, Tower 200, 6th Floor; phone: 259-1833).

Post Office – Central, 24-hour, self-service lobby (1401 W. Fort St.; phone: 226-8672); there is a Renaissance Center branch (Tower 200; phone: 259-4477).

Professional Photographer – *Ashley Photography* (phone: 645-5164); *Larry Peplin* (phone: 882-7057).

Secretary/Stenographer – *CDI* (phone: 259-7516); *Employer's Temporary Services* (phone: 372-7700).

Teleconference Facilities – *Hyatt Regency Dearborn, Pontchartrain,* (see *Best in Town,* below).

Translator – *Berlitz* (phone: 874-2777).

Typewriter Rental – *Dulin Office Machine* (phone: 527-8280).

Western Union/Telex – Many offices located around town (phone: 800-325-6000).

Other – *Fox Studios,* videotaping (phone: 526-2220); *Jet Services,* helicopter service to downtown and to *Hyatt Regency Dearborn* (phone: 459-0844).

SPECIAL EVENTS: The *Detroit Grand Prix* sends Indy-type cars thundering through the downtown canyons every June. This is also the month when hydroplanes race off Belle Isle during the annual *Thunderfest*. The friendship between Windsor and Detroit is celebrated in the *International Freedom Festival,* a series of events during *Fourth of July* week, highlighted by spectacular fireworks over the river. The *Montreux Jazz Festival* has become quite an annual event the week surrounding *Labor Day* weekend. Concerts are held in Hart Plaza, *Chene Park,* a riverside amphitheater, and at many other locations. Call

Detroit Renaissance (phone: 259-5400) for details on the *Grand Prix, Freedom Festival,* and *Jazz Festival. Michigan's Thanksgiving Day Parade,* a Detroit tradition since 1926, still marches on every "Turkey Day" (phone: 923-7400).

Note: Detroit suffers every *Halloween* when local thugs go on a "Devil's Night" rampage, torching scores of homes and businesses.

 MUSEUMS: Detroit's major museums — including the *Detroit Historical Museum, Detroit Institute of Arts,* and *Children's Museum* — are described under *Special Places.*

Four of the majestic homes created by Detroit's automotive wealth are open for public inspection on the Auto Barons Tour: Henry Ford's Fairlane mansion (Dearborn; phone: 593-5590); his son Edsel's home (where Henry II grew up), the Edsel & Eleanor Ford House (Grosse Pointe Shores; phone: 884-3400); the ornate riverfront entertainment estate of Lawrence P. Fisher, now the Bhaktivedanta Cultural Center in Detroit (phone: 331-6740); and Meadow Brook Hall in Rochester, which cost Matilda Dodge Wilson $4 million to complete in 1929 (phone: 370-3140).

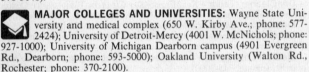 **MAJOR COLLEGES AND UNIVERSITIES:** Wayne State University and medical complex (650 W. Kirby Ave.; phone: 577-2424); University of Detroit-Mercy (4001 W. McNichols; phone: 927-1000); University of Michigan Dearborn campus (4901 Evergreen Rd., Dearborn; phone: 593-5000); Oakland University (Walton Rd., Rochester; phone: 370-2100).

 SPORTS AND FITNESS: Detroit wouldn't be Detroit without its top major league professional teams: the *Lions,* football; *Pistons,* basketball; *Red Wings,* hockey; and *Tigers,* baseball.

Baseball – Home base for the American League *Tigers* is *Tiger Stadium,* Michigan at Trumbull (phone: 962-4000).

Basketball – The 1990 NBA World Champion *Pistons* shoot hoops at the *Palace of Auburn Hills,* 2 Championship Dr. (phone: 377-0100).

Fishing – Fishing is pretty good in the Detroit River, especially around Belle Isle. There are hundreds of lakes in the area; we recommend Orchard Lake or Lake St. Clair.

Fitness Centers – The downtown *Westin* (phone: 568-8000), *Omni* (phone: 222-7700), and *Pontchartrain* (phone: 965-0200) hotels have spas for the exercise-minded. If you'd like to work up a sweat in the suburbs, the *Ritz-Carlton Dearborn* can't be beat (phone: 441-2000).

Football – The *Lions* play in the 80,000-seat, covered *Silverdome.* M-59 at Opdyke, Pontiac (phone: 335-4151).

Golf – Two of the better public courses are *Kensington Metropark* (2240 W. Buno Rd., Milford; phone: 685-1561) and *Pine Knob* (5580 Walden Clarkston; phone: 625-4430).

Hockey – *Red Wings* action is on the ice at *Joe Louis Arena,* Civic Center Dr. (phone: 567-6000).

Horse Racing – Thoroughbreds race at *Ladbroke DRC* (28001 Schoolcraft, Livonia; phone: 525-7300); *Hazel Park Harness Raceway* (1650 E. Ten Mile, Hazel Park; phone: 566-1595); *Northville Downs* (301 S. Center St., Northville; phone: 349-1000); *Windsor Raceway,* fall and winter harness racing (Hwy. 18, Windsor, Ont.; phone: 519-961-9545).

Jogging – The ideal spot is Belle Isle Park. To get there, run 2½ miles east along Jefferson and a half mile over the arched bridge; or take the Jefferson bus, then jog around the island's perimeter. A group called "People Who Run Downtown" meets every Tuesday at a downtown saloon before or after walking or jogging a route that varies each week (phone: 873-2725). An annual rite of fall is the *Detroit Free Press Mazda International Marathon* in Windsor and Detroit (phone: 222-6400).

Tennis – The City of Detroit operates several public courts. The best are at Palmer Park and Belle Isle. Call Parks and Recreation (phone: 224-1100) for schedule information.

THEATERS: Detroit's active theatrical life provides audiences with entertaining choices. There may be a Broadway-bound hit breaking in at the *Fisher Theater* year-round (Second at Grand Blvd.; phone: 872-1000). The *Birmingham Theater* (211 S. Woodward, Birmingham; phone: 644-3533) features straight drama and comedy, as does the *Meadow Brook Theatre* on the Oakland University campus. Its season runs from September to May (University Dr. east of I-75, Rochester; phone: 377-3300). Also very good are the *Hilberry Classic Theater* (4743 Cass; phone: 577-2972) and the *Attic Theater* (7339 Third Ave.; phone: 875-8284).

MUSIC: Just about any kind of music thrives in Detroit — symphonic, jazz, or soul. Detroit is the birthplace of Motown, the sound epitomized by the music of Stevie Wonder, the *Supremes,* and the *Temptations.* Today rockers like Bob Seger call Detroit home. Rock and soul concerts are played at the *Palace of Auburn Hills* — also the home of the *Pistons* (2 Championship Dr.; phone: 377-8200); *Cobo Arena* (Jefferson at Washington Blvd.; phone: 567-6000); *Joe Louis Arena* (Civic Center Dr.; phone: 567-6000); *Pontiac Silverdome* (M-59 at Opdyke, Pontiac; phone: 857-8000); *Masonic Auditorium* (500 Temple; phone: 832-2232); *Ford Auditorium* (Jefferson at Woodward; phone: 224-1055); *Royal Oak Music Theatre* (318 W. 4th St.; phone: 546-7610); and the *Fox Theatre* (2211 Woodward; phone: 567-6000). Maestro Neeme Järui leads the *Detroit Symphony,* whose concert season runs from September to May, at historic *Orchestra Hall,* which also offers other classical and dance and jazz concerts (3711 Woodward; phone: 833-3700). "*Brunch with Bach*" is presented Sundays at the *Detroit Institute of Arts* (5200 Woodward Ave.; phone: 833-2323). *Meadow Brook Music Festival* offers summer symphonies and pop and jazz artists (Oakland University campus; phone: 377-2010). Top-name entertainers perform at the outdoor *Pine Knob Music Theater* (Sashabaw, north of I-75, Clarkston; phone: 625-0511). The summer jazz series, *P'Jazz,* is held every Wednesday on the terrace of the *Pontchartrain* hotel (phone: 965-0200). *Music Hall Center for the Performing Arts* (phone: 963-7680) hosts traveling dance and music concerts. The *Masonic Auditorium* is the home of the *Michigan Opera Theater* (500 Temple; phone: 874-SING).

NIGHTCLUBS AND NIGHTLIFE: Dance to big band sounds at *Lido's on the Lake* (24026 E. Jefferson, St. Clair Shores; phone: 773-7770). *Midtown Café* (Birmingham; phone: 642-1133) and *Galligan's* (downtown; phone: 963-2098) are the places where singles mingle. At the *Soup Kitchen Saloon,* there's blues from Wednesdays through Sundays (1585 Franklin; phone: 259-1374). *Windsor's Top Hat* has lounge acts (73 University; phone: 963-3742). *Alexander's* has soothing decor and all that jazz daily except Sundays (4265 Woodward; phone: 831-2662); *Sully's* jazzes it up nightly (4758 Greenfield, Dearborn; phone: 846-5377); live jazz entertainment reigns at *Club Penta* (Fisher Bldg., W. Grand Blvd. at Second; phone: 972-3760); and *Club-Land* is a dance hall in an old Detroit moviehouse (2115 Woodward; phone: 961-5450). *Taboo* (1940 Woodbridge; phone: 567-6140) is Detroit's reigning New York–style disco. *Mark Ridley's Comedy Castle* presents national acts with local openers, and there's an open mike on Mondays (E. Fourth at Troy, Royal Oak; phone: 542-9900); bigger-name yuckmeisters such as Jay Leno, Paula Poundstone, and Paul Reiser (from TV's "My Two Dads") perform at *Chaplin's* (34244 Groesback, Fraser; phone: 792-1902).

BEST IN TOWN

CHECKING IN: By expensive, we mean between $90 and $130 for a double room. Our moderate selections are in the $65 to $90 range; inexpensive lodging (less than $65) is available at various chain hotels such as *Days Inn, Budgetel, Red Roof Inn,* and *Knights Inn.* For bed and breakfast accommodations, contact *Blanche House Inn* (506 Parkview; phone: 593-3366). All telephone numbers are in the 313 area code unless otherwise indicated.

Hyatt Regency Dearborn – Its 800 spacious, airy rooms overlook the landscaped park of the Ford World Headquarters in Dearborn. Round glass elevator pods, lit up like rockets, whisk guests to the upper floors. Nearby are *Fairlane Town Center Shopping Mall,* Greenfield Village, *Henry Ford Museum,* and a University of Michigan campus. Amenities include room service until midnight, concierge, 30 meeting rooms, secretarial services, A/V equipment, photocopiers, and express checkout. Michigan and Southfield Fwy., Dearborn (phone: 593-1234 or 800-233-1234; Fax: 313-3366). Expensive.

Omni International – Abutting the Millender Center of shops, restaurants, and apartments, this 25-floor hostelry with 258 spacious and imaginatively appointed rooms fills Detroit's need for more downtown hotel space. There's also an exercise room and health club, and restaurants. Other amenities include room service until midnight, concierge, 8 meeting rooms, secretarial services, A/V equipment, photocopiers, computers, and express checkout. 333 E. Jefferson, at the junction of RenCen and the Detroit-Windsor Tunnel (phone: 222-7700 or 800-843-6664; Fax: 313-222-6509). Expensive.

Radisson Pontchartrain – Detroiters call it "the Pontch." Built on the site of Ft. Pontchartrain, this landmark property has emerged from a $15-million face-lift of its public areas and 420 rooms. Heavy reds, greens, and velvets have given way to soothing mauves, jades, and plums and a decidedly residential feel. There also is a health club. *Top of the Pontch* is open for Sunday brunch. *Elaine's,* the fine dining room, serves continental fare; lighter meals can be taken in the *Garden Court,* with its greenhouse atmosphere. *P'jazz* concerts happen here every Wednesday during the summer. Amenities include 24-hour room service, concierge, 11 meeting rooms, secretarial services, A/V equipment, photocopiers, and express checkout. 2 Washington Blvd. (phone: 965-0200 or 800-333-3333; Fax: 313-965-9464). Expensive.

Ritz-Carlton Dearborn – From the outside, it looks like an imposing French château. All 11 floors, decorated in 18th- and 19th-century art and antiques, radiate unbridled warmth and elegance. Traditional decor defines the guestrooms, including those on the 2 executive floors. Fine dining is at *The Restaurant;* the *Grill and Bar* is a good steaks-and-chops place, with a wood-burning fireplace. There's also a full exercise room, including an indoor lap pool. Amenities include 24-hour room service, concierge, 7 meeting rooms, secretarial services, A/V equipment, photocopiers, computers, and express checkout. 300 Town Center Dr., across from Ford's headquarters, Dearborn (phone: 441-2000 or 800-241-3333; Fax: 313-441-2051). Expensive.

River Place Inn – This hostelry on the Detroit River occupies the one-time headquarters of a chemical company. There are 108 large guestrooms; top-floor luxury rooms; and a 3-level suite with Jacuzzi; and 2 restaurants including a British-inspired tavern. Its isolation and privacy make it popular with entertainers performing downtown. Complimentary shuttles to downtown, which is 10 minutes away. Other amenities include 24-hour room service, concierge, 4 meeting rooms, secretarial services, A/V equipment, photocopiers, and express checkout. 1000 Stroh River Place (phone: 259-2500 or 800-999-1466; Fax: 313-259-1248). Expensive.

Townsend – Here are 87 rooms (including executive and 2-room suites) in a surprisingly traditional building. A harpist holds court in the lobby and executive suites feature a formal dining room, living and sleeping area and 1½ baths. George Washington may never have slept here, but Paul McCartney, Michael Jackson, and Madonna have spent the night. Tasteful furnishings include marble bathrooms with brass fixtures; morning newspaper delivery; the *Rugby Grille* serves everything from beef to seafood. Use of local health club (transportation provided). Amenities include 24-hour room service, concierge, 6 meeting rooms, secretarial services, A/V equipment, photocopiers, and computers. 100 Townsend St., Birmingham (phone: 642-7900 or 800-548-4172; Fax: 313-645-9061; Telex: 798502). Expensive.

Troy Marriott – In Detroit's booming northern suburb, 350 rooms, including 4 suites, radiate from a skylight atrium. Convenient to K-Mart World Headquarters and the Pontiac *Silverdome. Stacy's Sea Grille* serves up delicious seafood. Amenities include room service until midnight, concierge, 16 meeting rooms, secretarial services, A/V equipment, photocopiers, and express checkout. 200 W. Big Beaver, east of I-75, Troy (phone: 680-9797; 800-777-4096; Fax: 313-680-9774). Expensive.

Westin Renaissance Center – This 1,400-room, 73-story round building has considerable drama in its public areas. The lobby takes up the first 8 stories, with fountains, trees, aerial walkways, specialty shops, and cocktail lounges. Three levels of bars and restaurants revolve. Unfortunately, the rooms are not nearly up to the standard of the public spaces. Amenities include 24-hour room service, concierge, 27 meeting rooms, and express checkout. At the east end of Hart Plaza, on Jefferson at St. Antoine (phone: 568-8000 or 800-228-3000; Fax: 313-568-8146; Telex: 755156). Expensive.

Radisson Plaza – A 392-room property, with indoor pool and health club, is at the doorstep of the office towers of Southfield. *Boquet's* restaurant and *Tango's* bar are popular. Amenities include 24-hour room service, concierge, 18 meeting rooms, secretarial services, photocopiers, computers, and express checkout. Prudential Town Center, Southfield (phone: 827-4000; 800-333-3333; Fax: 313-827-1364). Expensive to moderate.

Atchison House – Period antiques, lace panel curtains, and faux marble wall finishes adorn this lovely Italianate home in tree-shaded Northville, 35 minutes west of downtown Detroit. After a sip of sherry in the library, get cozy in an antique bed. All 23 guestrooms have private baths. Amenities include 1 meeting room and computers on request. 501 Dunlap, Northville (phone: 349-3340; Fax: 313-349-2905). Moderate.

Barclay Inn – Trendy suburban Birmingham draws its roots from this site, where John West Hunter, Birmingham's founder and first innkeeper, maintained a tavern and log cabins. The 128 rooms are divided between a 5-story tower where a Queen Anne style prevails and a motel-like building where washed pine furnishings and hunter green walls evoke a country flair. Tower hallways are a gallery of early Birmingham photos. Relax by the fireplace in the lobby with a complimentary breakfast of yogurt, fresh fruit, and scones; tea and cookies in the afternoon. Other amenities include 1 meeting room, A/V equipment, photocopiers, and computers. At Hunter and Maple Rds., Birmingham (phone: 646-7300 or 800-521-3509; Fax: 313-646-4501). Moderate.

Berkshire – A European-style operation, with amenities such as continental breakfast and newspapers delivered to each of the 109 rooms.

Amenities include 2 meeting rooms and photocopiers. 26111 Telegraph at 10½ Mile Rd., Southfield (phone: 356-4333 or 800-322-2339; Fax: 313-356-8544). Moderate.

Botsford Inn – The original 152-year-old stagecoach stop now has 75 spacious rooms and serves hearty American fare in the *Coach Room*. Amenities include a concierge desk, 3 meeting rooms, secretarial services, A/V equipment, photocopiers, and express checkout. 28000 Grand River Ave. at 8 Mile, Farmington Hills (phone: 474-4800; Fax: 313-474-9880). Moderate.

Dearborn Inn – On a 23-acre site, just a few hundred yards down the road from the historic *Henry Ford Museum* and Greenfield Village, and only a 20-minute journey from downtown Detroit, stands this Georgian-style mansion, built by Henry Ford in 1931 and later joined in 1937 by five reproductions of historic colonial homes and in 1960 by two motel-style wings. The charm and beauty of a bygone era have been re-created in the rooms and suites with early American-style furniture, hand-painted wallpaper, and old-fashioned hospitality. Guests can choose from 3 dining rooms, all of which offer tasty, albeit rather homogenous, American fare, and for those who wish to put history aside in favor of activity, there are tennis courts nestled between several of the colonial homes. Other amenities include valet, laundry, airport limousine, and baby-sitting service. Room service is available until midnight, and there are concierge and secretarial services, 12 meeting rooms, A/V equipment, and express checkout. 20301 Oakwood Blvd., Dearborn (phone: 271-2700 or 800-221-7236; Fax: 313-271-7464). Moderate.

Embassy Suites – "Rooms to roam" is the concept behind this all-suite hotel. Each of the 240 suites consists of a bedroom and parlor. Guests receive a free full breakfast cooked to order and complimentary cocktails. Indoor pool, sauna, whirlpool bath, and meeting rooms. Ideally situated if your business or pleasure is in the Southfield area. Amenities include room service until midnight, 9 meeting rooms, A/V equipment, photocopiers, and express checkout. 27754 Franklin Rd., Southfield (phone: 350-2000 or 800-EMBASSY; Fax: 313-350-2000, ext. 7033). Moderate.

Mayflower Bed & Breakfast – This cozy, family-owned inn offers full, complimentary breakfast to guests. Amenities include a concierge desk, 4 meeting rooms, and photocopiers. On the town square in quaint Plymouth. 827 Ann Arbor Trail (phone: 453-1620; Fax: 313-453-0775). Moderate.

Windsor Hilton – Just across the Detroit River and commanding a sparkling view of Detroit's skyline from all of its 307 rooms, it has mini-bars in every room and 2 executive floors with concierge service. Amenities include 24-hour room service, concierge, 20 meeting rooms, secretarial services, A/V equipment, photocopiers, and express checkout. 277 Riverside Dr. W. (phone: 962-3834, 800-HILTONS, or 519-973-5555; Fax: 519-973-1600; Telex: 06477948). Moderate.

EATING OUT: Detroit has a number of moderately priced restaurants serving everything from steaks, crêpes, and pheasant to natural foods and Coney Island hot dogs. And the nationalities represented include French, Middle Eastern, and Alsatian. Expect to pay $45 or more for two at expensive restaurants listed here; between $25 and $45, moderate; and under $20 in our inexpensive range. Prices do not include drinks, wine, or tips. All telephone numbers are in the 313 area code unless otherwise indicated.

Les Auteurs – Cozy bistro where pictures of great chefs and autographed menus make up the wall art. A constantly changing menu features vegetable sauces and other noteworthy items such as black bean cake with smoked chicken, tomato salsa, and sour cream. Inventive toppings of rock shrimp, fresh basil, and duck confit crown thin-crusted pizza. Chef Keith Famie's specials are listed on a blackboard above the open kitchen. Closed Sundays. No reservations. Major credit cards accepted. 222 Sherman Dr., Washington Square Plaza, Royal Oak (phone: 544-2887). Expensive.

Golden Mushroom – The menu changes with the mood of Milos Cihelka, one of the top chefs in town. Hope you're here when he's inclined to prepare his veal Oscar, calves' liver with green peppercorns, or roast rack of lamb persillade. Mushroom specials are displayed like jewelry at your table. Closed Sundays. Reservations advised. Major credit cards accepted. Ten Mile at Southfield (phone: 559-4230). Expensive.

Joe Muer's – Some people say this place serves the best seafood west of the Atlantic. Others say it's even better. Extravagant praise, no matter how sincere, can never substitute for firsthand experience, especially where seafood is concerned. Be prepared to wait in line, though. (A waiter will bring you a drink while you're standing in line.) Closed Sundays and holidays. No reservations. Major credit cards accepted. 2000 Gratiot (phone: 567-1088). Expensive.

The Lark – A charming country inn that features continental cooking. In fair weather, a mesquite barbecue is prepared outdoors. Closed Sundays and Mondays. Reservations necessary. Major credit cards accepted. 6430 Farmington Rd., W. Bloomfield (phone: 661-4466). Expensive.

1940 Chop House – Art Deco, supper-clubbish decor, and a menu to please any beef lover. Of 20 main courses, a dozen involve red meat — certified Angus beef from Kansas, succulent and seared over leaping flames by white-clad chefs in the exhibition kitchen. Open daily. Reservations advised. Major credit cards accepted. 1940 E. Jefferson near RenCen (phone: 567-1940). Expensive.

Opus One – One of the gems in a growing necklace of downtown-area restaurants, its finely tuned menu features breast of duck, roulades of salmon, sea bass in a subtle champagne sauce, salads that are arranged, not tossed, and inventive soups led by a crayfish bisque. The decor is classical, with tapestry-covered banquettes, varying shades of white, and etched glass. Open daily. Reservations advised. Major credit cards accepted. 565 E. Larned, Bricktown (phone: 961-7766). Expensive.

Rattlesnake – No, it is not on the menu. This lively, contemporary room, with wide windows looking out on the Detroit River, features highly acclaimed and ever-changing appetizers and sinful desserts. Main courses tend toward dishes like pickerel with spiced crust and green papaya, and pork with leeks, apples, and cider. Save room for the caloric ball of chocolate ice cream rolled in cocoa powder. Atmosphere can best be described as "theatrical." Main dining room and grill open daily for lunch and dinner. Reservations advised. Major credit cards accepted. 300 Stroh River Pl., foot of Joseph Campau (phone: 567-4400). Expensive.

Summit – Perched on the 72nd floor of the *Westin* and revolving to give diners a 360-degree view of Detroit, the river, and Canada. Char-grilled steaks, seafood, salads tossed right at your table, and a first-rate wine list. Open daily. Reservations advised. Major credit cards accepted. Renaissance Center (phone: 568-8000). Expensive.

Too Chez – Amid Pucci-like patterns, pictureless frames over the fireplace, and lamps made of magnum champagne bottles, diners are treated to chef Ed Janos's multi-ethnic menu. Try the assertively spiced orzo, a barley-like pasta cooked to a Thai spiciness in a purée of jalapeno peppers, and offered without charge to those who can eat the whole thing! Closed Sundays. Reservations advised. Major credit cards accepted. 27000 E. Sheraton, Novi (phone: 348-5555). Expensive.

Van Dyke Place – Detroit's most handsome dining spot in an old house decorated with walnut woods, marble fireplaces. The affordable menu features fixed-price dinners created by chef Patrick Dunn. Closed Sundays and Mondays. Reservations necessary. Major credit cards accepted. 649 Van Dyke Pl. (phone: 821-2620). Expensive.

Whitney – De rigueur dining in Detroit in an opulent jewel box of a midtown mansion, circa 1894. The owners insisted on American fare for an American house, and so the menu is replete with Michigan trout, Florida Keys shrimp, Maryland crabmeat, grilled or poached Maine lobster, California mussels, and farm-raised game. Save room for the chocolate taco: a raspberry mousse–filled walnut tuile (a super-thin cookie) topped with kiwi and grated white chocolate and napped in raspberry, lemon, and lime purée. Open daily. Reservations advised. Major credit cards accepted. Woodward at Canfield (phone: 832-5700). Expensive.

R.I.K.'s The Restaurant – A comfortable and unpretentious eatery, with open tile-trimmed kitchen and large arched windows, that offers contemporary Italian dishes including roasted peppers, imaginative pasta, and quail with orzo and chopped spinach. Open daily. Reservations advised. Major credit cards accepted. In the *Orchard Mall*, 6303 Orchard Lake Rd., West Bloomfield (phone: 855-9889). Expensive to moderate.

Cajun Quarter – Rich seafood gumbo, shrimp creole, blackened prime ribs, followed by sweet potato pecan pie. Sweetly Southern decor, too — pink walls, rosy table linens, and lace-paper doilies, with framed posters celebrating the food and music of New Orleans. And you only have to go as far south as Windsor, Canada (that's right, Canada is south of here), across the Detroit River. Open daily. Reservations advised. 3236 Sandwich St., Windsor, Ontario (phone: 519-258-8604). Moderate.

Charley's Crab – The seafood menu and the ragtime piano player are real crowd pleasers. Open daily. Reservations advised. Major credit cards accepted. 5498 Crooks Rd. at I-75, Troy (phone: 879-2060). Moderate.

La Cuisine – The chef of this mite-size French bistro whistles up heavenly three-mustard kidneys, tasty fish soup, and more from his kitchen smack in the middle of the room. Closed Sundays and Mondays. Reservations necessary. Most major credit cards accepted. 417 Pelissier, Windsor, Ontario (phone: 519-253-6432). Moderate.

Lelli's – Start with the best minestrone in town, served by black-tied waiters, in a romantic warren of dining rooms. Tenderloin, broiled red snapper, veal kidneys, and so on, but the tour de force is solid Italian fare. Closed Sundays. Reservations advised. Major credit cards accepted. 7618 Woodward (phone: 871-1590). Moderate.

One23 – A changing menu of contemporary American dishes is served in a skylit, bi-level dining room. Appetizers include mussels steamed in cider and rosemary, spicy green beans, and chicken sauté. Notable main dishes include plank-roasted Norwegian salmon and grilled spiced swordfish. Open daily. Reservations advised. Major credit cards accepted. 123 Kercheval, Grosse Pointe Farms (phone: 881-5700). Moderate.

Pontchartrain Wine Cellars – Where "cold duck" was invented, with a unique French/New York style. Closed Sundays. Reservations recommended. Major credit cards accepted. 234 W. Larned (phone: 963-1785). Moderate.

Très Vite – A bright, modern, urban café where the people watching is eclipsed only by snappy, contemporary cooking that features imported Italian pasta with interesting sauces and thin-crusted pizza topped with four different cheeses. Closed Sundays and Mondays. Reservations advised. Major credit cards accepted. 2203 Woodward in the *Fox Theatre* building, (phone: 964-4144). Moderate.

New Hellas – The hub of Detroit's 1-block Greek community is as Greek as Greek can be, with moussaka, calamari (squid), and baklava. Open daily until 3 AM. No reservations. Major credit cards accepted. 583 Monroe (phone: 961-5544). Inexpensive.

Wong's – Windsor's most popular Asian eatery got that way because of good food and the caring attention of owner Raymond Wong. Heaven, for lovers of this cuisine, is the luncheon buffet. Seafood — fresh abalone, mussels, and sea snails — is showing up more and more often on the voluminous menu. Choices range from Cantonese to Szechuan. Open daily. Reservations unnecessary. Major credit cards accepted. 1457 University Ave. W., Windsor (phone: 961-0212 or 519-252-8814). Inexpensive.

FT. LAUDERDALE

AT-A-GLANCE

SEEING THE CITY: The most commanding view is from the *Pier Top Lounge* of the 17-story *Pier 66* hotel (2301 SE 17th St.; phone: 525-6666). As the lounge makes one complete revolution each 66 minutes, a sweeping panorama unveils of the Atlantic Ocean and its beaches to the east, Port Everglades and Ft. Lauderdale International Airport to the south, the city's many canals, sprawling suburbs, and the Everglades to the west, and more canals and the Intracoastal Waterway to the north.

Boat Tours – Ft. Lauderdale is most easily and attractively seen by boat. One cruise vessel that plys the canals and river is the *Jungle Queen* at the Bahia Mar Yacht Basin (on Rte. A1A; phone: 462-5596). This boat, which offers 3-hour sightseeing tours twice daily, also takes riders down to Miami twice weekly for shopping sprees. From October to April, the *Carrie-B* (docked behind the *Pantry Pride* on Las Olas Blvd. and 5th St.; phone: 800-CARRIE-B), a new boat in the Ft. Lauderdale waters, runs 2-hour trips on the New River down to Port Everglades. *Blockbuster Cruises* (85 Las Olas Circle; phone: 524-2322) offers trips with a theme: sailing and shopping, murder mystery tours, starlight dining, and Broadway at sea.

Water taxis (1900 SE 15th St.; phone: 565-5507) are a popular way to travel from restaurant to hotel along the New River. Some taxis are open-air boats; the newer vessels are larger and air conditioned. A guided tour of the historic New River departs every Saturday morning at 10:30 from the *Guest Quarters* hotel (2670 E. Sunrise Blvd.; phone: 565-3800).

Tram Tours – Another wonderful way to sightsee is aboard the open-air *South Florida Trolley Tram Tours* (832 Military Rd.; phone: 426-3044), which winds its way through both the new and older sections of Ft. Lauderdale. Passengers can get on and off all day long or stay put for the 1½-hour tour. There's a trolley booth on Route A1A, south of Las Olas Boulevard.

SPECIAL PLACES: The best way to get around Ft. Lauderdale is by car.

Port Everglades – Because it has the deepest water of any port between Norfolk and New Orleans, Port Everglades attracts a lot of cargo and marine outfitting business, but it's also a popular port for luxury cruise ships, especially those that sail into the Caribbean, the Gulf of Mexico, or through the Panama Canal. Thanks to the remodeling of former warehouses and new construction, each of its eight passenger terminals boasts a different and bold design. Florida manatees and 120 species of tropical fish can be seen there. The port has one restaurant, *Burt & Jacks* (Berth 23, Port Everglades; phone: 522-5225), co-owned by Burt Reynolds. While there are no organized tours, visitors are free to roam around the port from 8 AM to 6 PM. State Rd. 84, east of US 1 (phone: 523-3404).

Discovery Center – An integral part of downtown Ft. Lauderdale's rejuvenated historic old town (formerly called Himmarshee Village) area, featuring 30 exhibitions in 4 buildings. The main facility is devoted to hands-on learning of things historic, artistic, and scientific; a second building houses the new Creativity Under the Sun exhibition. Tours are offered of the King-Cromartie House, a restored turn-of-the-century residence replete with antiques and set on the New River. (An entirely new Discovery Center is scheduled to be built across from the *Broward Center for the Performing Arts.* This complex will incorporate much of the old *Discovery Museum,* plus an IMAX theater.) Closed Mondays. Admission charge. 231 SW 2nd Ave. (phone: 462-4115).

Everglades Holiday Park – Savor what the famed ecological area is all about by bird watching, taking airboat rides and special tours, or by renting boats or RVs. There's also a campground. Open daily. No admission charge to the park. Admission charge for airboat rides. 21940 Griffin Rd. (phone: 434-8111).

Flamingo Gardens – This 60-acre botanical garden has exotic plants, a museum about the Everglades, orange groves, an island for flamingos, alligators, crocodiles, river otter, many birds of prey, and a tropical plant house. A guided tram tour takes visitors through a native hardwood hammock with stands of large, native oak, gumbo-limbo trees, and native fig trees, and through the groves and wetlands. An aviary, mangrove swamp area, and a pine forest are under construction. There's also a snack bar, a gift shop with nature books and crafts, and a fruit stall for purchasing and shipping citrus fruit. Open daily. Admisssion charge. 3750 Flamingo Rd., Davie (phone: 473-0010).

Sawgrass Mills Mall – This new 2.2 million-square-foot complex sports talking alligators and continuously running videos. It's billed as the world's largest outlet mall, with 200 specialty shops and 9 department stores. There's an *Ann Taylor* clearance center, a *Sears* outlet, *Marshalls,* and a *Joan & David* shoe outlet among the fray. Open daily. 12801 W. Sunrise Blvd.; Sunrise (phone: 800-FL-MILLS).

The Swap Shop – The largest flea market in the South, it is *the* place to find bargains on everything from electronic equipment to tomatoes. There also are concerts and a circus to distract you. Open daily. There are 2 locations (3291 W. Sunrise Blvd; phone: 791-SWAP) and 1000 N. State Rd., Margate (phone: 971-SWAP).

Butterfly World – A butterfly haven that allows visitors to walk among the fluttering creatures, which fly freely. These beauties are seen in all their stages of life, from larvae and pupae to cocoon and full adulthood. This 3-acre habitat has butterflies from all over the world, with a spectacular museum of mounted winged wonders. Open daily. Admission charge. 3600 W. Sample Rd., Coconut Creek (phone: 977-4400).

Atlantis the Water Kingdom – A 65-acre water theme park with a 6-story slide tower (which has 9 water slides), a 500,000 gallon wave pool, and a 9-hole golf course. One of the slides purports to be the fastest in all of Florida. Open March through October. Reservations necessary 48 hours in advance. Admission charge. 2700 Stirling Rd., Hollywood (phone: 926-1000).

Hugh Taylor Birch State Recreation Area – Just across the street from the beach is this lush, tropical park with 180 acres ideal for picnicking, playing ball, canoeing, biking, paddle boating, and hiking. Open daily. Admission charge. 3109 E. Sunrise Blvd. (phone: 564-4521).

John U. Lloyd Beach State Recreation Area – Many Ft. Lauderdale residents consider this to be *the* place for picnicking, swimming, fishing, canoeing, and other recreation. There are 244 acres of beach, dunes, mangrove swamp, and hammock (a raised area of dense tropical vegetation). Park rangers lead nature walks during winter months. Open daily. Admission charge. 6503 N. Ocean Dr., Dania (phone: 923-2833).

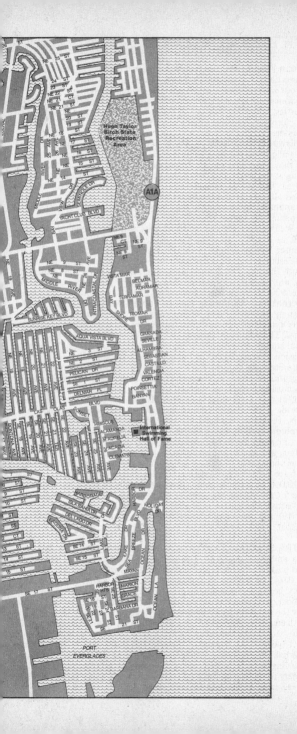

Ocean World – All the requisite aquatic creatures — sharks, alligators, sea lions, turtles, and dolphins — are featured here in continuous 2½-hour water shows. Visitors also may watch the dolphin show off in Davy Jones' Locker, a 3-story circular tank, or the more than 40 sharks, sea turtles, and other fish in the Shark Moat. Boat tours and deep-sea fishing also are available. Open daily. Admission charge. 1701 SE 17th St. (phone: 525-6611).

Hollywood Broadwalk – A 2.2-mile, 24-foot-wide concrete ocean promenade bordered by a bicycle path and lined with outdoor capes. Bikes may be rented on the Broadwalk, and there's often music and dancing at the bandstand. Since many French Canadians have settled in this area, half the promenade signs are in French. Lifeguard stations manned all year from 10 AM to 4 PM.

Stranahan House – One of the area's oldest museums — the restored 1913 home and Indian trading post of early settler Frank Stranahan. Open Wednesdays, Fridays, and Saturdays. Admission charge. 1 Stranahan Pl. at Las Olas Blvd. at New River Tunnel (phone: 524-4736).

Bonnet House – Built in the 1920s as a family retreat, this 36-acre private estate is one of the few remaining wildlife areas on the oceanfront in South Florida. The 2-story house and grounds have been preserved. Tours are offered. Open from May through November. Admission charge. 900 N. Birch Rd. (phone: 563-5393).

International Swimming Hall of Fame – Many of the world's top swimming and diving competitions are held here, but its newly refurbished Olympic-size pool with 10 lanes is open to the public when there's no meet. The adjoining museum, which also received a face-lift, houses unusual aquatic memorabilia from more than 100 countries. Open daily. Admission charge. 1 Hall of Fame Dr. (phone: 462-6536).

Topeekeegee Yugnee Park – With 40 acres, this is one of the area's larger parks. Visitors can enjoy all kinds of activities — swimming, boating, canoeing, picnicking, barbecuing, hiking, biking and water sliding. One of its two waterslides is another claimant to the title of the fastest in Florida. Open daily. Admission charge on weekends and holidays. 3300 N. Park Rd., just off I-95, Hollywood (phone: 985-1980).

Seminole Indian Reservation – The Native Village includes a museum, gift shop for Indian arts and crafts, demonstrations of alligator wrestling, and snake and turtle shows. Although commercial, for-profit bingo is not legal in Florida, it is here on the reservation. The bingo hall holds up to 1,400 people and often is full; winners have pocketed as much as $110,000 in a single game. Both open daily. There's an admission charge for the village and another for the bingo hall (this includes four bingo cards). The village is at 3551 N. State Rd. 7, Hollywood (phone: 961-4519); the bingo hall is at 4150 N. State Rd. 7, Hollywood (phone: 961-3220).

■ **EXTRA SPECIAL:** To experience fully the tropical beauty and laid-back ambience that is Ft. Lauderdale, drive east on Las Olas Boulevard past its chic boutiques and palm-lined streets. Continue through the Isles of Las Olas area, which is laced with canals and filled with fancy homes nestled among royal palm trees. Proceed on past the sailboat cove, where towering masts grope for the blue sky, and cruise over the small bridge to Route A1A, along the Atlantic Ocean. Turn north and drive along A1A and, at about 4 PM, stop at one of the hotel patio bars facing the ocean for a cocktail with the "end of the day" beach people. As it nears 5 o'clock, the beach will become nearly deserted, yet the ocean is filled with the multicolored sails of boats returning to safe harbor and cruise ships steaming out to distant corners of the world. Take off your shoes, walk along the sand at the water's edge — and let the images soak in.

SOURCES AND RESOURCES

 TOURIST INFORMATION: The Greater Ft. Lauderdale Convention & Visitors Bureau is in an easily accessible space downtown (200 East Las Olas Blvd.; Ft. Lauderdale, FL 33301). Stop in or call 765-4466 for information on accommodations, activities, attractions, sports, dining, shopping, touring, and special events. The Broward County Hotline (phone: 765-4468) is updated weekly and provides recorded information on dates, times, and additional sources of information about current events and visitor attractions. Contact the Florida state hotline (904-487-1462) for maps, calendars of events, health updates, and travel advisories.

Local Coverage – *Ft. Lauderdale News and Sun-Sentinel,* a morning daily, carries the following week's events in its Showtime section on Fridays.

Television Stations – WTVJ Channel 4–NBC; WPBS Channel 2–Public Television; WCIX Channel 6–CBS; WSVN Channel 7–FOX; WPLG Channel 10–ABC.

Radio Stations – AM: WNWS 790 (news/talk); WINZ 940 (news/talk). FM: WTMI 93.1 (classical music); WZTA 94.9 (classic rock); WFLC 97.3 (soft rock); WJQY 107 (easy listening); WLYF 101.5 (easy listening); WSHE 103.5 (album rock).

 TELEPHONE: The area code for Ft. Lauderdale is 305.
Sales Tax – The city sales tax is 6%, and there is a 3% hotel tax.

CLIMATE: With the exception of occasional days in late December through February, when it can be chilly, the area generally enjoys warm weather, with daily temperatures averaging 75F. Swimming is possible almost every day.

GETTING AROUND: Airport – Ft. Lauderdale/Hollywood International Airport is a 10- to 15-minute drive from downtown; taxi fare should run about $10 to $15. *Broward County Transit*'s No. 1 bus runs between the airport (pickup at terminals: Delta Dash pull-in area and next to terminal 3, both Lower Level) and the downtown bus terminal at NW 1st St. and 1st Ave.; fare is 75¢. *Airport Express* (phone: 527-8690) offers round-trip airport transfers to anywhere in Broward County from $6 to $13. Vans stop at the service desks outside the major terminals, beyond the baggage claim area.

Bus – *Broward County Transit* services most of the area. For information, call 357-8400.

Tri-Rail, a new double-decker train runs from Palm Beach south through Ft. Lauderdale to Miami, and connects with many other bus lines to deliver visitors to most of each city's major attractions. The train also travels to the airport in Broward (with a short shuttle ride), as well as to airports in Dade County and Palm Beach (phone: 800-TRI-RAIL).

Car Rental – Ft. Lauderdale is served by all the major national firms, two of which have their corporate headquarters in the city: *Alamo* (110 SE 6th St.; phone: 522-0000) and *General Rent A Car* (2741 N. 29th Ave., Hollywood; phone: 926-1700). There also are several regional agencies; check the yellow pages.

Taxi – While you can hail one on the street, it's best to pick one up at one of the major hotels and restaurants, or call for one. The major cab company is *Yellow Cab* (phone: 565-5400).

VITAL SERVICES: Audiovisual Equipment – *Central Audio Visual,* 7212 S. Andrews Ave. (phone: 522-3796).

Baby-sitting – *A-Baby Sitters* (phone: 564-4201) and *Lul-A-Bye Sitters Registry* (phone 565-1222).

Business Services – *Professional Office Service, Inc.,* 4520 NE 18th Ave. (phone: 772-6520).

Dry Cleaner/Tailor – *Cypress Creek Cleaners* (897 NE 62nd St.; phone: 771-1053); *Fashion Cleaners* (One W. Broward Blvd.; phone: 583-8225).

Limousine – *Airport Express* (phone: 527-8690); *Club Limousine Service* (phone: 522-0277).

Mechanics – *Cork's* (1041 NE 30th Court, Oakland Park; phone: 565-0630), for foreign cars; *Ocean Exxon* (3001 N. Ocean Blvd.; phone: 561-3120), for American makes.

Medical Emergency – *Holy Cross Hospital* (4725 N. Federal Hwy.; phone: 771-8000); *North Beach Hospital* (2835 N. Ocean Blvd.; phone: 568-1000).

Messenger Service – *All Florida Messenger & Delivery,* open 24 hours (622 NW 20th Ave.; phone: 973-3278); *Sunshine State Messenger Service,* also open 24 hours (6775 NW 15th Ave.; phone: 975-8100).

Pharmacy – *Cunningham Drugs,* Mondays through Fridays, 8 AM to 11 PM; weekends 8 AM to 9 PM, 3101 N. Ocean Blvd. (phone: 564-8424).

Photocopies – *Copyright,* 969 W. Commercial Blvd. (phone: 491-2679).

Post Office – A downtown location (330 SW 2nd St.; phone: 761-1172); there's also a main office (1900 W. Oakland Park Blvd.; phone: 527-2070).

Professional Photographers – *University Studios* (phone: 772-6644); *Woodbury & Associates* (phone: 977-9000).

Secretary/Stenographers – *Alpha Temporary Services,* 1001 W. Cypress Creek Rd. (phone: 776-6030).

Teleconference Facilities – *Marriott's Harbour Beach* (see *Best in Town,* below); *Ft. Lauderdale Marriott* (phone: 463-4000).

Typewriter Rental – *A & J Business Machines* (306 W. Oakland Park Blvd.; phone: 563-0438) has a 1-week minimum.

Western Union/Telex – Many offices located around town (phone: 800-325-6000).

 SPECIAL EVENTS: The *Seminole Indian Tribal Fair* normally is held during the first 2 weeks in February — it is a showcase of Indian crafts, entertainment, and food. During March, the *Florida Derby Festival* hits town: activities include a beauty pageant, the *Derby Ball* and parades, culminating in the race itself, Florida's richest thoroughbred race, with a purse of $500,000. The *Honda Golf Classic,* one of the biggest PGA tournaments, is held in late February or early March at *Eagle Trace;* it attracts the PGA's top players. In March, the annual *Las Olas Festival,* hosted by the *Museum of Art,* attracts 205 artists, who display their work in Bubier Park. Out in Davie, cowboys kick up their heels at the March *Orange Blossom Festival and Rodeo.* In April, seafood is king at the *Ft. Lauderdale Seafood Festival* at Bubier Park, where over 30 leading restaurants provide tastes of house specialties. Anglers get to test their skills in May during the *Pompano Beach Fishing Rodeo and Seafood Festival,* where more than $250,000 in cash is awarded for the largest catches. *Oktoberfest* falls (naturally) in October and features lots of German food, drink, and music. The *Ft. Lauderdale Boat Show,* the nation's largest in-water display of all types and sizes of watercraft, is held in November. Also in November is the *Promenade in the Park,* which showcases artwork, arts and crafts, food, and entertainment at Holiday Park, the *Greater Ft. Lauderdale Film Festival,* which shows more than 50 independent English language films, and the

Broward County Fair in Hallandale. The year's activities are capped by the month-long December *Sunshine Festival,* culminating in the Ft. Lauderdale and Pompano Beach boat parades, with processions of about 100 boats, festooned with colored lights and *Christmas* decorations, plying the Intracoastal Waterway, and a "Light up Lauderdale" laser show downtown.

 MUSEUMS: The *Discovery Center, International Swimming Hall of Fame,* and *Stranahan House* are described in *Special Places.* Other museums include the following:

Art and Culture Center of Hollywood – 1301 S. Ocean Dr., Hollywood (phone: 921-3275).

Ft. Lauderdale Historical Society – 219 SW 2nd Ave. (phone: 463-4431).

Museum of Art – 1 E. Las Olas Blvd. (phone: 525-5500).

Young at Art Children's Museum – 801 S. University Dr., Plantation (phone: 424-0085).

 MAJOR COLLEGES AND UNIVERSITIES: Broward Community College has three campuses (central, 3501 SW Davie Rd., Davie; north, 1000 Coconut Creek Blvd., Coconut Creek; and south, 7200 Hollywood Pines Blvd., Pembroke Pines; phone for all: 475-6500). The University Tower (220 SE 2nd Ave.; phone: 355-5200) is a relatively new facility shared by Broward Community College, Florida Atlantic University, and Florida International University.

 SPORTS: Baseball – Fans can watch spring training and preseason games during March. The New York *Yankees* play at *Ft. Lauderdale Stadium,* 5301 NW 12th Ave. (phone: 776-1921).

Diving – Diving is making a strong comeback in this part of Florida, due, in many ways, to the practice of sinking freighters and other large objects in the sea to create artificial reefs. While many people say these manmade reefs can't replace nature's delicate work, colorful fish certainly congregate around the sunken ships off the beaches in Pompano and Ft. Lauderdale. Numerous dive shops operate in the Ft. Lauderdale area; check the local yellow pages or go directly to the dive boats that depart from the Hillsboro inlet in the northern part of Ft. Lauderdale and from Port Everglades.

Fishing – There are lots of charter boat fishing operators at *Bahia Mar Yacht Basin,* across A1A from the beach (801 Seabreeze Blvd.; phone: 525-7174). Landlubbers fish 24 hours a day from the 1,080-foot Pompano Beach Fishing Pier (2 blocks north of E. Atlantic Blvd), and Anglin's Fishing Pier (2 Commercial Blvd.; phone: 491-9403).

Fitness Centers – *Nautilus Fitness Center,* with certified instructors, offers all the standard Nautilus exercise equipment plus saunas. 1624 N. Federal Hwy. (phone: 566-2222).

Golf – There are more than 76 golf courses in the area. Among those open to the public are *American Golfers Club* (3850 N. Federal Hwy.; phone: 564-8760); *Bonaventure* (200 Bonaventure Blvd.; phone: 389-2100); *Rolling Hills* (3501 W. Rolling Hills Circle, Davie; phone: 475-3010); and *Jacaranda* (9200 W. Broward Blvd., Plantation; phone: 472-5836).

Horse and Dog Racing – There's thoroughbred horse racing at *Gulfstream Park* (on US 1, Hallandale; phone: 454-7000), and harness racing at *Pompano Park Harness* (1800 SW 3rd St., Pompano Beach; phone: 972-2000). You can "go to the dogs" at *Hollywood Greyhound Track* (831 N. Federal Hwy., Hallandale; phone: 454-9400). Call for racing dates.

Horseback Riding – There are many stables in the area. Among the larger ones are *Bar-B Ranch* (4601 SW 128th Ave., Davie; phone: 434-6175); and *Stride-Rite Training Center* (5550 SW 73rd Ave., Davie;

phone: 587-2285). The county also operates stables at *Tradewinds Park* (3600 W. Sample Rd., Coconut Creek; phone: 968-3875).

Ice Skating – It seems incongruous in a tropical city, but Ft. Lauderdale residents love to ice skate. A favorite locale is *Sunrise Ice Skating Center,* 3363 Pine Island Rd. (phone: 741-2366).

Jai Alai – This Basque import is the area's most action-packed sport, with pari-mutuel betting adding spice. The season is year-round, except for 10 days in April and May. At *Dania Jai-Alai,* 301 E. Dania Beach Blvd., Dania (phone: 927-2841).

Nature Hikes – The Broward Parks & Recreation Department sponsors a different nature walk each Friday and Saturday, October through May. Call for a schedule (phone: 357-8101 or 536-PARK).

Rodeo – The "Wild West" can be found at the *Rodeo Arena* in Davie, where cowboys compete in bronco riding, calf roping, and other activities. Admission charge. 4201 SW 65th Way (phone: 797-1166).

Swimming – The most crowded beach is along "the Strip," from Sunrise Boulevard to Bahia Mar. The Galt Ocean Mile is quieter, with an older crowd. Perhaps the quietest strand is the stretch between Galt Ocean Mile and NE 22nd Street, and if you search you may find small pockets of peace in John U. Lloyd Beach State Recreation Area (6503 N. Ocean Dr.) in Dania or North Beach Park (3501 Ocean Dr.), in Hollywood. A favorite of locals is Deerfield Beach from the border of Broward and Palm Beach counties to SE 10th Street. This beach area has some of the best showers, and huge boulders in the water create coves.

Tennis – Most major hotels have tennis courts. There also are numerous courts open to the public. Among them are *Holiday Park Tennis Center* (701 NE 12th Ave.; phone: 761-5378); *Dillon Tennis Courts* (4091 NE 5th Ave., Oakland Park; phone: 561-6180); *Pompano Beach Tennis Center* (900 NE 18th Ave.; phone: 786-4115); and *George English Park* (110 Bayview Dr.; phone: 566-0622).

 THEATER: The area's major theaters are *Parker Playhouse* (707 NE 8th St.; phone: 764-0700), which stars name actors in Broadway productions, and *Sunrise Musical Theater* (5555 NW 95th Ave.; phone: 741-8600), which features Broadway musicals and individual stars in concert. The $50-million *Broward Center for the Performing Arts* (624 SW Second St.; phone: 522-5334) opened in early 1991, and features musicals, operas, drama, dance, and symphony concerts. Theatrical and cultural events also are staged at *War Memorial Auditorium* (800 NE 8th St.; phone: 761-5381) and *Bailey Hall* at Broward Community College (3501 SW Davie Rd.; phone: 475-6880). Playwright Vinnette Carol, who wrote *Your Arms Too Short to Box with God,* opened a theater in a converted church, the *Vinnette Carol Theater* (503 SE 6th St.; phone: 792-2424). For current offerings, check the newspapers.

MUSIC: The *Florida Philharmonic Orchestra* usually plays at the *Broward Center for the Performing Arts* (phone: 561-2997), which is also the site for performances of the *Opera Guild* (phone: 728-9700) during winter months; the latter often features visiting artists from New York and the *Greater Miami Opera Company. Gold Coast Symphony Orchestra* (1323 NE 17th St., Suite 668; phone: 522-0609) stages several major productions at various sites. Student and guest chamber, jazz, opera, and symphonic performances are staged throughout the year at Broward Community College (phone: 475-6884).

NIGHTCLUBS AND NIGHTLIFE: Most hotels and larger motels offer music and/or comedy acts nightly. The *Diplomat* (3515 S. Ocean Dr., Hollywood; phone: 457-8111) features well-known stars during the winter. Growing in popularity are comedy clubs such as *The Comic Strip* (1432 N. Federal Hwy.; phone: 565-8887), which showcases New York and Los Angeles comics. *Musician's Exchange*

Café (729 W. Sunrise Blvd.; phone: 764-1912) is the place to go for jazz, blues, and rock. For dance music, try *Riverwatch Lounge* in the *Marriott* (1881 SE 17th St.; phone: 463-4000); *Confetti's* (2660 E. Commercial Blvd.; phone: 776-4080); *Shakers* (4000 N. Federal Hwy.; phone: 565-3555); *Café 66* (2301 SE 17th St.; phone: 728-3500); *Squeeze* (401 S. Andrews Ave.; phone: 522-2068); *Yesterdays* (3001 E. Oakland Park; phone: 561-4400); and *Joseph's* (3200 Oakland Park; phone: 564-7788). There's dancing and dinner for an older crowd at *Stan's* (3300 E. Commercial Blvd.; phone: 772-3777).

BEST IN TOWN

CHECKING IN: Ft. Lauderdale's busiest period is winter, when reservations should be made as far in advance as possible. During high season a double room listed in the very expensive range could run $180 to $300 per night; a room in the expensive range will cost $150 to $180; in moderate, $95 to $145; and $90 to $115 in inexpensive. In the summer, occupancy (and room rates) drop. Note that a 3% tourist development tax and a 6% sales tax are added to all hotel bills. All telephone numbers are in the 305 area code unless otherwise indicated.

Marriott's Harbour Beach – The city's most expensive resort sits on 16 beachfront acres. Stunning public areas include 5 restaurants, 2 lounges, a pool bar, 5 tennis courts, and exercise facilities. There's also an 8,000-square-foot free-form pool with a waterfall and 50 cabanas. By contrast, the 624 rooms, including 35 suites are disappointing, especially in view of their price; however, suites are super. Free transport to the *Bonaventure Country Club* for golfers. Heavy meeting and convention clientele. Amenities include 24-hour room service, 29 meeting rooms, secretarial services, A/V equipment, and express checkout. 3030 Holiday Dr. (phone: 525-4000 or 800-228-9290; Fax: 305-766-6152; Telex: 6712056). Very expensive.

Palm-Aire – Ft. Lauderdale's original spa — over 1,500 acres with 191 rooms, 37 tennis courts, 4 championship and 1 executive golf courses, 2 racquetball courts, 1 squash court, and 4 dining rooms. Special 3- and 7-day packages may be booked at the spa, whose programs include beauty, health, relaxation, and total spa experiences. Other amenities include room service until 11 PM, concierge, 16 meeting rooms, A/V equipment, and photocopiers. 2501 Palm-Aire Dr. N., Pompano Beach (phone: 972-3300; 800-336-2108; Fax: 305-968-2744). Very expensive.

Bonaventure – One of the newer establishments in town, this lush 1,250-acre resort, complete with waterfalls, offers 2 golf courses, 5 swimming pools, 24 tennis courts, 5 racquetball courts, 1 squash court, horseback riding, indoor roller skating, and bowling. The spa has a full range of health and nutrition programs in separate facilities for men and women. There's even a resident nurse. The 500 rooms and suites have been built in 4-story structures, along with 4 restaurants and 2 lounges. Amenities include room service until 2 PM, 24 meeting rooms, concierge, secretarial services, A/V equipment, photocopiers, and express checkout. 250 Racquet Club Rd. (389-3300; 800-327-8090; Fax: 305-384-0563). Very expensive to expensive.

Pier 66 – Alongside the Intracoastal Waterway, this 17-story octagonal tower was the city's first luxury high-rise hotel. Multimillion-dollar expansion and refurbishing have greatly enhanced this property's appeal. There are 388 rooms, all with balconies, including 8 suites. Facilities include 2 tennis courts, 3 swimming pools with waterfalls, a 40-person Jacuzzi, a spa center, 7 restaurants, and lounges. A fleet of vessels of varying sizes is available for overnight lodging, business meetings, and sailing trips. The luxuriously furnished boats are moored at the hotel's own marina, and guests "rooming" aboard have full access to all the hotel's facilities. Amenities include 24-hour room service, concierge, 19 meeting rooms, secretarial services, A/V equipment, and photocopiers. 2301 SE 17th St. (phone: 525-6666 or 800-327-3796; Fax: 305-728-3541; Telex: 4416500). Expensive.

Embassy Suites – The chain's largest property in Florida offers 359 suites at prices equivalent to a standard hotel room. Facilities include a restaurant and lounge, pool, sauna, steamroom, and Jacuzzi. Breakfast and happy hour cocktails are free. Saluted by *Consumer Reports* magazine, the accommodations also feature a wet bar with refrigerator, microwave oven, coffeemaker, and dining table; complimentary beach shuttle service, free parking, and free 24-hour airport transportation are also available. Additional amenities include room service until 11 PM, 24 meeting rooms, A/V equipment, and express checkout. 1100 SE 17th St. Cswy. (phone: 527-2700; Fax: 305-760-7202). Expensive to moderate.

Ft. Lauderdale Marriott Norton – A 321-room property adjacent to an 8-acre aquatic preserve in the burgeoning Cypress Creek area, north of the city. Facilities include an outdoor pool, a health club with saunas and lockers, a gift shop, and parking for 450 cars. The 16-floor structure also features a restaurant, a lounge, a 5,082-square-foot Grand Ballroom, and 8 smaller meeting rooms. Room service is available until 11 PM, concierge, secretarial services, A/V equipment, and express checkout are also available. In the Cypress Park West business complex (phone: 771-0440 or 800-228-9290; Fax: 305-771-7519). Expensive to moderate.

Westin Cypress Creek – The Westin chain's first foray into Florida, this 15-story 293-room luxury property overlooks a 5-acre lagoon and features a health club, a large outdoor pool, and a lakeside pavilion; tennis and golf are a 5-minute drive away. There are 2 restaurants — one for fine dining, a second for casual food — and a bar complex. Two floors offer special concierge services. Other amenities include 24-hour room service, 20 meeting rooms, secretarial services, A/V equipment, and express checkout. 400 Corporate Dr., in the Radice Corporate Center (phone: 772-1331 or 800-228-3000; Fax: 305-491-9087; Telex: 5295590). Expensive to moderate.

Bahia Mar Resorting and Yachting Center – Nautically oriented hotel and marina, at the *Bahia Mar Yacht Basin* at the southern end of "the Strip," this resort and yachting center has 300 rooms, 2 restaurants, the *Schooners Lounge,* and 4 lighted tennis courts. Amenities include room service until 11 PM, concierge, 10 meeting rooms, secretarial services, photocopiers, and express checkout. 801 Seabreeze Blvd. (phone: 764-2233; Fax: 305-524-6912; Telex: 5145690). Moderate.

Ramada Beach – All of its 220 rooms have balconies that overlook either the Atlantic or the Galt Ocean Mile, and some are beautifully decorated in soothing rose and mauve tones. Its *Ocean Café* offers a mostly continental menu, and the lounge features live music and dancing on weekends during the winter months. On the beach, it has a heated pool, tiki bar (for hors d'oeuvres and cocktails), and offers sailboat rentals. Other amenities include room service until 2 PM, concierge, 4 meeting rooms, and photocopiers. 4060 Galt Ocean Dr. (phone: 565-6611 Fax: 305-564-7730). Moderate.

Sheraton Yankee – "Moored" directly on the beach, its unusual architecture makes this landmark look like a ship, and the nautical theme — which provides a warm, clubby feeling — is also carried through indoors, too. There are 505 rooms, 3 heated swimming pools, and a restaurant; 2 lounges provide entertainment. Amenities include room service until 11 PM, concierge, 1 meeting room, and express checkout. 1140 Seabreeze Blvd. (phone: 524-5551; Fax: 305-523-5376). Moderate.

Bahia Cabana – Small and unpretentious, nestled next door to the *Bahia*

Mar Yachting Center, it's informal and very Floridian. There are 116 rooms and apartments with kitchenettes; 3 swimming pools; a 36-person Jacuzzi; saunas; a dining room; and an outdoor patio bar/restaurant — a popular gathering spot for locals — that overlooks the marina. Amenities include a concierge desk, photocopiers, and express checkout. 3001 Harbor Dr. (phone: 524-1555; Fax: 305-764-5951). Inexpensive.

Riverside – Some 117 rooms in one of the city's oldest structures, it has a sedate ambience and cozy lobby, with chandeliers, armchairs, touches of wicker, and a fireplace. There is a restaurant, plus an intimate restaurant/lounge decorated with etched glass and a swimming pool amid tropical landscaping. Amenities include room service until 10:30 PM, 7 meeting rooms, limited secretarial services, A/V equipment, photocopiers, and express checkout. 620 E. Las Olas Blvd. (phone: 467-0671; Fax: 305-462-2148). Inexpensive.

EATING OUT: There are nearly 2,500 restaurants in Broward County. Many of these are well known, and most get quite crowded during the winter season, so it's always a good idea to make reservations. Casual dress is accepted in most restaurants, though a few of the more expensive ones prefer gentlemen to wear jackets. Expect to pay $60 or more for dinner for two in a restaurant listed in the expensive range; $35 to $50 in the moderate range; and $25 or less for inexpensive. Prices do not include wine, drinks, or tips. All telephone numbers are in the 305 area code unless otherwise indicated.

By Word of Mouth – This European café-cum-restaurant resides in the heart of the industrial district in downtown Ft. Lauderdale. The owner has not done any advertising since he opened the restaurant 10 years ago, but people hear about the abundant salads; sun-dried tomato, basil, garlic, and pesto pie; duckling soaked in apricot brandy; and the pastries. Closed Sunday through Tuesday for dinner. Reservations necessary. Major credit cards accepted. 3200 NE 12th Ave. (phone: 564-3663). Expensive.

Café Max – This trendy, California-style eatery is credited with pioneering nouvelle American cuisine in South Florida. The casual ambience and innovative menu are complemented by an excellent wine list — emphasizing California vintages — including many available by the glass. Open daily. Reservations advised. Major credit cards accepted. 2601 E. Atlantic Blvd., Pompano Beach (phone: 782-0606). Expensive.

Casa Vecchia – Fine Northern Italian food is served inside this lovely old house (built in the 1930s by the Ponds cold cream family), decorated with lots of plants, ceramics, and wrought iron. A courtyard adds to the charm, as does the view overlooking the Intracoastal Waterway. The restaurant can be reached by water taxi. Open daily. Reservations necessary. Major credit cards accepted. 209 N. Birch Rd. (phone: 463-7575). Expensive.

Down Under – The kitchen at this spot alongside the Intracoastal Waterway prepares an eclectic menu of French, American, and seafood dishes. The atmosphere and decor seem similarly haphazard — plants abound, the brick walls are lined with old posters, and the large rooms are filled with tables placed rather closely together. Open daily. Reservations advised. Major credit cards accepted. Can be reached by water taxi. 3000 E. Oakland Park Blvd. (phone: 564-6984). Expensive.

Mai-Kai – Large, rambling main room with Polynesian decor, it serves exotic drinks with its Polynesian, American and Cantonese food, and features Polynesian entertainment nightly (cover charge). The grounds boast lushly landscaped tropical vegetation. Open daily. Reservations advised. Major credit cards accepted. 3599 N. Federal Hwy. (phone: 563-3272). Expensive.

La Reserve – This French/continental dining place has a 2-tiered, beam-ceilinged, candlelit dining room with a sensational view of the Intracoastal Waterway. Adjoining it is the less formal bistro, *Ginger's,* available for private parties only. Open daily. Reservations advised. Major credit cards accepted. Oakland Park Blvd. at the Intracoastal Waterway (phone: 563-6644). Expensive.

Christine Lee's – It's a branch of the popular Miami Beach restaurant serving Szechuan, Mandarin, and Cantonese dishes. Surprisingly, it also has some of the best steaks in South Florida. Open daily. Reservations for three or more advised. Major credit cards accepted. 6191 Rock Island Rd., Tamarac (phone: 726-0430). Moderate.

La Ferme – Marie-Paul Terrier welcomes guests with a smile and closely watches over their well-being while husband Henri tends to the kitchen, whipping up traditional and nouvelle delights. The restaurant is small and cozy, with a French Provincial decor and lace tablecloths. Closed Mondays. Reservations advised. Major credit cards accepted. 1601 E. Sunrise Blvd. (phone: 764-0987). Moderate.

Pelican Pub – Downstairs, the casual, open-air restaurant serves food freshly plucked from the sea, presented on paper plates. Upstairs, the decor gets a bit fancier, but the food is just as fresh, with chicken and steaks added to the menu. Specialties of the house include a smoked fish spread and swordfish parmesan. Open daily. Reservations advised for parties of more than six people. Major credit cards accepted. 2635 N. Riverside Dr. (phone: 785-8550). Moderate.

Manero's – This family-run place is large, noisy, and crowded; the walls are adorned with autographed photos of many of the celebrities who have eaten here. Steaks and seafood are featured. Open daily. Reservations advised. Major credit cards accepted. 5681 W. Atlantic Blvd., Margate (phone: 971-4995). Moderate to inexpensive.

Big Louie's – A line of people are perpetually waiting at the doors of these cheery, casual eateries that serve solid Italian food and pizza with a choice of 21 toppings. Open daily. No reservations. Major credit cards accepted. Three locations: 1990 E. Sunrise Blvd. (phone: 467-1166), 2103 E. Commercial Blvd. (phone: 771-2288), and 3378 N. University Dr., Sunrise (phone: 572-2882). Inexpensive.

Cap's Place – Marilyn Monroe, John F. Kennedy, and Winston Churchill ate in this wonderful, old-Florida island restaurant. Founded in the 1920s, this old fishing shack was once the site for rum running, and held many a wild gambling party. Now it's strictly a seafood place. Diners are picked up by boat and taken for the 5-minute ride to Cap's Island off Lighthouse Point. Open daily. Reservations advised. Major credit cards accepted. 2765 NE 28th Court (phone: 941-0418). Inexpensive.

Carlos & Pepe's – The clientele at this popular hangout is eager and hungry; the setting is crowded but pleasant (light woods, green plants, and tile tables); and the menu is lighthearted Mexican (tacos, tortillas, and tostadas). Open daily. No reservations. Major credit cards accepted. 1302 SE 17th St. (phone: 467-7192). Inexpensive.

Ernie's Bar B Que – A local institution for 30 years, its ribs, chicken, pork, and beef are prepared in a special barbecue sauce. Try the fiery conch chowder. The decor has a rustic Key West style. Open daily. Reservations unnecessary. Major credit cards accepted. 1843 S. Federal Hwy. (phone: 523-8636). Inexpensive.

Papa Leone's – Papa Leone plays the organ every night at this small (only 18 candlelit booths and tables), old-fashioned, family-run, neighborhood Italian eatery. Closed Mondays. Reservations unnecessary. Only American Express accepted. Virtually invisible, it's next to *Publix* grocery store, at 2735 N. Dixie Hwy., Wilton Manors (phone: 566-1911). Inexpensive.

FT. WORTH

$$\boxed{\text{AT-A-GLANCE}}$$

SEEING THE CITY: Panoramic views of Ft. Worth turn up serendipitously over a hill or around a corner, but the best one is from the esplanade from the east entrance of the *Amon G. Carter Museum.* Get a king-size scoop of homemade ice cream from the *Front Porch* (across Camp Bowie Blvd.), then enjoy the rolling lawn of the *Kimbell Art Museum* as well as a spectacular view of downtown.

SPECIAL PLACES: One of the nicest things about Ft. Worth is that sightseeing is easy, with most of the city's attractions divided into the Stockyards District, the Cultural District, and the Downtown District. All the major museums are within walking distance of one another; the stockyard area is best seen on foot; and the botanical gardens and zoo are across the street from each other.

STOCKYARDS DISTRICT

Ft. Worth Stockyards – Wear your jeans to prowl around the north side of Cowtown. If any one area best embodies the city's latest promotional slogan, "Texas the way you want it to be," the Ft. Worth Stockyards is it. After years of neglect, this isolated enclave of history is in the full throes of a renaissance, its historical integrity preserved with National Historic District status. Once the center of Ft. Worth's cattle culture, the Stockyards area developed after the Civil War as a rest stop for cowboys driving their herds north to Kansas on the Chisholm Trail. Its turn-of-the-century heyday saw millions of cattle processed through the Armour and Swift meat-packing plants. Disaster struck the Stockyards many times during the first half of this century, but the district of saloons, hotels, and western outfitters that grew up in the area thrived until the packing industry's demise. In the 1960s and early 1970s, the area deteriorated into a near-slum.

A sluggish economy saved what was left after the meat packing plants were demolished; revived interest in things Texas — and considerable financial investment — brought the area back. Today, residents and tourists alike come to soak up the district's still authentic western flavor.

To get to the Stockyards, take Main Street north from downtown 2½ miles to the corner of North Main and Exchange Avenue. Park your car anywhere you can; everything is within walking distance. The Stockyards area includes the restored *Cowtown Coliseum,* which hosts live rodeo performances every Saturday night from April through September; the Livestock Exchange Building, housing, amidst the offices, several fine arts galleries; and dozens of stores where you can pick up a Stetson, a pair of lizard-skin boots, or a bridle for your bronco. Any Monday at 10 AM you can do some shopping at a cattle auction or people watch at the *Cattlecar Café,* a tiny place where the real Texas traders and other livestock folk just lean back and put their boots up while waiting for the café's home cooking. But most people come to the Stockyards to party: On weekend nights, the district is crowded with denim-clad folks meandering from one watering hole or country-and-western dance hall to the next. There are about 2 dozen nightspots from which

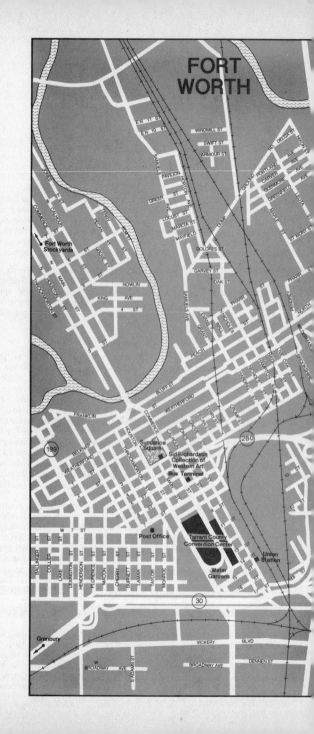

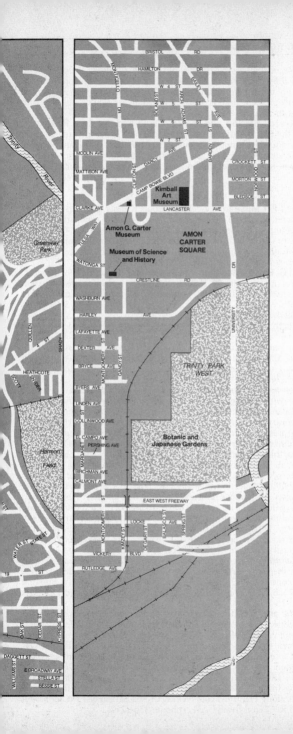

to choose, including the century-old *White Elephant Saloon,* not to mention *Billy Bob's Texas,* the "World's Largest Honky-Tonk," which literally holds several thousand people. And if you happen to get hungry, there's no problem finding a meal — so long as you're satisfied with Tex-Mex or steaks.

Stockyards Station and the Ft. Worth and Western Railroad – New at the Stockyards is this 19th-century–style depot ready to greet visitors riding the Tarantula Company's restored Ft. Worth and Western cars. The steam excursion train links the Stockyards District with the downtown 8th Avenue station and the historic Southside District (phone: 763-8297).

CULTURAL DISTRICT

Kimbell Art Museum – Architect Louis Kahn's last work (1973), it is considered one of the most important and beautiful small art museums in the country. Its permanent collection dates from pre-Columbian America to the early 20th century, with an emphasis on European art. Closed Mondays. Admission charge for special exhibits; otherwise free. 3333 Camp Bowie Blvd. (phone: 332-8451).

Amon G. Carter Museum – Best known for its paintings by Frederic Remington and Charles M. Russell, the museum also features an extensive collection of photography, sculpture, and paintings by many other 20th-century artists. Closed Mondays. No admission charge. 3501 Camp Bowie Blvd. (phone: 738-1933).

Ft. Worth Museum of Science and History – It includes the Hall of Medical Science, Man and His Possessions, and Computer Technology. Also part of the museum is the *Omni Theater,* a remarkable computerized 70mm multi-image projection and sound system — the largest of its kind in the world. Closed Mondays. Admission charge. 1501 Montgomery (phone: 732-1631).

Cattleman's Museum – Life-size scenes of life down on the ranch, complete with talking figures, make an unusual introduction to this newly expanded museum. Particular emphasis is on the historic and contemporary battles of ranchers and lawmen against cattle rustlers; the museum presents a complete picture of the life of a cattleman. Open daily. Admission charge. 1301 W. 7th St. (phone: 332-7064).

Ft. Worth Zoological Park – Part of Forest Park, with picnic tables and a small amusement park, the Ft. Worth zoo contains America's largest herpetarium, a lovely rain forest with rare and exotic birds, and an outstanding collection of mammals. New at the zoo is the exhibit called Texas!, with native flora and fauna such as longhorns, buffalo, and havalina (wild boars), as well as a barnyard area of domestic animals and a blacksmithy. Adjacent to the zoo is the longest miniature train ride in the country. It's a leisurely and scenic 5-mile trip covering the length of several parks. Open daily. Admission charge. 2727 Zoological Park Dr., off University Dr. (phone: 870-7050).

Log Cabin Village – Seven cabins from the 1850s have been restored and furnished with period antiques. Costumed "villagers" demonstrate typical pioneer crafts — weaving, quilting, etc. Open daily. Admission charge. 2100 Log Cabin Village La. near the zoo and botanical gardens (phone: 926-5881).

Botanic and Japanese Gardens – The Botanic Gardens encompass several acres for exploring and studying hundreds of different plant species and varieties of roses. Within are the Japanese Gardens, tranquil arrangements of trees and shrubs, bridges, pools, waterfalls, and teahouses. Closed Mondays. Admission charge for Japanese Gardens only. 3220 Botanic Garden Dr., off University Dr. (phone: 870-7686).

Thistle Hill – Built in 1903, this elegant old house is the last one remaining from the days when the rich cattle barons built their flashy mansions along Pennsylvania Avenue. Closed Saturdays. No admission charge. 1509 Pennsylvania Ave. (phone: 336-1212).

DOWNTOWN DISTRICT

Sundance Square – This charming square is formed by Commerce, Houston, 2nd, and 4th Streets downtown and is bordered by an interesting collection of boutiques, craft shops, restaurants, and art galleries. Main Street, which bisects the square, is notable for its red brick sidewalks, period streetlamps, and turn-of-the-century buildings. The well-known *Sid Richardson Collection of Western Art* (309 Main Street; phone: 332-6554), features more than 50 paintings by the western artists Frederic Remington and Charles M. Russell. *Fire Station No. 1*, (201-203 Commerce; phone: 732-1631) houses a museum showcasing the city's history with the exhibition "150 Years of Ft. Worth." Open Tuesdays through Fridays, 10 AM to 5 PM, Saturdays 11 AM to 6 PM, and Sundays 1 to 5 PM. No admission charge.

Water Gardens – The opening scenes of the science fiction movie *Logan's Run* were shot at this water wonderland, where some 19,000 gallons of water pour over pebbled concrete sculptures every minute. Open daily. No admission charge. South of the Convention Center between Commerce and Houston Sts.

Old Tyme Postique – The downtown post office has opened this permanent exhibit, which houses a collection of memorabilia, information, and merchandise (for sale) for philatelists. The building, built in the 1930s, has an interior of marble, bronze, and gold leaf. Open Monday through Friday from 10 AM to 6 PM. No admission charge. Lancaster and Houston Sts. (phone: 336-3018).

ARLINGTON

Six Flags Over Texas – About 30 minutes east of Ft. Worth, in Arlington, this famous amusement park features more than 95 rides, shows, and other attractions. Open daily June through August; weekends only in spring and fall. Admission charge. I-30 at Hwy. 360 (phone: 640-8900).

Wet 'n Wild – A great place to spend a blistering Texas day. Attractions include a body-surfing pool, water slides, inner tube rapids, and a children's play area. Open daily, June through August; weekends only, May and September. Admission charge. Across I-30 from *Arlington Stadium* at 1800 E. Lamar Blvd., Arlington (phone: 265-3013).

■ **EXTRA SPECIAL:** Ft. Worth may be typically Texan, but you really haven't seen the state until you've visited at least one of its small towns. Granbury, an easy 30 minutes southwest of Ft. Worth on Highway 377, has admittedly taken advantage of its charming eccentricities and attracted some tourist trade. But the appeal of the agricultural community has only been heightened. A limestone courthouse dominates a town square ringed with crafts shops, ice cream parlors, and restaurants, all in 19th-century buildings. In fact, Granbury is so full of Old West buildings that it's entered in the National Register of Historic Places. The *Granbury Opera House* (on the Square on Pearl St.) features drama, comedy, and music. (Reservations are advised: PO Box 297, Granbury, TX 76048; phone: 573-9191.) Surrounding Granbury is a manmade lake of the same name with beautiful camping and picnicking facilities; the Chamber of Commerce (phone: 573-1622) may provide further information. For a country-style buffet, try the local favorite, the *Nutt House* restaurant. "Country-style buffet" means you go through a line, cafeteria style, pick yerself up some grits (pronounced *gree*-uts), red beans, and maybe some ham, and set down at a long table. The *Nutt House,* like many establishments in Granbury, is closed Mondays (121 E. Bridge St.; phone: 573-9362).

For those fascinated by safaris, the *Fossil Rim Wildlife Center,* about a 1½-hour drive south from the Dallas/Ft. Worth Airport in Glen Rose, offers a safari camp where you can watch wildebeest, water buck, and the endangered oryx and addax. Nearly 30 other species are in residence here, including giraffes, zebras, gazelles, gemsbok, kudus, and antelope. For information, contact the *Foothills Safari Camp* (phone: 897-3398).

SOURCES AND RESOURCES

 TOURIST INFORMATION: For brochures, maps, and general information, contact the Ft. Worth Convention and Visitors Bureau (100 E. 15th St., Suite 400, Ft. Worth, TX 76102; phone: 336-8791). They may also be picked up at the *Sid Richardson Collection of Western Art* (309 Main St. Sundance Sq.; phone: 332-6554); the *Ft. Worth Museum of Science and History* (1501 Montgomery; phone: 732-1631); Fire Station No. 1, downtown (201-203 Commerce; phone: 732-1631), as well as at the visitors' information center (123 E. Exchange in the Stockyards District; phone: 682-4741); for information on special events, call 800-433-5747. Contact the Texas state hotline (800-8888-TEX) for maps, calendars of events, health updates, and travel advisories.

Local Coverage – The *Ft. Worth Star-Telegram* is published mornings, evenings, and Sundays. See Friday's issue for entertainment and restaurant listings.

Television Stations – KDFW Channel 4–CBS; KXAS Channel 5–NBC; WFAA Channel 8–ABC; KERA Channel 13–PBS.

Radio Stations – AM: KRLD 1080 (talk/news); KVIL 1150 (adult contemporary music); KESS 1270 (Spanish); KAAM 1310 (adult contemporary). FM: KSCS 96.3 (country); KEGL 97.1 (top 40); KLUV 98.7 (oldies); WRR 101.1 (classical).

Food – *Texas Monthly* magazine, publishes reviews of Ft. Worth's best restaurants. *D* magazine (as in Dallas) also lists many Ft. Worth restaurants.

 TELEPHONE: The area code for Ft. Worth is 817.

Sales Tax – There is a 7.5% sales tax on all purchases except food. Hotel room tax is 13%.

 CLIMATE: The official word is that Ft. Worth's average daily temperature during the spring is 65F; summer, 84F; fall, 66F; and winter, 47F. But don't let rumor or averages fool you: You can plan on summer scorchers and some pretty nippy winter days, sometimes (though rarely) with a touch of ice and snow.

GETTING AROUND: Airport – Dallas/Ft. Worth Airport (or D/FW), the country's largest, is usually about a 40-minute drive from downtown Ft. Worth; cab fare should run about $37. Bus transportation between D/FW, the downtown hotels, and the downtown *Greyhound* bus terminal is provided by the city-owned Airporter Bus Service and Park & Ride Terminal (phone: 334-0092); fare is $7; and *Supershuttle* (phone: 329-2000); fare is $18 from downtown ($11 from downtown hotels), door-to-door, and reservations are required.

Bus – *T Charter Service* provides bus service throughout Ft. Worth; it's free in the downtown area (pick up a pass when you board the bus). To check on routes and schedules, call 870-6200.

Car Rental – The major national agencies are represented.

Taxi – The best way to get a cab is to phone for one. Try *Yellow Cab* (phone: 534-5555).

Tours – For bus tours, call *Gray Line* (phone: 870-1112) June through August or *Trailblazing Tours* (phone: 624-8687) year-round for groups of 8 or more. There also are horse-drawn carriage tours of the downtown area, year-round, so let a Clydesdale show you the sights (phone: 870-1464). Take a tour of the Stockyards with Charlie McCafferty, longtime resident and founder of the North Ft. Worth Historical Society. Charlie knows how it was back in the Stockyards' heydey, and his 45-minute strolling tours are highly entertaining. Wednesdays at 11 AM. Admission for adults is $3; for children under 12, $1. Contact Charlie at the North Ft. Worth Historical Society (131 East Exchange Ave., Suites 111-114; phone: 625-5082). The Ft. Worth Convention and Visitors' Bureau also suggests two walking tours, the Western Heritage Trail, and the Museum and Garden Tour. Maps are available at their office in Water Garden Place (100 E. 15th St., Suite 400; phone: 336-8791; 800-433-5747).

Train – *Amtrak* serves Ft. Worth along two passenger routes, from Chicago via Houston and from St. Louis via San Antonio. 15th St. and Jones (phone: 332-2931).

VITAL SERVICES: Audiovisual Equipment – *AV Presentations* (phone: 589-2159).

Baby-sitting – *Luv-N-Care,* 4451 Boatclub Rd. (phone: 237-5683).

Business Services – *Kelly Services* (phone: 332-7807).

Dry Cleaner/Tailor – *Gunn's Quality Cleaners* (1001 W. Magnolia; phone: 927-8859); *Tom James Custom Clothiers* (1320 Lake St.; phone: 335-2186).

Limousine – *Candle Ridge* (phone: 294-8747); *Ft. Worth Limousine* (phone: 870-9783).

Mechanics – American cars: *Pep Boys* (4621 E. Lancaster; phone: 534-2227). For foreign cars: *Overseas Motors* (2824 White Settlement Rd.; phone: 332-4181).

Medical Emergency – *Harris Methodist Ft. Worth* (1301 Pennsylvania; phone: 882-3333); *Harris Methodist HEB* (1600 Hospital Pkwy.; phone: 685-4611).

Messenger Services – *Countdown Inc.* (213 One Tandy Center; phone: 263-4590; also 3007 S. Carrier Pkwy.; phone: 263-0381).

National/International Courier – *Federal Express* (phone: 800-238-5355); *DHL Worldwide Express,* in Dallas (phone: 214-471-1999).

Pharmacy – *Eckerd's Drugs,* open 24 hours, 2414 Jacksboro Hwy., in the *Town & Country Shopping Center* (phone: 626-8255).

Photocopies – *Alphagraphics,* 777 Main St., Suite C-90 (phone: 870-2660).

Post Office – Downtown station, 251 W. Lancaster Ave. (phone: 332-3260).

Professional Photographer – *Gittings Portraiture,* 6100 Camp Bowie Blvd., balcony level (phone: 732-2501).

Secretary/Stenographer – *Kelly Services* (phone: 332-7807).

Teleconference Facilities – *Ft. Worth Hilton, Hyatt Regency DFW* (see *Best in Town,* below).

Translator – *Berlitz* (phone: 335-4393).

Typewriter Rental – *Abel Office Machines* (phone: 926-2235).

Western Union/Telex – Many locations around the city (phone: 800-325-6000).

SPECIAL EVENTS: Any child who spent any time at all in the Ft. Worth Independent School District can attest that the highlight of the year comes during the 12 days in late January or early February when the *Southwestern Exposition and Livestock Show and Rodeo* comes to town. Schoolchildren have 1 day designated as *Stock Show Day* and receive free tickets, but the world's oldest indoor rodeo, midway, and stock show is fun for anyone. Contact the *Southwestern Exposition,* PO Box 150, Ft. Worth, TX 76101 (phone: 877-2420) for more information.

Ft. Worth's restored Main Street becomes a marketplace of food, arts and crafts, and entertainment during the *Main Street Ft. Worth Arts Festival* in April. Other special events are *Mayfest,* an annual celebration with food, music, and games on the banks of the Trinity River the first weekend in May; the *Chisholm Trail Roundup,* a 3-day festival of street dances, chili cook-offs, and gunfights staged in the Stockyards area the second weekend in June (phone: 625-7005); the *Shakespeare in the Park* series at the *Trinity Park Playhouse* in late June, when spectators bring picnic suppers and enjoy the free performances; *Pioneer Days,* a 3-day western winging held in September in the Stockyards (phone: 626-7921); *Oktoberfest,* the first weekend in October; and the *National Cutting Horse Futurity,* held the first week in December at *Will Rogers Coliseum* (phone: 335-0734), one of the premier western events in the country, with some of the highest monetary awards anywhere outside the racetrack.

 MUSEUMS: The *Amon G. Carter Museum,* the *Kimbell Art Museum,* the *Museum of Science and History,* the *Cattleman's Museum,* the *Old Tyme Postique,* and the *Sid Richardson Collection* are described under *Special Places.* Also of interest is the *Modern Art Museum of Ft. Worth* (1309 Montgomery; phone: 738-9215), a collection of 20th-century sculpture and paintings.

 MAJOR COLLEGES AND UNIVERSITIES: Texas Christian University has especially distinguished drama and music departments and offers performances year-round in *Ed Landreth Auditorium* (2800 S University Dr.; phone: 921-7000). Texas Wesleyan College is also in Ft. Worth (3101 E. Rosedale; phone: 534-0251), as is the Southwestern Baptist Theological Seminary, the largest Baptist seminary in the world (2001 W. Seminary Dr.; phone: 923-1921).

 SPORTS AND FITNESS: Baseball – The Texas *Rangers* play at *Arlington Stadium,* 1700 Copeland Rd., Arlington (phone: 273-5100).

Bicycling – The Department of Parks (2222 W. Rosedale; phone: 870-6000) provides maps of scenic biking trails that circle Forest and Trinity parks.

Fitness Centers – The coed *YMCA* downtown provides a pool, track, and all courts (512 Lamar; phone: 332-3281). Another fitness center is *Bally's President's* (6833 Green Oaks Rd.; phone: 738-8910).

Golf – There are 11 country clubs and 9 municipal courses in Ft. Worth. The *Colonial National Invitation* is held in May at *Colonial Country Club,* 3735 Country Club Circle (phone: 927-4200).

Jogging – Maps of the jogging trails around Forest and Trinity parks are available from the Department of Parks (2222 W. Rosedale; phone: 870-6000). The Trinity trail winds 8.2 miles through 3 city parks.

Tennis – The *Mary Potishman Lard Tennis Center* near Texas Christian University offers 22 outdoor and 5 indoor courts to the public. Open 9 AM to 10:30 PM Mondays through Thursdays, 9 AM to 9 PM Fridays year-round, except *Christmas Day.* Fee for 1½ hours of play outdoors is $2 before 5 PM, $2.50 after 5 and on weekends; $18 per indoor court. Reservation fee is $1 (3609 Bellaire; phone: 921-7960). The *McLeland Tennis Center* in southern Ft. Worth has 14 outdoor courts, 2 indoor courts, and 1 practice court, all lighted. Open from 9 AM to 9 PM Mondays through Fridays and from 9 AM to 6PM Saturdays and Sundays, November through February; 9 AM to 9 PM Fridays through Sundays, March through October. The fee for 1½ hours of play outdoors is $1.75 per person before 5 PM, $2.25 per person after 5 PM; $16 per indoor court. Reservation fee is $1. Instruction available (1600 W. Seminary Dr.; phone: 921-5134).

 THEATER: *Casa Mañana* ("the house of tomorrow") is probably Ft. Worth's best-known playhouse (3101 W. Lancaster at University Dr.; phone: 332-6221). A theater-in-the-round, it mounts a variety of dramatic productions. Others include the *William E. Scott Theater* (3505 Lancaster; phone: 738-6509); the *Circle Theater* (227 W. Magnolia; phone: 921-3040); *Stage West* (821 W. Vickery; phone: 332-6238); and the *Hip Pocket Theater*, which performs outdoors (1620 Las Vegas Trail N.; phone: 927-2833). The *Caravan of Dreams Theater* stages an eclectic repertoire of drama, dance, and film (312 Houston; phone: 877-3000). The *Jubilee Theater* (3114 E. Rosedale; phone: 535-0168) performs a cross-section of African-American theater on Fridays and Saturdays. The *Ft. Worth Ballet* gives performances at the *Ft. Worth/Tarrant County Convention Center* (1111 Houston; phone: 763-0207). The city makes much of the fact that it sustains a major ballet company, something that rival city Dallas has not been able to do.

MUSIC: The *Ft. Worth Opera* and the *Ft. Worth Symphony Orchestra* both perform at the *Ft. Worth/Tarrant County Convention Center* (1111 Houston; phone: 763-0207). The *Convention Center* also is the site of the *Van Cliburn International Piano Competition,* held every 4 years (May 22 to June 6, 1993, is the next competition). For general information, contact the Van Cliburn Foundation (phone: 738-6536). For ticket information, contact *Central Tickets* (phone: 214-988-7250), *Ticketron* (phone: 640-7500), or *Rainbow-Ticket Master* (phone: 787-1500). Ft. Worth's Grammy-winning *Texas Boys Choir* was once called the best in the world by composer Igor Stravinsky; concerts are given in a variety of places (phone: 738-5420). The *Schola Cantorum of Texas* is a 50-member chorus that also performs in different venues (phone: 737-5788). For information on the company's program schedule, call 738-6533 or the Ft. Worth Convention & Visitors Bureau (phone: 800-433-5747).

NIGHTCLUBS AND NIGHTLIFE: The *White Elephant Saloon* (106 E. Exchange; phone: 624-8273) is a popular watering hole that features barbecue, buffalo sweat margaritas, and country music; it's in the historic Stockyards area. *Billy Bob's Texas* (2520 Rodeo Plaza; phone: 624-7117) is a huge honky-tonk place with 42 bar stations, an arena for bull riding, and live entertainment Tuesday through Saturday evenings. Nationally known entertainers are featured on weekends. Also worth visiting in the Stockyards is the *Longhorn Saloon* (121 W. Exchange; phone: 624-4242). *Caravan of Dreams* (downtown at 312 Houston; phone: 877-3000), an avant-garde performing arts center, has a jazz and blues nightclub and a theater. It is the preeminent jazz club in the region, and its *Rooftop Garden and Grotto Bar* is the city's most unusual. The *Hop* (2905 W. Berry; phone: 923-7281) has a mixed bag of jazz, rock, and good food, and *J & J Blues Bar* (937 Woodward; phone: 870-2337) offers the best in regional blues.

BEST IN TOWN

CHECKING IN: At the hotels listed below, expect to pay $95 or more for a double room for a night in the expensive category, $50 to $90 for moderate; we found no establishments that met our standards in the inexpensive category. While Ft. Worth has no shortage of traditional hotels, another alternative, *Bed and Breakfast Texas-Style,* offers lodging and either continental or Texas-style breakfasts in private homes in the city's most desirable neighborhoods. Rates vary from budget to comfortable to deluxe, $20 to $60. (Write to *Ruth Wilson,* 4224 W. Red Bird La., Dallas 75237; phone: 214-298-5433). All telephone numbers are in the 817 area code unless otherwise indicated.

Hyatt Regency D/FW – Big, convenient, and busy, this attractive property in the airport complex is a good place to stay if you're planning to divide your time between Dallas and Ft. Worth — or to visit the amusement parks between the two cities. It has 1,390 rooms, 4 restaurants, access to 36 holes of golf, 10 racquetball courts, 7 tennis courts, and an outdoor swimming pool. Ask about summer family rates. There are 80 meeting rooms from which to choose for business functions, and other amenities include concierge and secretarial services, A/V equipment, photocopiers, and computers. Express checkout is a boon. D/FW Airport (phone: 214-453-1234 or 800-233-1234; Fax: 214-456-8668). Expensive.

Stockyards – Dating to cowboy boomtown days, this historic 3-story hotel reopened in 1984 after extensive renovations. Much is made of the time Bonnie and Clyde put up here. Smack in the middle of the Stockyards District, it's a popular choice among tourists since the *White Elephant Saloon,* numerous restaurants, and other attractions are all within walking distance. Check out the saddles that serve as barstools in the *Booger Red Saloon.* Three meeting rooms are available, also A/V equipment, photocopiers, secretarial services, and express checkout. 109 E. Exchange (phone: 625-6427; 800-423-8471 outside of Texas; Fax: 817-624-2571). Expensive.

Worthington – This lovely European-style hostelry is downtown, across the street from Sundance Square. There are 508 rooms, including 70 luxury suites, 2 outdoor tennis courts, indoor pools, fully equipped athletic club, 24-hour private dining service, and a fine restaurant called *Reflections.* Among the business services on call are A/V equipment, computers, a secretarial staff, and a concierge desk. Express checkout is another plus. 200 Main St. (phone: 870-1000, 800-772-5977 in Texas, 800-433-5677, in other states; Fax: 817-332-5679). Expensive.

Ft. Worth Hilton – It's right in the heart of downtown, near the *Convention Center,* and overlooks the Water Gardens. There are 435 rooms in twin high-rise towers, an indoor pool, and the *Greenery* restaurant. Around-the-clock room service available; 22 meeting rooms, A/V equipment, photocopiers, and express checkout. 1701 Commerce St. (phone: 335-7000 or 800-HILTONS; Fax: 817-335-3333). Expensive to moderate.

Hyatt Regency – A renovated old Texas hotel built in 1921, it has retained more of the city's original western flavor than any of the others. Three restaurants. Fourteen meeting rooms, A/V equipment, photocopiers, a concierge desk, and express checkout are available. One block north of the *Convention Center,* 815 Main St. (phone: 870-1234 or 800-233-1234;Fax: 870-1234, ext. 1555). Expensive to moderate.

Miss Molly's – For those who clamor for accommodations set in the Old West, this 8-room hostelry has a colorful past which includes its history as a bordello and then a boarding house. Each room is cleverly decorated and named in conjunction with its decor (the "Cowboy Room," the "Cattleman's Room"). There's the *Star Café* downstairs (see *Eating Out*), where you can get bountiful bites. 109½ W. Exchange (phone: 626-1522). Expensive to moderate.

Green Oaks Inn – A bit out of the way but conveniently across the street from an 18-hole golf course, this older hotel has 282 rooms, 2 swimming pools, and a winding brook that falls to a fish-stocked pond. Photocopiers and A/V equipment are at guests' disposal. Other business benefits are secretarial services and 16 meeting rooms. 6901 W. Freeway at State Hwy. 183 (phone: 738-7311; 800-772-2341 in Texas; 800-433-2174 elsewhere; Fax: 817-377-1308). Moderate.

Plaza Ft. Worth – Smack in the middle of a historic center alongside the Chisholm Trail, with a small historic cemetery in the parking lot, this hotel has been freshly redecorated in light, bright colors, and a spacious lobby has been added. Concierge and secretarial services, as well as A/V equipment, photocopiers, computers and 12 meeting rooms round out the amenities here. 2000 Beach St. (phone: 534-4801; 800-233-1441; Fax: 817-534-4801). Moderate.

Courtyard by Marriott – Located on the west side of town, this motel is part of Marriott's new idea to offer lodgings with a more homey atmosphere. Rooms are grouped around a central courtyard. Two meeting rooms are available, as is express checkout. 3150 Riverfront Dr. (phone: 335-1300; 800-321-2211; Fax; 817-336-6926). Moderate to inexpensive.

Days Inn Downtown – Conveniently located downtown, this 272-room hotel is redecorated in a Southwestern palette of rosy tan, beige, and white. Amenities found here are A/V equipment and 9 meeting rooms. 600 Commerce St. (phone: 332-6900; 800-325-2525; Fax: 214-332-6048). Moderate to inexpensive.

EATING OUT: In a city once called Cowtown, you'd naturally expect good beef, but natives pride themselves more on ferreting out superior Tex-Mex and chicken-fried steaks. Both are available in Ft. Worth, along with some better-than-average continental fare and a surprising assortment of ethnic eats. Expect to spend more than $50 for a meal for two in a restaurant listed as expensive; $30 to $50 for moderate; and less than $30 for inexpensive. Prices do not include drinks, wine, or tips. All telephone numbers are in the 817 area code unless otherwise indicated.

Carriage House – This longtime favorite of the Ft. Worth establishment combines a continental menu with a comfortably elegant decor. Open daily; Saturdays for dinner only. Reservations advised. Major credit cards accepted. 5136 Camp Bowie (phone: 732-2873). Expensive to moderate.

Tours – A mainstay of local continental cooking, it has moved from a shopping center into its own building, offering atmosphere more compatible with its food and a sparkling view of downtown from its upstairs bar. Open daily; brunch only on Sundays. Reservations advised. Major credit cards accepted. 3500 W. 7th St. (phone: 870-1672). Expensive to moderate.

Balcony – Dressy and romantic, it overlooks Camp Bowie Boulevard and serves continental cooking. Broiled lamb chops and lobster are the specialties. Closed Sundays. Reservations advised. Major credit cards accepted. 6100 Camp Bowie (phone: 731-3719). Moderate.

Saint-Émilion – Creatively prepared meats, fish, and fowl are featured at this country French bistro. Two- and four-course prix fixe meals are offered for dinner. Extensive wine selection. Closed Sundays. Reservations advised. Major credit cards accepted. 3617 W. 7th (phone: 737-2781). Moderate.

Star Café – This 2-story eatery, which is beneath *Miss Molly's* hotel, earned its fame in the Stockyards District with its chicken-fried steak smothered in gravy, along with its dense, delicious cottage fries. Closed Sundays. Reservations unnecessary. Some credit cards accepted. 111 W. Exchange (phone: 624-8701). Moderate.

Angelo's – Hearty barbecue with the finest of trimmings is all this Ft. Worth institution offers. But what more could one ask for than an icy beer and a paper plate heaped with tangy ribs (served after 4:30 PM only) or barbecued beef plus a scoop of potato salad, coleslaw, a pickle, some onion sauce, and bread. Closed Sundays. No reservations or credit cards accepted. 2533 White Settlement (phone: 332-0357). Inexpensive.

Benito's – The best place in Ft. Worth to sample a variety of Mexican dishes. The standard Tex-Mex combos are available, but the more authentic Mexican fare — *menudo* (tripe), homemade tamales, and chiles rellenos — hasn't been tamed for American taste buds. They're delicious. Open daily. Reservations advised. Major credit cards accepted, but no checks. 1450 W. Magnolia (phone: 332-8633). Inexpensive.

Carshon's – Split-pea soup and corned beef on rye aren't exactly the stuff of Ft. Worth's fame, but this spruced-up deli is touted statewide. Closed Mondays. No reservations or credit cards accepted. 3133 Cleburne Rd. (phone: 923-1907). Inexpensive.

Cattleman's Steak House – The portraits of blue-ribbon beef that grace the walls in this Stockyard stronghold are a little-needed reminder of each T-bone's heritage. Many of the cowboy customers are urban, but look carefully, since old-timers still like to splurge here. Open daily, dinner only Saturdays and Sundays. No reservations on Saturdays. Major credit cards accepted. 2458 N. Main (phone: 624-3945). Inexpensive.

Edelweiss – German food and an oompah band are the draws at this popular family place. The sauerbraten comes highly recommended. Closed Sundays and Mondays. No reservations. Major credit cards accepted. 3801A Southwest Blvd. (phone: 738-5934). Inexpensive.

Hedary's – Everything is fresh and flavorful at this Lebanese eatery, where customers may watch their dinners being prepared. Try the chicken with lemon, veal sausages, grilled lamb chops, and fresh pita bread. Closed Mondays. No reservations. All credit cards accepted. 3308 Fairfield in *Ridglea Center* (phone: 731-6961). Inexpensive.

Joe T. Garcia's – This famous North Ft. Worth dive serves Tex-Mex food family-style to crowds that arrive fully expecting to line up out front for more than an hour on weekends. The wait is eased (and the food improved) by a couple of stout, delicious frozen margaritas. Open daily. Reservations advised. No credit cards accepted. 2201 N. Commerce (phone: 626-4356). Inexpensive.

Juanita's – A tony Tex-Mex place in Sundance Square. One of the owners is June Jenkins, wife of Ft. Worth–raised author Dan Jenkins, and the place is named for his *Baja Oklahoma* heroine. Try a margarita and nachos at the bar before settling down to a Southwest meal. Classier than most Tex-Mex eateries. Open daily. Reservations advised. All credit cards accepted. 115 W. 2nd (phone: 335-1777). Inexpensive.

Massey's – No theory of evolution has been more often debated here than the origin of its chicken-fried steak. To date, it's an unsurpassed delight — tender beef and a crunchy crust topped with thick and creamy gravy. Open daily. Reservations advised. Major credit cards accepted. 1805 8th Ave. (phone: 924-8242). Inexpensive.

Paris Coffee Shop – Home-style cooking like grits 'n' gravy, homemade soup, and cornbread muffins are definitely de rigueur here. The clanging of dishes and table chatter provide the background music. Closed Sundays. Reservations unnecessary. Major credit cards accepted. 704 W. Magnolia Ave. (phone: 335-2041). Inexpensive.

Szechuan – If you hanker for Chinese food in Cowtown, this is the place — heaping portions, helpful service, and an extensive menu. The house specialties are heartily recommended. Open daily. Reservations advised. Major credit cards accepted. 5712 Locke (phone: 738-7300). Inexpensive.

HARTFORD

AT-A-GLANCE

SEEING THE CITY: The top of the Travelers' Tower offers the best view of the city, 527 feet above the madding crowd in the Travelers' Insurance Company building. There are 72 steps to climb before reaching the very top. Open weekdays from May until the last Friday in October, 10:30 AM to 3 PM. No admission charge, but call in advance. 700 Main St. (phone: 277-0111).

SPECIAL PLACES: Walking through Hartford can be highly enjoyable, especially since the city combines classical and contemporary architectural styles. Capitol Hill is a good place to begin.

Connecticut State Capitol – Guided tours daily, 9:15 AM to 1:15 PM. Open weekdays, 9 AM to 5 PM. 165 Capital Ave. (phone: 240-0222).

Baldwin Museum of Connecticut History – Three and a half centuries of Connecticut's heritage are packed into this museum with exhibitions tracing the growth of major manufacturers in the state. Most notable is the collection of Colt firearms. Closed Sundays and holidays. 231 Capitol Ave. (phone: 566-3056).

The Pavilion – This Palladian-style building at State House Square is the newest downtown landmark. Housing a warren of trendy shops and fast-food restaurants, its softly lit pink, rose, and aquamarine interior encourages strolling (phone: 241-0100).

Bushnell Park – Bushnell is to Hartford what Central Park is to New York. In fact, Frederick Law Olmsted, who designed Central Park, also worked on Bushnell. The Knox Foundation, a private charitable organization, has donated an antique carousel with Wurlitzer band organ to the Bushnell Park Carousel Society, a nonprofit corporation that sells annual $20 individual and $150 family memberships to support the carousel; members can then ride free. Non-members need only spend a quarter for a ride. Private parties can have the carousel to themselves for $150 per hour. Open mid-May to August, 11 AM to 5 PM; mid-March through mid-May and September, weekends only. Closed Mondays. Bounded by Trinity, Elm, Ford, Wells, and Jewell Sts. (phone: 728-3089).

Butler-McCook Homestead – Within strolling distance of downtown's modern hotels and corporate headquarters is the oldest private home in the city, built in 1792. It has an extensive collection of 18th-century furnishings, vintage American paintings, and a fascinating collection of Japanese armor and other curios. Open Tuesdays, Thursdays, and Sundays, noon to 4 PM, May 15 to October 15. Special Victorian *Christmas* display in December. Adults, $2; children under 17, $1. 396 Main St. (phone: 522-1806).

Center Church – In 1636, the Reverend Thomas Hooker of Cambridge, Massachusetts, led a group of 100 men, women, and children and 160 head of cattle to Hartford, at the time a Dutch trading post. On the site of the Old State House, in 1638, he preached a revolutionary doctrine: "The foundation of authority is laid, first, in the free consent of the people." Hooker's ideas were incorporated into Connecticut's royal charter in 1662, and the minister became known as the founding father

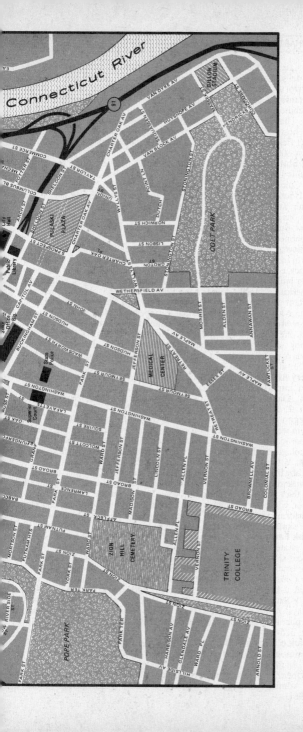

of the state. Outside the church is a cemetery, in use from 1640 to 1803. Open daily. First Church of Christ on Main St. (phone: 249-5631).

Hartford Civic Center – This "city within a city" has about 50 shops, 13 restaurants, the 407-room *Hartford-Sheraton* hotel, plus 79,000 feet of exhibition space for the *Boat Show,* the *Auto Show,* and other large events. The Hartford *Whalers* hockey team plays in a 16,200-seat arena, which hosts other sporting events and concerts in the off-season. For concert ticket information call 727-8080; for *Whalers'* tickets call 728-3366 or 800-WHALERS.

Old State House – At one time an active meeting house for states-men, this Federal building designed by Charles Bulfinch is now a mu-seum. Colonial furniture and other artifacts date to 1796, when the Old State House was built. Now privately owned, the museum also has a souvenir and craft shop. There also is information here about local attractions and special events. Open Mondays through Saturdays, 10 AM to 5 PM; Sundays, noon to 5 PM. No admission charge. Main and State Sts. (phone: 522-6766).

Wadsworth Atheneum – The oldest continually operating public art museum in the country, with eclectic collections of paintings, sculpture, ceramics, costumes, textiles, furniture, and firearms housed in five con-necting buildings, the *Atheneum* features one of the largest collections of American art in the country, with more than 1,000 objects. There are important works by the American artists Church, Sargent, Whistler, and Wyeth. Also represented are such European masters as Rembrandt, Picasso, Monet, and Miró. In the Stanley Gallery, the "No Kidding" section offers special exhibits for children. In the Matrix Galleries are changing shows of contemporary art. Admission charge except on Thursdays and Saturdays. Closed Mondays. Open 11 AM to 5 PM. 600 Main St. at Atheneum Sq. N. (phone: 278-2670).

Avery Art Memorial – Attached to the *Wadsworth Atheneum, Avery* has an important independent collection, including works by Rem-brandt, Daumier, Picasso, Goya, Cézanne, Whistler, Sargent, and Wyeth. 25 Atheneum Sq. N. (phone: 278-2670).

Morgan Memorial – Also part of the *Wadsworth Atheneum,* this museum was started by J. P. Morgan, a Hartford citizen who left home to make his fortune. Fine collections of Middle Eastern and Oriental archaeological relics, Meissen china, and firearms, especially those made by Colt, a local enterprise. 590 Main St. (phone: 278-2670).

Elizabeth Park – Another of Hartford's "firsts" is this botanical wonderland, the first municipally owned rose garden in the country. More than 900 varieties and 14,000 other plants are displayed every summer, while the greenhouses stay open year-round. Open-air concerts are performed in summer. In winter, the park's pond is a popular place for ice skating. Prospect and Asylum Sts.

Nook Farm – A 19th-century writers' community, the former Nook Farm estate contains several authors' houses. Mark Twain lived in a riverboat-shaped brick, stone, and wood 3-story house with brown and orange brick patternwork. Harriet Beecher Stowe, the author of *Uncle Tom's Cabin,* lived only slightly less elaborately in a brick house next door. A 2-hour tour takes you through both houses. Open Tuesdays through Saturdays, 9:30 AM to 4 PM; Sundays, noon to 4 PM. Closed Mondays. Admission charge. Mark Twain Memorial (351 Farmington Ave.; phone: 525-9317); Harriet Beecher Stowe House (77 Forest St.; phone: 525-9317).

Science Museum of Connecticut – Visitors to this progressive sci-ence museum are greeted by a life-size replica of a 60-foot sperm whale. Includes an aquarium, hands-on tank, mini-zoo, and planetar-ium. Open Tuesdays through Saturdays 10 AM to 5 PM, Sundays 1 to 5 PM. Admission charge. 950 Trout Brook Dr., West Hartford (phone: 236-2961).

■ **EXTRA SPECIAL:** For a diverting day trip that can include outdoor activities, visits to historic houses, and shopping for antiques, head west on Route 44. This scenic road travels over thickly forested Avon Mountain to the Farmington Valley. There, a plethora of natural attractions awaits, including canoeing, fishing, and exploring the hiking and cross-country ski trails in the Talcott Mountain State Park and Connecticut Blue Trail System. Heublein Tower, the area's key landmark, offers a panorama of five states to those who hike the 1½-mile trail starting at Route 185. Lining Route 44 are Avon, Farmington, and Simsbury — cozy New England hamlets with numerous crafts boutiques and antiques shops. Farmington's *Hillstead Museum* is an imposing neo-colonial mansion designed by architect Stanford White. The superb collection of early French Impressionists amassed by original owner Alfred Pope and the exquisite furnishings make it worth a visit (671 Farmington Ave.; phone: 677-9064). In Simsbury, dine in 19th-century elegance at the recently restored *Simsbury House,* which also has 35 guest rooms, each individually decorated with antique furnishings (731 Hopmeadow St.; phone: 658-7658). Farther south on Route 202 is Litchfield, a charming village of huge white mansions set around a classic New England village green. Just outside Litchfield, 3½ miles south on Route 63, is *White Flower Farm,* a perennial nursery that is a magnet for countless New England gardeners. Even for non-gardeners, it is worth a visit to see the display gardens, which peak in May and June; in July and August, a greenhouse full of magnificent English tuberous begonias share the limelight with fields of flowering shrubs and perennials. Open April through October. For more information, call 567-8789.

SOURCES AND RESOURCES

 TOURIST INFORMATION: The Greater Hartford Convention and Visitors Bureau (1 Civic Center Plaza, Hartford, CT 06103; phone: 728-6789 or 522-6766) distributes brochures, maps, and general tourist information. Contact the Connecticut state hotline (203-258-4290) for maps, calendars of events, health updates, and travel advisories.

Local Coverage – The *Hartford Courant* (the oldest daily newspaper in continuous circulation), morning daily; *Connecticut Magazine,* monthly; the *Hartford Advocate,* a free alternative news and entertainment publication, weekly; and *Hartford Monthly,* the city magazine, featuring events, restaurant, and entertainment listings.

Television Stations – WFSB Channel 3–CBS; WTNH Channel 8–ABC; CPTV Channel 24–PBS; WVIT Channel 30–NBC; WTIC–Channel 61, Fox.

Radio Stations – AM: WTIC 1080 (news); WPOP 1410 (news). FM: WDRC 102.9 (solid gold); WIOF 104 (adult contemporary music); WPKT 90.5 (public radio); WTIC 96 (rock).

 TELEPHONE: The area code for Hartford is 203.
Sales Tax – The city sales tax is 8%.

 CLIMATE: Hartford's humidity is a problem in the summer, when temperatures reach the 80s and 90s; winters are snowy, generally in the 20s and 30s; spring and fall are delightful.

GETTING AROUND: Airport – Bradley International Airport is about 12 miles from downtown Hartford. The drive usually takes 20 to 30 minutes, and taxi fare should run about $21. *Airport*

Taxi (phone: 627-3210) provides hourly bus service to the downtown area from 6:30 AM to 11 PM Sunday through Friday, 6:30 AM to 8 PM on Saturdays, for $8.

Bus – The state-owned *Connecticut Transit Company* operates the municipal bus service. 53 Vernon St. (phone: 525-9181).

Car Rental – All major national firms are represented at the airport as well as downtown.

Taxi – It's very difficult to get a cab in the street. Pick one up during the day in front of the *Sheraton Hartford* and *Summit* hotels, or call *Yellow Cab* (phone: 666-6666.)

Train – *Amtrak* trains to New York and Boston pull in and out of the Union Station Transportation Center (phone: 525-4580), which also serves *Greyhound Bus.* Outside the station is a colorful mural by Connecticut artist Gleve Grey.

VITAL SERVICES: Audiovisual Equipment – *Rockwell Communications* (phone: 528-9091); *Audio-Visual Rental Center* (phone: 296-4500).

Baby-sitting – *Care-At-Home,* 243 Farmington Ave. (phone: 728-1165).

Business Services – *Headquarters Companies* is at 1 Corporate Center (phone: 247-8300) and City Place (phone: 275-6500).

Dry Cleaner/Tailor – *M-Z Cleaners,* Cityplace, 14 Haynes St. (phone: 527-8511).

Limousine – *Center Limousine* (phone: 522-2442).

Mechanic – *Hartford Auto Repairs,* 12 S. Whitney St. (phone: 232-2236).

Medical Emergency – *Hartford Hospital,* 80 Seymour St. (phone: 524-2525).

Messenger Services – *ERI Courier,* 92 Walnut St. (phone: 728-0600).

National/International Courier – *Federal Express* (800-838-5355); *DHL Worldwide Courier Express* (phone: 627-7000).

Pharmacy – *Arthur Drug Stores,* 7:30 AM to 10 PM, 190 Farmington Ave. and Sigourney St. (phone: 527-1164).

Photocopies – *PIP,* 21 High St. (phone: 278-1561); *Pronto Printer,* 97 Pratt St. (phone: 247-5715).

Post Office – The central office is located at 185 Ann St. (phone: 249-6560).

Professional Photographer – *Capital Studios* (phone: 525-1175); *Creative Images* (phone: 528-7818).

Secretary/Stenographer – *H.Q. Headquarters Company,* word processing, telex, facsimile, conference rooms (phone: 249-7000).

Teleconference Facilities – *Holiday Inn* (see *Best in Town,* below).

Translator – *Accent* (phone: 236-2817); *Inlinuga* (phone: 236-2351).

Typewriter Rental – *Metro Office Machines,* 1-week minimum (phone: 528-4478); *George David Co.,* 1-week minimum (phone: 232-2192).

Western Union/Telex – Many offices located around the city (phone: 800-779-1111).

SPECIAL EVENTS: *A Taste of Hartford,* held at Constitution Plaza in the spring, is a giant block party with music, dancing, and booths set up by over 60 restaurants offering samples of their specialties. Hartford's *July 4th RiverFestival* features concerts, sporting events, and fireworks displays along the Connecticut River. The *Connecticut Family Folk Festival* fills Elizabeth Park on the city's west side with the sounds of guitars, fiddles, and dulcimers during the second weekend of August. *Kidrific* is a 2-day event held the weekend after *Labor Day,* specially designed for children and their parents. The festival includes a petting zoo, rides, and carnival games. The *Festival of Lights*

is held every year on Constitution Plaza the day after *Thanksgiving,* when thousands of tiny white lights are illuminated. Santa Claus always makes a dramatic appearance, arriving on top of the Connecticut Bank and Trust Building in a helicopter and descending in a window-washer's gondola that looks surprisingly like a sleigh.

 MUSEUMS: Museum aficionados will love the abundance of art and historical collections in Hartford. The *Avery Art Memorial, Baldwin Museum of Connecticut History, Butler-McCook Homestead, Morgan Memorial, Old State House, Science Museum of Connecticut,* and *Wadsworth Atheneum* are described above in *Special Places.* Another museum worthy of mention is:

Connecticut Historical Society – Open from noon to 5 PM; closed Mondays. Admission charge. 1 Elizabeth St. (phone: 236-5621).

MAJOR COLLEGES AND UNIVERSITIES: Trinity College (Summit, Vernon, and Broad Sts.; phone: 297-2000); St. Joseph College (Asylum Ave., West Hartford; phone: 232-4571); University of Hartford (200 Bloomfield Ave., West Hartford; phone: 243-4100).

SPORTS AND FITNESS: Fishing – For the best fishing, try Wethersfield Cove.

Fitness Center – The *YMCA* has a pool, squash and racquetball courts, and a track, 160 Jewell at Ann St. (phone: 522-4183).

Golf – There are 24 golf courses in the Hartford area. The best public course is in Goodwin Park. PGA tour pros compete in the *Greater Hartford Open* every July at the *Tournament Players Club* (Cromwell; phone: 635-5000).

Hockey – The NHL *Whalers* play at the *Hartford Civic Center* (phone: 800-WHALERS).

Jogging – The perimeter of Bushnell Park, across from the *YMCA,* is seven-eighths of a mile; other running courses include Goodwin Park, 1½ miles from downtown, with a 2-mile perimeter; and Elizabeth Park, 2 miles from downtown, with a 2½-mile perimeter.

Skiing – There's excellent cross-country skiing at the Metropolitan District Commission reservoir in West Hartford. Downhill enthusiasts like *Mt. Southington* (20 minutes south on I-84), *Powder Ridge Ski Area* (20 minutes south on I-91), and *Mt. Tom* (45 minutes north on I-91).

Swimming – The Connecticut River is acceptable for boating but is not clean enough for swimming, even though it may look tempting on a hot day. Hartford residents recommend swimming at the *YWCA* — there is an admission charge (135 Broad St.; phone: 525-1163) or *YMCA* (160 Jewell at Ann St.; phone: 522-4183).

Tennis – The best public courts are at Elizabeth Park, Prospect and Asylum Aves.; at the State Armory on Capitol Hill; there are indoor courts at *In-town Tennis,* 360 Broad St. (phone: 246-7448).

THEATER: For complete performance schedules, check the newspapers listed above. Hartford's main theater is the *Hartford Stage Company* (50 Church St.; phone: 527-5151); ballets are performed and touring companies frequently bring Broadway productions to *Bushnell Memorial Hall* (166 Capitol Ave.; phone: 246-6807).

MUSIC: Concerts, operas, and symphonies are performed at *Bushnell Memorial Hall* (166 Capitol Ave.; phone: 246-6807); and the *Goodspeed Opera House* (East Haddam, 30 minutes south on Rte. 9; phone: 873-8668). The *Civic Center* (1 Civic Center Plaza; phone: 727-8080) features rock concerts.

 NIGHTCLUBS AND NIGHTLIFE: Hartford's cafés are great places for listening to music. The selection varies from place to place, from night to night, so call ahead. At *Boppers* (22 Union

Pl.; phone: 549-5801), a DJ plays oldies but goodies from the back of a real 1957 convertible, parked in the center of the dance floor. For disco dancing, try *Goodnight Hartford* (187 Allyn St.; phone: 525-1919), where live rock bands perform on Wednesday nights, or the *Club Car* (S. Union Pl.; phone: 549-5444), which has an upstairs dance floor and video screens, Thursdays through Sundays ($5 cover); there is no cover to listen to jazz in the downstairs lounge. Just across from the *Civic Center, The Russian Lady* (191 Ann St.; phone: 525-3003) rocks with live music Thursdays through Saturdays; the rest of the week the club features dancing to top 40 dance hits ; there is a $3 cover. *Bourbon Street North* (70 Union Plaza; phone: 525-1014) is a popular yuppie hangout featuring live music and dancing to jazz and blues performers, Tuesdays through Saturdays, for a small cover charge. A comedy club operates in the back room of *Brown Thomson & Co.* (942 Main St.; phone: 525-1600) on Friday and Saturday nights, for an $8 cover; shows are at 8:30 and 11 PM.

BEST IN TOWN

CHECKING IN: Hartford has an unexceptional collection of comfortable hotels. The *Sheraton-Hartford, Summit,* and *Holiday Inn* offer in-room movies. Expect to pay $90 and up for a double room at places noted as expensive, $60 to $80 in the moderate category; we found no establishments that met our standards in the inexpensive category. For bed and breakfast listings and referrals, contact *Nutmeg Bed & Breakfast* (PO Box 1117, West Hartford, CT 06127; phone: 236-6698). All telephone numbers are in the 203 area code unless otherwise indicated.

J. P. Morgan – Located next to the *Civic Center,* this renovated and expanded former home of J. P. Morgan is now a 124-room luxury establishment. The banking titan's taste has been preserved with genuine antiques and turn-of-the-century reproductions, such as sleigh beds and period-style wallpapering in the lobby and hallways. The combination of contemporary and old-fashioned furnishings has produced an elegant ambience with modern amenities, including rooms with computer-compatible phone lines. Fine dining is offered at *Pierpont's* restaurant, as well as sandwiches and lighter meals at the *America's Cup Lounge.* Afternoon tea is served weekdays. Room service can be ordered around the clock. There are meeting rooms with a 125-person capacity, a concierge desk, A/V equipment, photocopiers, and express checkout. 1 Haynes St. (phone: 246-7500; Fax: 203-247-4576). Expensive.

Sheraton-Hartford – Connected to the *Civic Center,* this 388-room property gives the indoor sports enthusiast a wider range of facilities than any other Hartford hotel. The indoor heated pool has a lifeguard on duty. There's also a whirlpool bath, sauna, exercise room, recreation room, and café-bar. In-room movies also are available. Cribs for infants are free. There's a concierge desk, and A/V equipment, photocopiers, and computers are avialable for use. Meeting room capacity seats up to 800, and there is express checkout service. Trumbull St. at *Civic Center* (phone: 728-5151 or 800-325-3535; Fax: 203-522-3356). Expensive.

Avon Old Farms – Only 15 minutes from downtown, this gracious and elegant hotel offers all the benefits of a country setting, along with one of the region's premier restaurants, *Avon Old Farms Inn* (see *Eating Out*) just across the street. Many of the spacious 158 rooms have grand views of nearby Avon Mountain and picturesque Farmington Valley. Located on 20 acres of manicured grounds, it is near a public golf course and a health club. There is an outdoor pool, an exercise room and sauna, and hiking trails behind the hotel. A popular hiking route travels to the summit of Talcott Mountain, where you can enjoy a panoramic view from the top of the Heublein Tower. Meeting rooms for up to 200 are available; so, too, are A/V equipment and photocopiers. Express checkout will speed you on your way. Rtes. 10 and 44, Box 961, Avon (phone: 677-1651; Fax: 203-677-0364). Expensive to moderate.

Holiday Inn Downtown – On the fringe of downtown, with easy access to I-84 and I-91, this high-rise property was refurbished in 1989 and now has an outdoor pool and a health club with Nautilus equipment, and inexpensive parking. It's a popular choice among corporate travelers. Inexpensive parking is available. Although concierge service is limited, meeting rooms accommodate 450. Other conveniences are secretarial services, A/V equipment, and photocopiers. 50 Morgan St. (phone: 549-2400 or 800-HOLIDAY; Fax: 203-549-7849). Moderate.

Ramada–Capital Hill – A central hotel with basic conveniences at an attractive price, this is a good bet. Its 94 rooms have been refurbished, and there is a restaurant and café. Parking is free. Meeting rooms can hold up to 75. Other pluses are A/V equipment, photocopiers, and express checkout. 440 Asylum St. (phone: 246-6591 or 800-2-RAMADA; Fax: 203-728-1382). Moderate.

EATING OUT: The number and varieties of foreign cuisines available in the city are increasing gradually, but most of the best restaurants still feature traditional Hartford fare: Italian-American cooking, or the steaks-chops-seafood routine. For two people, expect to pay between $50 and $100 at restaurants designated as expensive; between $25 and $45 at those we've listed as moderate. Prices do not include drinks, wine, or tips. All telephone numbers are in the 203 area code unless otherwise indicated.

L'Américain – On the fringe of downtown, this eclectic dining place (inside a renovated factory) is a favorite of the local business community. Open daily. Reservations advised. Major credit cards accepted. 2 Hartford Sq. (phone: 522-6500). Expensive.

Avon Old Farms Inn – Once a colonial-era blacksmith shop, this inn has been serving meals since 1757, which makes it one of the oldest restaurants in the nation. It is across the street from the *Avon Old Farms* hotel. In the Old Forge Room, you can sit among antique smithy tools, and linger over veal, beef, and seafood specialties. A spectacular brunch is offered on Sundays. Open daily. Reservations advised. Major credit cards accepted. Rtes. 10 and 44, Avon (about a 15-minute drive from downtown Hartford; phone: 677-2818). Expensive.

Peppercorns Grill – A block from the *Wadsworth Atheneum,* this eatery offers a unique dining experience. The eclectic menu, esoterically described as "Interpretive Italian," features pasta specialties such as spicy fettuccine, and seafood dishes such as brochettes of scallops, shrimp, and calamari. Open daily. Reservations advised, particularly on weekends. Major credit cards accepted. 357 Main St. (phone: 547-1714). Expensive.

Carbone's – Northern Italian dishes are featured at this family-owned Hartford fixture that's been in the city's south end for more than 45 years. Closed Sundays. Reservations advised. Major credit cards accepted. 588 Frontline Ave. (phone: 296-9646). Expensive to moderate.

Brown Thomson & Co. – In the Richardson Building complex, which also includes a shopping mall, this antiques-encrusted restaurant offers the most extensive menu in town — 125 separate items. Sandwiches, Mexican food, and delicacies such as fried ice cream are included. This is where the young people of Hartford meet. A comedy club operates in the back room on Friday and Saturday nights, for an $8 cover;

shows are at 8:30 and 11 PM. Closed Sundays. Reservations unnecessary. Major credit cards accepted. 942 Main St. (phone: 525-1600). Moderate.

Congress Rotisserie – The long, sleek bar, black-and-white decor, and stylishly dressed clientele all let you know that this is one of Hartford's hottest eating establishments. From the spacious dining rooms you can watch chefs prepare spit-roasted chicken, duck, lamb, and (on weekends) salmon on the huge rotisserie. The menu also features a number of vegetarian dinner salads and pasta dishes. Selections from the bar include a choice of 16 different beers, many on tap. Open daily (the restaurant stays open later than most others in the city). Reservations necessary. Major credit cards accepted. 7 Maple Ave. (phone: 560-1965). Moderate.

Frank's – A favorite of state politicians, serving traditional Italian-American dishes. The manicotti is considered excellent and the veal superb. Especially busy before and after hockey games and *Civic Center* events, so make reservations. Specialties include fresh seafood delights, such as San Francisco *cioppino* (fish stew). The largest wine selection in the city. Open daily except Sundays in July and August. Reservations advised. Major credit cards accepted. In the CityPlace Complex at 185 Asylum St., across from the *Civic Center* (phone: 527-9291). Moderate.

Hot Tomato's – This popular downtown eatery in Union Station features Northern Italian specialties such as *giabotto* (chicken, veal, and hot sausage, with hot peppers and cheese) and shrimp piccata, made with lots of love — and garlic. The atmosphere is lively and cheeful. There's also a piano bar Thursdays through Saturdays. Open daily. Reservations unnecessary. Major credit cards accepted. 309 Asylum St. (phone: 249-5100). Moderate.

Max on Main – Currently the trendiest downtown dining spot, it calls itself an American bistro, perhaps because Saratoga water is served instead of Perrier. The fare is nouvelle American, featuring seafood and meat dishes made with locally grown ingredients. For lunch, try the chicken pot pie. Open daily. Reservations advised. Major credit cards accepted. 205 Main St. (phone: 522-2530). Moderate.

Spencer's Downtown Grill & Tavern – In the restored Linden apartment building (one of the city's most exclusive), this is actually two restaurants in one. The formal, Edwardian dining room features a continental bill of fare, while the *Tavern* serves lighter meals in a more casual atmosphere. There are also 4 billiards rooms and a garden patio. Live music at the piano bar Thursdays through Saturdays. Open daily. Reservations advised. Major credit cards accepted. 10 Capitol Ave. (phone: 247-0400). Moderate.

HONOLULU

AT-A-GLANCE

SEEING THE CITY: For an eye-popping view of the shoreline, take the outdoor glass elevator to the top of the *Ilikai* hotel (1777 Ala Moana Blvd.; phone: 949-3811). There are equally spectacular views from the *Hanohano Room* atop the *Sheraton Waikiki* (2255 Kalakaua Ave.; phone: 922-4422) and from *Nicholas Nickolas,* atop the *Ala Moana* hotel (410 Atkinson Dr.; phone: 955-4811). For another good perspective, visit the 10th-floor observatory in the Aloha Tower, with a panorama that stretches from the airport to Diamond Head (at the bottom of *Fort Street Mall;* phone: 537-9260). The popular Tantalus Lookout provides a sweeping perspective that takes in much of Honolulu, Waikiki, Diamond Head, and Manoa Valley, wherein lies the campus of the University of Hawaii. The lookout from Punchbowl Crater offers another panoramic perspective of the city, all the way from downtown Honolulu to Waikiki.

SPECIAL PLACES: Although it is now considerably overbuilt, Waikiki is nonetheless an interesting place to wander. We suggest getting to know your neighborhood first with a 3-mile walking tour.

Diamond Head – Guarding the southeasternmost boundary of Waikiki, this 760-foot volcanic crater is a world-famous landmark. You can climb around the slopes of Diamond Head along the tricky trail that begins at a gate off Makalei Place. It is also possible to drive into the crater through a tunnel to a state park inside, where there is a half-hour long hike to the summit, which passes by World War II bunkers. Open 6 AM to 6 PM. For park information, call the State Parks Dept. at 548-7455.

Kapiolani Park – This 220-acre park, named for the wife of Kalakaua, the last King of Hawaii, has enough to keep you busy for more than a few hours. Just off Monsarrat Avenue, the *Kodak Hula Show* (phone: 833-1661) is performed at 10 AM Tuesdays through Thursdays. Get there early if you want a good seat. Drift along toward the scent of the Kapiolani Rose Garden on the corner of Paki and Monsarrat. Other attractions in the park include the *Waikiki Aquarium, Honolulu Zoo,* tennis courts, beaches, jogging trails, and the *Shell,* featuring entertainment under the stars. Kalakaua Avenue, named after the good king, begins here. Pronounced Ka-la-*cow*-wah, it is the principal thoroughfare of Waikiki.

Waikiki Beach – Just outside the park, alongside Kalakaua Avenue, begins the famous, 2½-mile-long curve of Waikiki Beach, one of the most famous beaches and surfing spots in the world. The 2- to 5-foot waves that are standard along the shoreline for much of the year are perfect for novices and amateurs. (On the few days in the summer when they reach 10 feet, Waikiki's waves should be avoided by all but experts.) Several hotels along Waikiki — for example, the *Outrigger* (2335 Kalakaua Ave.; phone: 923-0711; ask for Beach Services) — provide instruction and surfboards.

International Marketplace – A great place to poke around outdoor

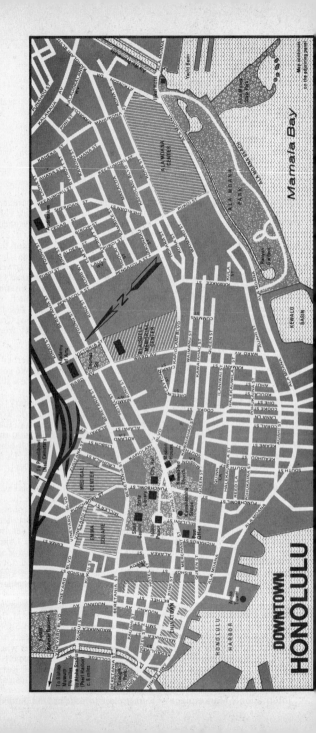

DOWNTOWN HONOLULU

Mamala Bay

Map continues
on the adjoining panel

Ala Moana Ship Park

Yacht Basin

ALA MOANA
PARK

ALA MOANA CENTER

Banyan
Garden

KEWALO
BASIN

HONOLULU
HARBOR

Aloha Tower

CHINATOWN

To Bishop
Museum,
Waikiki Stadium,
Pearl Harbor
c. 6 miles

To Punchbowl
Nat. Cemetery

Foster Botanic Garden

CULTURAL PLAZA

AALA
SQUARE

Academy
of Arts

Thomas
Sq.

THOMAS
SQUARE

NEAL BLAISDELL
MEMORIAL
CENTER

State
Library

State
Capitol

Iolani
Palace

Mission
House

Kawaiahao
Church

Kamehameha
Statue

Post
Office

N

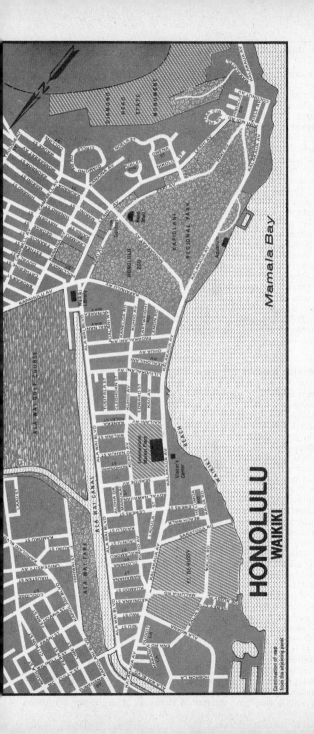

stalls underneath a giant banyan tree festooned with lanterns. (A souk, Hawaiian-style, is what we call it.) You can pick up all kinds of exotic junk and treasures you just can't live without. As we went to press, plans were being completed for a large *Convention Center* on the Marketplace acreage. 2330 Kalakaua Ave. (phone: 923-9871).

Royal Hawaiian Shopping Center – Stretching 3 blocks along the ocean side of Kalakaua Avenue, this 3-level outdoor mall is Waikiki's largest shopping complex, with everything from Hawaiian crafts to designer clothes, plus daily performances of music and Hawaiiana as well as several restaurants serving a variety of foods. 2201 Kalakaua Ave. (phone: 922-0588).

Ft. DeRussy Army Museum – Weapons used by ancient Hawaiians, weapons captured from the Japanese, and weapons used by US soldiers in campaigns from the Spanish-American to the Korean War are on display here. In addition, there are uniforms worn at various times by US forces as well as those of the enemy. The most fascinating items are the Hawaiian weapons made long ago from shark's teeth and the newspaper accounts of the US involvement in World War II following the invasion of Pearl Harbor. Closed Mondays. No admission charge. Kalia Rd. (phone: 955-9552).

Tantalus Drive – The country road that winds its way up Mount Tantalus provides some of the most beautiful urban scenery found anywhere. The panoramas from lookouts en route through lush rain forest include Waikiki, Diamond Head, downtown Honolulu, and the distant Waianae Mountains. A state park provides one of several places to relax, picnic, or hike.

DOWNTOWN

Mission Houses Museum – This museum complex contains the earliest American buildings in Hawaii. The frame houses, shipped around Cape Horn in pieces and then reassembled in 1821 by the first missionaries, used to be a school and a minister's home, as well as a mission. They contain furniture and artifacts more reminiscent of New England than Hawaii, as well as a rare archive of the islands' history. In the print house, constructed from coral, is a replica of the original printing press used to produce religious tracts and primers for schoolchildren, mostly in Hawaiian. On Saturdays, the Living History program populates the mission grounds with volunteers dressed in 19th-century garb. Open Tuesdays through Saturdays from 9 AM to 4 PM; tours offered from 9:30 AM to 3 PM. Open Sundays from noon to 4 PM. Closed Mondays. Admission charge. 553 S. King St. (phone: 531-0481).

Kawaiahao Church – Across from the *Mission Houses,* Kawaiahao Church also is known as the Westminster Abbey of Hawaii, and indeed, those remnants of the old Hawaiian royal and princely families who have retained their Congregational faith occasionally do use the church for baptisms, marriages, and funerals. It's the oldest church in Honolulu, built in 1842 on the site of Hawaii's first mission, which was a thatch-roofed hut standing close to an ancient and sacred *hao* (spring). Tall *kahilis* (feather-decorated staffs symbolic of royalty) placed on either side of the altar testify to its distinguished past. It was here that King Kamehameha III used the expression *Ua mau ke ea o ka aina i ka pono* ("The life of the land is perpetuated in righteousness"), which now is the state motto. Services are conducted in English and Hawaiian at 8 and 10:30 AM on Sundays. Open daily. King and Punchbowl Sts. (phone: 522-1333).

Chinatown – Chinatown is on the easternmost fringe of downtown and spills across the Nuuanu Stream into Aala Triangle Park. There are open-air meat, fish, and vegetable markets; herb shops selling age-old medications; and elderly people who still dress in traditional costume. This also is the "sin" quarter of Honolulu, where sleazy sex shows

compete for customers with family-style chop suey houses. Recent gen-
trification is under way, however, bringing new shops and galleries into
renovated turn-of-the-century buildings. A walking tour of Chinatown
with an optional lunch (a real bargain) takes place on Tuesdays at 9:30
AM, starting from the Chinese Chamber of Commerce, 42 N. King St.
(phone: 533-3181).

Mauna Kea Marketplace – Recently opened, the marketplace serves
as a commercial centerpiece for Chinatown's on-going renewal. The use
of Chinese architectural detail is particularly beautiful. The central
courtyard is filled with vendors, shops, restaurants, and food stalls which
offer a variety of Asian tastes. Maunakea and Pauahi Sts.

Hawaii Maritime Museum – Pier 7 is the home of the four-masted
Falls of Clyde and the outrigger voyaging canoe *Hokulea,* returned from
its three trans-Pacific voyages along Polynesian migration routes. There
also are displays related to Hawaii's maritime history, plus a library and
photo archive. Open daily. Admission charge. Pier 7, near Aloha Tower
(phone: 536-6373).

Iolani Palace – With elaborate surroundings, Iolani Palace sits in
state, receiving tribute from admirers. Highly revered by historians and
sentimentalists alike, the palace was the royal residence of monarch and
songwriter Queen Liliuokalani. In fact, she was imprisoned here following the 1893 revolution and wrote some of her famous songs, including
"Aloha Oe," while in detention. Iolani was built by her brother, King
David Kalakaua, between 1878 and 1882. In 1883, he placed a crown
on his own head in what is now *Coronation Bandstand,* where, every
Friday at noon, the *Royal Hawaiian Band* gives free, informal concerts.
Palace tours are given Wednesdays through Saturdays. Admission
charge. King and Richards Sts. (phone: 522-0832).

State Capitol – Built in 1969 and recently renovated, the capitol takes
its inspiration from the natural history of the islands. All of its features — columns, reflecting pools, courtyard — reflect aspects of Hawaii's environment. Outside the capitol stands a beautiful bronze statue
of Queen Liliuokalani and the controversial modern statue of Father
Damien, the hero of the leprosy settlement at Kalaupapa on the island
of Molokai. Open daily. Admission charge. 415 S. Beretania St. (phone:
548-2211).

OTHER SPECIAL PLACES

Ala Moana Center – This is one of the world's largest shopping
centers. Built in 1959, when Hawaii achieved statehood, and recently
expanded and updated for the 1990s, it has more than 220 stores selling
quality clothing, jewelry, fabric, and art made at home and imported
from other countries. The Food Court features a large selection of surprisingly good ethnic food outlets. Ala Moana Blvd. across from Ala
Moana Park.

***Arizona* Memorial –** More than a million people a year come to honor
the American sailors who perished on the USS *Arizona,* sunk when the
Japanese bombed Pearl Harbor on December 7, 1941. Something of a
surprise is the number of Japanese among the visitors. The only boat tour
of the memorial departs from the visitors' center daily except Mondays.
The National Park Service operates a large museum, with exhibitions
and films. *Paradise Cruises* (phone: 536-3641) departs from Kewalo
Basin (hotel transfers are included) for the half-day tour that passes the
memorial but does not allow for a visit. *Pearl Harbor Day* is commemorated every December 7, with a service at the memorial. The USS
Bowfin Pacific Submarine Museum (11 Arizona Memorial Place; phone:
423-1341) is adjacent to the visitors' center. Open daily. Admission
charge.

Bishop Museum – Near the beginning of Likelike (pronounced
Leekay-leekay) Highway, in the working class neighborhood called

Kalihi, this prestigious museum houses the greatest collection of Hawaiiana in the world. Founded in 1899, it is the center for most of the anthropological research done throughout Polynesia and the Pacific. In addition to excellent displays, the museum, which has been expanded recently, features daily performances of Hawaiian music and dance. Shows are also featured at the adjacent planetarium. Open daily. Admission charge. 1525 Bernice St. (phone: 848-4129).

Foster Botanic Gardens – Often overlooked by tourists, this cool, tranquil retreat in the middle of the city is a living museum of growing things. The No. 4 bus from Waikiki will bring you close to the garden at Nuuanu and Vineyard. Open daily. Admission charge. 180 N. Vineyard Blvd. (phone: 522-7065).

Honolulu Academy of Arts – Across Thomas Square from *Blaisdell Center,* the *Academy of Arts* has Oriental art and some European and American works. Interesting items include a Japanese ink and color handscroll dating to 1250, John Singleton Copley's *Portrait of Nathaniel Allen,* and Segna di Bonaventura's *Madonna and Child.* Lunch is served in the museum garden Tuesdays through Fridays at 11:30 AM and 1 PM. Thursday evenings dinner is served at 6 PM. Reservations necessary. Closed Mondays. No admission charge. 900 S. Beretania St. (phone: 538-3693).

Queen Emma's Summer Palace – This royal retreat in the cool highlands of Nuuanu Valley was the summer home of Kamehameha IV and Queen Emma, presented to them as a gift by the queen's aunt and uncle. Built sometime between 1847 and 1850, it is a simple building with Doric columns and a roof that overhangs a broad lanai (veranda). The building, which was abandoned when Queen Emma died in 1885, was rescued from wreckers by the Daughters of Hawaii, a civic group that has operated it as a museum since 1915. Both furnishings and artifacts are on display, including a Gothic-design cabinet, a gift of Queen Victoria's consort, Prince Albert; a stereopticon presented to Queen Emma by Napoleon III; and the christening robe made for the royal couple's only child, Prince Edward Albert, the last child born to a ruling Hawaiian monarch, who died tragically at the age of 4. Open daily. Admission charge. 2913 Pali Hwy. (phone: 595-3167).

National Memorial Cemetery of the Pacific – Also known as Punchbowl Crater, this cemetery is the Arlington of the Pacific. In prehistoric times it was the site of human sacrifices. Now, more than 26,000 servicemen lie buried among its 112 peaceful acres overlooking downtown Honolulu. Commercial bus and van tours visit Punchbowl, but if you're on your own, you'll need a car or taxi. A lookout from the crater's rim offers panoramic city views. Take Puowaina Drive to its end.

The Contemporary Museum – Hawaii's newest museum, on the Tantalus hillside with a beautiful view of the city, features contemporary sculpture, paintings, graphics, and more, most of it in well-displayed, changing exhibitions. There's a major permanent display of the works of David Hockney. In addition, a satellite gallery is in the news building of the Honolulu Newspaper Agency on Kapiolani Boulevard. Open daily from 10 AM to 4 PM; except Sundays, from noon to 4 PM; closed Mondays. Donations requested. 2411 Makiki Heights Dr. (phone: 526-1322).

Dole Cannery Square – A 60-year-old, still-operational pineapple cannery, with adjacent areas transformed into a visitors' center complete with shops and a hands-on children's museum. The best part of a visit is the escorted tour of the cannery itself, where the sweet smell of the spiky fruit hangs heavy in the air. Shuttle service links the cannery to Waikiki. Open daily. Admission charge. 650 Iwilei Rd. (just west of downtown Honolulu, off Nimitz Hwy.; phone: 531-8855).

■ **EXTRA SPECIAL:** Honolulu is the great jumping-off point for island-hopping expeditions. *Hawaiian Air* (phone: 537-5100) flies to the islands of Kauai, Maui, Hawaii,Molokai, and Lanai daily; *Aloha Air-*

lines (phone: 836-1111) serves all but Lanai; *Aloha Island Air* (phone: 833-3219) is the largest of several commuter airlines that fly among the islands. Commuter flights link both major airports as well as more isolated communities like Hana, Maui, or Waimea on the Big Island. On runs to Molokai, commuter fares are lower than those charged for the jet service of the majors. Kauai, the oldest of the islands, is known for golf at the *Princeville* and *Kauai Lagoons* resort courses, sunny Poipu Beach, and the spectacular beauty of Waimea Canyon and the Na Pali coast. Maui offers valleys, waterfalls, beaches, and the crater of the dormant Haleakala Volcano. The small Kapalua/West Maui Airport serves direct flights to Lahaina, Kaanapali, Kahana, Napili, and Kapalua resorts. The island of Hawaii, also called the Big Island, is the home of Mauna Loa and Kilauea, two of the most active volcanoes in the world, as well as Hawaii's premier archaeological sites including Puuhonua O'Honaunau and Paukuhoa heiau. On Lanai, only 17 miles long, the main draws are plenty of pineapples, two new resort hotels, and a sense of away-from-it-all isolation. Molokai, 37 miles long, a relatively untouched ranchers' island, offers tourists the opportunity to see a rural side of Hawaii, or visit the isolated leper's settlement at Kalaupapa, now administered as a National Historic Park. There also is a resort at Kaluakoi and several small condos and hotels along the east coast for those who wish to stay awhile.

SOURCES AND RESOURCES

TOURIST INFORMATION: For information, maps, and brochures, contact the Hawaii Visitors Bureau (2270 Kalakaua Ave., Suite 1108, Honolulu, HI 96815; phone: 923-1811). Call the Hawaii state hotline (phone: 808-923-1811) for maps, calendars of events, health updates, and travel advisories.

This Week, Spotlight Hawaii, and the pocket-size *Beach Guide* series are the best of the numerous free publications aimed at visitors, and they are available in most hotel lobbies. Also see our own *Birnbaum's Hawaii 1992.*

Local Coverage – *Honolulu Advertiser,* morning daily; *Honolulu Star-Bulletin,* evening daily; *Honolulu* magazine, monthly.

Television Stations – KHON Channel 2–NBC; KITV Channel 4–ABC; KGMB Channel 9–CBS; KHET Channel 11–PBS.

Radio Stations – AM: KSSK 590 (oldies and contemporary); KHVH 990 (news). FM: KHPR 88.1 (classical); KUMU 94.7 (easy listening); KPOI 98 (rock); KQMQ 96.3 (soft rock); KHHH 98.5 (jazz and popular music).

TELEPHONE: The area code for Honolulu and all of Hawaii is 808.

Sales Tax – There is a 4% sales tax in Honolulu and a statewide 5% hotel tax.

CLIMATE: In ancient times, the Hawaiians had no word for weather. They did, however, have words for two seasons — winter and summer. Winter, which runs from about October through April, means daytime highs reaching the mid-70s and low 80s, dropping into the low 60s at night. There can be several short rains in a day. You can count on 11 hours of daylight. Summer temperatures hover around the mid- to upper 80s; rains are less frequent, and you get about 13 hours of daylight, more vacation for your money.

GETTING AROUND: Airport – Honolulu International Airport is about a 20- to 25-minute drive from Waikiki (in moderate traffic), slightly less from the downtown area. Cab fare to

Waikiki should run $15 to $20; $12 to $16, downtown. *Airport Motor-coach* (phone: 926-4747) provides limousine service for $5 between the airport and Waikiki.

Bus – *TheBus,* as the municipal transit line is called, is the least expensive, most convenient way to get around Honolulu. You can get a map of bus routes at your hotel, at *Ala Moana Center,* or from the Honolulu Department of Transport, Mass Transit Lines (MTL), 811 Middle St. (phone: 531-1611).

Car Rental – There are several that provide quality service: *Tropical* (phone: 957-0800), *Budget* (phone: 922-3600), *National* (phone: 800-227-7368), *Avis* (phone: 834-5536), *Hertz* (phone: 836-2511), and *Dollar* (phone: 944-1544). Most serve four or five islands, and multi-island rates are offered. Check for special rates that are available when business is slow. Rental offices are at the airport and in Waikiki.

Helicopter Tours – *Papillon Hawaii Pacific* (phone: 836-1566) offers a series of aerial tours. *Cherry Helicopter* (phone: 833-4339) departs from the *Turtle Bay* resort on the north shore.

Taxi – Although taxis sometimes can be hailed on the street, most are on call. To be sure of getting a cab, call for one. Some reliable companies are *SIDA* (phone: 836-0011), *Charley's* (phone: 955-2211), and *Aloha State Taxi* (phone: 847-3566).

Trolley – The *Waikiki Trolley* provides open-air links in modified turn-of-the-century style every half hour daily between Waikiki (pickups at the *Hilton Hawaiian Village* and the *Royal Hawaiian Shopping Center*) and shops (*Ala Moana Center, Ward Warehouse, Ward Center, Maui Divers Hawaii Jewelry Design Center, Hilo Hattie's Fashion Center, Dole Cannery Square*) and attractions elsewhere in Honolulu (*Honolulu Academy of Arts,* Iolani Palace, Chinatown, *Maritime Museum, Mission Houses Museum*) between 8:30 AM and 4 PM. An all-day pass costs $10 (phone: 526-0112).

 VITAL SERVICES: Baby-sitting – *Aloha Baby-sitting* (phone: 732-2029) or check with the hotel concierge or activity desk.

Business Services – *Una May Young,* Suite 3206, Manor Wing, *Sheraton Waikiki Hotel,* 2255 Kalakaua Ave. (phone: 922-4422).

Dry Cleaner/Tailor – *Al Phillips the Cleaner,* 2310 Kuhio Ave. (phone: 923-1971).

Limousine – *Executive Limousine* (phone: 941-1999); *Silver Cloud Limousine* (phone: 524-7999).

Mechanic – *Toguchi Chevron Service Station,* 825 N. Vineyard Blvd. (phone: 845-6422).

Medical Emergency – *Queen's Hospital* at Discovery Bay, open to 10 PM (phone: 943-1111).

Messenger Services – *Courier Express* (phone: 955-0079); *ADDS Messenger Service* (phone: 946-1565 or 947-4228).

National/International Courier – *Federal Express* (phone: 359-3339); *DHL Worldwide Courier Express* (phone: 836-0441).

Pharmacy – *Pillbox,* open until 11 PM (1133 11th Ave.; phone: 737-1777); *Outrigger Pharmacy* (2335 Kalakaua Ave.; phone: 923-2529); any *Long's* drugstore (phone: 941-4433).

Photocopies – *Island Instant Printers* (2270 Kalakaua Ave.; phone: 922-1225); *Second Image* (2600 S. King St.; phone: 955-7498); *Ditto's,* open 24 hours (833 Kapiolani Blvd.; phone: 531-0544).

Post Office – Several locations: downtown (at 335 Merchant St. at Richards St.; phone: 541-1962); in Waikiki (330 Saratoga Rd.; phone: 941-1062); and at substations in the *Royal Hawaiian Shopping Center* (phone: 926-3710), the *Hilton Hawaiian Village* (phone: 949-4321), and at the airport (phone: 423-3930).

Professional Photographer – *David Cornwell* (phone: 949-7000); *Creative Focus* (phone: 942-0202).

Secretary/Stenographer – *Kelly Services* (phone: 536-9343).

Teleconference Facilities – *Kahala Hilton* (see *Best in Town,* below).

Translator – *Academia Language School* (phone: 946-5599); *A-1 Kanner Language Systems* (phone: 415-365-3046).

Word Processing/Typewriter Rental – *Pacific Business Machines,* 1- and 2-week minimums, depending on equipment (phone: 946-5059); *Alexander Brothers,* hourly in-office use or 2-week minimum rentals (phone: 837-7828); *Computer House,* rentals and repairs (phone: 472-7253).

Western Union/Telex – Many offices located around the city (phone: 942-2274).

Other – *Lyn's Video Rental* (phone: 941-1253); *Ditto's,* fax services (phone: 531-0544).

SPECIAL EVENTS: Special events are held year-round. Here are a few highlights:

January – The annual *Hula Bowl* College All-Star Football Classic is played in *Aloha Stadium* and the *Chinese New Year* is celebrated in Chinatown (sometimes in February).

February – Early in the month, the nationally televised 4-day *Hawaiian Open International Golf Tournament,* at the *Waialae Country Club* in the Kahala District (sometimes late in January).

June – On June 11, *Kamehameha Day* honors the conqueror of the islands with a long parade and floats.

July – In even-numbered years, the *Trans-Pacific Yacht Race* finishes off Diamond Head. *The Prince Lot Hula Festival* is held in a lovely outdoor setting at Moanalua Gardens.

September – The *Waikiki Rough Water Swim* is held over a 2-mile course, ending at Duke Kahanamoku Beach in front of the *Hilton Hawaiian Village* hotel. *Aloha Week* is Honolulu's biggest celebration. It features canoe races, luaus, balls, athletic events, parades and more. September also marks the beginning of symphony season.

October – The *Honolulu Orchid Society Show* is held at the *Neal S. Blaisdell Center,* with lei making and flower arranging demonstrations as well as floral displays.

December – December 7 is *Pearl Harbor Day,* commemorated by a service at the USS *Arizona* Memorial. Contestants in the *Honolulu Marathon* run from the Aloha Tower to the bandshell in Kapiolani Park. The *Triple Crown* of surfing competitions is held along Oahu's north shore. Late in November or early December, the *Pacific International Film Festival* presents a week of free movies. Streets are ablaze with *Christmas* lights between mid-December and *New Year's Eve* in the heart of downtown Honolulu.

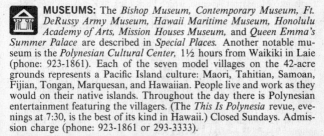

MUSEUMS: The *Bishop Museum, Contemporary Museum, Ft. DeRussy Army Museum, Hawaii Maritime Museum, Honolulu Academy of Arts, Mission Houses Museum,* and *Queen Emma's Summer Palace* are described in *Special Places.* Another notable museum is the *Polynesian Cultural Center,* 1½ hours from Waikiki in Laie (phone: 923-1861). Each of the seven model villages on the 42-acre grounds represents a Pacific Island culture: Maori, Tahitian, Samoan, Fijian, Tongan, Marquesan, and Hawaiian. People live and work as they would on their native islands. Throughout the day there is Polynesian entertainment featuring the villagers. (The *This Is Polynesia* revue, evenings at 7:30, is the best of its kind in Hawaii.) Closed Sundays. Admission charge (phone: 923-1861 or 293-3333).

MAJOR COLLEGES AND UNIVERSITIES: The University of Hawaii (in Manoa Valley; phone: 956-8855); Brigham Young University (at Laie; phone: 293-3211); Chaminade University of

Honolulu (phone: 735-4711); Hawaii Pacific College (downtown; phone: 544-0239); Hawaii Loa College (phone: 235-3647).

SPORTS AND FITNESS: Hawaii is one of the world's great centers for water sports. Surfing and swimming contests are held often. *Aloha Stadium* is the site of the *Hula Bowl* college football game each January; football and baseball games at other times are in Halawa Heights (phone: 486-9300). Basketball and boxing events are held at the *Neal S. Blaisdell Center,* 777 Ward Ave. (phone: 521-2911).

Bicycling – *Island Bike and Surf Rentals* (2084 Kalakaua Ave.; phone: 949-2453) is open from 8 AM to 5 PM. Closed Sundays.

Fishing – Fishing enthusiasts from all over the world flock to Hawaiian waters. Fishing boats can be chartered from *Coreene C's Sport Fishing Charters* (phone: 536-7472) or *Island Charters* (phone: 536-1555). Most boats leave from Kewalo Basin, at the end of Ward Avenue, on Ala Moana Boulevard.

Fitness Centers – The *YMCA* has a pool, racquetball court, sauna, exercise machines, and weights (401 Atkinson Dr., across from *Ala Moana Center;* phone: 941-3344). For a treat, set up an appointment with the massage (shiatsu) specialist at the *Sheraton Moana Surfrider* (2365 Kalakaua Ave.; phone: 922-3111).

Football – Enthusiasts of the sport can participate in the NFL Pro Bowl Dream Week, where amateurs are coached by and play with such football legends as Gale Sayers, Willie Lanier, Mel Blount, and Don Maynard. Everyone competes at the end of the week in a big pre-*Pro Bowl* football game at *Aloha Stadium* — and survivors get to attend the *Pro Bowl* game itself the next day. For information, contact *Dream Week, Inc.,* 2337 Philmont Ave., Huntingdon Valley, PA 19006 (phone: 215-938-1200 or 800-888-4376).

Gliding – *Hawaii Glider Rides* has 3-seat sailplanes departing about every 20 minutes daily from 10:30 AM to 5 PM at the north shore's Dillingham Airfield (phone: 677-3404).

Golf – There are numerous public golf courses on Oahu, with more in the planning stage. These include *Ala Wai,* the closest to Waikiki (phone: 296-4653); *Pali,* in Kaneohe (phone: 296-7254); *Sheraton West* course (phone: 695-9544) and *Makaha Valley Country Club* (phone: 695-7111), both in Makaha; The *Ko Olina* course (phone: 682-7324) near the Ewa district, west of Honolulu; and the *Turtle Bay Hilton* (phone: 293-8811), near Kahuku on the north shore.

Jogging – Run along Kalakaua Avenue to Kapiolani Park, where a group meets at the bandstand at 7:30 AM every Sunday from March through December for a short lecture and a run. The distance around the park is 1.8 miles; to tack on more mileage, continue along Kalakaua to Diamond Head Road and circle the base of Diamond Head. The road turns into Monsarrat Avenue, which leads back to Kalakaua (4½ miles altogether). Or take Diamond Head Road as far as Kahala Avenue, one of the island's most beautiful runs. Also popular, the 2-mile perimeter of Ala Moana Beach Park.

Kayaking – *Adventure Kayaking International* conducts a series of kayak tours, including 2-hour sunset and full-moon excursions, along the Diamond Head–Waikiki coast. They also offer day trips for beginners, starting at $45 a day, and 1- to 5-day overnight kayaking excursions to the Big Island and Molokai plus Tahiti and Fiji. Prices for overnight trips start at $150 a day and include kayaks, guides, gear, and food (but not air fare to or from the final destination). Excursions arranged for groups of 4 to 12 (children welcome, too). 53-352 Kam Hwy., in Ponaluu (phone: 924-8898 or 800 52-KAYAK).

Skin Diving – *Dan's Dive Shop* (660 Ala Moana Blvd.; phone: 536-6181) rents diving gear, offers instructions for beginners, and has brush-up courses for those with some experience. Out near Makaha, call *Lee-*

ward Dive Center (phone: 696-3414). On the north shore, call *Underwater Hawaii* (at the *Turtle Bay Hilton,* 57091 Kam Hwy., Kahuku, HI 96731; phone: 293-8811) for lessons, or *Surf and Sea* in Haleiwa (phone: 637-9887) for rentals. Snorkelers can take an inexpensive day trip to Hanauma Bay with *Hanauma Bay Snorkeling Tours* (phone: 944-8828). *Barefoot Charters* (phone: 522-1533) departs Kewalo Basin for half-day sails that include snorkeling in the marine preserve off Diamond Head (no tours are available on Wednesdays or Thursdays).

Surfing – The quest for the perfect wave attracts surfers from all over the world. Most hotels along Waikiki Beach have surfing instructors and concessions that rent surfboards, canoes, and catamarans. The most famous surfing beaches are Sunset, Ehukai, and Waimea, on the north side of the island. Major international competitions are held here in late November through early January.

Swimming – With Waikiki Beach generally very crowded, an alternative is to head to nearby Ala Moana or Diamond Head beach parks, or to beaches on the other side of the island. Equally spectacular settings include Sandy Beach and Makapuu, where just about everyone body-surfs; Waimanalo and Kailua, where swimming and windsurfing are popular; and on up the coast to Kahana and the legendary surfing beaches of the north shore. Many beaches are dangerous for swimming; stick to those with lifeguards.

Tennis – There are public courts at 40 places around Oahu. Try Ala Moana Park (phone: 522-7031), *Diamond Head Tennis Center* (phone: 971-7150), or *Kapiolani Tennis Courts* (no phone), or *Honolulu Tennis Center* (phone: 944-9696). The *Ilikai* hotel has 6 courts (1 lighted for night play), the *Hawaiian Regent* has 1 court, while the *Kahala Hilton* offers 6 courts (all night-lit) at the *Maunalua Bay Club.*

Windsurfing – *Aloha Windsurfing* (phone: 926-1185) and *Naish Hawaii* (phone: 261-6067) feature rentals and lessons in Waikiki or windward Oahu.

THEATER: You can get tickets at the door for most plays and musicals in Honolulu. The main theaters are *Blaisdell Memorial Center Concert Hall* (Ward and King Sts.; phone: 537-6191); *Diamond Head Theater* (Makapuu and Aloha Aves.; phone: 734-0274); and *Hawaii Performing Arts Company's Manoa Theatre* (2833 E. Manoa Rd.; phone: 988-6131). Also check for under-the-stars performances at the *Waikiki Shell* (phone: 521-2911).

MUSIC: The *Honolulu Symphony* plays at the *Blaisdell Center Concert Hall* (phone: 537-6191). Rock musicians appear at the *Blaisdell Center Arena* (phone: 521-2911) or sometimes at *Aloha Stadium* (phone: 486-9300) or the *Waikiki Shell* (phone: 521-2911). If the *Brothers Cazimero* are performing at the *Royal Hawaiian,* it's worth a visit.

NIGHTCLUBS AND NIGHTLIFE: With a large tourist industry to support it and a Hawaiian musical tradition to provide the raw material, the Kalakaua Avenue area swings from about 8 PM until 1 AM, with some clubs open until 4 AM, most nights of the week. Hawaii's most famous singer and entertainer, Don Ho, plays the *Hilton Dome,* as does illusionist John Hirokawa, whose mix of magic and Polynesian revue is one of Waikiki's most entertaining shows. Charo performs at the *Hilton's Tropics Room* (2005 Kalia Rd., in the *Hilton Hawaiian Village;* phone: 949-4321). The *Society of Seven* offers a Las Vegas–style revue that's become a Waikiki classic at the *Outrigger Waikiki* (2335 Kalakaua Ave.; phone: 923-0711). The *Brothers Cazimero* frequently perform at the *Royal Hawaiian's Monarch Room* and are the most popular and enduring of Hawaii's musical entertainers. There's also a piano bar at the *Sheraton Waikiki* (2255 Kalakaua Ave.; phone: 922-

4422), and, for a mix of pop and jazz, try *Trapper's* (at the *Hyatt Regency,* 2424 Kalakaua Ave.; phone: 923-1234). Popular discos include *Annabelle's* (atop the *Ilikai* hotel; phone: 949-3811); *Bobby McGees* (at the *Colony Surf,* 2885 Kalakaua Ave.; phone: 922-1282); *Rumours* (at the *Ala Moana;* phone: 955-4811); *Pink Cadillac* (478 Ena Rd.; phone: 942-5282); *Wave Waikiki* (1877 Kalakaua Ave.; phone: 941-0424); *Moose McGillycuddy's* (310 Lewers St.; phone: 923-0751); *Cilly's* (1909 Ala Wai Blvd.; phone: 942-2952); *Spats* (at the *Hyatt Regency Waikiki;* phone: 923-1234); *Maharaja* (at the Waikiki Trade Center, 2255 Kuhio Ave.; phone: 922-3030); and *Hula's* (2103 Kuhio Ave.; phone: 923-0669), with a mixed crowd ranging from punk to gay. The *Hard Rock Café* (1837 Kapiolani Blvd.; phone: 955-7383) attracts cognoscenti and commoners alike. At *Studebaker's,* in Restaurant Row (on the outskirts of downtown Honolulu), crowds line up to enter and enjoy music of the 1950s and 1960s with let-it-all-hang-out dancing by waiters and waitresses as well as patrons (500 Ala Moana Blvd.; phone: 526-9888). Check Oahu newspapers to find out where a favorite local funny man, Frank Delima, is appearing. His Imelda Marcos impression is worth the price of admission.

BEST IN TOWN

CHECKING IN: Honolulu hotels vary in personality, so do a bit of careful checking before picking one. Remember, it's not just a place to sleep; it also will serve as your tropical headquarters during your visit. Expect to pay $250 or more for a double at those places we've listed as very expensive; around $160 and up at hotels classed as expensive; between $70 and $150 at those designated moderate; under $70 at hotels listed as inexpensive. For a "superior double" room in a Waikiki condominium, expect to pay around $150 and up; for a standard condominium, the charge is $80 to $145 a night. Unless otherwise stated, the same rate applies for one to four people, though there often is a nominal (under $10) charge for each person after the first two. For bed and breakfast accommodations, contact *Bed & Breakfast Hawaii* (Box 449, Kapaa, HI 96746; phone: 822-7771), *Pacific Hawaii Bed & Breakfast* (970 N. Kalaheo Ave.; Suite A218, Kailua, HI 96734; phone: 254-5030), or *Bed and Breakfast Honolulu* (3242 Kaohinani Dr., Honolulu, HI 96817; phone: 595-7533). All telephone numbers are in the 808 area code unless otherwise indicated.

HOTELS

Aston Waikiki Beachside – This elegant remake of the *Waikiki Surfside,* completed last year, is decorated with Italian marble and antiques. Now Waikiki's most upscale hotel, it has 79 rooms, superb service, and is located directly across from the Kuhio section of Waikiki Beach. Amenities include a concierge desk, photocopiers, and CNN. 2452 Kalakaua Ave. (phone: 923-0266; 800-92-ASTON; Fax: 808-926-7380; Telex: 634479). Very expensive to expensive.

Halekulani – This contemporary mid-rise incorporates the old Lewers home, which served as the original hotel. Among its features are 456 rooms, a library, and an open-air, oceanfront lounge — *House Without a Key* — featuring Hawaiian music and fine views of Diamond Head and sunsets. Its restaurants, *Orchids* and *La Mer* (see *Eating Out* for both), are among Honolulu's best. Designed to reestablish Waikiki as a destination for the carriage trade, it is the essence of contemporary elegance. Room service is available around the clock. Among the business conveniences are 6 meeting rooms, concierge, secretarial services, A/V equipment, photocopiers, and computers. CNN and express checkout are also pluses. 2199 Kalia Rd. (phone: 923-2311; 800-367-2343; Fax: 808-926-8004; Telex: 8382). Very expensive to expensive.

Hawaii Prince – The second Hawaii property for Japan's Prince hotel chain (the other is on Maui). Attention to detail, carefully prepared cuisine, and panoramic views of the neighboring Ala Wai Yacht Harbor are the main justifications for upscale rates. On the western edge of Waikiki, it is just a short walk from Ala Moana Beach and Waikiki Beach. Twenty-four–hour room service is available, as are 6 meeting rooms. A concierge and secretarial services are on call. Other pluses are A/V equipment, photocopiers, CNN, and express checkout. 100 Holomoana St. (phone: 956-1111; 800-321-6284; Fax: 808-946-0811; Telex: 9460811). Very expensive to expensive.

Hilton Hawaiian Village – The $100 million devoted to upgrading the rooms, public areas, and the grounds of the 22-acre Hilton complex has been well spent, catapulting the decor out of the 1960s and into the 1990s. The result is a more open and appealing resort. With close to 2,600 rooms, it is Hawaii's largest hotel, as well as the western terminus of Waikiki Beach. Standing between the Duke Kahanamoku Lagoon and the beach, it boasts a colorful shopping center, its own post office, and a catamaran that offers both day and night cruises. The Rainbow Tower, with its 30-story rainbow mosaic (the *Golden Dragon* and *Bali Hai* restaurants (see *Eating Out*), and the Tapa Tower, with its 250 corner suites, have the best views. The Alii Tower (with the most luxurious rooms in the hotel) also has good views, plus its own pool and full concierge services. The village has lots that visitors want from a Hawaiian vacation — pools, beaches, fine dining, luaus, and Polynesian shows featuring Don Ho — but lacks the peace and serenity of rural Oahu. There are 32 meeting rooms, plus secretarial services, A/V equipment, photocopiers, and computers. A concierge desk, CNN, and express checkout are other pluses. 2005 Kalia Rd. (phone: 949-4321; 800-445-8667; Fax: 808-947-7914). Very expensive to expensive.

Kahala Hilton – Operated by Hilton International (which is now run by Britain's Ladbrooke group), this is one of the chain's prime showplaces. Queen Elizabeth II spent a couple of nights here, and King Juan Carlos of Spain came for part of his honeymoon with Queen Sophia. The main structure of this lavish hostelry is 12 stories high and overlooks an 800-foot stretch of beach that loses nothing by being manmade. Additional low-rise wings face the beach and the large lagoon in which dolphins, turtles, and penguins cavort. Rooms in the main building have semicircular lanais decorated with bougainvillea. Rooms have been recently refurbished and are elegant and spacious. The lobby offers handsome chandeliers and a stunning circular carpet — that manages to look plush and airy at the same time. Guests are greeted with chilled pineapple, and an orchid is laid on each pillow when beds are turned down in the evening. Besides ocean and pool swimming, the hotel provides kayaks and snorkeling equipment and can arrange deep-sea fishing and scuba diving. European efficiency at the executive level and island good humor at the service level are the keynotes here. They work together like a charm. There also are fine restaurants (see *Eating Out*). Business amenities include 3 meeting rooms, secretarial services, A/V equipment, photocopiers, and computers. CNN, 24-hour room service, concierge, and express checkout are also available. 5000 Kahala Ave., Kahala (phone: 734-2211; 800-367-2525; Fax: 808-737-2478; Telex: 397148). Expensive.

Sheraton Moana Surfrider – This beautifully restored Victorian hostelry has been standing at the edge of the Waikiki surf since 1901. Until its exotic neighbor, the *Royal Hawaiian,* was opened in 1927, the *Moana* was the only hotel in the area. Brass headboards, white wicker chairs, antique lamps, and Victorian armoires adorn many of the rooms. These touches, and in many cases a ceiling fan, manage to make you forget the more modern iconography of Waikiki outside. A recently completed multimillion-dollar face-lift has restored the hotel's turn-of-the-century charm. When making reservations, it is wise to specify a room in the old building, if that is what you want, as the Surfrider wing is more contemporary in style and decor. Rooms facing Kalakaua Ave. can be noisy. The new *Ship's Tavern* restaurant serves dinner nightly (see *Eating Out*). Among the amenities here are 24-hour room service, 7 meeting rooms, concierge, secretarial services, A/V equipment, photocopiers, computers, CNN, and express checkout. 2365 Kalakaua Ave. (phone: 922-3111; 800-325-3535; Fax: 808-943-0122). Expensive.

Ala Moana – Bright, sunny rooms highlighted by tropical colors and a full range of hotel services compensate for the fact that this 36-story property is not close enough to the Waikiki beaches to be in the swing. Rooms are quite attractive, thanks to a recent renovation. *Nicholas Nickolas* is its first-rate restaurant (see *Eating Out*). Concierge, CNN, and express checkout all are available, as are 7 meeting rooms, secretarial services, A/V equipment, photocopiers, and computers. 410 Atkinson Dr. (phone: 955-4811; 800-367-6025; Fax: 808-944-2974; Telex: 9474705). Expensive to moderate.

Diamond Head Beach – This 14-story structure on the beach is an attractive place in terms of price and location in Honolulu. Units range from hotel rooms to 1-bedroom apartments. Rooms are smallish but comfortable, with good-size lanais. Although there is little in the way of a lobby and no shops, pool, or tour desks, these are available close by, in the *New Otani*. Services include a concierge desk and photocopiers. CNN is available. 2947 Kalakaua Ave. (phone: 922-1928; 800-777-1700; Fax: 808-924-8980). Expensive to moderate.

Hawaiian Regent – Just across the road from the beach, the two tall towers possess little architectural distinction. The interiors, however, are a bit more appealing, with inner courtyards paved in tile and marble, and an outdoor-café atmosphere in the main lobby. The Ocean Terrace pool area is also inviting, and the rooms are large and comfortable. There are several first class restaurants in the hotel, including the prestigious *The Secret* (see *Eating Out*), which has a 6,000-bottle wine cellar. *The Library*, where there's not a book in sight, has some unusually good soft music starting at 8:30 PM. Business services include 12 meeting rooms, concierge, secretarial services, A/V equipment, photocopiers, computers, CNN, and express checkout. 2552 Kalakaua Ave. (phone: 922-6611; 800-367-5370; Fax: 808-921-5255). Expensive to moderate.

Holiday Inn Waikiki Beach – Although the rooms here provide the standard *Holiday Inn* level of style and comfort, this place boasts magnificent views of the ocean and Diamond Head. It also has a terrific site: just outside the hustle-bustle of the strip, next door to Kapiolani Park and the *Honolulu Zoo*, and across the street from the least crowded stretch of Waikiki Beach. Its *Captain's Table*, an easygoing eatery that looks out at the sea, is a good spot to sample your first mahimahi. Two meeting rooms are available for business needs, as well as A/V equipment, photocopiers, and CNN. 2570 Kalakaua Ave. (phone: 922-2511; 800-877-7666; Fax: 808-923-3656; Telex: 634226). Expensive to moderate.

Hyatt Regency – The two octagonal towers are a visual landmark among the concrete blocks along Kalakaua Avenue. The Great Hall, with its outdoor tropical garden, 3-story waterfall, and massive hanging sculpture, is a sightseeing spot in its own right. Each of its 1,234 rooms is furnished handsomely, and the art on the walls invariably is worth looking at. In the suites, which feature some exceptional antiques, there are also original oil paintings. Guests in the Regency Club, on the 39th and 40th floors, have their own private, complimentary bar and concierge. The pool deck is one of the most attractive in Waikiki, and the bars, cafés, and restaurants in the complex — they include *Musashi, Bagwell's, Furusato,* and *Spats* (see *Eating Out* for all) — and disco, and *Trapper's* (a jazz club) are among Waikiki's best. Amenities include 24-hour room service, 8 meeting rooms, A/V equipment, photocopiers, CNN, and express checkout. 2424 Kalakaua Ave. (phone: 923-1234; 800-233-1234; Fax: 808-926-3415; Telex: 7238278). Expensive to moderate.

Ilikai – This 3-pronged hotel on the *ewa* (western) edge of Waikiki includes Waikiki's best tennis facilities, with 6 courts, and pros available to provide instruction. The open area at the lobby level has pools, terraces, and fountains. The beach, Duke Kahanamoku Lagoon, and the yacht marina are just a stone's throw away. The 800 rooms are among the most spacious in Waikiki, and were renovated in 1991, when Nikko Hotels took over the hotel. Some rooms have kitchenettes. Atop the hotel sits *Annabelle's,* a disco reached via a spectacular ride in an exterior elevator that opens up vast panoramas of the Pacific as you ascend. Guests can request room service around the clock. Among the business conveniences are 12 meeting rooms, a concierge desk, secretarial services, A/V equipment, photocopiers, CNN, and express checkout. 1777 Ala Moana Blvd. (phone: 949-3811; 800-367-8434; Fax: 808-947-4523; Telex: 634555). Expensive to moderate.

New Otani Kaimana Beach – The location is the thing here: on the Diamond Head side of Kapiolani Park, just a few minutes away from Waikiki by foot or bus. The beach is right outside, and beautiful reefs are within easy snorkeling distance. The *Hau Tree Lanai* restaurant overlooks the beach and is edged by (and named for) large hau trees (see *Eating Out*). Oceanside rooms have stunning views. Families seem to like it here, and women traveling alone have found it a friendly, hospitable, and safe haven. There's a concierge desk, as well as secretarial services, 2 meeting rooms, A/V equipment, photocopiers, CNN, and express checkout. 2863 Kalakaua Ave. (phone: 923-1555; 800-657-7949; Fax: 808-922-9404; Telex: 7430470). Expensive to moderate.

Outrigger Reef – With 800 rooms, this is one of the largest of the more moderately priced hotels in Waikiki. All rooms and public areas have recently been upgraded, resulting in somewhat higher rates, although it remains well-priced when compared to its neighbors on the beach. Guests here seem to use their lanais more than those at any other hotel in the neighborhood; it's a friendly sight. Four meeting rooms, secretarial services, A/V equipment, photocopiers, computers, CNN, and express checkout are among the business amenities. 2169 Kalia Rd. (phone: 923-3111; 800-733-7777; Fax: 808-924-4957). Expensive to moderate.

Outrigger Waikiki – Recently fully renovated and refurbished, this beachfront property features extras like a beachside health club with an exercise room and lockers for beach-goers' convenience. Four restaurants are on the property, including *Monterrey Bay Canners* (see *Eating Out*). This is one of the better-priced Waikiki beachfront hotels. One meeting room is available for business needs, as well as secretarial services, A/V equipment, photocopiers, computers, and express checkout. 2335 Kalakaua Ave. (phone: 923-0711; 800-733-7777; Fax: 808-921-9749). Expensive to moderate.

Pacific Beach – Standing on the site of the summer home of Queen Liliuokalani, this property has a 280,000-gallon indoor oceanarium, which can be viewed from the hotel's bars and restaurants. Along with the swimming pool, there are tennis courts, shuffleboards, and a

Jacuzzi to ensure a feeling of well-being. A good buy. Other pluses are 7 meeting rooms, concierge, secretarial services, A/V equipment, photocopiers, computers, CNN, and express checkout. 2490 Kalakaua Ave. (phone: 922-1233; 800-367-6060; Fax: 808-922-0129; Telex: 633101). Expensive to moderate.

Royal Hawaiian – "The Pink Lady," as this flamingo-colored, 6-story landmark of Spanish-Moorish design is best known, is flanked by two other Sheraton properties that seem to stand in an adversary, rather than a neighborly, stance. This is one of the two grand old hotels in Waikiki (the *Sheraton Moana Surfrider* is the other). The pink color scheme runs, perhaps a smidgin too obviously, throughout the hotel. Most of the rooms have either a pink sofa, quilt, or drapes. Usually it works, sometimes it doesn't. In any case, once away from the bustle of the lobby, which attracts ten times more spectators than guests, this remains a hotel with distinctive charm. Room service is on call around the clock. There are 5 meeting rooms, secretarial services, A/V equipment, photcopiers, CNN, and express checkout. Reservations through the *Sheraton Waikiki,* 2259 Kalakaua Ave. (phone: 923-7311; 800-325-3535; Fax: 808-924-7098; Telex: 7431240). Expensive to moderate.

Sheraton Waikiki – With 1,852 rooms on 31 floors, this is the largest hotel tower in Hawaii. Lanais on the Pacific side loom over the ocean as precipitously as a cliff. It's a splendid sensation if you don't suffer from vertigo, and the sunsets can be memorable. Happily, subtle tans and casually tropical styling have replaced the garish greens and floral designs that made the rooms and lobby rather hard on the eyes. The *Sheraton* has all that's expected from a big hotel: There is never a dearth of taxis, it's a pickup point for every major tour operator, *TheBus* stops nearby, and there is just about every kind of restaurant you could crave, except a truly first class one. Ten meeting rooms, secretarial services, A/V equipment, photocopiers, computers, CNN, and AP wire service round out the business amenities. There's also a concierge desk and express checkout. 2255 Kalakaua Ave. (phone: 922-4422; 800-325-3535; Fax: 808-923-8785; Telex: 7430115). Expensive to moderate.

Ilima – Near the Ala Wai Canal, about 3 blocks from the *Royal Hawaiian Beach,* it offers the additional convenience of full kitchens in all rooms, as well as a restaurant, cocktail lounge, sauna, and pool. Business pluses include 1 meeting room, A/V equipment and photocopiers, and CNN. 445 Nohonani St. (phone: 923-1877; 800-876-5278 in California, 800-367-5172 in other states; Fax: 808-924-8371). Moderate.

Manoa Valley Inn – This is one of Hawaii's most complete bed and breakfast facilities, with 8 bedrooms in a beautifully restored turn-of-the-century Manoa Valley home, and it is highly recommended. Rates include an ample continental breakfast, afternoon pupus, and sunset cocktails. Bus connections to *Ala Moana Center,* and from there to all other parts of Oahu, also are available. Photocopiers, computers, and CNN are all offered here. About 2 miles from Waikiki, at 2001 Vancouver Dr. (phone: 947-6019; 800-634-5115; Fax: 808-946-6168). Moderate.

Outrigger Prince Kuhio – Quietly set on Kuhio Avenue, just 1 block from the beach, it manages to feel like a small hotel despite its 620 rooms on 37 floors. There are a maximum of 18 rooms to a floor, and each room is individually decorated and furnished, with its own wet bar and marble bathroom. The lobby is a graceful and airy place where complimentary coffee is poured from a silver samovar every morning. Rooms high on the Diamond Head side have stunning views of the crater. The top 3 floors are part of the exclusive *Kuhio Club.* There's a concierge desk, as well as 7 meeting rooms, secretarial services, A/V equipment, photocopiers, computers, CNN, and express checkout. 2500 Kuhio Ave. (phone: 922-0811; 800-733-7777; Fax: 808-923-0330). Moderate.

Outrigger Reef Towers – Although it is hard to believe that a street of concrete blocks can have character, the section of Lewers Street between Kalia Road and Kalakaua Avenue does — it's narrow and shaded by very tall, spindly coconut palms. One of the concrete blocks is the *Reef Towers*. Though gorgeous vistas are not a selling point here, some people find it an excellent buy. Rooms with kitchenettes are available. Photocopiers, A/V equipment, CNN, and express checkout are all available. 227 Lewers St. (phone: 923-3111; 800-733-7777; Fax: 808-924-6042). Moderate.

Waikiki Beachcomber – Whether you look toward the ocean, Diamond Head, or downtown, the lanais here are a pleasant spot for breakfast or cocktails. For the price, its rooms are surprisingly large, with separate dressing areas and capacious closets, and their layout and color scheme give them a feeling of coolness and comfort. The lobby has facilities for booking tours, and the hotel is a short walk from the beach. Room service is available until 9 PM, and there is a concierge, A/V equipment, photocopiers, and express checkout. 2300 Kalakaua Ave. (phone: 922-4646; 800-622-4646; Fax: 808-923-4889). Moderate.

Waikiki Joy – This 101-room hotel is convenient to Waikiki's shops, restaurants, and beach (a 3-block walk away). Rooms are furnished in contemporary colors and decor, and are outfitted with refrigerators (many have kitchenettes or complete kitchens), stereos, and in-bath Jacuzzis. The staff is friendly and knowledgeable, and the public area is attractively done up in marble. The pool is small, however, and lower floors may pick up some street noise. There's a concierge desk, and room service is available during meal times. Secretarial services, A/V equipment, photocopiers, CNN, and express checkout are pluses. 320 Lewers St. (phone: 923-2300; 800-733-5569; Fax: 808-955-1313). Moderate.

Waikiki Parc – Operated by the same Japanese company that owns the neighboring *Halekulani,* this place focuses on service and high-tech features such as computer-coded room locks on its 298 rooms. It's an easy walk to Waikiki Beach, a fact that isn't immediately obvious from its towering proximity to the *Halekulani* and the *Sheraton Waikiki*. Room service is available until 10 PM. There is a concierge desk, secretarial services, photocopiers, express checkout, and CNN, too. 2233 Helumoa Rd. (phone: 921-7272; 800-422-0450; Fax: 808-923-1336). Moderate.

Waikiki Shores Apartments – By a stroke of luck, this apartment hotel stands next to the *Ft. DeRussy Army Museum* and has an unobstructed view across the museum grounds. From each wide lanai there is a panorama of both ocean and mountains. Studios convert easily from living to sleeping accommodations, and suites have very comfortable, bright, and "homey" living rooms. Linen, cooking utensils, and dishes are provided. There are fully equipped kitchens and weekly maid service. Cost and location combine to make this one of the best buys on the beach, especially for families. 2161 Kalia Rd. (phone: 926-4733; 800-367-2353; Fax: 808-922-2902). Moderate.

Waikiki Terrace – Located adjacent to Ft. DeRussy, many rooms have spectacular views. It's also conveniently located within a short walking distance of central Waikiki's shops and beach. 2045 Kalakaua Ave. (phone: 955-6000; 800-445-8811; Fax: 808-943-8555). Moderate.

Waikikian – For many returning visitors, the torches that blaze outside each night signal that they are once more entering the fabled resort area. More torches line the narrow path that passes between the Polynesian cabanas that are the hotel's salient feature. These are decorated in Hawaiian motifs, with ceiling fans, rattan carpets, exposed timber ceilings, and wooden lanais, all contributing to the South Seas atmosphere. Some units also have kitchenettes. An adjacent 6-story contemporary building offers more conventional accommodations. The beach, a romantic lagoon, and a particularly attractive palm-fringed poolside area with a popular outdoor café called the *Tahitian Lanai* complete the amenities. Room service is available until 10 PM, and there's a concierge desk, photocopiers, and CNN. 1811 Ala Moana Blvd. (phone: 949-5331; 800-922-7866 Fax: 808-946-2843). Moderate.

Best Western Outrigger Edgewater – This small hostelry manages to look more like a seaside apartment house than a hotel and exudes an air of calm and quiet. For those who find the hurly-burly of large establishments either intimidating or just plain exhausting, this is the ideal spot at an ideal price. An added attraction is the *Trattoria,* a well-regarded Italian restaurant. Concierge, CNN, and express check-out are pluses. 2168 Kalia Rd. (phone: 922-6424; 800-733-7777; Fax: 808-922-6424; Telex: 634178). Moderate to inexpensive.

Colony's Coconut Plaza – Overlooking the Ala Wai Canal, this 84-room hotel is within a 10-minute walking distance of the beach. Rooms are appealingly decorated and offer panoramic views from comfortable lanais. The grounds include a small garden and fountain. Good service, complimentary continental breakfast, kitchenettes, restaurant, bar, and a heated pool are all pluses. Photocopiers are available. 2171 Ala Wai Blvd. (phone: 923-8828; 800-882-9696; Fax: 808-923-3473). Moderate to inexpensive.

Outrigger Waikiki Village – Brightly decorated with an emphasis on greens and blues, this member of the Outrigger chain is popular with young couples making a first visit to Hawaii. The poolside area is, if anything, busier than many others in the district, considering that the ocean is just 2 blocks away. Perhaps what attracts so many is its underwater viewing area. Some rooms have kitchenettes; all have CNN. Photocopiers are availble for guests' use. 240 Lewers St. (phone: 923-3881; 800-733-7777; Fax: 808-922-2330). Moderate to inexpensive.

Pleasant Holiday Isle – Right in the heart of Waikiki and just a block from the beach, this is a compact hotel where both the decor and the service are casually cheerful. This, plus reasonable rates, more than compensates for the fact that from most of the lanais, the view is less than indelible, and the street noise is occasionally audible. There's 1 meeting room, photocopiers, and CNN. 270 Lewers St. (phone: 923-0777). Moderate to inexpensive.

Quality Inn Waikiki – Just 1 block from 220-acre Kapiolani Park at the foot of Diamond Head, it has always enjoyed a good reputation for service and comfort. Some rooms in the older Diamond Head Tower and all the rooms in the newer Pali Tower have kitchenettes, although the newer accommodations tend to be larger and more subdued in decor. There are 2 swimming pools for people who find the 3-minute stroll to the beach too strenuous. 175 Paoakalani Ave. (phone: 922-3861; 800-221-2222; Fax: 808-924-1982). Moderate to inexpensive.

Royal Islander – Another stopping place where smallness is an advantage. The front desk personnel usually manage to remember guests' names. Recently renovated rooms are on the small side, though not oppressively so, and each has a lanai, refrigerator, and coffee-making facilities. Street noise may prove bothersome. The property is now managed by the Outrigger chain and is opposite the *Reef* hotel, behind which is the beach. 2164 Kalia Rd. (phone: 922-1961; 800-733-7777; Fax: 808-456-4329). Moderate to inexpensive.

Waikiki Parkside – Overlooking Ft. DeRussy and Ala Moana Boulevard, it offers CNN, complimentary indoor parking with shopping, restaurants, and the beach minutes away. One meeting room is available for business needs. 1850 Ala Moana Blvd. (phone: 955-1567; 800-237-9666; Fax: 808-955-6010). Moderate to inexpensive.

Royal Grove – A small apartment hotel with personality. Like the *Royal Hawaiian,* it is painted pink. There are very comfortable, cheerful studios as well as 1-bedroom units. CNN is available. Although the ocean, a block and a half away, is visible from some of the lanais, many people prefer to look out on the pool and tropical gardens. Most rooms have air conditioning and kitchenettes. There is maid service but no room service. 151 Uluniu Ave. (phone: 923-7691). Inexpensive.

Town Inn – This 26-room downtown property offers the basics at appropriate rates of $35 a day without air conditioning, $37 with it. Weekly rates also are available. Just beyond Chinatown in a totally un-Hawaiian setting. 250 N. Beretania St. (phone: 536-2377). Inexpensive.

Waikiki Surf – One of the "finds" of Honolulu. In a semi-residential part of Waikiki, it's friendly, clean, decorated in blue and green, quiet, and delightfully inexpensive. Some rooms have kitchenettes. Perhaps best of all, the 288-room *Waikiki Surf* has two companions — the 102-room *Waikiki Surf East* (422 Royal Hawaiian Ave.) and the 110-room *Waikiki Surf West* (412 Lewers St.) — owned and run by the same very friendly people. The original *Waikiki Surf* is at 2200 Kuhio Ave. (switchboard for all three: 923-7671; 800-733-7777; Fax: 808-921-4804). Inexpensive.

CONDOMINIUMS

Aston Waikiki Beach Tower – With only four 2-bedroom apartments to a floor (some can be divided to rent as 1-bedroom units), this is one of Waikiki's most exclusive rentable condominium. The views, particularly on floors 25 to 40, are magnificent, with large lanais offering front-row seats as the sun slides into the Pacific. Another prime asset is privacy — the perfect antidote to the street energy of Waikiki. Full concierge service, with the beach just across the street. 2470 Kalakaua Ave. (phone: 926-6400; 800-922-7866; Fax: 808-926-7380). Very expensive to expensive.

Aston Waikiki Sunset – Given the facilities, good-looking accommodations, and location just 2 blocks from the beach, this place is worth considering. Besides swimming in the large pool, guests can play tennis or shuffleboard. Daily maid service. 229 Paoakalani Ave. (phone: 922-0511; 800-922-7866; Fax: 808-923-8580). Expensive to moderate.

Colony Surf – A true Hollywood-style condominium right on the beach, it is one of the most delightful places to stay in Honolulu. Apartments are decorated in the plush, off-white tones that many people associate with seaside living. There are no lanais, but large windows with glorious views. Kitchens are modern and fully equipped, and there is daily maid service and adequate laundry facilities. The small, elegant lobby leads to *Michel's* restaurant (see *Eating Out*). Studios with lanais and kitchenettes are available in the adjacent *Colony East* hotel, which is owned and operated by the same company at the same address, but lacks the flair and views of the main building. 2895 Kalakaua Ave. (phone: 923-5751; 800-252-7873; Fax: 808-922-8433). Expensive to moderate.

Aston Banyan at Waikiki – One of the largest condos in Waikiki, it's a short walk from the beach, zoo, and Kapiolani Park. The living rooms are decorated handsomely and have attractive breakfast counters that separate them from the kitchen. The building contains a sauna, a large recreation area with tennis courts and a swimming pool, laundry facilities on each floor, and daily maid service. From the top floor on the Diamond Head side, you see beyond the crater to Maunalua Bay. 201 Ohua Ave. (phone: 922-0555; 800-922-7866; Fax: 808-922-0906). Moderate.

Aston Island Colony – Another high-rise looking out on the Koolau Mountains and the canal, it is decorated with bleached-wood furniture, light brown walls and textiles, and beige carpets, giving it a pleasantly restful appearance. It also has a restaurant, pool, sauna, and hydromassage facilities, as well as shuffleboard. Daily maid service. 445 Seaside Ave. (phone: 923-2345; 800-922-7866; Fax: 808-922-0991). Moderate.

Foster Tower – For location alone — right across Kalakaua Avenue from the beach — this is one of Waikiki's better buys, although decor in some rooms may be a bit dated. All rooms have color TV sets, and on the property are a restaurant, pool, and shops. No maid service. 2500 Kalakaua Ave. (phone: 523-7785; 800-367-7040; Fax: 808-537-3701). Moderate.

Imperial Hawaii – A short walk from the beach, the location is its primary asset, although rooms are nicely furnished and many of the lanais offer partial ocean views. Pool, shops, coffee shop, and sauna on property. 205 Lewers St. (phone: 923-1827; 800-367-8047, ext. 225; Fax: 808-923-7848). Moderate.

Pacific Monarch – Close to the *Kings Alley* shopping bazaar and a few minutes from the beach, the property offers spectacular views from its upper-floor 1-bedroom and studio units and the rooftop pool area. Laundry facilities and daily maid service. 142 Uluniu Ave. (phone: 923-9805; 800-777-1700; Fax: 808-924-3220). Moderate.

Royal Kuhio – Two blocks away from the beach and the *International Market Place,* it has upper-floor units that offer some of the best views of Diamond Head in Waikiki. On the 7th-floor deck are barbecue facilities, a pool, and shuffleboard. Weekly maid service. 2240 Kuhio Ave. (phone: 923-1747). Moderate.

Waikiki Lanais – With attractively furnished 1- and 2-bedroom apartments on one of Waikiki's quieter streets, this well-maintained condominium features a mix of vacation rentals and full-time residences that adds to its appeal, as does its location near the beach and the commercial heart of Waikiki. 2452 Tusitala St. (phone: 531-7595; 800-367-7042; Fax: 808-544-1868). Moderate.

EATING OUT: Strange as it seems, and disappointing though it is, there are few restaurants serving authentic Hawaiian food in Honolulu. However, there are a number of very good ethnic and continental eating places to sample. Overall, the quality of dining in the city is quite good, and there's an ample selection of restaurants where visitors can enjoy a delightful meal in pleasant surroundings. Expect to pay $100 or more for two people at those places we've described as very expensive; between $60 and $95 at those places listed as expensive; between $30 and $60 for moderate; and under $30, inexpensive. Prices don't include drinks, wine, or tips. All telephone numbers are in the 808 area code unless otherwise indicated.

Bagwell's – Luxury is the watchword here, with sculpted and etched glass and rich pastel hues combining to create a chic tropical atmosphere made all the more appealing and private by semicircular banquettes and raised dining platforms. The service is first class and, although always conscientious and friendly, it sometimes reaches a point where it can seem choreographed. The presentation is every bit as appetizing as the food itself, which includes such distinctive entrées as double breast of roast duck in a purée of island bananas, and broiled lamb chops dressed with a sauce of red bell peppers and caramelized garlic cloves. There also is a good selection of cheeses (unusual in Honolulu) and a distinguished wine list. Jackets are not necessary, but the atmosphere is such that a gentleman may feel more comfortable wearing one. Open daily for dinner. Reservations advised. Major credit cards accepted. In the *Hyatt Regency Hotel*, 2424 Kalakaua Ave. (phone: 923-1234, ext. 6100). Very expensive to expensive.

Black Orchid – Tom Selleck and the owners of *Nick's Fishmarket* have teamed up to manage this restaurant, serving mostly American cooking — both indoors and alfresco. There's also a dance floor and a large, beautifully designed lounge. Open weekdays for lunch, daily for dinner. Reservations advised. Major credit cards accepted. Restaurant Row (phone: 521-3111). Very expensive to expensive.

Chez Michel – The same Michel who lent his name to the *Colony Surf* hotel also created this place. He's retired, but the restaurant remains popular. Just outside the *Hilton Hawaiian Village* end of Waikiki in Eaton Square, it is lush with plants and boasts a rich French decor. The menu is varied, well prepared, and nicely presented. Open daily. Reservations advised. Major credit cards accepted. 444 Hobron La. (phone: 955-7866). Very expensive to expensive.

John Dominis – One of the best dining spots in Honolulu, albeit expensive, at the end of an unpromising street of warehouses and light industries on a promontory overlooking the Kewalo Basin and the Pacific. Inside the dining room, at a central island lavishly laden with fruits of the sea, a chef shucks oysters, steams clams, and makes broth. In saltwater pools spiny lobsters and fresh local fish clamber and swim around. Mainland specialties such as Maine lobster arrive fresh, but this is also the ideal place to sample island seafood: ono (wahoo), onaga (red snapper), and opakapaka (white snapper) are all available in season. The *cioppino* (seafood stew) and fresh fish cooked in tomatoes, herbs, and spices are unbeatable. Open daily for dinner. Reservations necessary. Major credit cards accepted. 43 Ahui St. (phone: 523-0955). Very expensive to expensive.

La Mer – The distinctive menu suits one of Hawaii's most refined restaurants. Start with an appetizer of grilled filet with steamed asparagus and orange sauce, then move on to roast duck with cherries marmalade and port wine sauce. The service is excellent and the decor an appealing blend of Oriental styles. Open daily from 6 to 10 PM. Reservations necessary. Major credit cards accepted. *Halekulani*, 2199 Kalia Rd. (phone: 923-2311). Very expensive to expensive.

Nick's Fishmarket – One of the best fish places in Honolulu. Don't let the earthy name confuse you; this is a plush establishment with individually controlled lighting systems for those customers seated at banquettes and rather too many staffers per customer — the attention can occasionally be stifling. Live Maine lobsters are available at substantial cost, but this is also the ideal place to sample fresh island fish, such as opakapaka, mahimahi, and ulua. The combination seafood Louis salad is enormous and beautifully prepared. Open daily for dinner. Reservations advised. Major credit cards accepted. In the *Waikiki Gateway Hotel*, 2070 Kalakaua Ave. (phone: 955-6333). Very expensive to expensive.

The Secret – Formerly the *Third Floor*, one of the top dining rooms in Honolulu consistently has won prizes for its cooking. Guests dine in a setting of high-backed rattan chairs with red velvet cushions, strolling musicians, a carp pool, and a fountain. Among the house specialties are medallions of veal forêt noire and rack of spring lamb. For dessert there are Polynesian fruits with kirsch, followed by well-made Irish coffee. Open daily for dinner. Reservations advised. Major credit cards accepted; there is a $15 minimum charge. In the *Hawaiian Regent Hotel*, 2552 Kalakaua Ave. (phone: 922-6611). Very expensive to expensive.

Bali by the Sea – Contemporary elegance, enhanced by a mix of cool whites and Mediterranean pastels, sets the scene for seaside dining. The food is excellent, with appetizers like coquille of shrimp and scallops with ginger sauce, enticing entrées such as Kaiwi Channel opakapaka with fresh basil, and a concluding irresistible dessert tray. Open daily for dinner. Reservations advised. Major credit cards accepted. Valet parking is available. *Hilton Hawaiian Village Rainbow Tower,* 2005 Kalia Rd. (phone: 949-4321). Expensive.

Crab Factory Sada – From soft shell to Alaskan king, from snow to Dungeness, crab is king here, and the fine preparation makes it worthy of a royal feast. Steamed, broiled, transformed into salads and soup, this is a real treat for crab lovers. Open daily for dinner. Reservations advised. Major credit cards accepted. 1360 S. King St., near the intersection with Keeaumoku St. (phone: 941-0043). Expensive.

Hy's Steak House – Entering this place is like walking into a magnificent Victorian private library, full of velvet chairs and etched glass. But the gleaming brass broiler inside a glassed-in gazebo, where steaks and chops are prepared with loving care, demonstrates that it is something more. Although the menu indicates that chicken and seafood are available, the main attraction is steaks, which are merely superb. Open daily for dinner. Reservations advised. Major credit cards accepted. 2440 Kuhio Ave. (phone: 922-5555). Expensive.

Maile – Guests descend through a minor jungle of anthuriums, yellow heliconia, and orchids into this restaurant beneath the lobby of the *Kahala Hilton,* where kimono-clad waitresses provide expert, unobtrusive service. The award-winning menu includes roast duckling Waialae (with bananas, peaches, litchi, and oranges) and fresh island chicken (poached in white wine with tarragon). Local fish treated somewhat exotically here include mahimahi glazed with banana and served on creamed mushrooms and baked kumu with fennel and a dash of Pernod. A classical guitarist or a pianist plays during dinner. Live dance music begins at 9 PM. Open daily for dinner only. Brunch is served Sundays from 10 AM to 12:30 PM on the Maile Terrace. Reservations necessary. Major credit cards accepted. *Kahala Hilton,* 5000 Kahala Ave., Kahala (phone: 734-2211). Expensive.

Michel's – At most beachfront spots in Honolulu, the cooking takes a back seat to the view. Not here. For a start, the decor does not suggest a mere extension of sand and ocean. The dining room is elegant and subdued. Although there are occasionally deft local touches, such as prosciutto served with papaya, most of the dishes tend to be continental. Even the opakapaka is served Véronique (with grapes) with a champagne sauce added. Jacket required for dinner. Open daily. Reservations necessary. Major credit cards accepted. In the *Colony Surf Hotel,* 2895 Kalakaua Ave., Diamond Head (phone: 923-6552). Expensive.

Musashi – This very elegant Japanese restaurant in the *Hyatt Regency Waikiki* features three styles of at-the-table preparation as well as a wide-ranging menu of Japanese specialties. Tabletop *teppanyaki* grill; cooked-in broth *shabu shabu* dishes; and cooked-in-sauce sukiyaki dishes are all prepared at the table. There's also an excellent sushi bar. Appealing multilevel decor includes small rock gardens and pools. Open daily for dinner. Reservations advised. Major credit cards accepted. 2424 Kalakana Ave. (phone: 923-1234). Expensive.

Nicholas Nickolas – Fine dining amid soft lights and elegance atop the 40-floor *Ala Moana* hotel, which affords magnificent views. The extensive menu focuses on both American and continental specialties, ranging from veal to lamb, with pasta, soups, salads, and catch-of-the-day entrées in between. Open daily from 5:30 to 11:30 PM, with live entertainment from 9:30 PM to 2:30 AM weekdays, to 3:30 AM on weekends. Reservations advised. Major credit cards accepted. 410 Atkinson Dr. (phone: 955-4466). Expensive.

Roy's – Owner Roy Yamaguchi combines French, Italian, and Asian cooking styles for first-rate results. Try the spiny lobster in macadamia nut butter, the thin-crusted pizza topped with Chinese-style chicken, pickled ginger, shiitake mushrooms and sprouts, or the mesquite-smoked Peking-style duck with candied pecans and passion fruit–ginger sauce. Open for dinner daily; open for brunch on Sundays only. Reservations necessary. Major credit cards accepted. 6600 Kalaniaole Hwy., Hawaii-Kai (phone: 396-ROYS). Expensive.

Ruth's Chris Steak House – Some of the best filets and New York steaks in town. Tender and perfectly prepared. Open Mondays through Saturdays for lunch, and daily for dinner. Reservations necessary. In Restaurant Row, near downtown Honolulu (phone: 599-3860). Expensive.

Ship's Tavern – The name's the same as the casual restaurant that once was housed here, but that's about all that's remained unchanged. The decor now is an appealing mix of gray, white, and celadon green, providing a perfect backdrop for Diamond Head and ocean views. The menu is well prepared, whether it's standards like New England clam chowder, or more unusual offerings like sautéed filet of veal in morel sauce. Dinner nightly. Reservations advised. Major credit cards accepted. *Sheraton Moana Surfrider Hotel* (phone: 922-3111). Expensive.

Andrews – The steamed clams in herbs and spices and the veal dishes are particularly noteworthy at one of Honolulu's less touted Italian restaurants. Linen, crystal, and silver set the tone for a relaxed evening in pleasant surroundings. Open daily for lunch and dinner. Reservations advised. Major credit cards accepted. *Ward Center,* 1200 Ala Moana Blvd. (phone: 523-8677). Expensive to moderate.

Bon Appetit – Perhaps Honolulu's best French dining place, it has the look of an elegant bistro in the French provinces with its cane-back chairs and light pink linen. The menu is imaginative and includes an unusual scallop mousse, bouillabaisse, and snails in puff pastry. Closed Sundays. Reservations advised. Major credit cards accepted. In the Discovery Bay complex at 1778 Ala Moana Blvd. (phone: 942-3837). Expensive to moderate.

Coasters – Nestled in a harborside setting at the back of the Hawaii Maritime Center, there's an excellent lunch and dinner menu, with appetizers such as clams casino and shellfish sausage nantua, plus a full range of seafood, veal, and steak entrées. Open for lunch and dinner daily. Reservations advised. Major credit cards accepted. At Pier 7, Hawaii Maritime Center (phone: 524-2233). Expensive to moderate.

Fursato – There are two branches of this Japanese restaurant in Waikiki. Each has its own menu and ambience; both are comfortable if not elegant. The kitchens generally offer a range of steaks, seafood, and sushi. Open daily for lunch and dinner. Reservations advised. Major credit cards accepted. *Hyatt Regency* (phone: 922-4991) and *Foster Tower* condominium (phone: 922-5502). Expensive to moderate.

Golden Dragon – Perhaps Hawaii's most elegant Chinese dining room, the food happily lives up to the surroundings. For example, one specialty, Imperial Beggar's chicken, is wrapped in lotus leaves with spices, then cooked for 6 hours inside a sealed clay pot to retain natural juices and flavor. Another specialty is the Peking roast duck, and be sure to leave room for pastry chef Gale O'Malley's celestial desserts. Thanks to the exquisite decorative flourishes, dining indoors is as appealing as alfresco. Open daily for dinner. Reservations advised. Major credit cards accepted. Valet parking available. *Hilton Hawaiian Village Rainbow Tower,* 2005 Kalia Rd. (phone: 949-4321). Expensive to moderate.

Hau Tree Lanai – The food is good, but the beachfront setting, especially at breakfast or at dusk, is its own reward. Open daily. Reservations advised. Major credit cards accepted. In the *New Otani Kaimana*

Beach, 2863 Kalakaua Ave. (phone: 923-1555). Expensive to moderate.

Matteo's – Low lighting, pleasant decor, and high-backed banquettes all conspire to make this a place for quiet dining. The service is good, as is the food which includes such highly recommended dishes as calamari, chicken, and veal. Open daily for dinner, from 6 PM to midnight; the bar is open until 2 AM. Reservations advised. Major credit cards accepted. In the *Marine Surf Hotel,* 364 Seaside Ave. (phone: 922-5551). Expensive to moderate.

Miyako – *Shabu shabu*–style cooking (meat, vegetables, and seafood prepared in boiling water at the table) is emphasized here. Seating is either in the main dining room with its rooftop, oceanside views, or in small tatami rooms where guests sit on mats on the floor. Two days' notice will procure the special Kaiseiki dinner of 7, 8, or 9 courses, all using the freshest produce, fish, and seafood available that day. Open daily for dinner. Reservations advised. Major credit cards accepted. *New Otani Kaimana Beach Hotel,* 2863 Kalakaua Ave. (phone: 923-1555). Expensive to moderate.

Orchids – Sliding French doors that open onto a green lawn and expansive views of Diamond Head and the sea are a perfect backdrop for crisp white linen and tables elegantly set with silver, crystal, and fresh flowers. Breakfast is a highlight, as is the Sunday brunch, though lunch and dinner also are first rate. Open daily. Reservations necessary. Major credit cards accepted. *Halekulani Hotel,* 2199 Kalia Rd. (phone: 923-2311). Expensive to moderate.

Pearl City Tavern – This Japanese-American place is famous for its *Monkey Bar,* at the back of which is a long glassed-in alley where denizens of the simian world prance and preen playfully. The Japanese dishes here tend to be better than the American, and the teriyaki and tempura are especially good. The middle-aged waitresses are downright motherly. Open weekdays for lunch, daily for dinner. Reservations advised. Major credit cards accepted. 905 Kamehameha Hwy., Pearl City (phone: 455-1045). Expensive to moderate.

Roy's Park Bistro – Master chef Roy Yamaguchi, whose first restaurant put Hawaii-Kai on the map with an exceptional Eurasian menu, goes Mediterranean in Waikiki, with amazing results. This is food to savor, accompanied by a wine list that is also worthy of praise. Open for breakfast, lunch, and dinner. Reservations advised. Major credit cards accepted. In the *Park Plaza Waikiki Hotel,* 6600 Kalaniaole Hwy., Hawaii-Kai (phone: 396-ROYS). Expensive to moderate.

Willows – One of the most famous restaurants in the state, and the place to sample traditional Hawaiian dishes. The celebrated poi supper offers many of these, including poi itself, steamed laulau, sweet potato, chicken luau, and lomilomi salmon. If all this seems too exotic, the curry dishes, leavened with coconut milk, are superb. This also is the perfect place for wearing an aloha shirt or muumuu for the first time; the rural tropical atmosphere of palm trees and thatch roofs seems to call for it, and strolling musicians provide the perfect accompaniment. Open daily. Reservations advised. Major credit cards accepted. 901 Hausten St. (phone: 946-4808). Expensive to moderate.

Zuke Bistro – This classy remake of a once-humble spot now offers a setting compatible with the high quality of the fish, meat, and poultry dishes cooked by the owner-chef. Be prepared for a bit of a wait at the table — each order is prepared from scratch, which takes time. Open daily for dinner, except Sundays. Reservations advised. Major credit cards accepted. 2171 Ala Wai Blvd. (phone: 922-0102). Expensive to moderate.

Baci – Linen, flatware, and crystal harmonize with the chic decor to provide an appropriate setting for the Italian specialties. Meals are complemented by a fairly priced selection of bottled wines. Open for lunch weekdays and dinner daily. Reservations advised for dinner and lunch groups. Major credit cards accepted. Ground level, Waikiki Trade Center, 2255 Kuhio Ave. (phone: 924-2533). Moderate.

Café Cambio – Contemporary Northern Italian cooking combines with Southern highlights like *cioppino* (fish stew) and an *antipasto misto*. The owner is from Turin, which ensures that his food is the real thing. Open for lunch Tuesdays through Fridays, dinner Tuesdays through Sundays. Reservations advised for lunch only. Major credit cards accepted. 1680 Kapiolani Blvd., next to the *Kapiolani Theater* (phone: 942-0740). Moderate.

Café Che Pasta – Homemade pasta is only part of a menu that includes fresh grilled fish, calamari, and other nouvelle-style dishes. The original eatery in Kaimuki established the good reputation that's maintained at this downtown branch. Open weekdays until 8 PM for lunch, snacks, and dinner. Reservations advised. Major credit cards accepted. 1001 Bishop St. (phone: 524-0004). Moderate.

Castagnola's – A New York–style Italian spot that has drawn rave reviews from the day it opened in the Manoa Marketplace. Delicate flavorings make for some good veal, pasta, and seafood dishes. Open daily except Sundays for lunch and dinner; lunch only on Mondays. Reservations necessary for dinner. Major credit cards accepted. 2752 Woodlawn Ave. (phone: 988-2969). Moderate.

Che Pasta – A casual café with good food. Pasta, veal, and chicken dishes are the specialties. Open daily for dinner. Reservations unnecessary. Major credit cards accepted. 3751 Waialae Ave. (phone: 735-1777). Moderate.

Coasters – A terrific eatery that nestles in a harborside setting at the back of the Hawaii Maritime Center. The excellent lunch and dinner menu includes appetizers such as clams casino and shellfish with sausages, plus a full range of seafood, veal, and stir-fry entrées. Open daily. Reservations advised. Major credit cards accepted. At Pier 7 near downtown Honolulu (phone: 524-2233). Moderate.

Il Fresco – High tech design and tables set with linen and crystal fit its location in the chic *Ward Center*. A varied menu features a variety of dishes, from blackened ahi (tuna) to pasta. Open daily. Reservations advised. Major credit cards accepted. *Ward Center* (enter on Auahi St.), 1200 Ala Moana Blvd. (phone: 523-5191). Moderate.

Great Wok – Cantonese-style Chinese cooking is prepared at your table, and the menu features such delicately flavored specialties as 1000 Happiness Lobster and Blush of Empress Shrimp. Open daily for lunch and dinner. Reservations advised. Major credit cards accepted. *Royal Hawaiian Center* (phone: 922-5373). Moderate.

Hala Terrace – A lovely lunchtime spot. Sit in the shade and watch the Pacific across one of the loveliest beaches on Oahu. Meals here are on the light side, so it's worth ordering vichyssoise or a spring salad to start with. Elegant sandwiches are the main item on the menu, in addition to which there are daily specials such as Kahuku prawns, which are delicious. Open daily for breakfast, lunch, and dinner. Reservations advised. Major credit cards accepted. *Kahala Hilton,* 5000 Kahala Ave., Kahala (phone: 734-2211). Moderate.

Horatio's – The nautical decor is most appropriate in this tavern overlooking the Kewalo Boat Basin. Among the house specialties worth trying are mahimahi stuffed with shrimp and crab, and beef Wellington glazed with Madeira sauce. Freshly baked Russian rye bread accompanies each entrée. Open daily. Reservations advised. Major credit cards accepted. *Ward Warehouse,* 1050 Ala Moana Blvd. (phone: 521-5002). Moderate.

Keo's Thai Cuisine – This is a fine place to sample Thai cooking, which can be flavorful and fiery, although the kitchen will prepare milder versions of its hot specialties if requested. Mint-flavored spring rolls make a delicious appetizer, and cold sweet tea is a good accompaniment for the spicier dishes. The setting is elegant and nearly drenched in orchids; the crowd, Honolulu's cognoscenti. Open daily for dinner. Reservations necessary. Major credit cards accepted. 441 Kapahulu Ave. (phone: 737-8240). Moderate.

Monterrey Bay Canners – The Waikiki branch of this restaurant, in the *Outrigger* hotel, offers a limited number of alfresco tables that take full advantage of the beachfront location. The best bet on the menu is one of the catch-of-the-day specials, which are reasonably priced and delicious. Open daily. Reservations advised for dinner. Major credit cards accepted. 2335 Kalakaua Ave. (phone: 922-5761). Moderate.

Murphy's – A pleasant eatery in the revitalized Merchant Square area and a good choice for people who are tired of exotic restaurant grub. From potato skins to salads and pasta, the menu offers many tasty specials. Live sports events are beamed in courtesy of a satellite dish. Open Mondays through Saturdays for lunch and dinner to 9 PM; Sundays, brunch only. Reservations advised. Major credit cards accepted. 2 Merchant St. (phone: 531-0422). Moderate.

Parc Café – Although the menu is limited to four entrées a night, plus a buffet, the food is delicious and the prices are reasonable. Prime ribs, pasta, chicken, and the catch of the day are usual fare. Sunday brunch is recommended. Open daily for lunch and dinner. Reservations advised. Major credit cards accepted. In the *Waikiki Parc Hotel,* 2198 Kalia Rd. (phone: 921-7272). Moderate.

Phillip Paolo's – Set in an eclectically decorated private home, a 5-minute drive from Waikiki, its Italian specialties — by owner-chef Phillip Paolo Sarubbi — earn the high praise they receive. Daily specials complement standard features like fettuccine Vigario (pasta with mushrooms and spinach in light basil cream sauce) and shrimp parmigiana. Open daily for dinner; Fridays for lunch and dinner. Reservations advised. Major credit cards accepted. 2312 Beretania St. (phone: 946-1163). Moderate.

Salerno – This is like a New York City neighborhood Italian eatery, where generous amounts of delicious food are served (order a half portion if you're not very hungry). Just over the McCully bridge from Waikiki. Closed Sundays. Reservations advised. Major credit cards accepted. 1960 Kapiolani Blvd., 2nd Floor (phone: 942-5273). Moderate.

Seafood Emporium – Flavorful food makes up for the relative austerity of decor that recalls New England; clearly, the pleasure here is not in adornment but in eating. Open daily for lunch and dinner. Reservations advised for dinner. Major credit cards accepted. *Royal Hawaiian Shopping Center,* 2201 Kalakaua Ave. (phone: 922-5547). Moderate.

Siam Inn – There has been high praise for this Thai place in the heart of Waikiki, where imported spices and fresh local produce and seafood are combined to advantage. Normally fiery Thai dishes are prepared with Western tastebuds in mind. Open daily for lunch and dinner. Reservations unnecessary. Major credit cards accepted. 407 Seaside (phone: 926-8802). Moderate.

Spats – Dinner in a well-known disco might not sound very promising, but don't let what goes on after 9 PM deter you from coming here. The decor recalls a rather lavish speakeasy, with beveled glass, highly polished wood, and waiters in cutaways and suspenders. Try the chicken alla cacciatore or shrimp *all' aglio e olio* (with garlic and oil). Fettuccine Alfredo is the star attraction among the pasta. Open daily. Reservations advised for dinner. Major credit cards accepted. *Hyatt Regency Hotel,* 2424 Kalakaua Ave. (phone: 923-1234). Moderate.

Sunset Grill – The style is California-casual; the food is cooked over kiawe wood to provide a distinctive flavor. Specialties include chicken, veal, lamb, and fish prepared on a rotisserie, grill, or in the oven. Open for lunch and dinner daily, breakfast on Sundays. Reservations unnecessary. Major credit cards accepted. Restaurant Row (phone: 521-4409). Moderate.

Swiss Inn – *Kahala Hilton* chef Martin Wyss has opened one of Hawaii's best restaurants in the suburban *Niu Valley Shopping Center.* It's well worth the 20-minute drive from Waikiki for standards like veal Florentine, trout amandine, and baked chicken. With 24 hours' notice, you also can order a meat or cheese fondue. Closed Mondays and Tuesdays. Reservations necessary. Major credit cards accepted. 5730 Kalanianaole Hwy. (phone: 377-5447). Moderate.

Trattoria – The chef doesn't overload the menu with tomato paste, and many dishes are cooked al burro — delicately, in butter — instead of doused in olive oil. The lasagna in this charmingly decorated restaurant is well worth tasting. So are *cotoletta di vitello alla parmigiana* and *pollo alla romana.* The *cannelloni milanese* is definitely a "don't miss." Open daily for dinner. Reservations necessary on weekends. Major credit cards accepted. *Outrigger Edgewater Hotel,* 2168 Kalia Rd. (phone: 923-8415). Moderate.

Yanagi Sushi – Two Tokyo-style sushi bars serve a sushi lover's abundance of specials. The atmosphere is upbeat, the decor simple but appealing, and the sushi first-rate. Open daily. Reservations necessary. Major credit cards accepted. 762 Kapiolani Blvd. (phone: 537-1525). Moderate.

California Pizza Kitchen – Italian specialties reign here, from calzone to eggplant parmigiana, and all dishes are cooked in ovens fueled with flavor-enhancing kiawe wood. Deservedly popular, it's also a very relaxed place to eat. Open daily. Reservations advised. Major credit cards accepted. 1910 Kalakaua Ave., 2nd Floor (phone: 955-5161). There is a branch in the *Kahala Mall* (phone: 737-9446). Moderate to inexpensive.

China House – The cavernous dining room of this Honolulu favorite often is full. If shark fin or bird nest soup is your thing, you can have it here. Four varieties of the former and three of the latter are offered. The dim sum is famous throughout the island and is served daily from 11 AM to 2 PM. Open daily. Reservations advised. Major credit cards accepted. At the top of the ramp from Kapiolani Blvd. in the *Ala Moana Center* (phone: 949-6622). Moderate to inexpensive.

Compadres – Delicious Mexican food, a comfortable setting, and good prices make this a hit at *Ward Center.* Mexican pizza is truly worthy of a cheese lover's praise. Open daily for breakfast, lunch, and dinner; closed Saturdays and Sundays for breakfast. Reservations advised. Major credit cards accepted. 2500 Kuhio Ave. (523-1307). Moderate to inexpensive.

Hard Rock Café – The Honolulu branch of this trendy international chain attracts a young crowd out to be part of "the scene." Food is good, crowds are standard day or night, and the noise level is decibels higher than that which allows comfortable conversation. But, then, that's intended to be part of the appeal. Guitars of famous rockers are part of the decor, as are other blasts of rock 'n' roll memorabilia, and patrons come as much to buy T-shirts and other signature souvenirs as to eat or drink. Valet parking. Open daily from 11:30 AM to midnight. No reservations. Major credit cards accepted. 1837 Kapiolani Blvd. (phone: 955-7383). Moderate to inexpensive.

Orson's – Downstairs is a coffee shop called the *Chowder House,* which serves fresh salads as well as seafood; upstairs, a dining room decorated with beautifully stained wood offers more fine seafood. Open daily for lunch and dinner. Reservations advised. Major credit cards accepted. *Ward Warehouse,* 1050 Ala Moana Blvd. (phone: 521-5681). Upstairs moderate; downstairs inexpensive.

Ryan's Parkplace – Popular for its pasta, vegetable, and fish dishes, desserts, and custom-brewed coffee. Open daily; dinner only on Sundays. Reservations advised. Major credit cards accepted. *Ward Center,* 1050 Ala Moana Blvd. (phone: 523-9132). Moderate to inexpensive.

TGI Friday's – The Honolulu version of the New York original features antique furnishings, a friendly bar, and surprisingly good food at modest prices (especially for the enormous portions served, which easily can be shared). Best known for its potato skins, this eatery also serves an array of quiche, omelettes, salads, desserts, and more. It's always lively and usually noisy. Open daily. No reservations. Major credit cards accepted. 950 Ward Ave. (phone: 523-5841). Moderate to inexpensive.

Bavarian Beer Garden – Bratwurst, knockwurst, sauerkraut, and warm German potato salad are among the house specialties. So, too, is dancing to a five-piece Bavarian band on the largest dance floor in Waikiki. Open nightly from 5 PM to midnight. No reservations, except for large groups. Major credit cards accepted. *Royal Hawaiian Shopping Center,* 3rd Floor (phone: 922-6535). Inexpensive.

Big Ed's Deli – This is the place to head if you've got a craving for New York–style pastrami or corned beef. Popular with the lunch crowd, it's much easier to go at dinnertime. Open daily from 7 AM to 10 PM, with breakfast and dinner selections at all hours. Reservations unnecessary. Major credit cards accepted. In *Ward Center* (phone: 536-4591). Inexpensive.

Bueno Nalo – The coconut wireless (as the local grapevine is called) gives this eatery high marks for its Mexican cooking — chiles rellaños, chimichangas, and such. It's a casual place, where guests bring their own wine or beer and wait for tables. Open Tuesdays through Fridays, 5 to 9 PM; Saturdays and Sundays from 3 to 9 PM. No reservations or credit cards accepted. 41-865 Kalanianaole Hwy., Waimanalo (phone: 259-7186). Inexpensive.

Caffe Guccini – The warm welcome at this low-key café is followed by fine pasta, rich cappuccino, and tempting desserts. Guests may bring their own wine or beer, but there's also a full bar. Open daily from 3 to 11:30 PM. Reservations unnecessary. MasterCard and Visa accepted. 2139 Kuhio Ave. (phone: 922-5287). Inexpensive.

Chinese Cultural Plaza – Though not quite as successful as planned, this ethnic enclave does offer a wide range of good Oriental restaurants and cuisines — Cantonese, Hakka, Mandarin, or Mongolian barbecue — as well as shops purveying Oriental bric-a-brac that are fun to browse through. Open daily. Reservations unnecessary. Most major credit cards accepted. 100 N. Beretania and River Sts. (phone: 521-4934). Inexpensive.

Emilio's – Just outside Waikiki, this little neighborhood-style pizza shop has very tasty pies and other Italian standards. Open daily. Reservations unnecessary. Major credit cards accepted. 1423 Kalakaua Ave. (phone: 946-4972). Inexpensive.

King Tsin – This spicy favorite serves up very tasty hot and sour soup. The crackling chicken is chopstick-lickin' good, as is the Hunan pork sautéed with broccoli. Open daily. Reservations advised. Major credit cards accepted. 1110 McCully St. (phone: 946-3273). Inexpensive.

Wo Fat – This granddaddy of Chinese restaurants in Honolulu will soon be 100 years old. Hong Kong chicken, beef in oyster sauce, and *Wo Fat* noodles draw people here from all over the island for lunch and dinner. Open daily. Reservations advised. Major credit cards accepted. 115 N. Hotel St. (phone: 537-6260). Inexpensive.

HOUSTON

AT-A-GLANCE

SEEING THE CITY: The revolving *Spindletop* restaurant atop the *Hyatt Regency* hotel turns on the Houston panorama. One revolution takes in all of Space City. To the south stands downtown, to the north an industrial area and the ship channel, industrial sprawl to the east, and Houston's residential neighborhoods to the west. Open 11 AM to 1 PM for lunch; 6 to 11 PM for dinner. All major credit cards accepted. 1200 Louisiana (phone: 654-1234).

Stationary, but splendid for a view of the downtown skyline, is Sam Houston Park (515 Allen Pkwy). Dominating the cityscape are the futuristic Pennzoil Towers, designed by Philip Johnson, and the city's other big oil headquarters, Shell and Tenneco.

SPECIAL PLACES: A car is a necessity for mobility in the Houston sprawl. Mass transit is unreliable and not always accessible. Several of the attractions are concentrated in a few areas, so you can park and walk, but otherwise, you'll be driving from place to place.

Museum of Natural Science – Each of the 13 halls in the largest such institution of the Southwest pertains to a different natural science including two subjects near and dear to the wallets of Houstonians — oil and space. You can learn how oil is formed, see a model of an offshore oil rig, or manipulate a working model of a fault — by turning a wheel you can create an earthquake. The space exhibit includes reproductions of the lunar Rover (the real one is still up there) and a model of the space capsule used by John Glenn. Not as endearing, but also on display, are Ecuadoran shrunken heads and a Diplodocus dinosaur skeleton. The *Museum of Medical Science* displays the human body — yours. You can listen to the rhythm of your heartbeat or test your lung capacity, or, if you're too modest to put yourself on display, skip it and visit the *Burke Baker Planetarium.* Open Mondays through Saturdays, 9 AM to 6 PM, Sundays, noon to 6 PM. Admission to the museum is $2.50 for adults, $2 for children under 12. There's an additional charge to the planetarium: $2 for adults, $1 for children under 12. The *Wortham IMAX Theatre,* installed at the museum at a cost of $6.5 million, features an 80-foot-wide and 6-story-high screen. It is only the second of its kind in Texas and one of 59 worldwide. Admission is $4.50 for adults and $3.50 for children under 12. Special rates for groups and senior citizens are available. 5800 Caroline St., in Hermann Park (phone: 526-4273 or 639-4629).

Houston Zoological Gardens – One of the best zoos around, this abounds with some rarely seen animals in unusual settings. Vampire bats, flying squirrels, and bush babies inhabit a red light district where time is reversed and you can see the bats feeding on blood at 2:30 in the afternoon. The Tropical Bird House has over 200 exotic birds in a rain forest. But our favorite is the Gorilla House, where the royal couple of the jungle swing in primordial splendor complete with waterfalls, vines, moats, and skylighting. There's also a children's zoo where kids can make contact with creatures from four regions of the world. Open daily

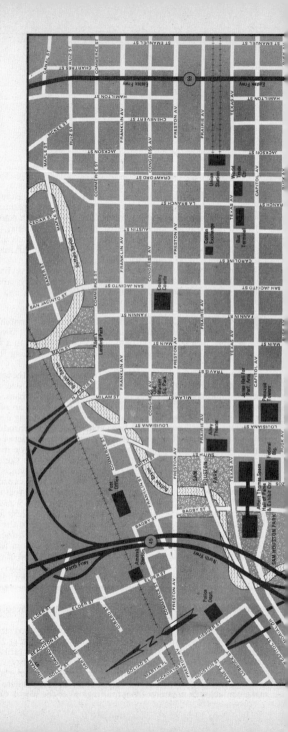

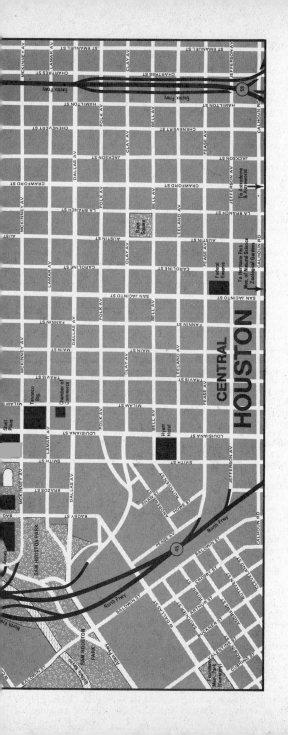

except Mondays from 10 AM to 6 PM. Children's Discovery Zoo is open from 10 AM to 5:45 PM, Tuesdays through Sundays. Admission $2.50 for adults, $2 for senior citizens, 50¢ for children between the ages of 3 and 12; free to all on city holidays. S. Main at Bissonnet in Hermann Park (phone: 523-5888 or 525-3300).

Children's Museum – Don't look for antique toys here. This is a modern, hands-on experience center designed for kids 3 to 12 years old. Children use computers to assemble dinosaurs and to work math and science problems. There's even a closed-circuit TV station, complete with costumes and sets, where kids can stage their own impromptu performances. For old-fashioned fun, they can play store in a nearly real setting, draw postcards, and cut out paper dolls. The major culture display changes each year. Open Tuesdays, Wednesdays, Thursdays, and Saturdays 9 AM to 5 PM, 1 to 5 PM Fridays and Sundays. Admission $2. 3201 Allen Pkwy. between Shepard and Waugh (phone: 522-6873).

Museum of Fine Arts – With neo-classical beginnings and finishing touches by Mies van der Rohe, this structure could house most any-thing — and it does, including the Ima Hogg collection of Southwestern Indian art with pottery and kachina dolls, an extensive collection of Frederic Remington's works, a pre-Columbian gallery, and a modern sculpture garden with Alexander Calder's *Crab.* Open Tuesdays, Wednesdays, and Saturdays from 10 AM to 5PM; Thursdays from 10AM to 9PM; and Sundays from 12:15 to 6 PM. Closed Mondays. Admission is $4 for adults, $1 for children under 13. Thursdays are free for all. 1001 Bissonnet (phone: 526-1361).

International Strip – On the main drag of Montrose, one of the city's oldest residential neighborhoods, natives and visitors come to browse through antiques shops, foreign bazaars, art galleries, boutiques, flea markets, and offbeat book shops. The art festivals held in October and April are the largest in the South. Sidewalk cafés and restaurants allow patrons to try dishes from around the world, linger in a wine tasting shop, or just hang out in a tree house bar. *A Moveable Feast* (2202 W. Alabama; phone: 528-3585) is great for health food sandwiches. Open Mondays through Saturdays from 9 AM to 10 PM and Sundays from 10 AM to 9 PM. The Strip is also the showplace for exotic nightlife. More sedate, but also in the neighborhood, is the Rothko Chapel (3900 Yupon; phone: 524-9839), a meditation chapel with works by Russian-born painter Mark Rothko. The Strip extends from the 100 to 1800 block of Westheimer.

River Oaks – If you're wondering where all that old oil money went, you'll find that no one's tried to hide it. Here are the palatial mansions and huge estates of Houston's super-rich, who still have it and flaunt it. River Oaks Blvd. between Westheimer and the *Country Club.*

Galleria Center – This stunning, glass-domed, 3-level edifice shows how the wealth is spread, Houston-style. Among the stores here are *Sakowitz* (a Houston native), *Neiman-Marcus, Lord & Taylor, Tiffany's,* and *Macy's;* across the street is *Saks Fifth Avenue.* There's also a skating rink on the ground floor. Open daily. 5015 Westheimer (phone: 622-0663).

Sam Houston Park – One of the few signs that there was an old Houston, this project of the Harris County Heritage Society, open 10 AM to 4 PM, encompasses a restored country church, homes, and shops, depicting the lifestyle of 19th-century Houstonians. The Kellum-Noble House, the oldest brick house in Houston, contains pioneer equipment and furnishings, and the Cherry House is a Greek Revival home fur-nished with American Empire antiques. Tours begin at the office (515 Allen Pkwy.). Open daily. Tour charge is $4 for adults, $2 for teens and senior citizens, and $1 for children 6 to 12. Allen Pkwy. and Bagby St. (phone: 655-9539).

Astrodome – Besides serving as home for the *Astros, Oilers,* and the University of Houston *Cougars,* this $36-million domed stadium, big enough to accommodate an 18-story building (standing) or 66,000 spectators, is Texas's most popular attraction. There are guided tours at 11 AM, 1, and 3 PM. Open daily. Admission charge is $3.25, or $2.75 for senior citizens. 4¾ miles southwest at I-610 and Kirby Dr. (phone: 799-9544).

Astroworld – Also part of Astrodomain, Houston's version of a theme park offers 70 acres of entertainment, including a cartoon-land section for small children, nighttime fireworks, and high-diving exhibitions. The Ultra-Twister roller coaster, opened in 1990, features a gut-wrenching 92-foot dive and a 360-degree rotating turn, both forward and backward. Another attraction is the Tidal Wave, an aqua-roller coaster guaranteed to soak both riders and spectators. One of the best times to visit *Astroworld* is during its Fright Nights just before *Halloween* when the park offers spook houses and magic shows. Open daily June through August, weekends during spring and fall. (Check locally for shortened or extended hours.) Admission charge. 9001 Kirby Dr., across from the *Astrodome* (phone: 799-1234).

San Jacinto Battleground – The 570-foot-tall San Jacinto Monument marks the spot where Sam Houston defeated Mexican General Santa Anna to win Texas's independence. The 460-acre state park also includes a *Museum of Texas History,* which traces the region's development from the Indian civilization through Texas's annexation by the US; it also houses the battleship *Texas,* veteran of both world wars. Admission to the battleship is $2 for adults, $1 for children under 16. No admission charge for the rest of the park. Farm Road 134, off Hwy. 225, 21 miles east of downtown Houston (phone: 479-2431).

Port of Houston – From an observation platform atop Wharf 9, visitors can see the turning basin area of this country's third largest port. To inspect some of the elaborate industrial-shipping developments, take an excursion along the ship channel aboard the MV *Sam Houston* (make reservations months in advance). No trips on Mondays or in September. No admission charge. Gate 8, off Clinton Dr. (phone: 225-4044).

Lyndon B. Johnson Space Center – Until you actually fly Trans-Universe to the moon, this is the closest you can get to the experience. This 1,620-acre campus-like facility was the training ground for the Gemini, Apollo, and Skylab astronauts and is the monitoring center for the NASA manned space flights. The visitors' center displays craft that have flown in space, moon rocks, and a lunar module, and the Mission Control Center houses some of the most sophisticated communications computer data equipment in the world. Visitors are welcome at the Control Center and the Skylab Training Room on guided tours, available by reservation. NASA films are shown throughout the day in the auditorium. Open daily. No admission charge. 25 miles SE of downtown Houston via I-45 (phone: 483-4321).

■ **EXTRA SPECIAL:** Just 51 miles south of Houston along I-45 is Galveston Island, a leading Gulf Coast resort area. Stewart Beach is the principal public beach, and there's good swimming, surfing, sailing, water skiing, and deep-sea fishing (reservations taken at boats on Piers 18 and 19 of the Galveston Yacht Basin). Seafood restaurants, art galleries, and restored turn-of-the-century homes are in the former vacation destination of the oil magnates clustered around Strand Blvd.

SOURCES AND RESOURCES

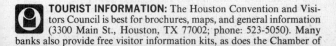

TOURIST INFORMATION: The Houston Convention and Visitors Council is best for brochures, maps, and general information (3300 Main St., Houston, TX 77002; phone: 523-5050). Many banks also provide free visitor information kits, as does the Chamber of

Commerce (1100 Milam; phone: 651-1313). Contact the Texas state hotline (phone: 800-8888-TEX) for maps, calendars of events, health updates, and travel advisories.

The revised edition of *Texas Monthly's Guide to Houston* by Felicia Coates and Harriet Howle (Mediatex Communications Corp.; $5.95) is a comprehensive guide.

Local Coverage – The *Post* and the *Chronicle,* both daily newspapers, are available at newsstands.

Television Stations – KPRC Channel 2–NBC; KUHT Channel 8–PBS; KHOU Channel 11–CBS; KTRK Channel 13–ABC.

Radio Stations – AM: KTRH 740 (news/sports); KPRC 950 (news/talk). FM: KTSU 90.9 (jazz/urban contemporary); KRTS 92.1 (classical); KLTR 93.7 (adult contemporary music).

Food – Check the *Texas Monthly Guide,* which lists the city's restaurants.

 TELEPHONE: The area code for Houston is 713.
Sales Tax – The sales tax is 8%.

 CLIMATE: In the summer, Houston is hot and humid. Winds from the Gulf of Mexico create warm summer nights, and keep the winters and the rest of the year relatively warm. But ice and (more rarely) snow sometimes shut down the city in winter.

GETTING AROUND: Airport – The city's main airports are Houston Intercontinental and William P. Hobby Airport. Those familiar with Houston traffic allow at least 45 minutes to reach either one from downtown (note that it is not unusual for rain, fog, or the nightly rush hour to double this time). *Yellow Cab* charges a flat rate of $26 for the trip between Intercontinental and downtown. Taxi fare into the city from Hobby should run about $15. *Airport Express* (phone: 523-8888) operates a shuttle service from Intercontinental ($8.70 for adults, and $4.35 for children under 12) to its four downtown terminals. Buses leave every half-hour, and tickets may be purchased at stands outside each terminal.

Bus – *Metropolitan Transit Authority of Harris County* serves downtown and the suburbs, but the system can be confusing. Minibuses run in the downtown shopping area. For route information contact the main office, 401 Louisiana (phone: 635-4000).

Car Rental – Because Houston is a huge, sprawling city whose backbone is its extensive freeway system, a car is the most practical mode of travel. Try to avoid being caught in Houston's rush hour, when traffic is impossibly snarled. All the major national firms serve Houston. Local service is provided by *Thrifty Rent-A-Car* at Hobby Airport (phone: 941-7484) and Intercontinental Airport (phone: 442-5000).

Taxi – Cabs can be ordered on the phone, picked up in front of hotels and terminals, or, with some difficulty, hailed in the street. Major companies are *United Taxicab* (phone: 699-0000) and *Yellow Cab* (phone: 236-1111). Be warned, however, that taxi rates are rather high.

VITAL SERVICES: Audiovisual Equipment – *Photo & Sound Co.* (phone: 956-9566).
    Business Services – *Abby Secretarial Service,* 6776 Southwest Freeway (phone: 789-7800).

Dry Cleaner/Tailor – *Imperial Laundry & Cleaners,* 3401 Harrisburg Rd. (phone: 223-1365).

Limousine – *Houston Executive Limousines* (phone: 928-5511); *Galleria Limousine & Travel Service, Inc.* (phone: 960-8790).

Mechanics – For American cars, *Lightsey's Auto & Diesel Repair* (7000 Synott; phone: 498-3535); for foreign cars, *Freeman's Auto Service* (4817 Bldg. A Ramus; phone: 681-9484).

Medical Emergency – *Ben Taub General Hospital,* 1502 Taub Loop (phone: 793-2600).

Messenger Services – *Astro City Courier* (phone: 827-8233).

National/International Courier – *Federal Express* (phone: 800-238-5355); *DHL Worldwide Courier Express* (phone: 442-4500).

Pharmacy – *Eckerd Drugs,* open 24 hours, 6011 Kirby (phone: 522-3983).

Photocopies – *Kinko's Copies,* pickup and delivery (1430 San Jacinto; phone: 654-8161); *Kwik Kopy Printing* (2122 Travis St. and other locations; phone: 659-2934).

Post Office – One is located downtown at 401 Franklin St. (phone: 226-3069).

Professional Photographer – *Dan Ford Connolly* (phone: 367-7156); *Memory Makers Video* (phone: 495-5136).

Secretary/Stenographer – *Olga Turner Temporaries* (phone: 977-6542).

Teleconference Facilities – *Inn on the Park* (see *Best in Town,* below).

Translator – *Berlitz* (phone: 529-8110); *Omni Intercommunications* (phone: 781-2188).

Typewriter Rental – *Brewington Typewriter Co.,* 1-week minimum (phone: 227-5282); *Hartwell's Office World,* 1-week minimum (phone: 777-2673).

Western Union/Telex – Many offices are located around the city (phone: 800-325-6000).

SPECIAL EVENTS: Check the publications noted above for exact dates. For 2 weeks in late February and early March, Houston cowboys come out in full force and descend on the *Astrodome* complex for the *Houston Livestock Show and Rodeo.* There's plenty of action — rodeo events and country and western concerts. During April and October, local and regional artists show their stuff in the *Westheimer Art Show,* an outdoor arts and crafts festival on Westheimer Road Most area hotels are filled for the 4-day *Offshore Technology Conference,* the world's biggest oil industry show, in late April and early May.

MUSEUMS: The *Children's Museum, Museum of Fine Arts,* and *Museum of Natural Science* are described under *Special Places.* Other notable Houston museums worth a visit:

Bayou Bend – Early American furnishings. 1 Westcott St. (phone: 529-8773).

Contemporary Arts Museum – 5216 Montrose at Bissonnet (phone: 526-3129).

MAJOR COLLEGES AND UNIVERSITIES: Among Houston's educational institutions are *Rice University* (6100 S. Main St.; phone: 527-8101), which has a good reputation for its engineering and science schools; *University of Houston* (4800 Calhoun Rd.; phone: 749-1011); and the *Texas Medical Center* (between Fannin St. and Holcombe Blvd.; phone: 797-0100).

SHOPPING: The *Galleria Center* (see *Special Places*) is still the most popular local shopping spot, where anything from the best shoeshine in town (a one-chair operation in *Cole's* hair salon on the lower level) to high-price items at *Tiffany's* and *Neiman-Marcus* can be found. Those shopping for real Texan western wear go to nearby *Stelzig's of Texas* (3123 Post Oak Blvd.; phone: 629-7779), the oldest family-owned store of its kind in Houston. The suburban area malls near such areas as Baybrook, Deerpark, Greenspoint, Memorial City, and Westbrook contain major chain stores including *Sears, Montgomery Ward, JC Penney,* and *Macy's.*

SPORTS AND FITNESS: Tickets to all professional games can be picked up at *Ticket Connection,* 2031 Southwest Fwy. (phone: 524-3687).

Ballooning – The *Rainbow's End Balloon Port* sends 'em up weekend mornings at dawn when the winds are calm. You can watch the balloonists rise to the occasion, and if they don't, join them for breakfast. 7826 Fairview (phone: 466-1927).

Baseball – The National League's *Astros* play at the *Astrodome* from April through October, I-610 and Kirby Dr. (phone: 799-9555).

Basketball – The NBA's *Rockets* play from November through April at the *Summit,* 10 Greenway Plaza (phone: 627-2115).

Bicycling – There are no outlets offering bicycles for rent in the entire city of Houston. But if you find one, bring one, or borrow one, there's a good bike trail running from the Sabine Street Bridge (just east of Allen's Landing) along Buffalo Bayou to Shepherd, and back along the Memorial side of the Bayou. The City of Houston Parks and Recreation Department offers a list of other bike routes. 2999 S. Wayside (phone: 845-1000).

Fishing – Best for fishing is Galveston, where you can wet a line in the Gulf of Mexico off piers or from deep-sea charters that leave from Piers 18 and 19 of the Galveston Yacht Basin.

Fitness Center – The *YMCA* has a pool, indoor and outdoor tracks, exercise classes, and handball and racquetball courts, 1600 Louisiana (phone: 659-8501).

Football – The *Oilers* play at the *Astrodome* (phone: 797-1000).

Golf – Best public course for the duffer is in Hermann Park (6201 Golf Course Dr.; phone: 526-0077). The most challenging of the municipal courses is in Brock Park (8201 John Ralston Rd., off Old Beaumont Hwy.; phone: 458-1350).

Jogging – Most running is done along a 3-mile loop in Memorial Park, 4 miles from downtown and reached on foot from Buffalo Bayou or by taking the No. 16 Memorial or the No. 17 Tanglewood bus. Other possibilities are Hermann Park, via South Main, and the well-used trails along Ellen Parkway.

Rodeo – The *Roundup Rodeo* in nearby Simonton offers real live rodeo followed by country-and-western dancing on a varied schedule. Westheimer Rd., 45 minutes west of the city (phone: 346-1534).

Swimming – There are 42 municipal pools in Houston, open from June through *Labor Day.* The Stude Park pool is conveniently located downtown. Most hotels also have pools. 1031 Stude St. (phone: 861-0322).

Tennis – The municipally run *Memorial Tennis Center* has 18 Laykold courts, showers, lockers, tennis shop, and practice court (600 Memorial Loop Dr.; phone: 520-7056, 861-3765, or 845-1119). There are free courts in most of the city parks.

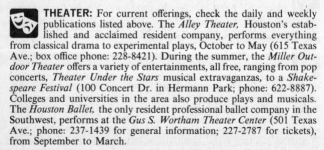 **THEATER:** For current offerings, check the daily and weekly publications listed above. The *Alley Theater,* Houston's established and acclaimed resident company, performs everything from classical drama to experimental plays, October to May (615 Texas Ave.; box office phone: 228-8421). During the summer, the *Miller Outdoor Theater* offers a variety of entertainments, all free, ranging from pop concerts, *Theater Under the Stars* musical extravaganzas, to a *Shakespeare Festival* (100 Concert Dr. in Hermann Park; phone: 622-8887). Colleges and universities in the area also produce plays and musicals. The *Houston Ballet,* the only resident professional ballet company in the Southwest, performs at the *Gus S. Wortham Theater Center* (501 Texas Ave.; phone: 237-1439 for general information; 227-2787 for tickets), from September to March.

MUSIC: *Jones Hall for the Performing Arts* is the home of the nationally acclaimed *Houston Symphony Orchestra* and offers concerts and performances throughout the year by internationally renowned guest artists and companies (615 Louisiana; phone: 237-1439). The *Houston Grand Opera* performs at the *Gus S. Wortham Theater Center* (501 Texas Ave.; phone: 237-1439 for general information; 227-2787 for tickets), from September to March. All give free performances at the *Miller Theater* in the summer. Big rock and occasional country-and-western concerts are held at the *Summit* throughout the year (10 Greenway Plaza; phone: 961-9003).

 NIGHTCLUBS AND NIGHTLIFE: Depending on what you want, you can unwind or recharge at one or more of Houston's nightspots. Current favorites for progressive country music, Texas-style, and local color: *The Rose on Richmond* (6367 Richmond; phone: 978-7673) or *Chipkickers* (3225 Farmers Market Road (FM) 1960 West; phone: 440-8882); for jazz, *Rockefeller's* (3620 Washington; phone: 861-9365); *Melody Lane Ballroom,* for ballroom dancing (3027 Crossview; phone: 785-5301); for disco, *R & R Bar* (5351 W. Alabama at Rice; phone: 840-9720), or *Studebakers* (2630 Augusta Dr.; phone: 783-4142). *Magic Island* (2215 Southwest Fwy.; phone: 526-2442) has big-name comedians and magicians (see *Eating Out*).

BEST IN TOWN

CHECKING IN: Houston's hotel industry rode the crest of the city's boom during the 1970s, with new — and usually luxurious — hotels springing up almost daily. As a result, hotels are now the most overbuilt segment of the city's real estate industry, and it is no longer impossible to get a room during the annual Offshore Technology Conference. But even though many hotels are having problems filling their available inventory of rooms, rates are still increasing. Expect to pay $100 or more a night for a double at a hotel we list as expensive, about $85 in the moderate range, and $50 to $65 in the inexpensive category. All telephone numbers are in the 713 area code unless otherwise indicated.

La Colombe d'Or – This converted mansion, next to St. Thomas University in the heart of Houston's Montrose area, is known for its haute French restaurant (see *Eating Out*). Now a member of the prestigious Relais & Châteaux group, it features 5 antiques-filled suites with private dining rooms, and also has a penthouse for $400 a night. The walnut paneling of the bar and public areas is enhanced with original artwork. There's an obliging concierge desk, plus business conveniences, such as secretarial services, A/V equipment, photocopiers, and 1 meeting room. Express checkout is also available. 3410 Montrose Blvd. (phone: 524-7999; Fax; 713-524-8923). Expensive.

Embassy Suites – All 2-room suites, with a complimentary full breakfast and 2-hour open bar daily. Free shuttle bus to Post Oak air terminal. There's an indoor pool, sauna, and a weight room. Meeting rooms can hold up to 300 people, and guests have access to photocopiers and A/V equipment. Other pluses are a concierge desk, CNN, and express checkout. 9090 Southwest Fwy. (phone: 995-0123; Fax: 713-779-0703). Expensive.

Inn on the Park – In the Riverway complex and part of the superb Four Seasons chain, the hotel overlooks a scenic bayou area populated by live swans and features an interesting sculpture garden. Amenities include 2 restaurants, a lounge, health club, 4 tennis courts, and garage. Twenty-four hour room service is available. A concierge desk, meeting rooms for up to 600, secretarial services, A/V equipment, photocopiers, CNN, and express checkout all can be found here. In Riverway at Post Oak La. and Woodway Dr. (phone: 871-8181; Fax: 713-871-0719). Expensive.

Lancaster – A small, elegant hostelry, set in a restored 1926 brick building with the air of a private British club. Oriental carpets and original oils fill the lobby; each of the 85 rooms and 8 suites is done up with antiques and a four-poster bed. Guests and the theater crowd (*Jones Hall for the Performing Arts* and the *Alley Theater* are across the street) enjoy the nouvelle accents on Gulf Coast seafood in the *Lancaster Grille.* Other features include a multilingual staff, concierge, 24-hour room service, meeting rooms for up to 200, A/V equipment, express checkout, and access to a health club. 701 Texas Ave. (phone: 228-9500 or 800-231-0336; Fax: 713-223-4528). Expensive.

Ritz-Carlton – Considered the top of the line in Houston. Formerly called the *Remington,* this establishment (built by Rosewood Hotels and now owned by Hadid Development) offers all the attention and amenities normally found in a top European hotel. There is a restaurant and grill, a bar, lounge, heated swimming pool, access to a health club, 24-hour room service, and more. Meeting rooms for up to 300, a concierge desk, secretarial services, A/V equipment, photocopiers, CNN, and express checkout. 1919 Briar Oaks Dr. (phone: 840-7600; Fax: 713-840-0616). Expensive.

Westin Oaks and Westin Galleria – Smack in the middle of the luxurious *Galleria Mall,* the ideal spot for a shopping spree. The *Oaks* (at 5011 Westheimer Rd.; phone: 623-4300 or 800-288-3000), with 406 rooms, is the older (but no less grand) facility. Really big spenders can splurge on its Crown Suite, a penthouse with 2 fireplaces, 2½ baths, and a banquet table for 14 — all for only $1,200 a night. Other features include a pool, cafés, entertainment and dancing, and access to ice skating, a running track, and indoor tennis. Free garage. Twenty-four hour room service is available, as are meeting facilities for up to 2,000, a concierge desk, secretarial services, A/V equipment, photocopiers, CNN, and express checkout. At the other end of the mall is the 489-room *Galleria,* 5060 W. Alabama (phone: 960-8100; Fax: 713-960-6549), which is every bit as fine. Both are expensive.

Wyndham – Located in the museum district, this Texas institution underwent renovations in 1990. Its beauty has been retained in the restored marble floors, 17th- and 18th-century French oak and ash paneling, and a 17th-century Aubusson tapestry. There are 315 wonderfully appointed guestrooms, and a 13,000-square-foot conference facility. Additional amenities include room service until 11 PM, concierge, limited secretarial services, A/V equipment, photocopiers, and express checkout. 5701 Main St. (phone: 526-1991; Fax: 713-639-4545). Expensive.

Allen Park Inn – Just outside the downtown area, this picturesque property is a favorite of film crews shooting in Houston. It's decorated with antiques throughout. A comfortable inn with a 24-hour restaurant, bar, and health club facilities. Amenities include meeting rooms for up to 150, A/V equipment, secretarial services, photocopiers, and CNN. 2121 Allen Pkwy. (phone: 521-9321; Fax: 713-521-9321). Moderate.

Rodeway Inn at Greenway Plaza – Another well-sited property with modest accommodations. The express checkout desk will speed you on your way. 3135 Southwest Fwy. (phone: 526-1071). Inexpensive.

There are several moderate to inexpensive motel chain facilities scattered about Houston, including *Ramada, Best Western, La Quinta, Days Inn,* and *TraveLodge.* Features and rates are standard for what one has come to expect from such chains. The deciding factor then is location: along the Katy Freeway or Southwest Freeway if you're visiting the outlying suburbs; along Buffalo Speedway or South Main to be near the *Astrodome;* inside Loop 610 of the Southwest Freeway to shop at the *Galleria;* North and Eastex freeways for the Intercontinental Airport area; and Galveston Freeway for Hobby Airport and — much farther out — the Johnson Space Center.

EATING OUT: Besides offerings of fine regional foods — chili parlors and Mexican restaurants abound — Houston has a great variety of cuisines, including seafood fresh from the Gulf of Mexico, continental, Chinese, Greek, and down-home Southern meals. Expect to spend at least $70 for a dinner for two at restaurants in the expensive range, $25 to $55 in the moderate range, and $20 or less in the inexpensive range. Prices do not include drinks, wine, or tips. All telephone numbers are in the 713 area code unless otherwise indicated.

Brennan's – A bit of New Orleans's Vieux Carré in Houston. Patio tables and a lovely pillared dining room are the setting for fine food. Louisiana-style and creole specialties make this branch as pleasurable as its counterparts in New Orleans, Dallas, and Atlanta. Open daily for lunch and dinner, with wonderful brunches on Saturdays and Sundays. Reservations advised. Major credit cards accepted. 3300 Smith (phone: 522-9711). Expensive.

La Colombe d'Or – Located in the hotel of the same name, many say this place serves the best French food in Texas. Chef Fabrice Beaudoin, one of four Relais Gourmand chefs in the country, prepares at least four specialties daily, such as roasted red snapper, grilled tuna, and grilled prime ribs, duck, or rabbit. Open Mondays through Fridays for lunch and dinner; Saturdays and Sundays for dinner only. Reservations advised. Major credit cards accepted. 3410 Montrose Blvd. (phone: 524-7999). Expensive.

Great Caruso – Singers belt out Broadway show tunes while diners enjoy continental cooking in a European opera house setting. The food is fine, the service superb, and the show (at no extra charge) is an added treat. Open for dinner Tuesdays through Sundays. Reservations necessary. Major credit cards accepted. 10001 Westheimer (phone: 780-4900). Expensive.

Harry's Kenya – Lushly formal (with a safari motif), this place is named for Harry Selby, the legendary African hunter who was the model for the Peter McKenzie character in Robert Ruark's novel *Something of Value.* Its excellent continental fare is enlivened with game dishes. Only a few steps from downtown hotels, complimentary shuttle service takes diners to performances at *Jones Hall,* the *Alley Theater,* and the *Music Hall.* Closed Sundays. Reservations advised. Major credit cards accepted. 1160 Smith (phone: 650-1980). Expensive.

Maxim's – Consistently fine food of the haute cuisine category, and what is probably the most extensive wine cellar in the Southwest. The decor is somewhat overwhelming, but once the meal begins, diners forget all about the pink and green overtones. The menu is weighted toward Gulf seafood, which is prepared well, but the beef is also prime. Chocolate mousse or brandy freeze for dessert are excellent. Closed Sundays. Reservations advised. Major credit cards accepted. 3755 Richmond (phone: 877-8899). Expensive.

Ruth's Chris Steak House – A true Texas establishment, redolent with the aroma of fine beef cooking; decorated with oil company paraphernalia and flashing the latest Dow Jones stock market reports, it's much appreciated for its prime cuts: filet, porterhouse, and strip steaks. Open daily; dinner only on Saturdays. Reservations advised. Major credit cards accepted. 6213 Richmond (phone: 789-2333). Expensive.

Tony's – Owner Tony Vallone is on hand most of the time to oversee this stronghold of elegance in this otherwise purposely informal city. Punctilious service by waiters in black tie, understated wood-paneled decor, and fresh flowers provide the backdrop for excellent continental food. The pâtés and salads are impeccable. Closed Sundays. Reservations advised. Major credit cards accepted. 1801 Post Oak Blvd. (phone: 622-6778). Expensive.

Uncle Tai's Hunan Yuan – Uncle Tai made his name and reputation in New York City, then headed south to start his own place, and people in Houston couldn't be happier. This family-run restaurant offers impeccable service, and the food is uniformly wonderful. Open daily. Reservations advised. Major credit cards accepted. 1980 Post Oak Blvd. (phone: 960-8000). Expensive.

Magic Island – As you insert a special pass card into a cobra's mouth to enter the magical elevator that lifts you through an Egyptian tomb, you know you're in for an unusual evening. The decor is suitable for a 19th-century séance, and for a price a psychic will tell your fortune. The food and service are mediocre, but the magic shows make up for it. The main show features big-name comedians, but it's the house magicians whose performance will leave you baffled and pleased. Closed Sundays. Reservations necessary. Visa and MasterCard accepted. 2215 Southwest Fwy. (phone: 526-2442). Expensive to moderate.

Bombay Palace – Indian fare is enjoying growing popularity in Houston, and this place is a great favorite. The best dishes prepared in the tandoor — the special Indian clay oven — are chicken, lamb, and prawns. Open daily. Reservations advised. Major credit cards accepted. 3901 Westheimer (phone: 960-8472). Moderate.

Cadillac Bar – The current Houston favorite for fine Mexican food. Try the *queso flameado con chorizo* (melted white cheese with sausage) with tender tortillas for starters. Ask about house specialties, which include such exotic dishes as mesquite-smoked kid. For those who can't decide, there's also a buffet. Open daily. Reservations advised. Major credit cards accepted. 1802 Shepherd at I-10 (phone: 862-2020). Moderate.

Ninfa's – A must for Mexican fare that seems to be on every local's list, so you may have to wait in line. But it's worth it, particularly for the *tacos al carbon* (tortillas wrapped around barbecued pork or beef) and *chilpanzingas* (ham and cheese wrapped in pastry, fried, and topped with sour cream). There are seven locations now, but the downtown site is still the best. Open daily. No reservations on weekends. Major credit cards accepted. 2704 Navigation (phone: 228-1175). Moderate.

Romero's – Tasty and interesting Italian and continental dishes are complemented by a good list of wines. Some favorites on the menu are veal piccata, blackened redfish, and angel-hair pasta with shrimp and crabmeat. Open daily; dinner only on Sundays. Major credit cards accepted. 2400 Midlane (phone: 961-1161). Moderate.

Captain Benny's Half Shell – Boiled shrimp, freshly shucked oysters, juicy crayfish in season, and lightly fried shrimp are all dished out to the crew of regulars who jam the place. You may have to stand, but you'll find the people watching and the food worth it. Closed Sundays. No reservations or credit cards accepted. 8506 S. Main (phone: 666-5469). Inexpensive.

Chili's – It's easy to guess the house specialty — the real hot stuff, served steaming, spicy, and thick, concocted from a secret Texas recipe. Otherwise, the jumbo hamburgers and homemade French fries make a solid meal at an easy price. Open daily. No reservations. Major credit cards accepted. 5930 Richmond (phone: 780-1654). Inexpensive.

Harlow's Hollywood Cafe – Open until 4 AM, this is the place to go after all the other nightspots have closed. Urban cowboys and New Wave dudes rub shoulders with the opera set here. Everything from deli sandwiches and Mexican dishes to Greek food and pre-dawn breakfast is found on the menu. Parking is hard to find, and you'll probably have to stand in line if you're not among the first to arrive, but it's worth it for people watchers. No reservations. Major credit cards accepted. 3100 Hillcroft (phone: 780-9500) Inexpensive.

James Coney Island – Here are hot dogs the way lots of folks like them to be served — with loads of chili and onions. About 12 locations around town, but the most fun spot is a 1950s-style diner with a free jukebox that plays top-40 tunes from 1959. Open daily. No reservations. No credit cards accepted. 5745 Westheimer (phone: 785-9333). Inexpensive.

Last Concert Café – This Tex-Mex eatery is one of Houston's best-kept secrets. It's located in a rough-looking industrial section, there's no name outside, and you have to knock to get in. But once inside, you'll enjoy lots of atmosphere, delicious food, and good entertainment on the patio. Open Mondays through Fridays for lunch, from 11 AM to 2 PM; Mondays through Thursdays for dinner, from 5 PM to 11 PM; and Fridays through Saturdays for dinner, from 5 PM to 2 AM. Reservations unnecessary. Major credit cards accepted. 1403 Nance (phone: 226-8563). Inexpensive.

Otto's – Aficionados argue over the merits of various styles of barbecue sauce. If you crave the East Texas sweet variety, ride over here and sample good beef, ribs, links, or ham awash in the delightful stuff. Open Mondays through Saturdays, from 11 AM to 9 PM. Reservations unnecessary. Checks, but no credit cards accepted. 5502 Memorial (phone: 864-2573). Inexpensive.

Ragin' Cajun – If you prefer the down-and-dirty spice and rice of Cajun cooking to highfalutin' creole sauces, then this is the place to go. It's a hole in the wall, but the atmosphere is great and the gumbo and red beans with rice are delicious. Open daily. Reservations unnecessary. Checks, but no credit cards accepted. 4302 Richmond (phone: 623-6321). Inexpensive.

INDIANAPOLIS

AT-A-GLANCE

SEEING THE CITY: Indianapolis has some breathtaking vantage points. The highest point is in Crown Hill Cemetery (3402 Boulevard Pl.; phone: 925-8231), at the grave of author James Whitcomb Riley. (John Dillinger and Benjamin Harrison also are buried at Crown Hill, which is a National Historic Site.) The Soldiers and Sailors Monument (Monument Circle, downtown) gives you the best overview of the layout of the city. No admission charge. The 13- x 13-foot model of the city at the Indianapolis City Center, a visitor and community information center, can help you get your bearings. To find out where a museum or monument is located, you press a button on the model's computer, and it will light up the corresponding site (201 S. Capitol Ave.; phone: 237-5200). The view from *Teller's Cage,* the 35th-floor restaurant at the top of the Indiana National Bank Tower (1 Indiana Sq.; phone: 266-5211) also is exceptional. Another stunning view is from the 28th floor of the City County Building Observatory (200 E. Washington St. between Delaware and Alabama Sts.; phone: 236-4345).

SPECIAL PLACES: You'll find Indianapolis an easy place to get around. Washington Street is the north-south dividing line; Meridian Street is the east-west dividing line. Numbered streets always run east and west, and the number of the street represents the number of blocks north of Washington Street. Most of the great places are spread out north of Washington Street.

Union Station – One of the state's most popular attractions is the revitalized historic Union Station. During the mid-1980s, the once-decrepit railroad terminal was transformed into an eating-entertainment-shopping area like *Faneuil Hall Marketplace* in Boston and *South Street Seaport* in New York. Centrally located across from the *Convention Center* and *Hoosier Dome,* the 3-block structure features nearly 75 eateries, shops, restaurants, and nightclubs. The highlight is the 276-room *Holiday Inn* — which purports to be the first ever placed in an existing structure — with even a few Pullman cars available for lodging (phone: 631-2221).

Eiteljorg Museum of American Indian and Western Art – The $14-million building, on the grounds of White River State Park, is a work of art in itself, and the $40 million collection, considered one of the finest of its kind in the country, features works by Frederic Remington, Georgia O'Keeffe, and Ernest L. Blumenschein. Closed Mondays. Admission charge. 500 W. Washington (phone: 636-9378).

Indiana State Museum – This entertaining museum relates the natural and cultural history of the state. Open daily. No admission charge. 202 N. Alabama, at Ohio (phone: 232-1637).

Scottish Rite Cathedral – A vast Tudor Gothic structure with a 54-bell carillon, two organs, and an interior that looks like 3-D lace turned into wood. Free tours on weekdays only. 650 N. Meridian (phone: 635-2301).

James Whitcomb Riley Home – Indiana's underrated poet laureate lived in this comfortable house between 1892 and 1916; the whole Lockerbie Street neighborhood has been restored to look as it might have then. Found on a cobblestone street, the home is considered one of the finest Victorian preservations in the country. Closed Mondays. Admission charge. 528 Lockerbie (phone: 631-5885).

Benjamin Harrison Memorial Home – This 16-room Victorian-Italianate mansion, built in 1875 for the 23rd president, has been fitted out with many of the original furnishings. Open daily. Admission charge. 1230 N. Delaware (phone: 631-1898).

Indianapolis Motor Speedway – Minibuses will take visitors around the 2½-mile oval on which the 500-mile race is held every year on the last Sunday in May. You also can visit the *IMS Museum,* where race cars from the early days are on display. Open daily. Admission charge. 4790 W. 16th (phone: 241-2500).

Indianapolis Museum of Art – By any standards, a truly remarkable museum. A new wing, the Mary F. Hulman Pavilion, houses the Eitel-jorg collection of African art. Its Krannert Pavilion contains a wide-ranging collection of American, Oriental, primitive, and 18th- and 19th-century European art. The adjacent Clowes Pavilion has rooms full of medieval and Renaissance art, plus some watercolors by Turner, ranged around a skylit, plant-filled courtyard. In the gardens are modern sculptures, including Robert Indiana's *LOVE,* and a wonderful, geometrical fountain. The grounds originally were the riverview estate of the Lilly family. Their mansion now shows off a collection of English, French, and Italian 18th-century decorative art. The 154 beautifully landscaped acres also feature a greenhouse, botanical gardens, and the biggest children's playhouse you've ever seen. Open daily. Admission charge for special exhibits; the pavilions are free. 1200 W. 38th St. (phone: 923-1331).

National Art Museum of Sport – Relocated to Indianapolis in January 1991 from West Haven, Connecticut, this 31-year-old museum collection houses the nation's largest collection of sports-related art. The city's newest collection sports paintings, sculptures, drawings, and prints from a 5th-century Greek bronze to contemporary works. No admission charge. 111 Monument Circle, mezzanine level (phone: 687-1715).

Children's Museum – The largest children's museum in the world. Kids and adults can explore the galaxies in the planetarium, ride a turn-of-the-century carousel, spelunk in a simulated limestone cave, and see a real mummy and the largest collection of toy trains on public display. Also featured are antique fire engines, a furnished Hoosier log cabin, folk art toys from around the world, and two major galleries filled with hands-on displays exploring the natural and physical sciences. Special programs are held regularly. Closed Mondays from *Labor Day* through *Memorial Day.* Admission charge. 3000 N. Meridian (phone: 924-5431).

Indianapolis Zoo – The $64-million, 64-acre world class Indianapolis Zoo, the nation's first major zoo in decades to be built from the ground up, opened in 1988. More than 2,000 animals are now housed in simulated natural habitats, including the new Deserts Pavilion featuring free-roaming lizards and birds, as well as the world's largest totally enclosed Whale and Dolphin Pavilion. Admission charge. (Admission discount the first Tuesday of every month, 9 to 11 AM.) 1200 W. Washington St. (phone: 630-2000).

Zionsville – A mid-19th-century restored village. The streets are now full of ritzy shops. Good for a long afternoon. 86th St. north to Zionsville Rd.

Conner Prairie Pioneer Settlement – Step back in time to 1836 and see the daily life of the era re-created. Interpreters portray villagers in this 25-building settlement: a doctor, a potter, a blacksmith, and an innkeeper talk as they perform their duties. Also on the premises is a restaurant featuring 19th-century country-style dinners, an old-fashioned *Fourth of July* bash, and *Christmas* by candlelight. Closed Mon-

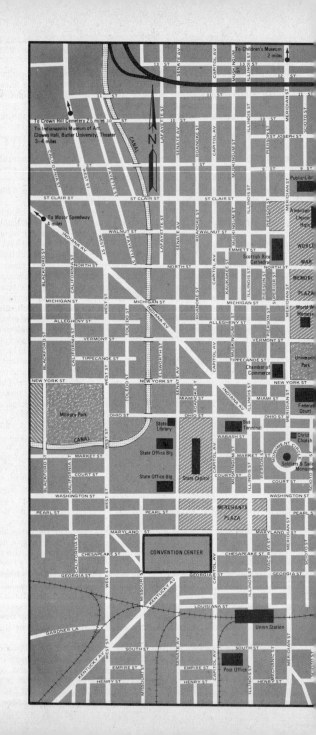

CENTRAL
INDIANAPOLIS

days. Admission charge. 13400 Allisonville Rd., about 20 miles northeast of Monument Circle via Rte. 37 and I-465 (phone: 776-6000).

Garfield Park Conservatory – More than 500 tropical plants are on display in addition to a large collection of cacti and a 15-foot waterfall. Closed Mondays. No admission charge. 2450 S. Shelby (phone: 784-3044).

Lilly Center – Through exhibitions, the research activities of the Eli Lilly Company — including genetic engineering — are highlighted. Some Lilly family memorabilia also is on display. No admission charge. 893 S. Delaware St. (phone: 276-3514).

SOURCES AND RESOURCES

TOURIST INFORMATION: The Indianapolis City Center (Pan American Plaza, 201 S. Capitol Ave., Indianapolis, IN 46225; phone: 237-5200, or 800-323-INDY) and the Indiana Tourism Development Division (1 N. Capitol, Suite 700; phone: 232-8860 or 800-289-6646) supply brochures and general tourist information. Contact the Indiana state hotline (800-289-6646) for maps, calendars of events, health updates, and travel advisories.

Local Coverage – *Indianapolis Star,* morning daily and Sundays; *Indianapolis News,* afternoon daily.

Television Stations – WRTV Channel 6–ABC; WISH Channel 8–CBS; WTHR Channel 13–NBC; WFYI Channel 20–PBS; WTTV Channel 4–Local.

Radio Stations – AM: WIBC 1070 (news); WYIC 1110 (easy listening). FM: WAJC 104.5 (news/jazz/classical); WFBQ 94.7 (album oriented); WENS 97.1 (adult contemporary music); WZPL 99.5 (top 40).

TELEPHONE: The area code for Indianapolis is 317.

Sales Tax – There is a 5% sales tax as well as a 5% hotel tax, and a 6% beverage tax in Marion County (Indianapolis).

CLIMATE: Indianapolis has typical midwestern weather — beautiful springs, steamy summers, mild autumns, and moderately cold winters with varying amounts of snow.

GETTING AROUND: Airport – Indianapolis International Airport is a 15-minute drive from downtown; taxi fare should run about $10. *AAA Limousine Service* (phone: 247-7301) offers frequent van service from the airport to most downtown hotels for $6 per person. *Metro Transit*'s No. 9 West Washington Street bus provides public tranportation between the airport and downtown; for the return trip, catch the bus on Washington between Illinois and Maryland Streets. The fare is 75¢ off-peak, $1 rush hours.; exact change is required.

You can get around by public transportation, but a car is more convenient since Indianapolis is a sprawling city.

Bus – Service has improved in recent years, and some lines operate 24 hours — but check before you go. *Metro Transit* (phone: 635-3344).

Car Rental – All the major national companies are represented here.

Taxi – Calling *Yellow Cab* (phone: 637-5421) is the surest way to get one.

VITAL SERVICES: Audiovisual Equipment – *Markey's Ideal Pictures,* 2909 S. Meridian (phone: 783-1155).

Baby-sitting – Most hotels can help you arrange for sitters. Failing that, contact *Kinder Care,* with several locations in the city (phone: 844-3096, main office).

Business Services – *Manpower Inc. of Indianapolis,* 251 N. Delaware (phone: 635-1001).

Dry Cleaner/Tailor – *Karstadt-Reed Cleaners* (1449 N. Illinois St.; phone: 634-5333); *Tuchman Cleaners* (Lockerbie Market Place, downtown; phone: 635-5810).

Limousine – *Indy Connection Limousine* (phone: 271-2522); *VIP Limousine Service* (phone: 635-2308).

Mechanics – *Kwik Auto Care* (134 S. Delaware St.; phone: 634-0928); *Chuck's Standard Service* (5061 E. Washington St.; phone: 357-5209); *Emergency Road Service* (phone: 923-3311); *Approved Auto Repair Service* (phone: 924-5687), affiliated with *AAA Motor Club*, gives locations and phone numbers of reputable shops.

Medical Emergency – *Urgent Care Center* (1919 N. Capitol Ave.; phone: 926-4471); *Methodist Hospital* (1701 N. Senate Ave.; phone: 929-8355).

Messenger Services – *Zipp Express* (3340 S. Shelby; phone: 782-9665); *Special Dispatch* (355 W. Merrill; phone: 683-0608).

National/International Courier – *Federal Express* (phone: 800-238-5355); *Emery Worldwide* (phone: 800-233-7233).

Pharmacy – *Hook's Drug Store,* open 24 hours (1744 N. Illinois St.; phone: 923-1491); they also have a downtown branch (175 N. Illinois St.; phone: 636-6664); *Reliable Drug Store* (310 N. New Jersey St.; phone: 639-4539).

Photocopies – *Quik Printing* (34 N. Delaware St.; phone: 637-8282); *Insty-Prints* (114 N. Delaware St.; phone: 635-2282).

Post Office – The central one is located at 125 W. South St (phone: 464-6000).

Professional Photographer – *B & L Photographers* (2105 N. Meridian St.; phone: 924-1615); *Cassell Productions* (2950 E. 55th Pl.; phone: 251-1201); *Banayote Photography* (4736 Pleasant Run Pkwy. N.; phone: 352-0310).

Secretary/Stenographer – *Bretz Inc.* (22 E. Washington St.; phone: 634-1545); *Manpower Temporary Services* (205 E. New York St.; phone: 635-1001).

Teleconference Facilities – *Holiday Inn North* (see *Best in Town,* below); *University Place Executive Conference Center and Hotel* (850 W. Michigan St.; phone: 269-9000).

Translator – *International Bureau of Translations, Inc.* (3254 N. Washington Blvd.; phone: 923-8670); *Prolingua* (6251 Winthrop Ave.; phone: 255-7055).

Western Union/Telex – Many offices are located around the city (phone: 800-325-6000).

SPECIAL EVENTS: The *Indianapolis 500-Mile Race* — the world's biggest single-day sporting event — is held at the *Indianapolis Motor Speedway* every *Memorial Day* weekend; myriad activities surrounding the *Indy 500* are held during May as part of the *500 Festival.* One Saturday night in June, thousands crowd Monument Circle downtown for the *Mid-Summer Fest,* a music fair. During July, *Indiana Black Expo,* the nation's largest exposition of black culture, history, and enterprise, takes place. The exuberant *Indiana State Fair* and the *Indiana Avenue Outdoor Jazz Festival,* featuring jazz, blues, and an array of food vendors, take place in August. The same month, Indianapolis hosts the *GTE/US Men's Hardcourt Championships* in a modern tennis stadium. The *National Championship Drag Races* are held at *Raceway Park* every *Labor Day* weekend. September brings the city's largest art fair, *Penrod,* and *Circlefest,* the city's largest festival of food and live entertainment. *Christmas on the Circle* is a month of festivities in the heart of the city.

MUSEUMS: The *Children's Museum, Conner Prairie Pioneer Settlement, Eiteljorg Museum of American Indian and Western Art, Indianapolis Museum of Art, National Art Museum of Sport,* and *Indiana State Museum* are described in *Special Places.*

MAJOR COLLEGES AND UNIVERSITIES: The combined campus of Indiana University–Purdue University at Indianapolis (IUPUI) is modern and beautifully designed (1100-1300 W. Michigan; phone: 274-5555). The campus of Butler University is farther north (at Sunset Ave. and W. 46th St.; phone: 283-8000). The *J. I. Holcomb Observatory and Planetarium* sits at the campus's north end (phone: 283-9333). There also are the private University of Indianapolis (1400 E. Hanna; phone: 788-3368) and Marian College (3200 Cold Spring Rd.; phone: 929-0123).

 SPORTS AND FITNESS: Baseball – The Indianapolis *Indians* of the AAA American Assocation is the Montreal *Expos'* top farm team. They play in *Bush Stadium* at 1501 W. 16th (phone: 632-5371).

Basketball – The NBA Indiana *Pacers* play in the *Market Square Arena,* 300 E. Market (phone: 639-2112).

Bicycling – The *Major Taylor Velodrome* (bicycle racing track) has a smooth, 28-degree, banked track open from mid-March to early November (except when sporting events are in progress), depending on the weather. Helmet and bicycle rental available for a nominal fee. 3649 Cold Spring Rd. (phone: 926-8356).

Fishing – Panfish at Eagle Creek Reservoir (7602 Walnut Point Rd.; phone: 293-5555). Farther out of town: Geist and Morse reservoirs and, about 2 hours south and much larger, Monroe Reservoir, near Bloomington.

Fitness Centers – The *National Institute for Fitness and Sport* is a professional-caliber center open to all (250 N. University Blvd.; phone: 274-3603). *Scandinavian Health and Racquet Club* (8831 Keystone Crossing; phone: 844-1515) also welcomes exercise devotees. The pool at the *YMCA* also is available (860 W. 10th; phone: 634-2478).

Football – The Indianapolis *Colts* of the NFL play in the *Hoosier Dome,* 100 S. Capitol (phone: 262-3389).

Golf – There are three good public courses near Riverside Park (3501 Cold Spring Rd.), and eight others around the city. For information on all of them, call the Parks and Recreation Department (phone: 924-9151).

Hockey – The Indianapolis *Ice* play at the *Coliseum,* State Fairgrounds (phone: 632-5151).

Ice Skating – November to March at Ellenberger City Park (5301 E. St. Clair; phone: 353-1600) and Perry City Park (541 E. Stop 11 Rd.; phone: 888-0070). Also, October through March at the *Coliseum* (State Fairgrounds; phone: 927-7536), and year-round at the *Carmel Skadium* (1040 3rd SW; phone: 844-8888). The *Indiana/World Ice Skating Academy and Research Center* is at Pan American Plaza, near Union Station. Indoor skating and skate rental are available to the public except when a competition is going on (phone: 237-5555).

Jogging – Take advantage of the walkways around the capital, at Capitol and Washington Street, in the early morning and evening. Joggers also use Military and University parks and the World War Memorial area downtown. Another possibility is the combined campus of Indiana University–Purdue University at Indianapolis (IUPUI; 1100 W. Michigan). Still other joggers use the IUPUI campus to the half-mile River Promenade, a pedestrian walkway at White River State Park.

Swimming – The *Indiana University Natatorium* (*IUPUI*), one of the premier aquatic facilities in the world, has two 50-meter pools. 901 W. New York St. (phone: 274-3517).

Tennis – One of the most popular spots is at the *Indianapolis Sports Center* (815 W. New York St.; phone: 632-3250). Most high school courts are open to the public. Municipal courts can be found throughout the city. For specific locations, call 924-9151.

THEATER: The professional *Indiana Repertory Theater* has grown by leaps and bounds in the last few years (140 W. Washington St.; phone: 635-5252). The new *American Cabaret Theatre* offers true European cabaret in a renovated ballroom at the historic Athenaeum Turners Building (401 E. Michigan; phone: 631-0334). Indianapolis also is home to the *Indianapolis Civic Theater* (1200 W. 38th; phone: 923-4597), the oldest continuously active civic theater in the US. Community theater can be found at the *Christian Theological Seminary* (1000 W. 42nd; phone: 924-1331). For dinner theater, *Beef & Boards* (9301 N. Michigan Rd. NW; phone: 872-9664) features stars of TV, Broadway, and Hollywood. In July and August there are musicals under the stars at *Starlight Musicals* (304 W. 49th; phone: 926-1581). *The Phoenix Theatre* (749 N. Park Ave.; phone: 635-7529) offers avant-garde and contemporary alternatives. The *Butler Ballet* performs primarily at *Clowes Hall* (phone: 283-9231).

 MUSIC: The *Circle Theater* is where the *Indianapolis Symphony Orchestra* plays most of its concerts (phone: 639-4300). The *Indianapolis Opera Company* plays at *Clowes Hall* (phone: 283-3531).

NIGHTCLUBS AND NIGHTLIFE: Like every other aspect of city life, nightlife in Indianapolis has grown. For dancing: *Ike & Jonesy's* (17 Jackson Pl.; phone: 632-4553); *Lauderdale's* is trackside at Union Station (phone: 638-8181). Sports fans catch the latest scores at the *Sports Bar* (231 S. Meridian St.; phone: 631-5838). Young singles patronize *Friday's* (3502 E. 86th; phone: 844-3355). *Crackers Comedy Club* (8702 Keystone Crossing; phone: 846-2500) features nationally known comedians Wednesdays through Saturdays; reservations advised. Comedy is also king (or queen) at *Indianapolis Comedy Connection* (247 S. Meridian St., 2nd Floor; phone: 631-3536), reservations necessary; and at the *Broad Ripple Comedy Club* (6281 N. College; phone: 255-4211), reservations necessary. There are also some promising nightclubs in the rejuvenated Union Station, across from the *Convention Center. Ltl Ditty's,* a participatory piano bar with two baby grands, is especially popular (Union Station; phone: 687-0068). Blues are featured Thursdays through Saturdays at the *Slippery Noodle Inn* — Indiana's oldest — ca. 1850 — bar (372 S. Meridian St.; phone: 631-6968). Jazz can be heard at *Madame Walker Urban Life Center* on Friday nights (617 Indiana Ave.; phone: 635-6915), at the *Chatterbox* (435½ Massachusetts Ave.; phone: 636-0584), and at the *City Taproom* (28 S. Pennsylvania St.; phone: 637-1334).

BEST IN TOWN

CHECKING IN: All the expected national chains are here — most of them immediately off I-465, which rings the city, or I-65, which runs diagonally through it. Very expensive rooms run from $130 and up for a double, expensive from $90 to $130, moderately priced rooms range from $45 to $80, and inexpensive run under $45. Rates are usually higher during *Indianapolis 500* weekend and other major sporting events. Call the Indiana Tourism Development Division (phone: 800-2WANDER) for a list of local bed and breakfast facilities. All telephone numbers are in the 317 area code unless otherwise indicated.

Canterbury – A small, European-style luxury hostelry, 2 blocks from Union Station, it offers 99 rooms, skylighted penthouse suites, and a Mercedes stretch limo (once owned by Frank Sinatra) to whisk guests to the airport. Its romantic *Beaulieu* restaurant specializes in French fare. Among the hotel's amenities are 24-hour room service, concierge, 5 meeting rooms, secretarial services, A/V equipment, photocopiers, computers, and express checkout. 123 S. Illinois St. (phone: 634-3000; Fax: 317-685-2519). Very expensive.

Embassy Suites Downtown – All of the accommodations are fully equipped suites — 360 of them — each with bedroom, living room, and kitchenette. There also is a pool, 2 hot tubs, and a sauna and steamroom. Complimentary services include full cooked-to-order American breakfast and limousine service to and from the airport. The first 3 floors of the building make up the *Claypool* court complex of shops and restaurants. There are 12 meeting rooms for business functions, as well as A/V equipment and photocopiers, and express checkout. Illinois and Washington Sts. (phone: 236-1800; Fax: 317-236-1816). Expensive.

Hilton at the Circle – The glass elevator that rises and falls through the 369-room hotel allows riders to look out at Monument Circle. Twenty-four hour room service is available. There's a concierge desk, 14 meeting rooms, A/V equipment, photocopiers, and computers. 34 W. Ohio (phone: 635-2000; Fax: 317-638-0782). Expensive.

Hyatt Regency Indianapolis – An imposing red brick edifice built around a 20-story central atrium lobby, it has 496 rooms, and several restaurants, lounges, and shops. A concierge desk, secretarial assistance, and express checkout are available, as are photocopiers, A/V equipment, computers, and 16 meeting rooms. 1 S. Capitol Ave., opposite the *Convention Center* (phone: 632-1234; Fax: 317-231-7569; Telex: 027357). Expensive.

Omni Severin – A blend of old and new across from Union Station, this historic 423-room establishment reopened in 1990 after a 2-year renovation and expansion. A 20-foot waterfall cascades in the atrium lobby. (Don't confuse this hotel with its franchise, the *Omni North*, about 25 minutes from town.) Amenities include room service until 11:30 PM; concierge; 17 meeting rooms; secretarial services; A/V equipment; photocopiers; computers; and express checkout. 40 W. Jackson Place (phone: 634-6664; Fax: 317-687-3612). Expensive.

Radisson Plaza – Within walking distance of some of the city's best shops and restaurants, it's convenient as well as comfortable. Amenities include a pool, Jacuzzi, exercise room, and men's and women's saunas. Try to dine at *Waterson's* restaurant (see *Eating Out*); if you can't make it, room service orders are accepted until 1 AM. Other conveniences include a concierge desk, 36 meeting rooms, secretarial services, A/V equipment, photocopiers, and express checkout. 8787 Keystone Crossing (phone: 846-2700 or 800-333-3333; Fax: 317-846-2700, ext. 402). Expensive.

Westin – Now the largest in the state (572 rooms), it opened in 1989 across from the *Indiana Convention Center*. The restaurant features an open grill and buffet, and the lobby lounge has an espresso counter. The 39,000 square feet of meeting and banquet space can handle receptions for up to 1,000 people. Room service is delivered around the clock. There are secretarial services, A/V equipment, photocopiers, computers, a concierge desk, and express checkout. 50 S. Capitol Ave. (phone: 262-8100 or 800-228-3000; Fax: 317-231-3928). Expensive.

Holiday Inn North – Features include a beautiful Holidome, a small sports complex with a pool, Jacuzzi, saunas, and other facilities for rest and relaxation. Twelve meeting rooms, secretarial services, A/V equipment, photocopiers, and express checkout are available. 3850 DePauw Blvd. (phone: 872-9790 or 800-HOLIDAY; Fax: 317-871-5608). Moderate.

Indianapolis Motor Speedway Motel – Next to the racetrack, it has many leisure-time pluses, including a golf course next to the *Speedway*

Museum, which is easily accessible, and an outdoor heated pool. There are 8 meeting rooms, photocopiers, and express checkout. 4400 W. 16th St. (phone: 241-2500; Fax: 317-241-2133). Moderate.

Tower Inn – Approximately 5 blocks from I-65, just north of downtown, and one of the best bargains in the area. Spacious rooms include sofas that open into queen-size beds. Meeting rooms handle up to 75 people. Round-the-clock room service is available. 1633 N. Capitol Ave. (phone: 925-9831). Moderate.

Days Inn South – The pleasant swimming pool makes the typical low rates especially noteworthy. On US 31 south and I-465 (phone: 788-0811 or 800-325-2525). Inexpensive.

EATING OUT: Indianapolis has always had more than its share of steak-and-baked-potato places and very few notable ethnic eateries. But this situation is changing. In addition to the variety of foods available at the places listed below, the revamped Union Station (phone: 637-1888) features over 40 eateries with every imaginable type of fare. You'll pay $40 and up for a meal for two in restaurants listed below as expensive, $25 to $30 at those marked moderate, and less than $20 at inexpensive places. Prices do not include drinks, wine, or tips. All telephone numbers are in the 317 area code unless otherwise indicated.

Benvenuti – Contemporary Italian food in an elegant, yet warm and comfortable setting. The menu changes daily. Open for lunch on weekdays and dinner Mondays through Saturdays. Closed Sundays. Reservations advised. Major credit cards accepted. 36 S. Pennsylvania (phone: 633-4915). Expensive.

Chanteclair sur le Toit – Entrées and desserts are flambéed at the table while strolling violinists entertain. Veal Oscar is among the continental specialties. Open for dinner only; closed Sundays. Reservations advised. Major credit cards accepted. At the *Holiday Inn–Airport,* 2501 S. High School Rd. (phone: 243-1040). Expensive.

Glass Chimney – Some of the city's best continental fare appears on the carefully set tables of this consistently fine establishment in a charming old house. Open daily for dinner; closed Sundays. Reservations necessary. Major credit cards accepted. 12901 N. Meridian (phone: 844-0921). Expensive.

Illusions – Magicians perform tableside at this unusual eatery that features steaks, prime ribs, pasta, seafood, and homemade pastries. Open for dinner only; closed Sundays. Reservations essential on weekends. Major credit cards accepted. 969 Keystone Way (phone: 575-8312). Expensive.

Jonathan's – English country accents fill the four dining rooms of this tasteful place specializing in American cooking, including a fine New York strip steak, roast pork, and prime ribs. Darts, backgammon, and chess are played in the Old English-style pub. Open for lunch and dinner daily; brunch served from 10:30 AM to 2 PM on Sundays. Reservations advised. Major credit cards accepted. 96th and Keystone Ave. (phone: 844-1155). Expensive.

New Orleans House – Visit this relatively plain establishment with a very empty stomach. Unless you're ravenous, it's impossible to do justice to the extravagant all-you-can-eat seafood buffet. Allow 2½ to 3 hours to consume your fill of oysters and clams on the half shell, chowders and creole dishes, crab legs and lobster. Open daily for dinner only. Reservations necessary. Major credit cards accepted. 8845 Township Line Rd. (phone: 872-9670). Expensive.

Peter's – Dining here is more than a nutritional experience. An exclusive, small (only 52 seats) place with a constantly changing menu, it features fresh seasonal Midwest dishes prepared with an innovative flair. Dinners include lamb, veal, Black Angus beef, game meats, and fresh fish. There's also an extensive wine list. Open daily. Reservations advised. Major credit cards accepted. 936 Virginia Ave. (phone: 637-9333). Expensive.

San Remo – The 20-minute drive from downtown is worth the effort for the Northern Italian dishes, elegant and cheery atmosphere, and excellent wine selection. Dinner is not complete without a dessert of *zabaglione*. Open daily. Reservations advised. In the *Holiday Inn North*, 3850 DePauw Blvd. (phone: 871-5630). Expensive.

Tower at the Heliport – One of the specialties of the house is the special dining package for couples that includes a ride in an executive helicopter before dinner. Open daily. Reservations essential. Major credit cards accepted. 51 S. New Jersey St. (phone: 262-3020). Expensive.

Waterson's – House specialties at this north-side hot spot include certified Angus steaks and fresh seafood. All desserts are prepared in the restaurant's bakery. Closed Sundays. Reservations advised. Major credit cards accepted. *Radisson Plaza,* 8787 Keystone Crossing (phone: 846-2700). Expensive.

Adam's Rib – Prime ribs are the specialty, but fresh fish is flown in daily, and the menu always lists one exotic viand like venison, rattlesnake, or antelope. The salad bar is one of the best in town. Open for dinner only; closed Sundays. Reservations advised. Major credit cards accepted. 40 S. Main, in Zionsville (see *Special Places;* phone: 873-3301). Expensive to moderate.

Fletcher's American Grill & Café – *Fletcher's* has two dining concepts: the *Grill* specializes in food grilled over mesquite charcoal and served in an informal setting; the *Café* specializes in new American cooking, in a more formal setting. Open daily. Reservations advised. Major credit cards accepted. 107 S. Pennsylvania St. (phone: 632-2500). Expensive to moderate.

St. Elmo's – A local tradition since 1902 for steaks, chops, the hottest shrimp cocktails this side of Hades, and fine wines. Open for dinner only; closed Sundays. Reservations advised. Major credit cards accepted. 127 S. Illinois (phone: 635-0636). Expensive to moderate.

Forbidden City – The menu here is extensive; in fact, it's several pages long. Chinese fare is the specialty; Hunan, Szechuan, and Mandarin dishes are prepared by a top chef and tastefully served in an elegant Oriental atmosphere. Open daily for lunch and dinner. Reservations advised. Major credit cards accepted. 2605 E. 65th St. at Keystone Ave. (phone: 257-7388). Moderate.

Hollyhock Hill – One of Indianapolis's several family-style spots, it serves steaks, fried chicken, and vegetables in generous portions. Open Tuesdays through Sundays for dinner, for lunch on Sundays. Reservations advised. Major credit cards accepted. 8110 N. College Ave. (phone: 251-2294). Moderate.

Key West Shrimp House – The seafood and steaks are as good now as when the place opened more than 40 years ago. Open for dinner except Sundays; open for lunch, weekdays. Reservations advised. Major credit cards accepted. 2861 Madison Ave. (phone: 787-5353). Moderate.

Milano Inn – The best place in town for Italian fare. Open daily for lunch and dinner. Reservations advised. Major credit cards accepted. 231 S. College Ave. (phone: 264-3585) Moderate.

Bar-B-Q Heaven, Inc. – Hickory-smoked ribs, rib tips, chicken, shoulder, corned beef, giant barbecue on a bun sandwiches, salads, and sweet potato pie. Carry-out and delivery of barbecue to downtown hotels and motels from 10 PM to 4 AM except Sundays. No reservations or credit cards accepted. 2515 Martin Luther King St. (phone: 926-1667). Moderate to inexpensive.

City Taproom & Grille – From hand-cut steaks, grilled chicken, and seafood to artichokes or hearty sandwiches, the camaraderie of this downtown pub is enhanced nightly with live jazz. Reservations advised. Major credit cards accepted. 28 S. Pennsylvania St. (phone: 637-1334). Moderate to inexpensive.

Mark Pi's China Gate – Mandarin, Hunan, and Szechuan dishes, reasonably priced and prepared without MSG. Reservations advised. Major credit cards accepted. 135 S. Illinois St. (phone: 631-6757). Moderate to inexpensive.

Parthenon – Surrounded by the boutiques of Broad Ripple Village, diners feast on absolutely authentic Greek and Middle Eastern cooking. The *spanokopita*, a pastry filled with spinach and feta cheese, is especially good. On Friday and Saturday nights, a belly dancer entertains the patrons. Open daily for lunch and dinner. Reservations advised. Major credit cards accepted. 6319 Guilford Ave. (phone: 251-3138). Moderate to inexpensive.

Shapiro's – Indianapolis's best deli, with food served cafeteria-style. Open daily for lunch and dinner. No reservations or credit cards accepted. 808 S. Meridian (phone: 631-4041). Moderate to inexpensive.

Acapulco Joe's – Potent spices and five flavorful cheeses make this Tex-Mex spot's servings of enchiladas, soft tacos, burritos, enchiladas, and tostadas a cut above the rest. Open daily. Reservations advised. Major credit cards accepted. 365 N. Illinois St. (phone: 637-5160). Inexpensive.

MCL Cafeterias – Ten locations in the city offer homemade fried chicken, vegetables, cinnamon rolls, and pies. Open daily. No reservations or credit cards accepted. For general information, call 257-5425. Inexpensive.

Paramount Music Palace – A lively family pizza place and ice cream parlor that features "the mighty Wurlitzer theater pipe organ," which plays all kinds of music. The sing-alongs and silent movies are also popular. Open daily for lunch and dinner. No reservations or credit cards accepted. I-465 at E. Washington St. (phone: 352-0144). Inexpensive.

KANSAS CITY, MO

CITY AT-A-GLANCE

SEEING THE CITY: One of the best views of Kansas City is from the Observation Tower on the 30th floor of City Hall (414 E. 12th St.; phone: 274-2000). Open weekdays from 8 AM to 4:30 PM. No admission charge. Even more dramatic is the view from atop the Liberty Memorial (100 W. 26th St.; phone: 221-1918), the great limestone column at the south edge of the downtown area, from which you'll see massive Union Station (second in size only to New York's Grand Central), the downtown skyline, and *Crown Center*. Closed Mondays. Open from 9:30 AM to 4:30 PM. Admission charges are $2 for the museum and $1 to ride the elevator up to the top.

SPECIAL PLACES: Kansas City's three major shopping complexes are self-contained units in which a visitor can be immersed for an entire day.

Crown Center – This $300-million development is the brainchild of the late Joyce Hall, founder of Hallmark Cards. We suggest starting out from the lobby of the super-elegant *Westin Crown Center* hotel, dominated by a tropical rain forest and waterfall that winds its way down the limestone hillside on which the hotel was built. Then move on to the shops, where more than 80 stores offer everything from fine art to frivolities. 2450 Grand (phone: 274-8444).

Westport – "Westward, ho!" used to echo across the field that is now *Westport.* It was here that pioneers outfitted themselves for the great journey west. Although times have changed, the tradition of seeking out supplies at *Westport* is implanted solidly in the consciousness of Kansas City residents. A lot of work has gone into restoring the old buildings, many of which date to the 1850s. Broadway at Westport Rd. (phone: 931-3440).

Country Club Plaza – A few blocks south of *Westport, Country Club Plaza* is an adult's *Disneyland.* More than $1 million worth of statues, fountains, and murals line the shaded walks of this spectacular Spanish- and Moorish-style residential shopping center with over 150 shops, restaurants, and nightclubs. West of 47th and Main Sts. (phone: 753-0100).

Town Pavilion – This architecturally striking vertical shopping center houses a large number of specialty stores and some enticing food options. An overhead walkway connects it to *The Jones Store,* Kansas City's last surviving downtown department store. Other national stores such as *The Limited* and *Paul Harris* are here. 1111 Main St.

Nelson-Atkins Museum of Art – The *Nelson* is renowned for its comprehensive collection of art, from the ancient Sumerian civilization (3000 BC) to works by contemporaries. Egyptian, Greek, Roman, and medieval sculpture and a reconstructed medieval cloister make this more than just a museum of Old Masters, although there are plenty of classics on the walls — Titian, Rembrandt, El Greco, Goya, the Impressionists, Van Gogh — as well as such contemporary works as the definitive Thomas Hart Benton collection. It also houses a notable Oriental art collection and the largest collection of works by British sculptor Henry

Moore in the US. Closed Mondays, major holidays. Admission charge, except on Saturdays. 4525 Oak St. (phone: 561-4000).

Swope Park – This 1,772-acre park has two golf courses, a swimming pool, picnic areas, a zoo, and the *Starlight Theater* (phone: 333-9481), where popular musicals and concerts are performed in the summer under the stars. Swope Pkwy. and Meyer Blvd.

Kansas City Stockyards – Although the great packing plants and most of the steers are long gone, you still can see what a Kansas City steak looks like on the hoof. Depending on how you react to the cattle-men in action, you may or may not look forward to a hefty meal of the beef that helped make Kansas City famous. There are frequent cattle auctions at the stockyards. Visitors are welcome at the Sales Pavilion of the Livestock Building on Wednesdays and Thursdays at 11 AM. 16th and Genesee (phone: 842-6800).

Benjamin Ranch – This western-style recreational complex has horse-drawn carts, wagons, and carriages. There are sleigh rides and hayrides, and horseback riding for those who want to ride the old Santa Fe Trail. Call 1 day in advance for a tour. Open 365 days a year 8 AM to dusk. 6401 E. 87th at I-435 (phone: 761-5055).

Worlds of Fun – This 140-acre family theme park has more than 60 rides. The adjacent *Oceans of Fun* (phone: 459-9283) is a huge aquatic park that's open in the summer. *Worlds of Fun* is open daily from June until early September; weekends only from mid-April to late May and in September and October. Admission charge. On I-435, just north of the Missouri River, at Parvin Rd. (phone: 454-4545).

Missouri River Excursions – A relaxing way to spend a few hours. Riverboat cruises leave from Kaw Point in Kansas City, Kansas, just a few blocks west of downtown. Cruises usually operate from April through mid-December. (phone: 281-5300).

■ **EXTRA SPECIAL:** Just 8 miles east of downtown Kansas City, in Independence, Missouri, is the *Harry S. Truman Library and Museum.* Remember "The buck stops here?" So should you if you're a Truman fan. Even if you're not, you might become one after a visit. Open daily 9 AM to 5 PM, except *Thanksgiving* and *New Year's Day.* Admission charge for adults; children under 15 and school-sponsored educational groups free. On US 24 at Delaware (phone: 833-1400). Just up the road a piece from the *Truman Library and Museum* is Ft. Osage, a reconstruction of the trading post established by explorer William Clark of the famous Lewis and Clark team. Open daily during daylight hours, March 15 through December 15. About 15 miles east of Independence on US 24, in Sibley, Missouri (phone: 816-881-4431).

SOURCES AND RESOURCES

TOURIST INFORMATION: The Kansas City Convention and Visitors Bureau has a 24-hour hotline (phone: 474-9600) for the latest information on city activities. It also provides brochures, maps, and a restaurant and hotel guide. The bureau is in the City Center Square Building (Suite 2550, 1100 Main St., Kansas City, MO 64105; phone: 221-5242 or 800-767-7700). Contact the Missouri state hotline (800-877-1234) for maps, calendars of events, health updates, and travel advisories.

Local Coverage – *Kansas City Star,* daily.

Television Stations – WDAF Channel 4–NBC; KCTV Channel 5–CBS; KMBC Channel 9–ABC; KCPT Channel 19–PBS; KSHB Channel 41; KZKC Channel 62; KYFC, Channel 50.

Radio Stations – AM: WDAF 610 (country music); KCMO 810

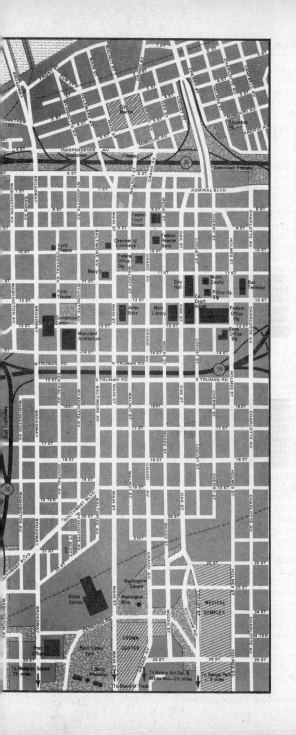

(news/talk). FM: KCFX 101.1 (classic rock, football coverage); KCUR 89.3 (NPR, classic, jazz); KLSI 93.3 (adult contemporary); KMBR 99.7 (easy listening); KBEQ 104.3 (contemporary hits); KXXR 106.5 (contemporary hits).

Food – *The Kansas City Star's* Friday Preview Section.

TELEPHONE: The area code for Kansas City, Missouri, is 816. **Sales Tax** – The sales tax is 6.675%.

CLIMATE: Kansas City's midwestern climate is notorious. It's fine in the spring and fall, but the winters are rough (frequently the thermometer doesn't rise above freezing in January), and the summers are hot and humid. Rain is particularly likely in spring.

GETTING AROUND: Airport – Kansas City International Airport is usually a 30- to 40-minute drive into the city; cab fare should run about $25 to $30. The green *KCI Airport Express* buses run from the airport to the major downtown and Plaza area hotels every 30 minutes, on the hour and half hour. Tickets are $9 to $11 and can be purchased at Gate 63 in Terminal C (take the inter-airport red buses to this terminal). Return schedules vary; ask for a timetable at your hotel or call 243-5950.

Bus – The Kansas City *Metro Bus* covers the downtown area, as well as the *Westport* and *Country Club Plaza* shopping and entertainment districts (phone: 221-0660).

Car Rental – The best way to see Kansas City is by car. Major rental firms are represented.

Taxi – Call *Yellow Cab* (phone: 471-5000).

Trolley – One of the best ways to see major sites is from the open-air trolleys that go from the Plaza, through *Westport* and *Crown Center* shopping centers, to downtown and back again. The trolleys (named Molly, Dolly, Polly, and so on) stop at the special trolley signs in the aforementioned shopping districts between March and December. A ride costs $3. The chatty drivers will fill you in on sights along the way. *Kansas City Trolley Corp.* (phone: 221-3399).

VITAL SERVICES: Audiovisual Equipment – *Hoover's Audio-Visual* (phone: 221-7663); *Kansas City Audio-Visual* (phone: 931-8940).

Business Services – *AAA Secretarial Service,* 406 W. 34th St. (phone: 531-4615).

Dry Cleaner/Tailor – *Royal Master Cleaners* (1501 Grand Ave.; phone: 842-3375); *English Cleaners* (3747 Broadway; phone: 531-1848).

Limousine – *American Limousine Service* (phone: 471-6050); *Mid-America Limousine Service* (phone: 346-4848).

Mechanic – *Glenn Freely Auto Repair,* 1922 Baltimore (phone: 421-2436).

Medical Emergency – *St. Joseph's Health Center* (1000 Carondelet Dr.; phone: 943-2711); *St. Luke's Hospital* (4400 Wornall Rd.; phone: 932-2171).

Messenger Services – *Express Delivery Service* (phone: 471-2340); *Flexfeet Couriers* (phone: 756-3505).

National/International Courier – *Federal Express* (phone: 661-0255); *Emery Worldwide* (phone: 800-645-3333).

Pharmacy – *Osco Drug Store,* 9 AM to 9 PM, 40th and Main Sts. (phone: 561-9680).

Photocopies – *Sir Speedy,* pickup and delivery (1101 Grand St.; phone: 421-7138); *Quik Print* (910 Walnut St.; phone: 421-3780).

Post Office – The central office is at 315 Pershing Rd. (phone: 374-9275).

Professional Photographer – *Wilborn & Associates* (phone: 531-

9000); *Jeff Brooks* (phone: 648-3133); *Swetnam & Associates* (phone: 421-6484).

Secretary/Stenographer – *AAA Secretarial Service,* pickup and delivery (phone: 531-4615); *The Grand Secretary* (phone: 221-1890).

Teleconference Facilities – *Ritz-Carlton* (see *Best in Town,* below).

Translator – *Transimplex Translators* (phone: 331-1863); *Languages on Wing* (phone: 842-2088).

Typewriter Rental – *Missouri Typewriter Co.,* 1-week minimum (phone: 363-5545).

Western Union/Telex – Many offices are located around the city (phone: 800-527-5184 or 800-325-6000).

 SPECIAL EVENTS: The *Renaissance Festival of Kansas City* runs for 7 weekends each fall, beginning *Labor Day*. The *Ren-Fest,* a popular re-creation of 16th-century life, features musicians, courtiers, knights, actors, acrobats, craftspeople, and lots of food and drink. It takes place on 40 wooded acres at the *Agricultural Hall of Fame* (Bonner Springs, just 20 minutes west of downtown on I-70; phone: 561-8005). The *American Royal Horse and Livestock Show* is held in November at *Kemper Arena* (1800 Genesee; phone: 421-6460). *Jazz Heritage Month* lasts throughout August, when local and international jazz performers jam throughout the city's clubs and parks.

 MUSEUMS: The *Nelson-Atkins Museum of Art* and the *Harry S. Truman Library and Museum* are described in *Special Places.* Other fine Kansas City museums include the following:

Agriculture Hall of Fame – I-70 to Bonner Springs (phone: 721-1075).

1859 Jail and Museum – 217 N. Main St., Independence (phone: 252-1892).

Kansas City Museum of History and Science – 3218 Gladstone (phone: 483-8300).

Liberty Memorial Museum – The country's only museum devoted to World War I. 100 West 26th St. (phone: 221-1918).

Shawnee Methodist Mission and Indian Manual Labor School – Indian Mission, 53rd and Mission Rd., Fairway, Kansas (phone: 913-262-0867).

Wornall House – Civil War restoration, 61 Terrace and Wornall (phone: 444-1858).

 MAJOR COLLEGES AND UNIVERSITIES: The University of Missouri–Kansas City, 51st and Rockhill Rd. (phone: 276-1000).

SPORTS AND FITNESS: Kansas City has major league baseball and football teams.

Baseball – The *Royals* take the field at the *Harry S. Truman Sports Complex,* I-70 and Blue Ridge Cutoff (phone: 921-8000).

Basketball – The fightin' *Kangaroos* of the University of Missouri–Kansas City play home games in *Municipal Auditorium,* downtown (phone: 276-2700).

Bicycling – Bikes can be rented in summer at *Shelter House One* in Swope Park, at the main entrance, Swope Pkwy. and Meyer Blvd.

Fitness Centers – *Woodside Racquet Club* offers pools, exercise equipment and aerobics classes (2000 W. 47th Plaza; phone: 831-0034); *Town & Country Health Club,* on the 5th floor of the *Westin Crown Center* hotel, has a pool, steam room, sauna, and coed whirlpool bath (1 Pershing Rd.; phone: 474-4400).

Football – The NFL Kansas City *Chiefs* call the *Harry S. Truman Sports Complex* home. I-70 and Blue Ridge Cutoff (phone: 924-9400).

Golf – The best is at *River Oaks,* 140 and US 71, in Grandview (phone: 966-8111).

Hockey – The Kansas City *Blades* of the International Hockey League play at *Kemper Arena* (phone: 421-6460).

Horseback Riding – *Benjamin Ranch,* 6401 E. 87th at I-435 (phone: 761-5055).

Jogging – Penn Valley Park, near the *Westin Crown Center* hotel (25th to 33rd St. and Pershing Rd.); Jacob L. Loose Park inner and outer loops, 1½ blocks south of the *Ritz-Carlton* hotel; Ward Parkway, a large, lovely boulevard (pick it up at the *Ritz-Carlton* and run south). An excellent jogging and exercise trail is in Mill Creek Park, just east of the Plaza.

Soccer – The Kansas City *Comets,* of the Major Indoor Soccer League, play at *Kemper Arena* (phone: 421-6460). The *Comets* led the MISL in attendance last year.

Tennis – There are more than 200 public tennis courts in the Kansas City metro area. Most are free. Swope Park has good courts at the picnic area north of the *Starlight Theater.* There are year-round courts at 4747 Nichols Parkway.

THEATER: For the latest information on theater and musical events, call 968-4100. The city's *Theater League* (phone: 421-7500) presents touring companies of Broadway hits in the *Midland Center for the Performing Arts* (1228 Main) and produces its own shows in the intimate *Quality Hill Playhouse* (10th and Central Sts.). Dramatic and musical productions are also booked into the *Music Hall* in the *Municipal Auditorium* (200 W 13th; phone: 421-8000); at the *Lyric Theater* (10th and Central; phone: 471-7344); and the *Folly Theatre* (12th and Central; phone: 474-4444). From July to September and January to March, the *Missouri Repertory Theatre* performs in the *Spencer Theater* (on the UMKC campus; phone: 276-2704). The *Starlight Theater* in Swope Park, an under-the-stars amphitheater, features musical comedy and concerts with top-name stars from May to mid-September (phone: 333-9481). Kansas City has two dinner playhouses, *Tiffany's Attic* (5028 Main; phone: 561-7529) and the *Waldo* (*not* Waldorf) *Astoria* (7428 Washington; phone: 523-1704). The newest addition to the city's theater inventory is the *American Heartland Theater* (in *Crown Center;* phone: 842-9999). Fans of off-Broadway shows should check out the *Unicorn Theater* (3820 Main; phone: 531-7529). There are two fine children's theaters: *Theater for Young America* (7204 W. 80th in suburban Overland Park; phone: 648-4600) and the *Coterie* (in the *Crown Center Complex;* phone: 474-6552).

MUSIC: For up-to-date data on concert happenings, call 968-4100 or check the newspapers. The *Kansas City Symphony* season, from November through May, features internationally known conductors and soloists. Performances are held on Friday and Saturday nights and Sunday afternoons in the *Lyric Theater* (11th and Central; phone: 471-7344). There are two opera seasons, in April and October at the *Lyric.* The operas are sung in English.

Jazz still thrives in Kansas City; call the Municipal Jazz Commission hotline (phone: 931-2888) for information on jazz events. Another good source of information on current musical offerings is the *Concert Connection* (phone: 276-2730), sponsored by the UMKC Conservatory of Music. To find out who's playing at the clubs, check the arts section of the Sunday *Kansas City Star* or pick up a copy of the *K.C. Pitch,* free at most record stores. You can consult the bimonthly magazine published by the Kansas City Jazz Ambassadors for local listings.

Milton's (805 W. 39th St.; phone: 753-9476) attracts dedicated jazz fans to this dark and atmospheric club once frequented by gangsters. *City Light* (7425 Broadway; phone: 444-6969) offers boisterous be-bop and jolting jazz of a more progressive bent. Ida McBeth electrifies *The Point* (917 W. 44th St.; phone: 531-9800) with her deep, powerful voice as she launches into well-worn jazz oldies or bawdy blues ballads. For swing, rhythm and blues, and contemporary jazz, *The Levee* (16 W. 43rd St.; phone: 561-2821) is an informal place to listen to the music, shake, and stomp. Upbeat jazz is hot at *The Phoenix* (302 W. 8th St.; phone: 472-0001) a small, upscale piano bar. After midnight on Saturdays, stop in at the *Mutual Musicians Foundation* (1823 Highland St.; phone: 421-9297) to hear local musicians, still in pursuit of the beat after their earlier shows around town, gather and play all night long. Famous jazzmen stop in regularly at this spot, which also functions as a nonprofit foundation that provides a support network for local jazz musicians.

NIGHTCLUBS AND NIGHTLIFE: In the last decade, Kansas City's after-dark scene has picked up so that now it's one of the liveliest in the Midwest. Because of its bistate location, liquor laws in Kansas City are a bit confusing. In Missouri, bars may remain open until 1 AM; clubs with cabaret licenses, until 3 AM. Bars are closed on Sundays, but hotels and restaurants may still serve liquor. Kansas City legalized the selling of liquor by the drink in the fall of 1986, and more counties are implementing this referendum each year. This means that in Kansas State you encounter taverns selling only 3.2 beer (lower alcohol content), restaurants with full-service bars, or private clubs requiring memberships. Singles action is liveliest at *Houlihan's Old Place* (4743 Pennsylvania; phone: 561-3141) and at the *Longbranch Saloon* (in nearby Seville Square, 500 Nichols Rd.; phone: 931-2755). Best bet for out-of-towners is to park in the *Country Club Plaza* or in *Westport* and barhop. There are dozens of clubs and bars — some with live entertainment — within easy walking distance of each other. *Westport* is very casual; the *Country Club Plaza* is a bit more formal, and some restaurant-bars require a coat and tie.

BEST IN TOWN

CHECKING IN: Expect to pay $100 and up for a double in hotels categorized as expensive, and $80 to $90 in those places designated as moderate. All telephone numbers are in the 816 area code unless otherwise indicated.

Allis Plaza – Built on what used to be known as "the strip," where jazz and bootleg gin flowed all night in the many clubs along its length, it has recaptured the spirit of this bygone era in its own ambience. Part of the major face-lift of the downtown *Convention Center* area, it has 572 rooms and suites, the *Coffee Shop,* and the *12th Street Bar* nightclub. Features include a nonsmoking floor, 2 outdoor tennis courts, and a health club with indoor pool, sauna, Nautilus and David equipment, and aerobics. A concierge desk, secretarial services, A/V equipment, photocopiers, computers, and express checkout are all here. 200 West 12th St. (phone: 421-6800). Expensive.

Hyatt Regency – Kansas City's fanciest hostelry has 731 luxury rooms and 42 suites. Facilities include a health club, a pool, and tennis courts, plus a covered walkway to the *Crown Center* shops. There are three restaurants, most notably the *Peppercorn Duck Club,* with its diversified menu, and *Skies* restaurant, which offers a revolving view of the city. Also, 15 meeting rooms (with A/V equipment and photocopiers available), a concierge desk, 24-hour room service, and express checkout. South of the downtown loop; McGee at Pershing Rd. (phone: 421-1234, 800-233-1234, or 800-228-9000). Expensive.

Ritz-Carlton – The former *Alameda Plaza* hotel has received a complete make-over. Many of the 374 elegantly appointed guest rooms have a commanding view of the nearby *Country Club Plaza.* Facilities include marble baths, twice-daily maid service, a concierge desk, 22 meeting rooms, secretarial services, photocopiers, 24-hour room service, and express checkout. 401 Ward Parkway (phone: 756-1500). Expensive.

Westin Crown Center – Built on a huge chunk of limestone known as Signboard Hill, because of the commercial embellishments that used to decorate it, this 730-room ultramodern property is part of the *Crown Center* complex. It integrates the limestone face of the hill into the lobby, where there is a winding stream, 5-story waterfall, and tropical rain forest. It has several restaurants, including *Trader Vic's,* and *Benton's Steak & Chop House.* There's 24-hour room service, 27 meeting rooms, A/V equipment, photocopiers, computers, and express checkout. 1 Pershing Rd. in *Crown Center* (phone: 474-4400 or 800-228-3000). Expensive.

Holiday Inn Crown Plaza – It has 296 rooms and is 2 blocks from the *Country Club Plaza,* 1 block from the *Nelson Gallery,* and smack-dab on the Main Street corridor. *Reunion,* a nostalgia-theme nightclub, indoor swimming, hydrotherapy pools, and a health club are among the offerings. Also express checkout, A/V equipment, photocopiers, computers, and 14 meeting rooms. 4445 Main (phone: 531-3000 or 800-228-9290). Expensive to moderate.

Doubletree – The once-sleepy bedroom community of Johnson County, Kansas, is now buzzing with business thanks to the industrial growth along I-435 and I-35 southwest of downtown Kansas City. Geared to the needs of visitors with business in that part of town. Fourteen meeting rooms, A/V equipment, photocopiers, and computers contribute to the list of business amenities, and there's also an express checkout desk. 10100 College Blvd. (phone: 913-451-6100 or 800-441-1414; Fax: 913-451-3873). Moderate.

Hilton Airport Plaza Inn – Ideal if you're more interested in traveling than downtown sightseeing. In addition to 360 comfortable rooms, there are 2 heated swimming pools — indoor and outdoor; a sauna, a whirlpool bath, a health club, putting green, and tennis courts, as well as 2 dining rooms, a coffee shop, and bar with entertainment. There are secretarial services, as well as A/V equipment, computers, and photocopiers to assist with your business requirements. There's also an express checkout desk. I-29 and NW 112th St. (phone: 891-8900 or 800-HILTONS; Fax: 816-891-8030). Moderate.

EATING OUT: Kansas City has great steaks and good French food. Its pride and joy, however, is barbecue. Visitors can select a high-price haute cuisine restaurant or one that will provide superb food at more moderate prices — although you'll find Kansas City prices reasonable everywhere. We recommend calling ahead for reservations at all the places listed below. Expect to pay $60 or more for dinner for two at those places listed as expensive; $35 to $55 at those places listed as moderate; under $30 at restaurants listed as inexpensive. Prices do not include drinks, wines, or tips. All telephone numbers are in the 816 area code unless otherwise indicated.

American – Often cited for its prominent role in popularizing "Heartland Regional Cuisine," this top-end choice, perched high above *Crown Center,* still upholds the loftiest standards. The impeccable service and grand scale, multi-level seating do justice to what's put on the table. Decor is French moderne; the menu features island oysters on the half shell with smoked carpaccio (thin slices of raw beef) in curry oil; grilled lamb loin in mint sauce; and roast pheasant with savoy cabbage and sweet potatoes. A dessert highlight is chilled maple rum mousse with bittersweet chocolate and shaved pralines. Open daily. Reservations essential. Major credit cards accepted. In the *Crown Center Hotel,* 2450 Grand Ave. (phone: 426-1133). Expensive.

Café Allegro – Owner Steve Cole has won a loyal following for his refreshing, inventive, cross-cultural cooking. The artsy dining rooms seem deceptively casual in light of the semi-formal style of service. Be on the lookout for grilled salmon with Chinese mustard glaze; veal tenderloin with roasted garlic and parmesan mashed potatoes, and roast duck with carmelized sweet garlic sauce. Open daily. Reservations necessary. Major credit cards accepted. 1815 W. 39th St. (phone: 561-3663). Expensive.

EBT – Extraordinary warmth and a strong sense of tradition are hallmarks of this dark, romantic suburban place. Named for a dear, departed downtown department store, it preserves many of the emporium's artifacts, including nine renovated brass elevator cars that can be reserved for intimate, private dining. The menu strikes a careful balance between classic and creative, a range that embraces veal Oscar and peppercorn strip steaks. Closed Sundays. Reservations advised. Major credit cards accepted. 1310 Carondelet Dr., I-435, south of Stateline Rd. (phone: 942-8870) Expensive.

Jasper's – Decades worth of dining awards do not lie. Kansas City's most honored restaurant lives up to its reputation for exquisite, French-influenced Northern Italian fare. Service hits the heights of haute; tuxedoed waiters have a reputation for hovering. Closed Sundays. Reservations necessary. Major credit cards accepted. 405 W. 75th St. (phone: 363-3003). Expensive.

Plaza III–The Steakhouse – This freshly minted steakery rose from the remains of an establishment that had had a far more diverse menu, but the specialization serves the diner well. Premium cuts are served in a setting that recaptures a half-real, half-imagined era of steakhouse opulence. Open daily. Reservations required. Major credit cards accepted. 4749 Pennsylvania Ave. (phone: 753-0000). Expensive.

Bristol Bar and Grill – Since 1980, this place has established itself as one of Kansas City's prime sources for fresh seafood. Its good reputation is bolstered by attentive service and a rich Edwardian ambience. Choicest seats are in curtained booths or under the back room's Tiffany leaded glass dome. The bar is a popular after-work watering hole for KC's upwardly mobile bunch. Open daily. Reservations advised. Major credit cards accepted. 4740 Jefferson in *Country Club Plaza* (phone: 756-0606). Expensive to moderate.

Savoy Grill – No K.C. restaurant matches this one in terms of longevity. It opened in 1903 and has catered to celebrities as diverse as Teddy Roosevelt and W. C. Fields. Seafood always has been a specialty, particularly dishes such as lobster thermidor and shrimp de Jonghe. White-jacketed waiters, venerable stained glass windows and well-preserved murals complete the classic picture. Open daily. Reservations advised. Major credit cards accepted. 219 W. 9th (phone: 842-3890). Expensive to moderate.

Venue – Art exhibits of local and national talents enliven the walls of this casually elegant eatery. Such fare as grilled marinated salmon on a bed of sticky rice, and sirloin tips sautéed in a veal sauce with mushrooms are accompanied by a huge bowl of fresh vegetables placed strategically in the middle of the table for everyone to share. Try the ice cream sandwich or the warm fig bar for dessert. On Friday evenings, live jazz, rock and roll, or country bands inspire customers to take a turn on the dance floor. Closed Sundays. Reservations unnecessary. Most major credit cards accepted. 4532 Main St. (phone: 561-3311). Expensive to moderate.

Coyote Grill – The grill's high-style Southwestern atmosphere takes surprisingly well to its location in a suburban shopping mall, and the food is routinely marvelous. Heading the list of specialties are such appetizers as barbecued shrimp enchiladas and squawking nachos topped with breast of chicken. Open daily. Reservations advised. Major credit cards accepted. 4843 Johnson Drive (phone: 913-362-3333). Moderate.

Prospect – Sunday afternoons are never quite complete without a bit of brunch at this bright, comfortable dining spot. Choices at the immense buffet range from the traditional scrambled eggs with fried potatoes and bacon to rumaki pâté and pizza. The atmosphere is unusually low-key, and the service is beautifully attentive; your coffee cup always seems to be magically refilled. Open Sundays only. Reservations advised. Major credit cards accepted. 1 Westport Sq. (phone: 753-2227). Moderate.

Golden Ox – In the heart of the stockyards, near *Kemper Arena,* this is a haven for the dedicated steak lover. Good, solid American cooking here, and arguably the best steaks in town, served with potato, garlic bread, and salad. Open daily. Reservations advised. Major credit cards accepted. 1600 Genesee (phone: 842-2866). Moderate to inexpensive.

Princess Garden – No better Chinese restaurant can be found in town, and chef Robert Chang's steady stream of Szechuan/Mandarin menu additions leaves others scrambling to keep up. The entire Chang family gets into the act, providing consistently superb service. Open daily. Reservations advised. Major credit cards accepted. 8906 Wornall Road (phone: 444-3709). Moderate to inexpensive.

Romanelli Grill – Modest owner Joe MacCabe says this is "just a neighborhood joint." And so it is, but it's one-of-a-kind. The colorful restaurant/bar, which dates to 1933, is best known for its catfish, onion rings, and barbecued baby back ribs. Closed Sundays. No reservations. MasterCard and Visa accepted. 7122 Wornall Road (phone: 333-1321). Inexpensive.

Stroud's – Trademark T-shirts still say, "We choke our own chickens." Far more believable, considering the volume of trade at this eatery, is that the chicken is fried in big black skillets and served with your choice of equally comforting side dishes, including lumpy potatoes, pan gravy, and homemade cinnamon rolls. Decor is early roadhouse (which is exactly how the place began); service is appropriately casual. Open daily. No reservations. Major credit cards accepted. 1015 E. 85th St. (phone: 333-2132). Inexpensive.

And finally, a note on barbecue: Kansas Citians are a peaceful lot, but you always can start a fight about who has the best ribs in town. Calvin Trillin, in his book *American Fried,* claimed that *Arthur Bryant's Barbecue,* on the east side of town, was America's best restaurant. Trillin's pronouncement may have been rib-in-cheek, but there's no doubt that, given their druthers, Kansas Citians would just as soon eat barbecue as anything else. Our advice is to check the phone book, snoop around and ask locals what they prefer — and why. There's a wide choice, from *Gates & Sons* to *Richard's Famous Bar-B-Q, Heyward's Pit, Zarda's,* and a dozen more. Most are differentiated by their sauces, which range from sweet and thick to thin and peppery. There's surely a perfect one for your taste. Don't forget the dental floss.

LAS VEGAS

AT-A-GLANCE

SEEING THE CITY: The *Skye Room* restaurant in *Binion's Horseshoe* hotel (128 E. Fremont St.; phone: 382-1600) offers a panoramic view of Las Vegas. As you ascend in the glass elevator, all of downtown Las Vegas glitters around you. As you reach the top, the expanse of surrounding desert appears, and your eye is drawn to the neon of the Strip, a long stream of hotels and casinos, and, to the west, the green heights of Mt. Charleston.

SPECIAL PLACES: Gambling is the name of the game in Las Vegas. The cultural aspects of the city are limited, but expanding, and its history has been all but obliterated by its rapid growth. But the surrounding area is rich in outdoor diversions that can fill your days with a wide variety of non-casino pleasures, leaving the nights for the air conditioned paradise of green felt, dazzling neon, and showgirl entertainment.

THE STRIP

If gambling is the game, the Strip is the place. Shining brightly in the desert sun, this 5-mile boulevard just south of town glows more intensely at night, ablaze with the glittering opulence of a seemingly never-ending stream of hotels. The sky's the limit here, and one after another of the big hotels offer it — the *Sahara, Circus Circus, Flamingo Hilton, Holiday Casino, Riviera, Sands, Caesars Palace, Tropicana, Dunes, Mirage,* and *Excalibur.* From slot machines, poker, and blackjack to the esoteric keno and baccarat of the casinos, to the production spectaculars with a cavalcade of stars in the main showrooms, to 24-hour breakfasts or dinners, it's all here and rolling around the clock. Las Vegas Blvd., just south of the city along US 91. Here are a few highlights:

Caesars Palace – Las Vegas's stab at ancient Rome, *Caesars Palace* outdoes its namesake in gaming. The only other similarities are the Romanesque names of casino areas and showroom, and the fact that cocktail waitresses and keno runners dress in distinctive minitogas. Otherwise, it's still one of the plushest in town. Superstars perform often; be sure to make reservations. 3570 Las Vegas Blvd. (phone: 731-7110).

Circus Circus – There's gambling on the ground and gamboling up above in this tent-shaped casino where trapeze and high-wire artists, clowns, acrobats, and dancers perform to the music of a brass band. The observation gallery at circus level is lined with food and carnival stands. Children are permitted in the gallery but not on the casino floor, so bring them along and everybody can have his or her own circus. Circus open 11 AM to midnight. No admission charge. 2880 Las Vegas Blvd. (phone: 734-0410).

Wet 'n Wild – A 26-acre family-oriented water playground with a surf lagoon, water chutes, rapids, flumes, and even pearl diving. Family rates and discount tickets are available at the Strip hotels. Open daily, May

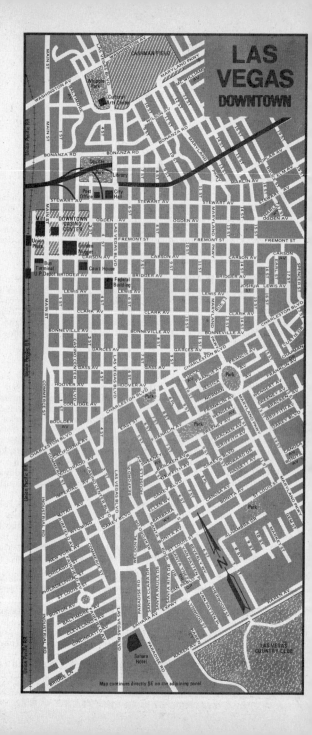

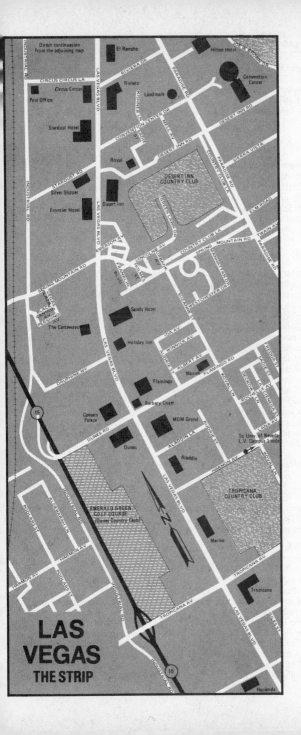

through October. On the Strip between the *Sahara* and *El Rancho* hotels (phone: 737-3819).

Convention Center – One of the world's major convention destinations, this is Las Vegas's center. This modern steel structure is a million-square-foot complex. On Paradise Rd., next to the *Las Vegas Hilton*, off the Strip (phone: 733-7818).

DOWNTOWN

Golden Nugget Hotel and Casino – The most spectacular hotel downtown and one of the most glamorous in Las Vegas. Attractions include the $50-million Town House Tower with just 27 duplex suites, *Elaine's* and *Stefano's* restaurants for fine dining, the 500-seat alfresco *Carson Street* restaurant, and a 500-seat theater-ballroom. The exterior of the building is encased in Italian marble. A must-see during any visit. 129 E. Fremont St. (phone: 385-7111).

THE OUTDOORS

Hoover Dam and Lake Mead – Completed in 1936, Hoover Dam is an awesome monument to man's engineering capabilities, a 726-foot-high concrete wall that tamed the mighty Colorado River and supplies electricity to Las Vegas and California. Daily tours. Modest admission charge; no admission for children under 15. Lake Mead, produced when the Colorado backed up behind the dam, is, at 115 miles long, one of the largest manmade lakes in the world. Fishing (bass, crappie, and catfish), swimming, and boating are available year-round. The visitors' center for Hoover Dam (phone: 293-1081) and headquarters of Lake Mead National Recreation Area (phone: 293-8907) are 30 minutes south of the city on Boulder Hwy. (US 93).

Mt. Charleston – Just 35 minutes north of the city, Mt. Charleston dramatically exhibits the effect of increased elevation with a wide variety of trees and wildlife. Plenty of cool fresh mountain air. During the winter months, snow covers the ground and temperatures often hover below freezing at the Lee Canyon ski slopes while vacationers swim in Las Vegas hotel pools just half an hour away. Tonopah Hwy. north to Rte. 39.

Red Rock Recreation Area – A beautiful desert locale featuring red and white hues of sandstone formations, and spectacular views of steep canyons. Just a few miles farther west, the Spring Mountain State Park has Old West buildings on a ranch that has belonged to such well-known capitalists as Howard Hughes and the German Krupp family (the armament folks). State rangers lead tours through the old buildings. W. Charleston Blvd., 15 and 20 miles west of the city.

■ **EXTRA SPECIAL:** Just 2 hours northwest of Las Vegas lies Death Valley, the hottest, driest, and lowest area in the US. It also is starkly beautiful. The high mountains surrounding the 120-mile-long valley have isolated it, and of the 600 species of plants that have been identified there, 21 grow nowhere else on earth. The variety of the colors and textures of nature in the raw is remarkable, from the jagged bluish rock salt formations of Devil's Golf Course, to the smoothly sculpted golden dunes of Mesquite Flat, to the rich reds and purples of Telescope Peak at sunrise. Scotty's Castle, an eccentric and intricate mansion built in the middle of this expanse by a Chicago millionaire, is the area's most incongruous wonder. Because of extremely high temperatures in the summer, the best time to visit the valley is from November through April. Tonopah Highway north (I-95) to Beatty, then take the Death Valley Junction cutoff straight into the park.

SOURCES AND RESOURCES

 TOURIST INFORMATION: The Las Vegas Chamber of Commerce is best for brochures, maps, suggestions, and general tourist information (2301 E. Sahara Ave., Las Vegas, NV 89104; phone: 457-4664). Contact the Nevada state hotline (800-NEVADA-8) for maps, calendars of events, health updates, and travel advisories.

Local Coverage – *Review Journal,* morning daily; *Las Vegas Sun,* evening daily. Several weekly entertainment guides are available at newsstands.

Television Stations – KVBC Channel 3–NBC; KLAS Channel 8–CBS; KLVX Channel 10–PBS; KTNV Channel 13–ABC.

Radio Stations – AM: KORK 920 (big band); KENO 1460 (oldies). FM: KOMP 92.3 (rock 'n' roll); KYRK 97.1 (top 40); KLUC 98.5 (top 40).

 TELEPHONE: The area code for Las Vegas is 702.

Sales Tax – A tax of 6% is levied on all purchases except groceries.

 CLIMATE: In the middle of the desert, Las Vegas summers are hot and dry. Winters are pleasant and mild (but cold at night), and outdoor activity takes place year-round.

 GETTING AROUND: Although Las Vegas is not really a large city, during the summer, the heat makes walking difficult. If you are going any farther than a hundred yards or so, you'll probably do better on wheels.

Airport – McCarran International Airport is a 20-minute drive and $8 cab ride from the Strip; allow 10 minutes and $5 more to reach downtown. *Whittlesea-Bell Co.* (phone: 384-6111) provides transportation to Strip hotels for $10; to downtown hotels for $16. For return service, call 2 hours before flight time. Plan to arrive at the airport at least an hour before flight time, since the distances between the main entrance and the check-in gates are great, and the newness of the facility — which has recently undergone a $300-million expansion — can cause a bit of confusion in matching passengers with their flights.

Bus – The *Las Vegas Transit System* covers the downtown area and the Strip. The discount commuter ticket offers a real savings if you expect to use the buses frequently. Route information is available at 1550 Industrial Rd. (phone: 384-3540). All fares are $1.10.

Car Rental – The large national firms serve Las Vegas, though the least expensive local service is provided by *Dollar Rent-A-Car* (at McCarran Airport; phone: 739-8408); *Abbey Rent-A-Car* (3745 Las Vegas Blvd. S.; phone: 736-4988); and *Allstate* (5175 Rent Car Rd.; phone: 736-6147).

Taxi – Cabs can be hailed in the street, ordered on the phone, or picked up at taxi stands in front of hotels. Major companies are *Whittlesea Cab* (phone: 384-6111); *Yellow Cab* (phone: 873-2227); *Checker Cab* (phone: 873-8012).

 VITAL SERVICES: Audiovisual Equipment – *Las Vegas Video Sound Rentals* (phone: 362-4660); *Nevada Audio Visual Services* (phone: 876-6272).

Baby-sitting – *Sandy's Sitter Service,* 24-hour service, 953 E. Sahara (phone: 731-2086).

Business Services – *Manpower Temporary Services,* 314 Las Vegas Blvd. N. (phone: 386-2626).

Dry Cleaner/Tailor – *Al Phillips, the Cleaner,* open 24 hours, 3659 S. Maryland Pkwy., in the *Maryland Square Shopping Center* (phone: 735-2805).

Limousine – *Bell Trans* (phone: 739-7990); *Lucky 7* (phone: 739-6277).

Mechanic – *Stiver's,* 2300 Western (phone: 385-2407).

Medical Emergency – *Humana Sunrise Hospital,* 3186 Maryland Pkwy. (phone 731-8000).

Messenger Services – *Armored Transport* (phone: 457-3934).

National/International Courier – *Federal Express* (phone: 800-238-5355); *DHL Worldwide Courier Express* (phone: 798-4090).

Pharmacy – *White Cross Drugs,* open 24 hours, 1700 Las Vegas Blvd. S. (phone: 382-1733).

Photocopies – *Kinko's* (4440 S. Maryland Pkwy.; phone: 735-4402); *PDQ,* (3820 S. Valley View; phone: 876-3235).

Post Office – Main office is near the airport (1001 E. Sunset Rd.; phone: 361-9212); there is a downtown office (301 E. Stewart Ave.; phone: 385-8944); and there's another along the Strip (1001 Circus Circus La.; phone: 735-2525).

Professional Photographer – *Photo Finish* (phone: 732-1878); *Positive Images* (phone: 791-3287).

Secretary/Stenographer – *Best Business Support Services* (phone: 737-3900).

Teleconference Facilities – *Caesars Palace, Las Vegas Hilton* (see *Best in Town,* below).

Translator – *Arriaga's Bilingual Services* (phone: 382-5497).

Typewriter Rental – *TAC,* 1-day minimum (phone: 736-2657).

Western Union/Telex – Many offices are located around the city (phone: 800-325-6000).

Other – The *Home Office* provides office space, photocopying, and typing services (phone: 873-5700).

Wedding Bells Are Always Ringing in Las Vegas – If you are at least 18 (16 with parental consent), and you feel a sudden urge to legally merge, it's easy to tie the knot on the spot. Just apply at the Las Vegas Marriage License Bureau; there's not even a blood test or waiting period. Pay a modest fee, say "I do," and the deed is done. They don't call this place the "Wedding Capital of the World" for nothing. Open round the clock on Fridays and Saturdays; till midnight Sundays through Thursdays. Clark County Courthouse, 3rd and Carson Sts. (phone: 455-3156; after hours, 455-4415).

 SPECIAL EVENTS: During the *Helldorado Festival,* held for 4 days in May, the city celebrates its Western heritage with rodeos, parades, beauty contests, and, for those who want some slower-paced action, a beard growing contest. The *Las Vegas Invitational Golf Tournament* takes place in October. The *Jaycees State Fair* takes place in August at the *Convention Center* and has carnival acts, magic shows, rides, livestock and craft exhibits. The *National Finals Rodeo* opens in early December at the *Thomas and Mack Center* for 10 days.

 MUSEUMS: Las Vegas hotels have commercial art exhibitions with works of well-known artists. *Herigstad's Gallery* (2290 E. Flamingo Rd. (phone: 733-7366) has art shows as well as works for sale. Open from 10 AM to 6 PM; closed Sundays. Also worth a visit is *Minotaur Fine Arts Ltd.* (in the *Fashion Show Mall;* phone: 737-1400). Open weekdays 9:30 AM to 9 PM, Saturdays 9:30 AM to 7 PM, Sundays 11 AM to 6 PM.

The University of Nevada at Las Vegas has a *Museum of Natural History* with collections of Indian artifacts and live desert reptiles. Open weekdays from 9 AM to 4:45 PM; closed Sundays. No admission charge. 4505 S. Maryland Pkwy. (phone: 739-3381).

The *Mineral Collection,* which is also on the campus, displays 1,000 specimens from the area and around the world. Closed weekends. No admission charge. Geoscience Hall, Room 103 (phone: 739-3262).

Other museums worth visiting are the *Las Vegas Art Museum* (3333 W. Washington Ave.; phone: 647-4300); the *Liberace Museum* (1775 E. Tropicana Ave.; phone: 798-5595); *Guinness World of Records Museum* (2780 Las Vegas Blvd. S.; phone: 792-3766); *Ripley's Believe It or Not Museum* (202 E. Fremont St.; phone: 385-4011); *Lied Discovery Children's Museum* (833 Las Vegas Blvd. N.; phone: 382-3445 or 382-5437); *Dolphin Environment* (in the *Mirage* hotel; 3400 Las Vegas Blvd. S.; phone: 791-3188); the *Lost City Museum of Archeology* (in the Valley of Fire area 20 miles north; phone: 397-2193); and the *Imperial Palace Auto Collection* (*Imperial Palace* hotel, 3535 Las Vegas Blvd. S.; phone: 731-3311).

 MAJOR COLLEGES AND UNIVERSITIES: The University of Nevada at Las Vegas is the largest school in the area, with an enrollment of 24,000; 4505 S. Maryland Pkwy. (phone: 739-3011).

SPORTS AND FITNESS: Las Vegas offers a wide variety of sporting events and fine facilities.

Basketball – The University of Nevada at Las Vegas has fielded one of the finest collegiate basketball teams in the nation for several years — they were the 1990 NCAA Champions. They play from November to February in the *Thomas & Mack Center,* an 18,000-seat arena. Tickets usually are available, but for really good seats your hotel bell captain or casino pit boss would be helpful (phone: 739-3900).

Betting – If you want to bet on almost any athletic event taking place outside of Nevada, numerous race and sports books dot the city. The most lavish facilities on the Strip are in *Caesars Palace* (3570 Las Vegas Blvd. S.; phone: 731-7110), the *Mirage* (3400 Las Vegas Blvd. S.; phone: 791-7111), the *Stardust* hotel (3000 Las Vegas Blvd.S.; phone: 732-6111), and the *Las Vegas Hilton* (3000 Paradise Rd.; phone: 732-5111). *Union Plaza's Book* tops the downtown locales (1 Main St.; phone: 386-2110).

Boxing – If punching is your bag, the major hotels promote many boxing matches. Major bouts between professional heavyweight contenders are held from time to time at *Caesars Palace,* the *Las Vegas Hilton,* and the *Mirage.*

Fitness Centers – The health club at *Caesars Palace* has a whirlpool bath, steam room, and exercise equipment, but no pool (3570 Las Vegas Blvd. S., 15th Floor; phone: 731-7110). The *Aristocrat Health Spa,* in the *Hilton,* has a sauna, whirlpool bath, and massage (3000 Paradise Rd., 3rd Floor on the pool deck; phone: 732-5111). A multimillion-dollar facility has been added to the *Desert Inn and Country Club* (3145 Las Vegas Blvd.S.; phone: 733-4444), the *Mirage* has men's and women's spa facilities, an exercise room and aerobics studios (3400 Las Vegas Blvd. S.; phone: 791-7111), and the *Golden Nugget* hotel sports a coed gym with sauna, whirlpool bath, and exercise equipment (129 E. Fremont St.; phone: 385-7111).

Golf – Dozens of courses dot the desert landscape. The *Sahara Country Club* (1911 E. Desert Inn Rd.; phone: 796-0016) and the *Desert Inn Country Club* (3145 Las Vegas Blvd. S.; phone: 733-4444) are the best. For lower prices, try the public courses. Best bet is the *Las Vegas Golf Club* (Washington Ave. and Decatur Blvd.; phone: 646-3003), which offers a reasonable challenge and good greens.

Jogging – It's possible to run right along the Strip between Flamingo Road and Spring Mountain, where there are no cross streets to slow the pace (about one-half mile each way); stay on the *Caesars Palace* side. Another possibility is Squires Park, one-half mile from downtown; or drive to Sunset Park, 7 miles from downtown, or Bob Baskin Park, W. Oakey Blvd. at Rancho Dr.

Tennis – Almost all the Strip hotels have good tennis facilities open to the public. Indoor courts are available at the *Studio 96 Tennis & Health Club,* 3890 Swenson Ave. (phone: 735-8153).

THEATER: For current performances, check the publications listed above. Outside of the entertainment at the Strip hotels, there are some old standbys, such as the *New West Stage Company* (phone: 876-6972), which presents its season at the *Charleston Heights Arts Center* (800 Brush St.); the *Actor's Repertory Theater* (phone: 647-7469); and the *Las Vegas Community Theatre* (phone: 794-3431); plus a number of local theater groups that all keep the curtains raised. The best bet for shows is the *Repertory Theater* at *Judy Bayley Theatre* (University of Nevada at Las Vegas campus; phone: 739-3641). The Clark County Community College and other local companies are featured in *Theatre Under the Stars,* outdoors at the *Spring Mountain Ranch* in late June and early July. The creative sets make fine use of the environment, and the acting is first-rate. Tickets can be purchased at the ranch (Spring Mountain Rd., 18 miles west on Charleston Blvd.; phone: 875-4141). The *Nevada Dance Theatre* performs at the *Judy Bayley Theatre* (phone: 739-3801).

MUSIC: Symphony concerts, opera, and jazz are featured throughout the year at *Artemus W. Ham Concert Hall* and the *Judy Bayley Theatre* on the UNLV campus. For tickets, call 739-3801.

NIGHTCLUBS AND NIGHTLIFE: When it comes to nightlife, Las Vegas is king. The city never sleeps, and can keep visitors who want to keep the same hours entertained all night. The Strip hotels offer a wide variety of entertainment. There are nightly production spectaculars, with dancing girls, lavish costumes and sets, and all kinds of specialty acts. *Jubilee* at *Bally's* (3645 Las Vegas Blvd. S.; phone: 739-4111) is the most extravagant. Other notables of this genre are *Splash* at the *Riviera* (2901 Las Vegas Blvd. S.; phone: 734-5110); *Folies Bergère* at the *Tropicana* (3801 Las Vegas Blvd. S.; phone: 739-2222); and *City Lites* at the *Flamingo Hilton* (3555 Las Vegas Blvd. S.; phone: 733-3111).

In the main showrooms of all the other hotels on the Strip, a constant parade of stars performs to audiences of 800 to 1,200 people. The *Union Plaza, Tropicana,* and *Flamingo Hilton* serve dinner at the early show. There's no cover charge, but the minimum runs about $10 to $35 per person for dinner shows and $6 to $35 for late "drinks-only" shows. The *Excalibur* serves a Renaissance dinner, with two shows a night — depicting the Arthurian legend — for $24.95, including dinner, drink, taxes, tip, and show. Keep a few things in mind when you are trying to get reservations: House guests get first priority for many shows, so consider staying at the hotel which has the show you most want to see. Always call in the morning, or better still, go in person. Most hotels do not take show reservations more than 1 day in advance. The reservation booths open at 10 in the morning and stay open till show time, and the earlier you get there the better. If you've been gambling a good deal, ask the pit boss for assistance, and if you haven't you might try tipping the bell captain and hoping for the best. Bring along a sweater for the indoors; powerful air conditioners are at work everywhere. And though dress is casual during the day; the showtime dress at night can be more formal and occasionally even elegant, but it's optional.

Often overlooked are the casino lounges, where lesser-known performers (many of whom soon become better known) perform for just the cost of your drinks.

Favorite non-hotel clubs are *Calamity Jayne's* (3015 Fremont St.; phone: 384-6336); *Botany's* (1700 E. Flamingo Rd.; phone: 737-6662); the *Shark Club* (75 E. Harmon; phone: 795-7525); and *Tramps* (4405 W. Flamingo Rd.; phone: 871-1424). Try the *Silver Dollar Saloon* (2501 E. Charleston Blvd.; phone: 382-6921) for live country-and-western music.

Las Vegas also presents the best-known burlesque/striptease artists in the world. Tops (or topless, more likely) is the *Palomino Club,* 1848 Las Vegas Blvd. N. (phone: 642-2984).

BEST IN TOWN

CHECKING IN: In Vegas, the hotel's the thing. The Strip (Las Vegas Blvd. South) is a 4-mile stream of hotel-casinos and motels, nearly matched in number — though usually not in quality — by the downtown "Glitter Gulch" area. Competition is fierce among the major hotels, and keeps room costs modest and on a par with one another. Expect to pay $95 and up for a double room per night in the expensive range; $40 to $60, moderate; around $20 to $35, inexpensive. All telephone numbers are in the 702 area code unless otherwise indicated.

Bally's – More grandiose than ever: 3,000 rooms. There are 6 restaurants, a shopping mall, the *Ziegfeld Room* for lavish production numbers, and the *Celebrity Room* for top-name entertainment. Big! Twenty-four hour room service, 42 meeting rooms, A/V equipment, photocopiers, CNN, and express checkout are some of the amenities offered here. 3645 Las Vegas Blvd. (phone: 739-4111; 800-634-3434; Fax: 702-739-4405). Expensive.

Caesars Palace – One of the images that immediately comes to mind when the subject of Las Vegas hotels is mentioned. Even the most basic of its 1,600 rooms are ornate, while the high roller suites are tributes to excess, with large classical statues to make you feel right at home — if you've just flown in from ancient Rome. The service is excellent, and the location — midway on the Strip — puts guests right in the middle of the action. It has big-name entertainment, cafés, bars, restaurants (see *Eating Out*), pool, tennis, golf privileges, meeting rooms, shops, and free parking. Reservations are a must during the summer, especially on holiday weekends. There are 40 meeting rooms for business needs, as well as A/V equipment and photocopiers. Express checkout, CNN, and 24-hour room service are other pluses. 3570 Las Vegas Blvd. S. (phone: 731-7110; 800-634-6001; Fax: 702-731-6636). Expensive.

Desert Inn – More a city itself than a hotel, the accommodations here are vast. There are 5 locations with rooms and suites (847 separate units altogether), each offering something unique. There's the Wimbledon, for example, a 7-story pyramid structure which practically sits on the golf course. Or, if you'd like to look out over the Strip and the mountains of Nevada, Augusta Tower can satisfy both desires. The dining facilities are numerous and just as varied, including the exquisite *La Vie en Rose* (see *Eating Out*). There are 6 meeting rooms (with A/V equipment and photocopiers available), a spectacular casino, several bars, a health spa, golf course, pool, tennis courts, CNN, and many shops, including separtate golf and tennis pro shops. There also is a *Hertz* rental car counter, if you should feel the need (but why?) to leave. Room service is available around the clock; express checkout. 3145 Las Vegas Blvd. S. (phone: 733-4444; 800-634-6906; Fax: 702-733-4774). Expensive.

Mirage – Among the newer Strip spots, this $630-million property has become the talk of the town. A volcano — complete with flames and smoke — explodes outside every 30 minutes. Set on 100 acres, the resort has 3,000 rooms, international dining in 8 restaurants, a spa and salon, shops, convention facilities, 15 meeting rooms, and a Polynesian-theme casino. Two natural habitats display dolphins and white tigers. Illusionists Siegfried and Roy perform here regularly and make everything from tigers to full-size elephants disappear. The hotel's photocopiers and A/V equipment are at guests' disposal, as are 24-hour room service and express checkout. 3400 Las Vegas Blvd. S. (phone: 791-7111; 800-627-6667; Fax: 702-791-7414). Expensive.

Golden Nugget – One of the glitzier of the downtown spots, combining an overall turn-of-the-century look with mountains of marble, brass, and crystal in its casino, spa, entertainment room, and restaurants. Amenities include 24-hour room service, a concierge desk, 12 meeting rooms, A/V equipment, photocopiers, CNN, and express checkout. 129 E. Fremont St. (phone: 385-7111; 800-828-6206; Fax: 702-386-8362). Expensive to moderate.

Las Vegas Hilton – With 3,100 rooms, it claimed the title of "Biggest in Vegas" until the coming of the *Excalibur.* More like a small city, with even a "children's hotel" to occupy younger guests while their parents attend to casino business. Off the Strip next to the *Convention Center,* it's not in the middle of the glitter, but neither is it in the center of traffic. With star entertainment, café, bars, restaurants (see *Eating Out*), large recreation center with pool, tennis, health club, putting greens and golf privileges, shops, and free parking. Business facilities include 41 meeting rooms, A/V equipment, CNN, and photocopiers. Twenty-four hour room service can easily provide you with a quick bite, and express checkout expedites your departure. 3000 Paradise Rd. (phone: 732-5111 or 800-HILTONS; Fax: 702-732-5249). Expensive to moderate.

Aladdin – The former owners ditched the Arabian theme and spent $30 million to give all its 1,100 rooms, 8 restaurants, and reception and public areas a more modern look. The *Florentine Room* (see *Eating Out*) features fine dining, and *Fisherman's Port* has a Cajun/seafood menu. Other facilities include the 7,000-seat *Aladdin Theater,* the Baghdad showroom, pools, meeting rooms, shops, and tennis courts. At presstime, the hotel was on the auction block. 3667 Las Vegas Blvd. S. (phone: 736-0111). Moderate.

Excalibur – The world's largest resort (4,032 rooms), it has castle-like decor and 4,500 employees decked out in clothing reminiscent of the time of King Henry VIII. Two dinner shows nightly offer Arthurian performances and royal feasting in Renaissance style. Room service is available until 11 PM. Other conveniences are photocopiers and express checkout. 3850 Las Vegas Blvd. S. (phone: 597-7777; 800-939-7777; Fax: 702-798-3388). Moderate.

Sahara – First stop on the Strip, and notable for its relatively tasteful decor and traditional style. This friendly sophistication characterized Las Vegas a long time ago but exists in fewer hotels each year. The service is personalized and generally excellent. Entertainment, café, bar, pools, health club, 25 meeting rooms (A/V equipment and photocopiers are available), CNN, and shops. 1,000 rooms. Express checkout and 24-hour room service are other pluses. 2535 Las Vegas Blvd. S. (phone: 737-2111; 800-634-6666; Fax: 702-791-2027). Moderate.

Stardust – Once the largest resort hotel on the Strip, it underwent a $100 million expansion in 1991 that brought its total rooms up to 2,500. One-third of its original rooms were refurbished, and the rest were torn down and replaced by a 32-story tower. There's a new landscaped pool and 6 restaurants. The amenities include 24-hour room service, 12 meeting rooms, A/V equipment, photocopiers, and express checkout. 3000 Las Vegas Blvd. S. (phone: 732-6111; 800-824-6033; Fax: 702-732-6525). Moderate.

Union Plaza – A large (1,020-room) place, with the most complete facilities downtown, at the entranceway to the downtown "Glitter Gulch" action. Facilities include a pool, tennis courts, café, bar, restaurant, shops, 11 meeting rooms, and a casino. Room service is available until 10:30 PM. 1 Main St. (phone: 386-2110; 800-634-6575; Fax: 702-382-8281; Telex: 684470). Moderate.

Circus Circus – Of all the hotels on the Strip, the only one really dedicated to family entertainment (at family prices). With a full-scale circus operating, complete with sideshows, there's something for everyone. Lots for the children — carousel, clown-shaped swimming pool; for the adults, the excellent *Steak House,* cafés, bars, meeting rooms, health club, sauna. 2,500 rooms. Among the extras are room service until 11 PM, photocopiers, and express checkout. 2880 Las Vegas Blvd. S. (phone: 734-0410; 800-634-3450; Fax: 702-734-2268). Inexpensive.

Motel 6 – Good clean accommodations at the best prices in town. The bargain is worthwhile since hotel-motel rooms get little use in Las Vegas, and most of the time you're in them, you're asleep. Also, you get a pool for your money. 758 rooms. 196 E. Tropicana (phone: 798-0728). Inexpensive.

EATING OUT: Probably the only sure bet in Vegas is the food. Between hotels, restaurants, and casinos there's plenty to eat, and the food is much better than standard hotel or nightclub fare. From the continental cuisine of the hotels' main restaurants to "all-you-can-eat" buffets, Las Vegas features quantity and quality. Though the offerings are basically American — steaks and seafood — there are a number of good ethnic restaurants. So eat up, and take advantage of the bargains in the casinos that are subsidized by gambling revenues; you're probably paying for them anyway. Our restaurant selections range in price from $55 or more for a dinner for two in the expensive range; $30 to $45 in the moderate range; and $20 or less, inexpensive. Prices do not include drinks, wine, or tips. All telephone numbers are in the 702 area code unless otherwise indicated.

André's – A French restaurant in an old home, it is a favorite of the crowd in the downtown area. Open daily; lunch served weekdays, dinner nightly. Reservations necessary. Major credit cards accepted. 401 S. 6th St. (phone: 385-5016). Expensive.

Aristocrat – Charming 80-seat dining spot featuring continental cooking in the Rancho Circle area. Open daily; lunch served weekdays, dinner nightly. Reservations essential. Major credit cards accepted. 850 S. Rancho Dr. (phone: 870-1977). Expensive.

Michael's – A gem of a restaurant in the Times Square section of the Strip. Among the offerings are shrimp served on frosted globes and double-dipped chocolate desserts. Outstanding service. Open daily. Reservations essential. Major credit cards accepted. *Barbary Coast,* 3595 Las Vegas Blvd. (phone: 737-7111). Expensive.

Le Montrachet – The pride of the *Las Vegas Hilton*'s dining dozen. Try the poached Dover sole with champagne sauce and truffles or the medaillons of veal or venison. Desserts are imaginative, rich, and very tempting. Dinner nightly. Reservations essential. Major credit cards accepted. 3000 Paradise Rd. (phone: 732-5111). Expensive.

Palace Court – Considered the ultimate in dining grace in Las Vegas, at *Caesars Palace.* Candelabra, vermeil flatware, and hand-blown crystal are the accoutrements of an unforgettable experience. Sommeliers pour wine from the hotel's distinguished wine cellar. Dinner nightly. Reservations essential. Major credit cards accepted. 3570 Las Vegas Blvd. S. (phone: 731-7110). Expensive.

Pegasus – An elegant dining room in one of only two major hotels (the other being the *St. Tropez*) without gaming. Specialties of the house include sautéed veal with sauce Périgaux and pâté, beef Wellington, and fettuccine baked in a paper bag with shellfish, accompanied by attentive service and background harp music. Open daily. Reservations essential. Major credit cards accepted. In the *Alexis Park Hotel,* 375 E. Harmon (phone: 796-3300). Expensive.

La Vie En Rose – This second-floor dining room overlooks the lush poolside vegetation. Boneless roast duckling, pheasant in sour cream sauce, and lamb in brioche are just a few of the menu entrées. The pride of the *Desert Inn,* this room's service is expensive — but worth it. Dinner nightly. Reservations essential. Major credit cards accepted. 3145 Las Vegas Blvd. S. (phone: 733-4444). Expensive.

Chin's – An expanded version of the original, now nestled in the glittering *Fashion Show Mall* on the Strip. It serves crisp salads, *Chin's* beef, and pudding. A special elevator delivers diners from the parking garage. Open daily. Reservations advised. Major credit cards accepted. *Fashion Show Mall* (phone: 733-8899). Expensive to moderate.

Hugo's Cellar – A basement restaurant, its decor creates a grotto effect and its menu is outstanding. Steaks, veal, seafood, and an imaginative salad cart are all exemplary, and there's a sommelier to help with the excellent wine list. Open daily. Reservations necessary. Major credit cards accepted. In the *Four Queens Hotel,* 202 E. Fremont St. (phone: 385-4011). Expensive to moderate.

Alpine Village Inn – Best are the portions of good Swiss and German food — the wurst plates of all varieties, and the huge kettles of thick, dark German chicken soup that are meant for two but could actually feed the entire Swiss Family Robinson. The restaurant also features a rathskeller with a piano player and lots of German beers. Open nightly. Reservations advised. Major credit cards accepted. 3003 Paradise Rd. (phone: 734-6888). Moderate.

Battista's Hole in the Wall – Plentiful Italian pasta for dinner, helped along by all the wine you can drink, and an occasional Italian aria by Battista himself, to create the proper mood. Open daily. Reservations unnecessary. Major credit cards accepted. 4041 Audrie, across from *Bally's* (phone: 732-1424). Moderate.

Bootlegger – Cozy, nestled in a quiet area about 3 miles from the Strip and specializing in Italian dishes. The sunken pit lounge area is a good place to relax after a day at the casinos. Closed Mondays. Reservations advised. Major credit cards accepted. 5025 S. Eastern Ave. (phone: 736-4939). Moderate.

Château Vegas – Continental cooking in elegant surroundings, backed up by soft music and a harpist. Best bets are the Italian veal and any of the steaks. Open daily. Reservations advised. Major credit cards accepted. 565 Desert Inn Rd. (phone: 733-8282). Moderate.

Claudine's – This posh room is part of the *Holiday Casino,* and a welcome relief from the gaudy atmosphere of much of the rest of the hotel. Specialties such as escargots bourguignon with herbed butter and sherry, and shrimp scampi provençale precede the excellent charcoal-broiled steaks. Closed Tuesdays and Wednesdays. Reservations advised. Major credit cards accepted. 3740 Las Vegas Blvd. S. (phone: 369-5000). Moderate.

Flamingo Room – A large, attractive, Art Deco room, dominated by a savory salad bar, overlooking the hotel pool and the "Bugsy Siegel" gardens. The extensive menu features American dishes. Open daily from 7 AM to 2 PM, and from 5 to 11 PM. Reservations advised. Major credit cards accepted. In the *Flamingo Hilton Hotel,* 3555 Las Vegas Blvd. S. (phone: 733-3111). Moderate.

Golden Steer – In a town that has to revise the phone books twice a year just to keep up with the comings and goings of things, 20 years in the same place attest to a strong tradition. The decor is luxurious western and the offerings topnotch, from the steaks (try the Diamond Lil prime ribs) to the toasted ravioli, and the extensive wine list. With a day's notice, they'll serve up a special delicacy: pheasant, goose, quail, chukar (partridge), or roast suckling pig. Open daily. Reservations advised. Major credit cards accepted. 308 W. Sahara Ave. (phone: 384-4470). Moderate.

Limelight – A lively family-run Italian establishment, serving such specialties as chicken Florentine, veal scaloppine marsala with demiglaze, and sea bass poached with chablis, leeks, and cream. Dinner nightly. Reservations advised. Major credit cards accepted. 2340 E. Tropicana (phone: 739-1410). Moderate.

Rafters – San Francisco–style restaurant, with some of the best seafood in town. Joe Thompson, a native of the Golden Gate city, has shipments flown in daily from Fisherman's Wharf. Try the splendid bouillabaisse, which comes topped with a whole soft-shell crab. Dinner nightly. Reservations advised. Major credit cards accepted. 1350 E. Tropicana (phone: 739-9463). Moderate.

Starboard Tack – For years, a local favorite. The *Port Tack,* also offers romance and good food in a larger setting with an attractive sunken fireplace, open 24 hours. Reservations advised. Major credit cards accepted. *Starboard,* 2601 Atlantic St. (phone: 457-8794); *Port,* 3190 W. Sahara Ave. (phone: 873-3345). Moderate.

Waldemar's – In a setting reminiscent of a German grotto, chef Waldemar prepares goulash, beef shashlik, and, for dessert, wife Janina's homemade plum cake, heaped with freshly whipped cream. Open daily for lunch weekdays, and dinner nightly except Sunday. Reservations advised. Major credit cards accepted. 2202 W. Charleston (phone: 386-1995). Moderate.

Vineyard – On the exterior of the *Boulevard Mall,* one of Las Vegas's three enclosed shopping malls, this quaint Italian eatery offers a fine antipasto salad bar and specialties such as chicken cacciatore and veal cutlet parmigiana. Open daily. Reservations advised. Major credit cards accepted. 3630 S. Maryland Pkwy. (phone: 731-1606). Inexpensive.

If all-you-can-eat sounds good to you, you can spend all your time in Las Vegas filling your plate. Virtually every Strip hotel and most of the downtown hotels have buffet breakfasts, lunches, and dinners where, for a couple of dollars or more, you can have as much as you can handle from an array of salads, fish, chicken, pasta, occasionally roast beef, and dessert. Best bets are the *Golden Nugget* (129 E. Fremont St.; phone: 385-7111); the *Fremont* (200 E. Fremont St.; phone: 385-3232); *Caesars Palace's Palatium* (3570 Las Vegas Blvd. S.; phone: 731-7110); the *Riviera* (2901 Las Vegas Blvd. S.; phone: 734-5110); the *Sahara* (2535 Las Vegas Blvd. S.; phone: 737-2111); *Holiday Casino* (3475 Las Vegas Blvd. S.; phone: 732-2411); *Frontier* (3120 Las Vegas Blvd. S.; phone: 794-8200); and the *Mirage* (3400 Las Vegas Blvd. S.; phone: 791-7111).

For something really special, try the weekend Champagne Brunch at *Caesars Palace* — a feast for the eyes as well as the tastebuds with its beautifully arranged selections of fresh pastries, fresh melons, eggs, bacon, ham, sausage, and all the champagne you can drink (3570 Las Vegas Blvd. S.; phone: 731-7110). Inexpensive. The Sterling Brunch at *Bally's,* served in *Caruso's* restaurant for $19.95, is exceptional. The all-you-can-eat entrées are presented in silver chafing dishes, the champagne is poured by white-gloved waiters, sushi and omelettes are made to order, and the dessert display is exquisite (3645 Las Vegas Blvd. S.; phone: 739-4111).

LOS ANGELES

$$\boxed{\textbf{AT-A-GLANCE}}$$

SEEING THE CITY: There are at least three great places to go for a fantastic view of Los Angeles. The most famous is Mulholland Drive, a twisting road that winds through the Hollywood Hills. Another is the top of Mt. Olympus, in Laurel Canyon, north of Sunset Boulevard. The 27-story, 454-foot City Hall Tower has a sweeping view of downtown, the mountains, and the Pacific Ocean. Open weekdays. City Hall, near south end of Los Angeles Mall (phone: 485-2891).

SPECIAL PLACES: A walk along Hollywood Boulevard from Vine Street to Highland Avenue will delight the heart of anyone who loves the era of those great movies that made Hollywood famous. However, Hollywood is no longer the physical center of film production, and its glamour is, sadly, long gone. X-rated movies now seem to outnumber the kinds of films that made the area world-renowned. Hollywood Boulevard usually bustles with tourists and a smattering of locals night and day. There is a lot to enjoy here, much of it at little or no cost.

OLD HOLLYWOOD: MEMORIES AND EMPTY BUILDINGS

Mann's Chinese Theatre – Known to movie fans around the world as *Grauman's Chinese Theatre,* this is probably the most visited site in Hollywood. If you wander down Hollywood Boulevard toward Highland Avenue looking for the Grauman's sign, you'll never find it, though. Several years ago, Ted Mann took over the theater and added it to his movie chain. As the new proprietor, he felt within his rights to take down the sign that had made Syd Grauman famous and replace it with his own. But he caused considerable controversy. The *Chinese Theatre* forecourt is world-famous for its celebrity footprints and handprints immortalized in cement. If you join the crowd of visitors outside the box office, you'll probably find imprints of your favorite stars from the 1920s to the present. If you buy a ticket to get in, you'll be treated to one of the world's most impressive and elaborate movie palaces. The ornate carvings, the very high, decorative ceiling, the traditionally plush seats, the heavy curtains that whoosh closed when the film ends, and the enormous screen itself are all part of a Hollywood that no longer exists. The *Chinese Theatre* is one of those movie theaters that give children some idea of what grandparents mean when they talk about how moviegoing has changed since their own childhoods. The less opulent *Chinese Twin* next door also shows films. 6925 Hollywood Blvd. (phone: 464-8111).

Hollywood Wax Museum – If the *Chinese Theatre* makes you nostalgic for the faces belonging to the celluloid souls, stop in at the *Hollywood Wax Museum.* If you've been leery of wax museums ever since you watched Vincent Price coat his victims in wax in the famous flick *House of Wax,* we hasten to reassure you that there is no such hanky-panky going on in the back rooms here. Marilyn Monroe, Jean Harlow, Paul Newman, Raquel Welch, Michael Jackson, Madonna, Mike Tyson, Sylvester Stallone as Rambo, and many more fill the star-studded display cases. There's also a horror chamber and a re-creation of *The Last Supper*. Open daily: weekdays to midnight, Fridays and Saturdays to 2 AM. Admission charge; no charge for children under 6. 6767 Hollywood Blvd. (phone: 462-8860; information: 462-5991.)

Hollywood Studio Museum – If nostalgia is what you seek, you also can find it at the largest single historical movie artifact in existence. Called the De Mille Barn, it was designated a California Cultural Landmark in 1956 and presently houses the *Hollywood Studio Museum*. Cecil B. De Mille used this structure, a rented horse-barn, as a studio when he made the first feature — *The Squawman* — ever shot in the town of Hollywood. Inside today are a replica of De Mille's office and stills from silent motion pictures. The outside of the building is interesting, too: When it was on the back lot of Paramount Studios, it often was used in Westerns, and for many years was seen as the railroad station in the "Bonanza" TV series. Open only Saturdays and Sundays, 10 AM to 4 PM. Admission charge (no charge for children under 6). 2100 N. Highland, across from the Hollywood Bowl (phone: 874-2276).

Paramount Pictures – At one time, RKO studios adjoined the Paramount lot. After RKO folded in 1956, its studio became the home of television's Desilu Productions, which in turn sold its property to next-door Paramount. Close to the Bronson Avenue intersection with Melrose is the famous Paramount Gate, the highly decorative studio entrance that many people will remember from the film *Sunset Boulevard*. The Gower Street side of today's Paramount was the old front entrance to RKO. At what used to be 780 Gower Street, you now will find simply an unimpressive back door to Paramount, painted in that dull, flat beige many studios use to protect their exterior walls. The door no longer bears its old marquee with distinctive Art Deco neon letters spelling out RKO, the numbers have been torn from the front steps, and the Art Deco front doors are gone. RKO is just a memory now. Paramount extends from Melrose Ave. on the south to Gower St. on the west, Van Ness Ave. on the east, and Willoughby Ave. on the north (phone: 956-5000).

Gower Street – This was once the center for so many small film studios that it became known in the film business as Gower Gulch. It was also nicknamed Poverty Row because so many of its independent producers were perpetually strapped for production money. Poverty Row's most famous studio was Columbia Pictures, which ultimately grew healthy enough to acquire most of the smaller parcels of studio real estate in the neighborhood. Columbia's old studios still stand at Gower Street and Sunset Boulevard, although Columbia moved out several years ago. It found a new home in Burbank at the Warner Brothers Studio, which was then renamed The Burbank Studios (TBS). The two film companies operate TBS as a rental facility for film and TV production today — not to be confused with the Turner Broadcasting System (TBS) television network. When Columbia vacated its Hollywood property, some of its sound stages were used for a time as indoor tennis courts. Today they have become film studios once more, available for rent to independent production companies.

Warner Brothers – During the late 1920s, when Warner's was introducing "talkies" to America, its pictures were filmed here. It also was the home of Warner's radio station at the time, KFWB. Today the old studio is the headquarters for KTLA-TV and KMPC radio. The stately southern mansion that served as Warner's administration building still stands on Sunset Blvd. and Van Ness Ave.

Max Factor Beauty Museum – The only museum in the world devoted to makeup is housed in the famous Max Factor Building, just off Hollywood Boulevard, where (since the 1930s) the stars came to have their faces painted, to have their hair styled, and to be fitted for wigs or toupees. The displays document the history of the company, which is synonymous with the history of makeup in film. One of the most unusual

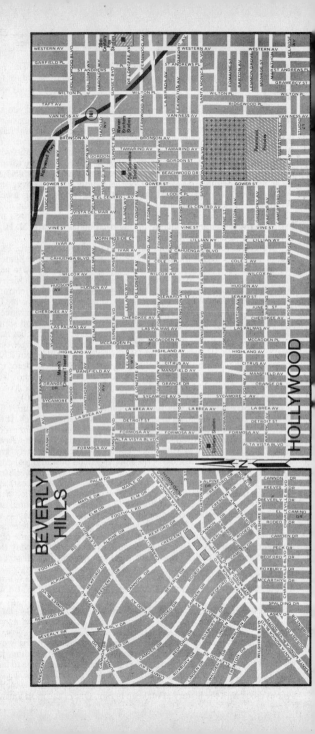

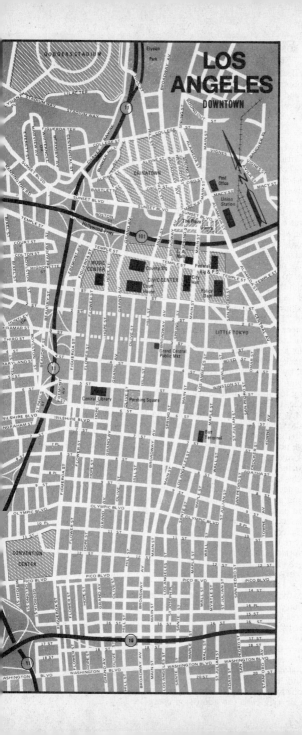

is a collection of special head blocks of famous stars, used to create wigs and toupees without the actors and actresses having to spend hours being fitted and styled. Open 10 AM to 4 PM, Mondays through Saturdays. No admission charge. Free parking. 1666 N. Highland Ave. (phone: 463-6668).

"HOLLYWOOD": ALIVE AND WELL

"Hollywood," meaning the film business, is no longer geographically in the district bearing that name. If your nostalgic walking tour of Old Hollywood has made you curious about modern production methods, we suggest a tour of one of the following Los Angeles studios:

Universal Studios Hollywood – The combination movie studio tour and theme park has been attracting more than 5 million people a year. In 1915, Universal Pictures established a mammoth studio on 420 acres of what was then a chicken farm. Land in the eastern part of the San Fernando Valley was very inexpensive, and Universal's founder, Carl Laemmle, was smart enough to buy a lot of it. As a result, the modern Universal, a division of MCA, found itself with more than enough room to make movies and television shows, as well as build a theme park. The Universal Studios Hollywood experience includes a guided tram tour through the back lot. Other highlights include a look at some of the 34 sound stages and other production facilities; a special-effects demonstration; a burning house; a collapsing bridge; and an earthquake simulation (called "The Big One") where the ground shakes beneath the wheels of passenger trams as riders experience shock waves in the high ranges of the Richter scale. You'll also see the house used in Alfred Hitchcock's *Psycho,* a street from *The Sting,* a flash flood, the parting of the Red Sea, an attack on the tour tram by the 24-foot "shark" from *Jaws,* another attack by a 30-foot-tall, computer-controlled King Kong, who tries to hurl your tram into a river, and the Doomed Glacier Expedition, where you get to plunge down an Alpine avalanche. If this isn't enough, there are other tricks and treats: *An American Tale,* a musical production; *The Riot Act,* a western stunt show; and *Back to the Future,* which reveals how the special effects were created for this movie series. If you're ready for all that, visit Universal Studios any day of the week. Admission charge; no charge for children under 3. Hollywood Fwy. to Lankershim exit, Universal City (phone: 818-508-9600).

Warner Brothers Studios – To take a look at real production rather than the Universal extravaganza, try these studios in Burbank — home of Warner Brothers as well as many independent production companies. Nothing on the tour is staged, so visitors watch whatever is happening on that particular day. Not only do you get to see some actual shooting whenever possible, you also see a lot of behind-the-scenes action — scenery construction, sound recording, and prop departments. Since tours are limited to 12 people (with children under 10 not permitted), reservations are required a week in advance. Open weekdays. Admission charge. 4000 Warner Blvd. (phone: 818-954-1744).

Beverly Hills – After a hard day on the lot, movie stars still living in Beverly Hills return to their mansions for a good night's sleep. Even during the sunshiny daylight hours, Beverly Hills is remarkably tranquil, with nary a person walking on the residential streets. Without a doubt the most affluent and elegant neighborhood in Southern California, Beverly Hills is a must-see. If you want to window-shop or purchase high fashion clothing, stroll along Rodeo Drive between Santa Monica and Wilshire Boulevards. If you want to make sure you don't succumb to an impulse to buy anything, go during the evening or on Sunday, when many stores are closed. *Gray Line* is one of several companies offering van and limousine tours (phone: 856-5900). During the week, an old-fashioned trolley, which departs from the *Regent Beverly Wilshire* hotel, tours Beverly Hills (no admission charge).

DOWNTOWN LOS ANGELES

To see a Los Angeles that most people don't know about, take a walking tour downtown.

The Plaza – If you ever wondered what the place looked like before shopping centers were created, step across the Plaza and marvel. The Plaza, a wide square, is the scene of monthly fiestas. The Old Plaza Church, which dates to 1822, has a curious financial history: It was partially paid for by the sale of seven barrels of brandy. The city's first firehouse is here, too; closed Mondays. Colorful local anecdotes are retold during a narrated walking tour of the Plaza, offered Tuesdays through Saturdays, 10 AM to noon. For information, contact El Pueblo de los Angeles State Historic Park on the Plaza, 845 N. Alameda St. (phone: 628-1274).

Olvera Street – Music from the Plaza fiesta spills into Olvera Street, a block-long pedestrian alley filled with colorful Mexican shops, restaurants, and spicy food stalls. The oldest house in Los Angeles is here — the 1818 adobe Avila House; closed Mondays. The first brick house also is here, but now it's a restaurant. There is a visitors' center in the 1887 Sepulveda House (both closed Sundays), and a free 18-minute film on the history of Los Angeles (phone: 628-0605).

Los Angeles Civic Center and Mall – An unusually quiet, well-landscaped city mall, with tropical plants, gentle splashing fountains, and sculpture half hidden among the lush greenery. It's the first mall of shops and restaurants to be built on City Hall property (at Main and Los Angeles Sts.). Stop in the rotunda to see a rotating art show. Make sure you get to the top of City Hall Tower at the south end of the mall for one of the best views of the city. Mall open daily (phone: 485-2891 and 485-2121).

Third and Broadway – Several places in this area are worth noting. First is the skylit, 5-story indoor court of the Bradbury Building, now a registered historic landmark. Open Mondays through Fridays, 8 AM to 5 PM. You can ride an old hydraulic elevator to the top balcony and walk down a magnificent staircase guaranteed to evoke visions of bygone splendors. Across the corner from the Bradbury Building is the *Million Dollar Theater* — Syd Grauman's first; it's currently a Spanish-language picture palace inside but it has a fascinating exterior. Just south of the theater is the entrance to the *Grand Central Public Market,* a conglomerate of stalls selling food from all over the world amid the sounds and smells of a Mexican mercado.

Little Tokyo – This is the social, economic, cultural, and religious center of the largest Japanese-American community in the US. There are four specialty shopping centers here, as well as the Japanese Cultural Center and many fine restaurants. 1st and San Pedro Sts. (phone: 620-8861).

Music Center – The best time to visit the *Music Center* is during a concert or performance, but it's worth seeing anytime. The *Ahmanson Theater* is the base for a branch of the *Center Theater Group* and hosts classical dramas, comedies, and international premieres with big-name stars. The *Mark Taper Forum,* a small, award-winning theater, houses the branch of the *Center Theater Group* that specializes in new works and experimental material. The glittering *Dorothy Chandler Pavilion,* a 3,200-seat auditorium, is the home of the *Los Angeles Philharmonic,* the *Joffrey Ballet,* and the *Los Angeles Master Chorale.* It's also the setting for most of the season of the *Los Angeles Opera Company.* The orchestra season runs from October to May; musical theater is presented generally in summer, when the orchestra moves to the *Hollywood Bowl.* Take the free guided tour of the theaters. 1st and Grand Sts. (phone: 972-7483 for tour information; 972-7211 for general information).

Chinatown – Chinatown has the usual assortment of restaurants, vegetable stores, and weird little shops selling ivory chess sets and acupuncture charts. The 900 block of N. Broadway.

Museum of Contemporary Art – This is one museum in two buildings: the *MOCA* at California Plaza, designed by Arata Isozaki, a modern art exhibit in itself, and the *Temporary Contemporary,* a renovated warehouse about 10 blocks away, on Bunker Hill downtown. Both house artworks from the 1940s to the present. Also, in *MOCA*'s *Ahmanson Auditorium,* there is a Media and Performing Arts Program, which looks at performance — contemporary dance, theater, film, and video — as an art form. Closed Mondays. Admission charge (except Thursdays from 5 to 8 PM). One ticket covers admission to both buildings on the same day. *MOCA:* 250 S. Grand Ave. at California Plaza (phone: 621-2766); *Temporary Contemporary:* 152 N. Central Ave. (phone: 626-6222).

MIDTOWN

Farmers Market – "Eat your liver." No, we're not quoting your mother, we're quoting Yossarian, the hero of *Catch-22* (book by Joseph Heller, movie by Mike Nichols). Yossarian used to say "eat your liver" all the time, and at the *Farmers Market* you can do just that. You also can eat anything else within the realm of gastronomic imagination. You'll find over 150 stalls of American, Mexican, Italian, Chinese, and vegetarian food, and any number of exquisite bakeries and fruit and candy shops. If you don't like to eat standing up, there are tables set among the aisles of this indoor, covered market. It's a great place to be hungry. Open daily. 6333 W. 3rd St. at Fairfax (phone: 933-9211).

Hancock Park – A midtown green space, the gift of an early oil magnate. The *Los Angeles Museum of Art* keeps building over remaining deposits where Hancock's oil pumps once bobbed. There are galleries of drawings, prints, photographs, and temporary exhibitions in the Frances and Armand Hammer Building and a dazzling, eclectic, permanent collection in the Ahmanson Building. Contemporary art is the focus of the Robert O. Anderson Building. The Oriental Pavilion for Japanese Art contains paintings, sculpture, and decorative arts. The *Leo S. Bing Theater* offers special films and concerts. Closed Mondays. Admission charge. 5905 Wilshire Blvd. (phone: 857-6000). The colorful *George C. Page Museum of La Brea Discoveries* displays some of the fossilized remains of prehistoric animals trapped in the tar pits, along with movies, dioramas, and a glassed-in laboratory where paleontologists work. Closed Mondays. Admission charge. 5801 Wilshire Blvd. (phone: 936-2230). Combination *Museum of Art/Page Museum* tickets available.

FARTHER AFIELD

Griffith Park – If you thought Texas had the biggest of everything, you're mistaken. This is the largest municipal park in the country. Griffith has three golf courses, a wilderness area and bird sanctuary, tennis courts, three miniature railroads, a carousel, pony rides, and picnic areas within its 4,043 acres. Not only that — this is where you'll find the famous Los Angeles Zoo, home to over 1,500 mammals, birds, and reptiles. Open daily, except *Christmas.* Admission charge except for children under 2 (5333 Zoo Dr.; phone: 666-4650). If you like railroads, you'll love *Travel Town,* a unique outdoor museum of old railroad engines, cars, railroad equipment, and fire trucks. The *Griffith Observatory* (2800 E. Observatory Rd.; phone: 664-1191) near Mt. Hollywood houses a 500-seat planetarium theater, a twin-refracting telescope, and the Hall of Science. Admission charge for planetarium shows. At the architecturally innovative *Gene Autry Western Heritage Museum,* memorabilia, films, and visual displays trace the history of the Western movement since the 1700s, prominently including the cinema's West. Closed Mondays. Admission charge (4700 Western Heritage Way, across from the zoo; phone: 667-2000). Most park facilities are open daily (phone: 665-5188).

Six Flags Magic Mountain – A 260-acre family theme park, featuring 100-plus rides, shows, and other attractions, this is the home of Bugs Bunny and his Looney Tunes friends in Bugs Bunny World. In addition to the mighty Colossus (a huge, wooden roller coaster) and the spine-tingling Revolution (a 360-degree vertical loop coaster), there's also the challenge of Roaring Rapids (a whitewater rafting experience), the Z Force mock starship ride, and a magic show run by the wily rabbit. Ninja, the West Coast's only suspended roller coaster, promises a delightfully terrifying trip. Newest is the 6-coaster Psyclone, a replica of Coney Island's Cyclone. The Viper is one of the world's largest — and LA's scariest — multiple-looped roller coasters. The dolphin show and a children's village and petting zoo are also worthwhile. Open daily from *Memorial Day* to *Labor Day,* weekends the rest of the year. Admission charge except for children under 3. Twenty-five minutes north of Hollywood on the Golden State Fwy., Magic Mountain exit in Valencia (phone: 818-367-2271 or 805-255-4100; for recorded information, 805-255-4111 or 818-367-5965).

Ports o' Call Village – Some 60 specialty shops here feature merchandise from around the world. You can relax by taking a boat or helicopter tour of Los Angeles Harbor and dining in your choice of 25 restaurants and snack shops. Open daily. Berths 76-79 at the foot of the Harbor Fwy., San Pedro (phone: 831-0287).

Redondo Beach Marina – A delightful waterfront recreation showplace, the marina offers boat cruises, and sport fishing. Open daily. 181 N. Harbor Dr., Redondo Beach. Take the Harbor Fwy. to the Torrance Blvd. exit and proceed west to the ocean (phone: 374-3481).

Forest Lawn Memorial Park – A major tourist attraction, Forest Lawn is a huge cemetery calling itself a memorial park; it advertises on huge billboards overlooking the freeways. Humphrey Bogart, Walt Disney, W. C. Fields, Clark Gable, and Bette Davis are buried here, among others. On the grounds you'll find copies of Michelangelo statues, including his *David,* a stained glass window depicting *The Last Supper,* and the largest religious painting in the world, Jan Styka's 195-by-45-foot *The Crucifixion.* And don't be surprised if you also find a real live bride and groom — some people like to get married here. Open daily. Donations appreciated. 1712 S. Glendale Ave., Glendale (phone: 818-241-4151).

Queen Mary – Now permanently docked in Long Beach (and owned by The Walt Disney Company). When she was launched in 1936, the *Queen* was the ultimate transatlantic travel experience of its time. She was "relaunched" in this picturesque harbor in 1971, after retiring from a long career on the high seas. You can tour the 81,000-ton ship from stem to stern and even can spend the night — nearly 400 converted staterooms now make up the *Queen Mary* hotel. Also at the site is Howard Hughes's *Spruce Goose,* the world's largest all-wood airplane. Open daily. Admission charge. Long Beach Fwy. to *Queen Mary* exit (phone: 435-3511).

Catalina Island – It's 1 hour by boat from Long Beach or 1½ hours from San Pedro to Catalina Island, where you can spend the day wandering around the flower-filled hills, looking at the ocean, swimming, sightseeing, playing golf, or riding horses. There are places to stay overnight, but be sure to reserve in advance during the summer. Boats to Catalina leave daily from Catalina Landing, 320 Golden Shore Blvd., Long Beach, and from the Catalina Terminal Building, foot of Harbor Fwy., Berths 95 and 96, San Pedro. Boats are operated by *Catalina Cruises* (phone: 514-3838) and the super-fast *Catalina Channel Express* (phone: 519-1212 or 519-7957), and depart from the Queen Mary terminal.

ORANGE COUNTY

Disneyland – For many people, this is the most compelling magnet in all of Southern California — and the inspired creation that forever changed the image of theme and amusement parks. If you've ever wished upon a star and longed to make your way toward the glittering spires of Fantasyland, a trip to this incredibly clean, colorful, and diversified amusement park is essential. More than 50 attractions delight visitors of all ages, from the ever-popular Pirates of the Caribbean to the intergalactic thriller Star Tours. You will undoubtedly encounter one of your favorite Disney characters promenading down Main Street, a re-creation of a typical 1890s American street. Our extensive guide to *Disneyland* can provide complete details about this still-expanding wonderland. 40 minutes from downtown LA, *Disneyland* is open daily. Admission charge. 1313 Harbor Blvd., Anaheim (phone: 714-999-4565).

Movieland Wax Museum – About a 10-minute drive from *Disneyland,* with more than 200 movie and television stars in wax, molded into stances from their most famous roles. The original props and sets from many films are here, too. At the Chamber of Horrors, 15 sets with wax figures re-create the special effects that made movies such as *Psycho* and *The Exorcist* famous. Open daily. Admission charge. 7711 Beach Blvd., Buena Park (phone: 714-522-1154).

Medieval Times – Across the street from the *Movieland Wax Museum* is a castle-like structure that houses an arena. It's an evening of 11th-century entertainment during which colorfully attired knights on horseback compete in medieval games, jousting, and sword fighting. The show comes with dinner (whole roasted chicken, spareribs, herb-basted potatoes, and various other finger foods, since people in those days didn't use forks). Open daily. Admission charge. 7662 Beach Blvd., Buena Park (phone: 714-521-4740 or 800-899-6600).

Knott's Berry Farm – The theme is the Old West. An old-fashioned stagecoach and authentic steam coach will take you around the grounds, past rides called the Whirlpool, Mountain Log Ride, Sky Jump, XK-1, Tumbler, Slammer, and Slingshot, as well as bumper cars. There also are a mine train, Montezooma's Revenge, the multiple-looped Boomerang roller coaster, Camp Snoopy (an entertainment area for kids), and the exciting Kingdom of the Dinosaurs. *Knott's Berry Farm* has top country-and-western artists performing frequently, and a great ice show at *Christmastime. Mrs. Knott's Chicken Dinner Restaurant* is older than the park. Open daily. Admission charge. 10 minutes from *Disneyland* at 8039 Beach Blvd., Buena Park (phone: 714-827-1776 or, for recorded information, 714-220-5200).

■ **EXTRA SPECIAL:** For one of the most spectacular drives in California, follow the Pacific Coast Highway (Rte. 1) north to Santa Barbara, about 95 miles from LA. Santa Barbara is a picturesque California mission town facing the Pacific, where bright bougainvillea burst with purple and magenta against classic white adobe Mediterranean-style architecture. A "red tile" walking tour zigzags through the historic district and runs along downtown State Street — Spanish to the last tile-enclosed trash bin and mailbox. The Spanish-Moorish courthouse is worth a visit for its opulent interior and the incomparable panorama from the tower. The city center owes its harmonious Spanish look to the strict architectural guidelines for reconstruction that were imposed after the devastating earthquake of 1925. Overnighters can opt for a hacienda-style hostelry, such as the *Four Seasons Biltmore* (phone: 805-969-2261); Charlie Chaplin's favorite hotel, the *Montecito Inn* (phone: 805-969-7854); an exclusive hideaway, such as the *San Ysidro Ranch,* with its excellent French *StoneHouse* restaurant (phone: 805-969-5046); the Victorian *Upham* hotel, with *Louie's,* its highly regarded restaurant serving California cuisine (phone: 805-962-0058); or one of many period bed and breakfast establishments. The *Cold Spring Tavern* (5995 Stagecoach Rd.; phone: 805-967-0066), about 10 miles northwest of Santa Barbara on Route 154, goes back to the old stagecoach days. Chili is popular at lunch. At dinner, the menu tends more toward chicken, steaks, and game. Open daily.

SOURCES AND RESOURCES

TOURIST INFORMATION: For free information, brochures, and maps, contact the Greater Los Angeles Visitors and Convention Bureau (515 S. Figueroa St., Los Angeles, CA 90012; phone: 624-7300). For the best (albeit most expensive) maps of the Los Angeles area as well as travel books, try *Thomas Bros. Maps & Books* (603 W. 7th St.; phone: 627-4018). Contact the California state hotline (800-TO-CALIF) for maps, calendars of events, health updates, and travel advisories.

The best individual city guides to Los Angeles are *LA/Access* by Richard Saul Wurman (Access Press; $11.95) and *Hidden LA and Southern California* by Ray Riegert (Ulysses Press Travel; $12.96). A more unusual guide is *Permanent Californians: An Illustrated Guide to the Cemeteries of California* by Judi Culbertson and Tom Randall (Chelsea Publishing Co.; $16.95), which describes the final resting places of many famous Californians and provides some interesting biographical notes.

Local Coverage – *Los Angeles Times,* morning daily; *Daily News,* published in the San Fernando Valley, morning daily; *Los Angeles* magazine, monthly; *California* magazine, monthly; *Angeles Magazine,* monthly; *LA Weekly,* a free newspaper with local listings of events about town.

Television Stations – KCBS Channel 2–CBS; KNBC Channel 4–NBC; KABC Channel 7–ABC; KTTV Channel 11–Fox; KCET Channel 28–PBS.

Radio Stations – AM: KKJZ 540 (jazz); KNX 1070 (news/sports); KRTH 101 (oldies). FM: KCRW 89.9 (public); KUSC 91.5 (public); KKGO 105 (classical); KPWR 105.5 (top 40).

Food – To keep absolutely up-to-date, check the restaurant listings in *Los Angeles* or *California* magazines or consult the concierge at your hotel. Another good resource is the Sunday "Calendar" section of the *LA Times.*

TELEPHONE: The area code for central Los Angeles is 213. The 818 area code covers the San Fernando Valley and the upper half of the San Gabriel Valley. The 805 area code covers the Ventura-Santa Barbara area; the 714 area code, Orange County. All telephone numbers are in the 213 area code unless otherwise indicated.

Sales Tax – There is a 6.75% sales tax and a 12% hotel tax.

CLIMATE: Summers are hot and dry, with temperatures reaching the 90s during the day, but cool enough for sweaters after sundown. In winter, there are occasional rainy days and hot days, with an average temperature of 68.

GETTING AROUND: It's always more convenient to have a car for exploring Los Angeles; however, there are buses, taxis, and tour operators.

Airports – Los Angeles International Airport (known as LAX) is the city's major airport and handles most international and domestic traffic. Especially helpful for business travelers are LAX's three business centers, in Terminals 1, 4, and 7. They have secretarial services, telexes, even conference rooms for up to 8 persons for a small charge. Also available here are automatic teller machines. For handicapped travelers, the airport provides van service with a wheelchair lift for transport between terminals or to and from outlying Parking Lot C (phone: 646-6402 or 646-8021).

The drive downtown from LAX takes about an hour, depending on traffic, and taxi fare should run about $25. Although city buses do stop at the airport, a more efficient alternative is one of the private transport companies. *Supershuttle* (phone: 777-8000) offers transportation by van from LAX to downtown hotels for $11. At the airport, *Supershuttle* and several other companies can be summoned through the courtesy phones in the baggage claim area or by calling 417-8988. For the return trip, call at least 4 hours ahead for a pickup at your hotel.

Bus – For route information on scheduled city buses, call the *Southern California Rapid Transit District* (phone: 273-0910 in the Beverly Hills/ West LA area; 626-4455 in Hollywood/central LA; and 818-781-5890 in the San Fernando Valley).

Car Rental – All major firms are represented throughout Greater Los Angeles. The least expensive is *Bob Leech Auto Rental* (4490 W. Century Blvd.; phone: 673-2727), with Toyota Tercels and Corollas at $19.95 a day with 150 free miles, 10¢ a mile thereafter. Sports coupes run $23.95 Free airport pickups and free drop-off at San Francisco International Airport. *Luxury Line* can snag you a Rolls Royce, Range Rover, or another suitably esoteric vehicle (300 S. La Cienega Blvd.; phone: 659-5555).

Taxi – Cabs *don't* cruise the streets in LA. Check at your hotel desk; different firms serve different areas. A few companies to try: *Bell Cab* (phone: 221-1112), *United Independent Taxi* (phone: 653-5050), and *LA Taxi* (phone: 627-7000).

Tours – *Star Line/Gray Line* (phone: 856-5900) is one of many companies offering tours of downtown LA (*Music Center,* Chinatown, Little Tokyo, Olvera St., and more) and the Hollywood–Beverly Hills area, as well as *Disneyland, Knott's Berry Farm,* and *Universal Studios Hollywood* (541 Hollywood Blvd., Hollywood; phone: 856-5900). There are tours that offer more than the usual sights, including tasteful trips through Southern California wine country, and the ghoulish *Graveline Tours,* which visit scenes of scandals, crimes, and misdemeanors in a renovated hearse (PO Box 931694, Hollywood, CA 90093; phone: 876-4286).

 VITAL SERVICES: Audiovisual Equipment – *Ametron Rents* (phone: 466-4321).

Baby-sitting – *Weston's Babysitters Guide* (8230 Beverly Blvd., LA; phone: 658-8792); *Community Service Agency* (18341 Sherman Way, Ste. 207, Reseda; phone: 818-345-2950).

Business Services – *Century Secretarial Service,* 2040 Ave. of the Stars, Ste. 400, Century City (phone: 277-3329).

Dry Cleaner/Tailor – *Sloan's Cleaners,* 201 N. Los Angeles St., across from City Hall (phone: 628-0603).

Limousine – *Carey Limousine* (phone: 275-4153, 272-0081); *Classic Fleet Limousine Service* (phone: 753-4384).

Mechanic – *Bliss & Bothwell Auto Service,* 2110 Kotner Ave. (phone: 475-8651).

Medical Emergency – *California Hospital* (1414 S. Hope St.; phone: 748-2411); *Cedars Sinai* (8701 Alden; phone: 855-6517).

Messenger Services – *Jet Delivery Inc.* (phone: 749-0123). Many hotels also can make arrangements.

National/International Courier – *Federal Express* (phone: 687-9767); *DHL Worldwide Courier Express* (phone: 973-7300).

Pharmacy – *Cadillac Pharmacy* (in *Kaiser Hospital*), open 24 hours daily, 6041 Cadillac Ave. and La Cienega Blvd. (phone: 857-2151).

Photocopies – *Barbara's Place,* 24-hour service Mondays through Thursdays; Fridays until 10 PM; and Saturdays from 10 AM to 4 PM (7925 Santa Monica Blvd., West Hollywood; phone: 654-5902); *Copy Print,* 24-hour service, pickup and delivery (404 S. Figueroa Ave., in the *Bonaventure* hotel; phone: 620-6279).

Post Office – Downtown, self-service lobby from 8 AM to 9 PM (900 N. Alameda St.; phone: 617-4641); in Beverly Hills (469 N. Crescent Dr.; phone: 276-3161); near LAX, *World Way* post office, self-service area open 24 hours (5800 Century Blvd.; phone: 337-8885).

Professional Photographer – *Vanguard Photography* (phone: 874-3980); *Atkinson Business Photography* (phone: 624-5950).

Secretary/Stenographer – *Century Secretarial Service* (phone: 277-3329); *HQ Headquarters Company,* word processing, telex, fax, conference rooms (phone: 277-6660 and 551-6666).

Teleconference Facilities – With the exception of the *Bel Air* and the *Beverly Hilton,* all hotels listed in the very expensive and expensive categories under *Best in Town* have teleconferencing facilities, as does the *New Otani.*

Translator – *Berlitz* (phone: 380-1144).

Typewriter Rental – *Office Machines Inc.,* convention rates can be arranged through hotels (phone: 484-9530).

Western Union/Telex – Many offices are located around the city (phone: 800-325-6000).

Other – *Word Shop,* for word processing, is one of the many agencies in the area (phone: 381-3801); many hotels also can make arrangements; *Seminars International,* seminar planning, production, and marketing (phone: 883-3330).

 SPECIAL EVENTS: There are more special events than we could possibly list here. For complete listings, check the local publications listed above or call the Greater Los Angeles Visitors and Convention Bureau (phone: 624-7300). Annual attractions include: The *Tournament of Roses Parade* and *Rose Bowl,* the traditional *New Year's Day* gridiron spectacle; *Los Angeles Open Golf Tournament,* Pacific Palisades, in February; *Los Angeles Marathon,* in March; *Disneyland's Easter Parade;* UCLA *Mardi Gras, Cinco de Mayo* celebrations throughout the area, the *California Strawberry Festival,* and *Manhattan Beach Art Festival,* in May; the *Playboy Jazz Festival,* at the Hollywood Bowl, in June; *Fourth of July* fireworks go off at *Anaheim Stadium* and Pasadena's *Rose Bowl,* as well as at the *Hollywood Bowl* and Burton Chase Park in Marina del Rey; *All-Star Shrine Football Game,* usually held in Pasadena's *Rose Bowl,* in July; *Festival of Arts and Pageant of the Masters,* Laguna Beach, also in July; *SeaFest,* Long Beach, in August; *International Surf Festival,* Redondo Beach, in August; *Los Angeles County Fair,* Pomona, in September; *Hollywood Christmas Parade* and the irreverent *DooDah Parade,* Pasadena, in November.

 MUSEUMS: The *Los Angeles County Museum of Art* and the *Museum of Contemporary Art* are described in *Special Places.* Other fine museums in LA are the following:

Armand Hammer Museum of Art – Rembrandts, Van Goghs, Cézannes, and Goyas are among the masterpieces that the late industrialist collected during his lifetime. Open daily. Admission charge. 10899 Wilshire Blvd. (phone: 443-7000).

J. Paul Getty Museum – Parking reservations are mandatory (if you're driving) at this replica of a Roman villa buried at Herculaneum. The museum houses permanent collections of Greek and Roman antiquities, European paintings (including Van Gogh's *Irises*), drawings, sculpture, illuminated manuscripts, decorative arts, and 19th- and 20th-century European and American photographs. A tearoom and the lovely grounds make for a wonderful afternoon outing. Closed Mondays. No admission charge, but admission is by reservation only. 17985 Pacific Coast Hwy., Malibu (phone: 458-2003).

Los Angeles Children's Museum – There are 18 hands-on exhibits and special workshops for children of all ages. Open daily. No admission charge for children under 2. 310 N. Main St. (phone: 687-8800).

Museum of Science and Industry – Science, mathematics, aerospace, energy, and health exhibits are featured. Open daily. No admission charge, except for IMAX theater (phone: 744-2014). 700 S. State, Exposition Park (phone: 744-7400).

Natural History Museum – Sixteen million artifacts and specimens feature world-famous animal dioramas, dinosaurs, the new Ralph W. Schreiber Hall of Birds, and dazzling gems, along with ever-changing, traveling exhibitions. Admission charge, except the first Tuesday of each month. Closed Mondays. 900 Exposition Blvd. (phone: 744-3466).

Norton Simon Museum of Art – The rich industrialist's multimillion-dollar collection. Five centuries of European art from the Renaissance to the 20th century. There's also Asian sculpture spanning a period of 2,000 years. Open Thursdays through Sundays. Admission charge. 411 W. Colorado Blvd., Pasadena (phone: 818-449-6840).

Richard Nixon Library & Birthplace – Opened in 1990, it includes the 52,000-square-foot Spanish-style library with exhibits chronicling the former president's life and career, plus the modest frame house in which Nixon was born in 1913. Open daily. Admission charge. 18001 Yorba Linda Blvd., Yorba Linda (phone: 714-993-3393).

Southwest Museum – Devoted to the anthropology of the Southwest. The museum contains some of the finest examples of Native American art and artifacts in the US. Closed Mondays. Admission charge. 234 Museum Dr., near *Dodger Stadium* (phone: 221-2163).

MAJOR COLLEGES AND UNIVERSITIES: There are many major university campuses spread through the LA area, in addition to dozens of colleges and junior colleges. The University of California (UCLA) is among the top-ranked universities in the nation. Known to college football and basketball fans for the *Bruins* teams (main campus at 405 Hilgard Ave.; phone: 825-4321). The University of Southern California (USC) is also a major institution, and with teams like the *Trojans,* is UCLA's arch-rival in sports (Exposition Blvd. and Figueroa St,; phone: 740-2311). California Institute of Technology, which excels in science and engineering, counts more than 20 Nobel laureates among its alumni and past and present faculty (main campus at 1201 E. California Blvd., Pasadena; phone: 818-356-6326).

SHOPPING: No single street on this planet so typifies consumer excess as Rodeo Drive in Beverly Hills. Few mortals will be able to afford the prices, but window shopping along this avenue for the affluent makes for as much fun as studying the boutiques along Paris's Rue du Faubourg-St.-Honoré, London's Bond Street, or New York's Fifth Avenue. In fact, many of the shop names are the same. Only a few are homegrown, such as the former *Giorgio,* now *Fred Hayman.* This supposed model for the title store of Judith Krantz's steamy novel *Scruples* sold its name and wildly successful fragrance to Avon. In addition, the recently opened *Two Rodeo,* a 2-block enclave, features Italianate cobblestone lanes that surround a piazza, travertine fountains, and an elaborate staircase that appears to be the twin of the Spanish Steps in Rome. The retail newcomers who have settled here represent the crème-de-la-crème in high fashion and jewelery. Here is a list of the top emporia along Rodeo and environs:

Alfred Dunhill of London – Tobacco and smoking accessories. 210-B N. Rodeo Dr. (phone: 274-5351).

Bally of Switzerland – High-style shoes for men (340 N. Rodeo Dr.; phone: 271-0666); and for women (409 N. Rodeo Dr.; phone: 275-3961).

Bijan – Where the rich and famous shop for men's clothing; by appointment only. 420 N. Rodeo Dr. (phone: 273-6544).

Carroll & Co. – Ivy-league clothing for men. 466 N. Rodeo Dr. (phone: 273-9060).

Cartier – Internationally renowned jewelers since 1847, with two locations on Rodeo (370 N. Rodeo Dr.; phone: 275-4272; and 220 N. Rodeo Dr.; phone: 275-4855).

Chanel – Clothes, scents, and accessories from the famous fashion house. 301 N. Rodeo Dr. (phone: 278-5500).

Charles Jourdan – Clothes, shoes, and accessories from the French firm. 201 N. Rodeo Dr., in the Two Rodeo complex (phone: 273-3507).

David Orgell – Crystal, china, antique and modern silver, and jewelry. 320 N. Rodeo Dr. (phone: 272-3355).

Dyansen Galleries – Fine art. 339 N. Rodeo Dr. (phone: 275-0165).

Elliott Katt's Books on the Performing Arts – Crammed with a tremendous selection of rare books pertaining to the performing arts, this amazingly informative shop is frequented by professionals in the movie and theater industries, as well as celebrities, who thumb through the vast casting and agency directories. Owner Katt stocks biographies of actors and directors, books on film, the scores of famous Broadway musicals, as well as how-to books on everything from how to write for television to how to get a job in the music business. 8568 Melrose Ave. (phone: 652-5178).

Frances Klein – Antique jewelry. 310 N. Rodeo Dr. (phone: 273-0155).

Fred Hayman – Chic clothing for both sexes; has a stand-up bar and complimentary drinks for shoppers in what used to be *Giorgio's*. 273 N. Rodeo Dr. (phone: 271-3000).

Fred Joaillier – Expensive jewelry, leather goods, and gifts. 401 N. Rodeo Dr. (phone: 278-3733).

Giorgio Armani Boutique – The designer's coveted clothes for men and women. 436 N. Rodeo Dr. (phone: 271-5555).

Gucci – Italian leather goods, jewelry, clothing, and accessories. 347 N. Rodeo Dr. (phone: 278-3451).

Harry Winston – Exquisite, expensive jewelry. 371 N. Rodeo Dr. (phone: 271-8554).

Hermès – Ultra chic and *cher* leather goods from France. 343 N. Rodeo Dr. (phone: 278-6440).

I. Magnin – California-bred specialty store. 9634 Wilshire Blvd. (phone: 271-2131).

Jurgensen's – Fine and fancy foods. 316 N. Beverly Dr. (phone: 858-7814).

Krizia – The Italian designer's boutique. 410 N. Rodeo Dr. (phone: 276-5411).

Louis Vuitton – Famous French handbags, accessories, and luggage. 307 N. Rodeo Dr. (phone: 859-0457).

Neiman Marcus – The specialty store for those who have almost everything. 9700 Wilshire Blvd. (phone: 550-5900).

The Rodeo Collection – A posh half-block mall, representing *Gianni Versace, Sonia Rykiel, Merletto, Fogal,* and *Furla,* among others. 421 N. Rodeo Dr. (phone: 858-7580).

Samuel French – This West Coast outlet for the oldest play publishers in the world (since 1833) has an extensive collection of drama books, biographies of film directors and stars, as well as a tremendous selection of plays. 7623 Sunset Blvd. (phone: 876-0570).

Scriptorium – Autograph gallery. Closed Mondays. 427 N. Canon Dr. (phone: 275-6060).

Sharper Image – The very latest in high tech toys. 9550 Santa Monica Blvd. (phone: 271-0515).

Superior Stamp & Coin – Gold coins and rare stamps. 9478 W. Olympic Blvd. (phone: 278-9740).

Tiffany & Co. – Fine jewelry in the famous blue boxes. 210 N. Rodeo Dr. (phone: 273-8880).

Williams-Sonoma – Dining table and kitchen outfitters. 317 N. Beverly Dr.

For specialty shopping with more native character, browse in several burgeoning areas, such as the following:

Melrose Avenue – It runs an eastward gamut from upscale to funky to weird, with Gallery Row found roughly between Doheny Drive and Fairfax Avenue. *LA Impressions* (8318 Melrose Ave.) specializes in Mexican art. At *Gemini Gel* (8365 Melrose Ave.), a superb maker and exhibitor of limited edition prints, customers watch the printing through upstairs gallery windows. At *A Star is Worn* (7303 Melrose Ave.) celebrity clothes, from the dress Barbra Streisand wore to the 1968 Academy Awards to Richard Gere's tie, are for sale. Antiques and gift shops, fashion boutiques, restaurants, and small theaters prosper all the way to La Brea Blvd.

Montana Avenue – This cornucopia of small shops that has sprung up between 7th and 17th Streets along this Santa Monica thoroughfare has become a window-shopper's delight. Among the pricey and super-specialized boutiques, there's silk lingerie at *Lisa Norman* (1134 Montana Ave.); bovine collectibles at *Udderly Perfect* (740 16th St. at Montana Ave.); ditto for cat lovers at *Montana Paws* (1025 Montana Ave.); and masks at *Thoraya* (1205 Montana Ave.). Take out superb bread and pastries at a branch of the *Il Fornaio* chain (1627 Montana Ave.); relax over lunch or tea at *Tour de Suisse* (1211 Montana Ave.); or join celebrities sipping cappuccino at *Oggi Café* (1518 Montana Ave.).

Lest anyone forgo the rather overwhelming experience of shopping in a mall, LA offers some of the finest, as well as some of the most eclectic merchandise marts in the country. Among the largest shopping complexes are *Beverly Center* (8500 Beverly Blvd.; phone: 854-0070), whose exterior was used for the film *Scenes from a Mall; Century City Shopping Center* (10250 Santa Monica Blvd.; phone: 277-3898); *Del Amo Shopping Center* (Hawthorne Blvd. and Carson St.; phone: 542-8525); *Glendale Galleria* (2148 *Glendale Galleria;* phone: 818-240-9481); and *Westside Pavilion* (10800 W. Pico Blvd.; phone: 474-5940).

SPORTS AND FITNESS: There is no question that Southern California is a paradise for sports lovers.

Baseball – The Los Angeles *Dodgers, Dodger Stadium* (1000 Elysian Park Ave.; phone: 224-1500); California *Angels, Anaheim Stadium* (2000 State College Blvd., Anaheim; phone: 625-1123 or 714-937-6700).

Basketball – The NBA *Lakers* play at the *Great Western Forum* (Manchester Blvd. and Prairie Ave., Inglewood; phone: 412-5000 for information; 673-1300 for tickets). The *Clippers* play at the *LA Memorial Coliseum and Sports Arena* (3939 S. Figueroa; phone: 748-6131).

Bicycling – Biking is great around the Westwood UCLA campus, Griffith Park, and on the oceanside, where there is a 19-mile bike path between the city of Torrance and Pacific Palisades.

Fishing – Power and sailing boats can be rented from *Rent-A-Sail* (13719 Fiji Way, Marina del Rey; phone: 822-1868). Fishermen catch halibut, bonito, and bass off the LA shores. Sportfishing boats leave daily from San Pedro, 22 minutes from downtown Los Angeles, site of the LA port, and from the Redondo Beach Marina in Redondo Beach.

Fitness Centers – *Nautilus and Aerobics Plus,* on the ground floor of the International Tower Building (888 Figueroa St.; phone: 488-0095), offers aerobics classes and has a Jacuzzi and sauna. It also has branches all over the metropolitan area. Many hotels have their own health clubs (see *Checking In*).

Football – Champions of the Big 10 and Pacific 10 college conferences meet in the *Pasadena Rose Bowl* every *New Year's Day*. UCLA plays its home games at the *Rose Bowl*, and USC plays at the *Coliseum* (3911 S. Figueroa; phone: 747-7111). The NFL *Rams* play at *Anaheim Stadium* (phone: 625-1123 or 714-937-6767).The NFL *Raiders* kick off at the *Coliseum*.

Hockey – The *Kings* make their home at the *Great Western Forum*, Manchester and Prairie, Inglewood (phone: 673-1300 or 480-3232 for tickets).

Horse Racing – If you like to spend your nights at the track, make tracks for *Los Alamitos*. There's harness, quarterhorse, and thorough-bred racing year-round during the *Orange County Fair Meet*. Take Free-way 605 south to Katella Avenue exit in Orange County (phone: 431-1361 or 714-995-1234). If you prefer daytime action, try *Hollywood Park* between mid-April and late July and from early November to *Christmas Eve*. Near Los Angeles International Airport between Manchester and Century Blvds. (phone: 419-1500). There's also thoroughbred racing at *Santa Anita Park* (Huntington Dr. and Baldwin Ave., Arcadia; phone: 818-574-7223), from late December to mid-April and October through November.

Jogging – Downtown, run around Echo Park Lake — during the day only — (a little less than a mile); get there by going up Sunset and taking a right onto Glendale. In Griffith Park, run in the woodsy Ferndale area near the Vermont Avenue entrance; get to the park via the Golden State Freeway and watch for the sign to turn off. In Westwood, UCLA has a hilly 4-mile perimeter course and a quarter-mile track. Four blocks from Century City, Cheviot Hills Park (at 2551 Motor Ave.) has a runners' course. And in Beverly Hills, jog in Roxbury Park (entrance at 471 S. Roxbury Dr. and Olympic) or along the 1½-mile stretch of Santa Monica Boulevard between Doheny and Wilshire. Jogging also is popular along the oceanside bike path between Marina del Rey and the Palos Verdes Peninsula, in Santa Monica's Palisades Park on Ocean Avenue, and along San Vicente Boulevard from Brentwood to Ocean Avenue.

Swimming and Surfing – The best beaches for swimming: El Porto Beach in Manhattan Beach, Will Rogers State Beach in Pacific Palisades, and Zuma Beach, north of Malibu. For surfing, Malibu Surfrider Beach, Hermosa Beach, El Porto Beach, and Zuma Beach are tops.

THEATER: There is no shortage of stages in LA, despite the overshadowing presence of the film industry. The *Center Theater Group* performs at the *Music Center*'s *Ahmanson Theater* and *Mark Taper Forum*. For information about either, call 972-7211. Also downtown is the *Los Angeles Theatre Center* (514 S. Spring St.; phone: 627-5599). The revived *State Theatre of California* is at the *Pasadena Playhouse* (39 S. El Molina Ave.; phone: 818-356-7529). Other Los Angeles theaters include the *Doolittle Theatre* (1615 N. Vine St., Holly-wood; phone: 462-6666); the *Shubert Theatre* (in the ABC Entertain-ment Center, 2020 Ave. of the Stars, Century City; for information and credit card reservations, call 800-233-3123); the *Odyssey Theatre Ensem-ble* in three small theaters (2055 S. Sepulveda; phone: 477-2055); and the *Pantages Theatre* (6233 Hollywood Blvd.; phone: 410-1062). Tickets for all major events can be ordered over the telephone through *Ticketron* (phone: 410-1062) or from *Ticketron* outlets at most *Tower Records* stores; call 642-4242 for the nearest location.

MUSIC: All kinds of music can be heard in LA's concert halls and clubs. The *Los Angeles Philharmonic* plays at the *Dorothy Chandler Pavilion, Music Center* (phone: 972-7211). The *Holly-wood Bowl* (2301 N. Highland Ave., Hollywood; phone: 850-2000) is a

17,630-seat hillside amphitheater that features famous guest entertainers as well as being the summer home of the *Philharmonic.* Leading popular performers in a wide range of musical styles play year-round at the *Universal Amphitheatre* (Hollywood Fwy. at Lankershim Blvd.; phone: 818-980-9421). The *Greek Theatre* (2700 N. Vermont Ave.; phone: 410-1062) is a 6,200-seat indoor theater with concerts by top names. The *Roxy Theatre* (9009 Sunset Blvd.; phone: 276-2222) is also good for concerts. For country-and-western music, check out the *Palomino Club* (6907 Lankershim Blvd., North Hollywood; phone: 818-983-1321). Rock and jazz buffs should try the *Palace* (1735 N. Vine, near Hollywood and Vine; phone: 462-3000), where the rock theater–dance club downstairs often has live shows as well as dancing. Upstairs, the *Palace Court* has live jazz on weekends.

NIGHTCLUBS AND NIGHTLIFE: Anything goes in LA, especially after dark. Swinging nightspots open and close quickly, since the restless search for what's "in" keeps people on the move. *Doug Weston's Troubador Club* pioneered a number of top rock music acts (9081 Santa Monica Blvd., West Hollywood; phone: 276-6168). Another place that seems to be able to hold its own is *Whisky A Go Go* (8901 Sunset Blvd.; phone: 652-4202). With Movietown's pool of talent, comedy clubs are a better bet than elsewhere. Among the options: *Improvisation,* the grandparent of them all (8162 Melrose Ave.; phone: 651-2583 and at 321 Santa Monica Blvd., Santa Monica; phone: 394-8664); the *Comedy Store* is another survivor (8433 Sunset Blvd.; phone: 480-3232); and the Chicago company *Second City* now has a second home in the nation's second city (214 Santa Monica Blvd., Santa Monica; phone: 451-0621). Other nightspots include *Roxbury's* (8225 Sunset, West Hollywood; phone: 656-1750), the latest "in" place for celebrities and the wanna-be crowd. There are 3 levels for entertainment such as live blues, a good restaurant, and an exclusive VIP. room. At *Vertigo* in downtown LA (333 S. Boylston; phone: 747-4849), a well-heeled crowd gathers on weekend nights to dine and dance until 4 AM. The *China Club* (1600 Argyle, Hollywood; phone: 469-1600) is a dark, Hollywood hangout for the young and restless, where the dancing is only superceded by looking cool. Mick Fleetwood's (of the rock group, *Fleetwood Mac*) 2-level blues supper club, *Fleetwood's* (8290 Santa Monica Blvd., West Hollywood), features "*cuisine de soleil*" and southside Chicago–style blues.

BEST IN TOWN

CHECKING IN: Los Angeles is the city where mere mortals stand the best chance of checking in alongside a movie star, although, obviously, it costs more for the possible privilege of rubbing shoulders with cinematic royalty. If you're looking for someplace simply to shower and sleep, you'll be happier at one of the smaller hotels or motels sprinkled throughout the area. Generally speaking, accommodations are less expensive in the San Fernando and San Gabriel valleys than in Hollywood or downtown. Expect to pay $200 and up for a double room at those places we've bracketed as very expensive; between $140 and $200 at those places listed as expensive; between $80 and $140 at moderate places; and under $80 at inexpensive places. (Be sure to ask about special "commercial" rates and "weekend" package deals.) For statewide bed and breakfast accommodations, contact *Eye Openers Bed & Breakfast* (PO Box 694, Altadena, CA 91001; phone: 684-4428 or 818-797-2055) or *California Houseguests International* (605 Lindley Ave., Suite 6, Tarzana, CA 91356; phone: 818-344-7878). All telephone numbers are in the 213 area code unless otherwise indicated. Twenty-four hour room service is the norm, unless otherwise demarcated.

Bel-Air – A beautiful California-Mediterranean–style expanse, splashed with purple and magenta bougainvillea and surrounded by splendid gardens (and a pond complete with swans), it has been completely renovated and now offers 59 rooms, 33 suites, and lovely public areas. Set on 11½ acres in a lushly overgrown canyon, it's as private as you're likely to want, and you'll need a car if you plan to leave the plush premises. (It's a member of the prestigious French Relais & Châteaux group.) Consider dining on the spot; the restaurant is excellent and beautiful. Meeting rooms accommodate up to 200, and other business services include secretarial assistance, photocopiers, and A/V equipment. There's also a concierge desk. 701 Stone Canyon Rd. (phone: 472-1211 800-648-4097, outside California; Fax: 213-476-5890; Telex: 674151). Very expensive.

Beverly Hills – The *Polo Lounge* is a famous watering spot for movie moguls and producers. Under the ownership of the Brunei Investment Agency, renovation (which is proceeding gently and gradually) is freshening up the 268 rooms without destroying the hotel's old charm. Room decor may vary slightly, but new colors are predominantly pastel, and bathrooms are richer with the addition of much marble and private Jacuzzis. Until the renovation is complete, however, be sure to ask for one of the newly done rooms. There's also the *Dining Room,* touting a celebrity menu — food personally recommended by the stars to the hotel. Among the items, there's Elizabeth Taylor's chili and Johnny Carson's whitefish. Show-biz action is pretty heavy at poolside. Stargazers can watch enraptured from a cabana while eating lunch and chatting on one of the poolside private phones. Other amenities include express checkout, concierge, secretarial services, A/V equipment, and photocopiers. 9641 Sunset Blvd., Beverly Hills (phone: 276-2251; 800-283-8885; Fax: 213-271-0319; Telex: 188580). Very expensive.

Checkers – Geared to the particular needs of the business traveler, this 190-room property in the center of Los Angeles's financial district has conference rooms, fax machines, 24-hour room service, secretarial and courier services, and interpreters. Rooms have multiline telephones with direct international dialing and call waiting capabilities. To ease the stress of the work day, this elegant hostelry also offers many non-commercial amenities, including a guest library for the mind, and a rooftop spa with sauna, steamroom, and exercise equipment for the body. And for mixing business with pleasure, *Checkers* restaurant, open for "power" breakfasts and lunches, as well as dinners, serves sophisticated American fare. A complimentary limo is available to downtown business locations. Four complimentary newspapers are available each day for guests' perusal. Additional conveniences include secretarial services, A/V equipment, photocopiers, and modems for computer and fax outlets are in all the rooms. There's also a concierge desk. 535 South Grand Ave. (phone: 624-0000 or 800-628-4900; Fax: 213-626-9906; Telex: 403525CHECKERS). Very expensive.

Doubletree – Across the road from Marina del Rey — the world's largest manmade small-craft harbor — this 338-room, seaside resort — with ocean and mountain views — is a short ride (by free shuttle) from the airport. Sailing, jogging, swimming, and bicycling are among the relaxing amenities. Two restaurants are on the property. Meeting rooms can accommodate up to 700, concierge, secretarial services, photocopiers, A/V equipment, and express checkout. 4100 Admiralty Way (phone: 301-3000 or 800-528-0444; Fax: 213-301-6890; Telex: 183365). Very expensive.

L'Ermitage – No relation to the restaurant of the same name, it has a

European ambience, 112 suites with kitchens, a rooftop Jacuzzi and pool, a piano lounge, and its own fine *Café Russe,* open only to guests and their guests. It is very well run and blissfully low key. Parking available. Business amenities include a concierge desk, secretarial services, A/V equipment, and photocopiers. 9291 Burton Way, Beverly Hills (phone: 278-3344; 800-424-4443; Fax: 213-278-8247; Telex: 4955516LEGG). Very expensive.

Four Seasons – In a residential area on the Los Angeles–Beverly Hills border, just a mile from Rodeo Drive, this luxurious property offers an unusual location. But then, there is very little about this hotel that could be considered "usual." With formal gardens and lifelike J. Seward Johnson statues outside, and marble floors, antiques, fresh flowers, and plants inside, it has the feel of a plush manor house, despite being a modern 16-story high-rise. The 285 rooms are more than ample, luxuriously appointed, and soothingly pastel, offering such amenities as a lighted makeup mirror in each bathroom, overnight clothes pressing, and shoe shines. On the fourth-floor rooftop terrace is a heated pool/spa area surrounded by palm trees and lounge chairs, with a small exercise area nearby. Topping off the impressive list are 2 restaurants, including *Gardens,* one of the more interesting hotel dining spots. Computer modems are located in all the rooms. Other conveniences include concierge, meeting rooms for up to 500, secretarial services, A/V equipment, photocopiers, and express checkout. 300 S. Doheny Dr. (phone: 273-2222; 800-332-3442; Fax: 213-859-3824; Telex: 00194364). Very expensive.

J. W. Marriott – On spacious grounds in Century City, this is Marriott's West Coast luxury flagship, in fashionable château style. The lobby is opulent yet intimate, with art objects, plants, and a resident live cockatoo. The hotel features 375 rooms, of which more than half are suites, and indoor and outdoor pools. Room decor runs to warm beige and peach. Among the extra-special touches: loofahs and natural sponges on tub edges. There's a concierge desk and express checkout. Meeting rooms hold up to 300, and secretarial services, A/V equipment, photocopiers, and computers all are on call. 2151 Ave. of the Stars (phone: 277-2777; 800-228-9290; Fax: 213-785-9240). Very expensive.

Park Hyatt – This 198-room property offers a relaxed yet sophisticated beachfront setting. Frette linen from Italy is a luxury, as are VCRs, marble baths, Jacuzzis, and speakerphones. Executive suites have wood-burning fireplaces and full ocean views. Fine seafood dining is found at *The Santa Monica Beach Club,* and the *Café Soleil,* on the beach promenade, offers indoor/outdoor casual dining. The up-to-date health spa and fitness center offers massages as well as beauty treatments. Business amenities include meeting rooms for up to 600, concierge, secretarial services, A/V equipment, photocopiers, computers, and express checkout. 1 Pico Blvd. Santa Monica (phone: 392-1234; 800-233-1234; Fax: 213-458-6478). Very expensive.

Peninsula Beverly Hills – European marble, polished wood, sumptuous antiques, and local artwork are just some of the impressive refinements. This property with 200 rooms, suites, and villas is the newest in Beverly Hills, situated in meticulously landscaped gardens with fountains. Suites are equipped with private fax machines, VCRs, and CD players. An additional 16 rooms and suites are located in 5 villas, some of which offer private terraces and fireplaces. A health spa features a weight room, lap pool, whirlpool, steam/sauna sundeck, and masseuses. There also is a terrace dining and 12 poolside cabañas equipped with telephones. The business center offers secretarial services, A/V equipment, photocopiers, and computers. On every floor, a 24-hour room attendant is at guests' beck and call. CNN and express checkout also are available. *The Living Room,* a lobby lounge, serves traditional afternoon tea, and *The Belvedere* is a top-notch continental restaurant. 9882 Santa Monica Blvd., Beverly Hills (phone: 273-4888; 800-462-7899; Fax: 213-858-6663). Very expensive.

Regent Beverly Wilshire – Just walk out the front door into the middle of the elegant Beverly Hills shopping district. The mood of this Regent group hotel is more businesslike and subdued (i.e., authentically elegant), less Hollywood flash than at spots like the *Beverly Hills.* In the tower wing, all the rooms are done in different color schemes, furniture styles, and themes. The renovated Wilshire Wing (our favorite) has 147 units, as well as 3 restaurants (the *Dining Room* is the best) and bars. There are 459 rooms in all, and the bathrooms are the best in LA. Meeting rooms hold up to 850. Other services include a concierge desk, secretarial assistance, photocopiers, A/V equipment, computers, and express checkout. 9500 Wilshire Blvd., Beverly Hills (phone: 275-5200 or 800-545-4000; Fax: 213-274-3709; Telex: 698220). Very expensive.

St. James's Club – An Art Deco gem, this lavishly restored apartment tower once played host to the likes of Clark Gable and Marilyn Monroe. To rub shoulders with today's celebrities (Joan Collins and Quincy Jones are members) and feel like English nobility in an exclusive club, non-members may check into the 18 rooms and 44 suites when available or buy a meal at the *Members' Room.* Fred Astaire in top hat and tails would have felt right at home in the stylish 1930s lobby, tapping down stairs carved out of a block of marble. Business amenities include concierge, meeting rooms that seat up to 200; secretarial services, A/V equipment, photocopiers, and express checkout. 8358 Sunset Blvd. (phone: 654-7100; Fax: 213-654-9287; Telex: 4979817). Very expensive.

Sheraton Grande – Pampering on a grand scale — the only hotel in town with personal butler service in every room, and other amenities beyond the call of duty. The 469 rooms are tastefully decorated, with plenty of living and work space. Conference and entertainment space is all first class and includes a ballroom, meeting rooms, teleconferencing, and, during the day, use of a 4-movie-theater complex in the building. There's a pool (but no health club), and each guest receives a complimentary membership to the *YMCA,* with its gym, running track, and courts, right across the street via a pedestrian bridge. Meeting rooms can accommodate up to 600, and there are secretarial and concierge services, A/V equipment, photocopiers, computer modems in all the rooms, video message system, and express video checkout. 333 S. Figueroa (phone: 617-1133; 800-325-3535; Fax: 213-613-0291; Telex: 677003). Very expensive.

Westwood Marquis – A favorite among businessfolk who appreciate quality. Originally built to house UCLA students, it has been converted to first class digs. The attractive high-rise holds 258 suites, and the bustling college town of Westwood is all around. The *Garden Terrace Room* is popular for Sunday brunch, and the elegant *Dynasty Room* (see *Eating Out*) serves classic California-cum-French food (dinner only). The UCLA running track is less than a half-mile away. There's also a lovely pool surrounded by cabañas. Secretarial assistance is available, as well as A/V equipment, photocopiers, computers, CNN, and express checkout. There's also a concierge desk. 930 Hilgard Ave., Westwood (phone: 208-8765; 800-421-2317; Fax: 213-824-0355; Telex: 181835MARQUIS). Very expensive.

Bel Age – A sister property to the fine *L'Ermitage,* this hotel also is European in tone. Its 198 suites are gracefully decorated with hand-carved rosewood and pecan wood furnishings complemented by pastel color schemes. *La Brasserie* is the hotel's casual café; *Diaghilev,* its more formal dining room, serves Franco-Russe cuisine. Other amenities include a heated rooftop pool. Meeting rooms can accommodate up to 500, concierge, secretarial services, A/V equipment, and photocopiers. 1020 N. San Vicente Blvd., West Hollywood (phone: 854-1111; 800-424-4443; Fax: 213-854-0926; Telex: 49555516LEGG). Very expensive to expensive.

Century Plaza – The 750-room hotel and the 322-room tower (which boasts spectacular views from spacious rooms and private balconies) are run separately, but share many facilities. This is a favorite spot for convention-goers; the hotel has a full-service business center. There are several fine restaurants on the premises, the best being the California-continental *La Chaumière* (see *Eating Out*), and plenty of shops to browse in. In Century City, near the ABC Entertainment Center, it offers complimentary town car service for trips within a 5-mile radius. Meeting rooms accommodate up to 2,000, and additional business services include a concierge desk, secretarial services, A/V equipment, photocopiers, computers, and express checkout. 2025 Ave. of the Stars, Century City (phone: 277-2000; Fax: 213-551-3355; Telex: 215554). Very expensive (the Tower) to expensive.

Marina International – Don't be misled by the less-than-grand exterior, for the meandering tile walkways eventually lead to spacious accommodations in wooden, shingled buildings. There are 135 rooms, but the wisest course of action is to request one of the 25 bungalows that are decorated in soothing pastels. Although there is no restaurant on the premises, there are plenty within walking distance, and a continental breakfast and light fare are available in the downstairs coffee shop. There is a pool and a Jacuzzi, as well as complimentary airport shuttle service. The meeting rooms offer space for 110, and there are secretarial services, A/V equipment, and photocopiers available for guests' use. 4200 Admiralty Way, Marina del Rey (phone: 822-1010; 800-421-8145 or 800-8-MARINA within California; 800-882-4000 elsewhere in the US; Fax: 213-301-6687). Very expensive to expensive.

Marina del Rey – This casual, California-style property is practically a peninsula, for it is surrounded by boats on three sides. The 160 pastel-decorated rooms and suites have patios and balconies that give guests a fine seat along the waterfront. Request a "Main Channel" room for the best views. There are 2 restaurants, a pool, and complimentary airport shuttle service. Meeting rooms seat up to 120. Other business conveniences include concierge, secretarial services, A/V equipment, photocopiers, and express checkout. 13534 Bali Way, Marina del Rey (phone: 301-1000; 800-8-MARINA within California; 800-882-4000 elsewhere; Fax: 213-301-8167). Very expensive to expensive.

Ritz-Carlton Marina del Rey – This California outpost borders the world's largest pleasure-craft harbor. There are sailboats for rent and a shore promenade, as well as 3 tennis courts, a swimming pool and fitness center, and 306 rooms with traditional decor. The club-like *Grill* serves dinner; all meals are provided in *The Café*, which has both indoor and outdoor seating with marina views. Afternoon tea and after-dinner cordials are served in the handsome library and lounge. Transportation to and from LAX is complimentary. Business conveniences include meeting rooms that hold up to 800, secretarial services, concierge, A/V equipment, photocopiers. computers, and express checkout. 4375 Admiralty Way, Marina del Rey (phone: 823-1700; 800-241-3333; Fax: 213-823-2403). Very expensive to expensive.

Beverly Hilton – Many fans say this is the best of the whole Hilton-managed lot (it's owned by Merv Griffin). It's not quite as convenient to downtown Beverly Hills as the *Regent Beverly Wilshire,* but if you plan to spend a lot of time in the hotel you'll be happy here, since this is another one of those self-contained establishments that cater to every need. *Trader Vic's* is a consistently good restaurant, and *L'Escoffier* offers good food plus entertainment and dancing. Meeting rooms hold up to 1,200, and there are secretarial services, a concierge desk, A/V equipment, photocopiers, computers, and express checkout. 9876 Wilshire Blvd., Beverly Hills (phone: 274-7777; 800-922-5432; Fax: 213-285-1313; Telex: 194683HILTONBVHL). Expensive.

Biltmore – The grande dame of downtown hotels offers dramatic interiors that combine the classical architecture typical of European palaces with contemporary luxury. There are 700 well-appointed rooms, an indoor pool, and Jacuzzi. Other pluses include the fine French restaurant *Bernard's* and the *Grand Avenue* bar, with great jazz nightly. Business amenities include meeting rooms that hold up to 1,000, concierge, secretarial services, photocopiers, A/V equipment, and express checkout. 506 S. Grand Ave. (phone: 624-1011; 800-245-8673; Fax: 213-612-1545; Telex: 677686). Expensive.

Hyatt Regency – Top-to-bottom renovation has reduced the scale of the Hyatt-signature atrium and created 2 restaurants, the *Brasserie* and the *Pavan* (serving Northern Italian fare). This 487-room super-modern place is another convention favorite. Meeting rooms that hold up to 6,600, secretarial services, concierge, A/V equipment, photocopiers, and express checkout. 711 S. Hope St. (phone: 683-1234; Fax: 213-629-3230). Expensive.

Loews Santa Monica – Loews' first venture on the West Coast, this 349-room property provides 20th-century comfort in a 19th-century setting, an era when the area flourished as a resort community. A 5-story atrium affords spectacular Pacific views; there also is an extensive fitness center, an indoor/outdoor swimming pool, a Jacuzzi, and the beach a few steps away. The decor is Victorian-by-the-sea, with antique ironwork, cool Pacific colors, and marine themes in paintings and sculptures by local artists. There are 2 restaurants, the contemporary Italian *Riva* and the more casual *Coast Café*, and a lobby bar that also serves afternoon tea. There are 5 meeting rooms, secretarial services, concierge, A/V equipment, photocopiers, and express video checkout. 1700 Ocean Ave., Santa Monica (phone: 458-6700; Fax: 213-458-6721). Expensive.

Le Mondrian – This contemporary 188-room establishment on the Sunset Strip pays homage to Piet Mondrian and attracts rock stars, models, and other Hollywood types. The suites provide stunning city views, and the decor is upbeat and sophisticated. There's a pool, a fitness center, a beauty salon and a restaurant that features Northern Italian cooking. The jazz lounge provides entertainment nightly. Guests can compose a personal brochure itinerary at the state-of-the-art computer center, which also has drafting tables and video editing equipment for project work. Additional amenities include a concierge desk, meeting rooms that hold up to 120, secretarial services, photocopiers, and A/V equipment. 8440 Sunset Blvd., West Hollywood (phone: 650-8999; 800-424-4443; Fax: 213-650-5215; Telex: 4955516). Expensive.

Radisson Bel Air Summit – This spot underwent an extensive renovation and now has added amenities and a light, breezy atmosphere. All 162 rooms have balconies, and there is a swimming pool, tennis court, cocktail lounge, and dining room. Free parking. Meeting rooms accommodate 400. Secretarial services are available, as are A/V equipment, photocopiers, and express checkout. 11461 Sunset Blvd. (phone: 476-6571; 800-333-3333; Fax: 213-471-6310). Expensive.

Ritz-Carlton, Huntington – Pasadena's Spanish-style landmark, razed after it was declared earthquake-unsafe, has risen like the Phoenix as interpreted by Ritz-Carlton — a country estate setting on 23 acres. The 1920s building has been reconstructed; the imposing Alamo Arch at the entrance is back, as are restored Japanese horseshoe gardens, 6 cottages, and leaded crystal chandeliers. Add the hotel chain's signature dark woods, art and antiques in 385 guestrooms, the Olympic-size pool, Jacuzzi and fitness center, 3 tennis courts, 3 restaurants, and 3 lounges. Business facilities include meeting rooms that seat 1,000, concierge, secretarial services, A/V equipment, photocopiers, computers, and express checkout. 1401 S. Oak Knoll Ave., Pasadena (phone: 818-568-3900 or 800-241-3333; Fax: 818-568-3159). Expensive.

Sheraton at LAX – This conference center is at the airport and features 810 rooms, comprehensive convention facilities, and *Landry's,* a fine restaurant with an excellent sushi bar. Additional amenities include meeting rooms that can hold up to 800, concierge, secretarial services, A/V equipment, photocopiers, computers, and express checkout. 6101 W. Century Blvd. (phone: 642-1111; Fax: 213-410-1276; Telex: 4720230). Expensive.

Sofitel Ma Maison – The tail wagged the dog in the decision to build a château-style hotel as the proper setting for the airy, plant-filled reincarnation of the noted *Ma Maison* restaurant (see *Eating Out*). The broad, carved staircase, country French furniture, and gaily patterned wall-and-window treatments create a fittingly homey atmosphere in this 311-room property called "My House." The bistro, *La Cajole,* is an approximate re-creation of an old Parisian artists' hangout. On the Beverly Hills–Los Angeles border, it offers complimentary limousine service once a day to *Mann's Chinese Theatre* (6925 Hollywood Blvd., phone: 464-8111) and to Rodeo Drive. Additional pluses are meeting rooms that can accommodate 440, secretarial services, a 24-hour concierge desk, A/V equipment, photocopiers, and express checkout. 8555 Beverly Blvd. (phone: 278-5444; 800-233-1234; Fax: 213-657-2816; Telex: 4974782SOFITEL). Expensive.

Stouffer Concourse – If it's Tuesday, this must be LA — a mile from the airport, this 750-room hotel announces the day of the week — on its carpets: Every midnight, the new day of the week appears on the elevators' carpets. With travelers often adjusting to time changes from places as far away as the Orient, this amenity could save a day. There is an outdoor swimming pool and a health club, the *Trattoria Grande,* and the *Charisma Café.* No surcharge on a collect, 800-number, or credit card call. Twenty-one suites have private outdoor Jacuzzis. The meeting rooms seat up to 1,300. Additional amenities include a concierge desk, A/V equipment, photocopiers, and express checkout. 5400 W. Century Blvd., Los Angeles (phone: 216-5858 or 800-HOTELS; Fax: 213 645-8053; Telex: 5106017169). Expensive.

Valadon – Formerly a pink Art Deco apartment building, this *L'Ermitage* relative is considered one of the best bargains (a relative term in LA) in the city. The 107 rooms are all suites; some have balconies and kitchenettes. A favorite place for people in the music business and movie industry, who often stay here for weeks. There is a rooftop pool, a Jacuzzi, and tennis courts. Meeting rooms accommodate up to 50, and there are secretarial services and photocopiers. 900 Hammond St., West Hollywood (phone: 855-1115 or 800-424-4443 Fax: 213-657-9192; Telex: 4955516LEGG). Expensive.

Westin Bonaventure – This 1,474-room giant is a major downtown convention hotel. Its cylindrical mirrored towers are an LA skyline landmark, and it is especially convenient for downtown activities. An $18 million renovation has greatly enhanced the property. This city within a city has 20 restaurants and lounges. Extras are a concierge desk, meeting rooms that seat 3,000, secretarial services, A/V equipment, photocopiers, computers, and express checkout. 404 S. Figueroa St. (phone: 624-1000; Fax: 213-612-4800; Telex: 677628). Expensive.

Le Rêve – With 80 suites, this is the smallest and most modest sister hotel of *L'Ermitage* and the *Bel Age.* The decor and atmosphere are country French. There is a rooftop swimming pool, a Jacuzzi, self-service laundry, and full room service from early morning until 11 PM, but no restaurant. Secretarial services are on call, and there's also A/V equipment. 8822 Cynthia St., West Hollywood. (phone: 854-1114;

800-424-4443; Fax: 213-657-2623; Telex: 4955516LEGG). Expensive to moderate.

Barnabey's – Possibly the best value in Southern California, with the charm of an English country inn, less than 3 miles from the airport and within walking distance of Manhattan Beach. All rooms are furnished with antiques and come with breakfast. Dine in *Barnabey's* restaurant and drink in *Rosie's Pub.* Complimentary 24-hour shuttle service to the airport, beach, and shopping. Room service is available until 10 PM. Meeting rooms seat 125, and A/V equipment and photocopiers are available for guests' use. Sepulveda Blvd. at Rosecrans Ave., Manhattan Beach (phone: 545-8466; 800-552-5285; Fax: 213-545-8621). Moderate.

Century Wilshire – In Westwood, the movie theater capital of LA and home of UCLA, this 99-room place offers kitchen units, complimentary coffee, and continental breakfast. No room service is available. There's a concierge desk, and secretarial services can be arranged. Photocopiers also are on the premises. 10776 Wilshire (phone: 474-4506; 800-421-7223, outside California; Fax: 213-474-2535). Moderate.

Hollywood Roosevelt – Once the social center of old Hollywood, this 322-room establishment now has renovated LA–Spanish charm, if not much of its former glamour. And traces of tinseltown still remain — photographs of movie celebrities grace the walls, the Hollywood sign is up the hill, and the star-studded Walk of Fame is right outside. For those who want to make themselves glamorous, a swimming pool, Jacuzzi, and weight room are on the premises. No room service is available. Meeting rooms can accommodate up to 300, and there is a concierge desk, A/V equipment, photocopiers, and express checkout. 7000 Hollywood Blvd., Hollywood (phone: 466-7000; Fax: 213-462-8056; Telex: 194404 HOLLYROOSVLAS). Moderate.

Mikado Best Western – The twisting canyon roads separating Hollywood from the San Fernando Valley are among the most scenic parts of LA. Set between Coldwater and Laurel canyons, where cottages and modern abodes and wood homes hang dramatically from cliffs, propped up only by stilts, the 58-room hostelry has a pool, a Jacuzzi, a restaurant, and a cocktail lounge. Guests receive complimentary American breakfast. No room service is available, but there are photocopiers for guests' use. 12600 Riverside Dr. (phone: 818-763-9141; 800-433-2239 within California; 800-826-2759 elsewhere in the US). Moderate.

New Otani – Conveniently within walking distance of the *Music Center,* it has 448 rooms featuring Japanese luxury and service in a lovely garden-like setting offers a soothing respite from the madness of downtown LA. The suites offer an authentic tatami room and futon bedding, as well as deep bathtubs. *A Thousand Cranes* is its serene Japanese restaurant (see *Eating Out*). Amenities include a shopping arcade and a Japanese health club, as well as meeting rooms that hold up to 750, concierge, secretarial services, A/V equipment, photocopiers, and express checkout. 120 S. Los Angeles St. (phone: 629-1200; 800-252-0197 within California; 800-421-8795 elsewhere in the US; Fax: 213-622-0980; Telex: 4720429). Moderate.

Figueroa – Downtown's best buy, this venerable, still gracious Spanish hotel has tile floors, patio dining, a pool, and 280 large guestrooms. The *Lobby Cafe* serves three meals a day; the *Music Room,* featuring American cooking, is open for dinner only. There is no room service. Photocopiers are available. 939 S. Figueroa St. (phone: 627-8971; 800-331-5151 or 800-421-9092 outside California; Fax: 213-689-0305). Inexpensive.

Safari Inn – If you're planning to visit the studios in Burbank, this will be more convenient than the Beverly Hills or downtown LA hotels. The spacious valley environment also provides more of a sense of being in the open. 105 rooms. Meeting rooms can accommodate up to 50, and there are photocopiers. 1911 W. Olive Ave., Burbank (phone: 818-845-8586; 800-STAHERE; Fax: 818-845-0054). Inexpensive.

EATING OUT: These days, Los Angeles may be the country's most exciting restaurant town. Only the purest of purists still go completely by Escoffier's book. Through and through, ethnic places abound in all price ranges, while imaginative chefs meld superb raw materials, ethnic ingredients, and nutritional caveats into pots of culinary gold. Though popularity with the show-biz crowd is often inversely proportional to the quality of a kitchen and the maître d's treatment of non-celeb guests, good manners are creeping back. Regrettably, dining in din is still in, even when the food is exquisite, but some new restaurants have rediscovered the joy of calm. Our choices are below. Expect to pay $70 or much more for two at those places we've listed as expensive; $35 to $70 at places in the moderate category; and under $30 at places in the inexpensive category. Prices do not include drinks, wine, or tips. All telephone numbers are in the 213 area code unless otherwise indicated.

Bice – Huge portions of classic Northern Italian trattoria fare are complemented by the sophisticated and international atmosphere. This Beverly Hills offspring from Milan attracts the kind of crowd who practically dress to match Adam D. Tihany's "nouvelle deco" decor. The pasta and risotto dishes are peerless, and there is a wide array of veal, seafood, and meat entrées. The service is attentive and unobtrusive. Open daily for dinner, Mondays though Saturdays for lunch. Reservations advised. Major credit cards accepted. 301 N. Canon Dr., Beverly Hills (phone: 272-BICE). Expensive.

Campanile – There really is a campanile atop this eatery where Charlie Chaplin once had a studio. Two *Spago* (see below) alumni have struck out on their own, serving American food with Italian influences. A first class bakery is on the premises. Serves breakfast and dinner; closed Sundays. Reservations essential (the farther in advance the better). Major credit cards accepted. 624 S. La Brea Ave. (phone: 938-1447). Expensive.

Champagne – The owner/chef is American, but the food is French — traditional, contemporary, and spa. The crispy Norwegian salmon and the veal shanks are most popular, and the restaurant is simple, elegant, and blissfully quiet. Lunch on weekdays; closed for dinner on Mondays. Reservations advised. Major credit cards accepted. 10506 Little Santa Monica Blvd. (phone: 470-8446). Expensive.

Le Chardonnay – Dark carved woods, arched mirrors, and delicate French tiles replicate a romantic Parisian bistro from the Belle Epoque. Chardonnays by the dozen star on the wine list, and the array of desserts would fill the windows of a Parisian pâtisserie. The menu is cosmopolitan, with an emphasis on French. Closed Sundays; open for lunch weekdays. Reservations advised. Major credit cards accepted. 8284 Melrose Ave. (phone: 655-8880). Expensive.

Chasen's – An LA institution for over 50 years. People come here more for echoes of old Hollywood than for the food, although specialties such as hobo steaks, chicken pot pie, and chili have become downright trendy. Dinner only; closed Mondays. Reservations advised. American Express accepted. 9039 Beverly Blvd. (phone: 271-2168). Expensive.

La Chaumière – Despite its location — the fifth floor of the tower at the *Century Plaza* hotel in a bustling area off Santa Monica Boulevard — this dining room evokes the charm of a French country manor, where diners can look out over the city while enjoying such California-French inspirations as cold lobster stew with Japanese cucumbers or roast rack of Sonoma lamb with dried figs and peanut sauce. In addition to some of the best California vintages, the wine list offers fine French and German selections as well. Open nightly for dinner, lunch on weekdays only. Reservations advised. Major credit cards accepted. 2055 Ave. of the Stars (phone: 551-3360). Expensive.

Chinois on Main – It took the Austrian-born owner Wolfgang Puck (proprietor of *Spago*, too) to combine Oriental and French into a delicious melting pot. The decor is *outré* and the din so loud you may not want to return without your earplugs. The food is superb, with unlikely orchestrations, such as goose liver with pineapple and plum-cinnamon sauce, and the Chinese-style whole fish stuffed with ginger. Dinner nightly, lunch Wednesdays through Fridays. Reservations essential. Major credit cards accepted. 2709 Main St., Santa Monica (phone: 392-9025). Expensive.

Le Dôme – One of the most interesting of LA's French restaurants. It opened as a brasserie with various grilled dishes (the thick veal chop is wonderful), but added more traditional haute cuisine in response to patron pressure. The atmosphere is chic, understated, comfortable. Closed Sundays. Reservations necessary. Major credit cards accepted. 8720 Sunset Blvd. (phone: 659-6919). Expensive.

Dynasty Room – California-French food is served in an atmosphere that showcases original artwork and artifacts from China's T'ang Dynasty. Baby abalone and pink-lip scallops on green beans with sauce *citronette* is just one of several winning combinations. Much of the restaurant's popularity is probably owed to its "menu minceur," which offers health-conscious dinners — appetizer, main course, and dessert — that total less than 500 calories. Open daily for dinner. Reservations advised. Major credit cards accepted. *Westwood Marquis Hotel*, 930 Hilgard Ave., Westwood (phone: 208-8765). Expensive.

L'Ermitage – Successfully combining French chic with California casual, it remains a fine, classic French dining spot. Among the many excellent choices on the menu are such familiar standards as chicken consommé and ravioli, medaillons of trout in cabernet sauvignon sauce, artichoke and truffle salad and, for a proper finale, Burgundy-style poached pear with homemade vanilla ice cream. This special place shouldn't be wasted on just an ordinary night, so celebrate something — anything — while you're here (maybe you could wave bon voyage to the $100 or so you two might part with for dinner). Dinner only. Closed Sundays. Reservations necessary. Major credit cards accepted. 730 N. La Cienega Blvd. (phone: 652-5840). Expensive.

Geoffrey's – The wings of Eros beat here, for whether you fall in love with the expansive views of the Pacific, the tasty food, or your dinner companion, it's nigh impossible not to find contentment here. Rich, roasted garlic soup topped with parmesan cheese, addictive rosemary muffins, and hearty braised veal ribs are the stars of the menu. The gallant service continues through the end of the meal, when ladies are offered a rose. Open daily. Reservations advised. Major credit cards accepted. 27400 Pacific Coast Hwy. (phone: 457-1519). Expensive.

Michael's – Now that prices have dropped closer to the level of LA's other high-priced restaurants, this pioneer eatery — where California nouvelle was first new — just may be affordable. The gorgeous garden and contemporary art add visual pleasure to the gustatory feats. Dinner nightly, lunch weekdays, brunch on weekends. Reservations advised. Major credit cards accepted. 1147 Third St., Santa Monica (phone: 451-0843). Expensive.

L'Orangerie – Under high ceilings and among the potted palms you'll find one of the city's most attractive dining rooms and some of the most exciting dishes as well. The mostly French menu offers soft scrambled eggs topped with caviar, Atlantic bass and other fish flown in from Brittany twice a week, and first class desserts like the apple tart or a puff pastry filled with raspberries and sweet cream. Open daily for dinner. Reservations necessary. Major credit cards accepted. 903 N. La Cienega Blvd. (phone: 652-9770). Expensive.

Patina – Wunderchef Joachim Splichal finally acquired his own place (in the former *Le St. Germain*) and the house has been packed ever since it opened. The interior is stark and elegant, with no art save the wall sconces in the lively West of the Bar room. Splichal has mastered the art of presenting layers of flavors that awaken the palate. A meal of free-range chicken, French string bean salad, or potato lasagne filled with earthy mushrooms and truffle sauce cannot be considered without one of the excellent desserts, such as the corn *crème brûlée*. Open weekdays for lunch; daily for dinner. Reservations necessary. Major credit cards accepted. 5955 Melrose Ave. (phone: 467-1108). Expensive.

Remi – Evocative of a tony seaside Italian restaurant (even though it's 3 blocks from the sea), and named for Venetian gondoliers' oars, ambrosial Venetian fare is served in a casually elegant atmosphere. The rich wood, gleaming brass, and nautical theme provide an airy backdrop for this eatery, which presents dishes such as whole fish infused with herbs and a wonderful selection of grappas. The outdoor tables are ideal for people watching on Santa Monica's Third Street Promenade. Open daily. Reservations necessary. Major credit cards accepted. 1451 Third St. Promenade (phone: 393-6545). Expensive.

Le Restaurant – A quaint and unassuming decor provides the backdrop for yet another of LA's fine French establishments. All entrées and appetizers are carefully prepared. Service is just as meticulous. Closed Sundays. Reservations necessary. Major credit cards accepted. 8475 Melrose Pl. (phone: 651-5553). Expensive.

Rex Il Ristorante – Filled with Lalique, oak paneling, and brass, this downtown eatery in an Art Deco building duplicates the dining room of the *Rex*, an Italian passenger liner popular during the 1920s. Each evening there's a six-course special dinner or à la carte dining. There's a full bar featuring soft dance music on the mezzanine level. Closed Sundays; open for lunch Thursdays and Fridays. Reservations necessary. Major credit cards accepted. 617 S. Olive (phone: 627-2300). Expensive.

St. Estephe – The Southwestern cooking fad may be fading, but the chef who raised it to artistic heights in the Southland is not. Both the food and the beauty of presentation are still worth the pricey tab and the trip to Manhattan Beach (near the LA airport). Closed Sundays and Mondays; open for lunch Tuesdays through Fridays. Friday and Saturday dinner reservations advised. Major credit cards accepted. 2640 Sepulveda Blvd., Manhattan Beach (phone: 545-1334). Expensive.

La Serre – At this garden-like stronghold of classic French cooking in the San Fernando Valley, the chef whips up unusual sauces, such as cream of whisky and coffee to accompany fish, and concocts a fragrant sorbet of homegrown mint, jasmine, and roses. Lobster with different sauces is the most popular choice. Closed Sundays; open for lunch weekdays. Reservations necessary. Major credit cards accepted. 12969 Ventura Blvd., Studio City (phone: 818-990-0500). Expensive.

Spago – Owner Wolfgang Puck (see *Chinois on Main* and *Eureka*) describes his unusual menu as California cuisine. Although entrées include roasted baby lamb, grilled salmon and tuna, and pasta that's made daily, this place is best known for its unusual and changeable pizza — with toppings like duck sausage, goat cheese, oregano, and tomato, or smoked lamb, eggplant, and roasted peppers. Baked in a wood-burning brick oven, they arrive at the table sizzling hot and crispy. Open daily. Tops among the trendy set, so it's necessary to reserve about 3 weeks ahead. Major credit cards accepted. 1114 Horn Ave. at Sunset Blvd. (phone: 652-4025). Expensive.

La Toque – A fine French restaurant, arguably (and if there's one thing devotees of fine food and wine like to argue about, it's this) the best in the city. Small, intimate, very romantic, with a menu rewritten daily. Since only the freshest ingredients are used, the menu changes to reflect seasonal availability and quality. Usually at least four fish dishes; another four or more meat dishes, including, each autumn, game. Plus an extensive wine list — about half California labels — with some real treasures (for instance, the 1974 Beaulieu Vineyards Cabernet Reserve). Closed Sundays; open for lunch weekdays. Only 20 tables, so reservations necessary. Major credit cards accepted. 8171 Sunset Blvd. (phone: 656-7515). Expensive.

Valentino – Devotees generally describe the food as Italian, and the homemade pasta certainly bears them out. But there's also a world of other choices on the eclectic menu — starters such as timballo (rolled baby eggplant) or crespelle (corn crêpes stuffed with seafood) and entrées like grilled fresh shrimp wrapped with swordfish and dressed with lime juice. The casually elegant spot boasts an impressive wine cellar: more than 50,000 bottles, including Italian, French, German, and California labels. Closed Sundays; open for lunch Fridays. Reservations necessary. Major credit cards accepted. 3115 Pico Blvd., Santa Monica (phone: 829-4313). Expensive.

Windsor – This award-winning place is noted for its wide variety of beef dishes. Though the atmosphere is somewhat formal, it's particularly popular with the *Dodger Stadium* crowds. Closed Sundays; closed for lunch Saturdays. Reservations advised. Major credit cards accepted. 3198 W. 7th St. (phone: 382-1261). Expensive.

I Cuigini – *Raviolini verde alle noci* (spinach ravioli filled with ricotta and chard, topped with a creamy walnut sauce), authentic Caesar salad, and great homemade breads are some of the tempting selections. Breads also are for sale at their bakery, located on the premises. Open daily. Reservations advised. Most major credit cards accepted. 1501 Ocean Ave. (phone: 451-4595). Expensive to moderate.

Ivy – A favorite venue for lunchtime power deals, it is an anomaly — an old brick farmhouse on bustling Robertson Boulevard, bordering Beverly Hills. Its rustic decor is the perfect setting for the eclectic (with a Southern accent) American menu. The owner grows herbs, peppers, deep-red beefsteak tomatoes, and citrus for the kitchen. Corn chowder with fresh tarragon, warm mesquite-grilled salad with chicken or shrimp, and twice-cooked Cajun prime ribs — first oven-seared and then grilled — are standouts on the changing menu. Desserts are the likes of which mama could only dream of making. Open for lunch and dinner daily. Reservations necessary. Major credit cards accepted. 113 N. Robertson Blvd. (phone: 274-8303). Expensive to moderate.

Ma Maison – The garden-like room is restful and service is attentive yet unobtrusive. The David Hockney covers of the menu, which changes daily, are for sale. The fare is French-Californian, expertly and lightly sauced. You would never guess that the flourless ravioli enveloped with goat cheese and herbs are made of turnips. Open for lunch and dinner; closed Sundays. Reservations advised. Major credit cards accepted. 8555 Beverly Blvd. (phone: 278-5444). Expensive to moderate.

Orso – While the outside decor is extremely unassuming, this popular Northern Italian trattoria more than compensates for its decor inside, with the charming patio framed by fica trees and candlelit tables. Earthy country salads, pizza with all-but-transparent crusts, grilled meats, and delicious calf's liver are served on attractive Italian pottery plates. There is an extensive wine list as well. Well-known actors frequent this spot, and the bar becomes lively after theater hours. Open daily. Reservations advised. Most major credit cards accepted. 8706 West 3rd St. (phone: 274-7144). Expensive to moderate.

Pacific Dining Car – Steaks — cut on the premises from aged, corn-fed beef — are the house specialty, although the menu also offers four types of fresh fish every day. The layout is a real dining car (plus an additional building) that's been at its downtown location since 1921. This is a good place for early dinner or late supper when you have tickets for a show at the *Music Center*. Open 24 hours daily. Reservations necessary. Visa and MasterCard accepted. 1310 W. 6th St. (phone: 483-6000). Expensive to moderate.

Trumps – A recycled gas station has become a simply furnished, trend-setting California dining place. The art show changes from time to time, while the exotic duck with black beans and pickled pumpkin is perennially popular. Open daily for dinner and late supper; Mondays through Saturdays for lunch and tea. Reservations necessary 2 or 3 days ahead. Major credit cards accepted. 8764 Melrose Ave., West Hollywood (phone: 855-1480). Expensive to moderate.

Bistro Garden – The very same Beverly Hills celebrities who have parked their Rolls-Royces up the street at the *Bistro* for years have made its sister restaurant the "in" spot. Lunch is especially chic with fare like baked sea scallops with a muscat-ginger sauce. Closed Sundays. Reservations necessary. Major credit cards accepted. 176 N. Canon Dr., Beverly Hills (phone: 550-3900). Moderate.

Border Grill – For those still uninitiated into the world of Mexican food, this is a great place to allay fears of too-spicy dishes that become bad memories. This slip of an eatery, which dishes out green corn tamales and soft tacos, is one of our favorites. Open daily. Reservations unnecessary. Major credit cards accepted. 7407½ Melrose (phone: 658-7495). Moderate.

Carroll O'Connor's Place – Hollywood celebrities have really taken to the actor's local branch of New York's *Gingerman* (formerly with the same name). At dinner, the specialties are a good choice, and the country pâté makes a fine starter. Open for breakfast Mondays through Fridays; open for lunch and dinner except Sundays. Reservations advised. Major credit cards accepted. 369 N. Bedford Dr., Beverly Hills (phone: 273-7585). Moderate.

Celestino – The young Italian chef draws on his Sicilian roots and Tuscan training for a limited menu with innovative twists, such as the highly praised seafood baked in a paper bag. The restaurant is airy and unpretentious. The art exhibit changes and so does the menu. Open daily for dinner, weekdays for lunch. There's a wonderful Sunday brunch, and late-night suppers Fridays and Saturdays until 1 AM, accompanied by jazz until 2 AM. Reservations advised. Major credit cards accepted. 236 S. Beverly Dr. (phone: 859-8601). Moderate.

C'est Fan Fan – A former chef of *Chinois on Main* transformed a sushi bar into a showcase for French/Chinese nouvelle cuisine. The exotic fare includes Peking duck with Maine lobster, and pan-fried Chinese Dungeness crab. Closed Mondays and closed weekends for lunch. Reservations necessary for dinner. Major credit cards accepted. 3360 W. First Street (phone: 487-7330). Moderate.

Chez Mélange – This South Bay eatery is true to its name, offering an international variety of victuals. There is a vodka, oyster, and caviar bar; a wine bar with tastings on Tuesdays; and a dining room, all in a former coffee shop of a motor inn. Open daily for breakfast, lunch, and dinner. Reservations advised. Major credit cards accepted. 1716 Pacific Coast Hwy., Redondo Beach (phone: 540-1222). Moderate.

Chez Sateau – The setting for this elegant French eatery is Arcadia in the San Gabriel Valley, home of *Santa Anita* racetrack and the lovely LA State and County Arboretum, where Tarzan used to swing from trees for the camera. Closed Mondays; open for lunch Tuesdays through Fridays, brunch Sundays. Reservations necessary. Major credit cards accepted. 850 S. Baldwin Ave., Arcadia (phone: 818-446-8806). Moderate.

Il Cielo – A brick cottage, with several romantic dining rooms (a fireplace glows in the winter), and a heated patio. Its Northern Italian food is excellent. During quiet hours the staff treats guests as if they were at a family reunion. On a balmy evening, eating in the garden feels like dining in Tuscany. Closed Sundays. Reservations advised. Major credit cards accepted. 9018 Burton Way, Beverly Hills (phone: 276-9990). Moderate.

Engine Co. No. 28 – This converted firehouse re-creates an American grill of 50 years ago, with an old-fashioned menu spiced up with modern touches, such as scallop ceviche and marinated lentil salad. Recipes created by firehouse cooks from around the country make up the weekly specials. Don't miss the spicy fries. Dinner daily, lunch weekdays. Reservations advised. Major credit cards accepted. 644 S. Figueroa St. (phone: 624-6996). Moderate.

Eureka – Another dining adventure from the creative culinary world of Wolfgang Puck (of *Spago* fame), only this time it's earthy fare at down-to-earth prices. Homemade sausages, smoked meats, pretzels, and Puck's own *Eureka* beer, are served in an unlikely setting in the heart of West LA's warehouse district. Despite the location and the modest cost, the place still attracts a Rolls Royce crowd. Open Mondays through Fridays for lunch and dinner; dinner only on Saturdays and Sundays. Reservations advised. Major credit cards accepted. 1845 South Bundy Dr., entrance on Nebraska St., West Los Angeles (phone: 447-8000). Moderate.

Fresco – It looks Italian, and the menu sounds Italian, yet both stretch tradition with twists such as lobster and spinach filling for cannelloni, and duck in port sauce wrapped in corn crêpes. Closed Sundays; open for lunch weekdays. Reservations advised. Major credit cards accepted. 514 S. Brand Blvd., Glendale (phone: 818-247-5541). Moderate.

Gilliland's – The owner is Irish but the product is Californian — with an Irish accent, such as soda bread on Sundays. Open daily for dinner, weekdays for lunch, Sunday brunch. Reservations necessary on weekends. Major credit cards accepted. 2425 Main St. (phone: 392-3901). Moderate.

Joss – The austere decor makes this a high-style showcase for unfamiliar regional Chinese delicacies, such as glazed ginger venison with *quei hua* wine. The waiter shows off the whole perfectly crisped, golden brown Hong Kong Pin-Pei chicken before carving and preparing it in the style of Peking duck on a side table. Tangerine beef marinated in liqueur and garnished with peel has a novel taste. Open daily for dinner; closed for lunch on weekends. Reservations advised. Major credit cards accepted. 9255 Sunset Blvd. (phone: 276-1886). Moderate.

Lawry's the Prime Rib – What's billed is what you get — delicious prime ribs with horseradish sauce, perfect Yorkshire pudding, mashed potatoes, and salad — at this reliable eatery. The room is paneled but bright, the better to see the immense portions. Dinner daily. Reservations advised. Major credit cards accepted. 55 N. La Cienega Blvd., Beverly Hills (phone: 652-2827). Moderate.

Mandarin – Northern Chinese cooking in elegant surroundings instead of the usual plastic, pseudo-Oriental decor. Not on the menu, but well worth remembering as an appetizer, is the minced squab wrapped in lettuce leaves; also, be sure to try the spicy prawns. Open daily for dinner; closed Sundays for lunch. Reservations advised. Major credit cards accepted. 430 N. Camden Dr., Beverly Hills (phone: 272-0267). Moderate.

Matsuhisa – The fare here — Japanese with Peruvian accents — is described by its chef as "new wave seafood." The most popular dishes are squid cut like pasta, with an asparagus topping, and seafood with soy, *wasabe*, and garlic. Open daily for dinner, weekdays for lunch. Reservations necessary 2 to 3 days in advance. Major credit cards accepted. 129 N. La Cienega Blvd. (phone: 659-9639). Moderate.

Mon Kee's – Amazing seafood combinations are the draw at this bus-tling Chinese dining spot which caters to downtown LA's business crowd, as well as tourists. "Live" lobster, 15 squid dishes (try the crispy squid with special salt), steamed or fried salt- and freshwater fish are the mainstays of the seafood menu, and for those not com-pelled by the above or the conch, clams, or oysters, there are dozens of traditional pork, poultry, beef, and vegetable dishes by which to be dazzled. Open daily. Reservations advised. Major credit cards ac-cepted. 679 N. Spring St. (phone: 628-6717). Moderate.

Musso & Frank Grill – It really is a grill, in Hollywood since 1919, and apparently not redecorated once (not that its regulars — film people, journalists, the moiling LA middle class — want it to change one iota). Orthodox American food and the kind of place the cachet of which is having no cachet; it's okay if you like nostalgia and surly waiters. Try the sand dabs and creamed spinach. Open for lunch and dinner; closed Sundays. Reservations advised. Major credit cards accepted. 6667 Hollywood Blvd. (phone: 467-7788). Moderate.

Pane Caldo Bistro – An unpretentious Italian *ristorante* with a great view of the city's famed hills. What it lacks in fancy appointments, it more than makes up for with careful food preparation, generous por-tions, and reasonable prices. A complimentary appetizer and basket of *focaccia* arrive with the menu to ease the difficult task of choosing from among Tuscan specialties such as warm bell-pepper salad, risotto specials, tagliatelle with porcini mushrooms, spinach tortelloni with butter and sage, osso buco, and a selection of 14 kinds of individual pizza. Try the ultra-rich *tiramisù* for dessert. Open daily for lunch and dinner. Reservations advised. Major credit cards accepted. 8840 Bev-erly Blvd. (phone: 274-0916). Moderate.

Parkway Grill – California cooking is served in a cozy, informal Pasadena eatery without the glitz and prices of *Spago*. The innovative cooking features mesquite-grilled fish and game, fresh pasta, and pizza lovingly baked in an oak-burning oven. Its late hours make it conve-nient for supper after the theater or a concert. Open daily for dinner, weekdays for lunch, and Sundays for brunch. Reservations advised. Major credit cards accepted. 510 S. Arroyo Pkwy. (phone: 818-795-1001). Moderate.

Siamese Princess – This Oriental eatery, which predates the Thai proliferation, looks like an antiques shop. European furniture and collectibles vie for space with Siamese gift items and photos of British, Thai, and show-biz royalty. The food, billed as "Royal Thai" and beautifully presented, ranks high above run-of-the-mill. Slivers of or-ange peel turn rice noodles into a delicacy. Dinner daily; lunch Tues-days through Fridays. Reservations necessary. Major credit cards accepted. 8048 W. 3rd St. (phone: 653-2643). Moderate.

A Thousand Cranes – Besides having such a beautiful name, this Japa-nese spot is well versed in the traditional art of serving beautiful food. It has several tatami rooms and a Western dining room. Open daily. Reservations advised. Major credit cards accepted. *New Otani Hotel,* 120 S. Los Angeles St. (phone: 629-1200). Moderate.

Tulipe – The space is simple, the better to focus attention on two chefs performing their culinary abracadabras in the open-view kitchen. The food is French: classic and contemporary. Open daily for dinner, and Tuesday through Friday for lunch. Reservations necessary. Major credit cards accepted. 8360 Melrose Ave., West Hollywood (phone: 655-7400). Moderate.

California Pizza Kitchen – This expanding chain is a *Spago* disciple's pop version of pizzeria à la California. Bright, sunny interiors with yellow ceilings and flowering plants show off the big, white-tiled wood ovens, which turn out the crusts for "design" toppings from Peking-style duck to goat cheese. Chrome-accented chairs and black tables recall Milan modern, but neither pizzerias nor pizza have ever been dressed like these in Italy. Pasta, salads, and desserts also are on the menu. Open mid-morning to late evening daily. Reservations unnecessary, but be prepared to wait. Major credit cards accepted. 207 Beverly Dr., Beverly Hills (phone: 272-7878) and other locations. Inexpensive.

Chicago Pizza Works – The pizza are deep-dish style and served with your choice of a wide range of toppings. Other offerings include lasagna, spaghetti, salads, and desserts. There also are over 100 beers from which to choose. Open daily. Reservations unnecessary. Visa and MasterCard accepted. 11641 W. Pico Blvd. (phone: 477-7740). Inexpensive.

Chin Chin – Delicious dim sum and traditional Chinese food, cooked without MSG, account for its ongoing popularity; so, too, its quick service and low prices. Takeout also is available. Open daily. Reservations unnecessary. Most major credit cards accepted. Four locations: 8618 Sunset Blvd., Sunset Plaza (phone: 652-1818); 11740 San Vicente Blvd., Brentwood (phone: 826-2525); 12215 Ventura Blvd., Studio City (phone: 985-9090); and 13455 Maxella Ave., Marina del Rey (phone: 823-9999). Inexpensive.

El Cholo – LA is glutted with places promising authentic south-of-the-border cooking, but this is the best, without question. Around for more than 60 years, its burritos and combination plates are real knockouts. Open daily. There's usually a wait even with reservations; they're advised anyway. Major credit cards accepted. 1121 S. Western Ave. (phone: 734-2773). Inexpensive.

Chopstix – A small chain turning out novel variations on Chinese themes, including Chinese pizza. Open daily for lunch and dinner (closes late). No reservations. Major credit cards accepted. Main location: 7229 Melrose Ave. (phone: 937-1111). Inexpensive.

Hamayoshi – One of the reasons Japanese diplomats request appointments to Los Angeles is this sushi bar for connoisseurs favoring flatfish of all kinds — a list not to be equaled at almost any other sushi house. The place is small and simple, and customers sometimes have to wait outside for a spot. Free parking. Open daily for dinner; for lunch weekdays. Reservations advised. Major credit cards accepted. 3350 W. 1st St. (phone: 384-2914). Inexpensive.

Katsu – Sushi artistry in both preparation and presentation, in a stark setting. How much you pay depends entirely on the number of tidbits you order, and you can check each one off on your own list at the table. Traditional Japanese dishes also are served. Dinner nightly; lunch weekdays. Reservations necessary. Major credit cards accepted. 1972 Hillhurst Ave. (phone: 665-1891).

Original Pantry – The decor is early greasy spoon — the food, waiters, and prices ditto — yet long lines at lunch have forced expansion after 66 years. A potful of raw vegetable sticks precedes big portions of basic food. If the mood for a big American breakfast strikes at 3 AM, one might even find a parking place outside. Open nonstop. Reservations unnecessary. No credit cards accepted. 877 S. Figueroa (phone: 972-9279). Inexpensive.

Twin Dragon – As inexpensive as Chinese food used to be, with a solid repertoire of topnotch Northern Chinese dishes. A lot of families bring their children here, but it's not too noisy. Open daily. Reservations advised. Major credit cards accepted. 8597 W. Pico Blvd. (phone: 657-7355). Inexpensive.

And finally, for dessert, try the luscious ice cream made by *Robin Rose,* at 215 Rose Ave. in Venice. Also sold in Old Pasadena (at 35 S. Raymond St.; phone: 818-577-7676); downtown in the Wells Fargo Center (333 S. Grand Ave.; phone: 687-8815); and in Brentwood (11819 Wilshire Blvd.; phone: 445-2771).

LOUISVILLE

AT-A-GLANCE

SEEING THE CITY: The *Spire* restaurant and cocktail lounge on the 19th floor of the *Hyatt Regency Louisville* revolves to show views of downtown Louisville, the Ohio River, and, when it's not too hazy, southern Indiana across the river. 320 W. Jefferson (phone: 587-3434).

SPECIAL PLACES: The best way to get around Louisville is by car. You can hop a trolley or walk around downtown, but attractions like *Churchill Downs,* historic homes, and the lovely surrounding countryside a few miles from the center of town require transportation.

Museum of History and Science – Space Hall, a 360-degree IMAX movie theater, the "mummy's tomb," and exhibitions on caves and the Ohio River Valley will appeal to children as well as adults. Open daily. Admission charge. 727 W. Main St. (phone: 561-6100).

Louisville Falls Fountain – In the middle of the Ohio River, "the world's largest floating fountain" creates 375-foot-high sprays, watery fleur-de-lis (the city symbol), and other special water and light effects. Daily, May through October. Best viewing is from Riverfront Plaza/Belevedere, north of Main St., between 4th Ave. and 6th St.

Kentucky Center for the Arts – Music, dance, and theater are on the bill at the city's performing arts center. There's also a restaurant and gift shop, and visitors are welcome. 5 Riverfront Plaza, at 6th and Main Sts. (phone: 584-7777).

Star of Louisville – An elegant way to see the area is aboard this 130-foot luxury yacht, which leisurely cruises the Ohio River. Well-prepared, abundant lunch and dinner buffets include dishes such as snow crab and New York strip steak. After dinner, diners can kick up their heels to a three-piece jazz-pop combo. There are 2-hour lunch cruises, 3-hour dinner cruises year-round; weekend cocktail cruises are offered spring through fall. 4th St. Wharf at the foot of 2nd St. on River Rd. (589-7827).

Humana Building – The Humana health care company conducted an international competition to design its new corporate headquarters; the result is New Jersey architect Michael Graves's 27-story pink granite tower. A 25th-floor curved terrace features a rotunda and loggia with a 50-foot waterfall, the latter a thematic tribute to the Ohio River. Free tours Saturdays, 10 AM to 1:30 PM. 500 West Main St.; use the 5th St. entrance for tours (phone: 580-3600).

Louisville Zoological Gardens – The zoo offers a pleasant afternoon outing for the whole family, but be prepared to do some walking. An up-close-and-personal polar bear exhibit and HerpAquarium (which includes amphibians and reptiles), with its simulated rain forest, are favorites of the crawling crowd. Closed Mondays in winter. Admission charge. 1100 Trevilian Way (phone: 459-2184).

Main Street Façades – West Main Street between 6th and 10th boasts the largest collection of 19th-century cast-iron façades found outside New York City. The Preservation Alliance offers a free map which details a walking tour of the area, and has custom-designed tours for groups. 7th and Main Sts. (phone: 583-8622).

Belle of Louisville – Board a 19th-century–style steamboat for a nostalgic, scenic cruise on the Ohio River. Afternoon cruises daily, *Memorial Day* through *Labor Day* weekend (except Mondays), with Saturday evening dance cruises. Tickets are available at the steamer office (4th Ave. and River Rd.) or in the boarding line at the foot of 4th Ave. (phone: 625-2355).

Farmington – Built according to Thomas Jefferson's plans, the 19th-century home of Judge John Speed is an outstanding example of Federal architecture. Open daily. Admission charge. 3033 Bardstown Rd. (phone: 452-9920).

Old Louisville – The homes in Old Louisville (2nd to 6th Sts. and Ormsby to Eastern Pkwy.) are fine examples of 19th-century Victorian architecture. You can visit the information center Mondays through Thursdays, year-round, for a free walking tour. 1340 S. 4th St. in Central Park (phone: 635-5244).

Locust Grove – Another fascination for architecture fans, this Georgian plantation was the last home of George Rogers Clark. Open daily. Admission charge. 561 Blankenbaker La. (phone: 897-9845).

Churchill Downs/Kentucky Derby Museum – By far Louisville's most popular attraction, the *Kentucky Derby* draws close to 100,000 people to *Churchill Downs* on the first Saturday in May. The twin-spired track is packed with fans sipping mint juleps, shedding a few tears at the sound of "My Old Kentucky Home," and if they're lucky, catching a glimpse of some of the world's most expensive horseflesh. If you can stand the unabashed sentimentality, the crowds, and the expense (accommodations are sold at a substantial premium on *Derby* weekend), the *Derby* is worth the trip — at least once. Reserved seats for the race are hard to come by (they're held by box owners), but all you need to join the general admission party in the infield is $20 — and a lot of nerve. For information, write to *Churchill Downs,* Derby Ticket Office, 700 Central Ave., Louisville, KY 40208 (phone: 636-4400).

There are several *Kentucky Derby* tour package offerings which are probably the best bet for anyone hoping to get to see this prestigious event. Contact *Travel Services, Inc.* (374 Starks Bldg., 455 Fourth Ave., Louisville, KY 40202; phone: 587-1234); *Wagon-lits Travel USA* (211 Holiday Manor Center, Louisville, KY 40222-6463; phone: 425-1078 or 800-866-9882); *Delta Queen Steamboat Co.* (Robin Street Wharf, New Orleans, LA 70130-1890; phone: 800-543-1949); or *Frontier Travel & Tours* (1923 N. Carson St., Suite 105, Carson City, NV 89701; phone: 800-647-0800).

The spring meet begins in May; closing dates vary. The fall meet varies from year to year. At other times the grounds are open. At the *Kentucky Derby Museum,* you can view racing memorabilia, watch a 360-degree panorama on the race, and through "hands-on" exhibits test your *Derby* trivia skills and explore the mysteries of pari-mutuel betting. Open daily except *Oaks Day* (the Friday before *Derby*), *Derby Day, Thanksgiving,* and *Christmas.* Admission charge. 700 Central Ave. (phone: 637-1111).

■ **EXTRA SPECIAL:** Kentucky history comes to life in Bardstown, about 40 miles south of Louisville. At My Old Kentucky Home State Park, visitors can tour the Federal mansion that inspired Stephen Foster to write what is now the state song. Open daily except Mondays in January and February; admission charge (phone: 348-3502). An outdoor drama, *The Stephen Foster Story,* is presented from June through September in the park. The *Oscar Getz Museum of Whiskey* chronicles the history of one of Kentucky's most famous products. Open daily, except Mondays in winter (phone: 348-2999). You can see how whiskey is made today at Maker's Mark Distillery, weekdays

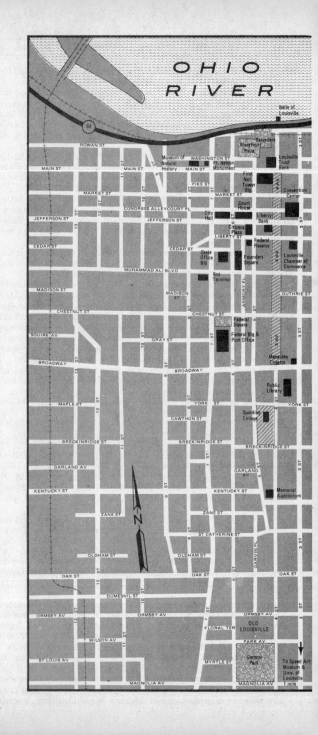

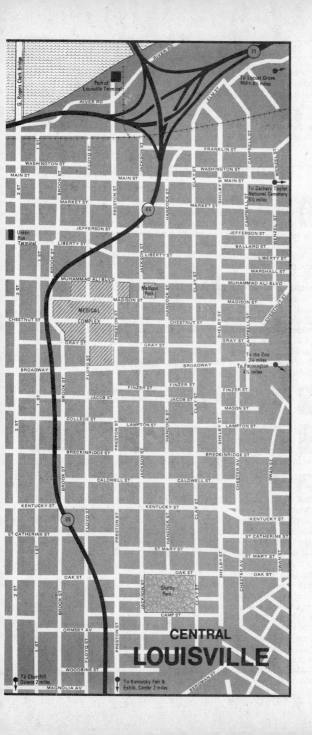

CENTRAL
LOUISVILLE

(phone: 865-2881). Traditional Kentucky food can be found at the *Old Talbott Tavern,* whose previous patrons include Abraham Lincoln and Andrew Jackson (phone: 348-3494). Take I-65 south out of Louisville, exiting to Route 245. En route to Bardstown, you'll encounter Clermont, where you can view a complete collection of Jim Beam decanters at the *American Outpost Museum,* open daily year-round (phone: 543-9877).

SOURCES AND RESOURCES

TOURIST INFORMATION: The visitors' information center (400 S. 1st St., Louisville, KY 40402; phone: 582-3732 or, from out of state, 800-626-5646) provides maps, brochures, and answers to any questions you might have about the city. There's also a visitors' information booth in the atrium of the *Louisville Galleria* (4th Ave. between Muhammad Ali Blvd. and Liberty St.; phone: 583-INFO). Contact the Kentucky state hotline (800-225-TRIP) for maps, calendars of events, health updates and travel advisories.

Local Coverage – *Louisville Courier-Journal,* morning daily (Friday's weekend section has highlights of the coming week's events); *Louisville* magazine, a monthly that includes a calendar of events. All are available at newsstands.

Television Stations – WAVE Channel 3–NBC; WHAS Channel 11–ABC; WLKY Channel 32–CBS; WKET Channel 68–PBS.

Radio Stations – AM: WHAS 840 (talk/sports/news); WAVG 970 (oldies/news/sports). FM: WFPL 89.3 (jazz/information); WUOL 90.5 (classical music); WLRS 102.3 (rock).

TELEPHONE: The area code for Louisville is 502.

 Sales Tax – There is a state tax of 6% on all purchases except groceries.

CLIMATE: The general tendency is toward mild winters, brief but exquisite springs and falls, and overbearingly humid, long, and polluted summers. But save the bets for the thoroughbreds; snow in April or a 60F day in December isn't too long a shot.

GETTING AROUND: Airport – Louisville's Standiford Field Airport, 5 miles south of downtown, handles only domestic flights. Depending on the traffic, the drive to the airport can take anywhere from 10 to 30 minutes and taxi fare will run about $13. The airport limousine service costs $5.50 and makes stops at a few downtown hotels, but most hotels in town offer courtesy vans to pick up registered guests. The city's *TARC* buses stop near the airport's main entrance and travel downtown for 35¢ or 60¢, depending on the time of day; for the return trip, buses can be picked up along the southbound side of 1st Street. For airport information, call 367-4636.

Bus – *TARC* bus system serves the downtown area adequately during the day but is limited in the suburbs and after dark downtown. Route information is available at the Transit Authority Office, 1000 W. Broadway (phone: 585-1234).

Car Rental – Most national firms have offices at the airport, and *Hertz* has an office downtown (at 329 West Broadway; phone: 589-0951).

Taxi – Cabs must be ordered by phone and are often slow to respond. The major company is *Yellow Cab* (phone: 636-5511).

Trolley – The *Toonerville II* provides free rides on 4th Avenue between Broadway and Main Street. Daily except Sundays (phone: 585-1234).

VITAL SERVICES: Audiovisual Equipment – *Hadden Co.* (phone: 634-4741); *Audio Visual of Louisville* (phone: 425-7317).
Baby-sitting – *We Sit Better of Louisville,* Starks Bldg., 455 4th Ave. (phone: 583-9618).

Business Services – *Private Secretary,* 604 Embassy Square Blvd. (phone: 499-5588).

Dry Cleaner/Tailor – *Meyers Dry Cleaning & Alterations,* 516 W. Main St. (phone: 587-8733).

Limousine – *Yellow Cab* (phone: 636-5517).

Mechanics – *Lee's Auto Service* (301 E. Breckinridge; phone: 583-6912); *Smith Imported Car Service* (1250 E. Broadway; phone: 583-4724).

Medical Emergency – *Humana Hospital University,* 530 S. Jackson St. (phone: 562-3015).

Messenger Services – *Zip Express* (phone: 587-3487); *Pony Express* (phone: 968-2200).

National/International Courier – *Federal Express* (phone: 800-238-5355); *DHL Worldwide Courier Express* (phone: 451-4691).

Pharmacy – *Walgreen's Drugs,* 8 AM to 7 PM Mondays through Saturdays; 11 AM to 5 PM on Sundays. 573 S. 4th St. (phone: 584-4342).

Photocopies – *Copy Boy* (518 W. Main St.; phone: 582-2679); *Kinko's Copies* (539 W. Market; phone: 584-0407).

Post Office – Downtown, 7th and York Sts. (phone: 454-1601).

Professional Photographer – *Lin Caufield Photographers* (phone: 636-3727); *Moseley Photography* (phone: 585-4042).

Secretary/Stenographer – *Secretaries Unlimited* (phone: 425-8786); *Private Secretary* (phone: 499-5588).

Translator – *International Language Institute* (phone: 589-1798); *EHK Company* (phone: 761-2611).

Typewriter Rental – *Advance Business Machines,* 1-day minimum (phone: 636-5566); *Kentucky Typewriter Company,* 1-week minimum (phone: 583-9805).

Western Union/Telex – Many offices located around the city (phone: 589-6040).

SPECIAL EVENTS: The week preceding the race, the *Kentucky Derby Festival* unwinds with a parade, music, hot-air balloons, and a race between the *Belle of Louisville* and *Delta Queen* steamboats. Many events are free (write to 137 W. Muhammad Ali Blvd., Louisville KY 40202; phone: 584-6383). The *Kentucky State Fair* is held in mid-August at the *Kentucky Fair & Exposition Center* (phone: 366-9592).

MUSEUMS: Museums not mentioned in *Special Places* include the following:
Rauch Planetarium – On the U. of L. campus, behind the museum (phone: 588-6664).

J. B. Speed Art Museum – 2035 S. 3rd St., next to the U. of L. Closed Mondays (phone: 636-2893).

Zachary Taylor National Cemetery – 4701 Brownsboro Rd. (phone: 893-3852).

MAJOR COLLEGES AND UNIVERSITIES: The University of Louisville, a 4-year state school, is the area's oldest educational institution. Between Eastern Pkwy. and Floyd St. south of 3rd St. (phone: 588-5555).

SHOPPING: The downtown *Galleria* combines 75 stores and a dozen restaurants under a glass roof (4th Ave. between Liberty St. and Muhammad Ali Blvd.; phone: 584-7170). Pottery collectors will want to stop at *Hadley Pottery* (1570 Story Ave. in Butchertown; phone: 584-2171) and at *Louisville Stoneware* (731 Brent Ave. off E. Broadway; phone: 582-1900) for hand-crafted dishes and decorative items. Antiques shoppers should try the cavernous assortment of architectural items at *Joe Ley's* (615 E. Main St.; phone: 583-4014) or the 50,000-square-foot *Louisville Antique Mall* (900 Goss Ave.; phone: 635-2852); or roam along Bardstown Road in the Highlands neighborhood. For authentic, high-quality Kentucky crafts, stop at the *Berea College Crafts* shop (140 N. 4th Ave. in the *Galt House* hotel; phone: 589-3707), or at *Kentucky Art and Craft Gallery* (609 W. Main St.; phone: 589-0102).

 SPORTS AND FITNESS: Baseball – The Louisville *Redbirds,* members of the American Association, play at the *Kentucky Fair and Exposition Center.* Off I-264 (phone: 367-9121).

Bicycling – Rent from *Highland Cycle* (1737 Bardstown Rd.; phone: 458-7832). Nearby Cherokee Park has good bike trails in hilly terrain.

College Sports – The University of Louisville's basketball and football teams play at the *Kentucky Fair and Exhibition Center,* off Watterson Expy. (I-264) (phone: 588-5151).

Fitness Centers – The *Louisville Athletic Club* has a lot to offer: a rooftop pool, exercise classes, steam room, sauna, whirlpool bath, and racquetball and squash courts; towels are provided, and there's a lounge and restaurant as well (5th and Muhammad Ali, at the red awning; phone: 583-3871; call ahead). The *YMCA* has a pool, gym, racquetball court, and indoor track (2nd and Chestnut; phone: 587-6700).

Golf – There are two good public 18-hole courses: *Iroquois Park* (Newcut Rd. and Southern Pkwy.; phone: 363-9520) and *Seneca Park* (Taylorsville Rd. and Cannons La.; phone: 458-9298).

Horse Racing – In addition to racing at *Churchill Downs* (May through July, November), the *Louisville Downs* has trotting races March through April and July through September. 4520 Poplar Level Rd. (phone: 964-6415).

Ice Hockey – The Louisville *Icehawks,* members of the East Coast Hockey League, play in *Broadbent Arena* at the *Kentucky Fair and Exposition Center.* The season runs from October through March (phone: 367-7797).

Jogging – For a 3-mile run, start at the *Hyatt Regency Louisville* on 4th Avenue. Run north to Main Street, turn right onto Main Street, turn left at 2nd Street, and head across Clark Memorial Bridge; then retrace your tracks.

Tennis – The *Louisville Tennis Center* has the best outdoor courts in the area. Open during spring and summer (Trevilian Way, across from the Louisville Zoo; phone: 452-6411). Indoor courts are available at the *Louisville Indoor Racquet Club* (8609 Westport Rd.; phone: 426-2454).

 THEATER: For current offerings, check the papers noted above. The *Actors Theatre of Louisville* (*ACT*), one of the nation's prominent theater companies and the birthplace of the Pulitzer Prize–winning *Crimes of the Heart,* performs traditional productions and avant-garde plays from September through May (316-320 W. Main St.; phone: 584-1205). *Stage One: Louisville Children's Theatre,* and touring repertory groups, including Broadway road shows, play at the *Kentucky Center for the Arts* (5 Riverfront Plaza; phone: 584-7777). The *Louisville Ballet Company* also performs at the *Center.*

 MUSIC: The *Louisville Orchestra* and the *Kentucky Opera Association* perform at the *Kentucky Center for the Arts,* 5 Riverfront Plaza (phone: 584-7777).

 NIGHTCLUBS AND NIGHTLIFE: Current favorites include the *Phoenix Hill Tavern,* which features popular music and a large rooftop beer garden (644 Baxter Ave.; phone: 589-4630); *Butch-*

ertown Pub for a variety of "hot" bands, plus a lively, friendly atmosphere (1335 Story Ave.; phone: 583-2242); and *Splash,* which offers dancing aboard a barge on the Ohio River (201 W. River Rd.; phone: 584-2000). For elegant, quiet, after-dinner drinking, try the *Seelbach Bar* in the *Seelbach* hotel (500 4th Ave.; phone: 585-3200).

BEST IN TOWN

CHECKING IN: Louisville's broad selection of accommodations ranges from standard large hotels to a resort-style motel with a lake and wave-making swimming pool. The expensive hotels cost about $125 to $150 per night for a double room; the cost of accommodations in the moderate category is from $70 to $100, and inexpensive hotels are in the $50 to $65 range. For bed and breakfast accommodations, contact *Kentucky Homes Bed & Breakfast,* 1431 St. James Ct., Louisville, KY 40208 (phone: 635-7341). All telephone numbers are in the 502 area code unless otherwise indicated. All hotels carry CNN unless noted.

Brown – Built in the 1920s, this architectural landmark has found new life after extensive renovations. From the marble-floored lobby and archway-adorned mezzanine to the *Crystal Ballroom* and warm wood interior of the *English Grille,* it's a step into Louisville history. Two restaurants (try a Hot Brown turkey sandwich, invented at the hotel), cocktail lounge. Their meeting rooms hold up to 1,400, and other business conveniences include a concierge desk, limited secretarial services, A/V equipment, and photocopiers. There is 24-hour room service and express checkout. 4th and Broadway (phone: 583-1234; 800-866-7666; Fax: 502-587-7006). Expensive.

Hyatt Regency Louisville – The contemporary atmosphere, spacious rooms, and attentive service mark this hotel in the heart of the downtown business district. Features include an 18-story atrium, the revolving *Spire* restaurant, pool, Jacuzzi, and tennis courts. Meeting rooms accommodate up to 1,200, and concierge, limited secretarial services, A/V equipment, and photocopiers are available. Express checkout will speed you along. 320 W. Jefferson (phone: 587-3434; 800-233-1234; Fax: 502-581-0133). Expensive.

Seelbach – Immortalized by F. Scott Fitzgerald in *The Great Gatsby,* this Beaux Arts showplace from the early 1900s has been thoroughly refurbished to offer the best of modern and period amenities. Elegantly furnished rooms, fine food in the *Oak Room* (see *Eating Out*), a comfortable bar, and respectful service are standard features here. The hotel offers 24-hour room service, meeting rooms for up to 600, concierge, A/V equipment, photocopiers, express checkout, and valet parking. Adjoining the *Galleria* shopping complex. 500 4th Ave. (phone: 585-3200; 800-333-3399; Fax: 502-585-3200, ext. 292). Expensive.

Old Louisville Inn – An elegant bed and breakfast establishment with massive columns in its lobby, 12-foot ceilings, and leaded glass windows. A complimentary breakfast includes popovers, blueberry muffins, pumpkin bread, and fresh fruit. 1359 S. Third St. (phone: 635-1574). Expensive to moderate.

Executive Inn – English manor decor sets the tone for this comfortably appointed motel adjacent to both the airport and the *Kentucky Fair and Exposition Center.* Amenities include a health club, barber/beauty shops, and fine food. Secretarial services, A/V equipment, and photocopiers are available, and meeting rooms for up to 400. Watterson Expy. at the fairgrounds (phone: 367-6161; 800-626-2706; Fax: 502-363-1880). Moderate.

Galt House – The view is wonderful; the hotel, which adjoins the Riverfront Plaza, overlooks the Ohio River. Facilities include 2 cocktail lounges, an outdoor swimming pool, on-site shops, and 3 restaurants, one of which, the *Flagship*, has a revolving section to make the most of a 25th-floor view. The food isn't quite as lofty as the scenery. Although there are limited secretarial services, there's A/V equipment, photocopiers, a concierge desk, and meeting rooms that seat up to 4,000. CNN is not available. 140 N. 4th St. (phone: 589-5200; 800-626-1814; Fax: 502-585-4266). Moderate.

Quality – Formerly the *Louisville-in-Towne*, this place offers good value, with all the standard features: pool, color TV sets, a restaurant, and a cocktail lounge. Meeting rooms for up to 300, A/V equipment, and photocopiers are the business pluses. 100 E. Jefferson St. (phone: 582-2481; 800-221-2222; Fax: 502-582-3511). Inexpensive.

Quality Inn Lakeview – This resort-style hotel features some unusual extras: a "Wave-Tek" ocean, which is really a huge swimming pool with mechanically created waves; a real 11-acre lake with boating, fishing, a floating bridal suite, and 10 lakefront villas. It also has health club access, baby-sitting service, and a restaurant and cocktail lounge. Business services include meeting rooms with a capacity for 750, limited secretarial services, A/V equipment, and photocopiers. Two miles north of downtown off I-65 at 505 Marriott Dr., Clarksville, Indiana (phone: 812-283-4411; 800-544-7075; Fax: 812-288-8976). Inexpensive.

EATING OUT: Our restaurant selections range in price from $60 to $100 for dinner for two in the expensive range, $35 to $60 in the moderate range, and $35 and below in the inexpensive range. Prices do not include drinks, wine, or tips. All telephone numbers are in the 502 area code unless otherwise indicated.

Oak Room – Antique furnishings combine with a continental menu and formal service to make dining here an elegant affair. Try the medallions of venison with quail or grilled swordfish. Open daily, including a sumptuous Sunday brunch. Reservations essential. Major credit cards accepted. *Seelbach Hotel,* 500 S. 4th Ave. (phone: 585-3200). Expensive.

610 Magnolia – The limited hours may exasperate you (it's open on weekends only and closed several months a year), but the deliciously daring menu (entrées change weekly at the chef's whim), delectable desserts (try the *boccone dolce,* three layers of meringue, strawberries, kiwi, chocolate, and mascarpone cheese), and charming atmosphere seem to be worth the trouble to legions of devoted fans. Open Fridays and Saturdays only. Closed January, February, and August. Reservations necessary (and tough to get). No credit cards accepted. 610 W. Magnolia Ave. (phone: 636-0783). Expensive.

Vincenzo's – Your palate will be pampered at this sure-to-impress restaurant. The food is Italian/continental (try the fettuccine Mondello, tomato pasta in a rich clam sauce, or any of the veal dishes — the sauces are superb); the atmosphere is classic European, and the attention is nonstop. Closed Sundays. Reservations recommended. Major credit cards accepted. 150 S. 5th St. (phone: 580-1350). Expensive.

Bristol – An informal bar and grill in the heart of downtown. Continental entrées include trout meunière and tenderloin seasoned in beer; lighter fare also is offered. Open daily. No reservations. Major credit cards accepted. *Kentucky Center for the Arts* (phone: 583-3342). Expensive to moderate.

Casa Grisanti – Whether you go for top-of-the-line veal scalopine, the asparagus ravioli, or cappellini with smoked salmon, you'll find the preparation and the service second to none at this Louisville institution of fine Northern Italian dining. Closed Sundays. Reservations advised. Major credit cards accepted. 1000 E. Liberty St. (phone: 584-4377). Expensive to moderate.

Café Metro – Urbane yet unpretentious, this creative eatery features a frequently changing lineup of entrées such as grilled swordfish with soy sauce, ginger, and sesame seeds, or quail stuffed with ground veal. Be sure to save room for dessert — try the Empress Carlotta or Chocolate Seduction. Closed Sundays. Reservations unnecessary. Major credit cards accepted. 1700 Bardstown Rd. (phone: 458-4830). Moderate.

Jack Fry's – Imaginative food (try the Indonesian grilled shrimp entrée, black-eyed pea burrito appetizer, or grilled-chicken Caesar salad) combined with a neighborhood-pub atmosphere. Good Sunday brunch. Open daily. Reservations advised. Major credit cards accepted. 1007 Bardstown Rd. (phone: 452-9244). Moderate.

Kienle's – The food is wonderful — and heavy. Wiener schnitzel, sauerbraten, and the homemade mushroom and cauliflower soups are highlights. Beer only. No jeans or children under 12. Closed Sundays and Mondays. Reservations advised. No credit cards accepted. Shelbyville Rd. Plaza (phone: 897-3920). Moderate.

Hasenour's – Steaks are the specialty, but the seafood and daily specials also are reliable in this popular neighborhood restaurant. There's a wide variety in both food and price, and the drinks are among the most masterfully mixed in town. Open daily. Reservations advised. Major credit cards accepted. 1028 Barret Ave. (phone: 451-5210). Moderate to inexpensive.

Ditto's Food & Drink – An informal eatery that specializes in scrumptious crabcakes and tasty pizza. Open daily. Reservations unnecessary. Most major credit cards accepted. 1114 Bardstown Rd. (phone: 581-9129). Inexpensive.

KT's – This popular eat-and-meet restaurant is usually busy and boisterous. Best are the light pasta dishes or burgers served with curly french fries. Open daily. Reservations unnecessary. Major credit cards accepted. 2300 Lexington Rd. (phone: 458-8888). Inexpensive.

MEMPHIS

AT-A-GLANCE

SEEING THE CITY: The best way to see Memphis is by drifting along the legendary Mississippi. Captain Jake Meanley's *Memphis Queen* paddleboat takes you along the river. The cruise takes about an hour and a half. It leaves daily from March through mid-December, from Memphis Downtown Harbor, Monroe Ave. and Riverside Dr. (phone: 527-5694).

SPECIAL PLACES: A natural place to start a tour of Memphis is by the riverbanks. From there, you can wander through downtown — stopping at Court Square, a delightful little park with a statue of Phoebe atop the center fountain — and then wend your way out to the suburbs.

Mud Island – Legend has it that Mud Island, measuring 1 by 5 miles, was formed by mud deposits clinging to a gunboat sunk during the Civil War. Residents are sure it was a Union gunboat, because, they say, Confederate gunboats were unsinkable. Now the site of a $63-million tribute to the history and heritage of the Mississippi, the island houses exhibits on the legends, music, and people of the Mississippi; a 5,000-seat outdoor amphitheater; a 5-block scale model of the river; and restaurants, shops, a river museum, marina, and picnic area. Mud Island recently underwent extensive renovations, and the amphitheater presents the best in local and national music, including rock, hillbilly, and rockabilly. Here also is the *Memphis Belle,* famed World War II B-17 bomber. Enter on Front St. between Poplar and Adams (phone: 576-6595); Mud Island is accessible by monorail.

Beale Street – Renovated buildings along this historic street, which saw the birth of the blues in the early 1900s, contain specialty shops, restaurants, bars, and offices. At the corner of Beale and 3rd is W. C. Handy Park, and at Beale and Main, Elvis Presley Plaza; both feature statues honoring these two international artists from Memphis. Don't miss *Lansky's* (at 126 Beale), where Elvis bought his clothes, or W.C. Handy's home (at Fourth and Beale).

Victorian Village – Homes and churches in this downtown area date to the 1830s and feature a variety of architectural styles, among them late Victorian, neo-classic, Greek Revival, French, and Italianate. The Fontaine House (phone: 526-1469) and the Mallory-Neely House (phone: 523-1484) are open to the public daily. 100 to 700 block of Adams St.

Overton Square – A 15-minute drive from downtown, the square has restaurants and bistros, jazz trios and rhythm and blues bands, specialty shops, an art gallery, and a professional theater. Madison at Cooper.

Libertyland – At the Fairgrounds, a mile from the square on East Parkway, this theme park reflects nostalgia and patriotism (its roller coaster is aptly named the Revolution). Open weekends beginning in the spring, daily from mid-June through August. Admission charge; children under 3 free. Fairgrounds (phone: 274-1776).

Memphis Pink Palace Museum and Planetarium – The museum is built of pink Georgia marble, and features exhibitions on the natural and cultural history of the mid-South, including a restored *Piggly-Wiggly,* the first self-service grocery store in the US. Closed Mondays. Admission charge. 3050 Central Ave. (phone: 320-6320).

Chucalissa Indian Village – A reconstructed village where Choctaw Indians live and work. Grass huts and a ceremonial house and museum are on the site, and Indian tools, weapons, and pottery are displayed. Closed Mondays. Admission charge. 6 miles south of downtown, adjoining Fuller State Park on Indian Village Dr. (phone: 785-3160).

Memphis Zoo and Aquarium – The complete range of lions, tigers, monkeys, and birds can be found in this well-designed city zoo. An aquarium adjoins the animal sections. Closed *Thanksgiving, Christmas Eve, Christmas,* and icy days. Admission charge except Mondays from 3 to 4:30 PM in winter and 3:30 to 5 PM in summer. Overton Park, off Poplar Ave. (phone: 726-4775, recording; for further information, 726-4787).

Graceland – Elvis Presley's home is the most popular site in Memphis. The white-columned southern mansion is open to the public, and Elvis fans can take a bus tour through the 14-acre estate, well shaded by oak trees, and pay respects at the graves of Elvis, his mother, father, and grandmother. Don't forget to look closely at the Musical Gate at the foot of the winding circular driveway. It has a caricature of Elvis with guitar and a bevy of musical notes in ornamental iron. Elvis's plane, the *Lisa Marie,* also is on display. Closed Tuesdays, November through February; and *Thanksgiving, Christmas,* and *New Year's Day.* Admission charge; make tour reservations in advance. 3764 Elvis Presley Blvd. in Whitehaven, South Memphis (phone: 332-3322 in Tennessee; 800-238-2000 elsewhere).

Sun Recording Studio – Elvis, Johnny Cash, Jerry Lee Lewis, Carl Perkins, and other recording artists cut their first records here. Restored and operated by the Graceland Division of Elvis Presley Enterprises. Tours daily from 10 AM to 6 PM. Admission charge. 706 Union (phone: 332-3322).

■ **EXTRA SPECIAL:** About 2½ hours away by car, Shiloh National Military Park lets visitors follow the sequence of the famous Civil War Battle of Shiloh, in 1862. Points of interest are clearly marked, and visitors can walk or drive along a 10-mile route. Pre-Columbian Indian mounds also are visible along the way. A 25-minute movie about the battle is shown in the visitors' center. Closed *Christmas Day* (Off US 64 in Shiloh; phone: 1-689-5275). On US 51, about 35 miles north at Henning, is the boyhood home of author Alex Haley (*Roots*), now a museum (200 S. Church St., Henning; phone: 738-2240).

SOURCES AND RESOURCES

TOURIST INFORMATION: The Memphis Visitor Information Center (207 Beale St., Memphis, TN 38108; phone: 576-8171), the Memphis Convention and Visitors Bureau (50 N. Front St., Morgan Keegan Tower, Memphis, TN 38103; phone: 576-8181), and the Memphis Area Chamber of Commerce (22 Front St.; phone: 575-3500) are all good places for general information. Contact the Tennessee state hotline (phone: 615-741-2158) for maps, calendars of events, health updates, and travel advisories.

Key magazine and the *Convention and Visitors Guide* are the best sources for information about Memphis activities.

Local Coverage – *Memphis Commercial Appeal,* morning daily; *Memphis* magazine, monthly; *Memphis Business Journal,* weekly.

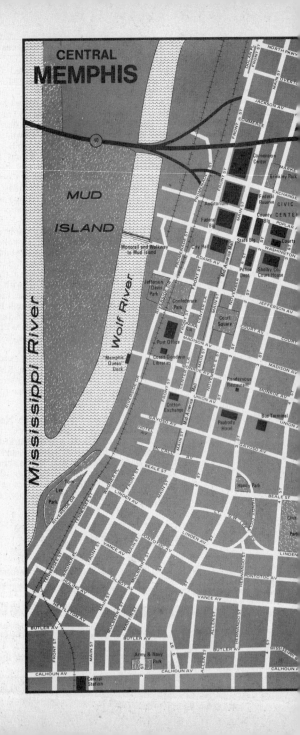

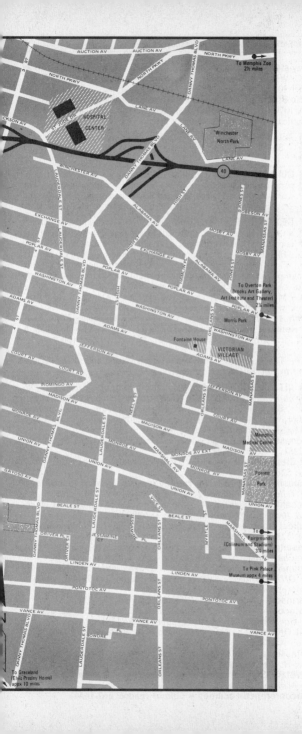

Television Stations – WREG Channel 3–CBS; WMC Channel 5–NBC; WKNO Channel 10–PBS; WHBQ Channel 13–ABC; WLMT Channel 30–Independent; WPTY Channel 24–Fox.

Radio Stations – AM: WHBQ 560 (country music); WMC 790 (talk); WDIA 1070 (rhythm & blues). FM: WEZI 54 (easy listening); WKNO 91 (classical/news); WEZI 94 (easy listening); WEGR 103 (rock).

 TELEPHONE: The area code for Memphis is 901.
Sales Tax – There is a city and state sales tax of 7¾%.

 CLIMATE: Memphis humidity is formidable. Even though temperatures seldom drop below the 30s in winter, it's wet. The worst month is February, when it occasionally snows. July and August get dripping hot, as the temperature climbs into the 90s and 100s.

 GETTING AROUND: Airport – Memphis International Airport is usually about a 30-minute drive from downtown and midtown; taxi fare should run about $14. The *Airport Limousine Service* (phone: 346-1300) meets incoming flights and takes passengers to the city for $6. When returning to the airport, call in advance for a pickup. Although public bus No. 20 stops at the terminal building, a transfer to bus No. 13 is required to get downtown. The fare is 95¢.

Bus – Memphis buses generally run between 5 AM and 8 PM during the week, with limited service on the weekend. Information, routes, from *Memphis Area Transit Authority,* 1370 Levee Rd. (phone: 274-6282).

Car Rental – The major national firms have agencies in Memphis. A reliable local firm is *Thrifty Rent-A-Car,* 2230 E. Brooks (phone: 345-0170).

Taxi – There are taxi stands near the bus station and at the airport. It's best to call *Yellow Cab* (phone: 577-7777).

 VITAL SERVICES: Audiovisual Equipment – *Memphis Communications Corp.,* 1381 Madison Ave. (phone: 725-9271).
Baby-sitting – *Crosstown Christian Daycare and Elementary School* provides 24-hour, 7-day service for children 15 months and older. 1258 Harbert (phone: 725-4666).

Business Services – *Services Rendered,* 2965 Summer St. (phone: 458-3228).

Dry Cleaner/Tailor – *Kraus Model Cleaners,* 1023 Linden Circle (phone: 528-0400).

Limousine – *Memphis Executive Limousine Service* (phone: 396-7733); *Yellow Cab* (phone: 526-2121).

Mechanic – *Ed Martin* (411 Monroe; phone: 527-8606); *OK Alignment & Brake* (3900 Jackson; phone: 382-4999).

Medical Emergency – *Baptist Memorial Hospital,* 899 Madison Ave. (phone: 522-5511).

Messenger Services – *American Courier Service* (phone: 360-9185); *Yellow Cab* (phone: 577-7700).

National/International Courier – *Federal Express* (phone: 345-5044); *DHL Worldwide Courier Express* (phone: 795-9911); *Purolator Courier* (phone: 615-292-7916).

Pharmacy – *Walgreen's,* 1801 Union (phone: 272-2006).

Photocopies – *Dawson's Printing Inc.* (347 S. Front St.; phone: 525-3311); *Gator Print* (118 Madison; phone: 523-2134).

Post Office – The main post office is located at 555 S. 3rd St. at Calhoun Ave. (phone: 521-2140).

Professional Photographer – *Frank Braden* (phone: 767-7897); *Brasher-Rucker Photography* (phone: 324-7447).

Secretary/Stenographer – *Diversified Services Agency* (phone: 794-5385); *Memphis Offices Inc.* (phone: 345-3900).

Teleconference Facilities – *Comsat* (phone: 367-1444).

Translator – *Language Services,* in Nashville, but work can be sent back and forth cheaply by *Purolator,* and interpreters will travel to Memphis (phone: 615-292-7916).

Typewriter Rental – *Dixie Rents,* 1-day minimum (phone: 327-1601); *Mid-South Office Machines,* 1-week minimum (phone: 276-6307).

Western Union/Telex: Many offices are located around the city (phone: 366-7690).

Other – *American Resource Systems,* word processing, photocopying, desk space (phone: 452-8130).

SPECIAL EVENTS: The *Volvo Tennis Championships* are held in February. The *Memphis in May International Festival* stretches from late April into early June. Highlights of the festival are the *International Children's Festival, International Cooking Contest* (barbecue), *Beale Street Musical Festival* and a *Sunset Symphony* on the banks of the Mississippi. *Great River Carnival* (formerly the *Cotton Carnival*) in early June, has parades, a midway, music and a riverside pageant. *Elvis International Tribute Week* is observed around August 17th, the day the "King" died. In September one of the ten largest fairs in the country, the *Mid-South Fair,* takes place. December heralds college football's *Liberty Bowl.*

MUSEUMS: The *Memphis Pink Palace Museum* is famous for natural history exhibitions (see *Special Places*). Other museums of note include the following:

Dixon Gallery and Gardens – (French and American Impressionist art), 4339 Park Ave. (phone: 761-5250).

Memphis Brooks Museum of Art – (American and European art), Overton Park (phone: 722-3500) (both are closed Mondays).

National Ornamental Metal Museum – 374 W. California Ave. (phone: 774-6380).

MAJOR COLLEGES AND UNIVERSITIES: Memphis State University (phone: 454-2040); Rhodes College (phone: 274-1800); University of Tennessee, Memphis (phone: 528-5500); Christian Brothers University (phone: 722-0200).

SPORTS AND FITNESS: Baseball – The Memphis *Chicks* (short for Chickasaw Indians, who once lived in the area) play at *Tim McCarver Stadium,* named for the Memphis-born former catcher for the Philadelphia *Phillies,* who is now a sports announcer on radio and TV. The *Chicks* are a Southern League farm club for the Kansas City *Royals. Tim McCarver Stadium,* Fairgrounds (phone: 272-1687).

Basketball – The Memphis *Rockers* play in the World Basketball League; their home base is at *Mid-South Coliseum* (phone: 726-6400).

Dog Racing – *Southland Greyhound Park* is across the Mississippi in West Memphis. Closed Sundays (phone: 735-3670).

Fishing – There are fish in the lakes, mostly bass, bream, crappies, and catfish. Sardis Lake is a good bet; Meeman-Shelby Forest, a 14,000-acre park with two large lakes.

Fitness Center – The *Peabody Athletic Club,* in the *Peabody* hotel, offers aerobics classes and a sauna, 149 Union (phone: 529-4161).

Golf – The $300,000 *PGA–Federal Express St. Jude Classic* is played in late July or early August at the Southwind, Hacks Crossing, and Winchester golf courses. The best public golf course is *Galloway,* 3815 Walnut Grove Rd. (phone: 685-7805).

Jogging – Run in Audubon Park on Park Avenue, and Overton Park on Poplar Avenue.

Swimming – Some of the lakes are polluted. The nearest good swimming pool is *Maywood,* just across the state line in Olive Branch, Mississippi. Admission charge. 8100 Maywood Dr. (phone: 601-895-2777).

Tennis – The best year-round public courts are at *Audubon Tennis Center* (4145 Southern; phone: 685-7907) and *John Rodgers Tennis Complex* (Midtown; phone: 523-0094).

 THEATER: *Playhouse on the Square* (51 S. Cooper; phone: 726-4656); *Theater Memphis* (630 Perkins Ext.; phone: 682-8323); *Orpheum Theater* (89 Beale St.; phone: 525-3000); *Circuit Playhouse* (1705 Poplar Ave.; phone: 726-5521).

 MUSIC: Big-name country and rock concerts are played at *Mid-South Coliseum* (Fairgrounds; phone: 274-7400) and *Dixon-Meyers Hall* at the *Cook Convention Center* (255 N. Main; phone: 523-7645). Headliners appear at the *Mud Island Amphitheater* from May through September (take the monorail on Front St. between Poplar and Adams; phone: 576-6595) and year-round at the *Orpheum Theater* (89 Beale St.; phone: 525-3000), year-round.

 NIGHTCLUBS AND NIGHTLIFE: Memphis blues originated on Beale Street, with W. C. Handy, and is performed nightly at *Rum Boogie* (182 Beale; phone: 528-0150). There's 1950s and 1960s music at *Proud Mary's* (326 Beale; phone: 525-8979). Other popular downtown nightspots include *Alfred's* (197 Beale; phone: 525-3711) and the *Anchor Bar* at *Captain Bilbo's* (phone: 526-1966), both in the *Beale Street Landing* shopping and restaurant complex (at the corner of Beale and Wagner). In midtown, the Overton Square area at Madison and Cooper, try the *Public Eye* (phone: 726-4040). Best bets elsewhere are *Etcetera* (4730 Poplar Ave.; phone: 761-2880); *Silky Sullivan's* (2080 Madison; phone: 725-0650); and *Bad Bob's Vapors* country and rock (1743 Brooks Rd. E.; phone: 345-1761).

BEST IN TOWN

CHECKING IN: There's an abundance of *Holiday Inns* (six, to be exact) — hardly surprising since the chain makes its headquarters in Memphis. Other chains, such as Ramada, TraveLodge, Hilton, and Sheraton, also are represented. Expect to pay between $60 and $100 (considered moderate) for a double at the hotels mentioned here. All telephone numbers are in the 901 area code unless otherwise indicated.

Peabody – In 1935, Mississippi author David Cohn wrote that "The Delta begins in the lobby of the *Peabody* and ends on Catfish Row in Vicksburg." Built in 1925, the 13-story, 400-room hotel reopened a decade ago after a $20-million renovation. A focal point of the elegant Renaissance lobby is a travertine marble fountain to which the *Peabody* ducks — trained mallards — march and swim each day. Sixteen square marble columns support a mezzanine balcony; the ceiling is graced by ornate woodwork and stained glass skylights. *Chez Philippe* is the hotel's fancy restaurant; *Dux,* its theme restaurant (see *Eating Out*). (Incidentally, neither restaurant serves duck.) For music and dancing, there's the *Skyway,* a rooftop nightclub. The *Plantation Roof* affords splendid views of the river and city. The hotel's lower level has a pool, snack bar, health club, beauty shop, barber shop, and shoeshine parlor. Room service responds around the clock, and there's an obliging concierge desk. Business pluses include secretarial services, A/V equipment, photocopiers, computers, and express checkout. 149 Union Ave. (phone: 529-4000; Fax: 901-529-4000; Telex: 9015558503). Expensive to moderate.

Holiday Inn Crowne Plaza – Part of the executive-oriented group of Holiday Inns, focusing on the affluent business traveler, and adjacent to the *Convention Center*. It offers 415 rooms, a pool, health club, and sauna. *Chervil's* is the ambitious restaurant, and there's a coffee shop and 24-hour room service. Amenities include meeting rooms with a capacity up to 400, concierge, A/V equipment, photocopiers, computers, and express checkout. 250 N. Main (phone: 527-7300; Fax: 901-527-7300). Moderate.

Omni Memphis – Formerly the *Hyatt Regency*, this circular, 27-story, all-glass structure is known affectionately as "the glass silo." On the eastern outskirts of town, the 400-room property has a swimming pool, café, and bar with nightly entertainment and dancing, free parking, free cots, and cribs. Pets welcome. Children under 18 free. Meeting rooms hold up to 1,350. Concierge and secretarial services are available, as well as A/V equipment and photocopiers. Express checkout. 939 Ridge Lake Blvd. (phone: 684-6664; Fax: 901-762-7411). Moderate.

EATING OUT: While it's true there are hundreds of fast-food franchise outlets in every section of the city, a visitor still can dine well, feast on some of the best barbecue anywhere, or enjoy home-cooked meals. Our restaurant selections range in price from $40 for two in the expensive category; around $25 to $30, moderate; under $20, inexpensive. Prices do not include drinks, wine, or tips. All telephone numbers are in the 901 area code unless otherwise indicated.

Dux – A delightful place in the *Peabody* hotel, serving American and continental cooking. Open daily for breakfast, lunch, and dinner. Reservations advised. Major credit cards accepted. 149 Union Ave. (phone: 529-4199). Expensive.

Folk's Folly – This is a steakhouse supreme, serving the largest bits of beef in Memphis. Vegetables are prepared Cajun-style. Try the sautéed mushrooms or fried dill pickles. Humphrey Folk, a John Wayne type, owns the place. According to local legend, he opened it to help out his girlfriend, who always wanted to run a restaurant. Open daily. Reservations advised. Major credit cards accepted. 551 S. Mendenhall (phone: 762-8200). Expensive.

Justine's – Often acclaimed as one of the nation's notable restaurants, and deservedly so. The French cooking here is first rate. Baking is done on the premises. A rather formal ambience prevails in this antebellum mansion, however. Jacket and tie are required. Closed Sundays. Reservations necessary. Major credit cards accepted. 919 Coward Pl. (phone: 527-3815). Expensive.

Captain Bilbo's – Have a drink at the bar and listen to nightly entertainment while viewing beautiful sunsets on the Mississippi River. And don't be surprised if an *Illinois Central Gulf Railroad* train rumbles past — the railroad track is only 22 feet from the restaurant's windows. Next, enjoy the excellent salad bar, seafood gumbo, steaks, and fish. Open daily. Reservations advised for groups of 12 or more. Major credit cards accepted. 263 Wagner (phone: 526-1966). Moderate.

Grisanti's – This Northern Italian eatery features spicy food and a chance to swap insults with owner, Big John Grisanti, a legend on the city's nightlife circuit. The cannelloni, manicotti, and veal are recommended highly. The blind can order from a braille menu. Closed Sundays. Reservations advised for 10 or more. Major credit cards accepted. 1489 Airways Blvd. (phone: 458-2648). Moderate.

Pete and Sam's – Pound for pound, the best all-around restaurant in town; serves dynamite Italian-American food. Order anything, the steaks are as good as the pizza. There are two locations, but try the original on Park Avenue. Open daily. Reservations advised. Major credit cards accepted. 3886 Park (phone: 458-0694). Inexpensive.

Rendezvous – In a basement in a back alley, this classic little place is chock full of Memphis memorabilia. It's as much a museum as a restaurant, and it serves the best barbecued ribs, beef, and pork in town. Closed Sundays, Mondays, and holidays. No reservations. Major credit cards accepted. General Washburn Alley, off S. 2nd and behind the *Ramada Inn* (phone: 523-2746).Inexpensive.

Memphis is a major league barbecue town, so everyone has his or her own favorite barbecue spot. One is *Gridley's* (5339 Elvis Presley Blvd. and 2 other locations about town; phone: 346-2260). Another is *John Wills Bar-Be-Q Pit* (2450 Central; phone: 274-8000). There's also *Smokey Ridge Barbecue* (near the airport at 4085 American Way; phone: 795-7534) and *Willingham's World Champion Bar-B-Que* (54 S. Holmes; phone: 324-7787). If you don't mind driving 40 miles for maybe the best barbecue of them all (for about $5), try *Bozo's* (at Mason, on Summer Ave. and Hwy. 70; phone: 294-3400).

MIAMI–MIAMI BEACH

AT-A-GLANCE

SEEING THE CITY: The *Rusty Pelican* (3201 Rickenbacker Cswy.) looks across Biscayne Bay at the spectacular Miami skyline; the *Roof Garden* restaurant atop the *Doral-on-the-Ocean* (4833 Collins Ave.) offers vistas of the bay and the Atlantic; *Crawdaddy's* restaurant (1 Washington Ave.), on the southernmost tip of Miami Beach, affords spectacular views of Government Cut, the throughway for the dozens of cruise ships that dock at the Port of Miami; and *Bayside Restaurant* (3501 Rickenbacker Cswy., Key Biscayne) has an outdoor seating area with views of downtown Miami.

Miami is largely a waterfront city, and one of the best ways to get to know it is by boat. Besides the *Island Queen,* which leaves from Miamarina (see *Special Places,* below), *Nikko's Gold Coast* cruises set sail out of Haulover Marina (10800 Collins Ave.; phone: 945-5461); the *Spirit* — with lunch, dinner, and "moonlight party" cruises at 2:30, 7, and 10:30 PM, respectively — departs from the *Fontainebleau Hilton* (4441 Collins Ave.; phone: 1-458-4999); and *Harrah's Belle,* a replica of a paddlewheel boat, offers sightseeing and dining cruises from the *Miami Beach Eden Roc* (4525 Collins Ave.; phone: 672-5911). *The Heritage of Miami* is a dramatic tall ship that offers 2-hour tours of Biscayne Bay. It is docked behind Bayside (phone: 858-6264) and is available for charters.

A bus tour of Miami highlights is given by *American Sightseeing Tours,* 4300 NW 14th St. (phone: 871-4992).

For a different view of the city, you can take *Miami Helicopter*'s flight over Miami Beach from Opalocka Airport. Open year-round (phone: 685-8223).

Tropical Balloons (phone: 666-6645) offers a 1-hour balloon tour of downtown Miami, Biscayne Bay, and the Everglades for $110 per person. There also are guided trolley tours that depart from *Bayside Marketplace* for $11 per person (phone: 374-TOUR).

SPECIAL PLACES: The best way to see Greater Miami is by car.
Port of Miami – Every week thousands of people depart on Caribbean cruises from here, making Miami the world's largest cruise port. Cruises aren't free, but watching the tourist-laden ocean liners turn around in the narrow channel that leads to the open sea is. Open daily. Ships leave Fridays, Saturdays, Sundays, and Mondays from 4 to 7 PM.

Bass Museum – Its Art Deco motif complements the outstanding collection of Renaissance, baroque, and rococo works. Admission charge except for children under 16. 2121 Park Ave., Miami Beach (phone: 673-7533).

Art Deco District – A drive or stroll through this area will convince you that you're in a decidedly different Miami, and will forever banish images of the city as a geriatric center. New and restored buildings, hotels, and cafés gleam with façades of shocking pink, bright turquoise, palpitating peach, and Day-Glo yellow. In the mid-1980s, local preservationists decided to upgrade the South Beach area, from Ocean Drive to

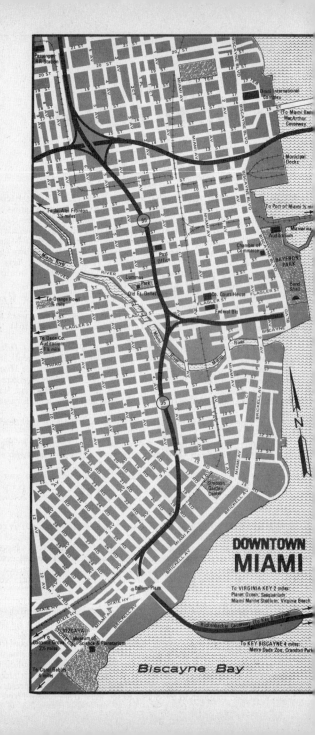

DOWNTOWN MIAMI

To VIRGINIA KEY 2 miles:
Planet Ocean, Seaquarium,
Miami Marine Stadium, Virginia Beach

To KEY BISCAYNE 4 miles:
Metro Dade Zoo, Crandon Park

Biscayne Bay

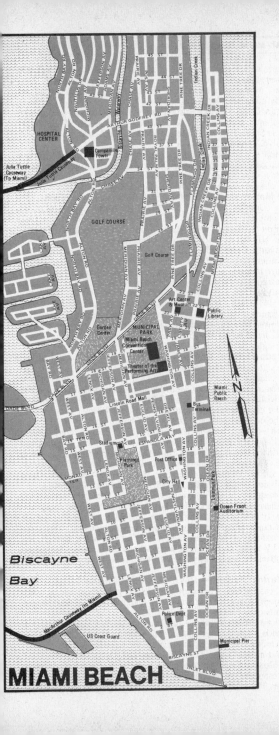

Lenox Court, which was in a state of almost complete ruin. Over 800 buildings were rehabilitated and redecorated in a combination of Bauhaus and art moderne styles, which was dubbed — though not all architecturally authentic — "Art Deco."

Bill Baggs Cape Florida State Park – A 406-acre spread of bike paths, woodlands, picnic areas, and a mile-long beach. The 45-foot lighthouse here is South Florida's oldest landmark. Admission charge. 1200 Crandon Blvd. (phone: 361-5811).

Miamarina – Sightseeing and charter boats berth in this downtown marina. You can board the *Island Queen* for a 2-hour circle cruise of Biscayne Bay, viewing waterfront estates and residential islands daily. Admission charge. 400 SE 2nd Ave. (phone: 379-5119).

Bayside Marketplace – On 20 acres of Biscayne Bay shoreline, this $93-million complex includes 165 shops, restaurants, entertainment areas, and a life-size reproduction of the HMS *Bounty,* built for the 1960 film *Mutiny on the Bounty.* Open daily. Admission charge to the *Bounty.* Entrance at NE 4th St. and Biscayne Blvd. (phone: 577-3344).

Little Havana, Calle Ocho (8th Street) – The real Latin flame burns in this community, founded by Cubans who left after Castro's takeover. Shops feature handmade jewelry, dolls, and works of art. Fruit stands, bakeries, restaurants, and coffee stalls offer authentic Latin food. Try *Málaga* (740 SW 8th St.; phone: 858-4224) or *Versailles* (3555 SW 8th St.; phone: 444-0240) for lunch or dinner — roast pork with rice and black bean sauce, then flan (a custard covered with caramel syrup) for dessert, followed by a cup of espresso at a sidewalk stall. You can watch cigars being hand-rolled by Cuban experts in exile at *Padron Cigars* (1566 W. Flagler St.; phone: 643-2117).

Metro-Dade Cultural Center – This huge $25-million downtown complex, designed by Philip Johnson, houses the *Center for the Fine Arts* (admission charge; phone: 375-1700), which features traveling exhibitions; the *Historical Museum of South Florida* (admission charge; phone: 375-1492), with exhibitions on Spanish exploration, Indian civilization, and maritime history; and the Miami-Dade Public Library (phone: 375-BOOK). The cultural center is at 101 W. Flagler St.

Metrozoo – Here, in Miami's cageless zoo, Bengal tigers lounge before a replica of a Cambodian temple; and the mountains, streams, and bridges inside the free-flight aviary evoke the natural habitat of the Asian birds inside. The air conditioned monorail whisks through the aviary. There is a special combined fare with *Metrorail* on weekends. Open daily. Admission charge. 12400 SW 152nd St. (phone: 251-0401).

Miami Seaquarium – Once you've learned all about the oceans, see who lives there at South Florida's largest tropical marine aquarium. Among the 10,000 creatures swimming around the tidepools, jungle islands, and tanks under a geodesic dome are killer whales, sharks, sea lions, and performing seals and dolphins. The real stars, though, are Flipper, of TV fame, and Lolita, a killer whale. Open daily. Admission charge. On Rickenbacker Cswy. across from *Planet Ocean* (phone: 361-5705).

Miami Marine Stadium – This 6,500-seat roofed grandstand on Biscayne Bay hosts Miami's big shows as well as powerboat races, water shows, outdoor concerts, and fireworks displays. Check newspapers. 3601 Rickenbacker Cswy. (phone: 361-6732).

Miccosukee Indian Village – Just 25 miles west of Miami, descendants of Florida's original settlers are maintaining the lifestyle of their forebears. Among the attractions are alligator wrestling, crafts demonstrations, and airboat rides. US 41 (phone: 223-8388).

Vizcaya Museum and Gardens – A palatial estate, where International Harvester magnate James Deering reaped his personal harvest. The 70-room Venetian palazzo, with 35 rooms open to the public, is furnished with European antiques, precious china, and artworks from the 15th to the 19th century and is surrounded by 10 acres of formal gardens. Closed *Christmas Day*. Admission charge. 3251 S. Miami Ave., just off US 1 (phone: 579-2708 or 579-4626).

Museum of Science and Space Transit Planetarium – Exhibitions on a coral reef and the Everglades are enlightening, and there's a participatory science arcade. The planetarium has several shows daily. If inspiration really strikes, search for the stars yourself with the Southern Cross Observatory telescope atop the building in the evenings. Open daily. Admission charge. 3280 S. Miami Ave. (phone: 854-4242).

Fairchild Tropical Gardens – Founded by a tax attorney with a touch of the poet in him, this might just be one of the most lyrical tax shelters imaginable — 83 acres of paradise with tropical and subtropical plants and trees, lakes, and a rare plant house with an extensive collection of unusual tropical flora. Tram rides are available through the grounds complete with intelligent commentary. Closed *Christmas Day*. Admission charge. 10901 Old Cutler Rd. (phone: 667-1651).

Parrot Jungle – More of the tropics, but this time, screaming, colorful, and talented. Not only do these parrots, macaws, and cockatoos fly, but they also ride bicycles, roller skate, and solve math problems. If you don't believe it, just wait till you see the flamingos on parade — all amid a jungle of huge cypress and live oaks. The coffee shop here is a great breakfast stop. Open daily. Admission charge. 2 miles south off US 1 at 11000 SW 57th Ave. (Red Rd.) and Killian Dr. (phone: 666-7834).

Monkey Jungle – The monkeys wander, run free, go swimming, and swing from trees while visitors watch from inside a wire cage. Naturally, some chimp stars perform, and there also are orangutans, gibbons, and an Amazonian rain forest with South American monkeys in natural habitats. Open daily. Admission charge. 14805 SW 216th St. (phone: 235-1611).

Orchid Jungle – Jungle trails wind through this huge orchid display, more species and colors than you thought existed. Open daily. Admission charge. South of Miami off US 1 in Homestead, 26715 SW 157th Ave. (phone: 247-4824).

Mary A. Heinlein Fruit and Spice Park – Some 20 tropical acres feature over 500 species of fruit, nut, and spice trees and plants. Guided tours by Parks Deptartment naturalists include samplings of seasonal fruits. Tours are conducted Saturday and Sunday afternoons for a nominal charge. Open daily. 35 miles southwest of Miami, at 24801 SW 187th Ave., Homestead (phone: 247-5727).

Miami Beach – At one time, this 8-mile-long island east of the mainland was renowned for its glittering seaside resorts, and that reputation has been restored, along with its unique architecture. Recent efforts at renewal and redevelopment have brought tourists back to the flashy *Fontainebleau Hilton* and the other big hotels that line Collins Avenue, the main drag. A $64-million beach renourishment program created a 300-foot strand extending from Government Cut to Haulover Inlet, and a beach boardwalk runs 1.8 miles from 21st to 46th Street. Miami Beach's Ocean Drive recently has been widened and spruced up. Today the street is lined with outdoor cafés, shops, galleries, and plenty of foot traffic. One Miami Beach attraction (besides the sun, sand, and star-studded nightlife) is the Miami Beach Garden and Conservatory, with a beautiful display of Florida's native flora (2000 Convention Center Dr.). The southern end of the island, between 5th Street and 20th, known locally as "South Beach," has been designated a National Historic District because of its many Art Deco buildings (see Art Deco District, above).

Spanish Monastery – The oldest building in the Western Hemisphere, this charming monastery, which today houses artworks, was first built in 1141 in Spain, dismantled, shipped, and rebuilt in Miami in 1954. Open daily. Admission charge. 16711 W. Dixie Highway, N. Miami (phone: 945-1461).

Coral Castle – This is testimony to lost love. Hand-built by a man who was jilted the day before his wedding, more than 1,000 tons of coral rock were dug by hand and fashioned into this unusual house complete with outdoor furniture, solar-heated bathtubs, and a maze of rooms. Open daily. Admission charge. 28655 US 1, Homestead (phone: 248-6344).

Holocaust Memorial – A $3 million memorial park dedicated to the survivors of the Holocaust. At the center of the park is the sculpture *Love and Anguish,* a 42-foot bronze outstretched hand that seems to reach out from the ground, symbolic of the concentration camp victims' struggle for survival. Open daily. No admission charge. Meridian Ave. and Dade Blvd., Miami Beach (phone: 538-1663).

Venetian Pool – Once a rock quarry that provided material for many of the stately coral rock homes in Coral Gables, the Venetian Pool has undergone an extensive face lift. A free-form lagoon with varying levels, waterfalls, and a surrounding of lush vegetation, it's a place for Esther Williams' fantasies. Open daily. Admission charge. 2701 Desoto Blvd., Coral Gables (phone: 442-6483).

■ **EXTRA SPECIAL:** For a refreshing change, drive south along US 27 through miles of Miami's little-known farmland. Stock up on fresh fruits and vegetables at numerous stands or go right out into the U-Pic fields and choose your own. Forty miles south of Miami (turnoff on US 1) is Everglades National Park, a unique and extremely diverse subtropical wilderness with some of the best naturalist-oriented activities anywhere in the world. This 1½-million-acre preserve features alligators, raccoons, manatees, mangroves, and thousands of rare birds, all in their natural habitats. Farther south along US 1 stretch the Florida Keys, a chain of islands connected by an Overseas Highway. Here is everything from the only living coral reef in the continental United States (which you can see in all its glory only by skin diving, snorkeling, or in a glass-bottom boat) at John Pennekamp State Park (the only underwater park in the country) in Key Largo to great fishing possibilities and better food: conch chowder, and Key lime pie.

SOURCES AND RESOURCES

TOURIST INFORMATION: The Greater Miami Convention and Visitors Bureau (701 Brickell Ave., Suite 2700, Miami, FL 33131; phone: 539-3000; Fax: 305-539-3113) is best for brochures, maps, and general tourist information. For information on fairs, art shows, and events in the area's parks, call the Parks and Recreation Department's information line (phone: 579-2568). Contact the Florida state hotline (904-487-1462) for maps, calendars of events, health updates, and travel advisories.

Local Coverage – *Miami Herald,* morning daily, publishes the Weekend section on Fridays with a schedule of upcoming events; *South Florida* magazine, monthly; *New Times,* an alternative weekly, includes "The Wave," a listing of weekly happenings; *New Miami* is a monthly business magazine.

Television Stations – WPBT Channel 2–PBS; WTVJ Channel 4–NBC; WCIX Channel 6–CBS; WPLG Channel 10–ABC.

Radio Stations – AM: WIOD 610 (news); WNWS 940 (news/talk); WINZ 1060 (talk). FM: WLUV 94.1 (soft rock, jazz); WTMI 93.1 (classical music); WMXJ 102.7 (oldies); WJQY 107.5 (easy listening).

TELEPHONE: The area code for Miami is 305.

Sales Tax – There is a 6% statewide sales tax and an 8% hotel tax.

 CLIMATE: Miami is warm all year, with average daily temperatures of 81F in summer and 69F in winter, and lots of sunshine. Summers can be prohibitively humid. Temperatures also can get cool indoors, where air conditioning prevails.

 GETTING AROUND: Airport – Miami International Airport is usually a 15-minute drive from downtown and about a half-hour from Miami Beach, longer during rush periods (8:30 to 9:30 AM and 4:30 to 6PM). Taxi fares average $12 to downtown, $16 to mid-Miami Beach. *Red Top* (phone: 526-5764) has van service every 20 to 30 minutes from the airport to hotels in downtown Miami for $6.75, to those in Miami Beach for $8. Call *Red Top* 24 hours in advance when returning to the airport; pickups are made 2 hours before flight time. The *Supershuttle* (phone: 871-2000) has van service to and from Miami International Airport for $8–$11.

Bus – *Metrobus* serves downtown Miami, Collins Avenue on Miami Beach, Coral Gables, and Coconut Grove fairly well, but service to other areas tends to be slow and complicated. For information on routes, schedules, and fares, call 638-6700.

Car Rental – Miami is served by the large national firms; rates here are among the least expensive in the country, but if you want a convertible during peak season, be sure to reserve one well in advance.

Metrorail – *Metrorail,* an elevated rail system, went into operation in 1984 from the *Dadeland* shopping mall in the Kendall area to downtown Miami, beyond to the Civic Center and Hialeah; fare, $1. The *Metromover* rail system is a 1.9-mile downtown loop that began service in 1986; fare, 25¢. For information, call 638-6700.

Taxi – You sometimes can hail a cab in the street, but it's better to order one on the phone or pick one up in front of any of the big hotels. Major cab companies are *Yellow Cab* (phone: 444-4444), *Super Yellow Cab* (phone: 888-7777), *Metro Taxi* (phone: 888-8888), and *Central Cab* (phone: 532-5555).

 VITAL SERVICES: Audiovisual Equipment – *Spire Audio-Visual* (phone: 576-5736).

Business Services – *Stephan Secretarial Services,* 3132 Ponce de León Blvd., Coral Gables (phone: 446-9500).

Dry Cleaner/Tailor – *La Salle Cleaners* (2341 Le Jeune Rd., Coral Gables; phone: 444-7376); *Mark's* (1201 20th St., Miami Beach; phone: 538-6104).

Limousine – *Red Top Sedan Service* (phone: 526-5764); *Club Limousine Service* (phone: 893-9850).

Mechanics – *Martino,* for foreign and American cars (7145 SW 8th St.; phone: 261-6071); *Lejeune-Trail Exxon,* for American makes (801 SW 42nd Ave.; phone: 446-2942).

Medical Emergency – *Jackson Memorial Hospital* (1611 NW 12th Ave., Miami; phone: 325-7429); *Mt. Sinai Medical Center* (4300 Alton Rd., Miami Beach; phone: 674-2200).

Messenger Services – *Sunshine State Messenger Service,* open 24 hours (phone: 944-6363); *Metro Messenger Service* (phone: 757-7777).

National/International Courier – *Federal Express* (phone: 371-8500); *DHL Worldwide Courier Express* (phone: 592-8795).

Pharmacy – *Robert's Drugs,* open 7 AM to midnight, 590 W. Flagler St.; phone: 545-0533).

Photocopies – *Sir Speedy* (1659 James Ave. in Miami Beach and other locations; phone: 531-5858); *Ace Industries* (54 NW 11th St.; phone: 358-2571).

Post Office – There is a downtown office (500 NW 2nd Ave.; phone: 371-2911); and an office in Miami Beach (1300 Washington Ave.; phone: 531-3763).

Professional Photographer – *Convention Photographers International* (phone: 865-5628); *Pelham & Friends* (phone: 371-2013).

Secretary/Stenographer – *Abacus Business Center,* English/Spanish (phone: 576-8310); *Girl Friday* (phone: 379-3461).

Teleconference Facilities – *Omni International* (see *Best in Town,* below); *Miami Beach Convention Center* (Miami Beach; phone: 673-7311).

Translator – *Berlitz* (phone: 371-3686); *Professional Translating Services* (phone: 371-7887).

Typewriter Rental – *Beach Typewriter,* 2-week minimum (phone: 633-6543); *A-1 Etron,* 2-week minimum (phone: 264-4652).

Western Union/Telex – Many offices are located around the city (phone: 358-0808, or 800-325-4045).

Other – *The Word Processing Center* (phone: 591-8365); *ABC Office Equipment,* (phone: 891-5090); *Florida Tent Rental,* tent pavilions for conferences or receptions, often set up at the Vizcaya estate (phone: 633-0199); *Florida Convention Services,* meeting and conference planners (phone: 758-7868); *Pearl's and Jessie's Catering* (20160 W. Dixie Hwy.; phone: 937-1511); *US Passport Agency* (51 SW 1st Ave., Miami; phone: 536-5395).

 SPECIAL EVENTS: Miami is the site of the annual *Orange Bowl Parade,* nationally televised from Biscayne Boulevard. each *New Year's Eve* as a prelude to the *Orange Bowl* football classic played on *New Year*'s night. Two of the country's largest boat shows are held here each year, the *Dinner Key Boat Show* in Coconut Grove, in October, and the *International Boat Show* at the Miami Beach *Convention Center* in February. Miami Beach hosts the *Art Deco Weekend* every January on Ocean Drive in the historic Art Deco district on South Beach, the *Festival of the Arts* each February, and the *Coconut Grove Art Festival* in the same month draws many away from the beach to stroll the shady lanes of this artists' haven. February also hosts the *Miami Film Festival,* a week of premieres of national and international films with visiting directors, producers, and stars. Also in late February or early March, the *Miami Grand Prix* attracts top racing drivers to the downtown "track" (on Biscayne Blvd. between Flagler and NE 8th Sts.; phone: 662-5660). In March, in Little Havana, natives and visitors alike head for Calle Ocho (8th St.) for *Carnaval Miami,* a 9-day festival featuring the largest conga line in the world. In April, the *Greater Miami Billfish Tournament* attracts more than 500 anglers vying for South Florida's richest fishing purse. In November, the *Miami Book Fair International* welcomes authors, publishers, booksellers, and street vendors to one of the world's largest week-long celebrations of the printed word.

 MUSEUMS: The *Bass Museum of Art,* the museums in the *Metro-Dade Cultural Center,* the *Museum of Science and Space Transit Planetarium,* and the *Vizcaya Museum and Gardens* are described in some detail in *Special Places.* Other museums to see:

Cuban Museum of Arts and Culture – The cultural heritage of Miami's Cuban community. 1300 SW 12th Ave. (phone: 858-8006).

Lowe Art Museum – 1301 Stanford Dr., on the University of Miami campus in Coral Gables (phone: 284-3535).

MAJOR COLLEGES AND UNIVERSITIES: The University of Miami in Coral Gables (1200 San Amaro Dr.; phone: 284-2211) has an enrollment of 17,000. Florida International University is a 4-year college with two separate campuses (SW 8th St. and 107th Ave., NE 151st St. and Biscayne Blvd.; phone: 554-2363). Miami Dade Community College, with three campuses, is the largest junior college in the country (11380 NW 27th Ave., 11011 SW 104th St., and 300 NE 2nd Ave.; phone: 347-3135).

SPORTS AND FITNESS: Baseball – Fans can watch preseason games of the Baltimore *Orioles,* whose spring training camp is in Miami; they often play the New York *Yankees,* who train in nearby Ft. Lauderdale (phone: 635-5395). The University of Miami *Hurricanes* play at *Mark Light Stadium* (on campus at 1 Hurricane Dr., corner of Ponce de León and San Amaro; phone: 284-2655). Good news for baseball fanatics: Miami has gotten the nod for a National League expansion team.

Basketball – The *Heat,* Miami's NBA entry, burns up the court at the *Miami Arena,* 721 NW 1st Ave. (phone: 530-4400, 577-HEAT).

Bicycling – Rent from *Dade Cycle Shop* (3216 Grand Ave. in Coconut Grove; phone: 443-6075). There are more than 100 miles of bicycle paths in the Miami area, including tree-shaded lanes through Coconut Grove and Coral Gables. A self-guided bicycle tour of Key Biscayne originates in Crandon Park. Dade County Parks & Recreation Department has information (phone: 579-2676).

Boating – Greater Miami is laced with navigable canals and has many private and public marinas with all kinds of boats for rent. Sailboats are available from *Dinner Key Marina* (Pan American Dr., Coconut Grove). Windsurfer and Hobie Cat rentals, some with free instruction, are available from *Easy Sailing* shops (on Key Biscayne; phone: 858-4001). The *Cat Ppalu* and *Pauhana,* two 49-passenger catamarans, are available for charter or sunset tours (phone: 888-3002). Charter boats for sport fishing are available at *Crandon Park Marina* (phone: 361-1281), *Miami Beach Marina* (phone: 673-6000), and *Miami Marina* downtown (phone: 374-6260).

Fishing – Surf and offshore saltwater fishing is available year-round. The boardwalks on the Rickenbacker, MacArthur, and Venetian causeways and the Haulover Beach Fishing Pier (10800 Collins Ave., Miami Beach; admission charge) are popular fishing spots. There's also plenty of freshwater action in canals and backwaters, including the Everglades and Florida Bay. Charter boats offer a half day and full day of deep-sea fish, snapper, grouper, yellowtail, pompano, and mackerel trips from *Crandon Park Marina* (phone: 361-1281) and *Haulover Marina* (10800 Collins Ave., Miami Beach; phone: 947-3525).

Fitness Centers – Staying in shape is no problem in Dade County. Try the *YMCA* (at the downtown World Trade Center; phone: 577-3091); it allows free visits for out-of-town guests. The *Downtown Athletic Club* (atop the Southeast Bank Building; phone: 358-9988) and *Body and Soul* (in Coral Gables; phone: 443-8688) also are good places.

Football – The NFL *Dolphins* and Dolphin-mania infect the entire city during the football season, so for good seats call the *Joe Robbie Stadium* in North Dade in advance (phone: 620-2578). The University of Miami *Hurricanes* play at the *Orange Bowl;* for tickets, contact the University of Miami ticket office (1 Hurricane Dr., Coral Gables; phone: 284-2655), or go to the *Orange Bowl.*

Golf – More than 35 golf courses are open to the public. Some of the best are *Kendale Lakes* (6401 Kendale Lakes Dr.; phone: 382-3930); *Miami Springs* (650 Curtiss Pkwy., Miami Springs; phone: 888-2377); *Bayshore* (2301 Alton Rd., Miami Beach; phone: 532-3350); *Palmetto* (9300 SW 152nd St., Miami; phone: 238-2922); and *Key Biscayne* (6700 Crandon Blvd., Key Biscayne; phone: 361-9129). There also are five 18-hole courses at the *Doral Ocean Beach* resort (see *Checking In*).

Horse and Dog Racing – Betting is big in Miami. *Hialeah* racetrack (2200 E. 4th Ave., Hialeah; phone: 887-4347) is worth a visit just to see the beautiful grounds and clubhouse and the famous flock of pink flamingos (they were in the opening of TV's "Miami Vice"). There also is thoroughbred horse racing at *Gulfstream Park* (901 S. Federal Hwy.,

Hallandale; phone: 944-1242) and at *Calder* (21001 NW 27th Ave.; phone: 625-1311). Greyhound racing is held at *Flagler* (401 NW 38th Ct.; phone: 649-3000) and at *Biscayne* (320 NW 115th St.; phone: 754-3484). Check the racing dates before heading to the track.

Jai Alai – From December through April there's jai alai (a Basque game resembling a combination of lacrosse, handball, and tennis) and betting action nightly at the *Miami Jai-Alai Fronton,* the country's largest. You can pick up tickets at the gate or reserve them in advance, 3500 NW 37th Ave. (phone: 633-6400).

Jogging – Run along South Bayshore Drive to David Kennedy Park, at 22nd Avenue, and jog the Vita Path; or jog in Bayfront Park, at Biscayne and NE 4th St. On Miami Beach, run on a wooden boardwalk that extends along the ocean from 21st to 51st Street, or run toward the parcourse on the southern tip of South Beach.

Nature Walks – There are nature walks at Fairchild Tropical Gardens and the Fruit and Spice Park, but the Parks & Recreation Department offers frequent guided tours through natural hammocks, tree forests, bird rookeries, and even through water (a marine walk and nature lesson and dousing are at Bear Cut, Key Biscayne). For information contact the Parks Department office (phone: 662-4124).

Skating – Hard-hit snowbirds can head north to Broward County for year-round ice skating at *Sunrise Ice Skating Center,* 3363 Pine Island Rd. (phone: 741-2366).

Swimming – With an average daily temperature of 75F, and miles of ocean beach on the Atlantic, Miami Beach and Key Biscayne offer some great places for swimming, all water sports, and another prime activity, sun worshiping. Some of the best beaches include the following:

> *Bill Baggs Cape Florida State Park.* This long beach with sand dunes, picnic areas, fishing, boat basin, restored old lighthouse, and museum is a favorite of residents. At Cape Florida, the far south end of Key Biscayne.
>
> *Crandon Park Beach,* a 2-mile stretch lined with shade trees, picnic tables, barbecue pits, ample parking. Drive to the far end for private cabanas rented by the day or week. Rickenbacker Cswy. to Key Biscayne.
>
> *Haulover Beach* is a long stretch of beautiful beach, good for surfing and popular with families. Marina, sightseeing boats, charter fishing fleets, restaurants, and fishing pier. A1A north of Bal Harbour.
>
> *Miami Beach.* Several long stretches of public beach at various places, including South Beach for surfers (5th St. and Collins Ave.), Lummus Park with lots of shaded beaches (South Beach on Ocean Ave.), and North Shore Beach with landscaped dunes and oceanfront walkway (71st St. and Collins Ave.). There are also small public beaches at the ends of streets in the midst of Hotel Row.

Tennis – Many hotels have courts for the use of their guests, and there are also public facilities throughout the county. Some of the best are the *Abel Holtz Tennis Stadium* (in Flamingo Park in Miami Beach) with hard and clay courts (1200 12th St.; phone: 673-7761); *Tamiami* (10901 Coral Way,; phone: 223-7076); *North Shore Center* (350 73rd St., Miami Beach; phone: 993-2022); and *Tropical Park* (7900 SW 40th St., Miami; phone: 223-8710).

 THEATER: For current offerings, check the publications listed above. The *Coconut Grove Playhouse* (3500 Main Hwy.; phone: 442-4000) imports New York stars in its classic season from October to May. The *Jackie Gleason Theater of the Performing Arts* offers touring plays and musicals, including some pre- and post-Broadway shows (1700 Washington Ave.; phone: 673-8300). The *Gusman Cultural Center* (174 E. Flagler St.; phone: 374-2444), and the *Dade County Auditorium* (2901 W. Flagler St.; phone: 545-3395) book theatrical and cultural events year-round. The *Miami City Ballet* (905 Lincoln Rd., Miami Beach; phone: 532-7713), headed by Edward Villella, is one of the country's best young companies and performs a full season beginning each fall.

MUSIC: Visiting orchestras and artists perform in Miami at the *Gusman Cultural Center* (174 E. Flagler St.; phone: 374-2444) and at *Dade County Auditorium* (2901 W. Flagler St.; phone: 545-3395), or in Miami Beach at the *Theater of the Performing Arts* (1700 Washington Ave.; phone: 673-8300). The *Greater Miami Opera Association* (1200 Coral Way; phone: 854-7890) stages a full complement of major productions in the winter season, as does the *New World Symphony* (101 E. Flagler St.; phone: 371-3005).

NIGHTCLUBS AND NIGHTLIFE: Miami's nightlife runs the gamut. For a Vegas-style "flesh and feathers" revue, head for the *Sheraton Bal Harbour* (9701 Collins Ave., Miami Beach; phone: 865-7511), or to *Les Violins* for a flashy show with a Cuban twist (1751 Biscayne Blvd.; phone: 371-8668). For live blues and a bit of history, stop in at *Tobacco Road* (626 S. Miami Ave.; phone: 374-1198), Miami's oldest bar. If jazz is your bag, try *Greenstreets* (2051 LeJeune Rd., Coral Gables; phone: 445-2131) or *Semper's* on Miami Beach (860 Ocean Drive; phone: 673-6730). The still-fashionable *Régine's* (2669 S. Bayshore Dr., Coconut Grove; phone: 858-9600) is in the *Grand Bay* hotel. For tunes from the 1950s and 1960s, two popular spots are *Studebaker's* in Kendall (8505 Mills Dr.; phone: 598-1021) and *Village Inn* (3131 Commodore Plaza; phone: 445-8721). The south end of Miami Beach is the latest "in" spot for nightlife. Head to *Deco's* (1235 Washington Ave.; phone: 531-1235) for throbbing dance tunes, *Club Nu* for chic crowds and dance music (245 22nd St.; phone: 672-0068), and *Club Boomerang* for live bands (323 23rd St.; phone: 532-1666). For nostalgia fans, Dick Clark has opened a new dance club, called — what else — *Dick Clark's American Bandstand* (Bayside Marketplace; phone: 381-8800), where you can dance to music which spans the decades from the 1950s to today.

BEST IN TOWN

CHECKING IN: Winter is the busy season, and reservations should be made well in advance. In winter, a double room in the very expensive range will run $195 and up per night; $145 and up in expensive; $120 and up in moderate. In summer, most hotels cut their rates, so shop around. For information about bed and breakfast accommodations, contact the Greater Miami Convention and Visitors Bureau (701 Brickell Ave., Miami FL 33131; phone: 539-3000; Fax: 305-539-3113). All telephone numbers are in the 305 area code unless otherwise indicated.

Alexander – An elegant, yet surprisingly homey, place metamorphosed from former luxury apartments. A chandeliered portico, a grand lobby with a curving stairway and antiques from the Cornelius Vanderbilt mansion in New York, and 211 spacious, antiques-filled suites are all impressive, as is *Dominique's* French restaurant (see *Eating Out*), with a main dining room overlooking the ocean. Roasted rack of lamb and exotic appetizers such as rattlesnake salad, alligator tails, and buffalo sausage are specialties. A $15-million expansion added a second restaurant and a ballroom. The grounds include an acre of tropical gardens, 2 lagoon swimming pools — 1 with its own waterfall — and

4 soothing whirlpool baths; a private marina and golf and tennis facilities are nearby. Room service is available until 11 PM; other amenities include a concierge desk, secretarial services, and 8 meeting rooms. 5225 Collins Ave., Miami Beach (phone: 865-6500 or 800-327-6121; Fax: 305-864-8525). Very expensive.

Fisher Island – Just off the southern tip of Miami Beach, this exclusive 216-acre island was once the private playground of William Vanderbilt. Now a private hideaway and elite resort refuge, the island has extravagantly furnished resort apartments, villas, and a couple of historic cottages available for transient rental — though the cost is significant. It's worth it to many for the island's unique serenity and distance from "the outside world." Facilities include a 9-hole golf course, superb tennis courts (including a couple of grass ones), a marina, 2 restaurants, and several shops. Secretarial services are available. Accessible only by private ferry (phone: 535-6020 or 800-624-3251; Fax: 305-535-6003). Very expensive.

Grand Bay – Run by the Aga Khan's CIGA chain and done in truly high style, the 181-room property overlooks Biscayne Bay and is near the equally tony *Mayfair Mall.* This is Miami's most elite hotel. It houses the fashionable *Régine's* nightclub, 3 restaurants (see *Eating Out*) and lounges, and a pool. There's around-the-clock room service, as well as 3 meeting rooms, a concierge desk, and secretarial services. 2669 S. Bayshore Dr., Coconut Grove, Miami (phone: 858-9600; Fax: 305-859-2026). Very expensive.

Mayfair House – This all-suite hotel, part of the *Mayfair Mall* complex in the heart of Coconut Grove, has 181 suites, each with a terrace, Jacuzzi, and a small dining area where a complimentary continental breakfast (with lots of tropical fruit) is served each morning. There is 1 restaurant, the private *Ensign Bitter's Dining Club* (for hotel guests only), and a rooftop pool with bar. Room service is available 24 hours a day. Other conveniences include concierge and secretarial services, 3 meeting rooms, and express checkout. 3000 Florida Ave., Miami (phone: 441-0000 or 800-433-4555; Fax: 305-447-9173). Very expensive.

Sonesta Beach – On the beach at Key Biscayne, this top class resort's facilities include a tennis club with 10 Laykold courts (3 lighted) and instruction by two pros, an Olympic-size swimming pool, a fitness center and an extensive children's program. In addition to the 300 rooms, there also are 4 restaurants and villas with from 2 to 5 bedrooms. Round-the-clock room service, secretarial assistance, 12 meeting rooms, and express checkout. 350 Ocean Dr., Miami (phone: 361-2021; Fax: 305-361-3096). Very expensive.

Biscayne Bay Marriott – On the marina, it offers 605 coral or mint-green rooms in the original building, a majority with bay views, and 150 rooms in the newer Venetia building. The brass and marble lobby is comfortably welcoming, and the 2 restaurants serve fresh seafood, as does the hotel's oyster bar. A third-floor skybridge connects the *Marriott* to the *Venetia* and to the *Omni International* shopping and hotel complex. Room service is available until 11 PM. In addition, there's a concierge desk, 4 meeting rooms, secretarial services, and express checkout. 1633 N. Bayshore Dr., Miami (phone: 374-3900 or 800-228-9290; Fax: 305-375-0597). Expensive.

Doral Ocean Beach – On the 18th floor of this 420-room high-rise is the *Doral Roof Garden* restaurant (worth the trip for the baby coho and chocolate linguine alone). Other highlights include a presidential suite, exclusive shops, Olympic-size pool, numerous water sports, tennis courts, an 80-foot executive yacht available for meetings, and a helipad. There is shuttle service to the country club (built around 5 championship 18-hole golf courses) and the spa. Relaxed elegance and friendly staff. There are 15 meeting rooms, and concierge and secretarial services. Room service can be summoned around the clock. 4833 Collins Ave., Miami Beach (phone: 532-3600; Fax: 305-534-7409). Expensive.

Fontainebleau Hilton – The famous Miami Beach landmark, on 18 acres of beachfront real estate, it's far more glitzy than glittering. The lagoon-like pool has a grotto bar inside a cave, and there are 12 restaurants and lounges, as well as a kosher kitchen. The *Dining Galleries* restaurant is especially popular for Sunday brunch. Fully equipped spa; 1,206 rooms; 7 tennis courts. Twenty-four–hour room service, concierge and secretarial services, and express checkout are offered. 4441 Collins Ave., Miami Beach (phone: 538-2000 or 800-HILTONS; Fax: 305-534-7821). Expensive.

Hyatt Regency – A 615-room riverside hostelry that's part of Miami's convention and conference complex in the heart of downtown. The top 2 floors feature Hyatt's Regency Club service, with complimentary continental breakfast, private lounge, and other extras. Two restaurants, one of which features a continental menu. Twenty-four–hour room service is available, as are 19 meeting rooms, secretarial and concierge service, and express checkout. 400 SE 2nd Ave., Miami (phone: 358-1234, 800-233-1234, or 800-228-9000; Fax: 305-358-0529). Moderate.

Inter-Continental Miami – Built in the grand old hotel tradition and in the city center. The 646 rooms have marble baths and Oriental furniture along with other luxurious appointments. Facilities include 4 restaurants (see *Eating Out*), a lounge, a swimming pool, tennis and racquetball courts, a jogging trail, and a 200-seat auditorium. Concierge desk, secretarial services, and 24-hour room service. 100 Chopin Plaza, Miami (phone: 577-1000, 800-332-4246, or 800-327-0200; Fax: 305-577-0384). Moderate.

Omni International – The 535-room hotel is part of the 10½-acre downtown complex that includes 165 shops, 10 movie theaters, 21 restaurants, an amusement area, a sun deck, and rooftop pool. Amenities include 24-hour room service, as well as concierge and secretarial assistance. There are 30 meeting rooms. 1601 Biscayne Blvd., Miami (phone: 374-0000 or 800-THE-OMNI; Fax: 305-374-0020). Moderate.

Place St. Michel – Charming, cozy, and elegant European-style small inn in the heart of Coral Gables. On the premises is *Stuart's,* a jazz bar, an excellent restaurant, a charcuterie, and a snack bar that is popular with the local lunch crowd. Room service is available until 11 PM, and there's an obliging concierge desk. 162 Alcazar Ave., Coral Gables (phone: 444-1666; Fax: 305-529-0074). Moderate.

Sofitel – A member of the French hotel chain, it is a relative newcomer to the States, and this sleek example is strictly international business in flavor. It offers 285 rooms, 2 French restaurants, a French bakery, lobby bar, health club, pool, Jacuzzi, and boating on a 100-acre fresh-water lake. Other amenities are 24-hour room service, a concierge desk, 8 meeting rooms, secretarial services, and express checkout. 5800 Blue Lagoon Dr., Miami (phone: 264-4888; Fax: 305-262-9079). Moderate.

EATING OUT: Much of Miami socializing centers around restaurant dining, so beware the long lines during the winter season (December through April), when snowbirds swell the ranks of regulars. Residents always make reservations. Expect to pay $70 or more for a dinner for two in the very expensive range; $50 to $60 in the expensive; $35 to $50 in the moderate; and under $30 in the inexpensive range. Prices do not include drinks, wine, or tips. Many establishments in the expensive category require that men wear jackets; it's wise to call ahead to inquire. All telephone numbers are in the 305 area code unless otherwise indicated.

Café Chauveron – Transplanted many years ago from New York City to Bay Harbor without the slightest disturbance of its famous soufflés, it's a French dining place in the grand manner. Everything is beautifully prepared, from *coquille de fruits de mer au champagne* to soufflé Grand Marnier. Docking space if you arrive by boat. Open daily but closed from June through early October. Reservations necessary. Major credit cards accepted. 9561 E. Bay Harbor Dr., Bay Harbor Island, Miami Beach (phone: 866-8779). Very expensive.

Dominique's – It's known for its outré dishes, such as rattlesnake and alligator, but regulars prefer the always excellent rack of lamb or filet of beef or veal, done in a classic French manner. For dessert, try the pistachio soufflé, named for a famous patron, Don Johnson. Open daily. Reservations necessary weekends and advised weekdays. Major credit cards accepted. In the *Alexander Hotel,* 5225 Collins Ave., Miami Beach (phone: 861-5252). Very expensive.

Pavillon Grill – For diners seeking creative cookery, here is American food with a decidedly nouvelle bent: Everglade frogs' legs cakes with chilled vermouth mayonnaise, marinated and mesquite-grilled lamb chops, lobster and chicken fanned over black beans and sweet red pepper sauce. The setting is stylishly formal, so men will need jacket and tie. Dinner only; closed Sundays. Reservations necessary. Major credit cards accepted. In the *Inter-Continental Hotel,* 100 Chopin Plaza, Miami (phone: 577-1000). Very expensive.

Chef Allen's – Regional South Florida cooking, using local produce and fish like yellowtail, tuna, and snapper. Specials include whole wheat linguine with lobster and Florida bay scallops *cilantro* (with coriander). Open daily for dinner. Reservations advised on weekends. All major credit cards accepted. 19088 NE 29th Ave., North Miami Beach (phone: 935-2900). Expensive.

Forge – Prime ribs and Java steaks are the specialties on the otherwise continental menu here, with an extensive wine list. This gaudily decorated restaurant is filled with Tiffany lamps, carved ceilings, and chandeliers. There's also a lounge with entertainment. Open daily. Reservations necessary. Major credit cards accepted. 432 Arthur Godfrey Rd., Miami Beach (phone: 538-8533). Expensive.

Gatti – In Miami Beach since 1924, this family-owned place remains in its original stucco house. The Northern Italian food is excellent and the service is attentive. Jacket required. Closed Mondays and May through October. Reservations advised. Major credit cards accepted. 1427 West Ave., Miami Beach (phone: 673-1717). Expensive.

Grand Café – This place oozes good taste, from the European elegance of the dining room and attentive service to the beautifully presented dishes, such as rack of lamb, she-crab soup, and black linguine (made with squid ink). Jacket required. Reservations necessary for dinner, advised for breakfast and lunch. Open daily. Major credit cards accepted. In the *Grand Bay Hotel,* 2669 S. Bayshore Dr., Coconut Grove (phone: 858-9600). Expensive.

Lucky's – Housed in the refurbished and lush Art Deco *Park Central* hotel, it is one of Miami's hottest spots. The menu hosts eclectic American bistro fare including roasted chicken breast, tortellini with steamed vegetables and tuna with sesame seeds and honey-lime glaze. Open Tuesdays through Sundays for dinner. Reservations advised. Major credit cards accepted. 640 Ocean Dr., Miami Beach (phone: 538-7700). Expensive.

Reflections on the Bay – The waterfront setting is spectacular, the glass and beam structure stunning, and the food carefully prepared and artistically presented. The menu changes frequently, but always features fresh ingredients and an intriguing Caribbean flair. Try the smoked mallard duck with fruit and summer greens; peppered prawns with callaloo greens and plantains; or spicy crabcakes with lobster sauce and okra. Open daily. Reservations advised. Major credit cards accepted. *Bayside Marketplace,* 401 Biscayne Blvd., Miami (phone: 371-6433). Expensive.

Vinton's – Spread across the ground floor of the old *La Palma* hotel, an elegant choice, with foot pillows and fresh flowers for the ladies and sorbet served midway through dinner to refresh the palate. Superb duck with raspberry sauce, salmon in sorrel sauce, and lots of fresh seafood. Some dishes flambéed tableside. Closed Sundays. Reservations advised. Major credit cards accepted. 116 Alhambra Circle, Coral Gables (phone: 445-2511). Expensive.

Caffè Baci – Northern Italian specialties, including scampi sautéed with herbs and lemon sauce and veal with orange sauce. In the heart of Coral Gables, a favorite lunch spot. Open daily. Reservations advised. Major credit cards accepted. 2522 Ponce de León Blvd., Coral Gables (phone: 442-0600). Expensive to moderate.

Café Tanino – What with white lights twinkling overhead, mirrors, fresh flowers, and peach and white napery, it is as festive as the Venice carnival prints on the walls. The food is pan-Italian, with dishes from Sicily and Naples as well as the north. Open daily. Reservations advised. Major credit cards accepted. 2312 Ponce de León Blvd., Coral Gables (phone: 446-1666). Moderate.

Casa Juancho – Country hams hang over the bar and troubadours stroll and serenade at this lively Spanish spot. The *parrillada en mariscos* (shrimp, scallops, squid, and lobster cooked on the big open grill) is a house specialty, as are the *tapas* (hors d'oeuvres), served straight from the bar. Open daily. Reservations unnecessary. Major credit cards accepted. 2436 SW 8th St., Miami (phone: 642-2452). Moderate.

Charade – Continental food in a charming Coral Gables landmark. Portions are large, and an oversize salad is included in the price of an entrée. Open daily. Reservations advised. Major credit cards accepted. 2900 Ponce de León Blvd., Coral Gables (phone: 448-6077). Moderate.

Christy's – This place feels like a private club, with its leather armchairs, brass sconces, and dark wood — and for the pinstripe-suit types who entertain here, it practically is. The aged Iowa steaks and Caesar salad are tops; lobster, veal, duck, and chicken are also first rate. Open daily. Reservations necessary. Major credit cards accepted. 3101 Ponce de León Blvd., Coral Gables (phone: 446-1400). Moderate.

English Pub – Dismantled in England and shipped here, it's dark, atmospheric, and. . .pubish. Prime ribs are the specialty. Open daily. Reservations advised. Major credit cards accepted. 320 Crandon Blvd., Key Biscayne, Miami (phone: 361-8877). Moderate.

Joe's Stone Crab – By now, this famous old (since 1913) South Beach restaurant is a Miami tradition, big, crowded, noisy, and friendly (get there by 6:30 or you'll have to wait). The stone crabs are brought in by *Joe's* own fishing fleet. People come here for serious eating, ordering tons of the coleslaw, hash brown potatoes, and Key lime pie that can keep dedicated diners in line for up to 2 hours. Open daily; closed from mid-May to mid-October. No reservations. Major credit cards accepted. 227 Biscayne St., Miami Beach (phone: 673-0365). Moderate.

Johnny's – A chic, casual newcomer to the hip South Beach scene. Owner Johnny Circharo lovingly prepares rack of lamb, pasta dishes, and seafood entrées. This is a favorite spot of *Miami City Ballet* dancers and night-time beachgoers. Open daily. Reservations advised on weekends. Major credit cards accepted. 915 Lincoln Rd., Miami Beach (phone: 534-3200). Moderate.

Le Manoir – Very good traditional French fare at reasonable prices in a former bakery. Big hit is the Friday night bouillabaisse. This spot is well-frequented by business executives. Closed Sundays. Reservations necessary. Major credit cards accepted. 2534 Ponce de León Blvd., Coral Gables (phone: 442-1990). Moderate.

Monty Trainer's – A casual atmosphere pervades this bayside eatery in Coconut Grove. Guests can arrive either by car or boat (100 dock spaces are available for diners), then enjoy a meal on a palm-fringed terrace or indoors. Its pricier twin, *Monty's Stone Crab* (at Mayfair in the Grove), serves those delectable crustaceans year-round (they're brought in from Virginia off-season), as well as a wide array of fresh seafood. Open daily. Reservations advised. Major credit cards accepted. *Monty Trainer's,* 2560 S. Bayshore Dr., Miami (phone: 858-1431). *Monty's Stone Crab,* 3390 Mary St., Miami (phone: 448-9919). Both moderate.

Savannah Moon – A beautifully designed eatery that features southern cooking at its most eclectic. Try the jambalayas, southern honey steaks, or the veal Vidalia (scallops of veal sautéed in sweet Georgia Vidalia onions). Open daily for dinner; Mondays through Fridays for lunch. Reservations advised. Major credit cards accepted. 13505 S. Dixie Highway, South Miami (phone: 238-8868). Moderate.

Strand – This Miami Beach hot spot caters to an artsy, chic clientele, and suffers from uneven service, but is still recommended for the opportunity to glimpse Miami's see-and-be-seen crowd. Try the fried goat cheese with marinara sauce, Caesar salad, and the (incredibly wonderful) meat loaf. Reservations advised weekends only. Major credit cards accepted. 671 Washington Ave., Miami Beach (phone: 532-2340). Moderate.

Toni's – Japanese standards and new Tokyo cuisine like grilled salmon and seafood pasta. The best sushi on South Beach. Open daily for dinner. Reservations advised on weekends. Visa and MasterCard accepted. 1208 Washington Ave., Miami Beach (phone: 673-9368). Moderate.

Yuca – The name is both a Miami acronym for Young Upscale Cuban Americans and a starchy vegetable that is a staple of Cuban cooking. The bilingual menu features nouvelle twists on Cuban standards — yuca croquettes, grouper with peanut sauce, and flan with berry sauce. The cooking and clientele rank as upscale Cuban. Open daily. Reservations necessary. Major credit cards accepted. 148 Giralda Ave., Coral Gables (phone: 444-4448). Moderate.

Mark's Place – Chef Mark Militello conjures up imaginative dishes like rare tuna steak edged with black and white sesame seeds, corn-fried oysters, a superior veal chop, and rich desserts. A cool, post-modern interior and an unobtrusive location have made this one of the city's hottest stops. Open daily. Reservations necessary. Major credit cards accepted. 2286 NE 123 St., N. Miami Beach (phone: 893-6888). Moderate to inexpensive.

News Café – An international newsstand-cum-bookstore-cum-sidewalk café that is an ideal spot for people watching or a pre-beach breakfast. The menu is light, with sandwiches, salads, and cheeses. Located across from the ocean in the heart of South Beach. Open daily. Reservations unnecessary. Major credit cards accepted. 800 Ocean Dr., Miami Beach (phone: 538-6397). Moderate to inexpensive.

Big Fish – Funky and friendly, this converted gas station on the working Miami River is a popular lunchtime eatery. The appeal is casual dining, a panoramic view of downtown, and fresh seafood on a menu chalked on a blackboard. Try the grouper sandwich on pita, with collard greens and black-eyed peas as accompaniments. Open daily. No credit cards or reservations accepted. 55 SW Miami Ave. Rd., Miami (phone: 372-3725). Inexpensive.

Centro Vasco – Next to jai alai, this is Miami's favorite Basque import. Specialties are *filet madrilene de Centro Vasco,* paella, and *arroz con mariscos.* A great sangria is made right at your table. Open daily.

Reservations advised. Major credit cards accepted. 2235 SW 8th St., Miami (phone: 643-9606). Inexpensive.

Málaga – This traditional Cuban eatery in Little Havana is a good place to get acquainted with the cuisine. Best are standards like fried whole snapper, spiced pork, or *arroz con pollo*. Flamenco shows downstairs start at 9:30 PM weekend nights. Open daily. Reservations advised. Major credit cards accepted. 740 SW 8th St., Miami (phone: 858-4224). Inexpensive.

Marshall Major's – Some people call Miami the Bronx with palm trees. Whether or not that's true, this deli ranks with New York's — pastrami, corned beef, home-style flanken, boiled chicken and vegetables, all served in huge portions. There's an Early Bird Special for dinner. Open daily. No reservations. Major credit cards accepted. 6901 SW 57th Ave., Miami (phone: 665-3661). Inexpensive.

Versailles – Authentic Cuban food and a lively ambience characterize this Little Havana landmark. A favorite of Latins and knowledgeable gringos. Wonderful Cuban sandwiches, black beans, and rice. Open daily till the wee hours. No reservations. Major credit cards accepted. 3555 SW 8th St., Miami (phone: 445-7614). Inexpensive.

Wolfie's – A Miami Beach institution that might be described as a deli, whose eclectic, 500-item menu carries everything from knishes to chicken parmigiana. Open daily. No reservations or credit cards accepted. 2038 Collins Ave., Miami Beach (phone: 538-6626). Inexpensive.

MILWAUKEE

 SEEING THE CITY: The 41-story First Wisconsin Center, Milwaukee's second-tallest building, anchors the eastern end of Wisconsin Avenue at Lake Michigan. Take the elevator to the 40th floor and walk one flight up to the deck. Open Monday through Friday from 2 to 4 PM. 777 E. Wisconsin Ave. (phone: 765-5733).

SPECIAL PLACES: The Milwaukee River divides the downtown area into east and west segments of unequal size (walking east you soon run into the beautiful Lake Michigan shoreline).

DOWNTOWN WEST

Wisconsin Avenue West – Walking west from the bridge along Wisconsin Avenue, Milwaukee's principal shopping street, you pass *Marshall Field* on the same site that John Plankinton, a pioneer butcher, started his career with one cow and boundless ambition. He became a millionaire, and gave a start to packing tycoons Philip Armour and Patrick Cudahy. The blocks between *Marshall Field* and the *Boston Store* have been converted into the *Grand Avenue* shopping mall.

Grand Avenue – Now the center of downtown shopping is the stretch of renovated buildings between Plankinton Avenue and N. 4th Street. The project brought the neighborhood back to life with its airy feel, a hub of fast-food restaurants called the *Spiesegarten,* and lots of different shops. Jugglers, mimes, pianists, choral groups, and other entertainers often perform at various locales throughout Grand Avenue (phone: 224-9720).

Joan of Arc Chapel – On the campus of Marquette University. This is the medieval chapel where Joan of Arc prayed before being put to torch — not here in Milwaukee, but in the French village of Chasse, whence the chapel was transported stone by stone. One of those stones reputedly was kissed by Joan before she went to her death, and is said to be discernibly colder than the others. Open daily except major holidays. Regular church services still held. No admission charge. 601 N. 14th St. (phone: 288-6873).

Milwaukee Public Museum – Has the fourth-largest collection of natural history displays in the country, plus a "Streets of Old Milwaukee" section, showing the city in the 19th century. The museum has some excellent dioramas: Northwest Coast, Great Plains, East Africa. Discreetly hidden away in an upstairs bedroom is the sink that once belonged to Kitty Williams, a famous Milwaukee madam. Open daily except major holidays. Admission charge. 800 W. Wells St. (phone: 278-2700).

Milwaukee County Historical Center – Built in a bank once run by beer barons, it is near the *MECCA Complex,* whose amenities include a sports arena and facilities for conventions and meetings. The *Bradley Center,* just to the north, is home to the city's professional basketball, hockey, and soccer teams. The museum has an archive and numerous exhibitions on the city's history, several of which are especially entertaining for children. Open daily. No admission charge. 910 N. 3rd St. (phone: 273-8288).

Père Marquette Park – Between the museum and the river, this park is named after the explorer-priest who stopped briefly in Milwaukee during a canoe trip through the Great Lakes area. Local legend insists that he landed here, although the site was then part of an extensive tamarack swamp along the Milwaukee River.

DOWNTOWN EAST

Wisconsin Avenue East – Wisconsin Avenue, east of the river, is a shopper's haven, with numerous fine stores. Shops on several nearby cross streets have been lovingly restored to their 19th-century origins. Across from the *Pfister* hotel is the *Milwaukee Club,* whose members are the city's ruling elite (phone: 276-0590).

Third Ward – Formerly an old warehouse district between the Milwaukee River and Lake Michigan, the neighborhood has made a great comeback. Artists' lofts, restaurants, shops, galleries, the *Milwaukee Institute of Art and Design, Milwaukee Magazine,* and *Theatre X* call the place home. Workers on Commission Row haul vegetables and fruit around BMWs and Toyota sports cars owned by the advertising and marketing execs who have moved into the district. For walking tour information, call the Historic Third Ward Association (phone: 273-1173).

Milwaukee War Memorial, Milwaukee Art Museum – On the lakefront, where Lincoln Memorial Drive crosses Wisconsin Avenue, the original building was designed by Eero Saarinen. The *Art Museum's* permanent collection includes Old Masters, contemporary art, and primitive painting and sculpture. It also runs the *Villa Terrace Decorative Arts Museum* (at 2220 N. Terrace Ave.). Outside, Lake Michigan provides a powerful backdrop for sculpture. The museum is closed Mondays. Admission charge. 750 N. Lincoln Memorial Dr. (phone: 271-9508).

Cathedral Square – Between Jackson and Jefferson Streets, this square dates to Wisconsin's territorial days. Except for the tower, St. John's Cathedral was nearly destroyed by fire in 1935. On the west side of the square, *Skylight Theater* offers musical plays and vest pocket operas. If you feel like a snack, turn left on Jefferson to No. 761, where *George Watts & Son's* interesting silver shop has a tea shop tucked away on the second floor (phone: 291-5120).

City Hall – Milwaukee's best-known landmark, this building with the tall tower (393 feet) was designed in 1895 so that taxpayers could drive their buggies up in the rain to pay real estate taxes without getting wet. In the tower above the arched entry, Old Sol, a 20-ton bell, gathers dust. In 1922, citizens complained about the noise of Old Sol tolling, and city fathers ordered it stilled. N. Water St. at Wells St.

OTHER SPECIAL PLACES

Annunciation Greek Orthodox Church – The last major building designed by Wisconsin-born architect Frank Lloyd Wright. You can tour the saucer-shaped structure daily except Sundays, by appointment only. Admission charge. 9400 W. Congress St. (phone: 461-9400).

Whitnall Park – One of the larger municipal parks in the country, Whitnall includes the 689-acre Boerner Botanical Gardens, with sunken gardens, nature trails, and exhibitions. Open daily. No admission charge. 5879 S. 92nd St., Hales Corners (phone: 425-1130). Also on the park grounds is the Todd Wehr Nature Center, a wildlife preserve for hikers and strollers. Open daily; closed Sundays in winter. No admission charge. 9701 W. College Ave., Franklin (phone: 425-8550).

Milwaukee County Zoo – Among the most famous zoos in the country, this one allows the animals to roam free in natural habitats. Kids

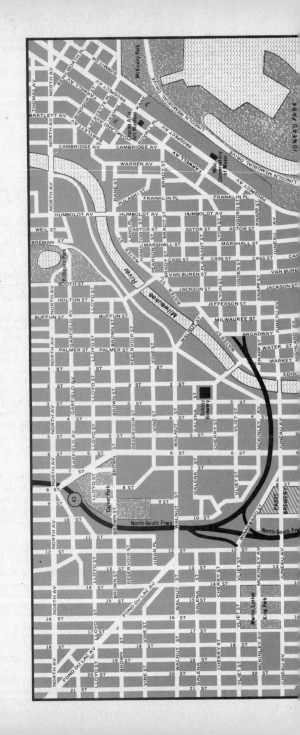

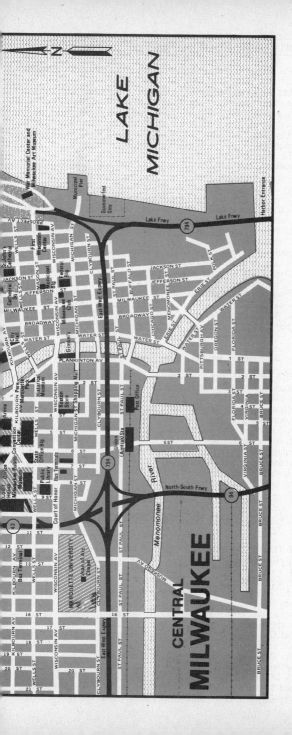

adore the miniature railroad and children's zoo. Open daily. Admission charge. 10001 W. Blue Mound Rd. (phone: 771-5500).

Schlitz Audubon Center – The 180 acres of undisturbed grazing area once provided pasture to brewery horses weary from pulling beer wagons. It's a good place to wander and wonder at days gone by. A 60-foot wooden tower built on a 100-foot bluff offers a bird's-eye view of the city and countryside. Be warned — there is no elevator. Closed Mondays. Admission charge; free to members of Audubon Center. 1111 E. Brown Deer Rd. (phone: 352-2880).

Neighborhoods – The Department of City Development recently launched a neighborhood promotion program that eventually will take in many of the city's interesting, out-of-the-way sights. Called *MKE Neighborhood Tours Ltd.,* the program aims to get visitors out of downtown and into the communities to sample the diversity of restaurants, shops, and people of Milwaukee. Already in place are itineraries for "The Mitchell Street Express," "Neighborhoods 94 West," "Neighborhood North," and "Riverwest." Discover the *Balkan Trading Company* (938 W. Lapham Blvd., phone: 643-7372) for homemade burek and Serbian smoked sausage; *Woodland Pattern Bookstore* (720 E. Locust St., phone: 263-4001), which offers readings and lectures; the *Comic Stop* (224 N. 35th St., phone: 933-0550) for comic books; and *Suzy's Cream Cheesecakes* (5901 W. Vliet St., phone: 453-2255), plus many more fascinating hideaways. For details, contact the Department of City Development (809 N. Broadway, Milwaukee, WI 53202; phone: 223-5796).

Harbor Cruises – *Iroquois Boat Line* (Clybourn St. Bridge dock; phone: 332-4194) offers 2-hour trips along the Milwaukee River. Daily from *Memorial Day* through *Labor Day.* The *Emerald Isle* also offers cruises of the harbor and the Milwaukee shoreline (phone: 786-6886).

■ **EXTRA SPECIAL:** For an interesting day trip, take I-94 west 78 miles to Madison, the state capital and home of the University of Wisconsin's 1,000-acre, Big Ten campus. Drop in at the information center at Memorial Union (on Park and Langdon Sts.) to pick up a map and find out what's happening on campus. There's more than enough to keep you busy, with an art center, geology museum, planetarium, observatory, and arboretum to see. The four lakes in Madison — Mendota, Monona, Waubesa, Wingra, and nearby Kegonsa — are great for fishing and swimming. If you continue driving west (toward the Iowa border), or due south toward Illinois, you'll find yourself in Wisconsin cheese country.

SOURCES AND RESOURCES

TOURIST INFORMATION: For information, maps, and brochures, contact the visitors' information center (828 N. Broadway; phone: 273-3950) and the Greater Milwaukee Convention and Visitors Bureau (510 W. Kilbourn Ave., Milwaukee, WI 53203; phone: 273-3950). The public service bureau in the lobby of the Journal Building (4th and State) also is helpful (phone: 224-2120). Contact the Wisconsin state hotline (800-432-TRIP) for maps, calendars of events, health updates, and travel advisories.

Local Coverage – *Milwaukee Sentinel,* morning daily; *Milwaukee Journal,* afternoon daily; *Shepherd Express Downtowner* and *Milwaukee Weekly,* weeklies; *Milwaukee* magazine, monthly.

Television Stations – WTMJ Channel 4–NBC; WITI Channel 6–CBS; WMVS Channel 10–PBS; WISN Channel 12–ABC.

Radio Stations – AM: WTMJ 620 (news, top 40); WBKV 1470 (adult contemporary); WAUK 1510 (country music). FM: WUWM 89.8 (jazz/

news); WKTI 94.5 (top 40); WKLH 96.5 (classic rock); WMYX 99 (mix of 1960s, 1970s, and 1980s).

 TELEPHONE: The area code for Milwaukee is 414.
Sales Tax – There is a 5% statewide sales tax.

 CLIMATE: Summer and fall are generally pleasant, but expect sudden change when the wind shifts to the east. In winter, be prepared for bitter winds. The sub-zero cold is formidable.

 GETTING AROUND: Airport – General Mitchell International Airport handles the city's domestic and international air traffic and is a 15-minute drive from downtown; taxi fare should run about $12. An economical share-a-ride program is available to those heading to the same destination; make arrangements through the Ground Transportation Coordinator, directly outside the baggage claim area. *Milwaukee County Transit* buses also provide service downtown for $1 (exact change required). *Airport Limousine* (phone: 272-1955) leaves every half hour for downtown hotels ($4.70) as well as hotels in the western and northern metro areas ($9.50).

Bus – During the summer, a shuttle bus runs from the lakefront to the courthouse, mostly along Wisconsin Avenue. For information on bus schedules, contact *Milwaukee County Transit System,* 1942 N. 17th St. (phone: 344-6711).

Car Rental – Most major car rental firms are represented. For a reliable local agency, contact *Selig Chevrolet* (10200 W. Arthur Ave., West Allis; phone: 327-2300) or *Econo-Lease* (3504 W. Wisconsin Ave.; phone: 933-1040).

Taxi – There are taxi stands at most major hotels, but we recommend calling *City Veterans Taxi* (phone: 933-2266) or *Yellow Cab* (phone: 271-1800).

 VITAL SERVICES: Audiovisual Equipment – *Midwest Visual Equipment Co.* (phone: 784-5880).
Baby-sitting – *Sara Care Services,* 9730 W. Bluemound Rd. (phone: 774-7272).

Business Services – *National Business Offices* (1033 N. Mayfair Rd.; phone: 259-9110; and at 2040 W. Wisconsin Ave.; phone: 933-0636); *National Bookkeeping Service* (759 N. Milwaukee St.; phone: 276-6655).

Dry Cleaner/Tailor – *One-Hour Valet Cleaners,* 12th and Wells Sts. (phone: 272-5808).

Limousine – *Andrus Limousine Service* (phone: 445-5060); *Arthur Livery Service* (phone: 475-5171).

Mechanics – *Midtowne Mobil Servicenter* (714 N. 27th St.; phone: 344-9229); *Bodden's Service* (136 N. Water St.; phone: 272-3777); for foreign cars, *Tosa Imports* (6102 W. North Ave.; phone: 771-2340).

Medical Emergency – *Mt. Sinai Hospital,* 950 N. 12th St. (phone: 283-6666).

Messenger Services – *Action Express* (phone: 549-3300); *Bonded Messenger Service* (phone: 933-4500).

National/International Courier – *Federal Express* (phone: 481-2599); *DHL Worldwide Courier Express* (phone: 800-225-5345).

Pharmacy – *Phillips' Juneau Village Pharmacy,* 8:30 AM to 9 PM Mondays through Saturdays; 9 AM to 5 PM on Sundays, 1125 N. Van Buren St. (phone: 272-0922).

Photocopies – *Minuteman Press* (710 N. Milwaukee St.; phone: 278-7997); *Anderson Graphics* (521 N. 8th St.; phone: 276-4445).

Post Office – The central office is located at 345 W. St. Paul Ave. (phone: 291-2530).

Professional Photographer – *John Nienhuis* (phone: 442-9199); *Pat Goetzinger* (phone: 645-4567).

Secretary/Stenographer – *National Business Offices* (phone: 933-0636).

Teleconference Facilities – *Hyatt Regency, Pfister, Marc Plaza* (see *Best in Town*, below).

Translator – *Berlitz* (phone: 276-4121); *Flagg & Associates* (phone: 278-8322); *Iverson Language Associates* (phone: 271-1144).

Typewriter Rental – *Teeter-Warsh Co.*, 1-day minimum (phone: 276-6436).

Western Union/Telex – Many offices are located around the city (phone: 800-325-6000).

SPECIAL EVENTS: For 5 weekends beginning at the end of January, *Winterfest*, Milwaukee's annual winter festival, takes place. *Summerfest* is held every June and July on the lakefront. Rock and jazz concerts are part of the celebrations. It is followed by a series of ethnic festivals featuring appropriate food and entertainment at the Henry W. Maier Lakefront Festival Park grounds. *Lakefront Festival of the Arts* is held outdoors near the *Milwaukee Art Center* in the middle of June with music, food, arts and crafts exhibits. The *Great Circus Parade*, revived in 1985, is now an annual July event. The *Wisconsin State Fair* takes place for 2 weeks in mid-August on the fairgrounds adjoining I-94, west of downtown. The weekend before *Thanksgiving*, *Holiday Folk Fair* features ethnic food, music and entertainment at *MECCA Complex*, Kilbourn Ave.

MUSEUMS: The *Milwaukee County Historical Center, Milwaukee Public Museum*, and *Milwaukee War Memorial and Art Museum* are described in *Special Places*. *Discovery World*, a museum of science, economics, and technology where visitors can manipulate exhibits, is open weekends in the main library building (818 W. Wisconsin Ave.; phone: 765-9966). Milwaukee has other museums a-plenty, among them:

Brooks Stevens Auto Museum – 10325 N. Port Washington Rd. (phone: 241-4185).

Charles Allis Art Museum – 1801 N. Prospect Ave. (phone: 278-8295).

Captain Frederick Pabst Mansion – 2000 W. Wisconsin Ave. (phone: 931-0808).

MAJOR COLLEGES AND UNIVERSITIES: Marquette University — 13,000 students (11th and 18th Sts. on Wisconsin Ave.; phone: 224-7250); University of Wisconsin–Milwaukee — 27,000 students (Kenwood Blvd. and Downer Ave.; phone: 963-1122).

SPORTS AND FITNESS: Baseball – The *Brewers* play at *County Stadium*, 201 S. 46th St. (phone: 933-9000).

Basketball – The Milwaukee *Bucks* and Marquette *Warriors* play at *Bradley Center*, 4th and State (phone: 227-0400).

Bicycling – Bikes can be rented from *East Side Cycle and Hobby Shop* (2031 N. Farwell Ave.; phone: 276-9848) and *Wilson Park Schwinn Cyclery* (2033 W. Howard Ave.; phone: 281-4720).

Fishing – Salmon and trout as big as 30 pounds are caught in Lake Michigan, from shore and breakwater. You can use launching ramps at McKinley Marina and near *South Shore Yacht Club* for $3 to $5. Half-day boat charters cost about $160 for a party of six, including bait and tackle, and are offered by numerous firms (see the yellow pages under Fishing Parties — Charter).

Fitness Center – The *YMCA* has a pool, track, sauna, weights, and massage (9250 N. Green Bay Rd.; phone: 354-9622); also downtown (915 W. Wisconsin Ave.; phone: 224-9622).

Football – Green Bay *Packers* play some of their games at *County Stadium*, 201 S. 46th St. (phone: 342-2717).

Golf – The best public golf course is at Mee-Kwon Park, 6333 W. Bonniwell Rd., Mequon (phone: 242-1310).

Hockey – The Milwaukee *Admirals* play at the *Bradley Center* (phone: 227-0550).

Ice Skating – In winter, many parks open rinks. For year-round ice skating (indoors), try *Wilson Park Center* (4001 S. 20th St.; phone: 281-4610) and *Eble Ice Arena* (19700 W. Blue Mound Rd.; phone: 784-5155).

Jogging – Run in Lake Front Park, near War Memorial Center, on the beach, sidewalk, or oval track.

Nature Walks – The Schlitz Audubon Center, at 1111 E. Brown Deer Rd., has plenty of nature walks, highlighted by an amazing variety of birds.

Polo – Sundays in summer Milwaukee's polo teams compete at *Uihlein Field*, Good Hope Rd. and N. 70th St. (no phone).

Skiing – Currie, Dretzka, and Whitnall parks have ski tows, and mostly beginners' trails. Cross-country skiers may use all county parks. The Whitnall Park trails are particularly good.

Soccer – The *Milwaukee Wave* professional soccer team plays at the *Bradley Center* (phone: 962-9283).

Swimming – Seven public beaches along the lakefront have lifeguards and dressing facilities. The water is usually chilly, even in August.

Tennis – Try *North Shore Racquet Club* (5750 N. Glen Park Rd.; phone: 351-2900) or *Le Club* (2001 W. Good Hope Rd.; phone: 352-4900). In warm weather, numerous county parks have courts available for nominal fee.

THEATERS: For complete listings on theatrical and musical events, see local publications listed above. *Milwaukee Repertory Theater,* in a former power station (on E. Wells St. just east of the Milwaukee River; phone: 224-9490), is linked to the *Wyndham Milwaukee Center,* which includes a hotel, office tower, and shops. The *Pabst Theater* (at 144 E. Wells St.; phone: 278-3663), which stages a variety of shows, also is connected to the center as part of what is called the Theater District. Across E. Kilbourn Avenue is the *Performing Arts Center,* home of *First Stage Milwaukee,* a children's theater. *Riverside Theater* (116 W. Wisconsin Ave.; phone: 271-2000) features stage shows by top performers. Other theaters include: *Skylight Comic Opera* (813 N. Jefferson St.; phone: 271-8815); *Theatre X* (158 N. Broadway; phone: 278-0555) for experimental drama; and the *Irish Fest Theater Company,* which presents works throughout the community, as well as regionally (phone: 258-9349).

MUSIC: *Milwaukee Symphony, Pennsylvania and Milwaukee Ballet,* and *Florentine Opera Company* perform at the *Performing Arts Center* (929 N. Water St.; phone: 273-7121). *"Music Under the Stars"* concerts are held in Washington and Humboldt parks on Friday and Saturday nights in July and August.

NIGHTCLUBS AND NIGHTLIFE: For jazz, visit *John Hawk's Pub* (Broadway and Michigan; phone: 272-3199). *Rumors* (in the *Marriott* at 375 S. Moorland Rd. in Brookfield; phone: 786-1100) has dancing to top 40 hits and caters to well-dressed young professionals; *La Playa* (atop the *Pfister* hotel; phone: 273-8222) has touch dancing, including the Latin *lambada,* plus a spectacular view. For dinner with piano music, try *Chip & Py's* (815 S. 5th; phone: 645-3435), closed Mondays. On Saturday nights, the *Brown Bottle Pub* (221 W. Galena; phone: 271-4444) has a machine that provides the background vocals and instrumentals of popular songs for customers who wish to belt out a tune or two. Located in the old taprooms of a Schlitz brewery, it also has a selection of 103 different ales and beers from which to choose.

BEST IN TOWN

CHECKING IN: Milwaukee's hotels range from the traditional, older *Pfister* and the modern *Hyatt Regency* to the functional *Grand* hotel, near the airport. Expect to pay between $80 and $105 for a double at those places designated expensive; between $55 and $75 in the moderate category; about $45 or $50 at inexpensive places. Several offer weekend bargain rates. All telephone numbers are in the 414 area code unless otherwise indicated.

Hyatt Regency – This $28-million, 18-story hotel was the first large property to be built in Milwaukee in many years and has helped to end a chronic shortage of rooms for conventions. And, by no coincidence, it is next to the downtown *Convention Center.* Topping the 485-room structure, with its atrium lobby, is the *Polaris,* a revolving restaurant (see *Eating Out*). Room service continues until 2 AM. Other amenities include 19 meeting rooms, concierge, A/V equipment, photocopiers, and express checkout. 4th and Kilbourn (phone: 276-1234, 800-233-1234, or 800-228-9000; Fax: 414-276-6338). Expensive.

Pfister – Catering to visiting and local elite since the 1890s. A multimillion-dollar restoration has brought this 330-room establishment back to the level that enchanted Enrico Caruso and several presidents. The bronze lions in the lobby are named Dick and Harry, by the way, and the best views of the lake are from rooms 8, 9, 10, or high up in the tower in the romantic lounge, *La Playa.* There also is a fine restaurant (see *Eating Out*). Round-the-clock room service arrives promptly. There are a concierge desk, 17 meeting rooms, photocopiers, computers, and express checkout. 424 E. Wisconsin Ave. (phone: 273-8222; Fax: 414-273-0747). Expensive.

Wyndham – In the heart of downtown, this facility is connected to the Theater District complex and is across the street from City Hall and the *Performing Arts Center.* The 10-story high-rise has 221 rooms, the *Kilbourn Café* for steaks and fowl, plus 2 nice bars. Rides in horse-drawn carriage are another feature. Eight rooms are available for business meetings, as well as 24-hour room service, a concierge desk, A/V equipment, photocopiers, and express checkout. 139 E. Kilbourn Ave. (phone: 276-8686; Fax: 414-291-4779). Expensive.

Marc Plaza – The largest hotel in Milwaukee since 1927, its 540 rooms have gone through extensive renovation during their long career. Updated facilities include a heated indoor swimming pool and sauna. Twenty-four hour room service is available, as are 16 meeting rooms, concierge, secretarial services, A/V equipment, photocopiers, computers, and express checkout. 509 W. Wisconsin Ave. (phone: 271-7250; Fax: 414-271-8091). Expensive to moderate.

Hilton Inn – Overlooking the Milwaukee River, this 164-room hostelry includes such amenities as king-size beds and an indoor pool. The adjoining *Anchorage* restaurant is noted for its seafood. There's 24-hour room service, 5 meeting rooms, and A/V equipment and photocopiers. On the Milwaukee River, near the Hampton Ave. exit of I-43 (phone: 962-6040 or 800-HILTONS; Fax: 414-962-6166). Moderate.

Marriott Inn – This place stands out among the many motels on the outskirts of town. It has 254 rooms (one especially equipped for paraplegics), an indoor heated pool, and a popular disco, *Rumors.* Room service will arrive until 11 PM, and there's an efficient concierge desk. In addition, there are 18 meeting rooms, secretarial services, photocopiers, and express checkout. 375 S. Moorland Rd., Brookfield (phone: 786-1100 or 800-228-9290; Fax: 414-786-1100, ext. 545). Moderate.

Grand – Near the airport, next to a convention hall, this property has 400 rooms, 2 heated swimming pools, and handball, tennis, and racquetball courts. If you're intrigued by one of Milwaukee's favorite sports, you'll be delighted to find out it's close to a bowling alley. Room service is available until 10:30 PM. Other services include 32 meeting rooms, secretarial services, A/V equipment, photocopiers, computers, and express checkout. 4747 S. Howell Ave. (phone: 481-8000; Fax: 414-481-8616). Moderate to inexpensive.

EATING OUT: Visiting Milwaukee without sampling the Wiener schnitzel would be like going to New Orleans's French Quarter and living on Big Macs. It was once said that visitors could get any kind of food in Milwaukee as long as it was German, but these days it's easy to feast at Polish, Chinese, Italian, Greek, Japanese, Serbian, and American restaurants as well. Expect to pay between $40 and $60 for two at those places listed as expensive; between $30 and $40 in the moderate category; under $20 in the inexpensive bracket. Prices don't include drinks, wine, or tips. All telephone numbers are in the 414 area code unless otherwise indicated.

English Room – This is the place if you suddenly develop an overwhelming craving for crêpes flambées or pheasant with truffles. Flaming dishes are prepared at your table with appropriate theatrical flourish. Open daily. Reservations necessary on weekends. Major credit cards accepted. In the *Pfister Hotel,* 424 E. Wisconsin Ave. (phone: 273-8222). Expensive.

John Ernst – Even older and still a favorite of members of the brewing aristocracy, serving since 1878. Decorated with steins, German clocks, and posters. You can get steaks, but to do as the local populace does, it's better to order "sauerbraten mit dumplings, ja?" Closed Mondays. Reservations advised on weekends. Major credit cards accepted. 600 E. Ogden Ave. (phone: 273-1878). Expensive.

Karl Ratzsch's – Ranked as one of Milwaukee's top dining spots for many years, specializing in Teutonic fare since the days when the city called itself the German Athens. Open daily. Reservations advised on weekends. Major credit cards accepted. 320 E. Mason St. (phone: 276-2720). Expensive.

La Rôtisserie and Polaris – These two restaurants are in the *Hyatt Regency* hotel. The former overlooks the 18-story lobby/atrium and specializes in duck roasted on a spit. The latter, revolving slowly atop the *Hyatt*'s roof, offers a more limited menu but a better view. Open daily. Reservations advised. Major credit cards accepted. 4th and Kilbourn (phone: 276-1234). Expensive.

Sanford – Three years ago, Sandy D'Amato converted this former grocery store (owned by his grandparents since 1915, and inherited by his parents) into a real charmer of a restaurant. His wife Angie supervises the dining room while chef Sandy works tirelessly to produce such culinary treats as basil flecked *cima Genovese* (a rolled veal roast) and shrimp cakes with carmelized onions and tamarind sauce. He's also a whiz at the grill, and daily changes on the menu attest to his skill. Closed Sundays. Reservations advised. Major credit cards accepted. 1517 N. Jackson St. (phone: 276-9608). Expensive.

Mader's – A family-run place going back to shortly after the century's turn, it's decorated in Bavarian style. For years, the late Gus Mader offered a reward to anyone who could finish his 3½-lb. pork shank. The prize? Another 3½-lb. pork shank, to be eaten at the same sitting. Open daily. Reservations advised on weekends. Major credit cards accepted. 1037 N. 3rd St. (phone: 271-3377). Expensive to moderate.

Old Town – At this Serbian spot you can dine to the tune of tinkling tamburitzas. Fine, you say, but what is Serbian food? Well you might ask. We did, and were delighted to find it means sizzling lamb dishes cooked somewhat spicier than similar Greek and Turkish dishes. Closed Mondays. Reservations advised on weekends. Major credit cards accepted. 522 W. Lincoln Ave. (phone: 672-0206). Moderate.

Toy's Chinatown – The family that owns this elaborate downtown Chinese dining spot has been serving Milwaukee residents for three generations, so when you eat here, you're not just getting egg rolls, you're getting tradition. Unless you order hundred-year-old duck eggs, you can be sure of fresh Cantonese dishes, like sweet and sour shrimp, spareribs, and chow mein. Open daily. Reservations advised on weekends. Major credit cards accepted. 830 N. 3rd St. (phone: 271-5166). Moderate.

Bavarian Inn – In a park owned by Germanic clubs, its dining room is open to the public daily except Mondays. The food is generally good, the atmosphere informal, and the Sunday buffet is one of the best bargains in town. You can help yourself to as much as you like. Be sure to bring a big appetite to do it justice. Soccer fields and a festival area on the grounds mean that there's usually something to see, as well. Reservations advised on weekends. Major credit cards accepted. Take the Silver Spring exit from I-43 north, turn south on N. Port Washington Rd., then west on Lexington to 700 W. Lexington Ave. (phone: 964-0300). Inexpensive.

Jake's Delicatessen – If corned beef on rye appeals to you more than goose à la Tivoli or souvlaki, this is the place. All kinds of people eat here, from local millionaires to penniless *kreplach* lovers. You can sit at a booth, at a counter, or take your pastrami sandwich with you in a paper bag. Try the specials — they're giant knockwurst-like sausages. Open daily. Reservations advised. No credit cards accepted. 1634 W. North Ave. (phone: 562-1272). Inexpensive.

Leon's Frozen Custard Drive-In – Besides their passion for cheese and beer, Milwaukeeans also love frozen custard. This place has been open since 1942, and is one of the favored spots for indulging in the creamy, frozen treat. Open daily. 3131 S. 27th St. (phone: 383-1784). Inexpensive.

Watt's Tea Shop – This cozy spot serves wonderful sandwiches and soups, and old-fashioned homemade desserts such as fresh fruit custard tarts, and freshly baked breads and muffins. 761 N. Jefferson St. (phone: 291-5120).

■ **THE BEERS THAT MADE MILWAUKEE FAMOUS:** If you're wondering where the smell of malt is coming from, follow your nose to one of the big breweries, where you'll be escorted through the facilities and given samples of the frothy wares (unless you're a child, in which case you only get to look): *Miller* (3939 W. Highland Blvd.; phone: 931-2337), *Pabst* (915 Juneau Ave.; phone: 223-3709), and a smaller one, *Sprecher's* (730 W. Oregon St.; phone: 272-BEER). All welcome visitors except on holidays, when everyone stays home testing the product.

MINNEAPOLIS–
ST. PAUL

AT-A-GLANCE

SEEING THE CITY: Although the IDS and Northwest Tower buildings are taller, the best view of the area is from the observation deck of the 32-story Foshay Tower (9th St. at 2nd Ave) in Minneapolis; closed in winter. St. Paul is built on seven hills, like Rome. Cherokee Park, overlooking the Mississippi River, affords a spectacular panorama of both cities. Another good view is that from Pennsylvania Avenue Hill.

SPECIAL PLACES: The most extraordinary feature of downtown Minneapolis and St. Paul is their interior skyways, an interconnected belt of pedestrian malls and escalators lacing in and out of shops, banks, and restaurants at the 2nd-story level. When it's below zero, you still can walk around comfortably without a coat. At street level, courtyards, gardens, fountains, and sculpture form attractive plazas. In Minneapolis, travelers may check in at one of five hotels connected to the skyway: *Radisson Plaza, Marriott City Center, Embassy Suites, Marquette,* and *Northstar.* St. Paul's skyway connects the *Radisson St. Paul* and the *St. Paul* hotel (see *Checking In*).

MINNEAPOLIS

Minneapolis Institute of Arts – Architecturally classical, the museum houses Old Masters, Chinese and Egyptian art, Revere silver, and historical exhibitions. In addition, its Society for Fine Arts presents classical films, recitals, and lectures. A model for other arts institutions around the country, the institute is also the home of the Minneapolis College of Art and Design and the *Children's Theater Company.* Open daily. Admission charge. 2400 3rd Ave. S. (phone: 870-3131).

Guthrie Theater – Internationally acclaimed for its superb productions, the *Guthrie* features a resident professional repertory company that presents ensemble productions of classical and modern drama. The contemporary theater building can seat more than 1,400 people in a 200-degree arc around an open stage. After a nationwide search for a hospitable metropolitan environment in which to locate a repertory theater, Sir Tyrone Guthrie selected Minneapolis. His choice has been borne out by the enthusiastic, loving support of audiences and patrons. The theatrical season generally runs from May to February; 1990 marked the theater's 25th anniversary. Concerts are given throughout the year. 725 Vineland Pl. (phone: 377-2224 or 347-1100).

Walker Art Center – Named after T. B. Walker, a local patron of the arts, the center, in the *Guthrie* building, complements the classical *Institute of Arts* by focusing on post-Impressionist and contemporary art. The *Walker* also features alternating exhibitions, innovative film programs, and concerts. Its restaurant is open from 11:30 AM to 3 PM. Closed Mondays. Admission charge. 725 Vineland Pl. (phone: 375-7600 or the box office, 375-7622).

Minneapolis Sculpture Gardens – To get to one of the country's

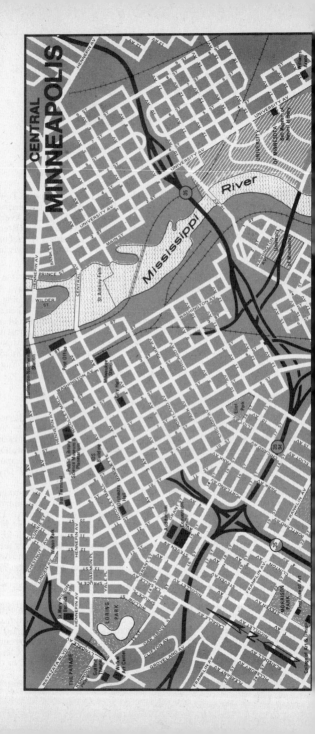

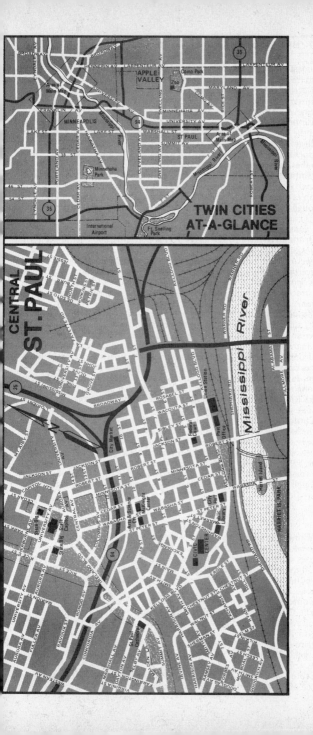

grandest monumental sculpture gardens, at the *Walker Art Center,* stroll from the *Nicollet Mall,* following Loring Greenway through Loring Park and across the Whitney Bridge. Pieces in the 7-acre park include such whimsical delights as *Spoonbridge and Cherry* by Claes Oldenburg and Coosje van Bruggen.

Minnehaha Park – In his poem "Hiawatha," Longfellow immortalized the "laughing waters" of Minnehaha Falls along the Mississippi. In addition to the splendor of the Falls, you can picnic near a statue of Minnehaha herself and brave Hiawatha. No admission charge. Minnehaha Pkwy. and Hiawatha Ave. S.

Minneapolis Grain Exchange – An ornate hall the size of a large school gym, the exchange is a loud, hectic place where futures and samples of actual grains are bought and sold. You can take a guided tour through the world's largest grain exchange, but you must make reservations in advance. Visitors' balcony open daily. Tours given on weekdays. No admission charge. 400 4th St. S. (phone: 338-6212).

Orchestra Hall – Music has had an appreciative audience in the Twin Cities since the turn of the century. The hall houses the *Minnesota Orchestra* (formerly the *Minneapolis Symphony*), which played its first concert in 1903 and has been playing classical and symphonic pop music to responsive audiences ever since. Though spartan in appearance, *Orchestra Hall* is renowned for its superior acoustics. 1111 Nicollet Ave. (phone: 371-5656).

Minnesota Zoo – Set in the rolling hills of Apple Valley, this 500-acre, state-funded zoological park provides a natural environment for Siberian tigers, musk oxen, moose, and other northern animals. There are many aquatic species in the aquarium, and a 5-story indoor tropical environment houses jungle fauna and flora. In winter, cross-country skiers can enjoy 10 kilometers of groomed trails that meander past musk oxen, caribou, and other Minnesota wildlife. Zoo lovers will find this one among the nation's best. Open daily. Admission charge. 12101 Johnny Cake Ridge Rd., Apple Valley, 25 minutes south of the city on Hwy. 35 (phone: 431-9200).

Canterbury Downs – Racing fans don't have to go far to see some of the Midwest's best quarter and thoroughbred horse action. *Canterbury Downs* is 1½ miles southwest of Valleyfair and Highway 100 in Shakopee, about 25 minutes south of the Minneapolis Loop. General admission, $3; grandstand seats, $2; clubhouse admission, $7.50. For general information, call 445-RACE. The season begins in spring and extends through mid-October, with varying post times. Ten races usually are offered daily.

ST. PAUL

Minnesota Museum of Art – Designed by Magnus Jemne, this magnificent Art Deco structure is now the museum's permanent home and houses contemporary art. Hours are from 1 to 4 PM Saturdays; from 11:30 AM to 4:30 PM Sundays; and from 10:30 AM to 4:30 PM weekdays. Open until 7:30 PM Thursdays. No admission charge. 305 St. Peter St. (phone: 292-4355).

Como Park – St. Paul has a multitude of parks. The largest is St. Paul's Como Park, which dates to Victoria's reign. A 70-acre lake, a small zoo, a golf course, a Japanese garden, and children's rides contribute to its popularity. In addition, there are special floral gardens, a year-round conservatory, and a lakeside pavilion where summer concerts are held. Open daily. No admission charge. Lexington Ave. at Como Ave. (phone: 488-7291 or 292-7400).

State Capitol – St. Paul is Minnesota's political center, and its capitol is one of the most important buildings in the state. Set on a hill, its giant dome — similar to one designed by Michelangelo in Rome — is one of the state's outstanding landmarks. More than 25 varieties of marble, limestone, sandstone, and granite were used to construct the building. Free guided tours given daily. The Minnesota Historical Society building is on the edge of the capitol grounds. Founded in 1849, 10 years before Minnesota became a state, the society houses records of pioneer days. Open daily. No admission charge. University Ave. between Wabasha and Cedar Sts. (phone: 296-3962).

Governor's Residence – This English Tudor residence, built in 1910–11, is on the National Register of Historic Sites. Donated to the state by the daughters of lumberman Horace Irvine, it is open for tours. Reservations required. No admission charge. 1006 Summit Ave. (phone: 297-2161).

St. Paul's Cathedral – The center of the Roman Catholic archdiocese, this cathedral is a replica of St. Peter's in Rome. Architecturally notable for its 175-foot-high dome and a central rose window, it has a special Shrine of the Nations, where visitors can meditate and pray. Open daily. No admission charge. 239 Selby Ave. (phone: 228-1766).

Science Museum of Minnesota – This $3.5-million complex combines a 635-seat theater for the performing arts, a 300-seat auditorium, an art gallery, an omnitheatre (see below), a rooftop lounge, and the pièce de résistance, the science museum. Featuring natural history, environmental, and geological exhibitions and films, the science center is immensely popular with residents. Open daily during the summer; closed Mondays in winter. Admission charge. 30 E. 10th St. (phone: 221-9488).

3M William L. McKnight Omnitheatre – Named after the founding father of the 3M Company, it is among the most advanced centers of its kind in the US. Part of the *Science Museum of Minnesota,* the high point of this new science complex is its "omnitheatre" — a floor-to-ceiling hemispheric screen surrounding the audience and tilted at 30 degrees so that viewers will see the screen in front of them rather than above, as in conventional planetariums. Closed Mondays. Admission charge. 505 Wabasha (phone: 221-9488).

Historic Ft. Snelling – The oldest landmark in the Twin Cities, one of the first military posts west of the Mississippi. Not very far west, however: Ft. Snelling sits high on a bluff overlooking the junction of the Mississippi and Minnesota rivers. You can see what life was like here during the 1820s. People in costume demonstrate early crafts, and parade in military formation. Fife and drum bands perform in summer. The history center is open weekdays year-round. The fort is open daily, May through October. No admission charge to the history center and museum; admission charge for the fort. Hwy. 5 and 55, 6 miles southwest of the city (phone: 726-9430 or 726-1171).

■ **EXTRA SPECIAL:** The St. Croix Valley, 25 miles northeast of Minneapolis–St. Paul, offers several stops for a day's outing. Stillwater, birthplace of Minnesota, is within easy striking distance of the Afton Alps, Welch Village, and Wild Mountain for skiers. In Stillwater, visit the *Grand Garage and Gallery* (on Main St.) with its shops and galleries. It has restaurants, but a better eating stop is *Brine's Meat Market and Lunchroom* (219 S. Main St.; phone: 439-1862) which has the *Employees Lunchroom* upstairs, open to anybody employed anywhere, with great bratwurst, pastrami, and chili. On the Wisconsin side of the tour is Somerset, which has one of the greatest summer activities in the entire world: tubing down the Apple River. You get carted upriver about 4 miles, plunked into an inner tube, and sent drifting back to Somerset. The river flows quickly over rapids at the outset, but widens and slows down, and the ride into town is tranquil.

SOURCES AND RESOURCES

TOURIST INFORMATION: Each Twin has its own tourist source: the Greater Minneapolis Convention and Visitors Association (1219 Marquette, Minneapolis, MN 55403; phone: 348-4313); and the St. Paul Convention and Visitors Bureau (55 E. 5th St., St. Paul, MN 55101; phone: 297-6985). A *Metro Area Visitors Guide* is also available from the convention and visitors bureaus in both St. Paul and Minneapolis and the Minnesota Office of Tourism. Contact the Minnesota state hotline (800-657-3700) for maps, calendars of events, health updates, and travel advisories.

Minnesota Explorer, a 24-page guide to events throughout the state published three times a year, is free from the Minnesota Office of Tourism, 375 Jackson St., 250 Skyway Level, St. Paul, MN 55101 (phone: 296-5029 or 800-657-3700).

Local Coverage – The *Star-Tribune,* daily; *St. Paul Pioneer Press,* daily. The *Reader* and *City Pages* (both distributed free in shopping centers and downtown hotels) list activities in the Twin Cities. *Mpls.–St. Paul* and *Twin Cities* magazines, available monthly at newsstands, give full details on what's what.

Television Stations – KTCA Channel 2–PBS; WCCO Channel 4–CBS; KSTP Channel 5–ABC; KARE Channel 11–NBC.

Radio Stations – AM: WCCO 830 (talk/news); KNOW 1330 (public); KSTP 1450 (talk/easy listening). FM: KSJN 91.1 (public); KS95 94.5 (top 40); KTCZ 97.1 (jazz).

Food – The *Twin Cities Directory,* published monthly, is distributed free throughout the metro area, especially at hotels. It contains reviews of restaurants and a listing of the month's events. The *Official Visitors Guide* (free from the St. Paul's Convention and Visitors Bureau) lists eateries, casual to elegant.

TELEPHONE: The area code for Minneapolis–St. Paul is 612.
Sales Tax – The sales tax in Minneapolis is 6½%; in St. Paul, 6%. There is no tax on clothing.

CLIMATE: In winter, be prepared for anything. The average temperature is 19F, but it can drop to 35F below zero, and snow has been known to fall as early as October. Summer temperatures are generally in the 70s and 80s.

GETTING AROUND: Airport – Minneapolis–St. Paul International Airport is a 15- to 20-minute drive from the downtown area of either Twin City; cab fare should run about $15 to $20. *Airport and Airline Taxi-Cab Corp.* (phone: 721-6566) provides metered cab transportation from the airport to Minneapolis hotels. *Metropolitan Transit Commission* buses 7C and 7D run between the airport and downtown Minneapolis, stopping along Washington Avenue every 40 minutes; to get to the airport from downtown St. Paul, take bus 9B on 6th St. and transfer to the 7C or 7D at Ft. Snelling. The fare is 75¢ to $1, depending on where you board. Limousines leave both the airport and downtown hotels in both cities about every 15 minutes. One-way fare: $5.50 (St. Paul) and $6.50 (Minneapolis); round-trip fare is $9.50 in both cities. One good company is *The Airport Express* (phone: 726-6400).

Bus – Minneapolis–St. Paul bus systems are a model of efficiency. They run from 6 to 1 AM. Express buses make the trip between Minneapolis and St. Paul in 20 minutes. Passengers' queries are handled by an extensive switchboard. *Metropolitan Transit Commission,* 560 6th Ave. N., Mpls. (phone: 827-7733). Fares are 80¢ off peak, $1 peak.

Car Rental – All major firms are represented. A good local agency is *Dollar Rent-A-Car,* at the airport (phone: 726-9494).

Taxi – As in many other cities, taxis are impossible to get when you really need them and plentiful when you don't. Most are radio-dispatched. There are some taxi stands. The largest cab company is *Yellow Cab* (2812 University Ave. SE, Mpls.; phone: 331-8294); they also have an office in St. Paul (167 Grand Ave.; phone: 222-4433).

 VITAL SERVICES: Audiovisual Equipment – *Blumberg Communications* (phone: 333-1271); *AVVT/ProCom* (phone: 456-9033).

Baby-sitting – The *YWCA* cares for children from 3 months to 5 years old; make reservations 24 hours in advance. Minimum sitting assignment is 4 hours (1130 Nicollet Ave., Mpls.; phone: 332-0501). There's also *New Horizon Child Care* (1385 Conway St., St. Paul; phone: 778-9441); *Ramsey County Day Care Referral* (phone: 298-4260); and *Jack and Jill Sitting Service* (1651 4th St., at White Bear Lake; phone: 429-2963).

Business Services – *A-1 Secretarial Services* (Pioneer Bldg., Suite 219, St. Paul; phone: 228-1907); *Executive Business Services* — for word processing and copying (1111 3rd Ave. S., Mpls.; phone: 332-5903).

Dry Cleaner/Tailor – *Dunrite Cleaners* (19 N. 6th St., Mpls.; phone: 332-4033); *Whiteway Cleaners* (286 W. 7th St., St. Paul; phone: 224-1391).

Limousine – *Silver Cloud Chauffeur Service* (phone: 894-1067); *Twin Star Limousine* (phone: 641-1385).

Mechanics – *Fisher Tire and Auto* provides excellent 24-hour road service at extremely reasonable prices (1022 Hennepin Ave., Mpls.; phone: 338-6953). *DJ's Towing* (842 University Ave., St. Paul; phone: 291-2637) provides complete auto repair and 24-hour towing at competitive prices.

Medical Emergency – *Hennepin County Medical Center,* 701 Park Ave., Mpls. (phone: 347-2121).

Messenger Services – *Action Messenger* (phone: 881-5100); *Courier Dispatch* (phone: 338-6300).

National/International Courier – *Federal Express* (phone: 340-0887); *DHL Worldwide Courier Express* (phone: 727-1100).

Pharmacy – *Loop Pharmacy* (Marquette at 10th St., Mpls.; phone: 333-2481); *Metropolitan Pharmacy* (825 S. 8th St., Mpls.; phone: 332-6522); *Moudry Apothecary Shop,* weekdays, 8 AM to 6:30 PM; Saturdays, 8 AM to 1 PM (364 St. Peter St., St. Paul; phone: 222-0571).

Photocopies – *Kinko's,* open evenings, has two Minneapolis locations (306 15th Ave., SE; phone: 379-8018; and 612 Washington Ave. SE; phone: 379-2452); and one St. Paul location (1665 Grand Ave.; phone: 699-9671).

Post Office – The central Minneapolis office has a mailbox in front for pickups and dispatch until midnight (100 1st St. and Marquette Ave.; phone: 349-4970). The central office in St. Paul has a 24-hour, self-service lobby (180 E. Kellogg Blvd.; phone: 293-3130).

Professional Photographer – *Marcus Photography* (400 First Ave. N., Studio 356, Mpls.; phone: 339-0258); *David Bank Studios* (phone: 333-1114); *Dellarson Studios* (phone: 224-2891).

Secretary/Stenographer – *Executive Secretary Ltd.* (phone: 333-0001); *A-1 Secretarial Services* (St. Paul; phone: 228-1907).

Teleconference Facilities – *Marquette, Sofitel, Radisson South* (see *Best in Town,* below), *World Trade Center* — *Conference Center* (phone: 297-1580).

Translator – *Berlitz* (phone: 920-4100); *AAA Worldwide Translation Center* (phone: 377-7989).

Typewriter Rental – *A-American Office Machines,* 1-day minimum (phone: 552-1043); *MTI Office Systems,* 1-week minimum (phone: 698-3629); *Wagner's Inc.,* 2-week minimum (phone: 644-3830).

Western Union/Telex – Many offices are located around the city (phone: 800-325-6000).

Other – For meeting and conference planning: *Uniglobe Travel* (phone: 941-1511) or *Meeting Concepts* (phone: 937-5955). Video and audiovisual productions for business training workshops: *Communications Workshop, Campbell-Mithurn* (phone: 347-1000). For word processing and copying: *Executive Business Services* (phone: 332-5903), *Travel Associates* (phone: 291-1222); *Group Travel Directions* (phone: 881-7811).

 SPECIAL EVENTS: The *Aquatennial Festival* in late July features sailboat races, a torchlight parade, and "Queen of the Lakes" beauty contest. The *Minnesota State Fair* runs for 12 days, ending *Labor Day* (at Midway Pkwy. and Snelling Aves., St. Paul). *St. Paul Winter Carnival,* late January through early February, is a citywide celebration. For football fans, *Superbowl XXVI* will be held here on January 26th of this year.

 MUSEUMS: The pride of Minneapolis–St. Paul is the Twin Cities' cultural wealth, and a visit to the many fine museums is well worth it. The *McKnight Omnitheatre,* the *Minneapolis Institute of Arts,* the *Minnesota Museum of Art,* the *Science Museum of Minnesota,* and the *Walker Art Center* are described in *Special Places.* Some others to see include the following:

Alexander Ramsey House – 265 S. Exchange St., St. Paul (phone: 296-8681).

American Swedish Institute – 2600 Park Ave., Mpls. (phone: 871-4907).

Bell Museum of Natural History – 10 Church St. SE, Mpls. (phone: 624-1852).

James J. Hill House – 240 Summit Ave., St. Paul (phone: 297-2555).

Landmark Center – 75 W. 5th St., St. Paul (phone: 292-3272).

Minneapolis Planetarium – 300 *Nicollet Mall,* Mpls. (phone: 372-6644).

Minnesota Museum of Art – 305 St. Peter, St. Paul, with additional galleries in the *Landmark Center,* 75 W. 5th St., St. Paul (phone: 292-4355).

Schubert Club Keyboard Instrument Museum – *Landmark Center,* 75 W. 5th St., St. Paul (phone: 292-3272).

 MAJOR COLLEGES AND UNIVERSITIES: About 60,000 students attend the University of Minnesota, one of the Big Ten; the campus sprawls across the east and west banks of the Mississippi. Escorted tours are available. University Ave. SE (phone: 624-6868).

SHOPPING: Bachman's Florists – Considered one of the country's largest floral outlets, they even offer tours of their nursery and garden center. There are special floral displays, showrooms, and greenhouses. 6010 Lyndale Avenue S., Mpls. (phone: 861-7600).

Bandana Square – Composed of specialty and apparel shops in a renovated railroad repair complex, the square is listed in the National Register of Historic Places. Five restaurants cater to hungry St. Paul shoppers. Be sure to visit the *Twin City Model Railroad Club* located in the square. 1021 E. Bandana Blvd., St. Paul (phone: 642-9505).

Byerly's – A food-shopping experience unlike any other — with wide, carpeted aisles and chandeliers — this is a place where cantaloupe thumpers and tomato squeezers can browse from cereal aisle to the imported crystal department, and even take cooking classes. The food store is open 24 hours a day, while some of the other departments close at 10 PM. 3777 Park Center Blvd., St. Louis Park, on Minneapolis's northwest side (phone: 929-2100).

Galtier Plaza – Located in St. Paul's historic Lowertown District, the plaza has a marketplace atmosphere. Shops, four movie theaters, the St. Paul *YMCA,* the area's largest comedy club, *Scott Hansen,* offices, underground parking, and a rooftop garden are among the occupants and facilities. Sibley Ave. between Fifth and Sixth Sts., St. Paul (phone: 292-0600).

 SPORTS AND FITNESS: Professional Sports – The 60,000-seat *Hubert H. Humphrey Metrodome,* (500 11th Ave. S., Mpls.) houses major league baseball and football teams.

Baseball – The Minnesota *Twins* play at the *Hubert H. Humphrey Metrodome,* 500 11th Ave. S., Mpls. (phone: 375-1116 for ticket information).

Basketball – The *Timberwolves* play in the *Target Center,* 600 1st Ave. N., Mpls. (phone: 337-3865).

Biking – There are bike trails around Lake Harriet, Lake Calhoun, and Lake of the Isles in Minneapolis; Lakes Como and Phalen in St. Paul. Bicycles may be rented from the *Bike Shop,* 213-217 Oak St. SE, Mpls. (phone: 331-3442).

Fishing – Twelve fishing lakes are in the Twin Cities metro area; the best is Lake Minnetonka (15 miles west on Hwy. 12.), which has 177 miles of shoreline. Within the city limits, Lake Calhoun has a fishing dock.

Fitness Centers – The *Medalist Sports Clubs* (Como and Snelling Aves., St. Paul; phone: 646-1165) and *Northwest Racquet, Swim and Health Clubs* (5525 Cedar Lake Rd., St. Louis Park; phone: 546-5474) have exercise equipment, sauna, whirlpool bath, and running tracks.

Football – The *Vikings* take to the field at the *Hubert H. Humphrey Stadium* (phone: 333-8828).

Golf – There are 18 courses in Minneapolis–St. Paul. Best is *Meadowbrook Golf Course,* 201 Meadowbrook Rd. at Goodrich Ave., Mpls. (phone: 929-2077).

Hockey – The *Met Center* (7901 Cedar Ave. S., Mpls.; phone: 989-5151) is the home of the *North Stars* hockey team.

Horse Racing – *Canterbury Downs,* 25 miles west of downtown Minneapolis, has thoroughbred and harness racing from mid-April through November (phone: 445-RACE).

Ice Skating – The cities clear, test, and maintain outdoor rinks on many of the lakes. Indoor ice arenas offer some free time for public skating. Consult the yellow pages directory for locations and numbers.

Jogging – An ambitious run leads to Lake of the Isles, 2½ miles from downtown, and from there to several other lakes: Cedar Lake to the west or Lakes Calhoun and Harriet to the south; the perimeter of each lake is about 3 miles. Another route is along the Mississippi on East or West River Road, by the University of Minnesota. In St. Paul, joggers take to the trails around Lake Como and Lake Phalen. The most popular and beautiful spot for runners in St. Paul is Summit Avenue and along the Mississippi River.

Skiing – Best are Afton Alps Ski Area, Welch Village, and Buck Hill.

Swimming – There are public swimming beaches at 23 lakes in and around the Twin Cities area. Open *Memorial Day* through *Labor Day.*

Tennis – There are many lighted, outdoor courts as well as indoor courts (ranging from $6.50 to $9 per hour) available throughout the cities.

THEATER: In addition to the *Guthrie,* Minneapolis–St. Paul has almost 100 theaters. The universities and colleges also produce plays and musicals. Best bets: *Guthrie* (phone: 377-2224), *Children's Theater Company* (phone: 874-0400), *Great American History Theatre* (phone: 292-4323), and *Penumbra Theater* (phone: 224-4601).

MUSIC: For a complete schedule of musical happenings, check the newspapers, especially *St. Paul Pioneer Press/Dispatch* on Thursdays; *Star-Tribune* Variety Weekend on Fridays. The *Twin Cities Reader* and the *City Pages* also offer calendar information. The copper-capped, glass-walled *Ordway Music Theater* (345 Washington St.; phone: 224-4222) presents performances by the *St. Paul Chamber Orchestra,* the *Minnesota Opera,* the *Schubert Club,* and the *Minnesota Orchestra,* as well as touring Broadway shows and other theater productions. There are outdoor summer concerts at Lake Harriet in Minneapolis and at Lake Como in St. Paul.

NIGHTCLUBS AND NIGHTLIFE: *Gallivan's Downtown* (354 Wabasha, St. Paul; phone: 227-6688) features professional entertainment. *The Manor* (2550 W. 7th St., St. Paul; phone: 690-1771) provides ballroom dancing Wednesdays through Saturdays. *Cleo's* (IDS Center, Mpls.; phone: 349-6250) offers a panoramic 50th-floor view and a Happy Hour buffet. Bob Dylan began his singing career in the West Bank area near the University of Minnesota, where there are a number of small clubs and cafés.
Rupert's (5410 Wayzata Blvd., Mpls.; phone: 544-5035) boasts a 10-piece band cranking out jazz, swing, and pop tunes Tuesdays through Saturdays, plus top Minnesota acts on Wednesdays. The *Dakota Bar & Grill* (phone: 641-1442) hosts the best jazz in the Twin Cities. Singles flock to *McCormick's Saloon and Deli* in the *Radisson University* hotel (615 Washington Ave., Mpls.; phone: 379-8888). The former Greyhound Bus Depot in Minneapolis is now the *First Avenue & 7th Street Entry* (29 W. 27th St.; phone: 332-1775) a nightclub featured in local rock star Prince's film *Purple Rain. The Fine Line Music Café* (318 1st Ave. N., Mpls.; phone: 338-8100) presents some of the best local talent to a "hip" audience. One of the hottest places in town for live music is the *Grand Slam* (110 N. 5th St., Mpls.; phone: 338-3383). *St. Paul's Hearthrob Café and Nightclub* (30 E. 7th St.; phone: 224-2783) draws a young, energetic crowd. Comedy-seekers can find laughs at *Scott Hansen* in Minneapolis (43 Main St.; phone: 331-5653).

BEST IN TOWN

CHECKING IN: There are a number of places near the Minneapolis–St. Paul International Airport, in the suburb of Bloomington, as well as some new and newly renovated hotels downtown. Expect to pay $90 or more for a double room in one of the hotels we've listed as expensive; $70 to $90 in the moderate range. *Days Inns, Best Western,* and *Quality Inns* are a few of the chains providing inexpensive (around $50) lodging. All telephone numbers are in the 612 area code unless otherwise indicated.

Hyatt Regency – In *Nicollet Mall,* just a short hop from the airport. There are 540 tasteful rooms and suites, and a Regency Club floor for extra-special service. The *Terrace* is the hotel's more casual eating spot; the *Willows* restaurant has fancier, continental fare; *Pronto* serves Northern Italian food (see *Eating Out*); the *Willows Lounge* features entertainment every night but Sunday. Room service responds around the clock. Twelve meeting rooms can accommodate up to 2,500, and other business pluses are a concierge desk, A/V equipment, photocopiers, and express checkout. 1300 *Nicollet Mall,* Mpls. (phone: 370-1234, 800-233-1234, or 800-228-9000; Fax: 612-370-1463). Expensive.

Luxeford Suites – An all-suite hotel at the edge of downtown, with a European feel. Each room has a wet bar, refrigerator, and microwave oven. A complimentary continental breakfast is laid out on the English sideboard of the club room, just off the lobby. There's also complimentary airport and downtown shuttle service, as well as free overnight shoeshines. Room service orders will arrive up to midnight. Other amenities include 3 meeting rooms, photocopiers, and express checkout. 1101 La Salle Ave., Mpls. (phone: 332-6800; Fax: 612-332-8246). Expensive.

Marquette – Connected to the interior skyway in the IDS Center and offering gracious, spacious accommodations in the middle of downtown. Presidents Ford and Carter have stayed here. There are a bar and restaurant, heated parking; 281 rooms. Among the amenities are room service until 2 AM, 11 meeting rooms, both concierge and secretarial services, A/V equipment, photocopiers, CNN, and express checkout. 710 Marquette Ave., Mpls. (phone: 332-2351 or 800-328-4782; Fax: 612-332-7007). Expensive.

Marriott City Center – This 32-floor glass tower (which is linked to the city's enclosed skyway system) is as modern and up-to-date as the many services it offers guests. It's particularly suited for those in town on business, since one whole floor is like a small convention center, with rooms appropriate for both small and large functions. The hotel also has 2 notable restaurants: *Gustino's* for Northern Italian food and the *Fifth Season* for American dishes from all around the country. Twenty-two meeting rooms are available for business functions, as well as a concierge desk, A/V equipment, photocopiers, and computers. Other pluses are CNN and express checkout. 30 S. 7th St., Mpls. (phone: 349-4000 or 800-228-9290; Fax: 612-349-9223). Expensive.

St. Paul – A beautifully restored Victorian hotel that's shining again after a $20 million face-lift. Crystal chandeliers sparkle in the lobby and elegant Biedermeier-style furniture decorates the guestrooms, some of which have lovely views over Rice Park. The newest on-site restaurants are the *St. Paul Bar & Grill* and *The Café*. The hotel is connected by a skyway to department stores, banks, boutiques, and travel agencies, and is across Rice Park from the *Ordway Theater*. Room service is on call until 11 PM; there are 9 meeting rooms, a concierge desk, A/V equipment, photocopiers, computers, and express checkout. 350 Market St., St. Paul (phone: 292-9292; Fax: 612-228-3810). Expensive.

Sofitel – The first North American link in the French hotel chain offers a concierge, the latest issues of Parisian magazines, and authentic croissants for breakfast. Many of the 287 deluxe rooms have bidets. Continental elegance includes an indoor heated pool, sauna, babysitting service, bars, and piano bar. Children under 12 admitted free, but for the rest of us it's pricey. Room service delivers until 1 AM. Thirteen meeting rooms, secretarial services, A/V equipment, and photocopiers round out the business amenities. Express checkout. I-494 and Hwy. 100, Bloomington (phone: 835-1900; Fax: 612-835-2696; Telex: 290215). Expensive.

Whitney – One of downtown Minneapolis's latest deluxe establishments, imaginatively created from a turn-of-the-century flour mill overlooking the Mississippi River. The building has 97 distinctive rooms, each adapted to the old building's unique style. Some are bi-level suites. *Whitney's Grill* is for formal dining. Located at 150 Portland Ave., Mpls. (phone: 339-9300). Expensive.

Radissons – The *Radisson South* is the tallest and largest hotel in Bloomington, with 578 rooms, an indoor heated pool, sauna, restaurants, bar, dancing, entertainment, shopping mall, and free parking (7800 Normandale Blvd.; phone: 835-7800). *Radisson St. Paul* has 485 rooms (2 for the disabled), a revolving rooftop restaurant, a café, lobby bar/lounge, indoor heated pool and garden court, entertainment, dancing, barber and beauty shops, sun deck, in-room movies (11 E. Kellogg Blvd.; phone: 292-1900). The *Radisson Plaza* has 357 rooms, including 18 for disabled guests, restaurants, a lounge, and access to Plaza VII exercise equipment, sauna, and whirlpool bath (35 S. 7th St., Mpls.; phone: 339-4900). Two other Radisson properties are the 222-room *Radisson Minnetonka* (12201 Ridgedale Dr., Minnetonka; phone: 593-0000), and the 308-room *Radisson University* (615 Washington Ave. SE, Mpls.; phone: 379-8888). All are expensive to moderate.

Sunwood Inn – Located in St. Paul's historic *Bandana Square* (and connected to it by an enclosed walkway), this actually is a renovated, historic railroad building. Retaining the original structural characteristics, the inn features tracks on the floor, huge entrances, exposed beams, and structural supports, each room has a different configuration. Historic photos throughout the building tell of the "good old days" of Minnesota railroading. Business amenities include 5 meeting rooms, A/V equipment, and photocopiers. 1010 Bandana Blvd. W., St. Paul (phone: 647-1637; Fax: 612-687-0294). Inexpensive.

EATING OUT: Almost any kind of food can be found in the Twin Cities area, from high-priced, exquisitely prepared continental dishes to Japanese food or a kosher delicatessen. In fact, Minneapolis–St. Paul is considered a great eating-out town. Prices range from $50 or more for a dinner for two in the expensive range, $30 to $50 in the moderate, and $25 or less, inexpensive. Prices do not include drinks, wine, or tips. All telephone numbers are in the 612 area code unless otherwise indicated.

Blue Horse – Winner of innumerable awards over the years, this gracious, intimate spot is consistently cited as one of the Twin Cities' finest. The chef devotes full, loving attention to every dish. The menu changes seasonally, and the wine list is extensive. Closed Sundays. Reservations necessary. Major credit cards accepted. 1355 University Ave., St. Paul (phone: 645-8101). Expensive.

510 – An evening couldn't be better spent partaking of the eight-course tasting menu at this elegant place next door to the *Guthrie Theater.* The preparation is French, and the results are largely terrific, whether it's veal chops with wild mushrooms, pork tenderloin with fig coulis, smoked goose, or one of the praiseworthy dessert soufflés. Closed Sundays. Reservations essential. Major credit cards accepted. 510 Groveland Ave., Mpls. (phone: 874-6440). Expensive.

Forepaughs – The charm and elegance of the Victorian age is preserved here, where French food is served in a gracious 19th-century former home. Free parking and shuttle service to the *Ordway Theater* are provided. Open daily. Reservations advised. Major credit cards accepted. 276 Exchange St., St. Paul (phone: 224-5606). Expensive.

Lowell Inn – The closest thing to a New England inn that you'll find in the Midwest. The menu includes beef fondue, and gigantic drinks are another special feature. Open daily. Reservations necessary. Major credit cards accepted. 102 N. 2nd St., Stillwater (a northeast suburb of St Paul; phone: 439-1100). Expensive.

Manny's – One of the best steakhouses in the Twin Cities, located in the *Hyatt Regency,* this dining spot has a rugged atmosphere, and a solid, "man's world" feel. But women are just as welcome to try the porterhouse steaks, veal, and swordfish. Open daily. Reservations advised. Major credit cards accepted. 1300 *Nicollet Mall,* Mpls. (phone: 339-9900). Expensive.

Minnesota Zephyr – For a moveable feast (literally), this elegant dining train relives the grand era of the 1940s as it leaves the Stillwater depot (45 miles away) and travels along the St. Croix River Valley. The 3-hour excursion includes a 4-course dinner. Boarding is at 6:30 PM weekdays and at noon on Sundays. A favorite getaway for Twin Citians; reservations are essential. Visa, MasterCard or Discover accepted. For more information, write: 601 Main St., PO Box 573, Stillwater, MN 55082 (phone: 430-3000). Expensive.

Murray's – Well known for its hickory-smoked shrimp appetizers, award-winning silver butterknife steaks, and homemade rolls and dressing. The decor is in the 1940s tradition, and there is music later in the evening. Open daily. Reservations advised. Major credit cards accepted. 26 S. 6th St., Mpls. (phone: 339-0909). Expensive.

New French Café – A white brick storefront provides a simple setting for some fine French cooking. The menu changes seasonally (look for duck and pheasant in winter, wild mushrooms in spring) but always includes fresh fish, gorgeous desserts, and the café's own bread, for which it's justly famous. Open daily for breakfast, lunch, dinner, late supper, and brunch on Saturdays and Sundays. Reservations advised. Major credit cards accepted. 128 N. 4th St., Mpls. (phone: 338-3790). Expensive.

Windows on Minnesota – Formerly the *Orion Room,* it's high atop the IDS Center, 50 stories up, and the view from three seating levels is magnificent. Specialties include rack of lamb, chateaubriand, wild rice soup, and Dover sole, and impressive tableside presentation enhances the spectacular setting. Open daily. Reservations advised. Major credit cards accepted. IDS Center, 80 S. 8th St., Mpls. (phone: 349-6250). Expensive.

Black Forest Inn – Near the *Institute of Arts,* the inn serves bratwurst and sauerkraut dinners, Wiener schnitzel, and other honest, substantial German fare. The restaurant evolved from a tavern that used to serve only beer and it still offers German brews which you can enjoy drinking in the outdoor beer garden. Open daily. Reservations advised. Major credit cards accepted. 1 E. 26th St., Mpls. (phone: 872-0812). Moderate.

Cherokee Sirloin Room – For good reason, the chef claims that he "steaks his reputation" on serving St. Paul's real meat eaters. Though the restaurant has had a name change (formerly *Cherokee's Beef*), top sirloins and tenderloins are still the specialties. Open daily. Reservations advised on weekends. Major credit cards accepted. 886 S. Smith, West St. Paul (phone: 457-2729). Moderate.

Dakota Bar & Grill – Featuring the Twin Cities' best jazz. Food ranges from down-home Minnesota-style steaks to lamb with wild rice, and fresh brook trout. Open daily. Reservations advised. Major credit cards accepted. 1021 E. Bandana Blvd., St. Paul (phone: 642-1442). Moderate.

Figlio – The cooking is Italian via California — pizza and pasta topped with unusual combinations, as well as fresh fish and meats from the wood-fired oven and grill in the open kitchen. It's a high-energy eatery and one of the hottest spots in the Twin Cities. Open daily. Reservations advised. Major credit cards accepted. 3001 Hennepin Ave. S., Mpls. (phone: 822-1688). Moderate.

Goodfellow's – Beautiful hardwood floors, a roaring fireplace, and a fine collection of contemporary art (including works by Frank Stella and Jim Dine) are almost peripheral to the creative dishes. Resident chef Tim Anderson was recently called one of the 10 best new chefs in America by *Food and Wine* magazine; deservedly. Coriander-crested New York strip steak, grilled salmon with a yellow pepper sauce, white chocolate brownies with Kona coffee ice cream and hot fudge, and blackberry walnut cake with whipped cream and hot blackberry sauce form the menu's mainstays. Closed Sundays. Reservations advised. Major credit cards accepted. 800 Nicollet Mall (phone: 332-4800). Moderate.

Lexington – This landmark spot has attracted politicians and business leaders for over half a century. The decor leans toward formal, the cooking traditional, with short ribs of beef, lamb shanks, prime ribs, lobster newburg. Closed Sundays. Reservations advised. No credit cards accepted. 1096 Grand Ave., St. Paul (phone: 222-5878). Moderate.

Pronto – In addition to Northern Italian fare of a very high standard, this smart-looking restaurant offers floor-to-ceiling views of the city greensward from both of its dining rooms. Go for the classics — carpaccio, *paglia e fieno, saltimbocca alla romana, zuppa inglese.* Sunday's brunch buffet is a hit, and deservedly so. Open daily. Reservations advised. Major credit cards accepted. *Hyatt Regency,* 1300 *Nicollet Mall,* Mpls. (phone: 333-4414). Moderate.

Café Brenda – Some call this sunny downtown spot a health food restaurant, but the fare is so tasty and sophisticated you forget it's also good for you. Try the Wisconsin rainbow trout, warming winter casseroles, and meal-size salads. Closed Sundays. Reservations advised. Visa and MasterCard accepted. 300 1st Ave. N., Mpls. (phone: 342-9230). Inexpensive.

Chi Chi's – No matter where one of these eateries springs up, you're certain to find folks lining up to partake of the Mexican food done with gringo know-how. Their popularity is due in no small part to the pleasant atmosphere (rotating fans, sprawling plants, and stucco walls), hefty margaritas and the chain's knack for using the freshest ingredients available. Specialties include chimichangas and Mexican fried ice cream. Expect a wait because the portions are large and reasonably priced. Open for lunch and dinner. Reservations advised. Major credit cards accepted. Five locations: 7717 Nicollet Ave., Richfield (phone: 866-3433); 389 N. Hamline, St. Paul (phone: 644-1122); 40 S. 7th St. (phone: 339-0766); 15550 Wayzata Blvd., Minnetonka (phone: 473-0770); and 7355 Regent Ave. N., Mpls. (phone: 561-0550). Inexpensive.

Ciatti's – There's a good selection of Italian dishes, including a variety of pasta served with different sauces, and a menu listing over 30 entrées; some non-Italian dishes also are available. Desserts, like the amaretto torte, are delicious. Open daily. Reservations advised. Major credit cards accepted. 1346 La Salle Ave. S., Mpls. (phone: 339-7747), and 850 Grand Ave., St. Paul (phone: 292-9942). Inexpensive.

Leeann Chin's – This cavernous space used to be the Union Depot. Now lofty columns, smoked mirrors, and a rosy beige decor provide a warm backdrop for stunning Oriental vases, jade, ivory carvings, and whimsical modern Chinese paintings. A buffet with everything from *fun kin* soup and cream cheese wontons to lemon chicken and almond cookie ice cream is served for both lunch and dinner. Open daily. Reservations advised. Major credit cards accepted. Union Depot Pl. at 4th and Sibley, St. Paul (phone: 224-8814). A branch, closed Sundays, is at 900 2nd Ave., Mpls. (phone: 338-3488). Inexpensive.

Mickey's Diner – This St. Paul institution has been serving the world's best omelettes 24 hours a day since 1939. Operated by the son of the founder, the diner still is kitty-corner from the Greyhound Bus Depot and attracts regular diners from all walks of life. Nothing fancy here, just straight, down-to-earth cookin'. Most of the help has been working here for years, and likely will call you "dearie." No reservations are required but there are only 4 booths and 17 counter stools (at 36 W. 7th St.; phone: 222-5633). The family also operates another *Mickey's Restaurant* with more space but the same ambience (at 1950 W. 7th St.; phone: 698-8387). Both are inexpensive.

What's the best place for barbecue? That question always has been followed by lively debate in Minneapolis. Current favorites include *Market BBQ* (1414 Nicollet Ave. S., Mpls.; phone: 872-1111), preferred by longtime residents for ribs cooked to dry, smoky perfection over a wood fire. And then there's *Rudolph's Bar-B-Que* (1933 Lyndale Ave. S., Mpls.; phone: 871-8969; 815 E. Hennepin Ave., Mpls.; phone: 623-3671; or 366 Jackson in St. Paul; phone: 222-2226), which took top honors in the National Rib Cook-Off in 1985 for its sloppy, piquant-sauced ribs served up with a great side of coleslaw.

NASHVILLE

AT-A-GLANCE

 SEEING THE CITY: The *Pinnacle* restaurant atop the *Holiday Inn-Crowne Plaza* downtown (7th and Union) makes a complete rotation each half hour, providing an excellent view of the city. The view is well worth the cost of lunch, dinner, or a drink. Call 259-2000 for reservations or information. Visitors also can get a good lay of the land by picking up a free brochure at the Nashville Area Chamber of Commerce (161 4th Ave. N.; phone: 259-4755), which outlines a walking tour of the downtown area.

 SPECIAL PLACES: Most of the outstanding attractions are clustered within a couple of miles of the downtown area, and ranged along the southern and eastern outskirts of the metropolitan area.

DOWNTOWN

Downtown Presbyterian Church – Designed by architect William Strickland and completed in 1848 after a fire destroyed the original (ca. 1808), it is a rare example of the Egyptian Revival architectural style popular in the mid-1800s. The highly-stylized interior, complete with desert clouds painted on the ceiling, was renovated in the 1880s. Open daily. No admission charge. 154 5th Ave. N. (phone: 254-7584).

Ft. Nashborough – A partial reconstruction of the pioneer fort where Nashville began back in 1779, when a small band of settlers under the leadership of James Robertson arrived on the west bank of the Cumberland River. Grounds are open daily. No admission charge. 170 1st Ave. N (phone: 255-8192).

Riverfront Park – This stretch along on the Cumberland appears to have been designed as an homage to concrete, but local bands play here on Saturday nights during the summer, and sheltered tables make for pleasant picnicking on cooler days. There's even a concrete walk that goes along the riverbank. The fireworks display on the *Fourth of July* attracts thousands of locals for a huge street party, complete with entertainment ranging from the *Nashville Symphony* to country and rock bands (phone: 862-8400 for entertainment information).

Ryman Auditorium – Home of the *Grand Ole Opry* between 1943 and 1974. Climb up onto its creaky wood stage and see mementos of the stars of days gone by. The *Ryman,* an irresistible magnet for country music lovers, was built in 1891 by a riverboat captain, Tom Ryman, who had found religion and wanted to help others do the same. Since restorations were completed in 1990, the *Ryman* now looks as it did when the *Opry* moved here in 1943. Open daily. Admission charge. 116 Opry Pl. (phone: 254-1445).

Tennessee State Capitol – Designed by architect William Strickland, who was entombed in the building after he died, at his request. Completed in 1859. Guided tours available. Open daily. No admission charge. 505 Deaderick (phone: 741-0830).

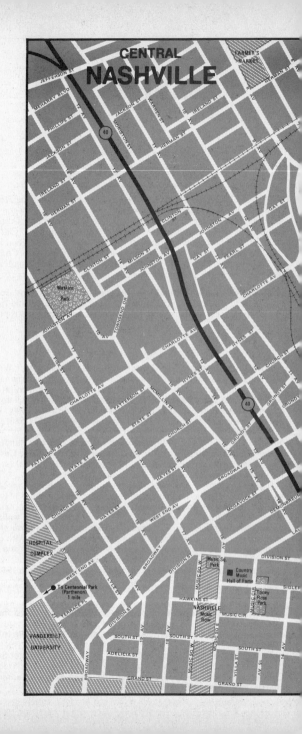

MUSIC ROW

Country Music Hall of Fame and Museum – Memorabilia of country music stars — Elvis Presley's solid gold Cadillac, comedienne Minnie Pearl's straw hat complete with dangling price tag, Chet Atkins's first guitar, rare film footage of Patsy Cline and earlier country singers, celebrates 60-plus years of the *Grand Ole Opry*. Special exhibitions feature current country stars or country music history. Open daily. Admission charge. Music Row at 4 Music Sq. E. (phone: 256-1639).

Studio B – Elvis Presley, Chet Atkins, Charley Pride, Eddy Arnold, and a score of other greats recorded for RCA at this famous studio in the 1950s and 1960s. Guides will tell you its history, talk about the Nashville recording industry, and let you act as a recording engineer at a "mix-down" session, in which the 16 tracks recorded by the artists are put onto 2 tracks before delivery to the record presser. Admission charge to Studio B is included in the *Hall of Fame* entry fee. Open daily. 17th Ave. at Roy Acuff St. (phone: 242-9414).

EAST

Grand Ole Opry – This long country-music-star-studded spectacular is well worth the planning it takes to get tickets. More than a third of the 60-odd acts under contract to the *Opry* will perform on a given night, and you're bound to like some if not all of them. There are shows Fridays at 7:30 PM and Saturdays at 6:30 and 9:30 PM year-round. Between *Memorial Day* and *Labor Day* there are also matinees Tuesdays, Thursdays, Saturdays, and Sundays, and two Friday evening shows. All seats are reserved, and if you don't have tickets, call the *Opry's* Information Center to see if any are available. Information Center, 2802 Opryland Dr. (phone: 889-3060).

Opryland USA – Music from Broadway and the hit parade and just about any other kind of melody that has ever been called music, including foot-tapping bluegrass, carry out the American-music-is-great motif at this family theme park. In addition to the shows, *Opryland* features a number of adventure and amusement rides. Open daily in summer, and weekends in spring and fall. Admission charge. Information Center, 2802 Opryland Dr. (phone: 889-6611 or 889-6700).

Hermitage – Once the home of President Andrew Jackson, this magnificent old plantation home is now a museum devoted to the Jackson family. Tulip Grove, a Greek revival house completed in 1836, is also on the grounds. The museum features artifacts from the time the Jacksons lived in the mansion, details of the home's restoration, and a 20-minute film about the Jacksons and their times. Self-guided audio tours or guided tours (allow 1½ to 2 hours) are available. Open daily; last tour at 4:30 PM, without fail. Admission charge. About a 30-minute drive from downtown in Hermitage (phone: 889-2941).

SOUTH

Belle Meade Mansion – Inside the century-old rock walls that edge the 24-acre estate, Belle Meade is just a shadow of its former self, but even its shadow is impressive: immense pillars and ornate plaster cornices outside and, inside, Adamesque moldings and a splendid double parlor. Open daily. Admission charge. Harding Rd. at Leake Ave., US 70S (phone: 356-0501).

Parthenon – A full-scale replica of the ancient Greek building; the building material is not marble but a steel-reinforced conglomerate. Its four bronze doors are the largest in the world. The interior features an impressive replica of the statue of Athena that graced the original Parthenon. Displays include reproductions of the Elgin marbles, plus pre-Columbian art and various changing exhibitions. Closed Sundays and

Mondays. Admission charge. In Centennial Park at 25th Ave. N. and West End Ave. (phone: 862-8431).

Travellers' Rest – The remarkably finely detailed home of John Overton, one of Nashville's first settlers, restored, expanded, and filled with furniture, letters, and memorabilia that tell the story of Tennessee's settlement and civilization. Open daily. Admission charge. 636 Farrell Pkwy. 6 miles south of downtown via Franklin Rd., which is US 31 (phone: 832-2962).

Tennessee Botanical Gardens and Cheekwood Fine Arts Center – *Cheekwood,* a Georgian mansion built in the 1930s, is now a museum with art shows and traveling exhibitions. You may be more impressed, though, by the elegant Palladian window, or the chandelier (once the property of a countess), or the swooping spiral staircase (which used to be a fixture of Queen Charlotte's palace at Kew in England). Outdoors: formal gardens, a wisteria arbor, wildflower gardens, a Japanese sand garden, greenhouses, horticultural exhibits, and an outstanding boxwood garden. Closed Mondays except in December. Admission charge. Forrest Park Dr., 7 miles west of town via West End Ave., then Belle Meade Blvd. (phone: 356-8000).

■ **EXTRA SPECIAL:** You'll see the announcements for tours of the homes of the stars on big billboards on the way into town, and even if you ordinarily hate group excursions, you may like these. While you're getting a glimpse into what makes Nashville tick, you also can enjoy some delightful southern-accented speech and the colorful language that seems to be the mark of Nashville citizenry. Each of the following offers several all-day, half-day, or evening tours: *Country Western/Gray Line* (2416 Music Valley Dr.; phone: 883-5555 or 800-251-1864); *Grand Ole Opry Tours* (2808 Opryland Dr.; phone: 889-9490); *Nashville Tours* (2626 Music Valley Dr.; phone: 889-4646); and *Stardust Tours* (1504 Demonbreun St.; phone: 244-2335).

SOURCES AND RESOURCES

TOURIST INFORMATION: For brochures, maps, general tourist information, and all kinds of other help, your best bet is to write the Nashville Area Chamber of Commerce (161 4th Ave. N., Nashville, TN 37219; phone: 259-4755); or to stop by the tourist information center at exit 85 on I-65N, just east of downtown. Contact the Tennessee state information (615-741-2158) for maps, calendars of events, health updates, and travel advisories.

The *Nashville Visitor's Guide,* on sale at most newsstands, is as comprehensive a city guide as you'll see anywhere.

Local Coverage – *The Tennessean,* morning daily; the *Nashville Banner,* afternoon daily. The former publishes a complete events listing on Fridays and Sundays; the latter on Thursdays. Both are available at newsstands. The *Nashville Scene,* a weekly paper available free at many stores and restaurants, publishes a comprehensive listing of area happenings, including a list of every nightspot in town.

Television Stations – WKRN Channel 2–ABC; WSMV Channel 4–NBC; WTVF Channel 5–CBS; WDCN Channel 8–PBS; WZTV Channel 17–FOX.

Radio Stations – AM: WSIX 980 (country music); WAMB 1160 (big band); WKDA 1240 (contemporary rock); WLAC 1510 (news/talk). FM: WPLN 90 (classical/public radio); WZEZ 93 (easy listening); WGFX 104.5 (rock hits); WRLT 100 (jazz/rock).

Food – Check the *Nashville City Guide* or the *Nashville Visitor's Guide* for complete restaurant listings. *Nashville Business and Lifestyle,* the local city magazine, also has listings and reviews.

 TELEPHONE: The area code for Nashville is 615.

Sales Tax – The city sales tax for most goods is 7¾%; the hotel tax is 11¾%.

 CLIMATE: Nashville's temperatures hover around the 80s and 90s in summer, dropping into the 40s and 30s (occasionally into the 20s or lower) between November and February. It gets humid in the summer, and you can expect thunderstorms from March through late summer. Expect rain in the spring and in October and November.

 GETTING AROUND: Airport – The Nashville Metropolitan Airport is a 15- to 20-minute drive from downtown (30 minutes or more during rush hours), and cab fare to downtown will run $15 to $20. Many hotels provide free transportation from the airport; check with your hotel when making reservations.

Bus – You need a car to manage conveniently. However, buses are available (route information, phone: 242-4433).

Car Rental – Major national car rental agencies can be found in Nashville. Four have rental offices at the Metro Airport; two more (*Thrifty* and *American International*) offer airport pickup.

Taxi – Nashville's principal cab companies are *Yellow* (phone: 256-0101) and *Checker* (phone: 254-5031).

 VITAL SERVICES: Audiovisual Equipment – *Consolidated Media Systems* (phone: 244-3933); *Allied Audio-Visual Services* (phone: 255-1000).

Baby-sitting – If you think you might need one, ask your hotel or motel to make the arrangements when you book your room.

Business Services – *Diamond Personnel* (1 Maryland Farms; phone: 377-3344); *Entech Services, Ltd.* (2120 Belcourt Ave., Suite 200; phone: 383-0607).

Convention Facilities – The *Nashville Convention Center* offers 118,675 square feet of exhibit space and 30,232 square feet of meeting room space. 601 Commerce St. downtown (phone: 615-259-7900).

Dry Cleaner/Tailor – *Dodge Cleaners* (201 21st Ave. N.; phone: 327-3144) and five other locations; many hotels and office buildings offer dry-cleaning services with pickup and delivery.

Limousine – *Imperial Limousines* (phone: 361-3055); *Nashville Connections* (phone: 889-7130).

Mechanics – People come from all the way across town to have their foreign and domestic cars fixed at *Garrett Amoco Service* (2600 Lebanon Rd., Donelson, near *Opryland;* phone: 883-1386). Also good for both foreign and domestic cars is *Wood's Garage* (108 28th Ave. N., by Centennial Park; phone: 327-3861).

Medical Emergency – *Vanderbilt University Hospital,* 22nd and Garland Aves. (phone: 332-3391).

Messenger Services – *Rapid Messenger & Delivery Service* (phone: 254-0807); *Accelerated Action Delivery Service* (phone: 361-3857).

National/International Courier – *Federal Express* (phone: 800-238-5355).

Pharmacy – *Farmers Market Pharmacy,* open 24 hours, 715 Jefferson St. (phone: 242-5561).

Photocopies – *PIP* has several locations (including 162 4th Ave. N.; phone: 254-7514); *Kinko's Copies* also has several locations (including 400 21st Ave. S.; phone: 327-4224).

Post Office – The central office is located at 901 Broadway (phone: 255-9446).

Professional Photographer – *Henry Schofield Studios* (phone: 383-3290); *Greg Kinney Photography* (phone: 297-8084).

Secretary/Stenographer – *Diamond Personnel* (phone: 377-3344); *Entech Services, Ltd.* (phone: 383-0607).

Teleconference Facilities – *Opryland* (see *Best in Town,* below).

Translator – *Language Services* (phone: 292-7916).

Typewriter Rental – *Business World,* weekly rates (phone: 244-7610); *Nashville Office Machines Co.,* 1-week minimum (phone: 329-3891).

Western Union/Telex – Many offices are located around the city (phone: 800-325-6000).

Other – *Meeting Services and Convention Consultants* (phone: 352-6900); *Events Resources,* meeting and convention planning (phone: 254-9300); *Events Unlimited* (phone: 329-3091).

SPECIAL EVENTS: The *Opryland Gospel Jubilee* brings gospel bands, choruses, and lots of extra music to the theme park every year over *Memorial Day* weekend (see *Special Places*). The annual *Tennessee Crafts Fair,* one of the largest shows of its kind in the south, is scheduled in Centennial Park on the first full weekend in May. (For information, write PO Box 12006, Nashville, TN 37212; phone: 665-0502). The second Saturday of May is the *Iroquois Steeplechase,* the day-long series of eight races that's the oldest amateur steeplechase meet in the US (Old Hickory Blvd. in Percy Warner Park, 11 miles south of Nashville. For information: PO Box 22711, Nashville 37202; or call 373-2130, beginning in February). The *International Country Music Fan Fair,* usually scheduled for the first week of June, brings thousands for 5 days of spectacular shows, autograph sessions, concerts and a *Grand Masters Fiddling Contest.* For more information, write to *Fan Fair* (2804 Opryland Dr., Nashville 37214; phone: 889-7503). In late September or October, there's the *National Quartet Convention,* 5 days of top-name gospel singing at the *Nashville Municipal Auditorium.* For information: *National Quartet Convention* (Dept. N, 54 Music Sq. W., Nashville 37203; phone: 320-7000). *Summer Lights,* a downtown festival held the weekend between the end of May and the beginning of June, lights up 12 city blocks from the historic Second Avenue "Market Street" area to Legislative Plaza. Local musicians of national and international stature are showcased along with street performers, visual arts exhibits, and other entertainment. Many notable Nashville restaurants offer specialties from street booths, and area shops have special outdoor stands. Produced by the Metro Nashville Arts Commission (phone: 862-6720). The annual *Fall Crafts Fair,* organized by the Tennessee Association of Craft Artists, is held on an October weekend in the *Convention Center.* (For information, write PO Box 120066, Nashville TN 37212; phone: 665-0502).

MUSEUMS: In addition to those described above in *Special Places,* the following are worth investigating:

Cumberland Museum and Science Center – A children's museum with live animal shows, science demonstrations, activities, and experiments to try. Closed Mondays. Admission charge except Tuesdays. 800 Ridley Ave. (phone: 259-6099).

Tennessee State Museum – In the *Tennessee Performing Arts Center,* with a branch devoted to military history in the War Memorial Building. Frequent exhibitions of local arts and crafts. No admission charge. 7th and Union Sts. (phone: 741-2692).

Van Vechten Gallery – Houses the Stieglitz Collection, over 100 works of 20th-century art donated to Fisk University by artist Georgia O'Keeffe after the death of her husband, photographer Alfred Stieglitz. Closed Mondays. Admission charge. Fisk University campus, 17th Ave. N. (phone: 329-8543).

MAJOR COLLEGES AND UNIVERSITIES: Of the dozen-plus colleges and universities in Nashville, Vanderbilt (West End at 21st Ave.; phone: 322-7311) is perhaps the most famous, as its nickname, "the Harvard of the South," would suggest. The city is also the home of Fisk University (17th Ave. N.; phone: 329-8500), one of the US's most noted predominantly black colleges, along with Tennessee State University (3500 Merritt Blvd.; phone: 320-3131).

SHOPPING: There's something offered for all tastes and interests in Nashville, from the small, exclusive shop to the large, encompassing mall. The city's three largest shopping malls are *Hickory Hollow* (I-24 at Bell Rd.), *Rivergate* (I-65 at Two Mile Pike), and the newest, *Bellevue Center* (I-40, Bellevue exit). Brave these on weekends only if you enjoy fighting crowds.

Davis-Kidd Booksellers – The best bookstore in town has a pleasant café built into its upper level where you can sip wine or herb tea and read your purchase. 4007 Hillsboro Rd. (phone: 385-2645).

Green Mills Mall – *Castner-Knott* and *Dillard's* department stores are found in this peaceful shopping environment, in addition to other exclusive shops including *Laura Ashley* (phone: 383-0131) and *Gadgette's* (phone: 386-9081), which has everything from high-tech wind chimes to unique telephones. 2126 Abbott-Martin Rd.

McClure's – The city's best department store has clothes for men, women, and children that you won't find anywhere else in town. 6000 Highway 1000, Belle Meade (phone: 356-8832) or 257 Franklin Rd. in Brentwood (phone: 377-3769).

Stanford Square – This collection of exclusive stores features clothing shops and *American Artisan* (phone: 298-4691), which sells interesting objets d'art and jewelry by local and national artisans. 4231 Harding Rd.

Antiques shops are all over the city, but several good ones are clustered on 8th Avenue near the intersection with Wedgwood. For a fun afternoon of browsing, try *White Way Antique Mall* (1200 Villa Place, behind the *White Way Cleaners* on Edgehill). *Architectural Antiques* has doors, windows, hardware, light fixtures, and other treasures salvaged from demolished buildings (110 2nd Ave. N.; phone: 254-8129).

SPORTS AND FITNESS: Baseball – The Nashville *Sounds,* a triple-A farm team for the Cincinnati *Reds,* play in *Greer Stadium* on Chestnut, between 4th and 8th Aves. S. (phone: 242-4371).

Fishing and Boating – Two manmade lakes — Old Hickory (phone: 822-4846) and Percy Priest (phone: 889-1975) — are a 20-minute drive from downtown, and several others are within an hour or so. Black bass, rock bass, striped bass, walleye, sauger, northern pike, crappie, bluegill, and sunfish are the standard catch. Call the Resource Management office at each lake for boat and equipment rental details. The Tennessee Wildlife Resources Agency (PO Box 40747, Ellington Agricultural Center, Nashville TN 37204; phone: 781-6500) can provide details about other lakes in the area.

Fitness Centers – The *Centennial Sportsplex* offers a fitness center with pool, weight rooms, aerobics programs, and an ice rink, which is open to the public. Open daily. Admission charge. 25th Ave. N., across from Centennial Park (phone: 862-8480).

Golf – There are ten public courses in Nashville. Best 18- or 27-holers are at *Harpeth Hills* (Old Hickory Blvd., off Rte. 431 S.; phone: 373-8202); *McCabe Park* (46th Ave. N. at Murphy Rd.; phone: 269-6951); *Nashville Golf and Athletic Club* (Moore's Lane in Franklin; phone: 370-3346); and *Shelby Park* golf course (20th Ave. and Fatherland St.; phone: 862-8474).

Jogging – Follow Church Street (which turns into Elliston Place) to

Centennial Park, about 1½ miles from downtown and near Vanderbilt University; or drive or take the West End Belle Meade bus (from 6th and Church, or Deaderick at 4th or 6th) to Percy Warner Park. Jogging in either area after dark is not recommended.

Stock Car Racing – Local racing on a five-eighths–mile track at the *Tennessee State Fairgrounds* every Saturday night from April through mid-October, Wedgewood Ave. between 4th and 8th Aves. S. (phone: 726-1818).

Swimming – *Wave Country* (on Two Rivers Pkwy.) near *Opryland* is the Southeast's largest surf-producing swimming pool. Open May through September. Admission charge (phone: 885-1052). Indoor swimming is available year-round at the *Centennial Sportsplex* (25th Ave. N. across from Centennial Park; phone: 862-8480).

Tennis – The major public facility is in *Centennial Park* (West End and 25th Aves. N.) where 13 courts are open from March through October. Admission charge. For more information, call 862-8400. Indoor tennis at *Nashboro Village Racquet Club* (2250 Murfreesboro Rd.; phone: 361-3242) also has outdoor clay courts, open during the summer months.

THEATER: For touring Broadway shows and regional companies: the *Tennessee Performing Arts Center* (505 Deaderick St.; phone: 741-2787). Lively children's theater and classics for adults: the *Nashville Academy Theatre,* the city's resident professional company (724 2nd Ave. S.; phone: 254-9103). The *Tennessee Repertory Theatre* performs five plays or musicals each year in the *Polk Theater* of the *Tennessee Performing Arts Center* (see above). Two small companies that perform recent works are *Actors Playhouse* (2318 West End; phone: 327-0049), with performances from September through May; and *The Circle Players* (phone: 383-7469), who present several plays each year, either at the *Johnson Theatre* of the *Tennessee Performing Arts Center* or at the *Alternate Circle Theater* (1703 Church St.). For dinner-theater, try *Chaffin's Barn Dinner Theater* (8204 Hwy. 100; phone: 646-9977).

MUSIC: The *Nashville Symphony Orchestra* holds concerts from September through May in the *Tennessee Performing Arts Center.* (The symphony box office is at 208 23rd Ave. N.; phone: 329-3033). On Friday and Sunday nights during June, July, and August, there are musical programs at *Centennial Park.* For information, call the Parks and Recreation Department's activities number (phone: 862-8400). Chamber music is offered at Fisk University, at the Blair School of Music on the Vanderbilt campus, and at *Cheekwood* on weekends (a beautifully restored early-20th-century mansion turned fine arts center, which also houses a restaurant and large botanical gardens; phone: 356-8000). Often it's free.

TV SHOW TAPINGS: The Nashville Network (TNN), a cable TV network originating in *Opryland,* tapes a number of programs before live audiences. For information about how to attend a TNN taping, contact the Nashville Network, Information Services (2806 Opryland Dr., Nashville, TN 37214; phone: 883-7000). The nationally syndicated "Hee Haw" variety show, which still airs around the South, is also taped at TNN's studios during June and October. Inquire by calling *Opryland* Customer Service (phone: 889-6700).

NIGHTCLUBS AND NIGHTLIFE: For music, this is a hard town to beat. Even motels can sometimes turn up good entertainers. Check newspapers and the *Nashville Visitor's Guide* for a thorough rundown of places to hear country music.

For the best in a concentrated area, however, visit Printer's Alley downtown, where, along with some striptease joints and seedy-looking bars, there are standouts like the *Captain's Table,* a silver and white linen tablecloth sort of place (phone: 256-3353), and *Boots Randolph's,* which features Boots (when he's in town), comedy acts, and a house band (phone: 256-5500). For bluegrass, try the *Bluegrass Inn* (184 2nd Ave. N.; phone: 244-8877) or the *Station Inn* (402 12th Ave. S.; phone: 255-3307). Hear local talent play jazz, rock, country, and folk music at the *Bluebird Café* (4104 Hillsboro Rd.; phone: 383-1461), which frequently hosts Writers' Nights to give local songwriters a chance to try out their compositions; *Boardwalk Cafe* (4114 Nolensville Rd.; phone: 832-5104); the *Bullpen Lounge* at the *Stock Yard* restaurant (901 2nd Ave. N.; phone: 255-6464); the *Cannery* (811 Palmer Pl.; phone: 726-1374); and *Exit/In* (Elliston Pl.; phone: 321-4400). The city's most active dance club is the *Ace of Clubs* (on 2nd Ave. downtown; phone: 254-2237), with good music (live bands on most nights) and a big dance floor. Most major hotels have entertainment in their lounges; the *Opryland* hotel has three lounges that offer good live country music. The *General Jackson* showboat offers dinner and an excellent musical show as well as entertainment in the lounge before dinner (phone: 889-6611 for reservations). *Zanies Comedy Showplace* (2025 8th Ave.; phone: 269-0221) features stand-up comedians nightly.

BEST IN TOWN

CHECKING IN: Along with some venerable (though refurbished) "Southern Belles," there are dozens of motels in Nashville — some parts of large chains, some parts of small chains, and a few independents. Prices generally range from $80 and up per night for a double room in an expensive hotel; $45 to $75 for accommodations in hostelries we've classified as moderate; and as low as $30 in an inexpensive place. All numbers are in the 615 area code unless otherwise indicated.

Hermitage – Built in 1910, this showpiece structure of Beaux Arts classic design is now a luxury hotel featuring 112 suites — with 3 phones and 2 color TV sets in each. It also has an oak-paneled bar, a fine dining room, and an outrageous Art Deco men's room that a few local ladies have been sneaked into for a peek. There's meeting space for 250, 24-hour room service, and express checkout. 231 6th Ave. N., downtown (phone: 244-3121 or 800-342-1908; Fax: 615-254-6908). Expensive.

Holiday Inn Crowne-Plaza – This 476-room property has glass elevators to whisk guests up through a vast skylit lobby. Also notable here are *Speaker's,* for casual dining, and *Pinnacle,* which rotates each half hour, providing a stunning view of the city. There are 9 meeting rooms, as well as limited secretarial service, a concierge desk, A/V equipment, photocopiers, and computers. Twenty-four–hour room service and express checkout. 623 Union St., downtown (phone: 259-1000, 800-233-1234, or 800-228-9000; Fax: 615-742-6056). Expensive.

Loews Vanderbilt Plaza – Now a member of the Loews family, this hostelry has 342 luxurious rooms, including 10 parlor suites and 3 executive suites. There's also a restaurant, café, game room and lounge, plus meeting facilities for up to 1,200. Amenities include health club facilities, 24-hour room service, concierge, express checkout, secretarial services, A/V equipment, and photocopiers. 2100 West End Ave. (phone: 320-1700; Fax: 615-320-0576). Expensive.

Opryland – Here are 1,891 rooms and 120 suites near the *Opry* and *Opryland* (but 20 minutes from downtown). Good entertainment at its *Stagedoor, Saloon, Cascade,* and *Staircase* lounges. The *Old Hickory Room* is one of the city's better (and more expensive) restaurants. The hotel also has a beautiful indoor conservatory with suspended walkways. Room service can be summoned 24 hours a day; there also are concierge services, 53 meeting rooms, A/V equipment, photocopiers, and express checkout. 2800 Opryland Dr. (phone: 889-1000; Fax: 615-871-7741). Expensive.

Stouffer's Nashville – A downtown high-rise with 673 rooms, next to the *Convention Center.* There is casual dining at the *Commerce Street Bar and Grill,* and the *Bridge Deli* features sandwiches. Adjacent to *Church Street Center,* a mall with shopping and more restaurants. There are 20 meeting rooms, 24-hour room service, concierge and secretarial services, A/V equipment, photocopiers, computers, and express checkout. 611 Commerce St. (phone: 255-8400 or 800-468-3571; Fax: 615-255-8163). Expensive.

Union Station – A National Historic Landmark, this hotel is located in what was originally the city's train station, which served the *Louisville and Nashville Railroad.* Recently converted, the property now offers 113 uniquely styled rooms along with 14 suites (two of which have 2 bedrooms). There are 2 restaurants, *Arthur's,* which serves fine continental food (see *Eating Out*), and *Greco's,* an Italian garden café. Sports facilities are available through a nearby fitness center. Other advantages include a concierge desk, A/V equipment, and photocopiers. 1001 Broadway (phone: 800-331-2123 or 615-726-1001; Fax: 615-248-3554). Expensive to moderate.

Hampton Inn Vanderbilt – This comfortable hotel with 163 rooms offers a hearty complimentary continental breakfast served in the lobby. Local telephone calls are free of charge. There's an exercise facility, an outdoor pool, and free parking. Photocopiers and A/V equipment also are available. 1919 West End Ave. (phone: 329-1144; Fax: 615-320-7112). There are 3 other locations in the Nashville area (phone: 800-HAMPTON for national reservations). Moderate.

Hermitage Landing Beach Cabins – On Percy Priest Lake, with aquatic activities — fishing, boating, swimming — at your doorstep. 20 units with kitchenettes (5 have fireplaces). Rte. 2 on Bell Rd. (phone: 889-7050). Moderate.

Holiday Inn Vanderbilt – Standard 300-room chain high-rise, close to Vanderbilt University and a horde of good restaurants, across the road from the Parthenon and Centennial Park and near some good nightspots. Amenities include a fitness center, secretarial services, A/V equipment, and express checkout. 2613 West End Ave. (phone: 327-4707; Fax: 615-327-8034). Moderate.

Knights Inn South – No-frills motel with 115 rooms; some units have kitchenettes. I-24 at Harding Pl. (phone: 834-0570). Inexpensive.

EATING OUT: Nashville is, as they say, a good eating town, with lots of small, unpretentious restaurants where you'll find fried chicken and shrimp, steaks, home-style vegetables, and the like. An inexpensive meal for two will cost $20 or less, a moderate one about $20 to $40, and an expensive one anywhere from $40 up. Prices do not include drinks, wine, or tips. All numbers are in the 615 area code unless otherwise indicated.

Arthur's – Seven-course continental dining (the menu changes daily) and plush decor characterize this chic eating place. Open daily. Reservations essential. Major credit cards accepted. *Union Station Hotel,* Broadway (phone: 255-1494). Expensive.

General Jackson – Based at *Opryland USA,* this showboat offers brunch and dinner cruises on the Cumberland River. Entertainment is topnotch, and the food — particularly brunch — also is good. Open daily, but the cruise schedule changes depending upon the time of year. Reservations essential well in advance. Major credit cards accepted. *Opryland USA* (phone: 889-6611). Expensive.

Julian's – Sophisticated French fare with seasonal specials along with the regular menu. In an old house, complete with white columns and plants. Diners can order à la carte or enjoy the prix fixe dinner. Open for dinner only; closed Sundays. Reservations essential. Major credit cards accepted. 2412 West End Ave. (phone: 327-2412). Expensive.

Mario's – Owner Mario Ferrari serves Northern Italian specialties, pasta, seasonal specials, interesting appetizers, and a variety of Italian veal dishes. Open for dinner only. Closed Sundays. Reservations essential. Major credit cards accepted. 2005 Broadway (phone: 327-3232). Expensive.

Ciraco's – Pasta, pizza, and a variety of veal dishes are available in either the intimate front room, with formal, white-tablecloth decor (where dishes and prices tend to be fancier), or in the back section, on plastic red-and-white-checkered tablecloths. Open daily for lunch and dinner. Reservations advised for the front room. Major credit cards accepted. 212 21st Ave. S. (phone: 329-0036). Expensive to moderate.

Faison's – Daily specials include fresh fish, pasta dishes, and soup, as well as a selection of specialty sandwiches. Yuppies pack in to soak up the eclectic atmosphere and well-executed entrées. Open daily for lunch and dinner; Saturdays, dinner only. Reservations required for groups of more than 7. Major credit cards accepted. 2000 Belcourt Ave. (phone: 298-2112). Moderate.

Garcia's of Scottsdale – Good Mexican food and margaritas, in an accessible location at the Harding Road exit off I-65. Open daily. Reservations advised for dinner on weekends. Major credit cards accepted. 4285 Sidco Dr. (phone: 331-9040). Moderate.

12th and Porter – Daily specials of fresh fish, either grilled or served in a sauce over fettuccine or rice. The eclectic menu also includes special pizza, calzone, plus beef and chicken dishes with interesting sauces. Casual, bohemian atmosphere. Closed Sundays. Reservations taken for large groups only. Major credit cards accepted. 114 12th Ave. N. (phone: 254-7236). Moderate.

Cakewalk – A small, pleasant café serving excellent and inventive lunches and dinners — fish and shrimp dishes, salads, quiche, and an attractive weekend brunch menu. Try any of the daily specials and soups. Open daily. Dinner reservations advised. Major credit cards accepted. 3001 West End Ave. (phone: 320-7778). Moderate to inexpensive.

Chinatown – An escape from the red plastic tablecloths found at almost every other Chinese restaurant in Nashville, it's a good spot for quiet conversation and tasty Hunan, Szechuan, and Mandarin food. Open daily. Reservations necessary. Major credit cards accepted. 3900 Hillsboro Rd. (phone: 269-3275). Moderate to inexpensive.

Siam Café – Excellent Thai food. If you're in a hurry, you can go through a cafeteria line and eat in the front section of the restaurant, but we recommend that you take the time to sit down in the quiet back section, order one of the day's specials, and try an appetizer or two. Open daily for dinner, daily for lunch except Sundays. No reservations. Major credit cards accepted. Directly off Nolensville Rd. at 316 McCall (phone: 834-3181). Moderate to inexpensive.

Cooker – This chain offers some of the best Southern cooking in town — nothing fancy, but plenty of big salads and stick-to-your-ribs main courses in a pleasant atmosphere. Open daily for lunch and dinner. No reservations, and expect a wait at peak hours. Major credit cards accepted. Several locations: 2609 West End Ave. (phone: 327-2925); 4770 Lebanon Rd., Hermitage (phone: 883-9700); 1195 Murfreesboro Rd. (phone: 361-4747). Inexpensive.

Elliston Place Soda Shop – Good lunches and dinners served by waitresses who look as if they're about to tell you to eat all your vegetables. The tile and chrome decor is beautifully intact from the 1940s. Closed

Sundays. Reservations unnecessary. No credit cards accepted. 211 Elliston Pl. (phone: 327-1090). Inexpensive.

Fuddrucker's – Good fast food in a busy setting that appeals to singles. Do-it-yourself burgers, hot dogs, wurst, and salads. Open daily. No reservations. Major credit cards accepted. 2020 West End Ave. (phone: 329-1331). Inexpensive.

Gaslight Beef Room – At *Opryland USA,* this steak-and-baked potato place is convenient if you're going to the *Opry.* Best are the homemade rolls. Open any time *Opryland* is open (see *Special Places*). Reservations unnecessary. Major credit cards accepted. 2802 Opryland Dr. (phone: 889-6611). Inexpensive.

Ham 'n' Goodies – Excellent homemade soup, salads, and sandwiches with Southern favorites such as honey-baked ham. Cakes and pies are available by the slice or whole. This fast food is home-cooked — eat in or take out. Centennial Park, a pleasant picnic spot, is only a couple of blocks down West End. Closed Sundays. Reservations unnecessary. MasterCard and Visa accepted. 2825 West End Ave. (phone: 329-0193). Inexpensive.

Loveless Motel – Fried chicken, homemade biscuits, and peach and blackberry preserves, plus country ham (salty, the way it's supposed to be) with gravy. Breakfast anytime. Closed Mondays. No reservations or credit cards accepted. Rte. 5, Hwy. 100 (phone: 646-9700). Inexpensive.

El Palenque – Locals come to this quiet, family-owned Mexican eatery for the comfortable, casual atmosphere. Open daily except Sundays for lunch and dinner. Reservations unnecessary. Major credit cards accepted. Hillsboro Rd. at Hobbs Rd. (phone: 386-3822). Inexpensive.

Swett's – Excellent Southern cooking, including home-cooked pork chops, barbecued chicken and ribs, meat loaf, and vegetables, ranging from traditional Southern green beans to stewed apples. Open daily. Reservations unnecessary. Discover, MasterCard, and Visa accepted. 28th and Clifton (phone: 329-4418). Inexpensive.

NEW HAVEN

AT-A-GLANCE

SEEING THE CITY: Once used by the Quinnipiac Indians for smoke signals, the 359-foot summit of New Haven's eastern cliff in East Rock Park still commands a panoramic view of the area — the city centered around the Green, the Yale campus, the harbor, and, on a clear day, 18 miles down Long Island Sound to Bridgeport.

SPECIAL PLACES: New Haven, the first architecturally planned city in the US, was designed for walking. Laid out in nine squares, New Haven is centered around the Green, still its main square. Almost everything of interest is nearby, in a 30-block area whose cultural and historic scope transcends its geographic limits.

The Green – The 16-acre square of grass, trees, and shrubbery in the city center remains today the focal point of New Haven activity as it was for early-17th-century settlers. Originally all public buildings were on the Green, as well as cows and pigs to keep the grass down. All the animals now are gone. The only buildings left are three churches, two of Georgian and Federal style and one Episcopal church of Gothic Revival, all built between 1812 and 1815.

New Haven Colony Historical Society and Museum – A large model offers a look at New Haven of 1640, and other collections span the city's historical development over the past three centuries. Closed Mondays. Admission charge. 114 Whitney Ave. (phone: 562-4183).

Yale Campus and Facilities – Named for Elihu Yale, East India trader and donor, the university, founded in 1701, is one of the most distinguished educational institutions in the world. The campus is lovely with its ivy-covered Gothic buildings, charming green courtyards, and examples of contemporary architecture. The best way to see the campus is to take a free university tour led by student guides well versed in college lore and anecdotes. The tour begins at the Old Campus with its Gothic and Romanesque structures, including the oldest of the ivy-covered buildings, Connecticut Hall, and proceeds to Memorial Quadrangle, Harkness Tower, Mory's, and the newer Yale structures such as the Ezra Stiles and Morse colleges and the Beinecke Rare Book Library. Open weekdays from 10 AM to 4 PM. Tours are given at 10:30 AM and 2 PM weekdays and at 1:30 PM on weekends throughout the year, starting at the University Information Office, Phelps Archway, 344 College St. (phone: 432-2300).

Peabody Museum of Natural History – Exhibits on evolutionary history: a huge skeleton of a brontosaurus, the famous *Age of Reptiles* mural by Rudolph Zallinger, the Hall of Mammals. Open daily. No admission charge weekdays from 3 to 5 PM. 170 Whitney Ave. (phone: 432-5050).

University Art Gallery – This fine collection includes John Trumbull's original paintings of the American Revolution and samples of ancient Greek and Roman art and architecture. Closed Mondays. No admission charge. 1111 Chapel St. (phone: 432-0600).

Yale Center for British Art and British Studies – Designed by Louis I. Kahn, it features works of Hogarth, Constable, Turner, Stubbs, and Blake. The paintings are hung in bright, open galleries that create the atmosphere of an English country house and provide optimal viewing. There are more British works here than anywhere outside Great Britain. From September through May, the museum sponsors concerts on Sunday evenings and Wednesday afternoons. Closed Mondays. No admission charge. 1080 Chapel St. (phone: 432-2800).

Shubert Performing Arts Center – This historic theater, once the preeminent staging ground for Broadway plays and musicals, has been restored to its original 1914 elegance, thus spurring a performing arts and retail renaissance in the College and Chapel Streets area. Productions include both national touring groups and local performers. 247 College St. (phone: 624-1825).

Palace Performing Arts Center – Directly across College Street from the *Shubert Center,* this concert hall complements New Haven's performing arts scene with an impressive musical performance schedule including everything from rock 'n' roll to classical. Children's shows also are regularly scheduled. 246 College St. (box office phone: 624-8497).

■ **EXTRA SPECIAL:** Some 60 miles east of New Haven on I-95 is the town of Mystic, where the fastest clipper ships and the first ironclad vessels were built in the 19th century. The town has been restored as a 19th-century seaport. You can stroll along the waterfront of the Mystic River or down the cobblestone streets lined with quaint seaport homes. The *Mystic Seaport Museum* (50 Greenmanville Ave., Mystic, CT 06355; phone: 572-0711) has an outstanding collection featuring the *Joseph Conrad,* one of the last square-riggers ever built, and the *Charles W. Morgan,* a large wooden whaling ship in service for more than 80 years, which celebrated its 150 birthday last year.

SOURCES AND RESOURCES

TOURIST INFORMATION: For general information, contact the Greater New Haven Chamber of Commerce (195 Church St.; phone: 787-6735) or the Cultural Affairs Department of the Mayor's Office (phone: 787-8956). You also can visit the Long Wharf Information Office (at Exit 46 of I-95; phone: 787-4282) from mid-April through mid-October. Yale has its own information center (at Phelps Archway, 344 College St.; phone: 432-2300), which offers hour-long architectural and historical walking tours of the campus weekdays at 10:30 AM and 2 PM, weekends at 1:30AM (free). Contact the Connecticut state hotline (phone: 258-4290) for maps, calendars of events, health updates, and travel advisories.

Enjoying New Haven, A Guide to the Area by Elizabeth Fledge and Eugenia Fayen (East Rock Press, Ltd., $8.95) is a good guide to the city.

Local Coverage – The *New Haven Register,* mornings and Sundays; the Friday *Register* and the *New Haven Advocate* (published Thursdays) list the coming week's attractions. The *Register* is available only at newsstands, and the *Advocate* is distributed throughout the city.

Television Stations – WFSB Channel 3–CBS; WTNH Channel 8–ABC; WVIT Channel 30–NBC; WEDH Channel 65–PBS.

Radio Stations – AM: WAVZ 1300 (oldies); WELI 960 (oldies, rock); WNHC 1340 (urban contemporary music). FM: WPLR 99.1 (rock).

Food – *Best Restaurants in Southern New England* by Patricia Brooks (101 Productions; $4.95) has many New Haven listings.

TELEPHONE: The area code for New Haven is 203.

Sales Tax – There is an 8% state sales tax on most consumer goods and a meals tax of 10%.

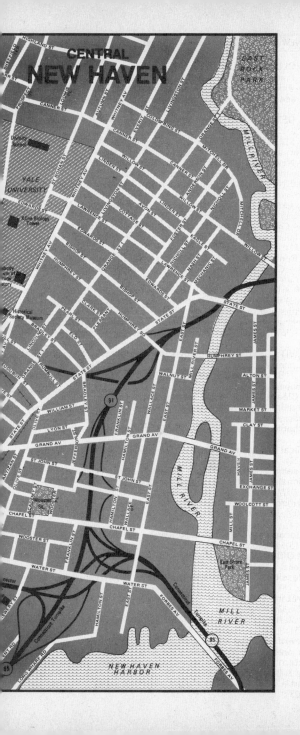

CLIMATE: Umbrellas are an important item in New Haven. On Long Island Sound, the city gets a lot of rain. The sea breeze, which gives some pleasant relief during the humid summers, the spring, and the fall, becomes raw during the cold and snowy winters.

 GETTING AROUND: Airport – Tweed–New Haven Airport is a 15-minute drive from downtown, and taxi fare will run about $12. The *Connecticut Transit* bus that heads this way is not recommended for those with luggage, since it stops 2 blocks away. Tweed–New Haven handles only domestic flights. Those with international connections can get to JFK and La Guardia airports in New York City and Newark International in northern New Jersey by contacting *Connecticut Limousine* (phone: 878-2222); the ride to any of the three from its terminal (on Brewery St. at Long Wharf) behind the New Haven post office) will take approximately 2 hours and cost from $30.

Bus – *Connecticut Transit* serves the downtown area and the suburbs. Route information and guides are available at 470 James St. (phone: 624-0151).

Car Rental – New Haven has offices of all the national firms.

Taxi – Cabs can be ordered on the phone. The largest company is *Metro Cab* (phone: 777-7777).

Train – New Haven is located on the main *Amtrak* line (phone: 777-4002) between New York and Boston. There is frequent service to those cities and to Hartford. Service to New York City and southern Connecticut is also offered by *Metro North Commuter Railroad* (phone: 800-638-7646). Trains leave from Union Station on Union Ave.

 VITAL SERVICES: Audiovisual Equipment – *HB Communications, Inc.* (phone: 234-9246); *Action Media* (phone: 865-7887). **Business Services** – *Audubon Copy Shoppe,* 48 Whitney Ave. (phone: 865-3115).

Dry Cleaner/Tailor – *Jet,* State St. (phone: 777-2546).

Limousine – *Hy's Livery Service* (phone: 934-6331); *Morgillo Limousine* (phone: 387-2081).

Mechanic – *Libby's Sales and Service,* 60 Printer's La. (phone: 772-1112).

Medical Emergency – *Yale New Haven Hospital,* 20 York St. (phone: 785-2222).

Messenger Services – *Royal Messenger Service* (phone: 488-6318).

National/International Courier – *Federal Express* (phone: 800-328-5355); *DHL Worldwide Courier Express* (phone: 653-5558).

Pharmacy – *Flexer's Pharmacy,* 9 AM to 7 PM (15 Broadway; phone: 865-1000); *Medical Center Pharmacy,* 7 AM to 7 PM (50 York St.; phone: 776-7064).

Photocopies – *Audubon Copy Shoppe* (48 Whitney Ave.; phone: 865-3115); *Kinko's,* open 24 hours (17 Broadway; phone: 782-6055).

Post Office – The main office is located at Federal Station, 150 Court St. (phone: 782-7110).

Professional Photographer – *Paul R. Anderson Photographer* (phone: 288-5059); *Gutrick Photographic Eye* (phone: 878-6884).

Secretary/Stenographer – *Olsten Services* (phone: 777-4477); *Diversified Employment* (phone: 397-2500).

Translator – *Berlitz* (phone: 787-4245); *Inlingua* (Hartford; phone: 236-2351).

Typewriter Rental – *Computer Products Center* (phone: 789-0267); *IBM,* monthly rate only (phone: 281-2300).

Western Union/Telex – Many offices are located around the city (phone: 800-325-6000).

Other – *Tyco Xerox Copy Center,* word processing services (phone: 562-9723).

SPECIAL EVENTS: The *New Haven Jazz Festival,* a series of concerts featuring well-known artists, runs from early July through mid-August. The 20-kilometer *Road Race* takes place annually on *Labor Day,* and the New Haven *Bed Race* is held in early September. The weekend before *Thanksgiving* of odd-numbered years (this year's game will be held on November 21), the Yale-Harvard football game takes place, with all the fanfare of a traditional rivalry, at the *Yale Bowl.*

 MUSEUMS: With Yale's fine collections and New Haven's Historical Society, the city touches all cultural bases. Two special collections reach interests further afield:

Beinecke Rare Book and Manuscript Library – Home of one of the few Gutenberg Bibles, dated 1455 and believed to have been the first printed volume in all of Western Civilization. There's also an unbelievably abundant collection of first editions and original letters and manuscripts from Gertrude Stein, Eugene O'Neill, William Shakespeare, and Charles Dickens, to name a few. This truly is a book lover's paradise. Closed Sundays. 121 Wall St. (phone: 432-2977).

Yale Collection of Musical Instruments – One of the world's finest collections of historical keyboard instruments, as well as a representative accumulation of Western European wind and string instruments. Open Tuesdays through Thursdays, 1 to 4 PM; closed in August and during all Yale University recesses. No admission charge. 15 Hillhouse Ave. (phone: 432-0822).

 MAJOR COLLEGES AND UNIVERSITIES: Yale University (see *Special Places*). Other educational institutions in the area are the University of New Haven (300 Orange Ave. in West Haven; phone: 932-7000) and Southern Connecticut State University (501 Crescent St.; phone: 397-4000).

 SPORTS AND FITNESS: Fitness Center – *The Downtown Health and Racquet Club* has racquetball, squash, and basketball courts, sauna, and Nautilus equipment. 230 George St. (phone: 787-6501).

Football – Yale has teams in all major sports, but the most followed are the *Bulldogs,* who play football at the *Yale Bowl* (Rte. 34, between Derby Ave. and Chapel St.). Call the Athletic Association for tickets (phone: 432-1400).

Hockey – The New Haven *Nighthawks* of the American Hockey League play from October to April at the *New Haven Coliseum,* 275 S. Orange St. (phone: 772-4330).

Horse Racing – Although there is no racetrack nearby, OTB has taken on a new meaning here with an $8 million racing theater, complete with a 24-by-32-foot screen and 40 betting windows. The "grandstand" seats 1,800. Open six afternoons (not Tuesdays) and six evenings (not Sundays) a week, it's called *Teletrack* (phone: 789-1943; in the Long Wharf area).

Jogging – Run along Whalley Avenue, which is hilly, to Edgewood Park, about 2 miles north; Amity Road provides a more rural setting; Fountain Street and Litchfield Road are other options. Every Monday at 6:15 PM a Fun Run leaves from Running Start, 93 Whitney Ave. and Trumbull St. (phone: 865-6244).

Skiing – Best facilities nearby are at *Powder Ridge* in Middlefield (21 miles on I-91 — exit 16 — to E. Main St. in Meriden); from there follow the signs to *Powder Ridge.*

Tennis – There are many good outdoor courts for the public in the city. Municipal courts at Bowen Field (Munson St. between Crescent St. and Sherman Ave.) and at Wilbur Cross High School (Orange St. and Mitchell Dr.) are free, while the *College Wood Courts* (Orange and Cold

Spring Sts.) charge a small fee. Yalies get preference at university courts, but the public is welcome. Derby and Central Aves.

 THEATER: For up-to-date offerings and performance times, check the publications listed above. New Haven is the home of a well-known professional repertory company, the *Long Wharf Theatre Company,* with productions of classics, musicals, contemporary works, and experimental theater, in a former warehouse in the meat and produce terminal. Closed in the summer (222 Sargent Dr.; phone: 787-4282). *Yale Repertory Theatre* (1120 Chapel St.; phone: 432-1234) also has experimental theater and classic plays. Under the direction of Lloyd Richards, its productions received great acclaim in recent years, and many moved on to Broadway. Richards recently resigned, and Stan Wojewodski is its new director. The *Shubert Theater* (247 College St.; phone: 624-1825) serves Broadway touring companies, and the *Palace Theater* (246 College St.; phone: 624-8497) features everything from jazz shows to wrestling.

 MUSIC: The *New Haven Symphony Orchestra* gives concerts from October through April at *Woolsey Hall* on the Yale campus. (For ticket information call 776-1444.) For information about the *Yale Chorus,* student groups, and visiting artists, call university information at 432-2300. Opera buffs should check out the *Shubert* (247 College St.; phone: 624-1825), which features opera when a Broadway touring company is not in residence.

NIGHTCLUBS AND NIGHTLIFE: Nightspots come and go in New Haven. For the yuppie crowd, *Bopper's of New Haven* (239 Crown St.; phone: 562-1957) offers a lively disc jockey, oldies from the 1950s and 1960s, and good dance music. Adding a touch of class to New Haven's nightlife is the *Palms,* the renovated ballroom of the old *Taft* hotel (261 College St.; phone: 776-3316). *Toad's Place* (300 York St.; phone: 777-7431) features national and local rock acts (The *Rolling Stones* and Bob Dylan have made surprise appearances here); disco dancing Wednesdays, Fridays, and Saturdays

BEST IN TOWN

CHECKING IN: Everything is easy to find in New Haven, but visitors will certainly be frustrated in their search for a grand old traditional hotel — it's simply not there. What does exist is as easy to find in New Haven as anywhere else — branches of the familiar chains, which offer double-room prices in all ranges. Hotels in the expensive category offer accommodations from $125 to $175; moderate, $80 to $95; and inexpensive, $55 to $65. For bed and breakfast accommodations, contact *Bed & Breakfast Ltd.* (PO Box 216, New Haven, CT 06513; phone: 469-3260). All telephone numbers are in the 203 area code unless otherwise indicated.

Inn at Chapel West – A welcome relief to travelers tired of the same old hotel chains. It offers 10 tastefully decorated rooms in a newly refurbished house in the heart of the downtown renovation. Rates include continental breakfast and parking. There are meeting rooms for up to 22, and photocopiers are available. 1201 Chapel St. (phone: 777-1201; Fax: 203-776-7363). Expensive.

Colony Inn – Comfortable, downtown, and as close to Yale as you can get without being enrolled, it has typical motel-style rooms with all amenities, a good restaurant (the *Colony Grille),* and a piano bar.

Guests may purchase a $5 pass to the *Paine and Whitney Gym* at Yale University, which includes a fitness center, racquetball court, and a swimming pool. Meeting rooms accommodate up to 250, and photocopiers are available. 1157 Chapel St. (phone: 776-1234; Fax: 203-772-3929). Moderate.

Holiday Inn – Also downtown, but farther away from Yale. Features 160 rooms with cable TV, live entertainment in its lounge, a restaurant, and an outdoor pool. Meeting rooms can hold up to 200, and A/V equipment, photocopiers, and computers are all available. Express checkout. 30 Whalley Ave. (phone: 777-6221; Fax: 203-772-1089). Moderate.

Park Plaza – This 19-story downtown property overlooks the Green and offers a rooftop restaurant (see *Eating Out*) with a panoramic view of New Haven at night, plus live entertainment and dancing. Contemporary in design, it is situated in the heart of the *Chapel Square Mall,* across from Yale. Rooms have views of Long Island Sound, and there is a heated pool and sundeck. Meeting room accommodations for up to 1,000, with A/V equipment and photocopiers available for business needs. Express checkout. 155 Temple St. (phone: 772-1700; Fax: 203-624-2683). Moderate.

Residence Inn – A new addition in town that caters especially to business travelers. All accommodations are suites with a full kitchen. The room rate includes a continental breakfast buffet and free van service around the city. Business amenities include meeting rooms for up to 25, A/V equipment, and photocopiers. 3 Long Wharf Drive (phone: 777-5337). Moderate.

Duncan – Small, old, and near Yale (so near, in fact, that students sometimes live here), it has rooms available for visitors, travelers, and the student-at-heart. 1151 Chapel St. (phone: 787-1273). Inexpensive.

EATING OUT: For folks who consider eating far more important than sleeping, New Haven is the place for you. What the city lacks in fancy overnight accommodations, it makes up for in an abundance and variety of restaurants. A 2-minute walk through the center of town will turn up several worthwhile eateries tucked away in basements and other unlikely corners. Because there are many potential diners in the city, restaurants are highly competitive, and prices generally are reasonable. Most of the restaurants are in the moderate ($20 to $30 for a dinner for two) to inexpensive range ($15 and under) though there are a few that are more expensive ($40 and up). Prices do not include tax, drinks, or tip. All telephone numbers are in the 203 area code unless otherwise indicated.

Delmonico's – The decor is strictly Valentino — from the posters on the wall to an occasional screening of an old silent film starring the sheik. And the food is Southern Italian. Inspired by the atmosphere, the chef has created two dishes designed to raise passions in the blood: fresh fish on a bed of linguine topped with a whole lobster, and a variety of meats mixed with peppers and onions, cooked in a secret sauce. Closed Sundays. Reservations advised. Major credit cards accepted. 232 Wooster St. (phone: 865-1109). Expensive.

Leon's – Family-run restaurant, its specialty is Italian food such as chicken Eduardo, prepared in a light butter and garlic sauce; the mussel and clam dishes also are good. Closed Mondays. Reservations necessary for large parties in private rooms only. Major credit cards accepted. 321 Washington Ave. (phone: 777-5366). Expensive.

Robert Henry's – Centrally located near Yale University in the beautifully restored Sherman Building, it brings more than a simple touch of class to downtown New Haven dining. Award-winning French chefs prepare a sophisticated menu combining the finest French culinary technique with only the freshest native ingredients. The menu changes frequently to keep pace with the chefs' creativity and the seasonal availability of fish, game, native vegetables, and herbs. All desserts are homemade, including the sorbets, ice creams, and chocolates. Elegant decor features original turn-of-the-century woodwork, marble, and hand-painted windows. No lunch on weekends. Reservations advised. Major credit cards accepted. 1032 Chapel St. (phone: 789-0100). Expensive.

Azteca's – A welcome addition to yet another reawakening New Haven neighborhood (the Upper State Street District), it offers the finest Mexican and Southwestern food in the area: tacos, enchiladas, chimichangas, and salads served in a cheerful, Southwestern ambience. Closed Sundays. Reservations advised. MasterCard and Visa accepted. 14 Mechanic St. (phone: 624-2454). Moderate.

Elm City Diner – An atypical Art Deco diner, favored by theatergoers for its late night, nouvelle cuisine menu. Piano bar Friday and Saturday nights. Open daily. Reservations unnecessary. Most major credit cards accepted. 122 Chapel St. (phone: 772-1800). Moderate.

Miya – A fine Japanese restaurant with the best sushi in town, as well as fresh fish specials, tempura, and teriyaki. One tatami room can be reserved for four or more. Open daily for dinner only. Reservations advised. Most major credit cards accepted. 68 Howe St. (phone: 777-9760). Moderate.

Scoozies – New Haven's hottest Italian place, offering generous portions of pasta and a fine wine selection in a bright, contemporary atmosphere. Two flights below street level, next door to the *Yale Repertory Theatre*. Open daily. Reservations advised. Major credit cards accepted. 1104 Chapel St. (phone: 776-8268). Moderate.

Top of the Park – This rooftop dining spot at the *Park Plaza* hotel overlooks the harbor, Yale University, and the Green, and specializes in prime ribs, veal, and fresh native seafood. A Sunday brunch is offered, as well as a buffet lunch on weekdays (except in summer). Live entertainment and dancing on weekends. Reservations advised. Major credit cards accepted. 155 Temple St. (phone: 772-1700). Moderate.

Hunan Wok – New Haven's best Chinese eatery, serving Hunan, Szechuan, and Mandarin cooking in a warm and friendly atmosphere. Takeout service also is available. Open daily. Reservations advised for Fridays and Saturdays. Major credit cards accepted. 142 York St. (phone: 776-9475). Moderate to inexpensive.

Gentree's Ltd. – A favorite with both students and townies, it offers a sumptuous California salad bar at lunchtime, all-you-can-eat barbecued ribs and chicken on Tuesday nights. Open daily. Reservations unnecessary. Major credit cards accepted. 194 York St. (phone: 562-3800). Inexpensive.

Leon's Picnic Basket – Part of the redesigned *Chapel Square Mall* with over a dozen eateries. The menu features stuffed croissants and deli sandwiches, salads, pastries, breads, and cookies. Seating is along a window wall overlooking the New Haven Green. Open daily. Reservations unnecessary. No credit cards accepted. *Chapel Square Mall* mezzanine. 900 Chapel St. (phone: 776-2938). Inexpensive.

Louis' Lunch – This tiny place, which looks like an English pub, claims to be the birthplace of the hamburger. Whether this is true or not, the burgers are great — big, juicy, and charcoal grilled. And don't ask for ketchup — they don't have it and to ask is considered an affront to the quality of the product. Open weekdays till 4 PM. No reservations or credit cards accepted. 263 Crown St. (phone: 562-5507). Inexpensive.

Modern Apizza – Baked in brick ovens, delicious pizza pies emerge — topped with everything from eggplant to crabmeat and clams. Other specialties include pasta dishes, submarine sandwiches, and calzones.

Closed Mondays. No reservations or credit cards accepted. 874 State St. (phone: 776-5306). Inexpensive.

Pepe's – Pepe claims to have invented the pizza. You might not believe him, but you'll have to agree that in an area where pizza making is a fine art, this place takes the pie. Closed Tuesdays. No reservations or credit cards accepted. 157 Wooster St. (phone: 865-5762). Inexpensive.

NEW ORLEANS

AT-A-GLANCE

SEEING THE CITY: The revolving bar in the *Top of the Mart* restaurant, on the 33rd floor of the World Trade Center, offers the best view of the city, the Mississippi River as it cuts the crescent shape of New Orleans, and the barges, ocean liners, and ferries as they move up and down the river. 2 Canal St. at the river (phone: 522-9795).

Bus Tours – There are four local tour companies that offer bus tours of the French Quarter, the Garden District, and the lakefront. Prices run about $20 per person for 3 to 4 hours. Two of the better companies are *New Orleans Tours* (phone: 487-1991) and *Tours by Isabelle* (phone: 367-3963).

Carriage Rides – Horse-drawn carriage tours take you through the French Quarter. Call *Old French Quarter Tours* (phone: 944-0446).

River Tours – On the Canal Street ferry you can ride back and forth to Algiers free. The *Bayou Jean Lafitte* motor vessel gives a tour from the Toulouse Street Wharf (behind Jax Brewery) through the bayou country to Bayou Barataria, home of the famous pirate. The paddlewheel steamboat *Natchez* has daily runs from the Toulouse Street Wharf up and down the river. A small paddlewheeler, the *Cotton Blossom,* makes three runs daily from the Canal Street docks to Audubon Zoo. Admission charge for all three (phone: 586-8777). The motorized, 3-decker *Cajun Queen* and the sternwheeler *Creole Queen* offer both daytime and dinner cruises, which depart from behind Riverwalk (phone: 524-0814). The *Voyageur,* a sightseeing boat, cruises from the foot of Canal Street into bayou country, with a stop at Chalmette Battlefield (phone: 523-5555). A high-speed catamaran, the *Audubon Express,* makes six daily trips between the aquarium and the Audubon Zoo (phone: 586-8777).

Streetcar Tours – Four vintage streetcars run the 1.5-mile stretch alongside the Mississippi River while tour guides answer your questions. 35¢. For more information call 569-2899.

Voodoo Tours – Voodoo, the ancient African religion that filtered into Louisiana in the early 1700s, is still widespread in New Orleans. When the government refused to recognize it as a religion and suppressed voodoo rites, practitioners went underground and voodoo became a cult. Today, there's a Voodoo Walking Tour of the French Quarter and the *Voodoo Museum;* a tour that lets you witness a voodoo ceremony; a Voodoo Ritual Swamp Tour at dusk; and other tours that wind through mysterious bayous, historic plantations, gardens, villages, Indian burial grounds, and fascinating swamp scenery and wildlife. Tours range from 2½ to 10 hours, and prices run from $15 to $55 (phone: 523-7685).

SPECIAL PLACES: Nestled between the Mississippi River and Lake Pontchartrain, New Orleans's natural crescent shape can be confusing. North, south, east, and west mean very little here; New Orleans residents keep life simple and use "lakeside" or "riverside" as directions.

VIEUX CARRÉ

Jackson Square – This stately square was once the town square of the French colonial settlement, and the scene of most of New Orleans's history, from hangings to the transfer ceremony of the Louisiana Purchase. Rebuilt in the 1850s with the equestrian statue of Andrew Jackson, the hero of the Battle of New Orleans, the square is a pleasant place to sit and watch New Orleans go by, against a setting of charming brick façades of the surrounding buildings. Heads no longer roll here, but frequent open-air jazz concerts do, and the only hangings are on the iron fence bounding the area, where local artists display their work, and some draw portraits. Traffic has been removed from the area, leaving a pedestrian mall. 700 Chartres (pronounced *Char*-ters) St., bordered by St. Ann, St. Peter, and Decatur Sts.

St. Louis Cathedral – Built in 1794, this beautiful Spanish building features towers, painted ceilings, an altar imported from Belgium, and markers in French, Spanish, Latin, and English for those buried in the sanctuary. Tours given daily except Sunday. Donations requested. 700 Chartres St., across from Jackson Square (phone: 525-9585).

Presbytère – Used as a courthouse during the Spanish colonial period, it is also part of the *Louisiana State Museum* and features exhibitions on Louisiana history. Closed Mondays and Tuesdays. Admission charge. Corner of Chartres and St. Ann Sts. (phone: 568-6968).

Pontalba Apartments – Built in the 1850s, this row of townhouses features distinctive cast ironwork on the balconies and a French-style arcade. Rich in New Orleans history, the apartments and shops have seen the comings and goings of the French aristocracy, Jenny Lind, Sherwood Anderson, and William Faulkner. Today, ice cream parlors and small shops line the ground floors, and some very fortunate New Orleans residents live above. Jackson Square at St. Ann and St. Peter Sts.

Moon Walk – Named for former Mayor Moon Landrieu, the name is a bit misleading. But this promenade alongside the Mississippi River shows "Ol' Man River" at its best as it winds its way along the crescent shape of the city (the only resemblance Moon Walk has with the moon). The Mississippi is deep and swift at New Orleans and the port, which can accommodate oceangoing vessels, is second in tonnage only to New York. Across the levee from Decatur St. at Jackson Square.

French Market – A farmers' market for 2 centuries, the *French Market* still has a colorful atmosphere with booths under large old arches offering everything in the way of fresh vegetables and fruits (try the Louisiana oranges, sugarcane, and the sweet midget bananas), meats, and fish including live crab, turtle, shrimp, catfish, and trout. The covered section has cafés, candy shops, and gift shops. *Café du Monde* (800 Decatur; phone: 581-2914) is a New Orleans institution featuring marvelous café au lait (half coffee and chicory, half hot milk) and *beignets* (square French donuts dusted with powdered sugar). The café never closes, and the market is open daily. Extending down Decatur St. from St. Ann to Esplanade.

Beauregard-Keyes House – Although George Washington never slept here, almost everyone else lived in this Federal house, including the novelist Frances Parkinson Keyes, chess player Paul Morphy, and Confederate General P.G.T. Beauregard; quite a few of another sort died here in a Mafia battle in 1909. The house has period furniture, a collection of dolls, and Keyes memorabilia. Closed Sundays. Admission charge. 1113 Chartres St. (phone: 523-7257).

Royal Street – There really was a streetcar named *Desire,* and from the 19th century and into the 1950s, it used to run along Royal Street to Canal. Though the streetcar is gone, desire for the old days remains and some of it can be fulfilled by a stroll down this street, famous for its antiques shops and highly distinctive architecture.

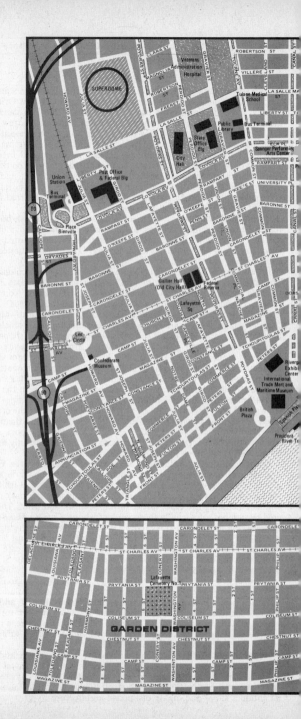

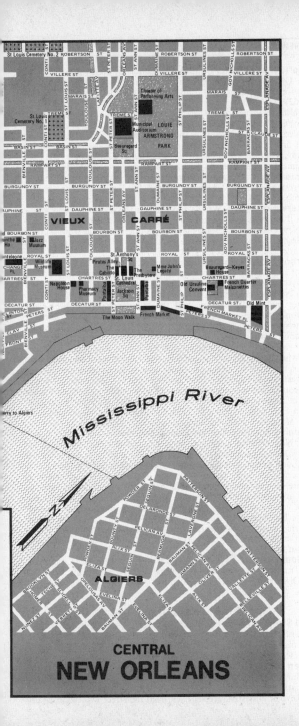

CENTRAL
NEW ORLEANS

Historic New Orleans Collection – Scholarly archives, a preserved French Quarter residence, gift shop, and historic exhibitions. Closed Sundays and Mondays. No admission charge. 533 Royal St. (phone: 523-4662).

Old Mint – Opened in 1982 and part of the *Louisiana State Museum,* the Mint contains a *Mardi Gras* exhibition, a jazz exhibit, and archives. Jazz lovers will find souvenirs of the patron saints of jazz — Louis Armstrong's first horn, Bix Beiderbecke's cuff links, and instruments played by members of the *Original Dixieland Jazz Band.* Fine displays trace the development of jazz from its African-American rhythms and the European brass band tradition to current progressive strains. Open Wednesdays through Sundays. Admission charge. 400 Esplanade Ave. (phone: 568-6968).

Preservation Hall – What's recorded in the jazz collection at the Mint still happens every night at *Preservation Hall;* featured is traditional New Orleans Dixieland played by a different band from a group of six. Sparse surroundings, but the real jazz thing. Open nightly. Admission charge. 726 St. Peter St. (phone: 523-8939).

Bourbon Street – Though the street was named for the French royal family, it actually has a lot more in common with the drink, which, along with anything else potable, can be found here in abundance (and New Orleans establishments have added many drinks to the bartender's list, including the absinthe frappe and the Hurricane). Round-the-clock honky-tonks offer live jazz, which gets wild in the wee hours, and live booze, which gets wicked the morning after. (It's legal to drink on the streets and plastic to-go cups are offered everywhere.) A hot strip since the postwar years, Bourbon Street also has lots of strip joints and peep shows, where, even if you stay outside, you'll get more of an eyeful than a peep as the hawkers swing the doors open to lure customers. Among the hottest spots is *Lafitte's Blacksmith Shop* (941 Bourbon St.) where pirate Jean Lafitte is purported to have had a smithy's shop, now a bar where the forge is still flaming; others are the *Old Absinthe House* (240 Bourbon St.), a barroom since 1826, for rhythm and blues, and *Lulu White's Mahogany Hall,* for Dixieland jazz (309 Bourbon St.).

St. Louis Cemetery Number One – The last stop in the Vieux Carré, this old New Orleans cemetery with its tombs designed by earlier architects is literally a diminutive necropolis. The marshy ground dictated aboveground burial, and the monuments are interesting for their structure, inscriptions, and number of remains inside (to solve overcrowding, tombs are opened, and the remaining bones are moved deeper into the vault to accommodate new arrivals). If you're interested, the caretaker will give you a tour. Among the prominent buried here are Etienne de Boré, the first Mayor of New Orleans; Paul Morphy, the chess player; and Marie Laveau, a 19th-century voodoo queen. Open daily. No admission, but small charge for tours. (It's best not to wander around alone.) 400 Basin St.

Voodoo Museum – African masks, artifacts, voodoo dolls, and manuscripts mark the development of voodoo in New Orleans from the 1880s. Open daily from 10 AM to dusk. Admission charge. 724 Rue Dumaine (phone: 523-7685).

DOWNTOWN AND THE GARDEN DISTRICT

Canal Street – Where the French Quarter ends, the business district begins, and the transition is sharp, from narrow cobblestone streets to a wide, main boulevard. The World Trade Center of New Orleans, a glass skyscraper, is the center for companies dealing in foreign trade.

Garden District – Above Canal Street and the business district is the lovely Garden District, once the center of 19th-century American aristocracy, still preserving its old style. The houses, mainly Victorian and Greek Revival in design, are set back from the street with wide, shady gardens of oak, magnolia, camellia, and palm trees. The district is a great place to stroll anytime (or take the St. Charles Avenue streetcar).

New Orleans Centre – In the heart of the business district, this "city within a city" links the *Superdome* and *Hyatt Regency* hotel with over 110 stores plus numerous eateries and offices. Cited as an architectural landmark, this new complex is expected to be an urban gathering place for shopping and dining (phone: 568-0000).

Aquarium of the Americas – Over 7,500 specimens of marine life are housed in an astonishing 17-acre underwater series of environmental exhibits that overlooks the Mississippi. Four major exhibits recreate undersea life in the Amazon Basin, the Caribbean Sea, the Gulf of Mexico, and the Mississippi River. Spectacular walking tours go through a transparent tunnel exposed to aquatic life, or along a jungle path, across a suspension bridge into an Indian gut. The *John James Audubon* (phone: 586-8777), a catamaran, runs several trips daily between the aquarium and the Audubon Zoo, 7 miles upriver. Open daily. Admission charge. 111 Iberville St. (phone: 595-3474).

CITY PARK AND LAKE PONTCHARTRAIN

New Orleans Museum of Art – This attractive Greek Revival building has fine permanent collections including the Samuel H. Kress Collection (Italian Renaissance and baroque masterpieces), 19th-century French salon paintings, works by Degas, pre-Columbian art, African art, Spanish colonial paintings, and a splendid collection of Fabergé. Closed Mondays. Admission charge. In City Park (phone: 488-2631).

Lake Pontchartrain – New Orleans's other body of water, this large saltwater lake has fishing from the sea wall as well as on the lake. Best is the drive over the Lake Pontchartrain Causeway, the longest overwater highway bridge in the world — 24 miles across open water, and for 8 miles in the center, you are completely out of sight of land; there's only Lake Pontchartrain as far as the eye can see. I-10 leads to the Causeway. Toll.

■ **EXTRA SPECIAL:** Somewhere out there in Louisiana country was once the heart of the Old South, and it still beats faintly along the banks of the Mississippi. A little over 100 years ago sugarcane was king in Louisiana, and large plantations established commercial empires, as well as an entire social system, around it. A few of these plantations have been restored and are open to visitors who want to see what that period was like, at least for the people on top. And the life that the Southern gentry created for themselves really is something to see. The most interesting plantations are within an hour's drive of New Orleans. *Houmas House* (72 miles west on River Rd.), which was used for the filming of *Hush, Hush, Sweet Charlotte,* looks just as a plantation should — a big, white mansion with stately columns and lovely grounds with huge, old oak trees and formal gardens. There is an excellent tour through the house, which has a circular staircase, rare antiques, a widow's walk for river gazing, and outside, *garçonnières,* little windmill-shaped structures where young men were sent to live independently when they came of age. San Francisco (42 miles west along River Rd.) is an attractive structure — Flamboyant Steamboat Gothic with lots of Victorian trim, elaborate ceiling paintings, and, over the front door, a mirror that reflects the Mississippi River. Other impressive plantations (and the following all welcome overnight guests) are *Oak Valley* (60 miles west on River Rd.; phone: 523-4351), whose magnificent miles of ancient oak trees predate the splendid brick edifice; *Asphodel Village & Plantation* (Jackson; phone: 654-6868); the *Destrehan Plantation,* the oldest intact structure in the lower Mississippi Valley (phone: 764-9315); and *Madewood* (2 miles from Napoleonville; phone: 524-1988), where Spanish moss hovers over an old graveyard and beautifully restored manor house and out-buildings.

SOURCES AND RESOURCES

 TOURIST INFORMATION: The New Orleans Tourist Information Center, in the French Quarter, provides a wealth of information on the city's attractions, including maps, brochures, and personal help (529 St. Ann St., New Orleans, LA 70116; phone: 566-5031). The Greater New Orleans Tourist and Convention Commission (1520 Sugar Bowl Dr., New Orleans, LA 70116; phone: 566-5011) has information about the outlying areas. Contact the Louisiana state hotline (phone: 800-33-GUMBO) for maps, calendars of events, health updates, and travel advisories.

New Orleans by Carolyn Kolb (Doubleday; $3.95) is the most comprehensive guide to New Orleans and the surrounding area. Another good source is *The Pelican Guide to New Orleans* by Tommy Griffin (Pelican; $2.95).

For up-to-date information about arts, cultural, or historical events call the New Orleans Hospitality Hotline (phone: 522-9200), from 10AM to 6 PM daily.

Local Coverage – The *New Orleans Times-Picayune,* daily; the *Gambit,* a free arts-oriented weekly; *Tourist News,* a monthly magazine distributed free in hotels and shops; *New Orleans Monthly,* a monthly city magazine; and *Where,* a free monthly magazine that lists hotels, restaurants, and shopping tips for tourists.

Television Stations – WWL Channel 4–CBS; WDSU Channel 6–NBC; WVUE Channel 8–ABC; WYES Channel 12–PBS.

Radio Stations – AM: WWL 870 (talk/news); WNOE 1060 (country music); WSMB 1450 (talk). FM: WEZB 97.1 (contemporary); WRNO 99.5 (rock); WLTS 106 (light rock).

Food – Check the *New Orleans Eat Book* by Tom Fitzmorris (New Orleans Big Band and Pacific Co.; $6.95).

TELEPHONE: The area code for New Orleans is 504.
Sales Tax – The city sales tax is 9%.

CLIMATE: New Orleans weather is subtropical with high humidity, temperatures, and substantial rainfall. Moderated by the Gulf of Mexico winds, summer temperatures hover around 90F, while winter temperatures rarely drop to freezing. Summers can get unbearably sticky.

GETTING AROUND: Airport – New Orleans International Airport is a 45-minute drive from the downtown area, and taxi fare is set at $18. The *Louisiana Transit Co.* (phone: 737-9611) runs an *Airport-Downtown Express* bus on a 10- to 25-minute schedule from downtown at the corner of Elks Place and Tulane Avenue; fare, $1.10. *Airport-Rhodes Transportation* (phone: 469-4555) also provides service from the airport to downtown hotels for $7, as well as *Airport Shuttle, Inc.* (phone: 592–1991), whose passenger vans depart from the airport every 15 minutes, picking up passengers in the Central Business District, French Quarter, Kenner, Metairie, amd Westbank.

Bus – *New Orleans Regional Transit Authority* provides efficient bus and streetcar service throughout the city. The St. Charles Avenue streetcar offers a scenic ride through the Garden District (board at Canal and Baronne Sts.). A streetcar line that runs along the riverfront and through the Central Business District and the French Quarter, from Julia Street to Esplanade, also makes a good sightseeing excursion. Complete information is available at the *Regional Transit Authority* office (101 Dauphine; phone: 569-2600), or by calling *RideLine* at 569-2700.

Car Rental – All of the major national car rental companies have offices in New Orleans. Be sure to reserve one well in advance for *Mardi Gras* week.

Taxi – Cabs can be ordered on the phone, hailed in the streets, or picked up at stands in front of hotels, restaurants, and transportation terminals. Major cab companies are *Yellow-Checker Cab* (phone: 525-3311) and *United Cab* (phone: 522-9771).

 VITAL SERVICES: Audiovisual Equipment – *AV Communications* (phone: 522-9769); *Jasper Ewing & Sons* (phone: 525-5257).
   Business Services – *Dictation Incorporated,* open 24 hours daily, 500 Valence St. (phone: 895-8637).

Dry Cleaner/Tailor – *Washing Well Laundryteria,* 841 Bourbon St. (phone: 523-9955).

Limousine – *Carey/Bonomolo Limousines* (phone: 523-5466 or 947-4162).

Mechanic – *Doody and Hank's Service,* 719 O'Keefe (phone: 522-5391).

Medical Emergency – *Tulane Medical Center,* 1415 Tulane Ave. (phone: 588-5711).

Messenger Services – *Barnett's Services* (phone: 734-0580); *Choice Courier Systems* (phone: 466-3111).

National/International Courier – *Federal Express* (phone: 523-6001); *DHL Worldwide Courier Express* (phone: 464-0231).

Pharmacy – *Walgreen's Drug Stores,* at two locations (900 Canal St.; phone: 523-7201; and 134 Royal St.; phone: 522-2736).

Photocopies – *Convention Copy Center,* pickup and delivery, fax service, offset printing (807 Convention Center Blvd.; phone: 524-2679); *Delta Reproductions,* pickup and delivery (826 Baronne St.; phone: 522-3157); *PIP* (324 Camp St.; phone: 523-3605; and 825 Common St.; phone: 524-2191).

Post Office – The downtown office is located at 1022 Iberville (phone: 589-1287).

Professional Photographer – *Convention Photography of Louisiana* (phone: 454-1225); *Commercial & Industrial Photographers* (phone: 368-6089).

Secretary/Stenographer – *Dictation Inc.,* 24-hour service (phone: 895-8637); *Marion Bernard,* public stenographer, *Fairmont Hotel* (phone: 525-2692 or 486-3158).

Teleconference Facilities – *Fairmont, New Orleans Hilton, Inter-Continental, Méridien, Westin Canal Place* (see *Best in Town,* below).

Translator – *Professional Translators and Interpreters* (phone: 581-3122).

Typewriter Rental – *Reboul's Business Machines,* 1-week minimum (phone: 561-1041); *Mule Durel Office Products,* daily, weekly, or monthly rental (phone: 529-7484).

Western Union/Telex – Many offices are located around the city (phone: 568-1440).

Other – *H.Q. Headquarters Company,* word processing, telex, fax machines, conference rooms (phone: 525-1175).

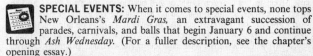 **SPECIAL EVENTS:** When it comes to special events, none tops New Orleans's *Mardi Gras,* an extravagant succession of parades, carnivals, and balls that begin January 6 and continue through *Ash Wednesday.* (For a fuller description, see the chapter's opening essay.)

As if *Mardi Gras* merriment were not enough, the Old River City begins to celebrate again soon after *Ash Wednesday.* Irish-Americans and Italian-Americans take to the streets on *St. Patrick's Day* and *St. Joseph's Day,* March 17 and 19, respectively. The *Tennessee Williams/*

New Orleans Literary Festival takes place in mid-March. The family-oriented *French Quarter Festival,* during the second weekend of April, has gained in popularity. It is a weekend of food, parades, and free musical entertainment in the Vieux Carré.

Since 1969, New Orleans has been driving home the point that there just ain't no better place for jazz than the *New Orleans Jazz and Heritage Festival,* held for 2 weeks each April and May. The top names in jazz perform at a number of places throughout the city, while all kinds of bands — ragtime, traditional New Orleans Dixieland, Cajun — and folk and blues musicians entertain at the *Fair Grounds* on weekends. All come together as jazz stars join in late-night jam sessions in the French Quarter. More than just music for the soul, the *Heritage* includes something for the stomach and plenty of it. All kinds of creole and Cajun food, the New Orleans specialties, are available on the *Fair Grounds.*

The *New Orleans Food Festival, Bastille Day,* and *La Fête* (phone: 525-4143), all held every July, celebrate the city's heritage with musical, sports, cultural, and culinary events.

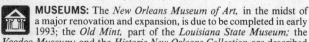

MUSEUMS: The *New Orleans Museum of Art,* in the midst of a major renovation and expansion, is due to be completed in early 1993; the *Old Mint,* part of the *Louisiana State Museum;* the *Voodoo Museum;* and the *Historic New Orleans Collection* are described above in *Special Places.* Other notable New Orleans museums include:

Confederate Museum – 929 Camp St. (phone: 523-4522).

Contemporary Arts Center – 900 Camp St. (phone: 523-1216).

Louisiana Nature and Science Center – 86-acre wildlife park with a planetarium. 11000 Lake Forest Blvd., New Orleans East (phone: 246-9381).

Pharmacy Museum – 514 Chartres St. (phone: 524-9077).

MAJOR COLLEGES AND UNIVERSITIES: Tulane University (6400 St. Charles Ave.; phone: 865-5000) is New Orleans's most prominent educational institution, known primarily for its medical and law schools. Loyola University (6300 St. Charles Ave.; phone: 865-2011) has an enrollment of over 10,000 students. The University of New Orleans (the Lakefront; phone: 286-6000) is the area's largest school.

SHOPPING: New Orleans offers an abundance of shopping opportunities. Local specialties in the French Quarter include gorgeous papier-mâché and porcelain masks for *Mardi Gras,* superb jazz posters and records, harlequin dolls, antiques (especially jewelry), and used books — try the *Librairie* (823 Chartres St.; phone: 525-4837) or *Old Books* (811 Royal St.; phone: 522-4003). While the Vieux Carré is something of a tourist trap, there are unusual handicrafts and bargains if you look hard enough. The quality of the shops jammed into its streets and the friendliness of their proprietors make it a magnet for shoppers seeking the unusual. For both shopping and dining, the *Jax Brewery Complex* (next to Jackson Square and the river) is a popular option, as is the *Rink,* an arcade of shops that once was the site of a skating rink (on Washington and Prytania Sts.). For Cajun and creole goodies, try the *New Orleans School of Cooking* (620 Decatur St.; phone: 947-0293). Outside the Quarter, there are art galleries and antiques shops on Magazine Street in the Garden District and boutiques in *Canal Place* and the Riverwalk (both at the foot of Canal St.), by the river. Large department stores also are on Canal Street and in several malls. The latest is the *New Orleans Centre,* with branches of *Macy's* and *Lord & Taylor,* plus 3 levels of the finest shops and eateries in the Central Business District.

SPORTS AND FITNESS: The biggest thing in New Orleans sports is the *Superdome,* the world's largest domed stadium. There are daily 45-minute tours of the 27-story arena (capacity:

76,000). It hosts the *New Year's Day Sugar Bowl* football classic (phone: 587-3810) and hosted *Super Bowl XXIV* in 1990.

Bicycling – Both City Park and Audubon Park have paved paths that are good for cyclists.

Fishing – On Lake Pontchartrain, and within easy distance of the Gulf of Mexico, New Orleans is a fishing paradise (for fishermen, not fish). The best spot is Empire, 52 miles south on Route 23, where you can rent boats or take a charter to go after king mackerel, white trout, and red snapper, at *Battistella's Marina* (phone: 657-9811). You can fish in Lake Pontchartrain for bass, speckled trout, and red fish off the seawall along Lake Shore Drive or rent a boat from *Ed Lombard's* bait center (at Chef Menteur).

Fitness Center – In the *Hilton,* the *Rivercenter Tennis Club* has a sauna, whirlpool bath, outdoor track, aerobic classes, and tennis and racquetball courts, 2 Poydras St., at the river (phone: 587-7242).

Football – The NFL's *Saints* play at the *Superdome* from August to December. Tickets are available at the box office (1500 Poydras St. at La Salle St.; phone: 522-2600). The Tulane University *Green Waves* play at the *Superdome* from late September through November (phone: 861-9283).

Golf – Golf is popular year-round, and the best courses for the public are the four 18-hole courses at City Park (Esplanade Ave. southwest of the French Quarter; phone: 483-9397) and the course at Audubon Park (473 Walnut; phone: 861-9511).

Horse Racing – There are two seasons for racing and pari-mutuel betting: winter season at *Fair Grounds Race Track* (1751 Gentilly Blvd.; phone: 944-5515) from *Thanksgiving Day* to mid-April; summer season at *Jefferson Downs* (Kenner La.; phone: 466-8521) from mid-April to early November.

Jogging – Audubon Park, 3 miles from downtown, has a popular 3-mile course; run or take the streetcar on St. Charles Avenue to get there.

Swimming – You can swim during the summer at the Olympic-size pool in Audubon Park, St. Charles Ave. (phone: 587-1920).

Tennis – City Park has 45 good public courts of various composition, open year-round; there's a small fee (phone: 483-9383).

THEATER: For up-to-date offerings and performance times, check the *New Orleans Times-Picayune* or the *Gambit,* a free, alternative paper distributed in stores and hotels on Fridays. New Orleans has several theaters that offer performances, some locally produced, others traveling shows. Colleges and universities in the area also produce plays and musicals. Best bets for shows: *Theatre of the Performing Arts* (801 N. Rampart St.; phone: 522-0592); *Saenger Performing Arts Center* (143 N. Rampart St.; phone: 888-8181); *Le Petit Théâtre du Vieux Carré* — the oldest continuously operating community theater in the nation, and host of the annual *Tennessee Williams Literary Festival* in March (616 St. Peter St.; phone: 522-9958).

MUSIC: Classical concerts and opera are heard at *Theatre of the Performing Arts* (801 N. Rampart St.; phone: 522-0592); *New Orleans Opera Guild* has 8 productions from September to May (phone: 529-2278); the *New Orleans Philharmonic Symphony* performs from September to May at the *Orpheum Theater* (129 University Pl.; phone: 525-0500). Jazz is the big story in New Orleans music, and when it comes to jazz, it's time for:

NIGHTCLUBS AND NIGHTLIFE: New Orleans is a night town, and the jazz gets better and the drinks stronger (at least it seems that way) as the night wears on. At any one time there is an astonishing array of jazz being played in the city: top names and talented local musicians playing traditional New Orleans jazz, progressive, blues, rock, or folk music.

There are more than 400 nightclubs in the city. Favorites are *Pete Fountain's* (in the *Hilton* on Poydras St.; phone: 523-4374), featuring the renowned jazz clarinetist; *Tipitina's* (501 Napoleon; phone: 895-8477), for blues, Cajun, rock, and rhythm and blues; *Snug Harbor* (626 Frenchmen; phone: 949-0696), for local favorites; *Storyville Jazz Hall* (1104 Decatur; phone: 525-8199), for a great variety of artists; *Lulu White's Mahogany Hall* (309 Bourbon St.; phone: 525-5595), for Dixieland music by the *Dukes of Dixieland;* and the *Maple Leaf Bar* (8316 Oak St.; phone: 866-9359), for ragtime, rhythm and blues, Cajun dancing on Thursday nights, and poetry reading on Sunday nights. *Preservation Hall* is the place for pure jazz (no drinks) by traditional New Orleans bands (726 St. Peter St.; phone: 523-8939). Favorite bars: *Napoleon House* (500 Chartres St.; phone: 524-9752); *Lafitte's Blacksmith Shop* (941 Bourbon St.; phone: 523-0066); *Old Absinthe* (400 Bourbon St.; phone: 525-8108); *Pat O'Brien's,* known as the home of the Hurricane (718 St. Peter St.; phone: 525-4823); *Harry's Place* (corner Dumaine and Chartres; phone: 524-7052); *Bombay Club* (1019 Dumaine St.; phone: 586-0972); and *Fritzel's,* a place frequented by Europeans (733 Bourbon St.; phone: 561-0432).

BEST IN TOWN

CHECKING IN: Hotels in New Orleans usually are more than just places to stay after spending a day (and half the night) seeing the city. Many of the hotels reflect the influence of French, Spanish, and/or Louisiana colonial architecture and often a full measure of charm. The service in these hotels is generally excellent. No matter where you stay or what you pay, make reservations well in advance, particularly during *Mardi Gras* season, from *Christmas* to *Ash Wednesday* (this includes *Sugar Bowl Week,* which precedes the football classic on *New Year's Day*). Slightly higher rates prevail during these periods. In general, however, the spate of hotel building that coincided with New Orleans's ill-fated *World's Fair* of 1984 has tended to keep the hotel business very competitive and rather reasonable — especially on weekends. Expect to pay $100 to $160 a night for a double room (and way up — particularly for suites) in the expensive range, $75 to $95 in the moderate scale, and $45 to $70 in the inexpensive category. Many of the more expensive hotels have excellent weekend promotional packages. All telephone numbers are in the 504 area code unless otherwise indicated.

Fairmont – They say New Orleanians wept when its predecessor, the *Roosevelt,* was sold to the Fairmont interests. But they weep no more. The owners have successfully wedded the charms of San Francisco and New Orleans and produced an efficient, 750-room hostelry. At the fine *Sazerac* restaurant, drinkers can sample the Sazerac cocktail or the famed Ramos gin fizz. The *Blue Room* has dinner dancing and top acts. *Bailey's* is a 24-hour restaurant-bar. There is a heated pool and 2 tennis courts. Business conveniences include 30 meeting rooms, a concierge desk, A/V equipment, photocopiers, computers, CNN, and express checkout. University Pl. (phone: 529-7111 or 800-527-4727; Fax: 504-522-2303). Expensive.

Inter-Continental New Orleans – An imposing presence in the business district, with 497 comfortable rooms, New Orleans musicians entertaining in the public rooms, and the *Veranda* restaurant. Twenty-four–hour room service is available, as is CNN, 20 meeting rooms, a concierge desk, and secretarial services. 444 St. Charles Ave. (phone:

525-5566, 800-332-4246, or 800-327-0200; Fax: 504-523-7310). Expensive.

Maison de Ville – This fine small inn in the French Quarter is actually a variety of accommodations: the main house, with wonderfully restored former slave quarters; and, most notable, the *Audubon Cottages* (named for the naturalist, who lived and painted here a century ago), each of which has a patio with access to a small swimming pool. It is in these cottages that the best of French Quarter ambience is felt. The hotel's restaurant, the *Bistro,* guided by an award-winning chef, has been acclaimed by both food critics and patrons (see *Eating Out*). Room service is available for lunch and dinner only. CNN. 727 Toulouse St. (phone: 561-5858 or 800-634-1600; Fax: 504-561-5858). Expensive.

Melrose – A lushly renovated Victorian house with polished wood floors and beautiful antiques that make this luxury bed and breakfast establishment cozy yet elegant. Fresh flowers and down pillows are found in each room. An additional plus is the limo that meets guests at the airport. Located on the northern edge of the French Quarter at 937 Esplanade Ave. (phone: 944-2255). Expensive.

Méridien – This 497-room hotel in the shopping district is directly along the *Mardi Gras* parade routes. The French atmosphere is thick, especially in the casual *La Gauloise* restaurant as well as in the more elegant and expensive *Henri* restaurant (See *Eating Out* for both). Health club, pool. Other facilities include 11 meeting rooms. Secretarial and concierge assistance is available, as well as 24-hour room service, CNN, and express checkout. 614 Canal St. (phone: 525-6500; Fax: 504-586-1543). Expensive.

New Orleans Hilton – Located downtown, this 1,602-room resort by the river offers a fine view and the *International Rivercenter,* an entertainment development that includes a cruise ship terminal, a tennis club, and a luxury shopping mall. The property also has a pool, health club, sauna, and garage. Pluses are *Le Café Bromeliad*'s Sunday champagne brunch; the *Rainforest* nightclub; *Pete Fountain's* nightclub, featuring the famous jazz clarinetist; *Winston's,* offering continental dining; and *Kabby's Seafood* restaurant, with a Sunday seafood brunch and Dixieland jazz. Support services include a concierge desk, secretarial assistance, and express checkout. The 10 meeting rooms hold up to 3,600. Room service delivers around the clock. CNN. 2 Poydras St. at the Mississippi River (phone: 561-0500 or 800-HILTONS; Fax: 504-568-1721). Expensive.

Omni Royal Orleans – On the site of the famous *St. Louis* hotel, amid the hustle and bustle of the Vieux Carré. The lobby is luxurious Italian marble, most of the 350 rooms rooms are elegantly furnished, and there is conscientious service. The hotel features the *Esplanade Lounge,* popular with the late-night crowd, *Café Royale, Touche-Bar,* a 3-level nightspot, the fine *Rib Room* for dining, a rooftop pool, a fitness center, shops, garage. Both secretarial and concierge services are available, as well as 24-hour room service. There are 6 meeting rooms for business tête-à-têtes. CNN. 621 St. Louis St. (phone: 529-5333 or 800-THE-OMNI; Fax: 504-523-5076). Expensive.

Pontchartrain – With 100 tastefully decorated rooms, each done individually, and suites with many French provincial antique furnishings, this is a favorite of celebrities and traveling dignitaries; its service is truly outstanding. An excellent restaurant, the *Caribbean Room* (see *Eating Out*), serves creole specialties, and there is a bar with a jazz pianist performing nightly. There's around-the-clock room service, as well as a concierge desk, secretarial services, and CNN. The 2 meeting rooms hold up to 300. 2031 St. Charles Ave. (phone: 524-0581; Fax: 504-524-1165). Expensive.

Soniat House – This remarkable pair of townhouses has been restored beautifully, and everything possible has been done to reinforce the feeling that guests are living in the New Orleans of 150 years ago. Rooms are filled with antique furniture, often including canopied beds and Victorian love seats. Room service is available for breakfast only. There's also a concierge desk. 1133 Chartres St. (phone: 522-0570 or 800-544-8808; Fax: 504-522-7208). Expensive.

Westin Canal Place – There are remarkable panoramic city views from the 11th-floor lobby of this establishment atop *Canal Place* — a shopping mall — with 438 top-quality rooms and suites of varying sizes and views. There is 24-hour room service, a concierge desk, CNN, and 8 meeting rooms available. 100 Rue Iberville (phone: 566-7006 or 800-228-3000; Fax: 504-523-2549). Expensive.

Windsor Court – Luxuriously British-style, with 58 deluxe rooms and 266 suites. Its afternoon tea is so popular that a reservation may be necessary. Every room, public and private, is richly decorated and comfortable. The *Grill Room* restaurant receives good reviews. Room service can only be ordered at specific mealtimes. Concierge assistance available. CNN. 300 Gravier St. (phone: 523-6000; Fax: 504-596-9513). Expensive.

Cornstalk – This old Victorian home is surrounded by a New Orleans landmark — a wrought-iron fence showing ripe ears of corn shucked on their stalks, ready for harvest, and pumpkin vines. The interior is something of a landmark, too — a grand entrance hall and lobby with antique mirrors and crystal chandeliers. The 14 rooms feature four-poster beds, and you can take continental breakfast there, in the front gallery, or on the patio. 915 Royal St. (phone: 523-1515; Fax: 504-525-6651). Expensive to moderate.

LaMothe House – Surrounded by moss-draped oaks on the Boulevard Esplanade at the edge of the French Quarter, this 150-year-old double townhouse exudes Old World charm with elaborate late Victorian furnishings and ambience. Careful attention to detail is a hallmark here. The 11 rooms and 9 suites are furnished with period antiques. Room service is available for breakfast only. 621 Esplanade Ave. (phone: 947-1161 or 800-367-5858; Fax: 504-943-6536). Expensive to moderate.

Monteleone – At the gateway of the Vieux Carré, this old 600-room property maintains a friendly atmosphere while offering the amenities of a larger operation. There are a rooftop pool and bar, revolving lounge, formal dining at *Le Chasseur,* a coffee shop, *Le Café,* an oyster bar, and a garage. Amenities include 24-hour room service, 6 meeting rooms, CNN, and concierge and secretarial services. 214 Royal St. (phone: 523-3341; Fax: 504-561-5803). Expensive to moderate.

Ste. Helene – A carefully preserved historic building, this guest house has a courtyard pool and 3 floors with 16 rooms, 7 with balconies overlooking the pool or busy Chartres Street. Conveniently located 2 blocks from Jackson Square and the popular *Napoleon House* bar/restaurant, it features reproductions of 19th-century antiques; each room has a full bath, color TV set, central air conditioning, and telephone. Room service is available for breakfast only. CNN. 508 Chartres St. (phone: 522-5014; Fax: 504-523-7140). Expensive to moderate.

Place d'Armes – Right off Jackson Square, this tastefully decorated hostelry has a lovely courtyard with a pool, fountains, magnolia and banana trees, and outdoor tables. There are 76 rooms and 8 antiques-furnished suites in eight 18th-century renovated buildings. Rooms have color TV sets (CNN is broadcast), and many have ceiling fans and balconies. Room service delivers breakfast only, and 1 small meeting room holds 30. 625 St. Ann St. (phone: 524-4531; 800-535-7791; Fax: 504-581-3802). Moderate.

Le Richelieu – A gem nestled at the end of the French Quarter, it offers

71 rooms and 17 suites, all pleasantly furnished. Refrigerators are found in 56 of the rooms, and most have brass ceiling fans. There is a lush, tropical patio with a pool, and the *Terrace Café and Lounge* is a popular gathering spot for locals. Room service is available until 9 PM. A concierge desk and CNN, too. 1234 Chartres St. (phone: 529-2492; 800-535-9653; Fax: 504-524-8179). Moderate.

Columns – An unusual spot in the Garden District, perfect for travelers who care less about creature comforts (not every room boasts a private bath) and more about immersing themselves in the ambience of early New Orleans. If the bar looks familiar, you know it from films like *Pretty Baby* and *Tightrope.* The St. Charles Avenue streetcar runs by the front door. 3811 St. Charles Ave. (phone: 899-9308). Moderate to inexpensive.

Holiday Inn Downtown-Superdome – The drawing card at this convenient location is its completely renovated 300-room hostelry. The *John James Audubon Room* restaurant serves standard New Orleans fare and the rooftop Olympic pool is a great perch for watching sunsets. Amenities include room service until 10 PM, a concierge desk, secretarial services, CNN, and 4 meeting rooms that hold up to 250. 330 Loyola Ave. (phone: 581-1600; Fax: 504-586-0833). Moderate to inexpensive.

French Quarter Maisonnettes – A converted Vieux Carré mansion with a carriageway drive of flagstones and a spacious patio, the inn is a quaint and friendly place to stay. Each of the 7 rooms is luxuriously private, some right on the patio. The owner presents each guest with a printed, personal folder listing places to go and offering advice and suggestions for activities. 1130 Chartres St. (phone: 524-9918). Inexpensive.

EATING OUT: The city abounds with more than 2,500 restaurants. Most are good. Many are excellent. And all reflect the distinctive cuisine of New Orleans, creole cooking — shaped through the years by the cultures of France, Spain, America, the West Indies, South America, African Blacks, and the American Indian. Seafood is king in creole recipes, and the nearby waters are a rich kingdom, providing crab, shrimp, red snapper, flounder, Gulf pompano, and trout. Vegetables in season, fowl, veal, and fresh herbs and seasonings are culinary staples that fill out the court and have made this strongly regional style a royal art. There are many fine expensive and moderately priced restaurants. Inexpensive restaurants and even department stores serve up New Orleans specialties, gumbo, po' boy (sandwiches), and red beans and rice on Mondays, a New Orleans tradition. Our selections range in price from expensive at $65 or more for a dinner for two, $35 to $45 in the moderate range, and $20 or less in the inexpensive range. Prices do not include drinks, wine, or tips. All telephone numbers are in the 504 area code unless otherwise indicated.

Henri – With food that lives up to its French counterpart in Alsace, this gem boasts rich entrees such as venison, salmon mousse, and sinful chocolate desserts. The service is superior. Open daily. Reservations necessary. Major credit cards accepted. *Le Méridien Hotel,* 614 Canal St. (phone: 527-6708). Very expensive.

Antoine's – Established in 1840, and one of the oldest restaurants in the country, it still offers a grand gastronomic experience. Specialties include tournedos with creole red wine sauce, *pompano en papillote,* oysters Rockefeller, *filet de boeuf Robespierre,* soufflé potatoes, and baked Alaska. Though the decor is somewhat sparse — white tiled floors and mirrored walls — there is a great wine cellar and picturesque private dining rooms. Closed Sundays. Reservations advised. Major credit cards accepted. 713 St. Louis St. (phone: 581-4422). Expensive.

Arnaud's – This once-noble Vieux Carré dining spot, founded in 1918 by Count Arnaud Cazenave, has rejoined the ranks of New Orleans's best. Its traditional menu has been shortened and strengthened. You can't miss with shrimp Arnaud (in a spicy *rémoulade*), trout meunière, and caramel custard. The dining areas were refurbished, but not at the expense of the old France–old New Orleans decor — crystal chandeliers and flickering gas lanterns. Open daily. Reservations advised. Major credit cards accepted. 813 Bienville St. (phone: 523-5433). Expensive.

Bistro at Maison de Ville – Tiny and wonderfully intimate, it's a favorite of locals. Wild game dishes, such as grilled breast of duck, sautéed sweetbreads, and venison. Lunch daily except Sundays; dinner nightly. Reservations necessary. Major credit cards accepted. 733 Toulouse St. (phone: 528-9206). Expensive.

Brennan's – Although the food is as good as ever, it's become so popular that the atmosphere is very hectic and the service declining. However, the saying goes that you haven't really had a full day in New Orleans unless you've started it with breakfast at *Brennan's* — poached eggs with hollandaise and *marchand de vin* sauce, creamed spinach, or New Orleans–style with crabmeat, turtle soup, and maybe bananas Foster (bananas with ice cream and liqueur) for a flaming dessert, and certainly café Brulot (coffee with curaçao and orange rind). Open daily. Reservations necessary. Major credit cards accepted. 417 Royal St. (phone: 525-9711). Expensive.

Caribbean Room – The *Pontchartrain* hotel's exceptional dining room serves French and creole dishes. The menu is imaginative, and specialties are beautifully presented — trout Véronique (poached and topped with green grapes and hollandaise sauce), crabmeat Biarritz (lump crabmeat with whipped cream dressing and topped with caviar), and, if you can go the distance, Mile-High Ice Cream Pie for dessert. An elegant brunch is served Sunday mornings. Jackets required. Open weekdays for lunch; daily for dinner. Reservations necessary. Major credit cards accepted. 2031 St. Charles Ave. (phone: 524-0581). Expensive.

Christian's – A quaint place known for its French and creole menu. The redfish *au poivre vert* (a broiled filet served with green peppercorn cream sauce) is recommended highly. Closed Sundays. Reservations necessary. Major credit cards accepted. 3835 Iberville (phone: 482-4924). Expensive.

K-Paul's Louisiana Kitchen – Though out of favor with many local diners and food critics who label it "overrated and overpriced," grouse about the lines at the door, community seating, and unpredictable hours, no New Orleans restaurant listing is complete without mention of this Paul Prudhomme eatery. In spite of the aforementioned misdeeds, it is still worth a visit for a *soupçon* of Cajun cooking. Lunch and dinner weekdays. No reservations. American Express accepted. 415 Chartres St. (phone: 942-7500). Expensive.

Le Ruth's – Owner and chef Warren Le Ruth spent his career in New Orleans preparing French and creole food, and his children now serve consistently fine dishes — oysters and artichoke soup, soft-shell crab with lump crabmeat and meunière sauce, veal Marie with crabmeat, frogs' legs meunière, homemade desserts, mandarin ice, and an exquisite almond torte. The restaurant bakes its own bread. Closed Sundays and Mondays. Reservations necessary. Major credit cards accepted. 636 Franklin St. in Gretna, 4½ miles across the Mississippi River Bridge from Canal St. (phone: 362-4914). Expensive.

Alex Patout's – One of Louisiana's most respected and innovative chefs presides over a popular French Quarter restaurant, especially good for lunch. Impeccably prepared "haute Cajun" dishes, such as duck smothered with oyster dressing, sweet potatoes with pecans, tasso (small bits of Cajun smoked ham) pasta with shrimp, and superb gumbos. Lunch weekdays; dinner nightly. Reservations advised. Major credit cards accepted. 221 Royal St. (phone: 525-7788). Expensive to moderate.

Brigsten's – A small place with a faithful following and a Cajun/creole menu that changes daily. Specialties of chef Frank Brigsten include rabbit with sautéed spinach and a zesty creole mustard, and duck with honey-pecan gravy. Reservations necessary. Major credit cards accepted. 723 Dante St. (phone: 861-7610). Expensive to moderate.

Emeril's – Emeril Lagasse of the *Commander's Palace* has opened this dining spot in the warehouse district. Nouvelle Cajun is the theme, and arrives à la fried oysters, crayfish-stuffed ravioli, and banana cream pie. Open daily. Reservations necessary. Major credit cards accepted. 800 Tchoupitoulas (phone: 528-9393). Expensive to moderate.

Galatoire's – No matter who you are or who you think you are, you stand in line on the sidewalk like everyone else when the house is full. But the wait is worth it. This favorite of New Orleans residents has great French and creole dishes, a distinctive atmosphere with ceiling fans and mirrored walls, and knowledgeable waiters. Specialties include trout Marguery with shrimp, shrimp remoulade, oysters en brochette, eggs Sardou (artichokes and spinach over poached eggs), and crêpes maison filled with currant jelly. Open for lunch and dinner; closed Mondays. No reservations or credit cards accepted. 209 Bourbon St. (phone: 525-2021). Expensive to moderate.

Masson's Restaurant Français – An elegant French restaurant near the lakefront that has a strong local following. Chef-owner Ernest Masson visits France frequently to bring back recipes for the latest in haute cuisine. He tries them out for a while and if they are *assez haute*, he adds them to the offerings on the already fine menu — oysters LaFourche, veal Vivian, and marinated rack of lamb. Closed Mondays. Reservations advised. Major credit cards accepted. 7200 Pontchartrain Blvd. (phone: 283-2525). Expensive to moderate.

Café Sbisa – Casual and artsy, this hangout is known for its mesquite-grilled dishes such as swordfish and shrimp and for its weekend musical entertainment. The entrées are a mixture of creole, French, and nouvelle American. Open daily for lunch and dinner. Reservations necessary on Saturday nights. Major credit cards accepted. 1011 Decatur St. (phone: 561-8354). Moderate.

Carmelo – Currently the hottest spot in town for Italian food and people watching. The eggplant parmigiana and the antipasto reaffirm that life is worth living, if only to eat here. Open daily. Reservations necessary on weekends. Major credit cards accepted. 541 Decatur St. (phone: 586-1414). Moderate.

Chez Helene – "Frank's Place," the short-lived TV show, was based on this place and its soul food. Entrées include stuffed bell peppers, gumbo, and fried chicken, and creole dishes like *étouffée* thick with crawfish. Open daily. Reservations advised. Major credit cards accepted. 1540 N. Robertson St. (phone: 945-0444). Moderate.

Commander's Palace – This longtime favorite in an old mansion in the Garden District has been operated for the past several years by a branch of the *Brennan's* restaurant family. The unusual "jazz brunch" offered on Saturdays and Sundays features traditional and exotic poached egg dishes accompanied by New Orleans jazz. Dinner specialties include crabmeat imperial, turtle soup, lemon crêpes, and filet mignon. Open daily. Reservations advised. Major credit cards accepted. 1403 Washington Ave. (phone: 899-8221). Moderate.

Copeland's – One of the attractive links in the New Orleans chain, this bar-type place has an extensive and affordable menu. Try Cajun popcorn (batter-dipped crawfish and shrimp) and onion mums (deep fried onions cut into the shape of chrysanthemums and dusted with Cajun spices). Open daily. Reservations necessary. Major credit cards accepted. 4338 St. Charles Ave. (phone: 897-2325). Moderate.

Feelings – A fetching local favorite renowned for its duck, fresh seafood specials, and peanut butter pie. Seafood-baked eggplant is always popular, along with a delicious appetizer of shrimp and crawfish *étouffée*. Piano music enhances Friday and Saturday nights and Sunday brunch. Lunch weekdays; dinner nightly. Reservations advised. Major credit cards accepted. 2600 Chartres St. (phone: 945-2222). Moderate.

La Gauloise – In the *Méridien* hotel, this casual bistro-style eatery has Cajun and creole specialties and an excellent Dixieland jazz brunch on Sundays. The crêpes-to-order dessert table alone is worth the trip. Open daily. Reservations necessary on Friday and Saturday nights. Major credit cards accepted. 614 Canal Street. (phone: 527-6712). Moderate.

Upperline – Off the beaten path, but always filled with diners who come here for the charcoal-grilled fish and the "Taste of New Orleans Creole Dinner," an entrée consisting of small portions of three different New Orleans specialties: blackened fish, chicken *étouffée*, and barbecued shrimp. Dinner nightly. Reservations necessary. Major credit cards accepted. 1413 Upperline (phone: 891-9822). Moderate.

Versailles – An eatery whose menu is a good mix of French, German, and creole. One fine appetizer is the *escargots en croute* (snails baked in a crust), classic snails *bourguignonne* served in a hollowed-out bun made of New Orleans French bread. Main course specialties include duck à la Flamande, rack of lamb *persillade* (parslied), veal *financière* with sweetbreads, bouillabaisse Marseillaise, and veal *farci* (stuffed) with crabmeat. On the ground floor of the Carol Apartments at the edge of the Garden District. Closed Sundays. Reservations advised. Major credit cards accepted. 2100 St. Charles Ave. (phone: 524-2535). Moderate.

Alonso's – This typical New Orleans neighborhood restaurant and bar specializes in seafood. The main attraction is the very large, very good, seafood platter. It contains the traditional hot seafood, plus a few seasonal items like crayfish or soft-shell crab, and some boiled shrimp or crab tossed in for good measure. Extremely crowded on Friday nights. Closed Sundays. No reservations or credit cards accepted. 587 Central Ave. (about 6 miles from Canal St.; phone: 733-2796). Moderate to inexpensive.

Central Grocery Company – Its grocery store has been here since 1906 and still stocks flour, beans, and other staples in barrels to sell by the pound. More popular, however, are the great take-out Italian sandwiches, cheeses, and salads. Open daily. No credit cards accepted. 923 Decatur (phone: 523-1620). Inexpensive.

Croissant D'Or – This small nook makes an excellent morning stop. Fresh French pastries are baked on the premises and are served with mugs of thick café au lait. Open daily. No reservations or credit cards accepted. 617 Ursulines St. (phone: 524-4663). Inexpensive.

Mandina's – Of the vast number of places that offer po' boy sandwiches, this small family-style spot does it best with Italian sausage and roast beef. The large servings of meatballs and spaghetti, gumbo, and jambalaya will not take too big a bite out of your pocket. Open daily. No reservations or credit cards accepted. 3800 Canal St. (phone: 482-9179). Inexpensive.

Ye Olde College Inn – In the university section, daily dinner plates, shrimp *rémoulade*, red beans and rice, oyster loaf, French-fried onion rings, and a good bar. The creole vegetables, especially the eggplant and stewed okra, are at the top of their class. Open daily. No reservations. Major credit cards accepted. 3016 S. Carrollton Ave. (phone: 866-3683). Inexpensive.

Gumbo, a culinary essential of Louisiana life, is a thick, spicy soup based on either seafood or chicken, and no two cooks make it exactly alike. According to locals, the best seafood gumbo is served at the *Gumbo Shop* (630 St. Peter St.; phone: 525-1486) and at *Ralph and Kacoo's* (519 Toulouse St.; phone: 522-5226). The best places to sample chicken gumbo are *Mr. B's* (201 Royal St.; phone: 523-2078) and *Bozo's* (3117 21st St., Metairie; phone: 831-8666). All are inexpensive.

NEW YORK CITY

AT-A-GLANCE

SEEING THE CITY: New York is, to put it simply, the most complex city in the world. People who have lived here all their lives don't even know all of it — its size and diversity challenge even the most ambitious. The best bet for the visitor who wants to feel the magic of New York and to understand how the city is laid out is to take it all in from several vantage points.

Brooklyn Promenade – Standing on this walkway at dusk, with the lights of Manhattan shimmering across the East River, you'll get an idea of the magnitude and beauty of the city. In lower Manhattan the towers of the World Trade Center rise before you, and the Brooklyn Bridge spans the river to your right. Farther north stand the Empire State Building and the UN Secretariat Building, landmarks of midtown. The easiest way to get here is via the *IRT* 7th Avenue subway line (No. 2 or No. 3 trains), Clark St. stop.

World Trade Center – The elevator to the observation deck of Two World Trade Center whisks you more than a quarter of a mile above the street. There is an enclosed deck on the 107th floor and a promenade on the roof above the 110th floor. Manhattan spreads out to the north, Brooklyn is to the east, to the west is New Jersey, and to the south lies New York Harbor, leading to the Atlantic Ocean. Open daily from 9:30 AM to 11:30 PM. Inclement weather and very strong winds may cause the roof promenade to be closed; check beforehand. Tickets are sold on the mezzanine level of Tower Two. Liberty and West Sts. (phone: 466-7397).

Empire State Building – Although many tourists prefer the newer and higher World Trade Center observation deck, the old queen of New York, who turned 60 in 1991, attracts more than 2 million people a year — the Art Deco design is far more romantic than anything in the World Trade Center (even if Deborah Kerr never kept her appointment with Cary Grant here in *An Affair to Remember*). You can feel the breeze from the 86th floor or ascend to the glass-enclosed 102nd floor. Don't be surprised if in the evening the top of the building is bathed in colored lights — it's the city's way to commemorate holidays and special occasions. Open daily from 9:30 AM to midnight (the last elevator is at 11:30 PM). Admission charge. 34th St. and Fifth Ave. (phone: 736-3100).

Views from Above and Below – Some of the most dramatic views of New York are visible when entering the city by car. The three western access routes have special features: the Holland Tunnel access road from the New Jersey Turnpike, leading into lower Manhattan, offers a panorama of the southern tip of the island; the Lincoln Tunnel access road offers a view of Manhattan's West Side; and the George Washington Bridge, linking New Jersey and the Upper West Side, has spectacular views of the Hudson, the city's long shore along the river, and the New Jersey Palisades, as well as being a work of art itself, best seen from a distance, from the river, or while driving north on the West Side Highway.

Tours – Many of the tour companies in the city will help you get your bearings before setting out on your own. *Gray Line* (900 8th Ave., between W. 53rd and 54th Sts.; phone: 397-2600), provides good bus tours. *Circle Line Sightseeing Yachts* offer an interesting 3-hour guided boat trip around Manhattan from early March until December 31. Boats leave from Pier 83 at the foot of W. 42nd St. and the Hudson River (phone: 563-3200). Most spectacular is *Island Helicopter*'s ride around Manhattan. Though the price is considerable ($36 to $89 for flights ranging from 8 to 30 minutes), you won't soon forget this trip. At E. 34th St. and the East River (phone: 683-4575). *The Manhattan Neighborhood Trolley* now includes Ellis Island among its escorted tours of popular sites (phone: 677-7268).

Seeing New York on foot is probably the best way to get acquainted with this complex city. A number of excellent walking tours are available, led by guides who are knowledgeable about everything from architecture and ethnic neighborhoods to literary history, the jazz circuit, movie locations, and noshing spots. Try *Adventures on a Shoestring,* which offers, year-round, 40 or more walking tours and other activities around Manhattan for $5 per tour (phone: 265-2663); also try the *Municipal Art Society* (phone: 935-3960), the *Museum of the City of New York* (phone: 534-1672), the *92nd Street YMHA* (phone: 996-1105), *New York Walk-About* (phone: 914-834-5388), or the ethnic *Lower East Side Tenement Museum's* Peddler's Pack tours (phone: 431-0233).

SPECIAL PLACES: Manhattan is a 12½-mile-long island stretching 2½ miles at its widest point. Avenues run north and south, streets run east and west. Fifth Avenue is the dividing line between addresses designated east and those designated west. For example, 20 E. 57th Street is in the first block of 57th east of Fifth Avenue; 20 W. 57th Street is in the first block west of Fifth Avenue. New York grew from south to north, street by street and neighborhood by neighborhood. The oldest parts of the city are around the docks in lower Manhattan and in the financial district.

The best way to discover the city and enjoy its incredible variety and ethnic diversity is by direct contact — walking through the neighborhoods. You will want to take taxis or public transport between areas — distances can be great — but, in general, the well-populated, active areas of the city offer an interesting environment for walking, so don't hesitate unless the neighborhood is unfamiliar, or it's late at night. The much-touted reputation of New Yorkers for aloofness and unfriendliness simply isn't true. Just watch what happens when you ask directions on a bus or subway (except during rush hours, when things are, admittedly, a bit primitive). We suggest a copy of *Flashmaps! Instant Guide to New York* (Flashmaps; $4.95), which has the most accessible and best-organized series of maps of New York neighborhoods we've seen. They're available at bookstores and newsstands around the city.

LOWER MANHATTAN

Statue of Liberty – Given by France as a symbol of friendship with the United States, this great lady has been guarding the entrance of New York Harbor since its dedication in 1886. To celebrate its centennial in 1986, "Liberty Enlightening the World" was given a major face-lift, and a new museum was added to its base. New lighting makes the statue even more dazzling than ever after dark. The *Circle Line* (phone: 269-5755) runs from Battery Park to Liberty Island every half hour from 9 AM to 3 PM; there is no admission charge to the statue or to the *American Museum of Immigration* (phone: 363-3200) at the base, though there is a fee for the boat trip. You can see the statue from a distance and the southern tip of the city by riding the *Staten Island Ferry,* still one of the world's great transportation bargains at 50¢. The Ferry Terminal is next to Battery Park (the South Ferry stop on the *IRT* 7th Ave. local line, No. 1 train).

Ellis Island – Visible from the Statue of Liberty or Battery Park, Ellis

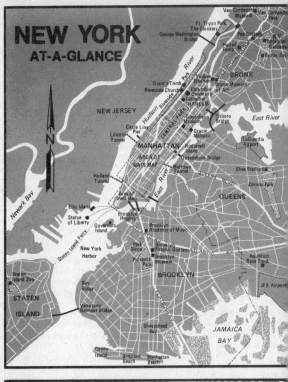

NEW YORK
AT-A-GLANCE

Van Cortlandt Park
Van Cortlandt Museum
Ft. Tryon Park
The Cloisters
George Washington Bridge
Pot Cortlandt
Hall of Fame
Botanical Garden
Bronx Zoo
BRONX
Yankee Stadium
Grant's Tomb
Riverside Church
Columbia University
Bronx Museum of Art
Cathedral
HARLEM
Guggenheim Museum
Tiboro Bridge
East River
Gracie Mansion
NEW JERSEY
Circle Line Pier
Lincoln Tunnel
LaGuardia Airport
MANHATTAN
Roosevelt I.
AREA OF MAIN MAP
Queensboro Bridge
Midtown Tunnel
Shea Stadium
Holland Tunnel
QUEENS
QUEENS BLVD.
Corona Park
Area of Inset Map
Ellis Island
Statue of Liberty
Brooklyn Heights
Governors Island
Brooklyn Academy of Music
New York Harbor
Park Slope
Brooklyn Botanic Gardens
ATLANTIC
Aqueduct Race Track
Prospect Park
Brooklyn Museum
JFK Airport
BROOKLYN
Bay Ridge
Verrazano Narrows Bridge
Staten Island Zoo
STATEN ISLAND
Sheepshead Bay
JAMAICA BAY
Coney Island
Brighton Beach
Manhattan Beach

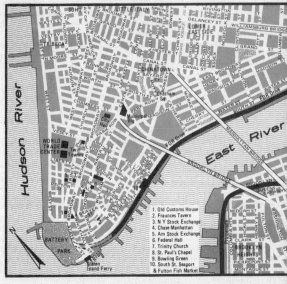

Hudson River
East River

SOHO
LITTLE ITALY
CANAL ST
RIVINGTON
SPRING
DELANCEY ST
WILLIAMSBURG BRIDGE
VESTRY
BROOME
TRIBECA
GRAND
LOWER EAST SIDE
HESTER ST
CANAL ST
ESSEX
N MOORE
FRANKLIN
CHINATOWN
EAST BROADWAY
WORTH
BAYARD
MADISON ST
HENRY ST
WORTH
Chatham Sq
CHAMBERS
Bow'ry
MARKET
CHERRY
Municipal Bldg
MADISON
SOUTH ST
FDR Drive
VESEY ST
WORLD TRADE CENTER
Twin Towers
LIBERTY
FDR Drive
BROOKLYN BRIDGE
MANHATTAN BRIDGE
RECTOR
East River
BATTERY PARK
Staten Island Ferry
BROOKLYN
QUEENS EXP'WY
MIDDAGH ST
CLARK ST
BROOKLYN HEIGHTS
PIERREPONT ST
MONTAGUE ST

1. Old Customs House
2. Fraunces Tavern
3. N Y Stock Exchange
4. Chase-Manhattan
5. Am Stock Exchange
6. Federal Hall
7. Trinity Church
8. St. Paul's Chapel
9. Bowling Green
10. South St. Seaport
    & Fulton Fish Market

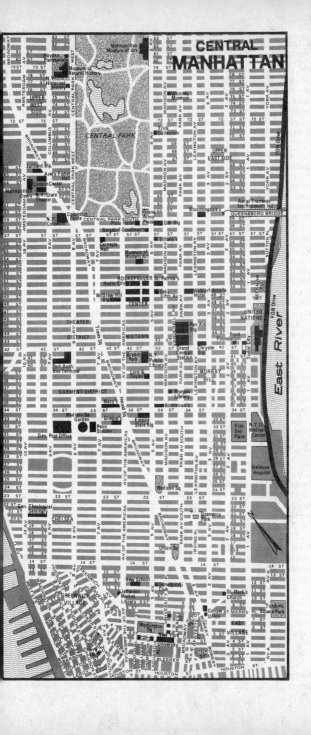

Island served as a processing center for immigrants from 1892 to 1954. More than 17 million people passed through this island on their way to a new life in the land of opportunity. These buildings were the sites of joy and heartbreak; many immigrant families were separated here when some members were refused entry to the US because of bad health or lack of money. A boat leaves from Battery Park (April through September). Ellis Island, now run by the National Park Service (phone: 732-1286), was recently reopened after a $156 million restoration, and the *Ellis Island Immigration Museum* in The Great Hall — the centerpiece of the immigration process — now is open to visitors. There are films, artifacts, oral histories, and thousands of period photographs to tell the tale of those who passed through these halls. Open daily. No admission charge (phone: 363-3200).

Governors Island – Now a Coast Guard base, the island's two pre-1800 structures are the Governor's House and Ft. Jay. Soviet leader Mikhail Gorbachev visited here in late 1988. The island is open to visitors only 2 days each summer. For specific information contact the Special Services Division, Building 110, Governors Island, NY 10004 (phone: 668-7255). Nearby, in Battery Park City is *South Cove,* a new 3-acre park that directly faces the Hudson River.

Battery Park – Twenty-one acres of green, overlooking New York Harbor, this is the spot for picnics on hot summer days. There's a statue of Giovanni da Verrazano, who piloted the *Dauphine,* the ship that reached Manhattan in 1524 (Verrazano later was killed by cannibals in the Caribbean). There's also a monument to World War II dead. Castle Clinton, built as a fort in 1812, has functioned as an opera house, an immigrant landing depot, and an aquarium at various times. Its latest incarnation is as a ticketing center for the Statue of Liberty ferry. Bordered by State St., Battery Pl., and the harbor (phone: 344-7220).

Battery Park to Wall Street – This area is a lovely and safe place to wander on weekends, when the empty streets emphasize the incongruity of the Merrill Lynch building and the World Trade Center surrounded by the 17th- and 18th-century buildings on Pearl Street, Bowling Green, and Hanover Square. Two buildings of particular note are India House, on the south side of Hanover Square (1837), and the old US Custom House (the new Custom House is in the World Trade Center), which was built in 1907 in neo-classical style. Another turn-of-the-century building houses *Delmonico's* restaurant (56 Beaver St.; phone: 422-4747), the meeting place of lower Manhattan's elite.

Fraunces Tavern Museum – This landmark building, the site of Washington's farewell to his officers in 1783, contains memorabilia of the American Revolution (including Washington's hat). Open weekdays from 10 AM to 4 PM. No admission charge on Thursdays. The *Fraunces Tavern* restaurant occupies the ground floor. At the corner of Pearl and Broad Sts. (phone: 425-1778).

New York Stock Exchange – A tree stands in front of the stock exchange to commemorate the tree under which the first transaction took place in 1792. Today, more than 1,600 corporations are listed on the big board. You can observe the action from a glass-enclosed gallery reached via the visitors' entrance at 20 Broad St. Open weekdays from 9:15 AM to 4 PM. No admission charge, but advance tickets are required (phone: 656-5167). Cameras are prohibited. The American Stock Exchange (86 Trinity Pl.) no longer has a visitors' gallery. If you want to see real emotion, head for the Coffee, Sugar, and Cocoa Exchange (4 World Trade Center; phone: 938-2800), which makes the Stock Exchange seem like a London tea party. Open weekdays from 9 AM to 3 PM. No admission charge.

Federal Hall – This National Historic Site served as the British headquarters during the Revolution and later was the seat of American government for about a year. George Washington was sworn in as president here in 1789. Open weekdays from 9 AM to 5 PM. No admission charge. At the corner of Wall and Broad Sts. (phone: 264-8711).

Trinity Church – Located on Broadway, at the head of Wall Street, this church was first granted a charter by William III in 1697. One of the citizens who aided in building the church was Captain Kidd, the notorious pirate who was hanged in London in 1701. The present building was completed in 1846, but the graveyard beside the church is even older. William Bradford, Jr., Robert Fulton, and Alexander Hamilton are buried here. For years, the Trinity Church steeple was the highest point on the New York skyline. Classical concerts are held year-round on Tuesdays at 12:45 PM in the church. At Broadway and Fulton Sts. (phone: 602-0800).

St. Paul's Chapel – The oldest public building in continuous use in Manhattan, this fine example of colonial architecture was erected in 1766 on what was then a field outside the city. George Washington worshiped here. Classical concerts are in the chapel on Mondays and Thursdays at noon. On the corner of Broadway and Fulton St. (phone: 602-0874).

Battery Park City – A $4-billion complex including apartments, tree-lined streets, public parks and squares, and a sumptuous centerpiece, the World Financial Center (not related to the neighboring World Trade Center). It's also home of the *Winter Garden* (not to be confused with the Midtown theater of the same name), where a variety of free concerts are held and artworks displayed amid towering Royal Palm trees in the soaring atrium. A true city within a city, this landfill development in the Hudson River is logically designed and decidedly not ostentatious. There are a wealth of other diversions: among them, a spa, a 1950s rock 'n' roll club, the acclaimed *Hudson River Club* restaurant (phone: 786-1500), and numerous shops. The views from the 1.2 mile Esplanade are spectacular, and the *Winter Garden* is a must. Browsing is free. The *Winter Garden* is open from 8 AM to midnight (phone: 416-5300). For general Battery Park City information, call 416-5300.

World Trade Center – A world in itself. At 1,350 feet each, its two towers are not the tallest buildings in the world (the CN Tower in Toronto is, at 1,821 feet), but close to it. In order to build the center, 1.2 million yards of earth and rock were excavated (they're now in the Hudson River). The concourse has shops and some excellent restaurants (see *Eating Out*), including the *Big Kitchen,* the *Market Dining Room,* and the 107th-floor *Windows on the World.* Not all World Trade Center businesses involve trade, but the Custom House is here, as are the Commodity Exchange and the Cotton and Mercantile Exchanges. Open daily. Charge for the observation deck. Bounded by West, Church, Liberty, and Vesey Sts. (phone: 466-4170).

City Hall – This is the third City Hall of New York; it was built in 1803 and contains the office of the mayor and the City Council chamber. The original construction cost half a million dollars, and in 1956 the restoration cost some $2 million (times change). The building was a site of great importance to New York's and America's history: Lafayette visited in 1824; Lincoln's body lay in state in 1865; and, in the 1860s, City Hall and Tammany Hall (Park Row and Frankfort St.) were controlled by Boss Tweed, the powerful corrupt politician who dominated New York politics until the 1870s.

Other city government buildings nearby include the Municipal Building on the northeast corner of City Hall Park, the United States Court House, across from Foley Square, the New York County Courthouse next door, the Federal Office Building on the other side of Lafayette St., and the Hall of Records. City Hall Park has a statue of Nathan Hale, the patriot of the Revolution who was executed here in 1776. Today, protestors of every persuasion gather in the park to "fight City Hall."

Open weekdays from 10 AM to 3 PM. No admission charge. In a triangular park between Park Row, Broadway, and Chambers St. (phone: 566-8681).

South Street Seaport and the Fulton Fish Market – In July 1983, stage one of the South Street Seaport renovation was completed, enlivening the area with new shops and restaurants and additional space for the *South Street Seaport Maritime Museum.* The Museum Block is an entire row of rejuvenated buildings (some dating to the 1700s) with room for exhibitions, shops, and offices. The Schermerhorn Row of renovated 19th-century warehouses is also alive with retail outlets and the South Street Seaport Museum Visitors Center. All of these changes have not substantially altered the area's famous old *Fulton Fish Market,* where, from about 2 to 8 AM, trucks still deliver fresh fish to the wholesale outdoor market. But the old market is now joined by another building called the *Fulton Market,* with restaurants, cafés, and food stalls. Among the many eateries are two of New York's oldest seafood restaurants, *Sweets* (2 Fulton at South St.; phone: 344-9189 or 825-9786; closed weekends), and *Sloppy Louie's* (92 South St.; phone: 509-9694). For years, these veterans of the *Fulton Fish Market* served the freshest seafood at rock-bottom prices in simple quarters. When the seaport was renovated, the restaurants moved into more sanitized surroundings, with proper dining rooms and higher prices — and, unfortunately, lost their boisterous atmosphere and earthy appeal. At least the portions remain hearty and the fish is as fresh as ever. Also of interest are the historic boats docked at Piers 15 and 16, where summertime pop and jazz concerts are staged. The 3-story *Pier 17 Pavilion* adds even more shops and restaurants to the riverside complex. Fulton St. between South and Water Sts.

Brooklyn Bridge – You can stroll from Manhattan to Brooklyn by crossing the Brooklyn Bridge on a pedestrian walk. You'll get a good view of the city, and a close look at this engineering feat. The 6,775-foot bridge, which spans the East River at a height of 133 feet and is considered by many to be one of the most beautiful bridges in the world, was completed in 1883 and cost $25 million. Many workers were seriously injured during its construction, and a number of people have since committed suicide by jumping from it. Always open. Free (unless someone succeeds in selling you title to the bridge). Take the *IRT* Lexington Ave. line (No. 4, No. 5, or No. 6 trains) to Worth St.–Brooklyn Bridge–City Hall station.

Chinatown – The best way to get the feel of New York's Chinese neighborhood is to hit the streets, especially Mott, Bayard, and Pell. More than 100,000 people live in this small area of crowded, narrow streets, and the Chinese population spills into neighboring Little Italy. Although the Chinese community here is not as large as the one in San Francisco, it is authentic. You'll know when you reach Chinatown by the pagoda-shaped telephone booths and stores that sell shark's fins, duck eggs, fried fungi, and squid. Herbs are lined up next to aspirin in the pharmacies. This is where the Chinese shop, and uptowners and out-of-towners follow their lead. Don't miss the good, inexpensive restaurants, the tea parlors, or the bakeries. Try the dim sum at lunchtime (steamed or fried dumplings filled with seafood, pork, or beef). Favorite spots among New Yorkers are *Peking Duck House* (22 Mott St.; phone: 227-1810), *Bo Ky* (80 Bayard St.; phone: 406-2292), and *Sun Hop Kee* (13 Mott St.; phone: 285-9856). Sundays are a good time to visit the area, but if you can, come during the *Chinese New Year* (held on the first full moon after January 21). The celebration is wild and woolly, with fireworks, dancing dragons, and throngs of people.

Little Italy – Italian music from tenement windows, old men playing *bocce,* old women dressed in black checking the vegetables in the markets, store windows with religious articles, pasta factories, and the ubiquitous odor of Italian cooking fill this neighborhood, which has the reputation of being one of the safest areas in the city. Mulberry Street is the center of Little Italy (stop at *Caffè Roma,* 385 Broome St., for an espresso), but the area stretches for blocks around and blends into parts of SoHo and Greenwich Village. Even Bleecker Street, toward 7th Avenue, has a decidedly Italian flavor, with bakeries selling cannoli and cappuccino sandwiched between Middle Eastern restaurants and stores selling Chinese window shades. Little Italy is thronged during the festivals of *San Gennaro* and *St. Anthony.* In late September, *San Gennaro* covers Mulberry Street from Spring to Park. *St. Anthony* fills Sullivan Street, from Houston to Spring, in mid-June. The festivals attract people from in and out of the city with game booths, rides, and most of all, enough food and drink (both Italian and "foreign") for several armies. Bordered by Canal and Houston Sts. and the Bowery and Ave. of the Americas.

Bowery – There is nothing romantic about New York's Skid Row. On this strip are people who are decidedly down on their luck — both old and young. If you drive west on Houston Street, you'll get a look at some of the inhabitants — they'll wipe your windshields whether you like it or not and expect some change for their trouble. Recently, however, the Bowery has had some new settlers; a few theaters and music places have moved in. The area also has some good places to shop; specialties include lamps and restaurant supplies. The stores have relocated here because of the proximity to one of the most interesting shopping markets in the world: the Lower East Side. Between 4th St. and Chatham Sq.

Lower East Side – This area is probably the largest melting pot in the city. Eastern European Jews, many of whom are Hasidim (an ultra-religious sect, recognizable by the men's earlocks, called *peyes,* and their broad-brimmed hats and long black coats), sell their wares — everything from designer fashions to bedspreads — for rock-bottom prices; you'll have to bargain if you want the best prices, and these merchants are formidable opponents. Everything is closed on Saturdays, the Jewish sabbath, but it's business-as-usual every Sunday, the busiest day. The area also is home to Hispanics, blacks, and various other minority groups; you will hear Yiddish, Spanish, and even some Yiddish-accented Spanish.

The Lower East Side was where the Eastern European Jews, fleeing czarist persecution and deadly pogroms, first settled during their massive migration from 1880 to 1918. Many of the streets, including Rivington, Hester, Essex, and Grand, still look much as they did then. To really get a taste of the area, try the food at the *Grand Dairy* restaurant (341 Grand St.; phone: 673-1904), knishes at *Yonah Schimmel's* (137 E. Houston St.; phone: 477-2858), hot dogs at *Katz's* delicatessen (205 E. Houston St.; phone: 254-2246), or the Romanian "broilings" at *Sammy's* (157 Chrystie St.; phone: 673-0330).

SoHo – The name stands for "South of Houston Street" (pronounced *How*-stun). SoHo leads a double life. On weekends, uptown New Yorkers and out-of-towners fill the streets to explore its trendy stores, restaurants, and art galleries. During the week, SoHo is a very livable combination of 19th-century cast-iron buildings, spillovers from Little Italy, off-off-Broadway theater groups, and practicing artists. At night, the streets are empty and you can see into the residential lofts of the old buildings; some are simple, open spaces, others are jungles of plants and Corinthian columns. *Fanelli's* (on the corner of Mercer and Prince Sts.) is one of the oldest bars around and a hangout for residents. Many artists are now moving to TriBeCa, which is south and west of SoHo and has better loft pickings. SoHo is between Canal and Houston Sts., Broadway and Hudson Sts.

TriBeCa – Long neglected, TriBeCa (the name stands for "*tri*angle *be*low *Ca*nal Street") was riddled with abandoned warehouses, cast-iron hulls, and lonely cobblestone streets, but is now enjoying a flashy come-back. The current artist residents have spawned a plethora of trendy art galleries on White and Franklin Streets and lower Hudson Street. This is where Robert De Niro has his film production studio, and there are also many discount clothing stores, nightclubs, restaurants, and theaters here. Historical oddities worth visiting include the *Bond* hotel (at 125 Chambers St.), reputedly Manhattan's oldest hotel; Stanford White's "Clocktower" building (at 346 Broadway); the Art Deco Western Union Building; and the *Market Diner* (at West and Laight Sts.) TriBeCa extends from Canal St. to Chambers St. and from West Broadway to the Hudson River.

East Village – Still the center of the New York counterculture, this section has become gentrified, with a growing number of art galleries, restaurants, and nightspots competing for space with poor artists and various ethnic groups (the largest of which is Ukrainian, but there also are Armenians, Czechs, Germans, Russians, Poles, Jews, Blacks, and Hispanics, many of whom live in low-income housing projects). Famous during the 1960s as the city's psychedelic capital, St. Mark's Place, between 2nd and 3rd Avenues, is still a lively block, lined with inexpensive restaurants and shops featuring styles from hippie to punk, and generally hopping (sometimes with the help of illegal substances) at all hours of the day and night. Two streets south is what could be considered two rows of Little India: numerous Indian restaurants line East 6th Street between 1st and 2nd Avenues. Astor Place, on the border of the East and West villages, is the site of liberal arts institute *Cooper Union* (good for free concerts and lectures) and the *Public Theater* (425 Lafayette St.; phone: 598-7150), Joe Papp's creation, where you'll find some of the best serious drama (both contemporary and classical) and experimental theater as well as progressive jazz. You can have a drink at *McSorley's Old Ale House* (15 E. 7th St.; phone: 473-9148), a fixture in the East Village for years. A few blocks north is the spiritual home of the village, St. Mark's-in-the-Bowery (on the corner of 2nd Ave. and East 10th St.). The church still sponsors community activities, especially poetry readings by some of the best bards in New York. The East Village has housed many writers, from James Fenimore Cooper (6 St. Mark's Pl.) to W. H. Auden (77 St. Mark's Pl.) to Imamu Baraka, born LeRoi Jones (27 Cooper Sq.). Bounded by Lafayette St. and the East River, Houston and 14th Sts. (Some parts of the East Village, especially east of Avenue A, remain seedy; don't wander here after dark unless you know where you're going.)

GREENWICH VILLAGE

You can — and definitely should — stroll around the West Village (as residents know it) at night. The area is filled with surprises. You've probably heard of Bleecker Street, the slightly tawdry gathering place of tourists and the high school crowd from the suburbs, or of Washington Square Park, with its musicians, mimes, and street people. But you might not have pictured Grove Court, the lovely and secluded row of 19th-century houses near the corner of Grove and Bedford Streets (where O. Henry lived), or the Morton Street pier on the Hudson River, from which you can see the Statue of Liberty on a clear day. But the Village is more than this. It is a neighborhood of activists, struggling to maintain control of their beloved community. There are meat packing factories from the 1920s, old speakeasies turned into restaurants, a miniature Times Square on West 8th Street, and immaculate (and expensive) brownstones on quiet, tree-lined streets. Get a map (you'll need it — there's nowhere else in Manhattan where West 4th Street could bisect West 12th) and wander. Or you can ask directions — villagers love to help and it's a nice way to meet them. You can eat, go to the theater, sip cappuccino in an outdoor café, hear great jazz, and find your own special places. Bounded by Fifth Ave. on the east, the Hudson River on the west, Houston St. on the south, and West 14th St. on the north.

Washington Square – A gathering place for students from New York University, frisbee aficionados, volleyball players, modern bohemians, and people who like to watch them all. The Arch is New York's answer to the Arc de Triomphe. Buildings surrounding the square include the New York University library, administration buildings, and law school. The north side of Washington Square has some lovely homes, including No. 7, where Edith Wharton lived. Bounded by extensions of W. 4th St., MacDougal St., Waverly Pl., and University Pl.

Bleecker Street – Strolling down Bleecker Street from La Guardia Place to 8th Avenue you'll pass outdoor cafés, head shops, falafel parlors, jazz clubs including the *Village Gate* (Bleecker and Thompson Sts.), Italian specialty stores, and myriad restaurants. You also should wander down some of the side streets, like Thompson, MacDougal (Bob Dylan's old stomping ground), and Sullivan. Have a cappuccino at *Caffè Dante* (79 MacDougal), then pay homage to Eugene O'Neill at the *Provincetown Playhouse* (133 MacDougal). Beyond 7th Avenue, the side streets become more residential; try Charles Street, West 10th Street, and Bank Street for examples of how the upper middle class lives in the Village. You'll also pass Christopher Street, the center of gay life in Manhattan (although the toughest part of it comes alive on West Street, by the West Side Highway, on weekend nights).

Fifth Avenue – Where the wealthy Villagers live. The *Salmagundi Club*, built in 1853 (at 47 Fifth Ave., near 12th St.), is the last of the imposing private mansions that once lined the avenue. On the streets between Fifth and the Avenue of the Americas (which the natives call 6th Avenue) you can see expensive brownstones. The New School for Social Research (66 W. 12th St.) has courses on everything from fixing a leak to ethnomusicology. From Washington Sq. North to 14th St.

Avenue of the Americas – New Yorkers know it as Sixth Avenue. One of the most unusual buildings in the village is the Jefferson Market Library (on 6th Avenue and 10th St.), with a small garden alongside. Built in 1878 in Italian Gothic style, it served as a courthouse for many years. Across the street is *Balducci's*, open daily from 7 AM to 8:30 PM (424 6th Ave.; phone: 673-2600), an Italian market with an incredible selection of exotic foods, plus meats, seafood, poultry, cheeses, breads, pastries, fresh fruit, and vegetables. *Famous Ray's of Greenwich Village* (465 6th Ave. at W. 11th St.; phone: 243-2253) — the place on the corner with the long lines — is considered the source of some of the best pizza in the city. (Note that many pizza places in the city have "Ray's" in their names, but this is the one that gets the raves.)

Farther west (between 6th Ave. and Hudson St. and W. Houston and Christopher Sts.) is a series of small winding streets with some especially interesting places to visit. At 75½ Bedford Street is the house in which Edna St. Vincent Millay and John Barrymore once lived (not at the same time) — it's only 9 feet wide. *Chumley's* (86 Bedford St.; phone: 675-4449) used to be a speakeasy during Prohibition and still has no sign on the door — but it does have good food and poetry readings inside. Commerce Street is a small side street lined with lovely old buildings, including the *Cherry Lane Theater,* one of the city's oldest. Morton Street, 1 block south, is often mistaken for Hester Street, because it was the site of the filming of *Hester Street,* a 1975 film about the Lower East Side's Jewish immigrants. (Hester Street begins in Little Italy.) Another block south is Leroy Street with St. Luke's Place, a row of 19th-century houses. No. 6 Leroy was built in 1880 and was the home of the city's flamboyant Mayor Jimmy Walker. If you walk to the end of the block and north on Hudson, you'll come to the *White Horse Tavern* (567 Hudson St.; phone: 243-9260), Dylan Thomas's hangout on his trips to New York City. Go in and have a drink.

14TH STREET TO 34TH STREET

Union Square – For many years, this was a place to avoid — particularly at night, when it was populated by drug pushers and other undesirables. Now it is in the midst of a major face-lift, and its open-air produce market on Wednesdays, Fridays, and Saturdays is beginning to hark back to the halcyon days of the 19th century, when the square was the core of upper-crust Manhattan life. There's even an upgraded subway station. A number of cafés, discos, theaters, antiques shops, and old bookstores fill the side streets; stop in at *The Coffee Shop* (29 Union Sq. W.; phone: 243-7969) or the more upscale *Union Square Café* (21 E. 16th St.; phone: 243-4020).

Gramercy Park – A few blocks north of Greenwich Village, Gramercy Park is one of the few places where visitors can experience the graciousness of old Manhattan. The park itself is open only to residents (they have their own keys), but on a sunny day you can see nannies with their privileged young charges sitting on the benches in the shadows of the 19th-century mansions that surround the park. Stop in for a beer on Irving Place at the cozy, historic *Pete's Tavern*, the oldest bar in America, where O'Henry penned *The Gift of the Magi* (129 E. 18th St.; phone: 473-7676). Teddy Roosevelt's birthplace (28 E. 20th St. on Gramercy Park; phone: 260-1616) is a museum, open from 9 AM to 5 PM Wednesdays to Sundays; $1 admission. Other well-known native sons and daughters include Herman Melville, Stephen Crane, and O. Henry. A few blocks north of Gramercy Park on Lexington Avenue are dozens of little East Indian shops selling splendid assortments of spices, saris, cotton blouses, jewelry, and food. E. 21st St. and Lexington Ave.

Chelsea – An eclectic residential neighborhood in the West 20s, between 7th and 10th Avenues, where you can find elegant brownstones next door to run-down, 4-story, walk-up tenements. The *Chelsea* hotel (222 W. 23rd St. between 7th and 8th Aves.) has earned an important place in literary history. Thomas Wolfe, Brendan Behan, Dylan Thomas, and Arthur Miller slept and wrote in its rooms. Andy Warhol made a 4-hour movie about its raunchier inhabitants. For a sojourn into tranquillity, step into the inner courtyard of General Theological Seminary, a gift to the city in 1817 by Clement C. Moore, author of "A Visit from Saint Nicholas." Open daily (except when special use is being made of it), noon to 3 PM weekdays, 11 AM to 3 PM Saturdays, and 2 to 4 PM Sundays. No admission charge. 175 9th Ave. (phone: 243-5150).

MIDTOWN (34TH STREET TO 59TH STREET)

West 34th Street – Still a major shopping street, this is the home of the traditional mercantile giant, *Macy's*, and scores of boutiques selling blue jeans, blouses, underwear, shoes, records, and electronic gear. The main shopping district runs along 34th Street from 8th Avenue east to Madison Avenue, with a number of smaller shops lining the street as far east as 3rd Avenue. The hub of 34th Street is *Herald Square*, where Broadway intersects the Avenue of the Americas (6th Avenue).

Madison Square Garden, Felt Forum, and Penn Station – A huge coliseum-arena, office building, and transportation complex. The *Garden*'s seats (20,000 maximum capacity) usually are fully packed when the New York *Knicks* (NBA basketball) or the New York *Rangers* (NHL hockey) play home games, when the *Ringling Brothers and Barnum & Bailey Circus* comes to town, or whenever there is a major exhibition, concert, or convention. The *Felt Forum*, a 5,000-seat subsidiary hall that's part of the *Garden* complex, is the site of boxing matches, concerts, and smaller exhibitions. Penn Station is *Amtrak*'s major New York terminal (for *Amtrak* information, phone: 582-6875). No guided tours. 1 Pennsylvania Plaza, W. 33rd St. between 7th and 8th Aves. (phone: 563-8300 for *Garden* and *Forum* information).

Garment District – The center of the clothing and fashion industries.

On any weekday during office hours, racks of the latest apparel are pushed through the terrifically hectic streets. Along 7th and 8th Aves. from 30th to 39th Sts.

Empire State Building – The first skyscraper in New York to be attacked by King Kong. The 102-story Art Deco edifice was erected in 1931 and became the symbol of the city for decades. There is an open-air observation deck on the 86th floor to which millions of tourists have been whisked over the years to gaze in awe at the surrounding New York skyline, and another, glass-enclosed viewing area on the 102nd floor. Open daily, 9:30 AM to midnight. Admission charge. W. 34th St. and Fifth Ave. (phone: 736-3100).

Jacob K. Javits Convention Center – This glass and steel monolith designed by I. M. Pei, covering 22 acres along the Hudson River, hosts the bigger synods and conventions that outgrew the old *New York Coliseum.* The complex runs for 5 blocks between 11th and 12th Avenues and encompasses 1.8 million square feet of space, making it one of the world's largest buildings. It has more than 900,000 square feet of indoor exhibition space, another 50,000 square feet outside, and a 15-story atrium. The kitchens produce banquet meals for up to 10,000, while the cafeteria serves 1,500 people an hour. State-of-the-art meeting facilities include a sophisticated audiovisual system and soundproofing throughout its 131 separate meeting rooms, with simultaneous interpretation in up to 8 languages. There's also a VIP lounge, a press room, a video information center, and a cocktail lounge. The only thing missing is a garage. 655 W. 34th St. (phone: 216-2000).

Times Square – Every *New Year's Eve,* Times Square is where thousands of New Yorkers and visitors welcome in the new year. Although the height of mad celebration reaches its pinnacle at that time, Times Square is always crowded. The quality of the crowds, however, leaves much to be desired. In spite of its reputation as one of the major crossroads of the world, Times Square is mainly the hangout of drug pushers, pimps, hookers, junkies, religious fanatics, and assorted street peddlers attempting to fence stolen goods. It is also the center of the city's tackiest sex industry. To the naked eye, it is nearly wall-to-wall porn shops and hard-core movies. Proposals for rehabilitation have been almost as numerous as the prostitutes on parade. A sign of a possibly brighter future came with the completion of the 50-story *Marriott Marquis* convention hotel, built — over protests from the theater community — on the site of the *Helen Hayes* and *Morosco* theaters (W. 44th St., where Broadway crosses 7th Ave.). This has led to a hotel renaissance that now includes the *Holiday Inn Crowne Plaza,* the *Macklowe,* the *Paramount,* and the *Embassy Suites* (see *Checking In* for all).

Broadway and the Theater District – Just north of Times Square, are the colorful marquees and billboards for which New York is famous. The lights are still pretty dazzling, twinkling on and off in a glittering electric collage. On most nights, the side streets are jammed with people from 7:30 to 11 PM. The legitimate theaters are mostly clustered between West 42nd and West 50th Streets to the east and west of Broadway. Sixty- to 90-minute backstage tours, conducted by directors, actors, and other theater pros, can be reserved by calling *Backstage on Broadway* (phone: 575-8065).

New York Public Library – A couple of blocks east of Times Square, this dignified Beaux Arts building is a good place to sit and catch your breath. Sit on the front steps, between the famous lion statues, or in the newly renovated Bryant Park, behind the library. Inside the library is New York's largest reference collection of books, periodicals, and exhibits of graphic art, as well as a gift store; there also are various exhibitions and public programs. Tours are given daily except Sundays at 11 AM and 2 PM. Closed Sundays. No admission charge. W. 42nd St. and Fifth Ave. (phone: 930-0501).

Grand Central Station – This magnificent Beaux Arts relic is worth seeing. It has recently been cleaned and spruced up, and more daylight illuminates the terminal. Even if you don't have time for the free 1-hour tour Wednesdays at 12:30 PM (phone: 935-3960), at least check out the zodiac dotting the immense vaulted ceiling. Main entrance on 42nd St. between Madison and Lexington Aves.

Chrysler Building – The princess of the skyline. Its distinctive, graceful spire, decorated with stainless steel, now sparkles with more than its usual brilliance since the installation of hand-blown fluorescent lights around its peak. Although it has long ceded the title of tallest on the skyline, this twinkling, Art Deco building of the 1930s remains, to many New Yorkers, the most beautiful of all. There are no tours or observatories, but a visit to the small lobby, with its exquisite inlaid elevator doors, is worth a trip. 405 Lexington Ave. at 42nd St.

Ford Foundation Building – If you happen to be wandering through New York at sunrise and climb the stairs between 1st and 2nd Avenues on 42nd Street, you'll see the bronzed windows of the Ford Foundation building catch the first rays of the sun, reflecting copper-colored light into the sky. At other times, the building is just as dramatic. Built around a central glass-enclosed courtyard containing tropical trees and plants, it is the only place in Manhattan where you can feel as if you're in a jungle. It's one of the great New York experiences — especially on snowy afternoons. Open weekdays. No admission charge. 320 E. 43rd St. (phone: 573-5000).

Tudor City – A nearly forgotten pocket of the city, this 1920s neo-Tudor apartment complex is one of its most romantic parts. An esplanade overlooks the East River and the United Nations. The home of many diplomats and UN employees, Tudor City serves as an international campus. (According to local legend, Tudor City used to be where executives and industrialists housed their mistresses in the 1930s and 1940s.) The long, curved staircase leading to the sidewalk opposite the United Nations is known as the Isaiah Steps because of the biblical quote carved into the wall. Between E. 41st and E. 43rd Sts. at Tudor City Place (near 1st Ave.).

United Nations – Although the UN is open all year, the best time to visit is between September and December, when the General Assembly is in session. Delegates from 160 nations gather to discuss the world's problems, and there are a limited number of free tickets available to the public. The delegates' dining room also is open to the public for lunch weekdays throughout the year. Overlooking the East River, it offers a lovely international menu and the chance to overhear intriguing conversations. Reservations are essential; pick up a pass in the lobby. There are guided tours of the UN. Open daily. Admission charge for tour. 1 Dag Hammerskjold Plaza, E. 45th St. and 1st Ave. (phone: 963-4440).

Rockefeller Center – A group of skyscrapers originally built in the 1930s, Rockefeller Center is best known for the giant *Christmas* tree in December, for its ice skating rink, for *Radio City Music Hall,* a theatrical landmark and home of the *Rockettes* (phone: 247-4777), and for the romantic *Rainbow Room,* where dinner for two becomes a Fred Astaire and Ginger Rogers fantasy. After dinner, visit the *Rainbow and Stars* for sophisticated cabaret entertainment (phone: 632-5000). Public opinion was generally dissenting when the Rockefeller Group was bought by Mitsubishi Estate Company in October 1989. However, the company actually has only a 15% interest in Rockefeller Center. There are tours of the center and the observation tower ($7.25) as well as tours of NBC television studios ($6) from 30 Rockefeller Plaza (the GE Building) daily except Sundays. Fifth Ave. between 48th and 51st Sts. (phone: 664-4000).

St. Patrick's Cathedral – A refuge from the crowds of Fifth Avenue, it's the most famous church in the city. Dedicated to Ireland's patron saint, it stands in Gothic splendor across the street from Rockefeller

Center in the shadow of the skyscrapers. Resplendent with gargoyles on the outside, stained glass windows and magnificent appointments on the inside, St. Patrick's is a good place for rest, contemplation, and prayer. Catholic services are held daily. Fifth Ave. between E. 50th and E. 51st Sts. (phone: 753-2261).

Sixth Avenue – Officially known as Avenue of the Americas, but no true New Yorker calls it that. Sixth Avenue between 42nd and 57th Streets is particularly breathtaking at dusk, when the giant glass and steel buildings light up.

Museum of Modern Art – A must. The masterpieces of modern art hanging on the walls include Wyeth's *Christina's World,* Monet's *Water Lilies,* and Van Gogh's *Starry Night.* A renovation project completed in 1984 gave *MoMA* twice as much gallery space and expanded study and library facilities. The most dramatic alteration was a 4-story glass Garden Hall overlooking the sculpture garden. The museum's permanent collection is installed in chronological order, and, by following a suggested route, visitors can see the history of modern painting, photography, and sculpture unfold. Closed Wednesdays except to members. Admission charge; on Thursday evenings, admission is on a pay-as-you-wish basis. 11 W. 53rd St. (phone: 708-9480).

Fifth Avenue – Although the street runs from Washington Square straight up to Spanish Harlem, when New Yorkers refer to Fifth Avenue they usually mean the stretch of the world's most sophisticated shops between Rockefeller Center at 49th Street and the *Plaza* hotel at the southeastern corner of Central Park at Central Park South (59th St.). *Saks, Gucci, Tiffany, Cartier, Bergdorf Goodman,* and, for children, *FAO Schwarz* make walking along the street an incredible test in temptation. Stop in at *Steuben Glass* on the corner of 56th Street and marvel at its permanent collection of sculpted glass depicting mythological and contemporary themes. And whether you decide to go in or not, *Trump Tower*'s gold façade is quite a spectacle, housing luxury apartments and some of the most exclusive (read expensive) stores in the city. Fifth Avenue is the dividing line between east and west in New York street addresses. It is the only New York avenue that runs perfectly straight along a north-south axis.

Grand Army Plaza – This baroque square, with its central fountain just across the street from the southeast corner of Central Park, faces the regal *Plaza* hotel, the General Motors Building, and the hansom cabstand where horse-drawn carriages (some guided by drivers in top hats and tails) wait to carry clients through Central Park. If you have a lover, be sure to arrange to meet here at least once. Be sure, too, to take at least one ride through the park in a hansom cab, preferably at dusk or very, very late. In the southern part of the plaza, Pomona, the Roman Goddess of Abundance, stands atop the Pulitzer Fountain. The recently regilded statue of General Sherman shines brightly (to many New Yorkers, too brightly) in the northern part of the plaza. Three times the quantity of gold used in the flame of the Statue of Liberty was used to brighten him. Bring your sunglasses! Central Park South and Fifth Ave.

Central Park – More than 50 blocks long but only 3 blocks wide, this beloved stretch of greenery designed by Frederick Law Olmsted and Calvert Vaux in the 1860s is now a National Historic Landmark. New Yorkers use it for everything — jogging, biking, walking, ice skating (at *Wollman Rink*), riding in horse-drawn hansom cabs, listening to concerts (including the *Free Concerts in the Park* series every summer, courtesy of the *New York Philharmonic*), and opera, watching Shakespearean plays, demonstrating against injustice, flying kites, boating, gazing at art, and playing all kinds of ball games. You should, however, avoid the park at night, and never go alone, even during the day. Central Park has been the object of much concern over the past year, and justifiably so, with the outbreak of many random, violent crimes. In other words, enjoy the incredible diversity of the park with caution. The Central Park Zoo (between E. 61st and E. 65th Sts. on Fifth Ave.) was taken over by the New York Zoological Society (phone: 861-6030), which also runs the Bronx Zoo, and $30 million worth of improvements were made in the habitats for this mid-Manhattan menagerie. It reopened in 1988 to rave reviews. Admission charge. Central Park is bounded by Central Park South (W. 59th St.) on the south, West 110th Street on the north, Fifth Avenue on the east, and Central Park West on the west. Urban rangers offer free walking tours of the park (phone: 860-1353), and there even are guides who describe which items growing in the park are edible. For information on park events, call 360-1333.

UPPER EAST SIDE

For the museum lover, upper Fifth Avenue offers "Museum Mile," including the *Metropolitan Museum of Art* and the *Guggenheim* (see below), and the *Cooper-Hewitt,* the *Frick,* the *International Center of Photography,* and the *Jewish Museum,* plus the *Whitney* on Madison Avenue (see *Museums*).

Metropolitan Museum of Art – Perhaps the finest museum this side of the *Louvre;* more than 4.5 million people visit every year. You easily could spend days walking through the impressive sections displaying the costumes, ceramics, metalwork, armor, mummies, paintings, drawings, sculpture, photographs, and mosaics of dozens of different periods and countries. The special exhibitions are really special. There is a good cafeteria and two superb, large gift shops. Films and lectures are presented throughout the year, and a distinguished concert series (phone: 570-3949) is held from September through May. Closed Mondays. Suggested admission: $6. Fifth Ave. at 82nd St. (phone: 535-7710 or 879-5500).

Solomon R. Guggenheim Museum – Designed in 1959 by Frank Lloyd Wright, this white circular building has spiraling ramps along its inner walls so you can travel through the collections by following the curves of the building. While it is given over primarily to exhibitions of contemporary art, some patrons feel that its architecture is more impressive than the collection it houses. The museum reopened in 1991 after extensive renovations, which included repairs to the exterior Wright spiral, and an additional annex, which more than doubles the exhibition space inside. Closed Mondays. Admission charge. 1071 Fifth Ave., between E. 88th and E. 89th Sts. (phone: 727-6200).

Yorkville and Gracie Mansion – An interesting ethnic neighborhood of mostly German and Eastern European families. There are plenty of restaurants, beer halls, and delicatessens selling Wiener schnitzel, sauerbraten, wurst, and kielbasa. Gracie Mansion, dating to 1799, is the official residence of the Mayor of New York and sits in a garden that is part of Carl Schurz Park alongside the East River. The park is popular with joggers and dog-walkers and is most attractive at dawn, when the eastern sky comes to life. Yorkville stretches from E. 80th to E. 89th Streets between Lexington and York Avenues. Gracie Mansion and Carl Schurz Park are at E. 88th St. and East End Ave. The mansion can be visited by appointment only, from April to October (phone: 570-4751).

Roosevelt Island – A self-contained housing development in the middle of the East River. Roosevelt Island, accessible from Manhattan by tramway, subway (the *Q* train weekdays, the *D* on weekends), or from Queens by bus, offers a unique view of midtown Manhattan. A loop bus encircles the island, which has restricted automobile traffic. Visitors also can stroll the attractive main street from end to end, stopping at shops and eateries along the way. A landscaped riverside promenade has benches for relaxing while enjoying the view. The aerial tramway leaves each side every 15 minutes daily except during rush hours, when it leaves every 7½ minutes. The tram costs $1.40. Manhattan terminal at E. 60th St. and 2nd Ave. (phone: 753-6626).

UPPER WEST SIDE

Lincoln Center – If you remember the scene from *Moonstruck* in which the characters played by Cher and Nicholas Cage meet for their first official date — a night at the opera — you have probably retained an image of the glowing lights of a fountain shooting into the air with an exuberance to match the excitement of a new love. That's the *Lincoln Center* fountain, and it's just as magnificent in real life. The pulsing water and light are dramatically framed by the *Metropolitan Opera House,* a contemporary hall with giant murals by Marc Chagall. The performing arts complex also contains *Avery Fisher Hall* (home of the *New York Philharmonic*), the *New York State Theater* (home of the *New York City Ballet*), the *Vivian Beaumont Theater,* the *Mitzi E. Newhouse Theater,* the Juilliard Building, and the *New York Public Library at Lincoln Center* and *Museum of the Performing Arts* (see *Theater* and *Music* sections, below). Guided tours through the major buildings are conducted daily and last about an hour. Admission charge for tour: $6.50 for adults, $5.50 for seniors and students, $3.50 for children aged 6 to 13. Free to children under 6. 140 W. 65th St. and Broadway, in the Lincoln Center Concourse (*Lincoln Center:* phone: 877-1800; *Metropolitan Opera Guild:* phone: 582-3512).

American Museum of Natural History – Although its $60 million face-lift won't be completed until 1995, the museum continues to be a cornucopia of curiosities. The anthropological and natural history exhibitions in the form of life-size dioramas showing people and animals in realistic settings have made this one of the most famous museums in the world. The dinosaurs on the fourth floor, which are slated to receive the brontosaur's share of the renovation budget, are the stars of the show. The Hall of South American Peoples displays more than 2,300 objects produced by aboriginal cultures of South America over a period of 12,000 years. Exhibitions include polychrome pottery, intricate gold and silver ornaments, and spectacular, brilliantly colored textiles. The popular *Naturemax Theater,* with its 4-story screen, often shows double features of nature films (phone: 769-5650). The museum has a cafeteria, a restaurant, and three gift shops. Free guided tours leave from the main floor information desk. Closed *Thanksgiving* and *Christmas.* Donations accepted; no admission Fridays and Saturdays after 5 PM. Central Park West and W. 79th St. (phone: 769-5000 or, for recorded information, 769-5100).

Hayden Planetarium – An amazing collection of astronomical displays on meteorites, comets, space vehicles, and other galactic phenomena. The sky show, in which constellations are projected onto an observatory ceiling, is one of the great New York sights. Subjects include lunar expeditions, the formation of the solar system, and UFOs. Open daily. Admission charge. W. 81st St. between Central Park West and Columbus Ave. (phone: 769-5920).

Cathedral of St. John the Divine – The largest neo-Gothic cathedral in the world, with a seating capacity of 10,000. It is irreverently nicknamed St. John the Unfinished, for a chronic shortage of funds has allowed only two-thirds of the impressive church to be completed since work began in 1892. Stonemasons, who most recently put down their trowels in the late 1930s, picked them up again in 1979, with plans to finish the interior of the crossing and the two towers' spires by the year 2000. There is a stunning collection of Renaissance and Byzantine art inside, and an exquisite time to see it all is on *Christmas Eve* at midnight mass. Guided tours of the cathedral and the stoneyard are conducted daily. The well-stocked gift shop rivals many for its variety of souvenir and gift items. Open daily. No admission charge. Amsterdam Ave. and W. 112th St. (phone: 316-7540).

Columbia University – The Big Apple's contribution to the Ivy League. Although more than 27,000 students attend classes here, the campus is spacious enough to dispel any sense of crowding. Around the campus are a number of interesting bookstores, restaurants, and bars. The *West End Café* (2911 Broadway and W. 113th St.; phone: 662-8830) is a long-standing student favorite, and it was from here that Jack Kerouac went forth to lead the Beat Generation of the 1950s. Free guided tours of the campus leave from 201 Dodge Hall every Tuesday and Thursday morning. Call ahead for reservations. Open daily. No admission charge. Broadway and W. 116th St. (phone: 854-2845).

Riverside Church – Perched on a cliff overlooking the Hudson River, Riverside is an interdominational Christian church with a functioning carillon tower and an amazing statue of the Angel Gabriel blowing the trumpet. The white building next to the church is known as "the God Box" because many religious organizations (among them, the National Council of Churches and the Interfaith Council on Corporate Responsibility) are based here. The carillon tower is open daily; free guided tours of the church Sundays at 12:30 PM. W. 120th St. between Riverside Dr. and Claremont Ave. (phone: 222-5900).

Grant's Tomb – Who is buried in Grant's tomb? Suffice it to say, You-Know-Who and his wife, Mrs. You-Know-Who, are entombed here in a gray building topped with a rotunda and set in Riverside Park. A word about the park: Don't wander in after dark. Grant's tomb is known officially as General Grant National Memorial. Closed Mondays and Tuesdays. No admission charge. Riverside Dr. and W. 122nd St. (phone: 666-1640).

Cloisters and Ft. Tryon Park – Without a doubt one of the most unusual museums in the country, if not the world. The *Cloisters,* a branch of the *Metropolitan Museum,* consists of sections of cloisters that originally belonged to monasteries in southern France. It houses an inspiring collection of medieval art from different parts of Europe, of which the *Unicorn Tapestries* are the most famous. Recorded medieval music echoes through the stone corridors and courtyards daily; medieval and Renaissance concerts are held on selected Sundays throughout the year. As part of its 50th anniversary celebration in 1988, the Cloisters Treasury on the ground floor was expanded. Set in Ft. Tryon Park along the Hudson River, the *Cloisters* offers a splendid view of the New Jersey Palisades, the George Washington Bridge, and the Hudson River. Closed Mondays. Suggested admission: $6. Closest intersection is Washington Ave. and W. 193rd St. (phone: 923-3700).

Harlem – Some visitors to New York — black or white — are uncomfortable at the thought of entering Harlem, and, like any unfamiliar place, it can be intimidating. But there is much to see here, and a visit can have the undeniable effect of shattering the monolithic association with threat and violence that attends most people's image of the community. Starting in earnest at 110th Street and stretching to about 160th Street, it is a community filled with neighborhoods of families as concerned about community problems as families in other neighborhoods throughout the city.

The nicest part of Harlem is the landmark block called "Strivers Row" — 138th Street between 7th and 8th Avenues — 2 blocks of turn-of-the-century brownstones, some designed by Stanford White. Quite a lot of Harlem, however, is undergoing a revival. *Mart 125* (at 260-262 W. 125th St.; phone: 316-3340) is a shopping center offering handicrafts from developing countries, and there always is a constant flow of activities held on Harlem's 10-block waterfront that includes Black, Latin, and Caribbean arts, music, entertainment, and food stalls. In August there is *Harlem Week,* 20 days of music, food, and cultural happenings, and in the fall, the *Harlem Jazz Festival.* The *Harlem Festival Orchestra* performs at the Church of The Intercession (550 W. 155th St.; phone: 283-6200). The famous *Apollo Theater* (253 W. 125th St.; phone: 749-5838) has been made over, condos are going up, and a multi-screen cinema has opened.

In the words of a New York police officer: "The best way to see Harlem is by driving or in a cab. Take a bus rather than a subway if you are using public transportation." Among the reliable tour operators are *Harlem Spirituals* (phone: 302-2594), *Harlem Tours* (phone: 410-0080), *Harlem Your Way* (phone: 690-1687 or 866-6997), and *Harlem Renaissance Tours* (phone: 722-9534). Worthwhile sights include the Morris-Jumel Mansion, once the home of Aaron Burr and Washington's headquarters (W. 160th St. at Edgecombe Ave.; phone: 923-8008); the Schomburg Center for Research in Black Culture (515 Lenox Ave. at W. 135th St.; phone: 862-4000); *Aunt Len's Doll and Toy Museum,* which offers a collection of more than 5,000 dolls, by appointment (6 Hamilton Terr. at 141 St.; phone: 281-4143); the Abyssinian Baptist Church (132 W. 138th St.; phone: 862-7474), where Adam Clayton Powell, Jr., preached; the *Studio Museum* (144 W. 125th St.; phone: 865-2420); and the *Black Fashion Museum,* the country's only museum devoted to black contributions to fashion (155-157 W. 126th St.; phone: 666-1320). For more information on Harlem, contact the Uptown Chamber of Commerce (phone: 427-7200) or the New York Convention and Visitors Bureau (phone: 397-8222).

BROOKLYN

Mention Brooklyn to most Manhattanites and you'll probably hear "Oh, I never go to Brooklyn" or some smart-aleck remark. People who do not know the borough think purely in terms of the book *A Tree Grows in Brooklyn* or 1930s gangster movies in which Brooklyn-born thugs make snide remarks out of the sides of their mouths while chewing on cigars. Actually, Brooklyn has a lot of trees (more than Manhattan) and some charming neighborhoods that are more European than American in character. Not only is it greener, it is also considerably more peaceful than Manhattan, even though it has more than 4 million people and bills itself as "the Fourth Largest City in America."

Brooklyn Heights – The most picturesque streets of classic (and expensive) brownstones and gardens can be found in this historic district. Not only does the Promenade facing the skyline offer the traditional picture-postcard view of Manhattan, but the area behind it retains an aura of dignity that characterized a more gracious past. Montague Street, a narrow thoroughfare lined with restaurants and shops selling ice cream, candles, old prints, flowers, and clothing, runs from the East River to the Civic Center, a complex of federal, state, and municipal government buildings. To get to Brooklyn Heights from Manhattan, take the *IRT* 7th Avenue line (trains No. 2 or No. 3) to Clark Street; or, better yet, walk across the Brooklyn Bridge and bear right. The district extends from the Brooklyn Bridge to Atlantic Avenue and from Court Street to the Promenade. For information on events in the Heights, contact the *Brooklyn Heights Association,* 55 Pierrepont St. (phone: 718-858-9193).

Atlantic Avenue – Lebanese, Yemeni, Syrian, and Palestinian shops, bakeries, and restaurants line the street, where purveyors of tahini, Syrian bread, baklava, halvah, assorted delicious foodstuffs, Arabic records, and books are also to be found. There is even an office of the Palestinian Red Crescent, an official branch of the International Red Cross that has been helping victims of the wars in Lebanon. Occasionally, women in veils make their way to and from the shops, some incongruously carrying transistor radios. The most active street scene takes place between the waterfront and Court Street along Atlantic Avenue.

Park Slope – An up-and-coming restoration district, the Slope resembles London's borough of Chelsea, with many beautiful, shady trees and gardens. It feels more like a town than part of the city, especially at night, when the only sounds are the birds and the wind rushing through the trees. A large part of Park Slope has been designated a historic district, and there are some truly impressive townhouses here. Grand Army Plaza, a colossal arch commemorating those who died in the Civil War, stands at the end of the Slope that extends along the western edge of Prospect Park. On Sundays, you can climb the inside stairway to the top — the view is stupendous. Seventh Avenue, 2 blocks from the park, is an intriguing shopping street where you can get old furniture, stained glass, ceramics, housewares, flowers, health food, vegetables, and toys. Saturday afternoons get pretty lively. To get to Park Slope from Manhattan, take the *IRT* 7th Avenue line (trains No. 2 or No. 3) to Grand Army Plaza or the *IND* D or Q train to the 7th Avenue exit.

Prospect Park and the Brooklyn Botanic Gardens – Prospect Park, an Olmsted and Vaux creation, has more than 500 acres of gracefully landscaped greenery with fields, fountains, lakes, a concert bandshell, an ice skating rink in winter, a bridal path, and a zoo. The Botanic Gardens (1000 Washington Ave.; phone: 718-622-4433) contain 50 acres of serene rose gardens and hothouses with orchids and other tropical plants, as well as an impressive bonsai collection, cherry trees, a Zen meditation garden, and hundreds of flowers and shrubs. Closed Mondays. No admission charge. From Manhattan, take the *IRT* 7th Avenue line to Eastern Parkway or take the *IND* D or Q train to Prospect Park.

Brooklyn Museum – In addition to its outstanding permanent anthropological collections on American Indians of both the northern and southern hemispheres, this museum hosts terrific traveling exhibitions. In the permanent collection are fine exhibits of Oriental arts, American painting and decorative arts, and European painting. The roster of artists whose work is permanently displayed includes Van Gogh, Rodin, Toulouse-Lautrec, Gauguin, Monet, and Chagall. It also is noted for its Egyptian and primitive art collections. Closed Tuesdays. Suggested donation: $4. From Manhattan, take the *IRT* 7th Avenue line to Eastern Parkway. 200 Eastern Pkwy. and Washington Ave. (phone: 718-638-5000).

Bay Ridge – Although Brooklynites have been fond of this Scandinavian waterfront community for years, it took the film *Saturday Night Fever* to bring it to national attention. Bay Ridge is dominated by the world's longest suspension bridge, the Verrazano-Narrows Bridge, which connects Brooklyn with Staten Island. (Some people say this bridge goes from nowhere to nowhere else, but they fail to appreciate its finer aesthetics.) Although chances are you won't see John Travolta tripping down 4th Avenue, you will see a lot of people who look like the character he played in the film, and you'll also get to see the bridge rising over the tops of houses, shops, restaurants, and discos. A bike path runs along the edge of the Narrows from Owls Head Pier, the pier of the now-defunct Brooklyn–Staten Island ferry, all the way to the Verrazano-Narrows Bridge. The pier has been renovated and is a great place for fishing, watching the ships come in, and looking at a wide-angle view of lower Manhattan. To get to Bay Ridge from Manhattan, take the *BMT* R train to 95th St.

Coney Island – If you've seen the classic film *The Beast from 20,000 Fathoms,* you no doubt remember the climactic final scene in which the beast is shot down from the top of a roller coaster called the Cyclone. As the monster falls, he destroys half of Coney Island. But fear not, gentle reader, Hollywood's illusion is a far cry from reality — although some disenchanted residents wish it were a lot closer to the truth. Now a long strip of garish amusement park rides, penny arcades, hot dog stands, and low-income housing complexes, Coney Island is jam-packed in summer, eerily deserted in winter. Weekends in the summer are the worst time to visit. Weekday evenings are considerably less frenetic. You can ride the Cyclone, one of the most terrifying roller coasters on the East Coast, and the Wonder Wheel, a giant Ferris wheel alongside the ocean; but the parachute jump, which is Coney Island's landmark and can be seen for miles, is no longer operational. The actual amusement park is called *Astroland Park* (phone: 718-372-0275 or 718-265-2100) and is open seasonally, 7 days a week, noon to midnight. There are honky-tonk bars along the boardwalk, where country-and-western singers compete with the sound of the sea. The famous belugas (white whales) are the stars of the *New York Aquarium* (Boardwalk and W. 8th St.; phone: 718-265-3400). If you get a sudden craving for Italian food, head for *Gargiulo's* (2911 W. 15th St.; phone: 718-266-0906) for some good Neapolitan dishes. The ultimate offbeat New York treat is to have hot dogs at *Nathan's* at 2 in the morning. The area's newest ethnic flavor is provided by Russian immigrants, and has been affectionately dubbed "Odessa by the Boardwalk." Surf and Stillwell Aves. Take *IND* F, D, or N trains to Stillwell Ave. from Manhattan. For further information, contact the Chamber of Commerce (phone: 718-266-1234).

Sheepshead Bay – More like a New England fishing village than part of New York; fishermen sell their catch on the dock in the early afternoon. Charter boats that take people out for the day leave very early in the morning. For the best view of the scene, cross the wooden footbridge at Ocean Avenue and walk along the mile-long esplanade. A few blocks south of the bay is Manhattan Beach, one of the smaller city beaches. Brighton Beach, a few blocks to the east, joins Manhattan Beach with Coney Island. To get to Sheepshead Bay from Manhattan, take the *IND* D or Q train to Sheepshead Bay.

THE BRONX

If you intend to visit the Bronx, don't ask for directions from someone from Brooklyn. Because of local prejudice, residents of these boroughs often look down on each other. With almost 2 million inhabitants, the Bronx is smaller than Brooklyn; it's the only borough in the City of New York that is on the mainland. Although all the points of interest listed here are safe for visitors, some sections of the Bronx are the most dangerous parts of New York City. The South Bronx has been nicknamed "Ft. Apache" by the police, and one officer advises staying clear of any place south of Fordham Road.

Bronx Zoo – One of the most famous in the world, the "habitat" zoo covers 250 acres inhabited by more than 4,000 animals. Elephants, tigers, chimps, seals, rhinos, hippos, birds, and buffalos are the favorites. Ride the *Bengali Express* monorail through Wild Asia, visit Jungle World, a children's petting zoo, or survey it all from the *Skyfair's* tramway. To get here from Manhattan, take the *IRT* 7th Ave. No. 2 express to Pelham Pkwy.; walk west to the Bronxdale entrance (for other routes, call the zoo). Open daily from 10 AM to 4:30 PM. Admission charge Fridays through Mondays; other days, donation suggested; parking, $4. At Fordham Rd. and Bronx River Pkwy. (phone: 367-1010).

New York Botanical Gardens – Adjoining the zoo to the north, the 250 acres of flowering hills, valleys, woods, and gardens are set in an unspoiled natural forest. The site comprises the only surviving remnants of the original woodland that covered the city. The Enid A. Haupt Conservatory (closed Mondays), a crystal palace with 11 pavilions — each with a totally different environment — is a special treat. Other highlights include a rose garden, azalea glen, daffodil hill, conservatory, botanical museum, and restaurant. Well worth the trip, especially in the spring. From Manhattan take the *IND* D train to Bedford Park station and walk 8 blocks east. (For information on other travel directions, call

220-8779.) Open daily 8 AM to 7 PM. Admission charge for the conservatory except Saturdays before noon; parking, $4. Southern Blvd. and 200th St. (phone: 220-8700).

Bronx Museum of the Arts – This museum's changing exhibitions have two themes: contemporary art and the artistic expression of the many ethnic groups who live in the borough. Classical music concerts, film programs, poetry readings, and dance performances are held throughout the year. From Manhattan, take the *IRT* No. 4 to 161st St. or the *IND* C or D to 167th St. Closed Fridays. Suggested donation: $2. 1040 Grand Concourse at 165th St. (phone: 681-6000).

Edgar Allan Poe Cottage – A tiny cottage, adequately cramped to inspire claustrophobia in anyone larger than a raven, sits incongruously in the middle of the Grand Concourse. Poe lived here during his last years; the cottage contains his personal belongings. Closed Mondays and Tuesdays. Admission charge. E. Kingsbridge Rd. at Grand Concourse (phone: 881-8900).

Wave Hill – A country mansion where Mark Twain, Teddy Roosevelt, and Arturo Toscanini once lived. It features a Gothic Armor Hall and beautiful gardens. Open daily. No admission charge weekdays. In the elegant, residential Riverdale section of the Bronx, 675 W. 252nd St. (phone: 549-3200).

Yankee Stadium – The home of the Bronx Bombers, and a sports landmark. Here, in this renovated 55,745-seat stadium, Babe Ruth, Lou Gehrig, Joe DiMaggio, and dozens of other baseball stars batted. Take the *IND* C or D trains or the *IRT* No. 4 from Manhattan to 161st St. Open during baseball season. 161st and River Aves. (phone: 293-6000).

Hall of Fame of Great Americans – Bronze-cast busts of great American presidents, poets, and people noted for achievement in the sciences, arts, and humanities. About 100 busts stand on podiums set atop columns. The landmark Hall is outdoors on the Bronx Community College campus; from Manhattan take the *IND* D train to 183rd St. or the *IRT* No. 4 train to Burnside Ave. Closed in winter, open daily the rest of the year. No admission charge. W. 181st St. and University Ave. (phone: 220-6450).

QUEENS

Manhattanites used to think of Queens as outer suburbia — until Manhattan's skyrocketing rents prompted many middle class folks to take a second look. Actually, Queens is less than 5 minutes away from Manhattan by subway and is the largest of the five boroughs. It boasts 118.6 square miles that include major sports facilities, 196 miles of waterfront, numerous parks, cultural centers, universities, two of the metro area's three airports, and even a growing motion picture industry. Queens also is one of the most ethnically diverse areas in the nation, though nationalities tend to congregate in specific pockets. Greeks have settled in Astoria; Hispanics in Corona and Jackson Heights; Asians in Flushing. The largest Hindu temple in North America is found on Bowne Street in Flushing, and Flushing's Chinatown now rivals Manhattan's. These neighborhoods offer a fascinating assortment of restaurants, groceries, and bakeries — Filipino, Italian, Peruvian, Ecuadoran, Colombian, Argentinian, Greek, German — and also sponsor a number of festivals featuring their own foods, crafts, music, and dancing. For information on these activities, call Queens Borough Hall (phone: 718-520-3270).

Queens's architectural ambience can change literally from block to block — from pretty Kew Gardens to opulent Jamaica Estates and Bayside Hills, and from the quiet row houses of Flushing to the Victorian houses in Richmond Hill, Old Woodhaven, and College Point. The earliest settlement in Queens dates to 1642. It was named for Queen Catherine of Braganza and was formally incorporated in 1898. Historical sites abound, including the Friends Meeting House (137-16 Northern

Blvd., Flushing; phone: 718-358-9636). Built in 1694, it is the oldest house of worship in the US.

Sports buffs flock to Queens to see the *Mets* at *Shea Stadium,* the horse races at *Aqueduct* and *Belmont,* and the *US Open Tennis Championships* at the *USTA National Tennis Center* at the *World's Fair* site in *Flushing Meadow Park.* There also are abundant facilities for golf, tennis, swimming, ice skating, horseback riding, boating, hiking, and bird watching. Lovers of the great outdoors enjoy the borough's wetlands and woodlands, including the 2-mile Pitobik Trail, Turtle Pond, and Alley Pond Creek (phone: 718-229-4000); Forest Park (phone: 718-520-5905/6/7); Jamaica Bay Wildlife Refuge (phone: 718-474-0613); and the Queens Botanical Gardens, in Flushing (phone: 718-886-3800).

Bowne House – This "shrine to religious freedom," dating from 1661, was the home of John Bowne, a Quaker credited with winning freedom to worship in the Dutch West Indian colony from Governor Peter Stuyvesant. The house is now a museum, featuring 17th- and 18th-century furnishings, pewter, and paintings. Open 2:30 to 4:30 PM, Tuesdays, Saturdays, and Sundays. Admission charge. 37-01 Bowne St., Flushing (phone: 718-359-0528).

Kingsland House – The sole survivor of what was once the prevalent architectural style in Queens, this Dutch colonial/English house dating to 1774 contains antique china and assorted memorabilia. Open 2:30 to 4:30 PM, Tuesdays, Saturdays, and Sundays. Donations encouraged. 143-35 37th Ave., Flushing (phone: 718-939-0647).

King Mansion – Built in 1730 for Rufus King, one of the signers of the Constitution, it is a fine example of Georgian-Federal architecture. The mansion currently is being renovated and tours are available by appointment only. Admission charge. Jamaica Ave. at 153rd St., Jamaica (phone: 718-291-0282).

American Museum of the Moving Image – Built on the site of the Famous Players–Lasky Studios, where the Marx Brothers films (among others) were produced, the museum offers filmmaking classes, lectures, and film series. An excellent permanent exhibit, "Behind the Screen: Producing, Promoting, and Exhibiting Motion Pictures and Television," includes displays of old movie sets, makeup displays, posters, costumes, and more. Closed Mondays. Admission charge. 34-31 35th St., Astoria (phone: 718-784-4520).

Flushing Meadows–Corona Park – The site of the *1939* and *1964 World's Fairs* and the original headquarters of the UN, the park is now a center for sports, cultural, and outdoor activities (phone: 718-699-4209). The *Queens Museum* has a variety of changing exhibitions as well as a permanent collection that includes a 15,000-square-foot scale model of New York City. Open from 10 AM to 5 PM Tuesdays through Fridays, noon to 5:30 PM weekends. Admission charge (phone: 718-592-2405). The park's *New York Hall of Science* opened in 1987; its permanent exhibitions include everything from laser displays to cow's-eye dissections. Open from 10 AM to 5 PM Wednesdays through Sundays. Donations encouraged (phone: 718-699-0005). The *Queens Theater-in-the-Park,* near *Shea Stadium,* presents musicals, plays, concerts, and dance ensembles (phone: 718-592-5700). There also is a children's zoo, open daily from 9:30 AM to 4:30 PM. Take the *IRT* No. 7 to Willets Point, Shea Stadium. No admission charge (phone: 718-699-4275).

STATEN ISLAND

Much closer to New Jersey than New York, Staten Island is the Big Apple's most remote borough and, with about 375,000 people, its least populous. This is the borough that keeps threatening to "secede" from the others in New York's union. Since the Verrazano-Narrows Bridge opened in 1964, Staten Island has been filling up with suburban housing developments and shopping centers. However, a few farms remain in southern Staten Island. To find them, take the bus marked Richmond Avenue at the ferry terminal. Getting around Staten Island by public transportation takes a long time. Driving is recommended if at all possible.

Staten Island Zoo – Considerably smaller than the Bronx Zoo, this zoo covers 8 wooded acreas near a lake in Barret Park. Its specialty is reptiles, and snakes of all descriptions. Open daily 10 AM to 4:45 PM. Admission charge: donation suggested. 614 Broadway and Clove Rd. (phone: 718-442-3101).

Jacques Marchais Center for Tibetan Art – One of the esoteric treasures of the city, this is also one of the best-kept secrets in the metropolitan area. A reconstructed Tibetan prayer hall with adjoining library and gardens with Oriental sculpture, the center sits on a hill overlooking a pastoral, un–New York setting of trees. *The Tibetan Book of the Dead,* other occult tomes, prayer wheels, statuary, and weavings are on display. Open only Fridays through Sundays in April, October, and November; extended hours May through September. Admission charge. 338 Lighthouse Ave. (phone: 718-987-3478).

Conference House – Now a national landmark, this manor house was built in 1670 and hosted such Revolutionary War notables as Benjamin Franklin. Crafts demonstrations usually are offered on the first Sunday of each month; call ahead. Open from 1 to 4 PM Wednesdays through Sundays. Admission charge. 7455 Hylan Blvd. (phone: 718-984-2086).

Richmondtown Restoration – A 96-acre park, with exhibits and crafts demonstrations which depict 3 centuries of local culture, harking back to the early Dutch settlers. Open from 10 AM to 5 PM weekdays, 1 to 5 PM weekends and holidays. Admission charge. 441 Clarke Ave. (phone: 718-351-1617).

SOURCES AND RESOURCES

TOURIST INFORMATION: The New York Convention and Visitors Bureau (2 Columbus Circle, New York, NY 10019; phone: 397-8222) is an excellent source for tourist information and assistance. Its office carries hotel and restaurant information, subway and bus maps, descriptive brochures, and current listings of the city's entertainment and activities, and it is staffed by multilingual aides. The New York Chamber of Commerce and Industry (200 Madison Ave., New York, NY 10016; phone: 561-2020) can mail informative brochures and pamphlets to people planning to move to the New York area. Some of the details may be out of date, but the literature can be helpful. For further information, contact the New York State Department of Economic Development, Division of Tourism (1515 Broadway, 51st Floor, New York, NY 10036; phone: 827-6250). A subscribers-only hotline called *Manhattan Intelligence* will give information on anything from where to pet a lion cub to more mundane items such as current cultural events, making restaurant reservations and finding a parking space for your car. Call 925-0900 for more information. Contact the New York state hotline (phone: 800-CALL-NYS) for maps, calendars of events, health updates, and travel advisories.

Visitors who require assistance in an emergency — anything from a lost wallet to a lost child — should stop at the *Traveler's Aid Services* office (158-160 W. 42nd St.; phone: 944-0013); open weekdays 9 AM to 6 PM (Wednesdays to 1 PM), weekends 9:30 AM to 3 PM. There is also a branch at the International Arrivals Building at Kennedy Airport, open weekdays 10 AM to 8 PM, weekends 1 to 8 PM (phone: 718-656-4870).

Numerous excellent guides to the city's architecture and history are available at most good-size bookstores.

Local Coverage – *The New York Times,* the *Daily News,* and *New York Newsday* all are morning dailies. The *New York Post* comes out twice daily, and the *Village Voice* weekly on Wednesdays. Other publications include the weekly *New Yorker* and *New York* magazines.

Television Stations – Channel 2–WCBS; Channel 4–WNBC; Channel 5–WNYW; Channel 7–WABC; Channel 9–WOR; Channel 11–WPIX; Channel 13–WNET (PBS).

Radio Stations – AM: WFAN 660 (sports/talk); WOR 710 (news/talk); WCBS 880 (news/talk); WQXR 1560 (classical music). FM: WBGO 88 (jazz); WXKR 92.3 (classic rock); WNYC 93.9 (classical); WQXR 96.3 (classical); WNEW 102.7 (rock); WNCN 104.3 (classical); WBLS 107.5 (urban contemporary).

 TELEPHONE: The area code for Manhattan is 212. The area code for Brooklyn, Queens, and Staten Island is 718. As of this July, the area code for the Bronx also will be 718. The area code for Long Island is 516.

Food – *Restaurants of New York,* by Seymour Britchky ($11.95); *Bryan Miller's New York Times Guide to Restaurants in New York City* (Times Books, $12.95); and Mimi Sheraton's *Favorite New York Restaurants* (Simon & Schuster; $9.95). All are updated annually.

The *New York Restaurant Hotline* can assist callers in selecting a dining spot according to the neighborhood, type of cuisine, ambience, and price range diners prefer. Callers should dial 838-6644 and indicate the type of restaurant desired by pressing the Touch Tone buttons as instructed. A voice recording will deliver brief descriptions of several eateries that meet the caller's specifications. *Menufax* is a similar service with information sent to the caller via fax machine (phone or fax: 800-545-MENU). Several restaurant choices, including addresses, phone numbers, and menus, are then faxed to the caller. There is no charge for either of these services.

Sales Tax – New York City's sales tax is 8.25%; hotel tax is 13.25%; restaurant tax is 8.5%.

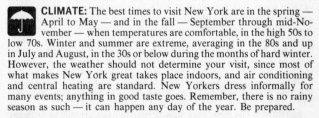 **CLIMATE:** The best times to visit New York are in the spring — April to May — and in the fall — September through mid-November — when temperatures are comfortable, in the high 50s to low 70s. Winter and summer are extreme, averaging in the 80s and up in July and August, in the 30s or below during the months of hard winter. However, the weather should not determine your visit, since most of what makes New York great takes place indoors, and air conditioning and central heating are standard. New Yorkers dress informally for many events; anything in good taste goes. Remember, there is no rainy season as such — it can happen any day of the year. Be prepared.

GETTING AROUND: Airports – New York City is served by three major airports: John F. Kennedy International (JFK) and La Guardia (for domestic flights) — both in the borough of Queens — and Newark International, across the Hudson in New Jersey. It takes 50 to 60 minutes to reach JFK from midtown Manhattan by cab and costs about $37. La Guardia from midtown is a 30- to 45-minute ride, with a fare of around $25. Newark International from midtown is the meter amount (usually about $40), plus $10 and tolls; one fare covers up to four or five passengers and their luggage (except trunks, which are 50¢ extra).

Quick and relatively inexpensive transportation is available via several bus lines. *Carey Transportation* (phone: 718-632-0506) provides service from 125 Park Avenue between 41st and 42nd Streets, the Air Trans Center at the Port Authority Bus Terminal, and the *Hilton, Sheraton*

City Squire, and *Marriott Marquis* hotels to JFK and La Guardia airports. Buses leave every 20 or 30 minutes. One-way fare to JFK is $9.50, $7.50 for La Guardia; *Carey* also runs a shuttle between these two airports ($8.50) *New Jersey Transit* handles service to Newark International out of the Port Authority Bus Terminal (8th Ave. between 40th and 42 Sts.; phone: 564-8484). Purchase tickets ($7) at the *Air Trans Center* desk on the ground floor of the terminal's North Main Wing. Buses depart every 15 to 30 minutes and the trip takes about a half hour. *Olympia Trails* (phone: 964-6233 in New York, 201-589-1188 in New Jersey) provides coach service every 20 minutes on weekdays from Newark International's North, A, B, and C terminals to the World Trade Center, Grand Central Terminal, and Penn Station, and hourly from La Guardia and Kennedy to the World Trade Center only; the fare is $7 one way, $12 round trip. The *Gray Line Air Shuttle* offers a share-ride service which operates among all New York airports and midtown hotels. Fares are $14 for Kennedy, $11 for La Guardia, and $16 for Newark. Arrangements can be made by your hotel, at the *Gray Line Air Shuttle* courtesy telephone by the airline baggage claim areas, or by calling 757-6840 or 800-451-0455. *Newark International Airport–New York City Mini Bus Service* (phone: 201-961-2535) is yet another alternative. It takes passengers from Newark to midtown Manhattan hotels for $12.

New York Helicopter (phone: 800-645-3494) offers daily flights from midtown's 34th Street Heliport to JFK or Newark in 10 minutes. One-way fare is $67 plus tax.

Pan Am's Water Shuttle (phone: 718-803-6600) sails hourly from Pier 11 at South and Wall Streets to La Guardia's Marine Air Terminal; the fare is $20 one way.

Bus – New York City buses run frequently. There are more than 220 routes and over 3,800 buses in operation. Although considerably slower than subways, buses bring you closer to your destination, stopping about every 2 blocks. The main routes in Manhattan are north-south on the avenues, and east-west (crosstown) on the streets, as well as some crisscross and circular routes. Check both the sign on the front of the bus and the one at the bus stop to make sure the bus you want stops where you are waiting. Be sure to have exact change for the fare, or, preferably, a subway token. It amounts to $1.15, no matter the length of your trip, and ask for a transfer, should you need one, when you board the bus. *Bus drivers do not make change, nor do they accept bills; but they do accept tokens.* Most bus routes operate 24 hours a day, 7 days a week, but a few do not run late at night or on Sundays. For information on buses to points outside Manhattan from the Port Authority Bus Terminal, call 564-8484. Free bus maps are available at Grand Central and Penn Stations or by sending a self-addressed, stamped #10 envelope to the *New York Transit Authority,* Room 875, 370 Jay St., Brooklyn, NY 11201, Attn.: Maps. For information, call 718-330-1234.

Subways – The New York subway system has a reputation for being dangerous, dirty, and confusing. The reality is not quite so harrowing as most people fear. The past 2 years have brought some new trains, tracks, and station improvements to this extensive underground network. Statistically, your chances of arriving at your destination unscathed are much better than they are aboveground. Its convenience and speed can't be duplicated by any other form of transportation, and the intelligence of its overall design is awesome. Pick up a free subway map at any token booth or at the New York Convention and Visitors Bureau.

Basically, there are three different subway lines, with express and local routes serving all city boroughs except for Staten Island (reached via the Staten Island Ferry). The most extensive line is the *IRT,* which originates in Brooklyn and traverses Manhattan en route to the Bronx. The *IRT* has two main divisions: the 7th Avenue line, which serves the West Side of Manhattan, and the Lexington Avenue line, which covers the

East Side. You can go from east to west (crosstown) on the shuttle (S) or *IRT* No. 7 train (which goes to Flushing, Queens) between Grand Central Station and Times Square, and the L train will get you crosstown at 14th Street. The *IND* serves Brooklyn, Queens, Manhattan, and the Bronx. The *BMT* serves Brooklyn, Queens, and Manhattan. The subway is the most heavily used means of city transportation (almost 4 million people ride it daily on 230 miles of track) and is mobbed during rush hours, weekdays from 7:30 to 9 AM and from 4:30 to 7 PM. The fare on New York City subways (and the Roosevelt Island tramway) is $1.15, no matter how far you travel. Tokens are required. Buy them at booths in the subway stations, and insert them in turnstiles to gain access to the trains. Buy a 10-pack of tokens to save time. The subway system operates 24 hours a day, although some schedules are cut back during the hours between midnight and 6 AM. At night, the lights outside many stations indicate accessibility: A red light means the station is closed; a yellow light indicates that a token is required for entry (no clerk on duty at the token booth); and a green light means both the station and token booth are fully open. For further information, call the *NY Transit Authority* (phone: 718-330-1234).

Car Rental – New York is served by all the major car rental companies as well as a host of small local firms.

Taxi – The handiest and most expensive way to get around the city is by cab. Cabs can be hailed almost anywhere and are required to pick you up and deliver you to your specified destination. Cabs can be identified by their yellow color and are available if the center portion of their roof light is on (if the *entire* roof light is on, it indicates that the cab is either off-duty or on call). Cabbies expect about a 20% tip. There is a 50¢ surcharge on some cab fares between 8 PM and 6 AM and all day on Sundays. New York also has dozens of services that provide sedans that can be called (known locally as "call cabs"). Fares run somewhere between yellow street cabs and limousines: among the companies that accept cash calls are *Dialcar* (phone: 718-743-8383); *Inta Boro* (phone: 344-4763); and *Love* (phone: 718-633-3338).

 VITAL SERVICES: Audiovisual Equipment – *Ace Sound Rental Co.* (13 E. 31st St.; phone: 685-3344); *Select Audio Visual* (902 Broadway at E. 20th St.; phone: 598-9800).

Baby-sitting – Ask at your hotel desk for recommended baby-sitting services.

Business Services – *QED Transcription Service* (phone: 563-0740) or *Wordflow* (phone: 725-5111) for taping and immediate transcription of meetings and seminars.

Dry Cleaner/Tailor – *S & A Cleaners & Tailors* (134½ E. 62nd St.; phone: 838-0630); *Newman Cleaners & Dyers* (914 7th Ave., between 57th and 58th Sts.; phone: 247-5207).

Limousine Service – *London Town Cars* (phone: 988-9700 or 800-221-4009, outside New York City); *Fugazy* (phone: 661-0100); *Chauffeurs Unlimited* (phone: 362-5354); *Gotham Limousine* (phone: 868-8860 or 800-227-7997); *Sotto Car and Limo Service* (phone: 431-9090 or 800-441-7646).

Mechanic – *Express Auto* (276 7th Ave.; phone: 242-5811); *Great Bear of the Garden* (363 W. 30th St.; phone: 563-4680). Both provide 24-hour road service and repairs.

Medical Emergency – *St. Luke's–Roosevelt Hospital Center* (428 W. 59th St. at 9th Ave.; phone: 523-4000); *Bellevue Hospital* (E. 27th St. at 1st Ave.; phone: 561-4347); *New York University Medical Center* (550 1st Ave.; phone: 340-7300); *St. Vincent's Hospital and Medical Center of New York* (7th Ave. and W. 11th St.; phone: 790-7000); *Lenox Hill Hospital* (100 E. 77th St.; phone: 439-2345); *Mount Sinai Hospital* (100th St. at Madison Ave.; phone: 241-6500).

Messenger Services – *Archer Courier Systems,* 24-hour service (phone: 563-8800); *Accurate Messenger Service* (phone: 688-5450).

National/International Courier – *Federal Express* (phone: 777-6500); *DHL Worldwide Courier Express* (phone: 718-917-8000).

Pharmacy – *Kaufman-Beverly Pharmacy,* open 24 hours, 557 Lexington Ave. at E. 50th St. (phone: 755-2266).

Photocopies – *Copyquick* (49½ E. 44th St.; phone: 983-5122); *Amal Printing* (630 5th Ave. in Rockefeller Center; phone: 247-3270); *Commerce Photo-Print Corp.,* open late and weekends by appointment (106 Fulton St., Wall Street area; phone: 269-2755).

Post Office – The central office has a 24-hour information window, at 33rd St. and 8th Ave. (phone: 967-8585).

Professional Photographer – *Matar Studio,* 101 Maiden La. (phone: 227-1792).

Secretary/Stenographer – *Esquire Reporting* (phone: 687-8010); *A Steno Service* (phone: 682-4990); *Ann H. Tanners Co.* (phone: 687-2870).

Teleconference Facilities – *New York Hilton, Waldorf-Astoria* (see *Best in Town,* below).

Translator – *Berlitz* (phone: 777-7878); *Lawyers & Merchants* (phone: 344-2930); *Lindner Translations* (phone: 269-4660).

Typewriter Rental – *Comet Office Products Center,* 2-week minimum (phone: 679-7004); *Circle Office Products,* office tables and chairs also, weekly rate only (phone: 265-4550).

Western Union/Telex – Many offices are located around the city (phone: 344-8910).

Other – *HQ, Headquarters Company,* word processing, telex, facsimile, conference rooms (phone: 949-0722); *International Conference Group,* meeting and conference planners (phone: 848-9200); *ETX Corp.,* simultaneous teleprocessing (phone: 557-5100); *L. Matthew Miller,* videotaping of meetings (phone: 741-8011); *Video Monitoring Service,* for broadcast information, tapes, and transcripts (phone: 736-2010); *Abet Rent-a-Fur* (phone: 989-5757); *Manhattan Passport,* a private concierge service providing travel arrangements and customized shopping and sightseeing tours, among other services (phone: 744-0203).

SPECIAL EVENTS: January–February, *Chinese New Year Celebration and Dragon Parade,* Chinatown; March 17, *St. Patrick's Day Parade,* Fifth Ave.; *Easter Sunday, Easter Parade,* Fifth Ave.; May, *Ninth Avenue International Festival;* May, *Washington Square Outdoor Art Show,* Greenwich Village; first Sunday in June, *Puerto Rican Day Parade,* Fifth Ave.; June, *JVC Jazz Festival,* throughout city; July 4th — *Macy's* fireworks along the East River; the 1992 *Democratic National Convention* will take place July 13-16 at the *Hilton* hotel; July–August, free *Shakespeare Festival, Delacorte Theater,* Central Park, and free performances, *NY Philharmonic, Metropolitan Opera,* all boroughs; August, *Harlem Week;* late August–September, *US Open Tennis Championships, USTA National Tennis Center,* Queens; September, *African-American Day Parade;* September, the 10-day *Festival of San Gennaro,* patron saint of the Neapolitans, Mulberry St., Little Italy; September–October, *New York Film Festival, Lincoln Center;* October, *Columbus Day Parade,* Fifth Ave.; October 31, *Halloween Parade,* Greenwich Village; November, *NYC Marathon;* November, *Veterans Day Parade;* November, *Macy's Thanksgiving Day Parade,* Broadway, Herald Square; December, *Christmas Tree Lighting,* Rockefeller Plaza; November–January, the *Great Christmas Show, Radio City Music Hall.*

For borough-by-borough information on parades, festivals, exhibits, and free events, call 360-1333 (Manhattan); 718-783-4469 (Brooklyn);

590-3500 (Bronx); 718-447-4485 (Staten Island); and 718-291-ARTS (Queens).

 MUSEUMS: The city boasts more than 150 museums. In addition to those described in *Special Places,* other notable New York museums include the following:

American Craft Museum – 40 W. 53rd St. (phone: 956-6047).

Asia Society – Changing exhibits of both ancient and contemporary Asian art. 725 Park Ave. at 70th St. (phone: 288-6400).

Center for African Art – 52-54 E. 68th St. (phone: 861-1200).

Cooper-Hewitt Museum – The *National Museum of Design* branch of the *Smithsonian Institution,* featuring a full range of decorative arts. 2 E. 91st St. (phone: 860-6868).

Forbes Magazine Galleries – World's largest collection of Fabergé Imperial *Easter* eggs, plus toy boats and soldiers. 62 Fifth Ave. at 12th St. (phone: 206-5548).

Frick Collection – The Pittsburgh industrialist Henry Clay Frick's collection of paintings, sculpture, porcelain, furniture, and antiques housed in a magnificent mansion. 1 E. 70th St. at Fifth Ave. (phone: 288-0700).

Guinness World of Records – In the Empire State Building, 350 Fifth Ave. (phone: 947-2335).

International Center of Photography – 1130 Fifth Ave. at 94th St. (phone: 860-1777) and 1133 6th Ave. at 43rd St. (phone: 768-4683).

Intrepid Sea–Air Space Museum – World War II aircraft carrier has exhibits on the Navy, pioneers of aviation, and technology. Permanently moored at Pier 86 in the Hudson River, W. 46th St. at 12th Ave. (phone: 245-0072 or 245-2533).

Jewish Museum – Housing a permanent collection of more than 14,000 artifacts, the exhibits cover 4,000 years of Jewish history. Closed Fridays and Saturdays. 1109 Fifth Ave. at 92nd St. (phone: 860-1888).

Lower East Side Tenement Museum – America's first urban "living history" museum. 97 Orchard St. (phone: 431-1889).

Museo del Barrio – Hispanic art. 1230 Fifth Ave. at 104th St. (phone: 831-7272).

Museum of American Folk Art – Columbus Ave. at 66th St. (phone: 977-7298).

Museum of the American Indian – 3753 Broadway at W. 155th St. (phone: 283-2420).

Museum of Broadcasting – A collection of over 40,000 radio and television programs and commercials. Drop by and relive a classic radio or television show. 1 E. 53rd St. (phone: 752-7684).

Museum of the City of New York – Free multimedia show "The Big Apple." Fifth Ave. at 103rd St. (phone: 534-0581).

Museum of Holography – 11 Mercer St. (phone: 925-0526).

New York Historical Society – 170 Central Park West at W. 77th St. (phone: 873-3400).

Noguchi Museum – This garden museum features more than 300 of Isamu Noguchi's works, including sculptures from stone, clay, and wood, paper lamps, and work plans for fountains and playgrounds. 32-37 Vernon Blvd., Long Island City, Queens (phone: 718-204-7088).

Pierpont Morgan Library – Old Masters drawings, early printed books, and music manuscripts, plus a public research library. 29 E. 36th St. at Madison Ave. (phone: 685-0610).

Whitney Museum of American Art – Permanent and changing exhibits of contemporary American art, including film and video exhibits and gallery talks. 945 Madison Ave. at E. 75th St. (phone: 570-3676). Branches in the Philip Morris Building (120 Park Ave. at E. 42nd St.;

phone: 878-2550) and at Equitable Center (787 7th Ave. at W. 51st St.; phone: 554-1113).

MAJOR COLLEGES AND UNIVERSITIES: New York City has a variety of leading institutions of higher education, some offering a broad-based liberal arts curriculum, others concentrating in areas of specialization, and all of them enriching New York as a center of culture and learning. Among them are Barnard College (Broadway at W. 117th St.; phone: 854-5262); Brooklyn College (Bedford Ave. and Ave. H; phone: 718-780-5485); the City College of City University (Convent Ave. at W. 138th St.; phone: 650-7000); Columbia University (Broadway and W. 116th St.; phone: 854-1754); Cooper Union (3rd Ave. and 7th St.; phone: 254-6300); Fashion Institute of Technology (227 W. 27th St. between 7th and 8th Aves.; phone: 760-7700); Fordham University (Columbus Ave. at W. 60th St.; phone: 841-5100, and E. Fordham Rd. at 3rd Ave., Bronx; phone: 579-2000); Hunter College (695 Park Ave.; phone: 772-4000); Jewish Theological Seminary of America (Broadway at W. 122nd St.; phone: 678-8000); Juilliard School of Music (Lincoln Center Plaza; phone: 799-5000); Mannes College of Music (105 W. 85th St.; phone: 580-0210); Marymount Manhattan College (221 E. 71st St.; phone: 517-0400); New School for Social Research (66 W. 12th St.; phone: 741-5600); New York Institute of Technology (1855 Broadway at 61st St.; phone: 399-8300); New York University (Washington Sq.; phone: 998-1212); Pace University (1 Pace Plaza; phone: 346-1200); Parsons School of Design (Fifth Ave. at 12th St.; phone: 741-8900); Pratt Institute (200 Willoughby Ave., Brooklyn; phone: 718-636-3600); Queens College (65-30 Kissena Blvd., Flushing, Queens; phone: 718-520-7000); Union Theological Seminary (3041 Broadway at Reinhold Niebuhr Pl. — W. 120th St.; phone: 662-7100); University of St. John's (Jamaica, Queens; phone: 718-990-6750); and Yeshiva University (500 W. 185th St. at Amsterdam Ave.; phone: 960-5400).

SHOPPING: This city is like no other for acquiring material possessions. It is the commercial center and the fashion capital of the country, and styles that originate here set the trends for fashionable folk from Portland, Maine, to Portland, Oregon. The scope of merchandise available approaches the infinite, and there's a price range for every budget.

Bloomingdale's, **A World unto Itself** – Known affectionately to New Yorkers as "Bloomie's" and considered by many to be the ultimate in Upper East Side chic; it's lost some of its cachet, though many still flock here. Whether you want satin running shorts or a sequined evening gown, you'll find it here. Saturdays on the main floor are something of a social event, particularly for suburban teenagers. E. 59th St. between Lexington and 3rd Aves. (phone: 355-5900 or 705-2073).

Antiques – Antiques Row is a district extending from 10th Street to 14th Street and west from Broadway to University Place. Many previously wholesale-only stores recently have opened to the public. Try *Howard Kaplan Antiques* (827 Broadway; phone: 674-1000) for Belle Epoque antiques. For French and continental 18th- and 19th-century furniture, *Reymer-Jourdan Antiques* (43 E. 10th St.; phone: 674-4470) is a good bet. Collectors of toy soldiers and miniatures should visit *Classic Toys* (69 Thompson St.; phone: 941-9129). Uptown, *Arts & Antiques* (1050 2nd Ave. at 56th St.; phone: 355-4400) has the largest and finest antiques center with a rich selection of clocks, jewelry, and furniture from around the world, in 104 galleries. *Place des Antiquaires* (125 E. 57th St.; phone: 758-2900) is a multi-level center of international art and antiques specializing in Art Nouveau, Art Deco, and Russian icons.

Bookstores – The publishing capital of the world, New York is a bibliophile's delight. Leaders among its outlets include *Barnes and Noble* (105 Fifth Ave. at 18th St.; phone: 807-0099; and 600 Fifth Ave. at 48th

St.; phone: 765-0590; and several other locations), which carries a wide selection at bargain prices. *B. Dalton* (666 Fifth Ave. at W. 52nd St.; phone: 247-1740; and at two other Manhattan locations), open daily, and *Doubleday* (724 Fifth Ave. at 56th St.; phone: 397-0550) carry a broad variety of new titles and trade books. The *Strand* (828 Broadway at E. 12th St.; phone: 473-1452) has 8 miles of shelves of old and used books and even some rare manuscripts. For an unusual selection of out of print books in an out-of-the-way location, visit *Isaac Mendoza Book Co.* (15 Ann St.; phone: 227-8777). *Rizzoli* (31 W. 57th St.; phone: 759-2424; and 454A W. Broadway; phone: 674-1616) is best known for its collection of art, music, and photography books. *Gotham Book Mart* (41 W. 47th St.; phone: 719-4448) specializes in contemporary literature and poetry, and sells books on theater and film. *Kitchen Arts & Letters* (1435 Lexington Ave. at E. 93rd St.; phone: 876-5550) is a bookstore and gallery exclusively devoted to food and wine. *Forbidden Planet* (821 Broadway at E. 12th St.; phone: 473-1576; with a branch at 227 E. 59th St.; phone: 751-4386) has the wackiest bunch of comics, science fiction, masks, and monsters you're liable to find this side of Mars. *New York Astrology Center* (63 W. 38th St., 5th Floor; phone: 719-2919) claims to have the country's largest selection of books on astrology. The *Complete Traveller Bookstore* (199 Madison at 35th St.; phone: 679-4339) and *Traveller's Bookstore* (75 Rockefeller Plaza at W. 52nd St.; phone: 664-0995) have enviable troves of travel literature. Architecture buffs should head to *Perimeter* (146 Sullivan St.; phone: 529-2275). And bookish-minded toddlers will be delighted by *Eeyore's Books for Children* (25 E. 83rd St.; phone: 988-3404; and 2212 Broadway at W. 79th St.; phone: 362-0634).

Boutiques and Specialty Shops – Fifth Avenue in the East Fifties and Madison Avenue in the East Sixties and Seventies are lined with boutiques that carry haute couture at haute prix, but looking is free. The names are an encyclopedia of style: *Versace, Kenzo, Sonia Rykiel, Daniel Hechter, Emanuel Ungaro, Saint Laurent, Armani, Valentino, Gucci, Tahari, Jaeger, Chanel,* and the like. Also on the cutting edge of fashion are the styles at *Charivari Workshop* (441 Columbus Ave. at W. 81st St.; phone: 496-8700; and at five other locations around town). For casual Italian sweaters in the latest styles, visit one of the city's many *Benetton* stores (there are a few on Fifth Avenue in the forties). For the finest in raincoats, there's *Burberrys* (9 E. 57th St.; phone: 371-5010) and *Aquascutum of London* (680 Fifth Ave. at E. 54th St.; phone: 975-0250). *Ashanti* (872 Lexington Ave. at E. 65th St.; phone: 535-0740) specializes in stylish clothes for larger women. Recent Parisian newcomer *Galeries Lafayette* (10 W. 57th; no phone at press time) adds French flair to the neighborhood with its collection of tony womenswear. *Polo/Ralph Lauren* (867 Madison Ave. at 72nd St.; phone: 606-2100), in the 19th-century Rhinelander Mansion, is a showcase for the designer's men's, women's, and boys' collections, as is *Louis, Boston* (131 E. 57th St.; phone: 308-6100). *Fendi* (720 Fifth Ave. at 56th St.; phone: 767-0100) features their exclusive label leather goods and clothes.

Indoor urban malls are a recent phenomenon in New York City; they arrived in 1984 with the glitzy *Trump Tower* (725 Fifth Ave. between 56th and 57th Sts.). The tenants in the tower's 6-story marble and mirrored atrium are among the world's most opulent (and most expensive) vendors: *Abercrombie & Fitch, Kenneth Jay Lane* (tony costume jewelry, including his "Barbara Bush" pearls), *Asprey's, Buccellati* (silversmiths), *Charles Jourdan* (men's and women's shoes), and *Martha* (for women's fashions).

Herald Center spans the block between West 33rd and 34th Streets on 7th Avenue; about 70 retail and restaurant outlets are in operation. The directory is far less exclusive than *Trump Tower*'s, but many prestigious names are in residence, such as *Ann Taylor, Alfred Dunhill,* and *Charles Jourdan.*

In lower Manhattan, Pier 17 at the *South Street Seaport* is another shopper's paradise.

China, Crystal, and Porcelain – *Villeroy & Boch* (974 Madison Ave. at 76th St.; phone: 535-2500), the 240-year-old European company, has just opened a retail store carrying a full line of elegant tableware. *Royal Copenhagen* (683 Madison at 61st St.; phone: 759-6457) has all that's best in contemporary crystal, porcelain, and their traditional blue and white fluted design. And for splendid glass sculpture, bowls, trays, and goblets, head for *Steuben Glass* (715 Fifth Ave. at 56th St.; phone: 752-1441).

Department Stores – *Macy's* (Broadway at 34th St.; phone: 695-4400) is the quintessential New York department store. You can buy what you need and choose from a large assortment of high-quality, stylish goods, but most people come here for the total experience of shopping — browsing, watching, and buying. *Macy's* basement emporium, the Cellar, is designed as a street lined with shops that carry everything from fruits and vegetables to housewares, and restaurants, including the *Cellar Grill*, which serves a variety of pizza, pasta, and grilled meats. *Lord & Taylor* (Fifth Ave. and 39th St.; phone: 391-3344) has stylish, rather conservative clothing and a bright, airy atmosphere that makes browsing enjoyable. *Saks Fifth Avenue* (Fifth Ave. and 49th St.; phone: 753-4000), newly renovated, is where you can be sure to get whatever is chic this season. *Bergdorf Goodman* (Fifth Ave. and 58th St.; phone: 753-7300) is the epitome of elegant shopping. In some haute couture salons, you sit in a parlor overlooking Central Park while salespeople bring merchandise for you to examine, then escort you to the fitting room. *Henri Bendel* (712 Fifth Ave.; phone: 247-1100) carries an impressive selection of trendy clothes, accessories, and miscellany at its elegant new location. *Barney's for Women* (7th Ave. at W. 17th St.; phone: 929-9000) is a major fashion player. *Abraham and Straus* (33rd St. at 6th Ave.; phone: 594-8500; and 420 Fulton St. in downtown Brooklyn; phone: 718-875-7200) carries a complete stock of moderately priced goods.

Jewelry and Gems – Diamonds are a girl's best friend, they say, and so as not to limit ourselves, we'll include emeralds, rubies, sapphires, gold, silver, and other precious metals. And so as not to discriminate, we'll include men, too. Without a doubt, the most famous of all luxury emporiums is *Tiffany & Co.* (727 Fifth Ave. at 57th St.; phone: 755-8000). If you must have something from *Tiffany's* but can't afford a necklace or ring, you can purchase a novelty like a silver bookmark or toothpaste roller. Across the street, *Bulgari* dazzles in its new prestigious corner boutique (5th Ave. and 57th St.; phone: 315-9000). *Harry Winston* (718 Fifth Ave. at 56th St.; phone: 245-2000) has display cases, but most of the jewels are kept in an inner sanctum. After conferring with a salesperson, the items you wish to see are brought for your inspection. *Cartier* (653 Fifth Ave. at 52nd St.; phone: 753-0111; and in *Trump Tower*; phone: 308-0840) is renowned for highly polished silver and some of the world's finest jewelry and accessories. *Fortunoff* (681 Fifth Ave., between 53rd and 54th; phone: 758-6660) has a variety of fine gems, sterling, gold, and porcelain in a wide range of prices. For bold Brazilian jewelry, stop in at *H. Stern Jewellers* (645 Fifth Ave. at 51st St.; phone: 688-0300; and also at several hotels). *Fred Leighton* (773 Madison at 66th St.; phone: 288-1872) is known for its exquisite antique and Art Deco designs. Known for quality and quantity in pearls is *Mikimoto* (608 Fifth Ave. at 49th St.; phone: 586-7153). Other noted jewelers are *David Webb* (445 Park Ave.; phone: 421-3030); *Van Cleef & Arpels* (744 Fifth Ave. at 57th St.; phone: 644-9500); *Black, Starr & Frost* (in the *Plaza Hotel*, Fifth Ave. at 59th St.; phone: 838-0720); and for watches, *Tourneau Corner* (500 Madison Ave. at E. 52nd St.; phone: 758-3265 and at Madison Ave. and 59th St.; phone: 758-6688).

If your budget is limited, do your gem shopping along 47th Street (the street sign here reads: "Diamond and Jewelry Way") between 5th and 6th Avenues. This is the heart of New York's wholesale jewelry district, and the best place to find sparkling stuff at mortal prices. And if you're planning to get married (or even reaffirm your vows), *1873 Unusual Wedding Bands* (Booth 86 at the *National Jewelers Exchange,* 4 W. 47th St.; phone: 221-1873) is a good place to stop; it has the largest collection of wedding rings in the city.

Kitchen Equipment – The Bowery is New York's kitchenware and lamp district, where large wholesale houses such as the *Federal Restaurant Supply Co.* (202 Bowery St.; phone: 226-0441) offer some commercial products at very reasonable prices. The *Bridge Co.* (214 E. 52nd St. at 3rd Ave.; phone: 688-4220) has 4 floors of kitchenware. You can find every possible domestic and imported item here, from cherry pitters to egg slicers. Selecting a single pot or pan could occupy several hours or a full day, given the number and variety on display. *Broadway Panhandler* has an enormous selection of cookware at affordable prices (520 Broadway at Spring St.; 966-3434). *Williams-Sonoma* (20 E. 60th St.; phone: 980-5155), of catalogue fame, has first-rate cookware and master chefs often do cooking demonstrations on the premises.

Luggage and Leather Goods – You'll have no trouble finding a wide selection of high- and low-priced luggage and leather goods in New York. *Hermès* (11 E. 57th St.; phone: 751-3181) is known the world over for spectacular silk scarves and ties, saddles and other fine leather goods in a variety of exotic skins, all at heart-stopping prices. *Louis Vuitton* (51 E. 57th St.; phone: 371-6111) has a large selection of leather goods (made in France) sporting the famous "LV" logo. However, if you prefer interlocking "G"s, visit *Gucci* (685 and 689 Fifth Ave. at 54th St.; phone: 826-2600). Another Italian wonder is *Bottega Veneta,* which is equally pricey (635 Madison Ave.; phone: 319-0303). For elegant, high-quality merchandise that's only slightly less costly, try *Crouch & Fitzgerald* (400 Madison Ave. at E. 48th St.; phone: 755-5888); *Mark Cross* (645 Fifth Ave. at 51st St.; phone: 421-3000); or *T. Anthony* (480 Park Ave. at E. 58th St.; phone: 750-9797). Along less expensive lines, you will run into several reasonable leather goods and luggage stores during your strolls around the West Side and the Lower East Side.

Men's Clothes – Manhattan has fashions to fit every man's taste, from the ultra-expensive glitzy chic at *Bijan* (by appointment only; 699 Fifth Ave. between 54th and 55th Sts.; phone: 758-7500), to *Billy Martin's Western Wear* (812 Madison Ave. at E. 68th St.; phone: 861-3100). *Brooks Brothers* (346 Madison Ave. at E. 44th St.; phone: 682-8800; and 1 Liberty Plaza downtown; phone: 267-2400), *Chipp Clothier* (342 Madison Ave., phone: 687-0850), *J. Press* (16 E. 44th St.; phone: 687-7642), and *F. R. Tripler* (366 Madison Ave. at E. 46th St.; phone: 922-1090) all offer expensive, high-quality conservative business suits and other classic menswear. *St. Laurie* (897 Broadway at E. 20th St.; phone: 473-0100) carries similar merchandise with slightly lower price tags. *Paul Stuart* (Madison Ave. at E. 45th St.; phone: 682-0320) offers an expensive but more *GQ* collection of top-quality clothing, while *Barney's* (106 7th Ave. at W. 17th St.; phone: 929-9000) has an eclectic array of goods that ranges from Hickey Freeman and Bill Blass to all the top European designers. For Italian alta moda in SoHo, try *Di Mitri* (110 Greene St.; phone: 431-1090). *Beau Brummel* (1130 Madison Ave. between 83rd and 84th Sts.; phone: 737-4200 and two other locations;) has everything for the fashion-conscious man. *Syms* (45 Park Place; phone: 792-1199) stocks fine discounted menswear on 5 floors. *Bergdorf Goodman Men* is the newest bastion for male chic (Fifth Ave. at 59th St.; phone: 753-7300).

Poster and Print Shops – *The Old Print Shop* (150 Lexington Ave. at E. 29th St.; phone: 683-3950) has a huge collection of early American prints, watercolors, and paintings ranging in price from $10 to $20,000. For contemporary theater posters and some collector's items, try the

Triton Gallery (323 W. 45th St., between 8th and 9th Aves.; phone: 765-2472). Rare movie posters are available at *Poster America* (138 W. 18th St.; phone: 206-0499) and *Jerry Ohlinger's* (242 W. 14th St.; phone: 989-0869). The *Gallery at Lincoln Center* (136 W. 65th St.; phone: 877-1800) has the largest collection of limited edition paintings and photographs celebrating the performing arts — dance, theater, and opera — plus the List Collection of original silk-screen posters.

Records and Tapes – There are a number of places where you can get good prices. *Tower Records* (692 Broadway and E. 4th St.; phone: 505-1500; and 1965 Broadway and 66th St.; phone: 799-2500) is the world's largest record store and is open until midnight every day of the year. *Sam Goody's* (51 W. 51st St.; phone: 246-8730; 666 3rd Ave. at E. 43rd St.; phone: 986-8480; and 220 East 42nd St., near the UN; phone: 490-0568) stocks new labels, classical, jazz, and foreign music as well as audio equipment. Two chain stores, *King Karol* and *Disc-o-mat,* carry a lot of labels at prices lower than standard retail stores. *Disc-o-mat's* main store is at 716 Lexington Ave. at E. 58th St. (phone: 826-3500). *King Karol's* main store is at 1521 3rd Ave. at 85th St. (phone: 988-9557). *J&R Music World* (33 Park Row; phone: 349-0062) has the best selection of new and hard-to-find jazz records at good prices. *House of Oldies* (35 Carmine St.; phone: 243-0500) specializes in discs from the past. *Gryphon Record Shop* (251 W. 72nd St., between Broadway and West End Ave.; phone: 874-1588) has 60,000 out of print records. *Colony Records* (Broadway and 49th St.; phone: 265-2050) or *Actors' Heritage* (262 W. 44th St.; phone: 944-7490), both have a well-edited selection of music, most notably Broadway cast albums. *HMV* (1200 Lexington St.; phone: 348-0800) has an excellent selection of jazz, blues, gospel, rock, pop, New Age, and comedy.

Sheets and Pillowcases – For good buys on top-brand and designer sheets and pillowcases, New York is definitely the place. At *Ezra Cohen* (307 Grand St.; phone: 925-7800) and *H & G Cohen Bedding Co.* (306 Grand St.; phone: 226-0818), you can find all the major brands at a 25% to 30% discount. *J. Shachter* (85 Ludlow St.; phone: 533-1150) specializes in making comforters from any fabric you wish. (All are closed Saturdays and open Sundays, typical of the stores on the Lower East Side.) *D. Porthault* (18 E. 69th St.; phone: 688-1660) is the French master of extraordinary table and bed linen in magnificent flower prints; *Sheridan Linens* (595 Madison Ave.; phone: 308-0120) sells fine bed linen from Australia, and is noted for design and color. *Descamps* (723 Madison Ave. between 63rd and 64th Sts.; phone: 355-2522) is another good shop for elegant French imports. *Léron* (750 Madison Ave.; phone: 753-6700), imports fine bed and table linen and lingerie.

Shoes – All of the expensive, top shoe designers are represented: *Ferragamo* (730 Fifth Ave. at 57th St., for men; phone: 246-6211; and 717 Fifth Ave. at 56th St., for women; phone: 759-3822); *Bally of Switzerland* (711 Fifth Ave. between 55th and 56th Sts.; phone: 751-9082; and at three other Manhattan locations for men; and 689 Madison Ave. at E. 62nd St., for women; phone: 751-2163); *Bruno Magli* (535 Madison Ave., for men only; phone: 752-7900); *Charles Jourdan* (725 Fifth Ave. in *Trump Tower;* phone: 644-3830; and 769 Madison Ave. at E. 66th St.; phone: 628-0133); *Carrano* (677 Fifth Ave.; phone: 752-6111, and 750 Madison Ave. at E. 65th St.; phone: 570-9020); and *Maud Frizon* (49 E. 57th St.; phone: 980-1460). For well-made men's boots and shoes, stock up at *McCreedy & Schreiber* (37 W. 46th St. between 5th and 6th Aves.; phone: 719-1552; and 213 E. 59th St. between 2nd and 3rd Aves.; phone: 759-9241). *Susan Bennis Warren Edwards* (22 W. 57th St.; phone: 755-4197) has outré American shoes. For the ultimate in fine leather, Italian walking shoes, and boots, for both men and women, go to *Tanino Crisci* (660 Madison Ave.; phone: 308-7778). Another venerable shop for Italian shoes and handbags is *Gucci* (685 Fifth Ave.; phone: 826-2600).

Sporting Goods – The most elegant sporting goods store is *Abercrombie & Fitch* (South Street Seaport; phone: 809-9000; and at *Trump Tower;* phone: 832-1001). *Herman's* (110 Nassau; phone: 233-0733; 135 W. 42nd St.; phone: 730-7400; 39 W. 34th St.; phone: 279-8900; and 845 3rd Ave. at E. 53rd St.; phone: 688-4603), New York's best-known sporting goods chain, has everything, but *Paragon* (867 Broadway at E. 18th St.; phone: 255-8036) says it has more, and at better prices. At either one, you can find just about every piece of sporting gear and wear under the sun. Serious joggers should stop in at the *Super Runners Shop* (*Herald Center,* at 7th Ave. between 33rd and 34th Sts.; phone: 564-9190) and three other locations. *Gerry Cosby's* (3 Penn Plaza; phone: 563-6464) outfits professional teams and offers top-of-the-line sporting goods and souvenirs. *Orvis* (355 Madison Ave.; phone: 697-3133) has fishing and hunting gear.

Thrift Shops – Most thrift shops carry a variety of merchandise, from men's and women's clothing to household items and appliances to furniture. The best area for thrifting in New York is the upper East Eighties along 1st, 2nd, and 3rd Aves. Unfortunately, many of the secondhand clothes stores in New York carry the price tags of fine antiques stores. Some interesting places to try are *Stuyvesant Square Thrift Shop* (1704 2nd Ave. at E. 96th St.; phone: 831-1830); *Irvington House Thrift Shop* (1534 2nd Ave. at E. 80th St.; phone: 879-4555); *Thrift Shop East* (336 E. 86th St. between 1st and 2nd Aves.; phone: 772-6868); and *Spence-Chapin Thrift Shop* (1430 3rd Ave. at E. 80th St.; phone: 737-8448).

Toys – Once immersed in the enchanting world of children's toys at *FAO Schwarz* (GM Bldg., Fifth Ave. at 58th St.; phone: 644-9400), adults have as difficult a time as children leaving empty-handed. It has every kind of toy — from precious antiques and mechanical spaceships to simple construction sets and building blocks. The prices are very high. The *Last Wound-Up* has wind-up toys in every shape, color, and size imaginable (889 Broadway; phone: 529-4197; and 290 Columbus Ave.; phone: 787-3388). *Penny Whistle Toys,* part-owned by Meredith Brokaw (wife of news anchor Tom Brokaw), has several locations offering everything from puppets and bubble machines to wooden blocks and educational toys (448 Columbus Ave.; phone: 873-9090; 1283 Madison Ave.; phone: 369-3868). The *Enchanted Forest* (85 Mercer; phone: 925-6677) and *Toy Park* (626 Columbus Ave.; phone: 769-3880) also have fine merchandise.

Trendy Gear – With a shift toward elegance, trendy fashions have been upgraded. Clothing with the unique combination of being both "in" and inexpensive can be found at *I. Buss* (738 Broadway; phone: 529-4655); *Parachute* (115 Wooster St.; phone: 925-8630); *Unique Clothing Warehouse* (704 Broadway between Waverly Pl. and Washington St.; phone: 674-1767); and *Camouflage* (139 8th Ave. at 17th St.; phone: 741-9118).

Uniquely New York – Probably nowhere else on earth could you find everything from earplugs to fine silver under one roof. *Hammacher Schlemmer* (147 E. 57th St. between 3rd and Lexington Aves.; phone: 421-9000), the first store to offer the pop-up toaster and microwave oven, has it all. And what it doesn't have, whether it's a *chotchka* or a real white elephant, it'll try to order. *Jenny B. Goode* (1194 Lexington Ave. at 81st St.; phone: 794-2492; and 11 E. 10th St.; phone: 505-7666) sells amusing nostalgia and contemporary adaptations (soft sculpture, mugs with gorgeous gam handles, watches disguised as giant Oreo cookies) that are a serendipitous delight. *Mythology* (370 Columbus Ave. at W. 77th St.; phone: 874-0774) has a wonderful selection of antique toys, modern robots, rubber stamps with hundreds of designs, unusual jewelry, and plastic food that looks good enough to eat. *Belle Epoch* (211 E. 60th St. at 3rd Ave.; phone: 319-7870) has very interesting tabletop antiques as well as a lovely collection of antique jewelry. *Dot Zero* (165 Fifth Ave. at 22nd St.; phone: 533-8322) is an adult toy store full of sophisticated gadgets. *Tropica* (170 E. 22nd St.; phone: 627-0808) is a kitschy island theme store with a panoply of tropical gifts.

The Annex is a flea market extraordinaire, that sells everything from antique jewelry to old books and prints to vintage clothing and decorative arts. It's held every weekend from 9 AM to 5 PM at 6th Ave. and 25th Street. *One Night Stand* rents designer gowns and accessories for formal parties, priced from $120 to $350 per evening (905 Madison Ave. at 72nd St.; phone: 772-7720). *Century 21* offers the ultimate discount experience; it's a vast, crowded emporium of European designer clothing and accessories, including Bally shoes, Valentino menswear, and Carolina Herrera dresses at as much as 50% below the retail price (22 Cortlandt St.; phone: 227-9092).

Round the world in a unique way with a trip to the *United Nations Gift Shop* (UN Bldg., 1st Ave. at E. 46th St.; phone: 754-7700), featuring handicrafts, ethnic clothing, native jewelry, indigenous toys — lots of beautiful things from many UN member states. Also visit *Liberty of London,* featuring the popular textiles and notions of one of Britain's leading stores (108 W. 39th St.; phone: 391-2150; and 630 Fifth Ave.; phone: 459-0080).

47th St. Photo (67 W. 47th St.; phone: 398-1410) is a bare-bones bargain center for cameras, computers, and other electronic gear with excellent discounts and a huge selection (some 5,000 items in stock). The tiny 2nd-floor headquarters, as well as its branches at 115 W. 45th St. and 116 Nassau St., tend to be chaotic with customers; know what you want before you go, because salespeople will not spend time helping you decide. Closed Friday afternoons and Saturdays; open Sundays.

Special Shopping Districts – The ultimate shopping experience is on the Lower East Side of Manhattan along Orchard Street, Delancey Street, and all the side streets. If you're up to it, you'll find incredible bargains in all manner of clothing and housewares; but finding them is only half the battle. Then you have to fight for them, and the haggling begins. The merchant says something along the lines of, "I couldn't give you this for a penny less than $12," to which you respond that it's not worth more than 50¢, and usually you come to terms — apparently unsatisfactory to both of you. A lot of the selling is done in a mixture of Yiddish, English, Russian, and Spanish — particularly the counting — and if you know any or all four, you'll do better than wholesale. Most stores are closed Saturdays, open Sundays. See *Special Places* for more on the Lower East Side.

 SPORTS AND FITNESS: New York is a sports-minded city, offering a great variety of spectator and participatory activities. It is the home of the *Yankees* and *Mets, Jets* and *Giants* (though the latter two play in New Jersey), *Knicks* and *Nets,* and the *Rangers, Islanders,* and the *Devils.* There are racetracks, tennis and basketball courts, bridle and bike paths, pool halls, bowling alleys, skating rinks, running tracks, and swimming pools, to name but a few venues.

Baseball – The season, April through early October, features the *Mets* (National League) at *Shea Stadium* (Flushing, Queens; phone: 718-507-8499), and the *Yankees* (American League) at *Yankee Stadium* (the Bronx; phone: 293-6000). Take the *IRT* No. 7 to the Willets Pt./Shea Stadium stop to the *Mets;* the *IRT* No. 4 or *IND* C or D trains to the 161st St. stop for the *Yankees.* Tickets usually are available at the many *Ticketron* outlets throughout the city (central ticket information, phone: 399-4444).

Basketball – The area features the *Knicks,* playing at *Madison Square*

Garden (phone: 563-8300), and the *Nets,* whose home is the *Brendan Byrne Arena* at the *Meadowlands Sports Complex* in East Rutherford, New Jersey, during the regular season from early November to late April. Buses leave from the Port Authority terminal (phone: 201-935-8500, for ticket and schedule information).

Bicycling – There are over 50 miles of bike paths in the city, with Central Park in Manhattan and Prospect Park in Brooklyn the two most popular areas. Most roadways within the parks are closed to traffic from May through October, except in rush hour on weekdays. They are closed on weekends year-round. Bikes can be rented in the parks or on nearby side streets.

Billiards and Bowling – Extremely popular with many New Yorkers. Pool halls and bowling alleys are plentiful throughout the city. Consult the yellow pages for the nearest location.

Boxing – Major bouts are still fought at *Madison Square Garden* (phone: 563-8300), and the *Daily News* continues to sponsor the *Golden Gloves* competition every winter.

Fitness Centers – *Sports/Dance/Fitness Training Institute* (428 E. 75th St.; phone: 628-6969) is a personal training center offering one-to-one training, small classes, and membership plans. Open 6:30 AM to 9 PM Monday through Friday, and by appointment on Saturdays and Sundays. On the West Side, the *Hudson Health Club,* in the *Henry Hudson* hotel, has a pool, track, steamroom, gym, and yoga and other classes (353 W. 57th St. near 9th Ave.; phone: 586-8630). Also consult the phone book for the various *Y's* around the city.

Football – During the September–December season, the *Jets* and the *Giants,* winners of the 1991 *Super Bowl,* play at *Giants Stadium* at the *Meadowlands Sports Complex* in East Rutherford, New Jersey (about 6 miles from midtown). Buses leave from the Port Authority terminal. Tickets to any of the NFL games are hard to get due to the great number of season subscribers. For *Giants* ticket information, call 201-935-8500; for *Jets* tickets, call 421-6600. Columbia University leads (in a very loose manner of speaking) the collegiate football scene, with its games played at *Baker Field* (phone: 280-2541, ext. 2546).

Golf – For up-to-date information on current golf tournaments, call the *Metropolitan Golf Assn.* (phone: 914 698-0390). The Department of Parks public information office (phone: 360-8141) can provide a complete list of public courses and how to get on them. On the unusual side, the *Midtown Golf Club* has a computer system that lets golfers practice their swing indoors. A player drives the ball into a screen (which projects different fairway views as you play), and an infrared camera above you measures the speed and angle of the drive to see where it would land if you were on an actual course. You can cover 18 holes in about 45 minutes. For more information, contact *Midtown* at 7 W. 45th St. (phone: 869-3636).

Hockey – Tickets are expensive and scarce during the early October to early April season, featuring the *Islanders,* at the *Nassau Coliseum* (phone: 516-794-9300), and the *Rangers,* at *Madison Square Garden* (phone: 563-8300). The *Devils* play at the *Meadowlands Arena* (phone: 201-935-3900).

Horseback Riding – Horses can be rented and boarded at the *Claremont Riding Academy* (175 W. 89th St. at Amsterdam Ave.; phone: 724-5100). There are almost 50 miles of bridal paths in the city, most in Central Park.

Horse Racing – Harness racing is at *Yonkers Raceway* (lower Westchester County, nightly except Sundays; phone: 562-9500) and at *Roosevelt Raceway* (Westbury, Long Island; phone: 516-222-2000). The *Meadowlands* (East Rutherford, New Jersey; phone: 201-935-8500) has both harness and flat racing nightly, except Sundays. Thoroughbreds also run during the day at *Aqueduct Race Track* (Queens; phone: 718-641-4700) or *Belmont Park Race Track* (Elmont, Long Island; phone: 718-641-4700). *Aqueduct* and *Belmont* are closed Tuesdays. Each track has a separate season; they are never open at the same time.

Ice Skating – From October to April, you can show off your figure eights at the famous Rockefeller Center rink (phone: 757-5730); from November through April at *Wollman Rink* (in Central Park; phone: 517-4800); and from early November through February at *Lasker Rink* (also in Central Park; phone: 397-3106). The small rink in front of the Rivergate Apartments (401 E. 34th St. at 1st Ave.; phone: 689-0035) is open from November through March. For information about skating conditions, call 397-3098 or 517-4800. Indoor skating year-round is at the Olympic-size *Skyrink* (450 W. 33rd St.; phone: 695-6555).

Jogging – Undoubtedly the most popular sport in New York, with enthusiastic runners in all the city parks; paths at Riverside Park (near W. 97th St.), around the Central Park Reservoir (85th St.), and the promenade along the East River (between E. 84th and 90th Sts.). It is unsafe to run at *any* of these places after dark. Either the *New York Road Runners Club* (phone: 860-4455) or New York Convention and Visitors Bureau (phone: 397-8222) can supply information on routes. The *Road Runners Club* also offers daily, guided 5-mile runs that depart at 6:30 AM from the General Sherman statue at Central Park's entrance at 59th Street, just west of Fifth Avenue, and covers scenic routes, including a lap around the Central Park reservoir. On Saturday, runners can participate in a 6-mile run that takes in such sights as Trump Tower, Rockefeller Center, the Empire State building, *Madison Square Garden,* Washington Square, SoHo, the World Trade Center, and *South Street Seaport*.

Roller Skating – Central Park on spring and summer weekends is one huge skating rink, with rentals available from *Peck & Goodie* (8th Ave. between 54th and 55th Sts.; phone: 246-6123). Don't skate in the park after dark.

Swimming – Several dozen indoor and outdoor pools are operated by the Parks Department. Indoor pools are open most of the year, except Sundays and holidays, and usually until 10 PM weekdays. Call the Parks Department public information office (phone: 360-8141) for particulars. Check the yellow pages for pools at the *YMCA* and *YMHA*.

Ocean swimming is a subway or bus ride away. Jones Beach State Park (Wantagh, Long Island, 30 miles outside the city) is the most popular. It is a beautifully maintained, enormous stretch of sandy beach, and includes surf bathing, swimming and wading pools, lockers, fishing, outdoor skating rinks, paddleball, swimming instruction, restaurants, and day- and nighttime entertainment. Beaches maintained by the city are Orchard Beach in the Bronx; Coney Island Beach and Manhattan Beach, Brooklyn; and Riis Park and Rockaway Beaches in Queens.

Tennis – Courts maintained by the Parks Dept. require a season permit. One of the larger privately owned clubs that will rent by the hour is the *Midtown Tennis Club,* 341 8th Ave. at W. 27th St. (phone: 989-8572). Check the yellow pages for other locations. The *US Open* is played at *The National Tennis Center* in Forest Hills every September.

THEATER: New York is a gold mine for the arts, and attracts the best and most accomplished talents in the world. There are devoted New York theatergoers who wouldn't dream of stepping inside a Broadway theater. They prefer instead the city's prolific off-Broadway and off-off-Broadway circuit, productions less high-powered but no less professional than the splashiest shows on Broadway. On the other hand, there are theater mavens who've never seen a performance more than 3 blocks from Times Square and who can remember every detail of the opening night of *A Chorus Line* (the final curtain came down after 6,137 performances). If their reminiscences don't have you running to the nearest box office for front-row seats to the season's biggest hit, you are made of stone.

Broadway signifies an area — New York's premier theater district, the blocks between Broadway and 9th Avenue running north of Times Square from 42nd Street — and a kind of production — the "big show" that strives to be the smash hit of the season and run forever. The glitter of the area has turned a bit tacky since the halcyon days of the Great White Way, but hopes are that a general reconstruction and renovation of 42nd Street will turn things around. In any case, the productions remain as stellar (and pricey) as ever.

Off-Broadway and off-off-Broadway signify types of theater (play-houses producing shows that qualify as off-Broadway are strewn from the Lower Village to the Upper West Side) that have developed in response to the phenomenon of Broadway. Off-Broadway productions are often smaller in scale, with newer, lesser-known talent, and are likely to feature revivals of classics or more daring works than those on Broadway. Off-off-Broadway is more experimental still, featuring truly avant-garde productions with performances in coffeehouses, lofts, or any appropriate makeshift arena. Off-Broadway often approaches the price of a Broadway ticket, though the price of a seat for an off-off-Broadway production is usually much less.

You should take advantage of all three during a visit. The excitement of a Broadway show is incomparable, but the thrill of finding a tiny theater in SoHo or the West Village in which you are almost nose to nose with the actors is undeniable. Planning your theater schedule is as easy as consulting any of the daily papers (they all list theaters and current offerings daily, with comprehensive listings on Fridays or Saturdays) or looking in the "Goings On About Town" column in *The New Yorker* or in Theater Listings in *New York* magazine, which lists current theater fare under headings of "Broadway," "Off-Broadway," and "Off-Off-Broadway."

Broadway tickets can be quite expensive (they average $30 to $60 — an occasional musical will charge as much as $100 — depending on where you sit and when you go), but that needn't be a deterrent to seeing as many shows as you can. The *TKTS* stands (47th St. at Broadway in Times Square and 2 World Trade Center in lower Manhattan; phone: 354-5800) sell tickets at half price, plus a service charge of a dollar or two, for a wide range of Broadway and off-Broadway productions; tickets are sold on the day of performance after 3 PM for evening shows, after noon for matinees. You must line up for the tickets — there are no reservations — and payment must be made in cash or traveler's checks.

To help ease the post-theater cab crush, two taxi stands operate in the Broadway area. Line up at 45th Street, west of Broadway (near Shubert Alley), and on 44th St., east of 8th Ave. (near the *St. James Theater*).

Theater Companies – *Circle Rep* (99 7th Ave. South; phone: 924-7100); *Hudson Guild Theater* (441 W. 26th St.; phone: 760-9810); *INTAR Theater* — Hispanic (420 W. 42nd St.; phone: 695-6134); *Irish Arts Center* (553 W. 51st St.; phone: 757-3318); *Jean Cocteau Repertoire* (330 Bowery; phone: 677-0060); *Jewish Repertory Theater* (344 E. 14th St.; phone: 505-2667); the *Joyce* (175 8th Ave.; phone: 242-0800); *La Mama ETC* (74A E. 4th St.; phone: 475-7710); *Manhattan Theatre Club* (*City Center,* 131 W. 55th St.; phone: 645-5590); *National Black Theatre* (2033 Fifth Ave., 2nd Floor; phone: 427-5615); *Pan Asian Repertory* (47 Great Jones St.; phone: 505-5655); *Playwrights Horizon Theater* (416 W. 42nd St.; phone: 564-1235); *The Public,* home of the *New York Shakespeare Festival* (425 Lafayette St.; phone: 598-7150); *Repertorio Español* (138 E. 27th St.; phone: 889-2850); *Ridiculous Theatrical Company* (1 Sheridan Sq.; phone: 691-2271); *Roundabout* (1530 Broadway; phone: 420-1360 or 420-1883); the *Vivian Beaumont Theater* and the *Mitzi Newhouse Theater,* both at *Lincoln Center* (phone: 239-6200); and *West-*

side Arts Theater (407 W. 43rd St.; phone: 246-6351). All can provide a schedule of offerings and performance dates. Alternatively, call the *Theatre Development Fund's* hotline (phone: 587-1111; out of state, 800-782-4369 or 800-STAGE-NY) or *New York* magazine's hotline, weekdays from 10:30 AM to 4:30 PM (phone: 880-0755). The *New York City Ballet* performs at the *New York State Theater* (phone: 870-5570). The *American Ballet Theater* presents its performances at the *Metropolitan Opera House* (phone: 362-6000). Both are located at *Lincoln Center for the Performing Arts* (Broadway and 65th St.).

MUSIC: New York is a world center for performing artists. It presents the best of classical and nonclassical traditions from all over the world, in a variety of halls and auditoriums, filled with appreciative, knowledgeable audiences.

Lincoln Center for the Performing Arts represents the city's devotion to concerts, opera, and ballet, and is on Broadway and 65th St. (general information, phone: 877-2011). It consists of *Avery Fisher Hall,* home of the *New York Philharmonic* (phone: 874-2424); *New York State Theater,* featuring the *New York City Opera* (phone: 870-5570); *Metropolitan Opera House,* for the opera (phone: 362-6000); *Damrosch Bandshell,* an open-air theater used for free concerts; the *Juilliard School* for musicians, actors, and dancers (phone: 799-5000); and *Alice Tully Hall,* home of the *Chamber Music Society* (phone: 362-1911). In addition, all the auditoriums in *Lincoln Center* present other musical events and recitals. While in the area, visit the *New York Public Library at Lincoln Center,* a unique library and museum of the performing arts (phone: 870-1630). Guided tours of *Lincoln Center* are available daily (phone: 877-1800, ext. 512).

Other major halls are *Carnegie Hall* — which celebrated its centennial in 1991 (at 57th St. and 7th Ave.; phone: 247-7800); *City Center* (131 W. 55th St.; phone: 581-7909); *Grace Rainey Rogers Auditorium* (Fifth Ave. and 82nd St.; phone: 570-3949), in the *Metropolitan Museum; Kaufmann Auditorium* (at the *92nd St. Y,* 92nd St. and Lexington Ave.; phone: 427-4410); *Symphony Space* (2537 Broadway at 95th St.; phone: 864-5400); and *Brooklyn Academy of Music* (30 Lafayette Ave.; phone: 718-636-4100). Also check music and dance listings in the newspapers *New York* and *The New Yorker* magazines. The *TKTS* booth in Times Square, which sells discount theater tickets, has a counterpart on West 42nd Street for those interested in buying half-price tickets to music and dance events on the day of the performance. The booth, open daily from noon to 7 PM, is on the 42nd Street side of Bryant Park (behind the New York Public Library, just east of 6th Ave.; phone: 382-2323).

Many pop, rock, rhythm and blues, and country artists perform at *Madison Square Garden* (7th Ave., at 33rd St.; phone: 563-8300) and at several clubs around the city. *Nassau Coliseum* (Hempstead Tpke., Uniondale, NY 11553; phone: 516-794-9300) holds large concerts on Long Island. The *Village Voice* offers a good listing of current and upcoming events.

NIGHTCLUBS AND NIGHTLIFE: The scope of nightlife in New York is as vast as the scope of daily life. Cultural trends strongly affect the kinds of clubs that are "in" at any given time and their popularity has a tendency to peak, then plunge rather quickly. Old jazz and neighborhood clubs, on the other hand, tend to remain intact, catering to a regular clientele. They offer various kinds of entertainment, and many stay open until the wee hours of the morning serving drinks and food. It is a good idea to call all the clubs in advance to find out when they are open and what shows or acts they are offering; or consult the Nightlife Directory listings in *New York* magazine. Many of the city's nightclubs with live entertainment and/or dancing have cover charges of about $10 and up; most accept major credit cards.

The current focus of the trendy crowd is on clubs that offer a kind of relaxed gentility. In addition to their lavish sound systems, many of these clubs also feature videos, live bands, several bars, and lots of room for dancing. Most popular are the *Ritz* (54th St. between 8th Ave. and Broadway; phone: 541-8900); the *Cat Club* (76 E. 13th St.; phone: 505-0090); *Limelight* (47 W. 20th St. and around the corner at 660 Sixth Ave.; phone: 807-7850), which had a face-lift that includes a cozy dining room for private parties; and the dance palace extraordinaire, the *Palladium* (126 E. 14th St.; phone: 473-7171).

One of the swankiest places in town is *Nell's* (246 W. 14th St. between 7th and 8th Aves.; phone: 675-1567). This Victorian-style nightclub has been immortalized by *People* magazine. *Warning:* It's very difficult to get in. Other trendy spots at press time include *M.K.* (204 Fifth Ave.; phone: 779-1340), a beautifully furnished multi-level club where you can dance, watch the beautiful people, or play pool on Friday and Saturday nights; on Thursdays, *M.K.* becomes *Caesar's* — same place, different crowd. Other posh spots include *The Living Room* (154 E. 79th St.; phone: 772-8488), in a brownstone setting that attracts a young-and-beautiful bar crush downstairs. An upstairs restaurant recently replaced its serious menu with trendier, "grazing" dishes (health food). *Tatou* (151 E. 50th St.; phone: 753-1144), a posh and cozy supper club with live jazz during dinner, metamorphoses into a disco later in the evening. The *Savoy Grill* (131 E. 54th St.; phone: 593-8800), modeled after the classic supper clubs of the 1940s, features good jazz and an equally good grill menu. *Grolier* (29 E. 32nd St.; phone: 679-2932) has the comfortable atmosphere of a men's club. *Big City Diner* (572 11th Ave. at 43rd St.; phone: 244-6033) has a 24-hour diner, an trendy restaurant which serves American cuisine, and a dance club which divides the 2 eateries.

Among the nightclubs with food and drink that feature live music — including rock, soul, rhythm and blues, reggae, jazz, and top 40 music — are *Sweetwaters* (170 Amsterdam Ave. at W. 68th St.; phone: 873-4100); and *Dan Lynch* (14th St. and 2nd Ave.; phone: 766-0911), a pub-style bar with live bands that play blues and jazz. Another favorite is *Rex* (579 6th Ave at 16th St.; phone: 741-0080). Don't be fooled by the façade of *Live Bait* (14 E. 23rd St.; phone: 353-2400); it looks as off-putting as it sounds. Inside the hip crowd, as well as the Cajun cuisine, is cutting-edge chic. Nearby, *Bar X* (28 E. 23rd St.; phone: 979-5731) attracts a similar group, who come to hang out and listen to the live music. Perhaps the coolest of this 23rd Street trio is *The Coffee Shop* (29 Union Sq. W.; phone: 243-7969), another "in" spot where the young gather and snack before tripping the light fantastic. The *Bitter End* (149 Bleecker St.; phone: 673-7030) and the *Bottom Line* (15 W. 4th St.; phone: 228-7880) often offer traditional blues folk, and jazz. Country music notables entertain, and are entertained, at the *Lone Star Café Roadhouse* (240 W. 52nd St.; phone: 245-2950) when they come to New York. The *Eagle Tavern* (355 W. 14th St. between 8th and 9th Aves.; phone: 924-0275) is good for country, bluegrass, and Irish music.

Even though discos are no longer the city's hottest spots, there are still a fair number of places where the beat goes on, such as *Régine's* (502 Park Ave. at E. 59th St.; phone: 826-0990). For dancing to a Latin beat, try the *Sounds of Brazil* (*S.O.B.'s*) supper club (204 Varick St.; phone: 243-4940). As for good, clean traditional ballroom fun with American and Latin live dance music, the famous *Roseland Dance City* (239 W. 52nd St.; phone: 247-0200) definitely deserves a whirl — it holds up to 4,000 dancers.

For a low-key, elegant evening of dancing to live music, a good show and dinner, try one of the city's supper clubs. *Au Bar* is a supper club with all the lofty but cozy accoutrements of London's Belgravia (41 E. 58th St.; phone: 308-9455). The *Rainbow Room* (30 Rockefeller Plaza; phone: 632-5100) reopened in late 1987 after a $20-million renovation that restored the splendor of its 1930s heyday. It has good cheek-to-cheek dance music and dazzling views of the city from the 65th floor of the RCA Building. The adjacent *Rainbow Promenade* is a café for midnight snacks and *Rainbow and Stars* showcases cabaret acts.

Among the small, intimate supper clubs with good food, a nice, informal atmosphere, and low-key, quality entertainment, we recommend the *Café Carlyle* — to hear the quintessential Bobby Short (in the *Carlyle Hotel,* 35 E. 76th St. at Madison Ave.; phone: 744-1600) — and the *Ballroom,* featuring the likes of Barbara Cook and Karen Akers (253 W. 28th St.; phone: 244-3005). Lively, casual "showcase" clubs, where singers, comedians, and performers of all kinds test their new material on reliably loud but not always appreciative audiences, include *Caroline's* (89 South St., Pier 17; phone: 233-4900); the *Improvisation* — the *original* one (358 W. 44th St.; phone: 765-8268); and *Catch a Rising Star* (1487 1st Ave.; phone: 794-1906).

The largest concentration of singles bars in New York can be found on 1st and 2nd (some on 3rd) Avenues, between 61st and 80th Streets. If you walk along either one of these you will probably find a likely looking place. Be sure to check out *Adam's Apple* (1117 1st Ave., between 61st and 62nd Sts.; phone: 371-8650), and *B. Smiths* (771 8th Ave. at 47th St.; phone: 247-2222), where the crowd is more interesting than the food. If you like sitting around a piano, listening to, requesting, and even singing your favorite tunes, the *Village Green* (531 Hudson St.; phone: 255-1650), *Knickerbocker Saloon* (33 University Pl.; phone: 228-8490), and *Oliver's* restaurant (141 E. 57th St.; phone: 753-9180) can fill the bill as well as satisfy your appetite.

The *Village Vanguard* (178 7th Ave. S.; phone: 255-4037), the *Village Gate* (Bleecker and Thompson Sts.; phone: 475-5120), *Sweet Basil* (88 7th Ave. S.; phone: 242-1785), and the *Blue Note* (131 W. 3rd St.; phone: 475-8592) feature top jazz artists. Some of the more casual, neighborhood-type jazz clubs with reasonable prices and a relaxed atmosphere are *Arthur's Tavern* (57 Grove St.; phone: 675-6879), the *Angry Squire* (216 7th Ave. at W. 22nd St.; phone: 242-9066), *Bradley's* (70 University Pl.; phone: 228-6440), and the *West End Jazz Room* (2911 Broadway at W. 114th St.; phone: 666-9160). For nostalgia and more traditional jazz sounds, try *Fat Tuesday's* (190 3rd Ave.; phone: 533-7902), or *Michael's Pub* (211 E. 55th St.; phone: 758-2272), where Woody Allen still plays his clarinet on Monday nights; reservations necessary.

Cabarets and floor shows have been making something of a comeback. *Café Versailles* (151 E. 50th St.; phone: 753-3884) is the place for gorgeous showgirls and flashy production numbers, while a supper club presentation of popular musical revues and off-Broadway shows are featured at *Steve McGraw's Cabaret Theater* (158 W. 72nd St.; phone: 595-7400). *Rainbow and Stars* (see above) is another elegant cabaret setting. *Forbidden Broadway* (211 E. 60th St.; phone: 838-9090) is an ever-changing satirical revue (and revue) of Broadway shows.

BEST IN TOWN

CHECKING IN: Host to more visitors than any other city in the world, New York is one of the hardest places to find an empty hotel room between Sunday and Thursday nights, even though a rash of new properties have opened. However, don't expect this increased supply to offset inflation's upward push on room rates in the foreseeable future. Do expect to pay $250 or more — often lots more — for a very expensive room for two in Manhattan; $150 to $200 for an expensive one; $100 to $150 for a moderately priced room; and $100 or less for an inexpensive one. These prices do not include meals. *Note:*

Many of these hotels offer special weekend packages for relatively low rates. The packages include a variety of amenities — from just a room to a room plus breakfast/dinner, champagne, theater tickets, and parking. Reservations always are necessary, so write or call for information well in advance.

Visitors who yearn to be in the thick of New York's theater district will find a flurry of new hotels springing up in the Times Square area. This lodging trend that began with the *Marriott Marquis* has spurred a wealth of hotel rooms — more than 5,000 at press time — in this bustling area. Among the newcomers: the *Macklowe,* the *Holiday Inn Crowne Plaza,* the *Paramount,* and *Embassy Suites* hotel (see below).

An alternative to taking a standard hotel room is to try bed and breakfast accommodations in private homes or in an apartment. This includes a continental breakfast, and costs from $54 to $115 per night for a double room. Unhosted, fully furnished apartments also are available, starting at $65 per night for a small studio. Monthly rates are available for both bed and breakfast accommodations and apartments. For information, contact *Urban Ventures* (PO Box 426, New York, NY 10024; phone: 594-5650); *At Home in New York* (PO Box 407, New York, NY 10185; phone: 956-3125 or 265-8539); the *Bed and Breakfast Network of New York* (535 Hudson St., New York, NY 10001; phone: 645-8134); and *Bed and Breakfast (and Books)* (35 W. 92nd St., New York, NY 10025; phone: 865-8740).

To reserve a suite in one of 9 different all-suite hotels around Manhattan. call *Manhattan East Suite Hotel* (phone: 800-637-8483). These accommodations are located in areas that range from the somewhat commercial (the *Southgate Tower* at 31st St. and 7th Ave.) to the posh (the *Surrey* at 76th St. and Madison Ave.); this chain represents a total of 1,633 suites around the city. Another option: Double rooms at many of the co-ed YMCAs throughout the city run about $48 a night.

All telephone numbers are in the 212 area code unless otherwise indicated. Twenty-four–hour room service and CNN (Cable News Network), are available in all hotels, unless otherwise noted.

Box Tree – Eccentric and unusual, housed in two East Side brownstones. For those who appreciate authentic luxury, this detail-oriented establishment is a good choice. Each of the 13 rooms is individually designed with different European furnishings. The restaurant serves French fare with an English accent, and is open Mondays through Fridays for lunch and dinner, Saturdays for dinner only, and Sundays for brunch. Photocopiers are available. 250-252 E. 49th St. (phone: 758-8320; Fax: 212-308-3899). Very expensive.

Carlyle – Long the leader among the most luxurious uptown hotels (it's where the Kennedy family traditionally stays), it's properly noted for its quiet and serenity — with prices that match the high level of service. Predominantly a residential hotel, it provides a very homey environment for the rich and respected. There is also a deluxe for-guests-only spa, complete with exercise machines, saunas, and personal trainers on the third floor. Concierge and secretarial services are accessible, as well as A/V equipment, photocopiers, and computers. Meeting rooms have a capacity of 200. Express checkout. 35 E. 76th St. (phone: 744-1600; Fax: 212-717-4682; Telex: 620692). Very expensive.

Drake Swissôtel – Thanks to the newly constructed grand entrance on Park Avenue, the familiar billing, "the only Swiss hotel on Park Avenue" takes on new meaning. A $52 million renovation has provided five high-speed elevators, twice the meeting space, an expanded *Caffè Suisse,* and completely refurbished guestrooms with individual safes, 3 phones with call waiting, personal computer and fax hookups, marble bathrooms, and even a working fireplace in the Presidential Suite. The popular *Drake Bar* has its own entrance on Park Avenue, and its French restaurant, the *Lafayette,* is still rated among the city's very best (see *Eating Out*). Business pluses here include meeting rooms that hold up to 300, photocopiers, A/V equipment, and computers. There's an obliging concierge desk, as well as secretarial services. Express checkout. 440 Park Ave. at E. 56th St. (phone: 421-0900 or 800-DRAKE-NY; Fax: 212-371-4190; Telex: 147178). Very expensive.

Embassy Suites – This 460-suite hotel has elegant lobby decor, well-appointed rooms, and an instantly attentive staff. All suites come equipped with a wet bar, microwave oven, and refrigerator. Business amenities include room service until 1 AM, a multilingual concierge desk, 8 meeting rooms, photocopiers, computers, A/V equipment, and express checkout. 1568 Broadway (phone: 719-1600 or 800-EM-BASSY; Fax: 212-921-5212). Very expensive.

Lowell – Little expense has been spared in turning this once undistinguished property into an authentic gem, an Art Deco delight — with mostly 1- and 2-bedroom suites. The cozy rooms are perfect for a modestly proportioned king or queen, and each suite has a working fireplace (a log costs $3.50). The overall feeling is one of being a guest in a very well-bred New York townhouse — on what could very well be the most stylish block in Manhattan. The only member of the prestigious Relais & Châteaux group in New York. The hotel's dining room is elegant and intimate. Room service is available until midnight. Concierge and secretarial services are business pluses, as are meeting rooms which accommodate 50, A/V equipment, and photocopiers. 28 E. 63rd St. (phone: 838-1400; Fax: 212-319-4230; Telex: 275750). Very expensive.

Mayfair Regent – Perfect for those who stay at the *Gritti* in Venice and the *Hôtel du Cap* in the south of France. There are just 80 rooms and 120 suites, plus the nonpareil *Le Cirque* restaurant (see *Eating Out*). Uncompromising elegance and superb service with a focus on detail: Their "Pillow Bank" has a budget of $100,000 merely to amass the finest pillows in the world; and guests can request an in-room putting green complete with golf balls. A favorite spot for afternoon tea, too. Concierge and secretarial services are handy, as well as A/V equipment, photocopiers, computers, and express checkout. Meeting rooms can hold up to 80. 610 Park Ave. at E. 65th St. (phone: 288-0800 or 800-223-0542 in New York State; 800-545-4000 for reservations for all *Regent* hotels; Fax: 212-737-0538; Telex: 236257). Very expensive.

Parc Fifty-One – The former *Grand Bay* hotel provides luxury lodgings in a part of town not traditionally associated with deluxe overnighting. The lobby has ornate marble columns and Oriental rugs, and the large guestrooms come with such amenities as 2 multi-line phones, 2 TV sets, and fax hookups. There's free limo service to Wall Street, valets to pack and unpack for you, and even an electronic paging service. The hotel's mezzanine café is a far quieter and more soothing place to dine than the crowded *Bellini by Cipriani* restaurant that holds court on the ground floor. Services such as a concierge desk and secretarial assistance, plus A/V equipment, photocopiers, and computers are a boon. Meeting rooms accommodate 32. Personal fax machines may be obtained upon request. 152 W. 51st St. at 7th Ave., in the Equitable Center (phone: 765-1900 or 800-237-0990 outside New York State; Fax: 212-541-6604; Telex: 147156). Very expensive.

Parker Meridien – Billing itself as New York's "first French hotel," this establishment provides guests with the atmosphere of a European hostelry. There are 600 tasteful rooms, plus apartments, bars, and *Le Restaurant Maurice,* serving nouvelle cuisine. The sports-minded will enjoy *Club Raquette* for racquetball, handball, and squash, and the rooftop running track that encircles the enclosed pool — where the views of Central Park are lovely. There's also a health club. Business assets include concierge and secretarial services, A/V equipment, photocopiers, and computers. Personal fax machines are obtainable. Meeting rooms can hold up to 250. Express checkout. 118 W. 57th St. (phone: 245-5000 or 800-543-3000; Fax: 212-307-1776). Very expensive.

Peninsula – This 250-room property is a grand hotel in the best Asian tradition, featuring oversize marble bathtubs, a health club with a jogging track, and a swank French restaurant and bistro — *Adrienne* and *Le Bistro*. Business pluses are the concierge and secretarial services, as well as A/V equipment, photocopiers, computers, and express checkout. Meeting rooms hold up to 120. 700 Fifth Ave. at W. 55th St. (phone: 247-2200; Fax: 212-903-3949; Telex: 4976154). Very expensive.

Pierre – The most luxurious stopping place in midtown, with the most august clientele. The elegance is low key, but consistent, and the rooms with a park view command the highest of already heady prices. Operated by the superb Four Seasons group, on one of the most attractive corners of the city. For many, it is the only place to stay in New York. Meeting rooms here accommodate up to 400. There's a concierge desk, and secretarial services, A/V equipment, photocopiers, and computers all are handy. Express checkout. Fifth Ave. at E. 61st St. (phone: 838-8000 or 800-268-6282; Fax: 212-826-0319; Telex: 127426). Very expensive.

Plaza – The only New York City hotel designated as a historic landmark, and usually the first name out-of-towners recall when they think of a luxurious urban hostelry. Erratic, but mostly elegant, it was the subject of much gossip in the Great Trump Divorce Sweepstakes — he bought it, she ran it. Stay tuned: In order to raise much-needed cash, at presstime Trump announced his intention of converting some of the guestrooms into condominiums. The concierge and secretarial services are efficient. Also helpful is the supply of photocopiers, computers, and A/V equipment. There are 20 meeting rooms, and guests can exit via express checkout. Fifth Ave. at W. 59th St. (phone: 759-3000; Fax: 212-759-3167; Telex: 236938). Very expensive.

Plaza Athénée – Small and sumptuous, this is the US edition of the celebrated *Plaza Athénée* in Paris. The Trusthouse Forte management strives to make the elegant edifice look as unlike a hotel as possible and prides itself on personal attention to its guests. There are 160 rooms and 34 suites, all furnished with French antiques. Amenities include both concierge and secretarial services, meeting rooms that accommodate up to 100, A/V equipment, photocopiers, and computers. Express checkout. 37 E. 64th St. (phone: 734-9100 or 800-225-5843; Fax: 212-772-0958; Telex: 6972900). Very expensive.

Regency – Where the movers and shakers of American business stay when they're in New York. The "Power Breakfast" began here, and more commerce is probably conducted in the dining room at breakfast than in all of the rest of the country during a normal business day. Its modern architecture does not detract at all from its appeal, and a recent basement-to-roof restoration and refurbishing has only added to its luster. Facilities include a health club and meeting rooms that hold up to 130. There also are photocopiers, A/V equipment, and computers. The concierge desk and secretarial services are sure to oblige. Express checkout. 540 Park Ave. at E. 61st St. (phone: 759-4100 or 800-23-LOEWS; Fax: 212-826-5674; Telex: 147180). Very expensive.

Rhiga Royal – New York's tallest hotel (54 stories high) is also the most luxurious of the all-suite properties, and caters to the corporate traveler. The 500 one- and two-bedroom suites are equipped with 2 TV sets, a VCR, a kitchen, 3 telephones, and computer hookups. There are a dozen meeting rooms, full-scale business and fitness centers, and even a shuttle to the Wall Street area. Aside from the meeting rooms that accommodate 430, there are concierge and secretarial services, A/V equipment, photocopiers, computers, and express checkout. 151 W. 54th St. (phone: 307-5000 or 800-937-5454; Fax: 212-765-6530; Telex: 2450170). Very expensive.

Ritz-Carlton – Finishing multimillion-dollar renovations this year, the 174 rooms and 40 suites at this classic property offer wonderful views of Central Park and the city skyline. Some of the suites have small terraces, and nonsmoking and handicapped access is available. Amenities include twice-daily maid service, terry robes in the rooms, 2-line telephones and phones in the bathroom, personal valet service, and complimentary limousines to Wall St. New facilities include 2 fitness centers with park views and a boutique which sells signature R-C goodies. Guests have access to nearby private exercise facilities. Contemporary continental/American food is served in the comfortable firelight of the *Jockey Club* restaurant, and the bar is a popular meeting place for both guests and New Yorkers. The meeting rooms can accommodate 250, and there also are photocopiers, A/V equipment, and computers to attend to guests' business needs. Both concierge and secretarial services are handy. Express checkout. 112 Central Park South (phone: 757-1900 or 800-241-3333; Fax: 212-757-9620; Telex: 971534). Very expensive.

St. Regis – This landmark establishment, built in 1904 by John Jacob Astor, recently reopened after a $100 million roof to sidewalk renovation, and is ready to resume its status as one of New York's grande dames. Now under the Sheraton hotels' banner, elegant Louis XV furnishings, oriental rugs and, marble bathrooms with double sinks are wonderful additions to the 365 rooms and 523 suites, all of which also are equipped with fax machines and two-line phones. The famous St. Regis Roof ballroom offers spectacular views of midtown Manhattan, and the equally renowned *King Cole* bar retains its look of yesteryear. There are 11 meeting rooms, a concierge, secretarial services, A/V equipment, photocopiers, computers, and express checkout. 55 and Fifth Ave. (phone: 767-0525; Fax: 212-787-3447). Very expensive.

Stanhope – Owned by the Japanese Tobishima group, this posh, upper Fifth Avenue address has 141 rooms, most of them 1- or 2-bedroom suites that all afford views of Central Park or Manhattan's spectacular skyline. Guests meet and relax in the hotel's opulent public rooms and enjoy a wide range of dining options, including an outdoor café in summer and afternoon tea in the sitting room. Complimentary limousine to midtown weekday mornings and evening transportation to *Lincoln Center, Carnegie Hall,* and the theater district. The concierge desk and secretarial services are useful, as are photocopiers, A/V equipment, and computers. Meeting rooms accommodate 170. Across from the *Metropolitan Museum* at 995 Fifth Ave. (phone: 288-5800 or 800-828-1123 outside New York; Fax: 212-517-0088; Telex: 6720662). Very expensive.

United Nations Plaza – In addition to its beautifully integrated modern design, from the sleek, green-tinted glass exterior through the dark green marble reception area to the top 10 floors, it also offers rooms with magnificent city views. Managed by Hyatt International, it has both a truly international staff and exceptional facilities — including a tennis court, heated pool, and exercise room. Meeting rooms here can hold up to 600, and there are concierge and secretarial services, and photocopiers. Express checkout. E. 44th St. at 1st Ave. (phone: 355-3400 or 800-228-9000; Fax: 212-702-5051; Telex: 126803). Very expensive.

Westbury – The tapestries at the entrance are Belgian; the soft pink carpeting in the marble lobby, Irish — as befits this tranquil, European-style hotel with its large international clientele (part of the Trusthouse Forte group). It still has its crystal chandeliers in the lobby and its brass doorknobs engraved with the hotel's address. Its *Polo* restaurant serves nouvelle cuisine. Concierge and secretarial services are easily accessible, as well as photocopiers, A/V equipment, and computers. Meeting rooms hold up to 500. 15 E. 69th St. at Madison Ave. (phone: 535-2000 or 800-225-5843; Fax: 212-535-5058; Telex: 125388). Very expensive.

Doral Tuscany – In the middle of attractive Murray Hill (between 40th and 34th Sts., on the East Side), it is a name not widely known outside the city. But guests who know it well treasure the high level of service and discreet atmosphere (there are 125 rooms). Its restaurant, *Time & Again,* is another neighborhood treasure. Meeting rooms can accommodate up to 150; A/V equipment, photocopiers, and concierge and secretarial services round out the list of business amenities. 120 E. 39th St. (phone: 686-1600 or 800-847-4078; Fax: 212-779-7822; Telex: 640243). Very expensive to expensive.

Essex House – Overlooking Central Park, this 40-story landmark (now owned by Nikko Hotels International) has undergone a $70 million restoration to its original 1931 grandeur. Reopened in the summer of 1991, its 594 guestrooms and bathrooms were enlarged and decorated in French and English country styles. In addition to an elegant restaurant which features French fare, there is a Japanese restaurant and a café which faces the park. Meeting rooms, too, take advantage of the park views. Other business facilities include complete secretarial services, 2-line hookups in the guestrooms, and fax machines. There's a helpful concierge desk, and meeting rooms with a capacity of 600. Photocopiers, A/V equipment, and computers are available. Express checkout. 160 Central Park South (phone: 247-0300 or 800-NIKKO-US; Fax: 212-315-1839; Telex: 125205). Very expensive to expensive.

Helmsley Palace – Yes, *that* Helmsley. This midtown property combines the landmark Henry Villard houses with a 51-story high-rise. The historic area has been restored beautifully, with elegant public rooms decorated in marble, crystal, and gold. The modern guestrooms are fine, but nothing very special. There are three entrances, one less hectic on 50th Street, one on 49th Street, and the other through wrought-iron gates on Madison Avenue. Meeting rooms hold up to 900, and there are photocopiers and A/V equipment. Concierge and secretarial services are available. Express checkout. 455 Madison Ave. at E. 50th St. (phone: 888-7000 or 800-221-4982; Fax: 212-355-0820; Telex: 640543). Very expensive to expensive.

Mark – Noted for understated elegance, its 100 rooms and 85 suites all feature a separate glass shower stall, tub, and vanity; cable TV sets, 2-line phones, pantry with refrigerator, sink, and stove; heated towel bars and heating lamps in bathrooms, overstuffed chairs, credenzas, and sofas, all in neo-classical Italian motif. Suites are large and offer a bidet, library, vanity, wet bar, large terrace, and separate living, dining, and bedroom areas. The elegant *Mark's* restaurant, with its antiques-filled club decor, is an East Side favorite. Quiet elegance throughout. Other pluses include concierge and secretarial services, A/V equipment, photocopiers, computers and meeting rooms that hold 300. Madison Ave. at E. 77th St. (phone: 744-4300 or 800-THE-MARK; Fax: 212-744-2749). Very expensive to expensive.

New York Helmsley – A shining glass skyscraper on 42nd Street, this executive-oriented facility has special services available for the business traveler — with secretaries, fax machines, photocopying, and 7 meeting rooms among them. For dining, there's *Mindy's,* a continental restaurant, and for drinks and piano music try *Harry's New York Bar.* Room service can be called upon until 1 AM. There's a concierge desk and express checkout. 212 E. 42nd St. (phone: 490-8900 or 800-221-4982; Fax: 212-986-4792; Telex: 127724). Very expensive to expensive.

New York Hilton & Towers – An enormous modern structure near

Rockefeller Center. One of New York's largest hotels, it's a bit antiseptic in ambience, but about as efficiently run as any hotel with more than 2,000 rooms can be. The well-equipped health club has saunas and even a video cassette player for your own workout tape. A favorite meeting and convention site. Pets allowed. Guests can order room service until 1 AM, and business amenities include 47 meeting rooms, concierge and secretarial services, A/V equipment, photocopiers, computers, and express checkout. 1335 Ave. of the Americas between W. 53rd and 54th Sts. (phone: 586-7000 or 800-HILTONS; Fax: 212-315-1374; Telex: 238492). Very expensive to expensive.

Omni Berkshire Place – Built in 1926, the old *Berkshire* hotel has been resuscitated by the Omni chain with dash and considerable understated flair. The rooms are still mostly on the small side, but they're tastefully furnished. Most impressive is the *Atrium Lobby,* a mirrored lounge accented with soft shades, creating a quite comfortable and intimate atmosphere. Gaining momentum on the culinary scene is the pretty *Rendez-vous* restaurant serving both classic French and nouvelle cuisines. The concierge desk and secretarial services are useful, as are the photocopiers, A/V equipment, and computers. Meeting rooms hold up to 180. Express checkout. 21 E. 52nd St. (phone: 753-5800 or 800-THE-OMNI; Fax: 212-355-7646; Telex: 7105815256). Very expensive to expensive.

Royalton – The management of ultra-hip *Morgans* set out to impress New York once again, this time with a 205-room property, a major boost to the ongoing rejuvenation of Times Square. The block-long lobby, with areas specifically designed for reading, conversation, billiards, and board games, is a popular gathering spot (and the restrooms have to be seen to be believed). Many of the rooms come with a wood-burning fireplace, sleeping loft, and living area, which includes a VCR, color TV set, and stereo cassette deck. Many of the baths sport a 5-foot round tub. Guests can opt for either casual or more formal dining, or just for pre-theater cocktails in the bar. Concierge and secretarial services, as well as photocopiers and express checkout, are among the options offered here. 44 W. 44th St. (phone: 869-4400; Fax: 212-869-8965; Telex: 213875). Very expensive to expensive.

Sherry-Netherland – It's a little less renowned than the *Plaza* and the *Pierre* (its immediate neighbors), but hardly less elegant. The location is superb, and this is a luxurious stopping place truly worthy of the description. Keep in mind that reservations can sometimes be a problem, because the hotel is largely residential. Fifth Ave. and E. 59th St. (phone: 355-2800 or 800-223-0522 outside New York State). Very expensive to expensive.

Vista International New York – The first hotel to be built in Manhattan's Wall Street vicinity in over 100 years, it sits between the World Trade Center towers facing New York Harbor. A full range of special services is available for business travelers in reliable Hilton International style. Other highlights include the indoor *Executive Fitness Center,* with a large lap pool and first-rate sports equipment; the *Greenhouse* and *American Harvest* restaurants, offering very good American regional specialties; and the *Tall Ships Bar,* a popular after-work meeting place. Twelve meeting rooms are available, as well as concierge and secretarial services, photocopiers, A/V equipment, and computers. Express checkout. 3 World Trade Center (phone: 938-9100 or 800-HILTONS; Fax: 212-321-2107; Telex: 6611030). Very expensive to expensive.

Waldorf-Astoria and Waldorf Towers – A legend on Park Avenue, divided between the basic hotel and the recently renovated, more exclusive and opulent (and more expensive) Towers. The degree of comfort delivered here is consistent with the hotel's reputation; it is also a popular convention property. *Peacock Alley* is a lively cocktail rendezvous, and the clock in the middle of the lobby may be New York's favorite meeting place. Business pluses include meeting rooms that accommodate up to 1,600, A/V equipment, photocopiers, computers, and express checkout. There's a helpful concierge desk, and secretarial services also are available. 301 Park Ave. at E. 50th St. (phone: 355-3000 or 800-HILTONS; Fax: 212-872-6380; Telex: 666747). Very expensive to expensive.

Barbizon – Not to be confused with the *Barbizon Plaza,* this East Side establishment was bought by the owners of *Morgans* and the *Royalton.* One of its former lives was as a residential hotel for women only. Its 368 room and café have been thoroughly refurbished. Guests will find an obliging concierge desk, meeting rooms that hold up to 150, photocopiers, and A/V equipment. Room service is available until midnight. 140 E. 63rd St. (phone: 838-5700 or 800-223-1020; Fax: 212-753-0360; Telex: 220060). Expensive.

Beekman Tower – Small and pleasantly old-fashioned, this all-suite hotel (convenient to the United Nations) has a cocktail lounge, the *Top of the Tower,* boasting splendid skyline views. Both concierge and secretarial services are available, as well as photocopiers, A/V equipment, and meeting rooms that have a capacity of 150. Room service orders are taken until 10 PM. 1st Ave. and E. 49th St. (phone: 355-7300 or 800-ME-SUITE; Fax: 212-753-9366). Expensive.

Grand Hyatt – Donald Trump's idea of how a glitzy New York City hotel should look: mirrored exterior glass and lots of shiny chrome. The centerpiece of the multilevel lobby is the tiered, marble fountain crowned by a 77-foot bronze sculpture. On the lobby's upper level is the *Sungarden,* a glass-enclosed bar and cocktail lounge that overhangs the hotel's entrance and the busy 42nd Street traffic. The 1,400 smallish rooms are still reminiscent of the old *Commodore* (from which this hostelry was created) although they now are dressed in rich, earthy tones that are brightened daily with fresh flowers. There are over 30 meeting rooms, and A/V equipment, photocopiers, and computers are useful for business needs. The concierge desk and secretarial services are easily accessible. Express checkout. 109 E. 42nd St. at Park Ave. (phone: 883-1234, 800-233-1234, or 800-228-9000; Fax: 212-697-3772; Telex: 64560). Expensive.

Holiday Inn Crowne Plaza – A razzle-dazzle, 46-story glass tower in the Times Square district that offers 770 guestrooms, 7 Crowne Plaza Club floors (VIP floors with special services), a fully equipped and staffed business center, and the 15th floor *Crowne Swim & Health Club* (which has the largest pool in Manhattan under a domed skylight). The *Broadway Grill,* with its California-style cuisine, is a neighborhood favorite. Definitely not a quiet, little, "hidden" place, but then, neither is the surrounding area. The business center offers secretarial services, A/V equipment, photocopiers, and computers. There's a helpful concierge desk, and 12 meeting rooms. Express checkout. 1605 Broadway at 49th St. (phone: 977-4000 or 800-HOLIDAY; Fax: 212-333-7393). Expensive.

Inter-Continental – A large (686 rooms), distinguished property with smallish guestrooms located on a busy East Side corner, 1 block south of the *Waldorf-Astoria.* A recent $3 million renovation resulted in spruced-up guestrooms that have 2-line phones with speaker capabilities. The new health club has saunas and steamrooms. The oak-paneled *Barclay* restaurant is one of New York's favorite luncheon haunts. Other amenities include concierge and secretarial services, photocopiers and computers, A/V equipment, and 16 meeting rooms. Express checkout. 111 E. 48th St. (phone: 755-5900, 800-332-4246; Fax: 212-644-0079; Telex: 968677). Expensive.

Loews Summit – This midtowner, convenient for businesspeople and conventioneers with East Side interests, has been given a new lease on life. After a $26 million renovation program, the big news is enlarged guestrooms and the addition of a spiffy new restaurant, the *Lexington Avenue Grill.* There's an ESP (Extra Special Patron) floor with a private lounge and concierge, as well as a fully staffed fitness center. Room service delivers until 2 AM. Business services include secretarial assistance, A/V equipment, photocopiers, and express checkout. There also are 12 meeting rooms. Lexington Ave. at 51st St. (phone: 752-7000 or 800-223-0888; Fax: 212-758-6311; Telex: 147181). Expensive.

Macklowe – The starkly chic decor of the 638 guestrooms in this 52-story tower in the Times Square area features high-tech electronics. There's a fitness center on site, as well as a 100,000-square-foot conference center (stocked with A/V equipment), built around an existing theater (the *Hudson*), which also can be used for meetings. Other business amenities include 38 meeting rooms, photocopiers, computers, a concierge desk, and express checkout. 145 W. 44th St. (phone: 768-4400; Fax: 212-768-0847). Expensive.

Marriott East Side – Formerly known as the *Halloran House,* this 665-room historic hotel has been redecorated and refurnished to shine with Old World charm. Built in the 1920s by A.L. Harmon, who designed the Empire State Building, it is a mix of Gothic, Byzantine, and Italian architectural styles. Among its many spectacular views of Manhattan and the East River, our favorite is the one on the 16th floor, from the *Fountain Room and Terrace* restaurant. There also are nonsmoking and Concierge Club floors. Room service is available until 11:30 PM. There are 9 meeting rooms, as well as A/V equipment and photocopiers. Express checkout. 525 Lexington Ave., between 48th and 49th Sts. (phone: 755-4000; Fax: 212-751-3440). Expensive.

Morgans – The ultimate contemporary hotel, without so much as a sign out front. This treasure features stereo cassette players and component TV sets with stereo sound which are standard in every room (VCRs and videotapes are available). Bathrooms are pure high tech, and artwork is by avant-garde photographer Robert Mapplethorpe. The only traditional touch here is the *Brooks Brothers*–style oxford cloth sheets and pillowcases. All things considered, it's not surprising that the hotel's 112 rooms, sleekly designed by André Puttman, are usually occupied by a trendy, young, international clientele. Concierge and secretarial services, as well as A/V equipment, photocopiers, and computers round out the business amenities. 237 Madison Ave. at E. 37th St. (phone: 686-0300 or 800-334-3408; Fax: 212-779-8352; Telex: 288908). Expensive.

New York Marriott Marquis – A predictably pedestrian convention hotel designed by John C. Portman, this 50-story, 1,876-room addition to Times Square tries to make up for a lack of distinction in room design with a 37-floor open atrium that is long on glitz, short on class. *The View,* a 3-tier rotating rooftop restaurant, overlooks the city, and the 8th-floor revolving lounge overlooks Broadway. There are 53 meeting rooms; other business pluses are concierge and secretarial services, A/V equipment, photocopiers, and express checkout. 1535 Broadway between W. 45th and 46th Sts. (phone: 398-1900 or 800-228-9290; Fax: 212-704-9030; Telex: 6973558). Expensive.

Sheraton Centre – This 50-story modern monolith is always busy; the rooms are quite comfortable and it's only a short walk to the theater. The top 5 floors, called the Sheraton Towers, are for more exclusive "business class" clients. Guests can request room service until 1 AM. Meeting rooms accommodate upwards of 2,000, and there are photocopiers, A/V equipment, computers, and express checkout. 7th Ave. at W. 52nd St. (phone: 581-1000 or 800-325-3535; Fax: 212-262-4410; Telex: 421130). Expensive.

Sheraton Park Avenue – Formerly the *Russell,* this is one of those "secret" hotels that regulars love to keep to themselves. The 150-room property on Park Avenue is convenient to Grand Central station and the garment center. The comfortable guestrooms have old-fashioned touches such as high ceilings and walk-in closets. There also are modern amenities, such as 3 phones and work areas in each room. *Russel's* is a fine dining restaurant; and the *Judge's Chamber,* which serves buffet lunch in a book-lined club setting, offers live jazz at night. Concierge and secretarial services can lend a hand, and there are 25 meeting rooms, A/V equipment, and photocopiers. Express checkout. 45 Park Ave. at 37th St. (phone: 685-7676 or 800-325-3535 Fax: 212-889-3193). Expensive.

New York Penta – Having undergone a $35-million renovation, accommodations in this Stanford White landmark building in the heart of Manhattan offer enhanced comfort. Executive meeting facilities make it a first class business hotel. Room service delivers until 10:30 PM, and there are 25 meeting rooms. Express checkout. 401 7th Ave. at W. 33rd St. (phone: 736-5000 or 800-223-8585; Fax: 212-502-8798). Expensive to moderate.

Roosevelt – This traditional favorite has recently changed ownership and undergone extensive redecoration and restoration. The accommodations are clean and comfortable, and the *Crawdaddy* restaurant has one of the area's most popular after-work bars. A good value (and prime location) for business travelers. Room service is available until 11 PM. There are 23 meeting rooms, as well as secretarial services, A/V equipment, and photocopiers easily accessible. Express checkout. Madison Ave. at E. 45th St. (phone: 661-9600; 800-223-1870 outside of New York State; Fax: 212-687-5064). Expensive to moderate.

Algonquin – Long a favorite among literary types, the hotel's reputation is most closely connected to the days of the literary "Round Table" in one of its fine restaurants. The personal attention accorded by the management is visible everywhere, and, if anything, the hotel has improved with age. It was recently acquired by a Japanese investment firm and a $20 million renovation of its 170 rooms has been completed. Amenities here include room service until 11 PM, meeting rooms that hold up to 150, A/V equipment, and photocopiers. 59 W. 44th St. between Fifth and 6th Aves. (phone: 840-6800 or 800-548-0345; Fax: 212-944-1419). Moderate.

Journey's End – This 29-story newcomer, completed in 1990, is noteworthy due to its excellent location (just east of Fifth Ave., across from the Public Library) and its reasonable rates are well below the city's standard charges. All 189 guestrooms are equipped with a work area and a cable TV set, and guests receive complimentary morning coffee and a copy of *USA Today.* There's a concierge desk, and photocopiers are available. 3 E. 40th St. (phone: 447-1500 or 800-668-4200; Fax: 212-213-0972). Moderate.

Mayflower – A favorite with ballet and concert buffs (it's close to *Lincoln Center*), as well as celebrities from the arts world. Guests enjoy a relaxed atmosphere and large, comfortable rooms with pantries that once served permanent residents. This place deserves to be better known. Room service delivers until midnight. The meeting rooms accommodate 100, and there are A/V equipment, photocopiers, computers, and express checkout. 15 Central Park West, between W. 61st and 62nd Sts. (phone: 265-0060 or 800-223-4164; Fax: 212-265-5098; Telex: 6972657). Moderate.

Milford Plaza Best Western – Out-of-towners usually come to Manhattan for Broadway's bright nightlife, and this place is smack in the center of New York's theater district. All kinds of money-saving tour packages are available, and while rooms are small, they're not a bad value for the price. *Mama Leone's* restaurant (legendary, but lousy) is in the hotel. The neighborhood, however, is the pits! Room service runs until 11 PM, and there are 8 meeting room and A/V equipment at guests' disposal. Express checkout. 270 W. 45th St. at 8th Ave.

(phone: 869-3600 or 800-221-2690; Fax: 212-944-8357; Telex: 177610). Moderate.

Paramount – Probably one of the most publicized new hotels ever to appear on the Manhattan scene, this latest Ian Schrager dazzler is actually a renovation of an old Times Square property. Designed by Philippe Stark, the tiny guestrooms — trompe l'oeil paintings give the illusion of space — are filled with oddly-shaped furniture. There's a theatrical, dual-level lobby for socializing, a 24-hour brasserie, a business center, and even a playroom for kids. Room service is available until midnight. There also are concierge and secretarial services, as well as meeting rooms that hold up to 50, photocopiers, and express checkout. 235 W. 46th St. (phone: 764-5500 or 800-225-7474; Fax: 212-354-5237). Moderate.

Salisbury – Owned by the Calvary Baptist Church (thus, no alcohol is permitted on the premises), it has a small, welcoming lobby and 320 newly painted, nicely sized pastel rooms (all with refrigerators and pantries, but no stoves). It's a favorite with musicians who like the hotel's location near *Carnegie Hall.* Room service only delivers until 7 PM. Meeting rooms seat 100, and A/V equipment is available. 123 W. 57th St. (phone: 246-1300 or 800-223-0680; Fax: 212-977-7752; Telex: 668366). Moderate.

Wyndham – Though admittedly overshadowed by better-known neighbors like the *Pierre, Plaza,* and *Sherry-Netherland,* this extremely convenient property has been fondly described as a posh country inn; a fine, small London hotel; and a private club. It's a particular favorite among actors. It takes a certain self-sufficiency to enjoy the special appeal of this place; there's no room service, the hotel restaurant is closed on weekends, and the front door is locked at night. We love it. 45 W. 58th St. between Fifth Ave. and Ave. of the Americas (phone: 753-3500; Fax: 212-754-5638). Moderate.

Empire – Recently renovated by its new owner, Metromedia, the 400 rooms all offer compact disc players, VCRs, Jacuzzis, and heated towel racks. Food is available from the *Empire Grill* around the clock. There's a concierge desk and photocopiers, as well as express checkout. 44 W. 63rd St. (phone: 265-7400 or 800-545-7400; Fax: 212-765-6125). Moderate to inexpensive.

Chelsea – A New York architectural and historic landmark where Dylan Thomas, Arthur Miller, Lenny Bruce, Diego Rivera, Martha Graham, and others have made their New York home. The atmosphere in this 19th-century structure is distinctly unmodern, unhomogenized, and unsterilized. There is a large permanent occupancy, with about 35 rooms available for transients. Rooms vary in structure, price, and facilities — some have a kitchen, a fireplace, and a bathroom, and others have none of the above. For the adventurous only; make reservations well in advance. 222 W. 23rd St. (phone: 243-3700; Fax: 212-243-3700). Inexpensive.

Gorham – The variety of room-and-bed combinations possible, together with the fact that all units contain a kitchenette, dining table, and color TV set, make this a great boon to families traveling with children. 136 W. 55th St. off Ave. of the Americas (phone: 245-1800; Fax: 212-245-1800; Telex: 286863). Inexpensive.

Olcott – By no means plush, but certainly comfortable and adequate, this is a typical New York residential hotel that offers some transient accommodations. Spacious facilities and a homey atmosphere are its advantages. Most rooms are suites, with a living room, bedroom, kitchen, and bathroom. Reservations should be made several weeks in advance. 27 W. 72nd St., only 1 block from Central Park (phone: 877-4200; Fax: 212-508-0511). Inexpensive.

Shoreham – On a fashionable block off Fifth Avenue, this small place has 75 good-size rooms that are pleasantly decorated and have modern bathrooms and cable TV. Although the hotel has no dining room, each guestroom has an electric coffeemaker and small refrigerator. 33 W. 55th St. (phone: 247-6700; Fax: 212-765-9741; Telex: 3767516). Inexpensive.

Wales – Comfortable and reasonably priced. it's in a very appealing residential neighborhood, close to Central Park and the *Metropolitan* and *Guggenheim* art museums. It offers more than 93 individually decorated rooms and suites, some with kitchenette or four-poster bed, all with cable TV. 1295 Madison Ave. at E. 92nd St. (phone: 876-6000; Fax: 212-860-7000). Inexpensive.

EATING OUT: New York City is, plain and simply, the culinary capital of the world. It is possible that there are more good French restaurants in Paris or more fine Chinese eating places in Taiwan, but no city in the world can offer the gastronomic diversity that is available in New York. If there is one compelling reason to come to New York, it is to indulge exotic appetites that cannot be satisfied elsewhere, and it is not unusual for dedicated eaters to make several pilgrimages to New York each year simply to satisfy their sophisticated palates.

Regrettably, New York's tastiest cuisine does not come cheap, though there are places to dine around the city where you need not pay the check in 30-, 60-, and 90-day notes. Currently, a new breed of American bistros is cropping up and challenging the reputation of New York restaurants for being overpriced and intimidating. Their simple approach toward both food and atmosphere is helping to redefine the way New Yorkers dine out. But, as in most things, you usually get what you pay for, and you should expect to pay about $150 for two at restaurants listed as very expensive, $100 or more for two in the restaurants that we've noted as expensive. Moderate restaurants will run between $70 and $100 per couple, and in inexpensive establishments, expect to spend from $30 to $70 for a 3-course meal for two. These price ranges do not include drinks, wine, or tips. All telephone numbers are in the 212 area code unless otherwise indicated.

■ **Note:** Unless otherwise noted, reservations are always necessary.

Le Bernardin – Gerard and Maguy de la Coze moved their headquarters from Paris to the sparkling Equitable Life Building, where they occupy subtly elegant premises. The menu is fiercely seafood-oriented, and no one prepares the products of the world's oceans more imaginatively or deliciously. Since the doors opened here in 1986, such unusual specialties as tuna tartare and sea urchin soup have become staples of the NYC restaurant scene, and it's worth a visit just to see what new wonders are swimming out of the kitchen. Lunch and dinner daily (prix fixe menu); closed Sundays. Major credit cards accepted. 155 W. 51st St. (phone: 489-1515). Very expensive.

Bouley – Like going to *grandmère*'s house in the French countryside — if she happened to be the best cook in the *ville.* In an out-of-the-way area, but well worth the effort, this spot is considered by many food critics to be among New York's best restaurants. The spectacular French (and American) fare — based on what's freshest at the market — is served without fuss. Reservations necessary at least 2 weeks in advance for Friday or Saturday dinner. Closed Sundays. Major credit cards accepted. 165 Duane St. (phone: 608-3852). Very expensive.

Le Cirque – The tables are too close together, the noise level can be deafening, and reservations are as hard to come by as an invitation to Buckingham Palace. Still, the remarkable continental food that comes out of the kitchen is enough to make legions of dedicated diners (which include the "A list" of the city's beautiful folk) put up with the less than perfect atmosphere. Everything on the menu is special and prepared perfectly. Remember, however, that the main reason for dining here is to taste the sublime *crème brûlée* for dessert. Nowhere in the world is it prepared better. Closed Sundays. Only American Express and Diners Club accepted. 58 E. 65th St. (phone: 794-9292). Very expensive.

Four Seasons – The *Pool Room* is perhaps the most beautiful dining room in the city, with a proprietorship that is not only creative but extremely able. This is arguably the best restaurant in the US, not just because of its accomplishments, but because of its innovation and boldness. Although the menu is interesting from top to bottom, desserts deserve special mention, and there's one called Chocolate Velvet that is simply ecstasy. Special "spa cuisine" provides careful calorie and sodium monitoring for the health-conscious. The *Grill Room* continues to be the luncheon favorite of New York's power elite, and is a good choice for dinner as well. Closed Sundays. Major credit cards accepted. 99 E. 52nd St. (phone: 754-9494). Very expensive.

La Grenouille – Soft green walls and glorious floral arrangements provide a romantic setting in which to sample such house masterpieces as *les grenouilles provençales* (frogs' legs); thin, sautéed calves' liver Bercy; and roast duck (prix fixe). Be prepared, however, for a very haughty, condescending attitude if you're not known to the staff. Closed Sundays and Mondays. Only American Express and Visa accepted. 3 E. 52nd St. (phone: 752-1495). Very expensive.

Lafayette – Supervised by chef Louis Outhier of Cannes's famed *L'Oasis,* this place has earned a wonderful rating from Michelin for 17 consecutive years for its exquisite French food. Open daily. Major credit cards accepted. Located in the *Drake Swissôtel,* 440 Park Ave. at E. 56th St. (phone: 832-1565). Very expensive.

Lutèce – Maintaining its mystique for over 3 decades as one of the world's finest restaurants, it remains what *The New York Times* dubbed a "culinary cathedral." Chef-proprietor André Soltner personally prepares the classic French fare in a simple East Side townhouse. Of all the premier restaurants in New York, this is the one most hospitable to strangers willing to pay the high price for deluxe French food. If you have the option, dine in the comfortable upstairs room, though the garden room downstairs is a treat in New York City. To sample the combination of classic dishes, innovative nouvelle creations, and Alsatian specialties, order the *menu de dégustation,* a tasting of six or seven small courses. Closed Sundays. Make reservations a month in advance. All major credit cards accepted. 249 E. 50th St. (phone: 752-2225). Very expensive.

Quilted Giraffe – Among the prime temptations at this highly regarded restaurant are entrées such as grilled Norwegian salmon and moist, crisp-skinned confit of duck with garlic potatoes. An alternative to the prix fixe dinner is a tasting menu offering five small courses. Similarly, the Grand Dessert provides a sampling of such pleasures as a hazelnut waffle with vanilla ice cream and maple sauce. The two intimate dining rooms have only 17 tables; for weekends, be sure to reserve about a month in advance. It also has the dubious distinction of being the most expensive restaurant in town. Open Mondays through Saturdays for dinner, Tuesdays through Fridays for lunch. Only American Express accepted. 550 Madison Ave. at 55th St. (phone: 593-1221). Very expensive.

"21" Club – The legendary atmosphere and unquestionable cachet are what lure most visitors, but when the original owners sold out, there was a discernible decline in camaraderie. A refurbishing spruced up the place, and the menu was overhauled — to the dismay of most former patrons. Happily, more than a touch of the old ambience (and favorite foods) has returned recently. Ties always are required, and if you're not a regular or a celebrity, sometimes the welcome isn't very warm. The upstairs dining room (open to the public for lunch) is more elegant and quiet, but those who wish to see and be seen usually adorn the section on the left as you enter the downstairs bar. Closed Sundays. Major credit cards accepted. 21 W. 52nd St. (phone: 582-7200). Very expensive.

Aquavit – In the landmark Rockefeller townhouse, this Scandinavian dining place is a current favorite with local foodies. It's actually two restaurants: a formal dining room set around an atrium and waterfall, with a prix fixe dinner; and a more casual room upstairs featuring simpler cooking. There are many varieties of salmon and game, such as arctic venison (reindeer) and snow grouse. Try the smorgasbord, caviar bank, and "aquavit chiller," consisting of 8 flavored vodkas. Open weekdays for lunch and dinner; Saturdays for dinner only; closed Sundays. Major credit cards accepted. 13 W. 54th St. (phone: 307-7311). Very expensive to expensive.

An American Place – Celebrated chef-owner Larry Forgione is regarded as one of the spearheads in the New American food preparation movement. Sample his American continental specialties and you'll discover why. Gastronomic delights include grilled free-range chicken with sunchoke gallette (Jerusalem artichokes in a cream sauce) and pan-roasted lamb with black pepper and cumin. Closed Sundays. Major credit cards accepted. 2 Park Ave. at E. 32nd St. (phone: 684-2122). Expensive.

Café Luxembourg – The interior here runs to Art Deco, bright lights, and noise, with everyone appearing to be looking around for someone famous. Not far from *Lincoln Center,* it is especially welcome to concertgoers. The fare is nouvelle, though the specials tend to be uneven. For the best look at the chic crowd, come after 8 PM. There's also a Sunday brunch featuring *boudin blanc,* a white pork sausage. Open daily. Major credit cards accepted. 200 W. 70th St. (phone: 873-7411). Expensive.

Il Cantinori – A welcome addition to New York's stable of Northern Italian restaurants, on one of the city's loveliest blocks. A beamed ceiling, terra cotta floor, and chairs of wood and straw create the charming ambience inside. Begin with *risotto nero* (a rice delicacy in squid ink) or *ravioli alla fiorentina* (dumplings of spinach and ricotta cheese) before an entrée of excellent fish or game. For dessert, try the restaurant's version of the popular Italian confection *tiramisù,* espresso-soaked ladyfingers and sweet mascarpone cheese. Open daily. Only American Express and Diners Club accepted. 32 E. 10th St. (phone: 673-6044). Expensive.

La Caravelle – Traditional bastion of classic French cuisine with all of the attendant hauteur, this is often the choice of New York's smartest set. Menus are unalteringly interesting, and the kitchen is not merely competent but innovative. The pre-theater menu is a bargain. Closed Sundays. Major credit cards accepted. 33 W. 55th St. (phone: 586-4252). Expensive.

Chanterelle – Its dingy SoHo corner has been abandoned, but not its commitment to seriously elegant dining. The prix fixe menu leans toward nouvelle dishes. Begin with seafood sausage, then choose from such entrées as salmon en papillote, rack of lamb, duck in sherry vinegar, or sautéed soft-shell crabs, all accompanied by crisp stir-fried squash mixed with zucchini blossoms and other vegetables. A cheese board is offered, and dessert might be chocolate pavé, a dense, rich, mousse-like cake. Closed Sundays and Mondays. Make reservations about 2 months in advance. Major credit cards accepted. 2 Harrison St., corner of Hudson (phone: 966-6960). Expensive.

Christ Cella's – A creditable eatery that specializes in sirloin steaks and seafood. The decor is unimpressive, the service is indifferently efficient, and it's a favorite of advertising and publishing types. Not quite up to its old standards, but still worth a visit. Closed Sundays. Major credit cards accepted. 160 E. 46th St. (phone: 697-2479). Expensive.

Coach House – Not as highly regarded as it once was, but still generally considered one of New York's best "American" restaurants. The black bean soup is a tradition here, as are the rack of lamb and the superb chocolate cake. Another attraction is its Greenwich Village location, across from some interesting Federal row houses. Closed Mondays. Major credit cards accepted. 110 Waverly Pl. (phone: 777-0303). Expensive.

Dock's Oyster Bar – There are two of these oversize seafood palaces, and each is packed at lunch and dinnertime. The sprawling raw bar attracts the young and the restless, while serious diners head for the crisply nautical dining area to tackle the lengthy menu that often includes seared and gingered tuna, tangy chowders, and a catch-of-the-day selection of seafood which regulars order with a side of sweet potato fries. Open daily. Major credit cards accepted. 2427 Broadway, between 89th and 90th Sts. (phone: 724-5588) and 633 Third Ave., at 40th St. (phone: 968-8080). Expensive.

Gloucester House – Among the most expensive seafood centers in the city. Fresh biscuits are a particular delight and help soften the blow of some frankly staggering prices. A fine place to dine, but a real budget-bender. Closed Sundays. Major credit cards accepted. 37 E. 50th St. (phone: 755-7394). Expensive.

Gotham Bar & Grill – A favorite of local food critics as well as a god-send to its legion of loyal fans. The space is cavernous (it was originally a warehouse), but an award-winning bi-level design and lofty decor simmer down the space to *grand-café* scale. Chef Alfred Portale's creations constantly amaze. Sample such dazzlers as grilled Muscovy duck breast with Szechuan peppercorns, apricots and turnips, grilled salmon, and artichokes à la Grecque. Open daily. Major credit cards accepted. 12 E. 12 St., between Fifth Ave. and University Place (phone: 620-4020). Expensive.

Manhattan Ocean Club – Both the lower-level and upstairs dining rooms of this fine seafood house near *Carnegie Hall* are reminiscent of a museum, with white walls, Grecian columns, and Picasso plates and prints displayed behind glass. The real attraction is the fresh, delicious fish and shellfish — the Hawaiian wahoo and melt-in-your-mouth kumomoto oysters are particularly good. The *pâtissier* is winning awards with such sumptuous treats as calvados ice cream on apple tarts. Open daily. Major credit cards accepted. 57 W. 58th St. (phone: 371-7777). Expensive.

Il Nido – A superb menu of Northern Italian specialties and the highest standards of service are the hallmarks of Adi Giovannetti's attractive, if somewhat cramped, East Side establishment. *Crostini di polenta* with a sauce of mushroom and chicken liver is the perfect starter, to be followed by *fritto misto* (mixed fried fish), *crostacei marinara* (shellfish in marinara sauce), or any of a host of other house specialties. Closed Sundays. Major credit cards accepted. 251 E. 53rd St. (phone: 753-8450). Expensive.

Palio – An elegant entry into New York's abundant inventory of fine Italian eateries. The street-level bar is surrounded by a mural of the exciting medieval horse race that gives the restaurant its name, and the upstairs dining room is spacious and elegant. Perfect for pre-theater dinners. Open nightly except Sundays for dinner; only weekdays for lunch. Major credit cards accepted. 151 W. 51st St., in the Equitable Center (phone: 245-4850). Expensive.

Remi – Surrounded by a wrap-around mural of Venice designed by co-owner Adam Tihany, diners indulge in such northern Italian fantasies as cuttlefish in its own ink over polenta, smoked prosciutto with greens and truffled olive oil, and ravioli Marco Polo with fresh tuna and ginger. A dessert favorite is the three-nut tart (pine, pecan, and walnut) with homemade ice cream. And if you've still got the heart and room, there are 45 kinds of grappa to follow the meal. Open daily. Major credit cards accepted. 145 W. 53rd St., between 6th and 7th Aves. (phone: 581-4242). Expensive.

River Café – Set on a barge on the Brooklyn shore of the East River, with spectacular views of the lower Manhattan skyline. One of the top American restaurants, with an especially good weekend brunch menu featuring lobster baked in horseradish oil with oyster risotto, poached eggs on smoked salmon waffles, and duck confit with roasted garlic and white beans. Open daily. Reservations necessary 2 weeks ahead. Major credit cards accepted. 1 Water St. (phone: 718-522-5200). Expensive.

Riveranda/Empress of New York – The food may not be the best in town, but the experience of dining on the city's only restaurant-yacht is worth the tab. It's delightful to have dinner and dance while cruising the Hudson River and New York Harbor past the glittering Manhattan skyline. There are luncheon and Sunday brunch cruises as well. Advance reservations and tickets necessary. Open daily in summer. Major credit cards accepted. Sailings from Pier 62 on the Hudson River at W. 23rd St. (phone: 929-7090). Expensive.

Russian Tea Room – With enough blinis to float diners down the Volga, this festive place is an almost obligatory stop for any visitor who plans to attend a concert at adjacent *Carnegie Hall.* Try the borscht or chicken Kiev, abide by the waiter's suggestions, or let your Slavic instincts have free rein. There is now a cabaret on Sunday nights. Open daily. Major credit cards accepted. 150 W. 57th St. (phone: 265-0947). Expensive.

Spark's – Nothing (except the food) is admirable: the entry to the dining room is the most cramped and uncomfortable in town, the decor is early bordello, and the service is oppressive at best. Still, the steaks are superb, the wine list is genuinely extraordinary, and it's a chance to experience at first hand the level of abuse that is an integral part of New York City life. Closed Sundays. Major credit cards accepted. 210 E. 46th St. (phone: 687-4855). Expensive.

Tavern-on-the-Green – The food is less famous than the decor and location just inside Central Park at one of New York's most beautiful dining establishments. In winter, the snow-covered trees trimmed with tiny white lights outside the *Crystal Room* make a dazzling display. Best of all at *Christmastime* (when reservations are a must a month in advance), but only slightly less spectacular in summer, when diners can sit in the outdoor garden. Open daily. Major credit cards accepted. Central Park West and 67th St. (phone: 873-3200). Expensive.

Terry Dinan's – The old *"21"* team from host to chef assuages the nostalgia of that restaurant's clientele for the *"21"* taste. Good uncomplicated American and continental fare is served in a comfortable, wood-paneled, club-like setting. Be sure to try the toasted pound cake with ice cream and hot chocolate sauce for dessert. Open daily. Major credit cards accepted. 10 Park Ave. at 34th St. (phone: 576-1010). Expensive.

Windows on the World – Somewhat overpriced (though interesting) menu that is extremely ambitious, but the food is less alluring than the best view of the city. Try to sit along the north wall, where you'll have all of glittering Manhattan spread out at your feet. If you don't care to spend the price of dinner, stop for a drink in the bar and enjoy the superb hors d'oeuvres. There's also a reasonably priced all-day Sunday buffet. The *Cellar in the Sky* room here serves an interesting prix fixe menu with a wide choice of wines — but no view. Open daily; for weekends, reservations a month in advance are advised. Major credit cards accepted. 1 World Trade Center (phone: 938-1111). Expensive.

Café des Artistes – Under the direction of restaurateur and raconteur George Lang, this West Side favorite is one of New York's most romantic restaurants. Appetizers and main dishes (French country-style) are all first rate, but the real lures are the desserts. Save room, for they've an unusual special offering that includes a sample of every dessert on the menu. For those with a sweet tooth, it's like visiting paradise. The most beautiful weekend brunch in town (reservations necessary). Open daily. Major credit cards accepted. 1 W. 67th St. between Columbus Ave. and Central Park West (phone: 877-3500). Expensive to moderate.

Oyster Bar – The place for oysters: On any given day, there will be 10 varieties from which to choose. There's also Maine lobster, North Atlantic salmon, Dover sole, mako shark steaks, pompano, pink snapper, swordfish, Florida stone crabs in season, and Mediterranean seafood. The huge volume assures fresh product. Open weekdays. Major credit cards accepted. Grand Central Terminal, lower level (phone: 490-6650). Expensive to moderate.

Palm – The best sirloin steaks in New York, in an atmosphere so unattractive that it's the restaurant's prime appeal. Sawdust covers the floor, and tables and chairs are refugees from a thrift shop, but the steaks are just great. The largest (and most expensive) lobsters in New York are served here. *Palm, Too,* across the street, is a branch serving identical food that takes care of the overflow. Closed Sundays. Major credit cards accepted. 837 2nd Ave. between 44th and 45th Sts. (phone: 687-2953). Expensive to moderate.

Parioli Romanissimo – Ensconced in an attractive East Side townhouse, the tables at this classy spot are among the most difficult to book in the city. Those who succeed dine on pricey but delicious Italian specialties. Opt for a meaty main course like veal chop *giardiniera* and then splurge on the chocolate torte for dessert. Service is notoriously chilly, and even when reservations are in hand, expect a wait. Closed Sundays and Mondays. Only American Express, Diners Club, and Carte Blanche accepted. 24 E. 81st St. (phone: 288-2391). Expensive to moderate.

Parker Parker's Lighthouse – In addition to a spectacular waterfront view just across the Brooklyn Bridge and sophisticated decor, there's an interesting selection of Cajun and seafood dishes. Open daily. Major credit cards accepted. 1 Main St. at Fulton Landing, Brooklyn (phone: 718-237-1555). Expensive to moderate.

Peter Luger – The best porterhouse and T-bone steaks in the country, lurking in the shadows under the Brooklyn side of the Williamsburg Bridge. The neighborhood is hardly fashionable, but the food is first class. No menu, but try the thick-sliced onions and tomatoes under the special barbecue sauce, and be sure to taste the best home fried potatoes the city has to offer. Open daily. No credit cards accepted. 178 Broadway, Brooklyn (phone: 718-387-7400). Expensive to moderate.

Time & Again – For a feeling of Edwardian luxury, this handsome, well-appointed place serves superb American food with a French accent. The spacious and elegant dining room is a throwback to a bygone era and the food is first-rate, with sumptuous specialties like tuna with ginger cream and seared prawns with avocado, papaya, and grapefruit. Open daily. Major credit cards accepted. In the *Doral Tuscany Hotel,* 116 E. 39th St. (phone: 685-8887). Expensive to moderate.

Water Club – The decor at this restaurant/barge in the East River is naturally nautical, but with restraint, since the view is decorative enough: river traffic and the twinkling lights of the Manhattan and Queens skylines. The menu, too, is nautical, with similar restraint. Appetizers range from oysters and smoked salmon to beluga caviar, entrées from Maryland crab cakes to Dover sole (with a delicately flavored beurre blanc) and lobster — but diners also can order pâté plus filet mignon. Open daily; Sunday brunch. Major credit cards accepted. It's tricky to get here, so take a cab. East River at 30th St., on the northbound service road of the FDR Drive (phone: 683-3333). Expensive to moderate.

America – The menu is as big (and varied) as its namesake — a staggering 175-plus dishes, representing every corner of the country and the ethnic groups that inhabit it — including dishes like the American-as-apple-pie Blue Plate Special and a peanut butter and jelly sandwich. The food ranges from good to fair, and the service is best described as leisurely. With its high, exposed ceiling and mural-covered walls, America looks like a warehouse-cum-loft, with an elevated bar that, despite its football field dimensions, is jammed most nights. Open daily. Major credit cards accepted. 9-13 E. 18th St. (phone: 505-2110). Moderate.

American Festival Café – In Rockefeller Center, cheery and very American. Reasonably priced and varied menu, including prime ribs, steaks, salad, roast chicken, and warm and cold seafood. Noted for its desserts, including Mississippi mud pie, New York cheesecake, and Key lime pie. Open daily. Major credit cards accepted. 20 W. 50th St. (phone: 246-6699). Moderate.

Azzurro – A tiny, modern storefront on the Upper East Side demonstrates the unexpected delicacy of Sicilian cooking. Grilled fish, fine pasta specials, and delectable vino santo. The waiters are all cousins; Mama is in the kitchen. Open daily. Only American Express and Diners Club accepted. 1625 Second Ave. between 84th and 85th Sts. (phone: 517-7068). Moderate.

Ballroom – When it opened a few years ago, this very pretty bistro in the Garment District introduced a new twist to Manhattan dining — the *tapas* bar. A changing, varied menu of *tapas* (Spanish for "appetizer") is spread along a lengthy bar, and patrons either nibble their way through dinner at the bar or head for the dining room, where waiters circulate with trays of *tapas*. There's also a very tempting menu of main courses, a reasonable and tasty buffet lunch, and a dessert table that's as much a feast for the eyes as for the taste buds. Cabaret-type entertainment is another reason to go. Closed Sundays and Mondays. Major credit cards accepted. 253 W. 28th St. (phone: 244-3005). Moderate.

Black Sheep – Utterly charming French country inn atmosphere with regional farmhouse cooking primarily from Provence and Burgundy. Owner Michael Safdiah, who studied under French master chefs, is especially proud of the duckling braised over an open fire with Armagnac, prunes, and apricots; the loin rack of lamb, Tuscan-style; and subtly flavored seafood specials. Vegetarian dishes are imaginative and tasty (try the artichokes with potatoes). A traditional Provençal aioli sauce (mayonnaise made with garlic, olive oil, and anchovies) served with crudités welcomes all diners. Extensive wine list. Open daily. Major credit cards accepted. 344 W. 11th St. (phone: 242-1010). Moderate.

Café Un Deux Trois – In this lively theater district bistro, patrons draw on the paper tablecloths with crayons while waiting to sample carefully prepared daily specialties that include fresh sea trout, steaks with pommes frites, and couscous with chicken, lamb, and chickpeas. Theatergoers should plan to dine early to be sure to make curtain time. Open daily from noon to midnight (to 11 PM Sundays). Reservations necessary for 5 or more. Major credit cards accepted. 123 W. 44th St. (phone: 354-4148). Moderate.

Carolina – Southern and Southwestern dishes grilled over hickory and mesquite are specialties. Although the red pepper shrimp can be disappointingly mild, the crab cakes are light and succulent, the corn bread flavorful, and the slaw creamy and delicious. The green chili soufflé is a tasty starter and the chocolate mud pie and tangy lime pie tempting finales. Note that the rear "garden room" can be noisy and traffic through the front room disconcerting; ask for a table to the right of the entrance. Open daily. Major credit cards accepted. 355 W. 46th St. near 9th Ave. (phone: 245-0058). Moderate.

Cent' Anni – This Little Italy gem serves down-to-earth Northern Italian fare in an unpretentious storefront setting. There are only 60 seats, so evenings tend to be both crowded and convivial as diners enjoy classic pasta. The name comes from the traditional toast, "May you live 100 years!" Open daily. American Express accepted. 50 Carmine St., between Bleecker and Bedford Sts. (phone: 989-9494). Moderate.

Florent – A classic 1940s diner which has been converted into a hip new French restaurant is the last word in trendy New York style. With so much to look at, one almost forgets to eat! No credit cards accepted. Open daily. 69 Gansevoort St., between Washington and Greenwich Sts. (phone: 989-5779). Moderate.

Gage & Tollner – Holding forth at this stand since 1889, it's worth a visit, if only to watch the gaslight glowing in the evening. Southern genius, chef Edna Lewis's specialties include lobster Newburg and crabmeat Virginia. Among the specialties are 15 separate styles of potatoes. Open daily. Major credit cards accepted. 374 Fulton St., Brooklyn (phone: 718-875-5181). Moderate.

Grotta Azzurra – Neapolitan specialties are served in a basement in the heart of Little Italy. Lobster fra diavolo exacts a high price, but it's worth the tariff. The garlic bread is like none other in this world, and it guarantees that you won't be bothered by vampires for years. Closed Mondays. No reservations, so be prepared to wait in line. No credit cards accepted. 387 Broome St. (phone: 925-8775). Moderate.

Hatsuhana – A Japanese restaurant that's still winning kudos from some of New York's toughest restaurant critics. The sushi, sashimi, and tempura are about the tastiest in town. Closed Sundays. Reservations necessary for dinner only. Major credit cards accepted. 17 E. 48th St. (phone: 355-3345). Moderate.

Jean Lafitte – As accurate an evocation of a cozy Parisian neighborhood bistro as exists in New York. For French folk feeling homesick, this will cure their blues. Excellent tripe, and the best place to sample an authentic choucroute (on specials only) or steak au poivre. Superb soups, which change daily, are a special treat during a cold New York winter. Open nightly for dinner; lunch on weekdays only. Major credit cards accepted. 68 W. 58th St. (phone: 751-2323). Moderate.

K-Paul's–New York – This sister restaurant of *K-Paul's Louisiana Kitchen* in New Orleans offers the city's best Cajun and creole specialties, along with extraordinarily friendly and welcoming service. Try the blackened prime ribs with mashed potatoes, crawfish *étouffée* with rice, and whenever available, their chocolate mocha cake for dessert. You are awarded stars at meal's end for your consumption. Open daily. Major credit cards accepted. 622 Broadway, between Bleecker and Houston Sts. (phone: 460-9633). Moderate.

Le Madri – A refreshing change of pace from the glut of so-so Italian restaurants. Delicacies such as fresh prawns stuffed with wild mushrooms and ricotta cheese, the antipasto with carmelized onions, and the osso buco are fabulous, and the apple tart with cinnamon ice cream is bound to leave you smiling at your dinner companion. Open daily. Major credit cards accepted. 168 W. 18th St. (phone: 727-8022). Moderate.

Montrachet – A downtown favorite, this spot is the creation of Drew Nieporent, a star on the city food scene. The cooking is best described as nouvelle French, with an emphasis on traditional flavors. Favorite dishes include duck in red wine sauce with mission figs, duckling with fresh ginger, and roast chicken with garlic and potato purée. In addition to an extensive à la carte menu, there also are three excellent prix fixe menus whose prices escalate as their selections increase. Closed

Sundays. American Express accepted. 239 W. Broadway, between Walker and White Sts. (phone: 219-2777). Moderate.

Odéon – In a gray cast-iron building, this refurbished cafeteria is in the midst of TriBeCa. Look for entrées such as squab with shiitake mushrooms and wild rice, and roast loin of lamb with white peppercorns. A dessert worth trying is crêpes with praline butter and apricot liqueur. Open daily; Sunday brunch. Major credit cards accepted. 145 W. Broadway (phone: 233-0507). Moderate.

Periyali – In this cool Aegean oasis, patrons enjoy traditional Greek fare prepared with an exceptionally light touch. Specialties include lima bean salad with *skordalia,* a tangy potato-based purée; baked sea bass with garlic, tomato, and white wine; and moussaka with grilled zucchini. For dessert, don't miss the luscious custard-filled *galaktoboreko.* Open weekdays for lunch and daily except Sundays for dinner. Major credit cards accepted. 35 W. 20th St. (phone: 463-7890). Moderate.

Pierre au Tunnel – Onion soup, mussels, frogs' legs, and minute steaks typify the French provincial dishes featured by this theater district bistro since 1950. Try the *noisette de veau* (loin of veal sautéed with fresh mushrooms and shallots) or *tripes à la mode de Caen* (tripe cooked with white wine and calvados). Closed Sundays. Only American Express, Visa, and MasterCard accepted. 250 W. 47th St. (phone: 582-2166). Moderate.

Provence – The perfect restaurant for its neighborhood. The spices and tomato-based sauces of southeastern France are nowhere better prepared, and the roast chicken with garlic gives a whole new meaning to the serving of fowl. A huge vat of aging brandy adorns the bar and provides a perfect digestif at the conclusion of a meal. In summer, the garden is an idyllic dining spot. Closed Mondays. Only American Express accepted. 38 MacDougal St. (phone: 475-7500). Moderate.

Quatorze – On the periphery of Greenwich Village, this is an attractive, convivial bistro. Diners may eat either at the marble-topped bar or in the pale yellow dining room with oak floor, white linen-draped tables, and a wall of red velvet banquettes. Try the chicory and bacon salad drenched in a hot vinaigrette dressing, then the grilled salmon in choron sauce or the grilled chicken. Choose the crispy, warm apple tart for dessert. The short wine list includes some interesting, reasonably priced offerings. Open daily. Only American Express accepted. 240 W. 14th St. (phone: 206-7006). Moderate.

Raga – A carved wooden gateway, tall carved columns, heavy silk fabrics, and antique musical instruments mounted on the walls provide the opulent setting for one of New York's finest Indian restaurants. Lobster Malabar, gosht vindaloo, and meat, poultry, and seafood specialties broiled in the stone tandoor are particularly good here. Most evenings musicians play the sitar, tabla, and flute for an unobtrusive background. Open daily. Major credit cards accepted. 57 W. 48th St. (phone: 757-3450). Moderate.

Sabor – Though tiny and unprepossessing, this eatery in the heart of Greenwich Village serves good simple, Cuban-based cooking: white bean soup, red snapper in green sauce, baked chicken scented with cumin, and shrimp in lime sauce. The baked coconut dessert, with cinnamon, sherry, and a dollop of whipped cream, is a must. Open daily. Major credit cards accepted. 20 Cornelia St. (phone: 243-9579). Moderate.

Sammy's Roumanian Steak House – The last survivor of a long, Lower East Side tradition of ethnic meat restaurants. Traditional Eastern European favorites are featured, as is old country music of a sort you're not likely to hear in any other establishment. The makings for egg creams are set right on the table — an experience you don't usually find this side of Minsk. Open daily. Only American Express and Diners Club accepted. 157 Chrystie St. (phone: 673-5526). Moderate.

Santa Fe – Less trendy than many of the new Mexican eateries that have sprung up around the city; there are no hanging plants, no neon signs, no ear-splitting conversational roar. Instead, crisp linen and salmon-colored walls hung with Mexican weavings provide a serene setting for nicely tart margaritas and well-prepared Southwestern dishes. Just a few blocks from *Lincoln Center*. Open daily. Major credit cards accepted. 72 W. 69th St. (phone: 724-0822). Moderate.

Shun Lee Palace – The late T. T. Wang was one of New York City's most talented Chinese cooks, and his menu here includes some exciting Oriental temptations. If you can somehow round up a group of 10 to dine together, you might be interested in ordering Wang's special Chinese feast. Open daily. Only American Express and Diners Club accepted. 155 E. 55th St. (phone: 371-8844). Moderate.

Shun Lee West – Same as above, this time very near *Lincoln Center*. Actually, this dining room is the better of the two *Shun Lee* emporia owned and run by Michael Tong, and its prices are about 15% lower. The adjoining *Shun Lee Café* serves Chinese dim sum. Open daily. Major credit cards accepted. 43 W. 65th St. (phone: 595-8895). Moderate.

TriBeCa Grill – A winning combination of celebrity and cooking. Stargazers come in hopes of seeing one of the co-owners: Robert De Niro, Sean Penn, Mikhail Baryshnikov, or Bill Murray. Serious diners flock to sample food director Drew Nieporent's menu, that includes such temptations as duck confit with crisp greens, *cavatelli* with plum tomatoes, basil, and pecorino cheese. Reservations necessary 3 weeks in advance. Open daily. Major credit cards accepted. 375 Greenwich St. at Franklin (phone: 941-3900). Moderate.

Tropica – The setting is an amalgam of every Caribbean island you've ever visited. The cooking is island-inspired; saucy and piquant, with an emphasis on freshly-caught seafood. Its location on the concourse level of Grand Central Terminal attracts overflow crowds of expense-account types at lunch, but things quiet down for the dinner crowd. Closed Saturdays and Sundays. Major credit cards accepted. Pan Am Building, 200 Park Ave., 45th St. and Vanderbilt Ave. (phone: 867-6767). Moderate.

Village Green – The owners of this 19th-century West Village row house have kept the 2-story dining room elegant yet cozy: linen-draped tables shining with crystal and silver, and a fire snapping away in the hearth. The menu is continental, the food always well prepared, and the service friendly. Closed Sundays and Mondays. Major credit cards accepted. 531 Hudson St. (phone: 255-1650). Moderate.

Zarela – Probably the city's best Mexican restaurant, this festive East Sider flourishes under the direction of its high-profile owner, Zarela Martinez, whose enthusiasm is as dynamic as her cooking. Menu selections range from the familiar to such eclectic dishes as roast duck with tomato and red chili sauce, and shrimp with tomato poblano salsa. There are spice levels for every palate, so the cautious needn't nurse fears. And there are tangy margaritas to shore up everyone's courage. Open weekdays for lunch, and Saturdays and Sundays for dinner. Most major credit cards accepted. 953 2nd Ave., near 50th St. (phone: 644-6740). Moderate.

Carnegie Delicatessen – The quintessential New York deli. The sandwiches are enormous, far too big to put in a normal human mouth. Corned beef and pastrami are king; waiters provide entertaining banter (to help pass the time). Communal tables; no atmosphere save the frantic 7th Avenue scene. Open daily. No reservations or credit cards accepted. 854 7th Ave. (phone: 757-2245). Moderate to inexpensive.

Harvey's Chelsea – Etched-glass windows, polished brass rails, and baroque wood paneling make this turn-of-the-century bar a delightful oasis in an otherwise dreary neighborhood. The best choice on the menu is the tasty fish and chips, accompanied by a frosty draft. Open daily. Only American Express accepted. 108 W. 18th St. (phone: 243-5644). Moderate to inexpensive.

Málaga – Delicious, reasonably priced Spanish specialties such as paella, shrimp in garlic sauce, and fish in salsa verde make this a neighborhood favorite. Try to sit in the front room, because the tin ceiling in the back room reverberates with noise when it's crowded. Open daily. Major credit cards accepted. 406 E. 73rd St. (phone: 737-7659 or 650-0605). Moderate to inexpensive.

Il Bocconcino – The celebrity photographs in the window date back to *la dolce vita* days, when Gilberto was a *papparazzo* in Rome. Now he and co-owner Giorgio run this modest but congenial Greenwich Village spot, with lace curtains, white tablecloths, and some murals of Italianate architecture to remind them of home. Sample the *bruschetta* (Roman garlic bread), then follow with pasta, chicken, veal, seafood, or pizza. Sidewalk tables in summer. Open daily. Major credit cards accepted. 168 Sullivan St. (phone: 982-0329). Inexpensive.

Café Mocca – Close your eyes and you're dining in downtown Budapest. Start with the gutsy goulash soup, go for the stuffed cabbage heaped with sauerkraut, and somehow leave room for the *palacsintas* (crêpes with jam) for dessert. A bargain at thrice the price. Open daily. Reservations advised for dinner. No credit cards accepted. 1588 Second Ave. at E. 82nd St. (phone: 734-6470). Inexpensive.

Carmine's – This eatery lures the hungry hordes with oversize portions of home-style food at reasonable prices. There's nothing "nouvelle" about this menu of Italian favorites reminiscent of Sunday dinner at mama's that includes such standbys as fried calamari, spaghetti with meatballs, and chicken Contadina (with sausage, peppers, and lots of garlic). Reservations are accepted only for parties over six; otherwise, be prepared to wait in a very long line. Open daily. Most major credit cards accepted. 2450 Broadway, between 90th and 91st Sts. (phone: 362-2200). Inexpensive.

Hard Rock Café – More a monument to rock 'n' roll than a restaurant, this funky spot — akin to the original in London — sports all manner of memorabilia: the guitars of Eric Clapton, Pete Townsend, and Bo Diddley, gold records of the *Rolling Stones,* and Prince's purple coat. Check out the 45-foot guitar-shaped bar and the 1959 Cadillac Biarritz jutting out from the second floor. The menu is your basic burgers and shakes; the music can be very loud. Popular with the younger set, the café draws between 1,500 and 2,400 patrons a day. Open daily. Major credit cards accepted. 221 W. 57th St. (phone: 489-6565). Inexpensive.

Hunan House – Among Chinatown's best, this pleasant place specializes in the subtly spiced food of the province of Hunan. Start off with fried dumplings or hot and sour soup, then have Hunan lamb, prepared with scallions; Changsha beef, done in a hot sauce with broccoli; or Confucius prawns with cashews. Open daily. No reservations. Only American Express and Diners Club accepted. 45 Mott St. (phone: 962-0010). Inexpensive.

Manhattan Brewing Company – A 3-level restaurant–cum–shopping complex features authentic barbecued, smoked, and grilled dishes — served at the *Tap Room* and the *Ocean Grill* — as well as a raw bar, liquor bar, and brewed-on-the-premises beers. Open daily. MasterCard, Visa, and American Express accepted. 40-42 Thompson St. (phone: 219-9250). Inexpensive.

Pamir – Small and family-run, this spot specializes in Afghan (much like Indian) cooking. The delicately seasoned lamb dishes are very good.

Closed Mondays. Only MasterCard and Visa accepted. 1437 2nd Ave. (phone: 734-3791). Inexpensive.

Serendipity 3 – Definitely not for kids only — this East Side classic has been packing them in for as long as most of us can remember. The front resembles an old-fashioned general store (but the merchandise is cutting-edge chic and trendy); the rear dining room is a cozy jumble of antique oak tables, Tiffany-style lamps, and old-time tin signs. Chocaholics delight in the bathtub-size hot fudge sundaes, and other favorites are the foot-long hot dogs and frozen hot chocolate. A great place to rest up after a *Bloomingdale's* shopping blitz. Open daily. Major credit cards accepted. 225 E. 60th St., between 2nd and 3rd Aves. (phone: 838-3531). Inexpensive.

Tennessee Mountain – Some of the meatiest baby back ribs in town come from this casual SoHo outpost. The gentle tomato-based sauce is also used to flavor the barbecued chicken, and don't miss the fried onion rings. Seafood also is served. Open daily; weekend brunch. Major credit cards accepted. 143 Spring St. (phone: 431-3993). Inexpensive.

Sunday brunch is a cherished tradition among New Yorkers (who usually take along a copy of the Sunday *New York Times*). Some popular brunch spots are *Sarabeth's Kitchen* (423 Amsterdam Ave.; phone: 496-6280; and 1295 Madison Ave.; phone: 410-7335); *Provence* (38 MacDougal St.; phone: 475-7500); *Man Ray Bistro* (169 8th Ave.; phone: 627-4220); *Odéon* (145 W. Broadway; phone: 233-0507); *Cadillac Bar* (15 W. 21st St.; phone: 645-7220); *Brasserie* (100 E. 53rd St.; phone: 751-4840); and *Florent* (69 Gansevoort St.; phone: 989-5779). Most of these cost under $20 per person. Hotel dining rooms with copious, and more costly, brunch buffets are the *Café Pierre* at the *Pierre; Ambassador Grill* at *UN Plaza; Peacock Alley* at the *Waldorf-Astoria;* and the *Palm Court* at the *Plaza.*

TAKING TEA: New Yorkers have become quite fond of the British tradition of afternoon tea, and a number of the city's poshest hotels have jumped on the bandwagon: the *Carlyle's Gallery,* the *Mayfair Regent,* the *Lowell,* the *Plaza's Palm Court,* the *Rotunda* at the *Pierre,* the *Helmsley Palace, Regency,* and *Stanhope* all offer superlative service to shoppers and browsers, with a variety of teas, scones, sandwiches, and condiments. Taking tea is a great way to experience the elegant ambience of these hostelries without having to stay the night. Tea for two usually is under $20; à la carte service is also available at some hotels.

For those who prefer cappuccino to China tea, *Caffè Roma* (385 Broome St.; phone: 226-8413) in the heart of Little Italy is one of the few remaining old-style coffeehouses still operating. Everything from espresso to egg creams is served daily from 8 AM to midnight.

OKLAHOMA CITY

AT-A-GLANCE

SEEING THE CITY: The *Eagles Nest* restaurant, on top of the 20-story United Founders Life Tower, offers a view of the city as well as fine seafood specialties (5900 Mosteller Dr.; phone: 840-5655). *Buggies for Rent* (phone: 235-1303) offers daily tours through downtown by horse-drawn carriage; tours also run Friday and Saturday nights, 6PM until midnight. *Territorial Tours Limited,* by Carol Jordan (1636 SW 79th. Ter., Oklahoma City, OK 73159) offers individual and group tours across the state. Most popular tours are offered through metro area, Guthrie, and Norman (phone: 681-6432).

SPECIAL PLACES: Most of the major attractions are not within walking distance. The city's *Masstrans* system provides bus service to all points of interest. For bus information, call 235-RIDE. You also can rent a car; all national car rental agencies are represented.

City Arts Center – Ongoing exhibitions, classes, and 1-day workshops (in art, dance, and professional writing). Open daily. 3000 Pershing Blvd., State Fairgrounds (phone: 948-6400).

Remington Park – This fancy racetrack even has something for the kids: an infield playground. Seasonal events begin in February, with quarter horse races scheduled from May to mid-July. Fall thoroughbred racing extends from late September to early December. Admission charge; special rates for seniors (62 and older). I-44 and Martin Luther King Blvd. (phone: 424-1000 or 800-456-9000).

National Cowboy Hall of Fame and Western Heritage Center – Hi-ho, Silver! Cowboys, real and fictional, line the halls of this outstanding museum. In addition to the extensive collection of Western art and sculpture, there are dioramas, relief maps showing migration paths, and a model Western village. Also represented are famous cowboys of the silver screen and heroes of the rodeo circuit. Open daily. Admission charge. 1700 NE 63rd St. (phone: 478-2250).

Oklahoma City Art Museum – One of the West's best fine art museums, with changing exhibits (every 6 to 8 weeks) of noted national and international artists. *Artsplace,* the downtown extension of the museum, displays the works of local and regional artists. Open daily. Admission charge. 3113 General Pershing Blvd. (phone: 946-4477) and 7316 Nichols Rd. (phone: 840-2759).

Kirkpatrick Center Museum Complex – A single price enables visitors to enjoy all the museums and galleries constituting this unique complex. In addition to the attractions listed below, the *Kirkpatrick Center* houses numerous exhibitions and historical collections. Open daily. Admission charge. 2100 NE 52nd St. (phone: 427-5461).

Air Space Museum – Over 500 exhibits, including the original 1912 Curtiss Pusher airplane and a reproduction of the space shuttle cockpit, tell the exciting story of aviation in Oklahoma and across the nation (phone: 427-5461).

Center of the American Indian – Donated to showcase Native American culture, the museum's permanent collection includes paintings, artifacts, crafts, and jewelry (phone: 427-5228).

CENTRAL
OKLAHOMA
CITY

International Photography Hall of Fame – Experience the world through the eyes of world-famous master photographers; of special note is the breathtaking photo-mural of the Grand Canyon (phone: 424-4055).

Omniplex Science Museum – One of the largest science and technology museums in the Southwest; hands-on participation is encouraged to make science fun for all ages (phone: 424-5545).

Kirkpatrick Planetarium – The most exciting way yet to discover the universe. Take a backyard look at the night skies on a voyage to the planets, stars, and galaxies (phone: 424-5545).

Enterprise Square, USA – A unique learning center that uses contemporary educational techniques, entertainment, and audience participation to communicate the fundamentals of the US economic system. Open daily. Admission charge. 2501 E. Memorial Rd. (phone: 425-5030).

Oklahoma City Zoo – Captivity seems to agree with the more than 2,000 animals, birds, and reptiles at one of the top ten zoos in the nation, perhaps because they're left to wander freely in natural settings. The zoo's newest attraction, Aquaticus, features live dolphin shows and marine life exhibits. A safari train transports visitors over 500 acres of exhibits. Open daily except *Christmas* and *New Year's Day.* Admission charge. Martin Luther King Blvd. and NE 50th St. (phone: 424-3344).

State Capitol – This is one of the few capitols in the nation that does not have a dome. It's also the only one with active oil wells on the grounds. The capitol complex consists of several buildings. Most interesting is the main building, of granite and limestone, with pillars and a wide staircase in front. A cowboy statue greets visitors entering the lobby, and murals of Oklahoma history hang in the halls. Open daily. Lincoln Blvd., between 22nd and 23rd Sts. (phone: 521-2011).

State Museum of Oklahoma – A fascinating collection of Indian artifacts chronicling Indian history from diggings that go back to AD 400 and to the days of Custer and Buffalo Bill. The library has one of the most complete archives of historical documents on American Indians in the US. Open daily. No admission charge. On the capitol grounds, in the Oklahoma Historical Society, 2100 N. Lincoln Blvd. (phone: 521-2491).

Frontier City Theme Park – Visitors enjoy thrilling rides and view exciting live and animated shows at this "western-style" theme park. Open daily, May through September. Admission charge. Rte. 35N and 122nd St. (phone: 478-2412).

White Water – At this amusement park, visitors can body-surf in the Wave Pool, take a slow ride over the rapids in an inner tube, or slide down the Bermuda Triangle (the tallest water slide in the world). Open May through September. Admission charge. 3908 W. Reno (phone: 943-9687).

Metro Concourse – Beneath downtown Oklahoma City is a network of tunnels and skywalks connecting dozens of unique restaurants and retail shops to hotels, office buildings, and the *Myriad Convention Center.* Stretching over 1½ miles, it is one of the most comprehensive enclosed pedestrian systems in the country. Open daily. No admission charge.

■ **EXTRA SPECIAL:** Myriad Gardens, one of Oklahoma City's unique attractions, is in the heart of downtown. Originally patterned after Tivoli Gardens in Copenhagen, this attractive park features spectacular landscaped hills, gardens, and waterfalls, enhanced by the Crystal Bridge — a huge glass and steel structure conceived as a greenhouse, containing exotic plants from all over the world. Live entertainment featured regularly on the *Water Stage* (phone: 297-3995). Open daily. No admission charge Mondays from 9 AM to noon. Other times: $2 adults; 75¢ children 4–12; and $1.50 for senior citizens.

SOURCES AND RESOURCES

TOURIST INFORMATION: Oklahoma City Convention and Visitors Bureau has brochures and maps (4 Santa Fe Plaza, Oklahoma City, OK 73102; phone: 278-8912 or 800-225-5652). Contact the Oklahoma state hotline (phone: 405-521-2413) for maps, calendars of events, health updates, and travel advisories.

Local Coverage – *Daily Oklahoman,* morning daily; *Journal Record,* daily for business and law news.; *Oklahoma Gazette,* weekly for feature and arts-related information.

Television Stations – KTVY Channel 4–NBC; KOCO Channel 5–ABC; KWTV Channel 9–CBS; OETA Channel 13–PBS.

Radio Stations – AM: WKY 930 (easy listening); KTOK 1000 (news/talk); KOMA 1520 (rock oldies). FM: KAIT 100 (rock); KEBC (country); KJYO 103 (top 40); KLTE (oldies); KMGL 104 (adult contemporary); KTNT (jazz).

Food – *Gazette* magazine, weekly.

TELEPHONE: The area code for Oklahoma City is 405.
Sales Tax – The city sales tax is 6¾%.

CLIMATE: The weather is very changeable. Changeable means that in winter it can be 12F in the morning and 45F or 50F in the afternoon. In the summer it sometimes gets up to 100F or higher, but the wind and low humidity keep it from being totally unbearable. The winds sometimes gust to 35 to 40 miles an hour.

GETTING AROUND: Airport – Will Rogers World Airport is a 15-minute drive from the downtown area; taxi fare should cost about $13. *Airport Express* (phone: 681-3311) provides transportation from the airport to downtown for $6 per person, plus $3 for each additional passenger.

Bus – *Masstrans* operates frequent buses; 300 E. California (phone: 235-RIDE).

Car Rental – Every major national firm is represented.

Taxi – There are taxi stands in front of the big hotels and at major intersections. For dependable service, call *Yellow Cab* (phone: 232-6161) or *Safeway Cab* (phone: 235-1431).

VITAL SERVICES: Audiovisual Equipment – *Fairview-AFX,* 3162 N. Portland (phone: 947-6711).

Business Services – *Kelly Services,* 6303 N. Portland, Suite 105 (phone: 946-4309).

Dry Cleaner/Tailor – *Grace Cleaners,* open 24 hours, 529 W. Main St. (phone: 235-2244).

Limousine – *Oklahoma City Limousine Service* (phone: 787-9475); *Airport Express* (phone: 681-3311).

Mechanic – *Ray's Tire and Auto Service,* 5201 N. Pennsylvania (phone: 842-1427).

Medical Emergency – *Presbyterian Hospital* (NE 13th ST. and Lincoln Blvd.; phone: 271-4064); *Ask-A-Nurse,* 24-hour hotline (phone: 232-6877).

Messenger Services – *Quick Way Delivery Service* (phone: 685-3708); *Executive Courier Service* (phone: 521-1566 or 525-3550).

National/International Courier – *Federal Express* (phone: 236-0004); *DHL Worldwide Courier Express* (phone: 495-1170 or 800-225-5345).

Pharmacy – *Eckerd Drugs,* 9 AM to 9 PM, 34th St. and Classen Blvd. (phone: 521-0996).

Photocopies – *PIP,* pickup and delivery service (905 NW 23rd St.; phone: 521-0851); *Archer Photo Group Copy Service,* pickup and delivery (711 N. Broadway; phone: 236-1607).

Post Office – The central office is located at 320 SW 5th St. (phone: 278-6300).

Professional Photographer – *Beats Photography* (phone: 751-1941).

Secretary/Stenographer – *Professional Suite* (phone: 236-1544); *Esther Secretarial Service* (phone: 943-8087).

Translator – *Language Associates of Oklahoma City,* translations, interpretations, and printing (phone: 946-1624); *Els Language Center,* translations (phone: 364-7170).

Typewriter Rental – *United Systems, Inc.* (phone: 523-2162).

Western Union/Telex – Many offices are located around the city (phone: 800-631-3193).

 SPECIAL EVENTS: *Wintertales,* storytelling festival, January; *Festival of the Arts,* April; *Red Earth,* the largest celebration of Native American culture on the North American continent, and *Aerospace America,* air show, June; *Festifall,* arts festival, September; *Oklahoma State Fair,* September; *World Championship Morgan Horse Show* and *Festival of the Horse,* October; *Oklahoma City Jim Thorpe Marathon Weekend,* November; *World Championship Quarter Horse Show,* December; *World Champion Barrel Racing, American Bicycle Association "Grand National,"* and *All-College Basketball Tournament,* December.

 MUSEUMS: In addition to the variety of museums described in *Special Places,* other Oklahoma City museums include the following:

1899er Harn Museum and Gardens – 312 NE 18th St. (phone: 235-4058).

45th Infantry Division Museum – 2145 NE 36th St. (phone: 424-5313).

Governor's Mansion – 820 NE 23rd St. (phone: 521-2342).

Museum of the Unassigned Lands – 4300 N. Sewell (phone: 521-1889).

National Softball Hall of Fame – 2801 NE 50th St. (phone: 424-5266).

Oklahoma Firefighters Museum – 2716 NE 50th St. (phone: 424-3440).

Oklahoma Heritage Center – 201 NW 14th St. (phone: 235-4458).

Oklahoma Museum of Natural History – 1335 Asp Ave., Norman (phone: 325-4711).

Overholser Mansion – One of 13 historic homes in Oklahoma designated as such by the Oklahoma Historical Society. Built in 1903 by Henry Overholser — dubbed "Father of Oklahoma City" — much of its original furnishings, as well as its charm, has been preserved. Tours given Tuesdays through Fridays on the hour, beginning at 10 AM, and on Saturdays and Sundays at 2, 3, and 4 PM. Closed on Mondays and holidays. No admission fee. 405 NW 15th St. (phone: 528-8485).

 **MAJOR COLLEGES AND UNIVERSITIES:** Central State University (Edmond; phone: 341-2980); University of Oklahoma (Norman; phone: 325-0311); Oklahoma State University (Stillwater; phone: 744-5000); Oklahoma City University (2501 NW Blackwelder; phone: 521-5000); Southern Nazarene College (6729 NW 39th Expy.; phone: 789-6400).

SPORTS AND FITNESS: Baseball – The AAA American League '89ers play at *All Sports Stadium,* Fairgrounds Park, 10th and May (phone: 946-8989).

Basketball – Last year was the premier season for the newly formed Oklahoma City *Cavalry* basketball team, members of the Continental Basketball Association (phone: 232-DUNK).

Fishing – Anglers will find excellent fishing at any of the beautiful lakes in the Oklahoma City area: Lake Hefner (Hefner Rd. & N. Portland), Lake Overholser (NW 36th & County Line Rd.), Lake Stanley Draper (I-240 & Douglas Blvd.), and Lake Thunderbird (Hwy. 9, east of Norman).

Fitness Center – The *YMCA* has a pool, track, weights, and squash, handball, and racquetball courts. 125 NW 5th St. (phone: 232-6101).

Football – College games are held at *Owen Stadium,* at the University of Oklahoma, where you'll find the Oklahoma City *Sooners* (in Norman; phone: 325-0311), and *Lewis Field* at Oklahoma State University, where the Oklahoma State *Cowboys* play (Stillwater; phone: 744-5746).

Golf – The best city course is at Lincoln Park, Eastern Ave. and NE 50th St.

Horse Racing – *Remington Park,* the state's first major pari-mutuel racetrack, is an $97-million facility featuring 153 days of thoroughbred, quarter horse, and mixed-breed racing. For information and schedules, call 424-1000 or 800-456-9000.

Jogging – It's possible to run in Memorial Park, at NW 32nd and Classen; in the park is a posted map showing 2- to 8-mile routes. Run around Lake Hefner, in Stars and Stripes Park, off Hefner Road, or the less traveled Lake Overholser, west of downtown and reachable only by car; or take the No. 11 or the No. 12 bus to Westwood and run around Woodson Park (1½ miles).

Sailing – There's good sailing on Lake Hefner, Lake Overholser, Lake Stanley Draper, and Lake Thunderbird.

Swimming – The Oklahoma City Community College *Aquatics Center* opened during the city's 1989 *US Olympic Festival.* The pool contains an 8-lane, 50-meter swimming pool and a separate 18-foot diving well with four springboards from three platforms. 7777 S. May St. (phone: 682-1611).

Tennis – Good public courts are at Memorial Park, 32nd and Classen, and Will Rogers Park, 36th and Portland.

THEATER: The *Lyric Theater* hosts a professional summer stock company that performs musicals from June through August (NW 25th and Blackwelder; phone: 528-3636). The *Jewel Box Theatre* (3700 N. Walker; phone: 521-1786) and *Carpenter Square Theater* (400 W. Main; phone: 232-6500) present innovative, contemporary productions year-round.

MUSIC: The *Oklahoma City Philharmonic Orchestra* plays at the *Civic Center Music Hall* (201 Channing Sq.; phone: 232-7575). Oklahoma City University's music school frequently sends opera singers to the *Metropolitan Opera* in New York City. Check out its performance schedules by calling 521-5000.

NIGHTCLUBS AND NIGHTLIFE: *Arthur's* is a lively nightspot in the *Hilton Inn Northwest* with dancing and complementary hors d'oeuvres (2945 NW Expressway; phone: 848-4811). *Russell's* is a Top 40 dance bar featuring live entertainment and a food buffet (in the *Marriott Hotel,* 3233 NW Expressway; phone: 842-6633), and *Jokers, The Comedy Club* features nationally acclaimed comedians (2925 W. Britton Rd.; phone: 752-5270).

BEST IN TOWN

CHECKING IN: Over 75 hotels and motels in Oklahoma City offer travelers a wide range of accommodations and prices. Expect to pay $80 and up for a double room at hotels listed as expensive and between $50 and $75 in the moderate category. All telephone numbers are in the 405 area code unless otherwise indicated.

Embassy Suites – More 236 (1- and 2-bedroom) suites opening onto balconies overlooking a central atrium are offered at this modern establishment. Dining room, spa, whirlpool bath, concierge, and free airport transportation also are available. Other amenities include 1 meeting room, A/V equipment, photocopiers, computers, and express checkout. Meridian and SW 18th (phone: 682-6000 or 800-EM-BASSY; Fax: 405-682-9835). Expensive.

Richmond Suites – Traditionally elegant, this all-suite hostelry has 49 units. Each suite includes handsomely furnished living areas, separate bedrooms, plus wet bar and refrigerator. Six boardroom suites are available, some with wood-burning fireplaces. The *Wellington* restaurant and club serves excellent continental fare. Room service is available until 9 PM; business conveniences include 3 meeting rooms and photocopiers. 31600 Richmond Square (phone: 840-1440; Fax: 405-843-4272). Expensive.

Waterford – Features include 196 rooms and suites that are graciously appointed with lovely cherry wood armoires and other traditional pieces. The *Waterford* restaurant offers formal continental dining; the *Veranda Room* serves lighter fare. For relaxation, guests enjoy a well-equipped health spa, including Nautilus, sauna, whirlpool bath, outdoor pool, tennis courts, jogging track, and squash courts. Free airport transportation. Room service is on call 24 hours a day. There are 10 meeting rooms, as well as secretarial assistance, photocopiers, computers, and express checkout. Excellent concierge service is available to 9th-floor guests. 63rd at Pennsylvania (phone: 848-4782; Fax: 405-843-9161; Telex: 796026). Expensive.

Marriott Oklahoma City – One of the city's newest, it offers modern decor along with the late-night hot spot, *Russell's*. Free airport transportation, spa, whirlpool bath, and a concierge. Secretarial services, meeting rooms with a capacity for up to 1,600, A/V equipment, and express checkout are all pluses. 3233 NW Expy. (phone: 842-6633 or 800-522-9440 in Oklahoma; 800-992-2009 outside the state; Fax: 405-840-5338). Expensive to moderate.

Sheraton Century Center – In the heart of downtown, this modern building has 400 rooms, in elegant decorator colors. Outdoor pool, disco, and restaurants. Room service is available around the clock from April through July. Concierge service is available on the 14th and 15th floors. There are 17 meeting rooms, A/V equipment, photocopiers, computers, and express checkout. 1 N. Broadway (phone: 235-2780 or 800-325-3535 Fax: 405-272-0369). Expensive to moderate.

Fifth Season Inn – Centrally located, it has beautifully decorated rooms opening onto a central atrium. Along with a full complimentary breakfast and cocktails, special services include a Jacuzzi, hot tub, sauna, and free transportation to the airport or *Remington Park* racetrack. Snacks and meals can be ordered from room service until midnight. Four rooms are available for business meetings, and A/V equipment, photocopiers, and express checkout are on hand. 63rd St. at Broadway Extension (phone: 843-5558; Fax: 405-843-5558, ext. 2641). Moderate.

Hilton Inn West – A popular gathering place for visitors as well as locals, there are 508 guestrooms, 3 bars (1 is a very good oyster bar), a restaurant, 4 pools (1 indoor), tennis, volleyball, and paddle tennis courts, an exercise room, and sauna. There are 16 meeting rooms, secretarial services, A/V equipment, photocopiers, computers, and express checkout. 401 S. Meridian (phone: 947-7681 or 800-HILTONS; Fax: 405-843-4829). Moderate.

Saddleback Inn – In the center of the I-40 and Meridian area, adjacent to many of the finest restaurants and city nightlife spots, it features a restaurant, lounge, outdoor pool, and spa. Free airport transportation. Room service can be ordered from 7 AM to noon, and from 5 to 9 PM. Business needs are served by 7 meeting rooms, A/V equipment, photocopiers, computers, and express checkout. 4300 SW 3rd (phone: 947-7000; Fax: 405-947-7000). Moderate.

EATING OUT: Oklahoma City is known for its steaks, but there is plenty of seafood listed on local menus. Restaurants are spread out across the city, rather than concentrated into one area. Expect to pay $40 for a meal for two at an expensive restaurant; between $15 and $20 at those we've classed as moderate; under $15 at the inexpensive ones. Prices do not include drinks, wine, or tip. About 30% of Oklahoma state is dry; the rest of the state, including Oklahoma City, serves liquor. All telephone numbers are in the 405 area code unless otherwise indicated.

Eagle's Nest – In addition to an elegant atmosphere and a magnificent view of the city, the menu features steaks, lobster, and veal. Open daily. Reservations advised. Major credit cards accepted. 5900 Mosteller Dr., United Founders Tower (phone: 840-5655). Expensive.

Michael's Supper Club – Elegant atmosphere, with a nightly piano bar. The menu features steaks, seafood, pasta, and veal. Open Mondays through Fridays for lunch and dinner; Saturdays, dinner only. Reservations advised. Major credit cards accepted. 1601 N. Western (phone: 842-5464). Expensive.

Haunted House – Dine in a relaxed atmosphere in a lovely old country inn serving steaks and seafood. Closed Sundays. Reservations necessary. Major credit cards accepted. 1 mile east of the *Cowboy Hall of Fame,* just off I-44 (phone: 478-1417). Expensive to moderate.

Hungry Peddler – Noted for its outstanding prime ribs and seafood specialties, it offers a deluxe salad bar and family atmosphere. Open daily. No reservations. Major credit cards accepted. 4500 W. Reno (phone: 947-0779). Expensive to moderate.

Alberta's Tea Room – Quiet atmosphere and fine food and service. The menu is the culmination of years of creative cooking, with homemade rolls, steaks, fresh shrimp in a luscious rémoulade sauce, and other specialties. Open for lunch only; closed Sundays. Reservations necessary for parties of five or more. Major credit cards accepted. *French Market Mall* at 63rd and N. May (phone: 842-3458). Moderate.

Applewoods – Moderately priced, excellent food in an elegant setting. All you can eat of the best apple fritters and dinner rolls found anywhere. Open daily. No reservations. Major credit cards accepted. 4301 SW 3rd (phone: 947-8484). Moderate.

Harrigans – The tastiest, widest variety of food in Oklahoma City: prime ribs, steaks, chicken, quiche, hamburgers, potato casserole, salads, homemade desserts, all served in attractive, brass-appointed dining rooms. Drinks served in club area. Open daily. No reservations. Major credit cards accepted. Three locations: 2125 N. Memorial (phone: 751-7322), 6420 NW Expy. (phone: 728-1329), and 2203 SW 74th (phone: 686-1012). Moderate.

Magnolia Café – Authentic Cajun-creole cooking, direct from Acadia, Louisiana. Live Dixieland band Friday and Saturday evenings create an entertaining atmosphere. Open daily. No reservations, except for large groups. Major credit cards accepted. 6714 N. Western (phone: 848-1026). Moderate.

Metro Wine Bar & Bistro – Casual country-French dining in a cozy atmosphere, with more than 200 vintages of wine from which to make a delicious selection. Sunday brunch is tops. Open daily. Reservations advised. Major credit cards accepted. 6418 N. Western (phone: 840-9463). Moderate.

Molly Murphy's House of Fine Repute – Waiters and waitresses here actually are performers who dress up like comic and storybook characters. The menu features steaks and chicken, and the Bacchus feast, a platter of steaks, chicken, vegetables, and fruit. Open daily. No reservations. Major credit cards accepted. 1100 S. Meridian (phone: 942-8588). Moderate.

Sullivan's – This is the place for straightforward American food — prime ribs, choice steaks, and seafood — prepared to perfection. Private dining rooms available. Open daily. Reservations advised. Major credit cards accepted. Corner of Reno and Meridian (phone: 943-5740). Moderate.

Texanna Reds – Sizzling mesquite-broiled fajitas and other Mexican specialties. Adult gameroom upstairs. Open daily. Reservations unnecessary. Major credit cards accepted. 4600 W. Reno (phone: 947-8665). Moderate.

Sleepy Hollow – The next best thing to eating a home-cooked meal. All meals are served family style. Entrées include chicken, steaks, shrimp, ribs, and catfish. Open daily. Reservations unnecessary. Major credit cards accepted. 1101 NE 50th (phone: 424-1614). Moderate to inexpensive.

Johnnie's Charcoal Broiler – Absolutely the best charcoal-broiled burgers in the region and excellent steaks served in a casual, family atmosphere. Open daily. No reservations or credit cards accepted. 2652 W. Britton Rd. (phone: 751-2565) and 421 SW 74th (phone: 634-4681). Inexpensive.

Oklahoma County Line – Barbecue is king here, a hearty variety stirred up from beef ribs, brisket, and smoked sausages. Prime ribs, pork loin, and duck and chicken are also well prepared. There's even homemade ice cream for dessert. Open daily. Reservations unnecessary. Major credit cards accepted. 1226 NE 63rd St. (phone: 478-4955). Inexpensive.

La Roca – Besides the attractive, casual atmosphere, devotees (as well as newcomers) also enjoy some of the best Mexican food north of the border. Closed Sundays. Reservations unnecessary. Major credit cards accepted. 412 S. Walker (phone: 235-0703). Inexpensive.

OMAHA

AT-A-GLANCE

 SEEING THE CITY: *Maxine's,* a restaurant and lounge atop the *Red Lion Inn,* offers the best view of Omaha — the metropolitan area, the Missouri River, and farther east to the small industrial town of Council Bluffs and the bluffs themselves, which are windblown deposits of soil that have formed steep hills, unusual for midwestern terrain.

SPECIAL PLACES: Omaha is spread out. You can walk around downtown or take the bus, but it's best to have a car to visit the places of interest on the outskirts of town, and in West Omaha, which is the thriving business center.

Central Park Mall – Reclaimed from a decayed commercial and warehouse district, this new urban park (completed in 1990) stretches a mile east to the Missouri River. Lined with an artificial stream, pond, and waterfall, the Mall is already the site of festivals and free concerts in nice weather. 14th and Douglas Sts.

Union Pacific Historical Museum – In *Union Pacific* National Headquarters, the museum recalls this line's colorful history as a transcontinental trailblazer, displaying everything from artifacts from the driving of the Golden Spike to Lincoln memorabilia (including a replica of his funeral car). Closed Sundays. No admission charge. 1415 Dodge St. (phone: 271-3530).

Old Market – Once Omaha's wholesale produce center, the market is now an ever-changing collection of small shops, restaurants, pubs, art and craft galleries, pinball arcades, and plant stores. Among the most interesting of the galleries is the *Artists' Cooperative,* which features contemporary and abstract prints, sculpture, and paintings by some of the area's best artists. The *Spaghetti Works* (phone: 422-0770) serves lunch and dinner — all the spaghetti and as much of the works (bread, salad, sauces) as you can eat for a song. 11th and Howard Sts.

Antiquarium – Near but not part of the *Old Market,* the *Antiquarium* has the real old stuff, from rare 19th-century manuscripts to over a half-million used books at bargain prices. Closed Sundays. 1215 Harney St. (phone: 341-8077).

Joslyn Art Museum – This monolithic chunk of pink marble, an Art Deco work in itself, holds one of the finest midwestern and western collections around, as well as exhibitions of international art through the ages. There's a fine collection of 19th-century European art, which includes works by Degas, Monet, and Renoir. During the summer, music programs are performed in the sculpture garden, and Sunday brunch is accompanied by classical music from October through May. Closed Mondays. Admission charge. 2200 Dodge St. (phone: 342-3300).

Boys Town – An internationally famous institution for homeless boys, it was founded in 1917 by Father Flanagan in the belief that there is no such thing as a bad boy, given a good Christian upbringing and education. Self-conducted tours of the campus, which has 65 buildings including grade and high schools, a trade school, gyms, a fine philatelic and

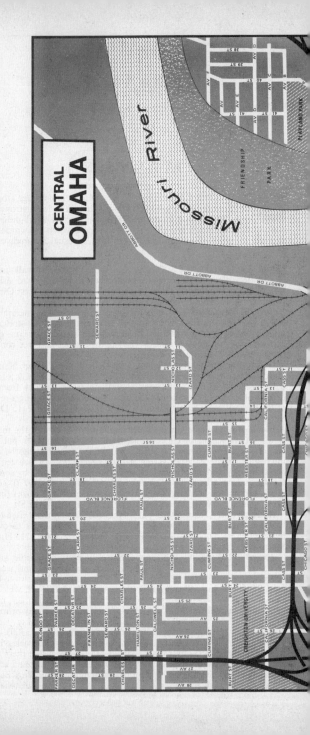

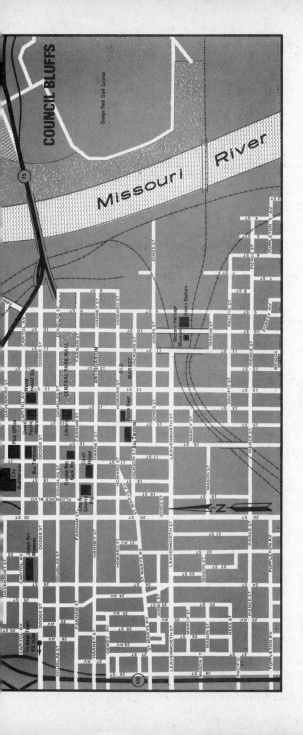

numismatic center, and 350 good boys. Open daily. No admission charge. 138th and W. Dodge Rd. (phone: 498-1140).

Henry Doorly Zoo – At 110 acres (bigger than either the San Diego or St. Louis zoos), there's plenty of space for more than 400 mammals, 670 birds, and 340 amphibians to make a home for themselves. The largest big cat complex in North America is here (a Sumatran tiger and Chinese leopards are on display), and the largest free-flight aviary in the zoo world. Visitors walk through a closed walkway on a 4-acre facility while birds fly around, above, and below the spectators. The new Lied Jungle, which will open late this year, is a re-creation of a tropical rain forest, and jungle inhabitants from Asia, Africa, South America, and Australia will live among its waterfalls and caves. Open daily from 9:30 AM to 5:30 PM from April 1 to October 31. The aquarium and Wild Kingdom pavilion, a hands-on learning center, stay open daily through the winter, from 9:30 AM to 4 PM. Admission charge. 10th and Deer Park Blvd. (phone: 733-8401).

■ **EXTRA SPECIAL:** Fifty miles southwest of Omaha along I-80 is Lincoln, the state's capital and second-largest city. The *University of Nebraska State Museum* (14th and U Sts., in Morrill Hall) has excellent displays of the geology and animal life of the Great Plains from prehistoric to modern times, as well as the world's largest mammoth. The 400-foot capitol is an impressive sight, visible for miles around, and features a glazed dome with the Indian Thunderbird design, topped by a 32-foot statue of *The Sower*.

SOURCES AND RESOURCES

 TOURIST INFORMATION: The Omaha Convention and Visitors Bureau (1819 Farnam, suite 1200, Omaha, NE 68183; phone: 444-4660) publishes brochures and maps of attractions that are available in all the hotels. For timely information on scheduled cultural events, call the bureau's Events Hotline (phone: 444-6800). Contact the Nebraska state hotline (800-228-4307) for maps, calendars of events, health updates, and travel advisories.

Local Coverage – *Omaha World-Herald,* morning and evening daily, publishes a Sunday *Entertainment* magazine, which lists the coming week's events.

Television Stations – KMTV Channel 3–CBS; WOWT Channel 6–NBC; KETV Channel 7–ABC; NETV Channel 12–PBS.

Radio Stations – AM: KFAB 1110 (adult contemporary music); KKAR 1180 (news/talk); KOIL 1290 (oldies). FM: KIWR 89.7 (classical/jazz/new age); KIOS 91.5 (National Public Radio; classical); KEFM 96.1 (contemporary hits); KGOR 99.9 (1960s and 1970s music).

Food – Weekend editions of the *Omaha World-Herald* are the best bet for current information.

 TELEPHONE: The area code for Omaha is 402.
Sales Tax – The sales tax in Omaha is 6.5%; across the river in Council Bluffs, shoppers pay a 5% tax.

 CLIMATE: Seasons are distinct and there is daily variety, perhaps a bit too much for some when the mercury drops to 15F below or rises to 105F above. Omaha is mostly sunny, with evening showers and thunderstorms occurring frequently between April and September.

GETTING AROUND: Airport – Omaha's Eppley Airfield is a 10-minute drive from downtown; cab fare should run about $7. Most hotels offer free airport shuttle transportation for guests.

Bus – *Metropolitan Area Transit* provides efficient service for the city and Council Bluffs. For route information contact *Metro Area Transit,* 2222 Cuming St. (phone: 341-0800).

Car Rental – Omaha has offices of the major national firms and inexpensive service is provided by *Thrifty,* 2323 Abbott Dr. (phone: 345-1040).

Taxi – Cabs can be picked up at taxi stands in front of major hotels or at the airport, or can be ordered on the phone. Major companies are *Happy Cab* (phone: 339-0110 or 331-8294); *Checker Cab* (phone: 342-8000); *Safeway Cab* (phone: 342-7474); and *Yellow Cab* (phone: 341-9000).

VITAL SERVICES: Audiovisual Equipment – *Audiovisual Inc.* (phone: 593-6500); *Modern Sound* (phone: 341-8476).

Business Services – *Professional Typing Services,* 900 S. 74th Plaza (phone: 397-0309).

Dry Cleaner/Tailor – *Omaha Lace Laundry French Cleaners,* pickup and delivery, 5007 Leavenworth (phone: 556-1522).

Limousine – *Old Market Limousine* (phone: 346-5512); *Accent Limousine Service* (phone: 399-9300).

Mechanic – *Anderson's Amoco Service,* 3423 S. 72nd St., (phone: 391-8611).

Medical Emergency – *Methodist Hospital,* 8303 Dodge St. (phone: 390-4424).

Messenger Services – *Express Messenger Systems* (phone: 734-4650); *Happy Cab Taxi-Pak* (phone: 339-0110 or 331-8294).

National/International Courier – *Federal Express* (phone: 800-238-5355); *DHL Worldwide Courier Express* (phone: 330-6806).

Pharmacy – *Kohll's Park Avenue Drug,* open 365 days a year, 8 AM to 11:30 PM, 2923 Leavenworth St. (phone: 342-6547).

Photocopies – *Kinko's,* free pickup and delivery with a $20 minimum (1006 S. 74th Plaza; phone: 399-8860); *Copycat Instant Print,* pickup and delivery (1501 Howard St.; phone: 341-0720).

Post Office – The downtown office is at 215 N. 17th St. (phone: 221-3866).

Professional Photographer – *James Soucie Photography* (phone: 334-8556); *Kriss & McCallum Photographers* (phone: 392-1419).

Secretary/Stenographer – *Melichar Secretarial Services* (phone: 393-6776); *Professional Typing Services* (phone: 397-0309).

Translator – *University of Nebraska at Omaha,* Foreign Language Dept., limited referral service, Spanish, French, German (phone: 554-4841); *Creighton University,* Modern Language Dept., limited referral service, French, Spanish (phone: 280-2508).

Typewriter Rental – *Honeymoon Rent-all,* 2-day minimum (phone: 331-6015); *All Makes Office Equipment,* 1-month minimum (phone: 341-2413).

Western Union/Telex – Many offices are located around the city (phone: 800-779-1111).

SPECIAL EVENTS: The *Ak-Sar-Ben World's Championship Rodeo* in late September features bull riding, calf roping, wild broncos, livestock collections, and country-and-western entertainers at *Ak-Sar-Ben Field,* 63rd and Center Sts.

MUSEUMS: In addition to the *Joslyn Art Museum* and the *Union Pacific Historical Museum* (see *Special Places*), you ought to visit:

Omaha History Museum – Closed Mondays. 801 S. 10th St. (phone: 444-5071).

Strategic Aerospace Museum – Open daily. 12 miles south on US 75 (phone: 292-2001).

MAJOR COLLEGES AND UNIVERSITIES: The University of Nebraska (Omaha at 60th and Dodge Sts.; phone: 554-2800), with an enrollment of 15,000, and the Medical Center (42nd St. and Dewey Ave.; phone: 559-4000) are both part of the University of Nebraska system. Creighton University (enrollment 5,000) is a private institution founded in 1878 by the Creightons, early settlers of the territory (2500 California St.; phone: 280-2700).

 SHOPPING: Regency Parkway, a 1-mile stretch that parallels Interstate 680 between West Dodge Road and Pacific Street, is the tie that binds a good part of Omaha's best shopping. *Westroads Mall* (102nd Street and West Dodge Road) is Omaha's biggest shopping center. Among its enticements are 3 department stores, 8 movie screens, and more than 140 specialty stores and services.

A short drive south on the parkway is *Regency Fashion Court,* a decidedly European enclave whose indoor avenues are dotted with high-fashion and decorator shops.

One Pacific Place, located at Regency Parkway's southern terminus, (at 103rd and Pacific St.), collects specialty stores (such as *Brookstone, Talbots,* and *Laura Ashley*) whose names are familiar across the country. Visitors also may want to check out the *Crossroads Mall* (at 72nd and Dodge St.). The mall has a skylight fabric roof, three department stores, and a fast-food court.

 SPORTS AND FITNESS: Baseball – The American Association's Omaha *Royals* play their home games at *Rosenblatt Stadium* from May to September (13th St. and Murphy Ave.; phone: 734-2550). In June, the stadium is the site of the NCAA *College World Series;* tickets available at *City Auditorium* (1804 Capitol Ave.; phone: 444-4750).

Dog Racing – The enclosed grandstand at *Bluffs Run* offers pari-mutuel bettors all-season comfort. Races daily except Mondays from early January through late December. Take the S. 24th St. exit in Council Bluffs off I-80 (phone: 712 323-2500).

Fitness Centers – The *YMCA* provides a pool, track, and racquetball courts, 20th St. and Howard (phone: 341-1600).

Golf – There are two excellent public golf courses: *Benson* (5333 N. 72nd St.; phone: 444-4626) and *Applewood* (6111 S. 99th St.; phone: 444-4656).

Horse Racing – For racing and pari-mutuel betting, *Ak-Sar-Ben* is ranked among the country's finest tracks. The season is from May through August, 63rd and Center Sts. (phone: 554-8800).

Jogging – Run in Memorial Park; on the University of Nebraska at Omaha or Creighton University campuses; or in the Dundee area, off Dodge, especially along Underwood Street, which is lined with lovely, old homes.

Tennis – Dewey Park has fine outdoor public tennis courts (500 Turner Blvd.; phone: 444-4980), and Hanscom Park offers indoor public courts (3200 Creighton Blvd.; phone: 444-5584).

 THEATER: For current offerings, check the publications listed above. The *Omaha Community Playhouse,* where Henry Fonda got his start, puts on a large variety of productions year-round, using amateur performers and a professional staff (6915 Cass St.; phone: 553-0800). The *Firehouse Dinner Theater* (514 S. 11th St.; phone: 346-8833) has professional local and outside actors who perform in comedies and dramas throughout the year.

MUSIC: The *Omaha Symphony* performs with featured guest artists from September to May, and *Opera/Omaha* presents three operas from November to April, both at the *Orpheum Theater* (409 S. 16th St.), a restored vaudeville palace. The *City Audito-*

rium has entertainment all year. Tickets for all *Orpheum* and *Auditorium* events are available at the *Auditorium Box Office* (1804 Capitol Ave.; phone: 444-4750), or at *Younkers'* stores ticket centers.

NIGHTCLUBS AND NIGHTLIFE: The *Howard Street Tavern* is a two-fisted bar with the best in blues, jazz, rock, and bluegrass music (11th and Howard Sts.; phone: 341-0433). *The Funny Bone* (705 N. 114th St.; phone: 493-8036) attracts nationally known comic talent. Other hot spots are *Arthur's* (8025 W. Dodge Rd.; phone: 393-6369) and *Chicago* (3529 Farnam St.; phone: 346-7300).

BEST IN TOWN

CHECKING IN: Several of the national chains have good representatives in Omaha. Our selections range in price from around $95 and up for a double room per night in the expensive category, $55 to $90 in the moderate range, and $50 and under, inexpensive. All telephone numbers are in the 402 area code unless otherwise indicated.

Embassy Suites – A Spanish-style building with a gleaming tiled fountain courtyard and an indoor garden. The 189 suites have kitchens, living rooms, hide-a-bed couches, and complimentary full breakfasts (until 8 AM). Facilities also include wet bars, a heated indoor pool, whirlpool baths, and a sauna. Free airport service. Business amenities include 6 meeting rooms, A/V equipment, photocopiers, and express checkout. 7270 Cedar St., 1½ miles north of I-80, exit 72nd St. (phone: 397-5141 or 800-EMBASSY; Fax: 402-397-3266). Expensive.

Omaha Marriott – Within walking distance of the city's largest shopping center, the *Westroads Mall,* it offers 301 rooms. Business pluses are secretarial services, meeting rooms that hold up to 600, A/V equipment, photocopiers, and express checkout. 10220 Regency Circle, just southeast of the I-680 Dodge St. exit (phone: 399-9000 or 800-228-9290; Fax: 402-399-0223). Expensive.

Red Lion Inn – Its location across the street from *City Auditorium* makes it Omaha's busiest convention hotel, with 414 rooms. The bar of the rooftop restaurant, *Maxine's,* offers a panoramic view of the city. Free parking in adjacent garage, as well as shuttle service from the airport. There are concierge and secretarial services available, as well as meeting rooms with a capacity of 1,250, A/V equipment, photocopiers, computers, and express checkout. 1616 Dodge St. (phone: 346-7600 or 800-547-8010; Fax: 402-346-5772). Expensive.

Dillon Inn – Offers upscale accommodations, but dispenses with a pool and other extras. Complimentary continental breakfast plus a 24-hour restaurant next door. *Westroads Mall* is directly across the street. There are meeting rooms that hold up to 50, as well as A/V equipment and photocopiers. 9720 W. Dodge Rd., just northeast of I-680 Dodge St. exit (phone: 391-5300 or 800-253-7503; Fax: 402-391-8995). Moderate.

Holiday Inn – Nebraska's largest hostelry (404 rooms) features 2 restaurants, 2 lounges with live entertainment, a "Holidome" (enclosed swimming pool), putting green, electronic games, shuffleboard, and bar. Four meeting rooms are available, as well as secretarial services, A/V equipment, photocopiers, and express checkout. 3321 S. 72nd St., just north of I-80, exit 72nd St. (phone: 393-3950 or 800-465-4329; Fax: 402-393-1809). Moderate.

Days Inn – In one of the city's busiest hotel areas, this chain's brand of basic motel hospitality includes color TV sets, complimentary continental breakfast, and a *Perkins' Cake and Steak* restaurant next door.

7101 Grover, just north of I-80, 72nd St. exit (phone: 391-5757 or 800-228-2000; Fax: 402-391-5757, ext. 100). Inexpensive.

New Tower Inn Best Western – Centrally located, with 330 rooms, it has good standard accommodations with modern furnishings and design. There is a domed indoor pool, saunas, whirlpool baths, and a cocktail lounge, as well as meeting rooms with a capacity for up to 300, and photocopiers. 7764 Dodge St. (phone: 393-5500 or 800-228-9075; Fax: 402-393-2240). Inexpensive.

EATING OUT: There really are a lot of cows out here, and when visitors eat out they quickly learn why. Omaha restaurant offerings run the gamut from prime ribs to hamburgers. Steaks are big here, and folks are proud of the local product — the beef is terrific. This is not fertile ground for vegetarians. Besides steakhouses, there are several ethnic eateries, plus a handful of continental restaurants. Our selections range in price from $60 up for a dinner for two in the expensive range, $35 to $55 in the moderate, and $30 and under in the inexpensive range. Prices do not include drinks, wine, or tips. All telephone numbers are in the 402 area code unless otherwise indiated.

Blue Fox – The continental menu with a sprightly Greek accent is the creation of owner/chef George Kokkalas. Everything — from appetizers to desserts — is made from scratch, and the fish and other seafoods are flown in fresh. The veal dishes and rack of lamb are very good. Closed Sundays. Reservations advised. Major credit cards accepted. 11911 Pierce Court; just off 119th and Pacific Sts. in the *Boardwalk Shopping Center* (phone: 330-3700). Expensive.

French Café – Of Omaha's restaurants that specialize solely in French food, this one adds a bit of glamour and buzzes with excited conversation. Specialties include onion soup, veal, rack of lamb, a daily fresh fish dish, rich desserts, and an extensive wine list, all served in an elegant, comfortable atmosphere. It's decorated with antiques, brassworks, and fresh flowers. Open daily. Reservations advised. Major credit cards accepted. 1017 Howard St. (phone: 341-3547). Expensive.

Indian Oven – Tandoori cooking, done over an open fire in a clay oven, makes this *Old Market*–area restaurant the city's most exotic. Carefully spiced Indian dishes, only some of which are "hot," range from *rogan josh,* a traditional North Indian lamb curry, to several chicken entrées and an even longer list of vegetarian dishes. Closed Mondays. Reservations advised. Major credit cards accepted. 1010 S. Howard St. (phone: 342-4856). Expensive to moderate.

Salvatore's – The menu offers a wide range of Italian dishes as well as other fine continental food. There's a good wine list, and the owner sometimes sings operatic arias. Closed Sundays. Reservations advised. Major credit cards accepted. 4688 Leavenworth St. (phone: 553-1976). Expensive to moderate.

Firmature's Sidewalk Café – At this green oasis within the city's most elegant shopping center, the all-encompassing menu ranges from lighter fare — omelettes, crêpes, and such — to steaks and seafood. Specialty of the house is Omaha's most coveted prime ribs. The New Orleans Brunch served on Sundays is worth skipping a sermon for. Open daily. Reservations unnecessary. Major credit cards accepted. 153 Regency Fashion Court (phone: 397-9600). Moderate.

Imperial Palace – An artfully decorated alternative to the usual Chinese storefront eating place, it has gained a reputation as Omaha's Oriental best. The menu embraces several of the cuisines of Northern China and the sinus-clearing specialties of Szechuan and Mandarin cooking. Open daily. Reservations advised. Major credit cards accepted. 11200 Davenport St. (phone: 330-3888). Moderate to inexpensive.

Mister C's – Although the decor here might be a little tacky — twinkling lights reminiscent of Italian street carnivals, an iridescent mural of Venice on one wall, a backlighted diorama of a Sicilian village on another — the food is quite good. Specialties are Omaha steaks; homemade soup appears on every table nightly except Saturdays, and strolling musicians always are on hand to play requests. It may well be the busiest steakhouse in Omaha, and despite its formidable capacity, there's often a wait to get in. Mister C himself greets one and all. Open daily. Reservations essential. Major credit cards accepted. 5319 N. 30th St. (phone: 451-1998). Moderate to inexpensive.

Neon Goose – This glitzy café/bar covers an entire block facing the city's old Union Station, just a short walk south of the *Old Market* area. Its menu runs from burgers to fresh seafood and it is known for a very good Sunday brunch. Closed Mondays. No reservations. Major credit cards accepted. 1012 S. 10th St. (phone: 341-2063). Moderate to inexpensive.

Bohemian Café – Besides an impressive collection of Jim Beam bottles, which speaks for itself, the café features a full line of Eastern European specialties, like boiled beef in dill gravy, sweet and sour cabbage, roast duck, liver-dumpling soup, and kraut. Open daily. Reservations unnecessary. Major credit cards accepted. 1406 S. 13th St. (phone: 342-9838). Inexpensive.

Gallagher's – The long menu runs the gamut from light to hearty fare — quiche to burgers. The elegant decor is set off by a stained glass skylight. Open daily. Reservations unnecessary. Major credit cards accepted. 10730 Pacific St. (phone: 393-1421). Inexpensive.

The Michaels' – When *mamacitas* do the cooking, they do it right. Consistently excellent Mexican food — spiced to sting, but not to start a fire — served in an unpretentious bar atmosphere. There's also a second location, called *Michaels at the Market.* Both are open daily. No credit cards or reservations are accepted at either *The Michaels',* at 1919 Missouri Ave. (phone: 733-9666) or *Michaels at the Market,* at 1102 Harney (phone: 346-1205). Inexpensive.

To corral a prime Omaha steak, try either of Omaha's classic steakhouses, *Johnny's* or *Ross'.* In both places all is the way it should be, big and heavy, from the cowtown decor, where huge tables and chairs leave plenty of room to rassle with the beef, to that pure slab of well-marbled pleasure itself, which can weigh in at as much as 20 ounces (not including the potato, spaghetti, bread, and salads that normally come along with the main ingredient). *Johnny's* (4702 S. 27th St.; phone: 731-4774). *Ross'* (909 S. 72nd St.; phone: 393-2030). Both closed Sundays. Reservations are advisable for both, and major credits cards are accepted. Expensive to moderate.

ORLANDO

SEEING THE CITY: For most visitors, the Orlando area's premiere panorama is the one from *Top of the World* in *Walt Disney World*'s *Contemporary Resort.* Whether you see it at sunset, when rosy light gilds the spires of Cinderella Castle, or at night, when tiny white lights glitter along the rooflines, it's absolutely stunning.

SPECIAL PLACES: *Walt Disney World* alone requires a minimum of 4 to 5 days — and even twice that time would not do total justice to all its shows, sporting facilities, restaurants, and other attractions (see below). When the rest of Orlando is also considered, it's easy to see how time really can fly during a visit hereabouts.

ORLANDO AND ENVIRONS

Florida Cypress Gardens – It's said that you'd have to visit 70 countries at different times of the year to see all of the 8,000 varieties of plants that can be viewed in a single day at this 223-acre attraction developed back in the mid-1930s. The famous water ski shows, in which athletes ski barefoot and backward, are also well worthwhile. There also is an Animal Forest, with displays of various species of exotic animals. Kodak's revolving Island in the Sky offers spectacular views from 150 feet up, and Cypress Junction, an elaborate model railroad exhibit, is well worth a look. More than Magic is a new show incorporating sleight-of-hand and elaborate laser effects. Open daily. Admission charge. Rte. 540, Winter Haven (phone: 813-324-2111, or 800-237-4826; 800-237-4826 in Florida).

Gatorland Zoo – In a couple of hours here you see thousands of alligators. Open daily. Admission charge. 14501 S. Orange Blossom Trail near Kissimmee (phone: 855-5496).

Sea World – The world's largest marine park ranks among Orlando's must-sees thanks to the high quality of the animal displays. Don't miss Shamu; New Visions, a show that employs a video screen in its exploration of the complex personality of killer whales; Sharks!, an exhibit which includes a film showing an incredible shark-feeding frenzy sequence and a glass tunnel that lets you walk "through" a huge pool full of sharks; and the Penguin Encounter, where more than 200 feisty penguins waddle, hop, leap, and dive to the delight of onlookers. Open daily. Admission charge. 7007 Sea World Dr., Orlando (phone: 351-3600).

Wet 'n Wild – Among connoisseurs of water slides, this aquatic play park full of water-based thrill rides gets top marks. Bring a bathing suit, and prepare for long lines on summer afternoons. Varying hours, depending on the season. Admission charge. 6200 International Dr., Orlando (phone: 351-3200).

Universal Studios Florida – Moviemaking comes to central Florida. Along with Disney–MGM Studios Theme Park, this attraction, which opened in June of 1990, lets visitors immerse themselves in the world of movie and television production. A sister attraction to the Universal Hollywood tour, the Orlando studios allow guests to witness a wide range of trade secrets while participating in scriptwriting, set design, casting, costuming, makeup, sound effects, editing, and special effects. Major attractions include Kongfrontation, Jaws, Earthquake: The Big One, E.T.'s Adventure, Ghostbusters: A Live Action Spooktacular, and the Fantastic World of Hanna-Barbera. The 444-acre property also offers a tour that re-creates scenes from some of Universal's most memorable films. There are more than 40 restaurants, including the *Studio Commissary, Schwab's Pharmacy,* and *Mel's Diner* from the movie *Alice Doesn't Live Here Anymore,* plus a branch of the *Hard Rock Café.* More than 30 shops feature one-of-a-kind movie memorabilia, collectibles, clothing, and movie- and television-theme merchandise. Admission charge. 1000 Universal Studios Plaza (phone: 363-8000).

WALT DISNEY WORLD

The fact that *Walt Disney World* attracts over 30 million visitors annually says just about everything that anyone needs to know about the basic appeal of Walt Disney's greatest dream-come-true. Less obvious is the sheer size of the place. For instance, the Magic Kingdom, the well-known rides and attractions area with the Cinderella Castle and other landmarks of American pop culture, occupies just 98 of the 27,400 acres of *WDW*'s property. EPCOT Center, which opened in the fall of 1982 to great fanfare, is more than twice as large, and the Disney–MGM Studios Theme Park is slated to double in size during the next 2 years. That still leaves 26,500 acres for the villas and hotels, shopping, a nonpareil swimming hole, a state-of-the-art water park, a nighttime entertainment complex, three golf courses, tennis courts, several lakes, and a huge nature preserve. The main telephone number at *WDW* is 824-4321.

Magic Kingdom – The glittering Cinderella Castle, the magical heart of the Magic Kingdom, sets the mood for this marvel of a park full of nooks and crannies, lush landscaping, restaurants, shops, shows, and "adventures" — boat rides, roller coasters, and other amusements that transcend themselves because they're incorporated into elaborate sets full of artificial plants, robotic people, and sound effects.

Top attractions include Pirates of the Caribbean and Jungle Cruise in the park's Adventureland section; the implacably cute Country Bear Vacation Hoedown and Big Thunder Mountain Railroad in Frontierland; the beautiful Haunted Mansion in Liberty Square; the wild Space Mountain in-the-dark coaster in Tomorrowland; a special celebration with Mickey Mouse at Mickey's Starland; Fantasyland's It's A Small World, with mechanical dolls and folk costumes; and the Hall of Presidents in Liberty Square, where a Disney-manufactured Abraham Lincoln stands up and talks as though he were Abe in the flesh.

During summer evenings and school holiday periods, be sure to see the Main Street Electrical Parade. The floats, made of metal frameworks studded with a million twinkling lights, are stupendous; the music, very tuneful. The fireworks presented after the first of the two runnings of this parade are equally impressive.

EPCOT Center – Something like a world's fair, but executed with the considerable technical skills, creativity, and financial resources of the Disney organization, EPCOT Center has two "entertainment worlds": Future World and World Showcase. Future World examines often controversial concepts such as energy and agriculture, while World Showcase brings nations of the world to life with the same extraordinary devotion to detail that makes the Magic Kingdom so enchanting. Appropriate entertainment, ethnic food, and lively shops stocked with wares made in the featured nations round things out.

At EPCOT Center, as in the Magic Kingdom, there are a few attractions that visitors simply must not miss. In Future World, these include the entire Living Seas pavilion, the ride inside the round ball known as Spaceship Earth, the Listen to the Land boat ride in The Land pavilion, the Journey into Imagination ride, the 3-D movie *Captain EO* (starring

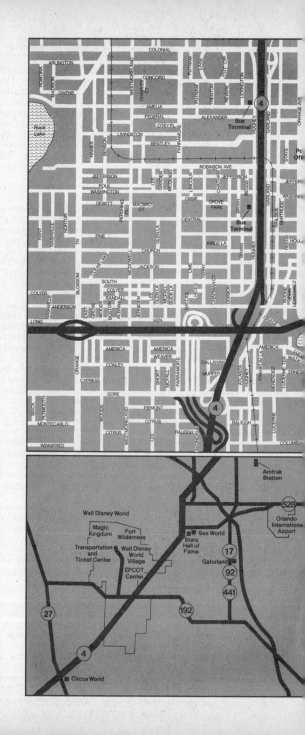

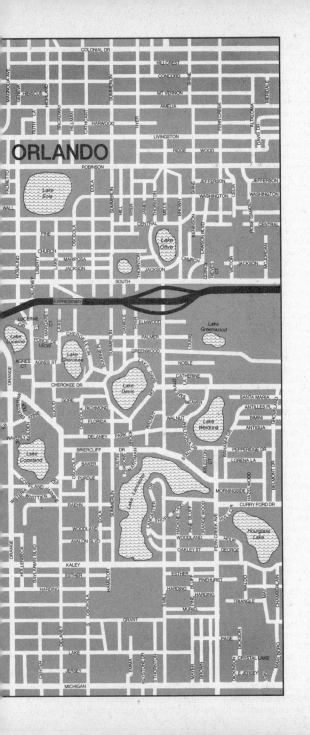

Michael Jackson), Body Wars, and Cranium Command in the Wonders of Life pavilion, the electronic funhouse known as the Image Works (in the Journey into Imagination pavilion), and the shows in the World of Motion, Horizons, and Energy pavilions. In World Showcase, make a point to see the movies in the Canada, China, and France pavilions, which take the travelogue to new heights, and the technologically diverting show at the American Adventure.

Disney–MGM Studios Theme Park – This major Disney attraction opened to rave reviews in May 1989, and it has been expanding ever since. For the first time in history, a fully functioning television and motion picture production facility offers guests the opportunity to spend a day at the movies — on both sides of the camera. The studios have several components. There's a backlot and soundstage tour like no other, where soundproof catwalks allow visitors to watch a movie or television show being filmed. Hollywood Boulevard, with its shops, restaurants, and Art Deco architecture, is reminiscent of old Hollywood. A ride-through attraction allows guests to see some famous film scenes: Gene Kelly in *Singin' in the Rain,* Julie Andrews and Dick Van Dyke in *Mary Poppins,* and Sigourney Weaver in *Aliens* come to life as Audio-Animatronic actors set in remarkably realistic movie set re-creations. A wonderful film starring Robin Williams and Walter Cronkite describes the animation process and guests are able to see animators at work. And to top off the excitement, the late Jim Henson's marvelous Muppets not only star in their own musical spectacular — "Here Come the Muppets," an extravagant swinging and singing show — but also star in the brand new *3-D Muppet Movie,* shown in a specially build Muppet theater. The recently acquired Teenage Mutant Ninja Turtle characters are an attraction, as well. A stunt theater, a variety of restaurants, and a sound effects studio round out the offerings. Star Tours, the much-acclaimed thrill attraction at California's *Disneyland,* is open as well. New attractions include the Honey, I Shrunk the Kids Adventure zone, inspired by the film, which features 30-foot-tall stalks of grass and a host of slides and props that make tall folk feel tiny; and the "Let's Make A Deal" television show, which is actually taped daily at the studios. During the next 5 years, additions will include Noah's Ark; Roger Rabbit's Hollywood, featuring the Toontown Trolley, the Benny the Cab ride, and the Baby Herman's Runaway Baby Buggy Ride; Dick Tracy's Crime Stoppers; and a replica of the original Disney Studios in Burbank.

Disney Village Marketplace – The shops here stock everything from baby bonnets to silk dresses, from thousand-dollar bottles of wine and toy soldiers to stuffed animals — and then some. You can sit on a bench and watch the boats on the lagoon — or rent one yourself on the spot. Best of all, for R&R, there's the wonderful *Baton Rouge Lounge,* aboard the gleaming white riverboat known as *Empress Lilly,* and *Cap'n Jack's,* across the lagoon, where you can get huge, tart, unique-to-*WDW* strawberry margaritas.

Typhoon Lagoon – The ultimate water-fun park. Set on a 50-acre site, it boasts the world's largest manmade watershed mountain, plus pools for snorkeling, surfing, swimming, and sliding.

River Country – It's next to impossible to go through childhood without developing a few fantasies about the perfect swimming hole. River Country is just such an animal, and it's full of curvy water chutes where even blasé grownups can't help but grin, even roar, with delight.

Discovery Island – Crisscrossed by footpaths, this tranquil 11½-acre landfall in Bay Lake is the home of dozens of birds — some in cages or huge aviaries, others running free; their chirps, tweets, crows, and caws nearly drown out the sounds of the little motorboats zipping across surrounding Bay Lake.

Hoop-Dee-Doo-Revue – Perhaps the most memorable of all *WDW*'s lively live entertainment is this dinner show, wherein a round of singing, dancing, and wisecracking keeps audiences whooping it up until their sides are as sore from laughing as their stomachs are full of country-style vittles. Reservations are required well in advance (phone: 934-7639).

Disney's Boardwalk – Slated to open this spring, this new attraction is designed in the tradition of the amusement areas of Atlantic City and Coney Island when they were in their prime. The 30-acre site features restaurants, shops, games, and live entertainment.

Pleasure Island – Adjacent to the *Disney Village Marketplace,* this complex features movies, nightclubs, restaurants, and shops that stay open well past midnight to fill the local void of late-night entertainment.

Behind the Scenes – There isn't a Magic Kingdom visitor around who wouldn't like to see Disney character costumes being made or talk to a Disney artist in person. The Wonders of Walt Disney World program makes precisely this kind of experience available to youngsters, and Disney Learning Adventures does the same for adults. For information, call 828-2405.

SOURCES AND RESOURCES

TOURIST INFORMATION: For details, contact the Orlando/ Orange County Convention and Visitors Bureau (7208 Sand Lake Rd., Suite 300, Orlando, FL 32819; phone: 363-5800) and Walt Disney World Co. (Box 10,000, Lake Buena Vista, FL 32830; phone: 824-4321). We immodestly believe that the best guide to the area is our own volume, *Steve Birnbaum Brings You the Best of Walt Disney World* (Avon Books & Hearst Professional Magazines, Inc.; $10.95). Contact the Florida state hotline (904-487-1462) for maps, calendars of events, health updates, and travel advisories.

Local Coverage – There are what's-doing sections in Friday's *Orlando Sentinel,* a daily, and in *Orlando* magazine.

Television Stations – WESH Channel 2–NBC; WCPX Channel 6–CBS; WFTV Channel 9–ABC; WMFE Channel 24–PBS.

Radio Stations – AM: WDBO 580 (news/talk/adult contemporary); WWNZ 740 (news/talk). FM: WDIZ 100.3 (rock); WSTF 101 (top 40); WBJW 105.1 (top 40).

TELEPHONE: The area code for Orlando is 407.
Sales Tax – The city sales tax is 6%, as is the hotel tax.

CLIMATE: Spring and fall enjoy temperatures averaging in the mid-70s. From November through March, warmer clothing is a must for evening. Summer can be hot and humid. Always pack something for unseasonably warm or cool weather.

GETTING AROUND: Airport – Orlando International Airport is 12 to 15 miles from the city's downtown area and 28 miles from the gates of *Walt Disney World.* Cab fare from the airport to Orlando averages around $12, $30 to *WDW.* *Mear's Motor Shuttle* (phone: 423-5566) provides transportation from the airport to the major downtown hotels for $10 and to *WDW* for $12. Reserve a seat upon landing at the airport; a van should depart about 20 minutes later. City buses run hourly between the airport and Orlando's downtown terminal at Pine and Central; the fare is 75¢. Call 841-8240 for more information.

Bus – *Gray Line* (phone: 422-0744) and *Rabbit* (phone: 291-2424) are among the operators providing transportation from hotels all over the city to the major attractions. Hotel desks can provide details.

Car Rental – Most major car rental firms are represented. Orlando has one of the largest number of fleet vehicles of any US city, and the rates (most with unlimited mileage) are relatively modest.

Taxi – *Mear's Transportation Group* (phone: 422-4561) has the largest taxi fleet in the city. *Ace Taxi* (phone: 859-7514) also serves the area.

VITAL SERVICES: Audiovisual Equipment – *Blumberg Communcations* (phone: 857-4747); *Photosound of Orlando* (phone: 898-8841); *Image Resources, Inc.* (phone: 645-4200).

Baby-sitting – At *Walt Disney World,* the *Polynesian Village Resort,* the *Grand Floridian Resort,* and the *Contemporary Resort* have child care facilities. *Kindercare,* the children's center at *WDW,* is suitable for youngsters age 2 through 12 (phone: 827-KIDS). The *Hilton at Walt Disney World Village* offers a "Youth Hotel" where children aged 3 through 12 can be accommodated. Also at *WDW,* the *Swan* and *Dolphin* hotels offer "Camp Swan" and "Camp Dolphin" for kids age 4 through 12.

Business Services – *Blumberg Communications* (7101 Presidents Dr.; phone: 857-4747); *Image Resources Inc.* (4546 36th St.; phone: 645-4200); and *Photosound of Orlando* (718 Virginia Dr.; phone: 898-8841).

Dry Cleaner/Tailor – *Acme Cleaners,* 7 AM to 6 PM, 600 NW Moreland St. (phone: 841-2301).

Limousine – *Carey/Admiral Limousine Service* (phone: 855-0442).

Mechanics – *College Park Auto Service* (2610 Edgewater Dr., Orlando; phone: 425-7372); *Car Care Center* (Floridian Way, *Walt Disney World;* phone: 824-4813).

Medical Emergency – *Orlando Regional Medical Center* (1416 S. Orange; phone: 841-5111); *Buena Vista Medical Center* (12500 Apopka Vineland Rd., immediately north of the *Disney Village Marketplace;* phone: 828-3434).

Messenger Services – *Magic Bee Services* (phone: 339-9667).

National/International Courier – *Federal Express* (phone: 800-238-5355); *DHL Worldwide Courier Express* (phone: 851-1432 or 800-225-5345).

Pharmacy – *Central Florida Pharmacy,* delivery service 9 AM to 6 PM Mondays through Fridays, 9 AM to 3 PM Saturdays (15 W. Columbia St.; phone: 422-8144); *Eckerd Pharmacy* (908 Lee Rd., off I-4; phone: 644-6908); prescriptions can be filled at the *Buena Vista Medical Center,* 12500 Apopka Vineland Rd., immediately north of the *Disney Village Marketplace* (phone: 828-3434).

Photocopies – *Sir Speedy* (7400 Southland Blvd., Suite 107; phone: 855-0398); *Superior Quick Print* (5744 International Dr.; phone: 345-8484).

Post Office – The main branch is at Orlando International Airport (phone: 850-6200); there is also a downtown branch (46 E. Robinson St. at Magnolia St.; phone: 843-5673).

Professional Photographer – *Bruce Wilson* (phone: 859-0930); *Image Creators — Robert Willmann* (phone: 380-0515).

Secretary/Stenographer – *Adia Personnel Services* (phone: 894-1324); *Associated Temporary Staffing* (phone: 894-7757); *Talent Tree* (phone: 851-6200).

Teleconference Facilities – *Walt Disney World Hotel Plaza (Buena Vista Palace* and *Hilton Walk Disney World),* and *Orlando Marriott* (see *Best in Town,* below); *Walt Disney World Conference Center.*

Translator – *International Planning, Inc.* (phone: 351-0504); *School of Modern Languages* (phone: 898-5555).

Western Union/Telex – Many offices are located around the city (phone: 800-527-5184).

 SPECIAL EVENTS: The *Scottish Highland Games* in January draw huge crowds for Highland dancing and bagpipe competitions. The *Winter Park Sidewalk Art Festival,* the third weekend of March, is one of the Southeast's most prestigious such events. The

Florida State Air Fair, held in nearby Kissimmee in October, has performances by the US Navy's *Blue Angels,* the Army's *Golden Knights,* or the Air Force's *Thunder Birds.* At *Walt Disney World,* beautiful decorations are put up at *Christmastime,* and there are parties and extra-large fireworks displays on *New Year's Eve.* The *Fourth of July* also occasions additional pyrotechnics.

MUSEUMS: Orlando has a handful of noteworthy small institutions:
Charles Hosmer Morse Museum of American Art – Noted for its collection of Tiffany stained glass. 133 E. Welbourne Ave. in Winter Park (phone: 644-3686).

Orlando Museum of Art – Permanent displays of paintings and sculpture and frequent special exhibits. 2416 N. Mills Ave. (phone: 896-4231).

Orlando Science Center – Houses the *John Young Planetarium.* 810 E. Rollins St. (phone: 896-7151).

MAJOR COLLEGES AND UNIVERSITIES: University of Central Florida (Alafaya Trail; phone: 823-2000); Rollins College (Winter Park; phone: 646-2000).

SPORTS AND FITNESS: Baseball – The Orlando *Sun Rays,* a Minnesota *Twins* farm team, play at *Tinker Field* during the summer (phone: 872-7593). The Houston *Astros* hold their spring training at *Osceola Stadium* in Kissimmee (phone: 933-5500). The Kansas City *Royals* prepare for the season at *Baseball City Stadium,* 28 miles southwest of Orlando (phone: 813-424-2424).

Basketball – The Orlando *Magic,* an NBA franchise, plays its home games at the $100 million *Orlando Arena* (phone: 896-2442).

Fishing – Bass anglers flock to Florida's third-largest lake, Tohopekaliga. To find out about nearby fishing camps, contact the Kissimmee–St. Cloud Convention and Visitors Bureau (phone: 847-5000).

Fitness Centers – The *YMCA* (433 N. Mills Ave., Orlando; phone: 896-6901), has an indoor pool, weight room, gymnasium with Nautilus equipment, outdoor track, and racquetball facilities. In addition, many hotels have health clubs for guests.

Football – The University of Central Florida *Knights* (phone: 823-1000) play at *Orlando Stadium* in the fall.

Golf – *Walt Disney World* currently has three public courses: *Magnolia* and *Palm* at the *Disney Inn* and *Lake Buena Vista* golf course (phone: 824-2270). Two more courses are slated to open this year. The courses at the *Hyatt Grand Cypress* hotel (adjacent to the Disney property) also are marvelous.

Jogging – Around Lake Eola in downtown Orlando, and on a trail at Ft. Wilderness and on the roads of *WDW.*

Swimming – Wet 'n' Wild and *WDW*'s River Country and Typhoon Lagoon (see *Special Places*) are good bets for a dip, and most hotels have pools. Within the boundaries of *WDW,* there are especially good-size pools at *Contemporary Resort* (phone: 824-1000), *Royal Plaza* (phone: 828-2828), and *Buena Vista Palace* (phone: 827-2727).

Tennis – It's possible to play on the many lighted *Walt Disney World* courts (where court reservations, lessons, rental rackets, and even a partner-finding service are available; phone: 246-2161). Or you can play for a small fee on Orlando parks' courts (phone: 849-2161). The *Grosvenor* resort, *Royal Plaza, Buena Vista Palace, Hilton at Walt Disney World Village, Hyatt Orlando, Peabody, Grand Cypress Hyatt Regency, Marriott's Orlando World Center, Orlando Marriott, Stouffer Orlando* resort, and *Swan* and *Dolphin* resorts at *Disney World,* are among the hotel establishments with courts for guests.

THEATERS: *Mark Two* features a buffet meal followed by a Broadway-style musical with a professional cast (3376 Edgewater Dr.; phone: 422-3191). At *King Henry's Feast,* a five-course repast is served in true Elizabethan style (no forks), while some of the Bard's characters perform (8984 International Dr.; phone: 351-5151). *Mardi Gras* offers a cabaret show with a New Orleans-style jazz band along with a four-course Louisiana dinner (8445 International Dr.; phone: 355-5151). The *Fort Liberty Wild West Dinner Show and Trading Post* serves up a four-course, Southern-style meal, accompanied by country-and-western music and an entertaining show (5260 US 92; phone: 351-5151). The *Civic Center of Central Florida* features musicals, dramas, and mysteries (1001 E. Princeton St.; phone: 896-7365).

MUSIC: Programs of dance, music, and theater are often presented at the *Mayor Bob Carr Performing Arts Centre* (401 W. Livingston St.; phone: 843-2577). Concerts, ice shows, and the circus are held at the *Orlando Arena* (600 W. Amelia St., phone: 849-2020)

NIGHTCLUBS AND NIGHTLIFE: Once a pair of decaying hotels in a depressed section of none-too-lively downtown Orlando, the *Church Street Station* complex of bars, shops, and restaurants is now a very popular place. A steep 1-year admission pass has made *Church Street* more attractive for locals than for tourists. There's Dixieland to keep things lively at vast, wood-floored *Rosie O'Grady's Good Time Emporium,* bluegrass and folk at the brick-floored, plant-and-wicker-decked *Apple Annie's Courtyard,* disco in *Phineas Phogg's Balloon Works,* ballroom dancing at *Orchard Garden,* traditional American and continental food at *Lili Marlene's,* oysters and other seafood at *Crackers Oyster Bar,* and barbecue and all the fixings at the *Cheyenne Saloon & Opera House.* Be aware that the charge for many specialty drinks includes the price of the glass (you turn it in at the gift shop for a refund). The *Church Street Station Exchange* featuring shops and restaurants is a recent addition to the complex, and it can be entered free of charge. Children are welcome. 129 W. Church St. (phone: 422-2434).

And *WDW* itself has a variety of nightspots, from the elegant, intimate *Empress Lilly Lounge* and the comfortable *Village Lounge,* which attracts jazz entertainers, to the mad, merry *Baton Rouge Lounge,* which features Disney's own more than competent musician-comedians. At Pleasure Island, try the *Comedy Warehouse,* the *Neon Armadillo,* or *Mannequins,* or catch a movie at the adjacent *AMC* theaters.

BEST IN TOWN

CHECKING IN: Most Orlando-area accommodations are clustered along International Drive and nearby Sand Lake Road at the Orlando city limits, 10 to 15 minutes' drive from *WDW;* along US 192, which runs east and west and intersects I-4 near *WDW* (actually in Kissimmee, and closer to *WDW*); and inside *WDW* itself. Expect to pay $125 to $250 for a double at those places designated as expensive; $80 to $120 for those identified as moderate; and $50 to $75 at inexpensive spots — occasionally less during quiet periods in winter. All telephone numbers are in the 407 area code unless otherwise indicated.

Walt Disney World–owned Properties – For both facilities and convenience, the hotels and villas owned by the Disney organization can't be beat, and the addition of the moderately priced *Caribbean Beach Resort* means that even budget-conscious travelers can enjoy staying right on the *Walt Disney World* property. Two new hotels, *Dixie*

Landings, a plantation-style resort, and *Port Orleans,* reminiscent of the architectural style of the New Orleans French Quarter, add 3,000 moderately priced rooms to the *WDW* inventory. The *Contemporary Resort,* a bustling high-rise with a pair of 3-story wings, has magical views, a lake's-edge location, 2 terrific swimming pools, and one of the biggest gamerooms anywhere. The *Polynesian Village,* on lushly landscaped grounds in several buildings by a lake, is only slightly more tranquil. Both are right on the monorail line — and exceptionally convenient to both the Magic Kingdom and EPCOT Center. The *Grand Floridian Resort* is between the *Polynesian Village* and the Magic Kingdom and also is on the main monorail route. Its Victorian style is reminiscent of old Florida, and it is the first authentic luxury (and very expensive) hotel at *WDW.* The understated *Disney Inn* is nearby, not on the monorail, but has a pleasantly relaxed atmosphere. The *Caribbean Beach Resort,* near EPCOT Center and the Disney–MGM Studios Theme Park, is composed of five brightly colored villages surrounding a 42-acre lake.

Not far from the *Caribbean Beach Resort* are two more Disney-owned hotels. The 634-room *Disney Yacht Club* and the 580-room *Disney Beach Club* have a New England theme and were designed by noted architect Robert A. M. Stern. Close to the array of shops at the *Disney Village Marketplace* are the *Walt Disney World Resort Villas,* where 1-, 2-, and 3-bedroom villas overlook a lake and a golf course. All of them are especially good values for families. The octagonal treehouse-type villas — built on top of a central "pole," surrounded by pines and peacocks, and equipped with kitchens — are utterly delightful. Also lovely are the luxurious trailers at *Fort Wilderness Campground,* which come complete with bathrooms, color TV sets, and fully equipped kitchens.

The Southeast's largest hotel and convention complex is now on Disney property as well. The *Swan* resort, which opened late in 1989, has 760 rooms, and the *Dolphin* (managed by Sheraton), which opened in 1990, has 1,510 rooms. The hotels share spacious convention facilities measuring some 200,000 square feet. There also are meeting facilites at the *Contemporary Resort,* the *Yacht Club* and *Beach Club* resorts, the *Disney Inn,* and the *WDW Conference Center.* For details about organizing a *Walt Disney World* meeting or convention, call 828-3200.

During the next 10 years, another seven Disney-owned hotels are slated for construction. All properties are expensive (the *Grand Floridian* is very expensive), except the *Caribbean Beach Resort, Port Orleans,* and *Dixie Landings,* which are moderate to inexpensive. For details, phone *WDW* Central Reservations (934-7639).

Walt Disney World Hotel Plaza – The seven hotels here, within walking distance of the *Disney Village Marketplace* and *Pleasure Island,* are nearly as convenient as the *WDW*-owned properties, and a couple of them are a bit less pricey. Our favorites in the complex are the *Buena Vista Palace,* which boasts 870 handsomely decorated rooms embellished with Mickey Mouse telephones and old-fashioned ceiling fans (as well as air conditioning), plus outstanding sporting facilities. The convention facility has more than 83,000 square feet of meeting space, with 33 meeting rooms, 45 suites, and 13 hospitality suites. A special entrance and check-in facilities are available for convention guests (phone: 827-2727 or 800-327-2990; Fax: 407-827-6034); the 814-room *Hilton at Walt Disney World* has a *Youth Hotel* that it recommends to guests with children. There are 51,000 square feet of meeting space, with 21 rooms and 2 ballrooms (phone: 827-4000; Fax: 407-827-6380); also attractive is the *Royal Plaza* hotel, a 17-story high-rise with a pair of 2-story wings, plus tennis courts and a good swimming pool (phone: 828-2828 or 800-248-7890; Fax: 407-827-3977). The *Howard Johnson*

Resort, another high-rise with a 6-story annex, is also handsome. There is a new conference center that can accommodate groups of up to 250 (phone: 828-8888 or 800-223-9930; Fax: 407-827-4623). Another good choice here is *Guest Quarters,* where all 229 suites feature a bedroom, living room, wet bar, refrigerator, built-in hair dryer, and 2 TV sets. There's also a pool, lighted tennis courts, and a gameroom. There is 1 meeting room that can accommodate up to 60 (phone: 934-1000 or 800-424-2900; Fax: 407-934-1011). All Disney hotels carry CNN (Cable News Network). Note that reservations for all of these properties can be made through *WDW* Central Reservations (phone: 934-7639). All are expensive.

Hyatt Regency Grand Cypress – This glittering, 750-room luxury hotel, with a 170-foot atrium lobby modeled after the *Hyatt Regency Maui* in Hawaii, is the star of a 1,500-acre complex that has more facilities than most visitors can ever use, including one of the largest free-form swimming pools anywhere. The golf course, restricted to guest use, is a Jack Nicklaus gem. Some 48 luxury villas surround the course's fairways. There is a concierge desk, 24-hour room service, and express checkout. Secretarial services, photocopying, A/V equipment, and computers can be provided. Meeting space consists of 57,000 square feet that can accommodate up to 2,500 people. At the villas, the Grand Cypress Executive Meeting Center offers meeting space for up to 160. 1 Grand Cypress Blvd., Lake Buena Vista (phone: 239-1234; Fax: 407-239-3800; for the villas, 239-9700; Fax: 739-7219). Expensive.

Marriott's Orlando World Center – Here is a 1,503-room, 27-story resort hotel that commands nearly 200 beautifully landscaped acres, just minutes away from *Walt Disney World*'s EPCOT Center. Features include a 6-story lobby atrium, 4 swimming pools, 12 lighted tennis courts, an 18-hole Joe Lee golf course, a fully equipped health spa, a gameroom, 10 restaurants and lounges, 24-hour room service, a concierge desk, and lots of specialty shops. The meeting facilities are vast, with 92,000 square feet on one level, and secretarial services, A/V equipment, photocopying, and computers all are available. World Center Dr., Orlando (phone: 239-4200 or 800-621-0638; Fax: 407-234-5777). Expensive.

Peabody Orlando – The only sister property of the well-known *Peabody* hotel in Memphis, this imposing 27-story, 891-room relative is International Drive's most luxurious. Facilities include an Olympic-size pool, 4 lighted tennis courts, a health club, a fitness trail, a gameroom, aerobics classes, 24-hour room service, and a concierge desk. The hotel is located directly across from the *Orlando/Orange County Convention Center,* but also has 54,000 square feet of meeting space right on site. A/V equipment, secretarial services, photocopying, and computers are available. The famous Peabody ducks are here, too: every day at 11 AM they waddle from a private elevator into the enormous lobby, down the red carpet, and into the marble fountain — a spectacle that attracts hotel guests and locals. Also a good restaurant (see *Eating Out*). 9801 International Dr. (phone: 352-4000; Fax: 407-351-9177). Expensive.

Sonesta Villa Resort – This full-service escape in a quiet setting on a tranquil lake is about 10 miles from *Walt Disney World* and 2 miles from *Sea World.* One- and two-bedroom villas which can accommodate up to 8 people range from $125 to $270 per villa per night. Located on over 90 acres of land, it offers a heated pool, 11 Jacuzzis, 2 tennis courts, a children's playground, a gameroom, and a small health club. 10000 Turkey Lake Rd. (phone: 352-8051; Fax: 407-345-5384). Expensive.

Stouffer Orlando – This $86-million, 782-room property rises 10 stories above an enormous atrium complete with free-flying birds and exotic fish. A fitness center, 6 tennis courts, pool, 4 restaurants, 24-hour room service, and a concierge desk round out the offerings. Meeting facilities include the 17,325-square-foot main ballroom, plus smaller ballrooms and 23 meeting rooms. 6677 Sea Harbor Dr. (phone: 351-5555 or 800-325-5000; Fax: 407-351-9991). Expensive.

Orlando Marriott – Arranged in 2-story stucco villas scattered around landscaped grounds, the 1,076 rooms here are popular with business travelers (it's convenient to the *Orlando/Orange County Convention Center*) but fine for any visitor in search of quiet. 8001 International Dr. (phone: 351-2420 or 800-228-8001; Fax: 407-345-5611). Moderate.

Park Plaza – Orlando's answer to New England's country inns has plenty of charm, even if the rooms don't always measure up to the palm-and-antique-decked lobby. 307 Park Ave. S., Winter Park (phone: 647-1072; Fax: 407-647-4081). Moderate.

Quality Suites Maingate East – Features 225 one- and two-bedroom suites, each with a full kitchen. Spacious bathrooms are a plus. 5876 W. Irlo Bronson Memorial Highway; Kissimmee (phone: 346-8040 or 800-848-4148; Fax: 407-396-6766). Moderate to inexpensive.

EATING OUT: The last decade's growth has attracted chefs from all over the world, so first class dining experiences are easy to find. Expect to pay between $50 and $80 for two at those places listed as expensive; between $40 and $50 in the moderate category; and under $40 in the inexpensive bracket — excluding drinks, wine, and tips. All telephone numbers are in the 407 area code unless otherwise indicated.

Chefs de France – Three of France's finest chefs — Paul Bocuse, Roger Vergé, and Gaston LeNôtre — firmly based the menu here on nouvelle cuisine, with very good results. Gleaming napery, sparkling brass, etched glass, and all manner of turn-of-the-century touches make the decor as appealing as the food. There's also a separate menu "for the little gourmet" (for kids under 12) at reduced prices. A first-rate bistro thrives upstairs. Open daily. Reservations necessary (they are available to *Walt Disney World* hotel guests by telephone — check with the hotel desk clerks; otherwise reservations are available only in person at EPCOT Center). Major credit cards accepted. World Showcase, EPCOT Center, *Walt Disney World.* Expensive.

Le Cordon Bleu – The unpretentious decor here gives no hint of the quality of the mushrooms filled with crabmeat and glazed with Mornay sauce, snails in garlic butter, rack of lamb, and other specialties at this favorite eating spot. Owner George Vogelbacher has been called the prince of pastry-makers. Closed Sundays. Reservations necessary on weekends. Major credit cards accepted. 537 W. Fairbanks, Winter Park (phone: 647-7575). Expensive.

Dux – At the *Peabody* hotel and named for the family of ducks that live in the lobby, the menu leans heavily toward American nouvelle. There are imaginative appetizers and entrées and a strong wine list. Closed Sundays. Reservations necessary. Major credit cards accepted. 9801 International Dr. (phone: 352-4550). Expensive.

Empress Room – Elegant (but cordial) service and Louis XV surroundings, replete with crystal and gold leaf, make this *WDW* room in the *Empress Lilly* riverboat a favorite among Orlando residents out for a big celebration. Jackets required for men. Open daily. Reservations necessary well in advance. Major credit cards accepted. *Disney Village Marketplace, Walt Disney World* (phone: 828-3900). Expensive.

Jordan's Grove – A stately, serene restaurant set under a canopy of oak trees. It has a homey warmth and an American nouvelle menu that changes often, sometimes daily. Expect the extraordinary here; it's not the place for a steak-and-potatoes meal. Closed Mondays. Reservations advised. Major credit cards accepted. 1300 S. Orlando Ave., Maitland (phone: 628-0020). Expensive.

Maison & Jardin – An elegant spot with high ceilings, widely spaced tables, and vast windows that take in the surrounding formal gardens, this restaurant that local wags have nicknamed "Mason Jar" serves ambitious fish, meat, and fowl preparations. Reservations advised. Major credit cards accepted. 430 S. Wymore Rd., Altamonte Springs (phone: 862-4410). Expensive.

Park Plaza Gardens – Garden-like awnings, skylights, and greenery make a lovely backdrop for tasty meals. Sunday brunch is particularly good. Open daily. Reservations advised for dinner only. Major credit cards accepted. 319 Park Ave. S., Winter Park (phone: 645-2475). Expensive.

Victoria & Albert's – In *Walt Disney World*'s *Grand Floridian Resort,* this small dining room seats only 53, and elegant touches include Royal Doulton china, Sambonet silver, and Schott-Zweisel crystal. The menu varies nightly. Open daily. Reservations advised. Major credit cards accepted. *Grand Floridian Resort, Walt Disney World* (phone: 824-2383). Expensive.

Chatham's Place – Two talented young chefs (who happen to be brothers) have moved from their tiny Windermere location to these larger quarters. The menu changes daily, and specials created in the open kitchen include roast duck with fresh raspberries; black grouper in pecan butter; and delectable five-onion soup. The chefs' mother serves as hostess, and their grandmother does all the baking (try her lemon cake). Closed Sundays. Reservations essential. Major credit cards accepted — and no smoking is allowed. 7575 Dr. Phillips Blvd. (phone: 345-2992). Expensive to moderate.

La Cantina – Orlando residents line up for as much as an hour for the huge steaks and Italian specialties here. Closed Sundays and Mondays. No reservations. Major credit cards accepted. 4721 E. Colonial Dr., Orlando (phone: 894-4491). Moderate.

Ming Garden – Sophisticated Mandarin, Szechuan, Hunan, and Cantonese dishes with an emphasis on Florida seafood. Decorated in shades of plum, with elaborate plum blossom chandeliers, the dining room is filled with greenery. Open daily for lunch and dinner. Reservations advised. Major credit cards accepted. 6432 International Dr., Orlando (phone: 352-8044). Moderate.

T.G.I. Fridays – A branch of this national chain is located at the *Crossroads Shopping Center,* near *Walt Disney World Hotel Plaza.* A variety of ethnic specialties, burgers, and salads are on the menu. Open daily. Reservations unnecessary. Major credit cards accepted. Crossroads Plaza, State Rd. 535 (phone: 827-1020). Moderate.

Pebbles – A café with a new American and Caribbean menu set amid lots of indoor greenery. Interesting appetizers include baked goat cheese served in a pool of tomato *concassée* (puréed) with garlic croutons. There are fresh seafood dishes daily and a variety of salads, pasta, and soup. Open daily. No reservations. Major credit cards accepted. Crossroad Plaza, State Rd. 535 (phone: 827-1111). Moderate to inexpensive.

Bubbalou's Bodacious BBQ – More of a joint than a restaurant, there are 20 picnic tables, red ruffled curtains, and baseball caps hanging from the ceiling lights. The food is hot, fast, fresh, and smoky. Closed Sundays. No reservations or credit cards accepted. 1471 Lee Rd., Winter Park (phone: 628-1212). Inexpensive.

Bubble Room – Kitsch — from the yellow-brick path leading to the front door to the waiters and waitresses known as Bubble Scouts. Most of the selections are classics: burgers, fish platters, chili. Desserts are obscenely huge. Open daily. No reservations. Major credit cards accepted. 1351 S. Orlando Ave., Maitland (phone: 628-3331). Inexpensive.

More Walt Disney World Restaurants – Most first-time visitors are surprised to discover just how far the *WDW* food offerings surpass the well-trod hamburgers-and-hot-dogs path — and then dive right into steak and kidney pie, fettuccine Alfredo, amaretto-flavored soufflés, or any number of other exotic foodstuffs served at EPCOT Center's World Showcase eateries. Another pleasure is that even cafeterias and fast-food stops have a bit of atmosphere that makes them just a little special. Where you eat at *WDW* will be determined by where you are at mealtimes. Below are a few of the more noteworthy spots.

In the Magic Kingdom, *Crystal Palace,* an old-fashioned glass-and-plant-filled cafeteria on Main Street, is very pretty. *Tony's Town Square Café* nearby serves delicious Monte Cristo sandwiches. *King Stefan's Banquet Hall* in Cinderella Castle has service by waitresses (but you must reserve in person, first thing in the morning).

EPCOT Center offers even greater variety. In Future World, try the *Farmers Market* in The Land, where each of a half-dozen stands serves soups or salads, barbecue, cheese items, baked potatoes, and other savory specialties. Upstairs, at the *Land Grille Room,* are unusual American foods and scrumptious cheese bread. At the Living Seas Pavilion, try the fresh seafood at the *Coral Reef* restaurant, complete with a panoramic view of a living underwater coral reef. *Stargate* serves unique breakfast pizza. In World Showcase, don't miss Canada's low-ceilinged, stone-walled *Le Cellier,* a cafeteria that offers a tasty Canadian pork and potato pie called tourtière; Italy's *Alfredo's,* for tasty Italian food; Germany's *Biergarten,* for its hearty food and oom-pah entertainment; Mexico's *San Angel Inn,* which takes Mexican food far beyond tacos; and China's *Nine Dragons,* where meals are prepared in a variety of provincial Chinese cooking styles. Dinner reservations, a must at many restaurants, must be made in person in Earth Station. (*Walt Disney World* hotel guests can make reservations by telephone; check with the hotel desk clerks.) Otherwise, arrive at the front gate a half hour before the published park opening, decide where to eat, and send the speediest member of your group to book your table when the park opens. (Be aware that by an hour later most restaurants are usually booked for prime dinner hours.) Lunch reservations can be made at the restaurant in person on the day of the seating or at Earth Station. Booking procedures sometimes change, so confirm the preceding information on arrival at *WDW* (phone: 824-4321).

At the *Contemporary Resort,* consider the viewful *Top of the World* for its bountiful breakfast and Sunday brunch buffets. The superb banana-stuffed French toast served in *Polynesian Village's Tangaroa Terrace* is worth a detour. At *Disney Inn's Garden Gallery,* there's delicious French-fried ice cream at lunch and dinner. At the *Grand Floridian,* the octagonal *Narcoosee's* offers seafood and steaks in a delightful setting.

The eateries at the *Disney–MGM Studios* offer trendy cuisine in an atmosphere reminiscent of Hollywood in the 1930s and 1940s. The *Hollywood Brown Derby* features the famous Cobb Salad, created by owner Bob Cobb in the 1930s. Try the Fettucine Derby, pasta in a parmesan sauce with chicken, red and green peppers, and filet of red snapper. And leave room for dessert! The *50's Prime Time Café* hails back to the favorite sitcoms of the 1950s. The decor is straight out of a suburban kitchen and the menu offers such standbys as alphabet soup, vegetarian chili, and Magnificent Meat Loaf, made with fresh veal and shiitake mushrooms and served with mashed potatoes and gravy. For reservations at both places, call 828-4000.

At the *Disney Village Marketplace,* the comfortable, unassuming *Village* restaurant has fine lake views. At Pleasure Island there's the *Portobello Yacht Club* for imaginative Italian fare and delicious small pizza, or the *Fireworks Factory* for barbecued ribs and chicken. Aboard the *Empress Lilly* riverboat, there's the charming *Fisherman's Deck,* with a picture-window view of a churning paddlewheel.

Travelers with children should make note of the special breakfasts with Disney characters in attendance (phone: 824-4321; 934-7639 for reservations). Moderate.

PHILADELPHIA

AT-A-GLANCE

SEEING THE CITY: You don't have to run up the steps of the *Philadelphia Museum of Art* the way Sylvester Stallone did in *Rocky.* You can walk up to get the same far-reaching view of the skyline. Inside is an impressive collection of paintings, drawings, sculpture, and graphic art from all periods and countries. Closed Mondays and holidays. Admission charge (for the museum, not the view). 26th and Parkway (phone: 763-8100).

A different, but equally appealing, view of Philadelphia is afforded from the observation deck of City Hall Tower. The vistas from this vantage point encompass the city, its surrounding rivers, and the New Jersey shoreline. Open weekdays from 9 AM to 5 PM. Tours at 12:30 PM or by appointment at 10:30 AM. No admission charge. At Broad and Market Sts. (phone: 668-3351).

You also can see Old Philadelphia by horse-drawn carriage. Tours depart from the carriage stand on Chestnut between 5th and 6th Streets daily, weather permitting. After 6 PM, carriages depart from New Market Square on 2nd Street, between Pine and South Streets. Charge for carriage tours (phone: 922-6840).

SPECIAL PLACES: Philadelphia's tight city blocks and narrow streets make it great for walking, not driving. Streets, laid out in checkerboard fashion, are easy to understand, but they are always choked with traffic. It's best to park your car at your hotel. Philadelphia's main places of interest are clustered in Independence Hall National Historical Park and around Fairmount Park in West Philadelphia.

INDEPENDENCE HALL HISTORICAL AREA

Visitors' Center – This is a good place to launch a tour of the historical area and pick up maps and brochures. There's also a half-hour film that provides helpful historical background. If you have driven your car, use the 2nd Street garage (behind the visitors' center between Chestnut and Walnut Sts.). Open daily. No admission charge. 3rd and Chestnut Sts. (phone: 597-8974).

Independence National Historical Park – "The most historic square mile in America." This is what everyone comes to see. Within the park, you'll find the major colonial and Revolutionary era buildings, which we've listed separately below. Open daily. No admission charge. The general park area runs from 3rd to 7th St. between Chestnut and Walnut Sts. (phone: 627-1776 for a 24-hour recording).

Independence Hall – When you think of Philadelphia, this is probably the first image that comes to mind. The solid tower, massive clock, and graceful spire are unmistakable. Early colonists called it the State House. Here, the Declaration of Independence was signed and, 11 years later, the Constitution was written. Open daily, with guided tours, beginning in the East Wing. No admission charge. 5th and Chestnut Sts. (phone: 597-8974).

Congress Hall – The first US Congress met here, between 1790 and

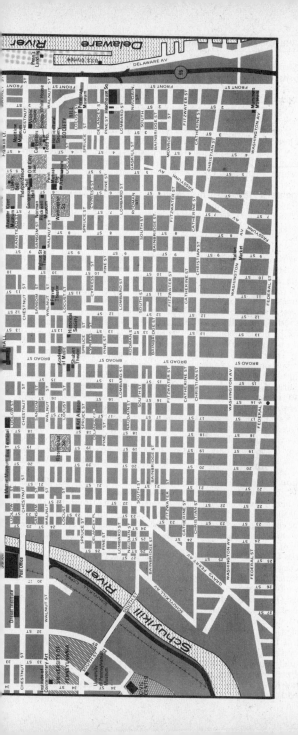

1800. George Washington delivered his final congressional address in these halls; here, too, the Bill of Rights was adopted. In 1800, the seat of federal government moved to the District of Columbia. Open daily. No admission charge. 6th and Chestnut Sts. (phone: 597-8974).

Old City Hall – The first US Supreme Court issued judgments from the bench inside this building. The court moved to new headquarters in Washington, DC, in 1800. Closed January through mid-March.

Independence Mall – Across the street from the Halls, this leafy stretch of grass, fountains, and tree-lined walks contains the glass pavilion housing the Liberty Bell. It was moved from Independence Hall so more people could see it. Open daily. No admission charge. Market and 5th Sts. (phone: 597-8974).

Carpenters' Hall – So named because it housed the Carpenters' Company Guild during the colonial era (before unions). The oldest building organization in the US still owns the hall, and early carpentry tools are on display. In 1774, the First Continental Congress met here. Closed Mondays; also closed Tuesdays in January and February. No admission charge. 320 Chestnut (phone: 925-0167).

Army-Navy and Marine Corps Memorial Museums – In Pemberton House and New Hall, respectively, the exhibitions and collections focus on Revolutionary War history in these military branches from 1775 to 1805. The buildings are on Carpenters' Court (leading back to Carpenters' Hall). Open daily. Closed January through mid-March. No admission charge. Chestnut, between 3rd and 4th Sts. (phone: 597-8974).

Second Bank of the United States – One of the earliest buildings designed by noted architect William Strickland, this early-19th-century building is an outstanding example of Greek Revival architecture. It houses "The Portraits of the Capitol City," which highlights people who were important in government, industry, the arts, and religion during the late 1700s. Open daily. Closed January through mid-March. No admission charge. Chestnut, between 4th and 5th Sts. (phone: 597-8974).

Todd House – Before she became Dolley Madison – wife of fourth president James, famed as First Lady and society hostess – she was Dolley Payne Todd, whose husband, the young Quaker lawyer John Todd, died in the yellow fever epidemic of 1793. Their home, built in 1775, is typical of middle class residences of the period. Free guided tours, by reservation only, must be arranged in person at the visitors' center on the day of the tour (see above). Open daily. 4th and Walnut Sts. (phone: 597-8974).

Bishop White House – While the Todd House reflects a middle class lifestyle, this home typifies the affluence of people such as Bishop William White, a politically active Episcopalian minister (from the 1770s to the 1790s) who served as rector of both Christ Church and St. Peter's. Must be combined with a tour of the Todd House. Sign up at the visitors' center. Open daily. No admission charge. 3rd and Walnut Sts. (phone: 597-8974).

Christ Church – Benjamin Franklin sat in pew 70, George Washington in pew 58. The original church was built in 1695; this, a larger one, was erected in 1745 and is significant both as an architectural structure and as a National Shrine. This Episcopal church holds weekly worship services. Open daily from 9 AM to 5 PM for tours. The church is closed on Mondays and Tuesdays from January through mid-March. Other times, tours are available by going directly to the church. Donation suggested. 2nd St. above Market St. (phone: 922-1695).

Christ Church Burial Ground – Throw a penny on the grave of Benjamin and his wife, Deborah Franklin – it's a Philadelphia custom. Open daily during the summer. Tours by appointment the rest of the year. Enter between 4th and 5th Sts. on Arch St. (phone: 922-1695).

Betsy Ross House – Where, tradition says, George Washington directed Elizabeth Ross, an upholsterer's widow, in the stitching of the first American flag. According to the Philadelphia Historical Commission, however, Betsy Ross never lived here and had nothing to do with the first US flag. Make up your own mind, after you've seen this tiny cottage filled with household items and memorabilia allegedly pertinent to that famous seamstress. Closed Mondays. No admission charge. 239 Arch (phone: 627-5343).

Elfreth's Alley – The oldest continuously occupied residential street in America, dating to 1690. Only 1 block long, 6 feet wide, it is lined with 200-year-old houses. Usually the first weekend in June, Elfreth's Alley holds its annual Fête Days with house tours and crafts shows. The Museum House, 126 Elfreth's Alley, is closed weekdays during January and February. North of Arch St., off 2nd St. between Arch and Race Sts. (phone: 574-0560).

Headhouse Square – Only survivor of the many middle-of-the-street markets that once flourished in the city. Built in 1775, it is surrounded by good restaurants and revitalized shops. In summer, it hosts crafts demonstrations and concerts. 2nd and Pine.

Franklin Court – Benjamin Franklin came to Philadelphia in 1723. In his later years Franklin resided in a brick house on this site. He died here in 1790. Although the house itself is no longer standing (it was demolished in 1812), three of the surrounding houses designed by Franklin are here, along with an 18th-century garden with a mulberry tree (planted by the National Park Service in 1976 because Franklin had one), a print shop, and a post office. An underground museum has Franklin stoves and a phone where you can "dial-an-opinion" from Benjamin Franklin. Open daily. No admission charge. Running from Chestnut to Market between 3rd and 4th Sts. (phone: 597-8974).

USS *Olympia* – The oldest steel-hulled American warship afloat, the *Olympia* was Commodore George Dewey's flagship at Manila Bay in the Spanish-American War. Open daily April through November; closed Tuesdays through Thursdays, December through March. Admission charge. Penn's Landing, near Delaware Ave. and Spruce St. (phone: 922-1898).

Penn's Landing Trolley – After leaving the USS *Olympia,* buy a ticket for a 20-minute ride on a restored trolley that served the Delaware Valley between 1904 and 1958. The conductor provides commentary as passengers ride along Delaware Avenue between the Society Hill and Queen Village areas and beside the Delaware River, where many tall ships are berthed. Weekends and holidays from April through December. Also check on extended summer schedule. Fare charge. Tickets valid for the entire day. Board at Delaware Ave. at Dock or Spruce St. (phone: 627-0807).

Boathouse Row – A collection of Victorian boathouses used by collegiate and club oarsmen. The hub of many national competitions. East River Dr., running along the east bank of the Schuylkill River, north of the *Museum of Art.* If you're driving just west of the museum on the Schuylkill Expressway (Route 76), or on the West River Drive after dark, don't miss the view across the river of the historic boathouses outlined in white lights.

WEST PHILADELPHIA

Fairmount Park – Approximately 8,000 acres of meadows, gardens, creeks, trails, and 100 miles of bridle paths for joggers, bicyclists, softball players, fishermen, and picnickers. For a small charge, pick up a detailed park map at Memorial Hall (42nd and Parkside; phone: 685-0000). Then be sure to take in the Japanese House and Garden (where tea is served in season), Glendinning Rock Garden, and, if children are along, Smith Memorial Playground. The *Fairmount Park Trolley Bus* (phone: 879-4044, for information), a replica of a Victorian conveyance, is a pleasant way of getting around the park and also seeing some of Philadelphia. It starts out at the visitors' center (16th and John F. Kennedy Blvd.). On Mondays and Tuesdays (daily December through March) there is a 2½-hour narrated tour of the Society Hill section of the city, Center City, and parts of the park, stopping at one of the seven restored historic mansions: Cedar Grove, Sweetbriar, Lemon Hill, Mount Pleasant, Strawberry, Woodford, and Laurel Hill. Wednesdays through Sundays, April through early December, the bus makes 90-minute rounds of the park with on-off privileges at all of the mansions. Don't miss the *Christmas* tour the first week in December, which takes in the mansions and Horticultural Society, decorated in colonial holiday styles. (Mansions closed Mondays. Admission charge. For guided tours, call 787-5449. It's best to arrange several weeks in advance.) Park open daily. No admission charge. The park begins at the *Philadelphia Museum of Art* and extends northwest on both sides of the Wissahickon Creek and Schuylkill River.

Philadelphia Zoo – Established in 1874, this is the nation's oldest zoo and is considered one of the best run. More than 1,600 animals, reptiles, and birds make their home within its 42 acres. There are several natural habitat displays, a children's zoo, and a safari monorail aerial tram. Don't miss the tree house, where children can interact with nature. Open daily, except *Thanksgiving, Christmas Eve, Christmas, New Year's Eve,* and *New Year's Day.* Admission charge except on Mondays from December through February. 34th St. and Girard Ave. (phone: 387-6400).

Philadelphia Museum of Art – Outstanding collections of all periods and schools, housed in a sweeping Greco-Roman building. It began as a building devoted to the decorative arts, and grew to include paintings and sculpture from the Renaissance, the 20th century, Europe, and America. This year, the exhibition "Love of the Gods," mythological paintings in 18th-century France, is on display from February to May. A collection of Picasso's still lifes will be exhibited from March through July. Closed Mondays and holidays. Admission charge except on Sundays until 1 PM. 26th and Parkway (phone: 763-8100).

Rodin Museum – Sculpture, sketches, and drawings make up the largest collection of Auguste Rodin's work outside France. An afternoon can easily be spent wandering through the halls and gardens. Foreign language tours are available by appointment. Closed Mondays, Tuesdays, and holidays. No admission charge; donations accepted. 22nd and Parkway (phone: 763-8100).

Franklin Institute Science Museum – Ben Franklin would have traded his kite for 1 day in this remarkable science museum, with *Fels Planetarium* and four huge floors jammed with hands-on exhibitions on anatomy, astronomy, aviation, electricity, physics, and more. The $72 million Futures Centerwing, opened in 1990, shows visitors the potentials of science and technology in the 21st century. The *Omniverse Theater* has a domed, 4-story OmniMax screen and 56 speakers which transport the viewer everywhere from within the human body to beyond the earth. *Philadelphia Anthem* presents an overview of the city. *Ben's Family* restaurant serves breakfast and lunch; the *Omni Café* offers lunch and dinner. Underground parking garage entrance off 21st Street. 20th & Benjamin Franklin Pkwy. (phone: 448-1200). Closed *Christmas* and *New Year's Day.* Admission charge. 20th St. and Parkway (phone: 448-1200; planetarium, 448-1292).

OTHER SPECIAL PLACES

City Hall – The most distinctive landmark in Philadelphia. Critics have called it "an architectural nightmare." Others praise its elaborate decor: sculpture, marble pillars, alabaster chandeliers, ceilings with gold leaf, carved mahogany, and walnut paneling. The Tower, at William Penn's feet, looks out to the Delaware and Schuylkill rivers. The business district fans out from City Hall. Guided tours of the restored Conversation Hall, the Mayor's reception room, city council chambers and caucus room, and the state supreme court chamber are offered weekdays at 12:30 PM or by appointment at 10:30 AM. No admission charge. Broad and Market Sts. (phone: 568-3351).

Rittenhouse Square – Named after David and Benjamin Ritten-house, who designed the first astronomical instruments in the US toward the end of the 18th century. Today, Rittenhouse Square is one of the loveliest, most elegant residential areas of the city. Handsome brown-stones and high-rise apartment houses surround a green park, where people from all over town congregate. Art shows, flower shows, and concerts take place here in spring and summer. 18th and Walnut Sts.

US Mint – Watch coins being minted at the largest facility of its kind in the world. This mint can produce 10,000 coins per minute. At each marked observation post, a pushbutton activates a taped commentary on the different stages of the minting process. Historic coins are exhibited in the Relic Room, and a special counter sells proof sets and medals. Accessible to people in wheelchairs. Closed Sundays, September through June, and on Saturdays, September through April, and selected holidays; coinage machines not in operation on weekends or federal holidays. No admission charge. 5th and Arch Sts. (phone: 597-7350).

Edgar Allan Poe House – The poet composed his epic to the raven and his chilling story *The Murders in the Rue Morgue* in these quarters. He lived here for 3 years, with his mother-in-law and young bride. A must for Poe addicts. Closed on Sundays, Mondays, and major holidays. No admission charge. 532 N. 7th (phone: 597-8780).

Pennsylvania Horticultural Society – The formal gardens of the 18th century are re-created here, with flowers, shrubs, and pruned trees typical of the era. This is the oldest horticultural association in the US, with a library devoted to botanical subjects. Open weekdays. No admission charge. 325 Walnut (phone: 625-8250).

Reading Terminal Market – Shoppers of all persuasions come to foray for fresh ground horseradish, study French brie, and snack at oyster bars. Check out the homemade soup and hot-from-the-oven shoo-fly pie. Ice cream at *Bassett's* is a must. Closed Sundays. 12th and Arch Sts. (phone: 922-2317).

Italian Market – Also known as *Rocky's* market. This is part of Sylvester Stallone's famous jogging trail, in South Philly. 9th St. and Washington Ave.

■ **EXTRA SPECIAL:** Even if you've never played the song "Washington at Valley Forge" on a kazoo, you've undoubtedly heard of the place. General George Washington and 11,000 Revolutionary troops re-treated to Valley Forge during the winter of 1777–78. The site of their camp and training grounds is now a state park. The visitors' center has a film and museum (open daily), and the park itself has a number of interesting historical buildings and brigade huts. There also is a 10-mile, self-guided auto tour; information is available at the visitors' center. Closed *Christmas*. No admission charge. Take the Schuylkill Expressway (Rte. 76) west to the Valley Forge exit (about 20 miles). Take Route 363 north to the park (phone: 783-7700).

For another kind of outdoor experience, visit Longwood Gardens, an expansive horticultural display where more than 11,000 different types of plants are carefully tended on 350 acres. Known for its old trees (some dating back to the late 1700s), the conservatories with ponds of Monet-like water lillies, picture-perfect orchids, and breath-taking fountains with wonderful summer light shows, Longwood Gar-dens also hosts more than 300 performing arts events annually, includ-ing concerts and theater productions. Pick up a calendar of events at the Philadelphia Visitors Center. The *Terrace Restaurant* (phone: 388-6771) offers both full-service and cafeteria-style dining. To reach the gardens in Kennett Square, some 30 minutes west of the city, take

Interstate 95 south to Route 322 west, then follow that about 8 miles to Route 1 south. Proceed another 8 miles to the entrance. Open daily: outdoor gardens 9 AM to 6 PM, conservatory 10 AM to 5 PM. Admission $8 for adults, $2 for children aged 6 through 14, and free for children under 6 (phone: 388-6741).

Just 5 miles north on Route 1 is the *Brandywine River Museum,* which houses three generations of Wyeth paintings (N.C., Andrew, and Jamie), along with works by Maxfield Parrish, Howard Pyle, and others. The museum is in a restored 19th-century grist mill with two glass towers where visitors can appreciate sweeping views of the Brandywine River. Outside is a nature trail, sculptures, and a wild-flower garden. An impressive display of model trains is shown during the Christmas holiday season. Open daily. Admission charge. Located at the intersection of Routes 1 and 100, Chadds Ford (phone: 459-1900).

SOURCES AND RESOURCES

 TOURIST INFORMATION: Right in the heart of the city, only steps from City Hall, is the Philadelphia Visitors Center, with maps, brochures, and other information. Ask specifically for a vacation kit containing the Official Visitor's Guide of restaurants, hotels, tours, maps, a seasonal "Calendar of Events," and other helpful information (16th St. at John F. Kennedy Blvd., or write: 1515 Market St., Philadelphia, PA 19102; phone: 636-1666 or 800-321-9563). Visitors may also request the *African-American Historical and Cultural Guide.* For a recording on what to see and where to go, call the Donnelley Directory Events Hotline (phone: 337-7777, ext. 2540; 24 hours). Contact the Pennsylvania state hotline (phone: 800-VISIT-PA) for maps, calendars of events, health updates, and travel advisories.

Disabled people can obtain information by calling the Mayor's Office for the Handicapped (phone: 686-2798); ask for the guide *Access to Philadelphia.* Foreign visitors can stop in at the Council for International Visitors (with 24-hour emergency language translation), Civic Center Blvd. at 34th St. (phone: 893-8415 weekdays from 9 AM to 5 PM; 735-7007 evenings and weekends.)

Local Coverage – The *Inquirer,* morning daily; the *Daily News,* afternoon daily; *Philadelphia* magazine, monthly.

Television Stations – KYW Channel 3–NBC; WPVI Channel 6–ABC; WCAU Channel 10–CBS; WHYY Channel 12–PBS.

Radio Stations – AM: WFIL 560 (oldies); KYW 1060 (news); WCAU 1210 (news/talk). FM: WHYY 90.9 (news/talk/public affairs); WXTU 92 (country); WFLN 95.6 (classical music); WMGK 103 (soft rock); WUSL 98.9 (black urban).

Food – *Philadelphia* magazine's restaurant listings or the *Official Visitor's Guide.*

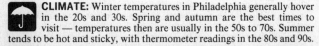 **TELEPHONE:** The area code for Philadelphia is 215.

Sales Tax – There is a 6% sales tax on most purchases, excluding many items of clothing.

CLIMATE: Winter temperatures in Philadelphia generally hover in the 20s and 30s. Spring and autumn are the best times to visit — temperatures then are usually in the 50s to 70s. Summer tends to be hot and sticky, with thermometer readings in the 80s and 90s.

 GETTING AROUND: Airport – Philadelphia International Airport is a 30-minute drive to Center City (up to an hour during rush periods); taxi fare should run about $18. The *SEPTA*

(*Southeastern Pennsylvania Transportation Authority*) *Airport Express* train (phone: 574-7800) makes the 20-minute trip to the city's main terminal, 30th St. Station, for $4. Trains stop at most of the airport terminals every half hour.

Bus, Rail, and Subway – SEPTA (*Southeastern Pennsylvania Transportation Authority*) will take you everywhere, by bus, trolley, train, or subway. A good *SEPTA* map showing routes for all public transportation is available at newsstands (call 574-7800 for information). The *Ben Franklin* line runs from the visitors' center at 3rd and Chestnut Street out to the *Museum of Art*, via the shopping thoroughfare along Chestnut Street, and the museum district at the Parkway. Buses and stops are marked with red kites (phone: 580-7800).

Car Rental – Philadelphia is served by all the national firms. *Thrifty Car Rental* is particularly worth noting: its inexpensive fleet ranges from mini-vans to executive no-smoking cars. Free shuttle service to and from airport (phone: 365-3900 or 800-367-2277).

Taxi – Costly, but for short hops to transport three or four people, it's worth it. Hail them in the street or do as Philadelphians do and pick them up in front of the 30th Street train station, the *Greyhound/Trailways* bus terminal, or the nearest hotel, which is where most of them wait for customers. Call *Metro Cab Company* (phone: 922-8400), *Quaker City Cab* (phone: 728-8000), or *United Cab Association* (phone: 625-2881).

 VITAL SERVICES: Audiovisual Equipment – *Williams, Brown & Earle,* film production supplies (phone: 923-1800); *Projection Inc.* (phone: 864-0456).

Business Services – *CPS Services,* typing and notary public weekdays from 8 AM to 5 PM, 1700 Walnut St., Suite 809 (phone: 985-9535).

Dry Cleaner/Tailor – *Academy Cleaners,* Mondays through Saturdays, same-day cleaning before 10 AM (1417 Locust St.; phone: 732-2627); *British Imperial,* open Mondays through Saturdays from 7 AM to 6 PM (1322 Locust St. at Juniper St.; phone: 545-6880) and other locations.

Limousine – *Ralph R. D'Abruzzo Limousine Service* (phone: 525-0144).

Mechanic – *Center City Service,* a 24-hour garage (427 N. Broad; phone: 922-7021); *Reggie's Citgo,* towing 9 AM to 9 PM (12th and Spring Garden Sts.; phone: 922-2110).

Medical Emergency – *Hahnemann University Hospital,* Broad and Vine Sts. (phone: 448-7963).

Messenger Services – *Quick Courier Service* (phone: 592-9933); *Rapid Delivery and Messenger Service,* same-day service (phone: 545-2781).

National/International Courier – *Federal Express* (phone: 923-3085); *DHL Worldwide Courier Express* (phone: 461-8111).

Pharmacy – *Penn Towers,* 8:30 AM to 6 PM weekdays, 9 AM to 2 PM Saturdays, 1821 JFK Blvd. (phone: 568-2366).

Photocopies and Printing Services – *Minuteman Press of Walnut Street,* 918 Walnut St. (phone: 925-5858).

Post Office – The central office is at 30th and Market Sts. (phone: 895-8000 or 895-8989 for 24-hour window service at the central office).

Professional Photographer – *Quaker Photo Service Co.,* photo lab processing only (1025 Arch St.; phone: 922-4444); *Standard Photo Service* (2031 Chestnut St.; phone: 561-0770).

Secretary/Stenographer – *HQ Headquarters Company,* provides word processing, dictation recorded via telephone, telex, fax service, photocopying, and office suites and conference rooms with full secretarial staff (18th and Market Sts.; phone: 569-9145); *Accurate Business Services,* typing and word processing service only (801 Arch St., Suite 603; phone: 592-9280).

Teleconference Facilities – *Holiday Inn* (Center City location); *Penn Tower* (see *Best in Town*, below).

Translator – *Berlitz*, written translation and oral interpretation, closed Sundays (phone: 735-8500); *ICOA Translations*, written into English only (phone: 875-0975).

Typewriter Rental – *American Business Machines* (phone: 482-5922).

Western Union/Telex – Many offices are located around the city (phone: 800-325-6000).

Other – *Meeting Planners* (phone: 494-2323).

SPECIAL EVENTS: The *Mummers Parade*, a Philadelphia tradition on January 1, is 8 hours of string bands strutting up Broad Street in elaborate "suits" (don't call them costumes). Spring comes to the city on the second week in March when the *Philadelphia Flower and Garden Show* is held at the Civic Center (34th and Civic Center Blvd.). During the first 2 weeks in May, many city residents open their homes and gardens for public tours as part of *Philadelphia Open House*. Make arrangements through the visitors' center (3rd and Chestnut Sts.; phone: 597-8974). Come fall, *Super Sunday*, usually the second Sunday in October, is a day of free culture at institutions along the Benjamin Franklin Parkway, with folk dancing, flea markets, music, food, and mobs of people. The *Philadelphia Craft Show*, held the first or second weekend in November at the 103rd Engineers Armory at Drexel University, is a jury show that displays and sells a wide variety of crafts by artisans from around the state. Fairmount Park holds its *Christmas* tour the first week in December, during which the mansions and Horticultural Society are decked out in colonial fashion for the holiday.

MUSEUMS: The *Philadelphia Museum of Art, Rodin Museum,* and the *Franklin Institute Science Museum,* described in *Special Places,* are only a few of Philadelphia's museums. Some of the other notable museums include the following:

Academy of Natural Sciences – Particularly known for its dinosaur exhibits. Open daily. 19th St. and the Parkway (phone: 299-1000).

Afro-American Historical and Cultural Museum – Closed Mondays. 7th and Arch St. (phone: 574-0380).

Athenaeum – Library featuring historic documents; architectural history and decorative arts of the 19th century. Research by appointment. Closed weekends. 219 S. 6th St., Society Hill (phone: 925-2688).

Attwater Kent Museum – Local history. Closed Sundays and Mondays. 15 S. 7th St. (phone: 922-3031).

Barnes Foundation – French Impressionist art. Open on Fridays through Sundays by appointment only. Closed in July and August. 300 N. Latch's La., Merion Station (phone: 667-0290).

Civic Center – Variety of exhibitions and events. 34th and Civic Center Blvd. (phone: 823-7400).

Fireman's Hall Museum – Closed Sundays and Mondays. 2nd and Quarry Sts. (phone: 923-1438).

Historical Society of Pennsylvania – Library and museum. Closed Mondays. 1300 Locust St. (phone: 732-6200).

Institute of Contemporary Art – University of Pennsylvania, 34th and Sansom Sts. (phone: 898-7108).

Library Company of Pennsylvania – Rare books. Closed weekends. 1314 Locust St. (phone: 546-2465).

Masonic Temple – Architectural wonder. Closed Sundays and major holidays. 1 N. Broad St. (phone: 988-1917).

Mummer's Museum – Mummer's memorabilia, history, and sound recordings. Closed Mondays. 2nd St. and Washington Ave. (phone: 336-3050).

Museum of American Jewish History – Closed Saturdays. 55 N. 5th St. (phone: 923-3811).

Mutter Museum – Medical history. Closed Saturdays through Mondays. 19 S. 22nd St. (phone: 563-3737).

Pennsylvania Academy of Fine Arts – The oldest art school and museum in the country. Closed Mondays. Broad and Cherry Sts. (phone: 972-7600).

Philadelphia Maritime Museum – Closed Mondays. 321 Chestnut St. (phone: 925-5439).

Please Touch Museum – Terrific hands-on exhibitions for children 7 years and under. 210 N. 21st St. (phone: 963-0667).

Port of History Museum – Closed Mondays and Tuesdays. Walnut St. and Delaware Ave. (phone: 925-3804).

Print Club – Prints and photography. Closed Sundays and Mondays. 1614 Latimer St., between Locust and Spruce Sts. (phone: 735-6090).

Norman Rockwell Museum – Extensive collection of *Saturday Evening Post* covers. In *Curtis Center* at 6th and Sansom Sts. (phone: 922-4345).

Rosenbach Museum and Library – Former private house containing porcelain, antiques, graphic art, and rare books. Closed Mondays. 2010 Delancey Pl., between Spruce and Pine Sts. (phone: 732-1600).

University of Pennsylvania Museum – Anthropology and archaeology exhibitions. Closed Mondays. 33rd and Spruce Sts. (phone: 898-4000).

Wagner Free Institute of Science – A Victorian building housing natural history exhibitions. Tuesdays through Fridays by appointment. 17th St. and Montgomery Ave. (phone: 763-6529).

MAJOR COLLEGES AND UNIVERSITIES: Philadelphia's colleges and universities are among the best in the country. Foremost is the University of Pennsylvania, founded by Benjamin Franklin in 1740 (34th and Walnut Sts.; phone: 898-5000). Others include Temple University (Broad St. and Montgomery Ave.; phone: 787-7000); Drexel University (32nd and Chestnut Sts.; phone: 895-2000); La Salle College (20th and Olney; phone: 951-1000); St. Joseph's College (5600 City Line Ave.; phone: 660-7000); Haverford College (370 W. Lancaster Ave., Haverford; phone: 896-1000); Swarthmore College (500 College Ave., Swarthmore; phone: 328-8000); Bryn Mawr College (Bryn Mawr; phone: 526-5000); Villanova University (Villanova; phone: 645-4500).

SHOPPING: For the best in department store shopping, head to the landmark *Wanamaker's* (Chestnut and Market Sts. at 13 St.) or *Strawbridge & Clothier,* one of the three anchor stores for the *Gallery* (9th and Market Sts.). The *Gallery* is the largest urban mall in the nation and has more than 200 stores and eating places. Running along Market Street from 9th to 12th, it connects with *SEPTA*'s Market East rail stop and several subway stations. The *Mellon Independence Center* (on Market St., between 7th and 8th) houses an assortment of upscale shops, as does the *Bourse,* a restored Victorian building (on 5th between Market and Chestnut Sts.). To see some of Philadelphia's most exclusive clothing shops and art galleries, walk along Walnut Street, beginning with *Nan Duskin* — for female finery (at Rittenhouse Sq.) — and capping the spree at *Polo/Ralph Lauren* (in the Bellevue section of Philadelphia at Broad St.). Philadelphia also is known for its jewelers' row, which dates back to the 1850s and is the second-largest diamond center in the country. Its heart lies between 6th and 8th, along Sansom Street. Similarly, an antiques row with both colonial and international crafts runs along Pine Street, between 9th and 12th. For the ultimate funky experience, don't miss a stroll down South Street from 10th to the river. You'll probably enjoy the people watching as much as the many boutiques and small restaurants.

SPORTS AND FITNESS: Whether you like to watch or do it yourself, there's enough sports activity to satisfy even the fanatics.

Baseball – From April to September, the *Phillies* chase the pennant at *Veterans Stadium,* Broad St. and Pattison Ave. (phone: 463-1000).

Basketball – Pro basketball's *76ers* pack them in at the *Spectrum,* Broad St. and Pattison Ave., from October to April (phone: 339-7676).

Bicycling – Rent year-round from the *Fairmount Bicycle Rental* (closed Sundays) behind the *Museum of Art* (Boathouse Row and E. River Dr.; phone: 225-3560). Some 10.6 miles of Fairmount Park are devoted to bike paths.

Boating – Within the city you can rent rowboats and canoes for the Schuylkill River at the *East Park Canoe House* on E. River Dr. (phone: 225-3560).

Fitness Centers – Your hotel facilities are your best bet.

Football – The NFL *Eagles* play at *Veterans Stadium,* Broad St. and Pattison Ave. (phone: 463-5500).

Golf – Try to get invited to a private country club. If you can't, your next best bet is to try the public city course at Cobbs Creek (7800 Lansdowne Ave.; phone: 877-8707). Nearby, the *Golf Corp. Sports Center* has a driving range and miniature golf (7900 City Line Ave.; phone: 879-3536).

Hockey – Hardest to get are tickets to the *Flyers,* who play at the *Spectrum* from October to April. Best bet is to try a center city ticket agency (or call 755-9700).

Horse Racing – *Philadelphia Park* has thoroughbred racing at Street and Richlieu Rds. (phone: 632-5770).

Jogging – In Fairmount Park, run along the banks of the Schuylkill River; enter the park at Eakins Oval.

Skiing – Everybody goes to the Pocono Mountains, 2 hours away in northeastern Pennsylvania. Best bets: *Camelback Mountain* (Tannersville; phone: 717-629-1661 or 800-233-8100 for ski report), *Big Boulder* (Lake Harmony; phone: 717-722-0101), and *Jack Frost* (Whitehaven; phone: 717-443-8425).

Tennis – The nation's number one indoor event, the *US Pro Indoor,* is held annually at the *Spectrum* in late January. The city owns more than 200 all-weather courts and Fairmount Park also has that many. Call the City Recreation Dept. at 686-3600, or the Fairmount Park Commission at 685-0053.

THEATER: Philadelphia no longer depends on Broadway-bound tryouts, although you can continue to see Broadway extravaganzas both at the *Forrest Theater* (1114 Walnut St.; phone: 923-1515), the *Shubert Theater* (250 S. Broad St.; phone: 732-5446), and at the *Walnut Street Theater* (9th and Walnuts Sts.; phone: 574-3550). A number of professional producing companies established themselves in the 1980s, allowing a host of first-rate plays and musicals, many with headlining performers, to be presented through regional theaters. Check offerings at the *Walnut Street Theater;* the *Wilma Theater* (2030 Sansom St.; phone: 963-0345); the *Society Hill Playhouse* (507 S. 8th St.; phone: 923-0210); and the *Annenberg Center* (3680 Walnut St.; phone: 898-6791), with its three theaters that house the *Philadelphia Drama Guild,* the *Annenberg Subscription Series,* and the *Philadelphia Festival Theater for New Plays.* The *Pennsylvania Ballet* performs at the *Academy of Music* (Broad and Locust Sts.; phone: 551-7014).

MUSIC: The *Philadelphia Orchestra,* under conductor Riccardo Muti, performs at the *Academy of Music,* a classic 1847 building (Broad and Locust Sts.; phone: 893-1930). In summer, they play at the *Mann Music Center* (Fairmount Park; phone: 567-0707), where rock concerts are also held. In summer, call 878-7707 for rock and pop

concert tickets. Free tickets to orchestra concerts are available at the visitors' center (16th and John F. Kennedy Blvd.) on the day of a performance. The *Opera Company of Philadelphia* and the *Soloists Chamber Orchestra of Philadelphia* also perform at the *Academy of Music* at various times throughout the year.

NIGHTCLUBS AND NIGHTLIFE: Philadelphians prefer cabarets to Las Vegas–type shows. Best bets: *Café Borgia* (406 S. 2nd St.; phone: 923-6660), a café with Left Bank ambience and sophisticated jazz; *Chestnut Cabaret* (3801 Chestnut St.; phone: 382-1201), ranging from rock 'n' roll to rhythm and blues; and *Middle East* (126 Chestnut St.; phone: 922-1003), with belly dancers. Comics perform upstairs from *Middle East* at *Comedy Works* (phone: 922-5997) and at the *Comedy Factory Outlet* (31 Bank St.; phone: 386-6911). For an enjoyable family or group activity, take a dinner (or lunch) cruise on *The Spirit of Philadelphia.* Sail along the Delaware as your waiters serve your meal and then perform a Broadway revue. Runs March through December (Pier No. 24 on Delaware Ave., north of Market St.; phone: 923-1419, or 923-4993 for groups of 20 or more).

■ **TAKE SOME PHILADELPHIA HOME WITH YOU:** "Tastykakes" are the things about which exiled Philadelphians dream most. The little packages of cakes and pies are available at most grocery stores. But the biggest local food thrill is Bassett's ice cream, available all around the city.

BEST IN TOWN

CHECKING IN: Hotels range from durable, famous places to sleek, new spots with loud, lively lobbies. But there are very few really good inexpensive hotels. Expect to pay $100 to $150 or more for a double in any of those places we've listed as very expensive; between $75 and $100, expensive; between $50 and $75, moderate. Most hotels offer weekend packages at significantly reduced rates. For bed and breakfast accommodations, contact *Bed and Breakfast Connections* (PO Box 21, Devon, PA 19333; phone: 687-3565 or 800-448-3619 outside PA) or *Bed & Breakfast of Philadelphia* (PO Box 252, Gradyville, PA 19039; phone: 358-4747 or 800-733-4747 outside of 215 area code). All telephone numbers are in the 215 area code unless otherwise indicated.

Barclay – Quiet, stylish, and stalwart, and only steps from Rittenhouse Square and the Walnut Street shops. Its continental restaurant is a favorite with the monied Main Line crowd. Though the 240 rooms are not regal, they are comfortable and tastefully furnished. Conference facilities for up to 300. There's also concierge, CNN, and 24-hour room service. Guests also have use of the adjacent *Rittenhouse Fitness Center.* 237 S. 18th St. (phone: 545-0300; Fax: 215-545-2896). Very expensive.

Four Seasons – The height of local elegance, with 371 authentically luxurious rooms and suites. Features include such touches as a mini-bar and a hair dryer in each room, twice-daily maid service, terrycloth robes, and a complimentary shoeshine, as well as 3 restaurants: the most gracious *Fountain* (See *Eating Out*), the *Swan Café*, and a courtyard café, open during the summer. The *Swan Lounge* features weekend entertainment. Other amenities include meeting rooms for up to 600, secretarial services, A/V equipment, photocopiers, computers, 24-hour valet and room service, concierge, beauty salon, CNN, and a health spa with pool, exercise room, sauna, and whirlpool bath. Express checkout. One Logan Sq. (phone: 963-1500 or 800-332-3442; Fax: 215-963-9506). Very expensive.

Hershey Philadelphia – A first class 450-room contemporary establishment in the center of the city, it features extensive meeting facilities that accommodate up to 500, secretarial services, A/V equipment, photocopiers, a restaurant, a cocktail lounge with nightly entertainment, and valet and room service, as well as a concierge desk. The athletically inclined can use the indoor pool, jogging track, racquetball courts, exercise room, and gameroom or relax in the suntanning salon, sauna, and whirlpool baths. Express checkout. Broad and Locust Sts. (phone: 893-1600; Fax: 215-893-1663). Very expensive.

Holiday Inn, Center City – Good location, near the Penn Center complex, within walking distance of major museums, a mile from Independence Mall. It offers 443 rooms, a restaurant, lounge, lobby bar, meeting facilities for up to 1,000, and an outdoor pool. Other conveniences include an exercise room, secretarial services, A/V equipment, photocopiers, around-the-clock room service, a concierge desk, and express checkout. 18th and Market (phone: 561-7500 or 800-HOLIDAY; Fax: 215-561-4484). Very expensive.

Holiday Inn, Midtown – Small, scrupulously maintained 161-room motor inn with a good location and an outdoor pool. Near theaters, and just a stroll away from all the best shops. Valet and 24-hour room service, restaurant and bar, CNN, and meeting facilities for up to 300. The use of a local health club is available for a small charge. Express checkout. 1305 Walnut (phone: 735-9300 or 800-HOLIDAYS; Fax: 215-732-2682). Very expensive.

Hotel Atop the Bellevue – One of the nation's grandest properties when it opened in the 1890s, it fell on hard times in the 1970s. After extensive renovations, however, this landmark reopened in 1989 in an 11-story retail/office complex. The 154 rooms and 18 spacious suites, decorated in turn-of-the-century style, offer many modern amenities: bathroom TV sets and hair dryers; an entertainment center with VCR, stereo, and mini-bar; and 3 phones with two lines each, and a computer hookup. Fine dining and nightly dancing are available in *Founders*. The *Library* lounge and *Ethel Barrymore Room* where afternoon tea is served are perfect for relaxing. In addition, guests receive a complimentary pass to the adjacent health club. There are meeting facilities for up to 1,200, A/V equipment, photocopiers, concierge and secretarial services, CNN, and 24-hour room service. 1415 Chancellor Court (phone: 893-1776 or 800-221-0833; Fax: 215-721-8518). Very expensive.

Latham – The 139 rooms are decorated with bright bedspreads, marble-topped bureaus, graceful French writing desks, and remote-control cable TV sets. Chocolates on the pillow at night are one of the ways the hotel pampers its guests. A Grand Tradition Hotel, it's a favorite of businesspeople who seek a central location and top service. There are 2 phones in each room, with call waiting and computer hookups, and a complimentary *Wall Street Journal* is delivered to rooms every business day. Guests may use a health club a block away. The hotel restaurant, *Bogart's* (see *Eating Out*), and the *Crickett Lounge* are places to see and be seen. Concierge, valet, and room service. Meeting rooms accommodate up to 60. Secretarial services are available, as well as A/V equipment, photocopiers, computers, and CNN. Express checkout. 17th and Walnut (phone: 563-7474 or 800-LATHAM-1; Fax: 215-563-4034; Telex: 831438). Very expensive.

Omni at Independence Park – Its grand marble lobby with working fireplace and its marvelous view overlooking Independence National Historic Park make this hotel special. Original watercolors of city scenes adorn the guestrooms, which have 2-line phones with voice mail and computer hookups, as well as VCRs (guests can use the hotel's film library). Complimentary coffee, danish, and the morning paper from guests' home cities (!) arrive with wake-up calls. Marble bathrooms are equipped with hairdryers and phones. The *Azalea* restaurant features regional Pennsylvania cooking. There's a lounge, 24-hour room service, a bilingual concierge, a health club with a lap pool, saunas, a Jacuzzi, and an exercise room. Meeting rooms accommodate up to 45. Express checkout and CNN. Towncar service with complimentary pickup is available at the 30th St. Station, as well as a pickup for a reduced charge at the airport. 4th and Chestnut Sts. (phone: 925-0000 or 800-THE OMNI; Fax: 215-925-1263). Very expensive.

Penn Tower – Slightly away from the mainstream with its location on the University of Pennsylvania campus next to the Civic Center, but close enough to most sites to remain convenient. It has 227 rooms, a restaurant, cocktail lounge, meeting rooms for up to 500, a concierge desk, and 24-hour room service. Secretarial services are at guests' disposal, as well as A/V equipment, photocopiers, and computers. Express checkout. Guests have use of athletic facilities at the University of Pennsylvania. Civic Center Blvd. at 34th St. (phone: 387-8333 or 800-356-PENN; Fax: 215-386-8306). Very expensive.

Rittenhouse – Appointed in classic European style, it has 87 rooms, 11 suites, and 183 condominiums for business travelers. Amenities include spacious marble bathrooms with tub and stall showers, phones with 2 lines and a computer hookup, a VCR, and twice-daily maid service. *Restaurant 210* provides elegant dining, and *Treetops Café* offers attractive pre- and post-theater menus. The *Cassatt Room* serves afternoon tea. A real advantage are the complimentary massages proffered by the in-house spa; guests can also enjoy the pool, sauna, workout equipment, and sun deck. The building complex also houses retail shops, a salon, a bank, and a florist. Business conveniences include 24-hour room service, both concierge and secretarial services, A/V equipment, photocopiers, computers, and CNN. The meeting rooms accommodate up to 500. 210 W. Rittenhouse Sq. (phone: 546-9000 or 800-474-1700; Fax: 215-732-3364). Very expensive.

Ritz-Carlton – Located in Liberty Place (the first 2 floors are devoted to retail shops and restaurants), this 290-room hotel has been designed and decorated in the style of the city's Federal period, with lots of moldings and wainscotting to make guests feel as if they are visiting a stately Main Line manse. Rooms have mini-bars, and marble bathrooms have phones and hairdryers. Guests can arrange to use the pool at a nearby sports club. There is an exercise and fitness center with Universal equipment, a massage room, and saunas. Two restaurants provide fine dining, and there are 2 lounge areas that serve afternoon tea. Meeting rooms accommodate up to 800, and other amenities include A/V equipment, photocopiers, computers, and secretarial services. Express checkout. 17th and Chestnut Sts. (phone: 563-1600 or 800-241-3333; Fax: 564-9559). Very expensive.

Sheraton Inn, Society Hill – In the historic district, within walking distance of Penn's Landing and Independence Mall. Its brick and wood decor lend colonial overtones to its rooms and lobby, where balconies overlook a verdant atrium. The hotel has 2 restaurants, an indoor pool, and health club. The 365 guestrooms have computerized snack bars (you select your items from a machine and they are billed to your room). Valet, concierge, and 24-hour room service are available. Meeting rooms seat up to 700, and there are photocopiers and A/V equipment. Express checkout. One Dock St., near Walnut (phone: 238-6000 or 800-325-3535; Fax: 215-922-2709). Very expensive.

Sheraton Inn, University City – Convenient to the University of Pennsylvania campus, with 377 rooms; an outdoor pool; a restaurant called *Smart Alex,* whose disc jockeys provide evening entertainment; and the *36th Street Deli,* which serves continental breakfast and lunch. Other amenities include 24-hour room service, photocopiers, CNN, and express checkout. Meeting rooms seat up to 500. Discounted parking. 36th and Chestnut Sts. (phone: 387-8000 or 800-325-3535). Very expensive.

Wyndham Franklin Plaza – Large and lavish, it's one of the city's best and only 4 blocks from City Hall, a few steps from the Parkway. Facilities include 720 modern rooms and 32 suites, racquetball courts, a fully equipped health club with indoor pool, underground parking, 3 restaurants, a lounge, valet and room service, and concierge. Extensive meeting space for up to 2,500. Secretarial services are available, as well as A/V equipment, and CNN. Express checkout. 17th and Vine Sts. (phone: 448-2000 or 800-822-4200; Fax: 215-448-2864). Very expensive.

Guest Quarters, Philadelphia Airport – One mile from the main terminal and 15 minutes from the city center, it offers 250 suites, each with living room, bedroom, and bath; also an exercise room and indoor swimming pool, whirlpool bath, and sauna; an 8-story atrium that includes the *Atrium Café* and *Lounge;* meeting and banquet facilities for up to 200 people; courtesy airport transportation and free hotel parking. There's 24-hour room service, as well as secretarial services, A/V equipment, computers, photocopiers, and CNN. Express checkout. 1 Gateway Center (phone: 365-6600 or 800-424-2900; Fax: 215-492-8471). Expensive.

Holiday Inn–City Line – A total of 350 rooms, plus an indoor/outdoor pool, exercise room, restaurant, lounge, limousine service to and from the airport, and free parking. It's also convenient to City Line shops and restaurants. There's a friendly all-night restaurant next door. Business amenities include meeting rooms for up to 400, A/V and photocopying equipment, and express checkout. City Line and Presidential Blvd. (phone: 477-0200 or 800-HOLIDAY; Fax: 215-473-2709). Expensive.

Howard Johnson's – A 2-story lodge near Valley Forge, with 168 refurbished rooms (some designated nonsmoking), cable TV (with CNN), and an outdoor pool; convenient to area restaurants. A complimentary continental breakfast is offered, and there are laundry facilities and meeting rooms that accommodate up to 20. Rte. 202, N. and S. Gulph Rd., King of Prussia (phone: 265-4500 or 800-654-2000). Expensive.

George Washington – We're certain George would have preferred staying at this motor lodge during his cold Valley Forge encampment. Its facilities include 135 rooms, and indoor and outdoor pools. Restaurant next door. Rte. 202 S. and Warner Rd., King of Prussia (phone: 265-6100). Moderate.

Quality Inn, Center City – With 279 rooms in the heart of the museum district and within walking distance of most major city attractions, the style is casual comfort. Amenities include a restaurant, lounge, outdoor pool, and free parking. There's meeting space for up to 60. 22nd and Parkway (phone: 568-8300 or 800-221-2222; Fax: 215-557-0259). Moderate.

EATING OUT: The city boasts quite a few outstanding restaurants. In fact, Philadelphia has been enjoying a restaurant renaissance in recent years, with both spacious and intimate places opening their doors, many offering very fine dining experiences. Expect to pay $75 or more for two in those places we've listed as very expensive; $50 to $70 in the expensive category; $20 to $45, moderate; under $20, inexpensive. Prices do not include drinks, wine, or tips. All telephone numbers are in the 215 area code unless otherwise indicated.

Le Bec Fin – Usually the best in town and, at its best, one of the finest restaurants in the country. Imaginative French food by Georges Perrier, the proprietor and master chef from Lyons. Constantly changing menu, but always a selection of lavish desserts. Prix fixe dinner, about $90 per person; lunch about $30 per person. Closed Sundays. Lunch served weekdays. Reservations essential. Make weekend reservations up to 3 months in advance as the restaurant seats only 75. Major credit cards accepted. 1523 Walnut (phone: 567-1000). Very expensive.

Deux Cheminées – This elegant dining spot, located in a 19th-century townhouse, features old Philadelphia decor, with Oriental rugs and polished hardwood floors. Master chef and owner Fritz Blank prepares nouvelle cuisine dishes. Open daily. Reservations advised. Major credit cards accepted. 1221 Locust St. (phone: 790-0200). Very expensive.

Fountain – Located in the *Four Seasons* hotel, this is one of Philadelphia's finest. Experience an evening of truly gracious dining accompanied by attentive service. Rich mahogany walls and picture windows overlooking the Benjamin Franklin Parkway add to the elegant setting. A changing menu features fine continental cuisine. An alternate low-sodium, low-cholesterol menu is available. Enjoy an extensive wine selection and the after-dinner trolley stocked with liqueurs and ports. Sunday brunch includes a combination buffet and à la carte menu selections. Open daily. Reservations advised (non-hotel guests must call 4 to 6 weeks in advance for Saturday nights). Major credit cards accepted. One Logan Square (phone: 963-1500). Very expensive.

Bogart's – Like the movie set of *Casablanca,* with wooden ceiling fans and tinkling piano. You won't find Bogie belting one down at the bar, but you will find continental dishes, some with fruit-flavored sauces that exhibit the chef's southern touch, and a well-dressed crowd. Open daily. Reservations advised. Major credit cards accepted. *Latham Hotel,* 17th and Walnut (phone: 563-9444). Very expensive to expensive.

Bookbinder's Seafood House – The better (and more expensive) of the two restaurants bearing this famous name. Happy, bustling, serving the same well-prepared, simple food, fresh from the ocean. Open daily. Reservations advised. Major credit cards accepted. 215 S. 15th (phone: 545-1137). Very expensive to expensive.

DiLullo Centro – Opened in 1985 in a renovated theater, this large establishment has world class atmosphere and small restaurant quality. Opulence is everywhere, from a bronze food-presentation table and glass elevator to Impressionist murals. The menu features a wide variety of homemade pasta as well as veal and seafood dishes and fresh pastries. Closed Sundays. Reservations advised. Major credit cards accepted. 1407 Locust St. (phone: 546-2000). Very expensive to expensive.

Top of Center Square – Expansive windows in each of the four dining rooms on the 41st floor of the Center Square building provide a panorama of the city. Request the east dining room to see the beautifully lighted City Hall and Billy Penn statue towering above. There is a varied and delicious menu of meats and seafoods. A favorite for business lunches. Open daily. Reservations advised. Major credit cards accepted. 1500 Market St. (phone: 563-9494). Very expensive to expensive.

Old Original Bookbinder's – Philadelphia's best-known restaurant, with mahogany and gleaming leather. Many love it, many hate it. The seafood is as much of a legend as many of the celebrities who dine here. Open daily. Reservations necessary. Major credit cards accepted. 125 Walnut St. (phone: 925-7027). Expensive.

Dickens Inn, Philadelphia – In the historic Harper House, whose architecture bespeaks the Federal period; the imported authentic period pieces from England create an English inn right out of Charles Dickens's day. In fact, Dickens's great-grandson Cedric Charles Dickens has given his stamp of approval on numerous visits. Begin an enjoyable evening by sipping a yard of ale and nibbling shepherd's pie in the inn's tavern. Then move on to the restaurant proper to choose from a menu that features traditional English cuisine, including the famous roast beef and Yorkshire pudding or a leg of lamb. Delicious desserts come from a bakery on the premises. The curiosity shop on the first floor is filled with Dickens memorabilia. Lunch and dinner daily. Reservations advised. Major credit cards accepted. 2nd between Pine and Lombard Sts. (phone: 928-9307). Expensive to moderate.

Downey's – A local favorite where diners come to relax and party, this Irish eatery in the heart of Society Hill is noted for both its corned beef dinners and liquored cakes. The continental menu includes a variety of steak dishes, and an oyster bar features seafood and soups. The wood and brass decor is complemented with Irish artifacts, including a mahogany bar brought over from a bank in Cork. A strolling string ensemble entertains during Sunday brunch. Open daily. Reservations advised. Major credit cards accepted. Front and South Sts. (phone: 629-0525). Expensive to moderate.

Garden – A continental menu with a French influence, along with fresh seafood and game in season, all served in a stylish old townhouse. Patrons can dine outdoors in the courtyard when the weather's good, or station themselves at the cozy Oyster Bar in the front room. Closed Sundays. Reservations advised. Major credit cards accepted. 1617 Spruce St. (phone: 546-4455). Expensive to moderate.

Sansom Street Oyster House – With a remarkable collection of several hundred oyster plates displayed overhead and highly polished wooden tables, the casual warmth of this place is a Philadelphia tradition. Superb Maryland crab cakes, as well as bread and rice puddings for dessert. Closed Sundays. Reservations advised. Major credit cards accepted. 1516 Sansom St. (phone: 567-7683). Moderate.

Apropos – A place for those seeking an upbeat bistro atmosphere with sophisticated ambience; but be warned — it can get noisy here. The menu ranges from mesquite-grilled chicken, fish, and meat entrées to lighter fare, such as salads, pasta, and sandwiches. All breads and desserts are freshly baked. Traditional and unusual pizza from a wood-burning oven. Live music Wednesdays and weekends. Dining is available in the large, open dining room or the glass-enclosed street café. Open daily. Reservations advised. Major credit cards accepted. 211 S. Broad St. (phone: 546-4424). Moderate to inexpensive.

Carolina's – It's vinyl-tablecloth and paper-napkin casual, with a local professional following and a lively neighborhood crowd at the bar. The menu features such home-style specials as veal loaf with mashed potatoes, grilled salmon steaks, and pork chops with mustard sauce, as well as salads, sandwiches, and fresh pasta. Open daily. Reservations advised. Major credit cards accepted. 261 S. 20th St. (phone: 545-1000). Moderate to inexpensive.

Marabella's – A contemporary Italian eatery featuring mesquite-grilled seafood, great pizza, and Italian delicacies including handmade pasta. Try the tortellini with goat cheese, sun-dried tomatoes, and olives; or a huge salad entrée of grilled chicken cutlet on a bed of radicchio, endive, and Bibb lettuce. Follow up (if you still can) with homemade chocolate truffle or ricotta cheesecake, or sample the *gelati,* Italian ice cream. Open daily for lunch and dinner. Reservations essential for lunch only. Major credit cards accepted. 1420 Locust St. in Academy House (phone: 545-1845). Moderate to inexpensive.

The Commissary – An upscale cafeteria in the city center with a simple menu — mostly salads, omelettes, and pasta. An adjoining market offers a take-out selection from coffee and muffins to sandwiches and ice cream. Open daily. Reservations unnecessary. Major credit cards accepted. 1710 Sansom St. (phone: 569-2240). Inexpensive.

Famous Delicatessen – Famous among Philadelphia residents, and for its celebrity customers, to which the picture-lined walls will attest. Monstrous hot pastrami, roast beef, and corned beef sandwiches. No-frill eating; the food comes on paper plates. Open Mondays through Saturdays until 6 PM; Sundays until 4 PM. No reservations. American Express accepted. 700 S. 4th St. (phone: 627-9198). Inexpensive.

H. A. Winston & Co. – Dozens of burger permutations in an atmosphere that's warm, cozy, and comfortable. Open daily. Reservations accepted only for parties of six or more. Major credit cards accepted. 1500 Locust St. (phone: 546-7232). Inexpensive.

Imperial Inn – One of the best-known spots in Chinatown. Its menu features Szechuan, Mandarin, and Cantonese dishes. Cantonese-style dim sum are offered during the more casual lunch hours; lights are dimmed and linen tablecloths are added at dinner. Parking is available at nearby 11th and Race Sts. Open daily. Reservations advised. Major credit cards accepted. 146 N. 10th St. (phone: 627-5588). Inexpensive.

Melrose Diner – With its 50-year history, fanatically devoted staff, and round-the-clock crowds, this is as much a Philly institution as the scrapple it serves. Food preparation is fastidious, right down to the refiltered water and the coffee specially brewed in a custom-made urn. Waitresses wearing coffee-cup-shaped pins with clock faces (the diner's logo; a tiny knife and fork form the hands) serve up scrapple (fried seasoned meat and corn meal) and eggs, cutlets, burgers, creamed chipped beef on toast, and other no-frills fare. The homemade desserts are popular take-out items. Open 24 hours. No reservations. No credit cards accepted. In South Philly at Broad St. and Snyder Ave. (phone: 467-6644). Inexpensive.

Pete's Pizza – Convenient to the *Franklin Institute, Please Touch,* and *Academy of Natural Sciences,* the menu here includes Philadelphia hoagies, grinders, and burgers in addition to pizza. It also claims to have the city's best *stromboli* (pizza dough filled with onions, peppers, meat, and sauce, folded over and baked with cheese on top). Open daily from 6 AM until 1 AM. No reservations or credit cards accepted. 116 N. 21st St. (phone: 567-4116). Inexpensive.

While in Philadelphia, don't forget to sink your teeth into a famous Philly cheesesteak — a sandwich loaded with steak, onions, cheese, and peppers. Try *Pat's King of Steaks* (1237 E. Passyunk Ave., S. Philadelphia; phone: 468-1546) for one of the best cheesesteaks in town. Open 24 hours, 7 days a week. Another favorite is *Jim's Steaks* (400 South St., phone: 928-1911), which also has great hoagies (also known as heros or sub sandwiches). Open daily. *Olivieri's* is the next best thing if you are in the *Reading Terminal Market* (12th and Arch Sts.; phone: 625-9369).

PHOENIX

AT-A-GLANCE

SEEING THE CITY: As you look out on Phoenix from South Mountain ponder on the words of an Indian prayer to Corn Mother and Sun Father: "Oh, it is good, you provide. It is the ability to think. It is the wisdom that comes. It is the understanding."

SPECIAL PLACES: Street numbers start at zero in the center of downtown. Central Avenue, the business and financial district, runs north and south, bisecting the city into east and west. Numbered avenues lie to the west of Central, numbered streets to the east.

State Capitol – The building will give an idea of what granite from the Salt River Mountains looks like when put to constructive use. It has now been restored to its original 1912 appearance (the time of statehood). The murals inside depict Arizona's discovery and exploration in the 16th century and life in the region through the 1930s. There also is an exhibit displaying an array of bola (string) ties, the official state neckware. Closed weekends and holidays. No admission charge. W. Washington and 17th Ave. (phone: 542-4675).

Heard Museum of American Culture and Art – A fascinating anthropological collection of artifacts from ancient Indian civilizations in Arizona. The kachina doll collection, donated by former Senator Barry Goldwater, is consistently interesting for neophytes as well as experts. Changing exhibitions feature contemporary American Indian sculpture, paintings, and drawings. The gift shop carries fine Indian jewelry, crafts, and artwork. Open daily except holidays. Admission charge. 22 E. Monte Vista (phone: 252-8840 or, for recorded information, 252-8848).

Phoenix Art Museum – Specializes in contemporary art from the Southwest; other collections lean toward North American art in general (including Mexican), with a small exhibition of Renaissance, 17th-, and 18th-century material. Closed Mondays and major holidays. Admission charge except Wednesdays. 1625 N. Central (phone: 257-1222).

Pueblo Grande Museum and Indian Ruins – On the site of a former Hohokam Indian settlement. By climbing to the top of a mound marked into seven stations, you can see the ruins which are believed to have been occupied from 200 BC to AD 1400, when the Hohokam vanished without a trace. Phoenix municipal archaeologists are continuing their excavations. Open daily except holidays. Admission charge. 4619 E. Washington (phone: 275-3452).

Desert Botanical Gardens – Half of all the varieties of cactus in the world are planted on the grounds, and self-guiding tours and booklets help identify the prickly flora. Open daily. Admission charge. Papago Park (phone: 941-1217).

Phoenix Zoo – When you're done walking around the Botanical Gardens, take a leisurely drive through desert rock formations to the Phoenix Zoo, which covers more than 125 acres in another section of Papago Park. (You can stop to picnic in the park.) Two of the most popular attractions are the oryx herd and Hazel, the gorilla. There are more than 1,200 animals altogether. Open daily. Admission charge. 5810 E. Van Buren (phone: 273-7771).

Scottsdale – This re-created western community with hitching posts is a haven for artists and art lovers. Scottsdale's Fifth Avenue is lined with galleries (see *Museums and Galleries*) featuring Indian art, handicrafts, and jewelry. Every Thursday evening from 7 to 9, October through May, the community sponsors an "art walk" through town. In Scottsdale, taking a walk is an aesthetic adventure. Take McDowell Rd. east to Scottsdale Rd. north.

Cosanti Foundation – The architect Paolo Soleri maintains a workshop here, with a model of Arcosanti, his megalopolis of the future. His sculpture and windbells are on display, too. Open daily except major holidays; call for tour information. Donation suggested. 6433 E. Doubletree Rd., Scottsdale (phone: 948-6145).

Taliesin West – The future owes much of its shape to the innovative imagination and technical expertise of the master architect Frank Lloyd Wright. His former office and school, Taliesin (pronounced Tal-ly-*ess*-en) West, offers the chance to see what goes into planning and designing those marvelous, ultramodern structures. Closed on rainy days and holidays; limited, varying hours from June to mid-October. Admission charge. Scottsdale Rd. north, to Shea Blvd. east, to 108th St. north, to Taliesin West in Scottsdale (phone: 860-8810).

Borgata – Not the place for bargain-priced jeans or a pound of sugar, it's one of the most opulent retail operations this side of Beverly Hills — and one of the most unusual anywhere. The Borgata houses about 50 boutiques and restaurants in a setting redolent of an old Italian village. It's well worth a visit, even if you can only afford to cast amazed glances at the price tags. Open daily. 6166 N. Scottsdale Rd., Scottsdale.

Heritage Square – This Victorian complex in the heart of downtown is a refreshing change in this relatively young city. Spend an afternoon in the museums, shops, restaurants, and open-air lathe house. Rosson House (1894) is particularly notable. Open Wednesdays through Sundays. Admission charge. 127 N. 6th St. (phone: 262-5071).

Arizona Center – Opened late in 1990, this downtown oasis became an immediate hit. Shops and restaurants line the L-shaped, 2-story center. Fountains, shade trees, and wide expanses of lawn help deflect summer's torrid heat. Open daily. 455 N. 3rd St.(phone: 271-4000).

The Mercado – Not a traditional Mexican open market, but a series of six buildings where Mexico's past blends easily with today's Southwest. This urban village, built to lure consumers downtown, is a colorful mix of restaurants, shops, office space, a community center, and a cultural museum. Open daily. Van Buren and Seventh Sts.

Rawhide's 1880s Western Town – Mosey on over to the valley's most authentic Wild West town, complete with gunfights, gold panning, a museum, a specialty zoo, steakhouse and saloon, and sunset cookouts. With the McDowell Mountains as a backdrop, it's a glimpse into how the West really was. Open daily. Admission charge. 23023 N. Scottsdale Rd. (phone: 563-5111).

***Dolly's Steamboat* on Canyon Lake** – A unique way to tour the desert. Board this nostalgic replica of a historic steamboat to cruise Canyon Lake, in the breathtaking Superstition Wilderness. Guides give an informal history and geography lesson along the way. Cruises depart at noon and 2 PM daily, with sunset charter rides available. Call for summer hours. Admission charge. 5106 E. Emilita, Mesa (phone: 827-9144).

■ **EXTRA SPECIAL:** For a picturesque day trip through open desert, take the Black Canyon Highway north, to Cordes Junction, then travel west through the old territorial capital of Prescott to Sedona, famous for its dramatic red cliffs. At Sedona, take a breathtaking drive up Oak Creek Canyon to Flagstaff, or complete the circle by driving back to Verde Valley, returning via the Black Canyon Highway. Be sure to stop in Jerome, the ghost town too ornery to die. A community

CENTRAL PHOENIX

of artists now lives in the old wooden buildings that cling precariously to the steep mountainside of this former copper mining town. Jerome has great curio and antiques shops specializing in mining paraphernalia and one of the best restaurants in Arizona, the *House of Joy,* open only on weekends. The food is continental, the prices are reasonable, and it's open only on weekends (so reservations are a must; phone: 634-5339).

SOURCES AND RESOURCES

TOURIST INFORMATION: For maps, brochures, and information, contact the Phoenix and Valley of the Sun Convention and Visitors Bureau (505 N. 2nd St., Phoenix, AZ 85004; phone: 254-6500) or the Arizona Office of Tourism (1100 W. Washington Ave., Phoenix, AZ 85003; phone: 542-8687). Contact the Arizona state hotline (phone: 602-542-8687) for maps, calendars of events, health updates, and travel advisories.

The best guide is *Phoenix Metro* magazine's *City Guide* (Phoenix Publishing; $3.95).

Local Coverage – *Arizona Republic,* morning daily; *Phoenix Gazette,* evening daily except Sundays; *Scottsdale Progress,* afternoon daily; *Mesa, Tempe and Chandler Tribune,* morning daily; *New Times, Business Journal,* and *Arizona Business Gazette,* all weekly; *Phoenix Metro* magazine, *Arizona Trend, Phoenix Home & Garden,* all monthly.

Television Stations – KTVK Channel 3–ABC; KAET Channel 8–PBS; KTSP Channel 10–CBS; KPNX Channel 12–NBC.

Radio Stations – AM: KTAR 620 (news/talk); KAMJ 1230 (contemporary); KLFF 1360 (big band music). FM: KZZP 104.7 (adult contemporary); KMEO 96.9 (easy listening); KSLX 100.7 (nostalgia).

Food – *100 Best Restaurants in Arizona,* by John and Joan Bogert (ADM; $3.95).

TELEPHONE: The area code for Phoenix is 602.
Sales Tax – The city sales tax is 6.7%.

CLIMATE: Try not to visit in summer (though hotel prices go down), when it's more than 100F. Fall, winter, and spring are dry, warm, and sunny. Temperatures range from daytime highs of between 60 and 80F to nighttime lows of about 35 to 50F.

GETTING AROUND: Getting around Phoenix is next to impossible without a car.

Airport – Sky Harbor International Airport is just a 10-minute drive from downtown, and, depending on the cab company, taxi fare will run from $7 to $14. (Fares vary widely, so be sure to agree on a price before getting into a cab.) *Supershuttle* (phone: 244-9000) offers transportation from the airport to downtown for $5 and to most other valley locations for $16 maximum. For rides to the airport, call 24 hours in advance. *Phoenix Transit* (phone: 257-8426) buses stop at terminals 3 and 4 at Sky Harbor every half hour. One goes downtown and one to the east valley. Fare is 85¢ and transfers are free.

Bus – There are buses, but service is sketchy, with interminable waiting periods, erratic schedules, very limited nighttime service, and few buses on Sundays. However, you can call *Phoenix Transit System* (phone: 257-8426) for schedule information.

Car Rental – All major national firms are represented. *Rent A Wreck* (phone: 252-4897) is among the least expensive.

Taxi – Call *Yellow Cab* (phone: 252-5071) or *Triple A* (phone: 437-4000).

VITAL SERVICES: Audiovisual Equipment – *Photo & Sound Co.* (phone: 437-1560); *Arizona Audio Visual Center* (phone: 860-9321).

Baby-sitting – *Ace Baby-sitting Service,* 3737 E. Turney Ave. (phone: 956-2848).

Business Services – *Alison's Secretarial Service,* 3270 E. Camelback Rd. (phone: 955-3542).

Dry Cleaner/Tailor – *Downtown Laundry & Dry Cleaning,* 308 N. 2nd Ave. (phone: 253-7245).

Limousine – *Arizona Limousines* (phone: 267-7097); *Valley Limousines* (phone: 254-1955).

Mechanic – *Western States Tire Co.,* 201 W. Van Buren (phone: 254-4131).

Medical Emergency – *St. Luke's Hospital* (1800 E. Van Buren; phone: 251-8183); Emergency medics and paramedics (phone: 245-1657).

Messenger Services – *Dial-a-Messenger* (phone: 954-6060).

National/International Courier – *Federal Express* (phone: 254-4662); *DHL Worldwide Courier Express* (phone: 244-9922).

Pharmacy – *Lahr Pharmacy,* open daily from 7 AM to midnight, 9220 N. Central Ave. (phone: 944-3326).

Photocopies – *Alphagraphics Printshop of the Future,* delivery service (3003 N. Central Ave.; phone: 254-6171); *Acme Blueprint* (1425 N. 1st St.; phone: 254-6171).

Post Office – The main office is located downtown, at 522 N. Central Ave. (phone: 253-4102).

Professional Photographer – *Ted Hill Photography* (phone: 946-7287); *Bill Lundwall Photography* (phone: 957-4515).

Secretary/Stenographer – *Northwest Secretarial Service,* pickup and delivery (phone: 866-0017).

Translator – *Berlitz* (phone: 265-7333).

Typewriter Rental – *ABC Business Machines,* 1-week minimum, typewriter stands and chairs as well (phone: 955-2050); *Arizona Typewriter Co.,* 1-week minimum (phone: 267-1631).

Western Union/Telex – Many offices are located around the city (phone: 800-325-6000).

Other – *AccuRent Computer Systems* (phone: 829-6500); *Use 'R Computers* (phone: 263-5599).

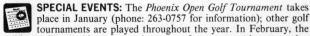 **SPECIAL EVENTS:** The *Phoenix Open Golf Tournament* takes place in January (phone: 263-0757 for information); other golf tournaments are played throughout the year. In February, the million-dollar Arabians prance into town for a spectacular equestrian event of pageantry at the *Arabian Horse Show and Sale* (phone: 264-5691). In March, the *Veterans Memorial Coliseum* (1826 W. McDowell; phone: 264-4808) is the site of the *Phoenix Jaycees Rodeo of Rodeos,* and the *Formula I Grand Prix Race* takes place in downtown Phoenix (phone: 800-872-4726 for tickets and information). In May, one of the city's most vibrant celebrations is the *Cinco de Mayo,* an annual holiday celebrating the Mexican victory over French troops in 1862. In October, the *Arizona State Fair* fills up the State Fairgrounds (phone: 252-6711) and the *Cowboy Artists of America* bring their works to town for this nationally recognized sale and exhibition at the *Phoenix Art Museum* (phone: 257-1880). November finds hundreds of colorful balloons dotting the turquoise skies in the annual *Thunderbird Balloon Race* at the American Graduate School of International Management in Glendale (phone: 978-7208). Watch for the month-long schedule of activities that begin in December for the *Sunkist Fiesta Bowl,* capped by a *New Year's* weekend that brings a parade, a national high school band pageant, and two of the country's top collegiate football teams together for a bowl title.

MUSEUMS: The *Heard Museum, Phoenix Art Museum,* and *Pueblo Grande Museum* are described in *Special Places.* Other museums worth a visit:

Arizona Mineral Museum – 1826 W. McDowell (phone: 255-3791).

Hall of Flame Museum – No kidding. A collection of firefighting paraphernalia from 1725. 6101 E. Van Buren (phone: 275-3473).

ART GALLERIES: Although Phoenix does have some interesting art galleries, most of the finest are in Scottsdale, within walking distance of one another. They exhibit a rich and vast array of art forms — paintings, sculpture, graphics — and many are devoted to American Indian art and contemporary western art. Some of the best are the following:

Artistic Gallery – Artists include the nationally acclaimed R. C. Gorman. 7077 E. Main St., Scottsdale (phone: 945-6766).

Elaine Horwitch Galleries – Contemporary sculpture and paintings by a wide variety of artists. 4211 N. Marshall Way, Scottsdale (phone: 945-0791).

Gallery McGoffin – The country's only batik gallery. 902 W. Roosevelt, Phoenix (phone: 255-0785).

Hand and the Spirit – Tapestries, ceramics, jewelry, and other American crafts. 4222 N. Marshall Way, Scottsdale (phone: 946-4529).

Lovena Ohl Gallery – Indian arts and crafts, from primitive to contemporary. 4251 N. Marshall Way, Scottsdale (phone: 945-8212).

Marilyn Butler Fine Art – Fritz Scholder is among the gallery's artists. 4160 N. Craftsman Court, Scottsdale (phone: 994-9550).

Suzanne Brown Gallery – Contemporary western art, from abstract to representational. 7156 E. Main St., Scottsdale (phone: 945-8475).

MAJOR COLLEGES AND UNIVERSITIES: The largest and most active campus is Arizona State University (Apache Blvd., Tempe; phone: 965-9011). Phoenix College (1202 W. Thomas Rd.; phone: 285-7418) and the American Graduate School of International Management (59th Ave. and Greenway Rd., Glendale; phone: 978-7011) sponsor concerts and activities, too.

SPORTS AND FITNESS: The year-round sun makes Phoenix ideal for watching or participating in outdoor athletics.

Basketball – The NBA Phoenix *Suns* play at *Veterans Memorial Coliseum* (1826 W. McDowell; phone: 258-6711), although a new downtown arena may be completed late this year. The Arizona State University *Sun Devils* play at the *University Athletic Center* on the campus in Tempe (phone: 965-2381).

Bicycling – Rent bikes from *Airplane and Bicycle Works,* 4400 N. Scottsdale Rd., Scottsdale (phone: 949-1978).

Dog Racing – *Greyhound Park,* 40th and E. Washington Sts. (phone: 273-7181).

Fishing – Trout, bass, and crappie can be caught at Apache Lake and Salt River.

Football – The NFL Phoenix *Cardinals* and the Arizona State *Sun Devils* play at *Sun Devil Stadium.* Call the ticket office for seat availability (phone: 965-2381).

Golf – There are about 90 courses in Phoenix, many of them at resorts that welcome transient players. The best public course is *Papago Park Municipal* (phone: 275-8428).

Horseback Riding – Hourly rentals at *Ponderosa Stable* (10215 S. Central; phone: 268-1261) and *South Mountain Stable* (10005 S. Central; phone: 276-8131). *All Western Stables* (10220 S. Central; phone: 276-5862) also rents horses by the hour.

Horse Racing – *Turf Paradise* (from October to May), 19th Ave. and Bell Rd. (phone: 942-1101).

Inland Surfing – If you've always wanted to surf but can't quite brave the force of the ocean, *Big Surf* in Tempe (1500 N. Hayden Rd.; phone: 947-2478) is a good place to break in. There are artificial beaches and waves, and you can rent the entire facility for parties. Closed Mondays except holiday weekends and October through March; open weekends only in September. Admission charge.

Jogging – An enclosed haven for fast walkers on scorchingly hot days is the air conditioned *Paradise Valley Mall* (Mondays through Saturdays 6 to 10 AM, Sundays 8:30 AM to noon) before it is officially open to shoppers; in northeast Phoenix at the intersection of Tatum and Cactus (phone: 996-8840). Under the sun run along the banks of the Arizona Canal (pick it up beside the *Biltmore* hotel) or the Grand Canal, reachable by jogging about a mile north along Central Avenue; Encanto Park, about three-quarters of a mile from downtown, also attracts runners.

Swimming – The Salt River is good for swimming, too. There are 23 municipal pools in Phoenix. Every large park has one. Try the pool at Coronado Park, N. 12th St. and Coronado Rd.

Tennis – *Phoenix Tennis Center* has 22 lighted courts for night games, 6330 N. 21st Ave. (phone: 249-3712). In all, there are more than 1,000 courts in the Phoenix area.

Tubing – Arizona's most popular summer sport. On any given weekend, as many as 20,000 residents strap beer-filled ice chests and their bottoms to old inner tubes and float down 5 or 10 miles of free-flowing Salt River, below Saguaro Lake, just north of Mesa. The trip is free and you can buy tubes — the bigger the better — at gas stations and stands along the route. This utterly relaxing pastime is called "tubing down the Salt." For tube rental and shuttle service, contact *Salt River Recreation,* Mesa (phone: 984-3305).

THEATER: There's quite a lot of drama in Phoenix and Scottsdale. Many plays take place on campuses, and world-renowned performers have come to play Shakespeare. Check the local publications listed above for schedules. The major theaters include: *Phoenix Little Theater* (25 E. Coronado Rd.; phone: 254-2151); *Herberger Theater Center* (222 E. Monroe St.; phone: 252-8497); *Gammage Auditorium* (a Frank Lloyd Wright building on the campus of Arizona State University in Tempe; phone: 965-3434); and *Scottsdale Center for the Arts* (Civic Center Plaza, Scottsdale; phone: 994-2787). *Arizona Ballet Theater* performs at *Scottsdale Center for the Arts* (7383 Scottsdale Mall; phone: 994-2787). Traveling dance troupes perform at *Gammage Auditorium* and the *Scottsdale Center for the Arts.*

MUSIC: The *Phoenix Symphony* (phone: 264-4754) and *Arizona Opera Company* (phone: 254-1664) play at *Symphony Hall* (225 E. Adams); the *Scottsdale Symphony* performs at *Scottsdale Center for the Arts* (7383 Scottsdale Mall; phone: 994-2787). Nationally known rock performers and classical musicians appear at *Gammage Auditorium* (phone: 965-3434). Rock groups also give concerts at *Veterans Memorial Coliseum* (1826 W. McDowell; phone: 258-6711). Good music also is found on college and university campuses (see "Major Colleges and Universities").

NIGHTCLUBS AND NIGHTLIFE: One of the most popular nightspots in Phoenix is *Oscar Taylor* (Biltmore Fashion Sq.; phone: 956-5705), which offers a great happy hour and a decor that's reminiscent of Chicago during Prohibition. Another good meeting place is *Timothy's* (6335 N. 16th St.; phone: 277-7634), where jazz artists appear nightly. If you crave a little Mexican food with your nightclubbing, don your dancing shoes and head to *Acapulco Bay Beach Club* (3837 E. Thomas; phone: 273-6077). And for margaritas and music that will knock your socks off, try *Depot Cantina* (300 S. Ash, Tempe; phone: 966-6677).

BEST IN TOWN

CHECKING IN: If you're going to Phoenix on business, you'll probably want to stay downtown. If it's a vacation, you can't beat the resorts, which offer full recreational activities and valley tours. Meals usually are included in the room rate at a resort, but be sure to check first. Expect to pay between $120 and $280 for a double room at an expensive resort; between $75 and $100 at an expensive hotel; $45 to $75 in moderate; and around $30 at an inexpensive listing. For bed and breakfast accommodations, contact *Bed & Breakfast in Arizona* (PO Box 8628, Scottsdale, AZ 85252; phone: 995-2831) or *Mi Casa, Su Casa* (PO Box 950, Tempe, AZ 85280; phone: 990-0682). All telephone numbers are in the 602 area code unless otherwise indicated.

Arizona Biltmore – The first, and still among the best in the valley, this 502-room resort is first class in every way. Golf and tennis facilities are outstanding, and so are the pools. Individual guests may be put off by the hordes of convention and meeting goers, who always seem to dominate the premises. The dining rooms serve fine continental food. Business amenities include a concierge desk, A/V equipment, photocopiers, secretarial services, computers, and express checkout. 24th St. and Missouri (phone: 955-6600; Fax: 602-954-0469; Telex: 165709). Expensive.

Boulders – Opened in 1985 by the Rockresort group (but no longer managed by them), this is a "rock resort" in another sense, too: It's set on 1,300 acres of desert foothills at the base of a towering pile of boulders. The 120 adobe-colored casitas blend beautifully with the surroundings, and each contains a room with a wet bar and working fireplace. There are also tennis courts, golf courses, and horseback riding. There's an obliging concierge desk, as well as 6 meeting rooms, A/V equipment, photocopiers, secretarial services, and computers available. Express checkout. Carefree, about 30 miles north of Phoenix (phone: 488-9009; Fax: 602-488-4118). Expensive.

Camelback Inn – Among the larger resorts in the state — 423 rooms, mostly in 2-story cottages. It's set among the beautiful Camelback Mountain foothills and has swimming pools, golf, and tennis facilities. The cowboy cookouts are great fun. Amenities include a concierge desk, A/V equipment, photocopiers, secretarial services, computers, and around-the-clock room service. Express checkout. 5402 E. Lincoln Dr., Scottsdale (phone: 948-1700; Fax: 602-951-2152). Expensive.

Camelview – Desert landscaping provides a placid retreat from the hustle-bustle of nearby downtown Scottsdale. There are 200 rooms, including suites and casitas, plus a pool, 8 lighted tennis courts, an exercise parcourse, and numerous other amenities. The main restaurant, *Café on the Lakes,* serves steaks and seafood. A concierge desk, 23 meeting rooms, A/V equipment, photocopiers, secretarial services, and computers make up the business conveniences. 7601 E. Indian Bend Rd., Scottsdale (phone: 991-2400 or 800-228-9822; Fax: 602-951-5072). Expensive.

Clarion Inn – Convenient to *Scottsdale Center for the Arts,* the *Scottsdale Mall,* and the town's numerous boutiques. An added bonus is the *Rotisserie Bar & Grill,* which features Southwestern cooking and a stylish piano bar that's open late every night but Sunday. Extra pluses are the concierge and secretarial services, 7 meeting rooms, A/V equipment, photocopiers, and computers. 7353 E. Indian School Rd., Scottsdale (phone: 994-9203; Fax: 602-941-2567). Expensive.

Embassy Suites – Run by a hotel chain whose goal is to provide guests with a homey atmosphere, and since 95% of the guests return, it appears that the management is successful. Accommodations are in 2-room suites with kitchens; breakfasts and late afternoon cocktails are free; and tipping is not permitted. Six locations: 5001 N. Scottsdale Rd., Scottsdale; 1515 N. 44th St., 2333 E. Thomas Rd., 2630 E. Camelback Rd., and 3210 NW Grand Ave., Phoenix; and 4400 S. Rural Rd., Tempe (phone: 800-362-2779). Expensive.

Hermosa Resort – Long one of the valley's most exclusive guest ranches and tennis resorts, it advertises that it is "not just a resort, it's an attitude." That sounds like hype until you check in and find rooms with gas-fired fireplaces, wet bars, Jacuzzis, and a staff that gives VIP treatment to every guest. The setting seems far removed from the rat race, but civilization is only minutes away — if you want it. 5532 N. Palo Cristi Rd., Paradise Valley (phone: 955-8614). Expensive.

Hyatt Regency – Play tennis after dark, swim, or relax those aching muscles in the whirlpool bath. This elegant, 711-room property has a fine restaurant and an overpriced coffee shop. Among the amenities are a concierge desk, 40 meeting rooms, A/V equipment, and computers, and secretarial services. There's also 24-hour room service and express checkout. 122 N. 2nd St. (phone: 257-1110 or 800-228-9000; Fax: 602-254-9472). Expensive.

Hyatt Regency Scottsdale – Built on the Gainey Ranch development, this $75-million, 497-room luxury resort offers all the basic recreational facilities (swimming pool with swim-up bar, 8 tennis courts, 27 holes of championship golf, health club, and Jacuzzi), as well as a few extras (lawn tennis and croquet). After all that exercise, guests can sate their hunger and quench their thirst at the 2 restaurants, entertainment lounge, or lobby bar. Twenty-four–hour room service is available, as well as a concierge desk, 21 meeting rooms, A/V equipment, photocopiers, secretarial services, computers, and express checkout. 7500 E. Doubletree Ranch Rd., Scottsdale (phone: 800-228-9000; Fax: 602-483-5511). Expensive.

Marriott's Mountain Shadows – With a 1,500-seat grand ballroom and 10 meeting rooms, it's no wonder this place is popular with convention groups and business travelers. And after all those meetings, guests can relax by taking advantage of the 3 pools, 2 Jacuzzis, 8 tennis courts, and three 18-hole golf courses. There are 2 informal restaurants, *Cactus Flower Café* and *Shells Oyster Seafood Bar.* Business amenities include a concierge, 10 meeting rooms, A/V equipment, photocopiers, secretarial services, computers, and express checkout. 5641 E. Lincoln Dr., Scottsdale (phone: 800-228-9290; Fax: 602-948-7111, ext. 1898). Expensive.

Phoenician – At the base of legendary Camelback Mountain, this $300-million property has 613 rooms, individual casitas, several restaurants, an 18-hole championship golf course and clubhouse, tennis, and health spa. It's had its financial problems, but new ownership (a 51%-49% partnership between the US government and the Kuwaiti Investment Corp.) should make operations more stable. Business amenities include a concierge desk, 30 meeting rooms, A/V equipment, photocopiers, secretarial services, computers, 24-hour room service, and express checkout. 6000 E. Camelback Rd., Scottsdale (phone: 941-8200; Fax: 602-947-4311). Expensive.

Phoenix Crescent – A 344-room establishment that caters to the business traveler. Features include a pool, tennis courts, a health club, and a restaurant, as well as a location that is convenient to the rapidly expanding North Phoenix commercial center. A concierge desk, 13 meeting rooms, A/V equipment, photocopiers, computers, and express checkout complete the list of business amenities. 2620 W. Dunlap Ave. (phone: 943-8200; Fax: 602-371-2856). Expensive.

Pointe at Squaw Peak – Lovely Southwestern decor characterizes this mountainside resort, which manages to remain almost fully booked even during the summer. *Pointe of View* (see *Eating Out*), which features Northern Italian cooking, is one of several good restaurants here. Room service is available around the clock; there's a concierge desk, 28 meeting rooms, A/V equipment, photocopiers, secretarial services, computers, and express checkout. 7677 N. 16th St. (phone: 997-6000 or 800-528-0428; Fax: 602-997-2391). Expensive.

Pointe at Tapatio Cliffs – Patterned after the successful *Pointe at Squaw Peak*, this mountainside resort has attractive Spanish-South-western architecture and luxurious amenities. The dazzling *Etienne's Different Pointe of View* restaurant is a high-tech mountaintop facility that serves fine French fare. Around-the-clock room service is availalbe; also concierge and secretarial services, 26 meeting rooms, A/V equipment, photocopiers, computers, and express checkout. 11111 N. 7th St. (phone: 997-6000 or 800-528-0428; Fax: 602-993-0276). Expensive.

Registry Resort – A good choice for those who want to go first class, this busy place borders several golf courses and has 3 pools, a complete fitness center, and nightly entertainment. Its *La Champagne* (see *Eating Out*) restaurant is considered one of the valley's best, and Sunday brunch in the *Phoenician Room* combines live music with a remarkable array of food. Amenities include a concierge desk, 12 meeting rooms, A/V equipment, photocopiers, secretarial services, computers, express checkout, and 24-hour room service. 7171 N. Scottsdale Rd., Scottsdale (phone: 991-3800; Fax: 602-948-9843). Expensive.

Ritz-Carlton – This 301-room hotel looks as if it was plucked right off the East Coast and plunked down in the desert. No cactus, no adobe-style architecture or kachina dolls here. Instead, it remains traditional, from the leaded glass chandeliers overhead to the plush Oriental rugs covering the floors. And just like other members of its group, the emphasis here is on service for well-heeled corporate travelers and affluent vacationers. Every whim is catered to by an attentive staff. Pluses here include 24-hour room service, concierge, 14 meeting rooms, secretarial services, A/V equipment, photocopiers, computers, and express checkout. 2401 E. Camelback Rd. (phone: 468-0700; Fax: 602-468-9883). Expensive.

Scottsdale Princess – Built on 450 acres of desert, this resort provides the best of the Southwest, with 363 rooms and 37 suites in its main building, plus 125 casitas. There's a full range of sports facilities, including two championship 18-hole golf courses (they play the *Phoenix Open* on the *TPC Stadium* course), 10 tennis courts (6 lighted), 3 heated pools, and a health club/spa with racquetball and squash courts, as well as restaurants (see *Eating Out*), lounges, bars, and shops. Among the amenities are concierge and secretarial services, 24-hour room service, 23 meeting rooms, A/V equipment, photocopiers, computers, and express checkout. 7575 E. Princess Dr., Scottsdale (phone: 585-4848 or 800-223-1818; Fax: 602-585-0091). Expensive.

Sheraton Phoenix – A Phoenix fixture, its 534 large rooms all have magnificent views and there's an old-time feeling at the quaint bar, with swimming pool, good coffee shop, and a good dining room. There's a concierge desk here, as well as 20 meeting rooms, A/V equipment, photocopiers, secretarial services, computers, and express checkout. 111 N. Central (phone: 257-1525, or 325-3535; Fax: 602-253-9755). Expensive.

Stouffer-Cottonwoods – It's easy to relax at this resort while admiring Camelback Mountain in the distance, sniffing the piñon-perfumed air, and basking in the bright Arizona sun. The 170 fresh and comfortable rooms have a Southwestern decor. A jitney connects the hotel with nearby shopping, and there's a pool, putting greens, and jogging trails. Golf and horseback riding also are nearby. Additional amenities are a concierge desk, 8 meeting rooms, secretarial services, around-the-clock room service, A/V equipment, photocopiers, and computers. Express checkout. 6160 N. Scottsdale Rd., Scottsdale (phone: 991-1414, 800-325-5000, or 800-HOTELS-1; Fax: 602-951-2434). Expensive.

SunBurst – Santa Fe decor enhances this place, which has as much to offer outdoors as in. Amenities include a free-form pool, a spa, a lively lounge, and a restaurant (the *Desert Rose*) with very good American and continental food. Concierge and secretarial services are available; as are 12 meeting rooms, photocopiers, A/V equipment, computers, and express checkout. 4925 N. Scottsdale Rd., Scottsdale (phone: 945-7666; Fax: 602-946-4056). Expensive.

Westcourt – Ultramodern, boasting more original artworks in its 284 luxury rooms and suites than many galleries. In the city next to the gargantuan *Metrocenter* — packed with shops and restaurants — it also has a dining room called *Trumps.* A/V equipment, photocopiers, and computers are available, plus 12 meeting rooms, concierge and secretarial services. Express checkout. 10220 N. Metro Pkwy. E. (phone: 997-5900; Fax: 602-997-1034). Expensive.

Wyndham Paradise Valley – This 20-acre, $40-million facility offers 380 rooms, including 27 suites, as well as 2 pools, a health club and spa, 2 racquetball courts, 6 tennis courts, and 2 restaurants, one of which features very creative American nouvelle cuisine. Computers, 18 meeting rooms, A/V equipment, photocopiers, concierge, secretarial services, and express checkout are all offered. 5401 N. Scottsdale Rd., Scottsdale (phone: 947-5400; Fax: 602-481-0209). Expensive.

Fiesta Inn – This venerable favorite is a true Southwest delight, with Mexican tiles and room-size fireplaces. Complimentary airport transportation, health club, and jogging trails are included. There's also a concierge desk, 7 meeting rooms, A/V equipment, photocopiers, and computers at guests' disposal. 2100 S. Prest Dr., Tempe (phone: 967-1441; Fax: 602-967-0224). Moderate.

Holiday Inn – Modern, with 292 rooms near the financial district, it also has 2 swimming pools, whirlpool bath, and a good restaurant. Pets are welcome. 3600 N. 2nd Ave. (phone: 248-0222 or 800-465-4329). Moderate.

Lexington – A good place for an extended visit. All 139 suites come with kitchens, continental breakfast, and hospitality hour. Discounts for long stays/relocation. 1660 W. Elliot Rd. (phone: 345-8585 or 800-53-SUITE). Moderate.

Travel Inn 9 – Smaller and quieter than the others, this 68-unit motel (with pool) also is kinder to your budget. 201 N. 7th Ave. (phone: 254-6521). Inexpensive.

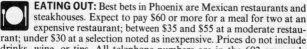 **EATING OUT:** Best bets in Phoenix are Mexican restaurants and steakhouses. Expect to pay $60 or more for a meal for two at an expensive restaurant; between $35 and $55 at a moderate restaurant; under $30 at a selection noted as inexpensive. Prices do not include drinks, wine, or tips. All telephone numbers are in the 602 area code unless otherwise indicated.

Avanti – This place has a 6-page menu of Northern Italian and continental dishes. Closed *Christmas.* Reservations advised. Major credit cards accepted. Two locations: 3102 N Scottsdale Rd., Scottsdale (phone: 949-8333); 2728 E. Thomas Rd., Phoenix (phone: 956-0900). Expensive.

La Champagne – Part of the prestigious *Registry Resort,* this ambitious restaurant offers American nouvelle and French cuisine, black tie service, an extensive wine list, and piano music. Closed Sundays and

Mondays. Reservations advised. Major credit cards accepted. 7171 N. Scottsdale Rd., Scottsdale (phone: 991-3800). Expensive.

Christopher's – Chef and owner Christopher Gross has a well-deserved local reputation for his well-prepared French dishes. Grilled sea scallops with Provençal vegetables, veal chop with carrot and onion potato purée, and sautéed venison with huckleberries and red wine sauce are just some of the selections that change each day. Open daily. Reservations advised. Major credit cards accepted. 2398 E. Camelback Rd. (phone: 957-3214). Expensive.

Golden Eagle – Although it's a pricey place, the view over the valley and the quick and attentive service make you feel it's worth it. The continental menu features some Southwestern specialties. Closed Sundays, *Christmas,* and *New Year*'s. Reservations advised. Major credit cards accepted. 201 N. Central, atop the Valley Bank Center, Phoenix (phone: 257-7700). Expensive.

La Hacienda – In the authentic-looking adobe mansion of the *Scottsdale Princess,* it features Mexican specialties as well as a roast of the day, which may be juicy lamb or crackling crisp suckling pig. The bar and lounge serve Mexican and Spanish *tapas* (hors d'oeuvres) during cocktail hours to the strains of live mariachi music. Open daily for lunch and dinner in season. Reservations advised. Major credit cards accepted. 7575 E. Princess Dr., Scottsdale (phone: 585-4848). Expensive.

Mancuso's – The decor at the Scottsdale location will transport you to an Italian Renaissance castle, and the continental dishes merit applause, as does the service. The prices of entrées include soup, salad, and more. Closed major holidays. Reservations advised. Major credit cards accepted. 6166 N. Scottsdale Rd., Scottsdale (phone: 948-9988). Also a branch at 4949 E. Lincoln Dr., Paradise Valley (phone: 840-8670). Expensive.

Palm Court – Tuxedoed waiters prepare much of the food at your table at this dining room in the *Scottsdale Conference Resort.* While gazing out on Camelback Mountain and Lake McCormick, you can select from the brief but tempting à la carte continental menu. Recommended are the Bibb lettuce salad, the lobster bisque, and the rack of lamb. Sunday brunch here is considered among the valley's finest. Open daily. Reservations advised. Major credit cards accepted. 7700 E. McCormick Pkwy., Scottsdale (phone: 991-3400). Expensive.

Pointe of View – Charcoal-broiled steaks and pasta are house specialties. The view affords an impressive panorama of the valley. Open daily. Reservations advised. Major credit cards accepted. 7677 N. 16th St., Phoenix (phone: 997-5859). Expensive.

Ruth's Chris Steak House – There's no cowboy atmosphere at all, but it does serve the best steaks in the state, in a sleek, contemporary dining room. Prices are high, but portions are gigantic. Closed *Christmas.* Reservations advised. Major credit cards accepted. 2201 E. Camelback Rd., Phoenix (phone: 957-9600). Expensive.

Tomaso's – The latest effort of a successful valley restaurateur, this eatery and its siblings are known for their Northern Italian specialties. Closed *Thanksgiving* and *Christmas.* Reservations advised. Major credit cards accepted. Three locations: 610 E. Bell Rd., Phoenix (phone: 866-1906); 3225 E. Camelback Rd., Phoenix (phone: 956-0836); and 1954 S. Dobson Rd., Mesa (phone: 897-0140). Expensive.

Vincent Guerithault on Camelback – Get a real taste of the Southwest in this elegant eatery headed by one of the finest chefs in the Southwest. You can order items like tacos and tamales anywhere, but never have they been prepared with such unique ingredients — try a duck tamale or a lobster corn pancake. Closed Sundays. Reservations advised. Major credit cards accepted. 3930 E. Camelback Rd., Phoenix (phone: 224-0225). Expensive.

Voltaire – The most popular entrée is sand dab — a white fish from the sole family that the chef blankets with egg batter and sautés in lemon butter — but the rack of lamb, medallions of veal, and boned breast of duck are just as gratifying. Closed Sundays, Mondays, and June through September. Reservations advised. Major credit cards accepted. 8340 E. McDonald, Scottsdale (phone: 948-1005). Expensive.

Christopher's Bistro – Christopher Gross, chef and owner of *Christopher's,* has extended his talents to the adjacent café (the two establishments share a communal kitchen). Dishes such as grilled mahi mahi with honey, cardamom, and couscous, osso buco with white beans and a roasted tomato, and grilled rib eye steak with peppercorns and roquefort chesse, as well as dessert soufflés made to order, crown the menu. Open daily. Reservations advised. Major credit cards accepted. 2398 E. Camelback Rd. (phone: 957-3214). Moderate.

El Chorro Lodge – Old Arizona charm at its best. By night, cozy up to the fireplace for a romantic interlude; by day, bask in the sun on the patio overlooking the majestic Camelback Mountain. No matter what time of day, don't miss the basket of hot sticky buns. Open daily, but closed during the summer. Reservations advised. Major credit cards accepted. 5550 E. Lincoln, Scottsdale (phone: 948-5170). Moderate.

Don & Charlie's – If your appetite is bigger than your budget, try this place. The menu's American dishes may seem standard, but just wait till they arrive at your table. Steaks are huge and perfectly cooked, and the meaty pork ribs are good, too. It boasts one of the best happy hour spreads in town. Closed on *Thanksgiving.* Reservations advised. Major credit cards accepted. 7501 E. Camelback Rd., Scottsdale (phone: 990-0900). Moderate.

Durant's – A fashionable place for everyone from politicians to local celebrities for 30 years. Enjoy the traditional appetizers before dinner, then choose an excellent steak or prime ribs entrée. Closed major holidays. Reservations advised. Major credit cards accepted. 2611 N. Central Ave. (phone: 264-5967). Moderate.

Eddie's Grill – American foods are prepared with a Mediterranean twist in a pleasant blend of cuisines. Served in lovely surroundings with koi ponds outside and a gazebo that houses a *tapas* bar for appetizers. For a romantic dinner, ask for a table in the wine cellar. Closed Sundays. Reservations advised. Major credit cards accepted. 4747 N. Seventh St. (phone: 241-1188). Moderate.

Famous Pacific Fish Co. – Good service and bargain prices are simply extras. This place is really special for its combination of Mexican mesquite charcoal broiling and fresh seafood. The nautical ambience is delightful, too. Don't miss the New England clam chowder, which may not be the "world's finest" (as the menu claims) but certainly comes close. Closed on major holidays. Lunch reservations advised. Major credit cards accepted. 4321 N. Scottsdale Rd., Scottsdale (phone: 941-0602). Moderate.

Monti's La Casa Vieja – A valley landmark. This spot serves some of the best steaks anywhere. It's always crowded, but the service is good and the side dishes are plentiful. Open daily. Reservations advised for lunch only. Major credit cards accepted. 3 W. First, Tempe (phone: 967-7594). Moderate.

Moroccan – It doesn't look like much from the outside, but inside, diners are transported to another place and time. The exotic menu features meat pastries topped with sugar and cinnamon, marinated vegetables, and an array of spicy lamb dishes. Entrées come with five courses and are eaten with the hands. For an added treat, there's Moroccan music and hip-rolling belly dancers. Open nightly. Reservations advised. Major credit cards accepted. 4228 N. Scottsdale, Scottsdale (phone: 947-9590). Moderate.

Pinnacle Peak Patio – No trip to Arizona would be complete without a visit to a real western cowboy steakhouse. This one's the oldest and most famous, with 2-pound porterhouses broiled over mesquite coals and served with sourdough bread and pinto beans. Don't wear a tie! Closed *Thanksgiving, Christmas Eve,* and *Christmas.* Reservations necessary for large groups only. Major credit cards accepted. 10426 E. Jomax Rd., Scottsdale (phone: 967-8082). Moderate.

Piñon Grill – Who said hotel restaurants had to be boring or uncreative? If you hunger for authentic Southwestern fare, head to the grill at the *Inn at McCormick Ranch.* The lakeside setting and the copper and cactus decor only enhance the fare from the topnotch and daring kitchen. Open daily. Reservations unnecessary. Major credit cards accepted. 7401 N. Scottsdale Rd., Scottsdale (phone: 948-5050). Moderate.

Steamers – It may seem impossible to find excellent seafood in the Southwest, but here it is. Try the Maine lobster, the Baltimore crab cakes, or the Boston clam chowder. It's also one of the most popular gathering places in the valley. Open daily. Reservations advised. Major credit cards accepted. 2576 E. Camelback Rd. (phone: 956-3631). Moderate.

T-Bone – A real out-of-the-way find that's never crowded. It has basically the same menu as *Pinnacle Peak* (see above), with a fantastic night view of the valley. Food is brought by entertaining, gun-totin' waitresses, and you can help yourself to a filling salad. Closed on *Thanksgiving, Christmas,* and the first 2 weeks in July. Reservations unnecessary. Major credit cards accepted. End of 19th Ave. south of Dobbins, Phoenix (phone: 276-0945). Moderate.

What's Your Beef – A valley favorite, serving beef and fresh fish; the super salad bar with fruit, vegetables, and breads is a big favorite. An adjoining bar offers entertainment nightly with no cover charge. Open daily. Reservations advised on weekends. Major credit cards accepted. 8111 E. McDowell, Scottsdale (phone: 998-1987). Moderate.

RoxSand – One of the most talked-about dining spots to open in the valley in years, this stylishly decorated place features "intercontinental" dishes that vary widely in price, complexity, and origin. There are enticing entrées from Italy, Korea, Mongolia, Morocco, Sweden, and Russia, but nothing beats the desserts. Closed on major holidays. Reservations advised. Major credit cards accepted. 2594 E. Camelback Rd., Scottsdale (phone: 381-0444). Moderate to inexpensive.

Aunt Chilada's – Authentic Mexican food is the specialty here. Try the Whole Aunt Chilada: chimichangas, bean burritos, tamales, guacamole, sour cream, and homemade flour tortillas served with fideo (Mexican pasta) instead of rice. Don't worry; it serves two. Closed *Thanksgiving.* Reservations advised. Major credit cards accepted. 7330 N. Dreamy Draw Dr., Phoenix (phone: 944-1286); 2021 W. Baseline Rd., Tempe (phone: 438-0092). Inexpensive.

Ed Debevic's Short Orders Deluxe – Step back in time to a 1950s diner, complete with a blue-plate special and wise-cracking, gum-snapping waitresses. Order the meat loaf sandwich with a real cherry Coke. It's as much fun and as good as you remember. Closed *Thanksgiving* and *Christmas.* Reservations unnecessary. Visa and MasterCard accepted. 2102 East Highland St. (phone: 956-2760). Inexpensive.

Honey Bear's BBQ – Tender chicken and pork are doused in a sweet spicy sauce. This stuff just slides off the bone, and their motto, "You don't need teeth to eat our meat," is close to the mark. Open daily. Reservations unnecessary. Major credit cards accepted. 5012 E. Van Buren St. (phone: 273-9148). Inexpensive.

El Norteno – This small take-out place is cramped and far from elegant, but the food more than makes up for the lack of atmosphere. It serves some of the best Mexican fare in Phoenix. Open daily. Reservations unnecessary. Most credit cards accepted. 1002 N. Seventh Ave. (phone: 254-4429). Inexpensive.

Los Olivos – A family operation for more than 3 decades, this is the valley's oldest Mexican eatery. Thoroughly modern decor belies its age, but the food explains its longevity. Try such house specialties as sour cream enchiladas and *carne asada,* then walk off the meal by strolling over to the adjacent *Scottsdale Center for the Arts.* Closed major holidays. Reservations accepted. Major credit cards accepted. 7328 E. 2nd St., Scottsdale (phone: 946-2256). Inexpensive.

Original Hamburger Works – If all you want is a good burger, wander over to the vicinity of Phoenix College and partake of giant hamburgers with all the fixin's. The decor is rustic 1880s, with advertising posters from the turn of the century on the walls. Closed *Thanksgiving* and *Christmas.* No reservations or credit cards accepted. 2801 N. 15th Ave., Phoenix (phone: 263-8693). Inexpensive.

Pink Pepper – A few years ago, the valley had only one Thai restaurant; now there are about 2 dozen. This ultramodern spot is the prettiest of the lot, and since it uses moderation when sprinkling on the spices, it's a good place for the uninitiated to try this often hot-as-fire food. The soup with lemon grass and coconut milk is tops, as are the meat dishes with Phonaeng curry. Open daily. Reservations advised. Major credit cards accepted. 2003 N. Scottsdale Rd., Scottsdale (phone: 945-9300). Two other locations: 4967 W. Bell, Phoenix (phone: 843-0070); 1941 W. Guadalupe, Mesa (phone: 839-9009). Inexpensive.

PITTSBURGH

AT-A-GLANCE

SEEING THE CITY: Go to the top of Mt. Washington via the Duquesne or Monongahela inclines for a sweeping 17-mile view of the confluence of the Allegheny, Monongahela, and Ohio rivers. Duquesne (75¢ each way) is at W. Carson St. (phone: 381-1665); Monongahela (60¢ each way), in operation since 1870, is at E. Carson St., behind the Freight House Shops of Station Square (phone: 237-1000). Exact change (75¢) is required. Pittsburgh's original blast furnace can be seen on the south side of the Monongahela River, between the two inclines.

For a more down-to-earth view, take one of several different cruises on the *Gateway Clipper* fleet, from the dock at Station Square. The captain aboard the 2-hour sightseeing cruise ($7.50 for adults, $4.25 for children 12 and under) will highlight points of interest along all three rivers. The *Goodship Lollipop* has clowns to keep children occupied while parents enjoy the sights on its 1-hour cruise (adults $5.25; children under 12, $3.25). Reservations are required for the dinner cruise ($17 to $27 per person), which leaves the dock daily at 7 PM. Specialty cruises include a tour of the river lock system and an excursion to *Waterford Race Track,* Wheeling, West Virginia. Some cruises are seasonal; call 355-7980 for information.

SPECIAL PLACES: There are four main sections of the city in which you'll find most of Pittsburgh's places of interest. The Golden Triangle encompasses the downtown area; the North Side, with its old homes, restored "Mexican War" streets, and parks; the East Side, with its museums and cultural institutions, and the South Side.

GOLDEN TRIANGLE

Though most of the major attractions are within walking distance, use the subway for quick crosstown transportation.

Point State Park – At the tip of the Golden Triangle, it covers 36 acres of broad walks and spacious gardens on the banks of the river junction, Point State Park contains Ft. Pitt Blockhouse, a 1764 fortification, and *Ft. Pitt Museum,* with exhibitions on the French and Indian War and early Pennsylvania history. The park is free and open daily (phone: 281-9284); the museum is open Wednesdays through Sundays. Admission charge.

PPG Place – The "crown jewel" in Pittsburgh's skyline is a plaza surrounded by six modern Gothic buildings, all with a mirrored glass façade, designed by Philip Johnson and John Burgee. On the ground floor of PPG 1 is the Wintergarden, open to the public for civic functions. An array of international food establishments and retail boutiques runs throughout buildings 2 through 6. Summer concerts are given in the plaza. Off Stanwix St.

Fifth Avenue Place – This striking new office building contains a collection of specialty shops, along with a food court on the second floor. The building is linked by a skywalk to *Joseph Horne Co.,* a family-owned department store that's been affiliated with Pittsburgh for more than a century. Penn and Liberty Aves.

One Oxford Centre – This office tower at Grant Street and 4th Avenue has 3 lower floors dedicated to designer shops including *Polo/ Ralph Lauren, Gucci,* and *Ann Taylor.* Several restaurants and nightclubs featuring live jazz are there when you've had your fill of shopping.

Civic Arena – Recognizable by its stainless steel roof — the largest retractable dome in the world — this is the home of the Pittsburgh *Penguins* hockey team and the Pittsburgh *Spirit* soccer team. The circus, ice shows, dog show, and top-name concerts also are held here. Bordered by Washington and Crawford Sts., Bedford and Centre Aves.

David L. Lawrence Convention Center – The city's exposition hall has 131,000 square feet of space and hosts the home show and the *Pittsburgh Folk Festival* every May. Call 565-6000 for a schedule of upcoming events. Penn Ave.

Benedum Center for the Performing Arts – Once an elegant movie palace of the 1920s, this theater has been restored into a glittering showplace. The backstage is bigger than New York's *Metropolitan Opera,* and is home to the *Pittsburgh Opera* and the *Pittsburgh Ballet,* as well as the *Civic Light Opera.* Penn and Seventh Aves. (phone: 456-6666).

Heinz Hall – A very classy movie theater in 1926, *Heinz Hall* is now an acoustically balanced, stately auditorium, home of the *Pittsburgh Symphony* (which currently enjoys international favor under the baton of Lorin Maazel), and host to performing arts troupes. Worth a look for its ornate decorations and gold leaf. Guided tours by appointment. Admission charge. 600 Penn Ave. (phone: 392-4800 for tickets).

Strip District – A noisy, hectic hub where the region's food wholesalers sell their produce. It can be a somewhat overwhelming place to visit, especially for those used to the antiseptic nature of supermarkets. In addition to the markets, everything from hole-in-the-wall cafés to a genuine Italian espresso bar line the streets. Stop in at the *Society for Arts in Crafts,* which displays and sells finely made local and international crafts. Penn Ave. and Smallman St.

SOUTH SIDE

Station Square – The beautifully restored *Pittsburgh and Lake Erie Railroad* complex includes an outdoor museum with antique rail cars and Bessemer converter, an elegant restaurant and saloon in the old station, and a complete shopping mall in the adjacent freight house. The *Gateway Clipper* dock also is here.

Carson Street District – A browser's Elysian Fields, which is home to many antiques shops, art galleries, bookstores, an old-fashioned hardware store, and a restored neighborhood movie theater. This renovated and reawakened area also boasts numerous good restaurants and nightclubs, where jazz and blues reign supreme. There's plenty of on-street parking. Cross Smithfield Bridge, south of Station Square.

NORTH SIDE

To get to the North Side from the Golden Triangle, cross the 6th Street Bridge, then proceed north to the *Allegheny Center Mall.* Crosstown buses leave from *Horne's,* at Penn Avenue and Stanwix Street.

Allegheny Observatory – With a 30-inch-diameter refractory lens — a very powerful telescope — this observatory is acclaimed as one of the world's best. Amateur astronomers can scan the heavens or partake of the illustrated lectures. Open Wednesday, Thursday, and Friday evenings by appointment, April through October. No admission charge. Riverview Park off Perrysville Ave. (phone: 321-2400).

Landmark Square – Almost hidden behind the bunker-like *Allegheny Center Mall* is the restored Old Post Office, home to the innovative *Pittsburgh Children's Museum* and the regional branch of the Carnegie Library. In the museum, tots and preteens can play with video equipment, operate puppets they know from TV, and participate in a kids'

CENTRAL PITTSBURGH

LANDMARKS

1. Fort Pitt Museum
2. Bank Center
3. David L. Lawrence Convention Center
4. Heinz Hall
5. Monongahela Incline
6. West Park Conservatory—Aviary
7. PPG Place
8. Buhl Planetarium
9. Cathedral of Learning
10. Carnegie Museum and Library
11. Mellon Institute
12. Phipps Conservatory
13. Historical Society of Western Pennsylvania
14. Frick Fine Arts Building
15. Pittsburgh Playhouse Theater Center
16. Penn. Central Station
17. Pittsburgh & Lake Erie Station
18. U.S. Steel Building
19. First Blast Furnace
20. "Mexican War" District

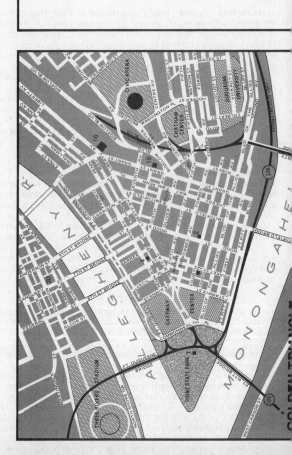

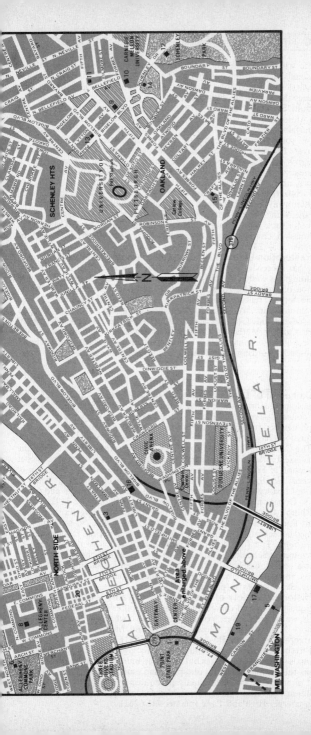

clinic where they are the doctor to an injured dummy. Open daily; seasonal hours. Admission charge (phone: 322-5059). Just steps away is the first Carnegie Public Library, opened in 1890. The building also houses the *Pittsburgh Public Theater.*

Buhl Science Center – This amazing center currently underwent renovations and it still has one of the best sky shows in the country. Entertaining exhibitions on astronomy and other branches of science allow you to pedal a bicycle to generate electricity, push a button to activate the rotation of planets in our solar system, and monitor voice patterns on an oscilloscope. There's also an Omnimax theater and a planetarium. Open daily. Admission charge. On the Pittsburgh North Shore, near *Three River Stadium* (phone: 237-3300).

Pittsburgh Aviary/Conservatory – Close to 260 species of birds chatter away in walk-through and enclosed exhibitions. A good place to escape from 20th-century urban America with the advantage that you can slip back into it once you've recharged your battery. Open daily. Admission charge. Ridge Ave. and Arch St., Allegheny Commons (phone: 323-7235).

Restoration Districts – In an effort to rescue its Victorian past, the city has succeeded in restoring the façades of many beautiful, historic buildings, as well as the old-time appearance of many streets. The renovation of Pali Alto, Resaca, Monterey, Taylor, Jacksonia, and Buena Vista Streets reflects the Civil War era. Several blocks away, across Brighton Road, are the restored homes along Beech Avenue. Former residents include Gertrude Stein and mystery writer Mary Roberts Reinhart. Calvary Methodist Church, at Beech and Allegheny, has a fine collection of original Louis Tiffany stained glass. The nearby Henry Hobson Richardson Church is an excellent example of the "brick oven" style.

EAST SIDE

Cathedral of Learning – Part of the University of Pittsburgh, this imposing 42-story Gothic tower is the only skyscraper of classrooms in the country. A special attraction is the 19 Nationality Rooms on the first floor, devoted to each of the city's major ethnic groups. Open daily. No admission charge. Bigelow Blvd. and 5th Ave. (phone: 624-6000).

The Carnegie – Cultural complex comprising the main branch of the Carnegie Libraries, a music hall, a museum of art with a magnificent collection of French Impressionist works, and the *Carnegie Museum of Natural History,* featuring 10,000 objects on display from all fields of natural history and anthropology. Closed Sunday mornings and Mondays. Donation suggested. 4400 Forbes Ave. (phone: 622-3172).

Phipps Conservatory – Rare tropical and domestic fragrant blossoms flourish in the greenhouses and gardens of this 2½-acre publicly owned conservatory. Annual flower shows are in spring, fall and during *Christmas.* The 13 greenhouses are only a fraction of the greenery of surrounding Schenley Park, which covers 422 acres. Schenley has a lake, tennis courts, baseball fields, a golf course, an ice skating rink, picnic areas, and nature trails. Conservatory (admission charge) and park open daily. Schenley Park (phone: 255-2375).

Historical Society of Western Pennsylvania – Curious bottles of antique glass, hand-carved furniture, and other memorabilia line the halls, walls, and shelves. You can peruse old documents on Pennsylvania history in the library. Closed Sundays and Mondays. No admission charge. 4338 Bigelow Blvd. (phone: 681-5533).

Pittsburgh Zoo – Not only does this zoo have more than 2,000 animals spread over 75 acres but there's an indoor Aquazoo as well, with tanks full of domestic trout and pike, and esoteric species like penguins and piranhas. Nocturnal animals are on display in the Twilight Zoo (a children's zoo that operates from May to October). Open daily. Admission charge. Highland Park (phone: 441-6262).

Frick Art Museum – A magnificent Renaissance-style building houses Old Masters from the Renaissance through the 18th century. Marie Antoinette's furniture is on display in an ornate living room. The eclectic collection comprises Russian silver, Flemish tapestries, and Chinese porcelains. Closed Mondays and Tuesdays. No admission charge. 7227 Reynolds St. and S. Homewood Ave., Point Breeze (phone: 371-0600).

Clayton – Near the Frick stands the restored home of its namesake, steel tycoon Henry Clay Frick, a onetime partner of Andrew Carnegie. Tours by reservation only. Closed Mondays. Admission charge. 72 Penn Ave. (phone: 371-0606).

■ **EXTRA SPECIAL:** For a change of scene, try the Laurel Highlands, just a 90-minute drive from the city. Take the Pennsylvania Turnpike to the Donhal exit. Follow Route 711 to Ligonier, where you'll find the *Compass Inn* (phone: 238-4983), an old coaching inn used by travelers in the 18th century. Lively tours are given Sundays from noon to 4:30 PM from the end of May to the end of October, with special candlelight tours in November and December; admission charge. Also nearby is Ft. Ligonier, a restored fort from the French and Indian War. Open daily from 9 AM to 5 PM from April 15 to November 15; admission charge (phone: 238-9701). The *Mountain Playhouse,* one of the oldest summer theaters in the country, is a half-mile north of Jennerstown on Route 985 off Route 30. Hungry theatergoers can dine next door at the excellent *Green Gables* restaurant. For reservations and information, call 814-629-9201.

SOURCES AND RESOURCES

 TOURIST INFORMATION: For information on places of interest and events contact the visitor information center in Gateway Center, the Golden Triangle. The information center is run by the Greater Pittsburgh Convention and Visitors Bureau (4 Gateway Center, Pittsburgh, PA 15222; phone: 281-7711), which offers a variety of city guides. For recorded information on daily events, call 800-255-0855 in Pennsylvania; 800-821-1888 elsewhere. Contact the Pennsylvania state hotline (phone: 800-VISIT-PA) for maps, calendars of events, health updates, and travel advisories.

Local Coverage – *Post-Gazette,* morning daily; *Press,* evening daily; *Business Times-Journal,* weekly; *Pittsburgh* magazine, monthly.

Television Stations – KDKA Channel 2–CBS; WTAE Channel 4–ABC; WPXI Channel 11–NBC; WQED Channel 13–PBS; WPGH Channel 53–FOX.

Radio Stations – AM: KDKA 1020 (contemporary/oldies); WTAE 1250 (talk); WKQV 1410 (news/talk). FM: WDUQ 90.5 (jazz); WBZZ 94.6 (top 40); WQED 89.3 (classical); WYDD 104.7 (top 40/jazz weekends).

Food – See the restaurant sections of *Pittsburgh* magazine.

 TELEPHONE: The area code for Pittsburgh is 412.
   Sales Tax – There is a 6% sales tax on everything except clothing.

CLIMATE: Pittsburgh has a moderate climate with frequent precipitation year-round. Summer temperatures climb into the 80s; winters drop into the 20s. About 200 days of the year are cloudy, and winters are wet.

 GETTING AROUND: Airport – Greater Pittsburgh International Airport is a 40-minute ride from downtown; taxi fare should cost about $25. *Airlines Transportation Co.* (phone: 471-2250) provides bus service every 20 or 30 minutes from the airport to the

Westin William Penn, Pittsburgh Hilton & Towers, and *Vista International* hotels for $8.

Bus – *Port Authority Transit (PAT)* provides efficient bus service (phone: 231-5707, for information).

Car Rental – All major national firms are represented.

LRT (Light Rapid Transit) Subway – *PAT* underground service has expanded to South Hills; it operates from downtown to South Hills, through Station Square, across the Monongahela River, from 5 AM (6:30 AM on Sundays), to 1 AM daily. Ultramodern trains run frequently during the day and every 15 to 30 minutes at night. They are free in the downtown Golden Triangle until 7 PM; all other route fares range from $1.25 to $1.50.

Taxis – *People's Cab* (phone: 681-3131; for 24-hour service, 441-5334) or *Yellow Cab of Pittsburgh* (phone: 665-8100).

Van Service – *Peoples Cab* (phone: 441-5334).

 VITAL SERVICES: Audiovisual Equipment – *Chujko Brothers Audio Visual Connection* (phone: 373-1011; airport location, 331-3308); *KVL Audio Visual, Inc. (Vista International Hotel;* phone: 281-3700).

Baby-sitting – All hotels have baby-sitting services. There are no independent child care services, however.

Business Services – *Allegheny Personnel Services,* Arrott Bldg. (phone: 391-2044).

Dry Cleaner/Tailor – *Galard's,* pickup and delivery, 119 Forbes Ave. (phone: 471-7686).

Limousine – *Allegheny Limousines* (phone: 731-8671); *Royal Limousine* (phone: 884-8306); the *Limo Center* (phone: 787-3421 or 800-523-5466 outside Pennsylvania).

Mechanic – *Goodyear Auto Center* (phone: 281-9318).

Medical Emergency – *Allegheny General Hospital* (320 E. North Ave.; phone: 359-3252); *Mercy Hospital* (1400 Locust; phone: 232-8111).

Messenger Services – *Fleet Feet Messenger Service* (phone: 261-2675); *Mercury Messenger Service* (phone: 391-2016).

National/International Courier – *Federal Express* (phone: 765-8900); *DHL Worldwide Courier Express* (phone: 262-2764).

Pharmacy – *Brooks Pharmacy,* 226 Sixth Ave. (phone: 281-1340).

Photocopies – *Matthews Printing,* 407 Wood St. (phone: 391-3393).

Post Office – Grant and 7th Sts. (phone: 644-4500).

Professional Photographer – *Associated Photographers* (phone: 321-4666).

Secretary/Stenographer – *Executive Office Services* (phone: 261-0900); *Add Stuff Business Centers* (phone: 566-2020).

Teleconference Facilities – *Pittsburgh Green Tree Marriott* (available with advance notice); *Pittsburgh Hilton* (see *Best in Town* for both, below).

Translator – The *Language Center, Inc.* (phone: 261-1101); *Berlitz* (phone: 471-6707).

Typewriter Rental – *Leslie Dresbol Typewriter Store* (phone: 781-1308); *Three Rivers Business Machines* (phone: 824-9940).

Western Union/Telex – Many offices are located around the city (phone: 288-0415).

Other – *Stetson Convention Service,* rentals include booths, furniture, and equipment (phone: 366-3103); *David L. Lawrence Convention Center* (phone: 565-6000).

SPECIAL EVENTS: The *Pittsburgh Folk Festival,* an ethnic fair and entertainment spectacular, takes place the weekend before *Memorial Day* weekend at the *David L. Lawrence Convention Center.* The *Three Rivers Arts Festival,* displaying the work of over 600 artists, spans 17 days in June. Performing arts and a film festival are a small part of the Carnegie-sponsored festivities. The *Shadyside Art Festival* takes place in Shadyside in early August. The festive *Three Rivers Regatta,* the first weekend in August, features the *Grand Prix of Formula I Boat Racing, Steamboat Races for the Mayors Cup,* the *Race of the River Belles,* and the not-to-be-missed *Anything That Floats* race. A hot-air balloon race, live music, and aerobatic and water-ski shows enliven the event. Schenley Park becomes a racetrack of yesteryear during the *Pittsburgh Vintage Grand Prix* the third weekend in August. And from the end of May through mid-August, the *Three Rivers Shakespeare Festival* stages three productions at the Stephen Foster Memorial. Point State Park is the site of celebrations over *July 4th* and *Labor Day* weekends.

 MUSEUMS: The *Buhl Science Center,* the *Carnegie,* the *Children's Museum, Ft. Pitt Museum, Frick Art Museum,* and *Historical Society of Western Pennsylvania* are described in *Special Places.* Other museums worth noting include the following:

Old Economy Museum and Village – 14th and Church Sts., Ambridge (phone: 266-4500).

Pittsburgh Center for the Arts – 5th and Shady Aves. (phone: 361-0873).

 MAJOR COLLEGES AND UNIVERSITIES: University of Pittsburgh (Forbes Ave., Oakland; phone: 624-4141); Chatham College (5th Ave. and Woodland Rd.; phone: 365-1100); Duquesne University (Blvd. of the Allies; phone: 434-6000); Carnegie-Mellon University (Schenley Park; phone: 578-2000).

 SPORTS AND FITNESS: Baseball – The Pittsburgh *Pirates* play at *Three Rivers Stadium,* Stadium Circle, North Side (phone: 323-5000).

Bicycling – There are no bike rental shops in town, but the county parks (like North and South parks) have rental facilities.

Canoeing, Kayaking – You can canoe and kayak through exciting whitewater rapids in the Laurel Highlands. *Canoe, Kayak and Sailing Craft* offers lessons and guided tours, 712 Rebecca Ave., Wilkinsburg (phone: 371-4802).

Fishing – The City Parks and Recreation Department runs a group fishing program at Panther Hollow in summer. You can rent rods and reels (phone: 255-2355).

Fitness Center – The *YMCA* has a pool, racquetball courts, track, and exercise classes, 304 Wood St. (phone: 227-3800).

Football – The *Steelers'* home grid is at *Three Rivers Stadium* (phone: 323-1200).

Golf – Three golf courses within the city limits offer good facilities. *Schenley Park* golf course, in Oakland, has 18 holes (phone: 521-9756), as does *North Park* golf course (off Rte. 19; phone: 935-1967). The *South Park* golf course (off Rte. 88; phone: 835-3545) has 27 holes.

Hiking – There are quite a few hiking programs. For information on Parks Dept. nature tours and programs for the handicapped, contact Schenley Nature Center (Schenley Park; phone: 681-2272). For information on hiking, backpacking, canoeing, and camping in the area, contact the *Sierra Club* (phone: 561-0203).

Hockey – The 1991 *Stanley Cup* champion *Penguins* play at *Civic Arena,* Washington Pl., Center and Bedford Ave. (phone: 642-1985).

Horse Racing – Fans have a choice of the *Meadows* (Washington, PA; phone: 563-1224) or *Waterford Park* (Chester, WV; phone: 304-387-2400).

Horseback Riding – Hit the trail in South Park. You can rent a horse or sign on for a hayride at *Valleybrook Stables* (phone: 835-9687). If you bring your own horse, you can board it at *Morning Star Stables* (phone: 655-9793).

Ice Skating – Gliding's good from October to March at an outdoor rink in Schenley Park (phone: 422-6547) or indoors year-round at *Great Southern Roller-Ice Arena* (341 Washington Rd., Bridgeville; phone: 221-7111).

Jogging – Point State Park, where the Allegheny and Monongahela meet; Schenley Park; and North Park (get there by car).

Scuba Diving – In Pittsburgh? Check it out. *Sub-Aquatics* gives a 36-hour course in essentials with tips on local lakes and water-filled quarries, 1593 Banksville Rd. (phone: 531-5577).

Swimming – There are swimming pools throughout the city. Ream Playground has a good one, Merrimac and Virginia (phone: 431-9285).

Tennis – The best municipal courts are at Mellon Park. There are excellent suburban courts at North and South parks.

THEATER: Pittsburgh's theatrical scene is pretty lively, especially in summer when *Park Players* and *Pittsburgh Puppet Theater* take to the parks. For information, call 255-2354. The *Pittsburgh Public Theater* (1 Allegheny Sq.; phone: 321-9800) and *Heinz Hall* (600 Penn Ave.; phone: 392-4800) are the city's most prestigious theaters. *Pittsburgh Professional Theater Company* (222 Craft Ave.; phone: 621-4445) produces plays for both children and adults. The *Benedum Center for the Performing Arts* (207 7th St.; phone: 456-2600) presents Broadway shows, drama, rock concerts, and films in its restored auditorium. The *Three Rivers Shakespeare Festival* (phone: 624-7529) livens the summer. *Syria Mosque* (4423 Bigelow Blvd.; phone: 621-3333) features popular artists and stage productions in an ornate theater. The *Pittsburgh Ballet Theatre* (2900 Liberty Ave.; phone: 281-0360) features classical and modern ballets. Other companies include the *Dance Alley* (phone: 621-6670) and the *Dance Council* (phone: 355-0330).

Carnegie-Mellon Theater Co. performs at *Kresge Theater* (Carnegie-Mellon University, Schenley Park; phone: 578-2407). *Chatham College Theater* presents modern classics (phone: 365-1100). There are dinner-theaters at *Apple Hill Playhouse, Lamplighter Restaurant,* Delmont (phone: 468-4545), and *Little Lake Dinner Theater* (Rte. 19S, Donaldson's Crossroads; phone: 745-6300, 745-9883). Half-price tickets for many performances are available on the day of performance at the *TIX Booth* (USX Plaza, downtown; phone: 642-2787).

MUSIC: The world-famous *Pittsburgh Symphony Orchestra* performs from September through May at *Heinz Hall* (600 Penn Ave.; phone: 392-4800). In summer, the air fills with music. The *American Wind Symphony* performs at Point State Park (phone: 681-8866). Jazz can be heard at the *Aviary,* string ensembles at the *Conservatory,* and folk music on *Flagstaff Hill.* The Parks Department coordinates schedules (phone: 255-2390). For jazz events, dial MUS-LINE. In the *Benedum Center for the Performing Arts,* the *Pittsburgh Opera,* in its 52nd year, performs the classics and the not-so-classic in lavish productions.

For fans of pop and rock, the city is a regular stop on the road-show circuit. The *Syria Mosque* and the *Civic Arena* are venues for popular performing artists. The new *Star Lake Amphitheater* is an outdoor performance area about 45 minutes from downtown where rock groups appear regularly during the summer (phone: 947-4700). Folk music enthusiasts can visit the *Calliope House* (phone: 687-7713) or attend the *Smoky City Folk Festival* in June.

NIGHTCLUBS AND NIGHTLIFE: *Chauncy's at Station Square* for the past 6 years has been voted the best dining and dancing spot in the city by *Pittsburgh* magazine. It's very dressy, and the crowd, food, and entertainment are tops. The DJ plays classics from the 1950s and 1960s nightly (phone: 232-0601). *Hyeholde Restaurant and Cabaret* is an elegant nightspot set on an estate in Coraopolis, 3 minutes from the airport. Features live cabaret; no reservations, cover, or minimum. Closed Mondays (phone: 264-3116). Jazz has its heyday at *The Balcony* (phone: 687-0110), *Cardillo's* (phone: 381-3777), *Oakland Holiday Inn* (phone: 682-6200), *James Street Tavern* (phone: 323-2222), and *Blue Note Café* (phone: 431-7080). The center for pop and rock music is *Grafitti* (phone: 682-4210) while the *Decade* (phone: 682-1211) and the *Artery* (phone: 361-9473) are local band hangouts.

BEST IN TOWN

CHECKING IN: With the city's second renaissance has come an influx of much-needed hotel space, mostly in the nearby suburbs of Greentree, Coraopolis, and Monroeville. All hotels listed below are downtown. For those listed in the expensive category, expect to pay $80 or more for a double; hotels in the moderate range cost from $40 to $50. All telephone numbers are in the 412 area code unless otherwise indicated.

Hyatt Pittsburgh – Conveniently near the *Civic Arena* and Exhibit Hall, all the 400 rooms here have been redecorated. The improvement is very apparent, and the top two Regency floors offer excellent accommodations. *Hugo's Rotisserie* serves a moderately priced lunch and buffet dinner, with roast duckling the specialty of the house. You can get an inexpensive meal at *QQ's Café.* Both open daily. There's also a concierge center, 14 meeting rooms, A/V equipment, computers in every room, CNN, and limited secretarial services. Express checkout. Chatham Center (phone: 471-1234, 800-233-1234, or 800-228-9000; Fax: 412-355-0315). Expensive.

Pittsburgh Hilton & Towers – Standing at the edge of Point State Park, overlooking the Monongahela and Allegheny rivers, it has undergone dramatic renovations recently. The lobby has been redesigned and computerized, and concierge service and parlor suites with wet bars have been added. Some of the 700 rooms, all totally refurbished, overlook the park. There is business seating for 2,800 in the ballroom, and the executive center has 5 conference rooms, with secretarial services, A/V equipment, computers, CNN, and express checkout. Gateway Center (phone: 391-4600 or 800-HILTONS; Fax: 412-391-0927). Expensive.

Ramada – Downtown's only all-suite property, formerly the *Bigelow,* has 200 studios and 1-, 2-, and 3-bedroom units. The quiet *Ruddy Duck* restaurant serves complimentary breakfast on weekdays. Fitness center next door. There are 21 meeting rooms, A/V equipment, and limited secretarial services. Concierge floor, CNN, and express checkout. Bigelow Square Plaza (phone: 281-5800 or 800-225-5858; Fax: 412-261-2932). Expensive.

Sheraton at Station Square – A 300-room riverside property with cocktail lounges and 2 restaurants: *River's Edge,* with a good seafood buffet on Fridays; and *Mr. C's,* which serves a sumptuous Sunday brunch. Near Station Square's shops and restaurants. CNN. Smithfield and Carson Sts. (phone: 261-2000 or 800-325-3535). Expensive.

Vista International – Pittsburgh's newest and most comfortable hotel has a contemporary design, with a 4-story atrium lobby, 614 rooms, and a fitness center. Guests can dine informally at the *Orchard Café* or more sumptuously at the *American Harvest* restaurant. Indoor parking, 24-hour room service, 20 meeting rooms, secretarial services, CNN, and an executive floor lounge are just some of the amenities. At

Liberty Center on Grant St. (phone: 281-3700 or 800-367-8478; Fax: 412-281-2652; Telex: 846642). Expensive.

Westin William Penn – A $30-million renovation a few years ago by Westin management has reinstated this property's status. Because the building was declared a National Historic Landmark, the exterior remains unchanged; the most striking alterations are found in the 595 enlarged and modernized rooms and the stunning lobby. There are 2 restaurants — one a coffee shop serving food all day, one for dinner only. Other conveniences include an on-site day-care center, concierge, 24-hour room service, a fitness center, express checkout, CNN, and 35 meeting rooms. Mellon Sq. (phone: 281-7100 or 800-228-3000; Fax: 412-281-34981 Telex: 866380). Expensive.

Pittsburgh Green Tree Marriott – Facilities that liven up this 467-room hostelry include a swimming pool, a putting green, a whirlpool bath, sauna, and exercise room. Guests can enjoy entertainment in 2 lounges, *Cahoots* and *Chats,* or dine at the *Prime House.* Additional amenities include meeting rooms with a capacity of 1,000, and business services such as secretarial assistance, computers, and photocopiers. CNN is available, and there's a concierge desk. Express checkout. 101 Marriott Dr., Crafton (phone: 922-8400 or 800-228-9290; Fax: 412-922-8981). Expensive to moderate.

Priory – Built in the 1880s as a residence for priests, this property has been lovingly restored and converted into an elegant Victorian inn. There are 24 rooms, long hallways, 12-foot ceilings, and a cozy courtyard. Shuttle service to downtown. There's also a restaurant on the premises. 614 Pressley Ave. (phone: 231-3338). Moderate.

EATING OUT: The city offers a wide choice of restaurants, with a variety of ethnic eateries all over town. These are, for the most part, highly rated, for they offer a quality of food and diversity of dishes far greater than those found at anonymous "continental" restaurants. Many places are dressier in the evening. Expect to pay $65 or more for two at a restaurant we've noted as expensive; between $35 and $50, moderate. Prices don't include drinks, wine, or tips. All telephone numbers are in the 412 area code unless otherwise indicated.

Christopher's – An unusual place with a fantastic view. Ride the exterior glass elevator up to dine luxuriously on steak Diane, chateaubriand, seafood, and specialties cooked tableside. Very dressy, with live entertainment on Friday and Saturday evenings. Closed Sundays. Reservations necessary. Major credit cards accepted. 1411 Grandview Ave., Mt. Washington (phone: 381-4500). Expensive.

La Forêt – This elegant place serves a blend of classical French and light California cuisines. Features changing menus monthly and an extensive wine list. A bit away from downtown but worth the trip. Dinners only; closed Mondays. Reservations advised. Major credit cards accepted. 5701 Bryant St., Highland Park (phone: 665-9000). Expensive.

Hyeholde – Just a few minutes from the Pittsburgh airport is a medieval castle, or at least what looks like one, with wooden beams, slate floors, European tapestries, and spacious grounds. The dinner menu changes daily but usually consists of classic dishes — filet mignon, trout, breast of fowl — prepared with the freshest ingredients. Bread and desserts are homemade, and don't pass up its acclaimed trifle. The wine list is the most extensive in the area. Closed Sundays. Reservations advised. Major credit cards accepted. 190 Hyeholde Dr., Coraopolis (phone: 264-3116). Expensive.

Ruth's Chris Steak House – Beef in all its American glory is the specialty at this popular dining place. Individual steaks are cut to order. Open daily. Reservations advised. Major credit cards accepted. 6 PPG Place (phone: 391-4800). Expensive.

Common Plea – One of the best downtown eateries, popular with city officials and lawyers and known for its house appetizers. The atmosphere is relaxed; the array of fresh seafood, splendid. Lunch weekdays; dinner daily. Reservations advised for lunch. Major credit cards accepted. 308 Ross St. (phone: 281-5140). Expensive to moderate.

Grand Concourse – This elegant remake of the old Pittsburgh and Lake Erie Railroad Terminal is where beautiful wood, stained glass, and gleaming brass surround diners who devour excellent seafood — oysters, shrimp, clams, crab — and especially a tangy seafood chowder that is served in a pewter tureen. Lunch and dinner daily. Reservations advised for dinner only. Major credit cards accepted. 1 Station Sq. (phone: 261-1717). Expensive to moderate.

Le Mont – Classic and contemporary, with French and Italian specialties and a spectacular view of the Golden Triangle. House specialties include prime ribs and veal. Dinner only; jackets required. Closed Sundays. Reservations advised. Major credit cards accepted. 1114 Grandview Ave., Mt. Washington (phone: 431-3100). Expensive to moderate.

Le Pommier – Classic French-country cooking is beautifully presented in this understated, classy spot on the South Side. There are also freshly made breads, baked on the premises. Open daily. Reservations necessary. Major credit cards accepted. 2104 E. Carson St. (phone: 431-1901). Expensive to moderate.

Juno Trattoria – A casual place specializing in regional Italian cooking and homemade pasta. Rated one of Pittsburgh's best new restaurants by *Pittsburgh* magazine. A wide variety of breads and pastries baked daily. Open for lunch and dinner and to midnight on weekends. Closed Sundays. Reservations advised on weekend nights and for parties of 5 or more. Major credit cards accepted. One Oxford Centre, downtown (phone: 392-0225). Moderate.

Mandarin Gourmet – Among the best of the Oriental restaurants that dot the town, the menu here is expansive and the service is polite. Open daily. Reservations necessary for groups of four or more. Major credit cards accepted. 305 Wood St. (phone: 261-6151). Moderate.

PORTLAND, OR

AT-A-GLANCE

SEEING THE CITY: Portland offers several exceptional vantage points from which to see the city, the valley in which it lies, and the mountains beyond. Pittock Acres Park, the grounds of the former Pittock Mansion (see below), sits 1,000 feet above the city (3229 NW Pittock Dr.). At your feet are the port, business section, the Willamette River, and the southeast residential areas. In the distance are the Cascade Mountains — Mt. Hood in Oregon, Mt. Rainier, Mt. Adams, and Mt. St. Helens in Washington. And visit Washington Park (400 SW Kingston.); the best view is from the International Rose Test Gardens, looking east toward mountains in the background.

SPECIAL PLACES: Portland was made for walking. Her founders frequently built homes in the west hills and walked to work along the waterfront. Especially on the west side, major points of interest are within walking distance of one another. Brochures describing self-guided walking tours are available from the Portland Visitors Association, 26 SW Salmon St.

WEST SIDE

Portland Center for the Performing Arts – The brightest dazzler on the city's roster of flourishing arts institutions is the 2,776-seat *Arlene Schnitzer Concert Hall* in the former *Portland Theater.* The ornate detail of the 1928 vaudeville–movie palace has been lovingly refurbished. Home of the *Oregon Symphony Orchestra,* the hall also holds pop, country, and jazz concerts; shows films, and hosts conventions. Next door are two plush smaller theaters. The *Oregon Shakespearean Festival* performs here, as do other local theater and dance groups. SW Broadway at Main (phone: 248-4335, for tours; 248-4496, for tickets).

Oregon Historical Society Museum – The museum has recently doubled its size; its exhibitions concentrate on Oregon history, before and after the arrival of the white man. Also a fine series of dioramas on Indian life, plus a research library with open stacks for browsing; pioneer craft demonstrations for children. Changing exhibitions vary from the Magna Carta to country quilts. Closed Sundays. No admission charge. 1230 SW Park (phone: 222-1741).

Ira Keller Fountain (and Civic Auditorium) – A series of pools and waterfalls a block wide, facing the *Civic Auditorium.* In hot weather, people splash around in its tons of swirling water. Designed by Lawrence Halprin, it is called *Ira's Fountain.* SW 3rd Ave at Clay. Though several blocks removed from its three sisters, *Civic Auditorium* is considered the fourth theater of the *Portland Center for the Performing Arts* (phone: 248-4496 for tickets).

Pioneer Courthouse – The first federal building in the Pacific Northwest, completed in 1875 and now restored to its original Victorian splendor. The interior includes a working post office, an elegant Victorian courtroom (where the US Court of Appeals meets), and adjoining rooms for the judges. The courtroom can be seen by asking the security guard to unlock the door. Enter at 555 SW Yamhill (no phone). Pioneer

Courthouse Square, an open city block across the street from the Pioneer Courthouse, has become the hub of downtown. This is a place for music, flowers, food, and fanfare.

Weather Machine – Check out the forecast every day at noon, when this whimsical mechanical sculpture predicts the weather for the following 24 hours with a trumpet fanfare and a spray of water. Up pops one of three metal sculptures: a gold leaf sun for fair skies; a blue heron for clouds and drizzle; a fire-breathing copper dragon for stormy weather. A series of lights indicates the temperature and air quality. Pioneer Courthouse Square.

Portlandia – The cookie-tin Portland Building (designed by the postmodern architect Michael Graves) is now crowned in glory. Over the main portico kneels a copper lady of heroic proportions. The new symbol of the city, the sculpture is by Raymond Kaskey. 1120 SW 5th Ave.

Old Town – When the Pioneer Courthouse was brand new, some folks thought it much too far from the downtown business section — a whole 6 blocks. Now "downtown" is called Old Town, a restored shopping and browsing area. Shops, largely in the *New Market Theater* and Skidmore Fountain Building, are filled with crafts, art, and antiques. Other shops are in the area from 1st to 5th Avenues, on both sides of Burnside. Artists from all over the state sell their work at the Saturday and Sunday markets, outdoors under Burnside Bridge, from 10 AM to 5 PM Saturdays, 11 AM to 4:30 PM Sundays; March through December 24.

Worth noting on Ankeny, south of Burnside: *Dan and Louis Oyster Bar* (see *Eating Out*), and *Le Panier* (on SW 2nd), whose Parisian chefs serve fresh French bread and croissants every day. North of Burnside, Couch Street, and beyond are numerous specialty shops. Best buys are Indian artifacts, toys, spinning and weaving supplies, original jewelry.

Washington Park – One of the city's oldest parks, it has 145 acres, all part of the 40-mile park system that thrives within the city limits. There are six points of special interest on the grounds: the Rose Test Gardens, the Japanese Garden, the Washington Park Zoo, the World Forestry Center, the Vietnam War Memorial, and Tera One, a totally solar home, as well as some magnificent views of the city and countryside. Plan to spend some extended periods of time here. The grounds are perfect for a picnic (*Elephant's Delicatessen* will prepare one for you; 13 NW 23rd Pl., phone: 224-3955), or you can eat at the cafes at *OMSI* or the zoo (see below).

The Washington Park Zoo comprises a special African exhibit; the new rain forest exhibit that opened in June 1991 simulates an African rain forest and houses animals indigenous to the forest; plus a special preservation and conservation of endangered species section for Asian elephants, the snow leopard, and penguins. A must see is the award-winning Cascade Exhibit, which displays the wonders of Oregon's Cascade Mountain Range and the animals that live within it. The World Forestry Center has displays and exhibitions on Oregon's largest industry. Admission charge. The entire complex is on SW Canyon (phone: 226-1561; Forestry Center, 228-1367).

The Rose Test Gardens offer hundreds of varieties of roses, all generously identified. June through September is the best time to see them. In summer, a zoo train runs from the gardens to the zoo (admission charge), which (among other displays) has a children's petting zoo. At the Penguinarium you can see Humboldt penguins at close range. Open daily.

Pittock Mansion – The imposing French Renaissance home built by Henry Pittock, a poor boy who made good as publisher of the *Oregonian* at the turn of the century. The grounds are open daily and are free; the house is open every afternoon from 1 to 5 PM, for a fee. The *Gate Lodge* serves lunch and tea on weekdays. 3229 NW Pittock Dr. (mansion, phone: 823-3624; lodge, 221-1730).

Tryon Creek State Park – The state's first metropolitan park, 2 miles

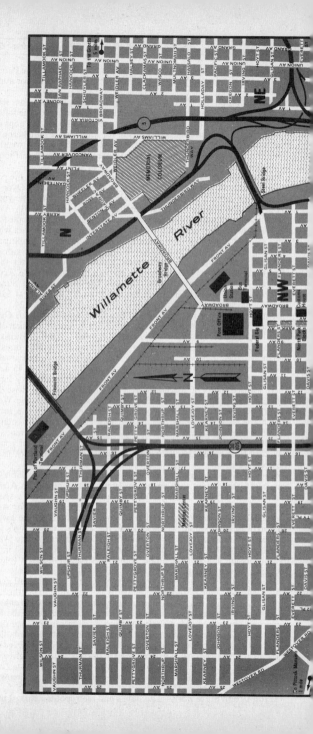

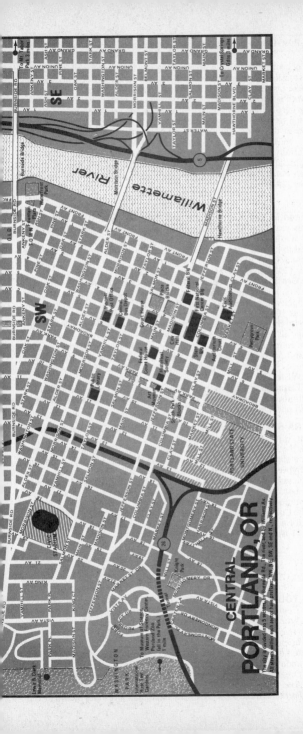

CENTRAL PORTLAND, OR

The city is divided into 5 sectors, by Burnside Rd., the river, and by Williams Av. All streets within each sector have prefixes: NW, NE, SW, SE and N. respectively.

Willamette River

SE

SW

OLD TOWN

WASHINGTON PARK

PORTLAND STATE UNIVERSITY

To Mt. Tabor Park 2 mi.

To Crystal Springs Gdns 3 miles

Burnside Bridge

Morrison Bridge

Hawthorne Bridge

Lewis & Clark Memorial

International Rose Test Garden

To Museum of Science, Western Forestry Center, Japanese Garden, Portland Zoo. All in the Park. 1 mile

Knight Park

Civic Stadium

Main Post Office

Central Bus Depot

Court House

Federal Bldg.

First National Center

Civic Hill

Civic Auditorium

State Office Bldg.

Art Museum

Historical Society

Public Library

South Park Blocks

Pettygrove Park

Mannford Park

south of central Portland, with 600 acres of wilderness for biking, hiking, and naturalists (horses are welcome, but there are none for rent). Adjoining Lake Oswego, at 11321 SW Terwilliger Blvd. (phone: 653-3166).

Powell's Books – Owner Mike Powell says visitors have been known to stop here before they go to their hotel! Among the reasons: more than a million new and used books, espresso, pastries, and readings by local authors at the *Anne Hughes Coffee Shop,* part of the store. One of the largest bookstores in the country, (it's a block long), *Powell's* has thoughtfully produced maps so that book lovers can find their way through the funky, cavernous store. Open 9 AM to 11 PM, Mondays through Saturdays; 9 AM to 9 PM on Sundays. 1005 W. Burnside St. (phone: 228-4651).

EAST SIDE

Oregon Museum of Science and Industry (OMSI) – Due to open late this year, this $31 million complex will be three times larger than its old Washington Park facility. An exhibition hall will present temporary exhibits, and there are hands-on exhibits for youngsters, a space wing, and large physics and chemistry labs. Open daily. Admission charge. 1701 SE Water St. (phone: 222-2828).

The Grotto – An outdoor chapel, built in a grotto with a 10-story cliff, monastery, and gardens at the top. The 64 acres of grounds are open for contemplation, quiet walks, solitude. Sunday mass is celebrated in the chapel at 10 AM. 8840 NE Skidmore (phone: 254-7371).

Crystal Springs Rhododendron Gardens – More than 2,000 rhododendron plants, maintained by the Portland chapter of the American Rhododendron Society. No Portlander would miss the gardens during April and May, when first the azaleas, then the rhododendrons, reach their peak. Adjacent is the campus of Reed College. SE 28th Ave. near SE Woodstock.

Mt. Tabor Park – Believed to be the only extinct volcano within a US city's limits. Some of the best views of the city are from here. Between Yamhill and Division, east of SE 60th Ave.

■ **EXTRA SPECIAL:** Sauvie Island, the largest island in the Columbia River, is just north of Portland on US 30. Devoted primarily to farmland, the island is ideal for biking, hiking, picnicking, fishing, or just lolling about for a day. Here, the Oregon Historical Society maintains the Bybee-Howell House, a restored pre–Civil War farmhouse, open to the public from June to *Labor Day* (free; donations appreciated). The last Saturday of September is the "Wintering-In" picnic and celebration at the house, when farmers sell harvest goods.

The Columbia River Highway runs east and west of Portland. Drive east for a view of the Columbia River Gorge, with its 2,000-foot cliff and 11 waterfalls.

SOURCES AND RESOURCES

TOURIST INFORMATION: The Portland Visitors Information Center at the Convention and Visitors Association is best for brochures, maps, general tourist information and personal help; if you arrive after hours, outdoor map dispensers and kiosks can provide a basic orientation. 26 SW Salmon (phone: 222-2223). Contact the Oregon state hotline (phone: 800-547-7842) for maps, calendars of events, health updates, and travel advisories.

The Oregon Welcome Center offers travel information at 12345 N. Union Ave. (phone: 285-1631).

The Portland Guidebook by Linda Lampman and Julie Sterling (The

Writing Works; $5.95) is the most comprehensive guide to Portland and its environs.

Local Coverage – *Oregonian,* morning and afternoon daily; *Willamette Week* offers a liberally opinionated study of the city.

Television Stations – KATU Channel 2–ABC; KOIN Channel 6–CBS; KGW Channel 8–NBC; KOAP Channel 10–PBS.

Radio Stations – AM: KGW 620 (talk radio); KXL 750 (news/talk); KUPL 1330 (country). FM: KGON 92.3 (rock); KINK 101.9 (adult contemporary); KMJK 106.7 (classic rock).

Food – Check *The Portland Guidebook* and the weekly newspaper restaurant reviews.

TELEPHONE: The area code for Portland is 503.
Sales Tax – At this writing, there is no sales tax in Oregon. But buyer beware — a sales tax measure is on the ballot in almost every election.

CLIMATE: The good news: It doesn't get too cold in Portland (snow is pretty rare); it doesn't get too hot here, either (summer temperatures above 90F only last 2 or 3 days). However, it certainly does rain. The months from October through May are the worst. June, July, August, and September are fairly clear, and the average temperature is in the 70s. That's the time when tourists visit the Portland area, so book ahead.

GETTING AROUND: Airport – Portland International Airport is a 20- to 30-minute drive from downtown, and cab fare should run $18 to $22. The *Raz Tranz Portland Airporter* bus (phone: 246-4676) provides transportation to downtown's major hotels for $5; $1 for children 6-12, children under 6, free. The trip takes about 45 minutes, 60 minutes during rush hour. Buses depart from in front of the airport every 20 minutes from 5:30 AM to midnight, every 30 minutes on weekends and holidays. *Tri-Met* city bus No. 12 also stops in front of the airport and connects to buses going downtown; the fare is 85¢ to $1.15.

Bus – Portland's *Tri-Met* system covers three counties; exact-change-only fare is zoned except within the 340-block downtown shopping area (including Old Town, major shopping malls, *Art Institute, Historical Center,* riverfront), which is free and called Fareless Square. Complete route and tourist information (and map of Fareless Square) is available from the downtown Customer Assistance Office, 1 Pioneer Courthouse Square (enter under the waterfall).

Car Rental – National and local firms are represented in abundance. Everything from rental Lincolns to *Rent-a-Wreck;* check the yellow pages. *General-Rent-A-Car* (7101 NE 82nd; phone: 257-3451) has one of the lowest weekly rates.

Light Rail – The bus system is complemented by *MAX,* the light rail network of streetcars serving downtown and the eastern suburbs. Schedules are available at light rail stops along the streets as well as at the Pioneer Courthouse Square transit office. Fares are the same as for buses, 85¢ and $1.15.

Taxi – Cabs must be called or picked up at taxi stations in front of the major hotels. They cannot be hailed in the street. Most hotels have direct phone connections to the two largest companies, *Broadway Cab* (phone: 227-1234); *Radio Cab* (phone: 227-1212).

VITAL SERVICES: Audiovisual Equipment – *Peter Corvallis Production and Audio-Visual Rentals & Services* (phone: 222-1664).

Baby-sitting – *Wee-Ba-Bee Child Care* (phone: 661-5966); *Rent-a-Mom of Oregon* (phone: 222-5779).

Business Services – *Business Service Bureau* (1208 SW 13th Ave.;

phone: 228-4107); *Association and Conference Services* (5100 SW Macadam, Ste. 250; phone: 222-3018).

Dry Cleaner/Tailor – *Bee Tailors & Cleaners* (939 SW 10th St.; phone: 227-1144); *Levines* (2086 W. Burnside; phone: 223-7221).

Limousine – *Oregon Limousine Service* (phone: 252-5882); *Classic Chauffeur* (phone: 238-8880).

Mechanics – *Tune Up Specialties* (8060 NE Glisan; phone: 252-8096); *Master Car Care Service by Firestone* (815 W. Burnside; phone: 228-9268).

Medical Emergency – *Good Samaritan Hospital* (1015 NW 22nd St.; phone: 229-7260); *Providence Medical Center* (4805 NE Glisan St.; phone: 230-6000).

Messenger Services – *American Messenger Service* (phone: 243-2275); *Pronto Select Messenger Co.* (phone: 239-7666).

National/International Courier – *Federal Express* (phone: 800-238-5355); *DHL Worldwide Courier Express* (phone: 800-225-5345).

Pharmacy – *Stadium Fred Meyer Pharmacy,* 9 AM to 10 PM Mondays through Saturdays,; 10 AM to 7 PM Sundays, 100 NW 20th Pl. and Burnside Rd. (phone: 226-7179).

Photocopies – *Kinko's,* open 24 hours (1525 SW Park Ave.; phone: 223-2056); *Pronto Print* (1101 NW Glisan St.; phone: 222-4771).

Post Office – The central office is located at 204 SW 5th Ave. (phone: 221-0202).

Professional Photographer – *Photo Art Commercial Studios, Inc.* (phone: 224-5665); *Conkling, Inc.* (phone: 281-1135).

Secretary/Stenographer – *Dorothy Bays Secretarial Service* (phone: 223-3201); *HQ, Headquarters Company* (phone: 221-0617).

Translator – *International Language Services* (phone: 292-2564).

Typewriter Rental – *Portland Typewriter Co.,* weekly and monthly rates (phone: 244-2000).

Western Union/Telex – Many offices are located around the city (phone: 800-325-6000).

Other – *Association & Conference Services* (phone: 222-3018); *CompuRent,* short- and long-term computer rentals; delivery available (phone: 241-7368).

 SPECIAL EVENTS: The *Portland Rose Festival,* featuring everything from beauty queens to bicycle races, runs during the first half of June. The *Mt. Hood Festival of Jazz* brings the best jazz musicians to town every August. *Wintering-In Celebration,* on Sauvie Island, is a harvest festival on the last Saturday of September.

 MUSEUMS: The *Oregon Historical Society Museum, Oregon Museum of Science and Industry,* and the *Pittock Mansion* are noted in *Special Places.* Other interesting museums include the following:

American Advertising Museum – One of the nation's best collections of persuasive media, from sandwich boards to videos. Through the evolution of advertising, much of our country's history and progress is revealed. Closed Mondays and Tuesdays. Admission charge. NW 2nd Ave. at Couch (phone: 226-0000).

Children's Museum for the City of Portland – The place to be on a rainy day. Kids amuse themselves with a children's grocery store, switchboard, cave, tunnel, and more. Closed Mondays. Admission charge. 3037 SW 2nd Ave. (phone: 248-4587 or 823-3171).

Oregon Art Institute – With an outstanding permanent collection of Northwest Indian art, the museum also features a representative group of Oregon's prolific contemporary artists and a wide variety of traveling shows. Also part of the *Institute* is the outdoor Sculpture Mall, the Pacific Northwest College of Art, and the Northwest Film and Video

Center. Closed Mondays. Admission charge. SW Park and Madison (phone: 226-2811).

Portland Carousel Museum – With more working carousels than any other US city, Portland also claims one of the only carousel museums. Inside, examine the intricately carved and painted horses; outside, ride the carousel away into magical nostalgic wonderlands. If he's there, ask the owner to tell you the story of how he acquired the carousels; it's a special treat. Open daily from 11 AM to 5 PM. Admission charge. NE Holladay St. between 7th and 9th Aves. (phone: 235-2252).

MAJOR COLLEGES AND UNIVERSITIES: The jewel in Portland's academic crown is Reed College (3203 SE Woodstock Blvd.; phone: 771-1112), a private, liberal arts college of the highest caliber. Other institutions of learning are the University of Portland (5000 N. Willamette Blvd.; phone: 283-7911); Lewis and Clark College (0615 SW Palatine Hill Rd.; phone: 768-7000); and Portland State University (724 SW Harrison; phone: 725-3000).

PARKS AND GARDENS: Even the freeways into Portland are divided by banks of wild roses and iris; the city is surrounded by green mountains and garlanded with 7,608 acres of parkland. Washington Park, Pittock Acres Park, Mt. Tabor Park, Crystal Springs Gardens, and Tryon Creek State Park are all described in *Special Places.* Other notable Portland parks include:

Council Crest Park – above Portland Heights, SW Fairmount Blvd.
Hoyt Arboretum – 400 SW Fairview Blvd.
Rocky Butte – I-84 east to NE 102nd.
Westmoreland Park – SE 22nd Ave. at Bybee.

SHOPPING: The absence of any sales tax makes Portland especially attractive to shoppers. The downtown shopping district is adjacent to Pioneer Courthouse Square. *Pioneer Place* (on SW Fourth Ave.; phone: 228-5800), with *Saks Fifth Avenue* among its 80 specialty stores in a glass-enclosed, 4-level pavilion, is the newest shopping development in the city. The *Galleria* (921 SW Morrison; phone: 228-2748), one of the city's first historic renovations, includes some 50 stores and restaurants within its 3 stories. East of downtown, the recently renovated *Lloyd Center* (phone: 282-2511) features more than 50 square blocks of shopping, near the *Oregon Convention Center.* Also, see "Old Town," under *Special Places.*

Healthy Pet Natural Nutrition Store – Organic catnip and futons for pets. 21 NW 23rd Place (phone: 222-5228).

Made in Oregon – Products made, caught, or grown in the state, including filberts, cranberry candy, Pendleton woolen goods, and Oregon wines. At several locations: Portland International Airport, 7000 Airport Way (phone: 282-7827); 9589 SW Washington Sq. Rd., Tigard (phone: 620-4670); *Galleria*, 921 SW Morrison (phone: 241-3630); *Clackamas Town Center*, 12000 SE 82nd Ave., #1117 (phone: 659-3155); 1028 *Lloyd Center* (phone: 282-7636); and Old Town, 10 NW First (phone: 273-8354).

Meier & Frank – The city's oldest department store. 621 SW 5th (phone: 223-0512).

Nordstrom – Department store known for fine-quality apparel. 701 SW Broadway (phone: 224-6666).

Norm Thompson – British shearling coats and other luxurious outdoorwear. 1805 NW Thurman (phone: 221-0764).

Powell's Travel Store – A large selection of books as well as all sorts of travel paraphernalia: money belts, journals, maps, and canteens. At Pioneer Courthouse Square, 701 SW 6th Ave. (phone: 228-1108).

The Real Mother Goose – A virtual woodland: wooden kaleidoscopes, carved wooden canes, furniture made from exotic woods plus handcrafted jewelry and garments that have been carefully woven, dyed, painted, and/or beaded by hand. 901 SW Yamhill (phone: 223-9510).

 SPORTS AND FITNESS: Baseball – The Portland *Beavers,* the top farm team for the Minnesota *Twins,* play at *Portland Civic Stadium,* April to September. Tickets are sold at the stadium, 1844 SW Morrison (phone: 248-4345 or 2-BEAVER).

Basketball – The NBA *Trail Blazers* play their home games at *Memorial Coliseum* from October through April (phone: 248-4496).

Bicycling – Rent from *Agape Cycle & Sports-Eastside* (2610 SE Clinton; phone: 230-0317). Numerous city and country rides are described in *The Portland Guidebook.*

Fishing – For chinook salmon, try the lower Willamette or Willamette Slough from March through early May. Steelhead are found in the Clackamas River, and its tributary, Eagle Creek, from December through February. But best of all (for fly fishermen) are the Washougal and Wind rivers in southwest Washington State, where you can do battle with the warrior steelhead.

Fitness Centers – The *YMCA* has a number of branches, including one in the Southeast (6036 SE Foster Rd.; phone: 294-3311); Northeast (1630 NE 38th St.; phone: 294-3377); and Metro Center (2831 SW Barbur Blvd.; phone: 294-3366).

Golf – The metropolitan area has 20 public courses. The best is *Forest Hills Country Club,* 20 minutes from downtown in Cornelius (a plus: it has showers; phone: 357-3347).

Horse and Dog Racing – For racing and pari-mutuel betting, *Portland Meadows Horse Race Track* (1001 N. Schmeer Rd.; phone: 285-9144), with a season from October to April; and *Multnomah Kennel Club Race Tracks* (220 3rd Ave., Fairview — 12 miles from city; phone: 667-7700), from May to September.

Jogging – Run up Broadway or 5th Avenue to Duniway Park, then follow the bike path along Terwilliger Boulevard; this route can range from 5 to 30 miles, as time or stamina permits. Upcoming running events are listed with the *Oregon Road Runners* (phone: 626-2348).

Skiing – The closest is *Mt. Hood Meadows;* better is *Mt. Bachelor,* 180 miles from Portland at Bend.

Tennis – The Park Bureau runs 7 indoor and dozens of outdoor courts. The indoor courts may be reserved by calling 233-5959 or 248-4200. Otherwise, first come, first served. The major tennis center is in Buckman Park, *Portland Tennis Center,* 324 NE 12th Ave. (phone: 233-5959).

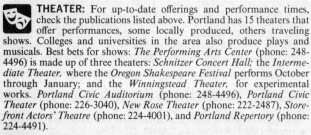 **THEATER:** For up-to-date offerings and performance times, check the publications listed above. Portland has 15 theaters that offer performances, some locally produced, others traveling shows. Colleges and universities in the area also produce plays and musicals. Best bets for shows: *The Performing Arts Center* (phone: 248-4496) is made up of three theaters: *Schnitzer Concert Hall;* the *Intermediate Theater,* where the *Oregon Shakespeare Festival* performs October through January; and the *Winningstead Theater,* for experimental works. *Portland Civic Auditorium* (phone: 248-4496), *Portland Civic Theater* (phone: 226-3040), *New Rose Theater* (phone: 222-2487), *Storefront Actors' Theatre* (phone: 224-4001), and *Portland Repertory* (phone: 224-4491).

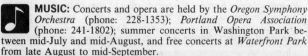 **MUSIC:** Concerts and opera are held by the *Oregon Symphony Orchestra* (phone: 228-1353); *Portland Opera Association* (phone: 241-1802); summer concerts in Washington Park between mid-July and mid-August, and free concerts at *Waterfront Park* from late August to mid-September.

NIGHTCLUBS AND NIGHTLIFE: Portland has become a genuinely great jazz town. Homegrown groups like the *Tom Grant Band* and the *Mel Brown Quintet* are gaining national attention. Current favorite clubs: *Brasserie Montmartre* (626 SW Park; phone: 224-5552), where the jazz is mellow weeknights and heats up on weekends; *Café Vivo* (555 SW Oak St.; phone: 228-8486), where Tom Grant can be found at the keyboard most weekends; and *Remo's Ristorante Italiano* (1425 NW Glisan; phone: 221-1150), an old firehouse now converted to a sophisticated supper club. Pop music, Dixieland, folk, and rock also are offered at Portland's many pubs, taverns, and nightclubs. Try *Starry Night* (8 NW 6th Ave.; phone: 227-0071), for danceable new wave; *Key Largo* (31 NW 1st Ave.; phone: 223-9919), for blues and rock; *Shanghai Lounge* (0309 SW Montgomery; phone: 220-1865), for rock music and for meeting everyone in town. The place to wear saddle shoes and string ties for rock 'n' roll of the 1950s and 1960s is *Bebop USA* (11753 SW Beaverton-Hillsdale Hwy.; phone: 644-4433). The *Goose Hollow Inn* (1927 SW Jefferson; phone: 228-7010) is a singularly Oregonian pub whose owner, the Mayor of Portland, frequently can be seen in the crowd of plaid shirts and raincoats.

BREW PUBS: Portland, with its many micro-breweries, boasts the most breweries of any US city. The largest is *Blitz Weinhard Brewing Co.* (1133 W. Burnside). Nearby are *Bridgeport Brewery Co.* (1313 NW Marshall St.), *Widmer Brewing Co.* (1405 NW Lovejoy St.), and the *Portland Brewing Co.* (1339 NW Flanders St.). In downtown Portland, there's the *B. Moloch/Heathman Bakery and Pub* (901 SW Salmon), and farther out of town are the *Hillsdale Brewery and Public House* (1505 SW Sunset Blvd.), and *Fulton Pub and Brewery* (0618 SW Nebraska St.). The McMenamin brothers have recently opened the *Mission Theatre & Pub* (1624 NW Glisan St.; phone: 223-4031) customers can view second-run films while they quaff a brew and munch on burgers.

■ **TAKE SOME PORTLAND HOME WITH YOU:** Fresh chinook and silver salmon are two of Portland's best-known exports, and airlines are accustomed to seeing passengers board an outbound flight with a cold fin under one arm. *Troy's Seafood Market* (816 NE Grand; phone: 231-1477) will supply fresh salmon and crab, specially packed to travel.

BEST IN TOWN

CHECKING IN: The choice of Portland hotels has become more interesting of late, and now it is possible to slumber in splendor as well as in comfort and convenience. Expect to pay $100 or more for a double room in one of the hotels we've categorized as expensive; $60 to $100 in the moderate range; and under $60 in the inexpensive category. For bed and breakfast accommodations, contact: *Northwest Bed & Breakfast* (610 SW Broadway, Suite 609, Portland, OR 97205; phone: 243-7616). All telephone numbers are in the 503 area code unless otherwise indicated.

Heathman – Adjoining the *Performing Arts Center* are 152 of the most luxurious rooms and suites in town. After a complete restoration and renovation (done by the same designer as San Francisco's *Stanford Court*), the hotel, listed in the National Register of Historic Places, has emerged as an authentic first class property. Rooms are decorated in floral chintz, and facilities include a complimentary video movie library for room use, a mezzanine bar, a library with signed editions from authors who have been guests, concierge, valet parking, free taxi passes to entertainment events, and access to a nearby health club. Its main restaurant is noted for its selections of fresh Pacific Northwest seafood and game. Additional amenities include around-the-clock room service, concierge and limited secretarial services, 8 meeting rooms, A/V equipment, photocopiers, and CNN. SW Broadway at Salmon (phone: 241-4100 or 800-551-0011; Fax: 503-790-7110). Expensive.

Portland Hilton – Sitting snugly between the major streets of the downtown shopping district, the recently renovated 455-room property sports a skylit atrium lobby with a bubbling pool, plants, and wood-sculpted trees, and a health club. *Alexander's* restaurant on the top floor offers good food with a glittery view. Amenities include room service, CNN, seasonal pool, and parking facilities. Business facilities include 29 meeting rooms, A/V equipment and photocopiers, and secretarial services. Other pluses are the concierge desk, 24-hour room service, and express checkout. 921 SW 6th (phone: 226-1611 or 800-HILTONS; Fax: 503-220-2565). Expensive.

Portland Marriott – More than a million dollars' worth of millwork went into this Northwest incarnation. It has 503 rooms, a concierge level, 2 lounges, 2 restaurants (one with a view of the Willamette River), banquet facilities, whirlpool bath, sauna, and exercise rooms. It also is the only downtown hotel with an indoor pool. There's a concierge desk, as well as 16 meeting rooms, A/V equipment, photocopiers, and CNN. Express checkout. 1401 SW Front Ave. (phone: 226-7600 or 800-228-9290; Fax: 503-221-1789). Expensive.

Riverplace Alexis – The city's newest inn is one of its smallest: only 74 rooms and suites clustered on the waterfront. (Ten condos are available for rent in the complex next door.) In the morning, guests awaken to views of the marina and to continental breakfast. Marble, brass, fresh flowers, and classic furnishings produce an easy elegance. Six suites have wood-burning fireplaces and wet bars. Concierge, 24-hour room service, access to adjacent health club. The *Esplanade* restaurant prepares Northwest regional dishes. Other conveniences are 5 meeting rooms, photocopiers, A/V equipment, limited secretarial services, CNN, and express checkout. 1510 SW Harbor Way (phone: 228-3233; Fax: 503-295-6161). Expensive.

Westin Benson – Built in 1913 by wealthy logger Simon Benson, this premier hotel has recently undergone a massive $17 million renovation to restore its original grandeur. The lobby maintains a feeling of Old World luxury, with its white Italian marble floor, walnut paneling, and tall transom windows. There are 290 rooms and suites, some of which include butler service. The *London Grill* restaurant (open daily) is quite good, as is the respectable *Trader Vic's* (closed Sundays). Concierge; access to health club; 24-hour room service. Valet parking. Thirteen meeting rooms are available for business functions, as well as photocopiers, secretarial services, and A/V equipment. CNN and express checkout. 109 SW Broadway (phone: 228-9611 or 800-228-3000; Fax: 503-226-4603). Expensive.

Red Lion Motor Inns – This giant complex on the Columbia River, just between Portland and Vancouver (Washington), is 10 minutes from the airport and comprises 3 inns: the *Red Lion Columbia River, Red Lion Jantzen Beach,* and *Red Lion Inn at the Quay* (on the Washington side) — with a total of 830 rooms. Fine restaurants, free parking, live entertainment, a large convention center, 2 grand ballrooms, and room service. Pool, tennis, and mini-golf at *Red Lion Jantzen Beach.* Other conveniences at the inns are concierge and limited secretarial services, 32 meeting rooms, A/V equipment and photocopiers, CNN, and express checkout. *Red Lion Columbia River,* 1401 N. Hayden Island Dr. (phone: 696-2565); *Red Lion Jantzen Beach,* 909 N. Hayden Island Dr. (phone: 283-4466); *Red Lion Inn at the Quay,* 100

Columbia St., Vancouver, WA 98660 (phone: 206-694-8341). Fax number for all is 503-283-4743. Expensive to moderate.

Mallory – A step down from the Jacuzzi tubs and poolside cabanas, but a comfortable, quiet 144-room hostelry that offers good accommodations and adequate restaurant facilities at a reasonable price. CNN. Just across the street from the *Civic Theater*. Free parking. 729 SW 15th Ave. (phone: 223-6311; Fax: 503-223-0522). Inexpensive.

EATING OUT: Portland shines pretty brightly as a dining place. The impact of a certain style of restaurant — small, personal, with creative cooking and inviting decor — has had dramatic effects on local eating habits. Residents are out of their own kitchens and around town as never before. Many new restaurants specialize in Pacific Northwest cooking, which puts to delicious use the abundant local seafood, farm fresh vegetables, and very good regional wines. Our restaurant selections range in price from $60 or more for a dinner for two in the expensive range, $30 to $55 in the moderate, and under $30 in the inexpensive range. Prices do not include drinks, wine or tips. All telephone numbers are in the 503 area code unless otherwise indicated.

Atwater's – Occupying the entire 30th floor of the US Bancorp Tower, one of the main lures is the only 360-degree view over all downtown. The kitchen does justice to the striking panorama, with a Northwest menu that relies on only the freshest local products. The menu undergoes revision seasonally. Dinner daily, plus brunch on Sunday. Reservations advised. Major credit cards accepted. 111 SW 5th Ave. (phone: 220-3600). Expensive.

L'Auberge – Admirers of grilled swordfish with cilantro pesto or spearfish in raspberry *beurre blanc* will find true contentment at this unstuffy French eatery that uses fresh Northwest ingredients. The dining room serves multi-course dinners from an eclectic menu. Open daily. Reservations advised. Major credit cards accepted. 2601 NW Vaughn St. (phone: 223-3302). Expensive.

Thirty-One Northwest – The second level of an urban shopping center is the unlikely location of this enclave of dusty rose elegance, where the salmon melts in your mouth and the vegetables never are overdone. This is the best of all possible escapes from the hubbub below. Closed Sundays. Reservations advised. Major credit cards accepted. 31 NW 23rd Pl. (phone: 223-0106). Expensive.

Zafiro's – With its small bar, chic, minimalist decor, and inventive continental menu, this has quickly become the city's newest and most popular dining spot. Entrées are often surprising combinations of Northwest ingredients with Old World and 1950s fare, such as lamb ragout on mashed potatoes. Open daily. Reservations advised. Major credit cards accepted (phone: 226-3394). Expensive to moderate.

Alexis – The place to be on *Greek Independence Day* (March 25), when Portlanders of all ethnic backgrounds join in the festivities. But a convivial atmosphere prevails every day at this casual, family-owned Greek eatery. A selection of the delectable appetizers, from stuffed grape leaves to spicy chunks of octopus, accompanied by a basket brimming with homemade bread can be a meal in itself. Dinner daily, lunch weekdays. Reservations advised. Major credit cards accepted. 215 W. Burnside St. (phone: 224-8577). Moderate.

Café des Amis – Lace curtains, candlelight, and delightfully personable waiters set the tone for this welcoming place. The menu is slightly French, more Pacific Northwest. Stuffed quail, *poussin* (baby chicken), fettuccine with mussels, salmon, and halibut are all done in a distinct style. Dinner only. Closed Sundays. Reservations advised. Major credit cards accepted. 1987 NW Kearny (phone: 295-6487). Moderate.

Cajun Café and Bistro – On historic Nob Hill, the current chef has introduced the best of Southwest cooking. Take your taste buds on a journey of serveral thousand miles at one sitting, sampling blackened seafood from the Pacific Northwest, plus jambalaya, or tuna and scallop brochettes. Dinner daily, lunch weekdays. Reservations advised. Major credit cards accepted. 2074 NW Lovejoy St. (phone: 227-0227). Moderate.

Chen's Dynasty – For Chinese specialties like stir-fried pork with pickled mustard greens and peanuts or cracked crab with Hunan black beans, this is the place. The menu of Oriental delights seems endless. Open daily. Reservations advised. Major credit cards accepted. 622 Washington (phone: 248-9491). Moderate.

Harborside – The eclectic, 100-item menu ranges from Cajun pizza to peanut butter truffle cake, with a stop at fresh salmon along the way. The proprietors miraculously manage very high quality throughout. Tables on three tiers give all diners a view of the waterfront. Open daily. Reservations advised. Major credit cards accepted. 0309 (really) SW Montgomery (phone: 220-1865). Moderate.

Jake's Famous Crawfish – Serving crawfish and other seagoing delectables since 1892, this place has occupied its current premises since 1908. Worth a visit for both quality food and interesting surroundings. Open daily. Reservations advised. Major credit cards accepted. 401 SW 12th St. (phone: 226-1419). Moderate.

Plainfield's Mayur – East Indian dishes prepared in full dramatic view at the tandoor, a deep clay oven with a 1,000-degree fire at the bottom. Tandoori chicken, lamb, breads, and other Indian specialties are served in the pleasant surroundings of an elegant old Portland home. Dinner daily except Sundays. Reservations advised. Major credit cards accepted. 852 SW 21st Ave. (phone: 223-2995). Moderate.

Der Rheinlander – A good spot to feed the kids on grand portions of good German food. Not the place to go for an intimate rendezvous, since it's filled with families who enjoy being serenaded by a strolling accordian player. Open daily. Reservations advised. Major credit cards accepted. 5035 NE Sandy Blvd. (phone: 249-0507). Moderate.

Ringside West – Portland's premier steakhouse has been serving the finest cuts of beef since 1944. The loyal patronage knows the longtime waiters by name, and vice versa. Though it's mostly known for steaks and prime ribs, some cognoscenti wouldn't dream of going anywhere else for fried chicken or hamburgers. The crisp onion rings are legendary. Dinner daily; lunch weekdays. Reservations advised. Major credit cards accepted. 2165 W. Burnside St. (phone: 223-1513). Moderate.

Zen – The food and attentive service are uniquely Japanese, and the sushi bar is a favorite with the locals. Dinner daily. Lunch weekdays. Closed Sundays. Reservations advised. Major credit cards accepted. 910 SW Salmon (phone: 222-3056). Moderate.

Bread and Ink Café – Snug in its neighborhood of antiques and apparel shops, this café serves up a delightful combination of Mediterranean and Mexican dishes. Omelettes are heavenly, and the cheese blintzes are possibly the best around. Open daily. Reservations unnecessary. Major credit cards accepted. 3610 SE Hawthorne Blvd. (phone: 234-4756). Inexpensive.

Casa-U-Betcha – Standard Mexican fare, well prepared, with a number of delicous house specialties and a low-cost children's plate. Dinner daily; lunch weekdays. Reservations advised for parties of 6 or more. Major credit cards accepted. 612 NW 21st Ave. (phone: 222-4833). Inexpensive.

Dan and Louis Oyster Bar – A Portland institution. Clams, crab, oysters — quickly, simply, and deliciously prepared. Opened in the days when restaurants didn't worry about decor, and it's still the same today (which means it has a distinct, turn-of-the-century style). No alcohol. Open daily. Reservations advised for five or more. Major credit cards accepted. 208 SW Ankeny (phone: 227-5906). Inexpensive.

Jamie's – Popular for hamburgers, salads, and sodas. Family atmosphere. Open daily. No reservations. Major credit cards accepted. NW 23rd Ave. and Kearney (phone: 248-6784). Inexpensive.

Mayas Tacqueria – Smells, tastes, and sounds in this comfortable, cozy eatery are reminiscent of the street cafés in Mexico City. Tacqueria-style cooking offers quick hot food that you can watch being prepared before your eyes. Open daily. No reservations or credit cards accepted. 1000 SW Morrison (phone: 226-1946). Inexpensive.

Old Wives' Tales – The menu features an eclectic mix of entrées, including Mexican, Middle Eastern, Italian, and vegetarian dishes. Children can adjourn to the playroom while adults enjoy espresso and dessert to the melodies of Windham Hill jazz or browse in the restaurant's library. Just across the Burnside Bridge from downtown. Open daily. No reservations. Major credit cards accepted. 1300 E. Burnside (phone: 238-0470). Inexpensive.

Papa Haydn – Select dessert first, then order a light meal that won't spoil it. There's almost always a crowd gathered around the pastry case, where delights ranging from "autumn meringue" to *boccone dolce* are on display. Dinners feature light, continental dishes, with an emphasis on seafood and chicken. Lunch and dinner Tuesdays through Saturdays; Sunday brunch. No reservations. Major credit cards accepted. 5829 SE Milwaukee Ave. (phone: 232-9440) and 801 NW 23rd Ave. (phone: 228-7317). Inexpensive.

Rose's Delicatessen – Delicate blintzes, delicious cakes, gigantic sandwiches. The food isn't kosher, but the atmosphere — and the quality of the sandwiches — is vintage New York City. Open daily. Reservations advised for prime meal times. Major credit cards accepted. 315 NW 23rd Ave. (phone: 227-5181). Inexpensive.

ST. LOUIS

AT-A-GLANCE

SEEING THE CITY: A tour of St. Louis must begin along the Mississippi River, where the city began, and the riverfront offers an irresistible focal point: Jefferson National Expansion Memorial, home of the Gateway Arch, soaring 630 feet above the levee. From its top, you can see most of St. Louis and miles of countryside beyond, on both sides of the river. Ride to the top of the Arch in one of two capsule trams, train-like vehicles running on special tracks to the 70-foot observation room, which affords a truly spectacular 30-mile view. While waiting for the tram, visit the *Museum of Westward Expansion,* also part of the national park (11 N. 4th St.; phone: 425-4465), see a film on the construction of the Arch in the *Tucker Theater,* or browse in the *Museum Shop,* on the plaza beneath the Arch. Admission to the museum is free with a $1 park pass, good for 7 days. Built in 1966 by architect Eero Saarinen, the Arch is so delicately engineered that its last segment — that bit of the arch that's farthest off the ground and connects the two columns — had to wait to be installed until the weather was perfect, so that the steel would neither contract nor expand a fraction until it was in place.

SPECIAL PLACES: Though it's most convenient to get around St. Louis by car, most areas lend themselves to a walking tour. You can park along the waterfront, for example, and explore on foot the levee, Laclede's Landing, and downtown. Neighborhood organizations offer various walking tours, such as the *Central West End House Tour* (phone: 376-2220), which peruses the city's mansions, and the *Lafayette Square Home Tour* (phone: 772-5724), which visits restored Victorian-era homes. For the less energetic, *Tram Tour* (516 Cerre St.; phone: 241-1400) offers a 2-hour narrated tram tour of the downtown area, which runs about every 30 minutes in summer; once in the morning and once in the afternoon in winter.

RIVERFRONT AND DOWNTOWN

The Levee – Moored on the river side of the cobblestone levee are St. Louis's most famous riverboats: the *Huck Finn* and the *Tom Sawyer* (phone for both: 621-4040), for day and night trips up and down the Mississippi. You'll also find the New Orleans–based *Delta Queen* (phone: 800-543-1949) and the *Robert E. Lee* (phone: 241-1282), luxurious sternwheelers from the golden era of steamboats, as well as the only floating *McDonald's* and the *Belle of St. Louis,* an excursion dining boat (phone: 342-7200 or 621-4040).

On the city side of the levee is Jefferson Expansion Memorial Parkway, with the Arch at its center, and in one corner, the Old Cathedral, which is, naturally, the oldest cathedral west (just west) of the Mississippi. It started as a log cabin in 1764 when the city was founded and took its present form in 1834. 2nd and Walnut Sts. (phone: 231-3250).

Laclede's Landing – In the 50 years after the Civil War, St. Louis became rich as well as famous, and the entire downtown section boomed and bloomed. What's left of the bloom is Laclede's Landing, a 10-block area just north of the levee on the far side of massive Eads Bridge with some fine examples of cast-iron-fronted buildings (Raeder Place, formerly the *Old Missouri* hotel at 806 N. 1st, is best of all). It's now the home of a new generation of restaurants and galleries, and one of the few areas in the city where liquor can be served until 3 AM. Some suggestions while wandering the area are *Kennedy's 2nd Street Company* (612 N. 2nd St.; phone: 421-3655), for a lunch of chili, burgers, and sandwiches, and a great place to hear local bands; *Mississippi Nights* (914 N. 1st St.; phone: 421-3853), which features local as well as national bands (the *Ramones* and the *Psychedelic Furs* have played here); the *Dub Club* (214 Morgan St.; phone: 231-CLUB) that hosts national and international reggae bands; the *Old Spaghetti Factory* (727 N. 1st St.; phone: 621-0276), for inexpensive Italian dishes and an old European decor; or, for a good catfish dinner or oyster appetizer, *2nd Street Diner and Fish Market* (721 N. 2nd St.; phone: 436-2222). For food as well as entertainment, try *Hannegan's Restaurant and Pub* (719 N. 2nd St.; phone: 241-8877) or *Bogart's on the Landing* (809 N. 2nd St.; phone: 241-9380).

Old Courthouse – At one time a site of slave auctions, this courthouse was just 2 years old in 1847 when an American slave named Dred Scott tested the legality of slavery by suing his owner. The case was heard here; when he lost, the course of slavery was set. Inside are displays of Old St. Louis and courtrooms where great lawyers such as Thomas Hart Benton tried their cases. Most interesting today is the building's cast-iron dome, completed in 1859, and the mural that adorns its interior. Open daily. No admission charge. 4th St. at Market (phone: 425-4465).

National Bowling Hall of Fame – A haven for bowling aficionados, it traces the history and development of bowling from 5200 BC to the present. Headquarters of the American Bowling Congress and the Women's International Bowling Congress. Old-time bowling alley, videodisc program, wide-screen theater, and restaurant. Admission charge. 8th and Walnut, across from *Busch Stadium* (phone: 231-6340).

Eugene Field House – Primarily an antique toy collection, with some artifacts of the famous St. Louis author Eugene Field, who wrote *Little Boy Blue*. At *Christmastime*, the house prepares a complete Victorian *Christmas* display. Closed Mondays. Admission charge. 634 S. Broadway (phone: 421-4689).

Campbell House – A stately mid-Victorian townhouse containing original furnishings. Open daily. Admission charge. 1508 Locust (phone: 421-0325).

Mercantile Money Museum – Here is everything you've ever wanted to know about money, including counterfeiting. A talking mannequin introduces you to the witticisms of Benjamin Franklin. Open daily. No admission charge. Mercantile Tower, 7th and Washington Sts. (phone: 425-2050).

St. Louis Centre – One of the country's largest urban shopping complexes, a 4-level glass-enclosed mall consisting of 150 shops and 20 restaurants that connects two of the city's largest department stores, *Dillard's* and *Famous-Barr*. Between 6th St., 7th St., Washington Blvd., and Olive Blvd.

Union Station – Eleven acres of history successfully masquerading as a shopping center. Originally built in the glory days of railroads, and once the busiest train station in the country, it has been restored at a cost of $135 million. Carefully preserved, it now features myriad exclusive shops and deluxe restaurants, a free theater, a luxury hotel, and authentic peeks into its rich past. A 10-screen movie theater operates at the far south end of Union Station. Old and new St. Louis meet here. 18th and Market Sts.

Dental Health Theatre – The props are 3-foot-high fiberglass teeth and a carpeted pink tongue, the characters are marionettes, and the show's all about teeth and dental health. This unique theater is a good

Mississippi R.

Map continues West after 2⅓ mile gap

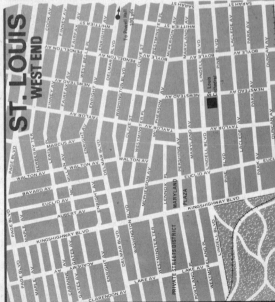

ST. LOUIS
WEST END

DOWNTOWN
ST. LOUIS

Map continues West after 2/3 mile gap

place to take the kids. Open weekdays from 9 AM to 4 PM; call ahead for show times. No admission charge. 727 N. 1st St., Suite 103, on Laclede Landing (phone: 241-7391).

Chatillion-DeMenil Mansion – Once the home of a renowned fur trapper and wilderness guide, this mansion, built in 1848, was saved from demolition when it was deemed an historical landmark. The interior is furnished in mid-Victorian style, with Greek architectural details. Closed Sundays and Mondays. Admission charge. 3352 DeMenil Place (phone: 771-5828).

St. Louis Public Library – This 1912 Italianate building contains an art gallery, the Julia Davis Afro-American History Collection, the Steedman Architectural Library, and extensive reference collections. Tours available. Closed Sundays. 1301 Olive St. (phone: 241-2288).

St. Louis Mercantile Library Association – Founded in 1846, this is the oldest circulating library west of the Mississippi River. Among its significant photo/print collection are works by George Caleb Bingham and George Catlin, painters who meticuluously documented the westward expansion. Also contained here are the old archives of the city newspaper. Closed Sundays. 510 Locust St. (phone: 621-0670).

St. Louis Sports Hall of Fame – A century of St. Louis sports is celebrated here, including photographs of yesterday's *Browns* and today's *Cardinals,* as well as football, soccer, and hockey displays. First baseman Stan Musial's glove is here, as well as other articles of clothing and equipment from the team, including the lockers where they stored their gear. In the *Hall of Fame Theater,* a film of the *Cardinals's* achievements is continuously played. Visitors can also play a computerized sports trivia game. Open daily. Admission charge. 100 Stadium Plaza (phone: 421-3263).

The Forum – Current art and photography shows, as well as a performing arts center, are housed here. There is also a small gift shop. Closed Saturdays and Sundays. No admission charge. 555 Washington Ave. (phone: 421-3791).

SOUTH ST. LOUIS

South St. Louis is primarily German, Italian, and Eastern European. The most determinedly ethnic neighborhood in the area is the Hill (between South Kingshighway and Shaw). From its *bocce* courts and front yard shrines to its green, white, and red hydrants, the Hill is 20 blocks of solid Italian consciousness — great for walking and snacking. Two suggestions: *John Volpi & Co.* (5256 Daggett; phone: 772-8550), closed Mondays, for salami, prosciutto, and Italian sausage; *Amighetti Bakery* (5141 Wilson; phone: 776-2855), closed Sundays and Mondays, for fresh bread and carryout "po' boys." This area is particularly noted for its fine Italian restaurants.

Anheuser-Busch Brewery – The makers of Michelob and Budweiser offer free 1-hour tours of the world's largest brewery and grounds, featuring, naturally, a healthy sampling of the King of Beers. Best on the tour: the stables, a registered landmark building, where the mighty Clydesdale horses reside when they're not on parade. Closed weekends and holidays. No admission charge. 610 Pestalozzi St. (phone: 577-2626).

Missouri Botanical Garden (Shaw's Garden) – After Henry Shaw got very rich with a hardware store in downtown St. Louis, he decided to repay the city by opening his Southside garden estate to the public. Since 1860 its reputation and its collection have grown apace. Highlights of the 79-acre park: the Climatron, a geodesic-domed tropical greenhouse; Seiwa-En, a beautiful Japanese garden where you can feed the huge school of *koi* (Japanese carp); and the Scented Garden, a special collection of scented plants for the blind that may be touched and handled, with descriptions and explanations in braille. Henry Shaw's home is open for tours. Other features include the *Boehm Porcelain Gallery,* a gift shop, and the *Garden View* restaurant. Open daily. Admission charge. 2101 Tower Grove (phone: 577-5100).

Soulard Market – Soulard is the name of both the market and the neighborhood which surrounds it. Since 1847, when the ground was given to the city to be used as a public farmers' market, *Soulard Market* has been open for business — busiest on Saturday mornings, when everything from live rabbits to homemade apple butter is for sale to city slickers. The outside stalls around the main building open whenever fresh goods — meat or poultry, vegetables, fruit, farmers' canned goods or home specialties — come into the city. Closed Sundays and Mondays; most active Fridays and Saturdays. 7th St. and Lafayette (phone: 622-4180).

CENTRAL WEST END

Named for its location near famous Forest Park at the western edge of the city limits, the Central West End (CWE) is St. Louis's most cosmopolitan and elegant section. A collection of small specialty shops, personable restaurants, and ornate mansions dot this historic neighborhood. Private "places" such as Portland and Westmoreland, beautifully maintained by residents, are worth exploring. Mississippi-born Thomas "Tennessee" Williams set *The Glass Menagerie* in a CWE Westminster Place apartment, where his family lived during the 1920s.

Maryland Plaza – A stroller's delight, between Kingshighway and Euclid Avenue. With the best people watching in town, this area is a magnet for politicians, media types, and other glitzy characters. A potpourri of shops and restaurants makes for good food and great buys, too. Visit *26 Maryland Plaza,* an arcade of boutiques featuring everything from seashells and antique clothing to herbs. For a bite to eat, if you have money enough left over, try *Duff's* (392 N. Euclid; phone: 361-0522), for a lunch of sandwiches and imported beer or the *Saint Louis Bread Company* (4651 Maryland Ave.; phone: 367-7636), which serves delicious sandwiches, fresh bread, pastries, and a variety of piping hot coffee. Sample *Dressel's* (392 N. Euclid; phone: 361-1060), for hearty Welsh pub fare (and the city's best selection of beer and ale). The Central West End also sports several establishments that can satisfy more hearty appetites, including *Balaban's* (405 N. Euclid; phone: 381-8085), for a dinner of seafood, French cuisine, or their unusual dinner crêpes, and *Culpeppers* (300 N. Euclid; phone: 361-2828), a trendy bar-café whose spicy chicken wings, club sandwiches, and soups are well known. For monthly shows of photography and contemporary art, stop by the *Greenberg Gallery of Contemporary Art* (44 Maryland Plaza; phone: 361-7600).

St. Louis Cathedral – It is not just the size of the cathedral — immense — that is awesome; it is the mosaics that adorn almost the whole interior space — beautiful, ethereal, light bearing; millions of pieces of stone and glass in thousands of shades depicting saints, apostles, and religious scenes. Considered one of the finest examples of mosaic-work in this hemisphere, and not to be missed. Tours conducted on Sundays (except *Easter*) at 1 PM. Lindell at Newstead (phone: 533-2824).

Fabulous Fox Theater – This restored 1929 movie palace now has all the gilt and glitz of its yesteryears. At night the house lights come on, and the *Fox* presents some of the biggest entertainment names in the country — Las Vegas–style shows and pop concerts at midwestern prices. Tours of the theater are given Wednesdays, Thursdays, and Saturdays at 10:30 AM for $2. 527 N. Grand Blvd. (phone: 534-1678, for entertainment information).

University City Area – This historic district on Delmar Avenue, known as the U. City Loop (where the streetcars turn around), just west of the Central West End, houses a "strip" of happenings: resale shops, modern boutiques, art galleries, and bookstores. Walkers should check out the pavement for stars containing famous St. Louisans' names. *Blue-*

berry Hill, a bar/restaurant where Chuck Berry, Elvis Presley, and Bo Diddly are held in esteem, serves Rock 'n' Roll beer (6504 Delmar; phone: 727-0880). The *Tivoli Theatre* (6350 Delmar; phone: 725-0220) features a repertory of foreign, classical, and modern films, as does the *High Pointe Cinema,* nearby, at 1001 McCausland (phone: 781-0800).

■ **EXTRA SPECIAL:** An hour south from St. Louis just off Route 55 is Ste. Genevieve, one of the oldest permanent settlements west of the Mississippi (established in 1735) and a town that has maintained its bounty of old homes with admirable care. A number of the oldest homes are open daily, as is an excellent old inn, *St. Gemme Beauvais* (78 N. Main St.; phone: 883-5744). It's a beautifully furnished, 8-room village inn with the best food in town. And not to be missed, if you are in the area during the second weekend of August: *Ste. Genevieve's Jour de Fête,* when all the old homes are open for a festive 2 days.

For the young, or just the young at heart, take a day trip to *Six Flags Over Mid-America,* a 200-acre theme park with Looney Tunes Town (where you can shake hands with Bugs Bunny), the shooting rapids of Thunder River, the Screamin' Eagle, and all sorts of unique shows and shops. Open daily, late May through late August, it's about a 20-minute drive from downtown (I-44 and Allenton Rd. in Eureka; phone: 938-4800 or 938-5300). Or visit the locale of Huck Finn and Tom Sawyer — Hannibal, Missouri (phone: 221-0114). Described as the "World's Most Famous Small Town," it was the home of Samuel Clemens, better known as Mark Twain. Another unusual attraction is Silver Dollar City. Tucked away in the heart of 2,000 acres overlooking Table Rock Lake, it is a unique community of good-time shows, old-time crafts, fun-time rides, and plenty of farm-fresh food in a variety of good restaurants.

Other nearby attractions: Meramec Caverns, one of the largest cave formations in the world and once a hideout of Jesse James. Camping and canoeing on the Meramec River are available April through October. The caverns themselves are open from March through December. Take I-44 west to the Stanton exit (phone: 468-3166). *Cahokia Mounds State Historic Site and Museum* (7850 Collinsville Rd., Collinsville, IL; phone: 618-346-5160) displays artifacts dating from AD 700 to 1450, when Indians inhabited the area, and conducts tours, craft classes, and a variety of seasonal events. Open daily from 9 AM to 5 PM. Donations accepted.

SOURCES AND RESOURCES

TOURIST INFORMATION: The St. Louis Convention and Visitors Commission (10 S. Broadway, Suite 300, St. Louis, MO 63102; phone: 421-1023 or 800-247-9791) publishes a free guide that lists special events (festivals, street fairs, house tours); it also has maps and other tourist information. A free Travel Plan Kit featuring a group tour manual, a 35-page visitor's guide, and a calendar of events is available. The St. Louis Visitors Center (308 Washington Ave. and Memorial Drive; phone: 241-1764) also has brochures, baseball schedules, and other information of interest. Contact the Missouri state hotline (phone: 800-877-1234) for maps, calendars of events, health updates, and travel advisories.

The St. Louis Annual Guide (published by *St. Louis* magazine; $3.50) is comprehensive. The *St. Louis Symphony Society* arranges special group (20 or more) tours of any part of the city, with proceeds going to the society's treasury (712 N. Grand Blvd.; phone: 533-2500). The *American Institute of Architects* has architectural maps of the city, pinpointing interesting buildings (phone: 621-3484). The *Landmarks Association* has information on neighborhoods and restoration projects (phone: 421-6474).

Local Coverage – *St. Louis Post-Dispatch,* daily (Thursday's edition carries a calendar of coming events); the *St. Louis American,* published each Thursday, the city's most informative black community newspaper; *St. Louis* magazine, monthly. The *St. Louis Business Journal* is a weekly update on the business scene, and the weekly *Riverfront Times* focuses on city happenings.

Television Stations – KTVI Channel 2–ABC; KMOV Channel 4–CBS; KSDK Channel 5–NBC; KETC Channel 9–PBS; KDNL Channel 30–UHF-Fox Network.

Radio Stations – AM: KUFA 550 (classic country); KOOL 590 (1950s music); KMOX 1120 (talk/sports); KGLD 1380 (oldies); KXOX 630 (news/talk); WCEO 590 (business news). FM: KWMU 90.7 (national news/music); KSD 93.7 (classic rock); KEZK 102.5 (easy listening); KMJM 107.7 (urban contemporary); KATZ 100.3 (jazz).

 TELEPHONE: The area code for St. Louis is 314.

Sales Tax – There is a 6% sales tax on general merchandise. In addition, restaurants charge a 1.5% tax, and hotels charge a 3.75% tourism tax.

 CLIMATE: St. Louis weather is unpredictable, with temperatures ranging from −10F to +103F. From mid-June through September, the heat and humidity are high, particularly in August. Dress coolly, but be aware that most places are air conditioned. Autumn is crisp, cool, and beautiful. Winters are very cold, with snow and ice. Spring is wonderful, but be prepared for occasional rain and very strong winds from April to June.

 GETTING AROUND: Airport – Lambert–St. Louis International Airport usually is a 30-minute drive from downtown (up to an hour during rush periods), and cab fares should run $18. The airport limo service to downtown costs $5.90 and leaves the airport every 15 minutes. The city's *Natural Bridge Airport* bus leaves for downtown from the air terminal's main entrance every 45 minutes to an hour and costs 85¢.

Bus – The *Bi-State* bus system serves most of the metropolitan area. Fare 85¢; 15¢ for transfers. Route information, maps, 707 N. 1st St. (phone: 231-2345).

Car Rental – St. Louis is served by all the major national companies; several have booths at the airport as well as around the city. A reliable local service is *Enterprise Leasing,* with nine locations around the city (phone: 231-4440).

Taxi – Cabs can be picked up at the major department stores and hotels, hailed in the streets, or ordered by phone. Major companies are *Laclede Cab* (phone: 652-3456); *Yellow Cab* (phone: 361-2345); *County Cab* (phone: 991-5300); *Allen Cab* (phone: 531-4545).

 VITAL SERVICES: Audiovisual Equipment – *Creve Coeur Camera and Video Center* (phone: 621-6157); *Bradley Business Services* (phone: 721-3842).

Baby-sitting – A number of agencies are listed in the yellow pages, but most will be more expensive than the nonprofessional organization that provides conscientious babysitters. *Missouri Baptist Hospital* (phone: 569-5193) supplies nursing students with good references and their own transportation; tightly run, relatively strict, and careful.

Business Services – *Bradley Business Service,* 34 N. Brentwood (phone: 854-9111).

Dry Cleaner/Tailor – *Erlich's Cleaners,* shoe repair also, 215 N. 10th St. (phone: 421-5506).

Limousine – *Jed Limousine Service* (phone: 991-0767); *Maxwell's Limousine Service* (phone: 576-5117).

Mechanic – Closest to the downtown area are *Stringer's Amoco Station* (7th and Russell; phone: 776-0092), with 24-hour service, and *Overturf's* (902 S. Broadway; phone: 436-2540).

Medical Emergency – *Barnes Hospital* (4949 Barnes Hospital Plaza; phone: 362-5000); *St. Louis University Hospital* (1221 S. Grand; phone: 771-6400).

Messenger Services – *National Courier Systems* (phone: 423-8484).

National/International Courier – *Federal Express* (phone: 367-8278); *DHL Worldwide Courier Express* (phone: 800-227-6177).

Pharmacy – *Walgreen's,* 24 hours 6733 Clayton Rd. (phone: 721-2033).

Photocopies – *Metro Blueprint* (917 Locust St.; phone: 231-5025); *PIP* (616 Olive St.; phone: 621-0991); *Brady Drake* (1113 Olive; phone: 421-1311).

Post Office – The main office is located at 1720 Market St. (phone: 425-5311). The airport mail facility (9855 Air Cargo Rd.; phone: 436-4550) is open all day, 7 days a week.

Professional Photographer – *Mind's Eye Commercial Photography* (phone: 426-6773); *DayPhoto* (phone: 231-3381).

Secretary/Stenographer – *Kelly Services* (phone: 421-4111); *Professional Business Center* (phone: 436-7335).

Teleconference Facilities – *Airport Marriott; Marriott Pavilion* (see *Best in Town,* below).

Translator – *Berlitz* (phone: 721-1070); *Calvin Communication Service* (phone: 725-9466).

Typewriter Rental – *Clayton Office Equipment Rentals,* 1-day minimum (phone: 427-4807).

Western Union/Telex – Many offices are located around the city (phone: 291-1010).

 SPECIAL EVENTS: The *International Festival* (phone: 997-1445) is held at *Steinberg Rink* in Forest Park during the 3-day *Memorial Day* weekend. Authentic music, dance, food, and crafts of 35 nationalities are featured. The *Huck Finn* and the *Tom Sawyer* riverboats are the contestants in the *Memorial Day Riverboat Race.* On the *Goldenrod Showboat,* St. Louis ragtimers host the *National Ragtime and Jazz Festival* (phone: 621-3311) in June. The *Japanese Festival* (phone: 577-5100) at Missouri Botanical Gardens is an annual summer celebration of Japanese culture through music, dance, food, and crafts. The *Veiled Prophet Fair* (phone: 367-FAIR) on the Arch grounds is a 4-day entertainment extravaganza, featuring a parade of 20 or more lavishly outfitted floats, fireworks, marathons, music, and air and water events, that takes place during the *July 4* holiday. German food and culture are celebrated during the *Strassenfest,* a weekend celebration usually held the end of July. The *Great Forest Park Balloon Race* (phone: 726-6896), an annual St. Louis tradition since 1904, begins in Forest Park and ends wherever the wind carries. Contact the visitors' bureau (phone: 421-1023) for exact dates.

 MUSEUMS: The story of the movement west is told in murals, graphic displays, and film sequences at the *Museum of Westward Expansion* under the Arch (see *Special Places*). Other museums of interest in St. Louis:

Dog Museum – Rotates selections from its permanent art collections. On hand are items depicting canines throughout history. A recent addition to the museum has helped to house the overflow of 19th-century English canine art, photography, and literature. Fido and Spot are permitted to visit the community room in the new building, with canine canvases and a film from the American Kennel Club on the finer attributes of the noble Clumber spaniel. Open Mondays through Saturdays from 9 AM to 5 PM, Sundays from 1 to 4 PM. Admission charge. 1721 S. Mason Rd., in Queeny Park in West County (phone: 821-DOGS).

The Magic House – Dares children to have a good time and learn something, too. Closed Mondays. Admission charge. 516 Kirkwood (phone: 822-8900).

McDonnell Douglas Prologue Room – At the world headquarters of the aerospace giant, the room displays some of McDonnell Douglas's achievements, including the first Gemini and Mercury space capsules ever built. Open daily (except Sundays) from 9 AM to 4 PM, June through August. No admission charge. McDonnell Blvd. and Airport Rd. (on the northeast side of the airport; phone: 232-5421).

Missouri Historical Society and History Museum – It's easy to get lost amid the colorful displays describing the history of St. Louis, the state of Missouri, and the American West. Of particular interest are the exhibits depicting 100 years of St. Louis advertising and of the *1904 World's Fair;* Charles Lindbergh memorabilia; and the extensive collections of firearms and period costumes. Open Tuesdays through Sundays from 9:30 AM to 4:45 PM. Guided tours offered on weekdays; make an appointment. No admission charge. Forest Park, Lindell Blvd., and De Baliviere (phone: 361-1424).

National Museum of Transport – The many vehicles on which Americans have relied, from horse-drawn buggies to Bobby Darin's dream car, are on display. The museum's train collection is heralded as one of the greatest collections of locomotives in the nation. Open daily (except holidays) from 9 AM to 5 PM. Admission charge. 3015 Barrett Station Rd., in West County (phone: 965-7998).

St. Louis Art Museum – This turn-of-the-century building, one of a few extant from the *1904 World's Fair,* has recently undergone a $32 million renovation. The museum is faithfully guarded by the 47-foot statue of King Louis, the Crusader. Open daily. No admission charge. Forest Park (phone: 721-0067). Closed Mondays.

St. Louis Science Center (McDonnell Planetarium) – The *McDonnell Planetarium* and the *Museum of Science and Natural History* are both part of one entertainment and educational complex. The planetarium features a *Star Theater,* hands-on science and natural history exhibitions, and a Discovery Room. A $34 million expansion has added a new building which houses the 330-seat *Omnimax Theater,* galleries devoted to ecological and technological themes, and a unique structure that shows an exhibit of the physics of highway construction and then plunges downward for a look at a Missouri mine and a city sewer. Open daily. Admission charge for special exhibits. 5100 Clayton Ave., Forest Park (phone: 289-4400).

St. Louis Wax Museum – Over 130 lifelike wax figures, including those of movie stars, presidents, sports celebrities, religious leaders, and public figures. Open daily (call for hours). Admission charge. 2nd and Morgan Sts. (phone: 241-1155).

Vaughn Cultural Center – Serves as a backdrop for many traveling African-American art and photography shows; also a resource for local and national African-American history. Open Mondays through Fridays, 8:30AM to 5 PM. Admission charge for specific exhibits. 525 North Grand Blvd. (phone: 535-9227).

MAJOR COLLEGES AND UNIVERSITIES: There are five major universities in the St. Louis area: St. Louis University, founded by the Jesuits in 1818 and the oldest college in the US west of the Mississippi (Grand at Lindell; phone: 658-2222); Washington University, founded by an ancestor of T. S. Eliot, too shy to name the school for himself (at the western end of Forest Park on a beautiful campus; phone: 889-5000); the University of Missouri, St. Louis (8001 Natural

Bridge Rd.; phone: 553-0111); Webster University (470 E. Lockwood in the quaint hamlet of Webster Groves; phone: 968-6900); and Southern Illinois University–Edwardsville (Edwardsville, IL, about 30 minutes east of downtown St. Louis; phone: 621-5168, in St. Louis).

PARKS AND GARDENS: Forest Park is one of America's largest city parks, along with New York's Central Park and the Portland, Oregon, park system, and it offers far too much to see in even a long day. Highlights are the zoo, whose exhibits — "Big Cat Country," the famous Monkey House, the walk-through Bird Cage — can be visited on foot or by zoo train. There is a grand Jungle of the Apes House. The newest addition is the $17-million state-of-the-art educational "Living World" center designed to teach the diversity and unity of life on earth. Admission charge. The Children's Zoo charges a modest admission price, and you must buy a ticket for the train; all else free (phone: 781-0900). The *Art Museum,* on Art Hill (closed Mondays), maintains a wide-ranging collection and hosts traveling exhibitions (phone: 721-0067). Laumeier International Sculpture Park (12580 Rott Rd.; phone: 821-1209) features huge outdoor sculptures in a woodsy setting. St. Louis RV Park (900 N. Jefferson; phone: 241-3330) is an urban park for recreational vehicles. Pool. Closed December through February. For information on the Missouri Botanical Garden, see *Special Places.*

SPORTS AND FITNESS: St. Louisans love their professional teams, and sports events are well attended.

Baseball – *Busch Memorial Stadium* (Broadway at Walnut St., downtown; phone: 421-3060) is the home of the National League *Cardinals.* Tickets are available at the stadium and from *Famous-Barr* and *Dillard's* department stores.

Bicycling – The largest biking event in St. Louis is the *Moonlight Ramble,* a 17-mile bike ride that starts at 2 AM on the last Sunday of every August and lasts until dawn. *American Youth Hostel* will have information (phone: 421-2044). For recreational biking, pick one of the many trails in the city's Forest Park; bikes can be rented at *Touring Cyclist* (1101 S. Big Bend Blvd.; phone: 781-9951).

Fitness Center – The revamped *Downtown YMCA* has a pool, racquetball courts, track, and exercise equipment (1528 Locust St.; phone: 436-4100). The *Marquette YMCA,* also downtown (314 N. Broadway; phone: 436-7070), offers a high tech exercise environment. No pool.

Golf – Forest Park has two public courses, 9 and 18 holes respectively. The 18-hole course has a reputation for being tough, but greens and tees are not in the best condition, though work is being done to improve the grounds. The 9-holer is in Ruth Park, 8211 Groby Rd., in St. Louis County. Modest fees (phone: 727-1800).

Hockey – The *Blues* play NHL hockey at the *Arena,* 5700 Oakland (phone: 644-0900).

Horse Racing – Thoroughbred racing at *Cahokia Downs* (Rte. 460, about 20 minutes from St. Louis; phone: 618-332-8481); harness racing at *Fairmount Park* (Rte. 40 East, Collinsville, IL; phone: 436-1517).

Jogging – Start at Wharf Street below the Gateway Arch and run the 2-mile stretch along the river; jog the 6-mile perimeter of Forest Park; or follow Wydown Road by the Washington University campus for about a 2-mile residential run.

Soccer – The St. Louis *Storm* play major league soccer at the *Arena,* 5700 Oakland (phone: 781-6475).

Tennis – Best for the visitor are the courts at *Dwight F. Davis Tennis Center* in Forest Park, open during daylight hours; permits for daily play obtained at the center (phone: 367-0220).

THEATER: For up-to-date offerings and performance times, check the publications listed above. Offerings include the fine *Repertory Theatre of St. Louis* (136 Edgar Rd.; phone: 968-4925); the *Fabulous Fox* (527 N. Grand Blvd.; phone: 534-1111), winter home of traveling Broadway shows and name entertainers; and the *Westport Playhouse* (600 West Port Plaza; phone: 878-2424), one of St. Louis's newest and most attractive theaters, for productions ranging from plays to well-known entertainers. The *Municipal Opera House* in Forest Park offers its summer stock program of musicals. About 1,400 seats every performance are free; line up outside the Muny about 6:30 PM (phone: 361-1900). *St. Louis Black Repertory*'s *23rd Street Theatre* (2240 St. Louis Ave.; phone: 231-3706) is entering its 15th season.

MUSIC: Concerts and opera from the *St. Louis Symphony* at *Powell Hall* (information, phone: 533-2500); *Opera Theater of St. Louis, Loretto-Hilton Theater* (phone: 961-0171); and *Sheldon Memorial* (3648 Washington; phone: 533-9900), one of the country's most acoustically perfect auditoriums. *American Theater* (416 N. 9th; phone: 231-7000) is a cabaret setting which hosts top-notch entertainment acts and musical groups.

NIGHTCLUBS AND NIGHTLIFE: After dark from Laclede's Landing to the suburbs, night crawlers can enjoy a variety of activities. Hear live jazz at *Gene Lynn's* (9th and Washington; phone: 241-3833) and *Just Jazz* in the *Majestic* hotel (1019 Pine St.; phone: 436-2355). Dance at *1227* (1227 Washington; phone: 436-3100) and *Zone 8* (75 Maryland Plaza; phone: 361-8801). Try *Rupert's* (5130 Oakland, south of Forest Park; phone: 652-6866), where the yuppies hang out. *Mississippi Nights* (914 N. 1st St.; phone: 421-3853), the only "nightclub" on Laclede's Landing, features a large dance floor and music from local as well as nationally known concert bands. For stimulating conversation and popular happy hours, there's *Café Balaban* (405 N. Euclid in the Central West End; phone: 361-8085), where St. Louis's old money rubs elbows (literally) with the nouveau riche; and *Cardwell's* (8100 Maryland, in the suburb of Clayton; phone: 726-5055), a mixture of business and cocktail chatter. Local and nationally known comedians appear at the *Funny Bone Comedy Club* (940 W. Port Plaza; phone: 469-6692).

BEST IN TOWN

CHECKING IN: Whether you want to be within walking distance of the levee, smack-dab downtown, on either end of Forest Park, or conveniently near Lambert Field Airport, high quality hotels are available. Prices range from $80 and up for a double in our expensive category, $55 to $75 in the moderate range. These prices do not include the 3.75% tourism tax tacked on to the 6% — and forever fluctuating — Missouri sales tax or the $2 fee on all hotel rooms (they call this a "Convention Center tax," and, for now, it is relevant only to downtown hotels). All telephone numbers are in the 314 area code unless otherwise indicated.

Adam's Mark – In the shadow of the Gateway Arch, with 17th-century Flemish tapestry, French crystal chandeliers, Russian lithographs, and an Italian marble lobby, it reflects the grand tradition of Europe's finest hotels. One of the city's best. A business center includes secretarial services, A/V equipment, and computers. Meeting rooms have a capacity of up to 1,000. There is also a concierge desk, 24-hour room service, and express checkout. 4th and Chestnut (phone: 241-7400; Fax: 314-241-6618). Expensive.

Airport Marriott – At Lambert Field Airport, half an hour from downtown, this 433-room spot features extensive recreational facilities — 2 pools, tennis courts, putting greens, sauna and exercise rooms — and is good both for businesspeople on short visits and families on the road who'd like to stretch after a day of travel. Meeting rooms can hold up to 1,500, and the business center features secretarial services and A/V equipment. Other amenities include shuttle service to various parking lots, concierge, around-the-clock room service, CNN, and express checkout. Free parking. I-70 at the airport (phone: 423-9700 Fax: 314-423-0213). Expensive.

Hyatt Regency – Formerly the *Omni International,* this is more than just a hotel, it's an event — part of the complex that includes the beautifully restored *Union Station,* originally built in 1894. Of its 546 rooms, 68 are in Head House, which actually was part of the station, and the remainder under the original roof of the train shed. All have phones and TV sets in the bathrooms. There are 2 restaurants, the elegant *Aldos* and the less formal *Station Grille,* and the *Grand Hall* bar. Surrounded by more than 11 climate-controlled acres of fine shops and marketplaces, it is truly an experience. Business services include meeting rooms that hold up to 1,500, secretarial assistance, computers, photocopiers, and A/V equipment. Other pluses are 24-hour room service, CNN, concierge, and express checkout. 1820 Market St. (phone: 231-1234; Fax: 314-436-4238). Expensive.

Majestic – Distinctively European, this 74-year-old National Historic Landmark sets the standard for fine service and the most luxurious accommodations in downtown St. Louis. Each of the 91 guestrooms or mini-suites is unique in design and appointments. Full-service concierge. Pampering from check-in to checkout includes evening turndown service. There also are meeting rooms that can accommodate up to 50, as well as 24-hour room service and CNN. Fine dining can be had in the *Richard Perry* restaurant (see *Eating Out*). 1019 Pine St. (phone: 436-2355; Fax: 314-436-2355, ext. 493). Expensive.

Marriott Pavilion – In the midst of rebuilt downtown St. Louis. The "Pavilion" of its title is the Spanish Pavilion, jewel of the *1964 New York World's Fair,* dismantled and moved to St. Louis by former Mayor Alfonso Cervantes amid great controversy. It now makes up the 2-story lobby of the 671-room property, where it is a great success. The hotel offers a coffee shop, 2 restaurants, a bar, a pool, a sauna, and free parking. A new business center has photocopiers, A/V equipment, and computers. Secretarial services are also on call. Meeting rooms can accommodate up to 1,000. The hotel offers a concierge desk, 24-hour room service, CNN, and express checkout. 1 Broadway (phone: 421-1776; Fax: 314-331-9029). Expensive.

Ritz-Carlton – This world class establishment recently set up shop in this midwestern hub (halfway between downtown and the airport) with 302 rooms, including 30 executive suites and 1 Ritz-Carlton Suite. Private concierge service is available, as well as a fitness and exercise center with an indoor climate-controlled pool. *The Restaurant* and *The Grill* are both full-service dining rooms. There is a complete range of business services available for guests' use, including secretarial assistance, A/V equipment, photocopiers, and computers. CNN, 24-hour room service, and express checkout are other bonuses. Located in the suburb of Clayton. Forsyth and Hanley (phone: 863-6300; Fax: 314-863-3525). Expensive.

Seven Gables Inn – With 32 charming European-style guestrooms and suites in the heart of Clayton's business district. This is the only Midwest member of the prestigious Relais & Châteaux group, and also is listed in the National Register of Historic Places. The Tudor-style, vintage 1916 inn was originally modeled after the house in Nathaniel Hawthorne's *House of the Seven Gables*. The award-winning *Chez Louis* restaurant (see *Eating Out*) and turn-of-the-century *Bernard's* bistro also are housed here. Three meeting rooms, with access to secretarial services, CNN, and a concierge desk are available. 26 North Meramec (phone: 863-8400 or 800-433-6590; Fax: 314-863-8846). Expensive.

Stouffer Concourse – Striking contemporary design, dramatic grand entrance with landscaped terraces, 393 well-appointed rooms, spa, fitness center, indoor and outdoor pool, superb restaurants, lounges, and exclusive club floors. CNN. 9801 Natural Bridge Rd. (phone: 429-1100). Expensive.

Cheshire Inn – Aspires to an image of an English country inn, 1 block west of Forest Park. Close neighbors are no longer surprised by the English double-decker bus that fetches hotel guests from the airport; the theme is embellished with reproductions of English antiques in its 110 rooms. Beware: Beds are set very high off the floor. Pool, good restaurant, free parking. Guests can request secretarial services and A/V equipment. CNN. Clayton Rd. at Skinker (phone: 647-7300; Fax: 314-647-0442). Moderate.

Clarion – For comfort as well as convenience, this impressive 855-room riverfront establishment is the place. In addition to luxury suites with Jacuzzi, features include indoor and outdoor pools, health club, game-room, 24-hour coffee shop, delicatessen, 2 bars, and the revolving *Top of the Riverfront* restaurant, which treats diners to a 360-degree panorama of the city. CNN. 200 S. 4th St. (phone: 241-9500; Fax: 314-241-6171). Moderate.

Clayton Inn – Modern, with 220 rooms, it's in one of St. Louis's wealthy suburbs. Good service, spacious rooms decorated in contemporary style, and fine facilities. There are 2 restaurants, including the *Top of the Sevens* (closed Sundays), with a panoramic view of the city, a piano bar, health club with indoor and outdoor pools, sauna, exercise room, and whirlpool bath. Seven meeting rooms; secretarial services are on call. CNN. In Clayton. 7750 Carondelet Ave. (phone: 726-5400; Fax: 314-726-6105). Moderate.

Drury Inn – Linking yesterday with today, it retains the elegance of the 1907 railroad *YMCA* building adjacent to *Union Station*. Above-average service makes this downtown hostelry a favorite of vacationers as well as businesspeople. Amenities include Quickstart breakfast, covered guest parking, free local phone calls, CNN, and an indoor swimming pool and whirlpool bath. There are 180 standard guest rooms and mini-suites. Other offerings include 4 meeting rooms, A/V equipment, and express checkout. 201 S. 20th Street, southwest of Union Station (phone: 231-3900; Fax: 314-231-3900). Moderate.

EATING OUT: Considering St. Louis's large Italian community, it is hardly surprising that the city's premier restaurant serves fine Italian food or that its name is *Tony's*. What is more surprising is the host of good restaurants that complement it and the wide variety of cuisines and reasonable prices charged. Our choices below are grouped into broad price categories — expensive, about $60 for a meal for two; moderate, $30 to $40; inexpensive, $15 to $25 — and are guaranteed to get you into the most interesting corners of the city for lunch or dinner. Prices do not include drinks, wine, tips, or the 1.5% restaurant tax added to the 6.1% St. Louis sales tax. All telephone numbers are in the 314 area code unless otherwise indicated.

Al's – Just north of Laclede's Landing, an unlikely but successful combination of riverboat decor and Italian (and American) dishes. Arguably, it has the best steaks in town as well as a very respectable rack of lamb and an excellent shrimp de jonghe (shrimp sautéed in marinara sauce). Dinner only; closed Sundays. No reservations necessary on Saturdays. Major credit cards accepted. 1st St. at Biddle (phone: 421-6399). Expensive.

Busch's Grove – This county landmark offers a club-like atmosphere and excellent barbecue. Open daily. Reservations necessary. Major credit cards accepted. 9160 Clayton at Price Rd. (phone: 993-9070). Expensive.

Chez Louis – Fine French food in fresh, contemporary surroundings. Try the fresh salmon baked in parchment. Open Mondays through Saturdays for dinner, lunch served weekdays only. Reservations advised. Major credit cards accepted. Located in the *Seven Gables Inn,* 26 N. Meramec (phone: 863-8400). Expensive.

Nantucket Cove – Fresh Maine lobster, fresh swordfish, red snapper, and oysters for a dime apiece are the lively specialties on the menu. Housed in a fashionable Central West End apartment building, this eatery has a cozy, New England fisherman's decor. Open daily. Reservations advised. Major credit cards accepted. 40 N. Kingshighway (phone: 361-0625). Expensive.

Premio – Italian dining with a great street-level view of downtown. Service with a flair. Open Mondays through Fridays for lunch and dinner; on Saturdays, dinner only. Reservations necessary. Major credit cards accepted. One Gateway Mall (phone: 231-0911). Expensive.

Richard Perry – Owner and master chef Perry has a long-standing reputation for his innovative cooking, and his Sunday brunches are delicious proof of his expertise. Sautéed trout with almonds and topped with poached eggs, sweet-potato fettuccine with shiitake mushrooms, and smoked chicken are among the outstanding dishes. The English club-like atmosphere, complete with cherrywood walls and hurricane-style wall sconces, is a complement to the fare. Open daily. Reservations advised. Major credit cards accepted. 1019 Pine St., in the *Majestic Hotel* (phone: 771-4100). Expensive.

Tony's – According to the *Wall Street Journal,* owner Vince Bommarito is the Vince Lombardi of the restaurant world — a stickler for detail and a perfectionist. What began as a spaghetti house has grown into a first-rate eatery, with waiters who study food and drink the way medical students cram for finals. Winner of the "Pasta Restaurant of the Year" award from the National Pasta Association, it takes no reservations, and the wait on Saturday night can last more than 3 hours. Dinner only; closed Sundays and Mondays. Major credit cards accepted. 862 N. Broadway (phone: 231-7007). Expensive.

La Veranda – The elegant and contemporary atmosphere is equally matched by the menu, whose highlights are smoked salmon, fried spinach, and pizza baked in a wood-burning oven. The service is extremely attentive. Open daily. Reservations advised. Major credit cards accepted. On the lower level of Union Stations's *Drury Inn,* 201 S. 20th St. (phone: 241-0707). Expensive.

Blue Water Grill – Don't be fooled by the small, simply decorated dining room. This place proffers delicious Southwestern food and delicately cooked fish dishes. Open daily. Reservations advised. Major credit cards accepted. 2067 Hampton Ave. (phone: 645-0707). Moderate.

Cardwell's – Seasonal dishes served in an atmosphere of relaxed elegance. Grilled meats cooked over pecan wood, mouth-watering pasta. Sunday brunch. Daily happy hour with complimentary hors d'oeuvres. Valet parking. Open daily. Reservations advised. Major credit cards accepted. 8100 Maryland, in the suburb of Clayton (phone: 726-5055). Moderate.

Cunetto's House of Pasta – On The Hill, where everything Italian prospers, and where the heart and soul of good food is pasta, hot, fresh, in a variety of styles, augmented by veal, steaks, and Italian specialties. Weekdays, lunch and dinner; Saturdays, dinner only. No reservations (long waits at dinnertime). Major credit cards accepted. 5453 Magnolia (phone: 781-1135). Moderate.

House of Jamaica – Jerked beef, pork, chicken, goat, and fish are done up in tasty fashion and served with Red Stripe beer (the Jamaican brew). The decor is very native, as is the service — slow. Open daily except Sundays for lunch and dinner. Reservations unnecessary. Major credit cards accepted. 6235 Delmar, in University City (phone: 725-4308). Moderate.

K.C. Masterpiece Barbecue & Grill – Kansas City's renowned barbecue palace has certainly made a name for itself in this town. Great ribs and sauce, and the wet fries smothered with spiced cheese are a must. Open daily. Reservations necessary. Major credit cards accepted. 611 N. Lindbergh Blvd. (phone: 991-5811). Moderate.

La Patisserie – The quiche and house coffee cake are the most sought-after treats at this European café. Weekends there may be a wait, but it's worth it. Open daily for breakfast and lunch only. Reservations accepted only on weekdays. Major credit cards accepted. 6269 Delmar (phone: 725-4902). Moderate.

Patty Long Café and Catering Co. – A creative menu sampling of French, Southwestern, and American (to name a few) dishes, blended with acute attention to detail, makes this one of the most talked about restaurants in town. Lunch Mondays through Saturdays, dinners Fridays and Saturdays only. Reservations advised for dinner. Major credit cards accepted. 1931 Park Ave. (phone: 621-9598). Moderate.

Riddles Penultimate Café – Modern American cooking with a dash of Cajun makes this a favorite among the business set and college students. The wine bar ranks high. Try the daily "chalkboard specials." Open for lunch weekdays, dinner daily; closed Mondays. Reservations advised on weekends. Major credit cards accepted. 6307 Delmar, in University City (phone: 725-6985). Moderate.

Two Black Cats – The decor is high-tech, and the food is very tasty. The onion soup is spicy, topped with baked cheese which threatens to burn the roof of your mouth, and the whisky bread pudding should not be forgotten. Open daily. Reservations advised. Most major credit cards accepted. 1405 Washington Ave. (phone: 421-CATS). Moderate.

Lettuce Leaf – A former business school professor decided to put his marketing theories into practice and opened up a few restaurants that serve tasty salads, sandwiches, and soup, and a very good cheesecake. Open daily. Reservations unnecessary. Major credit cards accepted. Three locations: 7823 Forsyth (phone: 727-5439); 107 N. 6th (phone: 241-7773); and 600 W. Port Plaza (phone: 576-7677). Moderate to inexpensive.

Miss Hulling's Cafeteria – A St. Louis tradition, serving healthful foods. The menu features 26 different salads. All breads and desserts are baked on the premises. Open daily except Sundays from 6 AM to 8:15 PM. No reservations. Major credit cards accepted. 11th and Locust Sts. (phone: 436-0840). Inexpensive.

Powers – A cozy restaurant/bar featuring grilled food (burgers, hot dogs, fries, chicken wings), salads, and soup. In downtown Clayton. Lunch and dinner. Closed Sundays. Reservations unnecessary. Most major credit cards accepted. 20 N. Central Ave. (phone: 862-8666). Inexpensive.

Salad Bowl Cafeteria – Home cooking, cafeteria-style, with a focus on the family. Open daily except Saturdays from 11 AM to 7:30 PM. No reservations. Most major credit cards accepted. 3949 Lindell Blvd. (phone: 535-4274). Inexpensive.

Shalimar Garden – A popular Indian eatery, whose large vegetarian selection includes hot, spicy dishes. The service is very slow, but the dishes will erase impatient memories. Open daily. Reservations advised. MasterCard and Visa accepted. 4569 Laclede Ave., in Central West End (phone: 361-6911). Inexpensive.

Uncle Bill's Pancake and Dinner House – A 24-hour place popular for its enormous, fluffy, home-cooked omelettes and gigantic burgers. A huge menu featuring breakfast, lunch, and dinner selections. Quick service. Closed Mondays. No reservations or credit cards accepted. 3427 S. Kingshighway (phone: 832-1973). Inexpensive.

SALT LAKE CITY

AT-A-GLANCE

SEEING THE CITY: From the top of Capitol Hill, you can look out over the whole city. For a less panoramic view, try the horse-drawn carriages through downtown Salt Lake City. Rates for one to six people are $25 for 30 minutes, $35 for 45 minutes, and $50 for 1 hour, and carriages will pick customers up anywhere in the downtown area. Contact *Carriage Connection*, 209 N. 400 West (phone: 484-7433).

SPECIAL PLACES: Salt Lake City's grid pattern is simplicity itself. Everything radiates from Temple Square. For example: 18 blocks south is 18th South, 5 blocks west is 5th West. Most of the city's attractions are within walking distance, except for the lake and the university.

CENTRAL CITY

Temple Square – The logical place to start a tour of the city, as it's the heart of the worldwide Mormon church. Enclosed within a 15-foot wall, the 10 acres of Temple Square's grounds draw about 4 million visitors a year. Within the grounds are the Salt Lake Temple, a granite structure that took 40 years to build; the dome-shape, acoustically perfect Tabernacle, home of the *Mormon Tabernacle Choir;* and an information center, where you can join any one of many free, daily guided tours. Public recitals on the great Tabernacle organ are held every day at noon. *Tabernacle Choir* rehearsals are open to the public on Thursday evenings. Organ recitals and choir rehearsals are free (phone: 240-2534).

Church Office Building – Across the street at Temple Square East is Utah's tallest structure, the Church Office Building, housing the general offices of the Church of Jesus Christ of Latter-Day Saints.

Family History Library – Formerly the Genealogical Library, it is used by thousands of people daily. It houses the world's largest genealogical collection, parish registers, biographies, and so on; chances are you or your ancestors are listed. Members of the staff will be happy to help you find out. Open Mondays from 7:30 AM to 6 PM, Tuesdays through Fridays from 7:30 AM to 10 PM, and Saturdays from 7:30 AM to 5 PM. 35 NW Temple (phone: 240-2331).

Museum of Church History and Art – This new building houses art exhibits and Mormon memorabilia. Open 9 AM to 9 PM weekdays, 10 AM to 7 PM weekends. There is no admission charge. 45 NW Temple (phone: 240-3310).

Beehive House – Built by Brigham Young as his official residence in 1854, *Beehive House* is now a museum run by the church. It was the first governor's mansion and is open Mondays through Saturdays from 9:30 AM to 4:30 PM; Sundays from 10 AM to 1 PM. Closed *Thanksgiving, Christmas,* and *New Year's Day.* The patriarch himself is buried half a block northeast in a quiet park. No admission charge. 67 E. South Temple St. (phone: 240-2671).

Capitol Hill – Capitol Hill contains the capitol, *Pioneer Museum,* and Council Hall, all within easy reach. The granite and marble capitol is a

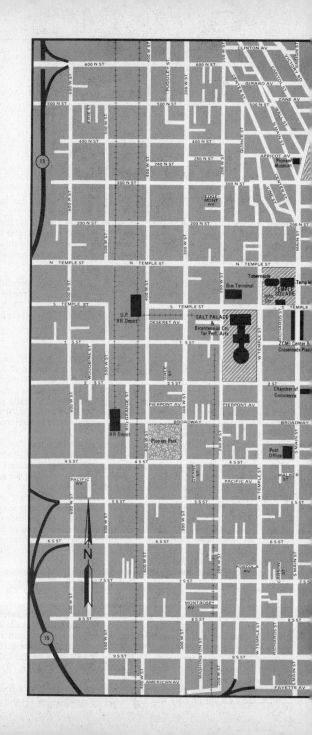

CENTRAL
SALT LAKE CITY

MEMORY PARK

DE SOTO ST
CORTEZ ST
GIRARD AV
E CAPITOL ST
BONNEVILLE BLVD
A ST
B ST
8 AV
C ST
8 AV
E ST
8 AV
F ST
8 AV
G ST
8 AV
H ST
8 AV
I ST
8 AV

PITH (VALLEY HILL)
State Office Bldg.
E CAPITOL ST
7 AV
D ST
7 AV
F ST
7 AV
H ST
7 AV
I ST
7 AV

State Capitol
6 AV
D ST
6 AV
F ST
6 AV
H ST
6 AV

Council Hall
Utah Travel Council
L SIDE AV
5 AV
A ST
5 AV
C ST
5 AV
E ST
5 AV
G ST
5 AV

4 AV
A ST
4 AV
B ST
4 AV
D ST
4 AV
E ST
4 AV
G ST
4 AV
H ST
4 AV

Church
Office Bldg.
3 AV
B ST
3 AV
D ST
3 AV
H ST
3 AV

N STATE ST
2 AV
A ST
C ST
2 AV
E ST
2 AV
G ST
2 AV

1 AV
A ST
1 AV
B ST
1 AV
D ST
1 AV
H ST
1 AV

Brigham Young Grave
Cath. of the Madeleine
Utah Hist. Soc. (Now Gov's Mansion)

S TEMPLE ST

Planetarium
SOCIAL HALL AV
ALAMEDA AV
6 EST

to University of Utah 3 miles:
Pioneer Memorial Theater,
Museum of Natural History,
Babcock Theater,
Museum of Fine Arts,
Museum of Earth Sciences

15 ST
3 E ST
15 ST
4 E ST
1 ST
5 E ST
7 E ST
BUENO AV

Federal Bldg.
HEATHER ST
S STATE ST
EDISON ST
2 E ST
2 S ST
2 S ST
S ST

BROADWAY
4 E ST
HORICHON ST
HAZEL ST
BROADWAY

3 E ST
4 S ST
4 S ST
4 S ST
4 S ST

Hall of Justice
Public Safety Bldg.
BLAIR ST
DENVER ST
5 E ST
HAZEL ST
PARK ST
GREEN ST
7 E ST

City Hall & Library
S STATE ST
5 S ST
3 E ST
STANTON AV
4 E ST
5 S ST
TROLLEY SQUARE
HAWTHORNE AV
HAWTHORNE AV
6 S ST
6 S ST
6 S ST
7 E ST

EDISON ST
2 E ST
COLFAX AV
IVERSON ST
COTTAGE AV
SEGO AV
5 E ST
PARK ST
LAKE ST

7 S ST
4 E ST
DENVER ST
7 S ST
6 E ST
7 S ST

LOWELL AV
DENVER ST
PARK ST

S STATE ST
EDISON ST
2 E ST
725 E ST
ROBERT ST
3 E ST
BLAIR ST
8 S ST
4 E ST
8 S ST
DENVER ST
8 S ST
5 E ST
GREEN ST
8 S ST
LAKE ST
8 S ST

To Pioneer Trail
State Park 4½ miles

9 S ST
2 E ST
9 S ST
4 E ST
9 S ST
DENVER ST
9 S ST
LIBERTY PARK

HUBBARD AV
BELMONT AV
BELMONT AV

splendid piece of Corinthian architecture, and it houses many exhibitions of Utah products and art. Council Hall, across the street to the south, was moved to the hill stone by stone and now houses the Utah Travel Council, where you can pick up brochures and maps (see *Sources and Resources;* phone: 538-1030). *Daughters of the Utah Pioneers Museum,* west of the capitol, has one of the most complete collections of pioneer relics in the West. Open Mondays through Saturdays from 9 AM to 5 PM; Sundays in June, July, and August from 1 to 5 PM; closed on major holidays. Donations accepted. 300 N. Main St. (phone: 538-1050).

Salt Palace and Salt Lake County Center for the Performing Arts – Almost anything goes on at the 28,000-seat *Salt Palace* — conventions, sports events, rock concerts (100 S. West Temple; phone: 363-7681 or 534-6370). The *Salt Lake County Arts Center* and a concert hall are on the same grounds. The *Capitol Theater,* a restored vaudeville playhouse and home of *Ballet West,* is nearby (50 W. 200th South; phone: 538-2253).

ZCMI Center and Crossroads Plaza – Returning to tree-lined Main Street, you'll find two of the largest downtown covered shopping malls in the West. The *ZCMI Center,* on the east side of the street (15 S. Main St.), has over 60 stores inside, some of which serve old-fashioned refreshments like phosphates and iron port (made with a shot of every soda flavor). Across the street to the west is the *Crossroads Plaza,* with 70 stores, numerous theaters, and fast-food eateries. 18 S. Main St.

MID-CITY

South Temple – Start at the Cathedral of the Madeleine, a Roman Gothic church completed in 1909, which has a beautiful series of German stained glass windows (331 E. South Temple). Farther along the street are dozens of exquisite old mansions built by mining magnates at the turn of the century. One of them, the marble, stone, and wood Governor's Mansion, has been restored and is at 603 E. South Temple.

Trolley Square – This interesting square has won national acclaim as a restoration project. Ingeniously rebuilt in abandoned trolley barns, this collection of shops, theaters, restaurants, and boutiques attracts a fascinating stream of people. Wandering artists and troubadors entertain in the turn-of-the-century entries and courtyards. Open daily. 5th South and 7th East Sts. (phone: 521-9877).

Liberty Park – Three blocks south on 7th East is 80-acre Liberty Park, with bowers, picnic areas, tennis and horseshoe courts, a swimming pool, a playground, the Tracy Aviary, an amusement park, and a boating center. 1302 South and 900 East Sts. (phone: 972-6714).

EMIGRATION CANYON

Pioneer Trail State Park – "This is the place," Brigham Young said when he and his entourage caught their first glimpse of the Valley of the Great Salt Lake. And this is where you'll now find Pioneer Trail State Park, with 12 renovated buildings from pioneer times, including the Brigham Young Farm Home and the Social Hall. This is also the site of This Is The Place Monument and visitors' center, with audio-visual exhibits showing the Mormon trek from Illinois to Utah. Tours of the buildings are available. The park is open daily except on *Martin Luther King Day, Presidents' Day, Thanksgiving, Christmas,* and *New Year's Day.* Guided tours through homes from *Memorial Day* weekend through *Labor Day* weekend only. Hours vary; call in advance (phone: 584-8391). Emigration Canyon, 2601 Sunnyside Ave.

GREAT SALT LAKE

Great Salt Lake – The most important natural feature of the region, the 73-mile-long lake is marshy, salty, sticky, and warm. As you approach it, it may look like nothing more than marshes and weird salt flats. Runoff causing the lake waters to rise and the beaches to flood was a major problem until 1987, when the state of Utah began pumping lake water out to the desert. Beaches have been constructed and the boat harbor at Great Salt Lake State Park (at the southern end of the lake) was saved. The rising waters have diluted the salt concentration, so while floating is still a unique experience, it's not the fantasy it once was. The water tastes awful and stings terribly if it gets in your eyes, so don't splash. We warn you, too, that the brine flies are sometimes ferocious. Showers, food, and sailboat and paddleboat rentals are available. 17 miles west on US 40, I-80.

■ **EXTRA SPECIAL:** The 848,000-acre Wasatch National Forest is one of the busiest forests in the country. In the High Uintas Primitive Area, it is full of mountain lakes, rugged spruce, dramatic canyons, and mountain peaks as high as 13,400 feet. The Utah State Fish and Game Department operates a winter elk feeding ground at *Hardware Ranch* in Logan (phone: 245-3131). There are camping and picnic grounds at Little Cottonwood and Big Cottonwood canyons, picnicking only in Mill Creek. Call the Salt Lake Ranger Station for information (phone: 524-5042). Those closest to the city are the most crowded. Hunting conditions are excellent here. Deer, elk, and moose can be hunted in the fall. A variety of trout swim the streams. Call the Utah Division of Wildlife Resources: 538-4700 for general information; 596-8660 for recorded fishing and wildlife viewing information; 530-1297 for recorded hunting information. In winter, skiers flock to Alta, 25 miles southeast of the city on Route 210; Brighton, 27 miles southeast on Route 152; and Snowbird, in Gad Valley, 2 miles from Alta (see *Sports*). To get to the eastern section of Wasatch, take US 40, and Routes 152, 210; to reach the northern part, follow US 89 and 91. For further information, contact the Supervisor's Office, Wasatch-Cache National Forests (125 S. State St., Salt Lake City 84138; phone: 524-5030 for campground information; 364-1581 for avalanche information).

SOURCES AND RESOURCES

TOURIST INFORMATION: For brochures and maps, write, call, or visit the Salt Lake City Convention and Visitors Bureau (180 S. West Temple, Salt Lake City, UT 84161; phone: 521-2863). For additional information on Salt Lake City and the state of Utah, contact the Utah Travel Council (Council Hall, Capitol Hill, Salt Lake City, UT 84114; phone: 538-1030). Information centers also are at Salt Lake City International Airport and Great Salt Lake State Park. For information on winter skiing and summer recreation, call 521-8102. Contact the Utah state hotline (801-538-1030) for maps, calendars of events, health updates, and travel advisories.

The best guide to Salt Lake City is the *Salt Lake Visitor's Guide,* a free magazine available from the convention and visitors bureau.

Local Coverage – *Salt Lake Tribune,* morning daily; *Deseret News,* evening daily; *Utah Holiday,* monthly magazine.

Television Stations – KUTV Channel 2–NBC; KTVX Channel 4–ABC; KSL Channel 5–CBS; KUED Channel 7–PBS; KBYU Channel 11–PBS; KSTU Channel 13–FOX; and KXIV Channel 14–Independent.

Radio Stations – AM: KALL 910 (adult contemporary music); KSOP 1370 (country); KSUN 1490 (news/talk). FM: KISN 97.1 (adult contemporary); KCPX 98.7 (top 40); KLVV 99.5 (adult contemporary); KSOP 104.3 (country).

Food – The *Dessert News* carries restaurant reviews and listings each Friday evening.

 TELEPHONE: The area code for Salt Lake City is 801.
  Sales Tax – The sales tax is 6.25%; hotel room tax is 3%.

 CLIMATE: Wintertime is for skiing. Spring is beautiful but fickle, with apricot blossoms sometimes covered in snow. Summer is hot and dry, with temperatures climbing into the 90s. Fall is gorgeous, especially in the nearby canyons.

 GETTING AROUND: Airport – Salt Lake City International Airport is a 15- to 20-minute ride from downtown; taxi fare should run $9 to $11. *Utah Transit Authority* buses run hourly from the airport terminals into the city center for 50¢. Special *Downtowner* buses run from the airport to downtown hotels on a regular basis.

Bus – For information on bus schedules in and around Salt Lake, call *Utah Transit Authority* (phone: 287-4636).

Car Rental – All major firms are represented; an inexpensive local alternative is *Payless Rent-a-Car* (1974 W. North Temple; phone: 596-2596 or 800-327-3631).

Taxi – The best way to get a cab is to call *Yellow Cab* (phone: 521-2100).

Trolley – An old-fashioned trolley circles the downtown area and major hotels, with pickup points at Trolley Square and Temple Square. Fare is 50¢. Contact the *Utah Transit Authority* (phone: 287-4636).

 VITAL SERVICES: Audiovisual Equipment – *Audio-Visual Services* (phone: 484-3344); *Inkley's Audio-Visual* (phone: 486-5985).

Business Services – *Aztec Typing Service,* 211 E. 3rd South (phone: 364-6806).

Dry Cleaner/Tailor – *Vogue Cleaners,* 906 S. 200 West, and other downtown locations (phone: 363-2627).

Limousine – *Presidential Limousine* (phone: 571-7737 or 800-674-2315).

Mechanic – *Andy Stevens Automotive,* 458 Montague Ave. (phone: 328-9222).

Medical Emergency – *LDS Hospital,* 8th Ave. and C St. (phone: 321-1180).

Messenger Services – *Pony Express Courier Services* (phone: 486-4906).

National/International Courier – *Federal Express* (phone: 800-238-3355); *DHL Worldwide Courier Express* (phone: 800-225-5345).

Pharmacy – *Smith's Food King Pharmacy,* open 9 AM to 10 PM Mondays through Saturdays; 10 AM to 6 PM Sundays, 402 6th Ave. (phone: 355-4617).

Photocopies – *Alpha Graphics* (122 S. Main St.; phone: 364-8451); *Aztec Copy* (205 E. 3rd South; phone: 364-6806).

Post Office – The central office is located at 230 W. 2nd South (phone: 530-5902).

Professional Photographer – *Dave Newman Photography* (phone: 272-8221); *Bill Shipler Photo* (phone: 582-3821).

Secretary/Stenographer – *Aztec Copy* (phone: 364-6806); the *Office Works* (phone: 350-9050).

Teleconference Facilities – *Salt Lake Hilton; Salt Lake Marriott* (see *Best in Town,* below).

Translator – *Foreign Translators & Interpreters* (phone: 485-8781); *Bilingual Services* (phone: 467-2766).

Typewriter Rental – The public library has typewriters available for 1 hour's use only, 2nd East and 5th South, second floor (phone: 363-5733).

Western Union/Telex – Many offices are located around the city (phone: 800-325-6000).

 SPECIAL EVENTS: In April and October, thousands of Mormons from all over the world converge on Temple Square for the conferences of the LDS Church. On July 24, Salt Lake City celebrates *Pioneer Day,* marking the arrival of the Mormon pioneers. Also in July, the *Japanese Obon Festival* is held at the Buddhist temple (211 W. 1st South). In September, the *Greek Festival* takes place at the Hellenic Memorial Building (279 S. 300 West). For information on other special events, call 521-2822.

 MUSEUMS: *Beehive House* is described under *Special Places.* *Hansen Planetarium* features exhibitions on astronomy and natural sciences, along with astronomy shows (phone: 538-2098). On the University of Utah campus are the *Utah Museum of Natural History* (phone: 581-6927) and the *Utah Museum of Fine Arts* (phone: 581-7332). Other notable museums are the *Salt Lake Arts Center* (20 S. West Temple; phone: 328-4201) and the *Museum of Church History and Art* (45 N. West Temple; phone: 240-3310).

 MAJOR COLLEGES AND UNIVERSITIES: The University of Utah campus has several theaters, a special events center, and two museums (see *Museums,* above). The university enrolls 25,-000 students. Between 14th East and 20th East, 1st South and 5th South (phone: 581-7200).

 SPORTS AND FITNESS: Baseball – The minor league Salt Lake *Trappers* play from mid-June to *Labor Day* at *Derks Field,* 65 W. 1300 South (phone: 484-9900).

Basketball – The NBA Utah *Jazz* play in the *Salt Palace,* 1st SW Temple (phone: 363-7681). Tickets usually sell out quickly, so try to reserve well in advance.

Fishing, Hunting, Camping, Backpacking, River Running – At Wasatch-Cache National Forest (phone: 524-5030), you can fish, hunt, camp, and backpack (see *Extra Special*). For hunting and fishing regulations, contact the Utah Division of Wildlife Resources (1596 W. North Temple; phone: 596-8660). For information on backpacking, river running, and primitive wilderness areas in general, call the Bureau of Land Management Office of Public Affairs (324 S. State St.; phone: 539-4001).

Fitness Centers – The *Deseret Gym* has a pool, sauna, steamroom, track, Nautilus exercise rooms, plus basketball, racquetball, and squash courts (161 N. Main; phone: 359-3911). *Sports Mall Metro* features a track, sauna, exercise equipment, aerobics, Nautilus, and classes, in addition to tennis, squash, racquetball, handball, and basketball courts (*Crossroads Plaza,* near the *Marriott;* phone: 328-3116).

Golf – There are 8 public courses in the Salt Lake Valley. The best is *Mountain Dell* (phone: 582-3812), in Parley's Canyon.

Hockey – The Salt Lake *Golden Eagles* (minor league) play at the *Salt Palace* (phone: 363-7681 for information, or 521-6120 for tickets).

Ice Skating and Sleigh Riding – *Bountiful Recreation Center* (150 W. 6th North, Bountiful; phone: 298-6120) for ice skating year-round, or *Triad Center* outdoor ice rink (350 W. South Temple, November through March; phone: 575-5423). *Sugarhouse Park* (21 S. 16th East; phone: 467-1721) for sleigh riding.

Jogging – Run in Memory Grove Park, half a mile from downtown, or in Liberty Park (1-mile perimeter), about 2 miles from downtown.

Skiing – Utah, "America's choice" for a *1998 Winter Olympics* bid, claims to have the "Greatest Snow on Earth," and downhill and cross-country skiers from all over the world enthusiastically attest to its excellence. The season runs from mid-November to May or June. For a recorded ski report, call 521-8102. The major ski resorts within half an hour's drive of Salt Lake City are the following:

Alta – The granddaddy of them all, in Little Cottonwood Canyon, has the best and most consistent snow conditions. 25 miles southeast of the city on Rte. 210 (phone: 742-3333).

Brighton – At the top of Big Cottonwood Canyon. The average annual snowfall here is 430 inches. 27 miles southeast on Rte. 152 (phone: 943-8309).

Deer Valley – Utah's newest and most stylish ski resort, where the number of skiers is limited, making for short lift lines. Reservations advised. 2 miles south of *Park City* (phone: 649-1000; 649-2000 for ski conditions).

Park City – The US ski team's national training center, with the longest night-skiing run in the nation. 20 miles east on I-80, up Parley's Canyon (phone: 649-8111 or 649-2000 for ski conditions).

Park West – The proposed site of the *1998 Olympic* freestyle events, 3 miles from Park City, is a favorite among local skiers. 4000 Park W. Dr., Park City (phone: 649-5400).

Snowbird – Also in Little Cottonwood Canyon, *Snowbird* is a jet set resort, with a spectacular tram lift to Hidden Peaks at 11,000 feet. The lift runs in summer, too. Gad Valley, 2 miles from *Alta* (phone: 521-6040).

Solitude – This Big Cottonwood Canyon resort favored by local skiers has new high-speed quad lifts and a Nordic center for cross-country skiing (phone: 534-1400).

Swimming – Beaches are open at the Great Salt Lake. Take I-80 west of town. For freshwater swimming try the *Raging Waters,* a huge aquatic park at 1200 W. 1700 South (phone: 973-9900).

Tennis – There are 17 parks in the city with tennis courts. The most popular are the 16 courts (14 lighted) at Liberty Park. Lessons are available spring and summer only (phone: 596-5036). The University of Utah has quite a few outdoor public courts.

THEATER: The *Pioneer Theater Company* on the University of Utah campus is an important regional theater featuring Equity actors in leading roles. The *Babcock Theater,* in the same building, stages more intimate productions (phone: 581-6961 for both). Downtown, the *Salt Lake Acting Company* produces lively drama (168 W. 500 North; phone: 363-0525). *Salt Lake Repertory Theatre* produces large-scale musical comedy shows (148 S. Main St.; phone: 532-6000). *Ballet West, Ririe-Woodbury Dance Company,* and *Repertory Dance Theater* perform at *Symphony Hall* and the *Capitol Theater.* Check local listings for other groups.

MUSIC: Salt Lake City has many concerts and dance events. For information, call 363-7681. The *Mormon Tabernacle Choir* rehearsals are open to the public on Thursday evenings (Temple Sq.). No admission charge. The *Utah Symphony Orchestra* performs at *Symphony Hall* and the *Capitol Theater.* Big-name rock and country artists perform at the *Salt Palace* (100 S. West Temple; phone: 363-7681).

NIGHTCLUBS AND NIGHTLIFE: *Room at the Top* in the *Salt Lake Hilton* (150 W. 5th South; phone: 532-3344) has a piano bar and fine food. The *Zephyr* (301 S. West Temple; phone: 355-9913) features live jazz and blues. More comfortable but less trendy is Salt Lake City's oldest private club, *D. B. Cooper's* (19 E. 200 South; phone: 532-2948). Utah liquor laws require that tourists buy a 2-week membership ($5) for clubs, which entitles you to bring four friends.

BEST IN TOWN

CHECKING IN: Since more than 10 million people a year visit Utah, it's logical to expect a decent selection of hotels in Salt Lake City. You won't be disappointed. Tourism is Utah's largest single industry, and accommodations are plentiful and varied. Expect to pay between $60 and $110 for a double room in those places we've listed as expensive; between $45 and $60 for those we've designated as moderate; and between $35 and $45 in inexpensive places. All telephone numbers are in the 801 area code unless otherwise indicated.

Inn at Temple Square – Formerly the *Temple Square* hotel, this recently refurbished establishment has a posh, old English atmosphere, rich tapestry fabrics, and mahogany furnishings. Meals are served in the *Carriage Court* restaurant, and there is a complimentary breakfast buffet. Its 90 rooms are all equipped with refrigerators, and suites come with Jacuzzis in oversize tubs. A bakery and ice cream parlor located downstairs are perfect spots to stop and snack. Free local phone calls and transportation to the airport. Room service is available until 10 PM. There are 3 meeting rooms, as well as A/V equipment, CNN, and photocopiers. 71 W. South Temple (phone: 531-1000; Fax: 801-536-7272). Expensive.

Little America – On the city's main thoroughfare, within walking distance of the downtown shopping area and *Convention Center,* this 850-room hotel has year-round swimming in an indoor-outdoor pool, plus another outdoor pool, wading pool, saunas, and weight-lifting room. Children under 12 stay free. Room service will deliver until midnight. Additional amenities include a concierge desk, 14 meeting rooms, A/V equipment, photocopiers, CNN, express checkout, and free bus service to the airport. 500 S. Main St. (phone: 363-6781 or 800-453-9450; Fax: 801-322-1610). Expensive.

Salt Lake Hilton – Exuding an aura of contemporary sophistication, this 351-room property has suites with sunken baths; there is an outdoor swimming pool, therapy pool, sauna, 3 dining rooms, and 1 nightclub. A package store on the premises sells liquor. Pets are welcome. Room service can be summoned until 11 PM. Both concierge and secretarial services are at guests' disposal, as well as A/V equipment, photocopiers, computers, CNN, and express checkout for guests staying on the concierge floor. 150 W. 5th South (phone: 532-3344 or 800-HILTONS; Fax: 801-532-3344, ext. 1029). Expensive.

Salt Lake Marriott – With 515 rooms, it has 2 restaurants, a lounge, an indoor pool, saunas, a liquor store, and direct access to the *Crossroads Mall.* Guests have privileges at an adjoining health spa for racquetball, squash, and tennis. Room service will arrive up to midnight. Business amenities include 17 meeting rooms, concierge and secretarial services, photocopiers, computers, A/V equipment, CNN, and express checkout. The 16-story structure is opposite the *Salt Palace* on the corner of West Temple and 1st South (phone: 531-0800 or 800-228-9290; Fax: 801-532-4127). Expensive.

Best Western Olympus – Formerly the *Tri-Arc,* this 13-story high-rise, built in an unusual arc, affords a view of the valley from every one of the 380 rooms. The panoramic view from the top floor is spectacular. Amenities include satellite TV and an outdoor pool. The *13th Floor Supper Club* and the *Café Olympus* restaurants are popular with residents (open daily). Around-the-clock room service is offered. There also are 15 meeting rooms, A/V equipment, photocopiers, CNN, and express checkout. Children under 14 stay free. 161 W. 6th South (phone: 521-7373; Fax: 801-524-0354). Moderate.

Carlton – A small (56 rooms), older place in the downtown area, it has a refrigerator and recliner in each room, plus sauna, Jacuzzi, and small exercise room. Other amenities include a complimentary breakfast (cooked to order), VCRs, and a film library through which visitors can browse. Room service, available only for breakfast, can be ordered until 11 AM. There alos are 3 small meeting rooms and CNN. 140 E. South Temple (phone: 355-3418 or 800-633-3500). Moderate.

Peery – The city's oldest, it is small (just 77 rooms) but elegant, with the charm of the early 1900s. Amenities include an outstanding café, complimentary continental breakfast, newspaper, shoeshine, Jacuzzi, and exercise room. There are 2 restaurants. Room service will respond until 10:30 PM. There's a concierge desk, as well as 4 meeting rooms, secretarial services, A/V equipment, CNN, photocopiers, and free airport transportation. 110 W. 3rd South (phone: 521-4300; Fax: 801-575-5014). Moderate.

Comfort Inn–Salt Lake Airport/International Center – Conveniently located just 7 miles from downtown and 2½ miles from the airport, it has 156 rooms (some of which do not allow smoking) and 4 executive suites. Other features: remote-control color TV sets, a heated pool (open in season), a hot tub (open year-round), a restaurant serving 3 meals daily, and complimentary coffee in the lobby. Room service is available when the restaurant is open. There are 2 meeting rooms, limited secretarial services, A/V equipment, photocopiers, and CNN. 200 N. Admiral Byrd Rd. (phone: 537-7444 or 800-535-8742; Fax: 801-532-4721). Inexpensive.

TraveLodge Salt Palace – Within walking distance of downtown, it features 130 rooms, an outdoor pool open year-round, a sauna, a whirlpool bath, and complimentary shuttle to the airport. Kids under 12 free. Additional conveniences are photocopiers, 1 meeting room, and express checkout. 215 W. North Temple (phone: 532-1000 or 800-255-3050). Inexpensive.

◼ EATING OUT: Salt Lake Valley restaurants offer a number of different cuisines, from continental to seafood, steaks, and chops. Expect to pay between $40 and $50 for two at those places we've listed as expensive; between $20 and $35 at those places designated moderate; under $20, inexpensive. Prices do not include drinks, wine, or tips. All telephone numbers are in the 801 area code unless otherwise indicated.

Special note: In a major concession to the tourist trade, Utah's liquor laws were revised in 1991. The old practice of "brown bagging," where customers brought their own alcohol to a restaurant, has been eliminated, as has the dispensing of mini bottles of liquor by dining establishments. Patrons can now imbibe after 1 PM, and there are twice as many restaurant liquor licenses available.

La Caille at Quail Run – One of Utah's finest dining spots, in a château (styled as an 18th-century French maison) a few miles from the city, serves food commensurate with its well-appointed surroundings. The dining room, overlooking the formal gardens of the estate, features French cooking and a popular Sunday brunch. Open daily for dinner, Sundays for brunch. Reservations necessary. Major credit cards accepted. 9565 Wasatch Blvd. (phone: 942-1751). Expensive.

La Fleur de Lys – A downtown place featuring traditional French food in an elegant, unhurried atmosphere. Open from 5:30 to 10 PM; closed Sundays. Reservations necessary. Major credit cards accepted. 165 S. West Temple, in Arrow Press Square (phone: 359-5753). Expensive.

Market Street Grill – A popular gathering spot, especially at lunchtime, it's in a handsomely renovated old building. The menu features fresh seafood (flown in daily) as well as steaks, prime ribs, and lamb. There's also an oyster bar (a private club; i.e., it serves liquor but you must buy a membership for $5). Open daily. No reservations. Major credit cards accepted. 60 Post Office Pl. (phone: 322-4668; oyster bar, 531-6044). Moderate.

Windows on the Square – In *Weinstock's* department store, it offers basic American food, good family atmosphere, and an unbeatable view of Temple Square (ask for a window seat). Open 11 AM every day except *Thanksgiving* and *Christmas;* closing times vary with store hours. Reservations unnecessary. Major credit cards accepted. In the *Crossroads Mall* (phone: 524-2677). Moderate.

Lamb's – In business since the early 1900s, this old-fashioned downtown eatery has become an institution. This is where the city's power brokers power lunch. A surprisingly extensive menu, good seafood. Open daily except Sundays from 7 AM to 9 PM. Reservations unnecessary. Major credit cards accepted. 169 S. Main St. (phone: 364-7166). Moderate to inexpensive.

Bird's Café – Pleasant dining, casual decor. Fresh fish, pasta, beef, and lamb are served with deft and tempting touches. Open for lunch and dinner daily; brunch only on Sundays. Reservations unnecessary. Major credit cards accepted. 1355 E. 21st South (phone: 466-1051). Inexpensive.

Café Pierpont – A south-of-the-border restaurant that caters to families, near downtown in a renovated old school. Try the fajitas or the huge mesquite-broiled T-bone. Open for lunch weekdays, for dinner daily. No reservations. Major credit cards accepted. 122 W. Pierpont (phone: 364-1222). Inexpensive.

Marianne's Delicatessen – For fans of German specialties, from homemade sausages to scrumptious desserts. Besides brimming delicacies to go, there are hot specials and a long list of sandwiches. Be prepared for a bit of a wait if you arrive between noon and 1 PM. Open Tuesdays through Saturdays for lunch from 11 AM to 3 PM; deli open 9 AM to 6 PM. No reservations. Major credit cards accepted. 149 W. 2nd South (phone: 364-0513). Inexpensive.

Old Spaghetti Factory – One of the more popular inexpensive eating places in town, it has lots of friendly ambience. You may find yourself surrounded by memorabilia and dining on an old brass bed or in a trolley car, with turn-of-the-century furnishings. Spaghetti comes in all styles, but try the clam sauce. Open daily. No reservations. Visa and MasterCard accepted. 189 Trolley Square (phone: 521-0424). Inexpensive.

SAN ANTONIO

AT-A-GLANCE

 SEEING THE CITY: The Tower of the Americas, San Antonio's most visible landmark, at 750 feet, offers the best vantage point from which to view the city and the surrounding countryside. From the revolving observation deck you see flatland stretching to the south and gently rolling hills to the northwest, leading to the Texas Hill Country. Directly below are the buildings of HemisFair Plaza, the site of the *1968 World's Fair,* and a tributary of the San Antonio River that cuts a horseshoe path through town and branches into HemisFair Plaza and *Rivercenter Mall.*

SPECIAL PLACES: The heart of San Antonio is great for walking, with the lovely Paseo del Río (River Walk) tracing the course of the river, and short distances between many of the attractions. Visitors can also take a slow-paced, horse-drawn carriage tour of downtown and the King William District. Carriages are available daily, from 10 AM to about 10 PM, and leave from the Alamo. Or, catch a 10¢ ride between the Alamo and Market Square aboard one of the trolleys operated by the public transportation system. Jump on 1 block south of the Alamo at the corner of Commerce and Alamo Streets. Other sights, including the missions along Mission Trail and the zoo, are best reached by car or bus.

CENTRAL CITY

The Alamo – Where Davy Crockett, Col. James Bowie, Col. Travis, and the 186 other Texas heroes fought against Mexican dictator Santa Anna and his force of 5,000 in Texas's 1836 struggle for independence. Established in 1718 by Spanish priests as the San Antonio de Valero Mission, the original mission has been restored and the site turned into a block-square state park that includes a museum with displays on the Alamo and Texas history, with an excellent weapon collection featuring derringers, swords, and an original bowie knife. Open daily. No admission charge. Alamo Plaza (phone: 225-1391). After visiting the Alamo, it's easy stroll along the Paseo del Río, which now reaches the west side of S. Alamo Street, directly across from the park; the steps from street level are bounded by a series of waterfalls that lead to the *Hyatt* hotel.

La Villita – This little Spanish town in the center of the city looks very much as it did 250 years ago, when it was San Antonio's first residential area. Girded by a stone wall and surrounded by banana palms and bougainvillea, the stone patios and adobe dwellings have been authentically restored and now house artisans' shops where many of the old crafts — glass blowing, weaving, dollmaking, and pottery — still are practiced. Among the buildings are the restored Cos House (1835), where General Cos, commander of the Mexican forces, surrendered to the Texians; and the *Old San Antonio Museum,* featuring displays on Texas history and pleasant outdoor cafés. Open daily. No admission charge. One square city block bounded by the river on the north, Nueva St. on the south, S. Alamo St. on the east, and Villita St. on the west. Main office, 418 Villita St. (phone: 299-8610).

Paseo del Río – A branch of the San Antonio River winds like a horseshoe through the central business district. Stone stairways lead down to the River Walk which, only 20 feet below street level, is as far from the world of the business district as you can get. Tall trees, tropical foliage, and banana palms line the walks, stretching 21 blocks, dotted with curio and crafts shops, night spots and cafés, and an increasing number of fashionable apartments. You can experience the 1½-mile-long section of river on a barge and, on some, dine aboard by candlelight. Make arrangements through the barge office, 430 E. Commerce St. (phone: 222-1701).

HemisFair Plaza and Urban Water Park – A legacy of the *1968 World's Fair,* HemisFair Plaza features the Tower of the Americas with its panoramic view of Texas countryside, a *Convention Center,* the *Lila M. Cockrell Theater for the Performing Arts,* shops, and several modern buildings that have exhibitions. The Institute of Texan Cultures examines the influence of 26 different ethnic groups — including the Mexicans, Germans, Polish, Hungarians, and Irish — who developed the state. There are films, slide shows, and exhibitions of artifacts including Mexican stone cooking equipment and examples of the dress of each of the groups. Closed Mondays. No admission charge. 801 S. Bowie St. (phone: 226-7651).

San Antonio Museum of Art – Rapidly gaining recognition as one of the Southwest's best museums, *SAMA* occupies the buildings that once housed the Lone Star Brewery Company. Its most recently acquired permanent display is Con Cariño (with affection), a Mexican folk art collection. Nelson A. Rockefeller's extensive private collection comprises the bulk of Con Cariño, reported to be the largest such collection in the US. Open daily. Admission charge. 200 W. Jones Ave. (phone: 226-5544).

El Mercado – Though the original marketplace has been renovated, it still is lined with Spanish buildings and retains its old market flavor, with Mexican merchants who do their best to lure you into shops offering handcrafted objects like baskets, piñatas, pottery, silver jewelry. Open daily. Market Square, 515 W. Commerce St. (phone: 299-8600).

Spanish Governor's Palace – The only Spanish colonial mansion remaining in Texas. Built in 1749 for the Spanish governors when Texas was a province of Spain, the palace has 3-foot-thick walls, a keystone above the door bearing the Hapsburg coat of arms, original Spanish furnishings, and a floor of native flagstone. Open daily. Admission charge. 105 Military Plaza (phone: 224-0601).

Hertzberg Circus Collection – If you're a circus fanatic, you'll go ring-crazy here with displays of over 20,000 artifacts tracing the development of the circus from its English origins to P. T. Barnum and the American three-ring extravaganza. Particularly strong in miniatures featuring the original carriage of Tom Thumb and an entire circus in one room. Closed Sundays. No admission charge. 210 W. Market St. in Library Annex (phone: 299-7810).

SOUTH SIDE

Missions – The Alamo was the first of five missions established under Spanish rule. All except the Alamo are still active parish churches and are located along the well-marked Mission Trail, starting at the southern tip of the city. The most notable to see are the following:

    Mission Concepción – Established in 1731, the oldest unrestored church in the country is nonetheless remarkably well preserved, with original frescoes painted by the padres and Indians using a mixture of vegetable and mineral dyes. Open daily. 807 Mission Rd. (phone: 229-5732).

    Mission San José – Called the Queen of the Missions, and established in 1720, it's the finest and largest example of early

CENTRAL
SAN ANTONIO

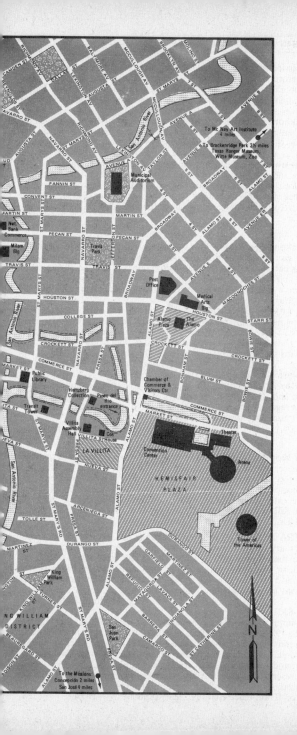

mission life. The original parish church, built of limestone and tufa, features Rosa's Window, an impressive stone carving, and is surrounded by a 6-acre compound including a restored mill, former Indian quarters, and a granary. Open daily. 6539 San José Dr., 6 miles south on US 281 (phone: 229-4770).

Buckhorn Hall of Horns and Texas Hall of History – Once an old shoot-'em-up saloon, *Buckhorn Hall* was transported lock, stock, and barrel by the Lone Star Brewing Company to tamer grounds. The collection is as wild as ever — some of the fastest guns in the West, and hunting trophies of everything imaginable from horns and antlers of elk, buffalo, and antelope to whole polar and grizzly bears. The *Texas Hall of History,* in an adjacent building, is a wax museum that features 14 dioramas of Wild West history. Open daily. Admission charge. 600 Lone Star Blvd. on the company's grounds (phone: 226-8301).

NORTH SIDE

Brackenridge Park – This 443-acre park includes the Southwest's largest zoo. Rock cliffs provide a backdrop for fine displays of animals in their natural settings. Over 3,000 specimens of 700 species are represented and best are Monkey Island, an outdoor hippo pool, open bear pits, and a children's zoo nursery. Open daily. Admission charge. 3903 N. St. Mary's (phone: 734-7183).

San Antonio Botanical Center – A living museum of diverse plant life, ranging from desert to tropical, is presented in lovely formal gardens on this 38-acre site near downtown. The gardens' centerpiece is the Lucile Halsell Conservatory, a 90,000-square-foot below-ground central courtyard surrounded by a complex of greenhouses. Open daily except Mondays from 9 AM to 6 PM; conservatory to 5 PM. Admission charge. 555 Funston (phone: 821-5115).

McNay Art Museum – Small but fine collections include works by Picasso and Chagall, among displays of international scope and exhibitions of regional artists. Closed Mondays. No admission charge. 6000 N. New Braunfels (phone: 824-5368).

WEST SIDE

Sea World of Texas – The world's largest marine entertainment showplace, on 250 acres of rolling hills 20 miles west of San Antonio. It features spectacular performances of killer whales, sea lions, and dolphins; professional water skiing and speed boat shows; concerts; and other events. Open daily *Memorial Day* through *Labor Day;* weekends only in fall and spring; closed in winter. Admission charge. 10500 Sea World Dr., reached by city bus service (phone: 523-3611).

■ **EXTRA SPECIAL:** The *Grey Moss Inn,* in Grey Forest, a wildlife sanctuary only a few minutes from downtown, offers outdoor dining on a shaded patio where you can have charcoal-broiled steaks, seafood, or chicken prepared on an open grill. Indoor dining centers around a fireplace (see *Eating Out*). Open daily for dinner only. Reservations strongly advised. Major credit cards accepted. Scenic Loop Rd., 12 miles from the Bandera Rd. Loop 410 Interchange (phone: 695-8301).

Dining aboard *The Texan,* a restored train with cars dating back to the 1930s, 1940s, and 1950s, is an expensive yet romantic adventure. The train makes a 3½-hour round trip to Hondo, 50 miles west of San Antonio, while passengers are served delicious meals in luxurious surroundings. Dining trips are made Wednesdays through Sundays, and reservations are necessary. The train departs the Southern Pacific Amtrak station in St. Paul Square near downtown at 1174 E. Commerce. Train office, 1000 N. Alamo (phone: 377-2900).

SOURCES AND RESOURCES

 TOURIST INFORMATION: General tourist information, brochures, maps, and events calendars are available at the San Antonio Convention and Visitors Bureau (121 Alamo Plaza, San Antonio, TX 78205; phone: 270-8700; or write: PO Box 2277, San Antonio, TX 78298). More convenient is the San Antonio Visitor Information Center, directly across from the Alamo (317 Alamo Plaza, San Antonio, TX 78205; phone: 299-8155). The *San Antonio Convention & Visitor's Guide* (free) is a good area guide. Contact the Texas state hotline (phone: 800-8888-TEX) for maps, calendars of events, health updates, and travel advisories.

Local Coverage – The *San Antonio Express-News,* morning and afternoon daily, and the *San Antonio Light,* morning and afternoon daily. Both papers are available at newsstands. Paseo del Río Association's *Reflexiónes* lists upcoming events and is available at the convention and visitors' bureau and in hotel lobbies.

Television Stations – KMOL Channel 4–NBC; KENS Channel 5–CBS; KLRN Channel 9–PBS; KSAT Channel 12–ABC.

Radio Stations – AM: KTSA 550 (pop music); KKYX 680 (country); WOAI 1200 (news/talk). FM: KCYY 100.3 (country); KQXT 102.7 (adult contemporary); KMIX 106.7 (adult contemporary).

TELEPHONE: The area code for San Antonio is 512.
Sales Tax – The sales tax is 8%; hotel room tax is 13%.

CLIMATE: Known as the place where "sunshine spends the winter," San Antonio winters are, naturally, sunny and mild with temperatures averaging above 50F. If you like hot weather, summers are blistering and humid, with temperatures over 90F and lots of sunshine except for an occasional tropical storm from the Gulf of Mexico.

GETTING AROUND: Airport – San Antonio International Airport is about a 15-minute drive from downtown; a taxi ride will run about $15. Buses run between the airport and downtown during certain hours in the morning and afternoon for 75¢; call *VIA Metropolitan Transit* (phone: 227-2020) for schedules. Limousine service is provided by most major hotels.

Bus – *San Antonio Metropolitan Transit System* serves all sections of the city. The basic fare is 40¢; second-zone (outside I-410) is an additional 10¢; and express buses are 75¢. Complete route and tourist information is available from the transit office, 800 W. Myrtle St. (phone: 227-2020).

Car Rental – All national firms are represented, but one of the best for the budget-minded is *Budget Rent-A-Car,* at San Antonio International Airport, 9245 John Saunders (phone: 828-5693).

River Taxi – The *Paseo del Rio* boat company operates a river taxi from hotels and various points along the river to the commercial center, $1.75 round-trip. They also offer a 45-minute boat tour during which a commentator describes the historical points of interest along the way. Admission is $1.75. Information: 430 E. Commerce, San Antonio, TX 78205 (phone: 222-1701).

Streetcar – Attractive reproductions of antique trolleys (on rubber wheels) follow five distinct tourist and traffic loops to and through major points of interest around the city. The fare is 10¢. Free maps are available from any visitors' center.

Taxi – Cabs may be ordered by phone or picked up at taxi stations in front of major hotels. Some will answer a hail in the street, most will not. Two of the largest companies are *Checker* (phone: 222-2151) and *Yellow* (phone: 226-4242).

 VITAL SERVICES: Audiovisual Equipment – *Donald L. Smith Co.* (phone: 224-2255); *AVW Audio Visual* (phone: 226-1376). **Baby-sitting** – *Northside Sitters Club,* 2500 Jackson Keller (phone: 341-9313).

Business Services – *Manpower Temporary Services,* 7550 I-10 West, Suite 300, in the Texas Commerce Building (phone: 342-2100).

Dry Cleaner/Tailor – *Famous Cleaners,* tuxedo rental, too, 1409 E. Commerce St. (phone: 227-16360).

Limousine – *Don's Limousine Service* (phone: 923-7556).

Mechanic – *American Car Care Center,* 400 S. Flores St. (phone: 226-4111).

Medical Emergency – *Baptist Memorial Hospital,* 111 Dallas St. (phone: 222-8431).

Messenger Services – *Consolidated Parcel Service* (phone: 654-4547); *Couriers of San Antonio* (phone: 225-8605).

National/International Courier – *Federal Express* (phone: 800-238-5355); *DHL Worldwide Courier Express* (phone: 800-225-5345).

Pharmacy – *Eckerd Drugs,* 24-hour prescription service, 6900 San Pedro Ave. (phone: 824-3237).

Photocopies – *Speedy Printing Service* (221 E. Travis St.; phone: 222-0341); *Minuteman Press* (110 Broadway; phone: 222-0002).

Post Office – The central office is located downtown at 615 E. Houston St. (phone: 227-3399).

Professional Photographer – *Dorothy Langmore, Inc.* (5800 Broadway; phone: 826-6300); *Frost & Associates* (phone: 734-2887).

Secretary/Stenographer – *HQ, Headquarters Company,* word processing, telex, fax machines, conference rooms (phone: 366-0366).

Teleconference Facilities – *Hilton Palacio del Río, Marriott on the River Walk, Plaza San Antonio, Sheraton Gunter, Marriott Rivercenter, Hyatt Regency* (see *Best in Town,* below).

Translator – *Berlitz* (phone: 681-7050); *Associated Translators and Interpreters* (phone: 691-1076).

Typewriter Rental – *American Typewriter & Office Equipment,* 1-week minimum (phone: 349-9026); *Executive Service Center,* 1-day minimum (phone: 349-3928).

Western Union/Telex – Many offices are located around the city (phone: 800-325-6000).

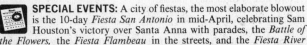 **SPECIAL EVENTS:** A city of fiestas, the most elaborate blowout is the 10-day *Fiesta San Antonio* in mid-April, celebrating Sam Houston's victory over Santa Anna with parades, the *Battle of the Flowers,* the *Fiesta Flambeau* in the streets, and the *Fiesta River Parade* with lighted floats on the river, a king and queen, and lots of food and drink for the subjects. The *Starving Artists Show* in early April has works of art by hungry local artists for nothing much more than $20; everyone is trying to make ends meet so he or she can eat at the fiesta. San Antonio celebrates the Mexican defeat of the French in the Battle of Puebla in true Mexican form during the *Cinco de Mayo* festival, at Market Square during the first weekend in May. The *Texas Folklife Festival,* staged the first weekend in August at the Institute of Texan Cultures, showcases ethnic customs and foods, crafts and games, and 30 cultures that helped shape Texas. In early December, *Las Posadas* is a Hispanic folklore drama re-enacting the Holy Family's search for shelter in Bethlehem. It is set against a dazzling River Walk backdrop of 60,000 red, blue, and green *Christmas* lights; mariachis herald the arrival of the pilgrims and a choir sings the traditional *posada* songs. *Fiesta de las*

Luminarias takes place on the first 3 weekends of December. Nearly 2,000 candles placed in sand-filled paper bags line the River Walk, symbolizing the lighting of the Holy Family's way to Bethlehem.

MUSEUMS: The *Alamo Museum,* the *Buckhorn Hall of Horns and Texas Hall of History,* the *Hertzberg Collection,* the *McNay Institute,* and the *San Antonio Museum of Art* are described in *Special Places.* Other interesting museums to visit:

Institute of Texan Cultures – Artifacts of various cultures that helped establish the Texan culture, including exhibits descibing the Indian, French, Spanish, German, Jewish, and African-American influences in the Lone Star State. Changing exhibits, special events, and tours. Closed Mondays. No admission charge. 801 S. Bowie (phone: 226-7651).

Pioneer Museum – Texas Rangers' history since their inception in 1823 is displayed. Closed Mondays and Tuesdays in winter. Admission charge. 3805 Broadway (phone: 822-9011).

San Antonio Zoo – Located in a rock quarry by the river, the zoo is surrounded by tall, limestone cliffs and pecan trees. There is a wonderful exhibit of koalas, as well as a remarkable African antelope collection and a vast variety of exotic birds. Elephant and camel rides are offered for children, and the zoo has the only whooping crane in captivity in the US. Open daily. Admission charge. 3903 N. St. Mary's St. (phone: 734-7183).

Witte Memorial Museum – Natural history museum with special exhibits about local history. Open daily. 3801 Broadway (phone: 226-5544).

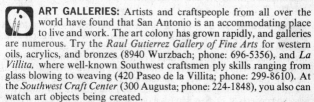

ART GALLERIES: Artists and craftspeople from all over the world have found that San Antonio is an accommodating place to live and work. The art colony has grown rapidly, and galleries are numerous. Try the *Raul Gutierrez Gallery of Fine Arts* for western oils, acrylics, and bronzes (8940 Wurzbach; phone: 696-5356), and *La Villita,* where well-known Southwest craftsmen ply skills ranging from glass blowing to weaving (420 Paseo de la Villita; phone: 299-8610). At the *Southwest Craft Center* (300 Augusta; phone: 224-1848), you also can watch art objects being created.

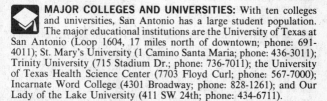

MAJOR COLLEGES AND UNIVERSITIES: With ten colleges and universities, San Antonio has a large student population. The major educational institutions are the University of Texas at San Antonio (Loop 1604, 17 miles north of downtown; phone: 691-4011); St. Mary's University (1 Camino Santa Maria; phone: 436-3011); Trinity University (715 Stadium Dr.; phone: 736-7011); the University of Texas Health Science Center (7703 Floyd Curl; phone: 567-7000); Incarnate Word College (4301 Broadway; phone: 828-1261); and Our Lady of the Lake University (411 SW 24th; phone: 434-6711).

SPORTS AND FITNESS: Baseball – The San Antonio *Dodgers* minor league team plays at *V. J. Keefe Field,* St. Mary's University (phone: 434-9311).

Basketball – The NBA *Spurs* play at the *Convention Center Arena* from October through March; tickets at the *Arena* in HemisFair Plaza (phone: 224-9578).

Fitness Center – The *YMCA* has a pool, track, weights, and handball and racquetball courts. 903 N. St. Mary's and Lexington (phone: 227-5221).

Golf – There are 19 courses in the city in constant use all year round. Best for visitors is *Olmos Basin Municipal Course,* 7022 McCullough (phone: 826-4041).

Jogging – Run along the River Walk early or late in the day; up Broadway to Brackenridge Park; or follow the Mission Trail, along Mission Road (the marathon route), to the missions.

Riding – *Brackenridge Stables* are ideal for urban cowboys wishing to ride along bridle paths in Brackenridge Park. 840 E. Mulberry (phone: 732-8881).

Swimming – There are 21 municipal pools open May through *Labor Day* (phone: 821-3000). Best is *Alamo Heights Pool* (229 Greeley St., phone: 824-2595). For serious lap swimmers, two 50-meter pools are open year-round: *Northside Aquatics Center* (7001 Culebra; phone: 681-4026) and *Blossom Athletic Center* (12002 Jones-Maltsberger; phone: 494-3775).

Tennis – *McFarlin Tennis Center* (1503 San Pedro Ave.; phone: 732-1223) is a municipal facility. Courts are $1.50 per person per hour before 5 PM, $2.50 afterward. Reservations advised.

THEATER: More than a dozen theaters offer a continuing and varied fare of traveling and locally produced shows, the most impressive of which is the *Majestic Theater* (216 E. Houston St.; phone: 226-3333). This incredibly ornate structure has been restored to its 1920s grandeur and hosts everything from traveling national theater companies to rock concerts. The area's colleges and universities also produce plays. For shows: *San Antonio Little Theater* (off the 1500 block of San Pedro; phone: 733-7258); *Harlequin Dinner Theater* (Ft. Sam Houston; phone: 221-5953); *Melodrama Playhouse* (300 HemisFair Plaza; phone: 271-0300); *Alamo City Theater* (339 W. Josephine; phone: 734-4646); and *Arneson River Theater* (Villita St. and the river; phone: 299-8610), where the stage and terraced hillside of the audience are separated by the river, and an occasional passing barge upstages the actors.

MUSIC: The *San Antonio Symphony* performs with guest stars from September through May. Offices at 109 Lexington Ave. (phone: 225-6161). The *Beethoven Maennerchor* and *Damenchor* are German choirs with more than a century's heritage in San Antonio. Outdoor concerts are held every third Friday, March through November, at the singing society's remodeled 1850s residence, Beethoven Home. (422 Peredia; phone: 222-1521). The *Fifth Army Band* stages free gazebo concerts at Ft. Sam Houston on the third Sunday of each month, May through August. Offices at Ft. Sam Houston (New Braunfels, and Grayson; phone: 221-6896).

NIGHTCLUBS AND NIGHTLIFE: Pop music, jazz, Dixieland, folk, rock, and country-western are all offered at San Antonio's many pubs, taverns, and nightclubs. For a little country, try the *Farmer's Daughter* (542 North W. W. White Rd.; phone: 333-7391). For jazz, try *Jim Cullum's Landing* (*Hyatt Regency;* phone: 223-7266) and *Dick's Last Resort* (406 Navarro on the River Walk; phone: 224-0026) for Dixieland jazz. You may want to try the nostalgia of *Larry Herman's Roaring 20's* (13445 Blanco Rd.; phone: 492-1353).

BEST IN TOWN

CHECKING IN: You can find all of the things you're probably looking for in San Antonio's hotels, like comfortable and convenient accommodations. Expect to pay $100 or more for a double room for a night in the expensive category and $65 to $90 in the moderate range. All telephone numbers are in the 512 area code unless otherwise indicated.

Fairmount – This cozy little landmark offers 36 elegantly appointed rooms, and a staff whose pampering makes you feel as if you've landed in Europe. Once a derelict building situated in a downtown renewal area, the hotel made moving history when it was rolled — all of its 3.2

million pounds intact — 6 blocks out of harm's way to its present site across the street from La Villita and HemisFair Plaza. The dining room offerings run the gamut from continental to Texas T-bone steaks. *Polo's* is a popular bar in which to while away a little time. The gift shop here features Texas-made items. Room service can be requested 24 hours a day. A concierge desk, 2 meeting rooms with a capacity for 72, photocopiers, and A/V equipment all are available. 401 S. Alamo (phone: 224-8800; 800-642-3363; Fax: 512-224-2767). Expensive.

Hilton Palacio del Río – Right on the riverside, at the liveliest corner of Paseo del Río, this place makes the best use of its prime location. The *El Comedor* dining room serves alfresco on the River Walk; half of the 484 rooms in this attractive Spanish-style building have river views; and there is an elevator stop that lets you off at river's edge. Also features a rooftop pool, free coffee in rooms, shops, and *Durty Nellie's* pub, where you can let loose with an Irish ditty. Nine meeting rooms can hold up to 700; other pluses are a concierge, car rental desk, and express checkout. The new business center offers secretarial services, photocopiers, computers, and A/V equipment. 200 S. Alamo St. (phone: 222-1400; 800-HILTONS; Fax: 512-270-0761; Telex: 767246). Expensive.

Hyatt Regency – Most of the 633 rooms in this 16-story establishment built around an atrium have views of the San Antonio River and Old San Antonio. For dining and drinking, there's the *Riverbend Saloon,* and *Chaps,* and the multilevel *River Terrace* lounge in the atrium. Pool. Services offered here include secretarial assistance, photocopiers and computers, A/V equipment, a concierge desk, and express checkout. There are also 23 meeting rooms, which have a capacity for 1,400. 123 Losoya (phone: 222-1234; 800-233-1234; Fax: 512-277-4925; Telex: 767249). Expensive.

La Mansión del Río – Combines a Spanish-style building with a restored 1852 building that originally was part of St. Mary's University. Nicely designed, with 335 rooms overlooking either the river or an inner courtyard and a pool. Features the *Capistrano Room* and *Las Canarias* restaurants and *El Colegio* bar. Room service caters to guests around-the-clock. Among the business accoutrements are a concierge desk, 22 meeting rooms with a capacity of 500, A/V equipment, and photocopiers. 112 College St. (phone: 225-2581; 800-531-7208; Fax: 512-226-0389; Telex: 767478). Expensive.

Plaza – A spacious garden property on nearly 5 acres, accented by tropical gardens, tall native Texas trees, and sparkling fountains. Its 252 rooms have balconies overlooking La Villita Historic District. The *Anaqua* restaurant (see *Eating Out*) has a distinctive international menu. Incorporated into the complex are 3 restored 19th-century bungalows, which are a functional part of the hotel's entertainment facilities. Pool, exercise rooms, sauna, and tennis courts. There is 24-hour room service, concierge and secretarial services, and express checkout, plus 15 meeting rooms which can hold up to 595, A/V equipment, photocopiers, and computers. 555 S. Alamo (phone: 229-1000; 800-421-1172; Fax: 512-229-1418; Telex: 0076381). Expensive.

St. Anthony – Richness envelops guests who enter the lobby, a by-product of the Empire chandeliers, Oriental rugs, marble, and hand-painted Mexican tiles, plus a rosewood and gold-leaf grand piano. This old landmark has been restored handsomely. The *Jefferson Manor* (one of the city's best) serves traditional American specialties in a setting that is a re-creation of a Monticello; there is a second restaurant, several bars, a rooftop garden, 24-hour room service, and a pool. In addition to 21 meeting rooms, which hold up to 350, there are secretarial services available, photocopiers, A/V equipment, and computers. 300 E. Travis St. (phone: 227-4392; 800-838-1338; Fax: 512-227-0915). Expensive.

Wyndham – This 328-room property has an exterior of polished pink granite and an attractive 2-story lobby with brass sculptures and a marble bar. With its 20,000 square feet of meeting space, it is a boon to business travelers; for relaxation, there are 2 large swimming pools, an exercise room and a sauna. Its 16 meeting rooms have a capacity for 370. Other helpful business services are express checkout, secretarial services, A/V and photocopy equipment, and computers. 9821 Colonnade (phone: 691-8888; 800-822-4200; Fax: 512-691-1635). Expensive.

Crockett – Behind the Alamo since 1909, it emerged from a $15-million renovation as one of the nicest of San Antonio's "old" hotels. Some of the 200 rooms are small, but all are beautifully decorated. The most impressive accommodations are the luxurious 7th-floor suites overlooking the Alamo grounds. *Lela B's* restaurant serves meat salads (turkey, duck, steak) and the like at lunch, weekdays, and continental fare for dinner, daily. Three meeting rooms hold up to 125. Secretarial services, photocopiers and A/V equipment, computer, and express checkout round out the list of business amenities. 320 Bonham (phone: 225-6500; 800-531-5537; Fax: 512-223-6613). Expensive to moderate.

San Antonio Marriott Rivercenter – Directly across the street from the *Convention Center* and nestled in a bend of the San Antonio River, it is one of the city's newest and largest properties. Most striking is its 7-story atrium with an indoor-outdoor heated swimming pool. *Gambits* on the River Walk, a 2-story nightclub, opens up onto the river; the *Cabrillo* features live entertainment; and the *Cactus Flower Café* has riverside dining on its patio. A complete business center is equipped with secretarial, computer, and media services. There are 20 meeting rooms with a capacity for up to 5,400. Other pluses are 24-hour room service, concierge, airline, and car rental desks, and express checkout. 711 E. River Walk (phone: 223-1000; 800-228-9290; Fax: 512-223-4092). Expensive to moderate.

Alamo Plaza – Formerly the *Emily Morgan,* its 177 rooms, including 11 plush suites with Jacuzzis, overlook the Alamo. *The Yellow Rose* is a modern coffee shop–style restaurant that serves good food. Among the amenities are 4 meeting rooms with a capacity for 100. Business services include secretarial assistance, photocopiers, and A/V equipment. Computers are also available on request. In addition, there are health club facilities and a swimming pool. 705 E. Houston St. (phone: 225-8460; 800-824-6674; Fax: 512-225-7227). Moderate.

La Quinta – Two blocks from the river, this 2-story Spanish building offers comfortable, convenient accommodations at good prices. Pool, TV sets, café. 130 rooms. The conference center offers secretarial services, A/V equipment, and photocopiers. 1001 E. Commerce St. (phone: 222-9181; 800-531-5900; Fax: 512-228-9816). Moderate.

Sheraton Gunter – Opened in 1909, it was twice declared a Texas landmark. A turn-of-the-century atmosphere still pervades the lobby, with its crystal chandeliers, marble floor, and dark mahogany paneling. More modern are the 326 high-ceilinged rooms with tile baths. International and Texas specialties are served in the *Café Suisse* restaurant; *Pâtisserie Suisse* is a European-style bakery; and there's dancing at *Padre Muldoon's,* a Victorian saloon. Business conveniences include secretarial assistance, photocopiers, computers, and A/V equipment. There's also 24-hour room service, a concierge desk, and 16 meeting rooms that hold up to 470. 205 E. Houston St. (phone: 227-3241; 800-22-CHARM; Fax: 512-227-9305; Telex: 767276). Moderate.

El Tropicano – Six blocks from the heart of downtown, at the north end of the River Walk; a good place from which to tour the river on foot or by river taxi. Fourteen meeting rooms hold up to 1,000. There's also a concierge and car rental desk. 110 Lexington Ave. (phone: 223-9461; Fax: 512-223-3662). Moderate.

EATING OUT: Some 26 ethnic groups pioneered Texas, and its current large military population has brought back a taste for exotic dishes from remote areas of the globe, resulting in a wide variety of restaurants. However, most folks would agree that San Antonio's best restaurants are Mexican. Non-Texans (outlanders, as they're called down here) generally are surprised (happily) by the prices. Our selections range in price from $50 or more for dinner for two in the expensive range, $25 to $45 in the moderate range, and under $20, inexpensive. Prices do not include drinks, wine, or tips. All telephone numbers are in the 512 area code unless otherwise indicated.

Anaqua Room – Splashing fountains, a historic courtyard, and superb culinary creations make this the premier hotel restaurant in San Antonio. Pan-fried crab cakes, baked grouper in macadamia nuts, and tequila-lime shrimp are specialties. Open daily. Reservations advised. Major credit cards accepted. *Plaza Hotel,* 555 S. Alamo St. in Arceniega (phone: 229-1000). Expensive.

Las Canarias – Add to highly-praised Southwestern treatments of prime ribs and paella festive doses of flamenco dancing or piano music and regal service for a memorable night. Open nightly Mondays through Saturdays; Sundays at brunch, too. Reservations advised. Major credit cards accepted. 112 College St. at St. Mary's in *La Mansion del Río Hotel* (phone: 225-2581). Expensive.

Fig Tree – Long, leisurely dinners with excellent service are the rule at this 19th-century adobe house. In the rare event that you have to wait for a table, have a drink on the balcony overlooking the San Antonio River. Specialties are seafood and beef. La Villita section, a few blocks from the Alamo. Open daily for dinner only. Reservations advised. Major credit cards accepted. 515 Paseo de la Villita (phone: 224-1976). Expensive.

Little Rhein – Possibly the city's priciest steakhouse, but undeniably the loveliest and most romantic. Texas caviar, a unique black-eyed pea dish, is complimentary, while pepper steak and lamb chops are top menu offerings. Its terraced riverside setting in an 1847 rock house is also a big draw. Open daily. Reservations advised. Major credit cards accepted. 231 S. Alamo St. (phone: 225-2111). Expensive.

La Louisiane – When it opened in 1935, this fine French and creole place offered full dinners for 75¢ to $1.25. Imminent failure was forecast by residents, who said it was too expensive for San Antonio. Today, a couple can go all out with an elegant $65 to $75 production that includes pompano *en papillote* (poached with oysters and shrimp in white wine sauce), frogs' legs sauté meunière, and three vintage wines; or some excellent dishes on a less grand scale. Over the years, the restaurant has won many national awards for its food and service. Closed Sundays and Mondays. Reservations advised. Major credit cards accepted. 2632 Broadway (phone: 225-7984). Expensive.

PJ's – A table at this sophisticated hangout is the best seat in town for watching the River Walk scene. The food is French nouvelle, with an emphasis on fresh fish and lightly sauced meats. The service, by tuxedoed waiters, wins constant praise. Diners get here by river taxi from the Casa Río boat dock. Closed Sundays. Reservations advised. Major credit cards accepted. 1 River Walk Pl., at St. Mary's (phone: 225-8400). Expensive.

Boudro's – A successful South by Southwest meeting, this popular River Walk place serves dishes that magically blend flavors from New Orleans and New Mexico together. Smoked salmon tacos, roasted corn soup, and blackened fish are just some of the excellent offerings.

Open daily. Reservations necessary for the river barge tables only. Major credit cards accepted. 421 E. Commerce St. on the River Walk (phone: 224-8484). Expensive to moderate.

Grey Moss Inn – To get to this historic inn in Texas hill country, you have to drive through some of the loveliest scenery around (see *Extra Special*). Mesquite-grilled steaks are the specialty. Open daily for dinner only. Reservations — and directions — essential. Major credit cards accepted. On Scenic Loop Rd., about 15 miles northwest of town (phone: 695-8301). Expensive to moderate.

Café du Vin – Wine is the star here. A gourmet food hall occupies one side of the building and a bright, pleasant café the other, where you can indulge in more than 21 varieties of wine. The food is American nouvelle, with dishes like blackened shrimp, veal tortellini, and bacon, lobster, and tomato sandwiches. Open daily. Reservations advised. Major credit cards accepted. Castle Oaks Village, 8055 West Ave. (phone: 349-4672). Moderate.

Cappy's – The kind of place where folks head after work on Fridays to let down their hair. It's comfy and familiar, with exposed brick walls and lots of natural wood, and choices include everything from light salads and burgers to more elaborate fish and meat entrées. Open daily. No reservations. Major credit cards accepted. Two locations: 5011 Broadway, Alamo Heights (phone: 828-9669), and 123 Northwest Loop 410 (phone: 366-1700). Moderate.

County Line – A cheery 1940s roadhouse is the setting for some of Texas's best barbecued ribs, beef, pork loin, and chicken, all smoked throughout the day. Just as sinful are the beans, potato salad, giant loaves of homemade bread, and fruit cobblers à la mode. Open daily. Reservations unnecessary. Major credit cards accepted. 606 W. Afton Oaks, near Loop 1604 and US 281 (phone: 496-0011). Moderate.

Crumpets – Soothing is the word for the atmosphere here: It's the classical music, quietly elegant room, and superlative desserts turned out by the restaurant's pastry shop next door. Try the buttercream cake or fresh fruit tart. Preceding dessert is some very good light continental fare. Open daily. No reservations. Major credit cards accepted. 5800 Broadway, Alamo Heights (phone: 821-5454). Moderate.

L'Etoile – This highly-rated, lively bistro turns out the kind of solid cooking that has given French food a good name — salmon in pastry shell, pâté, beef Wellington, and bouillabaisse. Inside, it's all light wood and soft colors under a skylit cathedral ceiling. There's also dining outdoors. Open daily. Reservations advised for dinner. Major credit cards accepted. 6106 Broadway, Alamo Heights (phone: 826-4551). Moderate.

Landry's Seafood Inn – A lucky seafood-basketball nut may connect on game night, enjoying fresh gulf seafood with a Cajun flair while rubbing shoulders with the NBA's San Antonio *Spurs*. Open daily. Reservations advised (although not accepted on game nights). Major credit cards accepted. 600 E. Market, backing onto the *Convention Center Arena* (phone: 229-1010). Moderate.

Mama's – Good food in a family atmosphere with everything from burgers to steaks. Specialty of the house is chicken-fried mushrooms. A volleyball court and basketball hoop are set up in the fenced backyard so kids can work off their energies while Mom and Pop have a leisurely after-dinner drink. Open daily till the wee hours. No reservations. Major credit cards accepted. 9907 San Pedro (phone: 349-2314). Moderate.

Cadillac Bar – An import from Nuevo Laredo, featuring dishes most often found in Mexican border towns. Beware of the salsa sitting innocently on the table; it has vaporized more than one palate. Ramos gin fizzes are the drink of choice; fish dishes are the best menu items. Strolling mariachis add to the atmosphere of this very friendly, informal eatery. Lunch and dinner daily except Sundays. No reservations. Major credit cards accepted. 212 S. Flores (phone: 223-5533). Inexpensive.

Church's Fried Chicken – Fast food with a hot twist — chicken and jalapeños. Both spicy and cheap. The headquarters of the national chain, San Antonio has more than 30 *Church's* so you can't miss them. Open daily. No reservations or credit cards accepted. Inexpensive.

Earl Abel's – After feeding hungry families for almost half a century, Earl has gotten pretty good at it. The place is a godsend for those who have been watching the ravenous animals at the nearby zoo. Offers big servings of standard American fare — freshwater catfish, a chicken liver dinner, a full line of hamburgers, big T-bones, and terrific homemade pecan pie. Open daily. No reservations. Major credit cards accepted. 4200 Broadway (phone: 822-3358). Inexpensive.

La Fogata – Authentic recipes and foods from Mexico. Cooking is exclusively by charcoal, and though the menu sounds exotic, the prices are down to earth. (No liquor is served.) Open daily. No reservations. Major credit cards accepted. 2427 Vance Jackson (phone: 340-1337). Inexpensive.

Mi Tierra Café and Bakery – When you tire of souvenir hunting at *El Mercado*, head for the heart of the market square for the real thing — great Mexican food at low prices. The cheese enchiladas are terrific, and the *cabrito* (kid) is good here too. Open 24 hours a day. No reservations. Major credit cards accepted. 218 Produce Row (phone: 225-1262). Inexpensive.

El Mirador – Citizens say the best (and most authentic) Mexican food in the city is served here. It's a special favorite at lunchtime on Saturdays, when the entire citizenry seems to visit. *Caldo Xochitl* (a chicken-cum-vegetable soup) is a special treat. Breakfast 6:30 to 10:45 AM. Closes at 4 PM on weekdays and 3 PM Saturdays. Closed Sundays. No reservations or credit cards accepted. 722 S. St. Mary's (phone: 225-9444). Inexpensive.

Schilo's Delicatessen – This downtown favorite has been around since the 1920s, and it's still where the locals go for stick-to-your-ribs German fare. Don't miss the potato pancakes or the heavenly cheesecake. Open daily except Sundays from 10 AM to 7 PM. No reservations. Major credit cards accepted. 424 E. Commerce (phone: 223-6692). Inexpensive.

Little House Café – The chilaquiles are diet-busters — corn tortilla chips are fried and served with eggs, salsa ranchero, and cheese. If you're adventurous, try the porkskin with eggs. Most expensive plate is under $4. Open Mondays through Fridays, 7 AM to 2 PM. Reservations unnecessary. No credit cards accepted. 107 S. Flores (phone: 225-3344). Very inexpensive.

SAN DIEGO

AT-A-GLANCE

SEEING THE CITY: The Cabrillo National Monument, where Juan Rodriguez Cabrillo first saw the West Coast in 1542, still offers the most spectacular view of San Diego. It's the second most visited national monument in the US — right after the Statue of Liberty. Museum and visitors' center open daily. Admission charge. Catalina Blvd. on the tip of Point Loma (phone: 557-5450).

SPECIAL PLACES: San Diego stretches from the fashionable northern suburb of Del Mar to the Mexican border: all in all, a span of more than 30 miles along the Pacific Coast. It's advisable to concentrate your sightseeing efforts in one particular area at a time. There's no way you can see everything in just a day. Each of the Big Four (Balboa Park, Old Town, San Diego Zoo, and *Sea World of California*) is an all-day proposition.

SAN DIEGO

Shelter Island – A manmade resort island in the middle of San Diego Bay lined with boatyards, marinas, and picturesque, neo-Polynesian restaurants. Between July and November, marlin sport fishers haul their giant catches into port here to be weighed and photographed. Stop off at Marlin Club Landing (2445 Shelter Island Dr.; phone: 222-2502). If the sight of these monsters makes you yearn for the tug of a giant fish on the line, sign on for a marlin expedition at any of the sport fishing marinas two blocks away on Fenelon Street. You also can fish for albacore and yellowtail. To get to Shelter Island, follow Rosecrans Street until you see signs pointing to Shelter Island.

Harbor Island – This is a superdeluxe, $50-million resort island. Actually, it started as a landfill project in 1961, when the US Navy offered surplus harbor muck to the Port of San Diego. The navy was deepening a channel through the bay and port officials accepted their offer and used the 3½ million tons of waste to create Harbor Island. You'd never know, to look at the place. Humble beginnings have yielded fancy beachside promenades, traffic-free malls, restaurants, and hotels. Take Rosecrans to Harbor Drive, then follow signs to Harbor Island.

Mission Bay Park – A 4,600-acre waterfront recreation area. Here you'll find manmade tropical islands, channels, and specific areas where you can water-ski, swim, and sail. There are golf courses, hotels, and restaurants here, too. The 2-mile stretch of Mission Beach, along the western edge of the park, is one of San Diego's oldest beach communities. The visitor information center is open daily. Take Route 5 to Mission Bay Drive exit. The information center is right off the exit ramp (phone: 276-8200).

Sea World of California – This 150-acre oceanarium is the highlight of the Mission Bay recreation complex. Performing dolphins, Shamu, the 3-ton killer whale, and Baby Shamu entertain regularly. The shows include performing sea lions and otters, and a water-light extravaganza. Penguin Encounter is a glassed-in bit of Antarctica, where penguins from Emperors to fledglings flourish at zero degrees. Backstage you can feed the dolphins and meet the walruses. Yes, there are sharks, too. Open daily. Admission charge. Mission Bay Park (phone: 226-3901).

Old Town San Diego State Historic Park – Historic buildings mix with commercial re-creations on the site of California's first permanent Spanish settlement, preserved by the State Department of Parks and Recreation. Tours, daily at 2 PM, leave the visitors' center (a good place to get an idea of what Old Town looked like 100 years ago). A diorama is on display. The Seeley Stables, with exhibits on Californian and western history and children's displays; the Stuart House, an early adobe structure where volunteers demonstrate candlemaking, spinning and weaving, and cook corn tortillas on adobe bricks; the Machado-Silvas House, another adobe structure; the Casa de Estudillo (see below); and an early dentist's office. (Buildings are closed on *Thanksgiving, Christmas,* and *New Year's Day.*) Living history programs take place on the fourth Saturday of each month. The *Bazaar del Mundo,* an area of shops and restaurants, also is in the park proper, plus an old-fashioned general store, tobacconist, and confectionery. For further information, contact the visitors' information center in Robinson-Rose House (Old Town Plaza; phone: 237-6770; for 24-hour information, call 293-0117). Old Town San Diego State Historic Park is bounded by Wallace, Juan, Twiggs, and Congress Sts. Some of the park's other highlights:

Old Town Plaza – The best way to see Old San Diego is by walking through it. Old Town Plaza (also known as Washington Square) used to be the scene of violent cockfights and bullfights. Duelists chose this as their site for shooting it out. No admission charge. San Diego Ave., Mason, Calhoun, and Wallace Sts. in Old Town San Diego State Historic Park. For general park information, call 237-6770.

Casa de Estudillo – A former *commandante* of San Diego, José Maria Estudillo, lived here while the city was under Mexican control. It was built in 1829. Open daily. Admission charge. San Diego Ave. and Mason St. (no phone).

San Diego Union Newspaper Museum – Still going strong, the *San Diego Union* started out in this small 1850s building. The newspaper is responsible for restoring it. Open daily. No admission charge. 2626 San Diego Ave. (phone: 297-2119).

Whaley House – The first brick house in San Diego, built by New Yorker Thomas Whaley. The house is supposed to be haunted by a man who was hanged on the grounds in 1852. Haunted or not, the house was the scene of many lively high society parties in its day. Ornate 19th-century furnishings still fill the halls. Closed Mondays and Tuesdays. Admission charge. 2482 San Diego Ave., in Old Town (phone: 298-2482).

El Campo Santo – At the southern end of San Diego Avenue is a cemetery containing the graves of many pioneers, soldiers, and bandits. One of the latter, Antonio Garra, actually was executed next to his grave. Unfortunately, many of the headstones are missing, but there's enough history here to make a visit compelling. San Diego Ave. and Noell St., in Old Town (no phone).

Heritage Park – A pocket of preserved Victoriana. The County Parks and Recreation Department has its offices in the Sherman-Gilbert House. There are several other mansions to explore. Open daily. No admission charge. Heritage Park Row, in Old Town (phone: 565-3600).

Mormon Battalion Memorial Visitors Center – This military museum marks the longest infantry march in US history: 1846 to 1847, when 500 Mormons left their home in Illinois and trekked more than 2,000 miles to San Diego. Only 350 made it. It also has a number of exhibitions of the Church of Jesus Christ of Latter-Day Saints and historical displays. Open daily. No admission charge. In Heritage Park at 2510 Juan St. (phone: 298-3317).

OLD TOWN SAN DIEGO

(Map labels: SAN DIEGO RIVER, 8, TAYLOR ST, HOTEL CIRCLE ST, Junipero Serra Museum, PRESIDIO PARK, PRESIDIO, Hinsite District, Casa De Estudillo, Old Town Plaza, Heritage Park, Mormon Memorial, SUNSET BLVD, 5, La El Campo, Santa 200 Yds.)

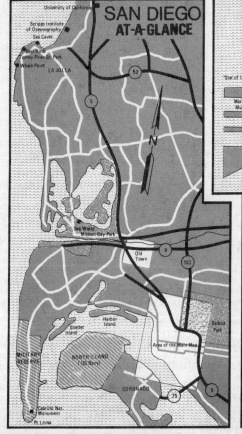

SAN DIEGO AT-A-GLANCE

(Map labels: University of California, Scripps Institute of Oceanography, Sea Caves, Seal Rock, Torrey Pines St. Park, Whale Point, LA JOLLA, 52, 5, Sea World, Mission Bay Park, Old Town, 8, 163, Shelter Island, Harbor Island, MILITARY RESERVE, NORTH ISLAND U.S. Navy, Area of the Main Map, Balboa Park, CORONADO, 75, 5, Cabrillo Nat. Monument, Pt. Loma, EMBARCADERO, HARBOR DR, Star of India, Maritime Museum, COR)

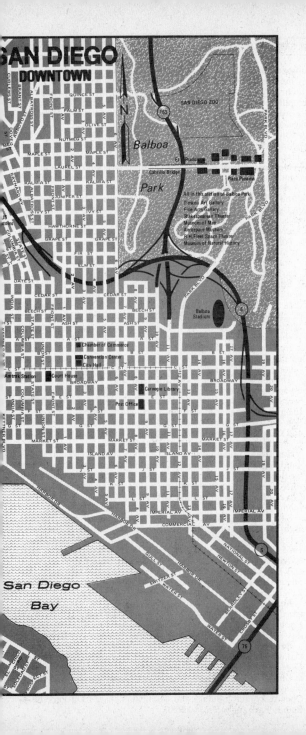

Junipero Serra Museum – Named after Fray Junipero Serra, this lovely museum, built in 1929, contains documents, books, and artifacts on the history of San Diego's early Spanish and Mexican period. The tower gallery is especially fascinating. The museum is on the site of the first European settlement in California. Closed Mondays. Admission charge. Presidio Park, in Old Town (phone: 297-3258).

Horton Plaza – The sparkplug project in San Diego's downtown redevelopment program, this multilevel, colorful, and confusing shopping plaza comprises major department stores, movie theaters, restaurants, entertainments, and 150 specialty shops. The *Omni* hotel abuts the plaza, and the legendary *U. S. Grant* hotel is across the street on Broadway. Stretching from Broadway to G St. between 1st and 4th Aves.

Balboa Park – A definite must — the cultural heart of the city. Within its 1,400 acres of lawns, groves, lakes, and paths are the world-famous San Diego Zoo, a complex of fine museums set in an area of the park known as the Prado (each listed below), restaurants, and a theater. Open daily. No admission charge to the park. Balboa Park Visitors Center, located in the House of Hospitality, provides a free map to the many museums, shops, restaurants, theaters, and sports facilities in the park. Park Blvd. (phone: 239-0512).

San Diego Zoo – Incomparable. One of the finest zoos in the world. For more than 75 years, San Diego has been home to more than 3,800 animals. The zoo covers over 125 acres, with animals ranging from Australian koalas to the only New Zealand kiwis in captivity in the country to Indonesian Komodo dragons. Very few of the animals are caged in. The Skyfari Aerial Tramway gives you a great bird's-eye view of everything. Guided bus tours leave frequently from the gate. Open daily. Admission charge. Balboa Park (phone: 234-3153 or 231-1515).

Timken Art Gallery – Controversial when it was built in 1965 because some people felt its modern bent clashed with the prevalent Spanish adobe architecture, the *Timken* houses French, Spanish, Flemish, and Italian Renaissance art, plus a world-famous collection of Russian icons. You'll find Rembrandt, Bruegel the Elder, and Cézanne on the walls. Open daily. No admission charge. 1500 El Prado, Balboa Park (phone: 239-5548).

San Diego Museum of Art – Donated by the Appleton Bridges family in 1926, the original section of the gallery was built to resemble the university at Salamanca, Spain. Two wings have been added since. Diego Rivera, Rubens, Rembrandt, and Dali are represented. Closed Mondays. Admission charge. Plaza de Panama, Balboa Park (phone: 232-7931).

San Diego Museum of Man – Concerning itself primarily with anthropology and archaeology, this museum bears the distinction of being the only remaining permanent structure from San Diego's *1915 Exposition*. Its Spanish colonial tower is remarkable in itself. Exhibitions focus on the Southwest Indians, pre-Columbian Maya, and Early Man. There's also an ethnic arts shop. Open daily. Admission charge except Wednesdays. El Prado, Balboa Park (phone: 239-2001).

Aerospace Historical Center – Containing the *San Diego Aerospace Museum* and the *International Aerospace Hall of Fame,* it has a notable collection of antique planes and gliders. Open daily. Admission charge. Ford Bldg., Balboa Park (phone: 234-8291).

Reuben H. Fleet Space Theater and Science Center – The first of its kind. Simulated space travel is the attraction here. Images projected on the 360° screen give you the impression you're moving in zero-gravity conditions. The *Science Center* also has exhibitions on astronomy and technology, and a free demonstration of lasers. Open daily, and evenings, too. Admission charge. Off Park Blvd., Balboa Park (phone: 238-1268).

San Diego Natural History Museum – More than a century old, this museum has a collection of birds that nest in the San Diego area, and sharks, whales, and fish who make their home in the surrounding seas. A Sefton seismograph measures tremors and earth movement. Open daily. Admission charge. Across from the *Fleet Space Theater,* Balboa Park (phone: 232-3821).

Japanese Friendship Garden – These 11½ acres contain a lake, tea garden, stone garden, meadow, and terrace. Closed Mondays, Wednesdays, and Thursdays. No admission charge. In Balboa Park, Near the *Spreckels Organ Pavilion* (phone: 232-2721).

Seaport Village – The city's expanding 24-acre waterfront complex of restaurants and specialty shops, built around three main plazas edging San Diego Bay, is designed to look much like a New England fishing village. A main attraction is the wonderfully restored Flying Horses Carousel, with its hand-carved wooden animals, originally constructed around 1900 for the amusement park at Coney Island, New York. It's nice to stroll through the village in the evening and have dinner in one of the restaurants here, or breakfast overlooking the water. The *Night Court* shopping complex opened in 1991, and is the largest bayfront retail and entertainment center in Southern California. The complex features over 65,000 square feet of shops, restaurants, bars, pubs, and nightclubs. *Seaport Village,* 849 Harbor Dr. at Pacific Hwy. (phone: 235-4013).

Embarcadero – Another interesting place to walk around. From the pier you can see the activities on North Island Naval Air Station across the bay, and watch cruise ships at anchor and the hundreds of sailboats cruising. Navy ships are open to visitors on weekends, off the Broadway Pier.

Maritime Museum – The oldest square-rigged merchantman afloat, the 125-plus-year-old *Star of India,* is berthed here, along with the turn-of-the-century ferryboat *Berkeley* and steam yacht *Medea.* Open daily. Admission charge. Broadway Pier at Harbor Dr. (phone: 234-9153).

LA JOLLA

Tidepools – La Jolla, a suburb with an uncommercial beach 12½ miles north of San Diego, offers opportunities to observe marine life in a natural setting. Visit the tidepools just beyond Alligator Head at La Jolla Cove at low tide to see a veritable profusion of hermit crabs, sea anemones, and starfish clambering over one another. Make sure you wear tennis shoes — the jagged rocks can cut your feet. From San Diego, take Route 5 to Ardath Road exit. Follow Ardath west until it becomes Torrey Pines Road. Take Torrey Pines west, turn right on Prospect and follow it to Coast Boulevard. Follow signs to La Jolla Cove.

Whale Point – If you visit La Jolla during December, January, or February, visit Whale Point. Every year the giant whales migrate south along this route. Since they've been doing this for the past 8 million years or so, we have no reason to believe they'll stop before you read this chapter. To get to Whale Point, follow the shore south from Alligator Head. Opposite the only large building on the beach, there's a small cove known as Seal Rock. From Seal Rock, you'll be able to see another cove, marked by a lifeguard stand and a wall. That's Whale Point.

San Diego Museum of Contemporary Art – Dramatically situated near the beach, between Seal Rock and Whale Point, the gardens and building are well worth a look. You'll find contemporary paintings and sculpture from all over the world. A good place to contemplate art and nature. Closed Mondays. Admission charge. Prospect and Silverado (phone: 454-3541).

Sea Caves – A natural formation of seven caves hollowed out by the waves. You reach them by walking along the cliffs facing the ocean. Take Coast Boulevard to the tunnel leading to Coast Walk.

Scripps Institute of Oceanography – One of the most highly esteemed marine study institutes in the world. You can stroll through the grounds, or relax on the Scripps beach. You can't walk on the pier, but the *Scripps Aquarium Museum* is open to the public. You can watch the fish being fed at 1:30 PM Wednesdays and Sundays. Open daily. Donation suggested. 8602 La Jolla Shores Dr. (phone: 534-6933 or 534-FISH).

Torrey Pines State Reserve – This 2,000-acre state nature reserve within the city limits literally is an oasis of wilderness in an urban environment. The unique-looking pine trees, which are the outstanding feature, date to the period when Southern California was less arid, and forests flourished. On the northern side of the park, Los Penasquitos Lagoon offers a spectacular vantage point for watching blue herons and rare egrets. Mule deer come to the southern part of the lagoon to feed. The visitors' center is housed in a 1923 adobe building. Try to arrive early in the day; the number of admissions is limited. Open daily. Admission charge. Torrey Pines Rd. (phone: 755-2063).

■ **EXTRA SPECIAL:** No tour of San Diego would be complete without a visit to Mexico. The bustling border city of Tijuana is just 17 miles south of downtown. Many visitors and residents drive there, park their cars on the US side of the border, and walk into Tijuana. (The Tijuana taxis are infamous for overcharging. Be sure to agree upon the fare before embarking on an adventure.) San Diego's trolley system is a good alternative to driving. The trip to Tijuana takes about 40 minutes and costs $1.50 each way. It's possible to hop on the trolley at various points along the route, but the trip originates at the *Amtrak* terminal (C St. and Kettner Blvd.), and terminates at San Ysidro (200 feet from the border). *Tijuana City Tour* buses pick up passengers at the trolley stop and, for an additional charge, will travel the main tourist attractions. Trolleys leave the main stations (in either direction) every 15 minutes from 5 to 1 AM daily; tickets are purchased at vending machines at all pickup points. For an interesting stopover, get off at Chula Vista Bay Station and take the shuttle bus to the Chula Vista Nature Interpretive Center. The living wetlands museum features marine flora and fauna. Tijuana has many crafts shops selling finely wrought ironwork, pottery, and jewelry. Prices are a fraction of those in the US. You may bring back $400 worth of goods duty-free, once every 30 days. Goods must be declared at retail value at the checkpoint for re-entering the US, but certain items — such as Mexican national treasures — are prohibited. Upon reentering, you may be asked for proof of citizenship (it often depends on how Latino and/or nervous you look), so it's wise to carry some sort of identification. Also, if you're driving into Mexico, it's wise to purchase insurance at one of the many insurance offices near the border. It can prevent unpleasant detention should you happen to have an accident while in Mexico. Conventional US auto insurance is not valid in Mexico. The Tijuana Cultural Center has an *Omnimax Theater,* which depicts Mexico's cultural heritage, a museum, a performing arts center, shopping, and a restaurant (Paseo de los Héroes; phone: 706-684-1111 or 706-684-1132). Tijuana also offers year-round thoroughbred racing at the *Caliente* track, dog racing, jai alai, and bullfighting. For more information, call the Tijuana Tourism and Convention Bureau (phone: 619-299-8518 or 800-522-1516).

A 1½-hour drive down a scenic toll road from Tijuana is Ensenada, a resort and major port. From Ensenada, the road stretches south to the most famous Mexican Pacific coast resort cities or to Baja California Sur. No visas or tourist cards are needed for US citizens in the border areas. You do need a tourist card to travel south of Ensenada. It's a good idea to always carry your passport, birth certificate, or voter registration card with you, as you are in a foreign country.

SOURCES AND RESOURCES

TOURIST INFORMATION: The San Diego Convention and Visitors Bureau (1200 3rd Ave., Suite 824, San Diego, CA 92101; phone: 232-3101) distributes brochures and maps. The main International Visitor Information Center is at Horton Plaza downtown, at 1st Avenue and F Street (11 Horton Plaza, San Diego, CA 92101; phone: 236-1212). Another information center is on E. Mission Drive, off Route 5 (phone: 276-8200). For maps and brochures on walking tours of the historic district, stop at the State Park Visitor Center at Old Town Plaza (phone: 237-6770). Contact the California state hotline (phone: 800-TO-CALIF) for maps, calendars of events, health updates, and travel advisories.

Barry Berndes's *The San Diegan* (San Diego Guide; $2.95) is the most complete guide to the area; write to *The San Diegan,* PO Box 99127, San Diego 92169, or call 275-2213.

Local Coverage – *Evening Tribune,* evening daily; *Union,* morning daily; *San Diego Reader,* weekly; *San Diego* magazine, monthly.

Television Stations – KFMB Channel 8–CBS; KGTV Channel 10–ABC; KPBS Channel 15–PBS; KNSD Channel 39–NBC.

Radio Stations – AM: KFMB 760 (adult contemporary music); KSDO 1130 (news/talk/sports); KSON 1240 (country). FM: KFSD 94.1 (classical); KIFM 98.1 (jazz); KCBQ 105.3 (rock).

Food – *K-Lynn Restaurant Guide,* by Lynn Heller and Kathy Glick, has listings of the best eateries in town (AM/PM Publishing; $6.50). *San Diego* magazine has the most reliable, up-to-date restaurant information, plus a terrific "Annual Dining Out" guide worth tracking down.

TELEPHONE: The area code for San Diego is 619.
  Sales Tax – The city sales tax is 7.25%. The tax on hotel rooms is 9%.

CLIMATE: Rainstorms are few and far between, and almost invariably occur in December, January, and February. During these months, the temperature might drop down into the high 40s at night. Daytimes generally are in the 60s. The rest of the year, you can expect bright days and cool evenings with daytime highs in the 70s, lows at night in the 50s. Bathing suits and tennis shoes are de rigueur all year round.

GETTING AROUND: Airport – San Diego International Airport is within sight of downtown. The cost of a cab ride between the airport and downtown varies but should run $6 or $7, $11 or $12 to Mission Valley. *San Diego Transit* (phone: 233-3004) bus No. 2 leaves from the airport every 20 minutes and runs along Broadway, downtown; fare, $1. *Peerless Shuttle* (phone: 279-8877), *SuperShuttle* (phone: 279-8877), and *Rainbow Ride Shuttle Service* (phone: 695-3830) also operate airport transfer service by mini-van.

Bus – The *San Diego Transit System* operates frequent buses connecting downtown with the suburbs (phone: 233-3004).

Car Rental – The best way to see everything at your convenience is by car. Most major national car rental firms are represented at the airport. For lower rates, try *Ladki International* (phone: 233-9333 or 800-245-2354).

Horse and Carriage – *Cinderella Carriages* (phone: 239-8080) picks up passsengers in front of *Croce's* in the Gaslamp District at Seaport Village and takes hour-long drives through different areas of the city.

Taxi – You can get a cab by calling *Yellow Cab* (phone: 234-6161); *Radio Cab* (phone: 232-6566); or *Checker Cab* (phone: 234-4477).

Trolley/Ferry – The *San Diego Trolley* originates at the *Amtrak* terminal (C St. and Kettner Blvd.). The *South Line* runs from the restored Spanish-style depot to the Mexican border, the *East Line* to the town of El Cajon, while the *Bayside Line* serves the *Convention Center* and coastal hotels and attractions. Tickets, available from machines at all 27 stops, cost 50¢ to $2, depending on distance (phone: 231-8549). The private *Old Town Trolley Tours* (phone: 298-8687) offers sightseeing loop tours of central San Diego with all-day on-and-off privileges and stops at or near many hotels. Tickets cost $12 for adults, $6 for children 6–12, and increase to $16 and $8 respectively, with additional travel on extension shuttles to Hotel Circle. There is a ferry (phone: 234-1111), which costs $3 round trip, between the Broadway Pier in San Diego and the Old Ferry Landing on Coronado, whence the *Coronado Trolley* makes the rounds of the island's major hotels (phone: 437-1861).

Water Taxi – Water taxis serve Coronado, the *Convention Center*, bayside hotels, shopping destinations, and attractions (phone: 437-1861). The fare is $5 to $8, depending on distance, with tokens available at hotels.

VITAL SERVICES: Audiovisual Equipment – *Audio-Visual West* (phone: 270-7800); *Meeting Services* (phone: 299-6042).
Baby-sitting – *Baby Sitter Service* (4138 30th St.; phone: 281-7755) or *Reliable Babysitter Agency* (3368 2nd Ave., Suite B; phone: 296-0856).

Business Services – *Economic Development Corp. of San Diego*, 701-B St. (phone: 234-8484).

Dry Cleaner/Tailor – *Exclusive Cleaners*, 7 AM to 5:30 PM, 3740 Park Blvd. (phone: 295-3156).

Limousine – *VIP Limousine Service* (phone: 299-7000); *Olde English Livery Service*, sedans also (phone: 232-6533).

Mechanic – *Jimmy on the Spot*, road service only (phone: 560-1140).

Medical Emergency – *University Hospital of San Diego County*, 225 W. Dickinson St. (phone: 543-6222).

Messenger Services – *United Couriers* (phone: 278-1000); *American Messenger Service* (phone: 233-0324).

National/International Courier – *Federal Express* (phone: 295-5545); *DHL Worldwide Courier Express* (phone: 275-3890).

Pharmacy – *Drug Fair*, open daily from 9 AM to 7 PM, Sundays 10 AM to 5 PM, 5161 Waring Rd. (phone: 583-7373).

Photocopies – *We Copy*, open to 9:30 PM, 5375 Kearny Villa Rd. (phone: 268-2880).

Post Office – The main office is at 2535 Midway Dr. (phone: 574-0477).

Professional Photographer – *Frank Mulligan* (phone: 444-5555); *Don Askew Photography* (phone: 569-6274).

Secretary/Stenographer – The *Word Center*, typing, word processing, photocopies (phone: 223-6070).

Teleconference Facilities – *Pan Pacific, San Diego Marriott, Sheraton Harbor Island, Sheraton Grande Torrey Pines, Westgate, Humphrey's Half Moon Inn, Hyatt Regency La Jolla at Aventine, Town and Country*, and *U.S. Grant* (see *Best in Town*, below).

Translator – *Translingua* (phone: 222-0369); *Inlingua* (phone: 453-4534 or 576-9696).

Typewriter Rental – *Mission Office Machines*, 1-day minimum (phone: 280-4565); *La Jolla Typewriter Co.*, 1-day minimum (454-6183).

Western Union/Telex – Many offices are located around the city (phone: 800-325-6000).

Other – *Pacific Infosystems*, word processing (284-6800).

SPECIAL EVENTS: San Diego is a summer festival almost all year. The exhilarating 23-mile race for the *America's Cup* will come to the city this year, with sailing competitors from around the globe. Challenge races will begin in January to determine which international contender will race against the American team in May. The listing below is only a selection of other events.

January – *Mission Bay Marathon* (sometimes in December) from Quivira Basin loop in Mission Bay (phone: 437-4667); *MONY Tournament of Champions* (PGA golf tournament), *La Costa Country Club* (Costa del Mar Rd., Carlsbad; phone: 438-9111).

February – *Shearson Lehman Hutton Open* at *Torrey Pines* golf course (La Jolla; phone: 281-4653); wildflowers bloom in the desert at Anza-Borrego State Park, February through April (phone: 767-5311).

March – *St. Patrick's Day Parade* (phone: 299-7812); *Ocean Beach Kite Festival* (phone: 531-1527).

April – *San Diego Crew Classic* (West Mission Bay; phone: 488-1039); *Bud Light La Jolla Grand Prix Bicycle Race* (phone: 279-1983).

May – *Cinco de Mayo Festival* (phone: 296-3161 or 296-3161); *Del Mar National Horse Show* (Del Mar Fairgrounds; phone: 259-1355 or 755-1161). This year, San Diego will host the *America's Cup* yacht race, with 21 competitors from 15 countries striving for the title.

June – *Del Mar County Fair* (*Del Mar Fairgrounds;* phone: 259-1355 or 755-1161); *Annual Camp Pendleton Rodeo* (Camp Pendleton, Area 16; phone: 725-4905).

July – *Festival of the Bells,* celebrating the founding of California's first mission, Mission San Diego de Alcala (101818 San Diego Mission Rd.; phone: 281-8449); *Mission San Luis Rey Fiesta* (at Mission San Luis Rey; phone: 757-3651); *Sand Castle Days* (at Imperial Beach Pier; phone: 429-4757); *World Championship Over-the-Line Tournament* (a beach softball game at Mission Bay; phone: 294-8484).

August – Annual celebration of America's *Finest City Week* (phone: 234-0331); *N.A.S. Miramar Air Show* (at the naval air station; phone: 537-4082); *Great American Bank Tennis Classic, San Diego Tennis and Raquet Club* (phone: 276-5683).

September – *Cabrillo Festival* commemorating the discovery of the West Coast (phone: 557-5450); *Fiddle and Banjo Contests* (Frank Lane Memorial Park in Julian; phone: 765-0564).

October – *Oktoberfest* (La Mesa Blvd.; phone: 465-7700); *San Diego Zoo Founder's Day,* free admission, first Monday in October (phone: 234-3153).

November – *Mother Goose Parade,* El Cajón (phone: 444-8712).

December – *Mission Bay Christmas Boat Parade of Lights,* from Quivira Basin to *Sea World of California* (phone: 488-0501); *San Diego Harbor Parade of Lights* (phone: 222-0301); *Las Posadas,* Mexican *Christmas* ceremony (Mission San Luis Rey; phone: 757-3651 or 757-3250); Old Town's *Las Posadas,* a *Christmas* candlelight procession honoring the Holy Family (phone:.237-6770); *Christmas on the Prado* (Balboa Park; phone: 239-2512).

 MUSEUMS: Balboa Park contains most of the city's museums: the *Timken Art Gallery, San Diego Museum of Art, San Diego Museum of Man, San Diego Aerospace Historical Center, Reuben H. Fleet Space Center, San Diego Automotive Museum,* and *San Diego Natural History Museum.* They and the *Maritime Museum, Junipero Serra Museum, San Diego Union Newspaper Museum,* Heritage Park, historic Old Town houses, *San Diego Museum of Contemporary Art,* and *Scripps Aquarium Museum* are given fuller descriptions in *Special Places.* Other Balboa Park museums include the *Musem of San Diego History, Centro Cultural de la Raza, San Diego Museum of Photographic Arts, San Diego Hall of Champions,* and *San Diego Railroad Museum.* In addition,

Palomar Observatory's giant telescope was, for many years, the most powerful in the world. It's still in use. Photographs of the cosmos are on display. Open daily. Admission charge. County Rd. S6, east of Escondido (phone: 742-3476).

MAJOR COLLEGES AND UNIVERSITIES: Scripps Institute of Oceanography (see *Special Places*) is only a part of the University of California at San Diego. The rest of the campus is at University City, La Jolla (phone: 534-2230). Other colleges and universities include the following: US International University (Pomerado Rd.; phone: 271-4300); San Diego State University (Alvarado Freeway; phone: 594-5200); University of San Diego (Alcala Park; phone: 260-4600).

SHOPPING: San Diego has its share of today's marketplaces, huge malls filled with cookie-cutter department stores, chain shops, eateries, and entertainment. Enclaves of commerce with more individuality, however, also are easy to come by — and get to. Museum shops are an excellent source of quality gifts and mementos. Theme "villages" have sprouted near other city attractions:

Bazaar del Mundo – Locals as well as tourists patronize this Old Town shopping center (2754 Calhoun St., between Taylor and Mason Sts.; phone: 296-3161). Be sure to check out *Ariana* (phone: 296-4989) for brightly colored hand-crafted jewelry, and ethnic and hand-painted silk and cotton apparel.

Marina Village – On the Quivira Basin in Mission Bay. 1842 Quivira Way (phone: 224-2481).

Old Ferry Landing – The counterpart of *Seaport Village* on the Coronado side caters to the tourist trade. 1201 First St. at B (phone: 435-8895).

Promenade at Pacifico Beach and *Belmont Park* – Located in Mission Beach, these two shopping spots are handy to beach resort hotels. The *Promenade* is at Ventura and Mission Blvds. (phone: 488-0668); *Belmont Park* is at 41550 Mission Blvd. (phone: 581-6275).

Seaport Village – A faux Victorian complex on San Diego Bay near the city center, 849 W. Harbor Dr. (phone: 235-4014).

The opening of *Horton Plaza* in 1985 (between Broadway and G St., and 1st and 4th Aves.; phone: 239-8180) brought shoppers back to downtown San Diego en masse. This mall, a glittering labyrinth in 48 shades of color, with passages and galleries, odd angles and curves, levels and half-levels, banners, awnings, whimsical sculptures, and plantings, contains nearly 150 shops and eateries, 7 movies, and 2 live theaters. Four department stores — *Nordstrom, Robinson's,* the *Broadway,* and *Mervyn's* — anchor the whole group. Designer boutiques here include *Laise Adzer, Louis Vuitton,* and *Laura Ashley. Storton's Men's Fashion Theatre* stocks good-quality Sunbelt clothes, and shirts are made to order at the *Custom Shop.* The most interesting art is on display in the 2-story *Dyansen's Gallery,* near the plaza entrance. Most entertaining are *Kite Country,* the *Nature Company* (with flora and fauna gifts and art objects), *Abercrombie & Fitch, Brookstone,* and *The Price of His Toys.*

Other regions around the city provide a variety of shopping enclaves, with specialty shops as well as national chains. In La Jolla, two streets vie for the title of San Diego's Rodeo Drive. Prospect Street runs on a bluff overlooking the Pacific and is the city's most pleasant street for shopping on foot. Art galleries and restaurants predominate. A fashion parade of boutiques on Girard Avenue, which intersects Prospect, culminates with *I. Magnin* on the west side of the street and *Saks Fifth Avenue* to the east. Among the intriguing establishments:

C.J. Felcher – A unique collection of antique and estate jewelry. 1237 Prospect (phone: 459-5166).

Jacques LeLong – Southern California–Western: studs and sequins on leather duds. 1141 Prospect St. (phone: 454-7760).

Ken Done – An Australian designer's showcase of bright and clever graphics on shirts, accessories, and stationery. 7872 Girard Ave. (phone: 459-6945).

London Associates Shells – Seashells above the seashore, as well as fossils, polished and often hand-crafted into jewelry. 1137 Prospect St. (phone: 459-6858).

Ports International – An oasis of classic ladies' fashions. 7844 Girard Ave. (phone: 454-9151).

Treasure House – Decorative arts from the Orient. 7886 Girard Ave. (phone: 456-2664).

SPORTS AND FITNESS: There's just about everything for everybody.

Baseball – The National League *Padres* (phone: 283-4494) play at *Jack Murphy Stadium*, 9449 Friars Rd. (phone: 525-8282).

Bicycling – *Hamel's Action Sports Center* (704 Ventura Pl., Mission Beach; phone: 488-5050); *Reid's Bike Rentals* (711 Pacific Beach Dr.; phone: 275-0765); *Rent A Bike Inc.* (1775 E. Mission Bay Dr.; phone: 275-2644); *Rent-R-Bikes USA* (746 Emerald St.; phone: 581-3665).

Fishing – The Oceanside Pier is one of America's longest wooden piers. There are piers at Mission Bay, San Diego Harbor, and Shelter Island. You do need a permit for deep-sea fishing. Write to the California Dept. of Fish and Game Resources Building (1350 Front St., Room 2041, San Diego, CA 92101; phone: 237-7311). Marlin, yellowtail, and sailfish run in the spring. A fishing license is required for those 16 and older. Licenses can be obtained for $6.25 a day at sporting goods stores and at many lakes.

Fitness Centers – *San Diego Sports Medicine Center* offers aerobics classes and workout equipment (6699 Alvarado Rd.; phone: 287-4446); *Shirley Sports and Health Center of Scripps Clinic* has a comprehensive fitness center (10820 N. Torrey Pines, La Jolla; phone: 554-FITT); the *YMCA* has a pool and weight room (5505 Friars Rd.; phone: 298-3576).

Football – The NFL *Chargers* (phone: 280-2111) and San Diego State *Aztecs* (phone: 283-7378) play home games at *Jack Murphy Stadium*.

Golf – For tournaments, see *Special Events,* above. *Torrey Pines* golf course (phone: 453-8148) alongside the ocean is the site of the annual *Shearson Lehman Hutton Open.* It's also the most famous of the more than 60 public courses in San Diego County. *Mission Bay* golf course is lighted up for night plays (Mission Bay Park; phone: 273-1221). Another course is the *Coronado* (2000 Visalia Row; phone: 435-3121).

Horse Racing – Thoroughbreds race at *Del Mar Race Track,* July to September (I-5 to Fairgrounds exit; phone: 481-1207), or contact *Del Mar Thoroughbred Club* (phone: 755-1141). The racetrack at Del Mar is closed on Tuesdays. There's also racing at *Caliente Race Track* (Tijuana; phone: 706-681-7811; see *Extra Special*).

Ice Skating – *Ice Capades Chalet* (4545 La Jolla Village Dr.; phone: 452-9110); *San Diego Ice Arena* (off Hwy. 15, 1001 Black Mountain Rd.; phone: 530-1825).

Jai Alai – This Basque import is played at *Fronton Palacio,* Tijuana, Fridays through Wednesdays (phone: 52-66-851612).

Jogging – Run along Laurel Street to Balboa Park, where there are six different courses, ranging from less than one-half mile to 9 miles. It's possible to jog along Harbor Drive in the direction of the airport, but avoid rush hours because of the fumes. Mileage (8 miles' worth) is marked around Mission Bay. In La Jolla, run along the shore and boardwalk or the La Jolla cove.

Sailing and Boating – The City Recreation Department rents motorboats and rowboats for use on lakes (phone: 236-5555). They also give sailing courses (phone: 488-1004). *Seaforth Mission Bay Boat Rentals* (1641 Quivira Rd., Mission Bay; phone: 223-1681) and *Coronado Boat Rentals* (1715 Strand Way, Coronado; phone: 437-1517) have sailboats, rowboats, and power boats as well as boats rigged for water skiing; they also rent fishing gear and windsurfing equipment. You can rent sailboats and take sailing lessons at *Harbor Island Sailboats* (2040 Harbor Island Dr., Harbor Island; phone: 291-9568) and at many beach resort hotels.

Skiing – The *Torrey Pines Ski Club* organizes trips to nearby mountains; write to PO Box 82087, San Diego, CA 92138.

Surfing and Scuba Diving – La Jolla Cove is the most popular scuba diving spot because the water is particularly clear. Boomer Beach, so named because of the rumbling sound of surf crashing to shore, is the bodysurfers' first choice. Surfboarders ride the waves at La Jolla Shores. Diving gear and lessons are available at *Diving Locker* (1020 Grand Ave.; phone: 272-1120).

Swimming – There are 70 miles of public beaches, not to mention Mission Bay Park's manmade lagoons. La Jolla and Torrey Pines State Park beaches are especially beautiful (see *Special Places*). There are ten municipal swimming pools: Kearney Mesa, Kearns Memorial Park, Vista Terrace, Swanson, King, Colina del Sol, Mission Beach Plunge, Memorial, Clairemont, and Allied Gardens. For information call the Aquatics Department of the City Recreation Office (phone: 490-0923). Don't miss the recently restored, historic "Plunge" waterslide at Belmont Shores.

Tennis – For special tennis tournaments, see *Special Events,* above. Public courts are at La Jolla Recreation Center (615 Prospect St.; phone: 454-2071); *Morley Field* (2221 Morley Field Dr., Balboa Park; phone: 298-0920); Standley Park (3585 Governor Dr.; phone: 452-LOVE); and Robb Field (2525 Bacon St.; phone: 531-1563).

Whale Watching – Watch the migrating sea mammals from Cabrillo National Monument, Whale Point in La Jolla, or go on a whale watching excursion from *H & M Landing* (2803 Emerson St.; phone: 222-1144) or *Fisherman's Landing* (2838 Garrison St.; phone: 222-0391), mid-December, January, and February.

THEATER: The *Old Globe Theatre* stages festivals every summer, featuring contemporary productions, as well as Shakespeare; the rest of the year, the company performs modern classics, musicals, and dramas at both the *Old Globe* and next-door *Cassius Carter Center Stage* (Balboa Park; phone: 239-2255). *San Diego Repertory Theatre* performs in the *Lyceum Theater* — two stages (*Horton Plaza;* phone: 235-8025). *Gaslamp Quarter Theatre Company* offers eight plays per season at the *Elizabeth North Theatre* (547 4th St.; phone: 234-9538) and *Hahn Cosmopolitan Theatre* (444 4th Ave.; 232-9608). The *La Jolla Playhouse,* at the Mandel Weiss Center of the University of California–San Diego campus, presents a variety of plays from May through November (phone: 534-6760). The *California Ballet* performs the *Nutcracker Suite* at *Christmas,* other classics the rest of the year, at venues around the metro area (phone: 560-6741).

MUSIC: *San Diego Symphony Hall* is the home of the *San Diego Symphony* (1245 7th Ave.; (phone: 699-4200). The *San Diego Opera Company* performs at the *Civic Theatre* (phone: 232-7636). Free organ concerts are played every Sunday afternoon at the *Spreckels Organ Pavilion* (Balboa Park). For jazz, visit the *Catamaran* (3999 Mission Blvd., Mission Beach; phone: 488-1081). *Croce's* restaurant (802 Fifth Ave.) features live jazz 7 nights a week, as does the *Palace Bar* at the *Horton Grand* hotel. Most rock concerts take place at the *San Diego Sports Arena.*

NIGHTCLUBS AND NIGHTLIFE: The *Halcyon* is a very popular disco in town (4258 W. Point Loma Blvd., Ocean Beach; phone: 225-9559), as is *Confetti* (5373 Mission Center Rd.; phone: 291-8635). The *Cannibal Bar* at the *Catamarand* hotel is a lively, young dance club. *Elario's* in La Jolla features top jazz performance on the top floor of the *Summerhouse Inn* (7955 La Jolla Shores Dr., La Jolla; phone: 459-0541). *Bacchanal* has live music nightly throughout the week during the summer and also offers a panoramic view from a circular dining room (8022 Clairemont Mesa Blvd.; phone: 560-8022). *Old Del Mar Café* (273 Via de la Valle, Del Mar; phone: 755-6614) is a popular venue for live jazz, country, and rock, as is the *Old Pacific Beach Café* (4287 Mission Blvd., Pacific Beach; phone: 270-7522). For comedy, try *The Comedy Store* (916 Pearl St., La Jolla; phone: 454-9176) and *The Improv Comedy Club and Restaurant* (832 Garnet Ave.; phone: 483-4522).

■ **WHEN THE SWALLOWS COME BACK:** Yes, the swallows come back to Capistrano. Every year, though not necessarily on March 19. Stop in at the Mission of San Juan Capistrano in March for a serenade. It's open daily and fascinating. Admission charge. Follow Route 5 north for 47 miles to the Capistrano exit (phone: 714-493-1424).

BEST IN TOWN

CHECKING IN: Spurred by the *Convention Center* in the redeveloping downtown and a boom in La Jolla, fine new hotels and resorts also are opening, with outdoor athletic facilities and spectacular views. Visitors seeking comfortable, reasonably priced accommodations will find them in all parts of San Diego. Those listed below are special in quality, character, or value. Expect to pay $130 and up for a standard double at those places noted as expensive; between $90 and $125, moderate; and under $90 at places listed as inexpensive. For accommodations at bed and breakfast establishments, contact *Bed & Breakfast Directory for San Diego* (PO Box 3292, San Diego, CA 92103; phone: 297-3130). All telephone numbers are in the 619 area code unless otherwise indicated.

Del Coronado – One of the world's most picturesque hotels. When it opened in 1888, it was the largest wooden building in the country and the first hotel in the world to have electrical lighting and elevators. Thomas Edison himself supervised the electrical installation. Today, this turreted, rambling, 700-room resort is a National Historic Landmark. The first floor ocean view lanai rooms are extraordinary, but other rooms in the historic building can be less impressive than the exterior architecture, and there is a modern annex that's downright pedestrian. Then there are those early morning flights buzzing out of the naval air station. . . There is a small spa, 2 pools, tennis courts, and a good restaurant (see *Eating Out*). Forty-four meeting rooms are available, and for businesspeople, such services as secretarial assistance, A/V equipment, photocopiers, and computers. A concierge desk is on call, as is 24-hour room service, and express checkout. On the Coronado Peninsula, 1500 Orange Ave. (phone: 435-6611; 800-468-3533; Fax: 619-522-8262;). Expensive.

Inn L'Auberge – The defunct *Tudor Del Mar* hotel, a favorite pre–World War II seaside hangout of Hollywood stars and *Del Mar* racetrack fans, has been reincarnated as a 123-room luxury resort in a cozy, flower-filled French provincial mode. The massive lobby fireplace is an exact replica of the original. Staff members meet guests arriving at the *Amtrak* station. Occasionally, private railroad cars will bring them from Los Angeles, for a hefty price. Other pamperings include multinational versions of continental breakfasts, afternoon tea, and weekend dinner dances. Pools, a health club, tennis courts, a European spa, and chic shops all are on the premises. Meeting rooms can hold up to 250, and there's a concierge, secretarial services, A/V equipment, photocopiers, and computers. 1540 Camino Del Mar, Del Mar (phone: 259-1515 or 800-553-1336; Fax: 619-735-4940). Expensive.

John Gardiner's Rancho Valencia – Reminiscent of early California haciendas, this secluded resort near Del Mar offers accommodations in 21 Spanish-style casitas, comprising 43 spacious suites with fireplaces and terraces. Known for its extensive tennis facilities and clinics, the property also boasts a pool and 2 Jacuzzis, a croquet lawn, and access to nearby golf courses in addition to its 18 tennis courts. The dining room, *La Parenade,* provides fine French/Southern Californian food prepared by chef Claude Segal. Room service is always on call. Meeting rooms can accommodate up to 150, and among the other business services are secretarial assistance, A/V equipment, photocopiers, and computers. There's also a concierge desk, and express checkout. 5921 Valencia Circle, Rancho Santa Fe (phone: 756-1123 or 800-548-3664; Fax: 619-756-0165). Expensive.

Le Meridien San Diego at Coronado – The French put up this fresh, airy, *très gai* luxury resort in a South Seas island setting, with tropical plantings, lagoons, and exotic birds on the Coronado Peninsula. The 300 rooms are bright, the atmosphere relaxing. An on-site spa soothes the strains of a full range of resort activities, and a spa menu is always available. Food at both the elegant *Marius* and the casual brasserie, *L'Escale,* is exquisite (see *Eating Out* for both). Cars can be rented at the hotel, and the *Coronado Trolley* and water taxi both pick up passengers here. Room service is available around the clock. The business center offers secretarial services, A/V equipment, photocopiers, and computers. There's express checkout, as well as a concierge desk. 2000 2nd St., Coronado (phone: 435-3000 or 800-543-4300; Fax: 619-435-3032). Expensive.

Pan Pacific – The cluster of green-glazed hexagonal towers that make up this 436-room property shares an atrium with similar hexagons of a sibling office complex. The hotel boasts a comprehensive business center, along with such leisure facilities as a swimming pool, Jacuzzi, and fitness equipment. Located conveniently near the beach and theaters. Complimentary airport transportation. Room service is on call around the clock. There are 14 meeting rooms, concierge, secretarial services, A/V equipment, photocopiers, and computers. Express checkout. 400 West Broadway (phone: 239-4500; 800-874-9100; Fax: 619-239-4527). Expensive.

San Diego Marriott – Two elliptical towers rise 25 floors above San Diego Bay and the hotel's own 19-acre marina. Inside are 1,355 rooms and suites, a shopping arcade, and half a dozen restaurants and bars. Also on the premises are a fitness center, 6 lighted tennis courts, and a large outdoor pool. An adjoining marina offers boats for rent. Meeting rooms accommodate up to 3,000, and additional business amenities include secretarial services, A/V equipment, photocopiers, and computers. Other pluses are 24-hour room service, concierge, and express checkout. 333 W. Harbor Dr. (phone: 234-1500 or 800-228-9290; Fax: 619-234-8678; Telex: 695425). Expensive.

Sheraton Grand on Harbor Island and Sheraton Harbor Island – This 1,060-room resort and convention hotel complex has tennis courts, saunas, a health club, a swimming pool, and complete meeting facilities, which accommodate up to 640. Room service is always available, and other amenities are concierge and secretarial services, A/V equipment, photocopiers, and computers. Express checkout. 1380 Harbor Island Dr. (phone: 291-2900 or 800-325-3535; Fax: 619-294-9627; Telex: 697877). Expensive.

Sheraton Grande Torrey Pines – Neighbor to La Jolla's biological research centers and the two *Torrey Pines* golf courses, this casually elegant, white Mediterranean-style establishment has 400 rooms overlooking the greens and the Pacific beyond. Facilities include a fitness center, swimming pool with Jacuzzi, privileges at the Sports & Health Center of the Scripps Clinic next door, plus a butler on each floor who will clean golf spikes or iron a shirt. The view alone is worth the price of admission. Free limousine service within a 6-mile radius. Room service is available around the clock. The business center provides secretarial services, A/V equipment, photocopiers, and computers. Meeting rooms can hold up to 1,500. There's also a concierge desk, and express checkout. 10950 N. Torrey Pines Rd. (phone: 558-1500 or 800-451-0772; Fax: 619-558-1131). Expensive.

U. S. Grant – Restored to its 1910 ambience, the grand property is a registered National Historic Place. The downstairs could be a museum. The lobby, with pillars and a green and white marble floor, is awesome, and public rooms glitter with gold leaf and chandeliers. The 280 rooms are discreetly luxurious and equipped with modern amenities, but vestiges of the past remain, such as windows that open. A health club is another concession to today. Light lunch and tea are served in the *Grant Grill Lounge,* and breakfast, lunch, and dinner at the excellent *Grant Grill* (see *Eating Out*). The central location in the redeveloping downtown can't be beat. Complimentary van transportation to and from the airport. There is a concierge desk, secretarial services, A/V equipment, photocopiers, 24-hour room service, meeting rooms that accommodate up to 1,300, and express checkout. 326 Broadway (phone: 232-3121 or 800-334-6957; 800-237-5029 outside California; Fax: 619-232-3626). Expensive.

Westgate – A 223-room property considered among the finest in the US. Its downtown location makes it convenient as well. Consistent with the $1 million worth of antiques decorating the premises, the hotel also offers superb service. The *Fontainebleau Room* is one of the most elegant eateries in town (see *Eating Out*). Additional conveniences are 24-hour room service, concierge, meeting rooms with a capacity of up to 500, A/V equipment, photocopiers, computers, and express checkout. 1055 2nd Ave. (phone: 238-1818 or 800-522-1564; 800-221-3802, outside California; Fax: 619-232-4526; Telex: 695046). Expensive.

Hyatt Islandia – This contemporary 423-room property is situated on 4½ lush acres overlooking Mission Bay and the Pacific. Guests are not far from *Sea World* and other San Diego attractions. A 17-story tower offers 260 spacious rooms with glass-enclosed patios. Upper floors boast terrific nighttime views. The Regency Club, on the top 2 floors, provides concierge service and complimentary continental breakfast and hors d'oeuvres. The Marina Suites are in a 3-story building overlooking the marina. The resort offers a huge, California-shaped swimming pool, an outdoor Jacuzzi, whale watching, deep-sea fishing, sailboat rental, and a jogging path; golf and tennis are nearby. There are 2 restaurants, 10 meeting rooms, concierge, secretarial services, A/V equipment, photocopiers, and express checkout. On San Diego's Mission Bay, 1441 Quivira Rd. (phone: 224-1234; 800-233-1234; Fax: 619-224-0348; telex: 697844). Expensive to moderate.

Omni San Diego – Adjacent to the whimsical, post-modern *Horton Plaza Shopping Center,* it has 450 rooms, an outdoor swimming pool, and 2 tennis courts, plus a health club. The interior is done in softened tones, the menu at the *Festival* restaurant features regional California cooking, and the early-bird dinner at the coffee shop is a tasty, smashing bargain, and 24-hour room service 24 hours a day. With theaters and shopping right outside the door, this place is in the thick of the action. Guests can order from the room service menu at any time. Business conveniences include meeting rooms that hold up to 650, secretarial services, A/V equipment, photocopiers, computers, and express video checkout. There's also a concierge desk. 910 Broadway

Circle (phone: 239-2200 or 800-THE-OMNI; Fax: 619-239-3266; Telex: 9102504553). Expensive to moderate.

La Valencia – The venerable, pink building on La Jolla's browse-able Prospect Street is a handsome Spanish *doña* bejeweled with wrought iron, tile, and flowers. Both an international 100-room hotel and a local meeting place, it offers garden dining under bright umbrellas, a sauna, fitness room, shuffleboard, Jacuzzi, and a pool. By popular demand, a communal jigsaw puzzle has reappeared in *La Salle Lounge*. Around-the-clock room service is available. There are 3 meeting rooms, as well as A/V equipment and photocopiers; concierge; express checkout. 1132 Prospect St., La Jolla (phone: 454-0771; 800-451-0772; Fax: 619-456-3921; Telex: 183959). Expensive to moderate.

Catamarand Resort – South Pacific in feeling, this renovated 318-room property features a lobby complete with a waterfall, ponds filled with koi, and a museum-quality collection of Polynesian artifacts. Throughout its 8½ acres of grounds, over 100 varieties of trees, exotic birds, and tiki torches create a Hawaiian-style ambiance. Don't miss the whimsical hippopotamus water fountain. There are six 2-story structures and a 13-story tower that overlooks Mission Bay. Many rooms come equipped with kitchens. The *Cannibal Bar* jumps at night with live entertainment and dancing, while *Moray's Bar* is a quieter haven. One of San Diego's finest restaurants, the *Atoll* (see *Eating Out*) is also lodged here. The *Bahia Belle,* an authentic paddle wheel riverboat, links the *Catamarand* with its sister hotel, the *Bahia.* Business services include meeting rooms for up to 1,000, secretarial services, A/V equipment, and photocopiers. There's also a concierge desk. 3999 Mission Blvd. (phone: 488-1081; 800-288-0770; Fax: 619-488-1081). Moderate.

Hacienda Old Town – This 150-suite hostelry has microwave ovens, refrigerators, and coffeemakers; outdoor barbecue grills are available for guests' use. A swimming pool and fitness center are on the premises, as well as a restaurant. Guests also can sign for their meals at the neighboring *Brigantine.* Other conveniences are the meeting rooms, which accommodate up to 100, A/V equipment, photocopiers, and concierge. 4041 Harney St. (phone: 298-4707 or 800-888-1991; Fax: 619-298-4707, ext. 2460). Moderate.

Horton Grand – Ironically, an old bordello rebuilt in rampant Victorian style is considered the city's most romantic hostelry. Joined by a sunny atrium is the hotel's second half, once a saddlery. The concierge dresses like a madam in a Western. Guilded mirrors swing open to reveal TV sets, and toilets flush with a chain from an overhead wood tank. Amenities are modern, the service cheerfully solicitous. The *Ida Bailey* restaurant (the original madam's name) has jazz on Friday and Saturday evenings in the bar. Room service will arrive until 11 PM. Meeting rooms hold up to 300, and secretarial services, A/V equipment, and photocopiers are available. There's a concierge desk and express checkout. 311 Island Ave. (phone: 544-1886; 800-999-1886; Fax: 619-239-3823). Moderate.

Horton Park Plaza – Another downtown National Historic Landmark, it's a tastefully converted former office building with a beautiful 2-level restaurant. All 65 units, named after famous authors, are suites with cable TV. There's an exercise room and a sun deck. Meeting rooms can hold up to 100, and there are photocopiers and A/V equipment. Express checkout. 901 5th St. (phone: 232-9500 or 800-443-8012; Fax: 619-238-9945). Moderate.

Humphrey's Half Moon Inn – On Shelter Island, overlooking the bay and the marina — with all its sleek and shining boats — this inn has 182 luxury rooms, a pool, putting green, and is within walking distance of boatyards and sport fishing operations. Also known for its jazz. The meeting rooms have a capacity of up to 1,000, and A/V equipment and photocopiers are available. 2303 Shelter Island Dr. (phone: 224-3411; 800-542-7400; Fax: 619-224-3478; Telex: 311926). Moderate.

Hyatt Regency La Jolla at Aventine – Architect Michael Graves designed the post-modern Roman motif. This 400-room hostelry is part of an 11-acre compound within La Jolla's Golden Triangle business area. The rooms are made with well-crafted woods and offer views of the ocean and hills from the upper floors. Each of the 4 independently operated restaurants features a different cuisine. There are colonnaded formal gardens, a 32,000 square foot sporting club and spa, 2 lighted tennis courts, racquetball and squash courts, and a lap pool surrounded by 31 private cabanas. An express video checkout speeds guests on their way. Room service is available around the clock. Business amenities include 18 meeting rooms, secretarial services, A/V equipment, photocopiers, and computers. There's also a concierge desk. 3777 La Jolla Village Dr., La Jolla (phone: 552-1234 or 800-233-1234; Fax: 619-552-6066). Moderate.

Somerset Suites – Here are 80 sunny apartments with fully equipped kitchens, close to Balboa Park and the lively restaurant row on 5th Avenue Pool, Jacuzzi, complimentary continental breakfast, and cable TV are among the amenities. Concierge service is on call, and there are photocopiers. 606 Washington St. (phone: 692-5200; 800-356-1787 in California; 800-962-9665 elsewhere; Fax: 619-299-6065). Moderate.

Clarion – Also convenient to Balboa Park, this renovated hotel looks like a sun-filled Mediterranean Tara. Several rooms and suites have libraries, and all suites come with white tile wood-burning fireplaces, incongruous but cozy. The pool is Olympic-size, and there is a spa and a restaurant. Complimentary full breakfast, parking, and shuttle to the airport and rail terminal. Meeting rooms accommodate up to 600. Other business conveniences include a concierge desk, A/V equipment, photocopiers, and express checkout. 2223 El Cajón Blvd. (phone: 296-2101; 800-423-1935 in California; 800-843-9988 elsewhere; Fax: 619-296-2101). Inexpensive.

Torrey Pines Inn – A spectacular location overlooking the Pacific and right on the two famous *Torrey Pines* golf courses. Surfers and hang gliders are visible from the hotel, and La Jolla's beaches are just out the door. Swimming pool and lounge with entertainment on the premises. 71 rooms. There is a concierge desk, meeting rooms that accommodate up to 300, secretarial services, A/V equipment, photocopiers, computers, and express checkout. 11480 Torrey Pines Rd., La Jolla (phone: 453-4420; 800-448-8355 in California; 800-44U-TELL elsewhere; Fax: 619-453-0691). Inexpensive.

Town and Country – One of the best in Mission Valley and among the largest hotels in the city, with over 1,000 rooms. A popular convention spot; facilities include pools, saunas, barber shop, beauty parlor, and a 24-hour coffee shop. Business conveniences include meeting rooms that accommodate up to 3,050, concierge and secretarial services, A/V equipment, photocopiers, computers, and express checkout. 500 Hotel Circle (phone: 291-7131; 800-542-6082 in California; 800-260-8USA elsewhere; Fax: 619-291-3585; Telex: 695415). Inexpensive.

EATING OUT: San Diego's range of restaurants has become more innovative and international. Naturally, seafood stars on many menus, and both locals and out-of-towners go for Mexican food here. Expect to pay $60 or more at those places listed as expensive; $30 to $55, moderate; under $30, inexpensive. Prices are for a meal for two, not including drinks, wine, or tips. All telephone numbers are in the 619 area code unless otherwise indicated.

Marius – Very simply, a first-rate dining experience. The great atmosphere and superb cooking strongly evoke Provence. The escargots, roast duckling with lavender honey and lemon, and seabass with a black olive purée are all concocted with a light hand and a touch of whimsy. At about $125 for dinner for two, the price is dear, but it costs much less than a trip to the south of France. Closed Mondays. Reservations advised. Major credit cards accepted. 2000 Second St., in *Le Meridien San Diego* (phone: 435-3000). Very expensive.

Anthony's Star of the Sea Room – One of the best on the West Coast. Overlooking San Diego Harbor, it serves fresh-from-the-ocean abalone, and other fish and shellfish. The clams Genovese often are ordered as an entrée. Open daily except major holidays. Reservations necessary a day or two in advance. Major credit cards accepted. 1360 N. Harbor Dr. at foot of Ash St. (phone: 232-7408). Expensive.

Avanti – A showcase for Northern Italian specialties in an Art Deco setting. The menu features continental dishes with an Italian accent, such as braised radicchio served with salmon and porcini mushrooms with beef filet. Open daily. Reservations advised. Major credit cards accepted. 875 Prospect St., La Jolla (phone: 454-4288). Expensive.

El Bizcocho – Haute French dishes, such as *magret de canard grillé, salade à l'orange et basilic* (grilled Muscovy duck breast cooked with oranges and fresh basil), and scallops poached with vegetables in a chervil and chive broth dominate the menu. The San Pasqual Mountains provide a dramatic backdrop. Open daily. Reservations advised. Major credit cards accepted. 17550 Bernardo Oaks Dr., in the *Rancho Bernardo Inn* (phone: 800-854-1065). Expensive.

Dobson's – Downstairs, the pub is crowded, cozy, and old-fashioned. The dining room above the bar seats 32 for delicious seafood and grilled dishes with a French flair, and the specialty of the house — mussel bisque topped with a pastry toque — is a big hit. Friendly host Paul Dobson is reputed to be a former bullfighter. No lunch on Saturdays. Closed Sundays. Reservations essential for the dining room. Major credit cards accepted. 956 Broadway Circle (phone: 231-6771). Expensive.

Fontainebleau Dining Room – Waiters wearing white gloves quietly serve French food in palatial surroundings. The dessert cart is fabulous. One of San Diego's best. Closed Sundays. Reservations necessary. Major credit cards accepted. *Westgate Hotel,* 1055 2nd Ave. (phone: 238-1818). Expensive.

George's at the Cove – Pleasant, with big windows overlooking the La Jolla cove, this dining spot features regional California cuisine which uses local produce and an excellent California wine list. Examples: prawns with *tapenade* (an olive paste), tuna with *wasabi* (a hot, Japanese mustard). Open daily for lunch and dinner; Sunday brunch. Reservations advised. Major credit cards accepted. 1250 Prospect St., La Jolla (phone: 454-4244). Expensive.

Grant Grill – A classic grill, specializing in fish, steaks, and roasts grilled on a spit in the kitchen. The dining room retains its original men's club atmosphere. Open daily, Sunday brunch. Reservations advised. Major credit cards accepted. *U. S. Grant Hotel,* 326 Broadway (phone: 239-6806). Expensive.

Lubach's – In the face of stiff new competition, this old favorite shows its staying power. Shrimp en brochette and calf's sweetbreads *financière* highlight a menu that includes some fabulous beef and duck dishes. Closed Sundays and holidays. Reservations advised. Major credit cards accepted. 2101 N. Harbor Dr. (phone: 232-5129). Expensive.

Top o' the Cove – Looking out onto La Jolla Cove, a favorite of show biz types from LA, and consistently voted the most romantic restaurant in the area. It features squab, venison, and fresh pasta dishes. Open daily. Reservations necessary. Major credit cards accepted. 1216 Prospect St., La Jolla (phone: 454-7779). Expensive.

Café Pacifica – A seafood place that has pulled ahead in popularity. The fish is fresh; the seasoning cosmopolitan in the modern manner. An alternative to Mexican in Old Town. Dinner nightly, lunch weekdays. Reservations advised. Major credit cards accepted. 2414 San Diego Ave. (phone: 291-6666). Moderate.

Chart House – This place is located in the old *San Diego Rowing Club* building, which is now a historic landmark. Besides the location and the outdoor deck overlooking the harbor (many customers arrive via the harbor, and dock for the evening), you'll find a fabulous, full oyster bar. Open daily for dinner. Reservations advised. Major credit cards accepted. 525 E. Harbor Dr., and 6 other locations, including Coronado and Shelter Island (phone: 233-7391). Moderate.

China Camp – Not the usual Chinese menu, specialties include "gold miner's chicken" and "beggar's hen," based on the recipes of the Chinese immigrants who came to California in 1849 to pan for gold. Dinner nightly, lunch weekdays. Reservations advised. Major credit cards accepted. Pacific Hwy. at Hawthorne (phone: 232-1367). Moderate.

Crown/Coronet Room – The dining room at the *Del Coronado* hotel gets high marks overall, especially for its Sunday brunches. Mexican and fresh-catch specials are featured at lunch. Open daily for breakfast, lunch, and dinner. Reservations strongly advised. Major credit cards accepted. 1500 Orange Ave. (phone: 435-6611). Moderate.

L'Escale – Located in *Le Meridien* hotel, this dining spot is fabulous for its outdoor luncheons served under white umbrellas, overlooking the bay. The emphasis is on fresh seafood and "Fitness Specials" that weigh in at 115 to 282 calories, but you'll have a hard time resisting the cheese twists and fresh bread. There's also a popular Sunday brunch. Open daily. Reservations advised. Major credit cards accepted. 2000 Second St. (phone: 435-3000). Moderate.

Fio's – This trendy, Northern Italian spot has been packed practically from the instant its doors opened. Of the two dining rooms, one is decorated with stunning murals of Siena's famous *Palio* by local artist Debra Sievers. There's an ever-changing menu, plus homemade pasta and pizza cooked in a wood-burning oven. Don't miss the *tiramasù* for dessert. Valet parking is a plus, since it is located in the heart of the Gaslamp District. Open Mondays through Saturdays for lunch and dinner; on Sunday, only dinner is served. Reservations advised. Most major credit cards accepted. 801 Fifth Ave. (phone: 234-FIOS). Moderate.

Il Fornaio – The menu here is as authentically Tuscan as the Carrara marble on its counters. Diners gaze at the Pacific from the terrace or window tables, or at a huge open kitchen with a genuine *girarrosto* spit from the counter seats. Coffee comes in many varieties, while hearty breads and delectable pastries are sold at the bakery counter. Open daily for lunch and dinner. Reservations advised. Visa and Master-Card accepted. 1555 Camino Del Mar (phone: 755-8876). Moderate.

French Side of the West – An instant hit, this 14-table country French restaurant had to expand after only a year of operation. The Burgundian chef prepares numerous tasty, fixed-price, five-course dinners with a dozen and a half entrées so proudly, he sometimes is moved to autograph the plate! Dinner only, daily. Reservations essential. Major credit cards accepted. 2202 Fourth Ave. (phone: 234-5540). Moderate.

Pacifica Grill – A more casual downtown sibling of the *Café Pacifica* overlooks the ground level of a warehouse fetchingly converted into a mini-mall next to the *Amtrak* terminal. The restaurant features familiar dishes concocted on the principle that anything goes as long as it's Southwestern. The wild mushroom fajitas with fresh herbs and Maui onions work beautifully, and the sourdough bread and coffee are exceptional. Dinner nightly, lunch weekdays. Major credit cards accepted. 1202 Kettner Blvd. (phone: 696-9226). Moderate.

Rainwater's – This neighbor of the *Pacifica Grill* reputedly serves the best steaks in town, along with fresh seafood. Late suppers are a boon to hungry theater- and concert-goers. Open daily for lunch and dinner. Reservations advised. Major credit cards accepted. 1202 Kettner Blvd. (phone: 233-5757). Moderate.

Atoll – Loudly lauded by local restaurant critics, this dining spot offers such dishes as lamb potstickers, and spinach salad with marinated scallops. The outrageous desserts, such as the chocolate marquis and the Southwestern lemon citrus tart, are not to be missed. Open daily. Reservations advised. Major credit cards accepted. 3999 Mission Blvd., in the *Catamarand* (phone: 488-1081). Moderate to inexpensive.

Alfonso's of La Jolla – The Mexican dishes here are probably the most popular in town. Try *carne asada Alfonso* or one of the burrito or taco combination plates. Ask for Alfonso's Secret — it changes every day, and it's not on the menu. Open daily for lunch and dinner. Reservations advised. Major credit cards accepted. 1251 Prospect St., La Jolla (phone: 454-2232). Inexpensive.

Anthony's Fish Grotto – If you're looking for a burger, don't come here, as this casual place serves only seafood. This is one of three in the popular chain of "grottoes." The other locations are in La Mesa and Chula Vista. Open daily. No reservations. Major credit cards accepted. 1360 N. Harbor Dr. (phone: 232-5103). Inexpensive.

Calliope's – A Greek café and take-out place, where both the aromas and the prices are pleasing. Marinated fish, fowl, and meats are roasted or skewered for the grill, there are phyllo specialties and classic Greek appetizers, salads, and daily vegetarian specialties. Open Mondays through Saturdays for lunch and dinner, brunch and dinner on Sundays. Reservations advised. Major credit cards accepted. 3958 Fifth Ave. (phone: 291-5588). Inexpensive.

Corvette Diner – A fire engine red classic Corvette holds the place of honor in this noisy, jumping 1950s bar and grill. It features excellent hamburgers with a variety of trimmings, mid-American nostalgic fare, and pure corn entertainment. Open from 11 AM to 11 PM weekdays, to midnight weekends. No reservations. $10 minimum on Visa and MasterCard. 3946 5th Ave. (phone: 452-1076, or 542-1001 for recording). Inexpensive.

French Pastry Shop – One of our favorite places for breakfast when we're headed for *Torrey Pines*. Lunch and dinner are just as good but the freshly baked breads and pastries somehow seem a bit tastier with morning coffee. Open daily. Visa and MasterCard accepted. 5550 La Jolla Blvd., La Jolla (phone: 454-9094). Inexpensive.

Hob Nob Hill – One of the most delightful places to have breakfast in the entire city, offerings include "The Three Musketeers," a slice of ham encased in 3 buttermilk pancakes, eggs Florentine, delectable pecan waffles, and Canadian blueberry hotcakes. Open daily for breakfast, lunch, and dinner. Reservations unnecessary. Major credit cards accepted. 2271 First Ave. (phone: 239-8176). Inexpensive.

Karinya – Pacific Rim cooking worth applauding makes this eatery worth a second visit. Dishes such as *meekrob,* sweet and spicy noodles, as well as shrimp, beef, and chicken prepared Thai-style with lots of cilantro and curry, are particular favorites. Open daily. Reservations advised. Most major credit cards accepted. 4475 Mission Blvd. (phone: 270-5050). Inexpensive.

Old Columbia Brewery and Grill – The first latter-day pub brewery in San Diego was a smash from the start. Guests in the spacious taproom and bar sample house brews, eat juicy burgers, and can order a few fancier items while watching the brewery's workings through a glass wall. Lunch and dinner daily. Reservations advised. Visa and Master-Card accepted. 1157 Columbia St. (phone: 234-2739). Inexpensive.

Old Town Mexican Café y Cantina – Perennial local Mexican favorite. *Carnitas* are the specialty. There is patio dining, and the bar stays open to 2 AM. Dinner nightly, lunch daily except Sundays, brunch Sundays. Reservations advised for parties of 10 or more. Major credit cards accepted. 2489 San Diego Ave. (phone: 297-4330). Inexpensive.

Point Loma Seafoods – Hickory-smoked fish attracts diners and gulls. Especially popular for take-out lunch. You pick up your meals, sit where you are, and throw what is left over to the birds. Lunch and dinner daily. Reservations unnecessary. No credit cards accepted. 2805 Emerson St. (phone: 223-6553 or 223-1986). Inexpensive.

Taco Auctioneers – Bidding isn't necessary, but this hip café warns diners that food fights are not allowed on the premises. Despite its eccentricities, the food is very, very good. *Enfrijoladas,* a dish of three corn tortillas with jack cheese, ranchero beans and avocados, is a favorite, as is the *sopa Mazatleca,* an excellent shrimp soup in a tomato broth. Open daily. Reservations unnecessary. No credit cards accepted. 1951 San Elijo Ave., Cardiff-by-the-Sea (phone: 942-8226). Inexpensive.

SAN FRANCISCO

AT-A-GLANCE

SEEING THE CITY: Coit Tower, on the summit of Telegraph Hill, offers a spectacular panorama of San Francisco and the surrounding area: to the north are the waterfront and San Francisco Bay, the Golden Gate Bridge, Alcatraz Island, and on the far shore, Sausalito; downtown San Francisco lies to the south; to the east are Berkeley and the East Bay hills; and Nob Hill and Russian Hill rise to the west. The tower itself, a 210-foot cylindrical column built in 1934 under the Works Progress Administration, is a striking landmark against the city's skyline; the funds came from a bequest by local eccentric and socialite Lilli Coit "to add beauty to the city (she) loved." Recently restored Depression-era frescoes depict scenes of California in political, economic, and social vignettes. Open daily. Admission charge to view lobby frescoes and ride the elevator to the top of the tower (follow Telegraph Hill Blvd. to the top from Lombard and Kearny Sts.). Twin Peaks is another excellent vantage point from which to view the city. (Follow Twin Peaks Blvd. to the top.) Several cocktail lounges offer fine views, too; among the highest, at 779 feet, is the *Carnelian Room,* the restaurant (don't go for the food) and bar atop the Bank of America Building (555 California St.; phone: 433-7500), open nightly for dinner and on Sundays for brunch.

SPECIAL PLACES: San Francisco is a compact city and easy to get around. Most of the attractions are concentrated within a few areas, and the mild weather year-round makes walking pleasant, but you can sightsee by almost anything that rides, flies, or floats, from cable cars and their motorized facsimiles to buses, bicycles, carriages, trains, boats, helicopters and hot-air balloons, to a beautifully preserved DC-3. Send $1 to the San Francisco Convention and Visitors Center (PO Box 6977, San Francisco, CA 94101) for the indispensable *San Francisco Book,* which lists many tour operators and videocassettes. The *Riders Guide–Auto Tape Tours* (484 Lake Park Ave., #255, Oakland; phone: 653-2553) has audiocassettes for do-it-yourself touring between Big Sur and the Napa and Sonoma valleys. The best way to see San Francisco is on foot. *City Guides* (Main Library, Civic Center, San Francisco 94102; phone: 557-4266) offers a free neighborhood walking tour daily that highlights the city's historical diversity. For example, the Gold Rush City trek explores the haunts of the original 49ers, and in Haight-Ashbury, the remnants of the Summer of Love in the 1960s are still evident in the psychedelic street attire worn by die-hards. "Cruisin' the Castro" is a walking tour of Castro Street, "the heart of gay America." The tour includes political and architectural highlights of the area; contact Trevor Hailey (375 Lexington St.; phone: 550-8110). For other unusual field trips including tours of cemeteries, windmills, and informative insider's tours, call *Near Escapes* (phone: 386-8687).

Winding streets, hills that rise and fall like giant tidal waves, the bay with its Golden Gate Bridge suspended across the sky like a timeless burnt-orange sunset — is it any wonder San Francisco has been the backdrop of so many Hollywood movies? A few movie highlights: The

Fairmont hotel (see *Checking In*), where the film famous frolicked, and Orson Welles unexpectedly faced William Randolph Hearst, the real-life inspiration for Welles's *Citizen Kane* (1941); across the street are the Brocklebank Apartments (1000 Mason St.), the elegant high-rise Kim Novak called home in Alfred Hitchcock's haunting *Vertigo* (1958); and Lauren Bacall's fabulous Telegraph Hill apartment in *Dark Passage* (1947) — the Art Deco building at 1360 Montgomery Street, with its etched-glass entrance, ocean liner motif, and silver-painted nautical murals that provided the perfect hideout for Bacall's favorite film fugitive, Humphrey Bogart. For a complete guided tour of the city's film locations contact *Showbus* (988 Market St., Suite 304; $22.50; reservations usually required.)

DOWNTOWN

Civic Center – This 7-square-block area encompasses several attractive buildings and a nicely designed fountain and plaza. Among the buildings are City Hall, a notable example of Renaissance grandeur with a 300-foot-high dome; the *War Memorial Opera House,* site of the signing of the UN Charter in 1945 and current home of the *San Francisco Opera* and *Ballet;* the *Civic Auditorium,* scene of cultural and political events since 1915; and the *Louise M. Davies Symphony Hall.* The War Memorial Veterans Building houses the *San Francisco Museum of Modern Art.* Its fine permanent collections include works by Matisse, Klee, Calder, and Pollock, while changing exhibitions include works by internationally known modern and contemporary artists. Closed Mondays. Open from 10 AM to 5 PM Tuesdays, Wednesdays, and Fridays; from 11 AM to 5 PM Saturdays and Sundays; open until 9 PM on Thursdays. Admission charge. McAllister St. and Van Ness Ave. (phone: 863-8800). Bounded by Van Ness Ave. and Hyde, McAllister, and Grove Streets, the Civic Center also is a good place to start the 49-Mile Drive, a well-marked trail that takes in many of the city's highlights. Just follow the blue, white, and orange seagull signs.

Union Square – Right in the shopping area, Union Square offers a respite from the crowds of people (though not from the hordes of pigeons). You can feed the birds, relax on the benches, and watch the fashion shows, concerts, and flower displays that are held here in good weather. The elegant *St. Francis* hotel is on the west side of the square, while the surrounding area contains sidewalk flower stands and the city's finest shops. One of the most interesting of these is *Gump's,* with its beautiful collection of jade among its many rare imports (250 Post St.; phone: 982-1616). Bordered by Geary, Post, Powell, and Stockton Sts.

Bank of California Museum – The bank maintains a *Museum of Money of the American West,* a collection of Gold Rush artifacts, silver ingots, and privately minted gold coins. Open weekdays during banking hours. No admission charge. 400 California St. (phone: 765-0400).

Wells Fargo History Museum – The history room features more of Old California, with photographs and relics from Gold Rush days, and the *Wells Fargo Overland Stage,* the wagon that brought pioneers west, as well as coins, placer, and hard rock gold from mother lode mines. Open weekdays from 9 AM to 5 PM. No admission charge. 420 Montgomery St. (phone: 396-2619).

Embarcadero Center – Between the financial district and the waterfront, this 8½-acre area of shopping malls, restaurants, and offices features several notable sculptures, including the Vaillancourt Fountain (100 abstractly arranged concrete boxes with water spouting from them) and a 60-foot sculpture by the late Louise Nevelson. At the foot of Market St.

Chinatown – The largest Chinese community outside of the Orient, Chinatown is an intriguing 24-block enclave of pagoda-roofed buildings, excellent restaurants, fine import shops featuring ivory carvings and jade

jewelry from the Orient, temples, and museums. Grant Avenue is the main thoroughfare — enter through an archway crowned with a dragon (Grant at Bush St.). Best to go on foot or take the California Street cable car, because the area is too congested for easy parking. The Old St. Mary's Church, built in 1854 of granite from China, is the city's oldest cathedral. It survived the 1906 and 1989 earthquakes, perhaps because of its warning on the façade above the clock dial: "Son Observe the Time and Fly from Evil" (Grant Ave. and California St.). More words of wisdom, as well as regional artifacts, including tiny slippers used for the bound feet of Oriental ladies, pipes from Old Chinatown opium dens, and photographs of some famed telephone operators who memorized the names and numbers of 2,400 Chinatown residents in the old days, can be found at the *Chinese Historical Society of America Museum* (650 Commercial St., between Kearney and Montgomery; phone: 391-1188). Open Tuesdays through Saturdays, noon to 4 PM. No admission charge. For information on walking tours of Chinatown, contact the Chinese Cultural Center (750 Kearny St., inside the *Holiday Inn;* phone: 986-1822), Tuesdays through Saturdays.

You haven't really experienced Chinatown fully until you've had dim sum, a brunch or luncheon feast of a variety of delicate morsels — chopped mushrooms in half-moons of rice dough, deep-fried sweet potato, meat dumplings; try either *Yank Sing* (427 Battery St.; phone: 362-1640) or the *Hong Kong Tea House* (835 Pacific Ave.; phone: 391-6365). Bordered by Kearny, Mason, and Bush Sts., and Broadway.

North Beach – There is no longer a beach here, but this traditional neighborhood remains colorful and diverse — mostly Italians, Basques, and Chinese. The area's great for strolling and eating — bakeries and bread shops sell cannoli, rum babas, marzipan, and panettone (a round, sweet bread filled with raisins and candied fruit). Numerous restaurants and cafés serve anything from espresso or cappuccino to complete dinners. For lunch or dinner, the *Washington Square Bar and Grill* (1707 Powell St.; phone: 982-8123) has great pasta, fresh fish, and veal, as well as a popular bar. Or if you want to make your own cup of coffee, you can pick up majolica espresso pots (and art imports) at *Biordi's* (412 Columbus Ave.; phone: 392-8096). At night, the district around Broadway offers everything from rock music and jazz to Italian opera on the jukebox at *Tosca Café* (242 Columbus; phone: 391-1244), to excellent shows by female impersonators at the legendary *Finocchio's* (506 Broadway; phone: 982-9388). An architecturally and gastronomically dazzling Chinese restaurant is *Brandy Ho* (450-452 Broadway; phone: 362-6268). One of the best times of year to visit North Beach is in early June, during the street bazaar, when local artists display their wares along Upper Grant Avenue. Other times, numerous galleries and studios exhibit crafts, paintings, jewelry, and unusual clothing. Washington Square is a nice place to sit in the sun or have lunch with the paisanos under the statue — ironically, not of the square's namesake — of Benjamin Franklin (Columbus and Union Sts.). Extends north and northwest from Chinatown to San Francisco Bay.

Japan Center – This attractive modern complex is the focal point in culture and trade of San Francisco's substantial Japanese community. The 5-acre area contains movie theaters, teahouses, restaurants, sushi and tempura bars, art galleries, shops selling everything from pearls to stereo equipment, a school where you can learn Japanese doll making and flower arranging, and the Japanese Consulate. With its 5-tiered Peace Pagoda in the center of a reflecting pool, the elegantly landscaped Peace Plaza is the scene of the April *Cherry Blossom Festival* and traditional Japanese celebrations, like the *Mochi-Pounding Ceremony* (in which much preparation and even more pounding result in delicious rice cakes). Speaking of pounding, the renovated *Kabuki Hot Springs and Japanese Spa* offers shiatsu massage, traditional Japanese baths, whirlpool baths, saunas, steambaths, and other services; the works will leave you feeling as fresh and crisp as a newly made rice cake (1750 Geary Blvd.; phone: 922-6000). Bounded by Laguna, Fillmore, Geary, and Post Sts.

FISHERMAN'S WHARF AND VICINITY

Fisherman's Wharf – This rambling waterfront section is both the center of the commercial fishing industry and California's largest tourist attraction after *Disneyland.* On the wharf at Jefferson Street, you walk through an open-air fish market where you can partake in an old San Francisco tradition; buy a loaf of freshly baked sourdough bread at *Boudin's Bread Company* (156 Jefferson St.; phone: 928-1849); and create the ultimate urban picnic by adding Dungeness crab purchased at one of the numerous sidewalk stalls. The fishing boats return in the afternoon and hoist their crates of fish to the pier at the foot of Jones and Leavenworth Streets. If you're up late (about 3 AM), there are few sights at that hour more impressive than the San Francisco fleet leaving the harbor for a day's catch. The wharf restaurants often are crowded and expensive, but try the huge *Alioto's;* the menu has been upgraded with Sicilian seafood recipes, and the cappuccino is as good as the best in Italy (No. 8 Fisherman's Wharf; phone: 673-0183). The wharf area has numerous sidewalk stalls selling handcrafted items, and many interesting sights also have sprung up here.

Pier 39 – Reconstructed with wood salvaged from other (demolished) piers, Pier 39 is a popular entertainment complex on the northern waterfront. A pleasant hour or two can be spent ambling through the plethora of shops — crafts, bakery, import, clothing, specialty, toy, jewelry, camera, fine food, crystal and silver, and many others. Meanwhile, mimes, jugglers, and other street performers provide continuous entertainment. For lunch or dinner, there's an international roster of foods from which to choose — Italian, Chinese, Swiss; grab a bite at one of the numerous stand-up, take-out fresh seafood booths; or simply indulge your sweet tooth at *Mendocino's Ice Cream.* Children can run off excess energy at the Pier's playground and park, or take a ride on the double-decker Venetian carousel at the end of the pier; weekend sailors and fishermen can charter boats at the marina. Pier 39, on the Embarcadero, just east of Fisherman's Wharf. (Parking garage across the way on Beach St.)

San Francisco Maritime National Historic Park – A huge, ship-shape building at the foot of Polk St., the park's *National Maritime Museum* is a treasure trove of memorabilia documenting shipping development from Gold Rush days to the present: with photographs, figureheads, massive anchors, shipwreck relics, and beautiful model ships. Open daily, 10 AM to 5 PM. No admission charge (Aquatic Park; phone: 556-3002). Berthed off nearby Hyde Street Pier, three old ships welcome the public. The *Balclutha* was a British cargo ship that rounded Cape Horn 17 times carrying rice and wine to San Francisco, worked as an Alaskan salmon trader, and even did a stint in Hollywood as a rather oversize prop in sea films. The *Eureka* used to shuttle passengers and cars across the bay during the early decades of the century. The antique automobiles displayed on the car deck are sure to delight car buffs. Aboard the schooner *CA Thayer,* "sailors" demonstrate raising sails and tying knots against the background of sea chanteys. Open daily. Admission charge (Hyde St. Pier; phone: 556-6435). *The Maritime Store* is full of books about the sea, plus maps and posters (phone: 775-BOOK).

Pier 45/USS *Pampanito* – A project of the National Maritime Museum Association. Historical photographs of this World War II submarine, including its role in the sinking of two Japanese ships with 2,000 British and Australian POWs aboard and the rescue of 73 survivors 2 days later, are on display on the pier. On board, a narrated tape guides visitors through the operations and life of a submersible, where every inch of space had to be put to life-and-death use. Open daily. Pier 45 (phone: 929-0202).

Bay Cruises – The *Blue and Gold Fleet* (Pier 39; phone: 781-7877) and the *Red and White Fleet* (Pier 43½, near Fisherman's Wharf, and Pier 41; phone: 546-2896 or 800-445-8880) cruise year-round past Alcatraz Island and the Golden Gate Bridge and then to the shoreline of Marin County, rimming the bay. Departures every day, all day. Admission charge. For evening vistas of the Bay Area from the water, *Hornblower Yachts* offers luxury dining cruises. Pier 33 (phone: 394-8900).

Alcatraz Island – This famed escape-proof federal penitentiary stands out grimly in the bay, 1½ miles from Fisherman's Wharf. Such notorious criminals as Al Capone, "Machine Gun" Kelly, and Doc Barker never returned from their stays here. The prison was closed in 1963 because of exorbitant operating costs and has been open to the public since 1973. The National Park Service runs tours of the prison block, where you see the "dark holes" in which rebellious prisoners were confined in solitude, and the tiny steel-barred cells. Two-hour tours depart daily on a first-come, first-served basis; tickets may be purchased in advance through *Ticketron*. Departs from Pier 41 (phone: 546-2896 or 800-445-8880).

Ghirardelli Square – Pronounced *Gear*-a-*del*li. Originally a woolen mill that turned out Union Army uniforms during the Civil War, then later a chocolate factory, the stately landmark red brick buildings here now house import shops which sell anything from Persian rugs to Chinese kites, plus outdoor cafés, art galleries, and fine restaurants. The *Mandarin* (phone: 673-8812 or 474-5438) serves excellent Chinese food; but perhaps sweetest of all is the *Ghirardelli Chocolate Manufactory* (phone: 771-4903), where you can watch chocolate being made and then eat the spoils afterward. If you're truly inspired, try the Golden Gate banana split, which tops all — three scoops of ice cream, three flavors of syrup, and a banana bridge rising above mountains of whipped cream. Open daily. Bounded by Beach, Larkin, North Point, and Polk Sts.

The Cannery – Modeled after Ghirardelli Square, this former Del Monte cannery is now a 3-level arcade featuring chic boutiques, restaurants, and an olive tree–shaded central courtyard where street musicians and mimes strut their stuff. Open daily. Bounded by Beach, Leavenworth, and Jefferson Sts.

Lombard Street – Often referred to as the most twisting urban street in the world, Lombard has eight switchbacks in a single block. Drive down slowly or, better yet, stroll, taking time to appreciate the lovely residential façades, colorful flowers, and lush plantings. Between Hyde and Leavenworth Sts.

GOLDEN GATE — THE PROMENADE AND THE PARK

Golden Gate Promenade – This 3½-mile shoreline trail is among the most spectacular walks (or jogging paths) in America. You meander from Aquatic Park past lush green trees, eroding rocky points, a classy yacht harbor in front of the *St. Francis Yacht Club,* a grassy park beside an old cobbled sea wall, all the while approaching that ultimate of spans, the Golden Gate Bridge. Near the seawall, the incoming tide fills the pipes of the Wave Organ, creating music by the sea. A number of interesting museums line the way. Ft. Point, completed in 1861 as the West Coast's only Civil War outpost, is now a National Historic Site. No admission charge (at the base of the Golden Gate Bridge, Presidio; phone: 556-1693). The *Presidio Army Museum,* established in 1776 as a Spanish garrison, has artifacts illustrating its whole history. Closed Mondays. No admission charge (Lincoln and Funston Aves.; phone: 561-4115). Most unusual is the *Palace of Fine Arts,* a grand Beaux Arts building constructed for the *Panama-Pacific Exhibition of 1915.* It houses the Exploratorium, a collection of 800 displays on science, technology, and the reaches and limits of human perception. Closed Mondays and Tuesdays. Admission charge (3601 Lyon St.; phone: 563-7337).

Golden Gate Bridge – The loftiest and one of the longest single-span suspension bridges ever constructed, the bright-orange Golden Gate marked its 50th anniversary in 1987 with a huge civic celebration that culminated in the permanent lighting of its towers. To enjoy a stunning view, follow the handicapped-accessible walk up to the toll plaza level, where you'll also find gardens landscaped with native flowering plants. From here you have several options: You can catch a bus back downtown; turn around, and walk back with the view of the city skyline accompanying you all the way; or follow in the footsteps of great coast trekkers across the Golden Gate Bridge and beyond — north along trails on the ridges and shoreline for 60 miles to Tomales Point. You can walk across the bridge (or under it); if you are driving, take the very first exit north of the bridge, park, and enjoy the terrific view of San Francisco.

California Palace of the Legion of Honor – A memorial for America's World War I dead, modeled after its namesake in Paris, this beautiful classic Greek building houses a fine collection of European art from medieval to Impressionist, represented by Monet, Manet, and Degas and Rodin sculptures. Closed Mondays and Tuesdays. Admission charge includes entry to the *de Young Museum* and the *Asian Art Museum* (see below). Lincoln Park (phone: 750-3600).

Golden Gate Park – Developed from 1,000 acres of rolling sand dunes, Golden Gate Park has all the amenities of a large recreation area. There are bike paths, hiking and equestrian trails, three lakes (where you can sail model boats, or rent real ones, or practice casting), sports fields, and a 25-acre meadow. The park also features a rose garden, a lovely rhododendron dell, the Strybing Arboretum — over 70 acres rich with 5,000 species of plants and trees from all over the world — and the Conservatory of Flowers, a greenhouse with lush tropical growth. (Arboretum and conservatory open daily. No admission charge. Along South Drive and Conservatory Drive, respectively.) The Japanese Tea Garden is a masterpiece of Oriental landscaping with a half-moon wishing-well bridge, a bronze Buddha, a temple, a teahouse serving jasmine and green tea, and, in the spring, magnificent blooms of cherry blossoms. Open daily. Admission charge. (Off South Dr. just west of the *de Young Museum.*) No such lyrical setting could be complete without music, and the Music Concourse offers this with free open-air *Municipal Band* concerts on Sunday afternoons when weather is good (between the *de Young Museum* and the California Academy of Sciences). The park also has three fine museums:

> **Asian Art Museum of San Francisco** – The bulk of this 6-century array of jade, bronzes, ceramics, paintings, woodwork, and art from India, Korea, China, Japan, and Southeast Asia was donated by Avery Brundage, the former president of the International Olympics Committee. Closed Mondays and Tuesdays. Admission charge. In Golden Gate Park (phone: 668-8922).

> **California Academy of Sciences** – The state's oldest scientific institution offers a wide variety of exhibitions ranging from the *Steinhart Aquarium,* with dolphins, piranhas, talking fish, penguins, and 14,000 other species, to the farthest reaches of space in the *Morrison Planetarium*'s changing shows. Open daily. Admission charge. On the Music Concourse (phone: 221-5100).

> **M. H. de Young Memorial Museum** – One of the West Coast's major art museums, it houses paintings, sculpture, and decorative arts from more than 300 cultures and an outstanding collection of American art. Closed Mondays and Tuesdays. Admission charge. 10th Ave. and Fulton (phone: 750-3600).

Cable Car Museum – This lovely brick building is the powerhouse for the current system and the storehouse for cable car history. The first cable car, invented in 1873 by Andrew Hallidie, and exact scale models of cars servicing all the various lines are on display here at their middle stop. Open daily. No admission charge. Washington and Mason Sts., near Chinatown (phone: 474-1887).

San Francisco Zoo – The Koala Crossing and an ultramodern Primate Discovery Center make a visit here particularly worthwhile. More than 1,000 birds and animals can be viewed on foot or from aboard the motorized tour train. Adjacent to the main zoo is the Children's Zoo, a 7-acre nursery where children can stroke barnyard animals or watch baby lions being bottle fed (phone: 661-7777). The spectacular primate center has dozens of exotic and/or endangered species, as well as a sophisticated discovery center full of hands-on experiments and informative, fun-to-do computer/slide programs. Open daily. Admission charge. Sloat Blvd. and 45th Ave. (phone: 753-7080).

SOUTH OF MARKET STREET

SoMa – Formerly the city's gritty warehouse district (the name stands for "South of Market"), this area has been transformed into a very trendy neighborhood with hip nightclubs, art galleries, and enough discount clothing outlets to satiate even the most obsessed shopper (see *Shopping*). *Shopper Stopper* (P.O. Box 535, Sebastopol, CA. 95472; phone: 707-829-1597) offers a 6½-hour shopping tour of the area conducted by fashion and color consultants. After you've worked up an appetite from all that shopping, head for *Max's Diner,* a 1950s-style diner and fountain (311 3rd St.; phone: 546-MAXS). The area is roughly bounded by Market, Embarcadero, China Basin, and Division Sts.

■ **EXTRA SPECIAL:** Within an hour's drive of San Francisco (north along US 101, Rte. 37, then Rte. 121) begins the number one wine-producing region in the US, the gently rolling Sonoma County and, beyond, the Napa Valley. The most interesting wineries for tours and tastings are Beringer (St. Helena), where you tour cellars dug into a hillside and then attend a tasting at Gothic Rhine House; the Christian Brothers (St. Helena); the Sterling Vineyards (south of Calistoga), with its striking Aegean-style architecture; Hans Kornell champagne cellars or Domain Chandon Yountville, where the bubbly costs $3 to taste and the restaurant is superb. Many eateries in this wine region offer intoxicating dining. *Truffles* in Sebastopol uses an array of exotic fresh mushrooms; and *Château Souverain* in Geyserville serves a corn-meal polenta with tomato fondue. The mild weather encourages not only grape production but also outdoor activity. Pick up some bread and cheese along Highway 29 en route to Bothe–Napa Valley State Park. Its 1,000 acres of broad-leaved trees, pines, and redwoods are lovely for picnicking, biking, and swimming in summer. In Yountville, you can shop on 3 levels at *Vintage 1879,* a bevy of specialty stores housed in a renovated brick warehouse, or take a hot-air balloon ride (contact *Adventures Aloft;* phone: 707-255-8688). Stop at *The Diner* (6476 Washington St., Yountville; phone: 707-944-2626) for lunch and a magnificent mocha milkshake. (At night, this place changes its name to *El Diner!*) Yountville's *Piatti* restaurant offers special pizza topped with bright orange flying fish roe. Calistoga, to the north, is a health spa with its own "Old Faithful" geyser, a 60-foot shower of steam erupting about every 40 minutes. *Dr. Wilkinson's Hot Springs* (1507 Lincoln Ave., Calistoga, CA 94515; phone: 707-942-4102) has refreshing mudbaths and mineral whirlpools. If time permits, try one of Napa Valley's charming bed and breakfast establishments, such as *La Residence* in Napa (4066 St. Helena Hwy. N., Napa, CA 94558; phone: 707-253-0337), or lovely resorts. *Meadowood* (900 Meadowood La., St. Helena, CA 94574; phone: 707-963-3646) and *Auberge du Soleil* (180 Rutherford Hill Rd., Rutherford, CA 94573; phone: 707-963-

1211) both have renowned restaurants. Or you may find you don't want to move from Sonoma County; with its rugged coastline, deep woods, and picturesque plains, it is an enticing place to spend the night. There are many charming bed and breakfast accommodations: Off Highway 101, but as peaceful as a sleepy small town, the *Vintners Inn* (4350 Barnes Rd., Santa Rosa, CA 95403; phone: 707-575-7350) is centrally located to vineyards in both Sonoma and Napa valleys. A few steps away from the inn is *John Ash & Company* (phone: 707-527-7687), one of Sonoma's best restaurants. If you want the elegance of a 1920s luxury hotel plus a fitness spa, try *The Sonoma Mission Inn* (18140 Hwy. 12, Boyes Hot Springs, CA; phone: 707-938-9000 or 800-862-4945). Smart travelers begin their day with the sourdough French toast at *The Big 3* (at the *Sonoma Mission Inn*). Once a graceful 1800s summer home, *Madrona Manor* (1001 Westside Rd., Healdsburg, CA 95448; phone: 707-433-4231) offers the ambience of life on a country estate.

South of San Francisco and about 1½ hours away (via US 101, then Rte. 156, then Rte. 1; or via the slow, scenic coastal Rte. 1 all the way) lies the Monterey Peninsula, an area rich in history and natural beauty. The town of Monterey was the military capital of California under three flags, and many of its adobe buildings survive in the State Historic Park. In Cannery Row, where gift shops and restaurants have taken over defunct sardine canneries, the *Monterey Bay Aquarium* is a spectacular re-creation of the region's marine life. The peninsula's pines and broad white beaches, bright with flowering succulents, are breathtaking. Famous for golf on Pebble Beach, the area attracts nature lovers who come to see monarch butterflies wintering in Pacific Grove, sea otters, seals, and the wild shorelands of Point Lobos State Preserve, south of Carmel. In this inexplicably *faux*-Bavarian resort town is a blessedly Mediterranean retreat with gorgeous gardens, the *La Playa* hotel (El Camino Real at 8th, Carmel-by-the-Sea, CA 93921; phone: 408-624-6476 or 800-582-8900) is the place to stay. Close to Monterey, in the heart of the Carmel Valley, is *Stonepine* (150 East Carmel/Valley Rd., Carmel Valley, CA 93924; phone: 408-659-2245), a French country château set on 330 acres.

SOURCES AND RESOURCES

TOURIST INFORMATION: The San Francisco Convention and Visitors Bureau (1390 Market St., or write to PO Box 6977, San Francisco, CA 94101; phone: 391-2000) is best for brochures, maps, general tourist information, and personal help. If you write ahead, it will send you (for $1) a valuable package of information, including a 3-month calendar of events. Call 391-2000 anytime for the lowdown on what's going on in town. Its downtown visitor information center on the lower level of Halladie Plaza (just downstairs from the cable car turnaround) provides multilingual services. 900 Market St. at Powell St. (phone: 974-6900). Contact the California state hotline (phone: 800-TO-CALIF) for maps, calendars of events, health updates, and travel advisories.

San Francisco at Your Feet by Margot Patterson Doss (Grove Press; $12.95) and *San Francisco: The Ultimate Guide,* by Randolph Delehanty (Chronicle Books, $14.95) are good walking guides; *San Francisco Access* by Richard Furman (HarperCollins, $16.95) is popular for its clarity and interesting layout.

Local Coverage – *San Francisco Chronicle,* morning daily; *San Francisco Examiner,* evening daily. Sundays, the two publish a joint edition, including a comprehensive entertainment section, the Datebook.

Television Stations – KRON Channel 4–NBC; KPIX Channel 5–CBS; KGO Channel 7–ABC; KQED Channel 9–PBS; KTVU Channel 2–FOX.

Radio Stations – AM: KFRC 610 (oldies); KCBS 740 (news); KGO 810 (news/talk). FM: KQED 88.5 (national public radio); KJAZ 92.7 (jazz); KKHI 95.7 (classical).

Food – Check *Jim Wood's Guide to San Francisco Restaurants* (Ten Speed Press, $9.95); *Epicurean Rendezvous* by Maia Madden (AM/PM Publishing, $6.95); and *Exploring the Best Ethnic Restaurants of the Bay Area* by Sharon Silva and Frank Viviano (S.F. Focus Books, $9.95).

 TELEPHONE: The area code for San Francisco is 415.
   Sales Tax – The basic sales tax is 7%, and the hotel tax is 11%.

 CLIMATE: Daytime temperatures average 60F to 65F in summer and 45F to 57F in winter (downpours are common between November and March). In summer, morning and evening fogs make parts of the day very cool; and while it is 65F in San Francisco, it can be in the 80s in the suburbs.

 GETTING AROUND: Airports – San Francisco International Airport is about 16 miles south of the city, a 30-minute drive when it's not rush hour. Taxi fare from downtown to the airport should run about $25. A number of shuttles operate to and from the airport for about $11 each way. Pick one up at the airport and reserve your return trip 6 hours ahead. *SFO Airporter* buses run every 20 minutes between the airport and downtown hotels for $6 one way, $10 round trip. *SAMTRANS* buses (phone: 800-660-4287) serve both the peninsula and downtown San Francisco (the Transbay Terminal at Mission and 1st Sts.). Buses depart from the airport every half hour during the day, hourly at night; the fare is $1.25. For more information on the airport's facilities, consult one of its teleguide terminals.

Oakland International Airport is a 30-minute drive from San Francisco's financial district during non-commuter hours; cab fare should run about $30. Bus transportation into downtown San Francisco is provided by *AC Transit* (phone: 839-2882) for $1.50. Rail service is available via the *Bay Area Rapid Transit* (*BART*) system (phone: 464-6000 or 788-2278); take a shuttle bus to the *Oakland Coliseum Arena* ($1), and then pick up *BART* to Montgomery St. in downtown San Francisco ($1.90). For airport information, call 444-4444.

BART – If you really want to move, this ultramodern, high-speed railway will whisk you from San Francisco to Oakland, Richmond, Concord, Daly City, and Fremont at up to 80 miles an hour. The system is easy to use, with large maps and boards in each station clarifying routes and fares. (The fares vary according to distance traveled.) For information, contact *Bay Area Rapid Transit,* 800 Madison St., Oakland (phone: 464-6000).

Bus – Efficient and inexpensive buses serve the entire metropolitan area. Bus maps appear at the front of the yellow pages in the telephone book. *MUNI* (*Municipal Transit*) Passports ($6 per day, $10 for 3 days) are good for rides on *MUNI* buses, streetcars, and cable cars. *MUNI* street and transit maps are available at bookstores for $1.50. For detailed route information, contact *MUNI* of San Francisco, 949 Presidio Ave. (phone: 673-MUNI).

Cable Car – The best way to travel up and over the hills of the city is aboard these famous trademarks; they are pulled along at 9½ miles an hour. There are three lines, and the most scenic is the Hyde Park line, which you can pick up at the turntable at Powell and Market Sts. It will take you over both Nob and Russian Hills to gaslit Victorian Park. For route information call 673-MUNI.

Car Rental – There are a few things to remember if you plan to drive in San Francisco: Cable cars and pedestrians always have the right-of-way; curb your wheels when parking on a hill to prevent runaway cars. The national firms all serve San Francisco. Least expensive is *Bob Leech Autorental* (at 435 S. Airport Blvd., South San Francisco — 5 minutes from the airport; phone: 583-3844), with Toyota Tercels and Corollas at $19.95 a day with 150 free miles, 10¢ for each mile thereafter. Free drop-off at LA International Airport.

Ferry – For outstanding views of the city, ride the *Golden Gate Ferry* (phone: 332-6600) from the terminal under the clock tower at the foot of Market Street. The 30-minute ride to Sausalito ($3.50 each way) takes you right past Alcatraz and almost within reach of the Golden Gate Bridge. A longer, equally breezy trip passes the now-defunct immigration center on Angel Island en route to Larkspur Landing ($3 one way). The *Red & White Fleet* (phone: 546-2805), departing from Piers 41 and 43½, offers ferry service across the bay to Oakland, Alameda, Sausalito, Tiburon, and Vallejo.

Streetcar – Five lines of the *MUNI Metro* streetcar system run under Market Street, one level above *BART,* and branch off toward various parts of the city. For route information, call 673-MUNI.

Taxi – Cabs can be hailed in the street, especially near hotels, or called on the phone. Major cab companies are *Yellow Cab* (phone: 626-2345); *Veterans Cab* (phone: 552-1300); *Luxor Cab* (phone: 282-4141).

VITAL SERVICES: Audiovisual Equipment – *McCune Audio/ Visual* (phone: 777-2700).

Business Services – *Red Carpet Services* (821 Market St.; phone: 495-1910). More and more hotels are offering business services in-house.

Dry Cleaner/Tailor – *Abell Martinizing,* 441 Eddy St., near Civic Center (phone: 776-6662).

Limousine – *Opera Plaza Limousines, Ltd.* (phone: 826-9630); *Carey Nob Hill Limousine* (phone: 468-7550).

Mechanics – *California Garage,* for American cars (1776 Green St. between Gough and Octavia Sts.; phone: 474-0279). *Foreign Car Repair,* for imports (6027 Geary between 24th and 25th Aves.; phone: 752-8305).

Medical Emergency – *St. Francis Memorial Hospital,* 1150 Bush St. (phone: 775-4321).

Messenger Services – *PDQ* (phone: 346-4229); *Western Messenger Service* (phone: 864-4100).

National/International Courier – *Federal Express* (phone: 877-9000); *DHL Worldwide Courier Express* (phone: 345-9400).

Pharmacy – *Bowerman Pharmacy,* 201 Jackson St. (phone: 433-4860).

Photocopies – *Blue Print Service Co.,* overnight service available (149 2nd St.; phone: 495-8700); *The Copy Factory,* 8:30 AM to 5:30 PM Mondays through Fridays (50 California St.; phone: 781-2990) and a branch is open 24 hours (2136 Palou Ave.; phone: 641-7500).

Post Office – The main branch is at 1300 Evans St. (phone: 550-6500).

Professional Photographer – *Gabriel Moulin Studios* (phone: 541-9454).

Secretary/Stenographer – *Ancha Business Center* (2500 Mason St., inside the *Sheraton;* phone: 627-6530); *Headquarters Co.* (phone: 781-5000).

Teleconference Facilities – *Hyatt Regency, Mark Hopkins, Fairmont, Campton Place, Donatello, Four Seasons Clift, Huntington, Pan Pacific* hotel, *Bedford, Villa Florence* (see *Best in Town,* below).

Translator – *Berlitz* (phone: 986-6464).

Typewriter Rental – *Holiday Office Machines,* hourly minimum (phone: 626-6344); *Guaranty Office Equipment,* 1-week minimum (phone: 781-3663).

Western Union/Telex – Many offices are located around the city (phone: 285-1384).

SPECIAL EVENTS: With a population so diverse that it supports 50 foreign-language newspapers, San Francisco is a city with festivals galore.

The *Chinese New Year,* a week-long celebration in January or February (depending on the full moon) begins with numerous private observances — settling of debts and honoring of ancestors — and then Chinatown goes public with festivals that draw thousands to the streets for the colorful *Dragon Parade,* featuring a block-long dragon, the *Miss Chinatown USA* pageant, marching bands, and elaborate fireworks. To buy reserved bleacher seats, contact the *Chinese Chamber of Commerce,* 730 Sacramento St. (phone: 982-3000).

The *Cherry Blossom Festival,* held on 2 weekends in April at Japan Center (Post and Buchanan Sts.; phone: 922-6776), features traditional tea ceremonies, flower arranging and dollmaking demonstrations, bonsai displays, and performances by folk dancers from Japan. The crosstown parade highlights the events with over 50 Japanese performing groups and intricate floats of shrines and temples.

Fleet Week celebrates the October birthday of the US Navy with a parade of ships under the Golden Gate Bridge and several days of open house on the vessels, plus aerial events, fireworks, and boat rides.

The *Grand National Livestock Exposition, Rodeo and Horse Show,* held in late October and early November at the *Cow Palace* (6 miles south of the city on Rte. 101), is one of the biggest events in the country, with all manner of rodeo events, equestrian competitions, and the best livestock in the West.

MUSEUMS: The city's major museums are all described in *Special Places.* Others worth a visit include the following:

African-American Historical and Cultural Society – Wednesdays through Sunday afternoons. Ft. Mason Bldg. C (phone: 441-0640).

Ansel Adams Center – Tuesday through Sunday afternoons. 250 Fourth St. (phone: 495-7000).

California Historical Society – Closed Mondays, and occasionally other days for private parties. 2090 Jackson St. (phone: 567-1848).

Craft and Folk Art Museum – Closed Mondays. Ft. Mason Bldg. A (phone: 775-0990).

Guiness Book of World Records Museum – Closed Mondays. 235 Jefferson St. (phone: 771-9890).

Mexican Museum – Wednesday through Sunday afternoons. Ft. Mason Bldg. D, Laguna St. and Marina Blvd. (phone: 441-0404).

Museo Italo-Americano – Wednesday through Sunday afternoons. Ft. Mason Bldg. C (phone: 673-2200).

MAJOR COLLEGES AND UNIVERSITIES: Two of the country's most prestigious universities are near San Francisco: University of California at Berkeley (Sproul Hall, Berkeley; phone: 642-6000) and Stanford University (Palo Alto; phone: 723-2300). San Francisco State University (1600 Holloway Ave.; phone: 338-1111) and the University of San Francisco (Golden Gate and Parker Aves.; phone: 666-6886) are in the city.

SHOPPING: Shopping the neighborhoods as well as downtown is easy in a compact city. For Japanese wares one can go to Japantown; for Chinese, Chinatown. With Ghirardelli Square, the Cannery, the Anchorage on Fisherman's Wharf, and Pier 39, San Francisco revived the age-old combination of marketplace and fun fair.

Embarcadero Center, between the waterfront and the financial district, is filled with shops and restaurants. *San Francisco Centre* is a stunning, polished stone structure with a huge, retractable skylight and spiral escalators; *Nordstrom* is the main department store here. When serious buying is the object — and money is not — the place to be still is Union Square and the streets that frame it. In the square are several major department stores: *Macy's, Saks Fifth Avenue, I. Magnin,* and *Neiman Marcus.* Specialty shops include firms from Britain, France, Italy, Denmark, and Switzerland, and native competitors. Not to be confused with Union Square is a stretch of Union Street on the old dairyland, Cow Hollow, and another on Fillmore Street. On Victorian Union Street, exotic and unusual gift shops predominate, while Fillmore's specialty is fashion, both new and vintage. For more bargains in high fashion, explore the factory outlets south of Market Street, which open to the public on weekends. A number of discount stores have opened up in the SoMa area; clothing prices are great, but shop decors usually are threadbare. Here's a window shopper's view of the famous, the classic, and the unusual:

UNION SQUARE

A. Sulka & Co. – Famous for ties, plus other pricey menswear. 188 Post St. (phone: 362-3450).

Alfred Dunhill of London – Classic menswear from a once-and-present tobacconist. 290 Post St. (phone: 781-3368).

Bally of Switzerland – Europe's most popular high-quality shoe chain for both men and women. 238 Stockton St. (phone: 398-7463).

Bogner – European sportswear. 400 Sutter St. (phone: 434-3888).

Cable Car Clothiers – Fine men's and womenswear; the cotton knit sweaters are outstanding. 1 Grant Ave. (phone: 397-4740).

Chanel Boutique – Two glittering stories with mirrors, black panels, chrome, and everything Chanel (plus salespeople who speak Japanese). 155 Maiden La. (phone: 981-1550).

Gucci – The Italian leather master, also beloved by the Japanese; for luggage, handbags, and other accessories. 2 Union Sq. (phone: 392-2808).

Gump's – Famous for its jade, art, jewelry, crystal, china, sculpture, furniture, stationery, and food. 250 Post St. (phone: 982-1616).

Hermès – High-priced silk scarves, leather, and other accessories. 212 Stockton St. (phone: 391-7200).

Jessica McClintock – Beaded, lacy original fashions for women and girls. 353 Sutter St. (phone: 397-0987).

Laura Ashley – Somewhat nostalgic Victorian ready-to-wear. 253 Post St. (phone: 788-0190) and 1827 Union St. (phone: 920-7200).

Louis Vuitton – Luggage and accessories with the familiar French initials. 317 Sutter St. (phone: 391-6200).

N. Peal Cashmere – Direct from London's Burlington Arcade: the finest sweaters on the same premises as another London import *Swaine Adeney,* which sells very correct men's clothing. 110 Geary St. (phone: 421-2713).

Obiko – One-of-a-kind women's clothing with an artistic bent by contemporary designers. 794 Sutter St. (phone: 775-2882).

La Parisienne – Antique postcards and posters from the Belle Epoque, fans from the 1920s, and jewelry. 460 Post St. (phone: 788-2255).

Shreve & Co. – One of San Francisco's oldest purveyors of the finest crystal and jewelry. 200 Post St. (phone: 421-2600).

Sidney Mobell – Anything and everything that can possibly be studded with jewels, including yo-yos, frisbees, and fax machines. 141 Post St. (phone: 986-4747).

Victoria's Secret – Romantic, frilly lingerie. 395 Sutter St. (phone: 397-0521) and 2245 Union St. (phone: 921-5444).

La Ville du Soleil – China, linen, antiques, books, and toys. 444 Post St. (phone: 434-0657).

Wilkes-Bashford – High-priced men's and women's clothing; sip imported water while making selections. 375 Sutter St. (phone: 986-4380).

MID-MARKET STREET

Bell'occhio – A unique and whimsical collection of dried flowers, antique and hand-dyed ribbons, unusual soaps, sachets, and eccentric little boxes. 8 Brady St. (phone: 864-4048).

Decorum – Art Deco furnishings. 1632 Market St. (phone: 864-3326).

House Party – Collectible objects, from salt shakers to sideboards, from the 1920s through the 1960s. 4 Brady St. (phone: 626-7072).

Red Desert – A wide range of cactus and succulent plants, which can be shipped throughout the country, and other finds from the desert. 1632 Market St. (phone: 552-2800).

Telaio – One-of-a-kind dresses, handmade silk scarfs, handbags, and jewelry. 10 Brady St. (phone: 626-7159).

Vero – Contemporary, dramatic objets d'art, jewelry, and gifts. 6 Brady St. (phone: 255-0707).

20th Century Furniture – American furniture, such as armchairs and highboys, from 1930 to 1960. 1612 Market St. (phone: 626-0542).

UNION STREET

Oggetti – Florentine papers and other gift items. 1846 Union St. (phone: 346-0631).

Paris 1925 – Antique watches and Art Deco jewelry. 1954 Union St. (phone: 567-1925).

Smile – Truly "tongue in chic": arts and crafts with a sense of humor. 1750 Union St. (phone: 771-1909).

FILLMORE STREET

Next to New Shop – The name says it all. 2226 Fillmore (phone: 567-1627).

Repeat Performance – Almost-new clothing. 2223 Fillmore (phone: 563-3123).

Seconds-to-Go – More good used clothing. 2252 Fillmore (phone: 563-7806).

The Way We Wore – Vintage clothing from the late 1800s through the 1950s. 2238 Fillmore (phone: 346-1386).

Zoe – Far-out, expensive women's clothes. 2400 Fillmore (phone: 929-0441).

SOUTH OF MARKET STREET (SoMa)

Coat Factory Outlet – Raincoats, wool coats, designer coats. 1350 Folsom St. (phone: 864-5050).

Discount Bridal – Brides-to-be travel cross-country for wedding dresses at sensational savings. 300 Brannon St. (phone: 495-7922).

Esprit – Young and funky sportswear. 499 Illinois St. (phone: 957-2550).

SPORTS AND FITNESS: The Bay Area has everything in professional sports.

Baseball – The San Francisco *Giants* play from April to October in *Candlestick Park* (Gilman Ave., on the southern edge of the city along Rte. 101; phone: 467-8000). The Oakland *A's* play at the *Oakland Coliseum Stadium* (phone: 638-0500).

Basketball – The NBA's *Golden State Warriors* play from October to March at the *Oakland Coliseum Arena* (phone: 762-2277).

Bicycling – Rent from *Avenue Cyclery,* near Golden Gate Park, which has good bike trails. 756 Stanyan St., 1269 9th Ave. (phone: 387-3155).

Fishing – Fine salmon fishing in the sea beyond the bay. Season is mid-February to mid-October; afternoon trips June through October. Charter boats leave daily early in the morning and return in the afternoon. For information contact *Sea Breeze Sport Fishing at Fisherman's Wharf* (PO Box 713, Mill Valley; phone: 381-3474). You also can cast off San Francisco's municipal pier at Aquatic Park, anytime. No license required.

Fitness Centers – *Fitness Break* (30 Hotaling Pl. near Washington and Montgomery Sts.; phone: 788-1681) has weekday aerobic workouts, noon and evenings; showers and lockers available. The *YMCA* (166 Embarcadero; phone: 392-2191) has a pool, sauna, and weight room, along with racquetball and handball courts.

Football – The San Francisco *49ers* play from August to December at *Candlestick Park,* Rte. 101, 8 miles south of San Francisco (phone: 468-2249).

Golf – There are fine public courses at Golden Gate Park (47th Ave. and Fulton St.; phone: 751-8987), Lincoln Park (34th Ave. and Clement St.; phone: 221-9911), and Harding Park (Skyline and Harding Pk. Blvd.; phone: 664-4690).

Horse Racing – *Bay Meadows* is the place, in San Mateo (phone: 574-7223). Seasons: quarter horse racing — third week of February through the third week of April; thoroughbred racing — first week of September through the first week of February. In the East Bay, *Golden Gate Fields* features thoroughbred racing from late January through late June (phone: 526-3020).

Horseback Riding – Rent from *Golden Gate Stables* (Kennedy Dr. at 36th Ave.; phone: 668-7360). Seven miles of equestrian trails wind through the park.

Jogging – Run along the Embarcadero to the Marina Green; jog back and forth across the Golden Gate Bridge (1½ miles each way) and enjoy the fore and aft views, as well as the one directly below. Take the No. 5 bus, which stops on Market, out to Golden Gate Park, where there are numerous dirt and concrete trails, not to mention plenty of other joggers. (It's not recommended to run alone in the park.)

Skating – Roller skating is very popular in San Francisco, especially in Golden Gate Park on Sundays, when traffic is detoured off the park's main roads. You can rent skates from *Magic Skates* (3038 Fulton St. at 6th Ave.; phone: 668-1117), right across from the park.

Swimming – Though much of San Francisco's waters are too rough and cold for swimming, Phelan Beach is good when the weather permits and the current is safe, at Sea Cliff Ave. and El Camino Del Mar. The *Sheehan* pool, (620 Sutter St.; phone: 775-6500) is open to the public daily throughout the year.

Tennis – Good public tennis courts are in Golden Gate Park on John F. Kennedy Dr. (phone: 753-7101).

Yacht Racing – The *Yacht Racing Association* holds several races each year in San Francisco Bay. Good observation points are the Marina and the Vista Point area on the north side of the Golden Gate Bridge (for information, call 771-9500).

 THEATER: The *American Conservatory Theater* is an excellent resident repertory company, which performs classical productions and modern plays from October to June. Temporarily turned out of its home at the *Geary Theater* because of 1989 earthquake damage, the company makes repairs while it performs at three smaller theaters: the *Stage Door* (420 Mason St.; phone: 749-2200), the *Orpheum Theater,* and the *Theater on the Square* (450 Post St.; phone: 433-9500); write for tickets to *ACT* Box Office (415 Geary St., San Francisco CA

94102; phone: 749-2228). The *Curran Theater* is best for musicals and often stages traveling Broadway productions (445 Geary St.; phone: 474-3800). The *Orpheum Theater* (1192 Market St.; phone: 474-3800) and the *Golden Gate Theater* (Golden Gate and Taylor Sts.; phone: 474-3800) also feature Broadway shows. At *Club Fugazi,* an old North Beach landmark, the camp cult classic *Beach Blanket Babylon Goes around the World* has been running for 17 years (678 Green St.; phone: 421-4222). If the tour inspires you to see the world through celluloid, visit *Castro,* a 1922 landmark theater — complete with an organist — that shows classic films (Castro and Market Sts.; phone: 621-6120). Or try the *Paramount* for its Friday night classic film series, which includes newsreels, cartoons, vintage trailers, and spin-the-wheel door prizes. The theater itself is a prize. Meticulously maintained, the Art Deco building is in the National Register of Historic Places (2025 Broadway in Oakland; phone: 465-6400). The *San Francisco Ballet,* the country's oldest company and among the finest, moves into the *War Memorial Opera House* with its *Nutcracker* production in December, followed by a repertory season from January through May (Civic Center; phone: 621-3838).

MUSIC: The *San Francisco Opera Company,* featuring celebrated guest artists, performs at the *War Memorial Opera House* (Civic Center; phone: 864-3330) from September to early December. Since tickets are difficult to get, it's best to write in advance (*War Memorial Opera House* Box Office, San Francisco CA 94102). The *San Francisco Symphony* season runs from September through May at *Davies Symphony Hall* in the Civic Center (phone: 431-5400), but the orchestra can be heard at other times, too, such as during its *June Beethoven Festival* or its July *Pops Concerts* in the *Civic Auditorium.* The *Midsummer Music Festival* is a free Sunday series of symphony, opera, jazz, and ethnic programs from mid-June to mid-August at *Stern Grove* (19th Ave. and Sloat Blvd.).

Tickets for most music, dance, and theater events can be obtained through *BASS* ticket centers (phone: 762-2277) and *Ticketron* (phone: 392-SHOW). In addition, half-price tickets to many events can be bought (cash or traveler's checks only) on the day of performance at the *STBS* booth on the Stockton Street side of Union Square, Tuesdays through Saturdays from noon to 7:30 PM, or the *STBS* booth at Embarcadero One, street level, Mondays through Fridays from 10 AM to 6 PM (phone: 433-STBS for recorded information).

NIGHTCLUBS AND NIGHTLIFE: San Francisco is alive at night and can keep you going whether you're inclined toward jazz or high camp. Much of the nightlife glitters around North Beach, but there's also plenty of activity all around the city. Current favorites: *Great American Music Hall* (859 O'Farrell; phone: 885-0750), for major jazz and folk artists; *Lascaux* (248 Sutter St.; phone: 391-1555), for jazz; *Finocchio's* (506 Broadway; phone: 982-9388), for female impersonators. For comedy: *Cobb's Comedy Club* (2801 Leavenworth St., in the Cannery; phone: 928-4320); and *Punch Line* (444 Battery St.; phone: 397-7573). For cabaret, try the *Plush Room* (940 Sutter St.; phone: 885-6800). For a view of San Francisco at night try *Top of the Mark,* in the *Mark Hopkins* hotel (1 Nob Hill; phone: 392-3434); *Oz,* a nightclub atop the *St. Francis* hotel (phone: 397-7000); or *Starlite Roof,* in the *Sir Francis Drake* hotel (phone: 392-7755). Dance to the Brazilian beat at *Bahia Tropical* (1600 Market at Franklin; phone: 861-8657). The district south of Market — known as SoMa — is the trendiest for dancing. Hot are *Club DV8* (55 Natoma St.; phone: 777-1419); the avant-garde *DNA Lounge* (375 11th St.; phone: 626-1409); and *Slim's* (333 11th St.; phone: 621-3330).

BEST IN TOWN

CHECKING IN: President Taft called San Francisco the town that knows how, and though he probably wasn't talking about hotels, his statement nonetheless applies. A pleasant embarrassment of riches confronts visitors, from luxurious mammoths to ritzy mid-size establishments to dozens of intimate "boutique" hotels, which mimic European small hotels of character. Expect to pay over $200 for a double room in the very expensive bracket; $140 to $200, expensive; $80 to $140, moderate; and under $80, inexpensive. For bed and breakfast lodgings, contact *American Family Inn/Bed & Breakfast San Francisco* (PO Box 349, San Francisco, CA 94101-0349; phone: 931-3083) or *Bed & Breakfast International* (1181-B Solano Ave., Albany, CA 94706; phone: 525-4569). Always ask about special packages and discounts. All telephone numbers are in the 415 area code unless otherwise indicated.

Campton Place – Half a block north of Union Square, this small property in the European tradition has 120 sumptuously decorated (if smallish) rooms and suites offering armoires, writing desks, remote-control cable TV, a telephone in the marble and brass bath, and even padded coat hangers. There's a roof garden for sunning and small receptions, and two conference rooms. On the lobby level, wonderfully innovative and impeccably prepared American dishes are served at breakfast, lunch, and dinner in the *Campton Place* restaurant (see *Eating Out*); cocktails and coffee are available in the adjacent bar. Other amenities include concierge, valet, telex and cable, as well as 24-hour room service, secretarial services, A/V equipment photocopiers, and computers. Express checkout. 340 Stockton St. (phone: 781-5555 or 800-235-4300; 800-647-4000 outside California; Fax: 415-955-8536; Telex: 6771185). Very expensive.

Fairmont – Just on the other side of the cable car tracks, but on Nob Hill neither side is the wrong one. Adjoining the distinctive old-fashioned main building is a modern tower topped by the *Crown Room,* which serves lunch, dinner, and Sunday brunch. Take the glass-sided elevator for a great view. For other treats try the *Squire Room* for continental dishes, the *Tonga Room* for Polynesian fare and dancing, *Mason's* restaurant, the *New Orleans Room* for nightly jazz, the *Bella Voce* coffee shop, and the *Sweet Corner* for ice cream. 596 rooms and suites. Amenities include around-the-clock room service, concierge and secretarial services, A/V equipment, photocopiers, and computers. Express checkout. California and Mason Sts. (phone: 772-5000; 800-527-4727; Fax: 415-781-3929; Telex: 9103726002). Very expensive.

Four Seasons Clift – This traditional favorite is polished to near perfection. An air of subdued elegance prevails, from the lobby sitting areas, reminiscent of an Edwardian salon, to the traditionally furnished guestrooms. No hotel in San Francisco provides friendlier service. The *Redwood Room* bar and lounge is a 1933 Art Deco original, paneled in redwood burl and set off with smart chandeliers, wall sconces, and Gustav Klimt prints. Its restaurant, the *French Room,* serves French food with an innovative California translation, plus a menu of low-calorie, low-cholesterol, low-sodium alternatives; it also has an award-winning list of predominantly California wines. Many of the 329 rooms are unusually spacious, with color TV sets and extension phones in baths; a gift shop and garage are also on the premises. Nonsmoking accommodations are available, as is 24-hour room service. There's a concierge and a business center, which offers secretarial services, A/V equipment, photocopiers, and computers. Geary and Taylor Sts. (phone: 775-4700 or 800-332-3442; Fax: 415-441-4621; Telex: 00340647). Very expensive.

Grand Hyatt San Francisco – With a grander name and a "down to the foundations" renovation, the hotel is almost brand new. The view from the lavish suites on the 34th floor is simply breathtaking. *Club 36* is a top-floor jazz boîte; *Nappers Deli,* off the plaza deck, is popular for weekday lunches; and the *Plaza* restaurant on the mezzanine is the place for Sunday brunch. 689 rooms. Among the business additions are 18 meeting rooms, including a ballroom which seats 600, secretarial services, A/V equipment, photocopiers, and computers. Twenty-four–hour room service and express checkout. 345 Stockton St. (phone: 398-1234 or 800-233-1234; Fax: 415-391-1780; Telex: 340592). Very expensive.

Hyatt Regency – Inside this futuristically designed structure is a 17-story atrium lobby with all the activity of a three-ring circus, plus glass elevators that whisk you to the top, where a revolving bar looks out on San Francisco. The 803 rooms are attractive and modern; amenities include convention facilities, shops, color TV sets, and, for a small extra fee, in-room movies. Nonsmoking floors are available. The lobby is particularly lively, with a classical guitarist playing most afternoons and a jazz trio nightly. Secretarial services are available, as are photocopiers, A/V equipment, and computers. Twenty-four–hour room service, a concierge desk, and express checkout. No. 5 Embarcadero Center (phone: 788-1234 or 800-233-1234; 800-233-1234, outside California; Fax: 415-398-2567; Telex: 170698). Very expensive.

Mandarin Oriental – This luxurious hostelry occupies the top 11 floors of the 48-story First Interstate Center, in the heart of the financial district, affording each of the 160 rooms unobstructed views of the city and portions of the bay. Decorated in soothing beige and blue, the rooms are graced with Oriental-motif art, fresh flowers, and marble bathrooms, each one complete with floor-to-ceiling windows, a robe, slippers, digital scale, and hair dryer. The larger rooms include screened sitting areas and floor-to-ceiling windows. The marble-walled lobby, the reception area, and the Business Center are all on the ground level. An outstanding restaurant, *Silks,* is on the second floor (see *Eating Out*). Room service is on call 24 hours a day. There are 3 meeting rooms, a concierge desk, secretarial services, A/V equipment, photocopiers, computers, and express checkout. There also are portable fax machines and 2-line phones in all the guestrooms. 222 Sansome St. (phone: 885-0999 or 800-622-0404; Fax: 415-433-0289; Telex: 5106001025). Very expensive.

Mark Hopkins – In the heights of extravagance at 1 Nob Hill, with some of the original gables and turrets of railroad magnate Mark Hopkins's 19th-century mansion and a guest list that has included everyone from Haile Selassie to Frank Sinatra. The 394 suites and rooms feature either classical or contemporary decor, commodious baths and closets, and possibly a grand piano (the Presidential Suite has one). The tower rooms have especially fine views, although the glass-walled *Top of the Mark* lounge offers the best 360-degree panorama of the city. The *Nob Hill* restaurant (open daily) serves noteworthy French food, with outstanding lamb and duck dishes, and wines from 34 states. Twenty-four– hour room service is available. There are 14 meeting rooms, as well as a concierge desk, secretarial services, photocopiers, computers, and A/V equipment. Express checkout. 1 Nob Hill (phone: 392-3434 or 800-327-0200; Fax: 415-421-3302; Telex: 340809). Very expensive.

Meridien – The epitome of commercial luxury, with a distinctly French atmosphere, this 36-floor, 675-room establishment is in the spruced-up South of Market (SoMa) area, just a block from the *Moscone Convention Center.* It features a fine restaurant, *Pierre,* which serves contemporary California-French dishes in an elegant lobby-level setting. There also is a brasserie, *Café Justin,* open from 6:45 AM to 11 PM, and 24-hour room service. Seventeen meeting rooms, a concierge desk, secretarial services, A/V equipment, photocopiers, computers, and express checkout are among the business amenities. 50 3rd St. (phone: 974-6400 or 800-543-4300; Fax: 415-543-8268). Very expensive.

Nikko – San Francisco's close ties with the Pacific Rim are nowhere more evident than in this striking hostelry, midway between Union Square and the theater district. The 525 rooms in this 25-story building include 2 traditional Japanese suites and 3 Nikko floors, with private lounges offering continental breakfast, an honor bar, and express checkout service. This is the only downtown hotel with a heated, glass-enclosed swimming pool, part of the extensive health club that includes a workout room, Jacuzzi, sauna, and massage rooms. A multilingual staff assists foreign visitors. Further business advantages include 24-hour room service, concierge, secretarial services, A/V equipment, photocopiers, and computers. 222 Mason St. (phone: 394-1111 or 800-NIKKO-US; Fax: 415-394-1156; Telex: 204910). Very expensive.

Park Hyatt at Embarcadero Center – All the makings of a home office away from home, including personal computers with data bases, are available in 360 luxurious rooms furnished in dark woods, fabrics, and leathers. Guest children are pampered with toys; afternoon tea is served in the reference library and the lounge; and fresh fruit, flowers, and bottled water are provided in the rooms. Here the complimentary transportation to and from points within the downtown area is in a Mercedes sedan (by appointment through the concierge). *Park Grill* serves all three meals, there is a caviar bar, and a lounge and outdoor terrace offer drinks and light meals. Exercise equipment is delivered to your room on request. Room service is available around the clock. Business facilities include 14 meeting rooms, concierge, secretarial services, A/V equipment, photocopiers, computers, and express checkout. 333 Battery St. (phone: 392-1234 or 800-233-1234; Fax: 415-421-2433; Telex: 330115). Very expensive.

Ritz-Carlton – Originally built in 1909 as the home of the Metropolitan Life Insurance Co., this historic landmark, with its white Greek columns and Ionic architecture, looks like the United States Treasury. And it may indeed be a treasure; under construction for 2 years, the entire interior was gutted to create 336 guestrooms, a full fitness center with an indoor pool, 2 restaurants and 2 lounges, and over 22,000 square feet of meeting space, including an outdoor courtyard. The decor is traditional with 18th- and 19th-century paintings and other artwork throughout. Room service is on call 24 hours. Other amenities include a concierge desk, secretarial services, A/V equipment, photocopiers, and computers. There's also CNN and express checkout. California and Stockton Sts. (phone: 296-7465 or 800-241-3333). Very expensive.

San Francisco Marriott – This 1,500-room establishment, 1 block from *Moscone Convention Center,* has its own good-size convention center. For relaxing, there is a complete health club and the largest indoor swimming pool in the city. Two lounges, a snack bar, and the *Fourth Street Deli* complement *Kinoko's Japanese Restaurant.* The 39th-floor *View Lounge* is the place to be at sunset. Room service is available round the clock. Secretarial services can be arranged, as well as A/V equipment, photocopiers, and computers. A concierge desk is on hand, and express checkout. 55 Fourth St. (phone: 896-1600 or 800-228-9290; Fax: 415-777-2799). Very expensive.

Sheraton Palace – A San Francisco landmark since 1875 and one of America's first grand hotels, with 552 rooms, it has recently been restored and renovated. The *Garden Court,* a huge, elegant room with a domed, leaded glass ceiling, crystal chandeliers, marble columns and floors, serves all meals, plus afternoon tea. Guestrooms are distinguished by antique furnishings and fixtures, along with such modern conveniences as robes, hair dryers, hookups for personal computers, and fax machines. The spa features an indoor pool, whirlpool, and sauna. Nonsmoking floors and handicapped-accessible rooms are available. Other highlights are 45,000 square feet of meeting space, 24-hour room service, concierge, secretarial services, A/V equipment, photocopiers, computers, and express checkout. Adjacent to the financial district. 2 New Montgomery St. (phone: 392-8600; Fax: 415-543-06711). Very expensive.

Sherman House – This ornate, white, 19th-century mansion, overlooking San Francisco Bay from Pacific Heights, has been transformed into one of the city's most luxurious small inns. Gaudy Victorian antiques, marble wood-burning fireplaces, four-poster beds swathed in tapestries, deep window seats, wet bars, TV sets and cassette systems, whirlpool baths, and down comforters are standard amenities in most of the 14 rooms and suites. One even has a large deck with a 300-degree bay view, and one of the three carriage house rooms has its own gazebo. Dining rooms that serve three meals daily look out on the bay and a formal garden designed by Thomas Church. A member of the prestigious Relais & Châteaux group. Business amenities include around-the-clock room service, small meeting rooms, secretarial assistance, A/V equipment photocopiers, and computers. 2160 Green St. (phone: 563-3600 or 800-424-5777; Fax: 415-563-1882). Very expensive.

Archbishops Mansion – Surrounded by San Francisco's most frequently photographed Victorian homes, this historic landmark was built in 1904 for the city's archbishop and is now a romantic, sophisticated bed and breakfast inn. Each of the 15 rooms (each one is named after an opera) is furnished with outstanding period antiques and Oriental carpets, and most have fireplaces. Amenities include embroidered linen, French-milled soaps, and a continental breakfast delivered to your room. Complimentary wine is served each afternoon in the parlor, accompanied by selections on a 1904 Bechstein Grand piano once owned by Noël Coward. There are 2 meeting rooms available for business needs, as well as a concierge desk, secretarial services, and photocopiers. A/V equipment can be arranged. 1000 Fulton St. (phone: 563-7872 or 800-543-5820). Expensive.

Donatello – One block west of Union Square, this elegant hotel offers 140 spacious rooms (including 9 suites), a serene atmosphere, and special touches such as plants, terry cloth robes, valet parking, conference rooms, and a concierge. On the mezzanine level is a restaurant — also called *Donatello* — which serves Northern Italian fare. Room service may be ordered until midnight. There are 2 meeting rooms, a concierge desk, and photocopiers. Secretarial services and A/V equipment can be arranged. 501 Post St. (phone: 441-7100 or 800-792-9837; Fax: 415-885-8842). Expensive.

Harbor Court – Parallel to the waterfront, this newly renovated landmark building, built right after the 1906 earthquake, has both Old World flavor and San Francisco Bay views. The original arches of this 132-room property, as well as the vaulted ceilings and architectural details, have been retained. Guests have use of a fully equipped health center located next door. Limousine service to the financial district each morning. Complimentary coffee and tea are served throughout the day in the upper lobby, and wine is offered in the evenings. 165 Stuart St. (phone: 800-346-0555). Expensive.

Huntington – A red-carpeted lobby, crystal chandelier, and white woodwork, give an elegant yet homey air to this former apartment building. A sleek, chauffeured Cadillac town car provides complimentary transportation within downtown. One of the best values on Nob Hill, each of its 140 rooms is distinctively decorated and comfortable, and many have outstanding views. The *Big Four* restaurant (the name refers to the four Gold Rush millionaires) looks like a turn-of-the-century men's club and serves fish, chops, and steaks. Deliveries from room service arrive until midnight. There are 4 meeting rooms, and such business amenities as a concierge desk, secretarial services, A/V equipment, photocopiers, and computers are available. Express checkout. 1075 California St. (phone: 474-5400 or 800-652-1539; 800-227-4683, outside California; Fax: 415-474-6227). Expensive.

Hyatt at Fisherman's Wharf – All the attractions of Fisherman's Wharf are located right on the doorstep of this 313-room property. Adults who need to pursue some quiet time can pack the kids off to Camp Hyatt (for children 3 to 15 years old), and work out in the fitness center, or try the heated pool and spa. The *Marble Works* serves all meals daily. The *North Point Lounge* is a sports bar with a Victorian setting. Twenty-four–hour room service is available. Business pluses include a concierge desk, secretarial services, A/V equipment, photocopiers, and express checkout. 555 Northpoint St. (phone: 563-1234 or 800-233-1234; Fax: 415-398-2650; Telex: 470733). Expensive.

Miyako – This 218-room establishment in Jápantown is the place for a plunge into the Orient — and a Japanese bath — especially during the *Cherry Blossom Festival.* The decor is Japanese, and both Japanese and Western suites with saunas are available, as is cable TV and a restaurant. Among the amenities here are 14 meeting rooms, A/V equipment, and secretarial services. Express checkout. 1625 Post St. (phone: 922-3200 or 800-533-4567; Fax: 415-921-0417; Telex: 278063). Expensive.

Pan Pacific – Glittering with rosy marble, brass, chrome, and glass, this 331-room property combines an American look with Asian-style service. Three valets per floor are prepared to unpack, press clothes, polish shoes, draw baths, and prop matchsticks against room doors (a toppled match signals that the guests may be out and their rooms should be tidied up). Computers with software and exercise machines can be rented for in-room use. The *Grill* (see *Eating Out*) equals the high standard set by several new hotel restaurants in the city, and the menu has an Asian influence. From 7 to 10 AM, Rolls-Royces continually shuttle guests free of charge to the financial district; in the evening, they deliver guests to dinner and the theater; and they also can be rented for airport pick-up or drop-off. Twenty-four–hour room service, concierge and secretarial services, A/V equipment, photocopiers, and express checkout are all available. 500 Post St. (phone: 771-8600 or 800-533-6465; Fax: 415-398-0267; Telex: 990264). Expensive.

Prescott – A long Oriental carpet on an Italian marble floor leads guests into the reception area of this 167-room establishment, 1 block from Union Square's famous shopping, theaters, and art galleries. Though in the heart of the city, the ambience is homey, with a Southern-style lobby "living room," complete with big country hearth fireplace and cases displaying California Indian artifacts. The *Postrio* restaurant is hot, with the clientele clamoring for chef Wolfgang Puck's interpretations of classic San Francisco fare (see *Eating Out*). Other amenities include complimentary wine and hors d'oeuvres in the living room; complimentary limousine service on weekday mornings to the financial district; and terry robes, hair dryers, cable TV, and stocked refrigerators in the rooms. Further advantages come in the form of room service until midnight, 2 meeting rooms, a concierge desk, secretarial services, A/V equipment, photocopiers, computers, and express checkout. 545 Post St. (phone: 563-0303 or 800-283-7322; Fax: 415-563-6831). Expensive.

Stanford Court – Built on the site of 19th-century Governor Leland

Stanford's mansion, this hotel is now owned by the Stouffer hotel chain. Designed in the tradition of Nob Hill elegance and with a touch of original flair, the drive-in courtyard is covered by a Tiffany-esque glass dome; the 402 rooms and suites have rattan furniture, canopied beds, etchings of old San Francisco, and private baths complete with miniature TV sets and heated towel racks. The restaurant, *Fournou's Oven*, specializes in contemporary American cuisine, with meats roasted over an oakwood fire. Breakfast and lunch are served in *The Pavillion*. The well-stocked wine cellar features private wine bins where patrons store their personal favorites. Coffee and tea are served in the lobby bar. Room service may be ordered round the clock. There are 4 meeting rooms, a concierge desk, secretarial assistance, A/V equipment, and photocopiers, and computers can be arranged. Express checkout. 905 California St. (phone: 989-3500 or 800-227-4736; Fax: 415-391-0513; Telex: 340899). Expensive.

Tuscan Inn – This unique 199-room hostelry strongly resembles a European seaside retreat. One step outside the door and lungs fill with the sea air; eyes view a panorama of sailing ships. Gold Rush artifacts are displayed in the lobby, and a hand-carved wooden mantle and antique chests add to the Old World aura. For business travelers, limousine service is provided daily to the financial district. The cable car turn-around, Pier 39, the Cannery, and Ghirardelli Square are within a block or two, and parking is available. *Café Pescatore* specializes in fish, pasta, and pizza. Business amenities include 24-hour room service, 3 meeting rooms, and a concierge desk. Secretarial services can be arranged; computers, photocopiers, and A/V equipment are available. 425 Northpoint St. (phone: 561-1100 or 800-648-4626; Fax: 415-561-1199). Expensive.

Westin St. Francis – This grand San Francisco landmark, since 1904, has entertained royalty, presidents, and international celebrities with its Old World charm. The 1,200-room establishment still keeps to its traditional theme of red velvet, glimmering crystal, and polished rosewood. At the top of the 32-story Tower are *Victor's* restaurant, featuring nouvelle cuisine, and the chic *Oz* disco; both have lovely panoramic views of the city. Back in the days when society ladies protested that handling coins soiled their white gloves, the hotel provided a coin-washing service for guests. This tradition continues on; you can relinquish your change and 2 hours later, you'll have coins that are so shiny that they seem freshly minted. The hotel's fitness center is open daily from 5 AM to 11 PM. There also are convention facilities and cocktail lounges on the premises. Room service is available 24 hours a day, and among the services available in the business center are secretarial assistance, A/V equipment, photocopiers, and computers. There's also a concierge desk and express checkout. Union Square (phone: 397-7000 or 800-228-3000; Fax: 415-774-0124). Expensive.

White Swan Inn – Converted from an old hotel, this 27-room English inn offers a personal welcome, lounge, and library with fireplaces, plus card rooms and a garden. Rooms are spacious and bright, amenities luxurious. Complimentary breakfast and afternoon tea, which also includes wine, sherry, and hors d'oeuvres. Valet parking. Also available are 1 meeting room and photocopiers. 845 Bush St. (phone: 775-1755; Fax: 415-775-5717). Expensive.

Inn at Union Square – Five floors of tranquillity in the middle of downtown San Francisco, this stylish spot has 30 rooms graced with Georgian antiques and brass fixtures, warm printed fabrics in pastel colors, down pillows, and thick terry bathrobes. The penthouse suite has a sauna, whirlpool bath, and fireplace. Each day of one's stay here is punctuated with breakfast (in bed, if you wish), tea and cucumber sandwiches, and wine and hors d'oeuvres. Guests can use a 2-bedroom suite for meetings. Secretarial services can be arranged, so too, computers. Photocopiers are available, and there's a concierge desk. No smoking is permitted in the hotel. 440 Post St. (phone: 397-3510 or 800-288-4346; Fax: 415-989-0529). Expensive to moderate.

Majestic – Convenient to midtown, this 5-story Edwardian mansion has been lavishly restored, with spacious rooms and suites upstairs and an elegant lobby lounge sharing the ground floor with the *Café Majestic* and its cozy adjacent bar. The sunlit restaurant won instant acclaim with its innovative California-French food served at lunch, dinner, and Sunday brunch. Additional amenities include room service, which is available only at meal times, valet parking, 2 meeting rooms, a concierge desk, and photocopiers. Limited A/V equipment also is on hand. 1500 Sutter St. (phone: 441-1100 or 800-869-8966; Fax: 415-673-7331). Expensive to moderate.

Mansion – This Queen Anne-style historical landmark will provide a stay unlike any other, with larger-than-life murals of local personages on some walls, a pervasive pig motif (ask for the story behind this one) on others (not in the 28 bedrooms, fortunately), a nightly musical hour or magic show that features Claudia the Ghost on piano, and a huge dining room dwarfed by a backlit stained glass window. Beyond (or despite) this, the French Foor and the service are excellent. There's also a concierge desk. 2220 Sacramento St. (phone: 929-9444 or 800-424-9444). Expensive to moderate.

Andrews – A renovated Victorian building that retained some original brass fixtures and beveled glass windows, as well as a sense of old-fashioned hospitality, in its 48 rooms. Continental breakfast included. *Fino,* located off the lobby, serves Northern Italian favorites at lunch and dinner. The front desk personnel double as concierge. 624 Post St. (phone: 563-6877; 800-622-0557 from within California; 800-227-4742 elsewhere; Fax: 415-928-6919). Moderate.

Bedford – Plain on the outside, cheerful with garden colors inside, this 144-room establishment is close to Union Square. There are still original late 1920s bathroom tiles and fixtures, and more modern amenities include a video library, valet parking, complimentary pre-dinner wine, and weekday morning limousine service to the financial district. The *4-Star Café* serves breakfast and dinner. Amenities include 2 meeting rooms, A/V equipment, and photocopiers. Express checkout. 761 Post St. (phone: 673-6040 or 800-227-5642; Fax: 415-563-6739). Moderate.

Canterbury/Whitehall Inn – Plenty of charm and greenery, including a florist's shop. The European-style lobby is filled with antiques and lots of people as well — most of whom are on their way to or from *Lehr's Greenhouse,* a tropical-garden restaurant with emphasis on seafood, steaks, and pasta; Sunday brunch is very popular. There's also an exercise club. The 275 rooms have cable TV, coffee makers, and refrigerators. Additional bonuses are 1 meeting room, photocopiers, and express checkout. 750 Sutter St. (phone: 474-6464; 800-652-1614 in California, 800-227-4788 elsewhere; Fax: 415-474-5856). Moderate.

Carlton – Just 5 blocks from Union Square, this 165-room property has all the charm of a large home. Complimentary wine is served each evening in the 1920s-style lobby. The hotel's café serves breakfast and dinner daily. Room service may be ordered during meal hours. One meeting room is available, as well as a concierge desk and photocopiers. 1075 Sutter St. (phone: 673-0242 or 800-227-4496; Fax: 415-673-4904; Telex: 470063). Moderate.

Diva – Italianate meets high tech on 7 floors with 108 stunning guest rooms, all furnished with chrome, glass, and bright lacquered furniture and fixtures. The bare floor in the lobby feels cold, and the ultramodern rooms look like a decorator's dream of a with-it office. The Italian theme softens with traditional down comforters and pillows, snacks and cold drinks in the mini-fridge, and complimentary continental breakfast that includes Italian coffee. Each room is equipped with a VCR, and there is an extensive library of classic and current video cassettes. The *California Pizza Kitchen,* a branch of the "designer-pizza" restaurant chain, fits in with the hip Italian theme. Perhaps best of all is the location: right near the theaters and just a couple of blocks from Union Square. There's 1 meeting room, and other business amenities include secretarial services, a concierge desk, photocopiers, A/V equipment, and computers. Express checkout. 440 Geary St. (phone: 885-0200 or 800-553-1900; Fax: 415-346-6613). Moderate.

Galleria Park – An affordable European-style hostelry in the heart of the shopping and financial district is just what the city needed. For starters, there's a third-floor park, a jogging track, an Art Nouveau lobby, and a 4-story atrium. Other features, like concierge, bar, morning coffee, wine on Fridays (TGIF), milk and cookies, Wednesday movies, and 2 restaurants (*Bentley's* for fresh seafood and *Chambord Brasserie*), make this place quite impressive for the price. 177 rooms (with refrigerators) and 20 suites. The rooms on the lower floors may induce claustrophobia. There are 3 meeting rooms, and secretarial services and computers can be arranged. A/V equipment and photocopiers also are available. 191 Sutter St. (phone: 781-3060 or 800-792-9639; Fax: 415-433-4409). Moderate.

Handlery Union Square – A family-run establishment that offers 377 rooms, a concierge, multilingual staff, a whole floor for nonsmokers, heated outdoor pool, sauna, restaurant, and ample parking. One room accommodates business meetings, and there are secretarial services, a concierge desk, limited A/V equipment, and photocopiers available. 351 Geary St. (phone: 781-7800 or 800-223-0888; Fax: 415-781-0269; Telex: 677050). Moderate.

Inn at the Opera – So close to the cultural pulse of the city that several of its 48 rooms and suites overlook the rehearsal studios of the *San Francisco Ballet.* All feature small refrigerators, microwave ovens, large baths, armoires and other antique furnishings, and unusual architectural details that distinguish each room. On the ground floor, *Act IV* resembles an English hunt club and serves breakfast and dinner until 10 PM, then post-theater lighter fare until after midnight. Twenty-four–hour room service is available. There's a concierge desk, and business amenities include secretarial assistance, A/V equipment, photocopiers, and computers. Express checkout. 333 Fulton St. (phone: 863-8400 or 800-325-2708; Fax: 415-861-0821). Moderate.

Juliana – Contemporary artwork on loan from local galleries adorns the walls of this small hotel on lower Nob Hill. Floral bed covers and upholstery give the 106 guestrooms a Laura Ashley look. *Vinoteca* serves all meals daily; coffee and tea are available in the lobby throughout the day; and wine is offered each evening. Other pluses are room service, which is available until 11 PM, 1 meeting room, secretarial services, A/V equipment, photocopiers, and express checkout. A block from Chinatown, 2 blocks from Union Square. 590 Bush St. (phone: 392-2540 or 800-382-8800; Fax: 415-391-8447; Telex: 470733). Moderate.

Kensington Park – Once the *Elks Club* headquarters, this 1924 building is now an elegant hotel with a liveried host; a marble lobby with a high, painted ceiling; and 84 spacious rooms furnished with mahogany Queen Anne reproductions, floral draperies, and down comforters. Complimentary coffee and croissants are served buffet style on each floor in the morning; afternoon tea, sherry, and cookies in the lobby. One room is available for meetings, and there's a concierge desk. A/V equipment can be arranged. 450 Post St., a block from Union Square (phone: 788-6400 or 800-553-1900; Fax: 415-399-9484). Moderate.

Monticello Inn – The Federal-style lobby and country colonial decor give it the feel of a large, gracious East Coast home. The 91 guestrooms all have partial-canopied beds, remote-control cable TV sets, and coffee makers. A complimentary continental breakfast is offered daily. The adjoining restaurant, the *Corona Bar & Grill,* serves innovative Southwestern cooking daily. Nonsmoking and handicapped-accessible rooms are available. There's a concierge desk on hand, and secretarial services and A/V equipment can be arranged. Photocopiers and express checkout also are available. 127 Ellis St. (phone: 392-8800 or 800-669-7777; Fax: 415-398-2650; Telex: 470733). Moderate.

New Richelieu – In downtown San Francisco, where old hotels never die, this one has been lovingly restored to the 1906 just-post-earthquake style of its birth. The lobby is rich with cardinal-red plush carpets, white settees, mirrors, dark woods, inverted dome chandeliers, and Tiffany-style stained glass. Period clothes are on display, as is the house cat, on its favorite settee. A lounge has a bar and piano. A small exercise gym is on the premises. The hotel offers complimentary afternoon tea, though there's no restaurant. Complimentary chauffeured limousine. Other amenities are around-the-clock room service, a concierge desk, and photocopiers. 1050 Van Ness (phone: 673-4711 or 800-227-3608; Fax: 415-673-9362; Telex: 6972047). Moderate.

Orchard – Built in 1907, this restored property near Union Square has an elegant European look. Italian custom-made rosewood furniture in 96 attractive rooms overlooking a garden. The *Sutter Orchard* restaurant serves delicious and reasonably priced breakfast and lunch, with unusually good coffee. A concierge desk, secretarial services, photocopiers, and computer hookups in rooms all are available. 562 Sutter St. (phone: 433-4434 or 800-433-4343; Fax: 415-433-3695). Moderate.

Petite Auberge – Near Union Square but closer to the heart of France, this less pricey Gallic sister of the *White Swan,* complete with an antique carousel horse in the foyer, manages to be both rustic and elegant. A sweeping staircase (and a small elevator for the less athletic) leads to 26 rooms on 5 floors, furnished with French country antiques. Full concierge service, a buffet breakfast, and afternoon tea are provided. Reserve a month or more in advance. Business amenities include A/V equipment and photocopiers. 863 Bush St. (phone: 928-6000; Fax: 415-775-5717). Moderate.

Regis – Thespian decor and memorabilia take center stage at this 86-room property, which also is conveniently across the street from two theaters and in close proximity to others. *Regina's,* an outstanding creole restaurant with late hours, is perfect for post-theater dinners. Furnishings are French and English antiques, beds are canopied, and, as in other "boutique" hotels, amenities are deluxe but prices aren't. Niceties such as 24-hour room service, 1 meeting room, concierge, secretarial services, A/V equipment, and photocopiers, are all on call. 490 Geary St. (phone: 928-7900 or 800-345-4443; Fax: 415-441-8788). Moderate.

Shannon Court – Irish in name, Spanish in style, it has painted wrought-iron and arched doors, and a prevalence of pink, peach, and primrose. This imaginative, if slightly kitschy, 173-room establishment is close to the theater district and attractively furnished (including phones in each room). Two suites have their own private portions of the rooftop terrace. The *Shannon Court Brasserie* keeps long hours for light snacks and meals. Also off the lobby is the elegant *La Mère Duquesne,* which exudes the ambience of expensive French, yet serves amazingly reasonable, classic prix fixe dinners (as well as à la carte). The conference room seats 50, and there are photocopiers, and a concierge desk. 550 Geary St. (phone: 775-5000 or 800-821-0493; Fax: 415-928-6813). Moderate.

Victorian Inn on the Park – Known as the *Clunie House,* it was built in 1897 in honor of Queen Victoria's *Diamond Jubilee* and now has guests reserving 2 or 3 weeks in advance for one of its 12 bedrooms. Inlaid oak floors, mahogany woodwork, charming period pieces, a handsome oak-paneled dining room (the complimentary continental breakfast features breads that are baked on the premises), and a lavish parlor (complimentary afternoon wine) are only some of the drawing cards of this registered historic landmark. Amenities include a concierge desk and express checkout. Across from Golden Gate Park, at 301 Lyon St. (phone: 931-1830). Moderate.

Villa Florence – Out front there is the hustle, bustle, and cable car clanging of Powell Street, and indoors the aroma of garlic and the pleasant noises from the trendy, first-rate restaurant, *Kuleto's*. This hostelry exudes overdone Italian atmosphere, with a trompe l'oeil mural that doesn't quite deceive the eye and Renaissance marble commingled with Art Nouveau. This ambience extends upstairs, to the 177 vividly decorated rooms. Two meeting rooms can accommodate up to 20. Limited secretarial services are available, as well as A/V equipment, photocopiers, a concierge desk, and express checkout. 225 Powell St. (phone: 397-7700 or 800-553-4411; Fax: 415-397-1006). Moderate.

Vintage Court – Everything is up-to-date in this 106-room boutique property, established in 1913. (A glass etching of the original building is in the mauve lobby with a cheerful fireplace.) A night's lodging for two costs less than dinner next door at *Masa's*, one of San Francisco's most famous and expensive French eateries (see *Eating Out*). Preferred restaurant seating is included with your room. Every afternoon in the lobby, the hotel serves complimentary California wine with fruit, cheese, and crackers; there also is free limousine service twice a morning to the financial district. The rooms (named for Napa Valley wineries) have bay-window seats, padded headboards, and bedspreads in floral or wine-grape motifs. The hotel's meeting room seats 15; A/V equipment and photocopiers are available. 650 Bush St. (phone: 392-4666 or 800-654-1100.; Fax: 415-392-4666, ext. 137). Moderate.

Washington Square Inn – Within walking distance of Ghirardelli Square and Chinatown. Only 15 rooms (11 with private bathrooms), each individually decorated, in a turn-of-the-century house in the North Beach area. Three rooms overlook Washington Square Park and are more expensive. Complimentary breakfast and afternoon tea. There's also a concierge desk. No smoking is permitted in the hotel. 1660 Stockton St. (phone: 981-4220). Moderate to inexpensive.

Beresford – For British charm at a reasonable price. Old-fashioned service, a writing parlor off the Victorian lobby, flower boxes in the street windows, and 114 pleasant rooms. Even the lamppost in front has a white and blue Wedgwood-esque frieze. The *White Horse* tavern uses fresh vegetables from the hotel's garden. 635 Sutter St. (phone: 673-9900 or 800-533-6533; Fax: 415-474-0449). Inexpensive.

Cornell – Everything but the name is French — atmosphere, furnishings, the manager's accent — in this lovingly spruced-up antique, with flower beds behind a picket fence, old reproductions of Cluny tapestries, a cage elevator, and rustic furniture in 50 rooms that include private bathrooms, phones, and cable TV. The *Restaurant Jeanne d'Arc*, filled with memorabilia honoring its namesake, serves dinner 6 days a week and complimentary breakfast. Ask about the special rate — under $500 for a double — for 7 nights and breakfasts, plus 5 dinners. A concierge desk and photocopiers are on call. 715 Bush St. (phone: 421-3154 or 800-232-9698; Fax: 415-399-1442). Inexpensive.

Golden Gate – Up the street is another renovated relic, owned and run by a very friendly couple, who are multilingual. Period photographs and the cage elevator hark back to the hotel's 1913 beginnings, but the small, comfortable rooms are fresh and bright, with flowered wallpaper and white wicker furniture or mahogany antiques. 14 rooms have private baths, 9 share 3 hall baths. Continental breakfast and afternoon tea are served in a cheery lounge with a fireplace. Concierge. 775 Bush St. (phone: 392-3702 or 800-835-1118; Telex: 5101001677). Inexpensive.

Pensione International – This refurbished 46-room establishment — complete with concierge — boasts an incredible location for the price (as little as $45 for a double with shared bath, $70 with private bath), plus color TV sets and complimentary continental breakfast. About halfway between Union Square and Japantown, it also is within easy walking distance of the theater district. 875 Post St. (phone: 775-3344). Inexpensive.

EATING OUT: San Francisco has about 4,300 eating places, serving a wide variety of food, from haute cuisine to ethnic fare, and taking fine advantage of the wonderful seafood and fresh produce so readily available from the ocean and the surrounding countryside. Along with the longtime favorites like *Ernie's* and *Jack's,* San Franciscans welcome trendy new restaurants that show up on the horizon at an astonishing rate. One notable trend is toward first-rate food in hotel restaurants, starting with *Campton Place* and extending to even newer establishments like *Silks* at the *Mandarin Oriental* hotel and the *Portman Grill.* At the other end of the spectrum are the neighborhood places that specialize in Chinese, Japanese, Vietnamese, Thai, or Mexican food at very affordable prices. Our restaurant selections range in price from $65 or more (sometimes much more) for a dinner for two in the expensive category; $40 to $60, moderate; $40 or less, inexpensive. Prices do not include drinks, wine, or tips. All telephone numbers are in the 415 area code unless otherwise indicated.

Acquerello – Attractive watercolor prints adorn the walls of this warm, intimate dining spot, which proffers traditional regional Italian dishes, not to mention an extensive list of Italian wines. Fresh breads and pasta are made on the premises. Closed Mondays. Reservations advised. Visa and MasterCard accepted. 1722 Sacramento St. (phone: 567-5432). Expensive.

Blue Fox – The setting may be downtown San Francisco, but the mood is definitely Northern Italian. Piedmontese-born restaurateur John Fassio has brought the foods of his region to these shores in grand style, giving such delicacies as *risotto* with quail, venison with white truffles, and pumpkin *gnocchi* with sage butter a home on the West Coast. Open for dinner only, Mondays through Saturdays. Reservations advised. Major credit cards accepted. 659 Merchant St. (phone: 981-1177). Expensive.

Campton Place – In the *Campton Place* hotel, but a legitimate magnet for diners in its own right. A relatively small room, decorated in soft shades of rose and gray, with a menu that is an outstanding example of American dishes done to perfection — without excessive fuss or fanfare. Breakfast, lunch, and dinner are served daily, and each is marvelous. Reservations at least a week in advance are necessary. Major credit cards accepted. 340 Stockton St. (phone: 781-5555). Expensive.

Chez Panisse – The temple of the so-called guru of California cuisine. Alice Waters gained national prominence when she began using the best, freshest local ingredients in variations on classic recipes at this 2-story, brown shingle house in the heart of Berkeley. Since only one meal is served in the downstairs dining room each evening, it's a good idea to call ahead to find out what it includes: perhaps spring lamb, grilled salmon, ravioli stuffed with potatoes, or something even more innovative. Upstairs, the more casual and less expensive *Chez Panisse Café* specializes in pizza, calzone, and imaginative salads and soups. To tell the truth, there's a lot of the "Emperor's New Clothes" about this place these days. Closed Sundays and Mondays. Reservations advised. Major credit cards accepted. 1517 Shattuck Ave., Berkeley (phone: 548-5525). Expensive.

Ernie's – Perhaps the best known name on the local scene. Dining here is a leisurely affair (at either lunch or dinner), so you have plenty of time to enjoy the atmosphere — Victorian yet tasteful. Traditional French dishes share the menu with nouvelle cuisine. Open daily. Reservations necessary. Major credit cards accepted. 847 Montgomery St. (phone: 397-5969). Expensive.

Fleur de Lys – Behind its heavy, ornate doors, the place shimmers with gold and red paisley fabric and mirrored panels. This is a bastion of French cooking — with California's natural flavors shining through; signature dishes include lobster soup with coconut milk and lemon grass, and lamb chops encased in a vegetable mousse. Among the highest priced in town, but habitués say it's worth it. Prix fixe dinners available. Open for dinner; closed Sundays. Reservations advised. Major credit cards accepted. 777 Sutter St. (phone: 673-7779). Expensive.

The Grill – Adjoining the atrium-style lobby of the *Pan Pacific* hotel, the contemporary elegance here is accented with silver and crystal. Diners enjoy California cuisine with a Pacific flair. Open daily for breakfast, lunch, and dinner. Reservations advised. Major credit cards accepted. 500 Post St. (phone: 929-2087). Expensive.

Masa's – Although Masa Kobayshi died in 1985, his namesake restaurant, headed by protégé Julian Serreno, still ranks as one of the city's finest. Masa was a master of perfect presentation, extravagant sauces, and creative combinations, and Serreno carries on that tradition. Dinner only, Tuesdays through Saturdays, 6 to 9:30 PM. Reservations necessary; call 3 weeks ahead. Only Visa and MasterCard accepted. 648 Bush St. (phone: 989-7154). Expensive.

Monsoon – Chef Bruce Cost, who is the author of two cookbooks on Asian cooking, shows off his expertise in the fresh, flavorful Chinese and Southeast Asian cooking served here. Under the watchful eye of a Chinese dragon on the ceiling, diners can taste tea-smoked duck with lotus rolls, salt-and-pepper spot prawns, and whole steamed catfish with Thai-style ginger and coconut sauce. Dinner daily. Reservations advised. Visa and MasterCard accepted. 601 Van Ness, Opera Plaza (phone: 441-3232). Expensive.

Postrio – "Post" refers to the street address and "Trio" to three chefs at this wildly successful brainchild of celebrated LA chef-restaurateur Wolfgang Puck. The eclectic food (with over a dozen main courses) is delicious and beautifully served. A Chinese cooking technique produces the crispest of fried quails. Open daily for breakfast, lunch, and dinner. Reservations essential long in advance. Major credit cards accepted. In the *Prescott Hotel;* 545 Post St. (phone: 776-7825). Expensive.

Silks – The bill of fare in this quiet, pastel-decorated dining room is California cooking with an Asian touch. The nightly prix fixe or à la carte menu might include salmon with black bean sauce or hot and sour soup with prawns and veal dumplings. Dinner and elaborate American breakfasts are served daily, and lunch is served weekdays. Reservations advised. Major credit cards accepted. Located in the *Mandarin Oriental Hotel,* 222 Sansome St. (phone: 986-2020). Expensive.

Stars – The stars have to do with the founding chef, Jeremiah Tower, a culinary luminary, as well as the patrons, all of whom are visible and audible in this large, glamorous establishment, divided into various levels for dining, drinking, and sampling seafood at the oyster bar. The changing menu might list an appetizer of marinated salmon or warm duck salad, Tower's stock-in-trade main course of grilled tuna served with baby vegetables, or fish and chips. The wine list numbers in the hundreds, including California wines from $15 and imports up to $900. It's slightly noisy, exciting, open late, and within walking distance of the *Opera House* and *Symphony Hall.* Open daily. Reservations necessary. Major credit cards accepted. 150 Redwood Alley, between Polk St. and Van Ness Ave. (phone: 861-7827). Expensive.

Lark Creek Inn – Chef Bradley Ogden, of *Campton Place* fame, now commands top-drawer reviews for his innovative way with traditional American cooking. Across the bay in Marin County, this dining spot is located in a creekside setting, complete with redwoods and gardens. Dinner nightly; closed for lunch on Saturdays. Reservations advised. Major credit cards accepted. 234 Magnolia Ave.; Larkspur (phone: 924-7766). Expensive to moderate.

Square One – Classic international dishes are the focal point for chef/owner Joyce Goldstein's ever-changing menu. Breads, pastries, and ice cream are all homemade, and the outstanding desserts and award-winning wine list complete the culinary experience. Open for lunch weekdays; dinner nightly. Reservations advised. Major credit cards accepted. 190 Pacific Ave. (phone: 788-1110). Expensive to moderate.

Zola's – Rustic country cooking is at its finest in this contemporary Mediterranean eatery. Among its tastiest offerings are *cassoulet, confit de canard,* and game, such as guinea hen with chestnuts and cabbage. Smoking is not permitted. Dinner only; closed Mondays. Reservations advised. Major credit cards accepted. 395 Hayes St. (phone: 864-4824). Expensive to moderate.

Zuni Café – The menu at this bright, casual, California-Mediterranean-style dining spot (with sidewalk tables, too) changes daily; it's based on the fresh, seasonal ingredients chef Judy Rodgers finds at the market each morning. Many dishes are cooked in a wood-burning oven and grill. There is also an oyster bar. Open for breakfast, lunch, and dinner; closed Mondays. Reservations advised. Major credit cards accepted. 1658 Market St. (phone: 552-2522). Expensive to moderate.

Buca Giovanni – Very Italian in decor and menu, this brick cellar is reminiscent of a Tuscan trattoria, as is the food. This longtime favorite with locals is strong on veal, pasta, and Italian wild mushrooms; all the pasta is made on the premises; and coffee is roasted in-house. Dinner only; closed Sundays. Reservations advised. Major credit cards accepted. 800 Greenwich St. (phone: 776-7766). Moderate.

Caffè Sport – Another nostalgic bit of Italy, with three sittings per evening for dinners served family style and the kind of food you find in the Old Country. Closed Sundays and Mondays. Reservations unnecessary. No credit cards accepted. 974 Green St. (phone: 981-1251). Moderate.

California Culinary Academy – In addition to teaching classic French cooking to prospective chefs, this school is open to the public to sample student creations. Three different dinning rooms offer varied fare: *Cyril's* serves Mediterranean soups, fish, and pasta dishes. Open for lunch only. No reservations. The *Academy Grill* serves traditional Americana, such as hamburgers. Open for lunch and dinner. No reservations. Sumptuous three-course meals are served Mondays through Thursdays in the *Carème,* the main dining area. A classical European buffet complete with pâtés and a plethora of desserts is served here Fridays. Open for lunch and dinner; closed weekends, except for a once-a-month Saturday night dinner-dance and Sunday brunch. Reservations necessary; lunch has three seatings. Major credit cards accepted in all rooms. 625 Polk St. near Turk (phone: 771-3500). Moderate.

Celadon – This elegant Chinese eatery is accented by graceful, highly polished chairs, Oriental decor, and celadon green carpeting. The food is Cantonese, which the Chinese consider their haute cuisine. A set multiple-course meal, such as the "Scholar's Dinner," shows off the chef's versatility. Open daily. Reservations advised. Major credit cards accepted. 881 Clay St. (phone: 982-1168). Moderate.

Le Central – Providing a variation on the continental theme, with bright lights, French art hung on brick walls, and the menu written on mirrors and blackboards. Food is in the best brasserie fashion: *cassoulet* (navy beans simmered with sausages, duck, pork, and lamb), *choucroute Alsacienne* (sauerkraut cooked in wine with bacon, pork, and sausage), and *saucisson chaud* (thinly sliced sausage with hot potato salad). Closed Sundays. Reservations advised for lunch and dinner. Major credit cards accepted. 453 Bush St. (phone: 391-2233). Moderate.

China Moon – In a cleverly disguised coffee shop setting, the owner/chef has succeeded in presenting her singular brand of Chinese food. In what other "Chinese" restaurant would you expect to find such appetizers as chili-spiked spring rolls, spicy lamb, fresh water chestnuts, and Peking antipasto plates side by side with a California wine list and Western-style desserts? No smoking permitted. Open daily for dinner; lunch served daily except Sundays. Reservations advised. Most major credit cards accepted. 639 Post St. (phone: 775-4789). Moderate.

Corona Bar & Grill – Mexican and Southwestern regional cooking receive a "nouvelle" twist in this popular eatery. The menu changes daily, with specialties such as a soup made from smoked snapper and mussels. Mexican artifacts with wood and brass furnishings give this a casual, Southwestern ambience. Open daily for lunch and dinner; brunch on weekends. Reservations advised. Major credit cards accepted. 88 Cyril Magnin (phone: 392-5500). Moderate.

Elite Café – Informal and very busy, it bills itself as a seafood place and has an oyster bar to prove it. But the tone is creole, and many other Southern specialties are on the menu. Dinner nightly and Sunday brunch. No reservations. Major credit cards accepted. 2049 Fillmore (phone: 346-8668). Moderate.

Empress of China – The Cantonese dishes served here are tasty (Peking duck is the house specialty), and the rooftop garden adds spectacular views to the dining experience. Located in the heart of Chinatown. Open daily. Reservations advised. Major credit cards accepted. 838 Grant Ave. (phone: 434-1345). Moderate.

Enoteca Lanzone – After gazing at Modesto Lanzone's contemporary art collection, perusing the wine library, with more than 200 varieties of grappa, and sampling some of the 110 kinds of olive oil and balsamic vinegars, be sure to order the superb pasta. One of the most intriguing dishes is *pansotti,* a concoction of delicate ravioli stuffed with spinach and ricotta and served with a creamy hazelnut sauce. Closed for lunch Saturdays and Sundays. Reservations advised. Major credit cards accepted. 601 Van Ness Ave., Opera Plaza (phone: 928-0400). Moderate.

Fog City Diner – This sleek chrome and neon spot serves creative appetizers called American dim sum — an array of American-style (from Cajun to Tex-Mex) treats, such as crab cakes and Buffalo chicken wings, meant to be passed around the table. Diners who prefer a plate to themselves can order entrées ranging from breast of chicken with roasted peppers and arugula pesto to grilled rabbit with ancho chili succotash. Like any self-respecting establishment that calls itself a diner, it also serves milkshakes, hamburgers, and similar fare, but even these are done differently. Open daily for lunch and dinner. Reservations advised. Most major credit cards accepted. 1300 Battery St. (phone: 982-2000). Moderate.

Il Fornaio – The Tuscan-style cooking, Carrara marble counters, Italian oil paintings, tile floors, Milanese lighting fixtures, and gleaming mahogany bring a bit of Italy to San Francisco. Choices range from a simple angel hair pasta with fresh tomato, basil, and garlic to a whole game hen oakwood-roasted in a clay pot. Fresh baked breads and other goodies are available for takeout. Open 7 AM to midnight daily. Dinner reservations advised. Major credit cards accepted. 1265 Battery St. (phone: 986-0100). Moderate.

Greens – Devotees consider this vegetarian eatery the best in the country. Things are always what they seem here; nothing masquerades as meat. The "greenery" includes sandwiches, pizza, pasta, chili, salad, and five-course prix fixe dinners on weekends. Lunch and dinner Tuesdays through Saturdays; brunch Sundays. Reservations advised. Only Visa and MasterCard accepted. Ft. Mason Bldg. A (phone: 771-6222). Moderate.

Hayes Street Grill – In a city famous for its seafood restaurants, this is one of the best. Everything is fresh; nothing is overcooked. There always is a long list of daily specials, along with great sourdough bread and an unusually good crème brûlée for dessert. A quintessential San Francisco dining experience. Open for dinner except Sundays; lunch served weekdays. Reservations advised. Visa, MasterCard, and Discover accepted. 320 Hayes St. (phone: 863-5545). Moderate.

Jack's – A landmark for nearly as long as San Francisco has been on the map. But because it is in the financial district, this eatery, with excellent continental food, is unknown to many visitors. All the grilled entrées are recommended, and for dessert, the banana fritters with brandy sauce are unbeatable. The decor is unpretentious, as are the prices (particularly the dinner special), and the service is good. Open daily. Reservations necessary. Only American Express accepted. 615 Sacramento St. (phone: 421-7355). Moderate.

Janot's – A stone's throw from formidable culinary competition, this French-Californian eatery manages top quality at medium prices. The atmosphere is nostalgic-modern, with the bricks, brass, and banquettes of yesterday in an up-to-date combination. The menu features such standards as steaks and calf's liver, imaginative French dishes, and scrumptious hot and cold salads. Lunch and dinner daily except Sundays. Reservations necessary. Major credit cards accepted. 44 Compton Pl. (phone: 392-5373). Moderate.

MacArthur Park – Fresh seafood, barbecued steaks and spareribs, and a good California wine list. Also serves one of the better breakfasts in town. Open daily. Reservations advised. Major credit cards accepted. 607 Front St. (phone: 398-5700). Moderate.

Mandarin – A Chinese palace with thick beamed ceilings, a delicate cherrywood lotus blossom carving, Mandarin antiques and embroideries — and excellent Chinese food, which you watch being barbecued in the Mongolian fire pit. Call a day in advance and order the Mandarin duck (a whole duck prepared with scallions and plum sauce). Open daily. Reservations advised. Major credit cards accepted. 900 North Point St., in Ghirardelli Square (phone: 673-8812). Moderate.

1001 Nob Hill – Housed in an elegant 1916 landmark building at the top of Nob Hill, the decor includes antiques, hand-crafted furnishings, beveled glass windows and doors, and whimsical paintings and murals. The cooking is a blend of Southern European and American with an Oriental flavor. Appetizers such as caviar pie and pan-fried oysters, and entrées, among them duck *confit* with cabbage and baby potatoes, plus an extensive selection of fine wines and a jazz pianist tinkering in the background complete the experience. Open nightly for dinner and until midnight at the cocktail lounge. Reservations advised. Major credit cards accepted. 1001 California St. (phone: 441-1001). Moderate.

690 – On the site of a defunct carburetor shop, this eatery derives its imaginative menu from chef Jeremiah Tower (of *Stars* fame), its red telephone booths from Britain, and its "tropical" dishes from Oriental,

Caribbean, Indian, and Moroccan influences. Open late. Dinner daily; lunch weekdays; brunch Sundays. Reservations advised. Major credit cards accepted. 690 Van Ness Ave. (phone: 255-6900). Moderate.

Splendido's – The interior is rustic and the food is a smash — Mediterranean-style cooking, such as grilled, roasted, and sautéed fish meat and game, as well as pasta and pizza. Reservations are an absolute necessity, as this is a luncheon haven for businessfolk. Lunch weekdays; closed for dinner Sundays. Major credit cards accepted. Embarcadero Center Four, podium level (phone: 986-3222). Moderate.

Tadich Grill – San Francisco's oldest restaurant (ca. 1849), and still going strong with what folks maintain is the freshest seafood in town. Best bets: baked avocado with shrimp diablo, rex sole, salmon, sea bass. Don't pass up the homemade cheesecake for dessert. Closed Sundays and major holidays. No reservations. Visa and Mastercard accepted. 240 California St. (phone: 391-2373). Moderate.

Tung Fong – This tiny teahouse in Chinatown serves remarkable dim sum, and weekend brunch is a wonderful experience. Carts come laden with Cantonese delicacies, such as a paper-wrapped chicken with barbecue sauce, dumplings with black-mushroom centers, and succulent spareribs. Both the pickled mustard greens and the hot black bean sauce are available by the bottle. Closed Wednesdays. Reservations advised. No credit cards accepted. 808 Pacific Ave. (phone: 362-7115). Moderate.

Yoshida-Ya – Stunning Japanese spot known for its excellent yakitori — a selection of meat, fish, and vegetables, all marinated, skewered, and grilled over charcoal. Upstairs is less crowded; as are weekends. Open daily. Reservations necessary. Major credit cards accepted. 2909 Webster at Union St. (phone: 346-3431). Moderate.

Garibaldi Café – An intimate double dining room tastefully decorated in high-tech neon and a clever kitchen make this place a standout. Always excellent specialties, such as roast pork loin stuffed with apricots and tortellini stuffed with veal, change daily. Open for lunch weekdays, and daily for dinner. Reservations advised. Visa, Discover, and MasterCard accepted. 17th and Wisconsin Sts. (phone: 552-3325). Moderate to inexpensive.

Balboa Café – A glass-enclosed San Francisco tradition, very popular, very crowded, and very noisy. It serves timeless American fare, including first class burgers, until 11 PM. Bar stays open until 2 AM. Open daily. Reservations necessary only for 6 or more. Major credit cards accepted. 31995 Fillmore St. (phone: 921-3944). Inexpensive.

Buena Vista – This saloon has built its reputation on great Irish coffee — which it claims to have introduced into the United States — and an extensive imported beer selection. The diverse clientele comes to drink, be merry, and then eat. Food is a secondary consideration. Community tables are half the fun. Overlooks the bay, with views of Alcatraz and Marin County. Open daily. No reservations. No credit cards accepted. 2765 Hyde St. (phone: 474-5044). Inexpensive.

Caffè Trieste – At this popular early morning hangout, customers start the day with strong Italian coffee and fresh sticky pastries. Around noon, the clientele arrive to eat simple meals, such as quiche or sandwiches — or simply to linger over cappuccino. Impromptu operatic arias are sung by the Giotto family on Saturday afternoons, and fresh coffee beans are sold at the next-door annex. Open daily. No reservations or credit cards accepted. 601 Vallejo (phone: 392-6739). Inexpensive.

Doidge's Kitchen – San Franciscans hungry for breakfast beat a path to funky, chic Union Street for marvelous omelettes, pancakes, and more unusual dishes — such as baked eggs wrapped in bacon and seasoned with vermouth. Open daily, only for breakfast and lunch.

Reservations advised. Only Visa and MasterCard accepted. 2217 Union St. (phone: 921-2149). Inexpensive.

Far East Café – Don't let the neon-lit exterior fool you — inside there are ornate Chinese lanterns and private, curtained booths. The extensive Cantonese and Mandarin menu features all the old classics and, if you call in advance, an excellent family banquet. Open daily. Reservations advised. Major credit cards accepted. 631 Grant Ave. (phone: 982-3245). Inexpensive.

Fly Trap – In the trendy SoMa district, this is a re-creation of a turn-of-the-century restaurant that earned its nickname from the squares of flypaper flapping over each table. The flypaper is gone, but the name has stuck; the menu has Californian flair and the nostalgic flavor of old San Francisco, with hearty original dishes. Dinner Mondays through Saturdays; lunch weekdays. Reservations advised. Major credit cards accepted. 606 Folsom St. (243-0580). Inexpensive.

Isobune – There's only counter service at this sushi and sashimi spot — but what counter service! Japanese-style wooden boats glide by bearing all sorts of Japanese wonders, and customers take what they want. Each dish contains two or three pieces of sushi and costs from $1.50 to $2. The tab is figured by counting plates. Count on a wait. Open daily. No reservations. Only Visa and MasterCard accepted. 1737 Post St. (phone: 563-1030). Inexpensive.

Khan Toke Thai House – The most ornate and, many think, the best Thai table in town. It goes to show that the best needn't be the dearest. Waitresses wear the national costume, and Thai dancers perform on Sundays. Open daily. Reservations advised. Major credit cards accepted. 5937 Geary (phone: 668-6654). Inexpensive.

Lavenue – American home cooking prepared with delicacy and expertise by Nancy Oakes, who also cooks for *Pat O'Shea*, the terrific neighborhood sports bar located next door. Mouth-watering entrées might include rack of lamb with ratatouille wrapped in a cabbage leaf and pan roasted breast of duck with sylvian berry sauce and sweet potato pancakes. Desserts range from snow white peach cobbler with vanilla ice cream to a crispy chocolate-stuffed banana split to deep-dish fresh-fruit pies. Open daily. Reservations advised. 3854 Geary St. (phone: 386-1555). Inexpensive.

Mario's Bohemian Cigar Store – Patrons are treated like relatives in this tiny, family-owned Italian eatery whose walls are covered with photos of regular customers. Not surprisingly, the owners prepare the food, which includes sandwiches made from *focaccia* (Italian pizza bread), desserts such as Italian cheesecake and apple turnovers. Because customers range in age from infants to at least 80, the menu offers grown-up cappuccino and "mini" versions for the kids (mostly steamed milk). Open daily. No reservations or credit cards accepted. 566 Columbus Ave. (phone: 362-0536). Inexpensive.

Miss Pearl's Jam House – The food is as colorful as the beach house setting, with such specialties as Jamaican jerked chicken and black-eyed pea fritters. Live steel drum music on the weekends. Lunch weekdays; dinner daily; Sunday brunch. Reservations advised on weekends. Visa and MasterCard accepted. 601 Eddy St. (phone: 775-5267). Inexpensive.

Pier 23 – With all the charm of an authentic waterfront dive but with food that makes up for the absence of fancy surroundings. A perfect lunch stop for weary Fisherman's Wharf sightseers. The menu generally features a few fresh seafood specials, as well as regular items like crab quesadillas and paella. Music nightly from 9:30 PM to 2 AM. Open daily for lunch; closed Sundays and Mondays for dinner; Sunday brunch. Reservations advised. Only Visa and MasterCard accepted. On the Embarcadero (phone: 362-5125). Inexpensive.

La Rondalla – *Christmas* decorations are left in place all year at this usually festive corner "Mexicatessen." A mariachi band makes Saturday nights particularly lively. Beyond all the tinsel is good, hearty food; specials, such as chiles relleños, are indeed special. Closed Mondays; on Sundays, brunch only. Reservations necessary only for 10 or more. No credit cards accepted. 901 Valencia St. (phone: 647-7474). Inexpensive.

Rory's – Here's an ideal spot to satisfy a weekend sweet tooth. Try the homemade ice cream in a variety of first rate flavors—espresso is our downfall—topped with phenomenal fudge, or ask for "twist-ins," and choose anything from Oreos to M & Ms folded in your favorite flavor. Open 11:30 AM to 11 PM Sundays through Thursdays; on Fridays and Saturdays from 11:30 AM until midnight. 2015 Fillmore St. (phone: 346-3692). Inexpensive.

San Francisco Bar-B-Q – The aroma of Thai spices wafts over Potrero Hill when the cooks fire up the grill to barbecue spareribs, chicken, duck noodles, salmon, trout, lamb, or even oysters. The meats can be ordered à la carte or as part of a dinner that includes sticky rice and grated carrot salad, with sourdough bread. A bowl of noodles comes cooked in sesame and soy, with crisp grilled pieces of duck. Just about everything on the menu can be ordered to go. Closed Mondays; closed Sundays for lunch. No reservations or credit cards accepted. 1328 18th St. (phone: 431-8956).

Sears Fine Food – A line forms outside for Sunday brunch at this San Francisco institution serving old-fashioned breakfasts. The pancakes are Swedish, the French toast is made with sourdough bread. The standard lunch menu includes non-standard items like lemon soufflé. Open for breakfast and lunch, Wednesdays through Sundays. No reservations or credit cards accepted. 439 Powell St. (phone: 986-1160). Inexpensive.

SANTA FE

AT-A-GLANCE

SEEING THE CITY: Visitors with lots of time and stamina should hike the trail up Tesuque Peak (12,040 feet) from the Aspen Vista Picnic Area. The trailhead is on the paved road to the Santa Fe Ski Area, a drive that also provides fine views for those who prefer to stay in the car.

SPECIAL PLACES: The downtown area of Santa Fe is very compact and can be explored on foot very easily. A car would be helpful for visiting the museums on Camino Lejo or for taking day trips to Taos, Acoma, and other nearby places of interest.

The Plaza – The Plaza has been the center of Santa Fe life for almost 4 centuries, ever since the day in 1610 when mounted Spanish soldiers in medieval armor first used it as a parade ground. Throughout the centuries the Plaza has been the scene of the most important public events in the city: markets, fiestas, proclamations, parades, and even, at one time, bullfights. An obelisk now marks the center of the lovely, tree-shaded square. Along the footpaths emanating from the obelisk are benches where weary shoppers rest, sightseers fiddle with their cameras, and office workers enjoy picnic lunches. The Palace of the Governors dominates the north side of the square; the three other sides are lined with shops, restaurants, and galleries.

Palace of the Governors – Built by Spanish settlers in 1609-10, eleven years before the Pilgrims landed at Plymouth Rock, this is the oldest continuously used public building in the country, serving as the seat of government for four "nations": Spain, Mexico, the Confederacy, and the US. Originally, all of the palace was made of mud except for the roof beams, or vigas. The walls, then as now, were adobe. The dirt floor was mixed with animal blood to pack it down and produce a sheen. Following the Pueblo Revolt of 1680, the Indians enlarged the structure and used it as a large pueblo. It again was occupied and further enlarged by the Spanish following the Reconquest in 1692. The palace became a museum in 1909, housing historical exhibitions for the *Museum of New Mexico*. This makes it a natural starting point for a tour of the city. Open daily from 10 AM to 5 PM. Closed Mondays during January and February. Admission charge; children under 16 admitted free. On the Plaza (phone: 827-6483).

Museum of Fine Arts – Next door, moving west from the palace, this museum houses a collection of more than 8,000 works of art. Changing exhibitions throughout the year feature 20th-century art and photography, prints, and sculpture with a strong emphasis on the Southwest. Completed in 1917, some 300 years after the palace, the building is an outstanding example of Pueblo Revival architecture. It became a model for the architectural style that still dominates Santa Fe, combining traditional adobe design and materials with modern comfort and efficiency. Open daily from 10 AM to 5 PM. Closed Mondays during January and February. Admission charge; children under 16 are admitted free. On the Plaza, W. Palace Ave. (phone: 827-4455).

Museum of International Folk Art – Housing the world's largest

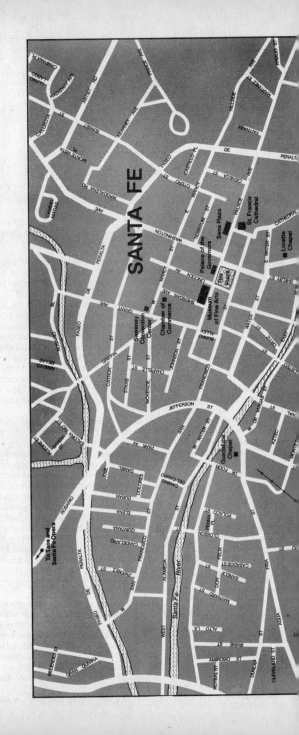

collection of folk art from around the globe, the museum was founded in 1953 by Florence Dibell Bartlett, who believed folk art to be a bond among the peoples of the world. The collection includes traditional costumes and textiles, masks, folk toys, items of everyday use, and Hispanic folk art from the Spanish colonial period. The famed Girard Foundation Collection, with selections from more than 100 countries, is on permanent exhibit. Open daily 10 AM to 5 PM. Closed Mondays in January and February. Admission charge; children under 16 are admitted free. 704 Camino Lejo, south of the Plaza, off the old Santa Fe Trail (phone: 827-6350).

Wheelwright Museum of the American Indian – Indian arts and artifacts (phone: 982-4636). *Note:* The *Case Trading Post* downstairs sells high-quality and award-winning Indian pottery, jewelry, and weavings. Open 7 days a week. 704 Camino Lejo (phone: 982-4636).

Museum of Indian Arts and Culture – As the exhibition facility for the adjacent 61-year-old Laboratory of Anthropology, its collection includes more than 50,000 pieces of prehistoric and historic basketry, pottery, textiles, jewelry, clothing, and other items crafted by the native peoples of the Southwest. Artifacts from this collection are shown in rotating exhibitions. With the inclusion of Southwest Indians on the staff and in the museum's many public programs, visitors see traditional art forms being carried forward in vibrant and innovative ways. The museum shop sells high-quality Native American jewelry, pottery, textiles, and baskets. Open daily from 10 AM to 5 PM. Closed Mondays in January and February. Admission charge; children under 16 are admitted free. Camino Lejo (phone: 827-6344).

Sena Plaza – East of the palace is this charming, tree-shaded and flower-brightened courtyard surrounded by the four wings of the 19th-century Sena hacienda. Once the home of Major José Sena, the 33-room adobe structure now is divided into shops and offices. E. Palace Ave. (For more information, call 988-5792).

St. Francis Cathedral – Directly across Palace Avenue, this structure built between 1869 and 1886 is the legacy of the French bishop Jean Baptiste Lamy, the most influential person in local history and the subject of Willa Cather's *Death Comes for the Archbishop*. The Romanesque style of the building is, like many of Lamy's ideas, imported and a little out of place. Its most interesting feature is the adobe chapel that existed here before the cathedral, most of which was incorporated into the larger structure built of local quarry stone. In continuous use since 1718, the chapel is dedicated to La Conquistadora (Our Lady of the Conquest), protector of the early Spanish settlers. The carved wooden statue of Conquistadora, said to be the oldest madonna in North America, was brought here from Mexico by the Spanish in 1625. 131 Cathedral Pl. (phone: 982-5619).

Barrio de Analco – The Santa Fe River is as slow, irregular, and inexpedient as the town it crosses, yet because it was the main source of water in the early days, almost all the homes were built along it. Noting how the town followed the path of the river, one 19th-century visitor described Santa Fe as "three streets wide and a mile long." Many of the old homes on the narrow streets in the Barrio de Analco (as the quarter on the other side of the river was called) have been preserved, particularly on East De Vargas. Although these homes are still private residences, visitors can stroll by for a look.

"Oldest House" – The foundations of this structure are thought to have been laid by the Pueblo Indians in the 13th century, although the tree rings in the ceiling beams only date to about 1750. However accurate the claim to be the "oldest house in the US," the western portion of this structure is in fact a good example of primitive adobe construction. Most early Santa Fe residents had similar dwellings, with low log ceilings, dirt floors, thick mud walls, and a corner fireplace for heating and cooking.

Closed on Sundays. No admission charge. 215 E. De Vargas; phone: 983-3883.

Chapel of San Miguel – This chapel is as old as the Palace of the Governors. Originally built in 1610–12, it was practically razed by the Pueblo Indians in the 1680 Revolt. When the Spanish rebuilt it in 1710, they covered over what remained of the earlier walls, placed the windows up high, and added adobe battlements to the roof. The most prominent feature of the interior is a fine old reredo, or colonial Spanish altar screen, made in 1798. Most of the paintings on the altar screen were done in Mexico in the 18th century. Old Santa Fe Trail and De Vargas St.

State Capitol – A bit south of San Miguel's Chapel is this unusual structure, which residents call the "Round House." It is intended by architects to evoke a Pueblo kiva (the ceremonial chamber in which religious rites are performed). Old Santa Fe Trail.

Canyon Road – One of the most romantic and picturesque streets in the US, it's also the oldest still in use; it was well established as a Pueblo trail long before the Spanish arrived. By the 18th century, residents were building adobe homes and cultivating farms along Canyon Road, which follows the river east from downtown. Sections of some of the current buildings date from that period, and the style of the street's architecture was established in a way that has not changed substantially since. In the early 20th century, Canyon Road became the center of the Santa Fe art colony. Though few artists can afford to live here today, the street still is zoned for "residential arts and crafts," limiting its use to galleries, studios, restaurants, and homes. It's an ideal place to see both the residential character of the old city and the latest work of Santa Fe artists.

Cristo Rey Church – Built in 1940, this church was designed by architect John Gaw Meem in classical Spanish mission style. Nearly 200,000 adobe bricks were used in its construction, all made from soil on the site — the traditional practice. One of the largest adobe structures in existence, it was scaled to house the most famous piece of Spanish colonial art in New Mexico, an ornately carved stone reredo (altarpiece), commissioned in 1760. Upper Canyon Rd.

■ **EXTRA SPECIAL:** Santa Fe is the best place in New Mexico (and perhaps in the entire Southwest) to shop for Indian art: jewelry, pottery, weavings, paintings, kachina dolls, beadwork, and baskets. As you travel, even a cursory browse will quickly reveal that Indian art can be very expensive: Pueblo pottery may cost several hundred dollars, while Navajo rugs can run into the thousands.

We recommend that you begin by visiting the area's museums — the *Wheelwright Museum of the American Indian* and the *Museum of Indian Arts and Culture* as well as the *Indian Pueblo Cultural Center* in Albuquerque. They all display the very distinctive work produced by the various tribes and you'll soon learn to recognize the traditional patterns and techniques each one employed. You'll become familiar also with the names of certain families or individuals who have become well known for a particular style. The museum shops at the *Indian Pueblo Cultural Center,* the *Palace of the Governors,* the *Museum of Indian Arts and Culture,* and the *Wheelwright Museum* (in the *Case Trading Post* downstairs) all carry fine Indian art as well as numerous books on the subject. They are also usually attended by salespeople who are willing to part with a few pointers about how to tell the real from the fake (some cheaper, imitation crafts are imported from Taiwan), what's special about the pieces they carry, and how to care for what you buy.

In addition to the museum shops, there are a number of stores and galleries along the Plaza and elsewhere in the city that sell Indian art. Among those to investigate are *Wind River Trading Co.* (112 E. Palace; 113 E. San Francisco), *Cristof's* (106 W. San Francisco),

Dewey Galleries, Ltd. (74 E. San Francisco), *Morning Star Gallery* (513 Canyon Rd.), *Mudd-Carr Gallery* (227 Otero), *Packard's Indian Trading Co.* (61 Old Santa Fe Trail), *Channing Dale Throckmorton* (53 Old Santa Fe Trail), *James Reid Ltd.* (114 E. Palace Ave.), and *Joshua Baer & Company* (116½ E. Palace Ave.). *Origins* (135 W. San Francisco) — chosen by *Women's Wear Daily* as one of the ten best boutiques in America — offers inspired ethnic clothing, jewelry, textiles, and collectibles from Santa Fe artists, as well as tribal art and contemporary designers from around the world. *Zaplin-Lampert Gallery* (651 Canyon Rd.) and *Fenn Galleries* (1075 Paseo de Peralta) have 19th- and early-20th-century American paintings, especially work by Taos and Santa Fe artists, and American Indian antiquities. *Linda Durham Gallery* (400 Canyon Rd.) represents contemporary artists with studios in New Mexico.

It's possible to buy pottery and jewelry directly from the Indians under the portico of the Palace of the Governors or by visiting the several pueblos in the area — Jemez, Zia, Santa Clara, San Ildefonso, Acoma, Zuni, and Taos. Two final bits of advice: Buy what you like when you see it; each piece is handmade and unique, and if you hesitate, it's unlikely you will find it elsewhere. Also, bring lots of cash if you shop in the pueblos, because Indians selling from their living rooms won't accept credit cards.

Visitors interested in art also should contact longtime Santa Fe resident Linda Morton, who runs an outfit called *Studio Entrada* (Box 4934, Santa Fe, NM 87502; phone: 505-983-8786), which takes people into local artists' studios for a peek behind the gallery glitz to meet artists, see works in progress, and buy on the spot. The year-round tours are limited to six adults and the circuit takes about 2½ hours, with Morton picking up visitors at their hotels and driving them around the city and its environs. The cost is $50 per person (two-person minimum), by appointment only, with 1 week's notice.

SOURCES AND RESOURCES

TOURIST INFORMATION: For a free copy of the Santa Fe Convention and Visitors Bureau's *Visitors Guide,* call 800-777-CITY, or pick one up at the *Sweeney Center,* also part of the Convention and Visitors Bureau (201 W. Marcy St., Santa Fe, NM 87501; phone: 984-6760). A better but more expensive alternative is the newsstand at *La Fonda* hotel (100 E. San Francisco), just off the Plaza, which carries all available guides and major works of fiction and nonfiction about the area. For a lively literary introduction to the city and vicinity, pick up Willa Cather's *Death Comes for the Archbishop* and John Nichols's *The Milagro Beanfield War,* a film version of which also is available on videocassette. Contact the New Mexico state hotline (phone: 800-545-2040) for maps, calendars of events, health updates, and travel advisories.

Local Coverage – The *New Mexican* is published daily; look at Friday's Pasatiempo section for information on events of the coming week. Do not, however, rely on the paper for restaurant recommendations.

Television Stations – KOB Channel 4–NBC; KNME Channel 5–PBS; KOAT Channel 7–ABC; KGGM Channel 13–CBS.

Radio Stations – AM: KZSS 610 (rock); KREO 920 (oldies); KFMG 1080 (rock); KRZY 1450 (country). FM: KHFM 96.3 (classical); KISS 97 (rock); KBAC 98.1 (contemporary music); KLSK 104 (jazz); KFMG 108 (rock).

TELEPHONE: The area code for Santa Fe is 505.
Sales Tax – The city sales tax is 5.825%.

 CLIMATE: Santa Fe's climate is shaped by both the Rocky Mountains and the Southwestern desert. The sun usually is shining, the air is very dry, and the sky is very clear and turquoise blue. During the day, the air temperature always feels warm, even when there's snow on the ground, although as soon as the sun sets the air cools quickly. The average daily temperature in the summer is about 80F and about 40F in the winter.

 GETTING AROUND: Airport – Santa Fe Municipal Airport is serviced by *Mesa Airlines* (phone: 800-MESA-AIR), which flies from Albuquerque and Denver to Santa Fe. Visitors usually fly into Albuquerque International Airport, about 65 miles south, and then either rent a car or rely on the bus service provided by a firm called *Shuttlejack* (phone: 243-3244, 982-4311 from Santa Fe). Departures are from the east end of the airport approximately every 2 hours; the trip costs $20 and takes about 75 minutes.

There is limited public transportation in Santa Fe, and although the downtown area is small enough to see enjoyably by foot, a car is needed to visit the farther-flung points of interest.

Car Rental – All the major car rental agencies are represented at Albuquerque airport. Cars may be rented in Santa Fe after arrival, but the rental offices are scattered. *Avis* has an office at *Garrett's Desert Inn* (311 Santa Fe Trail; phone: 800-331-1212 or 982-4361), and *Hertz* at the *Hilton Inn* (100 Sandoval; phone: 800-654-3131 or 982-1844).

Taxi – There is no central taxi stand, but you can call *Capital City Cab Co.* (1107 Early Rd.; phone: 989-8888).

 VITAL SERVICES: Audiovisual Equipment – *Camera Shop,* 109 E. San Francisco St. (phone: 983-6591).
Baby-sitting – *Sante Fe Kid Connection,* 1015 Valerie Circle (phone: 471-3100).
Business Services – *Plaza II Executive Center,* 125 Lincoln Ave., Suite 400 (phone: 984-8161).
Dry Cleaner/Tailor – *One Hour Martinizing,* 200 E. Water St. (phone: 982-8606).
Limousine – *Limotion VIP Limousine Service,* (phone: 982-5466).
Mechanic – *Automotive Repair Service,* 1212 Calle de Comercio (phone: 473-0031).
Medical Emergency – *St. Vincent Hospital* (455 St. Michael's Dr.; phone: 983-3361 or 989-5247 for emergency care); *Lovelace at Alameda* (901 W. Alameda; phone: 986-3656 or 986-3666 for emergency care); *Lovelace Multispecialty Clinic* (440 St. Michael's Dr.; phone: 982-2215).
Messenger Services – *Pigeon Express,* 1526 C. Pacheco (phone: 473-3447).
National/International Courier – *Federal Express* (Albuquerque; phone: 800-238-5355); *Airborne* (Albuquerque; phone: 842-4288).
Pharmacy – *Fraser Pharmacy,* 24-hour emergency service, 501 Old Santa Fe Trail (phone: 982-5524).
Photocopies – *Kinko's,* fax machine (333 Montezuma Ave.; phone: 982-6311); *The Paper Tiger* (120 E. Marcy St.; phone: 983-2839).
Post Office – Downtown, S. Federal St., off Paseo de Peralta (phone: 988-6351).
Professional Photographer – *Arnal Studio* (phone: 983-2410).
Secretary/Stenographer – *Kay Carlson* (phone: 982-3926); *Bell's Exec* (phone: 988-7374).
Translator – *Adelocorp* (phone: 984-2203).

Typewriter Rental – *Rocky Mountain Business Systems* (phone: 983-1181); *Santa Fe Business Products Inc.* (phone: 983-1549).

Western Union – Many offices are located around the city (phone: 982-2671).

 SPECIAL EVENTS: Summer is the performing arts season, with cultural events staged by the *Santa Fe Opera* and the *Santa Fe Chamber Music Festival* nightly in July and August. The annual *Indian Market* is held the third week in August in the Plaza; at this very popular event, Indians from the surrounding pueblos sell a wide variety of crafts — jewelry, pottery, sand paintings, weavings, kachina dolls, and so on. The *Fiesta de Santa Fe,* celebrated the weekend after *Labor Day,* originated in 1712. It opens with the ritual burning of a 40-foot marionette, called Zozobra, representing Old Man Gloom. After 2 days of parades, dancing, eating, and partying, the fiesta ends with mass at St. Francis Cathedral. The eight northern pueblos near Santa Fe have very different but equally interesting fiestas and other celebrations; the Santa Fe Convention and Visitors Bureau (phone: 984-6760 or 800-777-CITY) usually has information about the ones visitors are allowed to attend.

 MAJOR COLLEGES AND UNIVERSITIES: College of Santa Fe (1600 St. Michael's Dr.; phone: 473-6011); St. John's College (1160 Camino de Cruz Blanca; phone: 982-3691).

 SPORTS AND FITNESS: Camping and Hiking – For maps and advice about the Santa Fe area, write to the US Forest Service (PO Box 1689, Santa Fe, NM 87504; phone: 988-6940). For information about the Bandelier National Monument, write to the visitors' center (Bandelier National Monument, HCR 1 Box 1, Suite 15, Los Alamos, NM 87544; phone: 672-3861). Also refer to the book *Day Hikes in the Santa Fe Area,* published by the local chapter of the *Sierra Club.*

Fitness Centers – *Santa Fe Spa* (786 N. St. Francis Dr.; phone: 984-8727); *Carl Miller's Conditioning Center* (560 Montezuma; phone: 982-6760).

Golf – The *Santa Fe Country Club,* at Airport Rd. (phone: 471-0601), is popular.

Horseback Riding – *Camel Rock Ranch* (Hwy. 285 North, Tesuque Indian Reservation; phone: 986-0408), 10 miles north of downtown, offers trail rides, hayrides, and overnight trips through the 7,000-acre Tesuque Indian reservation year-round.

Horse Racing – The season at the *Downs,* just south of the city on I-25, extends from late May to *Labor Day,* with races on Wednesdays and weekends (phone: 471-3311).

Jogging – The most pleasant run is along the Santa Fe River, on Palace Avenue or Canyon Road. A more strenuous route is up Bishop's Lodge Road, into the Tesuque valley.

Skiing – Northern New Mexico usually has good powder from mid-December until early March and sunny spring skiing for several weeks after that. The *Santa Fe Ski Area* is close, moderate in size and challenge, and relatively uncrowded (phone: 982-4429). Advanced skiers often prefer the long, steep runs at the *Taos Ski Valley,* 1½ hours away (phone: 776-2916). Cross-country skiing lessons are available at *Ten Thousand Waves,* a Japanese bathhouse in the mountains, where you can enjoy a soak and a massage afterwards (phone: 982-9304). *Southwest Adventure Group* and *Santa Fe Adventures for Kids* (Sanbusco Market Center, 500 Montezuma; phone: 983-0876, 983-0111, or 800-766-5443) offer full or half-day cross-country and downhill packages for adults and children ages 7 to 12.

Tennis – There are 32 courts at nine locations around town (phone: 984-6864, for information). Non-guests sometimes are allowed to use the courts at the *Rancho Encantado* resort (for a fee).

MUSIC: The *Orchestra of Santa Fe* performs at the *Lensic Theater* downtown (phone: 988-4640) from September to May; in February the orchestra performs a *Bach or Mozart Festival,* alternating composers every year. A newer orchestra, the *Santa Fe Symphony* (phone: 983-3530), performs a similar season. In July and August the *Santa Fe Chamber Music Festival,* widely recognized for its posters reproducing the work of the late Georgia O'Keeffe, takes place at the *St. Francis Auditorium* in the *Museum of Fine Arts* (W. Palace Ave.). The 7-week festival begins in early July and features eminent artists from around the world (phone: 983-2075 or 800-96-BRAVO). The internationally acclaimed *Santa Fe Opera* offers lavish, adventuresome performances in a dramatic outdoor theater from late June to late August (phone: 982-3851). Lectures and backstage tours are available to the public. The theater is on Highway 84/285, about 7 miles north of town.

NIGHTCLUBS AND NIGHTLIFE: Santa Fe is not known for its throbbing nightlife; the summertime arts festivals can be exciting, but for the most part, it's a pretty quiet town. There are, however, some diversions. Maria Benitez, one of the world's great flamenco artists, dances most summer nights at the *Picacho Plaza* (phone: 982-5591). At *El Farol* (phone: 983-9912) jazz, blues, and other live entertainment draw in the crowds. *Vanessies* (phone: 982-9966) has a piano bar for those who want to sing along, and at *La Cantina* (phone: 988-9232) singing waiters and waitresses perform Broadway tunes. Live music (usually rock) and dancing can be found at *Club West* (213 W. Alameda; phone: 982-0099). If you're not up for dancing, consider soaking at *Ten Thousand Waves,* a Japanese bathhouse in the mountains with communal and private hot tubs, as well as massage, herbal wraps, and salt-glow facials (Ski Basin Rd.; phone: 982-9304).

BEST IN TOWN

CHECKING IN: Santa Fe sees a tremendous influx of visitors every summer, so it's best to book well in advance. Expect to pay up to $200 a day in the hotels listed in the expensive category, $60 to $100 in moderate, and under $50 in inexpensive. During the winter, rates usually are 10% to 25% lower. All telephone numbers are in the 505 area code unless otherwise indicated.

Inn of the Anasazi – This newly opened Revival Pueblo hotel is faithful to classic Santa Fe style; it is beautifully appointed, from the wood and stone floors, vigas, and kiva fireplaces to the Frette bed linen and hand-painted furnishings. Small yet elegant, the 60 rooms have all the luxuries of a world class hotel. Fax machines and computer modems are provided in the suites, and there are a library and wine cellar in which to browse. The extensive staff and even the masseuses are at your beck and call. Ancient ruins of the Anasazi and Northern Indian pueblos are located nearby, and there is access to fishing, hiking, rafting, and skiing. A good restaurant is on the premises, and room service is always available. There is a concierge desk, and secretarial services can be arranged. A/V equipment, photocopiers, and computers are all accessible, and meeting rooms accommodate up to 24. Express checkout. 113 Washington Ave. (phone: 988-3030 or 800-688-8100). Expensive.

Bishop's Lodge – Originally the retirement home of Bishop Lamy in the late 19th century, this quiet retreat of beautiful gardens and fruit trees is nested in the Sangre de Cristo on 1,000 acres prviately owned by a ranch-resort. This comfortable place has its own stables and breakfast horseback rides, tennis courts, pool, and sauna, trap and skeet shooting range, and an all-day program for children during the summer. The MAP tariff in the summer includes two meals a day, with ample buffets of American and continental food and a steak fry on Saturday nights. Open April through the beginning of January. And for those inclined to tie the knot, there's a historic chapel located on the property. Business services include meeting rooms that will accommodate up to 150, A/V equipment, and photocopiers. Bishop's Lodge Rd. (phone: 983-6377; Fax: 505-989-8739). Expensive.

Las Brisas de Santa Fe – Quiet, intimate, Southwest-style compound with 11 fully furnished 1- and 2-bedroom rental condominiums, within walking distance of the Plaza. The beautifully decorated units all have fireplaces. 624 Galisteo (phone: 982-5795). Expensive.

Eldorado – This 218-room property has handsomely furnished rooms with mini-bars and saltillo tile baths, while many suites boast wood-burning fireplaces and porches. There are remarkable mountain and city vistas, and guests can find everything from local art to *The New York Times* to real estate offerings in the extensive shopping gallery. The *Old House Restaurant* features superb New Mexican cooking. Other pluses are the heated rooftop Jacuzzi, saunas, and masseuses. For the celebrity-conscious, President George Bush and King Juan Carlos of Spain have been overnight guests. Meeting rooms can accommodate up to 1,400. There's also a concierge desk, limited secretarial services, A/V equipment, photocopiers, and express checkout. 309 W. San Francisco (phone: 988-4455; 800-955-4455; Fax: 505-988-4455). Expensive.

La Fonda – A Santa Fe landmark on the plaza, it's less notable for service than for a striking appearance and historic character: Though the present hotel was built in 1920, an inn (with the same name) has existed on this site since the opening of the Santa Fe Trail, almost 200 years ago. The refurbished rooms have Spanish colonial accents. There's an outdoor pool, plus 2 indoor Jacuzzis and massages by appointment. An outdoor bar, located in a bell tower, is open seasonally and offers city sunset views. Meeting rooms can hold up to 600. Other business conveniences include a concierge desk, A/V equipment, and photocopiers. 100 E. San Francisco St. (phone: 982-5511 or 800-523-0002; Fax: 505-982-6367). Expensive.

Grant Corner Inn – A small bed and breakfast place in an old home in the downtown area. This one may be the nicest of the neighborhood group, with 13 comfortable rooms and a terrific breakfast on the patio, which is also open to non-guests. 122 Grant Ave. (phone: 983-6678). Expensive.

Inn at Loretto – The exterior of this modern hostelry near the Plaza is distinctively Spanish pueblo in style, although the rooms are quite standard, with no surprises. It's named for the historic spot it occupies, that of the old Loretto Academy, established in the 1850s by Bishop Lamy and the Sisters of Loretto. Meeting rooms can hold up to 300. Business amenities include secretarial services, concierge, A/V equipment, photocopiers, and computers. 211 Old Santa Fe Trail (phone: 988-5531; Fax: 505-984-7988). Expensive.

Picacho Plaza – Formerly the *Sheraton* and now owned by Village Resorts, this recently remodeled hostelry offers 133 Southwestern-style rooms with hand-carved furnishings; many have private terraces. The hotel also manages 34 fully equipped condominiums with fireplaces, and outdoor spas. Highlights are a landscaped garden and a pool. The *Petroglyph* restaurant provides stunning views of the mountains. Nightly entertainment includes the renowned Spanish dancer Maria Benitez, who performs during the summer months. Perhaps even more famous is Father Pretto, who is possibly the world's only priest with a salsa band! Guests can use the 19,000-square-foot health club, which has racquetball courts, a lap pool, aerobics classes, and weights. Additional amenities include room service until 10 PM, meeting rooms that seat up to 250, A/V equipment, and photocopiers. 750 N. St. Francis Dr. (phone: 982-5591 or 800-441-5591; Fax: 505-988-2821). Expensive.

Rancho Encantado – The "Enchanted Ranch" is a gracious small resort in the Tesuque hills. Within the original adobe buildings are 22 Santa Fe–style rooms, the most attractive in the area, with fireplaces, vigas (decorative ceiling beams), Indian rugs, and hand-painted tiles. Any of the property's 36 condominiums also can be rented: 1 or 2 bedrooms, with living and dining rooms as well as a kitchen. The ranch offers facilities for a range of outdoor activities, such as horseback riding, tennis, archery, and swimming. Meeting rooms can accommodate up to 60, and there are photocopiers and A/V equipment available. Rte. 22 in Tesuque, 8 miles north of Santa Fe (phone: 982-3537; Fax: 505-983-8269). Expensive.

Santa Fe – This 131-room hotel, designed in the Pueblo Revival style, is located in the Guadalupe District less than a 10-minute walk to the plaza. The joint effort and partnership between the Picuris Tribe of northern New Mexico and the Santa Fe Hospitality Company is the first joint venture of its kind off the reservation trust lands. The 91 suites each have a separate living area and bedroom, with microwave ovens and mini-bars. Complimentary shuttle service to the plaza also is provided. Meeting rooms can accommodate up to 190, and there are photocopiers and A/V equipment available. There's also a concierge desk. Paseo de Peralta at Cerrillos (phone: 982-1200 or 800-825-9876). Expensive.

Inn of the Governors – Don't let the motelish exterior dissuade you, for this cozy, 100-room property has an extremely attentive staff and thoughtfully appointed accommodations. Classical music plays continuously in the inviting lobby. Rooms are furnished with contemporary rustic Southwest furniture and local art. Many rooms have wood-burning fireplaces and balconies. *Mañana* serves dinner nightly, and it has a piano bar and intimate outdoor dining around a huge fireplace. A concierge desk attends to guests, and meeting rooms that seat 50 and photocopiers are available. 234 Don Gaspar (phone: 982-4333 or 800-234-4534; Fax: 505-989-9149). Expensive to moderate.

Inn on the Alameda – This European-style hostelry is located at the base of Canyon Road, just 2 blocks from the plaza. Known for its intimate atmosphere, it offers 42 charming rooms (No. 308 has a fireplace), personal service, and elaborate continental breakfasts. Among the amenities are a concierge desk, meeting rooms that hold up to 40, A/V equipment, and photocopiers. 303 E. Alameda (phone: 984-2121 or 800-289-2122; Fax: 505-986-8325). Expensive to moderate.

Plaza Real – Located a half block from the plaza, this intimate, upscale establishment offers 56 rooms decorated in muted Southwestern tones. Most room are demi-suites with fireplaces and sitting areas, and some have balconies. Although there is no restaurant on the premises, the kitchen delivers a continental breakfast to your room. The cozy lobby has a fireplace. Meeting rooms can seat up to 75, and there's a concierge desk. Underground parking. 125 Washington Ave. (phone: 988-4900 or 800-279-7325; Fax: 505-988-4900). Expensive to moderate.

La Posada – A few blocks from the Plaza, this inn is spread out over 6 landscaped acres. The center of the complex is the Staab House, a Victorian home dating from 1882 that's been tastefully converted into a good restaurant and a popular lounge. Rates depend on the size and charm of the room, some of which are fairly conventional and some romantically Southwestern, with adobe fireplaces, vigas, and Indian rugs. A concierge desk responds to guests' needs, and A/V equipment, photocopiers, and meeting rooms that hold up to 80 are available. 330

E. Palace (phone: 986-0000 or 800-727-5276; Fax: 505-982-6850). Expensive to moderate.

St. Francis – Built in the 1920s and restored to its original style, this small downtown place features 83 rooms decorated in period furnishings and fixtures, the whole reflecting a simple, romantic elegance. Fifty can be accommodated in the meeting rooms. A/V equipment and photocopiers are available. There's also a concierge desk and express checkout. 210 Don Gaspar (phone: 983-5700 or 800-666-5700; Fax: 505-989-7690). Expensive to moderate.

El Paradero Bed & Breakfast Inn – Most of the 12 rooms and 4 suites in this cozy, 2-story adobe structure have private baths. Full breakfasts are served. Just a couple of blocks from the state capitol. 220 W. Manhattan Ave. (phone: 988-1177). Moderate.

Preston House – Another good bed and breakfast option downtown. Three of the 12 rooms have fireplaces. Two Queen Anne–style cottages and an adobe compound also are available for rent. 106 Faithway (phone: 982-3465). Moderate.

Pueblo Bonito Bed & Breakfast Inn – A downtown compound with 11 rooms and 4 suites decorated in Southwest style. All rooms have kiva fireplaces. Continental breakfast and afternoon tea included. 138 W. Manhattan Ave. (phone: 984-8001). Moderate.

El Rey Inn – The best bargain in town for Santa Fe charm; if downtown (instead of on motel row), prices would be at least double. Many of the individually decorated rooms have adobe fireplaces, vigas (decorated ceiling beams), and tile murals; some are solar heated and overlook a garden. A complimentary continental breakfast is included. There's also a playground, an outdoor pool, and a hot tub, which is open year-round. 1862 Cerrillos (phone: 982-1931). Moderate to inexpensive.

 EATING OUT: Expect to pay $40 or more for a meal for two (without drinks, wine, or tip) in a restaurant listed below as expensive; between $20 and $40 is moderate; and around $15 is considered inexpensive. All telephone numbers are in the 505 area code unless otherwise indicated.

La Casa Sena – This elegant yet cozy dining spot nestles in the historic Sena Plaza. Begin with a chilled margarita, and then segue into thin, blue corn muffins and *trucha en terracotta,* a fresh Rocky Mountain trout wrapped in vine leaves and baked in a clay dish which is cracked open at tableside. Open daily. Reservations advised. Major credit cards accepted. 125 E. Palace, Sena Plaza (phone: 988-9232). Expensive.

Comme Chez Vous – Third-floor dining with a summer balcony, after-dinner dancing and entertainment, and year-round views of the city. The fare is mostly French, and the rack of lamb is especially delicious. Open daily. Reservations advised. Major credit cards accepted. 116 W. San Francisco (phone: 984-0004). Expensive.

Compound – Santa Fe's best-known restaurant may no longer be depended upon to deliver consistently excellent meals on every occasion, but the (continental) food served usually is very good and there's a fine wine list. Housed in a converted 19th-century hacienda, the eatery provides a delightful dining environment. Jacket and tie required for men. Closed Sundays, Mondays and January and February. Reservations necessary. American Express accepted. 653 Canyon Rd. (phone: 982-4353). Expensive.

Coyote Café – Chef/owner Mark Miller, who established a national reputation in the San Francisco Bay area, runs this fashionable place which serves Southwestern nouvelle cuisine and uses regional ingredients in imaginative ways. Open daily. Reservations advised. Only Visa and MasterCard accepted. 132 W. Water (phone: 983-1615). Expensive to moderate.

Julians – Classic regional Italian food served in New Mexican elegance. Specialties include veal and exotic pasta dishes. Open daily for dinner. Reservations advised. Major credit cards accepted. 221 Shelby (phone: 988-2355). Expensive to moderate.

Pink Adobe – One of the city's best for many years, "the Pink" (as it's known) features an unusual menu that includes steaks, creole dishes, and New Mexican specialties. Try the steak Dunnigan, with green chili, or the chicken enchiladas with green chili and sour cream. The locals congregate in the *Dragon Room* bar over margaritas and other libations. Open daily. Reservations necessary. Major credit cards accepted. 406 Old Santa Fe Trail (phone: 983-7712). Expensive to moderate.

Santacafé – Locally popular for its casual elegance and fine food, it offers a sophisticated menu that changes daily with a selection of local and international dishes. Closed weekends for lunch. Reservations advised. Only Visa and Mastercard accepted. 231 Washington (phone: 984-1788). Expensive to moderate.

Shohko Café – One of several Japanese spots that have become very popular in Santa Fe, it offers what must be the only green chili tempura in the world. The rest of the menu includes more traditional dishes — sukiyaki, teriyaki, and so on — and there's a large, crowded sushi bar. Closed Sundays. Reservations advised for dinner. Only Visa and American Express accepted. 321 Johnson St. (phone: 983-7288). Expensive to moderate.

e.k. mas – The name is the phonetic spelling of "y que mas" — Spanish (not to mention appropriate) for "I want more." Small and charming, with an extensive wine list that complements the light international dishes. The emphasis is on fresh fish and seafood. Open 5 or 6 days a week for lunch and dinner — the schedule varies with the season. Reservations advised. Only Visa and MasterCard accepted. 319 Guadalupe (phone: 989-7121). Moderate.

El Farol – This longtime local favorite serves Spanish and Mediterranean *tapas* (hors d'oeuvres). The cozy bar is frequently crowded with locals. Curried chicken, pasta with manchego cheese, and marinated peppers are choices from the *tapas* menu. Nightly entertainment is eclectic; anything from jazz and flamenco to country blues. Open daily. Reservations advised. MasterCard and Visa accepted. 808 Canyon Rd. (phone: 983-9912). Moderate.

Maria's – A domain of powerful margaritas and mariachi music, not to mention delicious Mexican vittles. Diners can watch homemade tortillas patted out in the front room, or head to the cozy "cantina" in back for chicken fajitas, chiles relleños, homemade *posole,* green chili stew, and New Mexican barbecued ribs. An excellent wine list and scrumptious desserts are not easily forgotten. Open daily. Reservations advised. Major credit cards accepted. 555 W. Cordova Rd. (phone: 983-7929). Moderate.

La Tertulia – The classiest of the city's dining places, is housed in a converted convent and serves New Mexican fare. The native dishes tend to be mild but tasty, and the homemade sangria is excellent. Closed Mondays. Reservations necessary. Major credit cards accepted. 416 Agua Fria, near Guadalupe (phone: 988-2769). Moderate.

Old Mexico Grill – Tucked into a shopping center, this lively and popular eatery serves up sizzling fajitas, spicy paella, and *tacos al carbón* (mesquite-grilled chicken breast or sirloin, sliced and rolled into a taco shell, or a flour or corn tortilla). Closed Sunday lunch. Limited reservations are accepted, as most of the tables are left open for the walk-in crowd. Major credit cards accepted. 2434 Cerrillos Rd. (phone: 473-0338). Moderate to inexpensive.

Rancho de Chimayo – Generally agreed to be the best New Mexican–style restaurant anywhere, it's in an old adobe hacienda about 25 miles north of Santa Fe. The drive, the setting, and the food all are delightful. Those who especially like hot dishes should try carne adovada, pork cooked in red chile. The flan (custard with caramel syrup) may be the area's best. Closed Mondays in winter and for the month of January. Reservations necessary. Major credit cards accepted. Rte. 4 in Chimayo (phone: 351-4444 or 984-2100 from Santa Fe). Moderate to inexpensive.

Josie's Casa de Comida – A rare example of a dying breed — the small, plain, downtown luncheon café. The chiles relleños, enchiladas, and other regional dishes are terrific, and the more standard American lunches are pretty good, too. This place is so popular that people will line up and wait patiently on the street for a table. Lunch only. Closed weekends. No reservations or credit cards accepted. 225 E. Marcy St. (phone: 983-5311). Inexpensive.

Shed – The most popular place in town for lunch. There usually is a line after 11:30 AM, but the wait is pleasant in the front courtyard, originally the central patio of a large hacienda. The red chili served on blue corn enchiladas, tacos, and burritos is unmatched, the *posole* and beans very good, and the desserts fine. Lunch only. Closed Sundays. No reservations or credit cards accepted. 113½ Palace Ave. (phone: 982-9030). Inexpensive.

Tecolote Café – Despite the inauspicious location, it serves the best breakfast in town, complete with a basket of homemade biscuits and blueberry muffins. The Santa Fe omelette — filled with green chili and cheese — will get anyone moving. Open for breakfast and lunch. Closed Mondays. No reservations. Most major credit cards accepted. 1203 Cerrillos Rd. (phone: 988-1362). Inexpensive.

Tomasita's – At this local favorite, the selection of dishes is limited but the flavors are authentic, the portions large, and the service friendly. Unless you arrive early, the wait for a table can easily be as long as your dinner. Closed Sundays. No reservations. Visa and MasterCard accepted. 500 S. Guadalupe (phone: 983-5721). Inexpensive.

Tortilla Flats – Don't let the fast-food exterior deceive you; the New Mexican food is delicious and the service is friendly. Open daily for breakfast, lunch, and dinner. No reservations. Visa and MasterCard accepted. 3139 Cerrillos Rd. (phone: 471-8685). Inexpensive.

■ **Note:** For those with an urge to create their own Mexican culinary masterpieces, the *Santa Fe School of Cooking and Market* (116 W. San Francisco St., upper level, Plaza Mercado; phone: 505-983-4511) offers 2½-hour classes where you can learn to make *posole,* blue corn enchiladas, and sopapillas. Happily, you then get to consume the fruits (or in this case, enchiladas) of your labor. For $25, you attend the class and take home recipes. Reservations advised. Visa and MasterCard accepted.

SAVANNAH

AT-A-GLANCE

 SEEING THE CITY: Driving into Savannah across Talmadge Bridge offers a fine introductory view of the city. For a bird's-eye view of the Savannah River's busy cargo traffic, have lunch, dinner, or drinks at *Windows* restaurant (see *Eating Out*) in the *Hyatt Regency* hotel (2 W. Bay St.; phone: 238-1234).

For a delightful introduction, join *Carriage Tours of Savannah* for a day or night horse-drawn carriage ride around the historic district. As the horses clop gently through the old streets, guides enhance the mood with history, legends, and scandals of old Savannah (phone: 236-6756 for reservations). Cocktail and dinner cruises on the Savannah River are offered by the paddlewheel steamboats *Spirit of the Savannah* (phone: 238-1234) and the *Magnolia* (phone: 234-4011).

SPECIAL PLACES: Historic Savannah is appealingly negotiable on foot. We recommend at least four walking tours; and count on a minimum of 2 days to see everything. To see it from an insider's perspective, call *Square Routes* (phone: 232-6866), a dynamic little tour company that offers escorted walking tours of gardens, hidden shops, and private homes, spiced with amusing anecdotes and scandals of the past and present. For walking on your own, here are the city's most favored routes.

Riverfront Plaza – A logical place to start, Riverfront Plaza leads eastward along the Savannah River shoreline. Bordering the thriving seaport's 40-foot-deep channel, the 9-block, brick plaza is alive with commercial establishments in the 19th-century buildings which were formerly cotton warehouses. Waterfront browsers may be treated to a rock concert or a chamber music recital by a *Savannah Symphony* ensemble. A Riverfront Plaza day tour undoubtedly will whet the appetite for an evening excursion.

Bull Street – If you spend a morning at the plaza, the afternoon can be spent walking down Bull Street, from City Hall to Forsyth Park, 12 blocks south. Savannah's principal north-south street, Bull contains the city's five most beautiful squares. The 6-story City Hall, on River and Bay Streets, stands alongside two brass cannons captured from Cornwallis at Yorktown. The cannons were presented to the Chatham Artillery, a Savannah military unit, by George Washington, in 1791. East of City Hall, Factors Walk, with its iron bridges and narrow street, runs along the city side of the former cotton buildings. After passing City Hall, you will come to the US Customs House, built in 1852 on the same site where Georgia's founder, James Edward Oglethorpe, lived in 1733. It's also where evangelist John Wesley first preached in America. The five squares, not to be missed, are listed below:

Johnson Square – Here, two fountains flow and decks of azaleas are in dazzling flower in spring. Christ Episcopal Church, the first church established in the Colony of Georgia (1773), stands here, too. The present building dates to 1838.

Wright Square – The exquisite Ascension window of the Lutheran Church of the Ascension (1878) is known internationally as a work of art.

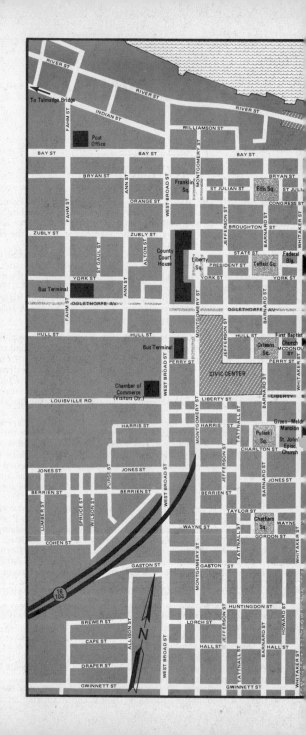

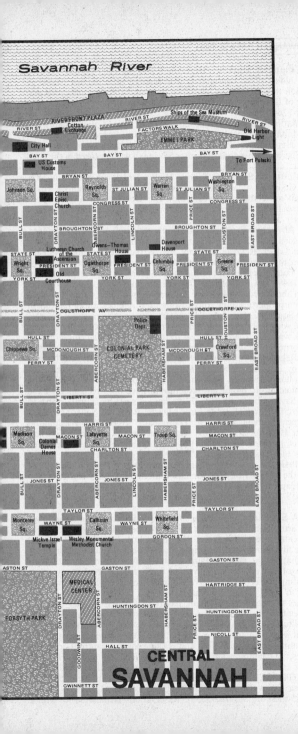

Chippewa Square – Here you'll find the First Baptist Church, the oldest of its denomination in Georgia; the Barrow Mansion, which now houses an insurance firm; and the *Savannah Theater,* one of the oldest theaters in continuous use in the country (phone: 233-7764).

Madison Square – The carillons and stained glass windows of St. John's Episcopal Church (1840) are well known to church lovers. Here, too, is the former Green-Meldrim mansion, which served as Sherman's headquarters after Savannah was captured in the Civil War.

Monterey Square – Temple Mickve Israel, consecrated in 1878 for Georgia's oldest Jewish congregation (1773), contains a Torah scroll more than 800 years old. The Gordon and Taylor Street houses facing Monterey Square are outstanding examples of historic preservations.

From Abercorn to St. Julian Street – Starting at Calhoun Square, at Abercorn and Gordon Streets, walk north toward *Massie School* (1885), a Greek Revival structure that is the public school system's education museum. Alongside stands Wesley Monumental Methodist Church. Four blocks north, at Lafayette Square, is the Colonial Dames House (1849). Two blocks east, beside Troup Square and on parallel Charlton and Macon Streets, are Savannah's two best examples of slum conversion properties, now tony townhouses. A block and a half north of Troup Square, Colonial Park Cemetery contains the graves of Georgia colonists, with priceless tombstone inscriptions. From the cemetery, it's a 2-block walk up Abercorn Street to the *Owens-Thomas House* (1816) at the corner of State Street, hailed as "America's finest example of English Regency architecture." Now a museum, the house was visited in 1825 by Revolutionary hero Marquis de Lafayette. One block east, facing Columbia Square, *Davenport House* (now also a museum) is the first architecturally important structure to have been reclaimed by the Historic Savannah Foundation. From here, it's a 3-block walk north to St. Julian Street, which splits three squares: Reynolds Square at Abercorn Street, Warren Square at Habersham Street, and Washington Square at Houston Street. This section has one of Savannah's largest clusters of restored 18th- and 19th-century homes. Facing Reynolds Square is the *Pink House* (ca. 1790), now a restaurant.

Ft. Pulaski – A national monument named for the Revolutionary hero killed in the 1779 Battle of Savannah. Built between 1829 and 1847, the fort was captured by Union forces in 1862. Open daily. No admission charge. US 80 near Savannah Beach (phone: 786-5787).

■ **EXTRA SPECIAL:** The *Savannah History Museum,* a multimillion-dollar attraction in the former train yards behind the Savannah Visitors Center, is a pleasant way to absorb a little history. Two theaters feature films, animated historical characters, and sound-and-light effects; Exposition Hall contains a 19th-century steam locomotive, a replica of the cotton gin (invented in Savannah), and many other interesting artifacts. Open daily. Admission charge (phone: 238-1779).

Hilton Head Island, a luxury resort area in South Carolina about 40 miles northeast of Savannah, has 16 golf courses, pretty beaches, deep-sea fishing, tennis courts, a private airstrip, and plenty of nightlife. Hilton Head has become overcrowded, and reservations are advised if you plan to stay overnight. *Sea Pines Plantation,* a resort community of private villas and a 204-room, oceanfront inn, has beaches, 3 championship golf courses (including famed *Harbour Town*), tennis courts, bicycle paths with rental facilities, swimming pools, marinas, and a 625-acre forest preserve. For information, contact *Sea Pines Plantation* (Hilton Head Island, SC 29928; phone: 800-845-6131 or 803-785-3333). Reservations islandwide for villas, condos, and homes, but not hotel rooms, may be made through the *Hilton Head Reservation Service* (phone: 800-845-7019). For information on Hilton Head activities, call the Chamber of Commerce (phone: 803-785-3673).

About 80 miles down the Atlantic coast from Savannah lie Georgia's "Golden Isles" — Sea Island, Jekyll Island, and St. Simons Island. Reached by causeway from Brunswick, Georgia, each has its own personality, and together they lay out an enormous spread of golf, tennis, beaches, lodgings, and dining. St. Simons offers the widest range of accommodations, shopping, and dining. Neighboring Little St. Simons is a privately owned, mostly primeval sanctuary, with a comfortably rustic lodge, dense forests, and 6 miles of unspoiled beaches and dunes (phone: 638-7472). Sea Island is the site of the fine *Cloister* hotel, with world class golf, elegant dining, and comfortable accommodations (phone: 638-3611). Jekyll Island's newest star is the *Jekyll Club* hotel, a gorgeously restored Victorian clubhouse, operated as a Radisson resort, where the elite once lodged (phone: 635-2600).

SOURCES AND RESOURCES

 TOURIST INFORMATION: Your first stop should be the Savannah Visitors Center (301 Martin Luther King Blvd.; phone: 944-0456). Housed in the railway station, which dates to the 1860s, the center has maps, information, tours, and a free slide show and is also the starting point for city tours. Before leaving home, write to the Savannah Convention and Visitors Bureau (222 W. Oglethorpe Ave., Savannah, GA 31499; phone: 944-0456 and 800-444-2427). Contact the Georgia state hotline (phone: 404-656-3590) for maps, calendars of events, health updates, and travel advisories.

Sojourn in Savannah by Betty Rauers and Franklin Traub (Historic Savannah Foundation; $3) offers detailed information on places of interest around town.

Local Coverage – *Savannah Morning News* and *Savannah Evening Press,* dailies.

Television Stations – WSAV Channel 3–NBC; WVAN Channel 9–PBS; WTOL Channel 11–CBS; WJCL Channel 22–ABC.

Radio Stations – AM: WBMQ 630 (oldies/talk); WSOK 1230 (gospel music/R&B); WCHY 1290 (country); WSGA 1400 (nostalgia). FM: WSVH 91 (classical and jazz); WCHY 94.1 (country); WAEZ 97.3 (adult contemporary).

 TELEPHONE: The area code for Savannah is 912.
Sales Tax – State and local sales tax is 6%. There is an additional hotel and motel tax of 6%.

 CLIMATE: Warm and sunny is the forecast for Savannah most of the year, with temperatures mostly in the 70s. From December through March, you can expect the mercury to drop into the 50s and 40s, and in the height of summer, to climb to the high 80s or low 90s. You also can be pretty sure of afternoon thunderstorms between June and September. Apart from the rains, however, the humidity hardly ever is higher than 60%.

GETTING AROUND: Airport – Savannah International Airport is about 11 miles from the downtown Historic District; taxi fare between the airport and downtown is a flat rate of $15 for one passenger, $3 for each additional passenger. *McCall's Limousine Service* (phone: 966-5364) operates between the airport and downtown and costs

$12 one way, $22 round trip. *Low Country Adventures* (phone: 966-2112) operates between the airport and Hilton Head Island, SC, resort area for $18 one way, $34 round trip.

Bus – *Chatham Area Transit* (CAT) operates the municipal bus system, 900 E. Gwinnett St. (phone: 233-5767).

Car Rental – *Avis* and *Hertz* have offices in town. *Thrifty Rent-a-Car* is a reliable local service (phone: 964-2341).

Taxi – Cabs can be hailed in the streets, downtown. Meter rate is $1.20 per mile. There are taxi stands at the main hotels, but you may prefer to call *Adam Cab* (phone: 927-7466).

VITAL SERVICES: Audiovisual Equipment – *Audio Visual Resources* (9-B Mall Ter.; phone: 355-2020); *Video Works* (342 Bull St.; phone: 238-2486).

Baby-sitting – *Angels and Imps,* 614 Jackson Blvd. (phone: 355-1068).

Business Services – *Norrell Services,* 7203 Hodgson Dr. (phone: 354-0044).

Dry Cleaner/Tailor – *Garrett Custom Dry Cleaning,* 4505 Bull St. (phone: 352-2274).

Limousine – *McCall's Limousine Service,* Savannah Airport (phone: 966-5364).

Mechanic – *Jackson Brothers Car Care* (phone: 236-0631).

Medical Emergency – *Memorial Medical Center,* Waters Ave. and 65th St. (phone: 356-8000).

Messenger Services – *Colonial Couriers of Savannah* (phone: 234-2161); *Savannah-Chatham Direct Delivery,* 1141 W. Gwinnett St. (phone: 236-3434).

National/International Courier – *Federal Express* (phone: 232-0068); *DHL Worldwide Courier Express* (phone: 800-225-5345).

Pharmacy – *Revco Medical Arts,* open 24 hours, *Medical Arts Shopping Center,* 4725 Waters Ave. at 63rd St. (phone: 355-7111).

Photocopies – *Chatham Repro-Graphics* (105 Eisenhower Dr.; phone: 352-2987); *Savannah Blueprint* (11 E. York St.; phone: 232-2162).

Post Office – The downtown office is located at 127 Bull St. (phone: 232-2601).

Professional Photographer – *Gerald Pollack & Associates* (111 E. 34th St.; phone: 238-0248); *Art Smiley & Associates* (10010 Abercorn St.; phone: 927-7888).

Secretary/Stenographer – *Norrell Services* (phone: 354-0044).

Teleconference Facilities – *Hyatt Regency* (see *Best in Town,* below).

Translator – *American Red Cross,* 422 Habersham St. (phone: 651-5300).

Typewriter Rental – *Independent Office Services,* 7805 Waters Ave. (phone: 352-1414).

Western Union/Telex – Many offices are located around the city (phone: 800-325-6000).

Other – *Convention Consultants of Savannah Delta,* convention planning and services (phone: 234-4088).

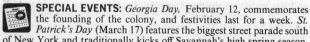

SPECIAL EVENTS: *Georgia Day,* February 12, commemorates the founding of the colony, and festivities last for a week. *St. Patrick's Day* (March 17) features the biggest street parade south of New York and traditionally kicks off Savannah's high spring season. Against a Technicolor background of millions of flowering azaleas, dogwood, and forsythia, the annual *Christ Episcopal Church Tour of Homes,* the end of March and early April, draws awestruck visitors into more than 3 dozen private mansions and gardens and to candlelight suppers at historic places around the city. *Night in Old Savannah,* the third weekend in April, is a 3-night festival of Dixieland and jazz and a culinary extravaganza prepared by the city's numerous ethnic communities. Also in April, the *Savannah Tour of Homes and Gardens* (phone: 234-8054) sponsors special walking tours, plus a shrimp boil, where guests peel and cook shrimp for dinner; Sunday dinner at *Mrs. Wilkes' Boarding House* (see *Eating Out*); and a barbecue in the old *City Market,* where guests can gorge on Brunswick stew and roast pig. *Christmas* is a special season, when homes, churches, and public buildings are dressed in colonial finery. Music, parades, and festivities punctuate the month of December, and the city ushers in the *New Year* with typical exuberance.

 MUSEUMS: Savannah is a treasury of historic and cultural elegance. On your way through the streets of the historic district, the *Telfair Academy of Arts and Sciences* (Barnard St.; phone: 232-1177) recommends itself as one of Savannah's outstanding museums. Other notable museums to visit:

Juliette Gordon Low Girl Scout National Center – 142 Bull St. (phone: 233-4501).

Savannah Science Museum – 4405 Paulsen (phone: 355-6705).

Ships of the Sea Maritime Museum – 503 E. River St. (phone: 232-1511).

Tybee Island Museum and Lighthouse – Tybee Island (phone: 786-4077).

 MAJOR COLLEGES AND UNIVERSITIES: Armstrong State College (11935 Abercorn St. Extension; phone: 927-5275); Savannah State College (Thunderbolt; phone: 356-2212). Both are 4-year colleges within the Georgia state university system.

SPORTS AND FITNESS: Savannah is at the head of one of the country's most popular vacationland areas. Names like Hilton Head, Sea Island, St. Simons, and Jekyll Island are all familiar to lovers of the outdoor life, and all are less than a day's drive from Savannah.

Bicycling – Cycling through the historic district can be an unforgettable experience. The *De Soto Hilton* hotel (phone: 232-9000) rents bikes.

Fitness Center – An outdoor pool, weight machines, indoor track, and tennis courts at the *YMCA* at 6400 Habersham (phone: 354-6223).

Golf – The *Sheraton Savannah* resort course, one of the best known in the South, also is open to the public on Wilmington Island (phone: 897-1612). The best municipal courses are at Bacon Park (Skidaway Rd. and Shorty Cooper Dr.; phone: 354-2625) and *Southbridge* golf club (415 Southbridge Blvd.; phone: 233-GOLF).

Jogging – Run around the perimeter of Forsyth Park, 1 mile, or along the waterfront in the early morning or evening when it isn't heavily trafficked; Lake Mayer, reachable by car, has an asphalt track. A jogging map is available at the *De Soto Hilton.*

Swimming and Fishing – Tybee Island (formerly Savannah Beach), nostalgically remembered as one end of a rollicking railroad that connected the mainland to the beach, has been a favorite haunt for many years. Here, you can indulge your penchants for swimming, fishing, surfing, crabbing, boating, picnicking, or beachcombing among the dunes. It's 18 miles from downtown Savannah.

Tennis – Best public tennis courts are at Bacon Park, Lake Mayer, Forsyth Park, and Daffin Park.

 THEATER: For complete performance schedules, check the publications listed above. *Savannah Civic Center* is the largest auditorium in the city, presenting touring Broadway productions, ballet, and dance theater performances (Orleans Sq.; phone: 234-6666). *Little Theater* (Chippewa Sq. downtown; phone: 233-7764) is another place for good drama. It occupies the historic *Savannah Theater,* the oldest theater in continuous use in the US.

MUSIC: The *Savannah Civic Center* is the home of the *Savannah Symphony Orchestra,* and offers the best concerts (in Orleans Sq.; phone: 234-6666).

 NIGHTCLUBS AND NIGHTLIFE: Riverfront Plaza is alive with discos and clubs. Four of the most popular are *Emma's* (phone: 232-1223), *Kevin Barry's Irish Pub* (phone: 233-9626), *Corky's* (phone: 234-0113), and *Hard-Hearted Hannah's* (phone: 232-3470).

BEST IN TOWN

CHECKING IN: Savannah has over 3,600 rooms for guests, most of them scattered among the motels within and around the fringe of the city. The city also has four hotels that offer a special elegance. Expect to pay between $80 and $100 or more for a double at those places we've listed as expensive; between $60 and $80 in the moderate range; under $50 for an inexpensive hostelry. For reservations at many of Savannah's historic inns, call these central services: *Savannah Historic Inns and Guest Houses* (phone: 233-7666 or 800-262-4667) and *R.S.V.P. Savannah* (phone: 232-7787 or 800-729-7787). All telephone numbers are in the 912 area code unless otherwise indicated.

Comer House – A grand Victorian mansion on one of the city's most picturesque squares, it offers guests the seclusion of 2 garden suites with kitchenettes and tours of the mansion's beautifully furnished main rooms. 2 E. Taylor St. (phone: 234-2923). Expensive.

DeSoto Hilton – In the heart of the historic district, this 264-room property blends modern pleasures with Savannah's Old World charms and retains much of the decor that made its predecessor the queen of the gaslight era's carriage trade. Amenities include the *Pavilion Room* for fine dining (see *Eating Out*), the *Red Lion* lounge, and recreation facilities. Liberty and Bull Sts. (phone: 232-9000 or 800-445-8667). Expensive.

Eliza Thompson House – This quaint 3-story 1847 townhouse in the Historic District has been restored and converted to an inn. Some of the 25 rooms are filled with antiques as well as with Savannah history books. Others also have fireplaces, kitchenettes, or private entrances. Complimentary sherry makes things even cozier. 7 W. Jones St. (phone: 236-3620). Expensive.

Gastonian Inn – One of the city's loveliest hostelries, it offers 13 rooms, rich in antiques and historic Savannah decor, in a pair of mid-19th-century townhouses. Many rooms have whirlpool baths. Tariffs include full Southern breakfast, afternoon tea, and late-night cordials. 220 E. Gaston St. (phone: 232-2869). Expensive.

Hyatt Regency Savannah – This 346-room property rises above Riverfront Plaza, giving guests a view of the oceangoing ships cruising in and out of the harbor. *Windows* restaurant, overlooking the river, has become a favorite dining spot (see *Eating Out*), along with the more casual *MD's Lounge* and *Patrick's Porch.* Guests can arrange tours and other activities at the concierge's desk in the lobby. Indoor parking. 2 W. Bay St. (phone: 238-1234 or 800-233-1234). Expensive.

Magnolia Place Inn – Facing Forsyth Park, in the heart of Savannah, it has 13 rooms, all with antique furnishings, Jacuzzis, and videodisc players. Limousine service. 503 Whitaker St. (phone: 236-7674). Expensive.

Mulberry Inn – Lavishly refurbished with 101 rooms and 28 suites, it is the classiest and most service-oriented of Savannah's historic inns. Facilities include a clubby bar, and a chintz-filled living room for afternoon tea. Rooms are furnished with bottled water, terrycloth robes, and down pillows. The Executive Conference Center has computers, Fax machines, and other commercial conveniences. 601 E. Bay St. (phone: 238-1200). Expensive.

Planters Inn – Built in 1920, this 7-story hotel recently has journeyed back in time to become a 19th-century-style inn, with antiques, Georgian furnishings, and all the modern comforts. The penthouse rooms even have working fireplaces. 29 Abercorn St. (phone: 232-5678). Expensive.

Radisson Plaza Savannah – The city's newest and largest downtown luxury hotel, which opened last year, has 384 guestrooms in an 8-story riverfront tower. A lighted boardwalk connects the hotel to Riverfront Plaza shops, restaurants, and nightclubs. Amenities include an upscale dining room, a café, 2 lounges, an indoor pool, and an exercise room. There's a concierge desk, plus secretarial services, A/V equipment, photocopiers, and computers. Express checkout. 100 General McIntosh Blvd. (phone: 233-7722 or 800-333-3333). Expensive.

Sheraton Savannah – Ten miles from Savannah on the Wilmington River, this was one of the Roaring Twenties' great resort properties, and succeeding owners have kept it in first class condition. Its 202 deluxe rooms are distributed among the 8-story hotel, a number of 2-bedroom condominiums, and some villas. It has a restaurant, nightly dancing, swimming pool, sauna, tennis, fishing, and boating. Its pride is its 18-hole golf course, one of the South's finest. A modified American plan is available. Wilmington Island Rd. (phone: 897-1612 or 800-325-3535). Expensive.

Best Western/Savannah Riverfront – This 142-room motel overlooks River Street. Its *Bottle Works* restaurant is open for all meals. There's a pool and a bar. 412 W. Bay St. (phone: 233-1011 or 800-528-1234). Moderate.

Courtyard by Marriott – Attractive, contemporary guestrooms and a good restaurant and bar make this an excellent suburban choice. 6703 Abercorn St. (phone: 354-7878 or 800-228-9290). Moderate.

Bed-and-Breakfast Inn – A restored 1853 townhouse that offers historic inn charm at reasonable prices. 117 W. Gordon St. (phone: 238-0518). Moderate to inexpensive.

Days Inn Savannah – Across the street from Riverfront Plaza, it's a good choice for families since there's a swimming pool, gameroom, and a 24-hour restaurant where kids under 12 eat for free. 253 attractive rooms. 201 W. Bay St. (phone: 236-4440 or 800-325-2525). Moderate to inexpensive.

Quality Inn/Heart of Savannah – Its romantic name and size (53 rooms) create a certain intimacy, in contrast to larger hotels. The two great things about it, though, are the complimentary continental breakfast and the price, about $40 for two. 300 W. Bay St. (phone: 236-6321 or 800-228-5151). Inexpensive.

EATING OUT: Savannah's restaurants range from elegant to home-style. Chefs at fine restaurants do wondrous things with fresh shrimp, oysters, flounder, and blue crabs. Two people can eat very well for about $50 to $60 (expensive). Anything between $30 and $40 is moderate; under $25, inexpensive. Prices do not include drinks, wine, or tips. All telephone numbers are in the 912 area code unless otherwise indicated.

45 South – Housed in a historic home built in 1852, complete with fireplaces and Native American art and artifacts, this upscale dining room serves delicious contemporary American fare. The rule here is that everything must be incomparably fresh. Broiled grouper in burgundy butter sauce, sautéed jumbo shrimp and sea scallops with black fettuccine, grilled tomato, and asiago cheese, and roast rack of lamb with garlic cream and madeira sauce, are satisfying choices. The menu changes monthly, and the attentive service appears invisible. Closed Sundays. Reservations advised. Major credit cards accepted. 20 E. Broad St. (phone: 233-1881). Expensive.

River's End Seafood – On the Thunderbolt yacht harbor, this lovely, dining room specializes in fresh local seafood, live Maine lobster, steaks, and prime ribs. Closed Sundays. Reservations advised. Major credit cards accepted. 3122 River Dr., Thunderbolt (phone: 354-2973). Expensive.

Windows – This exquisite dining room in the *Hyatt Regency Savannah* overlooks the Savannah River. Diners can watch merchant ships come and go while choosing from a continental menu featuring seafood, duck, and stir-fried Oriental dishes. Open daily; brunch only on Sundays; no lunch on Saturdays. Reservations advised. Major credit cards accepted. 2 W. Bay St. (phone: 238-1234). Expensive.

Elizabeth on Thirty-Seventh – In a lovely old Savannah mansion, the dining room has been widely acclaimed. Freshly prepared seasonal foods are offered along with sumptuous desserts. Lunch and dinner Mondays through Saturdays. Reservations advised. Major credit cards accepted. 105 E. 37th at Drayton (phone: 236-5547). Expensive to moderate.

La Toque – This popular dining spot features continental dishes and fresh local seafood. All entrées are cooked to order, and there's a good wine list. A specialty food shop, *Swiss Affair Ltd.,* also is on the premises and serves light dinners (omelettes, soup, and salads). Closed Sundays. Reservations advised. Major credit cards accepted. 420 E. Broughton St. (phone: 238-0138). Expensive to moderate.

Chart House – Loads of nautical paraphernalia, fine seafood and steaks, a cozy bar, and balconies overlooking the Savannah River and Riverfront Plaza make this one of the most popular dining spots in town. Dinner daily. Reservations advised. Major credit cards accepted. 202 W. Bay St. (phone: 234-6686). Moderate.

Cock'd Hat – Tucked away on a side street in the downtown Historic District, this inviting little restaurant and tavern serves excellent creole, Savannah-style seafood dishes, and first-rate beef. The proprietors always are on hand to make certain that all goes well. Lunch weekdays, dinner Mondays through Saturdays. Reservations advised. Major credit cards accepted. 9 Drayton St. (phone: 233-8952). Moderate.

Garibaldi's – An 1870s firehouse has been cunningly refashioned into a comfortable Italian café serving excellent pasta, veal, seafood, grilled duck, lamb, and lobster. Dining is enhanced by the decor: marbletop tables, lace curtains, mirrors and antiques. Dinner daily. Reservations advised. Major credit cards accepted. 315 W. Congress St. (phone: 232-7118). Moderate.

Johnny Harris – Specialties here are steaks, prime ribs, barbecue, and chicken. They do their own baking on the premises. In its third generation of continuous ownership, this is where the nationally marketed Johnny Harris Barbecue Sauce originated. Jacket and tie are required on Friday and Saturday nights, but surprisingly, reservations are unnecessary. Closed Sundays. Major credit cards accepted. 1651 E. Victory Dr. (phone: 354-7810). Moderate.

Pavilion – Another well-known Savannah spot, featuring traditional "Old South" recipes from land and sea, with a great buffet. Open daily. Reservations advised. Major credit cards accepted. *De Soto Hilton,* Bull and Liberty Sts. (phone: 232-9000). Moderate.

Sakura – Savannah's only authentic Japanese eatery. The tempura, teriyaki dishes, and sushi bar, not to mention the waterfront view, all are excellent reasons to dine here. Open Monday through Saturday for lunch; daily for dinner. Reservations advised. Major credit cards accepted. 21 E. River St. (phone: 233-0203). Moderate.

Sebastian's – In a restored old tavern, this cozy spot offers creative Low Country, American, and European dishes. Closed Sundays. Reservations advised. Major credit cards accepted. 321 Jefferson St., downtown (phone: 234-3211). Moderate.

Bodi's Café and Bakery – Cheery little suburban bake shop and café, a nice drop-in spot for lunch, continental breakfast, fresh croissants, breads, desserts, and wines. Open early morning to late night daily except Sundays. No reservations. Major credit cards accepted. 401 Mall Blvd. (phone: 354-3733). Inexpensive.

Crystal Beer Parlor – For the last half-century this place has been famous for its sandwiches, burgers, and casual, friendly atmosphere. Closed Sundays. Reservations unnecessary. Major credit cards accepted. 301 W. Jones St. (phone: 232-1153). Inexpensive.

Exchange Tavern – This is River Street's oldest restaurant, located in a riverfront landmark. Specialties include the Reuben sandwiches and Oompah's famous German potato salad, as well as fresh local seafood, and char-grilled steaks. There's live entertainment nightly. Open daily. Reservations unnecessary. Major credit cards accepted. 201 E. River St. (phone: 232-7088). Inexpensive.

Love's Seafood – On the Ogeechee River, south of the city, this simple seafood place for many years has been known for its shrimp, oysters, crabs, and channel catfish. Open for lunch and dinner daily except Mondays. No reservations. Major credit cards accepted. US 17S (phone: 925-2232). Inexpensive.

Mrs. Wilkes' Boarding House – One of Savannah's culinary landmarks. Mrs. Wilkes advertises by word of mouth, and while some people are critical, they admit that it is only because when they want home cooking they eat at home. When you walk in, you'll find set out on dining room tables food enough to stagger Sherman's army: grits, biscuits, sausage, and eggs for breakfast, or fried chicken, swordfish steaks, potatoes, rice, peas, cornbread, and other down-home treats for lunch. To serve yourself, just spread your arm in that proverbial boarding-house reach. Open weekdays for breakfast and lunch. No reservations or credit cards accepted. In the basement of 107 W. Jones St. (phone: 232-5091). Inexpensive by any standards — about $6 for all you can eat.

Palmers Seafood House – On Wilmington Island, just 15 minutes from downtown; many residents and visitors consider this the best place in the area for fresh seafood. The atmosphere is casual. Open daily. No reservations. Major credit cards accepted. 80 Wilmington Island Rd. (phone: 897-2611). Inexpensive.

Wall's BarBQ – Housed in a shack in an unpaved alley, this old Savannah favorite still dishes out the best deviled crab cakes in town. These piquantly seasoned patties cost $2 each and are available only on Fridays and Saturdays from noon to 6:30 PM. Take them out for gobbling elsewhere, since the shack's interior leans toward the gloomy. Only open Thursdays, Fridays, and Saturdays from 11 AM to 10 PM. No reservations or credit cards accepted. Between Houston and Price Sts. (phone: 232-9754). Inexpensive.

SEATTLE

AT-A-GLANCE

SEEING THE CITY: The best view of Seattle and the magnificent Washington landscape is from the top of the Space Needle (phone: 443-2111). The observation deck and revolving restaurant offer 360-degree views of the city, Puget Sound, Lake Washington, and beyond to the snow-covered peaks of the Cascade and Olympic mountains. Admission charge unless dining. Seattle Center.

SPECIAL PLACES: Don't be confused by the geographical designations in street addresses, like north or south. The directions that follow avenue names and precede street names (5th Ave. N. or N. 5th St.) give location in relation to downtown (where only street names and numbers are used).

Seattle Center – The legacy of the *1962 World's Fair,* this 74-acre area contains some of the city's finest facilities. Dominating the 50 buildings and the grassy plazas is the Space Needle, a futuristic steel structure that spires 605 feet upward from its tripod base. Among the other highlights are the *Food Circus* (Center House, 305 Harrison St.) where you can sample inexpensive international delicacies, two playhouses, the *Opera House* and *Arena* (adjoining buildings on Mercer St.), and *Fun Forest Amusement Park* (370 Thomas St.) for a variety of entertainment. Information for Seattle Center theater tickets and activities is at a booth in the Center House Building (5th Ave. N. between Denny Way and Mercer St.; phone: 684-7200).

Pacific Science Center – In the Seattle Center, this museum designed by Minoru Yamasaki features astro-space displays, models that teach children about anatomy, an operating oceanographic model of Puget Sound that simulates waves, a laserium that uses laser beams to form images, a reconstruction of a Northwest Indian longhouse, and a popular science playground with hands-on exhibitions for children. Open daily. Admission charge. 200 2nd Ave. N. (phone: 443-2001).

Seattle Aquarium – Next to the public fishing pier at Waterfront Park, the aquarium offers a close view of what's swimming in Puget Sound. In the domed viewing room — actually a 400,000-gallon tank — you are surrounded by octopus, starfish, dogfish sharks, rock cod, red snapper, scallops, shrimp, anemones, and sea pens. There also are tropical fish, a touch-me exhibition, and a wonderfully captivating family of sea otters. Open daily. Admission charge. Pier 59 (phone: 386-4320). All along the waterfront, there are seafood bars where you can pick up a good lunch.

Puget Sound Ferry Ride – If looking out at the sound and up at its marine life isn't enough, you can have the full sound experience by taking the 45-minute ride to Winslow or to Bremerton or as far as Victoria, British Columbia. Ferry Terminal (phone: 464-6400).

Pike Place Market – Founded in 1907, this public market is now a historic site full of lively vendors and a colorful array of produce, flowers, and fresh fish. There also are musicians, craftspeople, and specialty restaurants. Closed Sundays except in summer. 1st Ave. between Pike St. and Virginia St.

Seattle Art Museum – Designed by Robert Venturi, this museum has a vertically-fluted exterior with terra cotta, granite, and marble accents. Native American, Asian, African, and Oceanic art. Closed Mondays. Admission charge except Thursdays. 2nd Ave. between Union and University Sts. (phone: 625-8900).

Museum of History and Industry – Extensive collection of Pacific Northwest artifacts traces the history of Seattle's first 100 years. A mural depicts the fire that leveled the city in 1889, and the displays include almost everything that came afterward — mementos of the Gold Rush, old fire fighting equipment, a maritime display, and a Boeing exhibit that follows the company's development over the past 60 years. Open daily. Admission charge except Tuesdays. 2700 24th Ave. E. (phone: 324-1125).

Westlake Center – This $110-million retail and office project forms the heart of downtown Seattle. The airy 4-level glass and steel retail pavilion features upscale specialty shops, pushcarts, and the *Pacific Picnic* food court, offering ethnic dishes. It is flanked by a 25-story office tower and Westlake Park, with its granite plaza designed in contrasting colors to resemble a woven Indian basket. The center, open daily, is connected to the city's main department stores and is served by a monorail terminal. Pine St., between 4th and 5th Aves.

Pioneer Square – The site where the city was founded in 1852 has become a historic preservation area. The Victorian brick buildings house some of the city's favorite boutiques, galleries, and restaurants. When fire ravaged the district in 1889, the city rebuilt atop the rubble, leaving an underground town 10 feet below. *Bill Speidel's Underground Tours* guide visitors through the subterranean 8-block area, which has some storefronts, interiors, and old waterlines intact. Tours daily. Admission charge. Reservations advised (610 1st Ave.; phone: 682-4646). For Gold Rush nostalgia, visit the Klondike Gold Rush National Historic Park (117 S. Main; phone: 442-7220), which traces the history of Klondike gold fever with murals, exhibitions, movies, and a slide show.

International District – Seattle has a large Chinese and Japanese community concentrated in this interesting old section of the city. There is a Buddhist temple, many crafts shops, and Asian restaurants. Shop at *Uwajimaya* (6th Ave. S. and S. King; phone: 624-6248), the West Coast's largest Asian retail store, for gifts and specialty food items. The *Wing Luke Memorial Museum* features a permanent exhibition tracing the immigration of the Chinese to the Northwest from the 1860s on, a folk arts gallery, and a fine arts gallery. Closed Mondays. Admission charge. 407 7th Ave. S. (phone: 623-5124).

University of Washington Arboretum – Some 200 lakeside acres contain over 5,000 species of plant life from all over the world. Features one of the largest Japanese tea gardens outside Japan. Open all year. Admission charge to Japanese Garden. Lake Washington Blvd. between E. Madison and Montlake (phone: 543-8800).

■ **EXTRA SPECIAL:** Just an hour and a half south of Seattle is the spectacular Mt. Rainier National Park, with its 14,410-foot summit of the Cascade range. There are over 300 miles of trails, ranging from the super-rough, 90-mile Wonderland trail, which circles the peak, to short nature walks for mere earthlings. On the way home, stop at the *Wild Berry* restaurant in Ashford (phone: 569-2628) for a colossal club sandwich made with three slices of homemade whole wheat or rye bread and a jar of delicious mountain blackberry jam. Also on Route 161 is the Northwest Trek Wildlife Park (phone: 847-1903), where moose, elk, buffalo, mountain goat, and caribou roam free. The zoo belongs to the animals; visitors tour from a tram and are not allowed off. Admission charge.

Located 2 hours south of the city is Mt. St. Helen's, which erupted

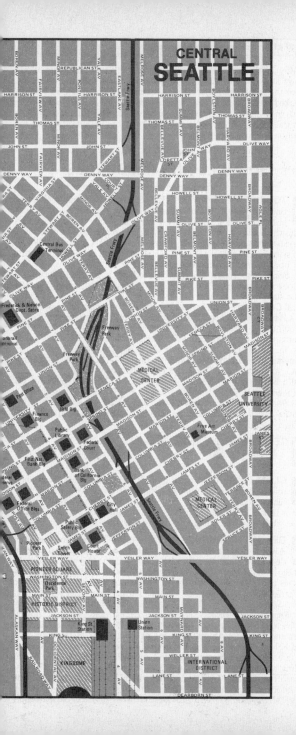

in May 1980. Drive along Highway 504, then take Interstate 5, and get off at exit 49, which will lead you directly to the visitors' center. From there you can make a tour of the slopes where Mt. St. Helen's wreaked the greatest havoc. Forests were swept away, and lakes were filled with molten mud, which changed the area dramatically. The visitors' center shows a film that describes the various stages of the eruption (phone: 274-4038).

SOURCES AND RESOURCES

 TOURIST INFORMATION: The Seattle/King County Convention and Visitors Bureau offers daily events schedules, maps, and information. Part of the press kit provided by this organization includes the *Seattle Visitors Guide,* which is also available at hotels and some restaurants. 666 Stewart St. (phone: 461-5840). Contact the Washington state hotline (phone: 800-544-1800) for maps, calendars of events, health updates, and travel advisories.

The Seattle Guidebook by Archie Satterfield, available at the Elliott Bay Book Co. (phone: 624-6600) for $10.95, is a good guide to Seattle and the surrounding area.

Local Coverage – *Seattle Post-Intelligencer,* morning daily, publishes What's Happening on Fridays with coming week's events; *Seattle Times,* afternoon daily, publishes Tempo magazine on Fridays. *The Weekly* is an opinionated yuppie-oriented newspaper. All are available at newsstands, including the *Seattle Visitors Guide* (for free), mentioned above.

Television Stations – KOMO Channel 4–ABC; KING Channel 5–NBC; KIRO Channel 7–CBS; KCTS Channel 9–PBS.

Radio Stations – AM: KIXI 880 (1940s, 1950s, and 1960s); KING 1090 (news/talk); KLSY 1540 (soft rock). FM: KLSY 92.5 (soft rock); KING 98.1 (classical music); KMGI 107.7 (adult contemporary).

Food – *Seattle's Best Places* by David Brewster (Sasquatch Books; $10.95).

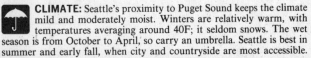 **TELEPHONE:** The area code for Seattle is 206.

Sales Tax – The city sales tax is 8.1%, except on groceries.

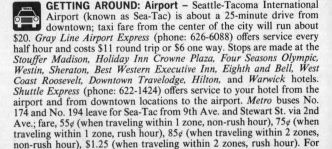 **CLIMATE:** Seattle's proximity to Puget Sound keeps the climate mild and moderately moist. Winters are relatively warm, with temperatures averaging around 40F; it seldom snows. The wet season is from October to April, so carry an umbrella. Seattle is best in summer and early fall, when city and countryside are most accessible.

GETTING AROUND: Airport – Seattle-Tacoma International Airport (known as Sea-Tac) is about a 25-minute drive from downtown; taxi fare from the center of the city will run about $20. *Gray Line Airport Express* (phone: 626-6088) offers service every half hour and costs $11 round trip or $6 one way. Stops are made at the *Stouffer Madison, Holiday Inn Crowne Plaza, Four Seasons Olympic, Westin, Sheraton, Best Western Executive Inn, Eighth and Bell, West Coast Roosevelt, Downtown Travelodge, Hilton,* and *Warwick* hotels. *Shuttle Express* (phone: 622-1424) offers service to your hotel from the airport and from downtown locations to the airport. *Metro* buses No. 174 and No. 194 leave for Sea-Tac from 9th Ave. and Stewart St. via 2nd Ave.; fare, 55¢ (when traveling within 1 zone, non-rush hour), 75¢ (when traveling within 1 zone, rush hour), 85¢ (when traveling within 2 zones, non-rush hour), $1.25 (when traveling within 2 zones, rush hour). For more information, contact the *Metropolitan Transit* office at 447-4800.

Bus – *Metropolitan Transit* provides extensive service in the metropolitan area with an added attraction: *Metro*'s Free Ride Service in the downtown-waterfront area. Route information is available at its office, 821 2nd Ave. (phone: 447-4800).

Car Rental – Seattle is served by the major national firms.

Monorail – The quickest and most exciting way to get from downtown to the Seattle Center is via the *World's Fair* monorail. Leaves every 15 minutes from Westlake Center.

Taxi – Cabs can be hailed in the street or ordered on the phone. Major companies are *Farwest* (phone: 622-1717) and *Yellow Cab* (phone: 622-6500).

VITAL SERVICES: Audiovisual Equipment – *Photo & Sound* (phone: 632-8461).

Business Services – *Secretarial Assistants,* Columbia Center (phone: 682-6072). JHD/Dry Cleaner/Tailor *Ange's French Cleaners,* 2000 9th Ave. (phone: 622-6727); *A-1 Tailors,* 1424 4th Ave., Suite 822 (phone: 625-1455).

Limousine – *Airebrook Limousine* (phone: 285-5505); *Washington Limousine,* sedans also (phone: 523-8000).

Mechanic – *Salmon Service Center,* 25th Ave. and 65th St. NE (phone: 523-9400).

Medical Emergency – *Virginia Mason Hospital* (925 Seneca St., phone: 583-6433); *Virginia Mason 4th Avenue* (walk-in clinic), 7 AM to 6 PM (1221 4th Ave.; phone: 223-6490).

Messenger Services – *Dependable Messenger Service* (phone: 728-4066); *Mail Dispatch* (phone: 762-2951).

National/International Courier – *Federal Express* (phone: 282-9766); *DHL Worldwide Courier Express* (phone: 763-4222).

Pharmacy – *Jordan Drugs & Grocery Center,* open from 7 AM to 2 AM (2518 E. Cherry St.; phone: 322-3050); *Pay 'n Save* (319 Pike St.; phone: 223-0512).

Photocopies – *Copy Co.* (616 6th Ave. S.; phone: 622-4050); *Lazer Quick* (412 Olive Way; phone: 622-4387).

Post Office – Downtown, 301 Union St. (phone: 442-6340).

Professional Photographer – *Wm. J. Murray* (phone: 441-2154); *Krogstad Photography* (phone: 682-9153).

Secretary/Stenographer – *Secretarial Assistants* (phone: 682-6072); *Business Service Center,* 1001 4th Ave. Pl. (phone: 624-9188).

Translator – *Berlitz* (phone: 682-0312).

Typewriter Rental – *McDonald-Klein Business Machines,* weekly rate only (phone: 524-3700).

Western Union/Telex – Many offices are located around the city (phone: 800-325-6000).

Other – *HQ, Headquarters Company,* word processing, telex, fax services, conference rooms (phone: 224-8700); *Globe Secretariat,* notary, word processing, 24-hour phone dictation (phone: 448-9441).

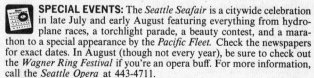

SPECIAL EVENTS: The *Seattle Seafair* is a citywide celebration in late July and early August featuring everything from hydroplane races, a torchlight parade, a beauty contest, and a marathon to a special appearance by the *Pacific Fleet.* Check the newspapers for exact dates. In August (though not every year), be sure to check out the *Wagner Ring Festival* if you're an opera buff. For more information, call the *Seattle Opera* at 443-4711.

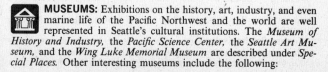

MUSEUMS: Exhibitions on the history, art, industry, and even marine life of the Pacific Northwest and the world are well represented in Seattle's cultural institutions. The *Museum of History and Industry,* the *Pacific Science Center,* the *Seattle Art Museum,* and the *Wing Luke Memorial Museum* are described under *Special Places.* Other interesting museums include the following:

Bellevue Art Museum – American and regional art. Bellevue Sq. (phone: 454-3322).

Frye Art Museum – Contemporary regional works. Terry Ave. and Cherry St. (phone: 622-9250).

Museum of Flight – This aviation museum features a soaring glassed-in gallery with more than 20 full-size planes suspended from the ceiling, including a DC-3 and the first supersonic jet. Admission charge. 9404 E. Marginal Way S., near Sea-Tac Airport (phone: 764-5720).

MAJOR COLLEGES AND UNIVERSITIES: The University of Washington, founded in 1861, is the area's oldest and largest educational institution (visitors' information center at 17th Ave. NE and NE 45th St.; phone: 543-9198). Also in the city are Seattle University (12th Ave. and E. Columbia St.; phone: 296-6000) and Seattle Pacific University (3rd Ave. W. and W. Nickerson St.; phone: 281-2000).

SHOPPING: *Westlake Mall* encompasses a number of upscale specialty shops, including *Fireworks Gallery* (400 Pine St.; phone: 682-6462), and access to Seattle's big three department stores, the *Bon, Frederick & Nelson,* and *Nordstrom.* At the *Pike Place Market* (1st Ave. between Pike St. and Virginia St.) shoppers can buy homegrown fresh and dried herbs, locally produced honey, and jams made from mountain berries. Fresh seafood can be packed in ice to take with you on the plane. Craftspeople sell silk-screened T-shirts, hand-painted jackets, hand-crafted jewelry, and photographs of the Seattle skyline. *Pioneer Square* is an 8-block area which features a concentration of art galleries, among its other shops:

Eddie Bauer – Clothing for your next hike or camping trip. 5th Ave. and Union St. (phone: 622-2766)

Elliott Bay Book Company – The staff here is extremely knowledge-able about the store's ever-expanding collection of new titles. At the *Elliott Bay Café* downstairs, authors give lectures and readings weekly. 101 S. Main St. (phone: 624-6600).

Fireworks Gallery – One-of-a-kind ceramic pieces, raku pottery, and a large selection of unique pins and earrings. 210 1st Ave. (phone: 682-8707).

Flying Shuttle – Exotic, hand-crafted jewelry, woven jackets, hand-knit sweaters, and whimsical folk art. 607 1st Ave. (phone: 343-9762).

Glass House – The only working glass studio in Seattle showcases large displays of glass goods. 311 Occidental Ave. S. (phone: 682-9939).

REI – Large selection of outdoor gear including everything from mountain bikes to ice axes. 1525 11th Ave. (phone: 323-8333).

SPORTS AND FITNESS: Seattle is in the big leagues, with three professional teams. The best bet is to order tickets by phone and later pick them up at the team's ticket office.

Baseball – The *Mariners*' season runs from April through September at the *Kingdome* (phone: 628-3555).

Basketball – The NBA *SuperSonics* play from October through April at the *Seattle Center Coliseum* (ticket office, at the west entrance; phone: 281-5800).

Bicycling – Rent from *Gregg's Green Lake Cycle,* 7007 Woodlawn Ave. NE (phone: 523-1822). Green Lake Park and Burke-Gilman Trail are good areas for biking.

Fishing – You can wet a line from the public pier of Waterfront Park or go after the big salmon by renting a boat or taking a charter into the deep sea from Pier 54 (Ivar's Pier) on the Seattle waterfront (phone: 292-0595).

Fitness Centers – *Fitness Limited* has a pool, Jacuzzi, sauna, steam-room, exercise equipment, and weights; athletic clothing is provided (2001 6th Ave., across from the *Westin* hotel; phone: 728-1500); The

YMCA has a pool, weight room, and track (909 4th Ave. and Madison; phone: 382-5000). The private *Seattle Club* (2020 Western Ave.; phone: 443-1111) is open to guests of several downtown hotels. Among the many facilities are racquetball courts, track, pool, Nautilus, massage, tanning, exercise classes, and a restaurant.

Football – The NFL *Seahawks* play from August through December at the *Kingdome,* 201 S. King St. (phone: 827-9777).

Golf – The city has three good 18-hole municipal courses: *Jackson Park* (1000 NE 135th St.; phone: 363-4747); *Jefferson Park* (4101 Beacon Ave. S.; phone: 762-4513); *West Seattle Municipal Course* (4470 35th Ave. SW; phone: 935-5187).

Horse Racing – *Longacres Park* is 11 miles southeast via I-5 and I-405 in Renton (phone: 226-3131). The season is from early April through September.

Jogging – Run the 3-mile course at Myrtle Edwards Park on the waterfront, at Alaska Way between W. Bay and W. Thomas. Or follow many Seattle residents and run around Green Lake (2.8 miles); to get there, take the No. 6 or No. 16 northbound bus from 3rd and Pine.

Skiing – Close by is *Alpental* (on the Snoqualmie Pass via I-90; phone: 434-6112). Also popular is *Crystal Mountain* (120 miles away near Mt. Rainier; phone: 663-2265).

Tennis – City parks have outdoor courts.

THEATER: For current offerings check the publications listed above. The *Seattle Repertory Theater* performs classical and modern productions from October through May at the *Bagley Wright Theater* at the Seattle Center (155 Mercer St.; phone: 443-2222). *Intiman Theatre Co.* performs at the *Seattle Center Playhouse* (155 Mercer St.; phone: 626-0782). Attend *A Contemporary Theater* (100 W. Roy; phone: 285-5110). The *5th Avenue Theater* (1308 5th Ave.; phone: 625-1900) features pop concerts and touring Broadway plays; and the restored *Paramount Theater* (907 Pine St.; phone: 682-1414) brings in top concert artists. The *Empty Space Theatre at First Stage* (107 Occidental Ave. S.; phone: 467-6000) showcases new plays. The *Bathhouse Theatre* (7312 W. Green Lake Dr. N.; phone: 524-9108) stages experimental productions, the *New City Theatre* (1634 11th Ave.; phone: 323-6800) features works by up-and-coming playwrights, and the *Group Theatre* (3940 Brooklyn Ave. NE; phone: 543-4327) focuses on ethnic plays.

MUSIC: The *Seattle Symphony* and the *Seattle Opera Association* perform at the *Opera House* from September through April. The *Opera*'s *Wagner Ring Festival* is in August, though it's not held every year. The ticket offices for both are in Center House, Seattle Center (for symphony, phone: 443-4747; opera, 443-4711).

NIGHTCLUBS AND NIGHTLIFE: Some of the area's hottest nightspots are *Jazz Alley* (6th and Lenora; phone: 441-9729) for jazz and *Swannie's* (222 S. Main St.; phone: 622-9353) for headline comedy acts. Another popular spot is *Celebrity Bar & Grill* (315 2nd Ave. S.; phone: 467-1111).

BEST IN TOWN

CHECKING IN: Seattle has an abundance and wide variety of accommodations. Those we rate as expensive begin at $90 for a double room; moderate, from $68. We could find no hotels that met our standards in the inexpensive category. For information about bed and breakfast accommodations, contact: *Pacific Bed & Breakfast*

Agency, 701 NW 60th St., Seattle, WA 98107 (phone: 784-0539). All telephone numbers are in the 206 area code unless otherwise indicated.

Alexis – For the sophisticated traveler who needs to be pampered, this 51-room hotel is the place. The management claims service to be its top priority and it shows, from the optional butler who will do your unpacking to the complimentary shoeshines. *Café Alexis* (see *Eating Out*) is special. Additional services include 24-hour room service, 1 meeting room, concierge and secretarial assistance, A/V equipment, photocopiers, and computers. 1st and Madison (phone: 624-4844; 800-426-7033; 206-621-9009). Expensive.

Four Seasons Olympic – A splendid restoration of a historic city landmark, it blends the old and new seamlessly. Highlights include the elegant guestrooms, the *Solarium,* a sparkling health spa; and the *Georgian* restaurant, a favorite for special occasions. Many of the city's most popular attractions are within walking distance. Room service is always on call. Business amenities include 15 meeting rooms, concierge and secretarial services, A/V equipment, photocopiers, computers, CNN, and express checkout. 411 University (phone: 621-1700 or 800-821-8106; Fax: 206-682-9633; Telex: 152477). Expensive.

Seattle Sheraton – With one of the region's most extensive permanent collections of contemporary Northwestern art, valued at more than $1 million, this is the place for those who enjoy culture along with their comfort. Many of the more than 2,000 original works, including a fantastic glass collection, are displayed in the lobby and other public spaces. Many of the 880 rooms offer great views. There is a pool room on the 35th floor (the Cirrus level); 3 restaurants, *Banners, Fullers, Gallery Seafood Bar* (see *Eating Out*), and *Gooey's Lounge;* shops; airport bus; and valet parking. Room service is available 24 hours a day. Business support services include concierge and secretarial assistance, A/V equipment, photocopiers, and computers. There are also 20 meeting rooms, CNN, and express checkout. 6th and Pike (phone: 621-9000 or 800-325-3535; Fax: 206-621-8441). Expensive.

Sorrento – This small first class spot, with just 76 rooms, offers many extras: terrycloth bathrobes, plants and potpourri in every room, a hot water bottle in your bed in winter, and complimentary limousine service into downtown. Dine at the highly acclaimed *Hunt Club* or enjoy English tea in the afternoon. Amenities such as a concierge desk, 4 meeting rooms, limited A/V equipment, and photocopiers are available. Terry Ave. and Madison St. (phone: 622-6400; 800-426-1265; Fax: 206-625-1059; Telex: 244206). Expensive.

Westin Seattle – Built in the heart of Seattle's shopping district and renovated in 1981, its two imposing 40- and 47-story towers are difficult to overlook. The 875 rooms offer spectacular views of Puget Sound, Mt. Rainier, and the Cascade and Olympic mountains. Restaurants include *Trader Vic's,* the *Market Café,* and the *Palm Court.* Shops, airport bus. There are both concierge and secretarial services on call here, as well as 24-hour room service, 18 meeting rooms, A/V equipment, photocopiers, and express checkout. 5th Ave. at Westlake (phone: 728-1000 or 800-228-3000; Fax: 206-728-2259; Telex: 152900). Expensive.

Inn at the Market – Accommodations in French country style above the *Pike Place Market.* Most of the 65 rooms feature a view of Elliott Bay. Guests enjoy complimentary coffee, limousine service around downtown, and *Campagne* restaurant for French country cuisine. Coffee shop; athletic facilities nearby. Business pluses are 1 meeting room, secretarial services, A/V equipment, photocopiers, and computers. 86 Pine St. (phone: 443-3600; 800-446-4484; Fax: 206-448-0631). Expensive to moderate.

Mayflower Park – In the downtown shopping district, adjacent to West-lake Center, providing accommodations in a convenient setting. Children under 17 stay free with their parents. Inexpensive parking, a coffee shop, and a cocktail lounge, *Oliver's*. Room service is available around the clock. Business support services include secretarial assistance, A/V equipment and photocopiers. There also are 9 meeting rooms. 4th Ave. and Olive Way (phone: 623-8700 or 382-6990; 800-426-5100; Fax: 206-382-6997). Expensive to moderate.

Pacific Plaza – An older hotel, smartly updated to appeal to business-people and others who want to be in the center of downtown at a reasonable price. It features 168 quiet rooms and complimentary continental breakfast. Secretarial services are available, as well as A/V equipment and computers. Express checkout. 400 Spring St. (phone: 623-3900; 800-426-1165; Fax: 206-623-2059). Moderate.

EATING OUT: Seattle's food industry did not really get moving until the *1962 World's Fair*. Being in the international spotlight spawned a wide variety of ethnic restaurants and boosted the quality of existing establishments. Our selections run from 70 and up for a dinner for two in the expensive range to $40 to $65 in the moderate and $35 or less in the inexpensive category. Prices do not include drinks, wine, or tips. All telephone numbers are in the 206 area code unless otherwise indicated.

Café Alexis – The atmosphere here has the intimacy of a friend's dining room, and while the fare occasionally borders on the experimental, the combinations work. Try the steamed clams and mussels in a spicy peanut–black bean sauce, or the roast duck with cardamom hazelnut sauce and apple catsup. Open daily. Reservations advised. Major credit cards accepted. *Alexis Hotel*, 1007 1st Ave. (phone: 624-3646). Expensive.

Canlis' – Features excellent dishes, including several cuts of charcoal-broiled steaks, poached fresh salmon in hollandaise sauce, pan-fried Quilcene oysters from nearby Quilcene Bay, and a sweeping view of Lake Union. Closed Sundays. Reservations advised. Major credit cards accepted. 2576 Aurora Ave. N. (phone: 283-3313). Expensive.

Fullers – In the *Seattle Sheraton*, this is one of Seattle's best, if not the best dining room in the city. Elegant peach- and buff-colored recessed booths showcase original artwork by Northwest artists. Villeroy & Boch china, crystal, elegant tableware, and hand-blown glass vases with fresh flowers are the prelude to splendid fare. The menu celebrates the special wealth of Northwest foods with selections such as gravlax (marinated salmon), baby leeks and herb port cream, veal chop with morels, or spinach salad with smoked duck. The wine list showcases the best the state has to offer, which is quite a lot. Closed Sundays. Reservations advised. Major credit cards accepted. 6th and Pike (phone: 621-9000 or 800-325-3535). Expensive.

Kaspar's – Overlooking Elliott Bay, this place — owned by Kaspar Donier, Swiss-born-and-trained chef — serves sophisticated Northwest and Southwest dishes. The Swiss onion soup is made with three different types of onions, port, and topped with melted gruyere. We recommend the sautéed sea scallops and the *Pike Street Market* mixed seafood grill. One of the quietest dining spots in Seattle. Open daily. Sunday brunch. Reservations advised. Major credit cards accepted. 2701 1st Ave. (phone: 441-4805). Expensive to moderate.

Ray's Boathouse – On the waterfront at Shilshole Bay, a great place to have a leisurely dinner while watching the sun go down behind the Olympic Mountains. Seafood offerings are fine and varied. Open daily. Reservations advised. Major credit cards accepted. 6049 Seaview Ave. NW (phone: 789-3770). Expensive to moderate.

Il Terrazzo Carmine – In the Merrill Place Building with its patio facing a reflecting pool, this is the perfect place for a summer drink or dinner. Choose between Italian and Northwest cuisine. Suggestions include ravioli with venison or local veal chop with artichokes and sun-dried tomatoes in wine sauce. Extensive Italian wine list, plus California and Northwest wines. Closed Sundays. Reservations advised, especially on weekends. Major credit cards accepted. 411 1st Ave. S. (phone: 467-7797). Expensive to moderate.

Café Sport – It's no accident that creativity reigns supreme here. Located in the *Pike Place Market*, the staff can choose from the freshest of seasonal fish and devise dishes at which diners marvel. Choices include baked King salmon glazed with mustard and garlic ginger with crème fraîche, charred rare tuna with wasabi aioli and tobiko caviar, and fresh Dungeness crab cakes. Open daily. Reservations advised. Major credit cards accepted. 2020 Western Ave. (phone: 443-6000). Moderate.

Cucina! Cucina! – A noisy, popular place where Italian bicycles and umbrellas hang from the ceiling. The tantalizing little pizza, spicy pasta dishes, and tender salmon are complemented by the view, which takes in much marine activity (including floatplanes). Closed Sundays. Reservations advised. Major credit cards accepted. 901 Fairview Ave. (phone: 447-2782). Moderate.

Metropolitan Grill – Aged beef, served a variety of ways, is the chef's specialty, as is the ever-popular salmon in this upscale steakhouse. Special *Seahawks* brunch during football season. Open daily. Reservations advised. Major credit cards accepted. 820 2nd Ave. (phone: 624-3287). Moderate.

Mikado – From its sushi bar through a dinner menu featuring shioyaki seafood, this is a true Japanese dining experience. Tatami rooms, where you feel a part of the culture, are available for 6 or more. Dinner only; closed Sundays. Reservations advised. Major credit cards accepted. 514 S. Jackson St. (phone: 622-5206). Moderate.

Rover's – In a romantic little house with a garden full of herbs and flowers, seasonal Northwest fare, such as salmon, pheasant, quail, venison, and rabbit, delights patrons nightly. Closed Sundays. Reservations advised. Major credit cards accepted. 2808 E. Madison St. (phone: 325-7442). Moderate.

Wild Ginger – Pacific Rim fare, with Vietnamese, southern Chinese, Korean, and Thai dishes on the eclectic menu. Try the sweet, succulent duck. The *satay* bar is a favorite hangout for sipping local beers and eating exotically seasoned, skewered seafood and meat. Open daily. Reservations advised. Major credit cards accepted. 1400 Western Ave. (phone: 623-4450). Moderate.

Al Boccalino – Carefully prepared southern Italian fare, fresh seafood, lamb, beef, and pasta in a cozy, *Pioneer Square* setting. Open for lunch and dinner. Closed Sundays. Dinner reservations necessary. Major credit cards accepted. 1 Yesler Way (phone: 622-7688). Moderate to inexpensive.

Ivar's Indian Salmon House – With views of Lake Union, sailboats, yachts, kayaks, and windsurfers, this is a favorite stop for out-of-towners. Designed to look like an Indian longhouse, it features heavy timbers, canoes hanging overhead, and totem poles inside. The menu includes alder-smoked salmon and black cod, prepared in Northwest Indian style, as well as mouth-watering prime ribs. Open daily. Reservations advised. Major credit cards accepted. 401 NE Northlake Way (phone: 632-0767). Inexpensive.

Trattoria Mitchelli's – The "Tratt" is great for an omelette and morning cappuccino, lunch, dinner, or late-night dining. Whether you choose a stool at the counter or a seat in the dining room, you'll enjoy the rich colors and warm ambience of a European café. The menu includes a tasty antipasto, Caesar salad, a range of pasta dishes, and a variety of rich desserts; specials are listed on chalkboards. Open daily except Mondays until 4 AM. No reservations on Friday and Saturday nights, Gallery Walk night (the first Thursday of each month, when galleries stay open late and people walk through the area), or during *Seahawks* games. Major credit cards accepted. 84 Yesler Way (phone: 623-3883). Inexpensive.

WASHINGTON, DC

$$\boxed{\text{AT-A-GLANCE}}$$

SEEING THE CITY: The 555-foot Washington Monument commands a panorama of the capital in all its glory. To the north stands the White House, below stretches the green Mall, with the Lincoln Memorial in the west and the Capitol perfectly aligned with it to the east. Beyond to the south and west flows the Potomac River, and across the river lies Virginia.

SPECIAL PLACES: In Washington, all roads lead to the Capitol. The building marks the center of the District. North/south streets are numbered in relation to it, east/west streets are lettered, and the four quadrants into which Washington is divided (NW, NE, SW, SE designated after addresses) meet here.

An easy way to get around the principal sightseeing area is by *Tourmobile.* These 88-passenger shuttle trams allow you to buy your ticket (good for all day) as you board, get on or off at any of the 18 stops, listen to highlights of the sights along the way, and set your own pace. *Tourmobiles* pass each stop every 30 minutes. For complete information contact the office at 1000 Ohio Dr. SW (phone: 554-7950).

Old Town Trolley Tours offers 2-hour group charter tours or individual tours of the District (phone: 269-3020). *Gray Line* offers narrated bus tours of the District and outlying areas (phone: 289-1905). Museum tours as well as special group tours emphasizing historic Washington are run by *National Fine Arts Associates* (4801 Massachusetts Ave. NW; phone: 966-3800). The *Spirit of Washington* runs sightseeing boats from March to December on the Potomac and from March to mid-October to Mount Vernon (6th and Water Sts. SW; phone: 554-8000 or 554-1542).

CAPITOL HILL AREA

The Capitol – The Senate and House of Representatives are housed in the Capitol, which is visible from almost every part of the city. When the French architect L'Enfant first began to plan the city, he noted that Jenkins's Hill (now called Capitol Hill) was "a pedestal waiting for a monument." And though Washington laid the cornerstone in 1793, the pedestal had to wait through some 150 years of additions, remodelings, and fire (it was burned by the British in 1814) to get the monument we know today. The 258-foot cast-iron dome, topped by Thomas Crawford's statue of Freedom, was erected during the Civil War; beneath it, the massive Rotunda is a veritable art gallery of American history featuring Constantino Brumidi's fresco *The Apotheosis of Washington* in the eye of the dome, John Trumbull's Revolutionary War paintings on the walls, and statues of Washington, Lincoln, Jefferson, and others. The rest of the building also contains many artworks, and though you are free to wander about, the 40-minute guided tours that leave from the Rotunda every quarter hour are excellent and provide access to the visitors galleries of Congress (congressional sessions start at noon). Open daily from 9 AM to 4:30 PM (last tour at 3:45). Between the first week of May and *Labor Day,* the Rotunda is open until 8 PM. No admission charge. You also can ride the monorail subway that joins the House and Senate wings with the congressional office buildings and try the famous bean soup in the Senate dining room. 1st St. between Constitution and Independence Aves. (phone: 224-3121). *Metro:* Capitol South.

Supreme Court Building – This neo-classical white marble structure, surrounded by Corinthian columns and with the inscription on its pediment "Equal Justice Under Law," was designed by Cass Gilbert and completed in 1935. Until then, however, the highest judicial body in the nation and one of three equal branches of government met in makeshift quarters in the basement of the Capitol. Now the Court receives equal treatment under the law and meets in an impressive courtroom flanked by Ionic columns when it is in session intermittently from the first Monday in October through June. Sessions are open to the public on a first-come, first-served basis. Open weekdays; courtroom presentations are on the half-hour from 9:30 AM to 3:30 PM except when court is in session. No admission charge. 1st St. between Maryland Ave. and E. Capitol St. NE (phone: 479-3000). *Metro:* Capitol South.

Library of Congress – These magnificent Italian Renaissance buildings house the world's largest and richest library. Originally designed as a research aid to Congress, the Library serves the public as well with 84 million items in 470 languages, including manuscripts, maps, photographs, motion pictures, and music. The exhibition hall displays include Jefferson's first draft of the Declaration of Independence and Lincoln's first two drafts of the Gettysburg Address. Among the Library's other holdings are one of three extant copies of the Gutenberg Bible, Pierre L'Enfant's original design for Washington, and the oldest known existing film — the 3-second *Sneeze* by Thomas Edison. The *Coolidge Auditorium* has regular concerts and literary events. For program and ticket information, call 287-6400. Forty-five-minute guided tours are offered on weekdays, 10 AM to 3 PM. Open weekdays from 8:30 AM to 9:30 PM, Saturdays from 8:30 AM to 5 PM, Sundays from 1 to 5 PM. No admission charge. 1st St. between E. Capitol and Independence Sts. SE (phone: 287-5458). *Metro:* Capitol South.

Folger Shakespeare Library – The nine bas-reliefs on the façade depict scenes from Shakespeare's plays, and inside you can find out anything you want to know about Shakespeare and the English Renaissance. The world's finest collection of rare books, manuscripts, and research materials relating to the foremost English-language playwright is here. The library, an oak-paneled, barrel-vaulted Elizabethan palace, also has a model of the *Globe Theatre* and a full-scale replica of an Elizabethan theater complete with a trapdoor (called the "heavens" and used for special effects). Visitors can see how productions were mounted in Shakespeare's day and how they are done today. Poetry, concerts, and plays by Renaissance and modern authors are presented here. The bookstore features the fine Folger series on the Elizabethan period as well as editions of Shakespeare's plays. Open 10 AM to 4 PM (tours 11 AM to 1 PM) daily except Sundays. No admission charge (phone: 544-4600). For information on attending a play, see "Theater," *Sources and Resources.* 201 E. Capitol St. SE (phone: 544-7077). *Metro:* Capitol South or Union Station.

Botanic Gardens – If you feel as if you are overdosing on history, the Botanic Gardens provides a pleasant antidote with its azaleas, orchids, and tropical plants — and we're not even going to tell you how big they are or where they're from. Open daily, 9 AM to 5 PM; until 9 PM from June through August. No admission charge. 1st St. and Maryland Ave. SW, at the foot of Capitol Hill (phone: 225-8333). *Metro:* Federal Center SW.

Union Station – This 82-year-old landmark recently was restored to its former Beaux Art grandeur. Modeled after the Diocletian Baths and the triumphal Arch of Constantine in Rome, its marble floors, granite

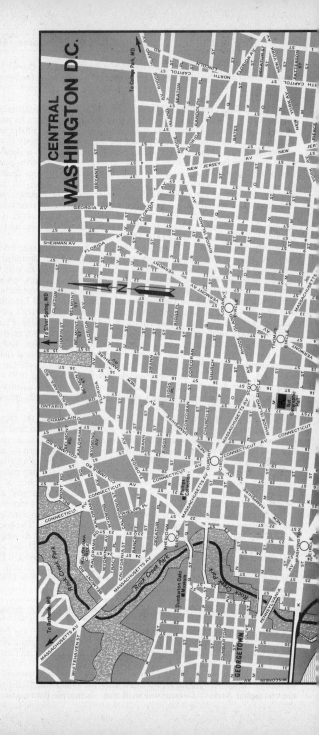

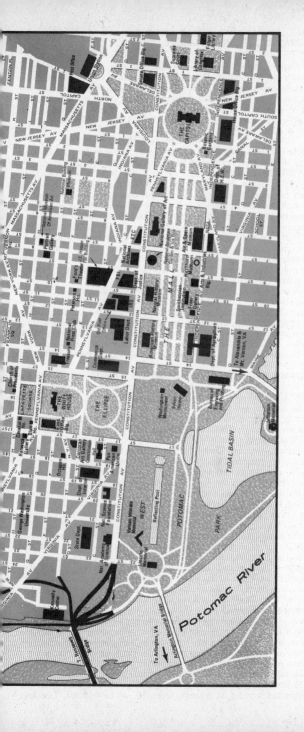

walls, bronze grilles, and classic statuary dazzle visitors. In front of *Amtrak*'s rail terminal is a complex of chic boutiques and dining areas. The main concourse, once the largest room under a single roof, has been divided into a series of levels and mezzanines for stores and eateries. The lower level houses movie theaters and a score of fast-food outlets. 50 Massachusetts Ave. NE (phone: 682-3767). *Metro:* Union Station.

THE WHITE HOUSE AREA

White House – Probably the most historic house in America because George Washington never slept here, though every president since has. It has been the official residence of the head of state since 1800. Designed originally by James Hoban, the White House still looks like an Irish country mansion from the outside; inside there are elegant parlors decorated with portraits of the presidents and first ladies, antique furnishings of many periods, and many innovations added by various presidents, like the revolving tray in the Green Room — an invention of Thomas Jefferson's that revolved between pantry and dining room, allowing him to serve such novelties as macaroni and ice cream and waffles without fear of eavesdropping servants. The five state rooms on the first floor are open to the public, and though you actually won't see the business of government going on, you'll be very close to it.

Visitors line up at the East Gate on E. Executive Ave. Open Tuesdays through Saturdays from 10 AM to noon. (Tickets, required during summer months, are available from the kiosk on the Ellipse.) Congressional tours of seven rooms, instead of the usual five, are available by writing to your congressman in advance. Be sure to specify alternate dates. Tuesdays through Saturdays from 8 to 10 AM. No admission charge. 1600 Pennsylvania Ave. NW (phone: 456-7041). *Metro:* McPherson Square.

Lafayette Square – If you do not enter the White House, you can get a fine view of it from this square, which was originally proposed by city planner L'Enfant as the mansion's front yard. Statues commemorate Andrew Jackson and the foreign heroes of the American Revolution — Lafayette, de Rochambeau, von Steuben, and Kosciusko. Flanking the square are two early-19th-century buildings designed by Benjamin Latrobe, Washington's first public architect. St. John's Church, constructed along classically simple lines, is better known as the Church of Presidents because every president since Madison has attended services here. Open daily. No admission charge. 16th and H Sts. NW (phone: 347-8766). The Decatur House, built for Commodore Stephen Decatur and occupied after his death by a succession of diplomats, is a Federal townhouse featuring handsome woodwork, a spiral staircase, and furniture of the 1820s. Open Tuesdays through Fridays, 10 AM to 2 PM; weekends, noon to 4 PM. Admission charge. 748 Jackson Pl. NW (phone: 842-0920). Near the southwest corner of the square at 1651-1653 Pennsylvania Ave. NW is Blair House, the president's official guesthouse since 1942 (not open to the public). *Metro:* Farragut W.

Ellipse – This grassy 36-acre expanse is the location of the zero milestone from which all distances in Washington are measured, the site of everything from demonstrations and ball games to the national *Christmas* tree. 1600 Constitution Ave. NW. *Metro:* Farragut W.

Corcoran Gallery of Art – If you think you've seen the Athenaeum portraits of George Washington before, you're probably not experiencing déjà vu. Check your wallet and with luck you'll see several more reproductions, and maybe a few of Jackson, too. This outstanding collection of American art contains some less familiar works as well, including a beardless portrait of Lincoln (a $5 bill won't help you here). The *Corcoran* also offers the opulent Grand Salon from the *Hôtel d'Orsay* in Paris, built by Boucher d'Orsay during the reign of Louis XVI and moved and reconstructed here in its entirety. Open 10 AM to 4:30 PM, Tuesdays through Sundays; until 9 PM on Thursdays. No admission charge. 17th St. and New York Ave. NW (phone: 638-3211). *Metro:* Farragut N. or W.

Renwick Gallery – The nation's first art museum, this beautiful French Second Empire building was designed by *Smithsonian* "Castle" architect James Renwick in 1859 to house W. W. Corcoran's art collection. Now run by the *Smithsonian Institution,* it is worth a visit for its changing exhibitions of contemporary American crafts and design. The gallery's other noteworthy sights are the entrance foyer, with its impressive staircase, and the 1870 Grand Salon, with overstuffed Louis XV sofas and potted palms. Open daily, 10 PM to 5:30 PM. No admission charge. Pennsylvania Ave. at 17th St. NW (phone: 357-3111). *Metro:* Farragut N. or W.

Daughters of the American Revolution Museum – Though any member of the DAR must prove that she is descended from those who served the cause of American independence with "unfailing loyalty," the museum is open to everyone regardless of the color of his or her blood. Exhibitions feature 33 period rooms, including the parlor of a 19th-century Mississippi River steamboat. There's also an extensive genealogical library. Open weekdays from 8:30 AM to 4 PM, Sundays from 1 to 5 PM (closed Saturdays). No admission charge. 1776 D St. NW (phone: 628-1776). *Metro:* Farragut W.

Octagon House – This stately red brick townhouse is a notable example of Federal architecture. The house in which President James and Dolley Madison lived for 6 months after the British burned down the White House in 1814 is maintained as a museum to give a picture of the high style of the early 19th century and features American antique furnishings from the Federal period. Open Tuesdays through Fridays from 10 AM to 4 PM, weekends noon to 4 PM. Donations suggested. 1799 New York Ave. NW (phone: 638-3105). *Metro:* Farragut W.

Organization of American States – In the Pan American Union Building. Its architects, Paul Cret and Albert Kelsey, have blended the styles of North and South America in this building of imposing formality and inviting elegance. Open 9 AM to 5 PM weekdays. The *Museum of Modern Latin American Art* is just behind the Aztec Garden. Open daily except Sundays from 10 AM to 5 PM. No admission charge. 17th St. and Constitution Ave. NW (phone: 458-6016). *Metro:* Farragut W.

THE MALL

This 2-mile stretch of green from the Lincoln Memorial to the Capitol forms something of the grand avenue envisioned by Pierre L'Enfant in his original plans for the city.

Lincoln Memorial – From the outside, this columned white marble building looks like a Greek temple; inside the spacious chamber with its colossal seated statue of Lincoln, sculpted by Daniel French, it is as inspiring. Carved on the walls are the words of the Gettysburg Address and Lincoln's Second Inaugural Address. National Park Service guides present brief talks at regular intervals. Open 24 hours a day. Memorial Circle between Constitution and Independence Aves. (phone: 426-6841). *Metro:* Farragut N.

Washington Monument – Dominating the Mall is the 555-foot marble and granite obelisk designed by Robert Mills (completed in 1884) to commemorate George Washington. The top (reached by elevator) commands an excellent panoramic view of the city. You can ride down or descend the 897 steps, where you see many stones donated by such groups as the "Citizens of the US residing in Foo Chow Foo, China." Open daily, 8 AM to midnight, from the first Sunday in April through *Labor Day;* 9 AM to 5 PM the rest of the year. No admission charge. 15th St. between Independence and Constitution Aves. (phone: 426-6841). *Metro:* Smithsonian.

Vietnam Veterans Memorial – Maya Ying Lin, while a Yale architecture student, designed this simple but immensely moving memorial to the American soldiers who died or are missing as a result of the Vietnam War. The two arms of the long, V-shaped, polished black granite walls point toward the Washington Monument and the Lincoln Memorial. On the 492-foot-long wall are inscribed the names of the men and women who were killed in the war or are still missing. A sculpture by Frederick Hart, depicting three soldiers, stands a short distance from the memorial. Constitution Ave. NW and Henry Bacon Dr. (phone: 634-1568).

US Navy Memorial Plaza – The plaza, dedicated in October 1987, has a statue of a lone US sailor overlooking the US portion of a granite world map. The visitors' center, which will open late this year, will include a gift shop, *IMAX* theater, and museum. Military bands perform during spring and summer evenings; pick up a brochure at any hotel or call for schedule. Pennsylvania Ave. between 7th and 9th Sts. NW (phone: 737-2300 or 800-821-8892).

Bureau of Engraving and Printing – If you're interested in money and how it is really made, the 25-minute self-guided tour that follows the entire process of paper currency production will prove enlightening if not enriching. Everything of a financial character from the 1-cent postage stamp to the $500-million Treasury Note is designed, engraved, and printed here. Though it costs only a penny to produce a single note, there are no free samples. Open weekdays, 9 AM to 2 PM. No admission charge. 14th and C Sts. SW (phone: 447-9709). *Metro:* Smithsonian.

National Archives – The repository for all major American records. The 76 Corinthian columns supporting this handsome building designed by John Russell Pope are nothing compared to the contents. Inside, in special helium-filled glass and bronze cases, reside the very pillars of our democracy — the Declaration of Independence, the Constitution, and the Bill of Rights. Open daily, 10 AM to 5:30 PM; extended hours April through *Labor Day* decided annually. No admission charge. Constitution Ave. between 7th and 9th Sts. NW (phone: 523-3000). *Metro:* Archives.

Jefferson Memorial – Dominating the south bank of the Tidal Basin, this domed temple-like structure (also designed by John Russell Pope) is a tribute to our third president and the drafter of the Declaration of Independence. The bronze statue of Jefferson was executed by Rudulph Evans, and inscribed on the walls are quotations from Jefferson's writings. This is the place to be for the most dramatic view of the cherry blossoms in early spring. Open daily. No admission charge. South Basin Dr. SW (phone: 426-6822). *Metro:* L'Enfant Plaza.

J. Edgar Hoover Building – If you want to find out a little more about an organization that already knows everything about you, take a tour of the FBI. In addition to a film on some past investigative activities, you'll get to see the laboratory and a firearms demonstration. Open weekdays, 8:45 AM to 4:15 PM. This popular tour takes 45 minutes. Line up early. No admission charge. Pennsylvania Ave. between 9th and 10th Sts. NW (phone: 324-3447). *Metro:* Metro Center or Gallery Place.

National Gallery of Art – One of the larger jewels in Washington's rich cultural crown, this gift to the nation by Andrew Mellon, financier and former Secretary of the Treasury, houses one of the world's finest collections of Western art from the 13th century to the present. Among the masterpieces in this huge and opulent white marble gallery are a grand survey of Italian painting including da Vinci's *Ginevra de' Benci* (the only da Vinci in the US), Fra Filippo Lippi's *The Adoration of the Magi,* Raphael's *Saint George and the Dragon,* works of French Impressionists, a self-portrait by Rembrandt, Renoir's *Girl With a Watering Can,* Picasso's *The Lovers,* and an extensive American collection. The 7-story East Building, designed by I. M. Pei, is something of an architectural masterpiece itself. An intriguing structure of interlocking triangular forms, it houses the Center for Advanced Study in the Visual Arts as well as exhibition halls. Several visits are necessary to see the whole gallery; there also are tours, films, lectures, and weekly concerts. Open Mondays through Saturdays from 10 AM to 5 PM, Sundays from noon to 9 PM. No admission charge. Between 3rd and 7th Sts. and Constitution Ave. NW (phone: 737-4215 weekdays; 842-6188 weekends). *Metro:* Judiciary Square Federal Center or Archives.

Smithsonian Institution – Before James Smithson died in 1829 he willed his entire fortune of half a million dollars "to found in Washington, an establishment for the increase and diffusion of knowledge among men." The wealthy English scientist had never even been to America and probably had no idea how much knowledge would be increased and diffused here in his name. Today the *Smithsonian* administers numerous museums, galleries, and research organizations; has an operating budget of over $90 million, a staff of over 4,000, and 75 million items in its total collection. The *Smithsonian*'s $73-million 3-floor complex just south of the Castle on Independence Ave. SW is a bit controversial because it is underground. Opened in autumn 1987, it houses two museums — the *Arthur M. Sackler Gallery,* featuring Asian art (including bronzes, jades, paintings, lacquerware, and sculpture), and the *National Museum of African Art* (see below), which was moved from its former Capitol Hill location. The third floor houses the International Center for exhibitions, and atop it all is the Enid A. Haupt Garden, a $3-million Victorian delight built around a 100-year-old linden tree. Entry to the museums is through kiosks in the garden. The Romanesque red sandstone building known as the Castle is the best place to get visitor information on any of the *Institution*'s activities. All buildings are open daily, 10 AM to 5:30 PM. Extended summer hours. No admission charge. 1000 Jefferson Dr. SW (phone: 357-2700, for information on all 14 Smithsonian museums). *Metro:* Smithsonian.

Among the *Smithsonian Museums* on the Mall are the following:

National Museum of African Art – The most extensive collection of African art in this country, and the only one dedicated exclusively to the arts of sub-Saharan Africa. Exhibitions include figures, masks, and sculptures in ivory, wood, bronze, and clay from 20 African nations; also color panels and audiovisual presentations on the people and environment of Africa. One gallery has an intriguing display concerning the influence of Africa's cultural heritage on modern European and American art. Delightful gift shop. Open all day weekdays and weekend afternoons. No admission charge. Quadrangle on the Mall, next to the *Sackler Gallery of Art* (phone: 357-4600). *Metro:* Smithsonian or Federal Triangle.

National Museum of Natural History – Only 1% of the museum's collection is on display but, with a total of some 60 million specimens, there's still plenty to see. Features eyefuls of the biggest and the best of most everything from the largest elephant on record — 12 tons from the African bush — to the precious Hope Diamond, at a hefty 44.5 karats, the largest blue diamond known (its only flaw is that it has brought tragedy to all its possessors). The Hall of Dinosaurs has mammoth skeletons. And there's even Martha, who died in the Cincinnati Zoo in 1914 and now is stuffed, the last of the extinct passenger pigeons. Open daily. No admission charge. Constitution Ave. at 10th St. NW. *Metro:* Smithsonian or Federal Triangle.

National Museum of American History – Everything that has to do with American ingenuity in craftsmanship, design, and industry can be found here, along with some things that bear only the most tenuous link. (That's where the real fun begins.) Hall after hall features such items as Eli Whitney's cotton gin, a gargantuan pendulum that was used by French physicist Jean Foucault to demonstrate the rotation of the earth, Radar's teddy bear (from the TV series "MASH"), Dorothy's ruby slippers (from the film *The Wizard of Oz*), and a full gallery of First Lady mannequins dressed in Inaugural Ball gowns. Open daily. No admission charge. Constitution Ave. at 14th St. NW. *Metro:* Smithsonian or Federal Triangle.

National Air and Space Museum – The largest of the *Smithsonian*'s museums, with displays of aircraft in its vast, lofty interior. Exhibitions include the Wright Brothers' plane, Charles Lindbergh's *Spirit of St. Louis,* the Apollo 11 command module, and a walk-through model of a Skylab orbital station. The films *To Fly, The Dream Is Alive, Living Player,* and *Flyers,* shown on a huge screen, are as spectacular as they are dizzying. Planetarium shows are presented in the *Albert Einstein Spacearium.* Open daily. No admission charge. Independence Ave. between 4th and 7th Sts. SW. *Metro:* L'Enfant Plaza.

Hirshhorn Museum and Sculpture Garden – Smaller but also superb is this collection donated in 1974 by a Latvian immigrant and self-made millionaire. The *Hirshhorn,* designed by Gordon Bunshaft, is worth a visit not only for its fine collection but also for the building itself, a circular concrete structure with an open core in which a bronze fountain shoots water 82 feet into the air. Displays include 19th- and 20th-century European and American works, and an attractive sculpture garden that features Rodin's *The Burghers of Calais* and Picasso's *Baby Carriage.* Open daily. No admission charge. Independence Ave. at 8th St. SW. *Metro:* L'Enfant Plaza.

Arts and Industries Building – Just east of the Castle, this is the second-oldest *Smithsonian* building on the Mall. The *Centennial Exhibition,* displayed in Philadelphia in 1876, has been re-created with marvelous displays of fashions, furnishings, and machinery. Open daily. No admission charge. Jefferson Dr. and Independence Ave. at 9th St. SW. *Metro:* Smithsonian.

DOWNTOWN

National Portrait Gallery and National Museum of American Art – Inside the *National Portrait Gallery,* an excellent example of Greek Revival architecture, many Americans who have gone down in the history of this country have gone up on the walls (in portrait form, that is). Among those hanging are all the American presidents, Pocahontas, Horace Greeley, and Harriet Beecher Stowe. The *National Museum of American Art* features American painting, sculpture, and graphic arts, including Catlin's paintings of the Indians and a choice group of works of the American Impressionists. Both museums (also administered by the *Smithsonian*) are open daily. No admission charge. 8th St. at F and G Sts. *Metro:* Gallery Place.

Ford's Theatre – The site of Lincoln's assassination in 1865 by John Wilkes Booth is a national monument, and in the 1960s it was restored and decorated as it appeared on the fatal night of April 14, 1865. In the basement is a museum of Lincoln memorabilia, including displays showing his life as a lawyer, statesman, husband and father, and president, and the clothes he was wearing when he was shot, the derringer used by Booth to shoot him, and the assassin's personal diary. Theater performances are held throughout the year. For theater tickets, call 347-4833. Open daily, 9 AM to 5 PM. Admission $1; no admission charge for those under 12, over 62, or handicapped. 517 10th St. NW (phone: 426-6924). *Metro:* Metro Center, 11th St. exit.

Peterson House – Directly across the street from the theater and museum is the house in which Lincoln died the morning after the shooting. The small, sparsely furnished house appears much the way it did in

1865. Open daily from 9 AM to 5 PM. No admission charge. 516 10th St. NW (phone: 426-6830).

GEORGETOWN

There's not much tobacco left in this area, once the Union's major tobacco port. It's particularly nice in the spring when it's pleasant to walk along the Chesapeake and Ohio Canal. The whole area's great for strolling. Beside the Canal (between Jefferson and 31st Sts.) the streets off Wisconsin Avenue house the city's social and political elite in beautiful restored townhouses with prim gardens and lovely magnolia trees. The main drags are Wisconsin Avenue and M Street, with boutiques and restaurants. Most of the action, including the city's hottest nightlife, takes place here. In the area at the top of the hill (along R St. east of Wisconsin Ave.), large 18th-century country estates survive and mingle with smaller row houses. The Dumbarton Oaks Garden has beautiful formal gardens, and in the *Dumbarton Oaks Museum* is a fine collection of early Christian and Byzantine art. The entrance to the museum is at 1703 32nd St. NW; the entrance to the gardens is at 31st and R Sts. NW. The museum is open Tuesday through Sunday afternoons; no admission charge. The gardens are open daily from 2 to 5 PM; admission charge from April to October (phone: 338-8278).

■ **EXTRA SPECIAL:** Just 16 miles south of Washington on George Washington Memorial Parkway is Mount Vernon, George Washington's estate from 1754 to 1799 and his final resting place. This lovely 18th-century plantation is interesting because it shows a less familiar aspect of the military-political man — George Washington as the rich Southern planter. The mansion, overlooking the Potomac, and the outbuildings that housed the shops that made Mount Vernon a self-sufficient economic unit have been authentically restored and refurnished. Some 500 of the original 8,000 acres remain; all are well maintained, and the parterre gardens and formal lawns provide a magnificent setting. There's also a museum with Washington memorabilia; the tomb of George and Martha lies at the foot of the hill. During the spring or the summer, start out early to avoid big crowds. Bicycle paths lead from the DC side of Memorial Bridge to Mount Vernon — a lovely ride along the Potomac. Open daily, 9 AM to 5 PM, March through October; to 4 PM the rest of the year. Admission charge (phone: 703-780-2000).

Also beautifully landscaped and overlooking the Potomac, but with many more tombs and monuments, is Arlington National Cemetery, a solemn reminder of this country's turbulent history. Here lie the bodies of many who served in the military forces — or in other ways served their country, among them Admiral Richard Byrd, General George C. Marshall, Robert F. Kennedy, Justice Oliver Wendell Holmes, and John F. Kennedy, whose grave is marked by an Eternal Flame. The Tomb of the Unknown Soldier, a 50-ton block of white marble, commemorates the dead of World Wars I and II and the Korean and the Vietnam wars and is always guarded by a solitary soldier. Changing of the guard takes place every hour on the hour (every half hour during summer months). The grounds of the cemetery once were the land of Robert E. Lee's plantation but were confiscated by the Union after Lee joined the Confederacy. Lee's home, Arlington House, has been restored and is open for public inspection. Cars are not allowed in the cemetery, but you can park at the visitors' center and go on foot or pay and ride the *Tourmobile* (phone: 628-48440). The house is open daily, 9:30 AM to 4:30 PM from October to March, to 6 PM the rest of the year (phone: 703-557-0613). The cemetery is open daily from 8 AM to 5 PM; April to September to 7 PM (phone:

703-692-0931). Directly west of Memorial Bridge in Arlington, Virginia. *Metro:* Arlington Cemetery.

SOURCES AND RESOURCES

TOURIST INFORMATION: The Washington Convention and Visitors Association (1212 New York Ave. NW, Washington, DC 20005) coordinates all Washington tourism information and runs the visitors' center (at 1455 Pennsylvania Ave. NW; phone: 789-7000). The center (open daily except Sundays, 9 AM to 5 PM) provides free maps and information on where to stay, eat, and shop. Volunteers from the Travelers Aid Society (phone: 347-0101) and International Visitors Information Service (phone: 783-6540) are on hand to assist foreign visitors. The Washington Visitors Association also has toll-free numbers for individual travelers (phone: 800-422-8644) and for meeting planners (phone: 800-635-MEET). Contact the District of Columbia's hotline (phone: 202-789-7000) for maps, calendars of events, health updates, and travel advisories.

Local Coverage – The *Washington Post,* morning daily; The *Washington Times,* morning daily; and *Washingtonian* magazine, monthly, all are available at newstands. *City Paper,* a free weekly highlighting cultural events in the area, is available in shops and restaurants. *Museum and Arts Washington* lists current museum exhibits, and *Regardie's* is a monthly business magazine.

Television Stations – WRC Channel 4–NBC; WJLA Channel 7–ABC; WUSA Channel 9–CBS; Channel 13–CNN; WETA Channel 26–PBS.

Radio Stations – AM: WFUD 930 (adult contemporary music); WNTR 1050 (news/talk); WTOP 1500 (news). FM: WPFW 89.3 (jazz); WKYS 93.9 (urban contemporary); WGAY 99.5 (easy listening); WAVA 105.1 (top 40); WCXR 105.9 (classic rock).

Food – *Best Restaurants and Others* by Phyllis Richman (101 Productions, $7.95) lists fine dining places in Washington, DC, and environs. *Washingtonian* magazine also has good restaurant listings.

TELEPHONE: The area code for the District is 202; for Maryland, 301; and for Virginia, 703.

Sales Tax – The city sales tax is 6%; there is an 8% tax on hotel rooms.

CLIMATE: Washington has four distinct seasons. Summers are Amazonian, falls New Englandish and lovely, winters cold with some snow and lots of slush, and spring — when the cherry blossoms bloom and all is sublime.

GETTING AROUND: Airports – Washington is served by three major airports. National is the city's primary facility, and the 20-minute drive to downtown by taxi will cost about $12 one way. The *Washington Flyer* (phone: 703-685-1400) provides limo service every half hour from National to most downtown and Capitol Hill hotels for $7. The *Metro's* blue and yellow lines connect downtown with the airport; Metro Center (11th and G Sts. NW; phone: 637-7000) is the system's main terminal.

Dulles International Airport is about 25 miles west of the city, in Virginia. The ride from downtown DC to Dulles usually takes about an hour, and cab fare should run about $35. The *Washington Flyer* (phone: 703-685-1400) leaves Dulles about every half hour for the *Mayflower,* the *Capitol Hilton,* and the *Washington Hilton* hotels; fare $12 one way, $20 round trip.

Baltimore/Washington International Airport (BWI) also serves the DC area and is a 45-minute trip from downtown by car. Cab fare from BWI to DC should run about $40. The *Washington Flyer* (phone: 703-685-1400) airport limo runs between BWI and the *Capitol Hilton* hotel for $22. *BWI Airport Transportation* (phone: 301-441-2345) also offers bus service from DC to BWI for $12.

Train – More than 50 *Amtrak* trains daily pull into historic Union Station on Capitol Hill, including the *Metroliner,* linking the capital to New York and other Northeast-corridor cities. For reservations and information, call 800-872-7245.

Bus – The *Metro Bus* system serves the entire District and the surrounding area. Transfers within the District are free; the rates increase when you go into Maryland and Virginia. For complete route information call the *Washington Metropolitan Area Transit Authority* office (phone: 637-7000).

Car Rental – All the national firms serve Washington.

Subway – The fastest way to get around Washington is by *Metrorail,* the subway system. The lines that are in operation provide a quick and quiet ride. New lines to the suburbs and other areas of the city open as they are completed, and buses deposit or pick up passengers at these stations. Transfers to the bus system are free. Be sure to pick up a transfer at your boarding station (not the exiting station). *Metro* hours are 6 AM to midnight, weekdays; 8 AM to midnight, Saturdays; and 10 AM to midnight, Sundays. For complete route and travel information and a map of the system, contact the *Washington Metropolitan Area Transit Authority* office, 600 5th St. NW (phone: 637-7000).

Taxi – Cabs in the District charge by zone. Sharing cabs is common, but ask the driver whether there is a route conflict if you join another passenger. Cabs may be hailed in the street, picked up outside stations and hotels, or ordered on the phone, but there is an extra charge of $1.50 for phone dispatch. By law, basic rates must be posted in all taxis. Major cab companies are *Yellow* (phone: 544-1212) and *Diamond* (phone: 387-6200).

Tourmobile – This shuttle bus operates in the downtown sightseeing area between the Lincoln Memorial and Capitol area (the Mall). Tickets can be purchased from the driver or from a booth near the tour sites. Passengers get on and off as often as they wish. The *Tourmobile* (phone: 628-4844) also goes to Arlington National Cemetery.

 VITAL SERVICES: Audiovisual Equipment – *Avcom* (phone: 638-1513); *Total Audio-Visual Systems* (phone: 737-3900).

Baby-sitting – *Kids First,* 15th and K Sts. (phone: 289-5437).

Business Services – *Echo Temporary Services,* 2020 K St. NW (phone: 457-1848).

Dry Cleaner/Tailor – *Central Valet,* shoe repair also, 1409 H St. NW (phone: 638-2606).

Limousine – *International Limousine Service,* multilingual drivers, sedans also (phone: 388-6800); *Congressional Limousine,* 24-hour service (phone: 966-6000).

Mechanic – *Call Carl,* gas 24 hours and repairs 7 AM to 5 PM (phone: 364-6360).

Medical Emergency – *George Washington University Medical Center,* 901 23rd St. NW; phone: 994-3884).

Messenger Services – *Central Delivery Service* (phone: 585-1000 or 589-8500).

National/International Courier – *Federal Express* (phone: 953-3333); *DHL Worldwide Courier Express* (phone: 684-8733).

Pharmacy – *Peoples Drug Stores,* open 24 hours, has several locations, including 1121 Vermont Ave. NW (phone: 628-0720).

Photocopies – *City Duplicating Center,* open evenings (1617 I St.

NW; phone: 296-0700); *Beaver Press,* pickup and delivery service (1333 H St. NW; phone: 347-6400; and 1800 M St. NW; phone: 466-4830).

Post Office – National Capitol Station, open from 7 AM to midnight, N. Capitol St. and Massachusetts Ave. (phone: 523-2337).

Professional Photographer – *Chase Studios* (phone: 338-2400).

Secretary/Stenographer – *Courtesy Associates* (phone: 347-5900).

Teleconference Facilities – *Four Seasons, Georgetown Inn, Loews L'Enfant Plaza,* (see *Best in Town,* below).

Translator – *Berlitz,* written translations only (phone: 331-1160); *International Translation Center* (phone: 296-1344); *IVIS Language Bank* (phone: 783-6540).

Typewriter Rental – *Shields Business Machines* (phone: 703-450-6161); *North's Office Machines* (phone: 466-2000); *A-1 Etron,* 1-week minimum to businesses only (phone: 277-8200).

Western Union/Telex – Many offices are located around the city (phone: 737-4260).

Other – *The Capital Informer,* convention and meeting planning (phone: 965-7420).

 SPECIAL EVENTS: Any town that inaugurates a new president every 4 years is in good standing when it comes to special events. The president takes the oath of office every 4th year on January 20. Usually the swearing-in is followed by a parade down Pennsylvania Ave.

In between inaugurations there's plenty to keep the District going for 4 more years. The publications above list exact dates. When you start noticing white single blossoms and a flood of pink double blossoms, it's *Cherry Blossom* time in Washington. In early April, a big festival celebrates the coming of the blossoms and the spring with concerts, parades, balls, and the lighting of the Japanese Lantern at the Tidal Basin.

Around the same time (give or take a few blossoms) is the *Easter Monday Egg Rolling,* when scads of children descend on the White House lawn; adults are admitted only if accompanied by a child.

House, garden, and embassy tours are given in April and May, allowing entrance to some of Washington's most elegant interiors. For information on the tours, see the Weekend section in Friday's *Washington Post.*

During the summer, the *American Folklife Festival* sponsored by the *Smithsonian Institution* sets up its tents on the Mall near the reflecting pool, and groups from all regions of the country do their stuff with jug bands, blues, Indian dance, and handicraft demonstrations.

The city is especially festive at *Christmas.* Special music programs are presented at the *Kennedy Center* and at many other spots around town.

 MUSEUMS: When it comes to museums, Washington is one of the nation's major showplaces, with the *Smithsonian Institution*'s outstanding museums leading the way. Described in some detail in *Special Places* are the *National Gallery of Art,* the *Smithsonian* (including the Quadrangle containing the *Arthur M. Sackler Gallery* and the *National Museum of African Art*), *Hirshhorn Museum, Freer Gallery of Art, National Air and Space Museum, Arts and Industries Building, National Museum of Natural History, National Museum of American History, National Portrait Gallery, National Museum of American Art,* the *Renwick Gallery,* and the *Corcoran Gallery.* Other notable museums include the following:

Columbia Historical Society – A museum devoted to Washington, DC, history, housed in the spectacular Victorian mansion of brewer Christian Heurich. Library open to the public Wednesdays, Fridays, and Saturdays from 10 AM to 4 PM; tours Wednesdays through Saturdays from noon to 4 PM. 1307 New Hampshire Ave. NW (phone: 785-2068).

Hillwood – Russian icons, portraits, and Fabergé creations are housed in the elegant former home of cereal heiress Marjorie Merriweather Post. Tours by appointment only; call well in advance for reservations. 4155 Linnean Ave. NW (phone: 686-5807).

National Building Museum – This museum in the old and wonderful Pension Building has permanent and changing exhibits relating to architecture, building, engineering, and design. Presidential inaugural balls are held in its Great Hall. 4th St. and Judiciary Sq. NW (phone: 272-2448).

National Geographic Society Explorers Hall – 17th and M Sts. NW (phone: 857-7588).

National Museum of Women in the Arts – In a former Masonic temple, this museum has a permanent collection of 500 pieces of pictorial, sculpted, and ceramic art spanning 400 years of women's work. New York Ave. and 13th St. NW (phone: 783-5000).

Phillips Collection – 19th- and 20th-century French and American modernist paintings plus changing exhibits. 1600 21st St. NW (phone: 387-0961).

Textile Museum – A diverse collection of fabrics from around the world, in a large former mansion. Open Tuesdays through Saturdays from 10 AM to 5 PM and Sundays from 1 to 5 PM. 2320 S St. NW (phone: 667-0441).

Washington Doll's House and Toy Museum – 5236 44th St. NW (phone: 244-0024).

Woodrow Wilson House – A memorial to our 28th president and his wife. 2340 S St. NW (phone: 673-4034).

SHOPPING: Washington has spruced up its shopping districts, inspired by a $100-million campaign to renovate the nation's main street, the stretch of Pennsylvania Avenue from the White House to the Capitol. The effort spilled over to nearby downtown, where a *Convention Center* was built, department stores were rebuilt and renovated, a mall installed, the *Willard Inter-Continental* hotel refurbished, and shops added. The city now sprouts pockets of well-known fashionable shops in its business and midtown area to complement other long-established shopping draws, such as trendy Georgetown, the bohemian Dupont Circle, and the Watergate complex (across from the *Kennedy Center for the Performing Arts*). For unique gifts, the city's myriad museums are the best bet. Most museums, shrines, and churches have their own shops, some offering reproductions of treasures at very affordable prices. Here's a sampling of what's available, by area:

Downtown – The *F Street Plaza,* a few blocks east of Pennsylvania Avenue, features Washington's traditional department stores (*Hecht Co.* and *Woodward & Lothrop*) as well as the glitzy shops at the National Press Building (at 13th and F Sts.). The collection of more than 80 specialty shops and restaurants on 3 glassed-in levels includes *Thornton's* British chocolate store and the *Sharper Image,* with expensive gadgets. Nearby, the *Willard Inter-Continental* hotel (at Pennsylvania Ave. and 14th St.) houses designer boutiques.

Dupont Circle – In the northern part of downtown, where Connecticut Avenue intersects Massachusetts Avenue, lies Dupont Circle. Browsers will discover art galleries, book shops, and boutiques, along with chic cafés and restaurants. *Kramerbooks & Afterwords* (1517 Connecticut Ave. NW) is known as a entertaining hangout, since the bookstore encourages its patrons to linger at the 24-hour café in back.

Georgetown – A second addition to *Georgetown Park Mall* (at Wisconsin Ave. and M St.) has nearly doubled the number (now over 100) of fine boutiques and restaurants that line the historic area. The two red brick buildings, built over 10 years ago, resemble the other Victorian structures in the neighborhood. Among its shops are *Abercrombie & Fitch, Liberty of London,* and an *FAO Schwarz* toy store. The eclectic collection of shops along Georgetown's streets includes *Hats in the Belfry* (1237 Wisconsin Ave. NW), the Irish shop *Threepenny Bit* (3122 M St. NW), and *Orpheus Records* (3249 M St. NW;), which specializes in obscure recordings. A few blocks north on Wisconsin Avenue are four intriguing shops: the *Phoenix* (Mexican jewelry, crafts, and clothing; 1514 Wisconsin), *Santa Fe Style* (crafts and art from the American Southwest; 1525 Wisconsin), *Little Caledonia* (unusual furnishings, fabrics, and stationery; 1419 Wisconsin), and *Appalachian Spring* (handmade crafts, quilts, and jewelry from all over the US; 1415 Wisconsin).

K Street/Business District – A few blocks to the northwest of downtown, the business district has blossomed with malls and shops. *International Square* (1850 K St. NW), set in a 12-story atrium with a cascading fountain, is filled with restaurants, fast-food eateries, and 30 retail shops. Just a few blocks away (at Connecticut Ave. and L St. NW), atop the Farragut North metro station, is the *Connecticut Connection*, a 3-story shopping and dining emporium. At the intersection of Connecticut Avenue and K Street north is an array of famous-name stores, ranging from Washington's own *Raleigh's* department store to *Burberrys Ltd.*

Museums – The *Smithsonian* museums are a good place to start looking for one-of-a-kind gifts, though nearly every monument, shrine, and church in Washington offers such a shop. The shop at the *National Museum of Natural History* (at 14th St. and Constitution Ave. NW) has everything from a reproduction of the Hope Diamond to First Lady dolls. The *Arts and Industries Building* (Jefferson Dr. and Independence Ave. at 9th St. NW) stocks items shown in the *Smithsonian* mail-order gift catalogue. Other finds and their respective museums include: NASA flight jackets, US rocket model kits, and astronaut freeze-dried dinners (*National Air and Space Museum*); contemporary jewelry (*Hirshhorn*); and busts of past presidents (*National Portrait Gallery*). *Dumbarton Oaks*'s (R and 23rd St. NW) private collection of Byzantine and pre-Columbian jewelry is reproduced for sale. The National Cathedral (Massachusetts and Wisconsin NW) has an extensive gift shop, and the National Geographic Society (17th and M Sts. NW) offers some of the best bargains around in atlases and maps.

The Pavilion – The *Old Post Office Pavilion* building at the Nancy Hanks Center, the city's oldest Federal building, was dedicated in 1899. Built in the fanciful Romanesque style with a bell tower and skylight, its restoration was begun in 1977 by Arthur Cooton Moore. Besides government offices, the *Pavilion* now contains shops, cafés, and restaurants on the lower floors. Its specialty shops include *Caswell & Massey*, *The Fudgery*, *Post Office Exchange* (T-shirts), and *Paper on Parade*. A performing arts stage offers free daily entertainment. Restaurants include *Blossoms* (raw bar) and *Fitch, Fox and Brown* (continental). 12th St. and Pennsylvania Ave. NW.

2000 Pennsylvania Avenue – A shopping area on the edge of the George Washington University campus. Incorporating townhouses and other buildings, it features a variety of specialty shops and *Cone E. Island* ice cream parlor. Between 20th and 21st Sts. NW.

Union Station – Washington's grand old rail terminal has been restored (see *Special Places*) and now features scores of shops, restaurants, and fast-food outlets. The 3-level complex houses such nationally known clothing and specialty shops as *Ann Taylor*, *Brookstone*, *Tannery West*, and *The Nature Company*. *Seasons Café* offers leisurely dining at relatively moderate prices and *Adirondacks* provides pricey fare in the lavishly appointed Presidential Suite, off the Main Hall. 50 Massachusetts Ave. NE (phone: 371-9441).

Washington Harbour – This expansive office/retail/residential complex on the Potomac River features unique architectural designs, with fountain-filled courtyards and specialty shops and restaurants. Visitors have access via a waterfront promenade which starts at Thompson's Boathouse and leads along the river to a park at the end of Wisconsin Ave. 3000 K St. (under the Whitehurst Freeway in Georgetown).

 MAJOR COLLEGES AND UNIVERSITIES: Washington has several universities of high national standing — American University (Massachusetts and Nebraska Aves. NW; phone: 885-1000); Gallaudet University — for the deaf (7th St. and Florida Ave. NE; phone: 651-5000); Georgetown University (37th and O Sts. NW; phone: 625-0100); George Washington University (19th to 24th Sts. NW, F St. to Pennsylvania Ave.; phone: 994-1000); and Howard University (2000 6th St. NW; phone: 636-6100).

 SPORTS AND FITNESS: Basketball – The NBA's *Bullets* hold court from October to April at the *Capital Centre* (Capital Beltway and Central Ave., in Landover, Md.; phone: 301-350-3400). Tickets are available at *Ticketron* outlets.

Bicycling – Rent from *Metropolis Bike & Scooter* (709 8th St. SE; phone: 543-8900). The towpath of the Chesapeake and Ohio Canal, starting at the barge landing in Georgetown, is a good place to ride.

Fitness Center – *Office Health Center* has separate exercise classes and whirlpool baths for men and women; its assistants all have master's degrees in health education or related fields; 1990 M St. and 20th, off Connecticut (phone: 872-0222).

Football – The NFL's *Redskins* play at *Robert F. Kennedy Stadium* from September to December. Tickets during the season are hard to come by and there usually is a waiting list for pre-season tickets, but if you're in town during late July or August for pre-season games, chances are much better. Try the *TicketCenter* (phone: 301-481-6000), or the stadium box office (E. Capitol and 22nd Sts. SE; phone: 547-9077).

Golf – The best public golf course is the *East Potomac Park* golf course. In East Potomac Park off Ohio Dr. (phone: 863-9007).

Hockey – The *Capitals,* Washington's pro hockey team, play at *Capital Centre* from October to April. Tickets are available at *TicketCenter* outlets or by calling 301-350-3400.

Jogging – Join plenty of others in making a round trip from the Lincoln Memorial to the Capitol (4 miles); also run in Rock Creek Park and in Georgetown, along the C&O Canal.

Skating – From November to April you can skate on the rink on the mall between 7th and 9th Sts. NW (phone: 371-5343).

Swimming – Year-round facilities are available at the *East Capitol Natatorium,* 635 North Carolina Ave. SE (phone: 724-4495).

Tennis – Washington has some fine public courts; the best bets are the District tennis facilities at 16th and Kennedy Sts. NW (phone: 722-5949).

 THEATER: The *Kennedy Center for the Performing Arts* (opened in 1971) gives the District its cultural cachet (it's off Virginia Ave. NW; phone: 467-4600). The center's *Eisenhower Theater* offers musical and dramatic productions, including Broadway previews and road shows (phone: 967-4600). The *Terrace Theater,* on the top floor, offers many different productions — modern dance, ballet, dramas, poetry recitals, and so on (phone: 254-9895). The *National Theater* presents major productions throughout the year (1321 Pennsylvania Ave. NW; phone: 628-6161). The *Arena Stage* and the *Kreeger Theater* host classical and original plays year-round (6th St. and Maine Ave. SW; phone: 488-3300), and the *Ford's Theatre* offers American productions (511 10th St. NW; phone: 347-4833). The *Folger Theatre Group* offers innovative interpretations of Shakespeare's plays as well as more contemporary works at the Folger Library's classical theater (201 E. Capitol St. SE; phone: 544-7077). Washington also has what one theater critic calls the "Off-off Kennedy Center movement" — a network of small avant-garde houses on or near the stretch of 14th Street NW above Thomas Circle: *Studio Theater* (1333 P St. NW; phone: 332-3300); *Woolly Mammoth Theater Company* (phone: 543-6211) and *Horizons Theater* (phone: 342-5503), which have separate stages at the same address (1401 Church St. NW); and *Source Theater* (1835 14th St. NW; phone: 462-1073). During the summer the *Olney Theater,* about a half-hour drive from the District, offers summer stock and well-known casts (Rte. 108, Olney, Md.; phone: 301-924-3400); and the *Wolf Trap Farm Park for the Performing Arts* presents musicals, ballet, pop concerts, and symphonic music in a lovely outdoor setting (bring a picnic; Rte. 7 near Vienna, Virginia, accessible via Dulles Airport toll road Rte. 267 and by subway to West Falls Church; phone: 703-255-1860). In winter, the *Barns at Wolftrap,* a 350-seat theater, holds performances indoors (phone: 703-938-2404). Unsold theater and concert tickets are available on the day of the performance at half price from the *TICKETplace* stand (in F Street Plaza, 12th and F Sts. NW; phone: 842-5387).

MUSIC: The *National Symphony Orchestra,* conducted by Mstislav Rostropovich, performs at the *Kennedy Center Concert Hall* from September through June (phone: 467-4600). The *Opera Society of Washington* (phone: 857-0900) presents four operas a year at the *Kennedy Center Opera House.* The *Juilliard String Quartet* and other notable ensembles perform chamber music concerts on Stradivarius instruments at the *Library of Congress Auditorium* (1st St. between E. Capitol St. and Independence Ave. SE, Thursday and Friday evenings in the spring and fall; for tickets, call 707-5502). During the summer there's music under the stars at *Wolf Trap Farm Park* (phone: 703-255-1860) and free concerts by the service bands on the plaza at the West Front of the Capitol or in front of the Jefferson Memorial. Consult newspapers for where and when. *Army and Navy Band* concerts are presented at different locations in the winter. For information on *Army Band* concerts call 703-696-3399; for *Navy Band* concerts, 433-2394.

NIGHTCLUBS AND NIGHTLIFE: For some, Washington is an early-to-bed town, but there's plenty of pub crawling, jazz, bluegrass, soul, rock, and folk music going on after dark. You just have to know where to look for it, and best bets are Georgetown, lower Connecticut Avenue, and the Capitol Hill areas. Current favorites: *F. Scott's,* one of the classiest bars in town (1232 36th St. NW; phone: 342-0009, evenings); *Blues Alley,* for mainstream jazz and Dixieland (1073 Wisconsin Ave. NW; phone: 337-4141); *Jenkins Hill,* for the District's longest bar, where everyone from public servants to students slake their thirst (223 Pennsylvania Ave. SE; phone: 544-6600); the *Dubliner Restaurant and Pub,* with old Irish and Celtic tunes and jigs (520 N. Capitol St. NW; phone: 737-3773); and *Cities,* a watering hole-cum-restaurant-cum-nightclub in what once was a 3-story auto dealership (2424 18th St. NW; phone: 328-7194). *Cities* is located in the heart of Washington's newest nightlife scene — Adams Morgan, a funky melange of bars, dance clubs, ethnic restaurants, and shops radiating from the intersection of Columbia Road and 18th Streets NW. In recent years Adams Morgan has come to rival Georgetown as "the" place to see and be seen after dark in the capital.

BEST IN TOWN

CHECKING IN: Washington currently enjoys a wealth of quality hotel establishments because of a building boom in the late 1980s. Still, accommodations at the best stopping places can dwindle fast, so reservations should be made in advance. Visitors in town for only a few days should stay downtown to make the best use of their limited time; weekends offer the best package deals. Inexpensive taxis, the *Metro* system, and buses facilitate getting around without a car, which is difficult and expensive to park. However, if you have a car, major motel chains have facilities at all principal entry points to the district — Silver Spring and Bethesda in Maryland; Arlington, Rosslyn, and Alexandria in Virginia. Expect to pay $125 and up (sometimes way up) for a double room in the expensive range, $75 to $100 in the moderate range, and $40 to $70 in the inexpensive category. For information about bed and breakfast accommodations, contact *The Bed and Breakfast League/Sweet Dreams & Toast* (PO Box 9490, Washington, DC 20016; phone: 363-7767). *Washington, DC, Accommodations* provides assistance with hotel reservations according to visitors' needs. This free service is available by calling 800-554-2220. All telephone numbers are in the 202 area code unless otherwise indicated. All accommodations receive CNN except where noted.

Canterbury – Near the downtown business district and not far from the White House, this small place has 99 suites with a stocked bar in each. Amenities include a complimentary continental breakfast, underground parking, nightly turndown service with a Godiva chocolate placed on your pillow, and *Chaucer's* restaurant. Lower weekend package rates are available. Room service is available until 10 PM. There's a helpful concierge desk, and business amenities include 6 meeting rooms, secretarial services, A/V eqiupment, photocopiers, and computers. 1733 N St. NW (phone: 393-3000; Fax: 202-785-9581). Expensive.

Four Seasons – On the edge of Georgetown, it looks a lot like a penitentiary from the outside, but the interior is bright and beautiful, and the appeal of its rooms has got visitors returning whenever possible. The *Aux Beaux Champs* restaurant also deserves high praise (see *Eating Out*). A traditional concierge offers many personal services including mail delivery. Around-the-clock room service is available as are 6 meeting rooms, secretarial services, A/V equipment, photocopiers, and computers. Express checkout. 2800 Pennsylvania Ave. NW (phone: 342-0444; Fax: 202-944-2076). Expensive.

Georgetown Inn – In the middle of one of Washington's most historic areas, this handsome brick building is unusually classy for a motor inn. All 95 rooms are well appointed with large beds and bathroom phones. Free parking. Room service can be ordered until 8 PM. 1310 Wisconsin Ave. NW (phone: 333-8900; Fax: 202-337-6317). Expensive.

Grand – A distinctive copper dome wedged between walls of brick and granite marks this West End hostelry. In architecture and ambience, it is reminiscent of a small European hotel: a white marble staircase cascades through the lobby, the inner courtyard is meticulously landscaped, and all 262 rooms feature Italian marble baths, 3 phones, remote-control TV sets, and working fireplaces in some suites. The elegant *Mayfair* serves *cuisine courante,* a step beyond nouvelle, with a menu that changes daily; the *Promenade Lounge* features lunch, brunch, and high tea in a more informal atmosphere. Besides a multilingual concierge and currency conversion service, there is 24-hour room service, valet and dry cleaning, valet parking, and Godiva chocolates accompanying the nightly turndown service. Other pluses include 10 meeting rooms, secretarial services, A/V equipment, photocopiers, computers, and concierge services. 2350 M St. NW (phone: 429-0100 or 800-848-0016; Fax: 202-429-9757). Expensive.

Hay-Adams – At an incomparable location just off Lafayette Square, within a silver dollar's throw of the White House. This 143-room hotel retains its Old World dignity and maintains the standards of the neighborhood with antique furnishings, a paneled lobby, a fine dining room (see *Eating Out*), cocktail lounge, and good service. Room service is available 24 hours a day. There's also a concierge desk, 5 meeting rooms, A/V equipment, photocopiers, and computers. 16th and H Sts. NW (phone: 638-6600; Fax: 202-638-2716). Expensive.

Jefferson – A clubby place and a favorite of the Bush family. Located near the White House and the shops on Connecticut Avenue, it has a low-key, traditional atmosphere and outstanding service. The *Jefferson* restaurant is a series of cozy alcoves, and the 68 rooms and 32 suites also offer intimacy. Jazz on Saturday and Sunday nights. There are 3 meeting rooms, concierge and secretarial services, A/V equipment, photocopiers, and computers. Twenty-four–hour room service and express checkout round out the amenities. 16th and M Sts. NW (phone: 347-2200; Fax: 202-223-9039). Expensive.

J.W. Marriott – A significant step above other members of this chain. Connected to a mall complex of 160 stores and the *National Theater*, it has 773 rooms, a pool, and a health spa. The Marquis floors (14 and 15) are especially nice. Room service is available around the clock. Among the business services are concierge and secretarial assistance, 15 meeting rooms, A/V equipment, photocopiers, computers, and express checkout. 1331 Pennsylvania Ave. NW (phone: 393-2000; Fax: 202-626-6991). Expensive.

Loews L'Enfant Plaza – This imposing, modernistic structure is one of Washington's best, occupying the top floors of an office complex. A huge fountain cascades on the plaza; below there is a large shopping mall with chic boutiques and a *Metro* station, and on the 12th story there's an outdoor swimming pool. The service is high quality, the location conveniently near the Mall. There are 372 rooms, 2 restaurants, and a cocktail lounge. Equally advantageous is an obliging concierge, secretarial services, 24-hour room service, A/V equipment, photocopiers, computers, 4 meeting rooms, and express checkout. 480 L'Enfant Plaza SW (phone: 484-1000; Fax: 202-646-4456). Expensive.

Madison – With 374 luxurious rooms, excellent service by a well-trained staff, amid gracious Federal decor; extras including interpreters, refrigerators, saunas, and bathroom phones. The *Montpelier Room* is quite a good restaurant. Open for buffet on weekdays and Sunday brunch. There are also 2 more informal restaurants and a cocktail lounge. In addition to 24-hour room service, there also are concierge and secretarial services available, as well as 15 meeting rooms, A/V equipment, photocopiers, computers, and express checkout. 15th and M Sts. NW (phone: 862-1600; Fax: 202-785-1255). Expensive.

Mayflower – Four blocks from the White House, this 724-room hotel hosted Calvin Coolidge's inaugural ball (it's undergone a very satisfying face-lift since then). The lobby and public areas are light, airy, and filled with flowers. Two excellent restaurants: the elegant *Nicholas* specializes in nouvelle cuisine with a wide variety of seafood, and the less formal *Café Promenade* has a buffet lunch and scrumptious desserts. The cocktail lounge also serves a light lunch. Room service is available 24 hours. There are both secretarial and concierge services, 20 meeting rooms, and A/V equipment, photocopiers, and computers to cater to guests' business needs. 1127 Connecticut Ave. NW (phone: 347-3000; Fax: 202-466-9082). Expensive.

Ramada Renaissance – Part of "Techworld," a recently built 2.5-million-square-foot multi-purpose complex across the street from the *Washington Convention Center*, its 801 rooms and 61 suites are decorated in a sophisticated contemporary style. The property also has a restaurant, swimming pool, and on-site parking. Twenty-four–hour room service, along with 19 meeting rooms, concierge and secretarial services, A/V equipment, photocopiers, and computers can be found here. 999 9th St. NW (phone: 898-9000; Fax: 202-289-0947). Expensive.

Ritz-Carlton – Restored to an elegance beyond even its original standard. This is as close to an evocation of a classic European hostelry as exists in Washington. There are 241 rooms, the *Jockey Club* restaurant (see *Eating Out*), the *Fairfax Bar,* as well as a ballroom and 7 meeting rooms. Standard business amenities, such as 24-hour room service, concierge and secretarial assistance, 7 meeting rooms, A/V equipment, photocopiers, and computers, are available. Express checkout. 2100 Massachusetts Ave. NW (phone: 293-2100 or 800-241-3333; Fax: 202-293-0641). Expensive.

Sheraton Carlton – Host to many presidents and dignitaries. Truman used to hold his affairs of state here while the White House was being redone, and Jimmy Carter announced his intention to run here. The hotel's Italian Renaissance lobby is elegant, the 215 rooms comfortable, and the bar good enough to win approval from Jimmy Breslin. There are 2 excellent dining rooms (Sunday brunch is terrific), and a cocktail lounge. Business services include secretarial and concierge assistance, 7 meeting rooms, A/V equipment, photocopiers, and computers. There's also 24-hour room service. 923 16th St. NW (phone: 638-2626; Fax: 202-638-4321). Expensive.

Vista International – François Mitterrand and Elizabeth Taylor are among those who have stayed at this 413-room hostelry, only 6 blocks from the White House. Its six 1-bedroom suites, designed by Givenchy, sport full-length mirrors, large private balconies, bathrooms in opalescent tile with Jacuzzis, and are completely separate from the rest of the hotel — sharing no walls with any other rooms (cost: $575 a night). Favorite recipes of past presidents are on the menu at the *American Harvest* restaurant; cardiovascular fitness gear is available at the health club. Secretarial and concierge assistance are available, and A/V equipment, photocopiers, and computers are on call for guests. Other pluses include 10 meeting rooms, 24-hour room service, and express checkout. 1400 M St. (phone: 429-1700 or 800-223-1146; Fax: 202-785-0786). Expensive.

Washington Court – A 268-room luxury property with a 4-story atrium; moderately priced restaurant, the *Café;* picturesque views; complimentary limousine service; and other amenities, such as TV sets and phones in both bedroom and bath, and exercise equipment delivered to rooms on request. There's also 24-hour room service, a concierge desk, secretarial services, A/V equipment, photocopiers, computers, and 15 meeting rooms. Two blocks from the Capitol, 525 New Jersey Ave. (phone: 628-2100; Fax: 202-879-7918). Expensive.

Watergate – Though this modern hotel-apartment-office complex doesn't look too historic, appearances can be deceiving (as can small pieces of tape). With 238 large contemporarily furnished rooms, indoor swimming pool and health club, the excellent *Watergate* restaurant (see *Eating Out*), cocktail lounge, *Les Champs* shopping mall with even more dining possibilities, and a location adjacent to the *Kennedy Center.* There's a concierge desk and 24-hour room service, and business amenities include secretarial services, A/V equipment, photocopiers, and computers. 2650 Virginia Ave. NW (phone: 965-2300; Fax: 202-337-7915). Expensive.

Westin – This link in the Westin chain is as elegant inside as it is outside. In addition to its lovely interior garden and 416 luxuriously appointed rooms — they even have bathroom speakers for the cable TV and 3 phones — there is a fine restaurant, the *Colonnade,* for formal dining, a more casual brasserie, and a lobby lounge in a glass loggia just off the garden. As if all this were not enough, there is a professionally staffed fitness center, complete with pool, Jacuzzi, sauna, squash courts, aerobics room, weights, and state-of-the-art exercise equipment, plus a beauty salon and juice bar. Children under 18 free. There are 14 meeting rooms, plus A/V equipment, photocopiers, computers, and secretarial services. Room service arrives around the clock, a concierge desk and express checkout. 24th and M Sts. NW (phone: 429-2400 or 800-228-3000; Fax: 202-457-5010). Expensive.

Willard Inter-Continental – Nine presidents-elect stayed at this Beaux Arts landmark while awaiting completion of the White House, and Charles Dickens and Julia Ward Howe were regulars, too. But the "crown jewel" of Pennsylvania Avenue fell into disrepair (and was almost razed during the late 1960s). Managed by Inter-Continental (and the recipient of a $70-million renovation and modernization of all public spaces and 394 rooms), it has been restored to its turn-of-the-century grandeur. Facilities include a mini-bar, direct-dial telephone, and hair dryer in all rooms. The hotel dining room, the *Williard Room*, is one of DC's most elegant eateries. *Café Expresso* is available for casual dining. Additional amenities include 24-hour room service, both concierge and secretarial services, 20 meeting rooms, A/V equipment, photocopiers, computers, and express checkout. Children under 16 free. Corner Pennsylvania Ave. and 14th St. NW (phone: 628-9100; Fax: 202-637-7326). Expensive.

Wyndham-Bristol – It's all suites — 240 of them. There's also the *Bristol Grill* restaurant, as well as the *Metro Café* for snacks and sandwiches. Cordials and chocolates that appear in the suites at night are among the appealing touches. Room service is available until midnight. There are 3 meeting rooms, a concierge desk, and express checkout. 2430 Pennsylvania Ave. NW (phone: 955-6400; Fax: 202-955-5765). Expensive.

Georgetown Dutch Inn – Near the C&O Canal and within a block of the best restaurants and shopping that Georgetown has to offer, this small inn has 47 housekeeping units. CNN is not available here. 1075 Thomas Jefferson St. NW (phone: 337-0900). Moderate.

Morrison-Clark Inn – Recently listed as one of the 10 best new inns by *Inn Review*, it served as the hostel for the *Soldiers, Sailors, Marines, and Airmen Club* from 1923 to 1984. A new addition added to the two historic buildings comprises 41 of the 54 tastefully decorated rooms. There also is an excellent restaurant. Room service can be ordered until 11 PM, and there's complimentary breakfast. A concierge desk, 3 meeting rooms, secretarial services, A/V equipment, photocopiers, and computers also are available. Located 1 block from the *Convention Center* and 4 blocks from *Metro Center* (*Metrorail* stop) at Massachusetts Ave. and 11th St. NW (phone: 800-332-7898; Fax: 202-289-8576). Moderate.

Tabard Inn – On a charming semi-residential street near the heart of the business district. Guests enjoy an ambience rare in an American city; there is a library and small dining room on the first floor. The rooms are furnished with antiques and some of them share baths. CNN is not available here, and room service is available for breakfast only. 1739 N St. NW (phone: 785-1277; Fax: 202-785-6173). Moderate.

Washington – One of the city's older properties offering an incomparable view from its rooftop restaurant. Always comfortable, but great during an inaugural parade. The 370 rooms feature TV sets and bathroom phones; nearby downtown shopping. Room service arrives until 10 PM. 15th St. and Pennsylvania Ave. NW (phone: 638-5900; Fax: 202-628-4275). Moderate.

Kalorama Guest House – Bed and breakfast (and complimentary afternoon sherry) in 6 comfortable turn-of-the-century row houses (in two different locations) decked out with antique furnishings. CNN is not available here. Four units in Kalorama, 1854 Mintwood Place NW (phone: 667-6369), and two units at Woodley Park near the National Zoo, 2700 Cathedral Ave. NW (phone: 328-0860). Moderate to inexpensive.

Windsor Inn – Small and unpretentious, in the trendy Adams Morgan district. A magnet for relocating embassy employees as well as government workers who prefer a modest, homey atmosphere. All 40 rooms have color TV sets and air conditioning; the staff is personable and attentive. Continental breakfast comes with a newspaper; and for a European touch, afternoon sherry is served. 1842 16th St. NW (phone: 667-0300 or 800-423-9111). Moderate to inexpensive.

Allen Lee – In the heart of the George Washington University campus near the downtown area. Most of the rooms don't have private baths, and you can't always count on hot water, but it's a popular spot with young people. CNN is not available here. 2224 F St. NW (phone: 331-1224). Inexpensive.

Harrington – A 310-room, older establishment in the center of Washington's commercial area, it has seen better days but provides clean accommodations and is within walking distance of the Mall. Popular with high school and family groups, who are drawn because the *Kitcheteria* makes feeding the troops easy and inexpensive. No CNN. 11th and E Sts. NW (phone: 628-8140). Inexpensive.

Rock Creek – This small, 54-room hotel is a well-kept secret. Not too far from downtown, adjacent to Rock Creek Park, it offers quiet lodging with few amenities. CNN is not available here. 1925 Belmont Rd. NW (phone: 462-6007). Inexpensive.

Windsor Park – Modest, but this 40-room property is within walking distance of the subway and near the French Embassy. Convenient and basic. 2116 Kalorama Rd., NW (phone: 483-7700). Inexpensive.

EATING OUT: Considering the international aspects of Washington — 2,000 diplomats and a large number of residents who have lived abroad and brought back a taste for foreign fare — it's not too surprising that the District can provide an international gastronomic tour de force. What is surprising is that this wasn't the case until just a few years back. The greatest local meals even 2 decades ago were served in private homes or in embassies (Jefferson was known to treat his guests to such delicacies as ice cream and imported French wines). The change began when the Kennedys brought a French chef to the White House, and this awakened a broad interest in food and spawned a restaurant boom that hasn't stopped yet. Though it's always helpful to have an ermine-lined wallet or, better yet, a generous expense account, those who have only the yen for good food needn't go hungry. Our restaurant selections range in price from $100 or more for a dinner for two in the very expensive restaurants to between $75 and $90 in expensive places, $40 to $60 in the moderate ones, and $35 and under in the inexpensive bracket. Prices do not include drinks, wine, or tips. Reservations are a must at the top-flight restaurants. All telephone numbers are in the 202 area code unless otherwise indicated.

Aux Beaux Champs – This handsome dining room in the *Four Seasons* hotel is distinguished by a highly creative menu that changes daily, stylish service, and a very cosmopolitan clientele. Open daily. Reservations advised. Major credit cards accepted. 2800 Pennsylvania Ave. NW (phone: 342-0444). Very expensive.

Galileo – A revitalized menu has proved invaluable in this dining establishment's major comeback. The grilled *porcini* mushrooms are a must, as is the pigeon with balsamic vinegar. The highlight among the pasta dishes is the exquisite ravioli. Open daily. Reservations necessary. Major credit cards accepted. 2014 P. St. (phone: 293-7191). Very expensive.

Jean-Louis – Named for its chef, this is a small (only 14 tables) and elegant restaurant with gracious service and fine nouvelle cuisine. Fixed price dinners. Closed Sundays. Reservations necessary. Major credit cards accepted. In the *Watergate Hotel,* 2650 Virginia Ave. NW (phone: 298-4488). Very expensive.

Le Lion d'Or – Reputed to have the finest French food in town, although some say that the service isn't up to par. Don't leave without tasting one of the spectacular desserts. Open Saturdays for dinner only; closed Sundays. Reservations necessary. Major credit cards accepted. 1150 Connecticut Ave. NW (phone: 296-7972). Very expensive.

Le Pavillon – Though this place may have the highest prices in town, French chef Yannick Cam offers nouvelle cuisine to those who know and appreciate the best. Closed Sundays. Reservations necessary. Major credit cards accepted. 1050 Connecticut Ave. NW (phone: 833-3846). Very expensive.

Cantina d'Italia – Still the longest running hit among Italian restaurants (Northern Italian cuisine), the changing menu offers new culinary delights but retains the old showstoppers like *fettuccine con salsa di noci* (homemade noodles with puréed walnuts, pine nuts, ricotta and parmesan cheese). The only drawback is the small and somewhat confining basement location. Closed Sundays. Reservations necessary. Major credit cards accepted. 1214A 18th St. NW (phone: 659-1830). Expensive.

Dominique's – Elegant French food, a lively and friendly atmosphere, and such exotic items as wild boar, rattlesnake, and buffalo. For a great bargain, try the pre- and post-theater prix fixe menu. Closed Sundays. Reservations necessary. Major credit cards accepted. 1900 Pennsylvania Ave. NW (phone: 452-1126). Expensive.

Jockey Club – This *Ritz-Carlton* restaurant is a favorite meeting and eating spot for local movers and shakers. The decor looks more like New York's *"21"* than the original (it once was managed by them). Open daily. Reservations necessary. Major credit cards accepted. 2100 Massachusetts Ave. NW (phone: 659-8000). Expensive.

Maison Blanche – The "in" spot during the Reagan years, where Washington's famous and powerful met amid an elegant Parisian dining room decor. Classical French dishes are served, but there are touches of "nouvelle" as well. An extensive list of lunch and dinner specials is offered daily. Closed Sundays. Reservations necessary. Major credit cards accepted. 1725 F St. NW (phone: 842-0070). Expensive.

Morton's of Chicago – One of the best places in Washington to get steaks with all the trimmings. Dinner only; closed Sundays. Reservations advised. Major credit cards accepted. 3251 Prospect St. NW (phone: 342-6258). Expensive.

I Ricchi – One of the city's hottest new eateries, Chef Francesco Ricchi concocts fabulous Florentine fare such as broad noodles tossed with hare sauce, leg of rabbit with rosemary, and quail stuffed with homemade sausage. This trattoria has a warm, clubby feeling. Open daily. Reservations necessary. Major credit cards accepted. 1220 19th St. (phone: 835-1059). Expensive.

Adams Room – There's not a better place to start the day than this beautiful room with views of the White House and Lafayette Square. Breakfast choices range from croissants and fresh berries to pecan waffles or corned beef and eggs. Open daily for breakfast and lunch. Reservations necessary. Major credit cards accepted. *Hay-Adams Hotel,* 16th and H Sts. NW (phone: 638-6600). Moderate.

American Café – A DC institution, popular for informal but imaginatively prepared meals of grilled fish, sandwiches, salads, and soup. There also are some luscious desserts and homemade breads. Open daily. Reservations unnecessary. Major credit cards accepted. Three of the establishment's eight locations: 1211 Wisconsin Ave. NW, Georgetown (phone: 944-9464); on Capitol Hill at 227 Massachusetts Ave. NE (phone: 547-8500); and National Pl., 1331 Pennsylvania Ave. NW (phone: 626-0770). Moderate.

Austin Grill – Tex-Mex food is the star here, along with the largest margaritas east of the Mississippi. Smoked duck quesadillas and the grilled pork chops baked with Mexican hot peppers are just two of the unbelievably good choices. Open daily. Reservations unnecessary. Major credit cards accepted. 2404 Wisconsin Ave. (phone: 337-8080). Moderate.

Bombay Club – This local Indian hangout has unusual specialties such as spiced lobster seasoned with mild curries, lamb entrées, and home-made chutneys. Closed for lunch both Saturdays and Sundays. Reservations unnecessary. Major credit cards accepted. 815 Conn. Ave. (phone: 659-3727). Moderate.

Clyde's – Frequented by Georgetown students and local preppy types, it serves omelettes, pasta, and steaks, but is known mostly for its terrific bacon cheeseburgers and its weekend brunch. There's also Guinness stout on tap that's served at just the right temperature. Open daily. Reservations advised, although none are taken for weekend brunch. Major credit cards accepted. 3236 M St. NW (phone: 333-9180). Moderate.

La Colline – Charming and reasonably priced, it serves adventurous French food and daily specials as well as wonderful desserts. Open daily. Reservations advised. Major credit cards accepted. 400 N. Capitol St. (phone: 737-0400). Moderate.

Germaine's – Varied Oriental menu — including Japanese, Korean, Vietnamese, and Indonesian foods. Specialties are lemon chicken and squirrel fish. Open daily. Reservations advised. Major credit cards accepted. 2400 Wisconsin Ave. NW (phone: 965-1185). Moderate.

Harvey's – A fixture in Washington since 1858, it's reputation for fine seafood is well deserved. Try the crab imperial, lobster and shrimp Norfolk, or the shad roe in season. Closed Sundays in July and August. Reservations advised. Major credit cards accepted. 1001 18th St. NW (phone: 833-1858). Moderate.

Hogs on the Hill – As the less-than-delicate name implies, the decor amounts to raw wood walls that are a porcine extravaganza; signs, posters, drawings, and other paraphernalia pay homage to the pig in all its splendor. The food, however, is sublime. Greens, red beans and rice, and French fries accompany barbecued ribs bathed in tangy sauce. There's also a take-out counter around the corner. Open daily. Reservations unnecessary. Major credit cards accepted. 732 Maryland Ave. NE (phone: 547-5443). Moderate.

Lafitte – Classic French and authentic creole specialties are served in an atmosphere reminiscent of 18th-century New Orleans. The chocolate raspberry torte is a must. Brunch only on Sundays. Reservations advised. Major credit cards accepted. 1310 New Hampshire Ave. NW (phone: 466-7978). Moderate.

Marrakesh – Minutes from Capitol Hill in a cumin-colored cube of a building, this spacious Near Eastern eatery has excellent traditional food accompanied by belly dancing. Open daily. Reservations advised. No credit cards accepted. 617 New York Ave. NW (phone: 393-9393). Moderate.

I Matti – *Galileo* owner Roberto Donna recently opened this popular eatery in the Adams Morgan section of town, offering both Northern Italian dishes and Italian nouvelle cuisine. Aromatic stews, pizza with paper-thin crusts, and meltingly wonderful ricotta cheesecake. Open daily. Reservations necessary. Major credit cards accepted. 2436 18th St. NW (phone: 462-8844). Moderate.

McPherson Grill – Contemporary American place featuring grilled seafood, meat, and poultry. Sandwiches, soup, and salads, as well as a variety of appetizers, are served at lunch. (Its sister restaurant, the *Occidental Grill,* is located at 1475 Pennsylvania Ave. NW; phone: 783-1475.) Closed Sundays. Reservations advised and major credit cards accepted at both places. 950 15th St. NW (phone: 638-0950). Moderate.

Old Ebbitt Grill – An old-timer in an elegant Victorian setting. Tasty appetizers lead off a menu ranging from hamburgers to filet mignon. Try the hot fudge sundae for dessert. Open daily. Reservations advised. Major credit cards accepted. 675 15th St. NW (phone: 347-4801). Moderate.

Old Europe – Features the best German wine list in the District with some French and American labels; standard German dishes as well. Open daily. Reservations advised. Major credit cards accepted. 2434 Wisconsin Ave. NW (phone: 333-7600). Moderate.

Suzanne's – Eponymous owner and chef Suzanne calls this tiny bistro occupying the second floor of a turn-of-the-century townhouse a "casual, friendly joint." There's nothing casual about the food, though, which is American contemporary (chicken salad with poblano chilies and salsa or stuffed veal *en papillote*) are excellent. Don't miss the desserts. Closed Sundays. Reservations advised. Only Visa and MasterCard accepted. 1735 Connecticut Ave. NW (phone: 483-4633). Moderate.

Tabard Inn – The nouvelle-influenced menu at this charmingly quirky inn is strong on fresh seafood such as grilled tuna and swordfish. Sunday brunch is a popular affair and a good excuse to try the terrific Bloody Marys. Open daily. Reservations advised. Only Visa and MasterCard accepted. 1739 N St. NW (phone: 785-1277). Moderate.

Au Pied de Cochon – An informal place for a good meal at a decent price 24 hours a day. If *pieds de cochon* (pigs' feet) aren't your style, try asparagus vinaigrette, coq au vin, and other bistro specialties. No reservations. Open daily. Major credit cards accepted. 1335 Wisconsin Ave. NW (phone: 333-5440). Moderate to inexpensive.

City Café – A warm, upbeat spot not far from Washington Circle in the West End with a blend of light and nouvelle dining. Individual pizza topped with sun-dried tomato, onion, and goat cheese, or chicken, tomato, and mozzarella are especially gratifying. Interesting soup, stir-fried scallops with vegetables, and hearty hamburgers are other worthy offerings. Open daily. Reservations advised. No credit cards accepted. 2213 M St. NW (phone: 797-4860). Inexpensive.

House of Hunan – Among the finest Oriental spots in the city. Unusual appetizers include shrimp balls and vegetable curls, and special main dishes are crisp whole fish Hunan-style, and honeyed ham. Open daily. Reservations necessary for dinner. Major credit cards accepted. 1900 K St. NW (phone: 293-9111). Inexpensive.

Iron Gate Inn – A former stable now dedicated to Middle Eastern food: shish kebab, couscous, and stuffed grape leaves. Speaking of which, there's a charming little grape arbor over the outdoor dining area where you can be served in warm weather. Open daily. Reservations advised. Major credit cards accepted. 1734 N St. NW (phone: 737-1370). Inexpensive.

Meskerem – The best of the Ethiopian eateries that line the Adams Morgan section of town. The dining room in front has conventional tables and chairs; in back there are woven straw tables called *mesobs*. Entrées arrive on huge plates of spongy Ethiopian bread, which is then torn off and used in lieu of utensils to scoop up the lamb, chicken, or vegetarian concoctions. Open daily. Reservations advised. Major credit cards accepted. 2434 18th St. (phone: 462-4100). Inexpensive.

Roma – Solid Italian family-style place, best in warm weather when the large outdoor garden is open and musicians and singers add to the relaxed ambience. All the old favorites are here from pizza to pasta. Open daily. Reservations advised. Major credit cards accepted. 3419 Connecticut Ave. NW (phone: 363-6611). Inexpensive.

Vietnam Georgetown – Small and intimate, this simple place serves the best Vietnamese food in town. Specialties include deep-fried crispy rolls, shrimp with sugarcane, and beef in grape leaves. Open daily.

Reservations unnecessary. No credit cards accepted. 2934 M St. NW (phone: 337-4536). Inexpensive.

For the sweet of tooth, Washington has a homegrown ice cream empire founded by renegade attorney Bob Weiss. *Bob's Famous Ice Cream* has stores on Capitol Hill (236 Massachusetts Ave. NE; phone: 546-3860), near the Cleveland Park *Metro* station (3510 Connecticut Ave. NW; phone: 244-4465), and in Bethesda (4706 Bethesda Ave.; phone: 301-986-5911). Bob's ice cream also is sold just above Georgetown at the *Ice Cream Shop* (2416 Wisconsin Ave. NW; phone: 965-4499).

INDEX

Index